KU-166-973

3RD EDITION

Information Technology for Management

TRANSFORMING BUSINESS IN THE DIGITAL ECONOMY

3RD EDITION

Information Technology for Management

TRANSFORMING BUSINESS IN THE DIGITAL ECONOMY

EFRAIM TURBAN
City University of Hong Kong

EPHRAIM MCLEAN
Georgia State University

JAMES WETHERBE
Texas Tech University

JOHN WILEY & SONS, INC.

ACQUISITIONS EDITOR	Beth Lang Golub
DEVELOPMENT EDITOR	Johnna Barto
SUPPLEMENTS EDITOR	Cynthia Snyder
EDITORIAL ASSISTANT	Jennifer Battista
MARKETING MANAGER	Jessica Garcia
SENIOR PRODUCTION EDITOR	Norine M. Pigliucci
COVER DESIGNER	Madelyn Lesure
TEXT DESIGNER	Kenny Beck
ILLUSTRATION EDITOR	Anna Melhorn
PHOTO EDITOR	Hilary Newman
PRODUCTION MANAGEMENT SERVICES	Suzanne Ingrao
COVER PHOTO	Christian Sarramon/CORBIS

This book was set in 10/12 Meridien Roman by TechBooks and printed and bound by Von Hoffmann Press.
The cover was printed by Von Hoffmann Press.

This book is printed on acid-free paper. ∞

Library of Congress Cataloging-in-Publication Data

Turban, Efraim.
Information technology for management: transforming business in the digital economy / Efraim Turban, Ephraim McLean, James Wetherbe.—3rd ed.
p. cm.
Includes bibliographical references.
ISBN 0-471-40075-0 (cloth : alk, paper)
Wiley International Edition ISBN: 0-471-21533-3
1. Management information systems, I. McLean, Ephraim R. II. Wetherbe, James C. III. Title.

T58.6.T763 2001
658.4'038'011—dc21

2001045647

Printed in the United States of America

10 9 8 7 6 5 4 3 2 1

Preface

THE DIGITAL AND WEB REVOLUTION. In the last few years we have been witnessing one of the most important events in human history thus far—the Web revolution. The Web is not only changing the way that we work, study, play, and conduct our lives, but it is doing so much more quickly than any other revolution (such as the Industrial Revolution), with impacts that are more far-reaching. Furthermore, all we have seen is the tip of the iceberg. It is difficult to predict all the implications. The Web revolution is facilitated by ever-changing information technologies.

Computerized systems in general and Web-based systems in particular can be found today in even the smallest businesses. It is almost impossible to run a competitive business without a computerized information system. Indeed, global competitive pressures and continuous innovations are forcing many organizations to *rethink* how they do business. To do so requires the ability to successfully incorporate *electronic commerce, knowledge management, customer relationship management, enterprise resource planning,* and *supply chain management* into an organization.

Information Technology for Management addresses the basic principles of MIS in light of these new developments. For example, one of the major changes occurring in IT is the ability to deliver systems over the Web, rather than to build them. This option, which is delivered by application server providers (ASPs), is a strategic option for the prudent managers of the digital economy. But does it fit all organizations? Such issues that resulted from the Web revolution are discussed in this text. Its major objective is to prepare managers and staff in the modern enterprise to understand the role of information technology in the digital economy.

Transforming Organizations to the Digital Economy

This book is based on the fundamental premise that the major role of information technology is to provide organizations with *strategic advantage by facilitating problem solving, increasing productivity and quality, improving customer service, enhancing communication and collaboration,* and *enabling business process reengineering.* By taking a practical, managerial-oriented approach, the book demonstrates that IT can be provided not only by information systems departments, but by end users and vendors as well. Managing information resources, new technologies, and communications networks is becoming a—or even *the*—critical success factor in the operations of many organizations, private and public, and will be essential to the survival of businesses in the digital economy.

Many introductory texts on information systems are geared toward yesterday's environment, where the important issues were the technology, the construction of information systems, and the support of traditional business functional applications. This book's approach is different. While recognizing the importance of the technology, system development, and functional transaction processing systems, we emphasize the *innovative* uses of information technology. The rapidly increased use of the Web, the Internet, intranets, extranets, and electronic commerce change the manner in which business is done in almost all organizations. This fact is reflected in our book: every chapter and major topic points to the role of the Web in facilitating competitiveness, effectiveness, and profitability. Of special importance is the emergence of the second-generation e-commerce applications such as m-commerce, c-commerce, and e-government. Also, the integration of ERP, CRM, and knowledge management with e-commerce is of a great importance.

Features of this Text

In developing the third edition of *Information Technology for Management,* we have tried to craft a book that will serve the needs of tomorrow's managers. During the process of revising and reorganizing this edition, we have been guided by certain recurring themes that are important to succeed in business in the digital economy.

This book reflects our vision of where information systems are going and the direction of IS education in business and e-business programs. This vision is represented by the following features that we have integrated throughout the book.

- ***Digital Economy Focus.*** This book was written with the recognition that organizations desire to transform themselves successfully to the digital economy. To do so companies need not only to use Web-based systems, but also to have an appropriate e-strategy and ability to plan click-and-mortar systems as well as new business models. Furthermore, they need to plan the transformation process, which is dependent on information technology.
- ***Managerial Orientation.*** Most IS textbooks identify themselves as either technology or socio-behavioral oriented. While we recognize the importance of both, our emphasis is on managerial orientation. To do so *we assembled all the major technological topics in five technology guides at the end of the book and on the book's Web site.* Furthermore, we attempted not to duplicate detailed presentations of behavioral sciences topics, such as dealing with resistance to change, or motivating employees. Instead, we concentrate on managerial decision making, cost-benefit justification, supply chain management, organizational restructuring, and CRM as they relate to information technology.
- ***Functional Relevance.*** Frequently, non–IS major students wonder why they must learn technical details. In this text the relevance of information technology to the major functional areas is an important theme. Also, we show, through the use of icons, the relevance of topics to accounting, finance, marketing, production/operations management, and human resource management. Furthermore, we show the relevance to public services and health care management, using icons. Finally, our examples cover small businesses and the international setting as well.
- ***Electronic Commerce and the Use of the Web.*** We strongly believe that electronic commerce and the use of the Internet, intranets, and extranets are changing the world of business. Not only is an entire extended chapter (5) dedicated to electronic commerce, but we demonstrate the significance of e-commerce in every chapter and major topic. The world of business is changing, and it is important that students understand these changes and their implications. For example, world-class companies such as General Electric, IBM, FedEx, Dell Computer, and Wal-Mart are introducing extremely innovative logistics systems supported by information technologies. This text tells you about all these innovations.
- ***Real-World Orientation.*** Extensive, vivid examples from large corporations, small businesses, government, and not-for-profit agencies will make concepts come alive by showing students the capabilities of information technology, its cost and justification, and some of the innovative ways real corporations are using IT in their operations.
- ***Failures and Lessons Learned.*** While most IT and MIS books introduce only the success of information systems, we present to the students the fact that many systems do fail. Every chapter of this book includes a discussion or example of failures, and the lessons learned from them. The case of FoxMeyer (on the Web site) shows how a large company was bankrupted as a result of misuse of IT.
- ***Solid Theoretical Backing.*** Throughout the book we present the theoretical foundation necessary for understanding information technology, ranging from Moore's law to Porter's competitiveness models including his latest e-strategy adaptation. Furthermore, we provide extensive references and many exercises to supplement the theoretical presentations.
- ***Most Current.*** The book presents the most current topics of information technology as evidenced by the many 2000 and 2001 citations. Topics such as mobile and collaborative e-commerce, extranets, chief knowledge officers and knowledge bases, CRM, Web-based supply chain systems, data warehousing, knowledge discovery and management, and information economics are presented both from the theoretical point of view and from the application side.
- ***Economic Justification.*** Information technology is mature enough to stand the difficult test of economic justification, a topic which is ignored by most textbooks. It is our position that investment in information technology must be scrutinized like any other investment, despite the difficulties of measuring technology benefits. In addition to discussion throughout the text, we are unique in devoting a complete chapter (13, "Information Technology Economics") to this subject.
- ***Integrated Systems.*** In contrast with many books that highlight isolated functional information systems, we emphasize those systems that support enterprise resources planning (ERP) and supply

chain management. Interorganizational systems are particularly highlighted, including the latest innovations in global e-exchanges.

• ***Global Perspective.*** The importance of global competition, partnerships, and trading is rapidly increasing. IT facilitates export and import, managing multinational companies, and electronic trading around the globe. International examples are highlighted in a special Global Index in the back of the book, and the book's Web site includes several international cases.

• ***Comprehensiveness and Ease of Reading.*** All major topics of information technology are covered, many with more details than you will find elsewhere. Furthermore, the book is very user friendly, easy to understand and follow, and it is full of interesting real-world examples and "war stories" that keep readers' interest at a very high level.

• ***Ethics.*** The importance of ethics is growing rapidly in the digital economy. Therefore we introduce the essentials of ethics as an appendix to Chapter 1. Then ethics is introduced in every chapter highlighted by icons in the margin. Finally, a primer on ethics is provided on the Web site.

Organization of the Book

The book is divided into five major parts composed of 16 regular chapters with five technology guides supplementing them.

Part I (IT in the Organization) introduces the drivers of the use of information technology in the digital economy. It also presents the foundations of information systems and their strategic use. Special attention is given to the role information systems play in facilitating Web-based business models and strategic information systems.

Part II (The Web Revolution) introduces the Web-based technologies and applications, starting with telecommunications networks and the role of the Internet, intranets, and extranets in contributing to communication, collaboration, and information discovery. Electronic commerce is presented in a most comprehensive way, followed by Web-based enterprise systems and supply chain management.

Part III (Organizational Applications) begins with the basics: IT applications in transaction processing and support of functional departments and operations. Planning for technology and the necessary organizational restructuring is discussed next, followed by a presentation of IT-supported knowledge management.

Part IV (Managerial and Decision Support Systems) discusses the many ways information systems can be used to support the day-to-day operations of a company, with a strong emphasis on the use of IT in managerial decision making. The three chapters in this part address some of the ways businesses are using information technology to solve specific problems and build strategic, innovative systems that enhance quality and productivity. Special attention is given to innovative applications of intelligent systems and to enterprise systems. The new approaches to data warehousing, analysis, and presentation are also highlighted.

Part V (Implementing and Managing IT) explores several topics related to the implementation, evaluation, construction, operation, security, and maintenance of information systems. We consider several issues ranging from the economics of information to outsourcing to the impacts of IT.

The five **Technology Guides** cover hardware, software, databases, telecommunications, and the essentials of the Internet. They contain condensed up-to-date presentations of all the material necessary for the understanding of these technologies. They can be used as a self-study refresher or as a basis for a class presentation. The technology guides are supplemented by a glossary, questions for review and discussion, and case studies, all of which are available on our Web site (*www.wiley.com/college/turban*).

Pedagogical Structure

We developed a number of pedagogical features to aid student learning and tie together the themes of the book.

• ***Chapter Outline.*** The outlines provide a quick indication of the major topics covered. Detailed outlines are provided at the beginning of the book.

• ***Learning Objectives.*** Learning objectives are provided at the beginning of each chapter to help students focus their efforts and alert them to the important concepts discussed.

• ***Opening Cases.*** Each chapter opens with a *real-world* example that illustrates the importance of information technology to modern corporations. These cases were carefully chosen to demonstrate the relevance, for business students, of the topics introduced in the chapter. They are presented in a format (problem, IT solution, results) that helps model a way to think about business problems, and are followed by a brief section (called Lessons Learned from this Case) that ties the important points of the opening case to the topic of the chapter.

- ***"A Closer Look" Boxes.*** These contain detailed, in-depth discussions of specific concepts or procedures, often using real-world examples. Some boxes enhance the in-text discussion by offering an alternative approach to information technology.
- ***"IT at Work" Boxes.*** These spotlight some real-world innovations and new technologies that companies are relying on to solve organizational dilemmas or create new business opportunities. Each box concludes with "for further exploration" issues.
- ***Highlighted Icons.*** Icons appear throughout the text to relate the topics covered within each chapter to some major themes of the book. The icons alert students to the related functional areas, IT failures, and ethical issues. Icons also indicate where related enrichment resources can be found on the book's companion Web site.
- ***Managerial Issues.*** The final section of every chapter explores some of the special concerns managers face as they adapt to an increasingly technological environment. Thought-provoking questions can serve as a springboard for class discussion and challenge business students to consider some of the actions they might take if placed in similar circumstances.
- ***Key Terms.*** All boldfaced new terms introduced within the chapter appear in a list at the end of the chapter and are defined in the end-of-book glossary.
- ***Chapter Highlights.*** All the important concepts covered in the chapter are listed at the end and linked by number to the learning objectives introduced at the beginning of each chapter to reinforce the important ideas discussed.
- ***End-of-Chapter Exercises.*** Different types of questions measure student comprehension and their ability to apply knowledge. Questions for Review ask students to summarize the concepts introduced. Discussion Questions are intended to promote class discussion and develop critical thinking skills. Exercises are challenging assignments that require students to apply what they have learned.
- ***Group and Role-Playing Activities.*** Comprehensive group assignments, including Internet research, presentation to classes, and role playing are available in each chapter. Students are asked to make competitive presentations and conduct debates.
- ***Internet Exercises.*** Over 100 hands-on exercises send the students to the most interesting Web sites to conduct research, investigate an application, or learn about the state of the art of a topic.
- ***Minicases.*** Real-world cases highlight some of the problems encountered by corporations as they develop and implement information systems. Discussion questions and assignments are included. Two types of minicases are available in each chapter. The shorter one is suitable for a class discussion without the need of any reading or Internet search. The longer one requires work on the Internet to be done at home by an individual or a group.
- ***Part Ending Cases.*** Longer real-world cases were chosen specifically for their ability to bring together many of the overriding concepts from each part of the text. These can be found on our Web site (*www.wiley.com/college/turban*).
- ***International Cases.*** Several cases from countries around the globe (including multinational corporations) are available on our Web site.

SUPPLEMENTARY MATERIALS

An extensive package of instructional materials is available to support this edition:

- ***Instructor's Manual.*** This manual presents objectives from the text with additional information to make them more appropriate and useful for the instructor. Chapter overviews provide an explanation of how each chapter fits in with previous chapters and the entire course. The manual also includes practical applications of concepts, case study elaboration, answers to end-of-chapter questions, questions for review, questions for discussion, and Internet exercises.
- ***Test Bank.*** The test bank contains approximately 1000 questions and problems (about 50 per chapter) consisting of multiple-choice, short answer, fill-ins, and critical thinking/essay questions.
- ***Computerized Test Bank.*** This electronic version of the test bank allows instructors to customize tests and quizzes for their students.
- ***PowerPoint Presentation.*** A series of slides designed around the content of the text incorporates key points from the text and illustrations where ap-

propriate. These were prepared by Emily Moody, a specialist in educational technology.

• ***Video Series.*** A collection of videos provides the students and instructors with dynamic and interesting business examples directly related to the concepts introduced in the text. The video clips illustrate the ways in which computer information systems are utilized in various companies and industries.

• ***Business Extra Web Site:* Wall Street Journal *Interactive and the On-Line Business Survival Guide.*** Wiley has teamed up with the *Wall Street Journal* to bring you instant access to a wealth of current articles dealing with all aspects of today's volatile business world. Use this resource to get up-to-date articles dealing with issues in information systems. The *On-Line Business Survival Guide* covers everything your students need to know to become master sleuths at finding critical information on the Internet. Each copy of the Survival Guide includes a special password for Wiley's *Business Extra Web Site* that allows students access to a series of relevant clippings from news wires and Dow Jones publications. For more information, go to *www.wiley.com/college/businessextra*.

• ***XanEdu.*** In a new partnership with XanEdu.com, Wiley now offers students the opportunity to read hundreds of articles related to the information systems industry with just the click of a mouse. Through the Wiley Web site students can get access to hundreds of articles that have been preselected from millions of articles found in thousands of publications. And students always get the most recent articles, as they are updated every 24 hours.

• ***The Turban Web Site.*** (*www.wiley.com/college/turban*). The Web site extends the content and theme of the text to provide extensive support for instructors and students. Organized by chapter, it includes cases, questions, and exercises for the technology guides, and downloadable PowerPoint slides, self-testing material for students, working students' experiences with using IT, links to resources on the Web, links to many of the companies discussed in the text, and a link to a unique supplement called "The Virtual Company."

• ***The Virtual Company.*** A Web-based case, The Virtual Company, features Internet and intranet sites for a simulated company that produces snowboards. Students are "hired" by the company as consultants and given assignments which require the students to use the information in the Internet and intranet sites to develop solutions and produce deliverables to present to the company. These exercises get the student into active, hands-on learning to complement the conceptual coverage of the text.

ACKNOWLEDGMENTS

Several individuals helped us with the creation of the third edition. Jay Aronson (University of Georgia) wrote the newly added Chapter 9, "Knowledge Management." Linda Lai (City University of Hong Kong) updated Chapters 2 and 14 as well as Technology Guides 1, 2, 3, and 5; and Narsi Bolloju (City University of Hong Kong) updated Chapters 4 and 13. Robert Davison (City University of Hong Kong) wrote the ethics appendix and updated all the ethical issues in the book. He also assisted in updating Chapter 16. Joe Walls (University of Michigan) updated Technology Guide 4. Particular thanks go to Wallace Wood (Bryant College), our "super reviewer" who took a last look at the final version of the proofs. Thanks to all for their contribution.

A recognition also goes to those who contributed to the second edition, especially to Ralph Westfall (California State University) and Kelly Rainer (Auburn University). Ralph wrote the chapter on information economics (Chapter 13) and contributed major portions to Chapters 8 and 14. Kelly created the technology guides to this book and updated the relevant technological topics. Also, we recognize the contribution of Kent Sandoe (California State University–Chico).

Many other individuals provided assistance in the creation of the third edition. First, dozens of students participated in the class testing of the material and helped develop exercises and find illustrative applications, and contributed valuable suggestions and annotations for the text. It is not possible to name all of them, but they all certainly deserve recognition and thanks.

Faculty feedback was essential to the development of the book. Many individuals participated in focus groups and/or acted as reviewers. Several others created portions of chapters or cases, especially international cases, some of which are in the text and others on the Web site.

We are grateful to the following faculty for their contributions to the *third edition*: Martin Bariff, Illinois Institute of Technology; Debabroto Chatterjee, Washington State University; Jason Chen, Gonzaga

University; Marlene Davidson, California State Polytechnic University–Pomona; John C. Di Renzo, Jr., Cameron University; Dennis Galletta, University of Pittsburgh; Chittibabu Govindarajulu, Drexel University; Randy Guthrie, California State Polytechnic University–Pomona; Shohreh S. Hashemi, University of Houston–Downtown; Gregory R. Heim, Boston College; Bobbie Hyndman, West Texas A&M University; Joan B. Lumpkin, Wright State University; Jane Mackay, Texas Christian University; Ravi Nath, Creighton University; Roger Alan Pick, University of Missouri–Kansas City; Mahesh S. Raisinghani, University of Dallas; Dolly Samson, Weber State University; Kenneth David Smith, Cameron University; Amita Suhrid, Keller Graduate School of Management; Peter Tarasewich, University of Maine; Stephen Thorpe, La Salle University; Thomas Triscari, Jr., Rensselaer Polytechnic Institute; Barbara D. Turner, Rowan University; Robert D. Wilson, California State University–San Bernardino; Wallace A. Wood, Bryant College; Jigish Zaveri, Morgan State University.

The following individuals helped us with the *second edition*: Christine P. Andrews, SUNY at Fredonia; Marzi Astanti, Winona State University; V. Bose, Texas A&M University; Marek Ejsmont, Keyano College (Alberta, Canada); George Fettes, Camosun College; David R. Fordham, James Madison University; Lisa Friedrichsen, Keller Graduate School; David Hale, University of Alabama; Fred G. Harold, Florida Atlantic University; Jeff Harper, Athens State College; Myron Hatcher, California State University, Fresno; Chin-Yuan Ho, National Central University (Taiwan); Change T. Hsieh, University of Southern Mississippi; Grace Johnson, Marietta College; Dorothy Leidner, Baylor University; James Linderman, Bentley College; Munir Mandviwalla, Temple University; Ji-Ye Mao, University of Waterloo; Vicki McKinney, University of Texas, Arlington; Derrick Neufeld, University of Manitoba; E. F. Peter Newson, University of Western Ontario; Floyd D. Ploeger, Southwest Texas State University; Larisa Preiser-Houy, California State University–Pomona; Mary Ann Robbert, Bentley College; Dolly Samson, Weber State University; Vijay Sethi, Nanyang Technological University (Singapore); Kathy Stewart, Georgia State University; Ted Strickland, University of Louisville; Edward Tsang, University of Essex (United Kingdom); and Liang Chee Wee, Luther College.

The following individuals participated in focus groups and/or acted as reviewers of the *first edition*: Mary Anne Atkinson, University of Delaware; Benedict Arogyaswamy, University of South Dakota; James Carroll, Georgian Court College; Paul Cheney, University of South Florida; Candace Deans, Thunderbird School, AGIM; Bill DeLone, American University; Phillip Ein-Dor, Tel Aviv University (Israel); Michael Eirman, University of Wisconsin-Oshkosh; Paul Evans, George Mason University; Deb Ghosh, Louisiana State University; Oscar Gutierrez, University of Massachusetts-Boston; Rassule Hadidi, Sangamon State University; Fred Harold, Florida Atlantic University; Jaak Jurison, Fordham University; Eugene Kaluzniacky, University of Winnipeg; Astrid Lipp, Clemson University; Jo Mae Maris, Northern Arizona University; E. F. Peter Newson, University of Western Ontario; Michael Palley, CUNY-Baruch College; Keri Pearlson, University of Texas; Bill Richmond, George Mason University; Larry Sanders, University of Buffalo; A. B. Schwarzkopf, University of Oklahoma; Henk Sol, Delft Institute of Technology (The Netherlands); Timothy Smith, DePaul University; Timothy Staley, DeVry Institute of Technology; Shannon Taylor, Montana State University; Robert Van Cleave, University of Minnesota; Kuang-Wei Wen, University of Connecticut; Anthony Wensley, University of Toronto (Canada); Jennifer Williams, University of Southern Indiana; G. W. Willis, Baylor University; Gayle Yaverbaum, Pennsylvania State University.

Also, we recognize those faculty who contributed cases to the first edition of the text: Kimberly Bechler, International Institute of Management Development (Switzerland); Christer Carlsson, Abo Akademi University (Finland); Guy Fitzgerald, University of London (United Kingdom); Young Moo Kang, Dong-A University (Korea); Ossi Kokkonen, Metsa-Serla Oy (Finland); Donald Marchand, International Institute of Management Development (Switzerland); David McDonald, Georgia State University; Boon-Siong Neo, Nanyang Technological University (Singapore); Nicolau Reinhard, University of Sao Paulo (Brazil); Chris Sauer, University of New South Wales (Australia); Scott Schneberger, Georgia State University; Pirkko Walden, Abo Akademi University (Finland); Leslie Willcocks, Templeton College, Oxford University (United Kingdom); and Ronaldo Zwicker, University of Sao Paulo (Brazil).

Many individuals helped us with the administrative work; of special mention are Grace Choi and Venus Ma of City University of Hong Kong and Judy Lang of Eastern Illinois University, who devoted considerable time to typing and editing. Hugh Watson of the University of Georgia, the Information Systems Advisor to Wiley, guided us through various stages of the project. Finally, we would like to thank the dedicated staff of John Wiley & Sons: Cynthia Snyder, Jeanine Furino, and Norine Pigliucci. A special thank you to Johnna Barto, Beth Lang Golub, Ingrao Associates, Shelley Flannery, and Ann Torbert, who contributed their considerable energy, time, and devotion to the success of this project.

Finally, we recognize the various organizations and corporations that provided us with material and permissions to use it.

Efraim Turban
Ephraim McLean
James Wetherbe

About the Authors

DR. EFRAIM TURBAN

Dr. Efraim Turban obtained his MBA and Ph.D. degrees from the University of California, Berkeley. His industry experience includes eight years as an industrial engineer, three of which were spent at General Electric Transformers Plant in Oakland, California. He also has extensive consulting experience to small and large corporations as well as to governments.

In his over thirty years of teaching, Professor Turban has served as Chaired Professor at Eastern Illinois University, and as Visiting Professor at Nanyang Technological University in Singapore. He has also taught at UCLA; USC; Simon Fraser University; Lehigh University; California State University, Long Beach; and Florida International University.

Dr. Turban was a Co-recipient of the 1984/85 National Management Science Award (Artificial Intelligence in Management). In 1997 he received the Distinguished Faculty Scholarly and Creative Achievement Award at California State University, Long Beach.

Dr. Turban has published articles in over 100 leading journals, including the following: *Management Science, MIS Quarterly, Operations Research, Journal of MIS, Communications of the ACM, Information Systems Frontiers, Decision Support Systems, International Journal of Information Management, Heuristics, Expert Systems with Applications, International Journal of Applied Expert Systems, Journal of Investing, Accounting, Management and Information Systems, Computers and Operations Research, Computers and Industrial Engineering, IEEE Transactions on Engineering Management, Omega, International Journal of Electronic Commerce, Organizational Computing and Electronic Commerce,* and *Electronic Markets.* He has also published 20 books, including best sellers such as *Neural Networks: Applications in Investment and Financial Services* (2nd edition) (co-editor with R. Trippi), Richard D. Irwin, 1996; *Decision Support Systems and Intelligent Systems,* (Prentice Hall, 6th edition, 2001); *Expert Systems and Applied Artificial Intelligence,* (MacMillan Publishing Co., 1992), *Electronic Commerce: A Managerial Approach,* (Prentice Hall, 2002) and *Introduction to Information Technology* (Wiley, 2001).

Professor Turban is currently on the faculty of City University of Hong Kong, Department of Information Systems, Faculty of Business Administration. Professor Turban's current major interest is electronic commerce, strategy, and implementation.

DR. EPHRAIM MCLEAN

Dr. Ephraim McLean obtained his Bachelor of Mechanical Engineering degree from Cornell University in 1958. After brief service in the U.S. Army Ordnance Corps, he worked for Procter & Gamble Co. for seven years, first in manufacturing management and later as a computer systems analyst. In 1965, he left P&G and entered the Sloan School of Management at the Massachusetts Institute of Technology, obtaining his master's degree in 1967 and his doctorate in 1970.

While at M.I.T., he began an interest in the application of computer technology to medicine, working on his dissertation at the Lahey Clinic in Boston. While there, he was instrumental in developing the Lahey Clinic Automated Medical History System. During the same period, he served as an instructor at M.I.T. and also assisted in the preparation of the books *The Impact of Computers on Management* (MIT Press, 1967); *The Impact of Computers on Collective Bargaining* (MIT Press, 1969); and *Computers in Knowledge-Based Fields* (MIT Press, 1970).

Dr. McLean left M.I.T. and joined the faculty of the Anderson Graduate School of Management at the University of California, Los Angeles (UCLA) in the winter of 1970. He was the founding Director of the Information Systems Research Program and the first Chairman of the Information Systems area, both within the Anderson Graduate School of Management. In fall 1987, he was named to the George E. Smith Eminent Scholar's Chair at the College of Business Administration at Georgia State University in Atlanta, Georgia.

Dr. McLean has published over 80 articles in such publications as the *Harvard Business Review; Sloan Management Review; California Management Review; Communications of the ACM; MIS Quarterly; Information Systems Research, Information & Management; Journal of MIS; Journal of Risk and Insurance; DATA BASE; InformationWEEK; Datamation; ComputerWorld;* and the *Journal of the American Hospital Association*. He is the co-author of *Strategic Planning for MIS* (Wiley Interscience, 1977) and co-editor of a book of programs entitled *APL Application in Management*. He was a founding Associate Editor for Research of the *MIS Quarterly* and is currently senior co-editor of the *DATA BASE for Advances in Information Systems*. He was twice on the national Executive Council of the Society for Information Management (SIM). In 1980, he helped organize the International Conference on Information Systems (ICIS) and was Conference Co-chairman in 1981 in Cambridge, Massachusetts; Conference Chairman in 1986 in San Diego, California; and Conference Co-chairman in 1997 in Atlanta, Georgia. He is currently Vice President for Affiliated Organizations of the Association for Information Systems (AIS).

In addition to university work, he has served as a consultant to such firms as the IBM Corporation, General Electric Company, Atlantic Richfield Company, Digital Equipment Corporation, BellSouth Corporation, the National Science Foundation, American Hospital Supply Corporation, McCormick & Company, Security Pacific National Bank, Pennsylvania Financial Corporation (now Primerica), and Citibank, N.A. of New York. He has also made executive presentations and conducted management workshops in Asia, Australia, Europe, South Africa, and throughout North America.

DR. JAMES C. WETHERBE

Dr. James C. Wetherbe is Stevenson Chair of Information Technology at Texas Tech University as well as Professor of MIS at the University of Minnesota where he directed the MIS Research Center for 20 years. He is internationally known as a dynamic and entertaining speaker, author, and leading authority on the use of computers and information systems to improve organizational performance and competitiveness. He is particularly appreciated for his ability to explain complex technology in straightforward, practical terms that can be strategically applied by both executives and general management.

Dr. Wetherbe is the author of 18 highly regarded books and is quoted often in leading business and information systems journals. He has also authored over 200 articles, was ranked by *InformationWEEK* as one of the top dozen information technology consultants, and is the first recipient of the MIS Quarterly Distinguished Scholar Award. He has also served on the faculties of the University of Memphis, where he was Fed Ex Professor and Director of the Center for Cycle Time Research, and the University of Houston. Dr. Wetherbe received his Ph.D. from Texas Tech University.

Brief Contents

Contents

3RD EDITION

Information Technology for Management

TRANSFORMING BUSINESS IN THE DIGITAL ECONOMY

PART I
IT in the Organization

CHAPTER

1

Information Technology in the Digital Economy

www.wiley.com/college/turban

LEARNING OBJECTIVES

After studying this chapter, you will be able to:

1. Describe the characteristics of the digital economy.
2. Recognize the relationships between business pressures, organizational responses, and information systems.
3. Identify the major pressures in the business environment and describe the major organizational responses to them.
4. Describe the role of information technology in organizational activities.
5. Define computer-based information systems and information technology.
6. List the essentials of networked computing and Web-based systems.

HOW BRISTOL-MYERS SQUIBB TRANSFORMED ITSELF TO THE DIGITAL ECONOMY

 THE PROBLEM

Bristol-Myers Squibb (BMS) is a world leader in the manufacture of pharmaceutical drugs as well as beauty and infant-food products. Its thousands of products are sold all over the globe. It sells to individuals and to businesses such as pharmacies, hospitals, large retailers, and more. It has many thousands of business partners, including suppliers from which its 30,000 purchasing agents worldwide buy raw materials and supplies. BMS operates in an extremely competitive environment. It has hundreds of direct competitors. With so many competitors, small and large, it is very difficult to keep all the business partners and customers happy, and to make money, and at the same time to move into the digital economy. However, this is exactly what BMS did.

www.bms.com

 THE SOLUTION

Bristol-Myers was collaborating with research institutions and universities through the Internet's precursor, the ARPNet. So it was natural for the company to embrace the Internet when it was commercialized. BMS is involved in many Web-based initiatives, all designed to transform the company into one that can maintain a competitive position in the digital economy. To do so, BMS is not only using Web-based systems but also overhauling its management structure, revamping its procurement and supply chain processes, and expanding its myriad Web sites. The goal is to reduce the company's reliance on costly and error-prone paper processing, banish expensive electronic data interchange (EDI) services by moving to the Internet, and forge tighter relationships with the wholesalers and retailers. The following are the company's major Internet-based activities.

- An Internet infrastructure for data communication replaces the current, expensive electronic data interchange (EDI) that used private networks.
- The company has established for both health-care professionals and patients an Internet-based health education database regarding diseases and available drugs.
- An e-procurement system makes possible purchases of equipment, PCs, and office supplies online. With this system, 30,000 purchasing agents now use standard procedures, and inexperienced employees can be guided through the now-standardized acquisition process. The system enables BMS to track end-user spending in the company, and in turn, lets IT managers channel users to preferred suppliers.
- BMS's human resources *portal* is a gateway to the organization's Web-site content. It makes human resources information easily available. Employees can view personnel information, administrative rules, and performance appraisals, and can enter changes in address, telephone number, and other such data.
- BMS business customers can buy goods and track orders online. Also, extensive customer service is provided online.
- BMS can use different sites to advertise its different products. For example, XtremeFX is a hair-color aimed at young adults. Using a new technology,

BMS set up a vivid Web site, with great publicity, to advertise this product. Visitors were encouraged to submit their own MP3 music files for possible inclusion as the background piece to the opening sequence at the XtremeFX Web site.

- Bristol-Myers Squibb's *supply chain*—all the activities related to the flow of materials from suppliers through manufacturing, distribution, and sales—is being automated. This enables BMS to reduce paper flow and better track the flow of information.
- The e-commerce system is integrated with an enterprise resource planning system that integrates all major business processes of the company.

THE RESULTS

It is difficult to estimate results at this early stage, but BMS's chief information officer (CIO) estimates $100 million annual savings just from e-procurement. Also, the move to a paperless transaction system has cut down on errors. For example, using electronic invoicing forms enables automated editing against catalog and reference material, resulting in significantly fewer errors.

Sources: Compiled from *Internetweek*, June 12, 2000, and from *bms.com*.

LESSONS LEARNED FROM THIS CASE

This case illustrates that fierce global competition drives even large corporations to find ways to reduce costs, increase productivity, and improve customer service. These efforts are best achieved by using Web-based systems, which are the major ingredient in the transformation to the digital economy. The major initiatives that the company embarked upon were:

1. Reduce costs by introducing an electronic procurement system and by smoothing the supply chain.
2. Increase sales by utilizing the Web, using many portals to better connect with retailers and end-customers.
3. Improve relationships with employees and customers. The company employs various e-commerce models, which were combined with restructuring of management processes.

In this chapter we describe the characteristics and concepts of the digital economy and how it is changing several business processes. In addition, we will explain the extremely competitive business environment in which companies operate today, the business pressures to which they are subject, and what companies are doing to counter these pressures. Futhermore, you will learn what makes information technology a necessity in supporting organizations and why any manager in the twenty-first century should know about it.

1.1 DOING BUSINESS IN THE DIGITAL ECONOMY

Electronic Commerce and Networked Computing

Bristol-Myers Squibb is an established "old-economy" company that is using new technology to enhance its operations. Its use of Web-based systems to support buying, selling, and customer service is an example of **electronic commerce (EC)**. Thus, this company is called a **click-and-mortar** company, meaning that it is adding some EC activities to its regular business. In EC, business transactions are done electronically over the Internet. EC is becoming a very significant global economic element in the twenty-first century (see Clinton and Gore, 1997, and Hamel, 2000).

The infrastructure for EC is **networked computing**, which is emerging as the standard computing environment in business, home, and government. Networked computing connects several computers and other electronic devices via telecommunication networks. This connection allows users to access information stored in many places and to communicate and collaborate with others from their desktop computers. While some people still use a standalone computer exclusively, or a network confined to one organization, the vast majority use networked computers. These may be connected to the global networked environment known as the **Internet**, or to its counterpart within organizations, called an **intranet**. In addition, some companies link their intranets to those of their business partners over networks called **extranets**.

This new breed of computing is helping some companies excel and is helping others simply to survive. Broadly, the collection of computer systems used by an organization is termed **information technology (IT)**, the focus of this book. Bristol-Myers Squibb is not the only company that uses IT, and electronic commerce in particular, to facilitate its business. As a matter of fact, almost all organizations, private or public, in manufacturing, agriculture, or services, use various types of information technologies, including electronic commerce, to support their operations.

Why is this so? The reason is simple: IT has become the major facilitator of business activities in the world today. (See for instance, Dickson and DeSanctis, 2001; Tapscott et al., 2000; and Gill, 1996.) IT is also a catalyst of fundamental changes in the structure, operations, and management of organizations (see Dertouzos, 1997), due to the capabilities shown in Table 1.1. These capabilities, according to Wreden (1997), support the following five business objectives: (1) *improving productivity* (in 51 percent of corporations), (2) *reducing costs* (39 percent), (3) *improving decision making* (36 percent), (4) *enhancing customer relationships* (33 percent), and (5) *developing new strategic applications* (33 percent).

TABLE 1.1 Major Capabilities of Information Systems

- Perform high-speed, high-volume, numerical computations.
- Provide fast, accurate, and inexpensive communication within and between organizations.
- Store huge amounts of information in an easy-to-access, yet small space.
- Allow quick and inexpensive access to vast amount of information, worldwide.
- Increase the effectiveness and efficiency of people working in groups in one place or in several locations.
- Vividly present information that challenges the human mind.
- Automate both semiautomatic business processes and manually done tasks.
- Speed typing and editing.
- Can be wireless, thus supporting unique applications.
- Accomplish all of the above much less expensively than when done manually.

The Digital Economy

The **digital economy** refers to an economy that is based on digital technologies, including digital communication networks (the Internet, intranets, and private value-added networks or VANS), computers, software, and other related information technologies. The digital economy is also sometimes called the **Internet economy**, the **new economy**, or the **Web economy**. In this new economy, digital networking and communication infrastructures provide a global platform over which people and organizations interact, communicate, collaborate and search for information. This platform includes, for example, the following, according to Choi and Whinston (2000):

- A vast array of digitizable products—databases, news and information, books, magazines, TV and radio programming, movies, electronic games, musical CDs, and software—which are delivered over the digital infrastructure any time, anywhere in the world.
- Consumers and firms conducting financial transactions digitally—through digital currencies or financial tokens carried via networked computers and mobile devices.
- Physical goods such as home appliances and automobiles, which are embedded with microprocessors and networking capabilities.

The term *digital economy* also refers to the convergence of computing and communication technologies on the Internet and other networks, and the resulting flow of information and technology that is stimulating e-commerce and vast organizational change. This convergence enables all types of information (data, audio, video, etc.) to be stored, processed, and transmitted over networks to many destinations worldwide. The digital economy is creating an economic revolution, which, according to the *Emerging Digital Economy II* (*ecommerce.gov*), is evidenced by unprecedented economic performance and the longest period of uninterrupted economic expansion in history. Here are some relevant statistics relating to this digital revolution in the United States:

- Information technology industries have been growing at more than double the rate of the overall economy. In 2000, they reached close to *9 percent of GDP,* up from 4.9 percent in 1985.
- IT industries by themselves have driven *over one-quarter of total real economic growth* (not including any indirect effects), each year between 1996 and 2000.
- Without information technology, overall inflation would have been *3.1 percent in 1997,* more than a full percentage point higher than the *2.0 percent* it actually was. Information technology has enabled the United States to enjoy a sustainable growth with almost no inflation in recent years.
- Companies throughout the economy are betting on IT to boost productivity. In the 1960s, business spending on IT equipment represented only 3 percent of total *business equipment* investment. By 2000, IT's share rose to *45 percent* of business spending per year.
- In 1999, over 8.5 million people worked in IT-related jobs across the economy. The average salary for these workers was *just under $49,000* per year, compared to an average of *$29,000* for the private sector as a whole.
- There were nearly 2.5 million Internet jobs in the United States in early 2000, up *36 percent* in just a 12-month period.

- Worldwide cost savings from the use of Internet applications, according to Giga Information Group, will reach *$1.25 trillion* in 2002, of which about $600 billion are in U.S. organizations.

Web-based electronic commerce (EC) systems are certainly providing competitive advantage to organizations. In a study conducted by Lederer et al. (1998), "enhancing competitiveness or creating strategic advantage" was ranked as the number-one benefit of Web-based systems. However, electronic commerce is not the only useful IT application. Computer-based information systems of all kinds have been enhancing competitiveness and creating strategic advantage on their own or in conjunction with EC applications (see Galliers et al., 1999).

The New versus the Old: Illustrative Examples

The changes brought by the digital economy are indeed significant. Let's look at a few examples that illustrate differences between the new economy and the old.

PHOTOGRAPHY. We begin with an activity that millions of people like to do, taking pictures.

Old Economy. You buy film at the store, insert it into your camera, and take pictures. Once you complete the film, sometimes weeks or months after you began the roll, you take it to the store (or mail it), for processing. You get back the photos and examine them, to see which you like. You go back to the store and pay for enlargements and duplications. You go home, put some of the photos in envelopes, and mail them to your family and friends. Of course, if you want to take moving pictures, you need a second, different camera.

New Economy. In first-generation digital photography, you follow the old-economy process up to the point of getting the pictures back from the photo lab. But when you have the pictures, you scan the ones you like. Then you can make reprints, enlarge them, or send them to your family and friends via e-mail.

In the second generation of digital photography, you use a *digital camera* that can also take videos. No film is needed, and no processing is required. You can see the results immediately, and you can enlarge photos and position and print them quickly. In minutes, you can send the pictures to your family and friends (see Figure 1.1). They can view the pictures on their personal computer, personal digital assistant (PDA), or cell phone. You can print pictures, or use them in a multimedia presentation.

In the third generation of digital photography, your digital camera is connected to a wireless device such as a palmtop computer or a cell phone. You are traveling, and you see interesting scenery or an athletic event. You take pictures, and within a few seconds they are sent to any destination on the Internet for viewing or reprints. Industrial cameras of this type are already in use (*New York Times,* December 14, 2000).

PROVIDING SERVICES WIRELESSLY. Companies provide many services to customers. The new economy is enabling companies to provide these services by wireless means.

Old Economy. Customers ask for services by writing, calling, or faxing a request. Traditionally the provider has sorted the requests and answered with a letter or by phone. However, the process is not always smooth: Telephone lines are frequently busy, calls are made to the wrong person, letters are slow or lost, customers do not get appropriate answers and have to ask again, and so on. Thus,

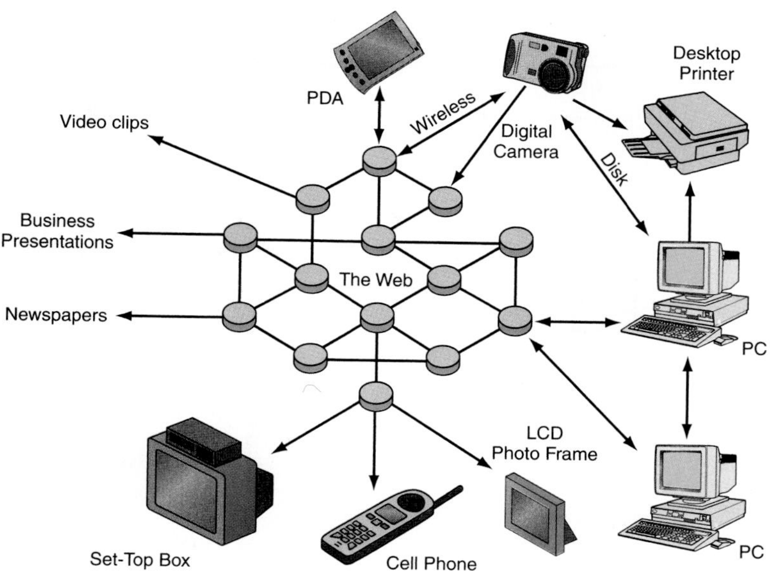

FIGURE 1.1 Taking photos with a digital camera.

customers often were very unhappy, and companies had to pay lots of money in providing their service.

New Economy. In the new economy, customer services are more direct and much closer at hand. You can log on the Internet from your cell phone to a company such as I-MODE in Japan, at any time and from any place. You can check your bank account, pay a bill, request a loan, or send a query. You get an answer in seconds for most of your questions. You can locate train timetables, or shopping and restaurant guides. You can find information about best-selling books and then buy them. You can get automatic notification in case of train or plane delays. You can get free entertainment, or see a recent movie for a small fee. Many more services, such as sending and receiving photos, are available. (For more, look at *nttdocomo.com/imode*.) Some services are even available on dashboard screens in cars.

www.nttdocomo.com/imode

SUPPLYING COMMERCIAL PHOTOS. Thousands of companies around the globe provide photos of their products to retailers who advertise them in newspapers, paper catalogs, or online. The new economy has changed the process by which these photos were supplied from a linear **supply chain** (the flow of materials from suppliers through manufacturing, distribution, and sales) to a hub.

Old Economy. In the old economy, the retailer sends to the manufacturer a request for a picture of the item to be advertised, say a Sony TV set. Sony then sends to a designated ad agency, by a courier, alternative pictures that the agency can use. The agency selects a picture, designs the ad, and sends it by a courier to the printer. There it is rephotographed and finally entered into production. An improvement introduced several years ago allows the ad agency to send the picture to a scanning house. There, a digital image is made, and that image is moved to the printer. Both the retailer and the ad agency may be involved in a quality check at various times, slowing the process. The cycle time per picture can be four to six weeks. The total processing cost per picture is about $80.

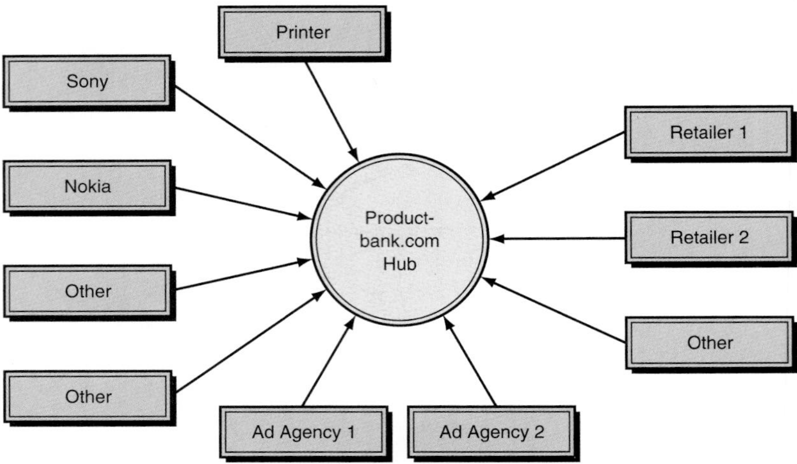

FIGURE 1.2 Changing a linear supply chain to a hub.

New Economy. Orbis Inc., a very small Australian company, changed the old-economy linear supply chain to a hub-like supply chain, as shown in Figure 1.2. In the new process, the manufacturer sends many digitized pictures to Orbis (*productbank.com.au*). Orbis organizes the pictures in a database. When a retailer needs a picture, it enters the database and selects a picture, or several alternatives. The choice is e-mailed with the picture's ID number to the ad agency. The agency enters the database, views the digitized pictures, and works on them. The final digitized pictures are e-mailed to the printer. The entire process takes less than a week at a cost of about $50 per picture.

www.productbank.com

In the examples above, and others at our Website, we can see the advantage of the new economy over the old one in terms of at least one of the following: cost, quality, speed, and customer service. What is amazing is the *magnitude* of this advantage. In the past, business improvements were in the magnitude of 10 to 25 percent. Today, improvements are measured in percentages of hundreds or even thousands. The new economy brings not only digitization but also new business models.

Business Models

The Internet is challenging the economic, societal, and technological foundations of the old economy. In essence a revolution is taking place. And like all successful revolutions, when it ends, the landscape will look significantly different. Entrepreneurs developing new models for business, the economy, and government.

A **business model** is a method of doing business by which a company can generate revenue to sustain itself. The model spells out how the company adds value, which consumers are willing to pay for, in terms of the goods and/or services the company produces in the course of its operations. Some models are very simple. Nokia makes and sells cell phones and generates profit from these sales. On the other hand, a TV station provides free broadcasting. Its survival depends on a complex model involving factors such as advertisers and content providers. Internet portals, such as Yahoo!, also use a complex business model.

Here are some examples of new business models brought about by the digital economy. Further examples and details can be found throughout the book, in Timmers (1999), Applegate (2001), and Turban et al. (2002), and at *digitalenterprise.org*.

NAME-YOUR-OWN-PRICE. Pioneered by Priceline.com, this model allows you to state a price you are willing to pay for a specific product or service. Using information in its database, Priceline will try to match your request with a supplier willing to sell on these terms. Customers may have to submit several bids before they find a price match for the product they want. Priceline's major area of operation is travel (airline tickets, hotels).

DYNAMIC BROKERING. In the digital age customers can specify requirements for a service or a product. These specifications are broadcasted over the Internet ("Webcasted") to service providers in an automatic invitation to submit bids. Bids can be offered, amended, and considered, all without any further input from the consumer. An example is GetThere.com, for travel services. A similar model is the *reverse auctions* used by organizations for procurement of materials and business services.

REVERSE AUCTIONS. If you are a big buyer, private or public, you are probably using a tendering (bidding) system to do your purchasing. Now tendering can be done online, saving time and money. Pioneered by General Electric Corp. (*gegxs.com*), tendering systems are gaining popularity. Several government entities are mandating electronic tendering as the only way to sell to them. Electronic reverse auctions are fast, they reduce administrative costs by as much as 85 percent, and products' prices can be 5 to 20 percent lower.

AFFILIATE MARKETING. **Affiliate marketing** is an arrangement in which marketing partners place a banner of a company, such as Amazon.com, on their Web site. Every time a customer clicks on the banner, moves to the advertiser's Web site, and makes a purchase there, the advertiser pays a 3 to 15 percent commission to the host site. In this way, businesses can turn other businesses into their *virtual commissioned sales force*. Pioneered by CDNow (see Hoffman and Novak, 2000), the concept is now employed by thousands of retailers or direct sellers.

GROUP PURCHASING. Anyone can pay less per unit when buying more units. Discounts are usually available for quantity purchases. Using the concept of **group purchasing**, a small business, or even an individual, can get a discount. EC brings in the concept of *electronic aggregation* for group purchasing, in which a third party finds the individuals or SMEs (small/medium enterprises), aggregates their small orders, and then negotiates (or offers a tender) for the best deal. Some leading aggregators are *etrana.com* and *apbs.com*. (We'll look at this topic again in Chapter 5.)

E-MARKETPLACES AND EXCHANGES. Electronic marketplaces have existed in isolated applications for decades. An example is the stock exchanges, some of which have been fully computerized since the 1980s. But, since 1999, thousands of electronic marketplaces, of different varieties, have sprung up (Chapter 5). E-marketplaces introduce operating efficiencies to trading, and if well organized and managed, they can provide benefits to both buyers and sellers. Of special interest are **vertical marketplaces**, which concentrate on one industry (e.g., *e-steel.com* in the steel industry).

In part, these new business models in the digital economy have sprung up in response or reaction to business pressures, which is the topic we turn to next.

1.2 Business Pressures, Organizational Responses, and IT Support

Environmental, organizational, and technological factors are creating a highly competitive business environment in which customers are the focal point. Furthermore, these factors can change quickly, sometimes in an unpredictable manner (see Tapscott et al., 1998, and Knoke, 1996). Therefore, companies need to react frequently and quickly to both the *problems* and the *opportunities* resulting from this new business environment (see Tapscott, 1999, and Drucker, 1995). Because the pace of change and the degree of uncertainty in tomorrow's competitive environment are expected to accelerate, organizations are going to operate under increasing pressures to produce more, using fewer resources.

Boyett and Boyett (1995) emphasize this dramatic change and describe it with a set of **business pressures**, or *drivers*. These business pressures are forces in the organization's environment that create pressures on the organization's operations. Note that here and throughout the book, in using the term "business" we refer not only to "for-profit" organizations, but also to public organizations and government agencies that need to be run like a business.

Boyett and Boyett maintain that in order to succeed (or even to survive) in this dynamic world, companies must not only take traditional actions such as lowering costs, but also undertake innovative activities such as changing structure or processes. We refer to these reactions, some of which are interrelated, as **critical response activities**. They can be performed in some or all of the processes of the organization, from the daily routine of preparing payroll and order entry, to strategic activities such as the acquisition of a company. A response can be a reaction to a pressure already in existence, or it can be an initiative intended to defend an organization against future pressures. It can also be an activity that exploits an opportunity created by changing conditions. Most response activities can be greatly facilitated by information technology. In some cases IT is the only solution to these business pressures (see Dickson and DeSanctis, 2001, and Callon, 1996).

The relationships among business pressures, organizational responses, and IT are shown in Figure 1.3. This figure illustrates a model of the new world of business. The business drivers create pressures on organizations, and organizations respond with activities supported by IT (hence the bidirectional nature of the ar-

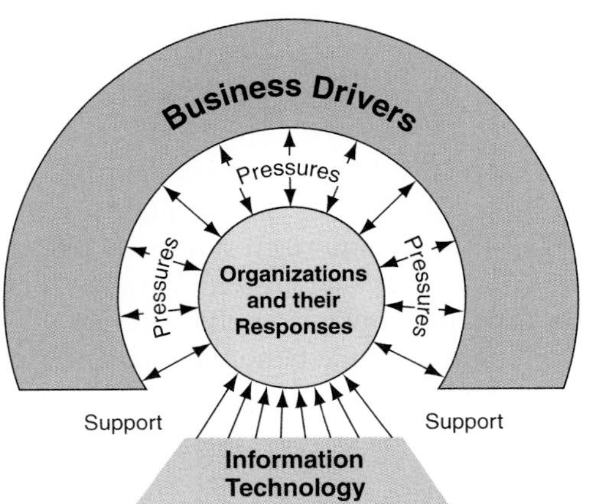

FIGURE 1.3 IT support to organizational responses.

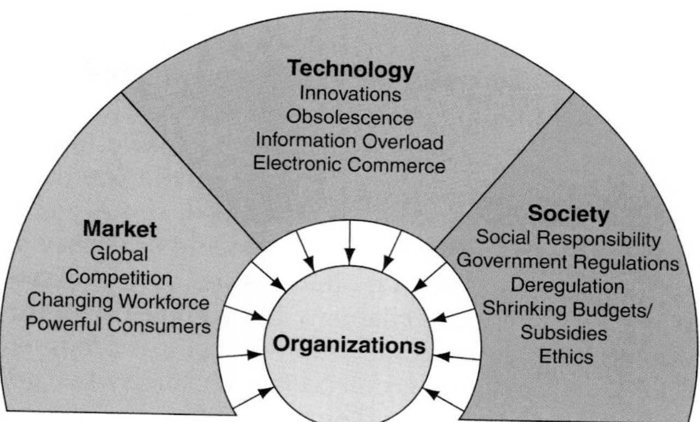

FIGURE 1.4 The major business pressures.

rows in the figure). The core of today's IT, as we will see throughout the book, is networked computing. Now, let's examine the components of the model in more detail.

Business Pressures

To understand the role of IT in today's organization, it is useful to review the major factors in the business environment that create pressures on organizations. The business environment refers to the social, technological, legal, economic, physical, and political factors that affect business activities. Significant changes in any part of this environment are likely to create pressures on organizations. Figure 1.4 presents a schematic view of the major pressures, which may interrelate and affect each other.

In this book, the business pressures are divided into the following categories: market, technology, and society. These are described next.

MARKET PRESSURES. The market pressures that organizations feel come from a global economy and strong competition, the nature of the workforce, and powerful customers.

Global Economy and Strong Competition. Within the last twenty or so years, the foundation necessary for a global economy has taken shape. Two important factors were the collapse of the Soviet Union, and moves toward a market economy in most countries, including China and Russia. Together, these have resulted in a fairly stabilized world political environment that makes possible a global economy (see Naisbitt, 1994). This move to globalization has been facilitated by advanced telecommunication networks and especially by the Internet (see Clinton and Gore, 1997; Lane, 1999; and Pine and Gilmore, 1999). Regional agreements such as the North American Free Trade Agreement (United States, Canada, and Mexico) and the creation of a unified European market with a single currency, the Euro, have contributed to increased world trade. Further, reduction of trade barriers has allowed products and services to flow freely around the globe.

One particular pressure that exists for businesses in a global market is the cost of labor. Labor costs differ widely from one country to another. While the hourly industrial wage rate (excluding benefits) is over $15 in some Western countries, it is only $1 to $2 in many developing countries, including those in Asia, South America, Eastern Europe, and Africa. The lowest labor cost for industrial employees can be found in China, India, and Thailand, where the hourly wage rate is 50 cents to $1.00. In addition, companies in developed countries usually pay high fringe benefits and environmental protection costs, which make their costs of doing business even higher. Thus, they have difficulty competing with developing countries in labor-intensive industries. Therefore, many companies have found it necessary to move their manufacturing facilities to countries with low labor costs. Such a global strategy requires extensive communication, frequently in several languages and under several cultural, ethical, and legal conditions. (For more on ethical issues in information technology, see Appendix 1.1 at the end of this chapter.) The complexity of the telecommunication system may greatly hinder competition unless it is properly supported by IT.

Global competition is especially intensified when governments become involved through the use of subsidies, tax policies, and import/export regulations and incentives. Rapid and inexpensive communication and transportation modes increase the magnitude of international trade even further. Previously confined within an industry or a region, competition is now becoming truly global.

Changing Nature of the Workforce. The workforce, particularly in developed countries, is changing rapidly. It is becoming more diversified, as increasing numbers of females, single parents, minorities, and persons with disabilities work in all types of positions. In addition, more employees than ever prefer to defer retirement. Information technology is easing the integration of this wide variety of employees into the traditional workforce. (For more, see the discussions of telecommuting in Chapter 4, and of support for the disabled in Chapter 16).

Powerful Customers. Consumer sophistication and expectations increase as customers become more knowledgeable about the availability and quality of products and services. On the Web, consumers can now easily find detailed information about products and services, compare prices, and buy at electronic auctions. As we mentioned earlier, in some cases they even can name the price they are willing to pay. Companies need to be able to deliver information quickly to satisfy these customers (Choi and Whinston, 2000).

Customers today also want customized products, with high quality and low prices. Vendors must respond, or lose business. For example, a large department store in Japan offers refrigerators in 24 different colors with a delivery time of just a few days. Dell Computer will take an order over the Internet for a computer, made to specifications of your choice, and will deliver that computer to your home within 72 hours. And Nike will let you design your own sneakers online and will make and ship them to arrive at your home in two weeks (*nike.com*). The old saying, "The customer is king" has never before been so true.

Customer Relationship Management (CRM). The importance of customers has created "competition over customers." This competition forces organizations to increase efforts to acquire and retain customers. An enterprisewide effort to do just that is called **customer relationship management (CRM)**. This topic will be addressed in detail in Chapter 7.

TECHNOLOGY PRESSURES. The second category of business pressures consists of those related to technology. Two major pressures in this category are technological innovation and information overload.

Technological Innovation and Obsolescence. Technology is playing an increased role in both manufacturing and services. New and improved technologies create or support substitutes for products, alternative service options, and superb quality. In addition, some of today's state-of-the-art products may be obsolete tomorrow. Thus, technology accelerates the competitive forces. Many technologies affect business in areas ranging from genetic engineering to food processing. However, probably the technology with the greatest impact is information technology (see Evans and Wurster, 1999, and Dertouzos, 1997).

Information Overload. The Internet and other telecommunication networks increase the amount of information available to organizations and individuals. Furthermore, the amount of information available on the Internet more than doubles every year, and most of it is free! The information and knowledge generated and stored inside organizations is also increasing exponentially. It looks as though the world is going to be drowned in a flood of information. Thus, the accessibility, navigation, and management of data, information, and knowledge, which are necessary for managerial decision making, become critical. The only effective solutions are provided by information technology.

SOCIETAL PRESSURES. The third category of business pressures consists of those related to society. These include social responsibility, government regulation/deregulation, spending for social programs, and ethics. The impact of societal pressures is on the increase, especially in developed countries.

Social Responsibility. The interfaces between organizations and society are both increasing and changing rapidly. Social issues that affect business range from the state of the physical environment to companies' contributions to education (e.g., by allowing interns to work in the companies or by sponsoring conferences). Corporations are becoming more aware of these and other social problems, and some are willing to spend time and/or money on solving various social problems. Such activity is known as organizational *social responsibility*. Table 1.2 lists some major areas of social responsibility related to business.

Government Regulations. Several social responsibility issues are related to government regulations regarding health, safety, environmental control, and equal opportunity. For example, companies that spray parts with paint must use paper to absorb the overspray. The paper must then be disposed of by a licensed company, usually at a high cost. Such regulations cost money and make it more difficult to compete with countries that lack such regulations. They also may create the need for changes in organizational structure and processes.

Government Deregulation. Government regulations are usually viewed as expensive constraints on all who are affected. Deregulation, on the other hand,

TABLE 1.2 Major Areas of Social Responsibility

- Environmental control (pollution, noise, trash removal, and animal welfare)
- Equal opportunity (hiring of minorities, women, the elderly, and the disabled)
- Employment and housing (the elderly, poor, teenagers, and unskilled)
- Health, safety, and social benefits to employees (the role of employer versus that of the government)
- Employee education, training, and retraining
- External relationships (community development, political, and other interfaces)
- Marketing practices (fairness, truth)
- Privacy and ethics

can be a blessing to one company but a curse to another that had been protected by the regulation. In general, deregulation intensifies competition.

Ethical Issues. **Ethics** relates to standards of right and wrong, and *business ethics* relates to standards of right and wrong in business practices. Organizations must deal with ethical issues relating to their employees, customers, and suppliers. Ethical issues are very important since they have the power to damage the image of an organization and to destroy the morale of the employees. Ethics is a difficult area because ethical issues are not cut-and-dried. What is considered ethical by one person may seem unethical to another. Likewise, what is considered ethical in one country may be seen as unethical in another.

The use of information technology raises many ethical issues. These range from the monitoring of electronic mail to the potential invasion of privacy of millions of customers whose data are stored in private and public databases. Ethical issues are very important in the digital economy. We consider ethical issues so significant that we have appended to this chapter a general framework of ethics in business and society (Appendix 1.1). Specific ethical issues are discussed in all chapters of the book (and are highlighted by an icon in the margin).

The environments that surround organizations are increasingly becoming more complex and turbulent. Advances in communications, transportation, and technology create many changes. Other changes are the result of political or economic activities. Thus, the pressures on organizations are mounting, and organizations must be ready to take responsive actions if they are to succeed. In addition, organizations may see opportunities in these pressures. Organizational responses to the increasing business pressures are described next.

Organizational Responses

In order to understand the impact of business pressures on organizations we will use a classic management framework, originally developed in the 1960s by Leavitt and later modified by Scott-Morton (Scott-Morton and Allen, 1994) and by the authors of this book. The framework is depicted in Figure 1.5.

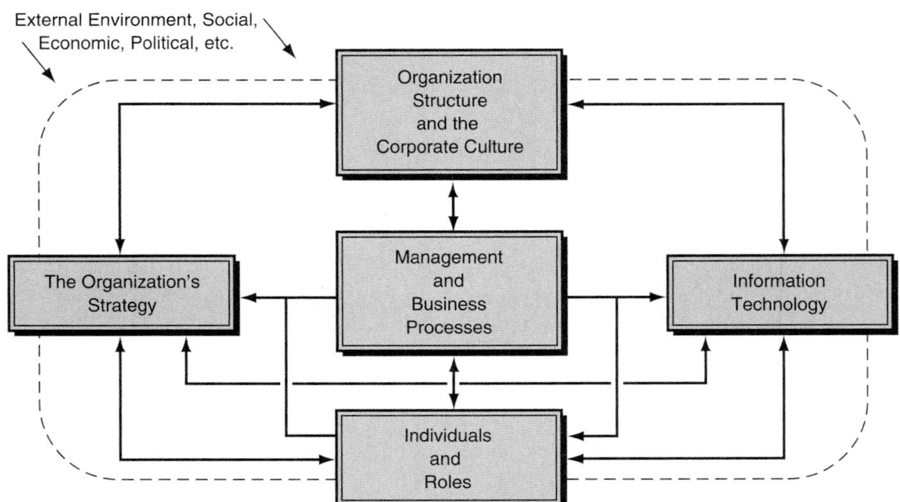

FIGURE 1.5 Framework for organizational and societal impacts of information technology. (*Source:* Compiled from M. Scott-Morton, "DSS Revisited for the 1990s," paper presented at *DSS 1986,* Washington, DC, 1986, and from M. Scott-Morton and T. J. Allen (eds.), *Information Technology and the Corporation of the 1990s,* New York: Oxford University Press, 1994.)

The figure shows that organizations are composed of five major components—one of which is IT. They are surrounded by an external environment, consisting of social, economic, and political forces. The five components of organizations are in a stable condition, called *equilibrium,* as long as no significant change occurs in the external environment or in any of the components. However, as soon as a significant change occurs, the system becomes unstable, and it is necessary to adjust some or all of the internal components. As you can see in the figure, the internal components are interrelated. For example, a significant change in an organization's strategy may create a need for change in the corporate structure. Unstable organizations may be unable to excel or even to survive. Therefore, organizations cannot afford to ignore destabilizing the components, but need to respond by what we call *critical response activities.* Such activities deal not only with long-term strategies, but also with the basic daily business activities.

In addition to changes within a company, there are changes within industries. A typical industry-level change in the digital economy is **disintermediation,** which refers to the elimination of intermediary organizations. Sales take place directly with customers, rather than via intermediaries. Such a situation is shown in Figure 1.6, where you can see that a direct sale can be made either from the manufacturer to the retailer, without a wholesaler; from the wholesaler to the customer, without a retailer; or from the manufacturer to the customer, eliminating all intermediaries. Therefore intermediary organizations must respond to the changes if they are to stay in business.

Traditional responses may not be effective with new problems. Therefore many old solutions need to be modified, supplemented, or eliminated. Organizations can also take *proactive* measures, to create a change in the market place. Such activities also include *exploiting opportunities* created by the external pressures. The major critical response activities are summarized in Figure 1.7.

Organizations' major responses are divided here into five categories: strategic systems for competitive advantage, continuous improvement efforts, business process reengineering (BPR), business alliances, and electronic commerce. (Many of the responses can be interrelated, so the categories sometimes overlap.)

STRATEGIC SYSTEMS. Strategic systems provide organizations with strategic advantages that enable them to increase their market share, to better negotiate with suppliers, or to prevent competitors from entering their territory (Callon, 1996). There are a variety of IT-supported strategic systems, as we will show in Chap-

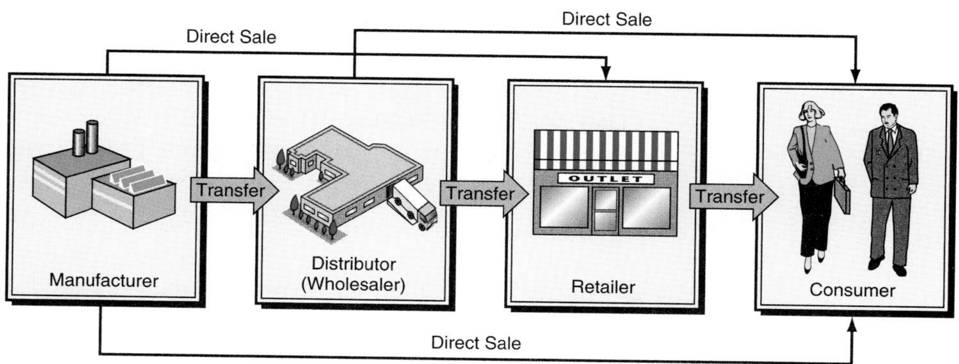

FIGURE 1.6 Disintermediation of distributors and/or retailers.

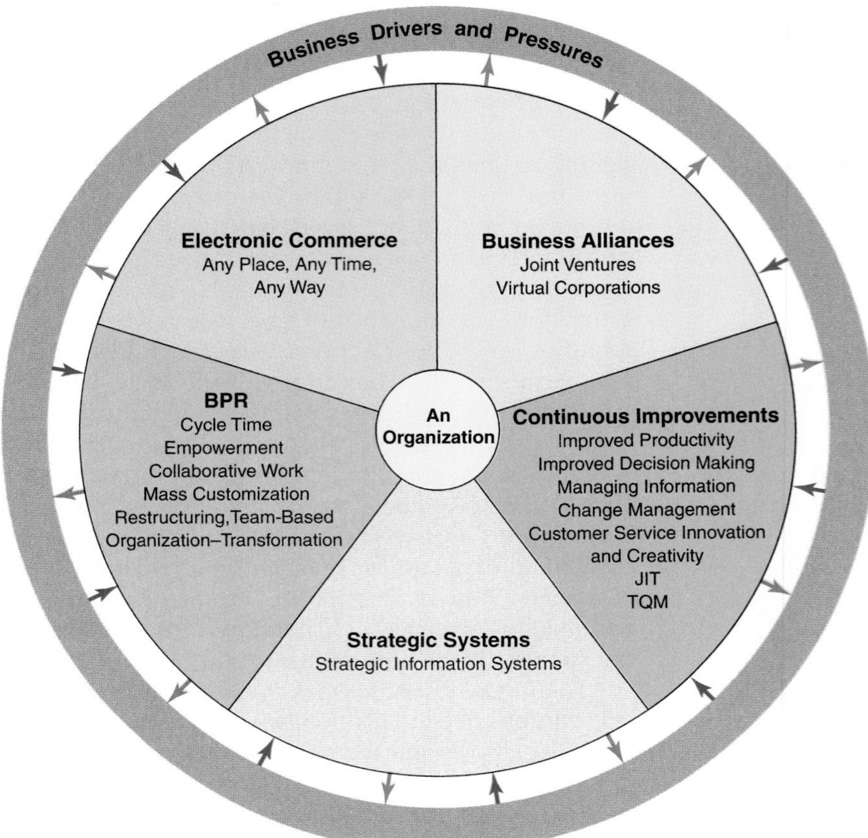

FIGURE 1.7 Critical response activities.

ter 3. A prime example is Federal Express's overnight delivery system. It enables the company to track the status of every individual package, anywhere in the system. Federal Express's system is heavily supported by IT. A major challenge with this kind of strategic system is the difficulty of sustaining competitive advantage. Most of FedEx's competitors duplicated the system. So FedEx moved the system to the Internet. However, the competitors quickly followed, and FedEx is now continuously introducing new innovations to keep or expand market share. For example, in 2000 it announced a plan to form a business alliance with the U.S. Postal Service, in which the USPS will use FedEx planes to ship mail and packages, and FedEx will be able to use post offices as collection centers.

CONTINUOUS IMPROVEMENT EFFORTS. Many companies continuously conduct programs that attempt to improve their productivity and quality. Examples of such programs are:

- ***Improved productivity.*** Productivity is the ratio of outputs to inputs. A firm can improve productivity by increasing output, reducing costs, increasing output faster than costs, and so on. IT is used extensively for productivity improvement, as we illustrate throughout the book and especially in Chapter 7.

- ***Just-in-time.*** The **just-in-time (JIT)** approach is a comprehensive production scheduling and inventory control system. It attempts to reduce costs and improve work flow by scheduling materials and parts to arrive at a workstation exactly when they are needed. JIT minimizes in-process inventories and waste and saves storage space. Although some just-in-time systems can be managed manually, IT makes it easier to implement large and complex JIT systems, as we'll describe in Chapter 7.
- ***Total quality management.*** **Total quality management (TQM)** is a corporate-wide organized effort to improve quality wherever and whenever possible. Information technology can enhance TQM by improving data monitoring, collection, summarization, analysis, and reporting. IT can also increase the speed of inspection, raise the quality of testing, and reduce the cost of performing various quality-control activities. Finally, IT can help avert quality problems before they arise.
- ***Knowledge management.*** Advances in computing and storage capabilities make it easier to create, store, process, and use knowledge. Knowledge management tells us how to do this efficiently and effectively, as shown in Chapter 9.
- ***Improved decision making.*** The term *management* implies making decisions. Appropriate decision making attempts to select the best, or at least a good enough, alternative course of action. This task becomes difficult in a frequently changing environment, when the number of alternatives can be very large and the impacts of the decision can be far reaching as well as difficult to forecast. Also, the cost of making wrong decisions can be very high. Decisions require information that is timely and accurate. IT plays a major role in providing such information, as well as in supporting difficult decision-making processes (see Chapter 10).
- ***Managing enterprise data.*** One of the major pressures described earlier was information overload. To deal with the problem, organizations need to build an appropriate IT infrastructure (Chapter 5, 8, and 11). They also must use effective methods to store, access, navigate, and properly use the vast amount of knowledge and information. In addition to effectively managed data and databases (Chapter 11), organizations need to find and properly interpret information. Intelligent systems are perhaps the most promising approach here (see Chapter 12).
- ***Innovation and creativity.*** Frequent environmental and technological changes require innovative organizational responses. Innovation and creativity can be facilitated by various information technologies, as we will see in Chapters 9, 10, and 12.
- ***Change management.*** Firms' responses to environmental changes may alter how organizations are structured and operated. Therefore, appropriate change-management methodologies are needed. Several information technologies can facilitate change-management activities such as training and presentations (see Chapters 7 and 9).
- ***Customer service.*** The increased power of customers and the stiff competition for them force organizations to improve customer service. In addition to the traditional activities of customer service, organizations are developing innovative Web-based approaches to satisfy customers. As we'll see in Chapters 4, 5, 6, 7 and 12, IT plays a major role in supporting customer service.

This important topic is also considered part of electronic commerce and of the business process reengineering approach, described next.

BUSINESS PROCESS REENGINEERING. Organizations may discover that continuous improvement efforts have limited effectiveness in an environment full of strong business pressures. Therefore, a relatively new approach called **business process reengineering (BPR)** is needed (Chapter 8). Business process reengineering refers to the introduction of a major innovation in an organization's structure and the way it conducts its business. Technological, human, and organizational dimensions of a firm may all be changed in BPR (see Hammer and Champy, 1993). BPR is one of the critical response activities to business pressures. See the appendix on BPR at the book's Web site.

Information technology plays a major role in BPR. It provides automation; it allows business to be conducted in different locations; it provides flexibility in manufacturing; it permits quicker delivery to customers; it creates or facilitates new business models; and it supports rapid and paperless transactions among suppliers, manufacturers, and retailers. The major areas in which IT supports BPR are the following.

- ***Reducing cycle time and time to market.*** Reducing the business process time (cycle time) is extremely important for increasing productivity and competitiveness (see Wetherbe, 1996). Similarly, reducing the time from the inception of an idea until its implementation—*time to market*—is important. Those who can be first in the market with a product, or who can provide customers with a service faster than competitors, enjoy a distinct competitive advantage. Information technology can be used to expedite the various steps in the process of product or service development, testing, and implementation, as shown in the *It at Work* box on the next page.
- ***Empowerment of employees and collaborative work.*** Giving employees the authority to make decisions on their own is a strategy used by many organizations as part of their response activities. Empowerment is related to the concept of self-directed teams. Management delegates authority to teams, who can execute the work faster and with fewer delays than unempowered workers (see Orsburn and Moran, 1999, and Lipnack and Stamps, 1997). IT allows the *decentralization* of decision making and authority but simultaneously supports a centralized control. For example, the Internet and intranets enable empowered employees to access data, information, and knowledge they need for making quick decisions. Computerized advisory systems, called "expert systems," can give experts' advice to team members whenever human experts are not available. In addition, computer networks allow team members to communicate with each other effectively as well as to communicate with other teams in different locations. Finally, a considerable amount of other needed information is publicly available on search engines such as *google.com* or *refdesk.com*.
- ***Customer-focused approach and CRM.*** Companies are increasingly becoming more customer oriented. Companies are finding it necessary to pay more attention to customers and their preferences, and so they are redesigning themselves to meet consumer demands. This can be done in part by changing manufacturing processes from mass production to *mass customization* (see Pine, 1999). In mass production, a company produces a large

IT at Work

WEB TECHNOLOGY IS SHORTENING THE TIME TO MARKET OF NEW DRUGS

www.fda.gov

The Food and Drug Administration (FDA) must be extremely careful in approving new drugs. At the same time, there is public pressure on the FDA to approve new drugs quickly, especially for high-profile diseases such as cancer and AIDS. The problem is that in order to assure quality, and minimize risk, the FDA requires companies to conduct extensive research and clinical testing. The development programs of such research and testing cover 300,000 to 500,000 pages of documentation for each drug. The subsequent results and analysis are reported in an additional 100,000 to 200,000 pages. These pages must then be reviewed by the FDA prior to approval of new drugs. Manual processing of this information significantly delays the work of the FDA, so the total process can take as long as 6 to 10 years.

Several software companies provide software that solves the problems. A pharmaceutical company that uses the software scans all its related documents into a database. The documents are indexed, and full-text-search-and-retrieval software is attached to the system. Using key words, corporate employees can search the database via the company's intranet. The database is also accessible, via an extranet, to the FDA employees, who no longer have to spend hours looking for a specific piece of data. It takes only a few seconds to access an image in the database. (See the screen at right.) Any viewed information can be processed or printed at the user's desktop computer.

The system not only helps the FDA but also the companies' researchers, who now can have any required information at their fingertips. Remote corporate and business partners can also access the system. The overall results: The time to market of a new drug has been reduced by up to a year. Each week saved can be translated into the saving of many lives. It can also yield up to $1,000,000 profit for the pharmaceutical company that gets FDA approval for a new drug. The system also reduces the time it takes to patent a new drug, thus protecting research and development efforts.

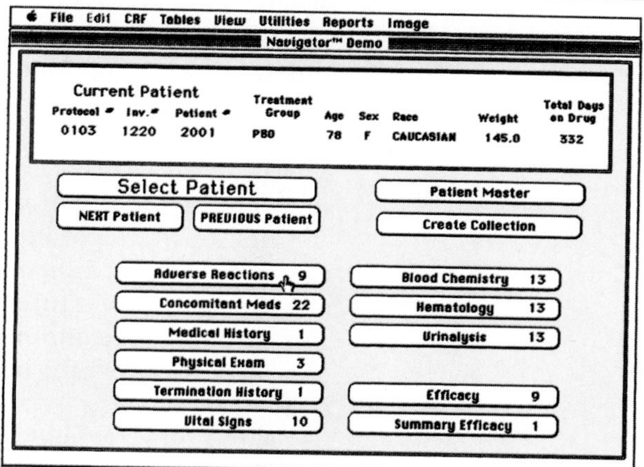

The Internet and intranets shorten time to market.

Recently, companies have been finding ways to further expedite the process. An example is ISIS Pharmaceuticals, a company that develops drugs for treating cancer. The company submits its reports to the FDA electronically, on a CD-ROM. This cuts the FDA's review time by several months. Furthermore, by using an intranet the company can expedite the internal preparation of the report. Smithkline Beecham quickens the process further by using an electronic publishing solution.

For Further Exploration: It is said that these systems help communication, collaboration, and discovery. Explain.

Sources: Condensed from *IMC Journal*, May–June 1993, pp. 23–25; *Inc. Technology*, No. 3, 1997, p. 48; *fda.gov*; and *openmarket.com/products/folio*.

quantity of identical items. In **mass customization**, a company produces items in large quantity but adapts each item to fit the desires of each customer. Information technology supports mass customization (see Chapter 8) and other customer-focused approaches. Details on CRM programs are provided in Chapter 7.

- ***Restructuring and team-based structure.*** One of the premises of BPR is that the organizational structure should fit the business processes. One way to attain this goal is to create many teams, each responsible for a complete business process. As we will see in Chapter 8, such a structure, called a **networked organization**, reduces or eliminates many of the problems created by business pressures. Networked organizations are frequently supported by IT.

BUSINESS ALLIANCES. Many companies realize that alliances with other companies, even competitors, can be very beneficial. For example, General Motors and Ford created a joint venture to explore electronic-commerce applications. There are several types of alliances: sharing resources, doing procurement jointly, establishing a permanent supplier-company relationship, and creating joint research efforts. Any of these might be undertaken in response to business pressures and usually is supported by IT.

One of the most interesting types of business alliance is the *temporary joint venture,* in which companies form a special company for a specific, limited-time mission. Such a venture is an example of a **virtual corporation**, which operates through telecommunications channels, usually without a permanent headquarters. This form of business organization could become common in the future. More details of virtual corporations are provided in Chapter 8.

A more permanent type of business alliance that links manufacturers, suppliers, and finance corporations is known as *keiretsu* (a Japanese term). *Keiretsu*-style collaboration refers to agreements in which the partners learn each other's needs and trust each other, usually signing long-term partnership contracts. This and other types of business alliances can be heavily supported by information technologies ranging from electronic data interchange to electronic transmission of maps and drawings.

ELECTRONIC COMMERCE. Still another form of organizational response to business pressures is electronic commerce. Doing business electronically is the newest and perhaps most promising strategy that many companies can pursue (see Turban et al., 2002). Several of the business models introduced earlier are in fact e-commerce. Chapter 5 will focus extensively on this topic, and e-commerce applications will also be introduced throughout the book.

Information Systems and Information Technology

While some critical response activities can be executed manually, the vast majority require the support of information systems. Before we provide more examples on the role of information systems and IT, let us briefly explore the terms *information system* and *information technology.*

WHAT IS AN INFORMATION SYSTEM? An **information system (IS)** collects, processes, stores, analyzes, and disseminates information for a specific purpose. Like any other system, an information system includes *inputs* (data, instructions) and *outputs* (reports, calculations). It *processes* the inputs and produces outputs that are sent to the user or to other systems. A *feedback* mechanism that controls the operation may be included (see Figure 1.8). Like any other system, an information system operates within an *environment.* An information system is not necessarily computerized, although most of them are. For more on systems, see Appendix 1.2 at the text's Web site.

Formal and Informal Information Systems. An information system can be formal or informal. Formal systems include agreed-upon procedures, standard inputs and outputs, and fixed definitions. A company's accounting system, for example, would be a formal information system that processes financial trans-

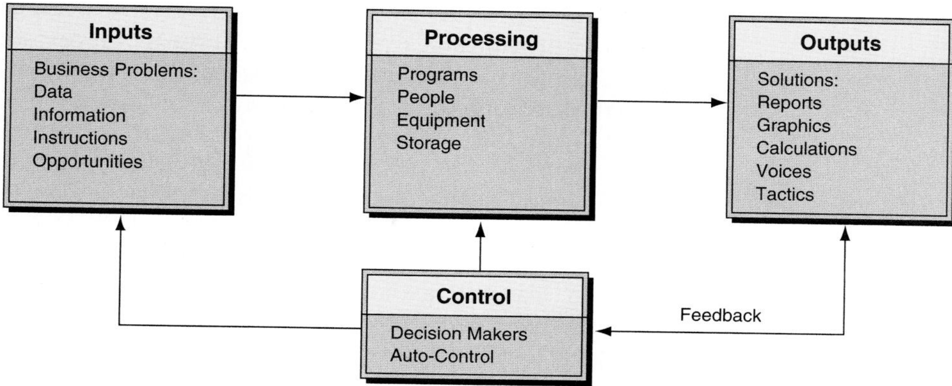

FIGURE 1.8 A schematic view of an information system.

actions. Informal systems take many shapes, ranging from an office gossip network to a group of friends exchanging letters electronically. It is important to understand the existence of informal systems. They may consume information resources and may sometimes interface with the formal systems. They may also play an important role in resisting and/or encouraging change.

WHAT IS A COMPUTER-BASED INFORMATION SYSTEM? A **computer-based information system (CBIS)** is an information system that uses computer technology to perform some or all of its intended tasks. Such a system can include a personal computer and software. Or it may include several thousand computers of various sizes with hundreds of printers, plotters, and other devices, as well as communication networks and databases. In most cases an information system also includes people. The basic components of information systems are listed below. Note that not every system includes all these components.

- ***Hardware*** is a set of devices such as processor, monitor, keyboard, and printer. Together, they accept data and information, process them, and display them.
- ***Software*** is a set of programs that enable the hardware to process data.
- A ***database*** is a collection of related files, tables, relations, and so on, that stores data and the associations among them.
- A ***network*** is a connecting system that permits the sharing of resources by different computers.
- ***Procedures*** are the set of instructions about how to combine the above components in order to process information and generate the desired output.
- ***People*** are those individuals who work with the system or use its output.

In addition, all information systems have a *purpose* and a *social context*. A common *purpose* is to provide a solution to a business problem. In the Bristol-Myers Squibb case, for example, the purpose of the system was to help reduce costs, improve customer service, and expedite administrative processes. The *social context* of the system consists of the values and beliefs that determine what is admissible and possible within the culture of the people and groups involved.

THE DIFFERENCE BETWEEN COMPUTERS AND INFORMATION SYSTEMS. Computers provide effective and efficient ways of processing data, and they are a necessary part of an information system (IS). An IS, however, involves much more than just computers. The successful application of an IS requires an understanding of the business and its environment that is supported by the IS. For example, to build an IS that supports transactions executed on the New York Stock Exchange, it is necessary to understand all the procedures related to buying and selling stocks, bonds, options, and so on, including irregular demands made on the system, as well as all related government regulations.

In learning about IS, it is therefore not sufficient just to learn about computers. Computers are only one part of a complex system that must be designed, operated, and maintained. A public transportation system in a city provides an analogy. Buses are a necessary ingredient of the system, but more is needed. Designing the bus routes, bus stops, different schedules, and so on requires considerable understanding of customer demand, traffic patterns, city regulations, safety requirements, and the like. Computers, like buses, are only one component in a complex system.

WHAT IS INFORMATION TECHNOLOGY? *Information technology,* in its narrow definition, refers to the technological side of an information system. It includes the hardware, databases, software, networks, and other devices. It can be viewed as a subsystem of an information system. Sometimes, though, the term *IT* is also used interchangeably with *information system.* Or it may even be used in a broad way to describe a collection of several information systems, users, and management for an entire organization. In this book, we use the term IT in this broadest sense. The purpose of this book is to acquaint you with all aspects of information systems/information technology.

Now that the basic terms have been defined, we present some examples of IS applications worldwide.

1.3 EXAMPLES OF INFORMATION SYSTEMS AT WORK WORLDWIDE

Millions of different information systems are in use throughout the world. The following examples are intended to show the diversity of applications and the benefits provided. At the end of each example, we list the critical response activities supported by the system. (More examples are shown at the book's Web site.)

Success Stories

As the examples in this section show, information systems are being used successfully in all functional areas of business. Beginning here, and throughout this book, we will call out, in the margins, the functional areas to which our real-world examples apply. Our purpose in doing this is to show how information technology is being integrated into accounting, production and operations management, human resources management, finance, marketing, public service, and health care.

Managing Accounting Information Across Asia. Le Saunda Holding Company (Hong Kong) manages 32 subsidiaries in four Asian countries, mostly in the manufacture, import, and sale of shoes (*lesaunda.com.hk*). Managing the financing and cash flow is a complex process. All accounting information flows to headquarters electronically. Sales data are electronically collected at point-of-sale (POS) terminals. Together with inventory data (which are updated automatically when a sale occurs), they are transferred to headquarters. Other relevant data, such as advertising and sales promotions, merchants, and cash flow, are also transmitted electronically and collected in a centralized database for storage and processing.

Integrating IT ...in Accounting

To cope with the rapid growth of the company, a sophisticated accounting software package was installed. The result was radical improvements in accounting procedures. For example, it now takes less than 10 minutes, rather than a day, to produce an ad-hoc special report. The company's accountants can now generate reports as they are needed, helping functional managers make quicker and better decisions. The system is also much more reliable, and internal and external auditing is easier. Headquarters knows what is going on almost as soon as it occurs. All these improvements have led to a substantial growth in revenue and profits for the firm. (*Source*: *lesaunda.com.hk*)

Critical response activities supported: Decision making, managing large amounts of information, improving quality, reduced cycle time.

Putting Community Health Care Online. Residents of Marysville, Kansas, a rural town of 12,000, enjoy a sophisticated health care system. This system connects the town's hospitals, insurance companies, clinics, local schools, ambulances, police, and the county health department into a seamless intranet-based data network. Here is how the system works.

Integrating IT ...in Health Care

Suppose a boy had an accident playing basketball at school. The school nurse calls for an ambulance and then enters the details of the injury on the intranet. A wireless system presents the details to the medics at the ambulance, so they can make appropriate preparations. The emergency room doctor also is alerted via the intranet. After reading the details, she checks the boy's medical history, including the immunization record available at the county's health department. Meanwhile, the medics have arrived at the scene and provide the most appropriate treatment. If needed, they can take photos and transmit them instantly to doctors via the Internet. The doctor provides appropriate transport instructions. The hospital is readied for the boy's arrival and is prepared to operate, should surgery be needed. (*Sources*: *Interactivework*, March 9, 1998, and *medgenix.com*, 2001.)

Critical response activities supported: Reduced cycle time, improved decision making of medics and doctors, distribution of information.

Integrating IT ...in Production & Operations Management, Marketing, and Accounting

www.mariner.mlb.com

Seattle Mariners Using Technology for Profitability. The Seattle Mariners baseball team is playing in a new stadium as of July 1999, a stadium that uses advanced information technologies to increase profitability. The stadium is wired with an integrated voice and data communication system. One of its major applications is to provide real-time inventory counts—so that hungry fans will never be without a hot dog or beer. All the cash registers are networked, and the concession vendors are equipped with wireless communication devices. All sales are monitored in real time, and replenishment is done according to these sales records, so shortages and lost revenues are eliminated. In addition to inventory control the enterprise network is used for the following purposes:

- Providing Internet access from certain "smart" seats, so you can find out what's going on outside the stadium at any time.
- Purchasing tickets for future games from kiosks that are scattered throughout the stadium.

- Producing a revenue report within hours after a game, rather than days.
- Frequent-attendance promotions, in which visitors can swipe smart cards through readers and get points for attending games.

The only downside of the new system is that if a main data center fails, the company may lose 50 percent of the concessions revenues that day.

Critical response activities provided: Decision making, increased sales, dissemination of information, electronic purchasing, improved supply chain.

Integrating IT ...in Marketing

www.campusfood.com

The Success Story of Campusfood.com. Campusfood.com's recipe for success was a simple one: Provide interactive menus to college students, using the power of the Internet to enhance traditional telephone ordering of meals. Launched at the University of Pennsylvania, the company took thousands of orders for local restaurants, bringing pizza, hoagies, and wings to the Penn community.

Founder Michael Saunders began developing the site in 1997 while he was a junior at Penn. With the help of some classmates, the site was launched in 1998. After graduation, Saunders began building the company's customer base. This involved registering other schools, attracting students, and generating a list of local restaurants from which students could order food to be delivered. Currently, this activity is outsourced to a marketing firm, and schools nationwide are being added to the list.

Financed through private investors, friends, and family members, the site was built on an investment of less than one million dollars. (For comparison, another company, with services also reaching the college-student market, has investments of $100 million.) Campusfood.com's revenue is generated through transaction fees; the site takes a 5 percent commission on each order.

When you visit *Campusfood.com,* you can:

- Search a list of local restaurants, their hours of operation, address, phone number and other information.
- Browse an interactive menu. The company takes a restaurant's standard print menus and researches each one in order to list every topping, every special, and every drink offered, along with the latest prices.
- Place an order (without being placed on hold), avoid miscommunications, and bypass busy signals.
- Get access to more specials and restaurant giveaways. The company is working to get even more meal deals available online exclusively to Campusfood.com customers.
- Get many additional features, including electronic payments.

(For more information see M. Prince, "Easy Doesn't Do It," *Wall Street Journal,* July 17, 2000. ©2000 Dow Jones & Company, Inc.)

Critical response activities supported: Customer service, improved cycle time, and innovative marketing method.

Information System Failures

So far we have introduced you to many success stories. You may wonder, though, is IT all success? The answer is absolutely not. There are many failures. We will show you some of these in most chapters of the book and in some cases present them on our Web site. We can learn from failures as much as we can learn from successes, as illustrated in the following *IT at Work* case.

IT at Work

Integrating IT ...in Government

THE MOTHER OF ALL FAILURES, THE 2000 U.S. PRESIDENTIAL ELECTION

Vote-counting machines have been used in the United States for decades in order to expedite the counting of votes and to ensure election integrity. Using information technologies such as optical readers, these machines counted millions of votes in many elections, without any major problem. All of this changed in November 2000, when it was found that the 20- to 30-year-old machines and the accompanying information processing and procedures generated the greatest election confusion ever encountered, followed by a lengthy and expensive legal and political battle.

What happened? When it became clear that now-President George W. Bush's victory margin in Florida, as counted by the machines, was slim, Vice President Gore attempted to prove that the machine count was inaccurate. Gore claimed that the count of the old machines, and their supporting information-processing procedures, did not reflect the *intention* of the voters. That is, the technology failed to do its job. So Gore wanted a manual recount of votes in specified counties in the state. The problem was that a manual count might bring the voting process back to the preautomation period, namely to the possibility of human errors, fraud, and ballot tampering.

What's the solution for the future? Introduce *digital-age voting machines,* which are in use in several countries. How do these machines work? Voting is done directly on a computer screen, or by using old-style punch card machines. The innovation of the digital age is that while the voter is still in the polling booth, and regardless of what type of machine he or she is voting on, a computer screen displays the vote, as recorded. Before leaving the booth, the voter is asked to verify the record shown on the screen. This is a simple procedure that we all use in other online settings—such as in conducting stock trading, banking, or shopping. It is called **nonrepudiation**, which means verifying the *intention* of the users and making sure that the user will not later deny the choice. With such a system, voters will not be able to later complain that the machine made a mistake. Once verified, the votes can be tabulated by computers very quickly.

As a matter of fact, in November 2000 the U.S. National Science Foundation (*nsf.gov*) was in the middle of a study about *digital voting.* One of the major problems in voting online is security, especially if voting is done from home. Other issues in online voting are privacy protection, and the possibility of fraud. In addition, there is the possibility that online elections could change the nature of politics and the power distribution between the federal government and the states. It is interesting to note that according to a senior expert at the prestigious Brookings Institution (*brookings.org*), the members of the U.S. Congress are too used to the old system and don't want to change to a new system, no matter what it is. This opinion was rendered in early 2000, well before the November election. It may be a different story today. (For further discussion, see *e-advocates.com; brookings.org;* Brown, 2000; and Hendren, 2000.)

For Further Exploration: Why may politics become personal if done online? Will more people vote if they can do it from home?

1.4 Information Technology Developments and Trends

In the previous section, we described the role of IT in supporting business activities. We also pointed out some of the capabilities (Table 1.1) that enable IT to play a support role. Next we will describe some of IT's developments and trends (see Chandra et al., 2000), and especially the move toward networked computing. But first imagine this scenario:

It's a Monday morning in the year 2003. Executive Joanne Smith gets into her car, and her voice activates a remote telecommunications-access workstation. She requests that all voice and mail messages open and pending, as well as her schedule for the day, be transmitted to her car. The office workstation consolidates these items from home and office databases. The message-ordering "knowbot" (knowledge robot), which is an enhanced e-mail messaging system, delivers the accumulated messages (in the order she prefers) to the voice and data wireless device in Joanne's car. By the time Joanne gets to the office, she has heard the necessary messages, sent some replies, revised her day's schedule, and completed a "to-do" list for the week, all of which have been filed in her virtual database by her personal organizer knowbot.

The virtual organizer and the intranet have made Joanne's use of IT much easier. No longer does she have to be concerned about the physical location of data. She is working on a large proposal for the Acme Corporation today; and although segments of the Acme file physically exist on several databases, she can access the data from her *wireless workstation* wherever she happens to be. To help manage this information resource, Joanne uses an *information visualizer* that enables her to create and manage dynamic relationships among data collections. This information visualizer has extended the graphical user interface to a three-dimensional graphic structure.

Joanne could do even more work if her car were able to drive itself. Although this kind of car is still in an experimental stage, it will probably be in commercial use sometime during the twenty-first century. As a matter of fact, a limited use of such cars is expected in California by the year 2010 (see Chapter 12).

The year-2003 scenario is becoming a reality even sooner, owing to important trends in information technology. These trends, which are listed in Table 1.3 and described below, fall into two categories: general and networked computing. Here we describe only selected trends. The rest are described in the Technology Guides near the end of the book and on the text's Web site.

GENERAL TECHNOLOGICAL TRENDS

General trends are relevant to any computing system. They include the following.

COST-PERFORMANCE RATIO: IMPROVEMENT BY A FACTOR OF AT LEAST 100. In about 10 years, a computer will cost the same as its costs today but will be about 50 times more powerful (in terms of processing speed, memory, and so on). At the same time labor costs could double, so the cost-performance ratio of computers versus manual work will improve by a factor of 100. This means that computers will have increasingly greater comparative advantage over people. This phenomenon is based on Moore's Law.

> **Moore's Law:** Gordon Moore, the co-founder of Intel, predicted in 1965 that the processing power of silicon chips would double every 18 months. And so it has, resulting in enormous increases in computer processing capacity and a sharp decline in cost (see Chapter 13).
>
> *Extension:* Moore's Law applies to electronic chips. A companion to Moore's law, according to McGarvey (2000) and *tenornetworks.com,* states that the performance of optical communication networks (see Technology Guide 4) is growing by a factor of 10 every three years.

OBJECT-ORIENTED ENVIRONMENT AND DOCUMENT MANAGEMENT. An *object-oriented environment* is an innovative way of programming and using computers that is expected to significantly reduce the cost of both building and maintaining information systems. **Object technology** enables the development of self-contained units of software that can be shared, purchased, and/or reused. These information assets can be used for various purposes within a single organization's information systems, or they can be used in a worldwide network of interorganizational

TABLE 1.3 Major Technological Developments and Trends

General

- The cost-performance advantage of computers over manual labor will increase.
- Graphical and other user-friendly interfaces will dominate PCs.
- Storage capacity will increase dramatically.
- Data warehouses will store ever-increasing amounts of information.
- Multimedia use, including virtual reality, will increase significantly.
- Intelligent systems, especially artificial neural computing and expert systems, will increase in importance.
- The use of intelligent agents will make computers smarter.
- Object-oriented programming and document management will be widely accepted.
- Computers will be increasingly compact.
- The use of "plug-and-play" software will increase.

Networked Computing

- Optical computing will increase network capacity and speed, facilitating the use of the Internet.
- Computers will be smaller, more portable.
- Mobile and wireless applications will become a major component of IT.
- Home computing will be integrated with the telephone, television, and other electronic services to create smart appliances.
- The use of the Internet will grow, and it will change the way we live, work, and learn.
- Corporate portals will connect companies with their employees, business partners, and the public.
- Intranets will be the dominating network systems in most organizations.
- Electronic commerce will grow rapidly, changing the manner in which business is conducted.
- Intelligent software agents will roam through databases and networks, conducting time-consuming tasks for their masters.
- Interpersonal transmission will grow (one-to-one, one-to-many, many-to-many).
- More transactions among organizations will be conducted electronically, in what is called business-to-business (B2B) commerce.

information systems. This environment includes object-oriented programming, databases, and operating systems that increase the capabilities of IT and its cost effectiveness (Chandra et al., 2000). The increased use of multimedia and object-oriented systems makes electronic document management one of the most important topics of IT.

Networked Computing

The technology of networked computing is emerging rapidly. This technology enables users to reach other users and to access databases anywhere in the organization and in any other place. The networks' power stems from Metcalfe's Law.

Metcalfe's Law: Robert Metcalfe, a pioneer of computer networks, claims that the value of a network grows roughly in line with the square of the number of its users. Thus, if you increase the number of users, say, from 2 to 10, the value will change from 2^2 (= 4) to 10^2 (= 100), or 25 times more. With 350 million Internet users, the value is $(350 \text{ million})^2$, an astronomical number.

Kelly's extension: The value of the Internet is much larger, according to Kelly (1999). The reason is that Metcalfe's law of n^2 is based on the idea of the telephone network, where the connections are point-to-point. On the Internet we can make multiple simultaneous connections between groups of people. So the potential value of the Internet is n^n, which is a much larger number.

MOBILE COMMERCE. **M-commerce (mobile commerce)** refers to the conduct of e-commerce via wireless devices. It is the commercial application of **mobile computing**, which is based on wireless networks (see Technology Guide 4). There is a strong interest in the topic because the number of mobile devices, according to industry research firms, is projected to top 1 billion by 2004. Furthermore, these devices can be connected to the Internet, enabling transactions to be made from anywhere and enabling many applications (see *A Closer Look* 1.1). For example, m-commerce can offer customers the location information of anything they want to purchase. This is a useful feature for customers but is even more important for merchants because it enables customers to act instantly on any shopping impulse. This wireless application is referred to as *location-based commerce,* or **l-commerce**. (For details see Chapter 5.)

THE NETWORK COMPUTER. In 1997, the *network computer* was introduced. This computer does not have a hard drive. Instead, it is served by a central computing station, and at a "dumb" (passive) terminal, it temporarily receives and can use applications and data stored elsewhere on the network. Also called "thin clients," network computers are designed to provide the benefits of desktop computing without the high cost of PCs. Prices of network computers are getting close to $200.

INTEGRATED HOME COMPUTING. Soon, home computing, television, telephone, home security systems, and other devices will be integrated and managed in one unit. Assuming such a unit will be easy to operate, the integrated system will facilitate telecommuting and the use of the Internet. These systems also provide the basis for smart appliances. **Smart appliances** refer to home appliances that are connected to the Internet and among themselves for increased capabilities. For example, Sharp Electronics demonstrated an intelligent microwave oven that can download recipes from the Internet and cook food according to instructions it receives remotely. (See Choi and Whinston, 2000.)

THE INTERNET. From about 50 million Internet users in 1997, there could be as many as 750 million by 2007. The wireless devices that access the Internet and the integration of television and computers will allow the Internet to reach every home, business, school, and other organization. Then the **information superhighway** will be complete. This is a national fiber-optic-based network and wireless infrastructure that will connect all Internet users in a country, and will change the manner in which we live, learn, and work. Singapore is likely to be the first country to have such a national information superhighway completely installed, as *A Closer Look* 1.2 discusses.

INTRANETS AND EXTRANETS. As the intranet concept spreads and the supporting hardware and software are standardized, it is logical to assume that most organizations will use an intranet for internal communication. Combining an intranet with the Internet, in what is called an *extranet,* creates powerful interorganizational systems for communication and collaboration. Intranets and the Internet are accessed via information portals.

A CLOSER LOOK
1.1 MOBILE AND WIRELESS APPLICATIONS

Mobile computing supports existing and entirely new kinds of applications. For example:

- ***Mobile personal communications capabilities,*** such as personal digital assistants (PDAs) and cell phones for networked communications and applications.
- ***Online transaction processing.*** For example, a salesperson in a retail environment can enter an order for goods and also charge a customer's credit card to complete the transaction.
- ***Remote database queries.*** For example, a salesperson can use a mobile network connection to check an item's availability or the status of an order, directly from the customer's site.
- ***Dispatching,*** like air traffic control, rental car pickup and return, delivery vehicles, trains, taxis, cars, and trucks.
- ***Front-line IT applications.*** Instead of the same data being entered multiple times as it goes through the value chain, it is entered only once and transmitted electronically thereafter.
- ***M-commerce.*** Users of wireless devices can access the Internet, conduct information searches, collaborate with others and make decisions jointly, and buy and sell from anywhere.

Wireless communications support both mobile computing applications and low-cost substitutions for communication cables. For example:

- Temporary offices can be set up quickly and inexpensively by using wireless network connections.
- Wireless connections to permanent office locations are often practical in difficult or hazardous wiring environments.
- Installing a wireless connection can replace leased lines that are used to connect local area networks (LANs), thus eliminating the costs of monthly line leases.

There are mobile and wireless application opportunities in many industries, such as:

- ***Retail.*** This has been a very successful application to date, particularly in department stores where there are frequent changes of layout. Also retail sales personnel can conduct inventory inquiries or even sales transactions on the retail floor with wireless access from their PCs or cell phones.
- ***Wholesale/distribution.*** Wireless networking is used for inventory picking in warehouses with PCs mounted on forklifts, and for delivery and order status updates with PCs inside distribution trucks.
- ***Field service/sales.*** Mobile computing can be used for dispatching, online diagnostic support from customer sites, and parts-ordering/inventory queries in all types of service and sales functions.
- ***Factories/manufacturing.*** Environments and applications include mobile shop-floor quality control systems or wireless applications that give added flexibility for temporary setups.
- ***Health care/hospitals.*** Health care personnel need to access and send data to patient records, or consult comparative diagnosis databases, wherever the patient or the health care worker may be located.
- ***Education.*** Pilot applications equip students with PCs in lecture halls, linked by a wireless network, for interactive quizzes, additional data and graphics lecture support, and online handout materials.
- ***Banking/finance.*** Mobile transactional capabilities can assist in purchasing, selling, inquiry, brokerage, and other dealings, using the Internet or private networks.

CORPORATE PORTALS. A **corporate portal** refers to a company's Web site that is used as a *gateway* to the corporate data, information, and knowledge. Corporate portals may be used both by employees and by outsiders, such as customers or suppliers. Employees have a password that allows them to access data through the portal that is not available to the public.

THE NETWORKED ENTERPRISE. The various components and technologies just described can be integrated together into an enterprisewide network that can be extended to all business partners. Netscape described this concept as follows:

A CLOSER LOOK
1.2 A NETWORKED INTELLIGENT COUNTRY

In Singapore, information technology is a national priority. This country of 3 million people became the first country with an advanced nationwide information infrastructure, which connects virtually every home, office, school, and factory. The computer evolved into an information appliance, combining the functions of the telephone, TV, computers, and more. The nationwide network provides a wide range of communication means and access to services.

Singaporeans are able to tap into vast reservoirs of electronically stored information and knowledge to improve their businesses and quality of life. Text, sound, pictures, videos, documents, designs, and other forms of media can be transferred and shared through the high capacity of the national fiber-optic telecommunication system, working in tandem with a pervasive wireless network. A wide range of new infrastructural services—linking government, businesses, and people—were created to take advantage of new telecommunications (see *s-one.gov.sg*).

The project is a joint government-industry venture based on five strategic thrusts:

1. Developing Singapore as a global hub for business, services, and transportation
2. Improving the quality of life for Singaporeans
3. Boosting the economic engine, increasing the competitiveness of the island's industries, and decreasing unemployment (see *ec.gov.sg*)

IT enables monitoring of operations at Singapore's ports, a major hub of business.

4. Linking communities locally and globally
5. Enhancing the capabilities of individuals

The *networked enterprise* comprises one seamless network, extending the corporate contacts to all the entities a company does business with. The networked enterprise provides two primary benefits:

- By creating new types of services, businesses can engage customers in a direct interactive relationship that results in customers getting precisely what they want when they want it, resulting in stronger customer relationships. Also, relationships with suppliers and other business partners are improved.
- By taking the entire product design process online—drawing partners and customers into the process and removing the traditional communication barriers that prevent rapid product design and creation—companies can bring products and services to market far more quickly. (*Source: www.netscape.com*, 1997.)

The networked enterprise is shown schematically in Figure 1.9. As a result of the technology pressures discussed earlier, companies that implement standards-based intranets can quickly create or join extranets, as we discuss in Chapter 5.

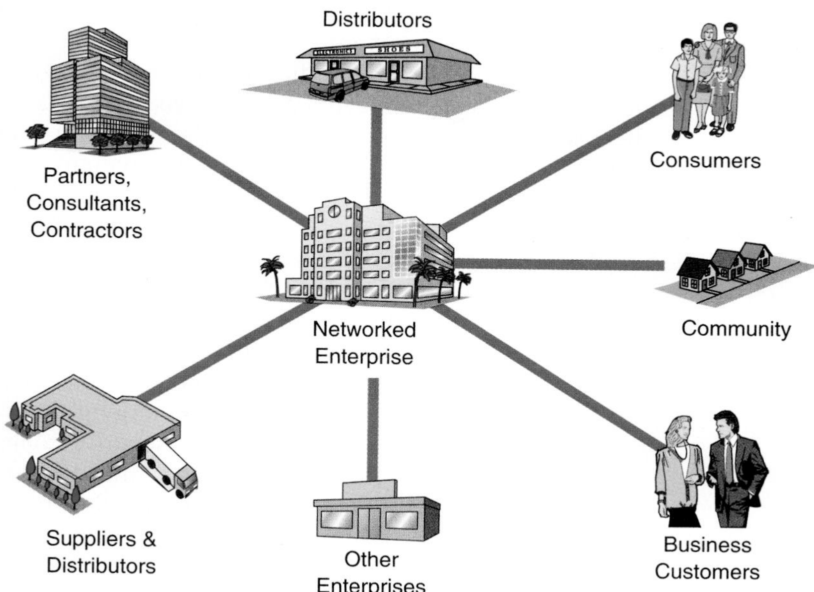

FIGURE 1.9 The networked enterprise.

OPTICAL NETWORKS. A major revolution in network technology is *optical networks*. These are high-capacity telecommunication networks that convert signals in the network to colors of light and transmit these over fiber-optic filaments. Optical networks are useful in Internet, video, multimedia interaction, and advanced digital services. (For more, see Technology Guide 4.)

All of these developments and prospects will increase the importance of IT both at home and at work. Therefore, to function effectively at home or at work, it makes sense to learn about IT.

1.5 Why Should You Learn About Information Technology?

We demonstrated in this chapter that we live in the digital age, and that the ways we live and do business are changing drastically. The field of IT is also growing rapidly, especially with the introduction of the Internet and EC, so the organizational impacts keep increasing. In this part of the chapter we describe some specific benefits you can derive from studying IT.

Being IT Literate On the Job and Off

This opening chapter stresses the role of IT as a facilitator of organizational activities and processes. That role will become more important as time passes. Therefore, it is necessary that every manager and professional staff member learn about IT not only in his or her specialized field, but also in the entire organization as well as in interorganizational settings.

Obviously, you will be more effective in your chosen career if you understand how successful information systems are built, used, and managed. You also will be more effective if you know how to recognize and avoid unsuccessful systems and failures. (Failures are shown throughout the book and in Chapter 13, and they are marked with a marginal icon like the one on page 24.) Also, in many ways, having a comfort level with information technology will enable you, off the job, in your private life, to take advantage of new IT products and systems as they are developed. (Wouldn't you rather be the one explaining to friends how some new product works, than the one asking about it?) Finally, you should learn about IT because of the many employment opportunities in this field.

Finding Employment Opportunities in IT

Addressing the issues listed in the previous sections requires considerable knowledge about IT and its management. However, being knowledgeable about information technology can also increase employment opportunities. Even though computerization eliminates some jobs, it also creates many more.

The demand for traditional information technology staff—such as programmers, systems analysts, and designers—is substantial. In addition, many well-paid opportunities are appearing in emerging areas such as the Internet and e-commerce, m-commerce, network security, object-oriented programming, telecommunications, multimedia design, and document management. The U.S. Department of Labor reported that among the twelve fastest-growing employment areas, four are IT-related. These four accounted in 2000 for about 50 percent of all additional jobs in the twelve areas. A study by the Information Technology Association of America (*itaa.org*) documented shortage of employees for about 350,000 IT positions in the United States. At about $60,000 per year, workers in the software and information services industries were the highest-paid U.S. wage earners in 2000, about twice that of the average worker in the private sector. Furthermore, earnings of IT employees were growing twice as fast as those in the entire private sector. Thus, salaries for IT employees are very high (see Table 1.4).

To exploit the high-paying opportunities in IT, a college degree in any of the following fields, or combination of them, is advisable: computer science, computer information systems (CIS), management information systems (MIS), electronic commerce, and e-business. Within the last few years, many universities have started e-commerce or e-business degrees (e.g., see *is.cityu.edu.hk* and *cgu.edu*). Many schools offer graduate degrees with specialization in information technology.

Majoring in an IT-related field can be very rewarding. For example, students graduating with baccalaureate degrees in MIS usually earn the highest starting salaries of all undergraduate business majors (more than $45,000 per year). MBAs with education in Internet technologies and e-commerce education were getting starting salaries of over $100,000/year, plus signing bonuses. Many students prefer a double major, one of which is MIS. Similarly, MBAs with an undergraduate degree in computer science or CIS have no difficulty getting well-paying jobs, even during recessionary times. Many MBA students select IS as a major, a second major, or an area of specialization. Finally, nondegree programs are also available on hundreds of topics. For details about careers in IT, see *techjourney.com* (see Career resources and also Technology careers at "Webwage").

FUTURE ORGANIZATIONAL LEADERSHIP. In the past, most CEOs came from the areas of finance and marketing. Lately, however, we see a trend to appoint CEOs who emerge from the technology area, or at least who have strong IT knowledge. This trend is likely to continue. Therefore, IT education is necessary for anyone who aspires to lead a firm in the future.

TABLE 1.4 IT Compensation by Job Titles (annual salaries, year 2000, 12 years' average experience)

Compensation by Job Title for Management Positions	
Vice President Information Technology	$125,000
Chief Information Officer	$110,000
Chief Technology Officer	$90,000
Senior Manager	$90,000
Compensation by Job Function for Staff Positions	
Enterprise Resource Planning	$73,000
Enterprise Application Integration	$73,000
Security	$70,000
Application Development	$66,000
Database Analysis and Development	$65,000
Data Center Management	$65,000
Compensation by Job Function for Management Positions	
Enterprise Application Integration	$90,000
Enterprise Resource Planning	$89,000
Application Development	$86,000
General IT Management	$80,000
Internet/Intranet	$80,000
Best Pay Raises for Management Functions (During 2000)	
Internet/Intranet	12.5%
Networking	10.6%
Telecommunications/Call Center	10.1%
Enterprise Application Integration	9.4%
General IT Management	9.1%
Database Analysis and Development	9.1%

Sources: Based on survey of 16,900 IT professionals conducted by *Information Week;* data extracted from *http://salaryadvisor.informationweek.com/ibi_html/iwsaloo,* and from *Techjourney.com* (search for IT Salary Advisor).

1.6 PLAN OF THE BOOK

A major objective of this book is to demonstrate how IT in general and Web systems in particular support different organizational activities. In addition, we will illustrate the role that networked computing plays in our society today and will play tomorrow. Furthermore, we describe how information systems should be developed, maintained, and managed.

We have divided the book into six parts. Figure 1.10 shows how the chapters are positioned in each part and how the parts are connected. The contents of the parts are described at the text's Web site.

Organizations and IT Support
Information Technology in the Digital Economy — Ch. 1
IT Concepts and Management — Ch. 2
Organization Responses:
Strategic Information Systems for Competitive Advantage — Ch. 3

The Web Revolution
Network Computing: Discovery, Collaboration, and Communication — Ch. 4
Electronic Commerce — Ch. 5
Supply Chain Management and ERP — Ch. 6

Organizational Applications
Transaction Processing — Ch. 7
IT Planning and BPR — Ch. 8
Knowledge Management — Ch. 9

Technology Guides
1. Hardware (at Web site)
2. Software (at Web site)
3. Databases
4. Telecommunications
5. The Internet (at Web site)

Managerial IT Support
Decision Support Systems — Ch. 10
Data Management — Ch. 11
Intelligent Support Systems — Ch. 12

Implementing and Managing IT
Information Economics — Ch. 13
Building Information Systems — Ch. 14
Managing Information Resources — Ch. 15
Impacts and Future — Ch. 16

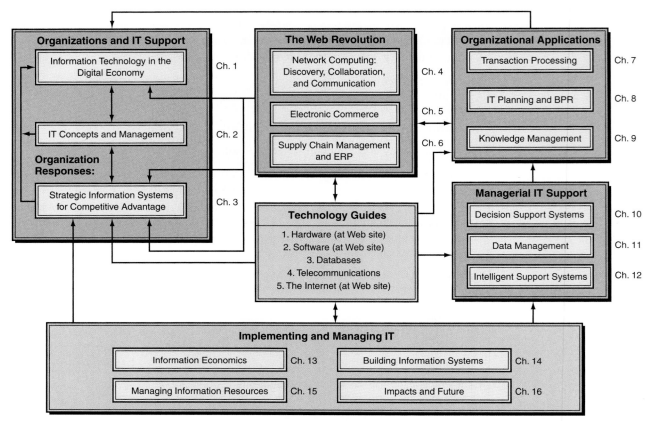

FIGURE 1.10 Plan of the book.

TECHNOLOGY GUIDES. The technology that is used for the infrastructure and the specific applications can be divided into five major categories: *hardware* (Technology Guide 1), *software* (Technology Guide 2), *databases and their management* (Technology Guide 3), *telecommunications and networks* (Technology Guide 4), and the *Internet* (Technology Guide 5). Technology Guides 3 and 4 can be found at the end of the book, and Technology Guides 1, 2, and 5 can be found on the Web site.

MANAGERIAL ISSUES

At the end of every chapter, we list some managerial issues relating to the topics covered in the chapter. For Chapter 1, these are as follows.

1. ***How can we recognize the opportunities for using IT and Web-based systems?*** These opportunities are highlighted and discussed in most chapters of the book, but especially in Chapters 3, 5, 6, 8, and 13.
2. ***Who is going to build, operate, and maintain the information systems?*** This is a critical issue because management wants to minimize the cost of IT while maximizing its benefits. Some alternatives are to outsource portions, or even all, of the IT activities, and to divide work between the IS department and the end users. Details will be provided in Chapters 13 through 15.

3. ***How much IT?*** This is a critical question related to IT planning. IT does not come free, but *not* having it may be much costlier. Chapters 8 and 13 deal with this issue.
4. ***How important is IT?*** In some cases, IT is the only approach that can help organizations. As time passes, the *comparative advantage* of IT increases.
5. ***Is the situation going to change?*** Yes, the pressures will be stronger as time passes. Therefore, the IT role will be even more important.
6. ***How about globalization?*** Global competition will have an impact on many companies. However, globalization opens many opportunities, ranging from selling products and services online in foreign markets, to conducting joint ventures or investing in them. IT supports communications, collaboration, and discovery of information regarding all the above.

7. ***What about ethics and social issues?*** The implementation of IT involves many ethical and social issues that are constantly changing due to new developments in technologies and environments. These topics should be examined any time an IT project is undertaken. Appendix 1.1 at the end of this chapter presents an introduction to ethics. Ethical issues are highlighted in most chapters throughout the book.
8. ***How can an organization transform itself to the digital economy?*** The transformation can be done on several fronts, as Bristol-Myers Squibb did. Management should study the opportunities, consider alternatives, and prioritize them. A prime area to start with is e-procurement (Chapters 5 and 6).

ON THE WEB SITE... Additional resources, including the Virtual Company, quizzes, cases, updates, additional exercises, links, demos, and activities, can be found on the book's Web site.

KEY TERMS

CHAPTER HIGHLIGHTS (Numbers Refer to Learning Objectives)

1 The world is moving to the digital economy, which can be viewed as a major economic, societal, and organizational revolution.

1 The digital economy is characterized by extensive use of information technology in general and the Internet in particular. These drive new business models that dramatically reduce cost and increase quality, customer service, and speed.

2 Many pressures surround the modern organization, which is responding with critical response activities supported by information technology.

3 An accelerated rate of change, complexity, and turbulence and a move toward a global economy today characterize the business environment. The competition faced by businesses is ever increasing.

3 Corporations are increasingly concerned about social responsibility.

3 Business alliances among organizations are spreading, largely due to the support of information technology.

3 Organizations are adapting a customer-focused approach in order to succeed.

3 Organizations are reengineering their business processes in order to cope with rapid environmental changes. IT plays an important role.

3 Organizations are changing their mode of operation by using IT-supported innovative approaches such as just-in-time, mass customization, and empowerment of employees.

4 The cost-performance advantage of information technology is increasing with time, due to increasing processing speed and storage capability.

4 Communication networks are the core of IT in the new economy.

4 Information technology is a major agent of change, supporting critical response activities.

5 Information technology refers to the network of all information systems in an organization.

5 An information system collects, processes, stores, and disseminates information for a specific purpose. A computer-based information system uses computers to perform some or all of these activities.

6 Networked computing via the Internet, intranets, and extranets is becoming the centerpiece of information technology.

QUESTIONS FOR REVIEW

1. Define an information system and list its major components.
2. Define digital economy and list its major characteristics.
3. Define a business model by giving an example of one.
4. What are the major pressures in the business environment?
5. List the major critical response activities used by organizations.
6. Define information technology.
7. What is a virtual corporation?
8. Define mobile commerce.
9. Define corporate portals.
10. What do we mean by empowerment of employees?
11. Describe mass customization.
12. What are Moore's law and Metcalfe's law?
13. What is time-to-market? Why is it so important?
14. Describe the concept of cycle-time reduction.
15. List the major capabilities of IT.
16. Define the Internet, an intranet, and an extranet.
17. Define networked computing and networked organizations.

QUESTIONS FOR DISCUSSION

1. Describe how information systems can support the just-in-time approach.
2. Review the examples of the new versus the old economy cases. In what way did IT make the difference?
3. Explain why IT is a business pressure and also an enabler of response activities that counter business pressures.
4. Why is m-commerce perceived as being able to increase IT applications?
5. Explain the relationship between empowerment of employees and IT.
6. Explain why the cost-performance ratio of IT will improve by a factor of 100, while performance is expected to improve by a factor of only 50.
7. Is IT a strategic weapon or a survival tool? Discuss.
8. It is said that networked computing changes the way we live, work, and study. Why?

9. Relate cycle-time reduction to improved performance.
10. Distinguish between network computers and networked computing.
11. Why is the Internet said to be the creator of new business models?
12. Explain why mass customization is desirable.

EXERCISES

1. Read the emerging *Digital Economy II* and other related reports at *ecommerce.gov*.
   a. Summarize the major points regarding the digital economy.
   b. How it is related to economic growth, productivity, and inflation?
   c. What are the relationships of the digital economy to IT policy?
2. Review the examples of IT applications in Section 1.3, and identify the business pressures in each example.
3. The market for optical copiers is shrinking rapidly. It is expected that by 2004 as much as 85 percent of all duplicated documents will be done on computer printers. Can a company such as Xerox Corporation survive?
   a. Identify all the business pressures on Xerox.
   b. Find some of Xerox's response strategies (see *Datamation,* June 1997, p. 42; and *Xerox.com, fortune.com,* and *forbes.com*).
   c. Identify the role of IT as a contributor to the business technology pressures.
   d. Identify the role of IT as a facilitator of the critical response activities.
   e. Review the role of the CIO in the revitalization project.
   f. Read about the problems of Xerox in 2000 and 2001 at *fortune.com* and *google.com.*

GROUP AND ROLE-PLAYING ACTIVITIES

1. Review the *Wall Street Journal, Fortune, Business Week,* and local newspapers of the last three months to find stories about the use of Web-based technologies in organizations. Each group will prepare a report describing five applications. The reports should emphasize the role of the Web and its benefit to the organizations. Cover issues discussed in this chapter, such as productivity, quality, cycle time, and globalization. One of the groups should concentrate on m-commerce and another on electronic marketplaces. Present and discuss your work.
2. Identify Web-related new business models in the areas of the group's interests. Identify radical changes in the operation of the functional areas (accounting, finance, marketing, etc.), and tell the others about them.
3. Enter *ecommerce.ncsu.edu/topics;* go to Net-centrism and read the latest "hungry minds" items there. Prepare a report regarding the latest in the digital age.

INTERNET EXERCISES

1. Enter the Web site of UPS (*ups.com*).
   a. Find out what information is available to customers before they send a package.
   b. Find out about the "package tracking" system; be specific.
   c. Compute the cost of delivering a 10″ × 20″ × 15″ box, weighing 40 pounds, from your hometown to Long Beach, California. Compare the fastest delivery against the least cost.
2. Surf the Internet (use *google.com, brint.com,* or a similar engine) to find information about:
   a. International virtual corporations (at least two examples).
   b. Virtual corporations in general.
3. Enter the Web site of Bristol-Myers Squibb (*bms.com*). Find out Web-based customer service activities BMS offers. Now enter *google.com* and find additional generic Web-based activities in the area of customer service. Prepare a report.
4. Enter *s-one.gov.sg*. Examine the progress in Singapore One's Network infrastructure. Also enter *ec.gov.sg* to monitor the e-commerce new initiatives.
5. Visit some Web sites that offer employment opportunities in IT (such as *execunet.com*). Compare the IT salaries to salaries offered to accountants. For other information on IT salaries, check *Computerworld*'s annual salary survey.
6. Prepare a short report on the role of information techology in government. Start with *ctg.Albany.edu, e-government.govt.nz,* and *worldbank.org/publicsector/egov*. Find e-government plans in Hong Kong and in Singapore (*cca.gov.sg;* check action plan).
7. Enter *x-home.com* and find information about the easy life of the future.

Minicase 1

Can Information Systems and the Internet Help a Small Business in Distress?

Sports for All, one of the most successful stores in Middletown, Illinois, is privately owned by Nancy Knowland. It employs 12 people and has sales of about $3 million per year. Nancy's family started the sporting goods store over 60 years ago. The store grew slowly over the years, attracting customers from several communities around Middletown. The store's strategy was to provide a large variety of products at low prices. Because of low expenses in Middletown (labor, taxes, rent), the store was able to compete successfully against both K-Mart's and Wal-Mart's sporting goods departments.

Lately, however, the situation has changed. Sports for All was losing customers to Wal-Mart because Wal-Mart was importing extremely inexpensive goods from sources that were not available to Sports for All. Furthermore, several customers opted to travel as much as 150 miles to St. Louis and pay higher prices for special products that were customized for them by a new and fashionable sporting goods store there.

Nancy became concerned last summer when total sales showed a clear trend of decline for four consecutive quarters. Yesterday, the monthly sales data was compiled and showed the lowest monthly sales level in 10 years. Nancy called in all the key people of the store for an emergency meeting.

Nancy's son, David, an MBA student at the University of Illinois, has been urging his mother for years to install a modern computerized information system in the store. Last summer, he purchased several computers and an accounting package and transferred most of the manual accounting transactions (billing, purchasing, and inventory) to the computer. The store also handles all of its correspondence on word processors. Nancy objected to further investment in computer systems, especially since profits were declining.

During the meeting, David proposed the installation of a sophisticated information system that would improve purchasing, inventory management, and customer service. "Some major manufacturers will not sell products to us because we are not on their electronic data interchange (EDI) system. We need to expedite the receipts of shipments and buy directly from manufacturers so we can be more responsive to customers. We also need to control costs and inventories," he explained. He also said that it is not enough to have Internet presence, but that it is necessary to build an e-commerce site. He urged the company to move the existing internal systems to an intranet, and to explore mobile commerce applications. Furthermore, he said, "we should explore the feasibility of joining group purchasing and an e-procurement marketplace."

Jim Park, who helps Nancy with finance and marketing, was not too enthusiastic. "David's proposal will cost more than $160,000, to begin with. Then we will have to infuse cash into the system every month, and it will not reduce our labor force by even one employee. We are just too small for these fancy machines. We will be better off applying this money toward advertising and providing special sales to attract customers," he said.

Questions for Minicase 1

As a consultant to Sports for All, complete the following:

1. Explain to management the changing business environment and why traditional actions such as an increase in advertising may not be effective.
2. Use the trends described in this chapter and the capabilities of IT to demonstrate to Nancy and Jim why the company may have to use IT in order to survive.
3. Why was David pushing the use of the Web?
4. What specific factors need to be considered in order to make a decision on whether or not to accept David's proposal?
5. Can a small business survive in the digital economy?

Minicase 2

Qantas Airways Responds with E-commerce

www.qantas.com

Rising fuel costs during 1999 and 2000 created a pressure on the airline industry. The fuel price increase came quickly, and was unanticipated. For Qantas Airways, Australia's largest airline, this was just the beginning of difficulties. The airline also had to deal with two new domestic competitors, Impulse and Virgin Blue, and with higher user fees at Sydney Airport. On top of this the airline faced the need to upgrade its fleet, replacing aging aircraft and buying new 500-seat planes. Also, the economy in Australia slowed down in 2000, and the Australian dollar was sinking. Finally, corporate clients managed to find or negotiate low ticket prices by using computerized planning models and the Internet. The problem was this: Could Qantas, the world's second-oldest airline, survive?

Qantas decided its salvation lay partially in IT. In addition to traditional responses such as buying fuel contracts for future dates, Qantas took major steps to get into e-commerce:

BUSINESS-TO-BUSINESS INITIATIVES

- Joined a purchasing business-to-business e-marketplace (called Airnew Co.), which links a dozen major airlines with suppliers of direct supplies: fuel, fuel services, general maintenance services, catering and so on. The marketplace operates with electronic catalogs and conducts different types of auctions.
- Joined another e-marketplace, called *corprocure.com*, together with thirteen other large corporations in Australia, for the purpose of buying indirect goods and services, such as office supplies, light bulbs, and airline maintenance services.
- Formed a Pan-Pacific e-selling marketplace that includes a full spectrum of travel services (air, hotels, cars, etc). It provides a chance for Qantas's business partners, such as travel agencies, to provide special and personalized services to their customers, at competitive prices. This e-marketplace will also sell direct to individual customers.

BUSINESS-TO-CONSUMER INITIATIVES

- Sent an e-mail to 2.4 million Qantas frequent flyers, inviting them to book direct online and rewarding them with bonuses and an opportunity to win $10,000 (Australian).
- Began providing information, including personalized information such as flight delays, to travelers via mobile phones and other wireless devices.

OTHER INITIATIVES

- Set up a portal for Qantas travel agents that provides information and online training (*gdstraining.qantas. com.au*).
- Established Qantas College Online, which offers dozens of courses online to help train 30,000 Qantas employees in 32 countries (*qfcollege.edu.au*). This is part of the airline's business-to-employees (B2E) initiative.
- Another B2E project is online banking services. The company operates a credit union with 50,000 members worldwide, and members make over 100,000 transactions a month at *qantascu.com.au*. Services are comparable with those of other commercial online banks.

STRATEGIC ALLIANCES

- Initiated several nontravel projects with Telstra (Australia's largest telecommunications company). Co-branding of credit cards and mobile phones are two examples of joint ventures undertaken.

Leading an old-economy company into the digital economy is not easy. It means interfering with power structures and fitting new-economy strategy with old-economy ways. But Qantas knew that this must be done, and did not expect results overnight. To implement all EC initiatives will take years and hundreds of millions of dollars. Yet, as early as 2003, Qantas expects to reap an estimated savings of $85 million (Australian) per year in reduced communications and advertising costs. Also, it expects to increase revenue by $700 million (Australian) annually from nontravel sales. Many airlines, including United Airlines (*united.com*) and CathayPacific (*cathaypacific.com*), are involved in similar projects.

Questions for Minicase 2

1. Identify all the business pressures cited in the case and additional business pressures you think might apply (see *fortune.com*, and *theeconomist.com*).
2. Identify the responses taken by Qantas. Look for additional responses at *qantas.com* (press releases) and in the Australia financial review (*afr.com.au*).
3. Relate Qantas's responses to the critical responses suggested in the chapter.
4. Which of the responses are supported by information systems?
5. Notice that Qantas has e-commerce buying and e-commerce selling projects. Find the benefits of such activities (use *cio.com, fortune.com*, and *ariba.com*).

Sources: Compiled from *Financial Review*, August 11, 2000; Australia *BRW*, August 25, 2000, and May 5, 2000; and Qantas's media releases, September 14, 1999.

REFERENCES AND BIBLIOGRAPHY

1. Anonymous, "The Net Imperative: A Survey of Business and The Internet," *The Economist,* 2000.
2. Applegate, L. M., "E-Business Models: Making Sense of the Internet Business Landscape," in G. W. Dickson and G. DeSanctis, *Information Technology and the Future Enterprise: New Models for Managers.* Upper Saddle River, NJ: Prentice-Hall, 2001.
3. Barrett, R., "Living in the Year 2025," *Interactive Week,* January 10, 2000.
4. Boyett, J. H., and J. T. Boyett, *Beyond Workplace 2000: Essential Strategies for the New American Corporation.* New York: Dutton, 1995.
5. Brown, D., "IS Virtual Voting Ready for Real-Time?" *Interactive Week,* January 10, 2000.
6. Callon, J. D., *Competitive Advantage Through Information Technology.* New York: McGraw-Hill, 1996.
7. Cambridge Technology Partners, *Business Models for the New Economy,* a white paper, Boston, 2000.
8. Chandra, J., et al., "Information Systems Frontiers," *Communications of the ACM,* January 2000.
9. Choi, S. Y., and A. B. Whinston, *The Internet Economy: Technology and Practice.* Austin, TX: Smartecon.com pub, 2000.
10. Clinton, W. J., and A. Gore, Jr., "A Framework for Global Electronic Commerce," *iitf.nist.gov/eleccomm/ecomm,* July 1997.
11. Dertouzos, M., *What Will Be: How the New World of Information Will Change Our Lives.* San Francisco: Harper Edge, 1997.
12. Devenport, T. H., *Information Ecology: Mastering the Information Knowledge Environment.* New York: Oxford University Press, 1997.
13. Dicarlo, L., "America's Most Wired Companies," *PC Computing,* December 1999.
14. Dickson, G. W., and G. DeSanctis, *Information Technology and the Future Enterprise: New Models for Managers.* Upper Saddle River, NJ: Prentice-Hall, 2001.
15. Drucker, D. F., *Managing in a Time of Great Change.* New York: Truman Tally Books, 1995.
16. Duvall, M., "The Internet's Big Pay-Off," *Interactive Week,* October 16, 2000.
17. Evans, P. B., and T. S. Wurster, *Blown to Bits: How the New Economics of Information Transforms Strategy.* Boston: Harvard Business School Press, 1999.
18. Galliers, D. E., et al., *Strategic Information Management.* Oxford, U. K.: Butterworth-Heinemann, 1999.
19. Gates, H. B., *Business @ the Speed of Thought.* New York: Penguin Books, 1999.
20. Gill, K. S. (ed.), *Information Society.* London: Springer Publishing, 1996.
21. Griffiths. P. M., et al. (eds.), *Information Management in Competitive Success,* New York: Pergamon Press, 1998.
22. Hagel, J., and M. Singer, *Net Worth.* Boston: Harvard Business School Press, 1999.
23. Hamel, G., *Leading the Revolution.* Boston: Harvard Business School Press, 2000.
24. Hammer, M., and J. Champy, *Reengineering the Corporation.* New York: Harper Business, 1993.
25. Hendren, J., "Armed to Send Chaos into Voting Oblivion," *New York Times,* December, 17, 2000.
26. Hoffman, D. L., and T. P. Novak, "How to Acquire Customers on the Web," *Harvard Business Review,* May–June 2000.
27. Jarvenpaa, S., and B. Ives, "The Global Network Organization of the Future: Information Management Opportunities and Challenges," *Journal of Management Information Systems,* Spring 1994.
28. Kalakota, R., and A. B. Whinston, *Electronic Commerce: A Manager's Guide.* Reading, MA: Addison Wesley, 1997.
29. Kelly, K., *New Rules for the New Economy.* New York: Penguin USA, 1999.
30. Knoke, W., *Bold New World: The Essential Road Map to the 21st Century.* New York: Rodensha America, 1996.
31. Lane, N., "Advancing the Digital Economy into the 21st Century," *Information Systems Frontiers,* Vol. 1, No. 3, 1999.
32. Lederer. A. L., et al., "Using Web-based Information Systems to Enhance Competitiveness," *Communications of the ACM,* July 1998.
33. Lipnack, J., and J. Stamps, *Virtual Teams.* New York: Wiley, 1997.
34. Mandel, M. J., et al., "The Information Revolution: Special Report," *Business Week,* June 13, 1994.
35. Mankin, D., et al., *Teams and Technology.* Boston: Harvard Business School, 1996.
36. McGarvey, J., "Net Gear Breaks Moore's Law," *Interactive Week,* April 17, 2000.
37. Naisbitt, J., *Global Paradox.* London: N. Breadly, 1994.
38. Orsburn, J. D., and L. Moran, *The New Self-Directed Work Teams.* New York: McGraw-Hill, 1999.
39. Pine, J. B., II, *Mass Customization,* 2nd ed. Boston: Harvard Business School Press, 1999.
40. Pine, J., II, and J. H. Gilmore, *The Experience Economy.* Boston: Harvard Business School Press, 1999.
41. Sahiman, W., "B-Schools, New Rules," *Harvard Business Review,* November–December 1999.
42. Schwartz, E. I., *Digital Darwinism.* New York: Broadway Books, 1999.
43. Scott-Morton, M., and T. J. Allen (eds.), *Information Technology and the Corporation of the 1990s.* New York: Oxford University Press, 1994.
44. Tapscott, D. (ed.), *Creating Value in the Network Economy.* Boston: Harvard Business School Press, 1999.
45. Tapscott, D., et al., *Blueprint of the Digital Economy.* Boston: Harvard Business School Press, 1998.
46. Tapscott, D., et al., *Digital Capital.* Boston: Harvard Business School Press, 2000.
47. Timmers, P., *Electronic Commerce.* Chichester, U.K.: Wiley, 1999.
48. Trout, J., and S. Rivkin, *Differentiate or Die.* New York: Wiley, 2000.
49. Turban, E., et al., *Electronic Commerce,* 2nd ed. Upper Saddle River, NJ: Prentice-Hall, 2002.
50. Wetherbe, J. C., *The World on Time.* Santa Monica, CA: Knowledge Exchange, 1996.
51. Wigand, R., et al., *Information, Organization, and Management: Expanding Markets and Corporate Boundaries.* New York: Wiley, 1997.
52. Wreden, N., "Business-Boosting Technologies," *Beyond Computing,* November–December 1997.

APPENDIX 1.1

ETHICS IN INFORMATION TECHNOLOGY MANAGEMENT*

Ethics is a branch of philosophy that deals with the analysis of decisions and actions with respect to their appropriateness in a given social context. Historical antecedents include the *Bible's* Ten Commandments, as well as elements of the philosophy of Confucius and Aristotle. As a discipline of study and practice, ethics applies to many different issues in information technology and information systems—and correspondingly, to many different people in industry and academia (managers, teachers, and students), both in the private and in the public sectors.

Ethics has been defined as involving the systematic application of moral rules, standards, and principles to concrete problems (Lewis, 1985). Some people believe that an ethical dilemma emerges whenever a decision or an action has the potential to impair or enhance the well being of an individual or a group of people. Such dilemmas occur frequently, with many conflicts of interest present in the information society. A variety of sets of ethical guidelines have been devised. But we must emphasize that what is unethical may not necessarily be illegal, and what is legal may not necessarily be ethical. Furthermore, whether an action or decision is considered ethical will depend on many contributing factors, including those of the social and cultural environment in which the decision is made and the action is implemented.

SOME GENERAL ETHICAL PRINCIPLES

Many different ethical principles have been developed throughout human history. Each of us needs to make an individual choice about which principles to follow. Nevertheless, it is useful to consider a selection of some well-known and widely accepted ethical principles here.

- ***The Golden Rule.*** A widely applied general ethical principle, which has versions in the *Bible* as well as in Confucian philosophy, is known as the *Golden Rule.* It generally reads like this: "In everything that you do, treat other people in the same way that you would like them to treat you." If you put yourself in the shoes of other people, and consider how you would feel if you were the object of a particular decision, then you should develop a good understanding of whether a decision is a good or fair one.
- ***The Categorical Imperative.*** "If an action is not suitable for everyone to take, then it is not suitable for anyone." This is Immanuel Kant's *categorical imperative.* If everyone undertook some action, what would be the consequence? Could society survive?
- ***The Slippery Slope Rule.*** "If an action can be repeated over and over again with no negative consequences, then no problem. But if such a repeated action would lead to disastrous consequences, then the action should not be undertaken even once." This is the *slippery slope rule.* Once you start down a slippery slope, you may not be able to stop before it is too late.
- ***The Utilitarian Rule.*** "The best action is the one that provides the most good for the most people." This is a form of *utilitarian rule.* It assumes that you are able to rank the various competing actions. Another version of the utilitarian rule can read as follows: "The best action is the one that leads to the least harm or costs the least. " For example, this rule might be used to answer the question, Should one build an airport in the middle of a crowded neighborhood—or away from people?
- ***No Free Lunch.*** Every object (tangible or intangible) has an owner. If you want to use it, you should compensate the owner for doing so. This is akin to the idea that there is *no free lunch*—everything has a price.

These ethical principles are very general in nature. In putting ethics into practice, there are always exceptions and conflicts, so-called "ethical dilemmas."

ETHICAL DILEMMAS

To illustrate the nature of an ethical dilemma, consider the following questions that relate to the copying/selling/distribution of software:

- Is it acceptable to buy a software product, but then to install it twice?
- How about if you install it, then give it to a friend for personal use?
- Alternatively, what if you install it and use a CD writer to create 100 copies — and sell them for profit to anyone who wishes to buy?
- What about making the software available on a Web site for others to download?
- What about trading software on the Web (consumer to consumer)?

You may be surprised to discover that there are no correct answers to these questions. Legally, it depends on the jurisdiction where you live and work. Ethically, it depends

*This appendix was contributed by Robert Davison, Department of Information Systems, City University of Hong Kong.

on the specific cultural and social circumstances of the environment in which you live and work.

The wide application of IT and the pervasive nature of the Internet have created many opportunities for activities that some people may judge to be unethical. Here are some more sample dilemmas from a selection of application areas:

- Does a company have the ***right*** to read its employees' e-mail?
- Does a company have the ***right*** to monitor the Web sites that its employees visit from company computers?
- Does an employee have the ***duty*** to use company resources only for company purposes/business?
- Does an employee have the ***duty*** to report the misuse of company resources?
- Does an individual have the ***right*** to data privacy?
- Does an individual have the ***duty*** to ensure that personal data held about him or her is at all times accurate and up-to-date?
- Does a software developer have the ***right*** to use disclaimers to minimize or eliminate responsibility for software failures?
- Does an end-user have the ***duty*** to respect the intellectual property vested in a product—by not decompiling and modifying it—even if the purpose is to improve the product?
- Does a data subject (for example, member of the public) have the ***right*** to access and to correct data records held by government agencies and departments (e.g., police, anticorruption agencies, taxing agencies)?
- Does a data user (for example, the government) have the ***duty*** to ensure that it responds promptly to data subjects' requests for access to that data?

From this selection of questions, two key issues emerge:

1. The fact that rights must be balanced by duties
2. The lack of concrete "correct" answers, due to legal and ethical differences in different societies

The appropriate relationship between rights and duties is clearly critical. Any understanding of this relationship will be informed by social and cultural circumstances. For example, the concept of individual privacy is more developed in Europe and in North America than in Southeast Asia, where current cultural (and political) systems favor the benefits to society rather than the individual. Similarly, privacy laws are far more developed in some jurisdictions (Canada, Sweden, the United Kingdom, Hong Kong) than in others (China, Mexico).

Issues that are generally considered to fall under the umbrella of information technology ethics are the following:

- Codes of ethics
- Intellectual property rights (primarily digital property, such as software, films and music, but also trademarks, patents, blueprints, and books)
- Accountability (for actions or nonactions)
- Personal and data privacy (including "dataveillance," electronic monitoring, and data accuracy and accessibility)
- Freedom of speech vs. censorship
- Ownership of information

We'll explore some of these issues in the sections that follow, and throughout the book. For further information about ethical issues relating to information systems and IT, see the list of Web sites in Table 1.1.1.

TABLE 1.1.1 URLs of Relevance to the IS/IT Ethics Debate

Organization/Ethical Concern	Address of Related Web Site
Centre for Professional and Applied Ethics	*valdosta.edu/cpae/*
Questions and answers on professional ethics	*members.aol.com/InternetEthics/*
Ethical principles in university teaching	*umanitoba.ca/academic_support/uts/stlhe/Ethical.html*
Ethical issues in the preparation and submission of research papers	*anu.edu.au/people/Roger.Clarke/SOS/ResPubEth.html*
Is IT Ethical? 1998 Ethicomp survey of professional practice	*ccsr.cms.dmu.ac.uk/resources/general/ethical/Ecv9no1.html*
European Group on Ethics in Science and New Technologies	*europa.eu.int/comm/secretariat_general/sgc/ethics/en/index.htm*
Centre for Computing and Social Responsibility	*ccsr.cms.dmu.ac.uk/*
Electronic Privacy Information Centre	*epic.org/*
The World Intellectual Property Association	*wipo.org/*
Software Piracy in Hong Kong and China—a study	*info.gov.hk/ipd/piracy.html*

CODES OF ETHICS

Codes of ethics involve the formalizing of some rules and expected actions. Violation of a code of ethics may lead to suspension of membership or termination of employment. In some professions such as law and medicine, membership in a professional society is a precondition of the right to practice, though this is generally not the case with information systems. Codes of ethics are valuable for raising awareness of ethical issues and clarifying what is acceptable behavior in a variety of circumstances. Codes of ethics have limitations, however, because of their natural tendency to generalize acceptable behavior—despite the variations in social and ethical values that exist in different communities. Certainly it would be arrogant to impose on people in Brazil the ethical standards developed in and appropriate for Norway, or indeed to do the reverse. Such impositions are unfortunately commonplace, and they tend to lead to outright rejection (rather than to higher ethical standards, which may be the intent). Nevertheless, a comparison of codes of ethics for the computing profession will reveal a perhaps remarkable degree of similarity. For a list of various computing organizations and the Web sites where their codes of ethics can be found, see Table 1.1.2.

INTELLECTUAL PROPERTY RIGHTS (IPR)

Intellectual property is the intangible property created by individuals or organizations. To varying degrees in different countries, intellectual property is protected under laws relating to copyright, patents, trademarks, and trade secrets. The copying of software is generally seen to be of greatest concern—at least to the software developers.

TABLE 1.1.2 Computing Organizations Worldwide and Their Web Sites

Organization	Address of Web Site
Association for Computing Machinery	*acm.org/*
Australian Computer Society	*acs.org.au/*
British Computer Society Society	*bcs.org.uk/*
Canadian Information Processing Society	*cips.ca/*
Computer Society of South Africa	*cssa.org.za/*
Hong Kong Computer Society	*hkcs.org.hk/*
Institute of Electrical and Electronics Engineers	*ieee.org/*
Singapore Computer Society	*scs.org.sg/*

Why is the topic of intellectual property rights (IPR) so important? One critical reason relates to the fundamental right to private property—especially property that represents the fruit of one's endeavors (see Locke, 1964). IPR protects the way in which the ideas are expressed, but not the ideas themselves. IPR may be seen as a mechanism for protecting the creative works of individual people and organizations. Yet this is problematic in societies that place less value on individual freedom and more on social order. In many developing countries, "individual claims on intellectual property are subordinated to more fundamental claims of social well-being" (Steidlmeier, 1993). In these countries, the welfare of society is considered to be more important than that of any individual.

Much of the discussion about IPR relates to the debate about rights and duties. Software developers demand the right of stringent legal protection for the fruits of their endeavors and compensation for resources expended in software development. Consumers are then deemed to have a duty to pay for that software and to respect the intellectual property, by not stealing (copying) it. Nevertheless, consumers may equally claim that the product they purchase should be free of defects (bugs), thus imposing a duty of quality (and professionalism) on software developers to ensure that a product is indeed bug-free and thus "fit for use."

ACCOUNTABILITY

Accountability is an issue closely tied to many codes of conduct. In general, *accountability* refers to the acknowledgment that a person (or group of people) takes responsibility for a decision or action, is prepared to justify that decision/action, and if necessary give compensation to affected parties if the decision/action causes negative effects, whether intended or otherwise. As the British Computer Society (2000) code states, "Members shall accept professional responsibility for their work." Accountability is important "because it shows that high-quality work is valued, encourages people to be diligent in their work, and provides foundations for punishment/compensation when, for example, software does not perform according to expectations or professional advice turns out to be unreliable" (Davison, 2000). It is important that we identify who should be accountable for a decision or action because computers and information systems are widely used in our society, and so the potential for disasters caused by poor-quality work is always present.

Although accountability is a valuable concept, its value may be diminished in a number of ways. It is common, for example, for computers to be made scapegoats for human failings. If you call your travel agent and ask to book an airplane ticket, and the travel agent says, "Sorry, the computer is down," then the computer is being blamed. Perhaps the computer really is down, or perhaps the agent is too busy or can't be bothered to serve you. And if the computer is down, why is it down? Has a human action

A CLOSER LOOK
1.3 SIX PRINCIPLES OF THE DATA PRIVACY ORDINANCE (HONG KONG)

1. ***Purpose and manner of collection.*** Data should be collected in a fair and lawful manner. Data users should explain to data subjects what data is being collected and how it will be used.
2. ***Accuracy and duration of retention.*** Personal data that has been collected should be kept accurate, up-to-date, and for no longer than is necessary.
3. ***Use.*** Data must be used only for the specific or directly related purpose for which it was collected. Any other use is conditional on consent of the data subject.
4. ***Security.*** Suitable security measures should be applied to personal data.
5. ***Information availability.*** Data users should be open about the kind of data that they store and what they use it for.
6. ***Access.*** Data subjects have the right to access their personal data, to verify its accuracy, and to request correction.

Source: Privacy Commissioner's Office (PCO), Hong Kong. More detailed information can be obtained at the Web site of the PCO: *pco.org.hk.*

caused it to be down? Is it a design flaw, a software bug, a problem of installation or of maintenance? Of course, we never know the answers to these questions. But this means that it is all too easy to blame the computer, perhaps apologize, and then claim that nothing can be done. All of these actions tend to help people to avoid being accountable for their actions and work.

It is also common, unfortunately, for software developers to deny responsibility for the consequences of software use—even when this use has been in accordance with the purpose for which the software was designed. Software developers assert that they are selling the right to use a software product, not ownership of the product itself. In parallel, developers employ legal disclaimers to reduce as far as they possibly can any liability arising out of a customer's use of the software. At the same time, customers may use the software only in a manner defined by the tight restrictions of a software usage license. In this way, the rights of the user are severely eroded, whereas those of the developers are maximized. If the software has design flaws (bugs) that cause negative consequences for users, users are not permitted to fix those bugs themselves. Nor, it appears, are developers bound by any duty to fix them, let alone compensate users for the inconvenience suffered or damage caused by those bugs.

DATA PRIVACY

In general, *privacy* can be defined as the right to be left alone (Warren and Brandeis, 1890). The notion of privacy has become one of the most contentious issues of the information age, due to the capability of computers to perform actions previously impossible or impractical. Agranoff (1993) defines *information (data) privacy* as the "claim of individuals, groups, or institutions to determine for themselves when, and to what extent, information about them is communicated to others." Nevertheless, the right to privacy is not absolute. It varies considerably in different cultures, as it has to be balanced by society's right to know.

One of the most detailed sets of data-privacy principles to emerge in the last few years has come from the Privacy Commissioner's Office (PCO) in Hong Kong. These principles, and the legislative measures that underwrite them, were created in the mid-1990s and officially promulgated in December 1996. A summary of the six data protection principles appears in *A Closer Look* 1.3. These principles are designed to enshrine the reasonable rights and duties of both the data subject (the person described by the data) and data users (those who possess data).

REFERENCES

Agranoff, M. H., "Controlling the Threat to Personal Privacy," *Journal of Information Systems Management,* Summer 1993.

British Computer Society, "British Computer Society Code of Conduct," *bcs.org.uk/aboutbcs/coc.htm,* 2000.

Davison, R. M., "Professional Ethics in Information Systems: A Personal View," *Communications of the AIS,* Vol. 3, No. 8, 2000.

Lewis, P. V., "Defining Business Ethics: Like Nailing Jello to the Wall," *Journal of Business Ethics,* Vol. 4, No. 5, 1985, pp. 377–383.

Locke, J., *Second Treatise of Civil Government.* New York: Bobbs-Merrill, 1964.

Steidlmeier, P., "The Moral Legitimacy of Intellectual Property Claims: American Business and Developing Country Perspectives," *Journal of Business Ethics,* Vol. 12, No. 2, 1993, pp. 157–164.

Warren, S. D., and L. D. Brandeis, "The Right to Privacy," *Harvard Law Review,* Vol. 193, 1890, pp. 193–220.

PART I
IT in the Organization

CHAPTER 2

Information Technologies: Concepts and Management

This chapter was revised by Linda Lai from the City University of Hong Kong.

LEARNING OBJECTIVES

After studying this chapter, you will be able to:

1. Describe various information systems and their evolution, and categorize specific systems you observe.
2. Describe transaction processing and functional information systems.
3. Identify the major support systems, and relate them to managerial functions.
4. Discuss information infrastructure and architecture.
5. Compare client/server architecture, enterprisewide computing, and legacy systems, and analyze their interrelationship.
6. Describe the major types of Web-based information systems and understand their functionality.
7. Describe how information resources are managed.
8. Describe the role of the information systems department and its relationship with end users.

BUILDING AN E-BUSINESS AT FEDEX CORPORATION

www.fedex.com

FedEx Corporation was founded in 1973 by Fred Smith. During 27 years of operation, FedEx earned myriad accolades and won over 194 awards for operational excellence. With a fully integrated physical and virtual infrastructure, FedEx's business model supports 24–48 hour delivery to anywhere in the world. As of 2000, FedEx operates one of the world's busiest data-processing centers, handling over 83 million information requests per day from more than 3,000 databases and more than 500,000 archive files. It operates one of the largest real-time, online client/server networks in the world. The core competencies of FedEx are now in express transportation and in e-solutions.

THE PROBLEM

Initially, FedEx grew out of pressures from mounting inflation and global competition. These pressures gave rise to greater demands on businesses to minimize costs of operation and to improve customer service. FedEx didn't have a business problem per se, but rather, has kept looking ahead at every stage for opportunities to meet customers' needs for fast, reliable, and affordable overnight deliveries, to stay ahead of the competition. Lately, the Internet has provided an inexpensive and accessible platform upon which FedEx has seen further opportunities to expand its business scope, both geographically and in terms of service offerings.

THE SOLUTION

In addition to e-Shipping Tools (which is a Web-based shipping application that allows its customers to check the status of shipments through the postal company's Web page), FedEx is now also providing integrated solutions to address the entire selling and supply chain needs of its customers. Its eCommerce Solutions provides a full suite of services that allow businesses to integrate FedEx's transportation and information systems seamlessly into their own operations. These solutions have taken FedEx well beyond a delivery company.

FedEx markets four eCommerce Solutions: FedEx PowerShipMC (a multicarrier hardware/software system), FedEx Ship Manager Server (a hardware/software system providing high-speed transactions and superior reliability, allowing an average of eight transactions per second), FedEx ShipAPI™ (an Internet-based application that allows customization, eliminating redundant programming), and FedEx Net-Return® (an Internet-based returns management system). This systems and technology infrastructure is now known as FedEx Direct Link. It enables business-to-business electronic commerce through combinations of global virtual private network (VPN) connectivity, Internet connectivity, leased-line connectivity, and VAN (value-added network) connectivity.

Figure 2.1 gives one simple example of a FedEx eCommerce solution. It shows how customers can tap into a whole network of systems through the Internet. When a customer places an order through a Web catalog, the order is sent to the FedEx Web server. Information about the order and the customer is sent to the merchant's PC, and a message is sent to the customer to confirm receipt of the order. From that point up to the point of delivery of the goods, both merchant and customer may check the status of the order via the Web. After the order is

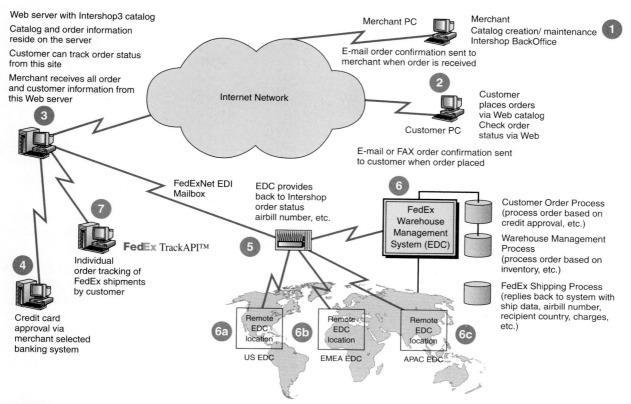

Customer places orders via Web catalog
Check order status via Web
Customer PC
E-mail or FAX order confirmation sent to customer when order placed
FedExNet EDI Mailbox
EDC provides back to Intershop order status airbill number, etc.
6
FedEx Warehouse Management System (EDC)
Customer Order Process (process order based on credit approval, etc.)
Warehouse Management Process (process order based on inventory, etc.)
FedEx Shipping Process (replies back to system with ship data, airbill number, recipient country, charges, etc.)
7
FedEx TrackAPI™
5
4
Individual order tracking of FedEx shipments by customer
Credit card approval via merchant selected banking system
Remote EDC location
6a
US EDC
Remote EDC location
6b
EMEA EDC
Remote EDC location
6c
APAC EDC

FIGURE 2.1 An example of a FedEx e-commerce solution. (*Source:* Based on a SIM 2000 award-winning paper written by William L. Conley, Ali F. Farhoomand, and Pauline S.P. Ng, at *simnet.org/library/doc/2ndplace.doc*. Courtesy of William Conley.)

received and acknowledged, the FedEx Web server sends a message to the merchant's bank to obtain credit approval. At the same time, the order is sent via electronic data interchange (EDI) to a FedEx mainframe that activates the warehouse management system. The order is processed (goods are picked and packed), the warehouse inventory system is updated, and the shipping process is synchronized. Information regarding the processing of the order is accessible at the three remote electronic data centers (EDC) located in the United States, the Europe/Mediterranean (EMEA) region, and the Asia Pacific (APAC) region.

THE RESULTS

FedEx's e-business model creates value for its customers in a number of ways: It facilitates better communication and collaboration between the various parties along the selling and supply chains. It promotes efficiency gains by reducing costs and speeding up the order cycle. And it transforms organizations into high-performance e-businesses.

Source: Based on a SIM 2000 award-winning paper written by William L. Conley, Ali F. Farhoomand, and Pauline S.P. Ng, *www.simnet.org/library/doc/2ndplace.doc*. Courtesy of William Conley.

LESSONS LEARNED FROM THIS CASE

Web server with Intershop3 catalog
Catalog and order information reside on the server
Customer can track order status from this site
Merchant receives all order and customer information from this Web server
3
Merchant PC

Catalog creation/ maintenance
Intershop BackOffice

E-mail order confirmation sent to merchant when order is received
Internet Network

In the network economy, how well companies transform themselves from traditional modes of operation to e-businesses will depend upon how well they can adapt their structure and processes to take advantage of emerging technologies.

FedEx has transformed itself into an e-business by integrating physical and virtual infrastructures across information systems, business processes, and organizational bounds. As more companies resolve to expand business online, FedEx's experience in building an e-business serves to show how a company can successfully apply its information technology (IT) expertise to pioneer "customercentric" innovations with sweeping structural annd strategic impact for an entire industry.

2.1 INFORMATION SYSTEMS: CONCEPTS AND DEFINITIONS

The opening case illustrates a Web-based interorganizational system with the following characteristics. These characteristics can be found in many information systems in the twenty-first century:

- Several different information systems can exist in one organization. As a matter of fact, FedEx's information system contains hundreds of smaller information systems.
- A collection of several information systems is also broadly referred to as an information system. Most of these systems are interconnected.
- Information systems are connected by means of electronic networks. If the entire company is networked and people can communicate with each other and access information throughout the organization, then the arrangement is known as an *enterprisewide system.*
- *Interorganizational information systems* (such as FedExNet) involve information flow in two or more organizations and are used primarily in e-business applications.
- An enterprisewide system or interorganizational information system is composed of large and small computers and hardware connected by different types of networks (such as virtual private networks, value-added networks, intranets, and the Internet). It also includes software, databases, data, procedures, and of course, people. These are the components of any information system.

These characteristics point to the complexities involved in organizing and managing information systems. Therefore, before one learns about IT and its management, it is necessary to define the major concepts and organize them in some logical manner. That is the purpose of this chapter.

Information systems are built to attain several goals. One of the primary goals is to economically process *data* into *information* or *knowledge*. Let us define these concepts:

- **Data** items refer to an elementary description of things, events, activities, and transactions that are recorded, classified, and stored, but not organized to convey any specific meaning. Data items can be numeric, alphanumeric, figures, sounds, or images. A *database* consists of stored data items organized for retrieval.
- **Information** is data that have been organized so that they have meaning and value to the recipient. The recipient interprets the meaning and draws conclusions and implications. Data processed by an *application program* represent a more specific use and a higher value added than simple retrieval from a database. Such an application can be an inventory management system, a university online registration system, or an Internet-based stock buying and selling system.

- **Knowledge** consists of data or information that have been organized and processed to convey *understanding, experience, accumulated learning,* and *expertise* as they apply to a current problem or activity. Data that are processed to extract critical implications and to reflect past experience and expertise provide the recipient with *organizational knowledge,* which has a very high potential value. Currently, *knowledge management* is one of the hottest topics in the IS field. (See Chapter 9.)

Data, information, and knowledge can be inputs to an information system; they can also be outputs. For example, data about employees, their wages, and time worked are processed to produce payroll information. Payroll information itself can later be used as an input to another system that prepares a budget or advises management on salary scales.

INFORMATION SYSTEMS CONFIGURATIONS. Information systems components can be assembled in many different configurations, resulting in a variety of information systems, much as construction materials can be assembled to build different homes. The size and cost of a home depend on the purpose of the building, the availability of money, and constraints such as ecological and environmental factors. Just as there are many different types of housing, so there are many different types of information systems. Therefore, it is useful to classify information systems into groups that share similar characteristics. Such a classification may help in identifying different systems, analyzing them, planning new systems, planning integration of systems, and making decisions such as the possible outsourcing of systems.

2.2 CLASSIFICATION OF INFORMATION SYSTEMS

Information systems can be classified in several ways: by organizational levels, major functional areas, support provided, and the IS architecture. Note that regardless of how they are classified, the structure of these systems is the same: Namely, each contains hardware, software, data, procedures, and people. Several major classification schemes are described next.

Classification by Organizational Structure

Organizations are made up of components such as departments, teams, and work units. For example, most organizations have a human resources department, a finance and accounting department, and perhaps a public relations unit. These components form an organization that may report to a higher organizational level, such as a division or a headquarters, in a traditional *hierarchical* structure. Although some organizations are reengineering themselves into innovative structures, such as those based on cross-functional teams, today the vast majority of organizations still have a traditional hierarchical structure.

One way to classify information systems is along organizational structure lines. Thus, we can find information systems built for headquarters, for divisions, for departments, for operating units, and even for individual employees. Such systems can stand alone, or they can be interconnected.

Typical information systems that follow the organizational structure are departmental, enterprisewide, and interorganizational. These systems are organized in a hierarchy in which each higher-level system consists of more systems from the lower level preceding it.

- ***Departmental information systems.*** Frequently, an organization uses several application programs in one functional area or department. An **application program** is a program designed to perform a specific function directly for the user or, in some cases, for another application program. For instance, in managing human resources, it is possible to use one application for screening applicants and another for monitoring employee turnover. Some of the applications might be completely independent of each other, whereas others are interrelated. The collection of application programs in the human resources area is called a *human resources information system*. That is, it is referred to as a single *departmental information system*, even though it is made up of several application subsystems. In large organizations, several departments in the same functional area may exist in different corporate locations. For example, a human resources department might exist at the corporate level as well as in each division. The designers of the IS then have two options: They can design a *divisional* information system that includes a human resources subsystem, or they can design a *centralized* human resources system for the entire corporation.
- ***Enterprise information systems (EIS).*** While a departmental IS is usually related to a functional area, the collection of all departmental applications when combined with other functions' applications comprises the *enterprisewide information system*. One of the most popular enterprise applications is *enterprise resources planning (ERP)*. ERP systems are systems that allow companies to replace their existing systems with a single, integrated system. This process involves planning and managing the use of the resources of an entire enterprise. ERP systems present a new model of enterprisewide computing (see Chapter 6 and Minicase 1 at the end of this chapter).
- ***Interorganizational systems.*** Some information systems connect several organizations. For example, the worldwide airline reservation system is composed of several systems belonging to different airlines. Of these, American Airlines' SABRE system (see Figure 2.2) is one of the largest. An **interorganizational information systems (IOS)** is a system connecting

FIGURE 2.2 A travel agent using an online reservation system such as SABRE (American Airlines) or APPOLO (United Airlines). The Internet also makes such systems available to corporations and individuals.

two or more organizations. Such systems are common among business partners and are extensively used for electronic commerce, frequently via an *extranet.* A special IOS is an international or multinational corporation, whose computing facilities are located in two or more countries. Interorganizational information systems play a major role in *electronic commerce,* as shown in the opening case to this chapter, as well as in supply chain management support.

Classification by Functional Area

Information systems at the departmental level support the traditional functional areas of the firm. The major functional information systems are the following.

- ***The accounting information system***
- ***The finance information system***
- ***The manufacturing (operations/production) information system***
- ***The marketing information system***
- ***The human resources management information system***

In each functional area, some routine and repetitive tasks exist that are essential to the operation of the organization. Preparing a payroll and billing a customer are typical examples. The information system that supports these tasks is called the *transaction processing system (TPS).* TPSs,* which are described in detail in Section 2.3, support tasks performed in all functional areas but especially in the areas of accounting and finance.

Classification by Support Provided

A third way to classify information systems is according to the type of support they provide, regardless of the functional area. For example, an information system can support office workers in almost any functional area. Likewise, managers, regardless of where they work, can be supported by a computerized decision-making system. The major types of systems under this classification are:

- ***Transaction processing system (TPS)***—supports repetitive, mission-critical activities and clerical staff.
- ***Management information system (MIS)***—supports functional activities and managers.
- ***Knowledge management system (KMS)***—supports all employees' need for corporate knowledge.
- ***Office automation system (OAS)***—supports office workers.
- ***Decision support system (DSS)***—supports decision making by managers and analysts.
- ***Enterprise information system (EIS)***—supports all managers in an enterprise.
- ***Group support system (GSS)***—supports people working in groups.
- ***Intelligent support system***—supports mainly knowledge workers, but can support other groups of employees, *expert systems* being the major technology.

Brief descriptions of these systems are provided in the following sections; they are also described in Chapters 7 and 9 through 12. Doke and Barrier (1994) provide an in-depth assessment of these and some other support systems.

---

*In the IS literature, the acronym *TPS* can be read either as singular or plural, as can many of the other acronyms related to information systems such as MIS and IS, but for the purpose of clarity and pedagogy, we differentiate in the book.

The Evolution of Support Systems

The first computers were designed to compute formulas for scientific and military applications during World War II. The first business applications began in the early 1950s, and the computers did repetitive, large-volume, transactions-computing tasks. The computers "crunched numbers," summarizing and organizing data in the accounting, finance, and human resources areas, in what is known as a **transaction processing system (TPS)**. These TPSs (see Chapter 7 for details) were easy to justify since they automated manual computations.

As the cost of computing decreased and computers' capabilities increased, it became possible to justify IT for less repetitive tasks than TPS. In the 1960s, a new breed of IS started to develop. Systems arrived that accessed, organized, summarized, and displayed information for supporting repetitive decision making in the functional areas. Such systems are called functional **management information systems (MISs)**. Geared toward middle managers, MISs are characterized mainly by their ability to produce periodic reports such as a daily list of employees and the hours they work, or a monthly report of expenses as compared to a budget. Initially, MISs had a *historical orientation;* they described events after they occurred. Later, they were also used to forecast trends, to support routine decisions, and to provide answers to queries. Today, MIS reports might include summary reports even for periods that are different from the periods of the scheduled reports.

The main types of support systems described in this book are shown in Table 2.1, together with the employees they support.

Support systems began to emerge in the late 1960s and early 1970s when networked computing and electronic communication became prevalent. Airline reservation systems are perhaps the best example of this development. Electronic communication is only one aspect of what is now known as an **office automation system (OAS)**. Another aspect, *word processing* systems, spread to many organizations in the 1970s. At about the same time, computers were introduced in the manufacturing environment. Applications ranged from robotics to computer-aided design and manufacturing (CAD/CAM).

By the early 1970s, the demand for all types of IT had begun to accelerate. Increased capabilities and reduced costs justified computerized support for a growing number of nonroutine applications, and the **decision support system (DSS)** concept was born. The basic objective of a DSS is to provide computerized support to complex, nonroutine decisions, as illustrated in the following *IT at Work.*

TABLE 2.1 Main Types of IT Support Systems

System	Employees Supported	Detailed Discussion in:
Office automation	Office workers	Chapters 4, 5, 7
CAD/CAM	Engineers, draftspeople	Chapter 7
Communication	All employees	Chapter 4
Group support system	People working in groups	Chapter 10
Decision support system	Decision makers, managers	Chapter 10
Executive information	Executives, top managers	Chapter 10
Expert system	Knowledge workers, nonexperts	Chapter 12
Neural networks	Knowledge workers, professionals	Chapter 12
Knowledge systems	Managers, staff, knowledge workers	Chapters 9, 12

IT at Work

GLAXO WELLCOME SAVES LIVES WITH DSS

Integrating IT

...in Health Care,
...in Production and Operations Management, and in Marketing
www.glaxowellcome.co.uk

Glaxo Wellcome of the United Kingdom is one of the largest pharmaceutical companies in the world. In 1996, the company found that a combination of two of its existing drugs, Epirir and Retrovir, were effective in treating some cases of AIDS. Doctors worldwide began writing prescriptions en masse almost overnight. Such a tidal wave of demand depleted the inventories of the two drugs in the pharmacies.

Glaxo needed to produce and ship Epirir and Retrovir quickly. But the increased demand, which is used to determine production, shipping schedules, and inventory levels, was too difficult to forecast.

To solve the problem, Glaxo developed a special enterprisewide networked information system based on relational online analytical processing technology (see Chapter 10). Essentially, this system processes data as soon as transactions occur. The system works with a vast amount of internal and external data stored in a data warehouse (Chapter 11). Using these data and DSS models, market analysts at Glaxo were able to track and size the sources of demand, generating summary reports and projections in minutes. The projected demand was inputted into DSS models to figure appropriate production plans, delivery schedules, and inventory levels along the supply chain.

As a result, Glaxo streamlined its distribution process so wholesalers and retailers around the world never ran out of the drugs. An added benefit was that operational costs were reduced. Also, the system provided Glaxo's employees with a tool that allows them to quickly and easily access information from different sources that is now stored in one place. In addition, the network allows for efficient internal and external collaboration and communication. Finally, the IT solution enabled the company to maximize the business opportunity and to save lives in the process.

For Further Exploration: Why was a DSS needed in this case, and why is quick data consolidation so important?

Source: Condensed from B. Friar, "Fast Data Relief," *Information Week,* December 2, 1996.

At first, the high cost of building DSSs constrained their widespread use. However, the microcomputer revolution, which started around 1980, changed that. The availability of desktop computers, which were easily programmable, made it possible for a person who knows little about programming to build DSS applications. This was the beginning of the era of *end-user computing,* in which analysts, managers, many other professionals, and even secretaries build their own systems.

Decision support expanded in two directions. First, **executive information systems** were designed to support senior executives. These were then expanded to support managers within the enterprise. Later these systems became **enterprise** (or **enterprisewide**) **information systems (EISs)**, supporting all managers in the enterprise. The second direction was the support of people working in groups. **Group support systems (GSSs)** that initially supported people working in a special decision-making room expanded, due to network computing, to support people working in different locations.

By the mid-1980s the commercialization of managerial applications of *artificial intelligence (AI)* began. Essentially, artificial intelligence is concerned with programming computers to do symbolic reasoning and problem solving. Applications of AI that are of special interest for organizations are **expert systems (ESs)**. Expert systems provide the stored knowledge of experts to nonexperts, so the latter can solve difficult problems. These advisory systems differ from TPS, which centered on data, and from MIS and DSS, which concentrated on processing information. With DSS, users make their decisions according to the information generated from the systems. With ES, the *system* makes the decisions for the users based on the built-in expertise knowledge.

Knowledge management systems (KMSs) are systems designed specifically to target professional and managerial activities by focusing on creating, gathering, organizing, and disseminating an organization's *knowledge* as opposed to data or information. The software that supports these systems connects people to documents and information, and people to people. It captures new information and converts it into new knowledge that propels the enterprise forward toward its goals. Knowledge management systems are more than just an organization's intranets or extranets; they specifically focus on collecting, organizing, and effectively distributing the core knowledge assets of the organization.

All of the above systems are very beneficial, but their support is fairly passive and limited. Even expert systems are unable to learn from experience. By the beginning of the 1990s, a new breed of systems with learning capabilities emerged. Systems such as **artificial neural networks (ANNs)**, *case-based reasoning,* and *genetic algorithms* can learn from historical cases. This capability enables machines to process vague or incomplete information, as shown in the following *IT at Work.*

IT at Work

Integrating IT ...in Law Enforcement

DETECTING BOMBS IN AIRLINE PASSENGERS' LUGGAGE

The Federal Aviation Administration (FAA) in the United States is making continuous efforts to improve safety and prevent terrorists from sneaking bombs aboard airplanes. Since it is practically impossible to open and search every piece of luggage, the FAA uses computer technologies in an attempt to find different types of explosives. One approach is to bombard each piece of luggage with gamma rays that are collected by a sensor and then interpreted. The FAA is using statistical analysis and expert systems to conduct the interpretation.

However, these technologies cannot detect all types of explosives. Since 1993, artificial neural networks have been added to improve detection effectiveness. The ANN is exposed to a set of historical cases (a training set); that is, it is shown pictures obtained by gamma rays. It is also told whether each specific piece of luggage contains an explosive or not. Once trained, the system is used to predict the existence of explosives in new cases. It can detect an explosive even if the explosive device is somewhat different from those used for training. The objective is not only to detect explosives successfully, but also to minimize false alarms caused by the fact that many things (including clothing) contain nitrogen, a major component of bombs.

For Further Exploration: It is said that two heads are better than one. Can the addition of ANN be considered an extra head? Why?

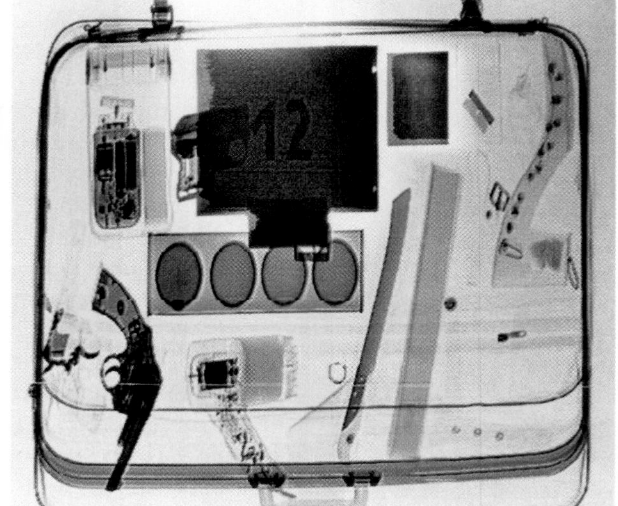

Color x-ray system used for airport security.

Source: Informal communication from Scan-Tech Security, Northvale, New Jersey (a developer of one of these systems), 1998.

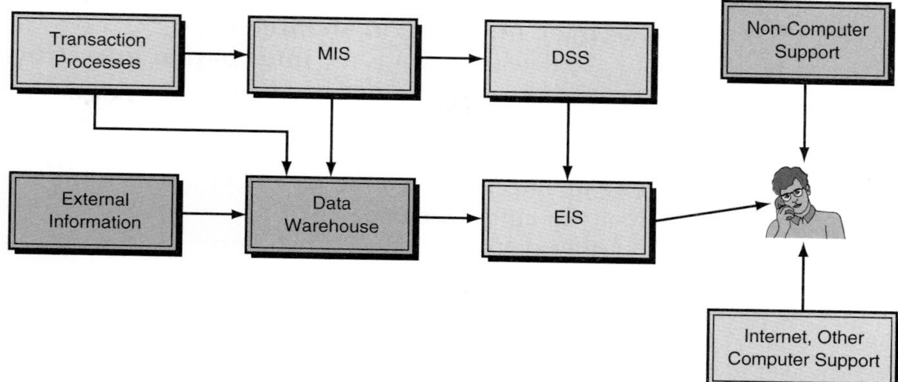

FIGURE 2.3 Interrelated support systems. The TPS collects information that is used to build the DSS and EIS. The information in the data warehouse and DSS can be used as an input to the EIS.

The relationship among the different types of support systems can be summarized as follows:

- Each support system has sufficiently unique characteristics so it can be classified as a special entity.
- The interrelationships and coordination among the different types of systems are still evolving.
- In many cases, two or more systems are integrated to form a hybrid information system.
- There is information flow among the systems. For example, MIS extracts information from TPS, and EIS receives information from data warehouses and MIS (see Figure 2.3).

A recent development in the evolution of support systems has been the development of data warehouses. A **data warehouse** is an additional database that is designed to support DSS, EIS, online analytical processing (OLAP), and other end-user activities, such as report generation, queries, and graphical presentation. It can provide an "executive view" of data and a unified corporate picture to the end users. It does this by combining the data from many operational systems and incompatible databases, without affecting the performance of the running operational systems. It can also provide the decision support system environment in which end users can analyze timely information, and it increases the ability of end users to exploit such information effectively. (This topic is discussed further in Chapter 11.)

INTEGRATION. Providing a computerized solution to a business problem may require integrating two or more of the systems mentioned above. For example, a decision support system combined with an expert system can be built to support a marketing promotion program. Therefore, it is more appropriate to view IS applications as a *matrix* in which the major functional areas are shown on the left side and the entities receiving support are at the top. The cells of the matrix are the areas in which specific applications are defined. Such a matrix is introduced in Section 2.5, where the concept of system architecture is presented.

Classification by System Architecture

How an information system is organized depends on what it is intended to support. Therefore, before designing an information system, a key task is to conceptualize the information requirements of the core business of the organization, including the way these requirements are to be met. This conceptualization is called the **information architecture**.

A related concept is the **information infrastructure**. It tells us how *specific* computers, networks, databases, and other facilities are arranged and how they are connected, operated, and managed. Architecture and infrastructure are interrelated aspects of IS design. An analogy is the *conceptual planning* of a house (the architecture) and the *specific components* such as the foundation, walls, and roof (the infrastructure).

Information systems can be classified according to three basic types of architecture:

1. A mainframe-based system
2. A standalone personal computer (PC)
3. A distributed or a networked computing system (several variations exist)

A brief description of these types is provided in Section 2.5

Now that we have introduced the different types of systems involved in the evolution of IT, let us look at some of the key systems in more detail.

2.3 TRANSACTION PROCESSING AND FUNCTIONAL INFORMATION SYSTEMS

Transaction Processing

Any organization that performs financial, accounting, and other daily business activities faces routine, repetitive tasks. For example, employees are paid at regular intervals, customers place purchase orders and are billed, and expenses are monitored and compared to the budget. Table 2.2 presents a partial list of business transactions in a manufacturing organization.

The information system that supports such processes is the *transaction processing system (TPS).* A TPS supports the monitoring, collection, storage, processing, and dissemination of the organization's basic business transactions. It also provides the input data for many applications involving other support systems such as DSS. Frequently several TPSs exist in one company. The transaction processing systems are considered critical to the success of any organization since

TABLE 2.2 Business Transactions in a Factory

Payroll	*Manufacturing*
Employee time cards	Production reports
Employee pay and deductions	Quality-control reports
Payroll checks	*Finance and accounting*
Purchasing	Financial statements
Purchase orders	Tax records
Deliveries	Expense accounts
Payments (accounts payable)	*Inventory management*
Sales	Material usage
Sales records	Inventory levels
Invoices and billings	
Accounts receivable	
Sales returns	
Shipping	

they support core operations, such as purchasing of materials, billing customers, preparing a payroll, and shipping goods to customers.

The TPS collects data continuously, frequently on a daily basis, or even in real time (as soon as they are generated, as in the Glaxo case). Most of these data are stored in the corporate databases and are available for processing. Further details on TPS are provided in Chapter 7.

Functional Management Information Systems

The transaction processing system covers the core activities of the organization. The functional areas, however, perform many other activities; some are repetitive while others are only occasional. For example, the human resources department hires, advises, and trains people. Each of these tasks can be divided into subtasks. Training may involve selecting topics to teach, selecting people to participate, scheduling classes, finding teachers, and preparing class materials. These tasks and subtasks are frequently supported by information systems specifically designed to support functional activities. Such systems are referred to as **functional MIS**, or just *MIS*.*

WHAT IS AN MIS? Functional information systems are put in place to ensure that business strategies come to fruition in an efficient manner. (This will be the topic of Chapter 7.) Typically a functional MIS provides periodic information about such topics as operational efficiency, effectiveness, and productivity by extracting information from the corporate database and processing it according to the needs of the user. MISs can be constructed in whole or in part by end users.

Management information systems are also used for planning, monitoring, and control. For example, a sales forecast by region is shown in Figure 2.4. This report can help the marketing manager make better decisions regarding advertisements and pricing of products. Another example is that of a human resources information system (HRIS), which provides a manager with a daily report of the percentage of people who were on vacation or called in sick as compared to forecasted figures.

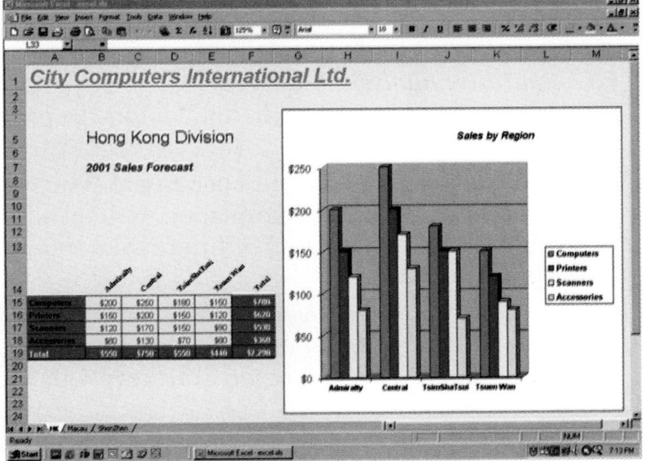

FIGURE 2.4 Sales forecast by region generated by marketing MIS.

*The term *MIS* here refers to a specific application in a functional area. MIS is also used to describe the management of information systems.

2.4 Operational, Managerial, and Strategic Systems and Hierarchy Support

Classification by the Activity Supported

Another important way to classify information systems is by the nature of the activity they support. Such support can be operational, managerial, or strategic.

OPERATIONAL SYSTEMS. *Operational systems* deal with the day-to-day operations of an organization, such as assigning employees to tasks and recording the number of hours they work, or placing a purchase order. Operational activities are short-term in nature. The information systems that support them are mainly TPSs, MISs, and simple DSSs. Operational systems are used by supervisors (first-line managers), operators, and clerical employees.

MANAGERIAL SYSTEMS. *Managerial systems,* also called *tactical systems,* deal with middle-management activities such as short-term planning, organizing, and control. Computerized managerial systems are frequently equated with MISs, because MISs are designed to summarize data and prepare reports. Middle managers also like to get quick answers to queries that an MIS can provide.

Managerial information systems are broader in scope than operational systems, but like operational systems, they use mainly internal sources of data. They provide the following types of support:

- ***Statistical summaries.*** Statistical reports include summaries of raw data such as daily production, weekly absenteeism rate, and monthly usage of electricity.
- ***Exception reports.*** To relieve managers of the information-overload syndrome, an information system can extract (or highlight) exceptions.
- ***Periodic and ad hoc reports.*** Users can get both statistical summaries and exception reports on a periodic basis or on demand. Users request ad hoc reports because they need information not available in the routine reports, or because they cannot wait for the scheduled periodic report. By means of these reports, managers can view current, or even real-time information, any time they wish to do so.
- ***Comparative analysis.*** Managers like to see performance values and other information compared to their competitors, to past performance, or to industry standards.
- ***Projections.*** In contrast to an operational system, which has only a historical orientation, managerial information systems also provide projections, such as trend analysis, projection of future sales, projection of cash flows, or forecast of market share.
- ***Early detection of problems.*** By comparing and analyzing data, managerial information systems can detect problems in their early stages. For example, statistical quality-control reports can reveal that a trend for reduced quality is developing.
- ***Routine decisions.*** Middle managers are involved in many routine decisions. They schedule employees, order materials and parts, and decide what to produce and when. Standard computerized mathematical, statistical, and financial models are available for the support of these activities.

- ***Connection.*** Functional managers need to interact frequently with each other and with specialists. The functional MISs provide e-mail and messaging systems which are not part of the operational systems. Whereas other managerial systems are confined to one company, e-mail can be extended to business partners, as in strategic systems.

STRATEGIC SYSTEMS. *Strategic systems* deal with decisions that significantly change the manner in which business is being done. Traditionally, strategic systems involved only **long-range planning**. Introducing a new product line, expanding the business by acquiring supporting businesses, and moving operations to a foreign country are prime examples of long-range activities. A long-range planning document traditionally outlines strategies and plans for five or even ten years. In the current electronic commerce environment, the planning period has been dramatically reduced to one to two years, or even months. From this plan, companies derive their shorter range planning, budgeting, and resource allocation. Today, however, strategic systems help organizations in two other ways.

...in Production & Operations Management and in Marketing

First, *strategic response systems* can respond to a major competitor's action or to any other significant change in the enterprise's environment. Although they can sometimes be planned for as a set of contingencies, strategic responses are usually not included in the long-range plan because they are unpredictable. IT is often used to support the response or to provide the response itself. When Kodak Corporation learned that a Japanese company was developing a disposable camera, for instance, the company decided to develop one too. However, the Japanese were already in the middle of the development process. By using computer-aided design and other information technologies, Kodak was able to cut its design time and beat the Japanese in the race to be the first to have the cameras in retail outlets.

Second, instead of waiting for a competitor to introduce a major change or innovation, an organization can be the initiator of change. Such *innovative strategic systems* are frequently supported by IT, as shown in Chapter 3. Federal Express's package tracking system is an example of such an innovative strategic system supported by IT.

New Strategic Systems (Electronic Commerce). As we saw in Chapter 1, *electronic commerce (EC)* has become a new way of conducting business in the last decade or so. In this new model, business transactions take place via telecommunications networks, primarily the Internet. E-commerce not only refers to buying and selling, but is also about enhanced productivity, reaching new customers, and sharing knowledge across institutions for competitive advantage. A variety of EC-supported strategic systems have been developed. An example is the FedExNet described in the opening case. It allows corporate IT to bring together different systems into a single, manageable environment that simplifies business processes and allows Federal Express to effectively service internal and external customers. Such strategic systems are indeed changing the manner in which business is done. Electronic commerce provides organizations with innovative and strategic advantages, thus enabling them to increase their market share, better negotiate with their suppliers, or prevent competitors from entering into their territory. We will provide e-commerce examples throughout the book, and Chapter 5 is devoted entirely to the topic.

The Relationship Between People and Information Systems

Top management usually makes strategic decisions. Managerial decisions are made by middle managers, and line managers and operators make operational decisions. The relationships between the people supported and the decision type are shown in Figure 2.5. The figure is organized as a triangle to also illustrate the number of employees involved. Top managers are few, and they sit at the top of the triangle.

As you can see, an additional level of staff support is introduced between top and middle management. These are professional people, such as financial and marketing analysts. They act as advisors to both top and middle management. Many of these professional workers can be thought of as knowledge workers. **Knowledge workers** are people who create information and knowledge as part of their work and integrate it into the business. Knowledge workers are engineers, financial and marketing analysts, production planners, lawyers, and accountants, to mention just a few. They are responsible for finding or developing new knowledge for the organization and integrating it with existing knowledge. Therefore they must keep abreast of all developments and events related to their profession. They also act as advisors and consultants to the members of the organization. Finally, they act as change agents by introducing new procedures, technologies, or processes. In many developed countries, 60 to 80 percent of all workers are knowledge workers.

Knowledge workers can be supported by a large variety of information systems. Such support systems range from Internet search engines that help them find information and expert systems that support information interpretation, to computer-aided design and sophisticated data management systems that help them increase their productivity and quality of work. Knowledge workers are the major users of the Internet. They need to learn what is new, to communicate with corporate managers and colleagues, and frequently to collaborate with knowledge workers in other organizations. Knowledge workers need to learn

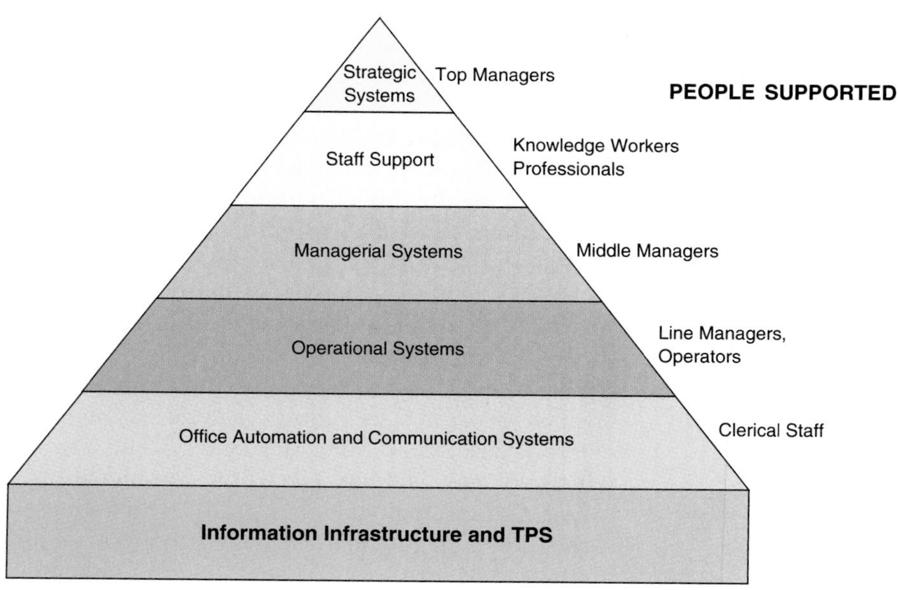

FIGURE 2.5 The information systems support of people in organizations.

and relearn. One way to assist them in improving their performance is through the use of expert systems. Expert systems can provide the knowledge of super experts and can facilitate training. The manner in which expert systems can be used is shown in the *IT at Work* story that follows.

IT at Work
EMBEDDED LOGIC

Integrating IT ...in Production and Operations Management

Since the early 1990s, expert systems have become so integrated that they have turned into parts of processes. Vendors sell them embedded in various products but seldom mention their presence. Programs are sold based on their functionality for a given application, not on whether they are "expert." The new "robot mind" becomes just part of the plumbing.

This self-effacement may have delivered expert systems to their true role, that of Web-based interfaces to corporate data resources. "Expert systems can personalize inquiries to the *n*th degree," says Tod Loofborrow, president and CEO of Authoira, an expert systems development company specializing in human resources and health-care information, whose systems let employees explore their benefits policies on the Web.

Akeel Al-Attar, of Attar Systems, thinks expert systems are a natural support system for e-commerce, since consumer "interviews" are rule bound and require much back-and-forth communication with corporate databases. He gives as an example a Japanese pump manufacturer and Attar Systems customer, Ebara Manufacturing, that produces several thousand kinds of pumps for many industries. Traditionally, customers would just ask for a pump. Sales personnel had to figure out what kind was needed. As products got more numerous and sophisticated, this manual system started to break down. Ebara fixed this problem with an online expert system. The system brings customers through a series of questions that connect their needs to specific products, often in less than a minute.

Al-Attar points out a subtle edge enjoyed by this new generation of "outward-facing" expert systems (systems that connect an organization to external entities). One reason why the programs of 10 years ago did not enjoy the success they expected, he suggests, was that they were internal systems; all they did was reduce costs. E-commerce applications, on the other hand, connect to the outside world and bring in revenue. While it might be true that a saved dollar contains the same number of pennies as an earned dollar, technologies that *make money* tend to get front-office attention. In the end, this may prove to be an even better marketing story than capturing the wisdom of experts.

For Further Exploration: What impacts have expert systems brought to industry? Will expert systems still play an important role in the e-commerce era?

Source: Extracted from Embedded Logic, *http://www.cio.com/archive/050100_revisit.html,* May 2000.

Another large class of employees is clerical workers, who support managers at all levels. Among clerical workers, those who use, manipulate, or disseminate information are referred to as *data workers.* These include bookkeepers, secretaries who work with word processors, electronic file clerks, and insurance claim processors. Clerical employees are supported by office automation and communication systems including document management, workflow, e-mail, and coordination software.

All of the systems in the support triangle are built on the information infrastructure. Consequently, all of the people who are supported work with infrastructure technologies such as the Internet, intranets, and corporate databases. The infrastructure that is shown as the foundation of the triangle in Figure 2.5 is described in the next section.

2.5 INFORMATION INFRASTRUCTURE AND ARCHITECTURE

Infrastructure

An *information infrastructure* consists of the physical facilities, services, and management that support all shared computing resources in an organization. There are five major components of the infrastructure: (1) computer hardware, (2) development software, (3) networks and communication facilities (including the Internet and intranets), (4) databases, and (5) information management personnel. Infrastructures include these resources as well as their integration, operation, documentation, maintenance, and management. Infrastructures are further discussed in Chapter 12, and in Broadbent and Weill (1997). If you go back and examine Figure 2.1 (which describes the architecture of the FedExNet), and substitute specific names instead of general ones, you will get a picture of the system's infrastructure.

Architecture*

Recall that an *information architecture* is a high-level map or plan of the information requirements in an organization. It is a guide for current operations and a blueprint for future directions. It assures us that the organization's IT meets the strategic business needs of the corporation. Therefore, it must tie together the information requirements, the infrastructure, and the support technologies, as shown in Figure 2.6.

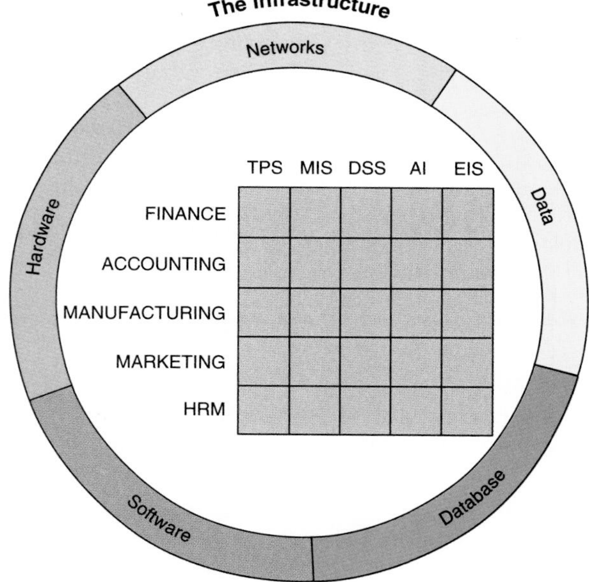

FIGURE 2.6 Schematic view of the information architecture, which combines the functional areas, the general support systems, and the infrastructure. The inside matrix includes specific applications in an organization. The outside ring includes the computing resources of the infrastructure.

*Information architecture needs to be distinguished from computer architecture (see Technology Guide 1). For example, the architecture for a computer may involve several processors, or special features to increase speed such as reduced instruction set computing (RISC). Our interest here is in information architecture only.

Remember the analogy of the architecture for a house. When preparing a conceptual high-level drawing of a house, the architect needs to know the purpose of the house, the requirements of the dwellers, and the building constraints (time, money, materials, etc.). In preparing information architecture, the designer needs similar information, which can be divided into two parts:

1. The business needs for information—that is, the organizational objectives and problems, and the contribution that IT can make. The potential users of IT must play a critical role in this part of the design process. An architect cannot plan without knowing the purpose of the house and the requirements of the owners.
2. The information systems that already exist in an organization and how they can be combined among themselves or with future systems to support the organization's information needs. If the architect is building an addition on the house, he or she needs to know how the new part of the house should fit with the old.

A system's architecture cannot be completed until the planning for the business is complete. However, IT architecture and business planning, for either a new business or the restructuring of an existing organization, are interrelated. This important topic will be revisited in Chapter 8.

AN INFORMATION ARCHITECTURE MODEL. The information architecture is a conceptual framework for the organizational IT infrastructure. It is a plan for the structure and integration of the information resources in the organization. Synnott (1987) proposes a model for information architecture, shown in Figure 2.7, which divides the information architecture into two major parts. The centralized portion serves the entire organization. It includes the business architecture (information needs of the organization), the data architecture, and the communications architecture. The decentralized (upper) portion focuses on an organizational function or on some service or activity (such as human resources, computers, end-user computing, and systems). Each entity in the upper part includes operational, managerial, and strategic applications.

GENERAL TYPES OF INFORMATION ARCHITECTURE. One way to classify information architecture is by the role the hardware plays. It is possible to distinguish two extreme cases: a mainframe environment and a PC environment. The com-

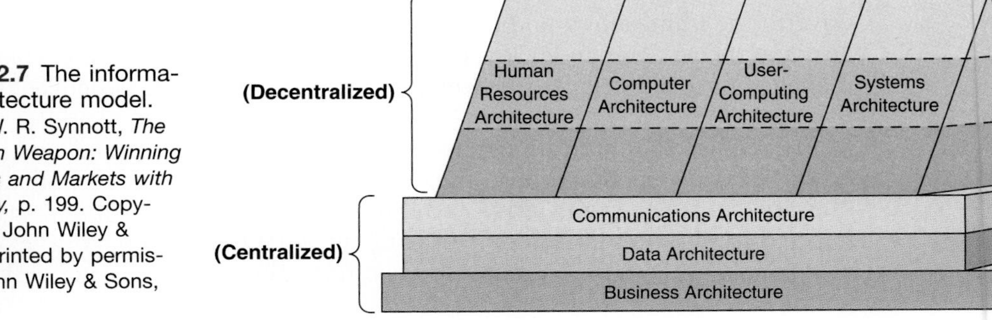

FIGURE 2.7 The information architecture model. (*Source:* W. R. Synnott, *The Information Weapon: Winning Customers and Markets with Technology,* p. 199. Copyright 1987 John Wiley & Sons. Reprinted by permission of John Wiley & Sons, Inc.)

bination of these two creates a third type of architecture, the distributed or networked environment.

1. ***Mainframe environment.*** In the mainframe environment, processing is done by a mainframe computer. The users work with passive (or "dumb") terminals, which are used to enter or change data and access information from the mainframe. This was the dominant architecture until the mid-1980s. Very few organizations use this type of architecture exclusively today. An extension of it is an architecture where PCs are used as smart terminals. A *smart terminal* (also called *intelligent terminal*) not only contains a keyboard and screen, but also comes with a disk drive so as to perform limited processing tasks when not communicating directly with the central computer. Yet, the core of the system is the mainframe with its powerful storage and computational capabilities. The network computers (NCs) that were introduced in 1997 are redefining the role of the centralized computing environment.
2. ***PC environment.*** In the PC configuration, only PCs form the hardware information architecture. They can be independent of each other, but normally the PCs are connected via electronic networks. This architecture is common for many small- to medium-size organizations.
3. ***Networked (distributed) environment.*** **Distributed processing** divides the processing work between two or more computers. The participating computers can be all mainframe, all midrange, all micros, or, as in most cases, a combination. They can be in one location or in several. **Cooperative processing** is a type of distributed processing in which two or more *geographically dispersed* computers are teamed together to execute a specific task. Another important configuration of distributed processing is the *client/server* arrangement, where several computers share resources and are able to communicate with many other computers via local area networks. When a distributed system covers the entire organization, it is referred to as an *enterprisewide system,* and its parts are frequently connected by an intranet. A distributed environment with both mainframe and PCs is very flexible and is commonly used by most medium- and large-size organizations.

This basic classification is analogous to a transportation system. You can travel three ways: First, you can use public transportation, such as a train or a plane. In this case, several riders share the vehicle and use it at specified times, and must obey several rules. This is like using a mainframe. Second, you can use your own car, which is like using a PC. Third, you can use both; for example, you can drive to the train station and take the train to work, or you can drive to the airport and take a plane to your vacation destination. This last arrangement, which is analogous to a distributed system, is flexible, providing the benefits of the other two options.

Thanks to communication networks and especially the Internet and intranets, *networked computing* is becoming the dominant architecture of most organizations. This architecture permits intra- and interorganizational cooperation in computing; accessibility to vast amounts of data, information, and knowledge; and high efficiency in the use of computing resources. The concept of networked computing drives today's new architecture. An example is provided in the *IT at Work* box that follows.

IT at Work

FLEXIBLE IT ARCHITECTURE AT CHASE MANHATTAN BANK

www.chase.com

Chase Manhattan Bank and Chemical Bank merged in 1996, creating the largest bank in the United States. The unified bank had to process 16 million checks daily across 700 locations in 58 countries. It also had to serve 25 million retail customers and thousands more institutional customers, with the customer base expected to grow by 6 to 10 percent a year. The problem was how to merge the different information systems of the bank and create an IT architecture that would support the bank's activities, including its future growth and additional planned acquisitions.

Previous mergers and acquisitions involving both Chase and Chemical had resulted in many problems in developing the IT architecture. "We needed to blueprint an architectural platform that provided operational excellence and customer privacy," says Dennis O'Leary, CEO and executive vice president of the new bank. "The platform also had to be functional and have the ability to integrate business at the retail, national, and global enterprise levels." One problem was the worldwide connectivity among more than 60,000 desktop computers, 14 large mainframes, 300 minicomputers, 1,100 T1 telecommunication lines, and more than 1,500 core applications.

A new architecture was constructed using the Internet and intranets. (Specifically, the new architecture was based on the TCP/IP model, as described in Technology Guide 5). An innovative three-layer system was designed. First is a global infrastructure; second are distribution networks that route traffic among business units; and third are numerous access networks. This flexible structure will allow the addition of more networks in the future. The global infrastructure is a network built on wide area networks, satellites, and related technologies. The architectural plan includes several security devices called *firewalls,* mainly in the distribution network layer. The access networks are the internal networks (now reformulated as intranets) of the different business units. They also have many client/server applications as well as mainframes. All the desktops are managed on Windows NT.

All of this massive networking has one goal: giving customers extensive real-time access to accounts and a view of their assets.

For Further Exploration: Why are banks so dependent on networks? Why is a three-layer system preferable to a single layer?

Source: Condensed from S. Girishankar, "Modular Net Eases Merger," *techweb.com/se/directlink.cgi,* CWK19970421S0005, April 1997.

Client/Server and Enterprisewide Computing

The Internet, intranets, and extranets are based on *client/server architecture* and *enterprisewide computing.* The principles of these concepts are briefly explained in this section, and details are provided throughout the book.

CLIENT/SERVER ARCHITECTURE. A **client/server architecture** divides networked computing units into two major categories, clients and servers, all of which are connected by local area networks and possibly by private wide area networks. A *client* is a computer such as a PC or a workstation attached to a network, which is used to access shared network resources. A *server* is a machine that is attached to this same network and provides clients with these services. Examples of servers are a database server that provides a large storage capacity and a communication server that provides connection to another network, to commercial databases, or to a powerful processor. In some client/server systems there are additional computing units, referred to as *middleware.*

The purpose of client/server architecture is to maximize the use of computer resources. Client/server architecture provides a way for different computing devices to work together, each doing the job for which it is best suited. For example, storage and heavy computation is more cost-effective on a mainframe than on a PC. Common office computing such as word processing is more conveniently handled by a PC. The role of each machine need not be fixed. A workstation, for example, can be a client in one task and a server in another. Another important element is *sharing*. The clients, which are usually inexpensive PCs, share more expensive devices, the servers.

There are several models of client/server architecture. In the most traditional model, the mainframe acts as a database server providing data for analysis, done by spreadsheets, database management systems, and other high-level programming languages, for the PC clients. For other models and more details see Technology Guide 2.

Client/server architecture gives a company as many access points to data as there are PCs on the network. It also lets a company use more tools to process data and information. Client/server architecture has changed the way people work in organizations. For example, people are empowered to access databases at will.

ENTERPRISEWIDE COMPUTING. Client/server computing can be implemented in a small work area or in one department on a LAN. Its main benefit is the sharing of resources within that department. However, many users frequently need access to data, applications, services, electronic mail, and real-time flows of data that are in different LANs or databases, so that they can improve their productivity and competitiveness. The solution is to deploy **enterprisewide computing**, a client/server architecture that connects data within an entire organization. This combination of client/servers and broad access to data forms a cohesive, flexible, and powerful computing environment. An example of such an architecture is provided in the FedExNet opening case.

An enterprisewide client/server architecture provides total integration of departmental and corporate IS resources. It thereby allows for a new class of applications that span the enterprise and benefit both corporate central management (providing controls) and end-user systems (providing empowerment). It also provides better control and security over data in a distributed environment. By implementing client/server computing as the architecture for enterprisewide information systems, organizations maximize the value of information by increasing its availability. Enterprisewide client/server computing enables organizations to reengineer business processes, to distribute transactions, to streamline operations, and to provide better and newer services to customers. In short, by using an enterprisewide client/server architecture, a corporation can gain a significant competitive advantage.

The client/server architecture can be implemented in different ways, depending on what hardware and software one is using, and what role the servers and the clients play (see Technology Guide 4). Many new IT developments are based on the client/server concept. These include enterprise group support technologies such as Lotus Notes/Domino, Microsoft Exchange, Netscape Communicator, and Microsoft Outlook (see Chapter 4) as well as the Internet and intranets.

Other Information Architectures

There are two other topics related to information architecture that we should discuss before we close this section. They are electronic data interchange and legacy systems. These form the foundation of all information architectures.

ELECTRONIC DATA INTERCHANGE (EDI). **Electronic data interchange (EDI)** is the electronic movement of specially formatted standard business documents, such as orders, bills, and confirmations sent between business partners. EDI is used primarily to electronically transfer repetitive business transactions. EDI contributes to the standardization of part of the information architecture between involved parties.

An EDI translator is necessary to convert the proprietary data into a standard format. In the past, EDI ran on expensive *value-added networks (VANs)*. These are private, data-only wide area networks used by multiple organizations to provide high capacity, security, and economies in the cost of network service. The VAN is, however, confined to data exchanges between large business partners. As a result, large companies doing business with thousands of small companies were unable to use EDI. However, the situation is changing rapidly with the emergence of *Internet-based EDI*, as we describe in Chapter 4. Internet-based EDI is an important technology for the new digital economy.

LEGACY SYSTEMS. **Legacy systems** are older, usually mature, information systems. Although legacy systems are usually less competitive and less compatible with modern equivalents, they are still, in some cases, part of the backbones of the overall IT infrastructure within an organization. They are usually pure mainframe or distributed systems in which the mainframe plays the major role and the PCs act as smart terminals. Newer legacy systems may include one or more LANs and even early client/server implementations.

Legacy systems were developed from the late 1950s through the 1980s for general-purpose business use in medium- to large-size companies. They were the primary mechanism for high-volume processing applications. Legacy systems are housed in a secured and costly data (or computer) center. They occupy one or several rooms and are operated by IS professional staff rather than by end users. Much of their work is routine, mainly in transaction processing. Some legacy systems are very large, including hundreds or even thousands of remote terminals networked to the mainframe processor. The role of legacy systems and the mainframe is changing rapidly (see Chapter 8).

2.6 WEB-BASED SYSTEMS

The concept of client/server architecture has dominated IT architecture for the past decade or so. But the specially structured client/server applications that were considered revolutionary in the mid-1990s may soon become obsolete due to the rapid development of **Web-based systems** such as the Internet and especially intranets and extranets. Although these technologies are based on the client/server concept, their implementation is considerably less expensive than that of many specially structured client/server systems. Furthermore, the conversion of existing systems to an intranet can be easy and fast, while the capabilities of an intranet can be more powerful. Therefore, as is shown throughout the book and especially in Chapters 4 and 5, the Internet, intranets, and sometimes extranets are becoming an indispensable part of most IT architectures. New Web-based architectures may replace old architectures, or may integrate legacy systems into their structure.

Technically, the term *Web-based systems* refers to those applications or services that are resident on a server that is accessible using a Web browser and is therefore accessible from anywhere in the world via the World Wide Web (WWW). The only client-side software needed to access and execute Web-based applications is a Web browser environment. An example of such an application would be an online store accessed via a Web browser such as Netscape or Internet Explorer. Additionally, two other very important features of Web-based functionality are (1) that the generated content/data are updated in real time, and (2) that they are universally accessible via the Web to users (dependent on defined user-access rights).

The Internet

The *Internet,* sometimes called simply "the Net," is a worldwide system of computer networks—a network of networks in which users at any one computer can, if they have permission, get information from any other computer (and sometimes talk directly to users at other computers). Today, the Internet is a public, cooperative, and self-sustaining facility accessible to hundreds of millions of people worldwide. Physically, the Internet uses a portion of the total resources of the currently existing public telecommunication networks. Technically, what distinguishes the Internet is its use of a set of protocols called *TCP/IP* (for Transmission Control Protocol/Internet Protocol). The Internet applications and technology are discussed in more detail in Technology Guide 4. Two recent adaptations of Internet technology, the intranet and the extranet, also make use of the TCP/IP protocol.

Intranets

The concept of an intranet is a natural progression in the marriage of the enterprise and the Internet. An *intranet* is the use of WWW technologies to create a private network, usually within one enterprise. It can be thought of as "a cloud within a cloud." Although an intranet may be a single LAN segment that uses the TCP/IP protocol, it is typically a network connected to the Internet. A security gateway such as a firewall is used to segregate the intranet from the Internet and to selectively allow access from outside the intranet.

Intranets have a variety of uses, as we discuss in Chapters 4 and 5. They allow for the secure online distribution of many forms of internal company information. Intranets are used for work-group activities and the distributed sharing of projects within the enterprise. Other uses include controlled access to company financial documents, research materials, and other information that requires distribution within the enterprise.

Extranets

The extranet is a further refinement of the intranet concept (see Chapter 4). *Extranets* can be viewed as external extensions of the enterprise intranet. They allow remote users to securely connect over the Internet or via private networks to the enterprise's main intranet. Typically, remote access software is used to authenticate and encrypt the data that pass between the remote user and the internal intranet. Extranets can also be the connection of two or more intranets to form a larger virtual network.

Extranets have uses beyond the intranet. They can allow remote access to the enterprise intranet for use by distant salespeople, online publishing personnel, remote work groups, and many others. Extranets can also allow two or more enterprises to share information in a controlled fashion. Extranets are playing a major role in the development of electronic commerce (see Chapter 5).

A sample relationship between the Internet and an enterprise intranet and extranet is shown in Figure 2.8.

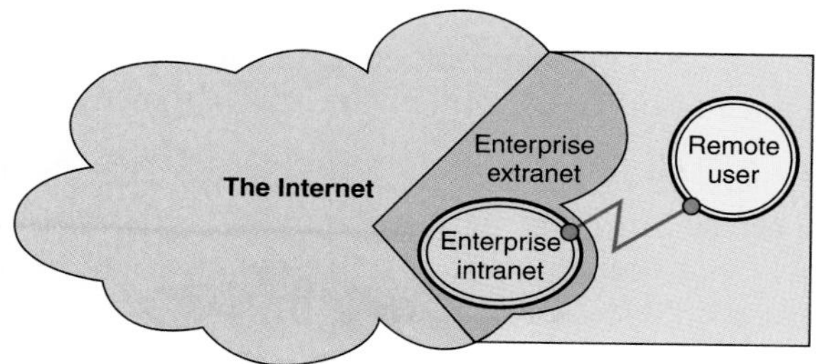

FIGURE 2.8 The Internet, an intranet, and an extranet.

E-Commerce and Storefronts

One of the natural outcomes of the Internet and the World Wide Web has been *e-commerce*. Electronic commerce is a very diverse and interdisciplinary topic, with issues ranging from technology, addressed by computer experts, to consumer behavior, addressed by behavioral scientists and marketing research experts (see Chapter 5). Web-based systems are the engines of e-commerce. They enable business and inventory transactions to be conducted seamlessly over the Internet twenty-four hours a day, seven days a week. The simple concept of the Web and e-commerce is that you can instantly reach millions of people, anywhere, anytime.

An *electronic storefront* is the Web-equivalent of a showroom (see Chapter 5). This is the Web site where an e-business displays its products. It contains descriptions, graphics, and even product reviews. Most electronic storefronts have the following common features and functions: catalog, shopping cart, checkout, transaction and payment processing, and automated fulfillment system.

Corporate Portals

Corporate portals (see Chapter 4) are also known as *enterprise portals*. These Web-based systems are developed on top of the enterprise's intranet applications. They provide aggregated information to organizational members from a single point of access. The function of corporate portals is often described as "corecasting," since they support decisions "core" (central) to particular goals of the enterprise. Portals have become a very powerful concept for intranets in particular. Some feel that the corporate portal is simply an extension of the corporate intranet, while others feel that it is in fact the next generation of this kind of intranet. Reasons for this latter view include the integration of grouped information, the unification of content, and the ability to scale down the bulk of information available in a corporate intranet. Corporate portals also help to personalize outside information.

Electronic Markets and Exchanges

Electronic markets (see Chapter 5) are rapidly emerging alongside Web-based systems as a vehicle for conducting business. An **electronic market** is a network of interactions and relationships over which information, products, services, and payments are exchanged. When the marketplace is electronic, the business center is not a physical building but a Web-based location where business interactions occur. In electronic markets, the principal participants—transaction handlers, buyers, brokers, and sellers—not only are at different locations but seldom even know one another. The means of interconnection vary among parties and can change from event to event, even between the same parties.

Electronic exchanges (see Chapter 5) are central Web-based locations where buyers and sellers interact dynamically, with buyer and seller going back and forth on a price. They were originally set as trading places for commodities. Since then a variety of exchanges have emerged for all kinds of products. *Vertical exchanges* position themselves as the hub for all buying, selling, and related services in a single market category, such as *home.boom.com.hk* for stock trading in Hong Kong and *milpro.com* for metalworking products. *Horizontal exchanges* focus on a specific function or need applicable to many different industries, such as purchasing office equipment or maintenance.

Mobile Commerce (M-Commerce)

Mobile commerce or *m-commerce* (see Chapter 5) is the buying and selling of goods and services through wireless handheld devices such as cellular telephone and personal digital assistants. Known as "next-generation e-commerce," m-commerce enables users to access the Internet without needing to find a place to plug in. The emerging technology behind m-commerce is mainly the *wireless application protocol (WAP),* which we describe in Technology Guide 4. WAP-enabled smart phones offer fax, e-mail, and phone capabilities all in one, paving the way for m-commerce to be accepted by an increasingly mobile workforce. As content delivery over wireless devices becomes faster, more secure, and scalable, there is wide speculation that m-commerce will surpass wireline e-commerce as the

IT at Work
WIRED EDUCATION

Integrating IT ...in Education

www.hbs.com

In an effort that began in 1995, Harvard Business School (HBS) has invested $10 million in a campuswide TCP/IP network designed specifically to run Web-based applications. Central to HBS's network infrastructure are dozens of intranets that are changing the culture of the 90-year-old institution in subtle yet significant ways, enhancing the school's already-strong sense of community and establishing a solid footing for the introduction of new academic services. Since September 1996, students have used a schoolwide intranet to conduct research, prepare class assignments, collaborate in study groups, communicate with professors—even get in touch with alumni.

During classes, professors can log into the HBS intranet, pull up case studies, and display them on classroom monitors. They can augment traditional class materials with real-time and multimedia information. They can also link to any Web sites as well as see video clips and hear company players comment.

For HBS students, the intranet is the communications backbone that holds together their academic community. This virtual community expands beyond the confines of the Cambridge, Massachusetts campus (near Boston) to include the more than 35,000 alumni who have volunteered to be contacted via e-mail by students about job searches. With all course material online, students use the intranet to get assignments and schedules, participate in study sessions, pull up archived e-mail messages from professors, and access research tools including OneSource and Dow Jones Interactive.

HBS decided in 1995 to make this big commitment to the Web in the form of developing an intranet. At that time, the school's five proprietary client/server LANs and seven different e-mail systems, strewn across campus, hardly befitted an institution that prides itself on being at the leading edge. The sequestered nature of the infrastructure created islands of information that could not be shared easily among the 200 faculty members. A current version of proprietary software had to be installed on client machines in order to access specific information. Tasks that should have benefited from technology were instead crippled by it.

Case studies—which are the mode of teaching at HBS—require group participation, collaboration, and research, and groups of HBS professors and students often work together in teams. For students, the new intranet is a means to get information that is customized for them. Today every course is online, and the intranet has expanded into dozens of intranets, each a collection of Web-based information and tools created for a specific user group. At HBS, each user has a password that enables access only to those intranets designed for him or her. In typical Harvard fashion, Dean Kim B. Clark holds fast to the quest for leadership position, but he admits HBS can and will do a lot more with its network. "Technology is crucial to the future of education," he says.

For Further Exploration: How can intranets help students to learn better? How can intranets help professors to teach better? How can intranets encourage collaborative learning?

Sources: Wire Education at *http://www.cio.com/archive/webbusiness/100198_hbs_content.html,* October 1998, and from *harvard.edu,* 2001.

method of choice for digital commerce transactions. See the *It at Work* on page 70.

Whether an organization uses mainframe legacy systems or cutting-edge Web-based ones, its information architecture and infrastructures are major information resources. These and other information resources are extremely important organizational assets that need to be managed. This topic is presented in Section 2.7.

2.7 MANAGING INFORMATION RESOURCES

A modern organization possesses several information resources. In addition to the infrastructures and architecture, many applications exist, and new ones are continuously being developed. (Remember that an *application* is a program designed to perform a specific function directly for the user or, in some cases, for another application program. Examples of applications include word processors, database programs, Web browsers, development tools, drawing, paint, and image editing programs, and communication programs.) Applications use the services of the computer's operating system and other supporting applications.

Application systems have enormous strategic value. Firms rely on them so heavily that, in some cases, when they are not working even for a short time, an organization cannot function. Furthermore, the acquisition, operation, and maintenance of these systems may cost a considerable amount of money. Therefore, it is essential to manage these information systems properly. The planning, organizing, implementing, operating, and controlling of the infrastructures and the organization's portfolio of applications must be done with great skill.

The responsibility for the management of information resources is divided between two organizational entities: the information systems department (ISD), which is a corporate entity, and the end users, who are scattered throughout the organization. This division of responsibility raises important questions such as:

- Which resources are managed by whom?
- What is the role of the ISD, its structure, and its place in the organization?
- What are the relationships between the ISD and the end users?

Brief answers to these questions are provided next.

Which Resources Are Managed by Whom?

There are many types of information systems resources, and their components may be from multiple vendors and of different brands. The major categories are hardware (all types of computers, servers, and other devices), software (development tools, languages, and applications), databases, networks (local, wide, Internet, intranets and extranets, and supporting devices), procedures, security facilities, and physical buildings. The resources are scattered throughout the organization, and some of them change frequently. Therefore, it may be rather difficult to manage IS resources.

There is no standard menu for the division of responsibility for the development and maintenance of IS resources between the ISD and end users. In some organizations, the ISD manages most of these resources, regardless of where they are located and how they are used. In others, the ISD manages only a few. The division depends on many things: the size and nature of the organization, the amount and type of IT resources, the organization's attitudes toward computing, the philosophy of top management, the maturity level of the technology, the amount and nature of outsourced IT work, and even the country in which the company operates.

Generally speaking, the ISD is responsible for corporate-level and shared resources, while the end users are responsible for departmental resources. Regardless of who is doing what, there are several activities involved in managing each resource. Thus, responsibilities range from planning and purchasing to application development and maintenance. Sometimes the division between the ISD and the end users is based on such activities. For example, the ISD may acquire or build systems and the end users operate and maintain them.

Because of interdependencies of information resources, it is important that the ISD and the end users work closely together and cooperate regardless of who is doing what. We discuss this below and in Chapter 15.

What Is the Role of the Information Systems Department?

The role, structure, and place of the ISD in the organization hierarchy and the department's leadership vary considerably. They depend upon the amount and importance of information resources to be managed, the extent of outsourcing, and the role that end users play. These issues will be described in Chapter 15. Here, we provide only some major observations.

1. The role of the ISD is changing from purely technical to more managerial and strategic (see Table 2.3).
2. As a result, the position of the ISD within the organization tends to be elevated from a unit reporting to a functional department, to a unit reporting to a senior vice president of administration or to the CEO.

TABLE 2.3 The Changing Role of the Information Systems Department

Traditional Major IS Functions
Managing systems development and systems project management
Managing computer operations, including the computer center
Staffing, training, and developing IS skills
Providing technical services
New (Additional) Major IS Functions
Initiating and designing specific strategic information systems
Infrastructure planning, development, and control
Incorporating the Internet and electronic commerce into the business
Managing system integration including the Internet, intranets, and extranets
Educating the non-IS managers about IT
Educating the IS staff about the business
Supporting end-user computing
Partnering with the executive level that runs the business
Actively participating in business processes reengineering
Proactively using business and technical knowledge to "seed" innovative ideas about IT
Creating business alliances with vendors and IS departments in other organizations

3. The role of the director of the ISD is changing from a technical manager to a senior executive, sometimes referred to as the *chief information officer* (CIO).
4. The internal structure of the ISD is changing to reflect its new role.
5. The ISD can be centralized or decentralized, or a combination of the two.
6. The ISD must work closely with external organizations such as vendors, business partners, research institutions, universities, and consultants.
7. The key issues in information systems management change with time. The ten most important issues for 1999 were researched by Palvia et al. (1999), and their relative importance was traced over time. These issues are listed in Table 2.4.

In early 2001, the major problem in information systems management was how to move an organization's IT systems to fit the digital age. All of these issues are covered in many places throughout this book.

Managing Relationships with End Users

The ISD and the end-user units must be close partners. Some mechanisms that build the required cooperation are:

- A *steering committee* that represents all end users and the ISD, sets IT policies, provides for priorities, and coordinates IS projects
- *Joint ISD/end-users project teams* for planning, budgeting, application developments, and maintenance
- ISD representation on the *top corporate executive committee*
- *Service agreements* that define computing responsibilities and provide a framework for services rendered by the ISD to end users
- *Technical and administrative support* (including training) for end users
- A *conflict resolution unit* established by the ISD to handle end-user complaints quickly and resolve conflicts as soon as possible

Details on these are provided in Chapter 15.

TABLE 2.4 Key MIS Issues for 1999

	Mean
1. Data and information resources	8.32
2. IS strategic processes	7.75
3. IS human resources	7.74
4. IS for competitive advantage	7.34
5. IS for organizational effectiveness	7.26
6. Software development processes	6.93
7. Telecommunications and networking	6.73
8. IS applications effectiveness	6.29
9. End-user computing and support	5.98
10. IS control	5.76

Source: Compiled from P.C. Palvia et al., "Information System Management Issues: Reporting and Relevance," *Decision Sciences*, Winter 1999, pp. 273–290.

MANAGERIAL ISSUES

1. ***The transition to networked computing.*** Converting the IT in organizations to networked computing may be a complicated process. It requires a client/server infrastructure, an Internet connection, and electronic commerce policy and strategy, all in the face of many unknowns and risks. However, this potentially painful conversion may be, in many organizations, the only way to succeed or even to survive. When to do it, how to do it, and what the impacts will be of such a conversion are major issues for organizations to consider.

2. ***From legacy systems to client/server to intranets.*** A related major issue is whether and when to move from the legacy systems to a client/server enterprisewide architecture. While the general trend is toward client/server, there have been several unsuccessful transformations and many unresolved issues regarding the implementation of these systems. The introduction of intranets seems to be much easier than that of other client/server applications. Yet, moving to any new architecture requires new infrastructure, and it may have a considerable impact on people, quality of work, and budget. These important issues are discussed in detail in Chapters 13 and 14.

   It should be noted that many companies need high-speed computing of high-volume data. Here the client/server concept may not be effective. In such cases, management should consider transformation of the legacy systems to new types of mainframes that use innovations that make the systems smaller and cheaper.

3. ***How much infrastructure?*** Justifying information system applications is not an easy job due to the intangible benefits and the rapid changes in technologies that often make systems obsolete. Justifying infrastructure is even more difficult since many users and applications share the infrastructure. This makes it almost impossible to quantify the benefits. Basic architecture is a necessity, but there are some options. Various justification methodologies are discussed in Chapter 13.

4. ***The role of the ISD.*** The role of the ISD can be extremely important, yet top management frequently mistreats it. By constraining the ISD to technical duties and considering it a second-class area, an organization may jeopardize its entire future. For appropriate roles of the ISD, see Chapter 15.

5. ***The role of end users.*** End users play an important role in IT development and management. The end users know best what their information needs are and to what degree they are fulfilled. Also, it is not economically feasible for the ISD to develop and manage all IT applications. Properly managed end-user computing is essential for the betterment of all organizations (see Chapters 8 and 14).

6. ***Ethical issues.*** Systems developed by the ISD and used and maintained by end users may introduce some ethical issues. The ISD's major objective should be to build efficient and effective systems. But, such systems may invade the privacy of the users or create advantages for certain individuals at the expense of others. See Appendix 1.1 to Chapter 1 and Chapter 16 for details.

ON THE WEB SITE... Additional resources, including the Virtual Company, quizzes, cases, updates, additional exercises, links, demos, and activities, can be found on the book's Web site.

KEY TERMS

Application programs *50*
Artificial neural network (ANN) *54*
Client/server architecture *65*
Cooperative processing *64*
Data *48*
Data warehouse *55*
Decision support system (DSS) *52*
Distributed processing *64*
Electronic data interchange (EDI) *67*
Electronic exchanges *69*
Electronic markets *69*
Enterprisewide computing *66*
Executive information system *53*
Enterprise information system (EIS) *53*
Expert system (ES) *53*
Functional MIS *57*
Group support system (GDSS) *53*
Information *48*
Information architecture *56*
Information infrastructure *56*
Interorganizational information system (IOS) *50*
Knowledge *49*
Knowledge management system (KMS) *54*
Knowledge workers *60*
Legacy system *67*
Long-range planning *59*
Management information system (MIS) *52*
Office automation system (OAS) *52*
Transaction processing system (TPS) *52*
Web-based systems *67*

CHAPTER HIGHLIGHTS (Numbers Refer to Learning Objectives)

1 Information systems can be organized according to business functions, the people they support, or both.

1 Interorganizational information systems (IOSs) connect two or more organizations and play a major role in e-business.

2 The transaction processing system (TPS) covers the core repetitive organizational transactions such as purchasing, billing, or payroll.

2 The data collected in a TPS are used to build other systems.

2 The major functional information systems in an organization are accounting, finance, manufacturing (operations), human resources, and marketing.

2 Management information systems refers to functional information systems. But MIS is also used to describe the field of IT.

3 The main general support systems are office automation systems, decision support systems, group support systems, knowledge management systems, enterprise information systems, expert systems, and artificial neural networks.

3 Managerial activities and decisions can be classified as operational, managerial (tactical), and strategic.

4 An information architecture provides the conceptual foundation for building the information infrastructure and specific applications. It maps the information requirements as they relate to information resources.

4 There are three major configurations of an information architecture: the mainframe environment, the PC environment, and the distributed (networked) environment.

4 The information infrastructure refers to the shared information resources (such as a corporate database) and their linkages, operation, maintenance, and management.

5 Legacy systems are older systems in which the mainframe is at the core of the system.

5 In a client/server architecture, several PCs (the clients) are networked among themselves and are connected to databases, telecommunications, and other providers of services (the servers).

5 An enterprisewide information system is a system that provides communication among all the organization's employees. It also provides accessibility to any data or information needed by any employee at any location.

6 Web-based systems refer to those applications or services that are resident on a server that is accessible using a Web browser. Examples are the Internet, intranets, extranets, e-commerce and storefronts, corporate portals, electronic markets and exchanges, and mobile commerce.

7 Information resources are extremely important, and they must be managed properly by both the ISD and end users.

7 In general, the ISD manages shared enterprise information resources such as networks, while end users are responsible for departmental information resources, such as PCs.

8 The role of the ISD is becoming more managerial and its importance is rapidly increasing.

8 Steering committees, service agreements, and conflict-resolution units are some of the mechanisms used to facilitate the cooperation between the ISD and end users.

QUESTIONS FOR REVIEW

1. Describe a TPS.
2. What is an MIS?
3. Explain the role of the DSS.
4. How does a KMS work?
5. Describe operational, managerial, and strategic activities.
6. Define data, information, and knowledge.
7. What information systems support the work of groups?
8. What is an enterprisewide system?
9. What is an information architecture?
10. Describe information infrastructure.
11. Discuss the evolution of support systems over time.
12. What is a Web-based system?
13. Define the Internet, intranet, and extranet.
14. What is mobile commerce?
15. List the information resources that are usually managed by end users.
16. Distinguish between a mainframe and a distributed environment.
17. Describe a legacy system.
18. What is a client/server system?
19. What mechanisms can be used to assure ISD and end-user cooperation?

QUESTIONS FOR DISCUSSION

1. Review the analogy between means of transportation and an information architecture. Show the equivalence, and indicate the major advantages and disadvantages of each of the three subsystems.
2. Discuss the logic of building information systems in accordance with the organizational hierarchical structure.
3. Distinguish between interorganizational information systems (IOS) and electronic markets.
4. Distinguish between information architecture and information infrastructure.
5. Explain how operational, managerial, and strategic activities are related to general support systems.
6. Relate the following concepts: client/server, distributed processing, and enterprisewide computing.
7. Web-based applications such as intranets and extranets exemplify the platform shift from client/server computing to Web-based computing. Discuss the advantages of a Web-based operating environment.
8. Some feel that the corporate portal is simply an extension of the corporate intranet, while others feel that it is in fact a next generation of this kind of intranet. What do you think?
9. Is the Internet an infrastructure, an architecture, or an application program? Why? If none of the above, then what is it?
10. There is wide speculation that m-commerce will surpass "wireline" e-commerce (e-commerce that takes place over wired networks) as the method of choice for digital commerce transactions. What industries will be most affected by m-commerce?

EXERCISES

1. Classify each of the following systems as one (or more) of the general support systems:
   a. A student registration system in a university.
   b. A system that advises farmers about which fertilizers to use.
   c. A hospital patient-admission system.
   d. A system that provides a marketing manager with demand reports regarding the sales volume of specific products.
   e. A robotic system that paints cars in a factory.
2. Review the list of key MIS issues in Table 2.4.
   a. Present these issues to IT managers in a company you can access. (You may want to develop a questionnaire.)
   b. Have the managers vote on the importance of these items. Also ask them to add any items that are important to them but don't appear on the list. Report the results. Try to explain the differences between your results and the original study.
3. Review the following systems in Chapter 1 and classify each of them according to the inside cells in the matrix in Figure 2.6. Try to match each system with at least one cell. (Note that a system can be classified in several ways.) The systems in Chapter 1 are:

   Bristol-Myers Squibb

   Le Saunda Holding

   Seattle Mariners

   FDA (*IT at Work*)
4. Review the following systems in this chapter and classify each of them according to the pyramid of Figure 2.7.

   FedExNet

   Glaxo Wellcome

   Bomb Detection by the FAA

   Harvard Business School

   J.C. Penney (Minicase 2)

GROUP AND ROLE-PLAYING ACTIVITIES

1. Observe a checkout counter in a supermarket that uses a scanner. Find some material that describes how the scanned code is translated into the price that the customers pay.
   a. Identify the following components of the system: inputs, processes, and outputs.
   b. What kind of a system is the scanner (TPS, DSS, EIS, MIS, etc.)? Why did you classify it as you did?
   c. Having the information electronically in the system may provide opportunities for additional managerial uses of that information. Identify such uses.
   d. Research and report on how such systems will be operating in the new digital economy. Describe them.
2. Divide the class into teams. Each team will select a small business to start (a restaurant, dry cleaning business, small software company, etc.). Each team will plan the architecture for the business's information system, preferably in consultation with Microsoft's or other vendor's Web site. Make a class presentation.

INTERNET EXERCISES

1. Enter the site of Federal Express (*fedex.com*) and find the systems innovations of the company from 1979 to 2001. Explain how the systems innovations contribute to the success of the company.
2. Surf the Internet for information about airport security via bomb detecting devices (review *IT at Work:* Detecting Bombs in Airline Passengers' Luggage). Examine the available products, and comment on the IT techniques used.
3. Visit the site of American Airlines (*aa.com*). Find out how American uses the Internet for advertisement, auctions, etc.
4. Enter the Web site of Hershey (*hersheyfoods.com*). Examine the information about the company and its products and markets. Explain how an intranet helps such a company compete in the global market.

Minicase 1

Web-based Information Systems in a Singaporean Hotel

Raffles Hotel, Singapore's colonial-era landmark and now a national monument, is the flagship of the Raffles Ltd., which manages 16 luxury hotels worldwide, including 2 in Singapore as well as 36 restaurants. Raffles Hotel is operating in a very competitive environment. To maintain its worldwide reputation, the hotel spent lavishly on every facet of its operation. For example, the hotel once stocked 12 different kinds of butter, at a high cost.

All this changed in 2001, when Raffles moved its purchasing and sales to the Web by creating a private online marketplace. Here is how it works:

To do business with Raffles, each of 5,000 potential vendors must log on to Raffle's electronic exchange. As for the purchasing, Raffles conducts reverse auctions (see Chapter 5) among qualified suppliers. This reduces the number of suppliers while increasing the quantity purchased, enabling lower purchasing prices. For example, butter is purchased now from only two suppliers. Also, negotiations can take place online.

The private exchange is strategically advantageous to Raffles in forcing suppliers to disclose their prices on the exchange, thus increasing competition among suppliers. To convince the purchasing agents at Raffles that their jobs were secure, they are encouraged to collaborate on the system. The company is saving about $1 million a year on procurement from eight high-volume suppliers for items such as toilet paper and butter alone.

The exchange is also used as a sell-side, allowing other hotels to buy Raffles-branded products like tiny shampoo bottles and bathrobes. Raffles-branded products are considered luxury products making the hotels purchasing the products look upscale.

Since each of Raffles hotels has its own information system as do all their trading partners, it is necessary to create a global, secured system that will connect all the parties. This is done via an extranet.

Questions for Minicase 1

1. Why is an extranet needed?
2. Which Web-based systems are likely to support this venture?
3. Is this an operational, managerial, or strategic system? Why?
4. Identify TPs and any functional systems that are involved in this venture.

Source: Compiled from I. Greenberg, *Asian Wall Street Journal,* May 21, 2001 pg. T1, and from *bexcom.com.*

Minicase 2

Two Faces of J.C. Penney

www.JCPenney.com

In 2000, Dallas retailer J.C. Penney enhanced an already strong e-retail position in time for the holiday rush by adding homegrown site features that let customers more quickly locate and pay for merchandise. With *JCPenny.com,* the company unveiled express checkout services that let customers zip through a purchase in as few as two clicks. It also inaugurated electronic gift certificates that can be redeemed online, plus improved order tracking to give customers more accurate delivery estimates. These features followed the early November launch of Mercado Search, a search engine that lets shoppers prowl J.C. Penney's site by product category and receive results ranked according to relevance. In the following year, the company is expecting to roll out specialized sites dedicated to name-brand merchandise, making it easier for customers to find certain products. All these steps are designed to boost an already strong online strategy.

(continued)

The success of JCPenney.com, in large measure, is a result of a customer service and logistics infrastructure built to support a multibillion-dollar catalog business that has been extended online. JCPenney.com plans to broaden its appeal by launching specialty sites to promote high-margin brands, including Sony, Levi Strauss, Nike, and Kitchen Aid appliances. The idea is to drive purchases of name-brand merchandise by providing more detailed information on those products, as well as direct links to the manufacturers. J.C. Penney is also conducting auctions on its Web site.

The company boasts strong integration between its Web site and its offline infrastructure that should help the site reach its aggressive sales targets. Anything purchased online can be picked up or returned at any J.C. Penney or Eckerd store. J.C. Penney has fourteen customer-service centers nationwide that handle catalog and phone inquiries, and employees have been cross-trained in e-mail. United Parcel Service (UPS) delivers most merchandise ordered online within 24 to 72 hours.

J.C. Penney serves customers via three sales channels—stores, catalogs, and Web sites. Integrating these three channels will eventually pay off, said Foreseter Research analyst Seema Williams. "As the number of online shoppers grows, the impact from multiple channels will be felt much more on J.C. Penney's bottom line," Williams said.

Despite the strong Web performance, e-commerce alone cannot turn around a company of J.C. Penney's size, experts said. "The Web is such a small part of their business; there's no way it's going to turn around the company," said an expert. "The Web is icing on the cake, but the biggest part of the company, by far, is struggling."

Questions for Minicase 2

1. How does a search engine help J.C. Penney to do a better job in customer service?
2. Does its existing legacy system help J.C. Penney.com accomplish its goal in promoting its online business?
3. What kind of information technologies can be used to help J.C. Penney to promote its business?
4. How does J.C. Penney use IT to accomplish its business strategies?
5. Visit *www.JCPenney.com* to see how J.C. Penney uses its storefront to provide customer services.
6. Visit *www.sears.com* and *www.marksandspencer.com,* and find out these companies' e-commerce strategies. Compare their strategies with those of J.C. Penny.

Source: Compiled from *Two Faces of J.C. Penney, http://www.internetweek.com/lead/lead_112400.htm,* November 2000.

REFERENCES AND BIBLIOGRAPHY

1. Alavi, M., and D. Leidner, "Knowledge Management Systems: Emerging Views and Practices from the Field," *Proceedings, 32nd Hawaiian International Conference on Systems Sciences (HICSS),* 1999.
2. Bingi, P., et al., "Critical IT Implementation Issues in Developed and Developing Countries," *Information Strategy: The Executive's Journal,* Winter 2000.
3. Brancheau, J. C., et al., "Key Issues in Information Systems Management: 1994–95, SIM Delphi Results," *MIS Quarterly,* June 1996.
4. Broadbent, M., and P. Weill, "Management by Maxim: How Business IT Managers Can Create IT Infrastructures," *Sloan Management Review,* Spring 1997.
5. Dickson, G. W. and G. DeSanctis, *Information Technology and the Future Enterprise: New Models for Managers.* Upper Saddle River, NJ: Prentice-Hall, 2001.
6. Doke, R. E., and T. Barrier, "An Assessment of Information Systems Taxonomies: Time to Re-evaluate," *Journal of Information Technology,* Vol. 3, 1994.
7. Duffy, D., "Chief Executives Who Get IT," *CIO Magazine,* July 15, 1999.
8. Harmon, P., M. Rosen, and M. Guttman, *Developing E-Business Systems and Architectures: A Manager's Guide.* San Francisco, CA: Morgan Kaufmann, 2000.
9. McNurlin, B., and R. Sprague, *Information Systems Management in Practice,* 4th ed. Upper Saddle River, NJ: Prentice-Hall, 1998.
10. Orfali, R., D. Harkey, and J. Edwards, *Client/Server Survival Guide,* 3rd ed. New York: Wiley, 1999.
11. Palvia, P. C., et al., "Information System Management Issues: Reporting and Relevance," *Decision Sciences,* Winter 1999.
12. Rajput, W., *E-Commerce Systems Architecture and Applications.* Cambridge, MA: Artech House, 2000.
13. Ross, J. W., and D. F. Feeny, "The Evolving Role of the CIO," in R. Zmud (ed.), *Framing the Domains of IT Management: Projecting the Future . . . Through the Past.* Cincinnati, OH: Pinnaflex Educational Resources, 2000.
14. Sinha, A., "Client-Server Computing," *Communications of the ACM,* July 1992.
15. Synnott, W. R., *The Information Weapon.* New York: Wiley, 1987.
16. Tiwana, A., *The Essential Guide to Knowledge Management: e-Business and CRM Applications,* Upper Saddle River, NJ: Prentice-Hall, 2000.
17. Turban, E., and J. Aronson, *Decision Support Systems and Intelligent Systems,* 6th ed. Upper Saddle River, NJ: Prentice-Hall, 2001.
18. Wreden, N., "Business Boosting Technologies" *Beyond Computing.* November–December 1997.
19. Zmud, R., *Framing the Domains of IT Management: Projecting the Future . . . Through the Past.* Cincinnati, OH: Pinnaflex Educational Resources, 2000.

PART I
IT in the Organization

CHAPTER

3

Strategic Information Systems for Competitive Advantage

LEARNING OBJECTIVES

After studying this chapter, you will be able to:

1. Describe strategic information systems (SISs) and explain their advantages.
2. Describe Porter's competitive forces model and how information technology helps companies improve their competitive positions.
3. Describe Porter's value chain model and its relationship to information technology.
4. Describe several other frameworks that show how IT supports the attainment of competitive advantage.
5. Describe the role of Web-based SIS and the nature of competition in the digital age.
6. Describe global competition and its SIS framework.
7. Describe representative SISs and the advantage they provide to organizations.
8. Discuss implementation issues, including possible failures of SIS.

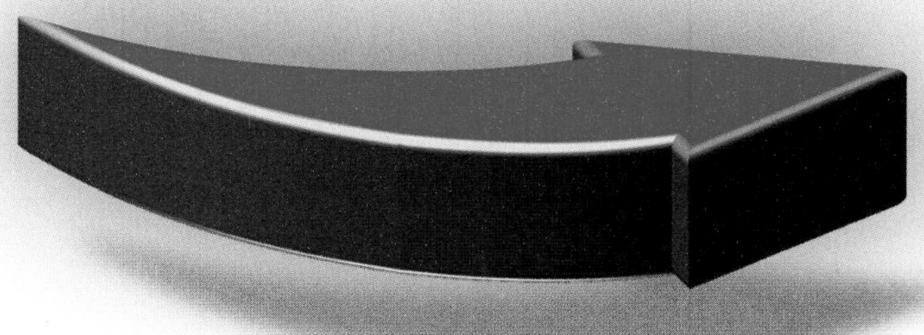

ROSENBLUTH INTERNATIONAL: COMPETING IN THE DIGITAL ECONOMY

THE PROBLEM

Rosenbluth International (*rosenbluth.com*) is a major global player in the extremely competitive travel agent industry. The digital revolution has introduced the following threats to Rosenbluth and other agencies in the industry:

www.rosenbluth.com

1. Airlines, hotels, and other service providers are attempting to displace travel agents by moving aggressively to electronic distribution systems (e.g., airlines are issuing electronic tickets, and groups of airlines are sponsoring selling portals for direct sale of tickets and packages).
2. Some travel service providers have reduced commissions caps (from $50 to $10) and have cut the commission percentage for travel agents (from 10 percent to 8 and then to 5 percent).
3. A large number of new online companies (such as *expedia.com*) are providing diversified travel services as well as bargain prices, mostly to attract individual travelers. These services are penetrating to the corporate travel area, which has been the "bread and butter" of the travel agents' business.
4. The competition among the major players is rebate based. The travel agencies basically give back to their customers part of the commission they get from travel service providers.
5. Innovative business models that were introduced by e-commerce, such as auctions and reverse auctions, were embraced by the providers in the industry, adding to competitive pressures on travel agencies (see Turban et al., 2002, Chapter 10).

All of the above business pressures threatened the welfare of Rosenbluth.

THE SOLUTION

The company responded with two strategies. First, it decided to get out of the leisure travel business, instead becoming a pure corporate travel agency. Second, it decided to rebate customers with the *entire* commission the agency receives and instead bills customers by service provided. Rosenbluth charges fees, for example, for consultation on how to lower costs, for development of in-house travel policies, for negotiating for their clients with travel providers, and for calls answered by the company staff. To implement this second strategy, which completely changed the company's business model, it was *necessary* to use several innovative information systems.

Rosenbluth uses a comprehensive Web-based business travel management solution that integrates Web-based travel planning technology, policy and profile management tools, proprietary travel management applications, and seamless front-line service/support. This browser-based service allows corporate travelers to book reservations anytime, anywhere—within corporate travel policy—in minutes. The specific tools that comprise this system are:

- ***DACODA (Discount Analysis Containing Optimal Decision Algorithms).*** This is a patented yield-management system that enables travel managers to decipher complex airline pricing and identify the most favorable airline contracts. Use of this system optimizes a client corporation's travel savings.

- ***Electronic Messaging Services.*** Electronic messaging enables clients to manage their travel requests via e-mail. Its main feature utilizes a Web-based template that permits clients to submit reservation requests, any time, without the need to pick up the phone. Additionally, a structured itinerary is returned to the traveler via e-mail.
- ***E-Ticket Tracking Solution.*** This system tracks, monitors, reports on, and collects the appropriate refund or exchange for unused e-tickets. As e-ticket usage grows, so do the number of unused e-tickets that need to be refunded or exchanged.
- ***Res-Monitor.*** This patented low-fare search system tracks a reservation up until departure time and finds additional savings for one out of every four reservations.
- ***A Global Distribution Network.*** This network electronically links the corporate locations and enables instant access to any traveler's itinerary, personal travel preferences, or corporate travel policy.
- ***Custom-Res.*** This global reservation system ensures compliance with client travel policies, consistent service, and accurate reservations.
- ***IntelliCenters.*** These advanced reservations centers use innovative telecommunications technology to manage calls from multiple accounts, resulting in cost savings and personal service for the corporate clients.
- ***Network Operations Center (NOC).*** This center monitors the many factors impacting travel, including weather, current events, and air traffic. This information is disseminated to the company's front-line associates so that they can keep clients aware of potential changes to their travel plans. The NOC also tracks call volume at all offices and enables the swift rerouting of calls if needed.

THE RESULTS

Using its IT innovations, Rosenbluth grew from sales of $40 million in 1979 in air sales, primarily leisure-oriented, in the Philadelphia, Pennsylvania area, to sales of over $3 billion in 1997. Today, the company has physical offices in 24 countries and employs about 4,500 employees. Since the introduction of the Web-based solution in 1997, sales increased to about $5 billion in 3 years (60 percent). The company not only survived the threats of elimination but also increased its market share and profitability.

Sources: Compiled from E. K. Clemons and I. H. Hann, "Rosenbluth International: Strategic Transformation" *Journal of MIS,* Fall 1999; and from information at *rosenbluth.com.*

LESSONS LEARNED FROM THIS CASE

This opening case is a vivid example of a company that has achieved competitive advantage in the digital era by using IT. Rosenbluth's experience illustrates the following points:

1. It is sometimes necessary to completely change business models and strategies to succeed in the digital economy.
2. Web-based IT enables companies to gain competitive advantage and to survive in the face of serious corporate threat.
3. Global competition is not just about price and quality; it is about service as well.

4. IT may require a large investment over a long period of time.
5. Extensive networked computing infrastructure is necessary to support a large global system.
6. Web-based applications can be used to provide superb customer service.
7. It is necessary to patent innovative systems to assure competitive advantage. Otherwise, competitors will copy the systems, and the advantage will disappear.

The most important lesson learned from this case is the double-sided potential of the Web: It can become a threat to an entire industry, yet it can also be an extremely important tool for gaining strategic advantage for an innovative company in the same industry. As a matter of fact, many executives who until 1998 were cynical about the strategic advantages of IT, have since then completely reversed their attitudes. They are seeing the potential of Web-based systems to provide competitive advantage to organizations. In a study conducted by Lederer et al. (1998), "enhancing competitiveness or creating strategic advantage" was ranked as the number-one benefit of Web-based systems. Web-based opportunities and risks are now attracting universal attention in executive boardrooms.

As a matter of fact, computer-based information systems of all kinds have been enhancing competitiveness and creating strategic advantage for several decades (e.g., see Griffiths et al., 1998, and Galliers et al., 1999). This chapter demonstrates, through numerous examples, how different kinds of strategic information systems work. We also present some classic models upon which strategic information systems have been built and utilized from the 1970s to this very day.

3.1 Strategic Advantage and Information Technology

Strategic Information Systems

Strategic information systems (SISs), like the one developed at Rosenbluth International, are systems that *support* or *shape* a business unit's competitive strategy (Callon, 1996, and Neumann, 1994). An SIS is characterized by its ability to *significantly* change the manner in which business is done. It can also change the goals, processes, products, or environmental relationships to help an organization gain a competitive advantage.

Competition, according to Porter (1985 and 1996), is at the core of a firm's success or failure. An organization's *competitive strategy* is the search for a **competitive advantage** in an industry, which gives it an advantage over competitors in some measure such as cost, quality, or speed. Competitive advantage leads to control of the market and to larger-than-average profits. A strategic information system helps an organization gain a competitive advantage through its contribution to the strategic goals of an organization and/or its ability to significantly increase performance and productivity.

Competitive advantage in the Web economy may be even more important than in the old economy, as will be demonstrated later in the chapter (in Section 3.5). Due to frequent changes in technologies and markets, and the appearance of new business models, industry structure and the nature of competition can change rapidly (Choi and Whinston, 2000). Companies with competitive advantage can benefit greatly at the expense of those that suffer from competitive disadvantage.

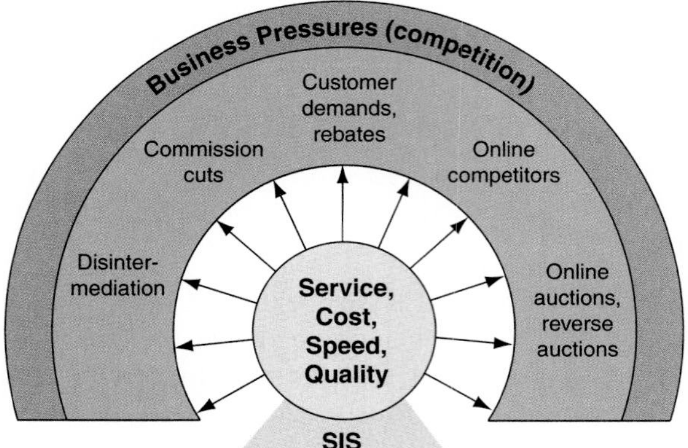

FIGURE 3.1 Strategic information systems at Rosenbluth—defending against business pressures and competition.

Let's examine Rosenbluth's competitive situation in light of the business pressures and organizational responses described in Chapter 1. As Figure 3.1 shows, there are five business pressures on the company. Rosenbluth's strategic response was (1) to eliminate the retailing activities, which were most likely to be impacted by the pressures, and (2) to change the revenue model from commission based to fee-for-service based. Such strategy requires extensive IT support, as discussed earlier.

Originally, strategic systems were considered to be *outwardly focused,* aiming at direct competition in an industry and visible to all. For example, strategic systems have been used to provide new services to customers and/or suppliers, with the specific objective of doing better than one's competitors. But since the late 1980s, strategic systems are also being viewed *inwardly:* They are focused on enhancing the competitive position of the firm by increasing employees' productivity, improving teamwork, and enhancing communication. These approaches may not be visible to the competitors. Rosenbluth used both approaches.

In order to better understand how SIS works, let us first discuss some generic aspects of strategic management.

A Key Element of Strategic Management—Innovation

The term *strategic* points to the long-term nature and to the large magnitude of the advantage an organization has over its competitors. *Strategic management* is the way an organization maps the strategy of its future operations. It has long been associated with long-range planning. Today, strategic management includes three complementary activities: **long-range planning**, **response management**, and proactive **innovation**. The topic of long-range planning is outside the boundaries of this book (see Luftman, 1996). Response management includes several of the critical response activities presented in Chapter 1. Here, we focus on innovation.

Innovation was one of the most important business concepts for the 1990s (see Davenport, 1993), and it is the key to success in the Web-based economy in the first decade of the twenty-first century. The Rosenbluth case at the beginning of the chapter demonstrated the importance of innovation for business success. Companies that can create strategic advantage by using Web-based IT are today's winners. When one company introduces a major successful visible innovation, other companies in the industry need to respond to the threat. Innovation is strongly related to information technologies, which can facilitate creativity and the generating of ideas, as shown in Table 3.1 (and as we will see in Chapters 10 and 12).

The Role of IT in Strategic Management

...in Production & Operations Management

Information technology contributes to the innovation needed in strategic management in many ways (see Kemerer, 1997, and Callon, 1996). Consider these six:

1. Information technology creates innovative *applications* that provide direct strategic advantage to organizations. For example, Federal Express was the first company in its industry to use information technology for tracking the location of every package in its system. Today, the company provides e-fulfillment solutions based on IT and is even writing software for this purpose (Bhise et al., 2000).
2. Information systems themselves have long been recognized as a competitive weapon (Ives and Learmouth, 1984, and Callon, 1996). Some of Rosenbluth's systems are patented and provide savings to customers. Such savings cannot be realized by competitors' systems.
3. IT supports changes such as *reengineering* that translate to strategic advantage. For example, IT allows efficient decentralization by providing speedy communication, and it streamlines and shortens product design time with computer-aided engineering tools.

TABLE 3.1 Areas of IT Related to Technological Innovations

Innovation	Advantage
New business models	Being the first to establish a new model puts one way ahead of possible competitors. The Web enables many innovative new business models, such as Priceline's "name-your-own-price" and eBay's online auctions. Using these models can provide strategic advantage.
New markets, global reach	Finding new customers in new markets. Using the Web, Amazon.com is selling books in almost 200 countries, all by direct mail. Rosenbluth International expanded to 24 countries backed by its communication systems.
New products	Constantly innovating with new competitive products and services. Electronic Art Inc. was first to introduce CD-ROM-based video games. MP3 Inc. enabled downloading of music from its Web site.
Extended products	Leveraging old products with new competitive extensions. When a Korean company was the first to introduce "fuzzy logic" in its washing machines, sales went up 50 percent in a few months.
Differentiated products	Gaining advantage through unique products or added value. Compaq Computers at one time became the leading PC seller after providing self-diagnostic disks with its computers. Dell Computer pioneered the concept of home delivery of customized computers.
Super systems	Erecting competitive barriers through major system developments that cannot be easily duplicated. American Airlines' reservation system, SABRE, became so comprehensive that it took years to duplicate; a super system always stays ahead of the competition. Caterpillar's multibillion-dollar equipment maintenance system is difficult to duplicate.
Customer terminals	Putting computer terminals in customers' offices can lock out the competition. American Hospital Supply did this during the 1980s, to great effect.
Computer-aided sales	Offering systems that provide computer support to marketing and sales. For example, a company might equip salespeople with wireless handheld computers that allow them to provide price quotations at the customer's location.

4. IT links a company with its business partners effectively and efficiently. For example, Rosenbluth's networks connect agents, customers, and providers around the globe, an innovation that allowed it to broaden its marketing range.
5. IT provides for cost reduction. For example, online stock brokerage is 90 percent cheaper than offline brokerage. Innovation in pricing is often the driving force in obtaining strategic advantage.
6. IT provides competitive (business) *intelligence* by collecting and analyzing information about products, markets, competitors, and environmental changes (see Guimaraes and Armstrong, 1997). For example, if a company knows something important before its competitors, or if it can make the correct interpretation of information before its competitors, then it can act first, gaining strategic advantage. Because competitive intelligence is such an important aspect of gaining competitive advantage, we look at it in some detail next.

Competitive Intelligence

Information about one's competitors sometimes can mean the difference between winning and losing a battle in business. Many companies continuously monitor the activities of their competitors. For example, Hertz monitors car rental prices of competitors on a daily basis, and Kraft, the giant food maker, closely monitors the performance of its competitors. Such activities to gather information on competitors are part of **competitive intelligence**. Such information gathering drives business performance by increasing market knowledge, improving internal relationships, and raising the quality of strategic planning.

Several technologies can be used for collecting competitive information. These range from the Internet to optical character recognition.

Integrating IT ...in Finance

However, it's not enough just to gather information on a competitor. Analyzing and interpreting the information is as important as collecting it. For these tasks, one can use IT tools ranging from *intelligent agents* (software tools that allow the automation of tasks that require intelligence; see Chapter 12) to *data mining* (searching in large databases for relationships among bits of data, using specialized logic tools). For example, Chase Manhattan Bank (New York) uses data mining to track several sources of information. Chase's goal is to determine the possible impact of the information on the bank, the customers, and the industry.

Research indicates that the percentage of companies using IT to support competitive intelligence has increased from 31 percent in 1993, to about 50 percent in 1997, to over 70 percent in 2000. This increase is primarily due to the use of the Internet.

THE INTERNET AND COMPETITIVE INTELLIGENCE. The Internet plays an increasingly important role in supporting competitive intelligence (see Teo, 2000, and Bell and Harari, 2000). Power and Sharda (1997) proposed a framework in which the Internet capabilities are shown to provide information for strategic decisions. According to the framework (see Figure 3.2), the external information required (upper left) and the methods of acquiring information (upper right) can be supported by Internet tools via processes such as organizational experience with the Internet and the strategic planning process.

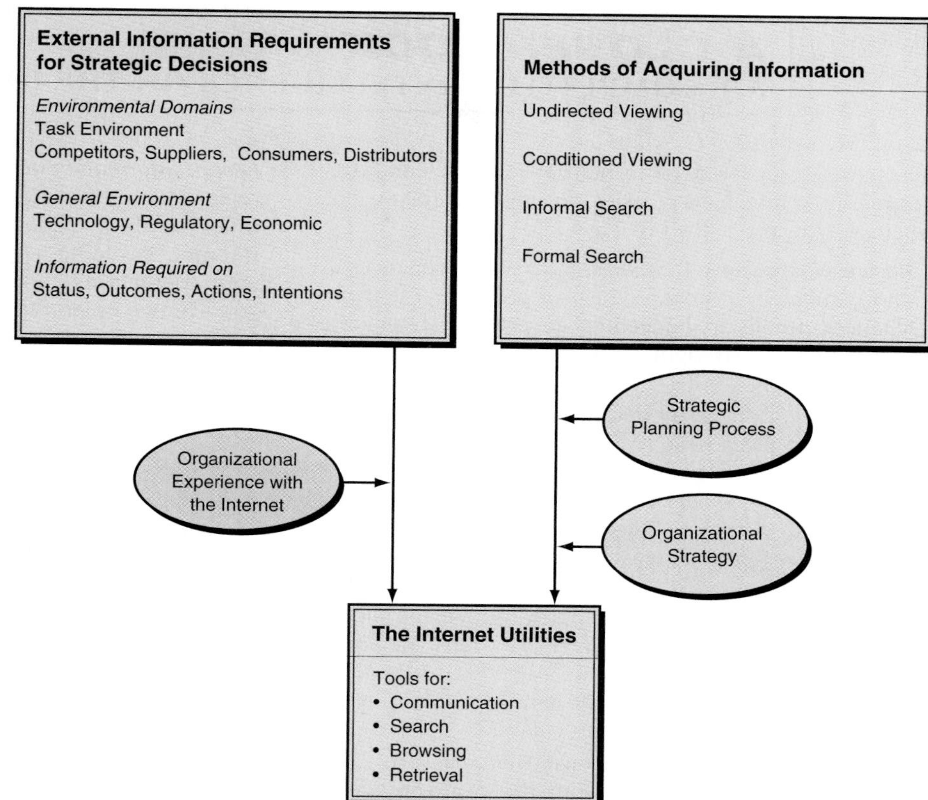

FIGURE 3.2 A framework for the Internet as a source of information for strategic decision making. (*Source:* Reprinted from *Long Range Planning,* 30, B. S. Pawar and R. Sharda, "Obtaining Business Intelligence on the Internet," 1997. With Permission from Excerpta Media Inc.)

Power and Sharda emphasize the search capability of the various tools of the Internet. Using these tools one can implement specific search strategies, as illustrated in *A Closer Look* 3.1 (page 88).

There is another aspect to competitive intelligence: *industrial espionage.* Corporate spies, which actually do exist in some industries, look for marketing plans, cost analyses, new products/services, and strategic plans. Such espionage can be unethical and illegal. Another type of industrial espionage is the theft of portable computers at airports, hotels, and conferences, which is a problem existing all over the world. Many of the thieves are interested in the information stored in the computers, not in the computers themselves. Protecting against such activities is an important part of maintaining competitive advantage. This topic is discussed in Chapter 15, and in McGonagle and Vella (1998).

Before we discuss how organizations apply IT to facilitate their competitiveness, it is necessary to introduce the concept of sustainable strategic advantage.

Sustainable Strategic Advantage

Competitive strategy aims to establish a profitable and *sustainable* position against the forces that determine industry competition. Strategic information systems (SISs) are designed to facilitate competitive advantage. Indeed, during the period from 1970 through the late 1990s, businesses implemented numerous successful IT-based strategic systems that lasted many years. However, in the first decade of the twenty-first century, it has become increasingly difficult to *sustain* an advantage for an extended period. Competitors can imitate systems in months rather

A CLOSER LOOK
3.1 COMPETITIVE INTELLIGENCE ON THE INTERNET

The Internet can be used to help a company conduct competitive intelligence easily, quickly, and relatively inexpensively in the following ways.

1. ***Review competitor's Web sites.*** Such visits can reveal information about new products or projects, potential alliances, trends in budgeting, advertising strategies used, financial strength, and much more (*dnb.com, lexis-nexis.com*).
2. ***Analyze related newsgroups.*** Internet newsgroups help you find out what people think about a company and its products. For example, newsgroup participants state what they like or dislike about products provided by you and your competitors. You can also examine people's reactions to a new idea by posting a question.
3. ***Examine publicly available financial documents.*** This can be accomplished by entering a number of databases. Most charge nominal fees. The most notable database of financial documents is the Securities and Exchange Commission EDGAR database. (See Internet Exercise 5 and *sec.gov/edgarhp.htm.*)
4. ***Do market research at your own Web site.*** You can pose questions to visitors at your site. You can even give prizes to those visitors who best describe the strengths and weaknesses of competitors' products.
5. ***Use an information delivery service to gather news on competitors.*** Information delivery services (such as Info Wizard, My Yahoo) find what is published in the Internet, including newsgroup correspondence about your competitors and their products, and send it to you. Known as *push technologies* (see Chapter 5), these services provide any desired information including news, some in real time, for free or for a nominal fee.
6. ***Use corporate research companies.*** Corporate research and ratings companies such as Dun & Bradstreet and Standard and Poor's provide information ranging from risk analysis to stock market analysts' reports about your competitors, for a fee. These are available electronically (e.g., *hoovers.com).*
7. ***Dig up the dirt on your competitors.*** Try *knowx.com* to find all the negatives on a company. For credit history, try *creditfyi.com.*
8. ***Find information about individuals.*** In addition to credit checking (e.g., TRW), try *Research.com* (cost $40/person).
9. ***Find out what are the going rates to pay employees.*** Try *wageweb.com* for free analysis.
10. ***Find corporation credit history.*** Dun & Bradstreet offers credit histories for some companies. Other places to look would be court records, banks, and credit bureaus.

than in years. In addition, new technological innovations today make yesterday's innovations obsolete. Furthermore, experience indicates that information systems, by themselves, can rarely provide a sustainable competitive advantage. Therefore, a modified approach is used.

Integrating IT ...in Marketing

Such an approach combines SISs with structural changes in the business, providing a **sustainable strategic advantage**, that is, a strategic advantage that can be maintained for some length of time. For example, Barnes and Noble not only started to sell on the Web, but created a completely independent organization to do so (*bn.com*). This strategy can work very well if the online and offline parts of a company can work in synergy. Barnes and Noble made a strategic move to regain market share lost to Amazon.com. The shift of corporate operations to a *strategic* orientation is significant, as illustrated in the McKesson example at the top of the following page.

Some studies have shown that more than 90 percent of executives surveyed strongly agree that IT has a significant impact on profitability, and even survival, by facilitating a strategic advantage. In order to understand the role of IT in providing strategic advantage, we next examine two classical strategic models.

IT at Work

McKESSON'S ECONOMOST AND WEB APPLICATIONS

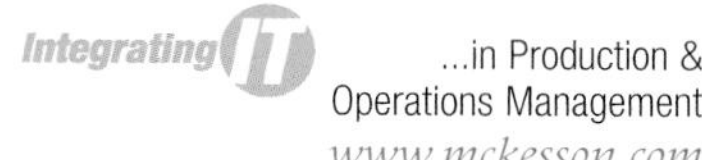

...in Production & Operations Management

www.mckesson.com

McKesson Drug Company is a wholesale drug distributor, operating in a very competitive market and known for its extensive use of IT. One example of its IT usage is Economost, its electronic order-entry system for prescription drug distribution.

McKesson had an important motivation to install Economost as early as 1975. Its primary customers were small, independent pharmacies at risk of going out of business because they were unable to compete with the large pharmacy chains. Economost was aimed at giving these pharmacies many of the advantages enjoyed by the large chains, thereby preserving their business.

Here is how the system works: The customer's order is phoned in, faxed, or preferably (as of 2000) transmitted electronically to McKesson's data center. The order is then acknowledged and transferred to an IBM mainframe for storage. Using their browsers, McKesson's regional distribution centers pull their shipment orders from the mainframe at regular intervals and deliver the drugs quickly to the pharmacies that placed the orders.

The IT has been combined with *structural changes.* The distribution centers are designed for maximum efficiency. For example, "pickers" walk through McKesson's warehouses, pushing carts on rollers and filling the orders. Warehouse shelves are arranged to correspond to pharmacy departments and are laid out to minimize the pickers' effort. Each distribution center has a minicomputer that runs the entire operation, from bar-code order-identification labels that are used to sort and route the products. Distant customers that are not tied directly to a warehouse are served from "mother trucks," which are sent to switching points where their content is transferred into smaller trucks for local deliveries.

The benefits to customers (pharmacies) include:

- More reliable order filling
- Reduced inventory holding costs
- Reduced transaction costs
- Faster delivery service

And the benefits to McKesson include:

- Rapid, reliable, and cost-effective customer order processing (the number of order-entry clerks has been reduced from 700 to 15).
- Sales personnel are no longer primarily order takers (their number has been cut in half).
- Productivity of the warehouse staff has increased by 17 percent, and the volume has increased substantially.
- Purchasing from suppliers has been reorganized to tightly match actual sales.
- Customers are loyal to McKesson because of the benefits they enjoy.

The impact of Economost for McKesson has been significant. Although the company's total market share has not significantly increased, Economost changed the manner in which business is done so that both McKesson and its customer pharmacies have been able to survive and McKesson's revenues have escalated.

In early 2001, McKesson implemented Web-based initiatives that offer a suite of comprehensive Internet-based applications to help customers manage their supply chain activities. In addition, the company created an information technology business, acting as a software provider and consultant to health care companies. The company offers Web-based solutions ranging from training to asset management. Some of these services are provided for free, others for a fee. Of special interest is *iMcKesson,* which allows physicians to order laboratory tests, view test results, prescribe medications electronically, and maintain patients' medical records.

For Further Exploration: Does Economost provide McKesson with a sustainable strategic advantage? Why or why not? Why is the company involved in the software business? What kind of information systems does McKesson use?

Sources: Clemons and Row, 1988; *cnnfn.com news,* June 12, 2000; and *mckesson.com,* 2001.

3.2 PORTER'S COMPETITIVE FORCES MODEL AND STRATEGIES

The Model

One of the most well-known frameworks for analyzing competitiveness is Porter's **competitive forces model** (1985). It has been used to develop strategies for companies to increase their competitive edge. It also demonstrates how IT can enhance the competitiveness of corporations. The model recognizes five major

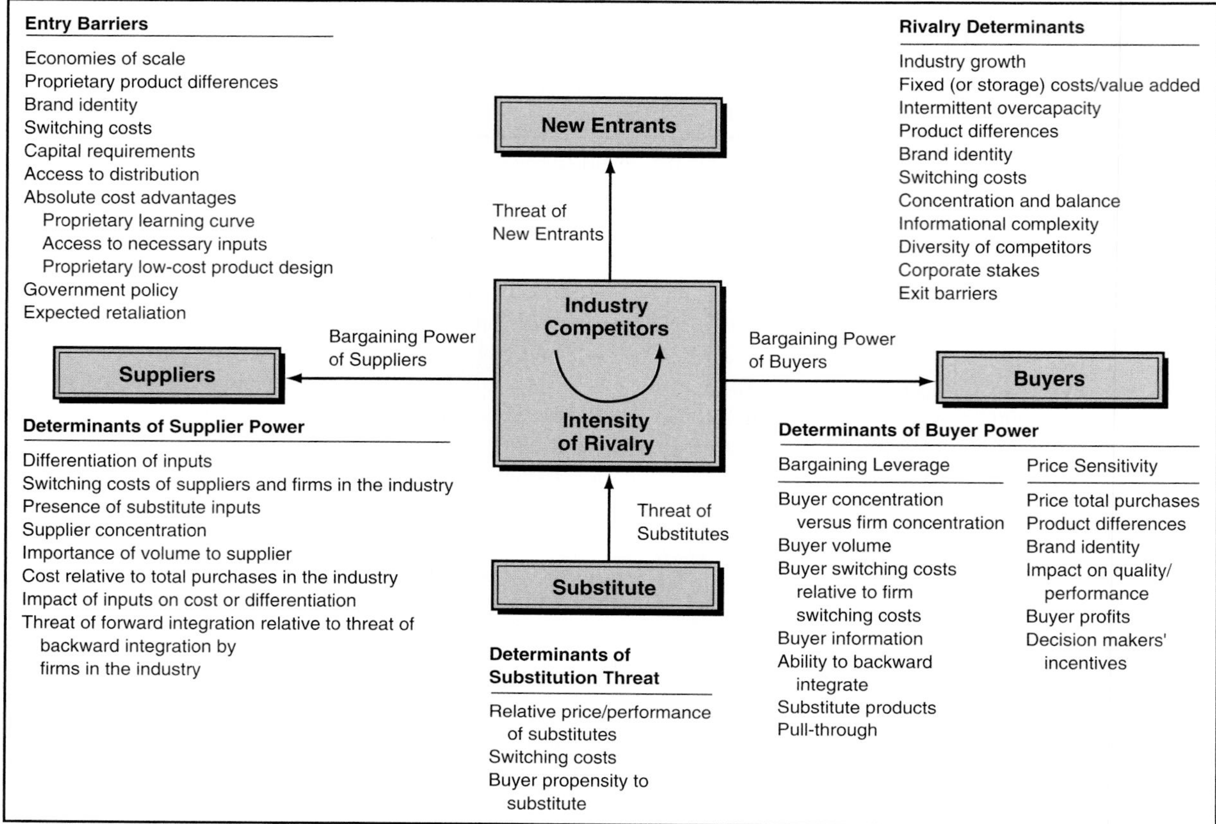

FIGURE 3.3 Porter's five forces model, including the major determinant of each force. (*Source:* Adopted with permission of the Free Press, a Division of Simon and Schuster, Inc., from *Competitive Advantage: Creating and Sustaining Superior Performance,* p. 6, by Michael Porter. © 1985, 1998 by Michael Porter.)

forces that could endanger a company's position in a given industry. (Other forces, such as those cited in Chapter 1, including the impact of government, affect all companies in the industry and therefore may have less impact on the relative success of a company within its industry.) Although the details of the model differ from one industry to another, its general structure is universal. The five major forces can be generalized as follows.

1. The threat of entry of new competitors
2. The bargaining power of suppliers
3. The bargaining power of customers (buyers)
4. The threat of substitute products or services
5. The rivalry among existing firms in the industry

The strength of each force is determined by several factors of the industry structure, which are shown in Figure 3.3. Most of the forces and determining factors that Porter identified in the early 1980s are still valid and are related to the pressures identified in Chapter 1.

Response Strategies

Porter (1985 and 1996) suggests how to develop a *strategy* aimed at establishing a profitable and sustainable position against these five forces. To do so, a company needs to develop a strategy of performing activities differently than a competitor. Porter proposed the following strategies.

- ***Cost leadership.*** Produce products and/or services at the lowest cost in the industry. An example is Wal-Mart, which, through business alliances supported by computers and by Web-based purchasing and inventory management, is able to provide low-priced products to its customers. The emergence of online retailing in the late 1990s made cost leadership a strategy for gaining online market share. Both Amazon and Barnes and Noble online discounted books by 30 to 40 percent, losing money in an attempt to acquire customers. A similar price war was conducted in the toy industry.
- ***Differentiation.*** Be unique in the industry. For example, provide high quality and services, such as Rosenbluth did. Wells Fargo Bank pioneered e-banking on a large scale before its competitors. Caterpillar and Otis Elevator provide their customers with an IT-facilitated product maintenance service that no competitor can match. Another differentiation strategy of special interest is Web-based mass-customization services, such as those offered by Dell Computer.
- ***Focus.*** Select a narrow-scope segment (niche market) and achieve either a **cost leadership** or a **differentiation** strategy in this segment. For example, several computer-chip manufacturers make customized chips for specific industries or companies. Such customization is supported by computers. Another example is frequent-flyer programs, which enable airlines to identify frequent travelers and offer them special incentives. Some airlines have several million customers registered in their program, which can be managed efficiently only with the help of computers. For example, major airlines enable members to self-track on the Web the status of their mileage accounts. Another example is *dogtoys.com* and *cattoys.com,* which offer online a large variety of pet toys that no other toy retailer offers.

ADDITIONAL RESPONSE STRATEGIES. Over the years, Porter (1996) and others have added to the list of response strategies. The major additional strategies are the following.

- ***Growth.*** Increase market share, acquire more customers, or sell more products. Such a strategy strengthens a company and increases profitability in the long run. Web-based selling can facilitate growth by creating new marketing channels, such as electronic auctions.
- ***Alliances.*** Work with business partners. This strategy creates synergy, allows companies to concentrate on their core business, and provides opportunities for growth. Alliances are particularly popular in electronic commerce (EC) ventures. Of special interest are alliances with suppliers, some of whom monitor inventory levels electronically and replenish inventory when it falls below a certain level. Alliances can be made among competitors as well. For example, in August 2000 Amazon.com and Toysrus.com launched a co-branded Web site to sell toys, capitalizing on each others' strengths. In spring 2001 they created a similar baby-products venture. Additional examples of alliances are provided in Chapters 5 through 7.
- ***Innovation.*** Develop new products and services, new features in existing products and services, and new ways to produce them. This strategy provides companies with a competitive advantage, as was done at Rosenbluth. Also included are innovative information systems applications. Of special interest are several new Web-based business models, such as reverse electronic auctions, which help companies to expand their customer base and sales.

- ***Improved internal efficiency.*** Improve the manner in which internal business processes are executed. Such improvements increase employee and customer satisfaction, quality, and productivity, while decreasing time to market. Improved decision making and management activities also contribute to improved efficiency. Web-based systems can improve the administrative efficiency of procurement, for example, by twenty- to thirtyfold.
- ***Customer-oriented approaches and CRM.*** Concentrate on making customers happy. Strong competition and the realization that the customer is king (queen) is the basis of this strategy. Web-based systems are especially effective in this area because they can provide a personalized, one-to-one relationship with each customer. This strategy was demonstrated in the opening case about Rosenbluth; it also will be shown in this section and in Chapter 5.

These strategies may be interrelated. For example, some innovations are achieved through alliances that reduce cost and increase growth. Cost leadership improves customer satisfaction and may lead to growth.

Examples of the various strategies can be found in Section 3.7 and throughout the book. In certain industries there may be a greater emphasis on one strategy than on another. For example, in the trucking industry cost leadership is critical, and companies are using innovative IT-based techniques to achieve it, as illustrated in the *IT at Work* (at the top of the following page).

Before we discuss how IT supports Porter's strategies, let us see how the generic model works.

How the Model Is Used

Porter's model is industry-related, assessing the position of a company in its industry. Companies can use the model for competitive analysis, to suggest specific actions. In most cases such actions involve the use of IT. We will use Wal-Mart as an example (see Figure 3.4, page 94) to demonstrate the four steps involved in using Porter's model.

- *Step 1:* List the players in each competitive force. An illustration of a competitive threat is online shopping, which may be offered by *e-tailers* (electronic retailers). In 1999, for example, Amazon.com started to sell online several items sold at Wal-Mart (e.g., toys, CDs, and gifts), competing directly with Wal-Mart.
- *Step 2:* Relate the major determinants of each competitive force (shown in Figure 3.3, page 90) to each player in the market. For example, for Wal-Mart, with respect to online shopping, we can check the switching cost for the buyers, the buyers' propensity to substitute, and the price advantage of the online shopping.
- *Step 3:* Devise a strategy with which Wal-Mart can defend itself against the competitive forces, based on the specific players and the determinants. For example, to counter online shopping, Wal-Mart can provide playgrounds for children, hand out free samples of products, and recognize frequent shoppers personally. Wal-Mart can also respond by imitating the competition. In fact, the company did just that by introducing Wal-Mart Online, which in 2001 was being expanded into a major marketing channel.
- *Step 4:* Look for supportive information technologies. An illustration of this step for online shopping is a technology for managing frequent shoppers. Wal-Mart uses a gigantic database, data-mining techniques, smart cards, and decision support capabilities to analyze shoppers' activities accurately and to act competitively in response. Wal-Mart uses IT extensively both to defend

...in Marketing

IT at Work

TRUCKING COMPANIES USE IT FOR GAINING COST LEADERSHIP

Integrating IT ...in Production & Operations Management

www.jbhunt.com; roadway.com

The trucking business is very competitive. Here are some examples of how IT has helped trucking companies achieve significant cost savings.

J. B. Hunt of Lowell, Arkansas, is a large truckload carrier. Its corporate PCs are connected to the fuel commodity market for real-time monitoring of fuel prices, which can fluctuate greatly and so harm the company's financial planning. The Web-based IT system can trigger the purchase of fuel at the lowest possible prices, which can result in significant savings since fuel costs represent 18 to 35 percent of the company's total operating costs. In addition, the system allows J. B. Hunt to pass on a very accurate fuel surcharge to its customers. The company offers several customers' Web services (*jbhunt.com*) and applications. Of special interest is the online "Proof of Delivery" documentation.

Roadway Express (*roadway.com*), another trucking company, owns several hundred gas pumps nationwide. Using computers, the company continuously compares vendors' prices and related gas-procurement expenses, so that it can purchase the least expensive gas available at any given time. The company offers Web-based customer services similar to those of J.B. Hunt.

Computers are also used by large trucking companies to monitor the productivity of their drivers and trucks. Using telecommunications and global positioning systems (GPS), companies can monitor the exact location of trucks at any given time, study their performance, communicate in a wireless system and thereby improve trucks' utilization. In addition, large trucking companies use DSS and EIS to optimize their operations. IT provides large trucking companies with a competitive edge against small companies.

Small companies can defend themselves by using *Web-based services* available to the industry. Examples of such services include: *logistics.com,* which helps find the cheapest fuel along the most efficient route; *transportation.com,* which offers operations and decision support; and *truckersb2b.com,* which is a comprehensive exchange for many trucking services. Small companies can also use a Web-based group-purchasing service to reduce the cost of gas and material and supplies by 5 to 15 percent.

Trucking companies are also adjusting themselves to the digital economy. An example is Schneider National (*schneiderlogistics.com*), which specializes in business-to-business (B2B) logistics. The company's transportation management system is connected to customers' computer systems, to enable them to find the cheapest and/or the fastest way to make B2B delivery. Schneider uses its 45,000 vehicles to make deliveries or contracts the jobs with UPS and FedEx.

For Further Exploration: How can trucking companies achieve cost leadership? Find the latest Web-based innovations used by major truckers. Are these competitive advantages sustainable?

Sources: Compiled from the Web sites of the companies cited and from *Interactive Week,* January 24, 2000.

---

itself against the competition and to create innovative services and cost reduction, especially along its supply chain. (We'll provide more specific examples in Chapter 6.)

EXAMPLES OF HOW THE MODEL IS USED. Here are some additional examples of businesses defending themselves against the five competitive forces listed by Porter.

- Extranets and electronic data interchange (EDI) can shrink order times and costs and thus increase the profitability of suppliers and their desire to do business with your company. For example, parts suppliers may help a buyer design a higher-quality customized part or a less expensive one, and/or they may be able to supply parts in a shorter time. Such an approach helped DaimlerChrysler to cut billions of dollars from the cost of its parts, which helped the company to compete in its industry as well as to reduce the bargaining power of its suppliers, as shown in the *IT at Work* case on page 94.
- Automobile manufacturers use computerized quality-control systems to make steel producers (the suppliers) more conscious of quality. With less steel rejected due to quality problems, steel producers develop closer relationships

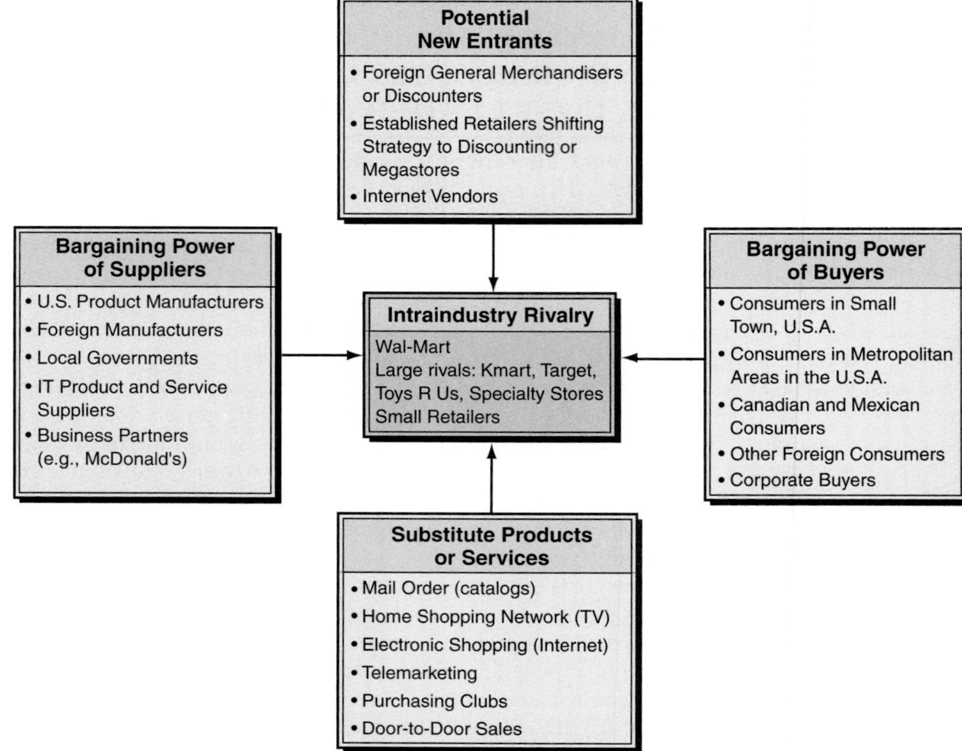

FIGURE 3.4 Porter's model for Wal-Mart. (*Source:* Adapted by Callon (1996) and reprinted by permission of *Harvard Business Review.* From "How Competitive Forces Shape Strategy" by Michael Porter, March–April 1979. © 1979 by the Harvard Business School Publishing Corporation; all rights reserved.)

IT at Work

DAIMLERCHRYSLER LINKS ELECTRONICALLY WITH SUPPLIERS—SAVES BILLIONS

Integrating IT ...in Production & Operations Management

www.daimlerchrysler.com

The automotive industry is very competitive. Chrysler (now DaimlerChrysler) has saved millions of dollars using the Internet and Lotus Notes. In 1989, Chrysler offered its parts suppliers a plan in which they would have an opportunity to share savings that resulted from cost-cutting suggestions the suppliers made. The program was not very successful when it was conducted manually. In 1993, Chrysler lost $2.6 billion.

Then, the program went online. Using Lotus Notes/Domino (see Chapter 4) and the Internet, the suppliers are able to submit proposals to Chrysler's purchasing agents. Furthermore, all communication among all participants is paperless and fast. Using electronic forms makes the filing of the suggestions easy. It also has become easy and fast to evaluate suggestions. To expedite the process, the proposers must first discuss the idea with the parts buyer. This discussion usually occurs electronically using a collaborating software such as that from *webx.com*. Only if the buyer is impressed is the proposal submitted. Using the workflow capabilities of Lotus Notes, the proposals are electronically routed to the appropriate evaluators.

In 1998 DaimlerChrysler started to use the Web-based Lotus/Domino to publish measurement reports to static HTML Web pages. Suppliers are now able to view the reports using an Internet browser. In 2000 DaimlerChrysler integrated its system with the industry e-procurement exchange Covisint (*covisint.com*).

For Further Exploration: What other collaborations could be done electronically between a car manufacturer and its suppliers? Is the current advantage to DaimlerChrysler sustainable? Find more information on the industry exchange.

Sources: Compiled from *knowledged Wharton,* June 14, 2000; *techweb.com/se/directlink.cgi?;* and from *Internet Week,* March 9, 1998.

with auto manufacturers and feel less likely to seek business elsewhere, thereby reducing their bargaining power with the car makers.

- Allowing the suppliers of funds to financial institutions (depositors and investors) to electronically transfer funds rapidly and easily is an example of influencing the bargaining power of suppliers through the use of IT, since the companies depend more heavily on such suppliers.
- Many companies provide their customers with free software and other computer services, thus increasing the customers' switching costs and reducing the customers' bargaining power. Rosenbluth provides such services on its Web site, as well as its propriety applications.
- Frequent-flyer (buyer) programs in the airline, hospitality, and retail industries and discount brokering in the securities industry have significantly changed rivalries among existing firms. Companies that have such programs have more loyal customers; thus, they are more preferred.

Ward and Griffiths (1997) provide a summary of the role of IT in each competitive force (see Table 3.2). Additional IT strategies have been proposed by others; some of these are described in Sections 3.4 to 3.6. Examples of IT facilitating additional strategies can be found in Section 3.7. A different way to analyze

TABLE 3.2 Impact of Competitive Forces and Role of IT

Key Force Impacting the Industry	Business Implications	Potential IT Effects
Threat of new entrants	Additional capacity Reduced prices New basis for competition	Provide entry barriers/reduce access by: • exploiting existing economies of scale • differentiating products/services • controlling distribution channels • segmenting markets
Buyer power high	Forces prices down Higher quality demanded Service flexibility required Encourages competition	Differentiate products/services and improve price/performance Increase switching costs of buyers Facilitate buyer product selection
Supplier power high	Raises prices/costs Reduces quality of supply Reduces availability	Implement supplier sourcing systems Extend quality control into suppliers' operations Do forward planning with suppliers
Substitute products threatened	Limits potential market and profit Imposes price ceilings	Improve price/performance Redefine products and services to increase value Redefine market segments
Intense competition from rivals	Increases price competition Spurs product development Makes distribution and service critical Customer loyalty required	Improve price/performance Differentiate products and services in distribution channel and to consumer Get closer to the end consumer—understand the use requirements

Source: J. Ward and P. Griffiths, *Strategic Planning for Information Systems,* 2nd ed. New York: Wiley, 1997, p. 86. Reprinted by permission of John Wiley & Sons, Inc.

competition and the role of IT is provided in Porter's *value chain model,* which is the subject of the next section.

3.3 PORTER'S VALUE CHAIN ANALYSIS MODEL

According to the **value chain model** (Porter, 1985), the activities conducted in any manufacturing organization can be divided into two parts: *primary activities* and *support activities.* The five **primary activities** are:

1. Inbound logistics (inputs)
2. Operations (manufacturing and testing)
3. Outbound logistics (storage and distribution)
4. Marketing and sales
5. Service

These activities constitute a supply chain.

The primary activities take place in a sequence from 1 to 5. As work progresses according to the sequence, *value* is added to the product or service in each activity. To be more specific, the incoming materials (1) are processed (in receiving, storage, etc.), and in this processing, value is added to them in what is called *inbound logistics.* Next, the materials are used in *operations* (2), where more value is added in making products. The products need to be prepared for delivery (packaging, storing, and shipping) in the *outbound logistics* (3), and so more value is added. Then *marketing and sales* (4) attempt to sell the products to customers, increasing product value by creating demand for the company's products. (The value of a sold item is much larger than that of an unsold one.) Finally, after-sales *service* (5) is performed for the customer, further adding value. All of these value-adding, primary activities result (it is hoped) in profit.

Primary activities are supported by the following **support activities**: (1) the firm infrastructure (accounting, finance, management), (2) human resources management, (3) technology development (R&D), and (4) procurement. Each support activity can support any or all of the primary activities; they may also support each other.

A firm's value chain is part of a larger stream of activities, which Porter calls a **value system**. A value system includes the suppliers that provide the inputs necessary to the firm and their value chains. Once the firm creates products, they pass through the value chains of distributors (who also have their own value chains), all the way to the buyers (customers), who also have their own value chains. All parts of these chains are included in the value system. Gaining and sustaining a competitive advantage, and supporting that advantage by means of IT, requires an understanding of this entire value system.

The value chain and value system concepts can be drawn for both products and services and for any organization, private or public. The initial purpose of the value chain model was to analyze the internal operations of a corporation, in order to increase its efficiency, effectiveness, and competitiveness. The model has since then been used as a basis for explaining the support IT can provide. It is also the basis for the *supply chain management* concept, which we will present in Chapter 6.

How the Model Is Used

The value chain model can be used in different ways. First, we can use it to do company analysis, by systematically evaluating a company's key processes and core competencies. To do so, we first determine strengths and weaknesses of performing the activities and the values added by each activity. The activities that add more value are those that might provide strategic advantage. Then we investigate whether by adding IT the company can get even greater added value and where in the chain its use is most appropriate. For example, Caterpillar uses EDI to add value to its inbound and outbound activities; it uses its intranet to boost customer service (see the Caterpillar case at the book's Web site). In Chapters 6 through 12, we show through many examples how IT supports the various activities of the value chain. The manner in which Frito-Lay uses IT to support the value chain is shown in the following *IT at Work* example.

IT at Work

FRITO-LAY CHIPS AWAY AT ITS COMPETITION

...in Production & Operations Management and in Marketing

www.fritolay.com

Frito-Lay, a subsidiary of PepsiCo, is the world's largest snack food producer and distributor. Frito-Lay is known for its extensive use of IT. Its strategic information system gives its managers the ability to visualize nearly every element of the company's value chain as part of an integrated whole. The SIS is a central nervous system that integrates marketing, sales, manufacturing, logistics, and finance. It also provides managers with information about suppliers, customers, and competitors.

Frito-Lay's employees in the field collect sales information daily, store by store, across the United States and in some other countries. They feed this information electronically to the company. By combining this vast amount of field data with information from each stage of the value chain, Frito's managers can better determine levels of inbound supplies of raw materials, allocate the company's manufacturing activity across available production capacity, and plan truck routing for the most efficient coverage of market areas. By checking what competitors do, Frito-Lay can make better pricing and inventory decisions. Frito-Lay employees also collect information about the sales and promotions of competing products or about new products launched by competitors at selected locations. This information enables the company to target local demand patterns with just the right sales promotion. This ability means that Frito-Lay can continuously optimize profit margins and reduce inventory costs. It can also use this information to identify and to react to environmental pressures and competitive forces. Wegmans, a large food retailer, collaborates with Frito-Lay in supply chain projects, which result in significant sales increases of Frito-Lay product at Wegmans' stores.

For Further Exploration: Why does Frito-Lay pay such close attention to the value chain? Who are the customers? Could smaller competitors use such a system? Is the strategy of collecting data on the competition ethical?

Sources: Compiled from Rayport and Sviokla, 1996, p. 78; and from *fritolay.com,* 2001. Also see "From Supply Chain to Collaborative Network: Case Studies in the Food Industry," Andersen Consulting (*wallon.Ascet.com,* 2000).

A second usage for the value chain model is to do an industry analysis, as shown for the airline industry in Figure 3.5. As in the company analysis, once the various activities have been identified, then it is possible to search for specific information systems to facilitate these activities. For example, in "Marketing and Sales," agent training can be conducted on the corporate portal.

Finally, the value chain model can be used either for an individual company or for an industry by superimposing different types of information systems that may help special activities. For example, EDI can help inbound and outbound logistics; virtual reality can help both advertising and product development.

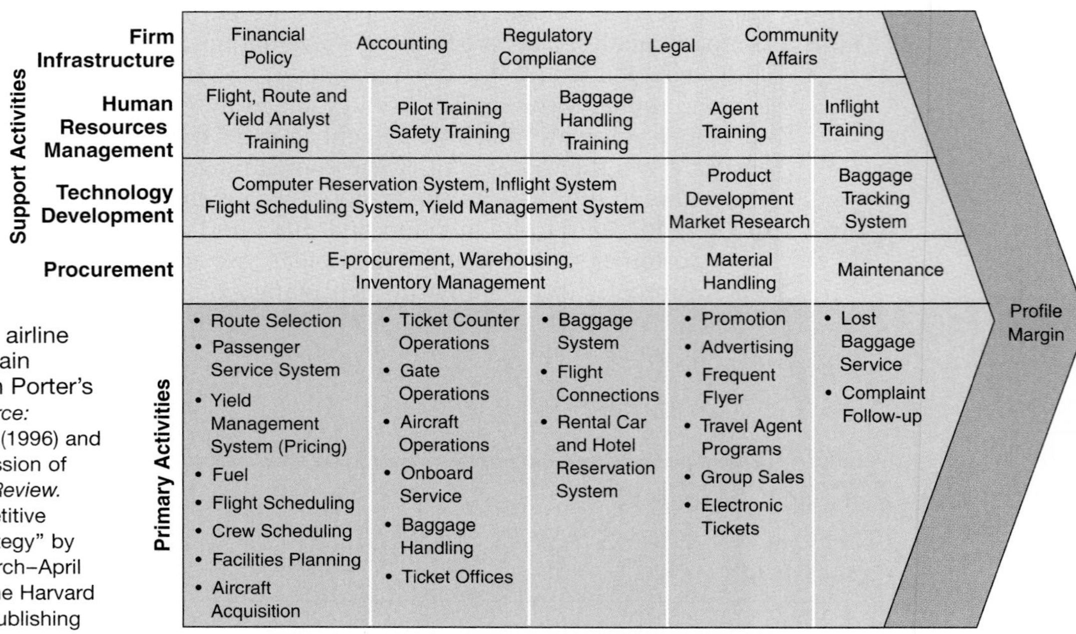

FIGURE 3.5 The airline industry value chain superimposed on Porter's value chain. (*Source:* Adapted by Callon (1996) and reprinted by permission of *Harvard Business Review.* From "How Competitive Forces Shape Strategy" by Michael Porter, March–April 1979. © 1979 by the Harvard Business School Publishing Corporation; all rights reserved.)

Porter's Models in the Digital Age

...in Marketing

The application of Porter's models is still valid today. But some adjustments may be needed to take into account the realities of business in the digital age. Consider a company such as Amazon.com. Some consider it a retailer competing against Wal-Mart. But according to *Interactive Week* (June 28, 1999, p. 70), this is not the case. Even though the two companies sell books, videos, and toys, they are not on a competitive collision course since they are after different customers and have different goals. So, who are Amazon's competitors? It depends. In books they compete mainly against Barnes and Noble Online, in toys against Kmart, Wal-Mart, and Sears, and in music against CDNOW.com. Could we use one illustration such as Figure 3.3 (page 90) to describe Amazon.com's competitive environment? Probably not. We might need several figures, one for each of Amazon's major products. Furthermore, due to alliances (such as between Amazon.com and Toysrus.com), the competition and the value chain analysis can be fairly complex and frequently in flux.

3.4 Strategic Information Systems Frameworks

A framework for a strategic information system (SIS) is a descriptive structure that helps us understand and classify the relationships among strategic management, competitive strategy, and information technology. One reason for the abundance of SIS frameworks is that there are many different types of information systems, as we saw in Chapter 2. Neumann (1994) advocates the use of SIS frameworks and provides a detailed description of (and references for) the most important ones. In this book, we present only a few of the more important frameworks, basically to illustrate their role in the study of SIS.

We introduce the following:

- Three frameworks that are related to Porter's models: Porter and Millar, Wiseman and MacMillan, and Bakos and Treacy
- McFarlan's application portfolio framework
- A customer resource life cycle framework
- A global business drivers' framework for multinational corporations

For other approaches, see Buchanan and Gibb (1998) and Lederer and Salmela (1996).

Porter and Millar's Framework

Porter and Millar (1985) concluded that competition has been affected by IT in three vital ways. First, industry structure and the rules of competition have changed as a result of new information technologies. Second, organizations have outperformed their competitors by using IT. Finally, organizations have created new businesses by using IT. Based on this conclusion, Porter and Millar developed a five-step framework that organizations can use to exploit the strategic opportunities IT creates (see *A Closer Look* 3.2). Note that almost exactly the same effects are observed in e-commerce (Choi and Whinston, 2000; Turban et al., 2002).

Porter and Millar have developed a matrix that indicates the high and low values of the interrelated information. They use this matrix to identify the role that information plays in product offerings, as well as the process used to deliver the product to customers. The framework enables managers to assess the *information intensity* in their businesses. **Information intensity** measures the

A CLOSER LOOK
3.2 PORTER AND MILLAR'S FIVE-STEP PROCESS

- **Step 1.** ***Assess information intensity.*** Organizations need to assess the information intensity of each link in each of their value chains. If customers or suppliers are highly dependent on information, then intensity is high, and strategic opportunities are likely to exist. Higher intensity implies greater opportunity.
- **Step 2.** ***Determine the role of IT in the industry structure.*** An organization needs to know how buyers, suppliers, and competitors might be affected by and react to IT.
- **Step 3.** ***Identify and rank the ways in which IT can create competitive advantage.*** An organization must analyze how particular links of the value chain might be affected by IT.
- **Step 4.** ***Investigate how IT might spawn new businesses.*** Excess computer capacity or large corporate databases can provide opportunities for spinoff of new businesses. Organizations should answer the following three questions:
  - What information generated (or potentially generated) by the business should be sold?
  - What IT capacities exist to start a new business?
  - Does IT make it feasible to produce new items related to the organization's current products?
- **Step 5.** ***Develop a plan for taking advantage of IT.*** Taking advantage of strategic opportunities that IT presents requires a plan. The process of developing such a plan should be business-driven rather than technology-driven.

Source: Compiled from M.E. Porter and V. E. Millar, "How Information Gives You Competitive Advantage," *Harvard Business Review,* July–August 1985. Reprinted by permission of *Harvard Business Review.*

level of information used in supporting business processes. The basic idea of the framework is to determine how specific IT applications can enhance various links in the value chain, whether in internal operations or in the external marketplace, and thus enable the business to achieve a strategic advantage. The framework relates the information intensity of a product's value chain to the information content of the product. A number of companies have used Porter and Millar's model successfully.

Wiseman and MacMillan Framework

Wiseman and MacMillan (1984) revised Porter's framework by adding four defense strategies, *innovation, growth, alliance,* and *time,* to Porter's three strategies. They then created a matrix in which the seven defense strategies are the rows and the columns are "suppliers," "customers," and "competitors." The cells in the matrix can direct IT applications. For example, in the cell of row *differentiation* and column *customer,* one can utilize Web-based mass customization. Thus, each cell in the matrix identifies the available IT strategies for an external industry force.

An important implementation question is how to find applications for the cells in this matrix. An example of a company that used this framework to find applications is GTE Corporation. The company employed a brainstorming procedure and identified more than 300 ideas for strategic applications of IT. (For other suggestions about how to find IT-based ideas, see Bergerson et al., 1991; Boynton et al., 1993; and Callon, 1996.)

Bakos and Treacy Framework

Bakos and Treacy (1986) proposed a causal framework of competitive advantage. According to their model, the two major sources of Porter's competitive advantage are bargaining power and comparative efficiency (see Figure 3.6). These sources of competitive advantage are caused by five specific items: search-related costs, unique product features, switching costs, internal efficiency, and interorganizational

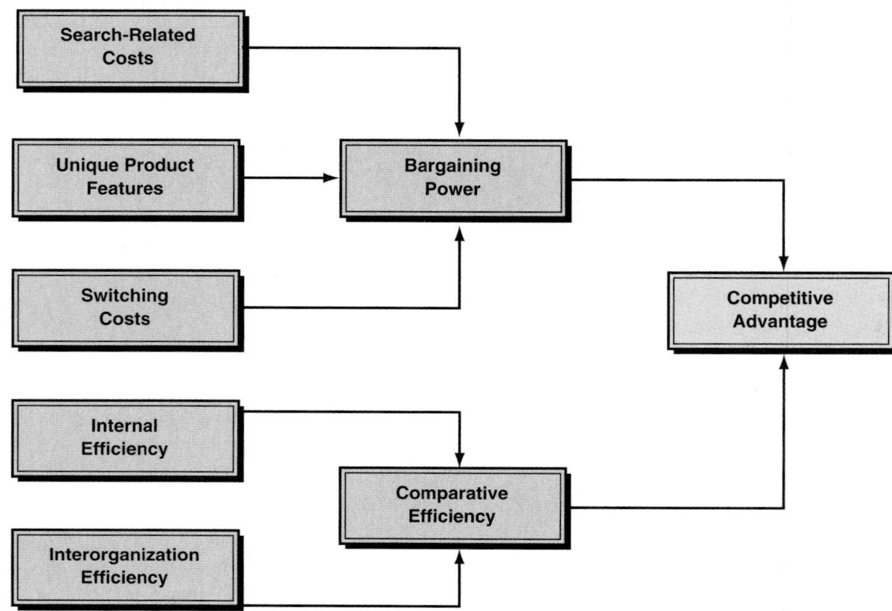

FIGURE 3.6 Bakos and Treacy's causal model of competitive advantage. [*Source:* "Information Technology for Corporate Strategy, *MIS Quarterly,* June 1986. © 1986 by the Management Information Systems Research Center (MISRC) by the University of Minnesota and the Society for Information Management (SIM). Reprinted by permission.]

efficiency. Initially, IT efforts were aimed at increasing comparative efficiency. Lately, however, IT is also dealing with the other items, such as impacting search and switching costs by use of the Web.

Let us consider how IT can support the five activities (shown on the left side of Figure 3.6) that drive bargaining power and comparative efficiency from the point of view of a company planning a defensive strategy.

Integrating IT ...in Marketing

1. IT can create or enhance unique product features. For example, Mattel enables customization of its Barbie dolls over the Web. Similarly, Rosenbluth's systems provide unmatchable cost reduction for their customers.
2. IT can increase the switching cost to a company's customers when certain IT-based services are provided (e.g., a Web-based tracking system).
3. IT contributes to internal efficiency; it is known for its effectiveness in reducing costs and increasing productivity, as shown throughout the book.
4. IT can increase interorganizational efficiency through *synergy,* enhancing business partnerships, joint ventures, and other alliances. This is done by using EDI, extranets, and vertical exchanges for procurement (see Chapter 5).
5. IT can create new business models, such as reverse auctions and vertical exchanges, or can support new business models, such as "fee for service," which replaced commissions as the revenue model of Rosenbluth. In doing so, improved internal efficiency, interorganizational efficiency, and search-related costs all contribute to competitive advantage.

McFarlan's Application Portfolio Analysis Framework

F. W. McFarlan developed a framework (1984) with which organizations can analyze their mix of existing, planned, and potential information systems. The framework, which can be applied to any type of application, including e-commerce, can be viewed as a four-cell matrix. Applications are classified into a collection (portfolio) of the following four categories:

- ***High potential:*** applications that may be important in achieving *future* business success (such as intelligent systems or human resources planning)
- ***Key operational:*** applications upon which the organization *currently* depends for success (such as inventory control, accounting receivable, personnel duties)
- ***Strategic:*** applications that are critical for *future* business strategy (e-procurement, extranet, enterprise resource planning)
- ***Support:*** applications that are *currently* valuable and desirable (but not critical) for business success (such as video conferencing and multimedia presentations)

Note that the classification is done according to *current* and *future* contributions as perceived by management. Note also that the positioning of the applications may vary from company to company. For example, online training, which we listed as a support application, would be a key operational application for a software vendor.

McFarlan's framework is important for allocating funds to IT initiatives, especially to costly ones. Figure 3.7 (page 102) shows, for example, how one airline classified its current e-commerce projects.

Customer Resource Life Cycle Framework

The customer resource life cycle (CRLC) framework, set forth by Ives and Learmouth (1984), focuses on the relationship with customers. The idea behind CRLC is that an organization differentiates itself from its competition in the eyes of the

Strategic E-procurement, electronic ticketing, agents' management	**High Potential** Intelligent data mining, e-mail, direct marketing
Key Operational Online scheduling, online parts ordering, online maintenance	**Support** Frequent-flyer account tracking, online credit union, online training, wireless SMS information

FIGURE 3.7 McFarlan's application portfolio model. (*Source:* F. W. McFarlan, "Information Technology Changes the Way You Compete," *Harvard Business Review,* May–June 1984.)

customer. Therefore, concentrating on the customer relationship is the key to achieving a strategic advantage.

CRLC postulates that the customer goes through 13 fundamental stages in the relationship with a supplier and that each stage should be examined to determine whether IT can be used to achieve a strategic advantage. (See Table 3.3 for a list of the stages.) This approach is used, for example, in developing electronic commerce systems. For example, Gonsalves et al. (1999) used the model to analyze the impact of the Web on competitiveness. The CRLC concept is one of the foundations upon which customer relationship management (CRM) is based (see Chapter 7).

3.5 WEB-BASED STRATEGIC INFORMATION SYSTEMS

Many of the strategic information systems of the 1970s through the 1990s that involved business partnerships were based on privately owned networks. Some of the systems described in Section 3.7 are of this nature. Such systems can be called *organizational information systems* (OIS), which are considered a part of electronic commerce. Of special interest were the EDI-based systems.

Several of the electronic markets (or exchanges) that emerged in the 1990s used private lines and/or EDI. An example is Citus Belgium (*citus.be*). Citus acts as a hub between customers and suppliers, hosting suppliers' catalogs electroni-

TABLE 3.3 Stages in the Customer Resources Life Cycle

Stage	Description
1.	Establish customer requirements.
2.	Specify customer requirements.
3.	Select a source; match customer with a supplier.
4.	Place an order.
5.	Authorize and pay for goods and services.
6.	Acquire goods or services.
7.	Test and accept goods or services.
8.	Integrate goods into and manage inventory.
9.	Monitor use and behavior.
10.	Upgrade if needed.
11.	Provide maintenance.
12.	Transfer or dispose of product or service.
13.	Keep financial records of purchases (accounting).

cally. Using a pioneering technology, the company gained incredible competitive advantage, by significant cost reduction and the building of a loyal customer community (see Timmers 1999). Citus's success was so great that it became a target for acquisition and was purchased by EDS Corp.

However, privately owned networks and EDI generally are expensive to implement. Furthermore, EDI requires the use of agreed-upon standards, conversion software, and complex operating procedures. Therefore, the adoption rate of this type of SIS was slow, as the following *IT at Work* case shows.

IT at Work

MOBIL MOVES ITS EDI TO AN INTRANET AND THEN THE WEB

Integrating IT ...in Production & Operations Management

www.exxon-mobil.com

Mobil Oil (now Exxon Mobil) is the largest marketer of lubricants in the United States. Sales are made through about 300 small regional distributors. Prior to 1995, all orders were submitted by telephone, postal mail, and fax, and then were processed manually. This was expensive, slow, and error-prone.

In 1995 the company introduced an EDI system over private data transmission lines (an intranet). The system was to be used to place orders, submit invoices, and exchange business documents. However, the system was complex to use and expensive to operate. Therefore, only a few distributors used it. The processing cost on the system was $45 per order, not much of an improvement over the manual system, which was still in operation. Furthermore, the Mobil IT staff had to maintain and operate the EDI system.

In 1997 the company transformed its system to a Web-based, business-to-business (B2B) system. In a short time the new system was fully adopted by all users, permitting Mobil to reduce the processing cost to $1.25 per order. This cost savings enabled Mobil to reduce prices, which led to increased market share. In addition, the system has enabled Mobil to better manage its inventories, so fewer shortages exist and customers now receive better service. Finally, distributors' administrative costs declined, so the distributors have become more loyal to Mobil.

For Further Exploration: Can the strategic advantage be sustained? What other innovations can help Exxon Mobil better work with its distributors?

Sources: Compiled from *PC Week,* April 11, 1997, and from *Internet Business,* November 1998.

Today, new SISs, like Exxon Mobil's system, are predominantly Web-based, providing competitive advantage in a fierce competitive environment.

Competition in the Web Economy

The focus on Web-based strategic systems is not surprising, since the Web is changing the nature of competition and even industry structure. Consider the following.

...in Marketing

- Bookseller Barnes and Noble and other companies have created independent online divisions, which are competing against the parent companies. Such companies are termed "click-and-mortar" companies, because they combine both "brick-and-mortar" and e-commerce operations.
- Any company that sells direct to consumers is becoming a distributor (wholesaler or retailer), competing against its own traditional distributors.
- The variable cost of a digital product is close to zero. Therefore, if large quantities are sold, the product's price can be so low that it might be given away, for free. For example, some predict that commissions for online stock trading will go to zero for this reason.

Integrating IT ...in Production & Operations Management

- Competitors are getting together and becoming more willing to share information. Examples are the vertical exchanges owned by industry leaders. The "Big Three" auto manufacturers, for example, operate the auto exchange (*covisint.com*). Similar exchanges exist in the paper, chemical, and many other industries. These exchanges are designed to pressure suppliers to reduce prices. (See Chapter 7 in Turban et al., 2002.)

In some cases it is not a specific SIS that changes the nature of competition, but it is the Web technology that renders obsolete traditional business processes, brand names, and even superior products. Let's look at one example.

www.brittanica.com

Technology Changes Competition for Britannica. For generations *Encyclopaedia Britannica* was known for its world's-best content and brand name. However, in 1997 the company lost so much money that it was liquidated and sold for a fraction of its book value. What happened?

Integrating IT ...in Marketing

Microsoft started to sell a much-less-known encyclopedia, *Funk & Wagnalls*, on CD-ROMs for $50, under the name *Encarta*. Later on, the CD-ROMs were given away free with Microsoft PCs. In contrast, *Britannica*'s price was about $2,000. Furthermore, Encarta was media-rich. It included video clips, voices, and many pictures.

Britannica's sales declined rapidly. To compete, the company created a media-rich CD-ROM version, which was given free with the printed version. Without the print version, the CD-ROM was sold for $1,000. But very few people were willing to pay $1,000 when a competing product was available essentially for free.

What killed *Britannica* was not Microsoft. It was the new technology and the customers' desire to use their PCs, a CD-ROM, and the Internet. And indeed the new *Britannica* has restructured itself as an Internet portal, giving free access to the encyclopedia. (See Venkatraman, 2000, and *britannica.com*.)

Examples of Web-based SISs

The Web can provide strategic advantage both to individual companies and to groups of companies.

FOR INDIVIDUAL COMPANIES

Integrating IT ...in Marketing

Electronic Auctions. Electronic auctions are used extensively by companies as an additional marketing channel, to increase market share. An example is Dell Computer, which auctions both new and used computers mainly to individuals and small businesses. For details, see *dellauction.com*.

Electronic Biddings. The consumer product market is extremely competitive. General Electric is one of the few U.S. companies to successfully compete with Japanese companies by using an electronic bidding system. (See Chapter 5 for details.)

Buyer-Driven Commerce. A new business model introduced by Priceline.com enables businesses and individuals to "name-your-own-price." Buyers indicate the price they are willing to pay for products and services, and selling companies can choose whether to meet these bids. Sellers affiliating with Priceline.com can sell more, and buyers gain the advantage of paying less for the goods and services they want.

Integrating IT ...in Production & Operations Management

Single-Company Exchange. Large companies, especially multinational ones, are creating exchanges where their suppliers can trade. For example, Caltex Corporation uses a central exchange for procurement, payment, and logistics for its many suppliers of indirect materials (e.g., office supplies, repair items, etc.). (See more details of this system in Section 3.7.)

...in Marketing

Direct Sales. Large companies such as Cisco, Intel, Dell, and IBM are selling billions of dollars' worth of products directly to their customers, saving millions of dollars by eliminating intermediaries.

FOR GROUPS OF COMPANIES

...in Production & Operations Management

Industry (Vertical) Consortiums. The major players in many industries (steel, paper, insurance, oil, cars, and mining) are creating vertical exchanges operated and controlled by the major players in the industry. These exchanges are used primarily for purchasing and are designed to reduce the bargaining power of suppliers.

Horizontal Consortiums. Similar consortiums are organized for the purpose of purchasing maintenance, replacement, and operations (MRO) items. In Australia all the largest corporations are organized in an e-purchasing exchange (see *corprocure.com*).

Still other examples of Web-based SISs are the following.

- ***Call Centers.*** These systems provide superb customer service. The call center of Lands' End, Inc. (*landends.com*) is an example. (For more details on Web-based call centers, see Chapters 4, 5, and 7.)

...in Production & Operations Management and in Marketing

- ***Tracking Systems.*** One of the early systems in this category was that of FedEx, which offers customers the ability to track via the Web the progress of shipments. An example of an innovative tracking system is that of Ford Motors. This system allows customers to track, in real time, the status of a customized car while it is being made for them by Ford.
- ***Intelligent Agents.*** By using Web-based intelligent agents, online companies can scan and sense their environments and carry out some sort of operation or task (see Li et al., 2000, and Kvassov, 2000). (See Chapter 12.) The information gathered by intelligent agents not only is collected at a reasonable cost, but its quality is very high since the agents can visit large numbers of sources.

...in Marketing

- ***Web-based Cross Selling.*** *Cross selling* is an effective marketing strategy by which certain products or services are offered (or "pushed") to customers at the time a customer is contacted for a sale of a related product. Prior to the Internet, cross selling was done mainly by salespeople. For example, when you made a deposit in a bank, you were told about other banking services. Such recommendations were often costly to the vendor or ineffective.

  Today, not only will a Web-based selling system automatically offer a related product, but if the system knows something about the customer, the offer can be personalized. An example is the partnership of Barnes & Noble Online (*bn.com*) with Lycos.com. Each time you search a topic using Lycos's search engine, a banner from Barnes & Noble appears on the right side of the screen, with suggested related books. For example, if you request from Lycos a search on "strategic information systems," the *bn.com* banner will say, "Strategic Information, GO." When you click on this banner you will be linked directly to Barnes & Noble Online's page that lists 86 books on the topic (February 2001).

3.6 A FRAMEWORK FOR GLOBAL COMPETITION

Many companies are operating in a global environment. First, there are the fully global or multinational corporations. Second, there are the companies that export or import. Third, a large number of companies face competition from products created in countries where labor and other costs are low, or where there is an abundance of natural resources. Other companies have low-cost production facilities in these same countries. Finally, electronic commerce facilitates global trading by enabling even small companies to buy from or sell to business partners in other countries. Thus, globalization is rapidly increasing.

Doing business in a global environment is becoming more and more challenging as the political environment improves and telecommunications and the Internet open the door to a large number of buyers, sellers, and competitors worldwide. The increased competition forces companies to look for better ways to do global business, and IT is frequently evaluated as a potential solution. Porter and Youngman (1995), for example, propose an approach that focuses on employment policies and government regulations. A more general approach is presented next.

A Global Business Drivers Framework

Ives et al. (1993) proposed a comprehensive framework that connects IT and global business. According to this framework, the success of companies doing business in a competitive global environment depends on the alignment of the information system and the global business strategy. This connection is demonstrated by Rosenbluth International, whose strategy enables it to compete with local travel agencies in 24 countries, and by Caterpillar Corporation, which employs a business strategy of strong support to dealers and customers worldwide by means of its effective global information system.

The success of multinational firms and companies engaged in global activities, in a highly competitive global market, thus strongly depends on the link between their information systems and their business strategy. Information managers must be innovative in identifying the IT systems that a firm needs in order to be competitive worldwide and must tie them to the strategic business imperatives.

The global business driver framework provides a tool for identifying business entities, such as customers, suppliers, projects, and orders, that will benefit most from an integrated global IT management system. The basic idea is to apply IT through a firm's **global business drivers**. These are business factors that benefit from global economies of scale or scope and thus add value to a global business strategy. Typical business drivers are: risk reduction, availability of skilled and/or inexpensive workforce, quality products/services, location of materials, supply and suppliers, location of customers, and a country's infrastructure. The idea of the global business drivers framework is to look at the drivers in terms of current and future information needs and focus on worldwide implementation.

Advances in Internet availability and electronic commerce (EC) are of special interest to global traders. First, many of the business drivers can be facilitated by the Internet, which is much cheaper and more accessible than private communication networks. Second, the Internet and EC are answers to several of the analysis questions related to global business drivers. Analysis of some global business drivers is available at the book's Web site.

3.7 STRATEGIC INFORMATION SYSTEMS: EXAMPLES AND ANALYSIS

The frameworks presented in the previous sections suggest strategies that companies can use to gain strategic advantage. In this section, we provide examples of how companies use, and how IT supports, the response strategies.

Classic SIS

Several SISs developed in the 1970s and 1980s are cited as classic illustrations of the power of IT. Representative examples are given in Table 3.4.

Other Representative Strategic Information Systems

In this section, we present and analyze specific examples of how IT has successfully supported the various strategies that companies use to gain competitive advantage.

Computerized Total Quality Management at Florida Power and Light. Florida Power and Light (FPL) is the largest U.S. utility, and it has one of the best information systems in the industry. It is also a leader in implementing *total quality management* and was awarded the prestigious Deming Prize, Japan's highest award for quality.

www.fplgroup.com

...in Production & Operations Management

FPL's IT includes many interesting applications. One is the Generation Equipment Management System (GEMS), which tracks generators at 13 power plants. When a generator goes down, GEMS diagnoses the problem and recommends a remedy. Once the remedy has been approved, GEMS automatically budgets the repair, orders the parts, and issues work orders over the corporate intranet. GEMS also predicts mechanical breakdowns, allowing preventive maintenance work to be scheduled. This system has cut downtime from 14 to 8 percent, saving about $5 million per year and increasing customer satisfaction.

TABLE 3.4 Classic Strategic Information Systems

System	Description
Otis Elevator—centralized call center, self-diagnosing elevators' malfunctions and maintenance analysis needs	Offered computerized diagnosis of malfunctions and dispatching of repair people within 30–40 minutes, and computerized analysis of failures and repairs for improved design and maintenance. Centralized call center (now Web-based) provides superb customer relationship management (CRM). Wins lucrative elevator maintenance contracts.
Baxter International (formerly American Hospital Supply)—terminals in customers' hospitals	Pioneered installation of computer terminals in hospitals for electronic ordering, which significantly reduced delivery time; made ordering from competitors seem inconvenient, slow, and error-prone. Preceded competitors by 2 years.
Merrill Lynch—cash management accounts system	Pioneered one report per customer for all financial services (brokerage, credit cards, banking, etc.). Differentiated itself by providing superb CRM years before competitors.
American Airlines—computerized reservation system (SABRE)	Installed PC-based reservation system in travel agents' offices. System used also by many small airlines that cannot afford such a large system. New capabilities (now Web-based) are added frequently, some enhancing agents' offices. Travel services are provided both by *easysabre.com* and *travelocity.com.*

Sources: Compiled from Callon (1996), Neumann (1994), and Ward and Griffiths (1997).

FPL has implemented over 20 different quality-control applications. These programs have reduced customer complaints by over 50 percent and have helped FPL improve its financial position. Another application that has led to increased customer satisfaction is the Trouble Call Management System. It collects complaints from blacked-out customers and analyzes the causes of the malfunctions. This analysis helped reduce the average blackout time from 70 to 48 minutes.

Recognized all over the world for its computerized quality control programs, FPL created a subsidiary, Qualtec Inc., that sells quality-control software to other companies, including nonutilities. (*Sources: fplgroup.com,* 2001, and private communication with FPL, 2001.)

Integrating IT ...in Health Care

www.geisinger.org

An Intranet and the Web Give Geisinger a Shot in the Arm. Health maintenance organizations (HMOs) have grown rapidly in the United States as an approach to containing health-care costs. However, HMOs face strong competition among themselves and from physicians' groups. The rapid growth of some HMOs creates problems of inefficient operation and poor customer services, as was the case at Geisinger, a rural HMO in Danville, Pennsylvania.

The company, which grew through mergers and acquisitions, had 40 different IT legacy systems that needed to be upgraded and integrated. An innovative approach required use of an intranet to deal with the complexity of this integration. Not only does its intranet allow Geisinger to integrate its systems, but it also allows the HMO to offer innovative services such as "Tel-a-Nurse," which provides ways for patients to communicate with nurses. Patients can easily ask medical questions via a telephone or the HMO's Web site.

Moreover, Geisinger installed a clinical management system to work with its intranet. Medical personnel can use digital cameras to take pictures of patients' injuries. Having these pictures accessible through the intranet reduces unnecessary reordering of tests and x-rays. As of 2001, pictures taken by a nurse in a rural area, or at the scene of an accident, can be transmitted by a wireless connection, as an e-mail attachment, to expert physicians in hospitals.

The intranet is also used for human resources management, routine paperwork, and library systems. Geisinger's radiology department, which performs diagnostic procedures such as x-rays, mammograms, and MRIs, has placed an electronic information kiosk in its waiting rooms. Patients can click on the homepage to find a list of several dozen common procedures, described in nontechnical terms, which are performed in the various departments. Also, the Web is used for patient education.

Geisinger, which was named the premier network healthcare organization of 1996, uses its intranet and Web site to improve its quality, creativity, and innovation. Moreover, utilization of its intranet helps the company reduce costs and unnecessary medical work. (*Sources:* Compiled from *PC Week,* February 3, 1997, pp. 27, 39, and from *geisinger.org.,* 2001.)

Integrating IT ...in Production & Operations Management

www.caltex.com

Caltex Uses B2B Extranet to Compete. Caltex Corporation is a major multinational company that sells gasoline and petroleum products. Thousands of gasoline stations and other facilities affiliated with Caltex used to purchase different supplies from some 7,000 suppliers. This situation drastically changed in 2000 with the introduction of a centralized e-purchasing corporate exchange.

Companies that want to supply Caltex must go online on one of the most advanced supply chain management systems in the world. This electronic procurement, payment, and logistics system is deployed worldwide. The online system requires suppliers to build electronic catalogs with the Ariba software. These catalogs are aggregated on Caltex's server so they can be used by any Caltex purchasing agent. Here are some of the system's benefits:

- It reduced the number of suppliers from 7,000 to 800, due to the ability to easily interact with remote suppliers.
- It presents the negotiated prices to all Caltex buyers in comparison tables.
- It reduces expensive, unplanned emergency buying at local offices.
- It is able to automatically handle international trade issues: customs documentation, duties, language translation, and currencies conversion.
- It makes possible coordination in spending across Caltex's geographical boundaries.
- It offers smooth integration with back office transactions.
- It can drive down costs, via bidding and requests for quotes (RFQs).
- It reduces the need for third-party intermediaries for sourcing of supplies.

The system is especially useful in Asia, Africa, and the Middle East, which do not have the effective infrastructure of North America. It enables Caltex to more effectively compete in a competitive market place by handling complex business environments, such as multiple currencies, multiple tax regimes, the movement of goods across borders, poor electronic infrastructure, and unavailability of door-to-door delivery systems in some countries. (*Sources:* See *caltex.com* and *ariba.com.*)

Integrating IT ...in Production & Operations Management

www.singaport.gov.sg

The Port of Singapore Competes by Using Intelligent Systems Over Its Enterprise Portal. The Port of Singapore, the second largest container port in the world, is facing strong competition from neighboring ports in Malaysia, Indonesia, and the Philippines. In these neighboring countries, labor, space, utilities, and services are significantly cheaper. The Port of Singapore automated many of its port services to reduce costs.

Its most innovative applications are the intelligent systems designed to reduce the cycle time of unloading and loading vessels. This cycle time is most important to ships since their fixed cost is very high; the longer they stay in port, the higher the cost. For example, an intelligent system is used to expedite trucks' entry into and exit from the port. As a result of using neural computing, the time is down to 30 seconds per truck instead of 3 to 5 minutes in other countries. Expert systems plan vessel loading, unloading, and container configuration, so cycle time can be as little as 4 hours (versus 16 to 20 hours in a neighboring port). Expert systems also are used for improved resource allocation that makes customers happy while reducing costs. Several other intelligent systems are available to planners, crane operators, and managers over the enterprise portal. (*Sources:* L. L. Tung and E. Turban, "Expert Systems Support Container Operations in the Port of Singapore," *New Review of Applied Expert Systems,* March 1996; and corporate sources in Singapore, July 2000.)

Integrating IT ...in Marketing and in Production & Operations Management

www.volvo.com

Volvo Speeds Cars to Buyers via a Global Network. Selling new cars is becoming more difficult as global competition intensifies and regional trade agreements expand. Volvo of North America (now a subsidiary of Ford Motor Company) is known for its quality cars, but they are relatively expensive. Also, delivery times were slow, so customers were going to competitors. Volvo undertook a new strategy involving a complex network for both internal operations and external dealer applications.

The creation of a global communication network between dealers in the United States and Canada and Volvo headquarters in Sweden allows customer orders to be placed on the Web in real time. This allows for quicker fulfillment and also reduces inventories of cars and parts. Volvo believes that the system helps the company understand who its customers are and what they really need. Overall, delivery time has been reduced from 12 to 16 weeks to 4 to 6 weeks for customized cars. The cost of doing business has also significantly declined, along with the cost of making the car. Volvo's $35 million IT investment is expected to pay for itself in less than five years.

This system has been such a hit that faster delivery of customized cars is now offered by all major car manufacturers. In certain cases delivery time has been reduced from 3 months to 2 weeks. IT is used not only to facilitate the supply chain, but also to enable customers to track, via the Web, the status of their car at any given time while it is in production. For example, in spring 2000 Ford Motors installed a tracking system using UPS technology. (*Sources: PC Week,* February 3, 1997, pp. 71, 78; and Slater, 1999.)

Integrating IT ...in Production & Operations Management

www.cat.com

Caterpiller Rolls Over Its Competitors. Caterpillar Corporation, a world leader in manufacturing of heavy machines, had been struggling with its Japanese competitors. After sustaining heavy losses in the 1980s, Caterpillar (CAT) introduced several IT-based initiatives, at a cost of $2 billion. These included computer-aided manufacturing and robots to cut costs, computerized inventory management, supply chain management Web-based initiatives (including e-procurement of raw materials), a global intranet that connects employees and dealers in over 1,000 locations, EDI for fast communication with business partners, and a Web-based computerized parts service for quick repairs.

Also of a special interest is a sensory intelligent system that CAT attaches to its products after they are sold. The system monitors performance and detects potential failures. Once a problem is detected, the information is passed via the Web to the equipment's owner, along with a cost estimate. Repairs can be made very quickly. The success of the intelligent system was so great that CAT's major competitor, Komatsu of Japan, shifted its strategy to avoid head-to-head competition with CAT. (*Sources:* See *Harvard Business Review,* March–April 1996, p. 89. Reprinted with permission of *Harvard Business Review.* For more details, see the Caterpillar case at the book's Web site.)

Integrating IT ...in Finance

www.dub.com

Dun and Bradstreet Corporation Evaluates Credit Via the Web. Dun & Bradstreet (D&B) is a credit clearinghouse that provides risk analysis to manufacturers, wholesalers, and marketers in several industries. D&B maintains and updates a database of credit ratings on several *million* businesses worldwide. Customers who pay D&B for the credit analysis of other companies used to complain about inaccuracies (it is difficult to update the material constantly), inconsistencies (such as different interpretations by different risk analysts), and slow response time. A new Web-based expert system is now capable of handling more than 95 percent of all requests. As a result, response time has been reduced from about three days to a few seconds (provided via the Web), and the credit recommendations are more accurate. As soon as there are changes in a business's data, the expert system reevaluates the implications for creditworthiness and informs its clients, if needed.

Clients communicate with D&B via the Internet or a value-added network. Once a report is purchased from D&B it can be placed on the buyer's intranet

TABLE 3.5 Company Examples and Competitiveness Strategies

Company	Cost Leadership	Differentiation (Quality, Speed, Customization etc.)	Growth	Alliances	Innovation	Internal Efficiency	Customer Orientation
American Airlines		X	X	X			
American Hospital Supply				X			
Caltex				X	X	X	
Caterpillar		X			X	X	X
Dun and Bradstreet		X					X
Florida Power & Light						X	X
McKesson		X		X		X	X
Merrill Lynch		X					
Otis Elevator		X			X		
Rosenbluth	X	X			X	X	X
Seven Eleven (Minicase 2)		X	X	X	X		X

and accessed by all authorized employees. D&B also provides Web-based access to its corporate database, which includes powerful search engines. Together, these various Web-based systems help the company maintain its position as a leading information provider. (*Source: dbn.com.* Also, see Internet Exercise 5 at the end of this chapter.)

SUMMARY. The relationships between the competitiveness strategies presented earlier in the chapter and some of the company examples are summarized in Table 3.5.

3.8 IMPLEMENTING AND SUSTAINING SIS

Implementing strategic information systems may be a complex undertaking due to the magnitude and the complex nature of the systems. In this section we will briefly look at several related issues: (1) SIS implementation, (2) SIS risks and failures, (3) finding appropriate SIS, and (4) sustaining SIS and strategic advantage.

SIS Implementation

Most SISs are large-scale systems whose construction may take months or even years. In later chapters we will discuss at more length various important issues relating to SIS implementation: Chapter 8 covers the development process of such systems, which starts with IS generic planning. Chapter 13 addresses the methodologies of how to justify strategic information systems, whose sometimes-intangible benefits may be difficult to value. Finally, Chapter 14 discusses in detail the general topic of systems development and implementation.

Risks and Failure

The magnitude and complexity of the continuous changes occurring both in technology and in the business environment may result in partial or even complete failures of SIS. When SISs succeed they may result in huge benefits and profits. When they fail, the cost can be extremely high. In some cases, SIS failure can be so high that a company may even go bankrupt as a result. For example, FoxMeyer, a large distributor of drugs in the United States, filed for bankruptcy in 1996 and was sold in 1998 after failing to implement a SIS that included electronic ordering, inventory management, automated transaction processing, logistics, and scheduling. The failure occurred despite the use of a major IT consulting firm and the leading enterprise resources planning (ERP) software.

Finding Appropriate SIS

Identifying appropriate strategic information systems is not a simple task. Two major approaches exist: One approach is to start with known problems or areas where improvements can provide strategic advantage, decide on a strategy, and then build the appropriate IT support. This is a *reactive approach.* It is basically what Rosenbluth International did. The second approach is to start with available IT technologies, such as EDI or e-procurement, and try to match the technologies with the organization's current or proposed business models. This is a *proactive approach.* In either case a SWOT (strengths, weaknesses, opportunities, threats) analysis or McFarlan framework may be appropriate.

Sustaining SIS and Strategic Advantage

The strategic information systems of the 1970s and 1980s enabled a number of companies to enjoy a competitive advantage for several years before competitors imitated their systems. For example, Federal Express's package tracking system was copied by UPS, DHL, and others after three to five years. The SISs of the 1970s and 1980s were primarily *outward systems,* which are visible to competitors. Due to advances in systems development, outward systems can now be quickly duplicated, sometimes in months rather than years. Also, innovations in technology may make even new systems obsolete rather quickly.

Therefore, the major problem that companies now face is how to *sustain* their competitive advantage. Ross et al. (1996) suggest the three IT assets—people, technology, and "shared" risk and responsibility—as a way to develop sustainable competitiveness. Porter (1996) expanded his classic competitive forces model to include strategies such as growth and internal efficiency that facilitate sustainability. We here present some ways to accomplish competitive sustainability with the help of IT.

One popular approach is to use *inward systems* that are not visible to competitors. Companies such as General Motors and American Airlines, for example, use intelligent systems in a number of ways to gain strategic advantage, but the details are secret. It is known that several companies (such as John Deere Corp.) are using neural computing for investment decisions, but again the details are not known. The strategic advantage from use of such inward systems is sustainable as long as the systems remain a secret, or as long as competitors do not develop similar or better systems. One way to protect outward systems is to patent them, as Rosenbluth did.

Another approach is to develop a comprehensive, innovative, and expensive system that is very difficult to duplicate. This is basically what Rosenbluth did, as did Caterpillar Corporation.

Finally, a third approach is to combine an SIS with structural changes. We alluded to this possibility in differentiating competitive advantage from strategic advantage. This is basically what is attempted in business processes reengineering and organizational transformation, which are described in Chapter 8.

MANAGERIAL ISSUES

1. ***Implementing strategic information systems can be risky.*** The investment involved in implementing an SIS is high. Frequently these systems use new concepts. Considering the contending business forces, the probability of success, and the cost of investment, a company considering a new strategic information system should undertake a formal risk analysis.
2. ***Strategic information systems require planning.*** Planning for an SIS is a major concern of organizations, according to Earl (1993). He surveyed 27 companies and reported on major SIS planning approaches. Exploiting IT for competitive advantage can be viewed as one of four major activities of SIS planning. The other three (which will be discussed later in the book) are aligning investment in IS with business goals (Chapter 8), directing efficient and effective management of IS resources (Chapters 13 and 15), and developing technology policies and architecture (Chapter 8).
3. ***Sustaining competitive advantage is challenging.*** As companies become larger and more sophisticated, they develop sufficient resources to quickly duplicate the successful systems of their competitors. For example, Alamo Rent-a-Car now offers a frequent-renter (Quick Silver) card similar to the one offered by National car rental. Sustaining strategic systems is becoming more difficult and is related to the issue of being a risk-taking leader versus a follower in developing innovative systems.
4. ***Ethical issues.*** Gaining competitive advantage through the use of IT may involve actions that are unethical, illegal, or both. Companies use IT to monitor the activities of other companies and may invade the privacy of individuals working there. In using business intelligence (e.g., spying on competitors), companies may engage in tactics such as pressuring competitors' employees to reveal information or using software that is the intellectual property of other companies without the knowledge of these other companies. Companies may post questions and place remarks about their competitors with Internet newsgroups. Many such actions are technically not illegal, due to the fact that the Internet is new and its legal environment is not well developed as yet, but many people would certainly find them unethical.

ON THE WEB SITE... Additional resources, including the Virtual Company, quizzes, cases, updates, additional exercises, links, demos, and activities, can be found on the book's Web site.

KEY TERMS

Competitive advantage *83*
Competitive forces model *89*
Competitive intelligence *86*
Cost leadership *91*
Differentiation *91*
Global business drivers *106*
Information intensity *100*
Innovation *84*
Long-range planning *84*
Primary activities *96*
Response management *84*
Strategic information system (SIS) *83*
Support activities *96*
Sustainable strategic advantage *88*
Value chain model *96*
Value system *96*

CHAPTER HIGHLIGHTS (Numbers Refer to Learning Objectives)

1 Strategic information systems (SISs) support or shape competitive strategies.

1 SIS can be outward (customer) oriented or inward (organization) oriented.

1 Strategic management involves long-range planning, response management, and technological innovation.

2 Cost leadership, differentiation, and focus are Porter's major strategies for gaining a competitive advantage. Other strategies exist. All of the competitive strategies can be supported by IT.

3 Porter's value chain model can be used to identify areas in which IT can provide strategic advantages.

4 Different frameworks can be used to describe the relationship between IT and attainment of competitive advantage and to match IT applications with corporate strategies.

5 The Web revolution enabled many SISs to be delivered via the Web. Many conventional SISs are changing to Web-based.

6 Multinational corporations and international traders need a special IT approach to support their business strategies.

7 Strategic information systems can be found in all types of organizations around the globe.

8 Some SISs are expensive and difficult to justify, and others turn out to be unsuccessful. Therefore, careful planning and implementation are essential.

QUESTIONS FOR REVIEW

1. What is an SIS?
2. Describe the three dimensions of strategic management.
3. List the major benefits of SISs.
4. Describe Porter's value chain model and its view regarding competition.
5. List the five forces in Porter's competitive forces model.
6. Describe McFarland's application portfolio model.
7. Explain the meaning of cost leadership, differentiation, and focus.
8. Describe the global business drivers model.
9. Compare the value chain to the value system.
10. List the major variables that provide a competitive advantage in the Bakos and Treacy framework.
11. Describe the customer resource life cycle framework.
12. List some Web-based SIS applications.

QUESTIONS FOR DISCUSSION

1. Identify the information technologies used in McKesson's *IT at Work* story.
2. A major objective of the Rosenbluth strategy was to create a very close relationship with the customer. Relate this objective to Porter's two models.
3. Discuss the relationship between the critical organizational responses of Chapter 1 and a *differentiation* strategy.
4. Provide three examples (at least one Web-based) of IT being used to build a barrier to entry for new competitors or new products.
5. Discuss the idea that an information system by itself can rarely provide a sustainable competitive advantage.
6. Give two examples (one of which is Web-based) that show how IT can help a defending company *reduce* the impact of the five forces in Porter's model.
7. Give two examples (one of which is Web-based) of how attacking companies can use IT to *increase* the impact of the five forces in Porter's model.
8. Why might it be difficult to justify SIS, and why is it that some systems do not work?
9. Explain what unique aspects are provided by the global business drivers model.
10. What is the importance of business intelligence in SIS? What role does the Internet play in intelligence gathering?

EXERCISES

1. Review the applications in Section 3.7 and relate them to Porter's five forces.
2. One of the forthcoming areas for intensive competition is selling cars online (see Slater, 1999). Examine the strategy of the players cited in the paper (available at *cio.com*). Identify the related new business models and relate them to the strategies promoted in this chapter.
3. Study the Web sites of Amazon.com and Barnes & Noble online (*bn.com*). Also, find some information about the competition between the two. Analyze Barnes & Noble's defense strategy using Porter's model and Porter's 1996 extension. Prepare a report.
4. Identify the major competitors of Rosenbluth International. Visit three Web sites (e.g., *cmxtravel.com, press-plan-travel.co.uk,* and *carlson.com*), and compare their strategies and offerings to those of Rosenbluth.
5. Review the Rosenbluth opening case, and answer the following questions: (a) How can the two strategies counter the five threats listed in the problem statement? (b) The company's initial SISs were copied by the competition. Now some of Rosenbluth's SIS are patented. Why? Can competing IT systems be developed even if patents exist?

GROUP AND ROLE-PLAYING ACTIVITIES

1. Assign group members to each of the major car rental companies. Find out their latest strategies regarding customer service. Visit their Web sites, and compare the findings. Have each group prepare a presentation on why its company should get the title of "best customer service provider." Also, each group should use Porter's forces model to convince the class that its company is the best competitor in the car rental industry.
2. The competition in retailing online is growing rapidly as evidenced in goods such as books, toys, and CDs. Assign groups to study online competition in the above industries and more. Identify successes and failures. Compare the various industries. What generalizations can you make?
3. Assign group members to each of the major airlines. Read Callon's (1996) chapter on the competition in the airline industry. Visit the Web sites of the major airlines. Explain how they deal with "buyers." What information technologies are used in the airlines' strategy implementation? Have each group make a presentation explaining why its airline has the best strategy.
4. Assign each group member to a company to which he or she has an access, and have each member prepare a value-chain chart. The objective is to discover how specific IT applications are used to facilitate the various activities. Compare these charts across companies in different industries.
5. Assign members to UPS, FedEx, DHL, and the United States Postal Service (see *Internet Week,* March 9, 1998). Have each group study the e-commerce strategies of one company. Then have members present the company, explaining why it is the best.

INTERNET EXERCISES

1. McKesson Drugs is the largest wholesale drug distributor in the world. Visit the company Web site (*mckesson.com*). What can you learn about its strategy toward retailers? What is its strategy toward its customers? What e-commerce initiatives are evidenced?
2. Enter the Web site of Dell Computer (*dell.com*) and document the various services available to customers. Then enter IBM's site (*ibm.com*). Compare the services provided to PC buyers at each company. Discuss the differences.
3. Research the online toys competition. Visit the sites of *toysrus.com, lego.com, KBKids.com,* and also check toy sales online by *sears.com, amazon.com,* and *walmart.com.* Finally, examine *dogtoys.com.* Prepare a report with your findings.
4. Enter some EDGAR-related Web sites (*edgar-online.com, hottools.com, edgar.stern.nyu.edu*). Prepare a list of the documents that are available, and discuss the benefits one can derive in using this database for conducting a competitive intelligence (see Kambil and Ginsburg, 1998).
5. Enter *dnb.com,* go to Products, then USA, and access the free database trial. Find three other services offered by D&B Corp. Prepare a short report on your experience. To whom would such a service be most valuable?

Minicase 1

www.tfa.nl

New Entrants to the Dutch Flower Market: Electronic Auctions

The Dutch auction flower market in the Netherlands is the largest in the world, attracting sellers from dozens of countries such as Thailand, Israel, and East African states. Some 3,500 varieties of flowers are sold in 120 auction groups. The auctions are semiautomated; buyers and sellers must come to one location where the flowers are shown to the buyers. The auctioneer of each variety of flower uses a clock with a large hand which he starts at a high price and drops until a buyer stops the clock by pushing an ordering button. Via an intercom, the quantity is clarified, and the clock hand is reset, at the high price, for the next batch of flowers. The process continues until all flowers are sold.

In September 1994, the Dutch growers who own the auction organization, called the Dutch Flower Auctions (DFA), decided to ban foreign growers from participating during the summer months in order to protect the Dutch growers from low prices from abroad. By March 1995 some foreign growers, together with several local buyers, created a competing auction called the Tele Flower Auction (TFA), limited to the Netherlands and a few neighboring countries. TFA is an *electronic auction* that enables its initiators to penetrate the Dutch flower market. Here is how it works:

In the TFA, buyers can bid on flowers via their PCs from any location connected to the network. The process is similar to the traditional one, and the auction clock is shown on the PC screen. The buyers can stop the clock by pushing the space bar. The auctioneer then converses with the buyers by telephone, a sale is concluded, and the clock is reset. The flowers are not physically visible to the buyers. However, a large amount of relevant information is available, for example, the time flowers are picked up, quality, and arrival time to the Netherlands. The buyers are alerted to a specific auction, in real time, when their item of interest is auctioned.

Initial results indicated that buyers and growers are enthusiastic about TFA. While prices are about the same as in the regular auctions, the process is much quicker, and the after-sale delivery is much faster than in other markets. Delivery starts within 30 minutes after the sale; nearby buyers can receive their purchases within a half hour; for buyers in other European countries, delivery takes longer. A major issue with the online auction could be the quality of the flowers, since the buyers cannot see them; but the quality is actually better since there is less handling (no need to bring the flowers to an auction site), and the growers stand behind their products. As a result, there is enough trust so that everyone is happy.

The TFA has gained considerable market share at the expense of existing organizations—a real new-entrant success story. Using IT, the new entrant quickly built a competitive advantage. While some minor competitors decided to install a similar system in order to compete immediately, it took the major Dutch Growers Association more than a year to cancel the import restrictions and implement their own electronic clearinghouse for flowers.

Questions for Minicase 1

1. Why was the TFA successful?
2. How can the TFA sustain its success while competitors are copying its new concept?
3. The cancellation of the import restrictions is not working too well for the Dutch Growers Association. Advise the CEO of the association what to do.
4. Can this concept be extended to the Internet? If so, how can real-time flower auctions be implemented?

Sources: A. Kambil and E. Van Heck, "Reengineering the Dutch Flower Auctions," *Information Systems Research,* March 1998; E. Van Heck, et al., "New Entrants and the Role of IT—Case Study: The Tele Flower Auction in the Netherlands," *Proceedings of the 30th Hawaiian International Conference on Systems Sciences,* Hawaii, January 1997; also see *Electronic Markets,* December 1997.

Minicase 2

7-Eleven Japan: A Technology Company with Convenience Stores

www.sej.co.jp

Ito-Yokado Company is Japan's most profitable retailer. In 1974, Ito-Yokado bought the franchise rights to 7-Eleven in Japan from Southland Corporation (Houston, Texas). The first 7-Eleven store opened in Japan in May 1974, and by 2000 the Japanese franchise had grown to over 6,000 stores. In the meantime, 7-Eleven's parent company—Southland—was also expanding its operations. However, heavy debt forced it to seek bankruptcy court protection from its lenders. In an attempt to raise cash, Southland was forced to sell assets. In 1990, Ito-Yokado Corporation purchased 70 percent of Southland Corporation.

While 7-Eleven in the United States was losing a considerable amount of money, 7-Eleven Japan made over 40 percent profit on its sales. Such a high level of profit is extremely unusual, not only in Japan but also in other countries. What enabled a franchiser of 7-Eleven to achieve such a high profit margin while its parent company was filing for bankruptcy? The answer is a *consumer-focused* orientation based on information technology.

In the early 1990s 7-Eleven Japan created a \$200-million information system for its stores. The purpose of the system was to (1) discover who the customers are and what they want and (2) create a sophisticated product-tracking system. How does the system work? In selected stores, clerks key in *customer information,* such as gender and approximate age, when purchases are made. In this way, the company knows who buys what, where, and at what time of day, so it can track customer preferences. Clerks also key in information about products requested by customers that are not included in the store's inventory. Such information leads to stocking the appropriate products and even to the customization of products, manufactured by specially created companies in Japan.

The information system is also used for other purposes, such as monitoring inventories. By implementing the *just-in-time approach,* in which inventory arrives at stores just as it is needed, a minimum inventory is kept on the shelves. This reduces the costs of investing in and keeping inventory, as well as the cost of spoilage. Also, because stores know customer's preferences, they seldom run out of stock. In addition, most stores have arrangements with their suppliers for quick delivery of products they sell, and so they do not need large inventories. Other uses of the information system are to (1) electronically transmit orders to distribution centers and manufacturers (via satellite), (2) determine which products to keep in each store (70 percent of the products are replaced each year), (3) determine how much shelf space to allocate to each product, and (4) track employee performance (for rewarding high performers).

In addition, the company maintains a high level of quality. A team of 200 inspectors visits the 7-Eleven stores regularly. Even the company's president occasionally drops into stores incognito to check quality. Quality control data are collected and analyzed continuously by a computerized decision support system at headquarters. Brands that do not meet strict quality requirements are immediately discontinued. Quality is extremely important in Japan, where fresh hot meals are sold at convenience stores.

As a result of its information system, 7-Eleven Japan has extensive knowledge of its market. It maximizes sales in limited space and optimizes its inventory level. Also, knowing exactly what the customers want helps the company to negotiate good prices and high quality with its vendors, who support the just-in-time approach. (About 20 manufacturers have special factories that make only or mostly 7-Eleven products.)

7-Eleven Japan has also created a time-distribution system that changes the product mix on display in its stores at least twice a day, based on careful and continual tracking of customers' needs. The company knows that customers' needs in the morning are completely different from those in the evening. Space is very expensive in Japan, and the stores are small. So the system allows them to display the most appropriate items at different hours of the day.

The company is in the process of reshaping its U.S. operations. The Japanese are interested in changing the U.S. way of doing business before they improve the U.S. information systems. Thus, they are concentrating on transforming 7-Eleven into a high-quality, profitable, and truly *convenience* store operation.

In late 1997, 7-Eleven was the first convenience store chain to introduce Internet access terminals in their Seattle area stores. These terminals allow customers who do not have computers to access the Internet by paying a user fee to 7-Eleven. In 1998 it introduced a computerized system to track inventory and forecast sales in the United States. In 1999 it introduced multimedia-based Internet kiosks in its Japanese stores for ordering from the stores' site, with capabilities to pay for the goods in the stores. The stores are also used as a receiving station for the merchandise ordered.

Questions for Minicase 2

1. 7-Eleven competes with both other chains of convenience stores and independent stores. What competitive advantages can you identify in this case?
2. Use the Internet to find the major competitors of 7-Eleven in Japan, the United States, and other countries where 7-Eleven is active. Describe the competition faced by the company.
3. Which of Porter's five forces are countered by the 7-Eleven system described here?
4. Which strategies of those suggested in the various frameworks are noticeable in this case?
5. Which of the business pressures discussed in Chapter 1 are evidenced in this case?
6. Which of the corporate response activities of Chapter 1 are evidenced in this case?
7. Does the procedure of collecting customers' information infringe on their privacy? Why or why not? Is it unethical? Should customers have the right to anonymity, or to check that information collected on them is accurate?
8. Surf the Internet to find information about recent IT-related initiatives of 7-Eleven, both in Japan and the United States. Relate them to "gaining strategic advantage."

Sources: Based on stories in *Business Week,* January 1992 and September 1, 1997, and on *businesswire.com,* September 15, 1997. See also stories at *forbes.com,* 2000, and at *fortune.com,* 2000.

REFERENCES AND BIBLIOGRAPHY

1. Bakos, J. Y., and M. W. Treacy, "Information Technology and Corporate Strategy: A Research Perspective," *MIS Quarterly,* June 1986.
2. Bell, C. R., and O. Harari, *Deep! Deep! Competing in the Age of the Road Runner.* New York: Warner Books, 2000.
3. Bergerson, F., et al., "Identification of Strategic Information Systems Opportunities: Applying and Comparing Two Methodologies," *MIS Quarterly,* March 1991.
4. Bhise, H., et al., "The Duel for Doorstep," *McKinsey Quarterly,* No. 2, 2000.
5. Boynton, A. C., et al., "New Competitive Strategies: Challenges to Organizations and Information Technologies," *IBM Systems Journal,* Vol. 32, No. 1, 1993.
6. Buchanan, S., and F. Gibb, "The Information Audit: An Integrated Strategic Approach," *International Journal of Information Management,* February 1998.
7. Callon, J. D., *Competitive Advantage Through Information Technology.* New York: McGraw Hill, 1996.
8. Choi, S. Y., and A. B. Whinston, *The Internet Economy: Technology and Practice.* Austin TX: SmartEcon Pub., 2000.
9. Clemons, E. K., and M. Row, "A Strategic Information System: McKesson Drug Company's Economost," *Planning Review,* September–October 1988.
10. Clemons, E. K., and I. H. Hann, "Rosenbluth International: Strategic Transformation," *Journal of MIS,* Fall 1999.
11. Curry, J., and J. Ferguson, "Increasing the Success of Global Information Technology Strategic Planning," *Proceedings of the 33rd Hawaiian International Conference on Systems Sciences (HICSS),* Hawaii, 2000.
12. Davenport, T. H., *Process Innovation: Reengineering Work Through Information Technology.* Boston: Harvard Business School Press, 1993.
13. Earl, M. J., "Experiences in Strategic Information Systems Planning," *MIS Quarterly,* March 1993.
14. Galliers, R., et al. (eds.), *Strategic Information Systems: Challenges and Strategies in Managing Information Systems,* 2nd ed. Woburn, MA: Butterworth-Heinemann, 1999.
15. Gonsalves, G. R., et al., "A Customer Resource Life Cycle Interpretation of the Impact of the Web on Competitiveness," *International Journal of Electronic Commerce,* Fall 1999.
16. Gottschalk, P., and N. J. Taylor, "Strategic Management of IS/IT Functions: The Role of the CIO," *Proceedings, 33rd HICSS,* Hawaii, 2000.
17. Griffiths, P. M., et al. (eds.), *Information Management in Competitive Success.* New York: Pergamon Press, 1998.
18. Guimaraes, T., and C. Armstrong, "Exploring the Relationships Between Competitive Intelligence, IS Support, and Business Change," *Competitive Intelligence Review,* Vol. 9, No. 3, 1997.
19. Ives B., and G. P. Learmouth, "The Information System as a Competitive Weapon," *Communications of the ACM,* December 1984.
20. Ives, B., et al., "Global Business Drivers: Aligning IT to Global Business Strategy," *IBM Systems Journal,* Vol. 32, No. 1, 1993.
21. Kambil, A., and M. Ginsburg, "Public Access Web Information Systems: Lessons from the Internet EDGAR Project," *Communications of the ACM,* July 1998.
22. Kambil, A., and E. Van Heck, "Reengineering the Dutch Flower Auctions," *Information Systems Research,* March 1998.
23. Kemerer, C. (ed.), *Information Technology and Industrial Competitiveness: How IT Shapes Competition.* Boston: Kluwer Academic, 1997.
24. Kvassov, V., "Strategic Decisions and Intelligent Tools," *Proceedings, 33rd HICSS,* Hawaii, 2000.
25. Lederer, A. L., and H. Salmela, "Toward a Theory of Strategic Information Systems Planning," *Journal of Strategic Information Systems,* Vol. 5, 1996.
26. Lederer, A. L., et al., "Using Web-based Information Systems to Enhance Competitiveness," *Communications of the ACM,* July 1998.
27. Loebbecke, C., and P. Powell, "Competitive Advantage from IT in Logistics: The Integrated Transport Tracking System," *International Journal of Information Management,* February 1998.
28. Luftman, J., *Competing in the Information Age: Strategic Alignment in Practice.* London: Oxford University Press, 1996.

29. McFarlan, F. W., "Information Technology Changes the Way You Compete," *Harvard Business Review,* May–June 1984.

30. McGonagle, J. J., and C. M. Vella, *Protecting Your Company Against Competitive Intelligence.* Westport, CT: Quorum Books, 1998.

31. Miller, J., et al., *Millennium Intelligence: Understanding and Conducting Competitive Intelligence in the Digital Age.* Medford, NJ: *infotoday.com,* 2000.

32. Mintzberg, H., et al., *Strategy Safari: A Guided Tour Through the Wilds of Strategic Management.* New York: Simon and Schuster, 1998.

33. Neumann, S., *Strategic Information Systems—Competition Through Information Technologies.* New York: Macmillan, 1994.

34. Porter M. E., et al. (eds.), *Global Competitiveness Report 2000.* Boston: Harvard University Press, 2000.

35. Porter, M. E., *Competitive Advantage: Creating and Sustaining Superior Performance.* New York: Free Press, 1985.

36. Porter, M. E., "What Is a Strategy?" *Harvard Business Review,* November–December 1996.

37. Porter, M. E., "Strategy and the Internet," *Harvard Business Review,* March 2001.

38. Porter, M. E., and V. E. Millar, "How Information Gives You Competitive Advantage," *Harvard Business Review,* July–August 1985.

39. Porter, M. E., and J. A. Youngman, *Keeping America Competitive: Employment Policy for the Twenty-first Century.* Lakewood, CO: Glenbridge Publishing, 1995.

40. Power, B. S., and R. Sharda, "Obtaining Business Intelligence on the Internet," *Long Range Planning,* April 1997.

41. Prakash, A., "The Internet as a Global Strategic IS Tool," *Information Systems Management,* Summer 1996.

42. Rayport, J. F., and J. J. Sviokla, "Exploring the Virtual Value Chain," *Harvard Business Review,* November–December 1996.

43. Ross, J. W., et al., "Develop Long-Term Competitiveness Through IT Assets," *Sloan Management Review,* Fall 1996.

44. Slater, D., "Car Wars," *CIO Magazine,* September 15, 1999.

45. Teo, T. S. H., "Using the Internet for Competitive Intelligence in Singapore," *Competitive Intelligence Review,* 2nd quarter, 2000.

46. Tung, L. L., and E. Turban, "Expert Systems Support Container Operations in the Port of Singapore," *New Review of Applied Expert Systems,* March 1996.

47. Turban, E., et al., *Electronic Commerce: A Managerial Perspective,* 2nd ed. Upper Saddle River, NJ: Prentice-Hall, 2002.

48. Van Heck, E., et al., "New Entrants and the Role of IT—Case Study: The Tele Flower Auction in the Netherlands," *Proceedings, 30th HICSS,* Hawaii, January 1997.

49. Venkatraman, N., "Five Steps to a Dot-Com Strategy: How to Find Your Footing on the Web," *Sloan Management Review,* Spring 2000.

50. Ward, J., and P. Griffiths, *Strategic Planning for Information Systems,* 2nd ed. Chichester: Wiley, 1997.

51. Wiseman, C., and I. MacMillan, "Creating Competitive Weapons from Information Systems," *Journal of Business Strategy,* Fall 1984.

52. Yoffie, D. B. and M. A. Cusumano, "Judo Strategy: The Competitive Dynamics of Internet Time," *Harvard Business Review,* January–February 1999.

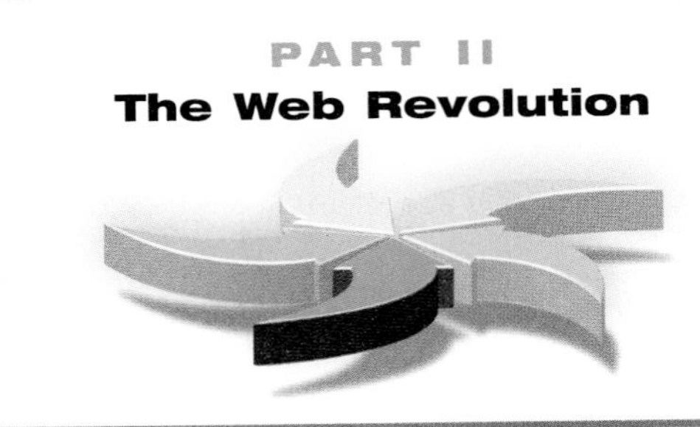

CHAPTER 4

Network Computing: Discovery, Communication, and Collaboration

LEARNING OBJECTIVES

After studying this chapter, you will be able to:

1. Understand the concepts of the Internet and the Web, their importance, and their capabilities.
2. Understand the role of intranets, extranets, and corporate portals in organizations.
3. Identify the various ways in which communication is executed over the Internet.
4. Demonstrate how people collaborate over the Internet, intranets, and extranets using various supporting tools, including voice technology and teleconferencing.
5. Describe groupware capabilities.
6. Describe and analyze the role of software agents for the Internet/intranets.
7. Analyze telecommuting (teleworking) as a technosocial phenomenon.
8. Consider ethical issues related to the use of the Internet.

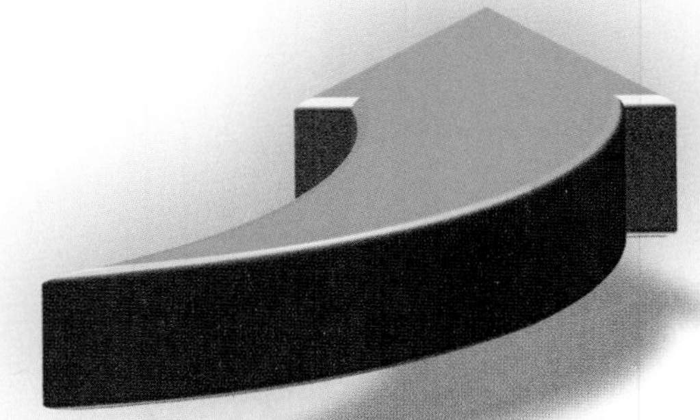

This chapter was revised by Narasimha Bolloju of City University of Hong Kong.

NATIONAL SEMICONDUCTOR CORPORATION

THE PROBLEM

The semiconductor (or chip) industry is one of the most competitive global industries. The rivalry among Japan, Korea, Taiwan, and the United States is fierce, and prices are continuously being driven down. When the economy is weak, demand for computers weakens, resulting in price cuts and losses to the chip manufacturers.

One way to survive is to customize products. National Semiconductor Corporation (NSC) (*national.com*) has over 10,000 products. However, this creates a problem for customers: When customers need a chip, they provide specifications to several chip manufacturers, collect catalogs and samples from the manufacturers, and then contact them for prices and technical details. This takes a considerable amount of time and effort.

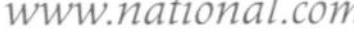

www.national.com

Connectivity problems due to different hardware, software, and communication standards had forced NSC to resort to the telephone, fax, and regular mail to communicate and collaborate with its customers. The communication channels that were available prior to the Internet were either regular telephone lines or private communication lines, both of which were expensive. Electronic data interchange (EDI) was in use, but it was limited to transaction processing and was carried on an expensive value-added network (VAN). Transmission of pictures, charts, and diagrams, a major part of the NSC product catalog, was a very difficult task. NSC found it just too expensive and cumbersome to handle communication and collaboration with customers over its old system.

THE SOLUTION

NSC introduced an innovative solution. The company posts detailed descriptions of its 10,000 products on its corporate *portal.** The portal allows NSC's customers to access product information 24 hours a day. *Browsing* through the information, customers are able to download the documents they need. The Web site is also used by the company's employees to search out information quickly and accurately, and to receive more direct feedback from customers.

NSC's Web site uses innovative technologies such as a *search engine* that can help find a matching product for a customer, based on product specifications. It also uses custom software that can extract information from existing databases and automatically format it in the *HTML* programming language. (HTML helps in preparing documents that appear on the Internet; see Technology Guide 5.)

NSC customers can also build personalized Web sites (titled "My Bill of Materials"). These personalized sites can host information related to customer projects and their requirements, and any other pertinent information. Customers can select the information to be made accessible to NSC. Through the personalized Web sites, NSC delivers the latest product information of interest to individual customers. This application is part of the corporate *extranet* system. The arrangement also allows NSC to watch the inventory level of chips at customers' facilities. (NSC is allowed to enter a portion of customers' intranets in order to track these data.) The Internet links enabled Tektronix Inc., for example, to

*Note: The Internet terms italicized in this case are defined in Technology Guide 5 or in Chapter 5. For an Internet dictionary and tour guide, see *whatis.com*.

discontinue paper files of past and current inventory parts. Product specifications and availability are automatically updated and linked to Tektronix's system. This, in turn, has enabled NSC to reengineer its distribution system. NSC can manage customers' inventory and automatically ship products to them when the inventories are low.

The search process is supported by an *electronic form* that is easily filled in by customers, and by a menu of *hyperlinks* to related products and services. The system is used both by customers and by NSC engineers. Its benefits are:

- Reducing the sample-ordering process by days or weeks.
- Expediting the design of new products.
- Increasing the exposure of NSC products by a factor of ten. (Customers are now downloading ten times as many documents as they did previously using just e-mail.)
- Providing more information to the customers.
- Providing direct and expeditious feedback from customers.
- Increasing quality and productivity.
- Improving the company's relations with its business partners.
- Increasing profitability and competitiveness.

The NSC Web site offers design assistants and simulators to guide customers in designing their products. Using this facility, customers can input their system specifications, find the devices that fit the specifications, validate design by simulation, and order the required parts. NSC also provides behavioral models and software to support the design process. NSC's design-assistant tool kit (Webench 2.0) is estimated to save National's customers $50 million in the first year.

 THE RESULTS

The Internet solution enables NSC to use *electronic catalogs* instead of paper ones, thus saving the company typesetting, printing, and mailing expenses. The electronic catalog also can be kept much more current than paper catalogs could. In addition, customers can view these catalogs from their own sites and download detailed documents in order to analyze products more closely. The Internet's electronic mail capabilities allow rapid communication between NSC engineers and customers. Recently added software and hardware, such as videoconferencing and screen sharing, let NSC engineers collaborate with customers electronically, allowing them to work on the same documents from different locations. All this is done at a relatively low cost.

NSC's sales and profitability increased significantly in 1996 and 1997 due to the Internet solution. Since 1997, the company tracks its visitors' movements in its site, trying to predict their buying habits. In 1998, NSC earned the best extranet application award from *Internetweek* and *Network Computing*.

Sources: C. Corcoran, "National Semiconductor Uses Web to Ease Support Services," *Infoworld*, July 22, 1996; *Internetweek*, March 9, 1998; and *national.com/news/item/0,1735,563,00.html*, October 16, 2000.

 LESSONS LEARNED FROM THIS CASE

The NSC opening case demonstrates the increasing role that the Internet, intranets, and extranets play in organizations, and their potential benefits. Using various Web-based applications, NSC enabled its employees to work very closely with its customers, to speed up design, and to cut costs. NSC made full use of Web technologies both for internal and external applications. Customers use the Web to discover information, to communicate with NSC's employees, and to collaborate with the technical staff.

In this chapter we learn about the major capabilities of network computing to support discovery of information, communication, and collaboration activities in organizations. We also learn how organizations are exploiting network computing for distance learning and telecommuting.

4.1 Network Computing—An Overview

An Overview of the Internet

Many aspects of the way we work and live in the twenty-first century and beyond will be determined by the vast web of electronic networks dubbed the **information superhighway** or the Internet. As you know from Chapter 1, the **Internet** is a *global network of computer networks.* It links the computing resources of businesses, government, and educational institutions using a common computer communication protocol, TCP/IP (described in Technology Guide 5). Because of its capabilities, the Internet (frequently referred to as "the Net") is rapidly becoming one of the most important information technologies today. It is clearly the most widely discussed IT topic of the new century.

The Internet is a network of networks, a predecessor of the information superhighway, discussed in Chapter 1. A large portion of the information superhighway in developed countries is already constructed. However, to wire the United States completely with fiber-optic lines that will reach every individual and organization may take 50 years and cost $500 billion. Smaller countries will do this much sooner. Singapore, a small island with population of less than three million, has a national digital network largely based on fiber optics. Japan, France, and Germany plan to complete their national networks by 2015. South Korea and China are implementing several national projects. While fiber-optic lines are supporting high-speed communication over the Internet, wireless networking is gaining popularity for flexible communication in *wide area networks* in cities and *local area networks* in buildings. Such wireless networks are greatly increasing worker mobility in many organizations.

Future versions of the superhighway will allow larger volume and a more rapid flow of information. Eventually we may see several information superhighways. It is probable that the original concept of a scientific-educational system will be separated from the commercial one. For example, in order to support advanced network applications and technologies, over 180 U.S. universities, working in partnership with industry and government, are working on a project named **Internet2** (*internet2.edu*). On Internet2, advanced next-generation applications such as remote diagnosis, digital libraries, distance education, online simulation, and virtual laboratories will enable people to collaborate and access information in ways not possible using today's Internet (Choi and Whinston, 2000).

Completing the information superhighway will not be a simple undertaking. In addition to the high cost and the question of how it will be financed, there are a number of other issues and factors that could slow or limit its development, such as technological obstacles, privacy, security, ethics, government regulations, or political considerations for information crossing national borders. The project also faces many conflicting interest groups, especially telephone companies, cable TV operators, cable manufacturers, and the manufacturers of telecommunications hardware and software.

Internet Application Categories

The Internet supports applications in the following major categories:

1. ***Discovery.*** Discovery involves browsing and information retrieval. As demonstrated in the opening case, it provides customers the ability to view documents and download whatever they need. Discovery on the Internet, intranets, extranets, and through corporate portals is discussed in Section 4.2.
2. ***Communication.*** The Internet provides fast and inexpensive communication channels that range from messages posted on bulletin boards to complex information exchanges among many organizations. It also includes information transfer (among computers) and information processing. E-mail, chat groups, and *newsgroups* (Internet chat groups focused on specific categories of interest) are examples of major communication media presented in Section 4.3 and in Technology Guide 5.
3. ***Collaboration.*** Due to improved communication, electronic collaboration between individuals and/or groups is on the rise. Several capabilities can be used, ranging from screen sharing and teleconferencing to group support systems, as we will illustrate in Section 4.4. Collaboration also includes resource-sharing services, which provide access to printers and specialized servers. Several collaboration tools, called groupware, can be used on the Internet and on other networks.

The World Wide Web is the most widely used application on the Internet. Other applications on the Internet include e-mail, telnet (provides remote logic), and ftp (file transfer programs).

The Net is also used for education and entertainment. People can access the content of newspapers, magazines, and books. They can locate any material catalogued by the U.S. Library of Congress, can download documents, and do research. They can correspond with friends and family, play games, listen to music, view movies and other cultural events, and even visit many major museums and galleries worldwide. Figure 4.1 illustrates some of the technologies that the Internet will bring into people's homes.

Moreover, the Net's ever-increasing capabilities allow companies to conduct many types of business activities on the Net. These **electronic commerce (EC)** activities range from just advertising to rendering a full range of customer services. As discussed in earlier chapters, e-commerce is booming. Some of the tools developed for the Internet are covered in Technology Guide 5. These tools can be used not only on the Internet, but also on an *intranet* (network used within an organization) and on an *extranet* (an intranet extended to provide access to other organizations. *A Closer Look* 4.1 (page 125) outlines how organizations are using the Internet, intranets, and extranets to gain competitive advantage.

The *discovery, communication,* and *collaboration* capabilities available on the Internet at low cost provide for a large number of useful applications. In the next three sections of this chapter, we discuss these three capabilities of network computing. Many applications are presented here, in Chapter 5, and throughout the book.

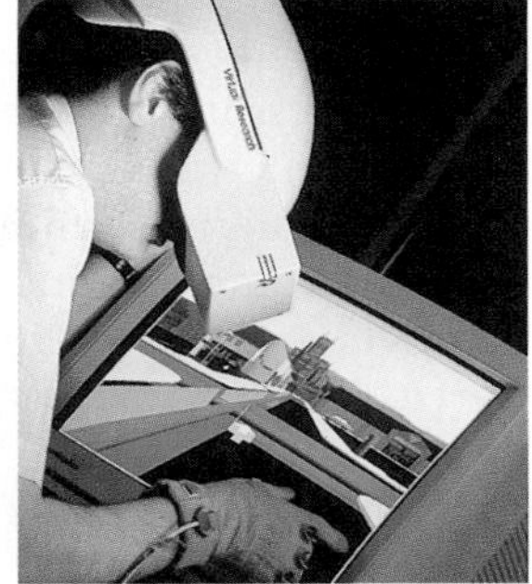

FIGURE 4.1 What the information superhighway may bring to your home.

A CLOSER LOOK
4.1 HOW TO USE THE INTERNET, INTRANETS, AND EXTRANETS TO GAIN COMPETITIVE ADVANTAGE

The Internet, intranets, and extranets can be used in various ways in a corporate environment in order to gain competitive advtange. Some of these applications are listed below.

1. ***Management systems.*** Managers view daily progress reports from sales managers nationwide; invoke database queries through self-explanatory menus; electronically distribute reports in HTML and/or publish from the original database; post project assignments for collaborative viewing by work groups; make team goals and management charts available online, enterprisewide; post meeting minutes of various committees/teams for review by all interested employees.
2. ***Collaborative workgroups and interdepartmental communication.*** Planners, designers, engineers, and marketing people interactively collaborate in designing or reengineering a product. Programmers access a list of toolkit components for software design.
3. ***Online reference.*** Factory workers access instructions and maintenance procedures. Sales representatives view the latest product information, promotions, discounts, and rebates, or read more details on specific customers, suppliers, or company policies. Employees view benefit programs or company policies.
4. ***Interactive communication.*** Researchers automatically distribute surveys to employees, customers, or suppliers, and automatically gather the results into a database. Employees sign up for events immediately after reading an online announcement.
5. ***Training.*** A medical student studies a training lesson that includes a moving picture of a fetal ultrasound scan and the sound of the child's heart beat. A new employee clicks through an online orientation seminar and completes an online quiz.
6. ***Customer support.*** A help desk operator views a centralized menu that provides direct, single-point, clickable online access to all of the company's printed documentation. A customer service representative views detailed customer or supplier information while on the phone, retrieves invoices or purchase orders from an imaging database, and views quick reference guides or written procedures for specialized orders. A company presents a virtual trade show with booths and exhibits that exist only on the Web or an online version of a real trade show.

Source: Condensed from R. Bernard, *The Corporate Intranet,* 2nd ed. (New York: Wiley, 1998). Reprinted by permission of John Wiley & Sons, Inc.

4.2 DISCOVERY

The Internet

The Internet permits users to access information located in databases all over the world. Although only a small portion of organizational data may be accessible to Internet users, even that limited amount is enormous. Many fascinating resources are accessible, ranging from the content of most major libraries and museums to the archives of cities and public hospitals. The discovery capability can facilitate education, government services, entertainment, and commerce. Discovery is done by *browsing* and *searching* data sources on the Web.

The amount of information on the Web is at least doubling every year. This makes navigating through the Web and gaining access to necessary information more and more difficult. *Search engines* and *directories* are two fundamentally different types of information search facilities available on the Web. A **search engine** (e.g., Altavista, Google) maintains an index of hundreds of millions of Web pages and uses that index to find pages that match a set of user-specified keywords. Such indices are created and updated by software robots called **softbots**. A **directory** (e.g., Yahoo!, About.com), on the other hand, is a hierarchically organized collection of links to Web pages. Directories are compiled manually, unlike indexes, which are generated automatically.

Search engines and directories often present users with links to thousands or even millions of pages. It is quite difficult to find information of interest from such a large number of links. One of the most effective solutions to this problem is the automation of routine activities conducted over the Internet by means of **software agents**, also called **intelligent agents** (Weiss, 1999; Murch and Johnson, 1999). These are computer programs that carry out a set of routine computer tasks on behalf of the user and in so doing employ some sort of knowledge of the user's goals. The topic of intelligent agents is discussed more fully in Chapter 12. Here we present only a few examples of Internet-based agents, which appear under names such as *wizards, softbots,* and *knowbots*. Four major types of agents available for help in browsing and searching are Web-browsing-assisting agents, FAQ agents, Internet softbots, and indexing agents.

WEB-BROWSING-ASSISTING AGENTS. Some agents can facilitate browsing by offering the user a tour of the Internet. Known as *tour guides,* they work while the user browses. For example, WebWatcher helps find pages related to the current page, adding hyperlinks to meet the user's search goal and giving advice on the basis of the user's preference (Joachims et al., 1997).

NetCaptor (*netcaptor.com*) is a Web browser with a simple-to-navigate window interface that makes browsing more pleasurable and productive. NetCaptor opens a separate tabbed space for each Web site visited by the user. Users can easily switch between different tabbed spaces. The CaptorGroup feature creates a group of links that are stored together so the user can get single-click access to multiple Web sites. The PopupCaptor feature automatically closes pop-up windows displayed during browsing. NetCaptor also includes a utility, called Flyswat, to turn certain words and phrases into hyperlinks. Clicking on these links opens a window with links to Web sites with relevant information.

Another example is Letizia (*lieber.www.media.mit.edu/people/lieber/Lieberary/Letizia/Letizia-Intro.html*). This agent monitors the user's activities with a browser. Using various heuristics, or rules of thumb built into the agent, it tries to anticipate additional items that might be of interest to the user. A similar agent is

Netcomber Activist from IBM. This agent monitors your surfing through the Yahoo! catalog. It builds your interest profile, and then can recommend newspapers for daily reading, and so on. For more details on Web browsing assistants see O'Leary (1996), Murch and Johnson (1999), and Lieberman et al. (1999).

FREQUENTLY ASKED QUESTIONS (FAQ) AGENTS. *FAQ agents* guide people to the answers to frequently asked questions. When searching for information, people tend to ask the same or similar questions. In response, newsgroups, support staffs, vendors, and others have developed files of those FAQs and an appropriate answer to each. But there is a problem: People use natural language, asking the same questions in several different ways. The agent (such as FAQFinder) addresses this problem by indexing large numbers of FAQ files. Using the text of a question submitted in natural language, the software agent can locate the appropriate answer. GTE Laboratories developed an FAQ agent that accepts natural-language questions from users of Usenet News Groups and answers them by matching question–answer pairs (Whitehead, 1994).

AskJeeves (*askjeeves.com*), another FAQ assistant, makes it easy to find answers on the Internet to questions asked in plain English. The system responds with one or more closely related questions to which the answers are available. Parts of such questions may contain drop-down menus for selecting from different options. After the user selects the question that is closest to the original question, the system presents a reply page containing different sources that can provide answers. Due to the limited number of FAQs and the semistructured nature of the questions, the reliability of FAQ agents is very high.

SEARCH ENGINES AND INTELLIGENT INDEXING AGENTS. Another type of discovery agent on the Internet traverses the Web and performs tasks such as information retrieval and discovery, validating links or HTML, and generating statistics. Such agents are called *Web robots, spiders,* and *wanderers.*

Indexing agents can carry out a massive autonomous search of the Web on behalf of a user or, more commonly, of a search engine like Google, HotBot, or Altavista. First, they scan millions of documents and store an index of words found in document titles, key words, and texts. The user can then query the search engine to find documents containing certain key words. Figure 4.2 shows a comparison of index sizes as of November 1, 2000.

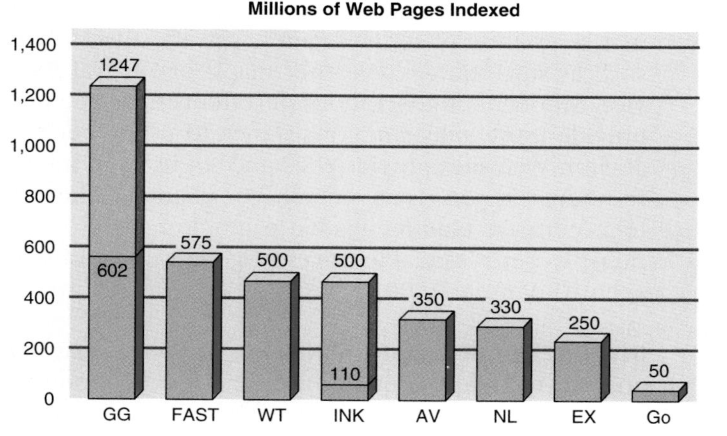

FIGURE 4.2 Search engines' index-size comparison. (*Source:* Compiled from *searchenginewatch.com/reports/size,* November 2000. Reprinted with permission from *http://www.internet.com* Copyright 2001 INT Media Group, Incorporated. All rights reserved. Search Engine Watch and *internet.com* are the exclusive Trademarks of INT Media Group, Incorporated.)

Special indexing agents are being developed for knowledge sharing and knowledge acquisition in large databases and documents. *Metasearch engines* (such as *Spider, Savvy Search, Metacrawler, All in One,* and *Web Compass*) integrate the findings of the various search engines to answer queries posted by the users. The following *IT at Work* example provides an insight into a specific application of search and indexing technology in education.

IT at Work

CATCHING CASES OF PLAGIARISM AT SCHOOLS

www.turnitin.com

The Internet provides abundant information to students who may be tempted to download material and submit it as their own work. Some companies (e.g., Plagiarism.org) are offering Internet-based anti-plagiarism technology to identify cases of plagiarism. Here's how the process used to find cases of plagiarism works:

- Instructors register their classes at the TurnItIn.com Web site (*turnitin.com*), and request their students to upload term papers or manuscripts into databases designed for specific courses.
- Each manuscript is converted into an abstract representation using a proprietary technology.
- Each manuscript is then checked against a database of other manuscripts collected from different universities and classes and from all over the Internet. The cases of gross plagiarism are flagged, and an originality report, accessible only to the instructor, is generated for each paper.
- The manuscript collection databases are constantly updated through a series of automated Web robots that scour the Internet for rogue term paper mills.

For Futher Exploration: Do you support using antiplagiarism technology to catch cases of cheating at school? Elaborate on your reasons. Can you think of any other means of finding cases of plagiarism?

Source: plagiarism.org, 2000. Courtesy of iParadigms, developers of Plagiarism.org and Turnitin.com.

INTERNET SOFTBOTS. Search agents suggest locations on the Web to the user. Such suggestions are based on a relatively weak model of what the user wants and what information is available in the suggested location. *Internet softbots,* originally developed at the University of Washington (Etzioni and Weld, 1994), attempt to determine more specifically what the user wants, and they also understand the contents of information services so they can better focus a search. The first generation of softbot agents was effective only with structured information such as stock quotes, weather maps, or Federal Express's package tracking service. Subsequent generations of softbots have been designed for applications that provide more substantial assistance to users. For example, a number of online auction Web sites provide assistance to users in the form of "biddingbots," which resubmit bids on users' behalf. For example, the BiddingBot, a multiagent system, employs bidding agents to monitor prices of goods in several online auctions, to get reasonable prices of goods, and to place bids on behalf of a leader agent (Ito et al., 2000).

INTERNET-BASED DATA MINING. The term *data mining* refers to sophisticated analysis techniques for sifting through large amounts of information. Data mining permits new patterns and relationships to be revealed through the use of software that can do much of the mining process (see Chapter 11). Intelligent agents are a key tool in discovering such previously unknown relationships, especially in complex data structures. *Query-and-reporting tools,* on the other hand, demand a predefined database structure and are most valuable when asking specific questions to confirm hypotheses.

Web mining is the application of data mining techniques to discover actionable and meaningful patterns, profiles, and trends from Web resources. The term Web mining is used to refer to both Web-content mining and Web-usage mining. *Web-content mining* is the process of information discovery from millions of Web documents. *Web-usage mining* is the process of analyzing Web access logs and other information connected to user browsing and access patterns on one or more Web localities.

Web mining is used in the following areas:

- Information filtering (e-mails, magazines, and newspapers)
- Surveillance (Internet competitors, patents)
- Mining Web-access logs
- Assisted browsing
- Services that fight crime on the Internet

In e-commerce, Web mining is critical, due to the large number of visitors to e-commerce sites (about 2 billion during the Christmas 2000 season). For example, Amazon.com provides a list of other books purchased by the customers who have purchased a specific book. By providing such mined information, the Web site minimizes the need for additional search by the customers. (For further discussion, see Parsa, 1999.)

Web mining is an important part of data mining. According to Etzioni (1996), it can perform the following functions:

- ***Resource discovery:*** Locating unfamiliar documents and services on the Web
- ***Information extraction:*** Automatically extracting specific information from newly discovered Web resources
- ***Generalization:*** Uncovering general patterns at individual Web sites and across multiple sites

Some of the agents described earlier can assist in these activities. For example, WebCrawler and MetaCrawler can facilitate resource discovery. Internet Learning Agent and Shopbot are Web miners that rely on a combination of test queries and domain-specific knowledge to learn descriptions of Web services automatically. The learned descriptions are then used to extract information.

Miner3D (*miner3d.com/m3Dweb/features.html*) is a Web-mining tool that displays hundreds and even thousands of search hits on a single screen. The actual search for Web pages is performed through any major search engine, and this tool presents the resulting search hits in the form of a 3D graphic instead of displaying links to the first few pages. It is possible to jump instantly to the selected Web pages. Tools like this support access to information in large sets of search results that would otherwise require a significant amount of effort and time. For details on a number of Web mining products see *kdnuggets.com/software/web.html*.

Intranets

An **intranet** (*internal Web*) is a network designed to serve the internal informational needs of a company, using Web concepts and tools. It provides Internet capabilities, especially easy and inexpensive browsing. Using a Web browser, a manager can see resumes of employees, business plans, and corporate regulations and procedures; retrieve sales data; and review any desired document. Using hyperlinks to expedite searches for material in a database, employees can use an intranet to check availability of software for particular tasks and test the software from their workstations.

Intranets also provide communication and collaboration capabilities. They are frequently connected to the Internet, enabling the company to conduct e-commerce activities, such as cooperating with suppliers and customers, checking a customer's inventory level before making shipments, and more. (Such activities are facilitated by *extranets,* as described later in this chapter and in Chapter 5.) Using screen sharing and other groupware tools, the intranets can be used to facilitate the work of groups. Companies also publish newsletters and deliver news to their employers on their intranet.

Information that can be accessed via an intranet is kept fairly safe, within the system's firewalls. A **firewall** is a device that acts as a gatekeeper between the firm's intranet and external networks (like the Internet). All outgoing requests for information go to a special computer, which hides the sender's machine address but passes on the request. All incoming information is also checked by the firewall computer. Employees can venture out onto the Internet, but unauthorized users cannot come in. This arrangement lets companies speed information and software safely to their own employees and business partners. (For further discussion of firewalls, see Chapter 15.)

Intranets have the power to change organizational structures and procedures and help reengineer corporations. According to a story in *Datamation* (Geoffrey, 1996), when reengineering fails, it does so for three major reasons: (1) it is a top-down process resisted by employees who fear layoffs; (2) massive personnel retraining is necessary; and (3) participation of several departments is needed. Intranets can be useful to rectify the situation, because (1) they support a participative bottom-up process, (2) they are easy to use and facilitate information sharing and cooperation, and (3) they can usually support a diversity of computer platforms in different departments. Intranets can be implemented using different types of local area network (LAN) technologies (see Technology Guide 4). The *It at Work* on the opposite page illustrates how a hospital intranet can be used effectively with a wireless LAN.

Intranets are used in all types of organizations, from businesses to health care providers to government agencies to educational institutions. Examples of several more intranets follow.

KPMG Is Counting on Immediate Business Intelligence. In 2000, Financial Times Electronic Publishing implemented its online news and information service, FT Discovery, to be used by 10,000 intranet users at KPMG Peat Marwick (a worldwide accounting firm). FT Discovery is integrated into the KPMG corporate intranet to provide immediate access to critical business intelligence from over 4,000 information sources. A "Corporate Navigator" is integrated into the intranet to provide in-depth advice on where to go for information on the issues and companies of interest to KPMG (*idm.internet.com/articles/200007/ic_07_26_00e. html,* July 2000).

Saying Aloha (Hello) to Information. All the Hawaiian islands are linked by a state educational, medical, and other public services network (*htdc.org*). This ambitious

IT at Work

WIRELESS LANS SPEED HOSPITAL INSURANCE PAYMENTS

The Bridgeton, a holding company that operates four hospitals in New Jersey, is using wireless LANs to process insurance paperwork. The goal is to reduce the number of claims being denied by insurers. Nurses log on to the network using notebook computers to access the hospital's intranet.

The network environment broadcasts data over a distance of about 120 feet from nursing workstations. Nurses can move with their notebooks from the station into patient rooms while maintaining a network connection. When a nurse takes a notebook computer from one nursing station to another, the radio card in the notebook computer goes into a roaming mode similar to a cellular phone.

The company is getting a good return on investment, savings in six-figure dollar amounts, for a moderate cost of setting up the network (about $200 for each notebook computer radio card and $750 for each of 28 wireless access points).

For Further Exploration: What are the disadvantages of using a wireless LAN?

Source: Compiled from *Computerworld*, April 10, 2000, p. 74.

intranet provides quality services to residents of all the islands (*Interactive Week*, January 12, 1998).

Integrating IT ...in Marketing and Production & Operations Management

www.sundanceresort.com

An Intranet on the Slopes. A June 1996 fire destroyed much of Utah's Sundance Ski Resort's IT infrastructure. An intranet was built to replace it. Sundance's intranet runs such functions as reservations, billings, e-mail, guest requests, catering, food services, and food inventory. In addition, the network allows the resort to improve customer service by distributing customer information like guest photos and personal preferences to hostesses and managers. The intranet has also improved efficiency in internal operations by facilitating better collaboration and communication among the staff (*Computerworld*, January 27, 1997).

Extranets

An intranet's infrastructure is confined to an organization's boundaries, but not necessarily geographical ones; intranets can also be used to connect offices of the same company in different locations. The Internet is an infrastructure that is used to connect various organizations. Another type of infrastructure that connects different organizations is an **extranet**. An extranet is an infrastructure that allows secure communications among *business partners* over the Internet. It offers limited accessibility to the intranets of the participating companies as well as the necessary interorganizational communications, using Internet technology. The use of extranets is rapidly increasing due to the large savings in communication costs that can materialize. Extranets enable innovative applications of business-to-business (B2B) e-commerce (see Chapter 5). The National Semiconductor Corporation case study at the beginning of this chapter illustrates how NSC's customers could save time and effort in design by using design assistance offered through extranets. Finally, extranets are closely related to improved communications along the supply chain (for details see Chapter 6 and Technology Guide 4).

Corporate Portals

With growing use of intranets and the Internet, many organizations encounter difficulties in dealing with information overload at different levels. Information is scattered across numerous documents, e-mail messages, and databases on different systems. Finding relevant and accurate information is often time-consuming and requires access to multiple systems, many with their own applications. As a consequence, organizations lose a lot of the productive time of their employees.

One solution to the problem of scattered and duplicative data is portals. Kounadis (2000) defines a **corporate portal** as a personalized, single point of access through a Web browser to critical business information located inside and outside of an organization. Portals provide gateways to corporate data, information, and knowledge. Through an intranet-based environment (e.g., Web browser), they provide access to relevant information from disparate IT systems and the Internet, using advanced search and indexing techniques.

In contrast with *Internet portals* (such as Yahoo!), which are the gateway to the Internet, corporate portals provide single-point access to an organization's information and applications available on the Internet, intranets, and extranets. Corporate portals are an extended form of intranets that offer employees and customers an organized focal point for their interactions with the firm. A special category of portals, called *affinity portals*, are being built to support communities such as labor minors, hobby groups, and political parties (Tedeschi, 2000). These are more like corporate portals, in that they offer a single-point access for an organization or a community, than they are like Internet portals.

Many large organizations are already implementing portals. Their goals in doing so are to cut costs, free up time for busy executives and managers, and add funds to the bottom line (*Informationweek.com*, May 2000). The following *IT at Work* takes a look at the corporate portals of some well-known companies.

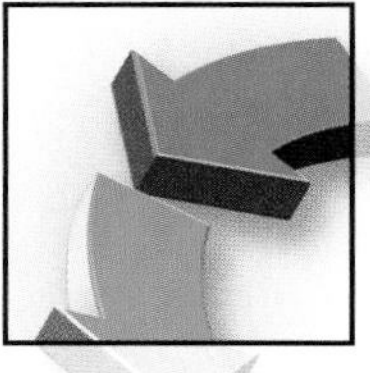

IT at Work
OPENING SOME CORPORATE PORTALS

Integrating IT ...in Human Resources and Production & Operations Management

www.pg.com; www.dupont.com; www.staples.com

The IT division at Procter & Gamble Co. (P&G), a consumer products company, began developing a system for sharing documents and information over the company's intranet. The scope of this system soon expanded into a Global Knowledge Catalogue to support the information needs of all 97,000 P&G employees worldwide. Although the system helped in providing required information, it also led to information overload. In order to solve this problem, P&G developed a corporate portal to provide to each employee personalized information that can be accessed through a Web browser. Employees no longer need to navigate through 14 different Web sites to find the information they need. P&G's corporate portal now can deliver to its employees marketing, product, and strategic information, and industry-news documents, from over one million Web pages, organized in thousands of Lotus Notes databases. Employees can gain quick access to information through customized preset views into various information sources and links to other up-to-date information.

Chemical maker DuPont & Co. began implementing an internal portal to bring order to millions of pages of scientific information stored in information systems throughout the company. The initial version of the portal was intended for daily use by over 550 employees. Through the portal, they would record product orders, retrieve progress reports for research products, and access customer-tracking information. DuPont plans to extend the portal from this relatively small initial user group to some 20,000 to 60,000 employees in 30 business units in various countries.

Staples is a retailer of office supplies and furniture. Its corporate portal, launched in February 2000, is used by 3,000 of its executives, knowledge workers, and store managers. Staples is expecting that the portal will grow to support 10,000 of the company's 46,000 employees as the interface to business processes and applications. The portal is used by top management, as well as by managers of contracts, procurement, sales and marketing, human resources, and retail stores. It is also used for internal business by Staples' three business-to-business Web sites. The portal offers e-mail, scheduling, headlines on the competition, new product information, internal news, job postings, and newsletters.

For Further Exploration: Describe how the corporate portals are supporting organizational activities in the above companies.

Source: Compiled and reused with permission from CMP Media LLC, *Information Week*, May 1, 2000.

Figure 4.3 depicts a corporate portal framework based on Aneja et al. (2000) and Kounadis (2000). This framework illustrates the features and capabilities required to support various organizational activities using internal and external information sources. For a closer look at guidelines used to define corporate portal strategy see *A Closer Look* 4.2 (page 134).

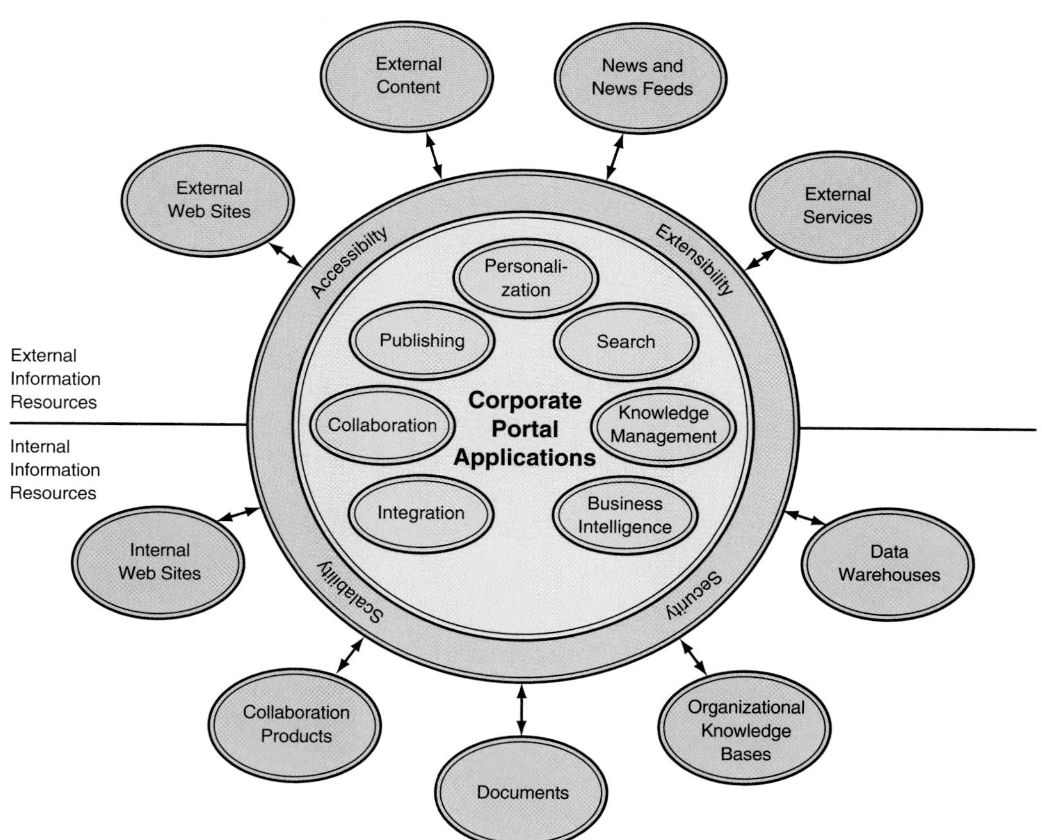

FIGURE 4.3 A corporate portal framework. (*Sources:* Compiled from A. Aneja et al., "Corporate Portal Framework for Transforming Content Chaos on Intranets," *Intel Technology Journal,* Q1, 2000, and from T. Kounadis, "How to Pick the Best Portal," *e-Business Advisor,* August 2000.)

A CLOSER LOOK
4.2 KEY STEPS TO CORPORATE PORTAL STRATEGY

- Identify the content that is or will be available, and identify where this content resides.
- Use existing systems, resources, and repositories.
- Include both structured and unstructured information.
- Organize content into categories that can be browsed and searched.
- Integrate search functionality across multiple information repositories.
- Build a platform for publishing/subscribing to content.
- Deliver personalized content and services to users based on their performances and roles.
- Develop the corporate portal in phases.
- Create online communities to connect people and enable collaborative work.
- Develop an architecture that allows for extended functionality.
- Sustain a collaborative portal by institutionalizing it within daily business operations and weaving it into long-term strategies.
- Purchase an integrated portal product rather than building custom portal functionality.

Source: Compiled from A. Aneja et al., "Corporate Portal Framework for Transforming Content Chaos on Intranets," *Intel Technology Journal,* Q1, 2000.

According to a survey by the Delphi Group, over 55 percent of its 800 respondents had begun corporate portal projects, with about 42 percent of them conducting the projects at the enterprisewide level (*Datamation,* July 1999). The top portal applications, in decreasing order of importance, were:

- Knowledge bases and learning tools
- Business process support
- Customer-facing sales, marketing, and service
- Collaboration and project support
- Access to data from disparate corporate systems
- Internal company information
- Policies and procedures
- Best practices and lessons learned
- Human resources and benefits
- Directories and bulletin boards
- Identification of experts
- News and Internet

The Delphi Group also found that poor organization of information and lack of navigation and retrieval tools contributed to over 50 percent of the problems for corporate portal users. (For further details see *www.delphigroup.com/pubs/corporate-portal-excerpt.htm.)*

4.3 COMMUNICATION

Communication is an interpersonal process of sending and receiving symbols with messages attached to them. Through communication, people exchange and share information as well as influence and understand each other. Most managers spend as much as 90 percent of their time communicating. Managers serve as "nerve centers" in the information-processing networks called organizations, where they collect, distribute, and process information continuously. Since poor communication can mean poor management, managers must communicate effectively among themselves and with others, both inside and outside of organizations. The Internet has become a major supporter of interactive communications. People are using Internet phone, videoconferencing, radio, TV, and more.

Factors Determining the Uses of Information Technologies for Communication

Several factors determine the IT technologies that could be used to provide communication support to a specific organization or group of users. The major ones are the following:

- ***Participants.*** The number of people sending and receiving information can range from two to many thousands.
- ***Nature of sources and destinations.*** Sources and destinations of information can include people, databases, sensors, and so on.
- ***Location.*** The sender(s) and receiver(s) can be in the same room, in different rooms at the same location, or at different locations.
- ***Time.*** Messages can be sent at a certain time and received almost simultaneously. In such a case, communication is synchronous. Telephones, teleconferencing, and face-to-face meetings are examples of **synchronous (real-time) communication**. **Asynchronous communication**, on the other hand, refers to communication in which the receiver gets the message sometime after it was sent.
- ***Media.*** Communication can involve one or several media. Today's IT can handle several types of media such as text, voice, graphics, pictures, and animation. Using different media for communicating can increase the effectiveness of a message, expedite learning, and enhance problem solving. Working with multiple media may, however, reduce the efficiency and effectiveness of the system (its speed, capacity, quality) and may significantly increase its cost.

A TIME/PLACE FRAMEWORK. A framework for classifying IT communication support technologies has been proposed by DeSanctis and Gallupe (1987). According to this framework, communication is divided into four cells, as shown in Figure 4.4 (with a representative technology in each cell). The time/place cells are as follows:

1. ***Same-time/same-place.*** In this setting, participants meet face-to-face in one place and at the same time. An example is communication in a meeting room.
2. ***Same-time/different-place.*** This setting refers to a meeting whose participants are in different places but communicate at the same time. A telephone con-

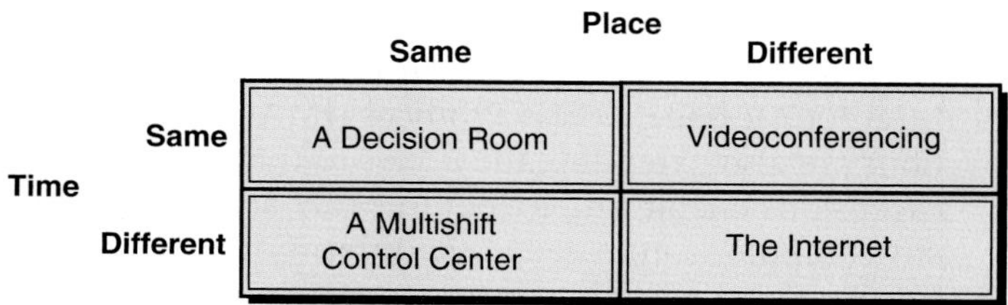

Place
Same
Different
Same
Time
Different
A Decision Room
Videoconferencing
A Multishift Control Center
The Internet

FIGURE 4.4 A framework for IT communication.

ference call, desktop videoconferencing, chat rooms, and instant messaging are examples of such situations.

3. ***Different-time/same-place.*** This setting can materialize when people work in shifts. The first shift leaves electronic or voice messages for the second shift.
4. ***Different-time/different-place.*** In this setting, participants are in different places, and they send and/or receive messages (for example, via the Internet) at different times.

Businesses require that messages be transmitted as fast as they are needed, that the intended receiver properly interprets them, and that the cost of doing this be reasonable. Communication systems that meet these conditions have several characteristics. They allow two-way communication: Messages flow in different directions, sometimes almost simultaneously, and messages reach people regardless of where they are located. Efficient systems also allow people to access various sources of information (such as databases). IT can meet these requirements through the electronic transfer of information using tools such as e-mail.

Electronic discussion forums are providing a highly efficient way to communicate and share business knowledge and expertise among large groups of people. They are also enabling groups of people that share common interests to exchange information and opinions. (For a comprehensive list of Web-based discussion forum software, see *strom.com/places/wc.html*.)

Next, we discuss e-mail. (Other specific communication tools and technologies are described in Technology Guide 5.)

Electronic Mail

Electronic mail (e-mail) is the most-used service of the Internet. E-mail systems have been used for many years as an internal medium of communication. For example, IBM's PROFS (Professional Office System) has enabled employees to communicate with each other all over the world. With the Internet, e-mail is able to connect people in different organizations who are working on different local area networks and using different hardware, operating systems, and communication systems. People can use such e-mail systems from home or on the road, over regular telephone lines. Wireless e-mail connects remote users with corporate e-mail systems via paging technology and the Internet. This capability allows mobile users such as salespeople and repair people to enter the corporate e-mail system quickly, to send and receive messages, and to initiate communication in workgroups.

E-mail can be enhanced to provide valuable services. Several extensions and facilities are now being incorporated into e-mail programs. TalkToMe, for example, is a talking program that can read your e-mail messages in addition to reading Web pages, documents, and reminders (*talk-to-me.net*). Moodwatch, an extension to the Eudora e-mail application, acts as an emotion monitor that recognizes aggressive language in e-mail you are writing and informs you about it as a rating of a message before it is sent (*www.eudora.com/email/features/moodwatch.html*). Moodwatch can also alert you to potentially offensive incoming messages.

The standard server-based e-mail protocols are Post Office Protocol (POP) and Internet Message Access Protocol (IMAP). In addition to these, many organizations are also extending the access to their e-mail systems through the Web. Such extensions enable employees to easily access e-mail using *any* Web browser from *any* computer connected to the Internet. United Airlines, for example, outsourced its corporate messaging system for easy and flexible access using any Web browser.

INSTANT MESSAGING SERVICES. **Instant messaging** services allow users to identify and exchange instant messages with other online users in real time. ICQ is the most popular instant messaging tool on the Internet. It informs the users who is online at any time and enables users to contact them. ICQ provides facilities such as chat, sending messages and files, and playing games. AOL's Instant Messenger, Microsoft's MSN Messenger Service, and Yahoo! Messenger are some popular instant messaging services. A problem with these services, however, is that the users must use the same messaging service in order to communicate.

MESSAGING IN WIRELESS ENVIRONMENTS. Messaging in wireless environments, such as with a product called *i-mode* (*nttdocomo.com*), offers access to the Internet from cellular phones. Subscribers of i-mode can send and receive e-mail, and access the Internet directly from their cellular phones. DoCoMo's i-mode supports m-commerce transactions (e.g., mobile banking, ticket reservations, stock trading), entertainment (e.g., karaoke reservations, network games, fortune-telling), database access (e.g., restaurant guide, telephone directory, business dictionary), and various other services such as viewing news and weather. Short Messages System (SMS) allows users to send short text messages (up to 160 characters, in 2000) to and from their cellular phones. Using applications such as MSN Messenger and ICQ, one can also send SMS messages to cellular phones from PCs connected to the Internet. The number of subscribers of NTT DoCoMo's i-mode service approached 15 million in late 2000.

SOFTWARE AGENTS. Software agents are programs that execute mundane tasks for the benefit of their users. **E-mail agents** assist users with the often time-consuming task of managing their e-mail. E-mail agents, for example, monitor what each user routinely does with his or her e-mail and learn from those actions. When a new situation occurs, the agent analyzes the features of the situation and suggests an action to the user (read, delete, forward, or archive).

Several e-mail agents help users handle large numbers of messages. For example, American Finance and Investment, Inc. uses intelligent agents to control its e-mail flood. This application reduced the number of employees answering e-mail from four to one. (For details see Gotcher, 1997.) An example of an e-mail agent's output is shown in Figure 4.5 (page 138).

Automatic e-mail distribution systems apply work flow tracking techniques to manage the flood of e-mail sent to customer support. Verizon's inResponse system, for example, automatically reponds to an incoming message, routes the message to the appropriate internal agent or customer service representative, and tracks the agent's response to the customer. Such systems are popular in automatic response to customers' inquiries, which is a part of Web-based call centers. A representative vendor in this area is Adante (*adante.com*). (For further details on such systems see Gaskin, 1999.)

UNIVERSAL MESSAGING SYSTEMS. Universal messaging systems enable users to access their e-mail, voice mail, and fax messages from a single number over the phone or the Internet from anywhere in the world. E-mail and fax messages can be transformed from text to speech so that users can receive them as voice messages over the phone. Users can also send messages to digital mobile phones and pagers. A universal messaging service, 2bSURE (*2bSURE.com*), provides access to voice mail, fax, and e-mail to its subscribers through a single number in Australia, the United States, and in over 10 countries in Asia.

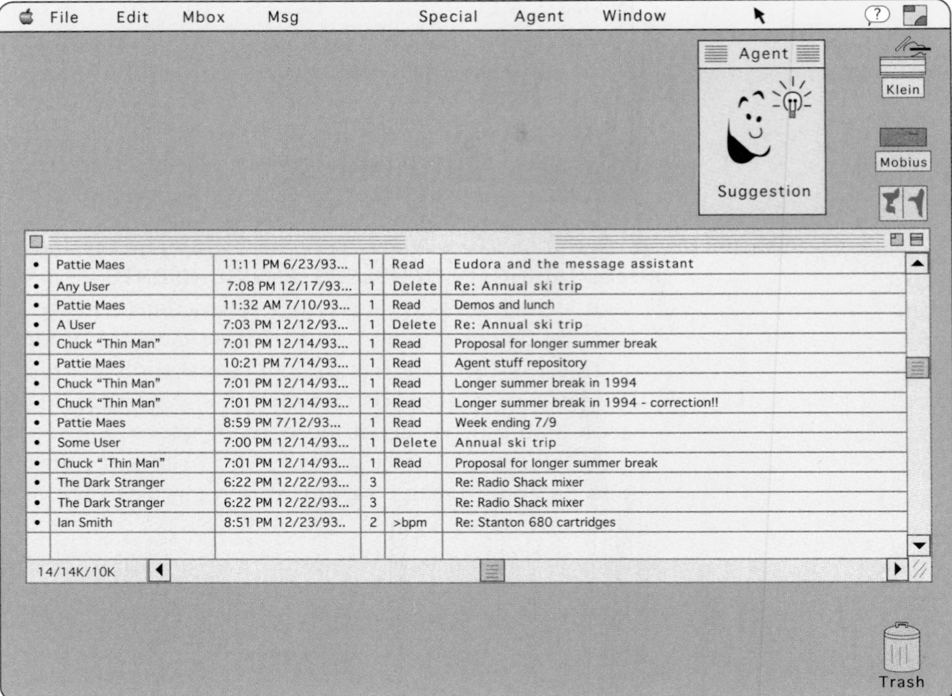

FIGURE 4.5 The e-mail agent makes recommendations to the user (middle column). It predicts what actions the user will perform on messages, such as which messages will be read and in which order, and which messages will be deleted, forwarded, archived, and so on. (*Source:* P. Maes, "Agents that Reduce Work and Information Overload," *Communications of the ACM,* July 1994, p. 34. P. Maes © 1994 Association for Computing Machinery, Inc. Reprinted by permission.)

Web-based Call Centers

Effective personalized customer contact is becoming an important aspect of customer support through the Web. Such service provided through Web-based call centers complements the existing self-service options. In this context, enabling Web collaboration and simultaneous voice/Web contact can differentiate a company from its competitors. There are at least four categories of capabilities—e-mail, interactive text chat, callbacks, and simultaneous voice and Web sessions. (For possible choices for Web-based call centers, see Drury, 1999.) WebsiteAlive (*websitealive.com*), a Web-based call center support product, delivers live customer-service capabilities for any online company. Further details are provided in Chapter 7.

Peer-to-Peer (P2P) Networking

Peer-to-peer networks are systems that include a large number of small computer systems used for information exchange and sharing resources. Napster (*napster.com*) is an application of this concept that supports swapping of CD-quality music files over the Internet. The central directory of Napster tells you which users are offering what music files. When a user wants to download a file, he or she will take it directly from another user's computer.

At the time of this writing, Napster services were provided to users free of charge, and are used by millions. Obviously the users are happy to get free quality music. But the publishers and artists are losing their royalties. In fall 2000, Bertelsmann AG, a large music publisher, announced that it is teaming up with Napster, because of its widespread popularity, to develop a new music distribution system for the Internet file-swapping service that will guarantee payments to artists.

Peer-to-peer networking tools based on Gnutella technology (e.g., BearShare) dispense with the centralized database and facilitate sharing of files over the

Internet. Peer-to-peer also helps in sharing of resources over the Internet, which may be otherwise idle. For example, Intel is using armies of desktop computers that are lying idle around the world, instead of buying huge central computers, for big number-crunching jobs.

Chat Rooms

Electronic chat refers to an arrangement whereby participants exchange messages in real time. The software industry estimates that among several hundred thousand Web sites, there are millions of chat rooms.

A **chat room** is a virtual meeting ground where groups of regulars come to gab. The chat rooms can be used to build a community, to promote a commercial, political, or environmental cause, to support people with medical problems, or to let hobbyists share their interest. And since many customer-supplier relationships have to be sustained without face-to-face meetings, online communities are increasingly being used to serve business interests, including advertising (see *roguemarket.com* and Chapter 5).

A vendor frequently sponsors a chat room. Chat capabilities can be added to a business site for free by letting software chat vendors host your session on their site. You simply put a chat link on your site and the chat vendor does the rest, including the advertising that pays for the session.

Chat programs allow you to send *messages* to people who are connected to the same channel of communication *at the same time*. It is like a global conference call system. Anyone can join in the online conversation. Messages are displayed on your screen as they arrive, even if you are in the middle of typing a message. You can even use voice chat, which, like voice e-mail, is free of charge, even if it is long distance. Two major types of chat programs exist: (a) Web-based chat programs, which allow you to send messages to Net users using a Web browser and visiting a Webchat site (e.g., *chat.yahoo.com*), and (b) an e-mail-based (text only) program called *Internet Relay Chat (IRC)*. A business can use IRC to interact with customers, provide online experts' answers to questions, and so on.

Electronic Voice Communication

The most natural mode of communication is voice. When people need to communicate with each other from a distance, they use the telephone more frequently than any other communication device. Voice communication can now be done on the computer using a microphone and a sound card. You can even talk long distance on the Internet without paying the normal long distance telephone charges. For example, dialpad.com offers free long distance calls through the Internet to regular telephones in U.S. cities from anywhere in the world. Voice and data also can work together to create useful applications. For example, operators of private branch exchanges (PBXs) are letting callers give simple computer commands using interactive voice response. See Chapter 12, Table 12.5 for different types of voice technology applications.

Voice technologies have the following advantages:

1. Hands-free and eyes-free operations increase the productivity, safety, and effectiveness of operators ranging from forklift drivers to military pilots.
2. Disabled employees can enter voice data to command a computer to perform various tasks.
3. Voice terminals are designed for portability. Workers do not have to go to the computer. They can communicate with the computer from their work areas, even when they are on the move, using telephone lines and/or wireless equipment.

4. Voice terminals are more rugged than keyboards, so they can operate better in dirty or moving environments.
5. Speed: It is about two-and-a-half times faster to talk than to type.
6. In most circumstances, fewer errors in voice data entry are made compared to keyboard data entry, assuming a reliable voice recognition system is used.

There are many other applications of voice technologies. Here is a sampling:

- ***Interactive voice recognition.*** Interactive voice recognition, one of the most popular applications, enables a computer to recognize the content of incoming telephone calls.
- ***Voice annotation.*** A combination of recorded voice messages with e-mail, spreadsheet, and other applications, voice annotation can be used to add comments to documents. Prerecorded voices of experts can add background information, or users can enter a request for advice or explanations on their PC. A computer program orders the telephone system to dial the user, who can then pick up the phone to receive recorded instructions.
- ***Automated attendant.*** An automated attendant system transfers calls, monitors them for completion, streamlines call flow, and shortens call hold times. Applications are in call routing, call screening, and receptionist backup.
- ***Voice mail.*** **Voice mail** is a computerized system for storing, forwarding, and routing telephone messages. Applications include personal greetings, front-end beepers and pagers, departmental messaging, message broadcasting to groups, and emergency notifications.
- ***Audiotext.*** Audiotext plays and records information in any sequence and/or in response to touch-tone input.

More advanced applications of voice technology such as natural language speech recognition, voice synthesis, and voice portals, are described in detail in Chapter 12.

4.4 COLLABORATION

One of the abiding features of a modern organization is that people collaborate to perform work. **Collaboration** refers to mutual efforts by two or more individuals who perform activities in order to accomplish certain tasks. Group members work together on tasks ranging from designing products and documents, to teaching each other, to executing complementary subtasks. Also, people work with customers, suppliers, and other business partners in an effort to improve productivity and competitiveness. Finally, group members participate in decision making. In all of the above cases they need to collaborate. Collaboration can be supported electronically by several technologies (see Smith and Rist, 1998).

Group work is increasing in importance. Indeed, it is a cornerstone in some BPR projects and in e-commerce. Also, group work is needed in virtual corporations as well as in multinational organizations. The use of group work is also increasing due to the support provided by IT, especially the support provided to groups whose members are in different locations. To understand such support, let us first examine how groups work.

The Nature of Group Work

The term **work group** refers to two or more individuals who act together to perform some task. The group can be permanent or temporary. It can be in one location or several. Members can meet concurrently or at different times. The group can be a committee, a review panel, a task force, an executive board, a team, or a department.

THE CONVENTIONAL APPROACH. For years, people have recognized the benefits of collaborative work. Typical benefits that relate to decision making are listed in Table 4.1. But despite the many benefits of group interaction, groups are not always successful. The reason is that the process of collaborative work is frequently plagued by dysfunctions, as listed in Table 4.2.

To reconcile these differences, researchers have worked for many years to improve the work of groups. If we could eliminate or lessen some of the causes of group dysfunctions, the benefits of group work would be greatly enhanced.

NEW APPROACHES TO GROUP WORK. Many approaches have been developed to attempt to solve the problems inherent in group work. Two representative methods are the *nominal group technique* and the *Delphi method.*

The **nominal group technique (NGT)** is a group communication method that includes a sequence of activities: (1) silent generation of ideas in writing, (2) round-robin listing of ideas on a flip chart, (3) serial discussion of ideas, (4) silent listing and ranking of priorities, (5) discussion of priorities, and (6) silent reranking and rating of priorities. The rankings obtained from the last activity are consolidated by the group facilitator. (See Lindstone and Turroff, 1975, for more details.)

The **Delphi method** is used with a group of experts who do not meet face-to-face and do not know who the other group members are. The experts provide individually written opinions on an issue, along with supporting arguments and assumptions. These opinions are then distributed as anonymous feedback to all participants along with a second round of questions. The questions and feedback

TABLE 4.1 Benefits of Working in a Group

- Groups are better than individuals at understanding problems.
- People are accountable for decisions in which they participate.
- Groups are better than individuals at catching errors.
- A group has more information (knowledge) than any one member and, as a result, more alternatives are generated for problem solving.
- Synergy can be produced, so the effectiveness and/or quality of group work can be greater than the sum of what is produced by independent individuals.
- Working in a group may stimulate the participants and the process.
- Group members have their egos embedded in the decision they make, so they will be committed to its implementation.

TABLE 4.2 Dysfunctions of Group Process

- Social pressures to conform ("groupthink") may eliminate superior ideas.
- Group process can be time-consuming, slow, and costly.
- Work done in a group may lack appropriate coordination.
- Some members may dominate the agenda.
- Some group members ("free riders") may rely on others to do most of their work.
- The group may compromise on solutions of poor quality.
- The group may be unable to complete a task.
- Unproductive time is spent socializing, getting ready, waiting for people, or repeating what has already been said.
- Members may be afraid to speak up.

continue in writing for several rounds, becoming increasingly more specific, until consensus among the panel members is reached, or until the experts no longer change their positions.

Both methods take time and organizational resources and require a trained facilitator or coordinator, and each eliminates only a few dysfunctions of the group process. So, their success is limited. The limited success of the new approaches to group work has created an opportunity for information technology to support groups electronically. The name for the supporting software products is *groupware.*

Groupware

Groupware refers to software products that support groups of people who share a common task or goal and collaborate on its accomplishment. It provides a way for them to share opinions and resources. Groupware implies the use of networks to connect people, even if they are in the same room. Many groupware products are available on the Internet or an intranet, enhancing the collaboration of a large number of people worldwide. Ozer et al. (1996) have identified 41 different approaches and technologies for the support of groups on the Internet. Major features available for collaboration and conferencing support in groupware are listed in Table 4.3.

Groupware products come either as a standalone product supporting one task (such as e-mail), or as an integrated kit that includes several tools (e-mail, workflow, etc.). In general, groupware technology products are fairly inexpensive and

TABLE 4.3 Major Features in Collaboration and Conferencing Tools

GENERAL
- Built-in e-mail
- Browser interface
- Joint Web-page creation
- Sharing of active hyperlinks
- Support of workgroups
- File sharing (graphics, video, audio, or other)
- Built-in search functions (by topic or keyword)
- Synchronous
- Videoconferencing
- Audioconferencing
- Shared whiteboard
- Text chat

ASYNCHRONOUS
- Threaded discussions
- Users can receive/post e-mail
- Users can receive activity notification via e-mail
- Users can collapse/expand threads
- Users can sort messages (by date, author, or read/unread)
- Chat session logs
- Bulletin boards

Source: Compiled from S. Gray, "Collaboration Tools," *Syllabus,* 1999. Courtesy of *Syllabus Magazine* © 1999.

can be easily incorporated into existing inforn systems. The Internet, intranets, extranets, and private communication provide the infrastructure needed for the hardware and software of groupw e software products are either Web-based, which is the trend today (Smi ist, 1998), or they are not related to the Internet and work with other n

Because groupware technologies are compute makes sense to integrate them with other computer-based or comp ed technologies. Integrating several technologies can save time and sers. Here are some examples:

- PictureTel Corporation (*picturetel.com*), in an allianc Lotus, developed an integrated desktop video telec uses Lotus Notes. Using this integrated system, Read NY) has built several applications combined with vid developer ities. This product is now available on the Internet. ct that
- Netscape Communicator (Web-based), LiveLink fron ville, based), Microsoft Exchange, Novell GroupWise, and Lot bil- scribed in detail below) have developed a set of compr tools in an effort to provide tools that support many gro *InfoWorld,* March 2, 1998.)

In this section we present the major groupware technologies laboration and conferencing.

Groupware Technologies

WORKFLOW SYSTEMS. **Workflow systems** are business proces tools that place system controls in the hands of user departments. They flexible and can be designed to automate almost any information processi The primary purpose of workflow systems is to provide users with tracking, r ing, document imaging, and other capabilities designed to improve business processes. The *IT at Work* example on page 144 demonstrates a workflow system.

There are three major types of workflow software: *Administrative workflow software* focuses on the tracking of expense reports, travel requests, and messages. *Ad hoc workflow software* deals with the shaping of product brochures, sales proposals, and strategic plans. And *production workflow software* is concerned with tracking credit card mailings, mortgage loans, and insurance claims.

There are many workflow software packages on the market. Some are Internet-based and may be combined with e-mail. Others use a shared database or a file on a server that people can log into. Notable software in the latter category is Lotus Notes. An innovative application of workflow is its use in supply-chain optimization, which greatly improves customer-supplier relationships. (See Stricker et al., 2000, for details.)

SCREEN SHARING. Another technique to support group work is **screen sharing**. In collaborative work, members are frequently in different locations. Using special software, it is possible for them to work on the same document, which is shown on the screen of each participant. For example, two authors can work on a single manuscript. One may suggest a correction and execute it so the other author can see the change. Collaborators can work together on the same spreadsheet (only one of them needs to have the spreadsheet software), or on the resultant graphics. Changes can be done by using the keyboard or by touching the

IT Work

. WORKFLOW SYSTEM TO GE CURRENCY FLOWS

www.dresdner-bank.dc

Dresdne ... any, has automated the way it hand ... of currency orders. It allocates these ... ey originate from within a single ... trading rooms worldwide, using a ... Limit Order Application (LORA) ... ilt on top of Microsoft Exchange, has ... elephone and fax-based processes.

... in problems that Dresdner Bank sought ... system was the allocation and uptake of ... different trading rooms around the world. ... ow more efficient trading across the differ- ... es, for instance, making it easier for traders to ... rankfurt order in New York after close of busi- ... rmany. Three types of bank staff—traders, con- ... nd administrators—use this system as follows:

- ... hen an order is received, it is placed into an elec- ... ronic folder by the controller. All order folders are held in a "public" file and can be viewed by the relevant staff.
- When a trader accepts an order, he or she is responsible for that order from that moment on. Although the order can still be canceled or reversed at this stage, the details of price and order quantity cannot be changed. The status of the order is displayed, and any order is locked when accessed, to prevent anyone from altering it. (Even small changes in the details of an order could result in huge profits or losses for the bank or its clients.)
- When the order is executed, or if it is canceled or reversed or it expires, then it is sent to a subfolder to be archived.

The bank dropped an initial plan of implementing global common folders that could be accessed by any of its 1,000 traders, in any location. It did so because of resistance from the traders, who did not like the idea of relinquishing local control and allowing other traders to process or execute their orders. Instead, the bank has implemented a system of local folders that reside within the branch of origin and can be read but not accessed by traders elsewhere. Traders can decide whether orders are to be passed to other locations.

With LORA, users can respond more quickly and accurately to customer queries, as they are able to view the precise status of orders on the computer screen. There is also improved control, with responsibility for any order always assigned to a specific staff member. Special consideration was given in designing the user interface to meet stringent requirements with respect to efficiency and ease of use.

LORA has been built mainly using Visual Basic, with provisions to extend the system to allow reuse of existing components. The system was implemented in about six months. It supports the bank's 500 dealers in Frankfurt, with plans to implement it in other branches.

For Further Exploration: How do workflow application systems differ from typical transaction-oriented application systems? What type of processes can be best supported using workflow systems?

Source: Compiled from *www.microsoft.com/europe/industry/financialservices/casestudies/473.htm*, 2000.

screen. This capability can expedite the design of products, the preparation of reports and bids, and the resolution of conflicts.

WHITEBOARDING. IT allows you to create what is called a *virtual whiteboard.* Whiteboarding with a computer works like the real-world version with markers and erasers, with one big difference: Instead of one person standing in front of a meeting room drawing on the whiteboard, all participants can join in. Throughout the meeting, each user can view and draw on a single document "pasted" onto the electronic whiteboard. You also can save digital whiteboarding sessions for later use. Some products let you insert graphics files that can be annotated by the group (e.g., CoolTalk, from Netscape communication). (See Haskin, 1997.)

Take, for example, an advertisement that needs to be cleared by a senior manager. Once the proposed ad has been scanned into a PC, both parties can see it on their screens. If the senior manager does not like something, he or she can use a stylus pen and highlight what needs to be changed. This makes communication between the two parties both easier and clearer. The two parties can also share applications. For example, if party A works with Excel, party B can see A's screen and make amendments to it even if party B does not have Excel. Desktop videoconferencing can also be used by advertising agencies to show their clients creative concepts and ideas. A client can make changes online that can be seen immediately by the advertising agency. Marketers can also use it to make remote presentations to customers.

Computerized real-time whiteboarding makes a lot of sense given the way people like to work. It's about sketching out ideas, and sharing ideas quickly. And it's a medium with which many people are familiar.

COLLABORATIVE WEB BROWSING. Collaborative Web browsing agent Let's Browse assists a group of people in browsing by suggesting new material likely to be of common interest (Lieberman et al., 1999). This agent is built as an extension to the Web browsing agent Letizia. While a Letizia agent scouts for pages around the user's current page, the Let's Browse agent detects the presence of users, automates "channel surfing" browsing, displays user profiles, and explains its recommendations to the group. Collaborative Web browsing agents improve the effectiveness and efficiency of information search by groups of people (e.g., a project team).

Real-Time Collaboration Tools

The Internet, intranets, and extranets offer tremendous potential for real-time and synchronous interaction. *Real-time collaboration (RTC)* tools help companies bridge time and space to make decisions and collaborate on projects. RTC tools support synchronous communication of graphical and text-based information. These tools are being used in distance training, product demonstrations, customer support, e-commerce, and sales applications.

RTC tools can either be purchased as standalone tools or used on a subscription basis. Many vendors are offering these tools on a subscription basis in one of the three following models:

1. ***Server model.*** All users must install and configure software on each client computer to access in-house-server-based RTC tools. Example products of the server model include CentraOne (*centra.com*), LearnLink 4.5 (e-learning at *learnlink.com*), and Sametime 2.0 (*lotus.com/home.nsf/welcome/sametime*).
2. ***Service model.*** Users access the service through a Web browser. Examples of service model products include Conference Center 2000 (*placeware.com*), and WebEx Meeting Center (*webex.com*).
3. ***Hybrid models.*** Users access the tools on their own server through a browser. Example products of the hybrid model include MeetingPlace (*latitude.com*), NetMeeting 3 (*microsoft.com/windows/netmeeting*), and PictureTalk Distance Selling Server (*pixion.com*).

For further details on the above RTC tools, see Coleman and Ward (1999).

The *IT at Work* at the top of the next page illustrates the use of a service-model real-time collaboration tool at Ricoh Canada.

Various standalone real-time collaboration tools are also in popular use. One of the best-known of the RTC tools is Lotus Notes. **Lotus Notes/Domino Server**

IT at Work

WEBEX MEETING CENTRE AT RICOH CANADA

...in Marketing

www.ricoh.com

Ricoh Canada, a leading supplier of office automation equipment, found that sending sales representatives all over the country for demonstrations of new products had become too expensive. Ricoh was spending as much as $20,000 each quarter for sending three people from one coast to the other. A team of marketing staff and IS personnel evaluated several products capable of supporting presentations in real-time over the Internet and selected WebEx Meeting Center.

Ricoh's sales representatives use WebEx to hold meetings with other sales staff and with dealers twice a month to brief them on marketing campaigns and new products. The service department is also using WebEx to train technicians on skills such as taking machines apart and adding accessories.

Using WebEx to communicate more effectively, Ricoh has made its workforce more competitive and more effective, and also has increased customer satisfaction.

For Further Exploration: What other uses of service-model RTC tools can you think of?

Source: www.webex.com/home/services_stories-ricoh.html, 2000.

was the first widely used integrated groupware. It enables collaboration by letting users access and create shared information through *specially programmed* Notes documents. Notes provides online collaboration capabilities, workgroup e-mail, distributed databases, bulletin whiteboards, text editing, (electronic) document management, workflow capabilities, consensus building, voting, ranking, and various application development tools. All these capabilities are integrated into one environment with a graphic menu-based user interface. Notes fosters the virtual corporation and creates interorganizational alliances. By the end of 1999, there were over 50 million Notes users worldwide ("Lotus Announces Over 50 Million Users of Lotus Notes," January 17, 2000, *lotus.com*).

Many applications have been programmed (written) in Lotus Notes. This includes Learning Space, a package for supporting distance learning. Lotus Development Corp. also provides TEAMROOM, to which decision makers can subscribe for online conferencing, and both QuickPlace and Sametime Collaboration, which have instant virtual meetings, whiteboarding, live documents, application sharing, and one-to-one instant messaging.

Netscape Collabra Server, a component of SuiteSpot, provides collaboration services through discussion groups, shared multimedia documents, and a Web browser interface. Anytime/anyplace virtual meetings can be structured within Collabra. It includes open e-mail, groupware, editing, calendaring, document access, and Web browsing. Like most groupware, Collabra does not include seamless, embedded databases. However, all major database systems provide HTML documents for querying and dynamic Web-based reporting.

Microsoft NetMeeting is a real-time collaboration package that includes whiteboarding (relatively freeform graphics to which all participants can contribute simultaneously), application sharing (any Microsoft Windows application document), remote desktop sharing, file transfer, text chat, data conferencing, and desktop audio and videoconferencing. The application sharing is a vast improvement over what was simply called whiteboarding a decade ago. The NetMeeting client is included in Windows 98 and 2000.

Novell's GroupWise offers a wide range of communication and collaboration capabilities integrated with document management capabilities including e-mail, personal calendaring, group scheduling, imaging, automated workflow, and electronic discussions. GroupWise simplifies communications through a single access point, the Universal Mailbox, for all types of messages, calendar information, and documents. Users of GroupWise can gain access to their personal Universal mailboxes through notebook computers when they are away from their desktops. The WebPublisher component enables users to publish documents on the Internet and intranets.

Teleconferencing

Teleconferencing is the use of electronic communication that allows two or more people at different locations to have a simultaneous conference. There are several types of teleconferencing (Storm, 1997). The oldest and simplest is a telephone conference call, wherein several people talk to each other from three or more locations. The biggest disadvantage is that it does not allow for face-to-face communication. Also, participants in one location cannot see graphs, charts, and pictures at other locations. While the latter disadvantage can be overcome by using a fax, this is a time-consuming, expensive, and frequently poor-quality process. One solution is video teleconferencing, in which participants can see each other as well as the documents.

VIDEO TELECONFERENCING. In a **video teleconference**, participants in one location can see participants at other locations. Dynamic pictures of the participants can appear on a large screen or on a desktop computer. Originally, video teleconferencing was the transmission of live, compressed TV sessions between two or more points. Video teleconferencing (or *videoconferencing*) today, however, is a digital technology capable of linking various types of computers across networks. Once conferences are digitized and transmitted over networks, they become a computer application. (For details, see Storm, 1997.)

With videoconferencing, participants can share data, voice, pictures, graphics, and animation. Data can also be sent along with voice and video. Such **data conferencing** makes it possible to work on documents together and to exchange computer files during videoconferences. This allows several geographically dispersed groups to work on the same project and to communicate by video simultaneously. The major benefits of video teleconferencing are given in Table 4.4.

TABLE 4.4 The Benefits of Teleconferencing

- Provides the opportunity for face-to-face communication for individuals in different locations.
- Supports several types of media during conferencing, including voice and radio.
- Improves employee productivity and cuts travel costs.
- Conserves the time and energy of key employees and increases the speed of business processes (including product development, contract negotiation, and customer service).
- Improves the efficiency and frequency of communications.
- Makes available different types of systems to provide flexibility to meet different needs.
- Saves messages in the computer to reconstruct specific parts of a meeting for future purposes.
- Makes it possible to hold classes at different locations.

Video mail is an example of videoconferencing as a computer application. It is similar to voice mail; however, the voice and image components of video mail can be created from portions of conferences and stored on a file server.

The first generation of computerized video teleconferencing was conducted in special rooms with large screens, cameras, and recorders. The second generation has moved to the desktop, using special equipment such as a PC videophone and local area networks (LANs) in conjunction with other desktop facilities.

However, several factors limit the growth of video teleconferencing. These include a lack of standards, the cost of setup and maintenance, lack of connectivity, problems with network security, and network capacity. Technological developments are reducing the seriousness of these factors as time passes. Companies such as PictureTel, Fujitsu, and Creative Technology market several interesting teleconferencing products. Many of these products can now work on the Internet. Some of them use analog telephone lines and run either as standalone units or across a LAN. The digitally based products provide better quality, but they are more expensive.

In military and security applications, desktop videoconferencing can be used as a remote surveillance tool. The video camera can capture movements that can then be interpreted by security personnel located elsewhere. A particular benefit here is that a single frame of the video can be captured and enlarged to spot security breaches. An application in transportation is similar. Traffic officers, stationed strategically along highways during peak traffic hours, can transmit maps showing congested areas and decide how to divert traffic.

Businesses can conduct videoconferencing and collaborative work sessions over the Internet or corporate intranets easily and inexpensively, with a quality that approaches that of TV. The latest technological innovations permit both business-to-business and business-to-consumer applications. Banks, insurance agents, and others can conduct videoconferencing sessions over the Internet with a customer at home. Banks in Alaska use *video kiosks* in sparsely populated areas instead of building underutilized branches. The video kiosks operate on the banks' intranet and provide videoconferencing equipment for eye-to-eye interactions.

4.5 DISTANCE LEARNING AND TELECOMMUTING

Web-based systems enable many applications related to discovery, communication, and collaboration. Two important applications are presented in this section—distance learning and telecommuting.

Distance Learning

Distance learning (DL) occurs when learning is performed with tools or technologies designed to overcome the restrictions of either same time or same place learning. Bunker (1999) and Matthews (1999) provide the history and capabilities of DL. Distance learning has unlimited potential to revolutionize learning at universities and colleges, public and private schools, and on-the-job training. When television was invented in the 1920s, it was heralded as a device that would revolutionize education. Radio was used in the 1920s and 1930s for distance learning programs. Video distance learning systems have been in operation for decades. Now that technology has evolved, television, or rather videoconferencing and collaborative computing through the Internet, can finally fulfill its destiny by providing support tools to enable distance learning.

The Internet/Web and videoconferencing and collaborative computing tools customized to the classroom environment enable inexpensive and widespread distance learning. Distance learning has developed into a substantive sector of higher education around the world over the last few decades. It is becoming an increasingly popular alternative to traditional degree programs and workshops. DL is a nontraditional way of delivering education and focuses on working professionals whose primary requirement is the element of convenience. Student profiles of distance learners have changed dramatically over the last two decades. As the economics of education and socioeconomic trends evolve, students are completing their college educations in nontraditional ways (Matthews, 1999). By 2001, over 2,000 educational institutions worldwide offered DL courses, not including the comparable if not larger number of independent companies offering remote education courses. These numbers are growing daily (Larsen, 1999).

Most major colleges and universities utilize technology to offer a variety of DL programs. In 1999, in the USA, more than 300 accredited major colleges and universities, including Stanford and Harvard, offered DL-delivery degrees in over 800 fields. Also, *cvc.edu*, a coalition of major California universities, offers 2000 courses online. For information about specific distance learning programs, see *Petersons.com, ECollege.com, icdl.open.ac.uk,* and *usdla.org* (Larsen, 1999). For experiences in moving courses and partial courses to online DL environments, see Berger (1999), Boisvert (2000), Dollar (2000), and Schell (2000).

DISTANCE LEARNING COURSEWARE. There are hundreds of **courseware** packages that enable distance learning. These range from more general collaboration tools (like Lotus Notes, Microsoft NetMeeting, Novell GroupWise, and GroupSystemsV) to specialized tools (like the popular Lotus Learning Space and WebCT) (Chaffee, 1998). Learning Space (written in Lotus Notes/Domino Server) is a powerful collaborative support tool that handles most aspects of online learning in a Web environment.

Mottl (2000) describes another courseware package, LearnLinc Virtual Classroom (from LearnLinc Corp.). LearnLinc lets online instructors control class presentations using synchronized multimedia and content over the Web. It also offers application sharing, electronic hand raising, and a "glimpse" feature that lets instructors acquire a screen capture of any student's desktop. The instructor can use one-way streaming video and audio (streaming multimedia allows users to view or listen to a clip without completely downloading the entire file) or prerecorded communications, as well as two-way audio in multicast audio conferencing. See the "2000 Buyer's Guide of Tools for Conferences, Meetings, and Distance Learning" (1999) for a list of available tools.

ONLINE CORPORATE TRAINING. Because of the current IT labor shortage, the frequent changes in technology, and the high cost of training, more and more organizations are training their employees online. Web-based learning technologies allow IT organizations to keep their staff members up to date with the latest innovations in IT. In 1999, private industry spent $58 billion on employee training (Markel, 1999). Driven by the demand for cheaper, more interactive courses, online learning is fast becoming the standard operating procedure: Traditional classroom use is projected to drop dramatically from its 77 percent share of the training market in 2000 to 51 percent by 2003. Conventional classroom instruction costs (in 2000) are about $75 an hour, with full-week programs costing $3,000 to $5,000. Computer-based training costs about half that, without travel costs or class size restrictions.

Web-based or online courses will account for 50 percent or more of all training by 2002 (from 17 percent in 1998). Training via the Web can run 24 hours per day, every day ("24/7"). Web-based training (WBT) can be faster and cheaper than classroom training. IBM estimates a savings of $500,000 for every 1,000 hours of training not done in the traditional classroom. International Data Corp. (IDC) predicts revenue from Internet-based training program sales to grow at a compound annual rate of 64.5 percent through 2003. Advanced electronic learning requires real-time, two-way communication via either audio or videoconferencing tools that let students and instructors interact and provide feedback. With most Web training, students view a live or recorded class, and participation is limited to posts on bulletin boards and e-mail discussions.

Reed (1999) suggests the following strategies to help improve communication and learning while using videoconferencing technology:

- Set expectations and establish protocols.
- Involve students from the beginning.
- Use visual aids.
- Provide supporting materials.
- Punctuate lectures with small group activities.
- Reduce distractions.
- Encourage dialogue.

EVALUATION OF DISTANCE LEARNING. Distance learning is a form of collaboration and knowledge management that can be done in a 24/7 framework. It is critical to assess the impact of Web-based courses in terms of benefits and costs (Gaud, 1999). Most student experiences are positive (see Dollar, 2000; Pitcher et al., 2000; Schell, 2000). Students tend to learn more using groupware and especially when it spans distance. There are several factors that are important in distance-learning situations: High levels of student motivation, a strong work ethic, and intensive student support measures typically result in success for distance learners (Reid, 1999). The most important factor for achieving success in distance learning is the degree to which instructors and support staff are able to encourage students to undertake responsibility for their own learning (Reid, 1999).

Both students and faculty must understand how the collaborative technology impacts on how they perform coursework (Berger, 1999). Some issues revolve around training, determining which technology to use and how, what to distribute and when, what standards to use for files that students submit, and so forth.

Distance learning is radically changing education, and the socioeconomic and technological changes should be examined as the learning behaviors and expectations of learners change. There is a sharply growing demand for flexible and adaptive learning environments that are independent of time and geography (Meso and Liegle, 2000). Despite the disadvantages, distance learning is growing dramatically due to the increased demand for it.

Telecommuting

By **telecommuting**, or *teleworking*, employees can work at home, at the customer's premises, or while traveling, using a computer linked to their place of employment. The first telecommuters were typists and bookkeepers. Today, a growing number of professionals do a significant portion of their work at home or on the road. Almost all groupware technologies can be used to support telecommuting. Regular and overnight mail, special messengers, and fax are still used to support telecommuting, but they are relatively slow and expensive. The Internet is gradually replacing them. Telecommuting, which is used by many corporations in large cities, is also appealing to small entrepreneurs (see *IT at Work,* below).

Telecommuting has a number of potential advantages for employees, employers, and society. However, there are also potential disadvantages. The major disadvantages for the employees are increased feelings of isolation, loss of fringe benefits, lower pay (in some cases), no workplace visibility, with, in turn, the potential of slower promotions, and lack of socialization. The major disadvantages to employers are difficulties in supervising work, potential data security problems, training costs, and the high cost of equipping and maintaining telecommuters' homes. Despite these disadvantages, the use of telecommuting is on the increase. Some experts predict that in 10 to 15 years, 50 percent of all work will be done at home, on the road, or at the customer's site. On the other side are those that believe that the growth of telecommuting will be very slow due to its disadvantages and employers' resistance to change. For a detailed list of advantages and disadvantages of telecommuting, see Nilles (1998). Major reasons for failure of telecommuting programs and possible preventive measures are presented in Table 4.5 (page 152).

Telecommuting can be used on a temporary basis. For example, during the 1996 Summer Olympics, Atlanta employers anticipated that the 750,000 additional cars of spectators would create a traffic nightmare. So, many Atlanta companies set up temporary data transmission network lines to save employees from traffic snarls. Vendors cooperated: Symantec and U.S. Robotics offered companies free software to provide remote access to corporate networks. The Olympics offered many employees and companies their first taste of telecommuting.

IT at Work

HANDLING CRUCIAL FILES ON THE ROAD

Integrating IT ...in Marketing

www.netdocuments.com

Mellissa McNatt, regional sales director for a Web-based company, makes sales calls twice a week. McNatt needed to exchange letters and PowerPoint presentations with her customers. Not being able to attach large files to e-mail messages due to objections from her customers, she had to resort to a slow process of sending printouts of drafts through the U.S. mail.

McNatt found a solution to her problem on the Internet at NetDocuments (*netdocuments.com*), which offers document storage at its site. Registered users of NetDocuments can create folders and subfolders into which they can upload their documents. With this facility McNatt is able not only to access her documents but also to share them with her customers through a feature called NetEnvelopes. This feature allows the registered users to set up accounts for others and designate with whom the users want to share documents.

Using NetDocuments to handle crucial files on the road, McNatt expects to cut down her cycle of contact with prospective customers from seven or eight days to two days.

For Further Exploration: Are there any disadvantages or limitations for telecommuters in using solutions like NetDocuments?

Source: Compiled from "Telecommuting—Bold Storage," *Inc.,* March 15, 2000.

TABLE 4.5 Reasons for Failures of Telecommuting Programs and Preventive Measures

Reasons for Failure (in decreasing order of importance)	Preventive Measures
Insufficient support infrastructure: Teleworkers often work extended hours or in a different time zone; they cannot bring their workstations for technical support nor can support staff troubleshoot remote computers.	Train telecommuters on remote workstation configuration and maintenance; train support staff on the remote access environment, and consider expanding technical support hours.
Insufficient security policies: Teleworkers require full access to all system resources from home.	Revise security policies to address the issues regarding employees working from home.
Union difficulties: Unions may feel that telecommuting interferes with their representation and collective bargaining power.	Construct a telecommuting program that is acceptable to both the enterprise and union.
Quantifiable productive gains aren't achieved: Changes in productivity are difficult to measure.	Rewrite performance mesurements for all eligible job roles to focus on objective, output-oriented goals and train managers to use those new measurements.
Teleworker productivity declines: Telecommuter productivity decreases during the first six to ten weeks due to insufficient training and inexperience.	Minimize the impact and duration of the productivity decline with proper training.
Overall productivity declines: Overall productivity decreases as the workgroup disintegrates without sufficient tools to support online and offline collaboration.	Encourage communication by publishing working schedules and home office contact numbers. Modify workgroup processes to take advantage of collaboration tools.
Employee morale drops: Without formal policies on eligibility, available equipment, etc. a telecommuting program can result in lower employee morale.	Establish policies that outline eligibility requirements.
Budget overruns: A full-time telecommuter can cost more than an office-bound worker in terms of equipment, support, and voice and data communications.	Perform a thorough cost-benefit analysis at the beginning and allocate sufficient funds.
Legal morass: The organization must ensure that it is in compliance with all local, regional, and national regulations.	The legal department should provide guidance in all stages of the program and should review the policies.
Management reprisal: It is difficult to get volunteers for the program's pilot or deployment stage due to employee fear that management will look harshly at people who do not work in the office.	Managers must be convinced of the benefits and should be trained in how to work with telecommuting employees.

Source: Compiled from "Transcend the Top Ten Telecommuting Traps," *Byte,* July 1998. *BYTE by BYTE MAGAZINE.* Copyright 1998 by CMP MEDIA. Reproduced with permission of CMP MEDIA in the format Textbook via Copyright Clearance Center.

The opportunity to work at home helps women or single parents with young children assume more responsible managerial positions in organizations. This could lead to better pay for women who can devote more attention to business while they still carry on duties at home. Telecommuting also helps health care employees and physicians to treat patients from a distance. This is especially important in rural areas and during disasters or military conflicts.

TELECOMMUTING AND PRODUCTIVITY. Why would productivity go up if people work at home? Strangely enough, reduced absenteeism has been cited by many organizations as a reason for increased productivity. Paul Ruper, Associate

Director of New Ways to Work, claims absenteeism can be reduced by telecommuting because it eliminates "sort-of" illnesses. He refers to those mornings when an employee wakes up and feels just "sort of blah." The trip to work and a whole day at the office is not going to make him feel any better, so he stays home. A telecommuter in the same situation is likely to try to get some work done, though perhaps he does so unshaven and in a bathrobe.

Telecommuting forces managers to manage by results instead of by overseeing. Telecommuting forces both employees and managers to ask some serious questions about the real purpose of a job. This process, although difficult, could make both the manager and the employee reduce misunderstandings about work. The employee will have a clear understanding of his or her responsibilities and thereby be accountable for his or her actions. For more on teleworking, see Shin et al., 2000.

Even though many employees are attracted to telecommuting, it is not for everybody and should not be mandatory. Some employees need to work with others, and for those employees telecommuting may not be an option. Also, not all jobs can be done while telecommuting, and not all managers can participate. The American Telecommuting Association (ATA) provides information, developments, ideas, and lists of equipment required for supporting teleworkers (*knowledgetree.com/ata.html*). Khalifa and Davison (2000), based on a survey of over 100 telecommuters in North America, identify key factors that contribute to the decision to telecommute.

Using a sample of 316 telecommuters from 18 companies, Guimaraes and Dallow (1999) found the importance for the success of telecommuting programs of carefully considering the characteristics of supervisors, employees, tasks, and work environments, as well as management support and problems encountered. Studying the telework environment for distributed software engineering, Higa et al. (2000) found that effective adoption of e-mail by teleworkers could benefit distributed work in distributed organizations through enhanced work productivity. For a detailed study of a company that combined salesforce automation with a telecommuting program to improve organizational performance see Watad and DiSanzo (2000).

4.6 SOME IMPLEMENTATION AND ETHICAL ISSUES

Of the many issues involved in implementing network computing environments, ethics and management issues will be discussed here.

Ethics on the Net

Several ethical, legal, and security issues have been raised as a result of the use of electronic networks in general and the Internet in particular. For example:

- Does an employer have the right to look at your e-mail without your permission?
- Is someone's desire to download pornographic images from a newsgroup protected by freedom of speech and privacy laws?
- Should someone post critical comments about a product, service, or person to a newsgroup?
- Should a network provider be held liable for the content of the traffic on the network?

Whenever there are no specific answers to such questions and their legal dimensions are vague, ethics become an important factor. Here are some representative issues:

1. ***Privacy and ethics in e-mail.*** The increased use of e-mail raises the question of privacy. While letters are sealed, e-mail material is open (unless encrypted). Many organizations are monitoring e-mail (which they have the right to do in most states); this raises questions of invasion of privacy (see discussion in Chapter 16). Other issues include the use of e-mail at work for personal purposes and for sending and receiving material that is not related to work. (For privacy protection tips see *PC World,* February 1997, pp. 223–229.)
2. ***Right to free speech.*** The dissemination of information such as pornographic and racist material via e-mail, newsgroups, electronic bulletin boards, and public networks may offend some people. But dissemination of such information in the United States is believed to be a right protected by the U.S. Constitution. At the time of this writing, the degree of freedom in the online world, and who should be liable for transmissions that are illegal, is still very much in debate. Legislation has been proposed that would require providers to create filters allowing adults to keep children from accessing inappropriate material. In fact, the commercial online providers have largely done so. The Internet, however, remains entirely accessible for anyone with a direct connection.
3. ***Copyright.*** The material you access on the Internet may be marked as being in the public domain; in that case it can be used by anyone for any purpose. Some material is marked as "copyrighted," which indicates that you need permission for anything other than a "fair use." *Fair use* refers to use for educational and not-for-profit activities. If you make a profit from copyrighted material, you should pay the copyright owner some royalties.

   Much of the material on the Internet is not marked as either in the public domain or copyrighted. Therefore, at least from an ethical point of view, it should be considered copyrighted. This includes software: You cannot legally copy any licensed software. However, *freeware* on the Internet can be downloaded and distributed. *Shareware* can be downloaded for review but you are expected to pay for it if you decide you want to use it.
4. ***The privacy of patients' information.*** In the United States, several specialized healthcare networks exist, such as Telemed, a network that tracks tuberculosis patients in order to prescribe the most suitable drugs. These systems could be abused. How do patients know they are getting qualified advice? What if personal medical records fall into the wrong hands? The growth of computerized networks makes medical confidentiality harder to preserve. The problem is how to strike a balance between the benefits of health information systems and their potential ethical problems.
5. ***Internet manners.*** It is very easy to offend people or tread on their toes when you cannot see their faces or you do not know who they are. Two well-known behaviors on the Internet are spamming and flaming. **Spamming** refers to indiscriminate distribution of messages, without consideration for their appropriateness. Some people spam newsgroups repeatedly. Spamming is frequently answered by **flaming**, which refers to sending angry messages. The Internet can become a war zone between spammers and flamers. Both sides may be equally guilty of ruining newsgroups. Flamers are known for

A CLOSER LOOK
4.3 HOW TO BEHAVE ON THE INTERNET—REPRESENTATIVE NETIQUETTE

Never respond rashly to provocation on the Internet. Although "flame wars" have often broken out on unmoderated mailing lists and Usenet newsgroups, they are generally frowned on. If you must respond, do it offline (that is, in private e-mail, not to the group as a whole).

Criticize ideas, not people. Try to be as constructive in your criticism as possible.

Watch or monitor for a while any mailing list or newsgroup you want to participate in, to get a feel for the tone and to avoid asking "newbie" (newcomer) questions. Do your homework before asking questions. Look for the relevant Frequently Asked Questions (FAQ) files to avoid asking questions that have already been answered.

Think carefully before sending a message. Remember that you are making your reputation internationally through the messages you send out.

Stay on the topic of the newsgroup or mailing list. No matter how strongly you feel about a subject, it is not appropriate to send information or opinions about it to unrelated groups.

Do not "shout." (Typing messages in ALL CAPS is shouting.) A single word in uppercase for emphasis is fine, but no more.

Don't post commercials. Ads have their place in the online world, but make sure you understand just where that place is. The vast majority of usenet groups eschew ads. Indeed, posting an advertisement in the wrong place will surely provoke a flame attack and worse.

Know whereof you speak. Don't pass along unsubstantiated rumors or anything you yourself don't believe to be true.

Don't be the skunk at the picnic. If you don't accept the underlying premise of a discussion group, don't disrupt it; just go away. An atheist, for example, needn't bother joining a conference of nuns who are debating church matters.

Apply the Golden Rule: Do unto others in cyberspace as you would do unto them face to face, which is, of course, as you would want them to do unto you.

their attacks on inexperienced visitors to newsgroups as well as on those that make spelling errors. A *spam shield* can stop spamming (for examples see *siegesoft.com, spamcop.com,* and *stopspam.org*).

There are certain rules, called **netiquette** (network etiquette), governing Internet manners. Some of these rules are shown in *A Closer Look* 4.3.

Likewise, it is far easier to take offense because online interaction excludes the nuances of body language, rhythm, mood, and context. E-mail users developed an expressive language that can be used to overcome this problem. A sample is shown in *A Closer Look* 4.4 (page 156).

6. ***Monitoring employees' use of the Internet.*** Some companies use special software that monitors time spent on the Internet, by employee and by site address. The objective is to eliminate abuse of access during working hours and the accessing of "indecent" sites. It seems to be a good idea, but is it ethical? Other companies simply disconnect sites they do not want their employees to visit. It sounds good, but what about freedom of speech? Is freedom of speech an absolute right, or does it also involve associated responsibilities?

 MANAGERIAL ISSUES

Providing timely, relevant, and correct information is a critical factor for the success of almost any organization. In implementing IT to support communication and collaborative work, the following issues may surface.

A CLOSER LOOK
4.4 AN UNOFFICIAL SMILEY GUIDE

Smileys are simple but creative drawings of expressions. They are very often used in electronic messages in place of facial and tonal expressions. For example, if I say, "Get lost!" you may think that I am really angry at you. But if I say, "Get lost :-)" you know I don't really mean it. The remark becomes something like a joke between us and I am really giving you a pat on your back. There may be more than one explanation for each Smiley, and some are more obvious than others. You can design your own Smileys too. Some typical Smileys are listed below. (*Note:* If you cannot see the "faces," turn this page clockwise 90 degrees.)

:-)	Basic smiling smiley
:)	Smiley midget
:-X	A big wet kiss
:-x	My lips are sealed
:-D	A big smile
;-)	Winking
<:-O	Eeek!
8-O	Omigod!!
:-o	Shocked
**-(	Too many shocks
%-(	Confusion
&-|	Tearful
:'-(	Crying
:-(	Frowning
:-*	Kissing
#-)	Partied all night
%-|	Been working all night
%+{	Lost a fight
8-)	Wears glasses
(:-{~	Bearded
:=~)	Has a cold
:^D	"Great! I like it!"
|-{	"Good grief!"
>-<	Absolutely livid!!
0:-)	Angel

1. ***Security of communication.*** Communication via networks raises the issue of the integrity, confidentiality, and security of the data being transferred. The protection of data in networks across the globe is not simple (see Chapter 15).
2. ***Data crossing national borders.*** Governments cannot or do not wish to control data crossing their borders via regular mail. However, it is easier to control data crossing national borders electronically. Such control, which is commonly justified as a protection of citizens' privacy, is sometimes done to preserve jobs.
3. ***Congestion.*** Some people believe the increased use of the Internet will clog it, and therefore that companies should develop a plan to limit the use of the Internet. Others believe that technological developments will solve the capacity and security problems of the Internet.
4. ***Control of employee time and activities.*** "Surfing the Net" is an exciting, yet time-consuming activity. Employees may be tempted to conduct private surfing during work hours. Control can be achieved by limiting the information that employees have access to, and by using special monitoring software. Providing guidelines is simple and fairly effective.
5. ***Questionnaires and referenda.*** An increasing number of researchers and pollsters are using the Internet for conducting marketing surveys or running national referenda on political issues. Some researchers have questioned the reliability and validity of such surveys because of possible response biases.
6. ***Organizational impacts.*** Technology-supported communication may have major organizational impacts. For example, intranets and groupware force people to cooperate and share information. Therefore, their use can lead to

significant changes in both organizational culture and the execution of business process reengineering. Further impacts may be felt in corporate structure and the redistribution of organizational power.

7. ***Telecommuting.*** Telecommuting is a compelling venture, but management needs to be careful. Not all jobs are suitable for telecommuting, and allowing only some employees to telecommute may create jealousy. Likewise, not all employees are suitable telecommuters; some need the energy and social contact found in an office setting.
8. ***Cost-benefit justification.*** The technologies described in this chapter do not come free, and many of the benefits are intangible. However, with the introduction of intranets and other competing products, the price of many networking technologies is decreasing.
9. ***Legal issues.*** There are many unresolved legal issues. For example, international groups are struggling over jurisdiction of trademarks and names on the Web. In one instance, when Carl's Jr. Corporation, a fast-food chain, applied for a Web site by this name (for which it has the trademark), it found the name had been granted to a youngster named Carl Junior. Other examples are the use of the Internet for misrepresentation, fraud, and other illegal transactions (see Chapter 5).
10. ***Controlling access to and managing the content of the material on an intranet.*** This is becoming a major problem due to the ease of placing material on an intranet and the huge volume of information. Flohr (1997) suggests tools and procedures to manage the situation.

ON THE WEB SITE... Additional resources, including the Virtual Company, quizzes, cases, updates, additional exercises, links, demos, and activities, can be found on the book's Web site.

KEY TERMS

Asynchronous communication *135*
Chat room *139*
Collaboration *140*
Corporate portals *132*
Courseware *149*
Data conferencing *147*
Delphi method *141*
Directories *126*
Distance learning (DL) *148*
Domino Server *145*
E-mail agents *137*
Electronic commerce (EC) *124*
Electronic mail (e-mail) *136*
Extranet *131*
Firewall *130*
Flaming *154*
Groupware *142*
Information superhighway *123*
Instant messaging *137*
Intelligent agents *126*
Internet *123*
Internet2 *123*
Intranet *130*
Lotus Notes *145*
Netiquette *155*
Nominal group technique (NGT) *141*
Peer-to-peer networks *138*
Screen sharing *143*
Search engines *126*
Softbot *126*
Software agents *126*
Spamming *154*
Synchronous (real-time) communication *135*
Teleconferencing *147*
Telecommuting (teleworking) *150*
Video teleconference *147*
Video mail *148*
Voice mail *140*
Workflow systems *143*
Work group *141*

CHAPTER HIGHLIGHTS (Numbers Refer to Learning Objectives)

1. Information superhighways will enable us to integrate voice, text, and other interactive media and bring them into every home, school, and business.

1. The Internet is a network of many networks. It is the predecessor of the information superhighway.

2. Intranets are an implementation and deployment of Web-based network services within a company.

2. Intranets and extranets have the power to change organizational structures and procedures.

3. There are four ways of supporting communication in meetings: same-time/same-place, same-time/different-place, different-time/same-place, and different-time/different-place.

3. Electronic mail allows quick communication across the globe at minimal cost.

4. Electronic meeting systems, computer-supported co-operative work, groupware, and other names designate various types of computer support to groups.

4. Video teleconferencing utilizes several technologies that allow people to communicate and view each other as well as view and transfer documents.

4. Voice technologies can be used to increase productivity and usability of communication.

5. Lotus Notes is a major integrated software that supports the work of dispersed individuals and groups.

6. Software agents help to carry out mundane tasks on the Internet such as searching, browsing, and sorting e-mail.

7. Distance learning and telecommuniting are supported by network computing.

8. Ethical behavior on the Internet is critical to its success. You need to know what is right and wrong.

QUESTIONS FOR REVIEW

1. List the major advantages of the Internet.
2. Define an intranet.
3. Define discovery, communication, and collaboration.
4. Describe corporate portals and their benefits.
5. Distinguish corporate portals from information (Internet) portals.
6. What are some major benefits of working in groups?
7. Are there any major limitations to working in groups?
8. Define telecommuting and describe its benefits.
9. Describe the time/place framework.
10. List software agents' applications regarding the Internet.
11. Describe differences between intranets and extranets.
12. Define groupware.
13. Describe the major capabilities of real-time collaboration tools.
14. List the major capabilities of teleconferencing.
15. Define e-mail and describe its capabilities.
16. Define workflow systems.
17. Describe software agents.
18. List the major Internet-based agents.
19. Define Internet, information superhighways, and Internet2.
20. Define voice technology and list its uses.
21. Define flaming and contrast it with spamming.
22. Define netiquette.

QUESTIONS FOR DISCUSSION

1. Identify some commercial tools that allow users to conduct browsing, communication, and collaboration simultaneously.
2. Explain why the topic of group work and its support is getting increased attention.
3. Explain the advantages of electronic mail over regular mail.
4. Relate telecommuting to networks.
5. Distinguish between flaming and spamming. How are they related?
6. It is said that collaboration tools can change organizational culture. Explain how.
7. How can computers support a team whose members work at different times?
8. Based on what you know about Lotus Notes, can it support different-time/different-place work situations?
9. Relate flaming to netiquette.
10. Discuss the role of Web-based call centers and their contribution to competitive advantage.
11. Describe how agents can help people find specific information quickly.
12. Explain the advantages of using Web-based e-mail over server-based e-mail.

EXERCISES

1. From your own experience or from the vendor's information, list the major capabilities of Lotus Notes/Domino. Do the same for Microsoft Exchange. Compare and contrast the products. Explain how the products can be used to support knowledge workers and managers.
2. Visit *picturetel.com* and sites of other companies that manufacture conferencing products for the Internet. Prepare a report. Why is it called video commerce?
3. Marketel is a fast-growing telemarketing company whose headquarters are in Colorado, but the majority of its business is in California. The company has eight divisions, including one in Chicago. (The company has just started penetrating the Midwest market.) Recently the company was approached by two large telephone companies, one in Los Angeles and one in Denver, for discussions regarding a potential merger.

   Nancy Miranda, the corporate CEO who was involved in the preliminary discussions, notified all division managers on the progress of the discussions. Both she and John Miner, the chief financial officer, felt that an immediate merger would be extremely beneficial. However, the vice presidents for marketing and operations thought the company should continue to be independent for at least two to three years. "We can get a much better deal if we first increase our market share," commented Sharon Gonzales, the vice president for marketing.

   Nancy called each of the division managers and found that five of them were for the merger proposal and three objected to it. Furthermore, she found that the division managers from the West Coast strongly opposed discussions with the Colorado company, and the other managers were strongly against discussions with the Los Angeles company. Memos, telephone calls, and meetings of two or three people at a time resulted in frustration. It became apparent that a meeting of all concerned individuals was needed. Nancy wanted to have the meeting as soon as possible in spite of the busy travel schedules of most division managers. She also wanted the meeting to be as short as possible. Nancy called Bob Kraut, the chief information officer, and asked for suggestions about how to conduct a conference electronically. The options he outlined are as follows.

   1. Use the corporate intranet. Collect opinions from all division managers and vice presidents, then disseminate them to all parties, get feedback, and repeat the process until a solution is achieved (similar to the Delphi method).
   2. Fly all division managers to corporate headquarters and have face-to-face meetings there until a solution is achieved.
   3. Use the Web for a meeting.
   4. Fly all division managers to corporate headquarters. Rent a decision room (a facility designed for electronic meetings) and a facilitator from the local university for $2,000 per day and conduct the meetings there.
   5. Conduct a videoconference. Unfortunately, appropriate facilities exist only at the headquarters and in two divisions. The other division managers can be flown to the nearest division that has equipment. Alternatively, videoconferencing facilities can be rented in all cities.
   6. Use a telephone conference call.

   Answer the following questions:

   a. Which of these options would you recommend to management and why?

   b. Is there a technology not listed that might do a better job?

   c. Is it possible to use more than one alternative in this case? If yes, which technologies would you combine, and how would you use them?

GROUP AND ROLE-PLAYING ACTIVITIES

1. You are a member of a team working for a multinational finance corporation. Your team's project is to prepare a complex financing proposal for a client within one week. Two of the team members are in Singapore, one is in Seoul, South Korea, one is in London, and one is in Los Angeles. You cannot get the team members together in one place. Your team does not have all the required expertise, but other corporate employees may have it. There are 8,000 employees worldwide; many of them travel. You do not know exactly who are the experts in your company.

   Your company has never prepared such a proposal, but you know that certain parts of the proposal can be adapted from previous proposals. These proposals are filed electronically in various corporate databases, but you are not sure exactly where. (The company has over 80 databases, worldwide). Finally, you will need a lot of external information, and you will need to communicate with your client in China, with investment groups in Japan and New York, and with your corporate headquarters in London.

   If the client accepts your proposal, your company will make more than $5 million in profit. If the contract goes to a competitor, you may lose your job.

   Your company has all the latest information and communication technologies.

a. Prepare a list of tasks and activities that your team will need to go through in order to accomplish the mission. (Look at *knowldgespace.com.*)
b. Describe what information technologies you would use to support the above tasks. Be specific, explaining how each technology can facilitate the execution of each task.

2. The world of the Internet is growing very fast, and it keeps changing. The task for the group is to report on the latest developments on the Internet's uses. Members of the group will prepare a report to include the following.
   a. New business applications on the Internet.
   b. New books about the Internet.
   c. Information about new software products related to the Internet.
   d. New managerial and technological issues related to the Internet.

   Also, send an e-mail message about a topic of concern to you to the White House and include the reply in your report.
3. Assign each group member to an integrated group support tool kit (Notes, GroupWise, Communicator, etc.). Have each member visit the Web site of the commercial developer and obtain information about this product. As a group, prepare a comparative table of the major similarities and differences among the kits.
4. Assign each team to a college collaborative tool such as Blackboard, WebCT, etc. Establish common evaluative criteria. Have each team evaluate the capabilities and limitations of its tool, and convince each team that its product is superior.

INTERNET EXERCISES

1. Your friend wishes to pursue graduate studies in accounting in the United States. She is especially interested in two universities: the University of Illinois (U of I) and the University of Southern California (USC). Use the Internet to find information that will help her choose between the two universities. Such information should include, *but not be limited to,* the following:
   a. The types of degree programs in accounting offered by the two universities.
   b. The admission procedures and school calendar.
   c. Coursework and dissertation requirements of the programs under consideration.
   d. The costs of tuition and other expenses associated with the programs.
2. You plan to take a three-week vacation in Hawaii this December, visiting the big island of Hawaii. Using the Internet, find information that will help you plan the trip. Such information includes, *but is not limited to,* the following:
   a. Geographical location and weather conditions in December.
   b. Major tourist attractions and recreational facilities.
   c. Travel arrangements (airlines, approximate fares).
   d. Car rental; local tours.
   e. Alternatives for accommodation (within a moderate budget) and food.
   f. Estimated cost of the vacation (travel + lodging + food + recreation + shopping + . . .).
   g. State regulations regarding the entrance of your dog that you plan to take with you.
   h. Shopping (try to find an electronic mall).
3. Your friend manufactures canned food products (vegetables, beef) and wants to export them to Mexico. He has heard about the North American Free Trade Agreement (NAFTA) and wishes to find out how it may affect his business prospects. Surf the Internet to find information that will help your friend address his concerns about NAFTA. Such information includes, *but is not limited to,* the following:
   a. The nations involved in NAFTA.
   b. The scope of NAFTA (with specific reference to food products).
   c. The time-table for the provisions of NAFTA (what went or goes into effect when).
   d. The expected benefits to the participants in NAFTA.
   e. Implications of NAFTA for businesses located in your state.
   f. Implications of NAFTA for businesses located in a food-exporting country (e.g., Australia).

   Collect information on NAFTA and prepare a report recommending whether your friend should pursue this project.
4. Visit *cdt.org.* Find what technologies are available to track users' activities on the Internet.
5. Visit the ON Technology Corporation Web site (*on.com*). Describe the capabilities of the current version of Site Manager. Download the Site Manager demo software, try it with a group, and report your findings. Visit and download the demo of "The Meeting Room" from Eden

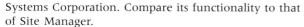

Systems Corporation. Compare its functionality to that of Site Manager.

6. You are assigned the task of buying desktop teleconferencing equipment for your company. Using the Internet:
   a. Identify three major vendors.
   b. Visit their Web sites and find information about their products and capabilities.
   c. Compare the least expensive products of two vendors.
   d. Find a newsgroup that has an interest in video teleconferencing. Post new questions regarding the products selected (for example, what are the users' experiences?).
   e. Prepare a report of your findings.
7. Both Microsoft Explorer and Netscape Navigator have the capability for telephony; all you need is a sound card, microphone, and speakers on your PC. (If you do not have these browsers, access the VocalTec Web site at *vocaltec.com/*, and download and install its fully functional Internet long-distance telephone software). Get a friend in another city to do the same. Contact each other via the Internet using your computer as a telephone. What are the advantages and disadvantages of using the Internet for telephone service? Compare your experience to that of making a standard telephone call.
8. Visit *albion.com/netiquette/netiquiz.html* and take the online quiz about netiquette.

Minicase 1

Marine Forces Reserve Streamlines Communications Using the Web

www.marforres.usmc.mil

Like organizations in the private sector, the Marine Forces Reserve (MARFORRES) is always seeking ways to make its operations more efficient. MARFORRES trains 14,000 reserve personnel at any given time, for a war or national emergency, in 200 locations around the United States. Reservists are at their training centers only one weekend a month. This created a communication problem.

The number of simple administrative requests from the 100,000 reservists was difficult to manage. Until 1997 even relatively simple requests from reservists, especially those not at bases, could take months to process. The delays caused frustration and loss of productivity among the reservists during their training.

The solution was the creation of a Web site and an internal communication system, based on Lotus Notes/Domino, for the 200 training centers. The system includes both e-mail and groupware, and it contains several Notes applications that both solve the communication problem and facilitate the reduction of the administrative personnel. One of the first areas addressed was the hierarchical communications bottlenecks. Reservists now submit requests electronically. Using workflow software, the requests are automatically routed to the proper authorities. If more information is needed, a request is instantly routed back to the sender. The reservists can track the status of their requests at any time. The results were staggering: Processes that had been taking six months were now down to three days!

In order to reduce administrative overhead, MARFORRES replaced the manual system with Notes databases in which all directives are stored and changed centrally. Other applications include: e-mail for the internal system, a platform for decisions, and planning and awareness tools (e.g., to plan training exercises and to manage the number of people, where they are to be transported, and other cost and logistics issues).

Lotus Notes is also used for internal collaboration. The MARFORRES knowledge-sharing database (R-NET) allows technical experts to answer users' questions.

The entire system was rapidly deployed. User training for the permanent staff on Marine bases was facilitated by computer-based, video-based, and self-paced courseware at each of the 200 sites.

The MARFORRES Web site (*marforres.usmc.mil*) is integrated with Lotus Domino server. This Web site provides considerable information to the 100,000 reservists in any location in the world. By 2000, the site had become a major portal for the Marine Forces Reserve, including recruiting information and MARFORRES news.

Sources: Compiled from *Lotus Solutions*, Winter 1998, pp. 10–11, and *marforres.usmc.mil*, 2001.

Questions for Minicase 1

1. Communication among the 200 training centers and the MARFORRES headquarters is conducted over dedicated military lines. In each training center there is one

(continued)

Lotus Notes server. However, there is only one Domino server at the headquarters. Why?

2. Examine some of the capabilities of Notes. What other applications can you envision at MARFORRES? You may want to check *lotus.com* for the newest capabilities of Notes and Domino.
3. Training in Lotus Notes takes 2 to 3 days, but it is automated at MARFORRES. Why?
4. Which of Notes' capabilities do you think is used by the reservists and which by the bases' permanent staff? Why?
5. Log on to the MARFORRES Web site. What information/services available on the Web are related to the Notes system? Why?
6. How can Notes contribute to the reduction of the administrative personnel at MARFORRES?

Minicase 2

Business Intelligence Portal Speeds Product Research and Development at Amway

www.amway.com

Through thousands of independent agents all over the world, Amway sells more than 450 home, nutrition and wellness, and personal products. In order to do it effectively, the research and development (R&D) department at Amway must develop new products in a streamlined and cost-efficient manner. The R&D department consists of 550 engineers, scientists, and quality-assurance staff, working on more than 1,000 projects at a time.

Fast and easy access to information about current products is required for supporting the design activity. Such information includes product specifications, formulas, design criteria, production schedules, costs and sales trends. Providing this wide array of information was difficult because the required data resided in at least 15 disparate repositories such as a data warehouse and supply chain and accounting systems in different departments. When scientists needed production or financial data, for instance, they had to request paper reports from each department, which sometimes took days to be processed.

Amway developed a business intelligence and knowledge management portal, called Artemis, tailored to the R&D division. Artemis is a browser-based intranet application that enables R&D staff to quickly find the required information. It also includes knowledge management features such as collaboration and a database for locating company experts. Using Lotus' agent and full-text search engine technology, Artemis pulls data from disparate corporate sources and generates dynamic reports in response to user queries.

Artemis started with the goal of saving each R&D employee one hour per week. Structured product data from legacy systems is abstracted by Artemis and is used for creating dynamic reports from users' search criteria. Time required to access information dropped from days to seconds or minutes, enabling fast what-if investigations needed by product developers.

The first challenge was gaining corporate buy-in at Amway. Though everyone agreed with Artemis' goal, information gatekeepers across Amway were hesitant to relinquish control. A simple working prototype of the portal was presented to a supply chain executive committee to overcome the first challenge. Amway's development partner, marchFIRST, suggested that Lotus Domino would best leverage existing resources such as the intranet and data warehouse. Domino's strong security features, easy integration with legacy systems, built-in agents, and a fast search engine, along with powerful knowledge management capabilities, were all instrumental in making Artemis a success.

With a budget of less than $250,000, Amway's IT support group and the users worked with marchFIRST to complete Artemis over three phases of eight to twelve weeks each, going live in January 2000. The portal runs on a fast, dedicated server. Each night, Domino sends agents out to a data warehouse and builds or updates an information document for each Amway product stored in a database. R&D staff do full-text searches against this database to locate products they're interested in, then Domino queries the data warehouse for details. The only non-Domino part of Artemis is an inexpenive ($800) utility, called PopChart Live, used to create the trend and pie charts within the final document the user sees.

Artemis' collaborative features include a time-accounting function for the R&D staff. Used to help calculate R&D tax credits allowed by the Internal Revenue Service, this system has a gated section where managers can analyze big-picture R&D trends. Artemis' event-reporting database also tracks project content and status. Domino's strong messaging alerts staffers via e-mail when their projects are updated.

After a staged roll out, all 550 R&D staffers now have access. Initial user surveys indicated that 60 percent are saving 30 minutes or more per week. This is expected to rise as links to more information are added and users gain comfort with the system.

Lessons learned from Amway's portal project include the following:

- Don't assume you know what business users need.
- An iterative development cycle works best.
- Query rank-and-file users on their thinking and business needs.
- Conduct a number of user meetings and do much paper prototyping before you begin to code.
- Don't forget to add business intelligence nuggets for management, such as executive-level reporting, to foster high-level support for the project.

Sources: Condensed from C. Abbott, "At Amway, BI Portal Speeds Product R&D," *DM Review,* October 2000, and from *amway.com.*

Questions for Minicase 2

1. Describe how the information access problems affected the R&D department in developing new products.
2. Describe the role of the business intelligence portal in R&D at Amway.
3. How did Amway plan the implementation of the business intelligence portal?
4. Enter *amway.com* and examine Amway's corporate structure. What kind of groupware can help the company's salespeople?
5. Find a couple of business intelligence and knowledge management portals and compare those with Artemis.

REFERENCES AND BIBLIOGRAPHY

1. Aneja, A., et al., "Corporate Portal Framework for Transforming Content Chaos on Intranets," *Intel Technology Journal,* Q1, 2000.
2. Berger, N. S., "Pioneering Experiences in Distance Learning: Lessons Learned," *Journal of Management Education,* Vol. 23, No. 6, December 1999.
3. Bernard, R., *The Corporate Intranet,* 2nd ed. New York: Wiley, 1998.
4. Boisvert, L., "Web-based Learning: The Anytime Anywhere Classroom," *Information Systems Management,* Vol. 17, No. 1, Winter 2000.
5. Bunker, E., "History of Distance Education," Center for Excellence in Distance Learning (CEDL), Lucent Technologies, *lucent.com/cedl/,* 1999.
6. Chaffee, D., *Groupware, Workflow and Intranets: Reengineering the Enterprise with Collaborative Software.* Boston: Digital Press, 1998.
7. Choi, S. Y., and A. B., Whinston, *The Internet Economy: Technology and Practice.* Austin: TX: SmartEcon Publishing, 2000.
8. Coleman, D., and L., Ward, "Taking Advantage of Real-Time Collaboration Tools," *IT Pro,* July–August 1999.
9. Corcoran, C., "National Semiconductor Uses Web to Ease Support Services," *Infoworld,* July 22, 1996.
10. DeSanctis, G., and B. Gallupe, "A Foundation for the Study of Group Decision Support Systems," *Management Science,* Vol. 33, No. 5, 1987.
11. Dollar, G., "Web-based Course Delivery: An Empirical Assessment of Student Learning Outcomes," *Proceedings of the Americas Conference of the Association for Information Systems,* Milwaukee, WI, August 2000.
12. Drury, J., "Realistic Choices for Web-based Call Centers," *Business Communications Review,* June 1999.
13. Etzioni, O., "The WWW: Quagmire or Gold Mine?" *Communications of the ACM,* November 1996.
14. Etzioni, O., and D. S. Weld, "A Softbot-based Interface to the Internet," *Communications of the ACM,* Vol. 37, No. 7, 1994.
15. Flohr, U., "Intelligent Intranets," *Byte,* August 1997.
16. Gaskin, J. E., "Software Helps Manage E-Mail Flood," *Interactive Week,* January 25, 1999.
17. Gaud, W. S., "Assessing the Impact of Web Courses," *Syllabus,* November–December 1999.
18. Geoffrey, J., "Intranets Rescue Reengineering," *Datamation,* December 1996.
19. Gotcher, R., "AFI Turns e-mail Deluge into a Profitable Sales Resource," *Infoworld,* December 8, 1997,
20. Gray, S., "Collaboration Tools," *Syllabus,* January 1999.
21. Guimaraes, T., and P., Dallow, "Empirically Testing the Benefits, Problems, and Success Factors for Telecommuting Programs," *European Journal of Information Systems,* Vol. 8, 1999.
22. Haskin, D., "Meetings Without Walls," *Internet World,* October 1997.
23. Higa, K, et al., "Understanding Relationships Among Teleworkers' E-mail Usage, E-mail Richness Perceptions, and E-mail Productivity Perceptions Under a Software Engineering Environment," *IEEE Transactions on Engineering Management,* May 2000.
24. Ito, T., et al., "BiddingBot: A Multiagent Support System for Cooperative Bidding in Multiple Auctions," *Proceedings of the Fourth International Conference on Multi-Agent Systems (ICMAS),* 2000.
25. Joachims, T., et al., *Proceedings of IJCAI97,* August 1997.
26. Khalifa, M., and R., Davison, "Exploring the Telecommuting Paradox," *Communications of the ACM,* Vol. 43, No. 3, March 2000.
27. Kiser, K., "10 Things We Know So Far about Online Training," *Training,* Vol. 36, No. 11, November 1999.
28. Kounadis, T., "How to Pick the Best Portal," *e-Business Advisor,* August 2000.

29. Larsen, N. C., "Distance Learning: Linking the Globe through Education," *World Trade,* Vol. 12, No. 12, December 1999.

30. Lieberman, H., et al., "Let's Browse: A Collaborative Browsing Agent," *Knowledge-Based Systems,* Vol. 12, December 1999.

31. Lindstone, H., and H. Turroff, *The Delphi Method: Technology and Applications.* Reading, MA: Addison-Wesley, 1975.

32. Markel, M., "Distance Education and the Myth of the New Pedagogy," *Journal of Business and Technical Communication,* Vol. 13, No. 2, April 1999.

33. Matthews, D., "The Origins of Distance Education and its Use in the United States," *T.H.E. Journal,* Vol. 27, No. 2, September 1999.

34. Meso, P. N., and J. O. Liegle, "The Future of Web-based Instruction Systems," *Proceedings of the Americas Conference of the Association for Information Systems,* Milwaukee, WI, August 2000.

35. Mottl, J. N., "Learn at a Distance," *Informationweek,* No. 767, January 3, 2000.

36. Murch, R., and T. Johnson, *Intelligent Software Agents.* Upper Saddle River, NJ: Prentice-Hall, 1999.

37. Nilles, J. M., "Managing Telework: Strategies for Managing the Virtual Work Force," *New Wiley,* 1998.

38. O'Leary, D., "AI and Navigation on the Internet and Intranet," *IEEE Expert,* April 1996.

39. Ozer, J., et al., "Collaboration on the Web," *PC Magazine,* October 6, 1996, pp. 100–230.

40. Parsa, I., "Web Mining Crucial to e-Commerce," *DM News,* December 7, 1999.

41. Pitcher, N., et al., "Video Conferencing in Higher Education," *Innovations in Education and Training International,* August 2000.

42. Reed, J., "Using Video Conferencing Technology in Teaching," *Syllabus* (*syllabus.com*), January 1999.

43. Reid, K. A., "Impact of Technology on Learning Effectiveness," Center for Excellence in Distance Learning (CEDL), Lucent Technologies, *lucent.com/cedl,* 1999.

44. Schell, G. P., "The 'Introduction to Management Information' Course Goes Online," *Proceedings of the Americas Conference of the Association for Information Systems,* Milwaukee, WI, August 2000.

45. Shin, B., et al., "Telework: Existing Research and Future Directions," *Journal of Organizational Computing and Electronic Commerce,* Vol. 10, No. 2, 2000.

46. Smith, G. S., and O. Rist, "Collaboration (Groupware)," *Internetweek,* January 19, 1998.

47. Sterne, J., *Customer Service on the Internet: Building Relationship, Increasing Loyalty, and Staying Competitive,* 2nd ed. New York: Wiley, 2000.

48. Storm, D., "Videoconferencing," *Internet World,* September 1997.

49. Stricker, C., et al., "Market-based Workflow Management for Supply Chains of Services," *Proceedings of the 33rd Hawaiian International Conference on Systems Sciences (HICSS),* Hawaii, 2000.

50. Tedeschi, B., "A Fresh Spin on 'Affinity Portals' to the Internet," *New York Times on the Web,* April 17, 2000.

51. "Tools for Conferences, Meetings, and Distance Learning," *Presentations,* Vol. 13, No. 12, December 1999.

52. Watad, M. M., and F. J., DiSanzo, "Case Study: The Synergism of Telecommuting and Office Automation," *Sloan Management Review,* Vol. 41, No. 2, Winter 2000.

53. Weiss, G., *Multiagent Systems: A Modern Approach to Distributed AI.* Cambridge, MA: MIT Press, 1999.

PART II
The Web Revolution

CHAPTER

5

Electronic Commerce

LEARNING OBJECTI

After studying this chapter, y

1. Describe electronic con benefits, limitations, an
2. Describe the major appl in the B2C area, includi
3. Discuss the importance a research and customer se
4. Describe B2B models and r chain management.
5. Describe e-commerce in service
6. Describe other e-commerce applica (auctions, C2C, m-commerce, and e-government).
7. Describe the e-commerce infrastructure, extranets, and EDI.
8. Compare the various electronic payment systems, describe the role of smart cards, and discuss e-payment security.
9. Discuss legal and ethical issues related to e-commerce.
10. Describe failure factors of e-commerce.

L CORPORATION EMBRACES THE WEB

THE PROBLEM

Corporation, the world's largest producer of microprocessor chips, sells its prod- s to thousands of manufacturers. Competition in the chip market is intense. In- creates customized catalogs and sends them to its potential customers together ith information on product availability. Until 1997 it was all done on paper. Fur- hermore, orders from Intel's thousands of customers, distributors, and business partners worldwide were received by fax and phone, making the distribution process slow, expensive, and frequently not up to date. In 1997 some departments launched their own electronic order handling, which resulted in incompatible and inefficient systems.

THE SOLUTION

In 1998, Intel established its Web-based e-business program. The program focuses on online ordering for a range of products. Order placing is the major part of the program but not the only part. Intel's order site also features self-service order tracking and a product documentation library. This library of Intel products replaces the work of customer service representatives who previously sent information manually to customers.

In its e-business program, Intel specifically targeted small and mid-size customers, the majority of which operate outside the United States. These companies had previously communicated with Intel mostly by phone and fax, whereas larger companies typically were connected to Intel via electronic data interchange (EDI) networks. Eleven of Intel's larger customers also were connected in fall 1998 to a system called Supply Line Management, which lets Intel link across the Internet to customers' plants in order to track parts consumption.

By 2001 Intel was using various Web-based portals to deliver personalized information to its customers and employees. New applications include procurement of material and services from suppliers. Intel claims that it is doing e-business more than any other company in the world.

THE RESULTS

The e-business initiatives enhance Intel's competitive advantage by giving its customers better tools for managing transactions. At the same time the system brings substantial tangible savings. For example, the company has been able to eliminate 45,000 faxes per quarter to Taiwan alone.

Sources: Compiled from *InternetWeek,* November 23, 1998, pp. 1, 98; from "Intel Goes E-Business," *intel.com/eBusiness/enabling/ebusiness.htm* (Dec. 28, 1999); and from *intel.com,* press releases (2001).

BUYING CHEMICALS VIA CHEMCONNECT

www.chemconnect.com

THE PROBLEM

The market for industrial chemicals and plastics is very fragmented. For most products there are thousands of buyers and hundreds of sellers. Some products can substitute for each other, the quantities sold are not large, and buyers repeat their purchasing at long intervals. A large number of retailers and wholesalers intervene, charging high commissions, in a very inefficient and inconsistent (in terms of pricing) market. Very few buyers and sellers in the market are happy with it.

THE SOLUTION

Buyers and sellers of chemicals and plastics can now meet in a large Internet marketplace called ChemConnect. Using this network, global industry leaders, such as British Petroleum, Dow Chemical, BASF, Hyundai, and Sumitomo, find new markets and trading partners around the globe.

ChemConnect provides a trading marketplace and an information portal to 12,000 members in 125 countries (membership is free). In 2001, more than 60,000 products were traded in this public e-marketplace. This unbiased, third-party market offers three trading places: (1) A *public exchange floor.* Here, members can post items for sale or bid anonymously, at market prices. (2) The *commodities floor.* This space allows some 200 companies to buy, sell, and exchange commodity products, online in real time through regional trading hubs. (3) *Corporate trading rooms.* In these private online auctions, members negotiate contracts and spot deals (one-time, as-needed purchases) in timed events managed by ChemConnect.

In the three trading spaces, up-to-the-minute market information is available and can be translated to 30 different languages. Members pay transaction fees only for successfully completed transactions. Business partners provide several support services, such as financial services for exchange members. A large catalog organizes, by category, offers to sell and requests to buy, including starting prices and shipping terms.

The exchange works with certain rules and guidelines that ensure an unbiased approach to the trades. There is full disclosure of all legal requirements, payments, trading rules, etc. (Click on "Legal info and privacy issues" at the Web site.)

THE RESULTS

ChemConnect is growing rapidly, adding members and trading volume. Although it is too early to assess the full impact of this exchange, it is clear that the customers like it. Very few leave, and many more join every week. The site shows a buy-side savings of 20 to 30 percent and sell-side premiums of 9 to 50 percent. The major savings are due to lower commissions, more efficient market prices, and integrated supply-chain services provided by approved partners.

LESSONS LEARNED FROM THESE CASES

These two opening cases illustrate two different ways of conducting business in the digital economy. The Intel case illustrates business-to-business (B2B) activities, where trading is done between businesses. (B2B accounts for about 85 percent of all EC volume.) Intel is both buying and selling electronically. In addition Intel provides customer services online. (Intel has several other EC initiatives that are not described here, as most large corporations do.) We call the model exemplified by the Intel case a **company-centric e-marketplace**. This model has either one seller and many buyers, or one buyer and many sellers. The ChemConnect case introduced the concept of an **electronic exchange** (also known as an e-exchange or more simply, an exchange), where many buyers, many sellers, and other business partners congregate electronically. ChemConnect is a third-party market maker, which provides a platform to sell, buy, conduct auctions and bids, and more. In both cases, the objective is to do business better, faster, and cheaper, to share information, and to provide superb customer and partner services.

In this chapter we present, in a condensed form, the essentials of electronic commerce, which is a widely varied and ever-changing topic. (A complete, book-length coverage is available in Turban et al., 2002.) Topics covered in this chapter include the benefits of EC; direct retail marketing and advertising, market research, and customer service; the essentials of B2B, intrabusiness (B2E), and service industry applications; the emerging areas of mobile commerce, auctions, and consumer-to-consumer EC; the payment systems that support EC; and legal, ethical, and public policy issues.

5.1 FOUNDATIONS OF ELECTRONIC COMMERCE

The two opening cases illustrate a new way of conducting business, called **electronic commerce (e-commerce, or EC)**. As we've seen in previous chapters, EC involves making business transactions via telecommunications networks, primarily the Internet. Electronic commerce may occur between businesses and consumers (such as takes place when a consumer orders a book from Amazon.com) or between businesses. It can also be done between a government and other parties, between individual consumers, and between a company and its employees (B2E).

The term electronic commerce is viewed by some as being fairly narrow, referring only to transactions conducted in an **electronic marketplace**. Thus, many instead use the term **e-business** (or **e-biz**) to refer to a broader definition of EC that involves not just buying and selling, but also servicing customers, collaborating with business partners, and conducting electronic transactions within an organization. We use the various terms interchangeably in this book.

Electronic commerce is a diverse, interdisciplinary topic, with issues ranging from technology, addressed by computer experts, to consumer behavior, addressed by behavioral scientists and marketing research experts. In this section we survey the foundations of electronic commerce, including history, a conceptual framework, benefits, various models, and infrastructure requirements.

History and Scope

Electronic commerce applications began in the early 1970s with such innovations as electronic transfer of funds. However, the applications were limited to large corporations and a few daring small businesses. Then came electronic data interchange (EDI), which expanded EC from financial transactions to other kinds of transaction processing. This development extended the types of participating companies from financial institutions to manufacturers, retailers, and services. Since the commercialization of the Internet and the introduction of the Web in the early 1990s, EC applications have expanded rapidly. Over the last years we have witnessed many innovative applications, from large-scale direct marketing to auctions and electronic procurement. In fact, buying food from a vending machine with a smart card or with a cellular phone is also considered EC. Today, almost every company in the United States has a Web site, many with thousands of pages and diversity of applications.

The Electronic Commerce Framework

Many people associate EC with having a presence on the Web. While presence and the related advertisement is important, e-commerce is much broader than that. The framework pictured in Figure 5.1 shows the content of the field of EC and the relationship among its major components. The top of the figure shows

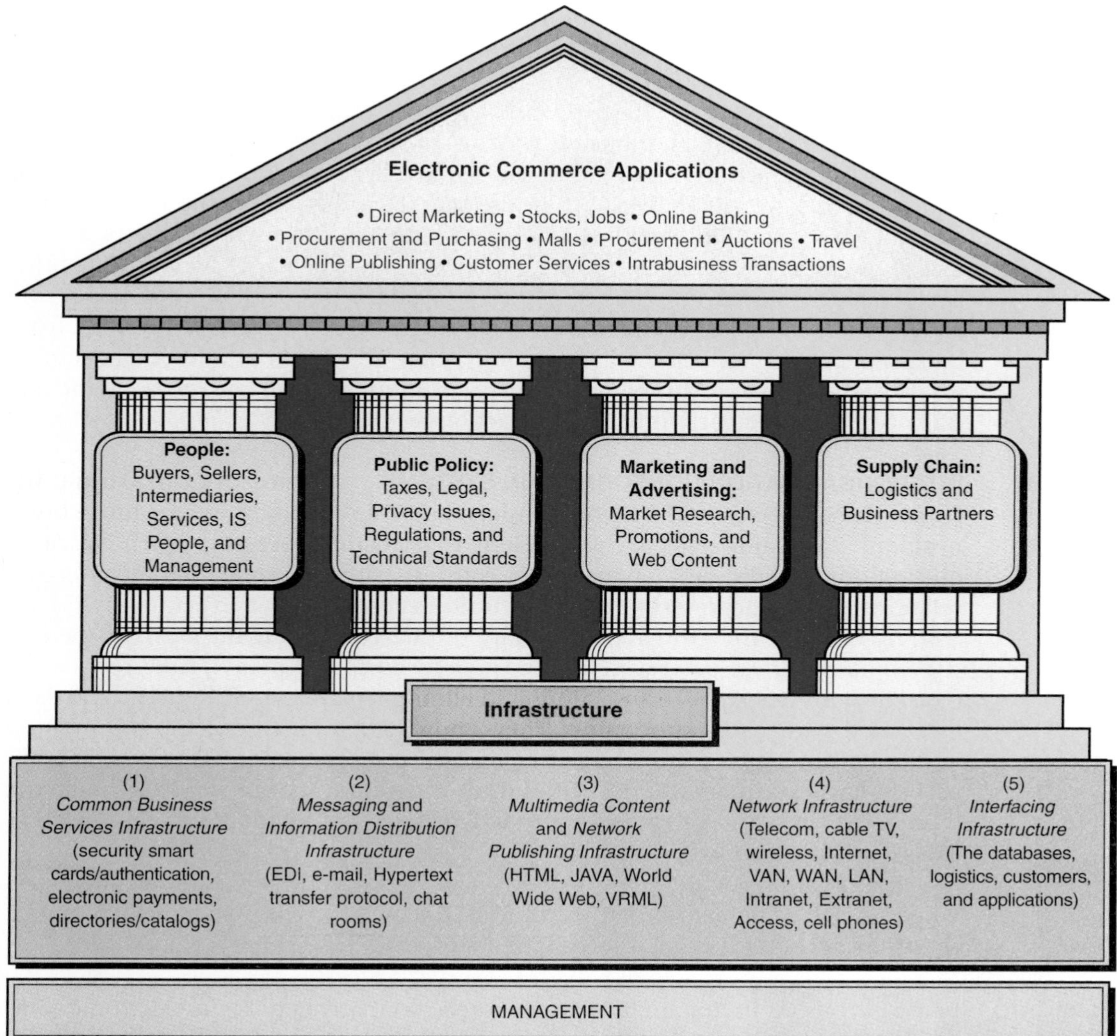

FIGURE 5.1 A framework for electronic commerce.

the major applications of EC. These include direct marketing, home banking, shopping in electronic stores and malls, buying stocks, finding a job, conducting auctions and bids, collaborating electronically with business partners around the globe, and providing customer service.

These applications are supported by four major support categories (shown as supporting pillars in the figure): (1) people and participating organizations; (2) public policy, standards, and regulations, including security and protocols; (3) marketing and advertising, including marketing research; and (4) supply chain management and logistics, including business partners. To deliver EC applications it is necessary to have several types of infrastructure (lower part of picture). Finally, EC management coordinates all of the above and makes decisions on strategy, outsourcing, joint ventures, and the like.

Electronic Markets and Interorganizational Information Systems

The field of EC can be divided into two segments: electronic markets and interorganizational information systems. Lately there has been a trend to combine the two.

ELECTRONIC MARKETS. Electronic markets are rapidly emerging as an important vehicle for conducting business. An *electronic market,* or e-marketplace, is a network of interactions and relationships where information, products, services, and payments are exchanged. When the market is electronic, the business center is not a physical building but a network-based location where buyers, sellers, and other partners meet electronically to conduct business interactions. The principal participants not only are at different locations but seldom even know one another. The means of interconnection vary among parties and can change from event to event, even between the same parties. The market handles all the necessary transactions, including the transfer of money. Electronic markets include B2C, company-centric, and B2B transactions

INTERORGANIZATIONAL INFORMATION SYSTEMS. An **interorganizational information system (IOS)** involves information flow among two or more organizations. Its major objective is efficient transaction processing, such as transmitting orders, bills, and payments. In contrast with electronic markets, here all relationships are predetermined; there is no negotiation, just execution. IOSs are a direct result of the growing desirability of interconnecting business partners to streamline business processes. The reasons to do so are many: They reduce the costs of routine business transactions and eliminate paper, inefficiencies, and costs associated with paper processing. They improve the quality of the information flow by reducing or eliminating errors. They compress cycle time in the fulfillment of business transactions regardless of geographical distance. They make the trading process easy for users, and they facilitate coordination and collaboration along the supply chain.

Interorganizational systems are used exclusively for B2B applications, whereas electronic markets exist in the B2B and B2C cases. As indicated earlier, the trend recently has been to combine the two.

Benefits and Limitations of Electronic Commerce

Few innovations in human history encompass as many benefits as electronic commerce. The global nature of the technology, the low cost, the opportunity to reach hundreds of millions of people, the interactive nature, the variety of potential applications, and the resourcefulness and rapid growth of the Internet result in many benefits to organizations, individuals, and society. These benefits are just starting to materialize, but they will increase significantly as EC expands.

BENEFITS TO ORGANIZATIONS. The major benefits of EC to organizations are:

- E-commerce allows a vendor to *reach a large number of customers, anywhere* around the globe, at a very *low capital outlay and operating cost.*
- Companies can procure materials and services from other companies *rapidly* and can do so 5 to 20 percent *less expensively* than they could otherwise.
- Marketing distribution *channels* can be *drastically cut* or even eliminated, simultaneously making products cheaper and vendors' *profits higher.* Ultimately, some intermediaries are eliminated, allowing direct *one-to-one marketing* and sales.

- E-commerce *decreases the cost* of creating, processing, distributing, storing, and retrieving paper-based information by as much as 90 percent.
- E-commerce allows *reduced inventories* and overhead by facilitating a "pull"-type supply chain. In a *pull* system the process starts with the customer's order and uses just-in-time production and delivery processing. This allows *product customization* and *lower inventory costs.*
- Customer services and relationships are facilitated by *interactive, one-to-one* communication, at a low cost.
- E-commerce may *reduce the time* between the outlay of capital and the receipt of products and services.
- E-commerce *lowers telecommunications cost,* as the Internet is much cheaper than value-added networks (VANs).
- E-commerce enables innovative business models that *increase competitiveness and profitability.*
- *Advertisement* can be *media-rich,* be *changed* frequently, reach *large audiences,* and be *customized.*

Electronic commerce can also help small businesses to compete against large companies. For example, Egghead Software closed all of its physical stores in 1998 and moved completely to the Web because of its inability to compete in the conventional marketplace with large software distributors, such as CompUSA. Egghead added items other than software to its product mix, and in 1999 merged with the online auction company Onsale, adding another distribution channel. This example demonstrates a case of a changing *business model.* New and modified business models are greatly facilitated by EC.

BENEFITS TO CONSUMERS. EC's major benefits to consumers are:

- E-commerce frequently provides customers with *less expensive* products and services by allowing them to shop in many places and conduct quick, online comparisons.
- E-commerce provides customers with *more choices.* They can select from many vendors and from more products.
- E-commerce enables customers to shop or do other transactions *24 hours a day,* year round, from almost any location.
- Customers can receive relevant and *detailed information* and *other services* in seconds, rather than in days or weeks.
- E-commerce enables consumers to get *customized products and services,* from PCs to cars, at competitive prices.
- E-commerce makes it possible for people to *participate in virtual auctions.* Thus, customers can obtain unique products and collectors' items that might otherwise require them to travel long distances to a particular auction place at a specific time.
- E-commerce allows customers to *interact* with other customers and with vendors in *electronic communities,* to exchange ideas and share experiences.

BENEFITS TO SOCIETY. EC's major benefits to society are:

- E-commerce is a major facilitator of the digital economy, which enables the United States and other countries to enjoy extended economic growth, with low inflation, resulting from high productivity.
- E-commerce enables more individuals to *work at home* and to do *less traveling,* resulting in less traffic on the roads and *lower air pollution.*
- E-commerce allows some goods to be sold at lower prices, so less-affluent people can buy them, *increasing their standard of living.*
- E-commerce enables people in developing countries and rural areas to *enjoy products and services that otherwise are not available to them.* This includes opportunities to learn professions and earn college degrees, or to receive better medical care.
- E-commerce *facilitates delivery of public services,* such as government entitlements, reducing the cost of distribution and fraud, and *increases the quality* of the social services, police work, health care, and education.

LIMITATIONS OF ELECTRONIC COMMERCE. The spread of EC has been slowed somewhat by some limitations, which can be classified as *technical* and *nontechnical.* These limitations are listed in Table 5.1.

As time passes, these limitations, especially the technical ones, will lessen or be overcome. Also, appropriate planning can minimize the impact of the limitations. Despite these limitations, very rapid progress is occurring in electronic com-

TABLE 5.1 Limitations of Electronic Commerce

Technical Limitations

1. Lack of universally accepted standards for quality, security, and reliability.
2. Insufficient telecommunications bandwidth.
3. Still-evolving software development tools.
4. Difficulties in integrating the Internet and EC software with some existing (especially legacy) applications and databases.
5. The added cost of special Web servers in addition to the network servers.
6. Expensive and/or inconvenient accessibility to the Internet for some.

Nontechnical Limitations

1. Many legal issues as yet unresolved, including the issue of taxation.
2. National and international government regulations and standards are not developed for some circumstances.
3. Difficulty of measuring some EC benefits, such as Web advertisements. Methodologies for justifying EC are in their infancy.
4. Many sellers and buyers are looking for EC to stabilize before they take part in it.
5. Customer resistance to the change from a real to a virtual store. People do not yet sufficiently trust paperless, faceless transactions.
6. The perception that electronic commerce is expensive and unsecured. As a result, many do not even want to try EC.
7. In many EC activities, lack of a critical mass (sufficient number) of sellers and buyers needed for profitable EC operations.

merce, especially in fields such as auctions and sales of stocks, books, CDs, and computers. Also, corporate procurement and direct sale to businesses, as well as B2B marketplaces, are expanding. As experience accumulates and technology improves, the ratio of EC benefits to cost will increase, resulting in an even greater rate of EC adoption.

Models of Electronic Commerce

There are various types or models of e-commerce, as indicated in the following list. B2B e-commerce accounts for about 85 percent of all EC volume. The remaining types make up the other 15 percent.

- ***Business-to-business (B2B).*** These are transactions where the buyers and sellers are organizations.
- ***Business-to-consumers (B2C).*** In this case the sellers are organizations; the buyers are individuals.
- ***Consumer-to-businesses (C2B).*** In this case consumers make known a particular need for a product or service, and organizations *compete* to provide the product or service. (An example is Priceline.com, where the consumer names the price and suppliers try to fulfill it.)
- ***Consumer-to-consumer (C2C).*** In this case an individual sells products or services to other individuals. A special case of this is *peer-to-peer (P2P).*
- ***Intrabusiness (intraorganizational) commerce.*** In this case an organization uses EC internally to improve its operations. A special case of this is known as *B2E* (business to its employees).
- ***Government-to-citizens (G2C) and others.*** In this case the government provides services to its citizens via EC technologies. Governments can do business with other governments as well as with other organizations.
- ***Collaborative commerce (c-commerce).*** In this type of EC, business partners collaborate electronically. Such collaboration frequently occurs between and among business partners along the supply chain. In Chapter 6 we will demonstrate how retailers and manufacturers forecast demand together.
- ***Mobile commerce (m-commerce).*** When e-commerce is done in a wireless environment, such as using cell phones to access the Internet, we call it *m-commerce.*

EC Infrastructure

For the activities represented in the various EC models, companies use diverse infrastructures. Of special interest are the Internet, intranets, EDI, and extranets. Some companies use only one of the above; others use them all. Let's examine how this is done in a hypothetical company, Toys Inc. As shown in Figure 5.2 (p. 174), Toys Inc. has a corporate intranet for conducting all its internal communication, collaboration, dissemination of information, and accessing of databases. It uses a corporate extranet (shown on the left side of the figure) to communicate with its large business partners (suppliers, distributors, noncorporate retail stores, salespeople, liquidators). In addition, Toys Inc. is connected to the toy industry extranet (upper-right portion of Figure 5.2), which includes other manufacturers, professional associations, and large suppliers.

The company may also be networked to additional extranets. For example, some major corporations may allow Toys Inc. to connect to their intranets, via their extranets. Toys Inc. is also connected with its banks and other financial

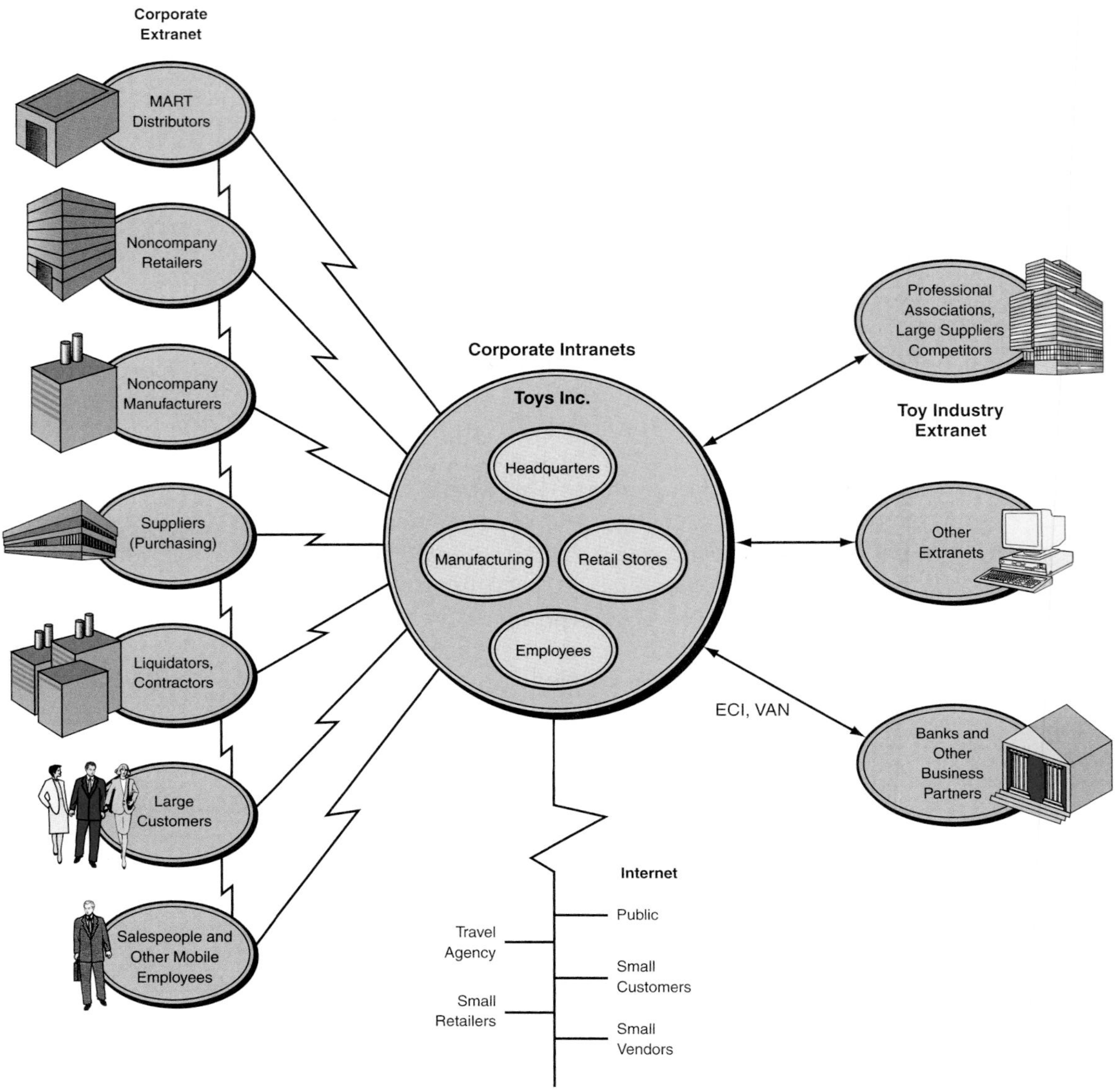

FIGURE 5.2 How a company uses the Internet, intranet, and extranets.

institutions (loan providers, stock issuers) over a highly secured EDI that runs on a VAN. The company also uses the VAN-based EDI with some of its largest suppliers and other business partners. An Internet-based EDI is used with smaller business partners that are not on the corporate EDI or extranet. Finally, the company communicates with individual customers, public agencies, and others over the Internet.

Many companies are moving toward a similar network configuration. Today, it is almost impossible to do business without being connected through an EDI, extranets, and the Internet to one's business partners. These topics will be revisited in Section 5.7.

5.2 DIRECT RETAIL MARKETING AND ADVERTISEMENT

There are many potential applications of EC that will foster trading between businesses and individual customers (B2C). The projected 750 million Internet users within 3 to 7 years could generate a huge volume of business-to-consumer transactions. Because of limited space, we can describe here only some of the major categories of such applications.

For decades, home shopping from catalogs has flourished, and television shopping channels have been attracting millions of shoppers since the 1980s. However, paper catalogs become quickly outdated, and television shopping is limited to what is shown on the screen. These limitations of conventional home shopping can be overcome by electronic retailing.

Electronic Retailing

With electronic commerce you can buy from home, 24 hours a day, 7 days a week. The Web offers you a wide variety of products and services, including the most unique items, usually at lower prices. In addition, you can get very detailed information on products in seconds, and you can easily search items and compare prices. Finally, you can easily interact and communicate with vendors and other shoppers. **Electronic retailing** is direct sale (B2C) through electronic storefronts or in electronic malls, usually designed around an electronic catalog format. Some companies such as Wal-Mart Online sell to corporations as well (B2B), usually at discounts for large quantities.

STOREFRONTS AND MALLS. In electronic retailing, there are several selling channels: solo electronic storefronts, electronic malls, shopping portals, and metamalls.

Electronic Storefronts. Solo **electronic storefronts** maintain their own Internet name and Web site. They may or may not be affiliated with electronic malls. Electronic retail stores may be extensions of physical stores, such as Disney Online, The Sharper Image, and Wal-Mart Online. Others are new businesses started by entrepreneurs who saw a niche on the Web. Examples of pioneering sites are *wine.com*, *amazon.com*, and *hothothot.com*. There are two types of storefronts: *general* and *specialized*. Specialized storefronts sell one or a few products (flowers, wines). The general stores sell many products. Amazon.com began as a specialized storefront, selling books, but has since expanded to a general storefront.

Electronic Malls. An **electronic mall**, also known as a **cybermall**, is a collection of individual shops under one Internet address. The basic idea of an electronic mall is the same as that of a regular shopping mall: to provide a one-stop shopping place that offers many products and services. With a keystroke, browsing people become potential shoppers as they explore cybermalls. As is true of regular shopping malls, a vendor that locates itself in a mall gives up a certain amount of independence: Its success depends on the popularity of the entire collection of stores as well as on its own efforts. On the other hand, malls generate streams of prospective customers who otherwise might never have stopped by the store.

Representative cybermalls are: Downtown Anywhere (*da.awa.com*), HandCrafters Mall (*cactushill.com*), America's Choice Mall (*choicemall.com*), *shopnow.com*, and Shopping 2000 (*shopping2000.com*). Each of these malls may include thousands of vendors. For example, *shopnow.com* listed over 30,000 stores in 1999.

Of special interest is the Internet Shopping Network (*internet.net*), a futuristic mall.

A cybermall may supply the same look and feel to all its tenants, or it may just link its tenants' own electronic home pages. Some malls offer prizes and entertainment to draw shoppers and encourage them to stay. For example, America's Choice Mall offers a "5-minute multimedia tour" contest for success stories about products, services, or leasing associated with the mall. An overview of mall shopping and a list of major malls is available at *cybermall.com*.

Shopping Portals. Several of the Internet portals offer extensive shopping services. Examples are: *shopping.yahoo.com*, *aol.com/shopping*, *eshopmsn.com*, and *shopping.altavista.com*. Most of the shopping on these portals is done via affiliation. It is basically a referral service.

Metamalls. In an attempt to make shopping easier, the next logical step is to provide one-stop shopping over multiple malls. This concept is referred to as **metamalls**. Metamalls allow customers to shop in different malls using one search engine to find items. In addition, customers are able to pay *only once*, for purchases made in different malls, in a highly secure system. The metamall can provide other services such as comparative pricing and finding substitute products. An example of a pioneering metamall is Metaland of Korea (*metaland.com*). Major department stores, banks, and manufacturers sponsor Metaland.

WHAT DO PEOPLE BUY MOST ONLINE? Goods that are sold most often online are: computers and computer-related items, books and magazines, CDs, cassettes, movies, videos, clothing and shoes, toys, and food. Services that are sold most often online include: travel services, stocks and bonds trading, electronic banking, insurance, and job matching. (Online service industries are presented in Section 5.5.)

DIRECT SALE VS. USE OF AN INTERMEDIARY. **Business-to-consumer (B2C)** electronic commerce can be done in two major ways: (1) companies can sell direct from the manufacturer or service-provider to the customer; those that sell direct typically use a storefront or a company-based auction place; or (2) companies can use an intermediary, such as a mall.

Selling Direct to Customers. Some companies have sold direct to customers for decades, avoiding distributors. Fuller Brush and Avon are examples. Most recently, Dell has sold computers direct to customers. However, most companies have used distributors and retailers to reach customers, seeing these channels as the best way to reach large numbers of customers. Some companies use both methods. With the advent of television and telemarketing, more companies moved to direct marketing, avoiding expensive intermediaries. Direct marketing has another advantage—the ability to personalize products and services. An example of company that has successfully used direct marketing in this way is Dell Computer.

The Internet provides an unprecedented opportunity to sell direct to customers. And indeed several companies, like Dell, have succeeded in direct selling. Other examples are *happypuppy.com*, which started as a way to sell electronic games developed by its founders, and *hothothot.com*, which started by selling hot sauces made by the company. In both cases, the companies became virtual retailers, or **e-tailers**, selling the products of others as well.

Sometimes electronic retailing is used as an additional distribution channel for companies that also sell through traditional channels. Lego, the giant Danish toy maker, is selling some of its products (Mindstorms, Robotics) online, and only in about a dozen countries. Lego decided not to offend its many distributors by offering more of its products online. In this way, Lego is trying to avoid a **channel conflict**—a situation in which manufacturers become distributors and thus compete with their established distribution channels.

ELECTRONIC INTERMEDIARIES. Most of the B2C volume is generated by the use of electronic *intermediaries,* which sell others' products (or services) online. Selling by retailers overcomes the channel conflict mentioned above. Two types of intermediaries exist online: (1) pure online e-tailers such as Amazon.com and CDNOW, and (2) the so called **"click-and-mortar" retailers**, which sell both offline and online.

E-Tailers. The excitement about Internet commerce that started in 1995 was accompanied by extended media coverage and high expectations. Stories about e-tailers doubling their sales every few months encouraged entrepreneurs to create more and more e-tailers, backed by seemingly unlimited venture capital. Everyone wanted to be the next Amazon.com. (See the *IT at Work box,* below.) Several companies succeeded in gaining a substantial share of the e-market. Names such as Amazon.com, egghead.com, CDNOW, and peapod.com became well known. However, most of these companies started to fail in 2000, for reasons to be discussed later.

Click-and-Mortar Retailers. A large number of traditional "brick-and-mortar" retailers are selling on the Internet as well. Typical examples of click-and-mortar retailers are Wal-Mart online, ToysRUs.com, and Barnes and Noble.com. In such cases the online operation competes with the offline business, creating possible conflicts in resource allocation and pricing of products.

IT at Work

THE ONE-STOP (MEGA) E-TAILER: AMAZON.COM

www.amazon.com

Amazon.com got its start selling books. Soon it found that the infrastructure created to sell books and the experience gained from doing so could be used successfully for additional products (such as CDs, jewlery, and gifts). Amazon carefully selected only products that sell well on the Internet.

In 2000, Amazon changed its business model by signing long-term agreements with other e-tailers. These agreements turn Amazon into an entry point for other e-tailers that need a brand name. The first example was living.com, a furniture e-tailer. The concept was simple: A customer who entered Amazon and searched Amazon's "Furniture" menu was referred to *living.com.* (Unfortunately, living.com failed just a few months after it collaborated with Amazon, so neither company really got to see how well this partnership would work.) A similar arrangement exists between Amazon and *cardirect.com* and between Amazon and *toysrus.com.* In the latter case, Amazon became part owner of ToysRUs online. Their 10-year agreement could become a model for other click-and-mortar companies that prefer to separate their online business from the brick-and-mortar one. Under the agreement, ToysRUs designs products, does market research, and procures the toys. Amazon advertises, takes orders, and fulfills the orders.

For Further Exploration: Do you think there are any logical limits to this business model? What do you think Amazon.com should be looking for in e-tailing partners? What kinds of e-tailers should be looking to partner with Amazon?

Advertising Online

Opening a storefront is necessary but is seldom sufficient to attract visitors and buyers. Being in a mall may generate additional traffic. But a necessary solution to attract visitors and customers, in either case, is to advertise.

INTERNET ADVERTISEMENT. *Advertisement* is an attempt to disseminate information in order to affect a buyer-seller transaction. Traditional advertisement on TV or in newspapers is impersonal, one-way mass communication. Using telemarketing to reach individual customers personalizes advertisement and marketing. But when done on the phone, or with direct mail, advertising can be expensive, slow, and ineffective at times. *Internet advertisement* redefines the meaning of advertisement. It is media-rich, dynamic, one-to-one, and interactive, and it can reach large numbers of people at relatively low cost.

Why Internet Advertisement? The major reasons for advertising on the Internet are as follows:

- Ads can be updated any time with a minimal cost, so they can always be timely.
- Ads can reach very large numbers of potential buyers all over the world.
- Online ads are frequently cheaper in comparison with television, radio, newspaper, or billboard ads. Traditional ads are expensive since their costs are determined by space occupied (print ads), how many days (times) they are shown, and position (front page in newspaper, prime TV time), etc.
- Web ads can efficiently use text, audio, graphics, and animation.
- The use of the Internet itself is growing very rapidly, so the audience for Internet advertising is growing.
- Web ads can be interactive and targeted to specific interest groups and/or individuals.
- Customers can move easily and quickly from viewing an ad to getting details and to ordering.

To better understand why businesses would choose to advertise on the Internet, see Table 5.2, which compares the benefits and the shortcomings of the major advertisement media.

There are several advertisement methods on the Internet. The most common ones are banners, e-mail, and URL placement.

Banner Advertisement. As you drive along a highway, you see countless billboards on the sides of the road. The same is true as you make your way along the information superhighway. A *banner* is an electronic billboard. As you surf your way through the Internet, banners are everywhere. Banner advertisement is the most commonly used form of advertising on the Internet.

Typically, a banner contains a short text or graphical message promoting a product or a vendor and urging the viewer to connect to its Web site ("click on the link"). Banners may contain video clips and sound. Advertisers go to great lengths to design a banner that catches consumers' attention. Designers of banners pay a lot of attention to the content, media, and size of the image in the banner. Because long downloading times may cause a viewer to become impatient and move on even before the banner is fully displayed, the size of the banner and its multimedia content should be carefully controlled.

There are two types of banners: *keyword banners* and *random banners.* **Keyword banners** are banners that appear when a predetermined word is queried

TABLE 5.2 Benefits and Shortcomings of the Major Advertisement Media

Medium	Benefits	Shortcomings
TV	• Intrusive impact—high awareness getter. • Ability to demonstrate product and feature "slice of life" situations. • Time is sold in multiprogram packages. • Very "merchandisable" with media buyers.	• Ratings fragmenting, rising costs, "clutter." • Heavy "downscale" audience skew. • Time is sold in multiprogram packages. Networks often require major upfront commitments. Both limit the advertiser's flexibility.
Radio	• Highly selective by station format. • Allows advertisers to employ time-of-day or time-of-week to exploit timing factors. • Copy can rely on the listener's mood or imagination.	• Audience surveys are limited in scope, do not provide socioeconomic demographics. • Difficult to buy with so many stations to consider. • Copy testing is difficult, few statistical guidelines.
Magazines	• Offer unique opportunities to segment markets, demographically and psychographically. • Ads can be studied, reviewed at leisure. • High impact can be attained with good graphics and literate, informative copy.	• Reader controls ad exposure, can ignore campaign, especially for new products. • Difficult to exploit "timing" aspects.
Newspapers	• High single-day reach opportunity to exploit immediacy, especially on key shopping days. • Reader often shops for specific information when ready to buy. • Portable format.	• Lack of demographic selectivity, despite increased zoning—many markets have only one paper. • High cost for large-size units. • Presumes lack of creative opportunities for "emotional" selling campaigns. • Low-quality reproduction, lack of color.
Internet	• Internet advertisements are accessed on demand 24 hours a day, 365 days a year, and costs are the same regardless of audience location. • Accessed primarily because of interest in the content, so market segmentation opportunity is large. • Opportunity to create one-to-one direct marketing relationship with consumer. • Multimedia will increasingly create more attractive and compelling ads. • Distribution costs are low (just technology costs), so the millions of consumers reached cost the same as one. • Advertising and content can be updated, supplemented, or changed at any time, and can therefore always be up-to-date. Response (clickthrough rate) and results (page views) of advertising are immediately measurable. • Ease of logical navigation—you click when and where you want, and spend as much time as desired there.	• No clear standard or language of measurement. • Immature measurement tools and metrics. • Although the variety of ad content format and style that the Internet allows can be considered a positive in some respects, it also makes apples-to-apples comparisons difficult for media buyers. • Difficult to measure size of market, therefore difficult to estimate rating, share, or reach and frequency. • Audience is still relatively small.

Source: Based on N. Meeker, "The Internet Advertising Report," Morgan Stanley Corporation, 1997.

from a search engine. This type of banner is effective for companies who want to narrow their target audience. **Random banners** appear randomly. A main purpose for using random banners could be to introduce new products, or to keep a well-known brand, such as Amazon.com or IBM, in the "public eye."

A 1998 study by AOL showed that 9 out of 10 people responded favorably to banner advertisement. About 50 percent of the viewers recalled ads immediately after seeing them (*adage.com*, March 15, 1998).

A major advantage of using banners is the ability to customize them to the target audience. If the computer knows who you are or what your profile is, advertisers can send a banner that matches your interests. At minimum, the advertiser can target a market segment. Another advantage of banners is that they enable advertisers to use a *forced advertising* marketing strategy. Customers are forced to see the banners that come into view before the content the customer was searching for. A major disadvantage of banner advertising is the high overall cost. Although Internet advertising is cheaper than TV or newspaper advertising, banner advertisement is expensive compared to other online ads. Another major drawback of using banners is that they allow only limited information to be conveyed. Also, the ratio of people clicking on banners to pages viewed is declining. Hence advertisers need to think of creative but short messages to attract viewers.

E-Mail Advertisement. E-mail is emerging as a cost-effective marketing channel with a better and quicker response rate than other advertisement channels. Marketers develop or purchase a list of e-mail addresses, use them as a customer database, and then send advertisements to customers—via e-mail. A list of e-mail addresses can be a very powerful tool that enables marketers to target a group of people with similar profiles, or even specific individuals.

E-mail advertising can be used in various ways. The most common usage is to send advertisement material to potential buyers. The recipient can then be linked to a Web site to receive more information and to place an order. E-mail can also be used for customer service. Customers can e-mail queries to a company and get answers. Also, a company can send information about new products or services it thinks the recipient may have an interest in.

What happens, though, when every marketer starts inundating prospects and customers with e-mail, in what is referred to as **spamming**? How will consumers respond? What must marketers focus on to ensure e-mail marketing success? The answers to these and similar questions will determine the success of e-mail marketing. Unfortunately, the answers to these questions are not always known. However, if the reactions of consumers to telemarketing calls are any indication, there may be some pressure for government regulation of unrequested e-mail (anti-spamming regulation). Also, customers can block e-mail from any source. Programs such as *junkbusters.com* and *getlost.com* can block banner ads as well.

In light of this, marketers employing e-mail must take a long-term view and work toward the goal of motivating consumers to continue to open and read messages they receive. This is especially important as even today nearly one-third of consumers read e-mail only from senders with whom they have a relationship. As the volume of e-mail increases, consumers' tendency to screen messages will rise as well.

URL Advertisement. The major advantage of using a *URL* (universal resource locator) as an advertising tool is that it is free. Any company can submit its URL to a search engine and be listed. Also, by using a URL the company can lock in a targeted audience and filter out uninterested viewers because of the key word function. However, the URL method has several drawbacks. First, due to intense competition, even if a company is placed at the top of the list generated by a search engine, its position can quickly be occupied by others. To overcome this limitation, a company may decide to register with several search engines. However, with several thousand search engines to choose from, each of which indexes its listing differently, deciding which ones to register with becomes complex. Professional consultants are ready to help (for a fee) to optimize the chance to make the top of the list and thereby maximize exposure.

Online Events and Promotions (Sponsorship). A Web site without visitors has little value. There are several ways to attract visitors to a site and induce them to buy. Here we will discuss some of the strategies involved in attracting visitors. Contests, quizzes, giveaway samples, and coupons are as integral a part of Internet commerce as they are in offline commerce. There are dozens of innovative ideas in use. Here are some examples:

1. Yoyodyne Inc. conducts giveaway games, discounts, contests, and sweepstakes, whose entrants agree to read product information of advertisers ranging from Major League Baseball to Sprint Communication. For example, Yoyodyne organized a contest in which H&R Block, the tax-preparer, paid $20,000 toward the winner's federal taxes. Yoyodyne also offers multisponsor games.
2. Netzero and others offer free Internet access in exchange for viewing ads.
3. Both *egghead.com* and *lucent.com* use real people to talk to you over the phone about your interests, and then they "push" ads to your computer.
4. Cybergold (now part of *mypoint.com*), Goldmine (*goldmine.com*), and others connect you with advertisers who *pay you* money or give you discounts in exchange for reading ads and exploring the Web.
5. Riddler (*riddler.com*) provides an opportunity to play games in real time and win prizes. People also play games at the site for fun alone.
6. Netstakes runs sweepstakes that, in contrast with contests, require no skill. You register only once and can randomly win prizes (see *webstakes.com*). Prizes are given away in different categories. The site is divided into channels, each with several sponsors. The sponsors pay Netstakes to send them traffic. Netstakes runs online ads, both on the Web and in e-mail lists that people requested to be on.
7. Other ideas include giving free PCs to qualified customers (*freepc.com*), paying a penny a page for viewing ads (*gotoworld.com* and *tripod.com*), and giving free samples and coupons (*clickrewards.com*).
8. Two Web sites, *hotcoupons.com* and *supermarkets.com*, offer consumers any discount coupons they want. All consumers have to do is select the store where they plan to redeem the coupons, and print them. In the future, transfer of coupons directly to the virtual supermarket (such as *peapod.com* or *netgrocer.com*) will be available so that you can receive discounts on the items you buy there.

In general, the marketing principles behind running promotions on the Internet are similar to those used for running offline promotions (Aronson et al., 1999; Chase et al., 1998; O'Keefe, 1997; and Sterne, 1999).

Other Forms of Internet Advertisement. Online advertisement can be done in several other ways including chat rooms, newsgroups, and kiosks. Of special interest is advertisement to members of **Internet communities** (see Chapter

16). Community sites such as *geocities.com* offer a targeted advertisement opportunity, where members can buy the advertised products at a discount. There are also ads that link consumers to other sites that might be of interest to the community members. Targeted ads may also go to members' personalized Web pages.

In addition, advertisement on Internet radio is just beginning, and soon advertising on Internet television will commence. With the surge in wireless phones connected to the Internet, ads are also starting to appear on cellular phones.

SOME ADVERTISEMENT ISSUES. Numerous issues surround Internet advertisement. We present here, in brief, several important issues related to designing Internet advertising. In addition, there are numerous other implementation issues, such as how to design ads for the Internet, where and when to advertise, and how to integrate the online and offline ads. For details on those and other topics, see O'Keefe, 1997; Meeker, 1997; and Sterne, 1999.

Customizing Ads. Because there is so much information on the Internet for customers to view, filtering the irrelevant information by providing *customized ads* can be beneficial to customers and advertisers alike. BroadVision's Web site (*broadvision.com*) is an example of a customized ad platform. Its software, named One-to-One, allows the rapid creation of secure and robust visitor-centered Web sites. The heart of One-to-One is a customer database, with registration data and information gleaned from site visits. Using this software, a marketing manager can customize display ads based on users' profiles. For examples of how to customize ads, see the demos at *micromass.com* and *bcentral.com*.

Segmentation. With increased used of marketing databases, companies started to classify customers by age, gender, location, and other characteristics. Each group is called a *segment*. America Online, for example, divides its millions of customers into over 200 segments. Companies may sell to interested advertisers the e-mail addresses of people in various segments. Segmentation is not as effective as a one-to-one personalized approach, but it is much cheaper.

Webcasting. Another model of customized ads can be found in *webcasting*. For example, *webcast.com* provides a free Internet news service that broadcasts personalized news and information. This is an information "push" strategy, and the technology that makes it possible is called **push technology**. When a user establishes his or her system, the user selects the type of desired information, such as sports, news, headlines, stock quotes, and so on. The webcasting company then sends the user the information he or she wants ("pushes" it at the user), but at the same time also sends customized banner ads.

Permission Marketing. Traditional telemarketing interrupts consumers when they are doing somethng else, such as eating dinner. This does not leave them with a positive feeling, nor does it put them in the mood to buy the product or service being marketed. As consumers gain increasing control of information, marketers must be increasingly clever about finding ways to communicate their brand messages. **Permission marketing** is one answer. It offers consumers incentives to voluntarily accept advertising and e-mail. How is it done? Ask people what they are interested in, ask permission to send them information, and then do it in an entertaining, educational, or interesting manner.

Permission marketing is the basis of many Internet marketing strategies. For example, some 1.7 million Net users receive American Airlines e-mails each week. Users of this marketing service can ask for notification of low fares to exotic (or not-so-exotic) places. In addition, users can easily unsubscribe at any time. Permission marketing is also extremely important for market research (e.g., see *mediametrix.com*).

In one particularly interesting form of permission marketing, *AllAdvantage.com* built a customer list of 5 million people who are happy to receive advertising messages whenever they are on the Web. This is because they are being paid $0.50 an hour to view these messages while they do their normal surfing. They also are paid $0.10 an hour for the surfing time of any friends they refer to AllAdvantage. AllAdvantage charges advertisers for space in the view bar on user screens, but instead of pocketing all the money they collect, they split it with customers. Furthermore, from the referrals it gets from customers, AllAdvantage is able to further increase its customer base.

Viral Marketing. The customer referrals at AllAdvantage are an example of one type of viral marketing. **Viral marketing** refers to word-of-mouth marketing, which has been used for generations, but whose *speed* and *reach* are multiplied many fold by the Internet. It is one of the new models being used to build brand awareness at a minimal cost. It has long been a favorite strategy of online advertisers pushing youth-oriented products. The main idea in viral marketing is to have people forward messages to friends, asking them, for example, to "check this out." You can distribute a small game program, for example, which comes embedded with a sponsor's e-mail, that is easy to forward. By releasing a few thousand copies, vendors hope to reach many more thousands.

Examples abound: *coshopper.com*, a Singapore auction site, allows users to type in friends' e-mail addresses; Coshopper then e-mails those friends with details about its service. Similarly, in the 2000 U.S. Presidential election, the Bush campaign Web site urged supporters to bring in new backers via e-mail. The person in each state who recruited the most support won an autographed picture of then-Governor Bush and a commemorative Bush-Cheney 2000 jacket. In July 2000, the promoters of Lee Jeans posted fictitious home pages of three "dorky" people on its site, hoping that people would forward the funny pictures to others. Then, the company began to use the same characters in its printed ads. This approach was also used by the founder of Hotmail, which grew at its inception from zero to 12 million subscribers in just 18 months. Viral marketing also was used successfully by blueskyfrog.com to give away five free SMS cell phone messages for every friend you bring in. Within a few months, this Australian company had over a million subscribers.

Unfortunately, though, several e-mail hoaxes have spread via viral marketing also. A danger of viral advertisement is that a destructive virus can be added to an innocent advertisement, related game, or message. However, when used properly, the innovative approach of viral marketing, known also as **advocacy marketing**, can be both effective and efficient. For details, see Helm (2001).

MEASURING THE EFFECTIVENESS OF ADVERTISEMENTS AGAINST THEIR COST. Justifying advertising expenses is a difficult task. Therefore the pricing of ads on Web sites becomes an important issue in EC. The major methods of charging for ads are the following:

1. The most common measure used to determine ad payments is ad view (or impressions). An *ad view* is the number of times users see a banner ad during a specific time period. It is analogous to paying for TV ads by the number of viewers (exposure).

2. Another measure by which ads are charged is paying only when a customer clicks on a banner and moves to the advertiser's Web home page. This method is preferred by some large advertisers, such as Procter & Gamble.
3. Some advertisers prefer to pay only if the customer clicks on a banner, moves to the advertiser's site, and while there seeks product leads or fills out questionnaires. This is a more accurate measure than the previous two methods.
4. Finally, the amount of actual purchases made on the Web is the most precise measure. In this method, companies pay a commission of 3 to 15 percent for customers who click on the banner, move to their site, and actually make a purchase. This method is used in what is called **affiliate programs**. Companies such as Amazon.com and CDNOW.com have many thousands of affiliates.

It's often hard to measure the effectiveness of a particular ad. With online advertisement, this problem is even tougher. It is difficult to know what are the real benefits of Internet ads to advertisers because:

- It is difficult to relate the number of ad views to actual purchases. One problem is that 100 ad views can be recorded by one person visiting the site 100 times or by 100 users visiting it once each. Obviously, there is a major difference between the two.
- The number of *unique visitors* at a site during a specific time can be calculated by recording some form of user registration or identification. This overcomes the problem cited above.
- It is not known whether visitors who do not buy online while visiting a site will buy offline later. Such purchases may or may not be related to the online advertising.

ELECTRONIC CATALOGS. Printed catalogs have been a medium of advertisement for a long time. Electronic catalogs on CD-ROM and on the Web are newer, and more powerful. The merchants' objective in preparing **online catalogs** is to advertise and promote products and services to customers who use the catalogs as a source of information. With the help of search engines, customers can quickly search electronic catalogs and can compare products very effectively. Electronic catalogs consist of a product database, a directory, search capability, and a presentation function.

In the early stage of online catalogs, most were a replication of text and pictures from the vendors' printed catalogs. Today, electronic catalogs are dynamic, customized, and integrated with selling and buying procedures such as order taking and payment.

Comparing Online Catalogs with Paper Catalogs. Table 5.3 contrasts the advantages and disadvantages of online catalogs with those of paper catalogs. Online catalogs have significant advantages, but one big disadvantage: Customers need computers and the Internet in order to access online catalogs. However, since Internet access is becoming available from cell phones, kiosks, TV, and inexpensive computers, we can expect many paper catalogs to be replaced by, or at least be supplemented by, electronic catalogs.

Customized Catalogs. A *customized catalog* is a catalog assembled specifically for a client company, usually a customer of the catalog owner. It can be also tailored to individual consumers in certain cases. There are two approaches

TABLE 5.3 Comparisons of Online Catalogs with Paper Catalogs

Type	Advantages	Disadvantages
Paper Catalogs	• Easy to create a catalog without high technology. • Reader is able to look at the catalog without a computer system. • More portable than electronic catalog.	• Difficult to promptly update changed product information. • Only a limited number of products is displayed. • Limited information is available through photographs and textual description. • No possibility for advanced multimedia such as animation and voice.
Online Catalogs	• Easy to update product information. • Able to integrate with the purchasing process. • Good search and comparison capabilities. • Able to provide timely, up-to-date product information. • Provision for global range of product information. • Possibility of adding voice and motion pictures. • Cost savings. • Easy to customize. • More comparative shopping. • Ease of connecting order processing, inventory processing, and payment processing to the system.	• Difficult to develop online catalogs; large fixed cost. • Customer needs skill to deal with computers and browsers.

to customized catalogs. The first approach is to let the customers identify the interesting items out of the total catalogs, as is done by One-to-One from *broadvision.com.* In this approach, customers do not have to deal with irrelevant topics.

The second approach is to let the system automatically identify the characteristics of customers, based on their transaction records, and build catalogs accordingly. For collecting data on individuals, *cookie* technology is used to trace the transactions. A **cookie** is a small data file placed on users' hard drives when they first visit a site, which can later be used to track users' actions and preferences. However, to generalize the relationship between the customer and items of interest, such technologies as *collaborative filtering* (see Turban et al., 2002) or *data mining* are needed. (See Chapters 4 and 11.) This second approach, of letting the system define customer characteristics, can be effectively combined with the first one. Customized catalogs are used mainly in B2B, as will be described in Section 5.4.

The Impact of EC on Traditional Retailing Systems

What is the impact of EC on traditional retailing systems? Let's look at two representative issues: the elimination of traditional distribution channels and the rise of new ones, and the impact of EC on distribution strategy.

DISINTERMEDIATION AND REINTERMEDIATION. In the traditional distribution channel, there are intermediating layers, such as distributors, wholesalers, and retailers, between the manufacturers and the consumers. In Japan, for example, there sometimes exist ten layers of intermediaries, which add a 500 percent markup to cost. The presence of the Internet as a marketing and product-selection vehicle is making customers question the value offered by traditional distribution channels. Using the Internet, manufacturers can sell directly to customers and provide customer support online. In this sense, the traditional intermediaries may be eliminated. We call this phenomenon **disintermediation**.

Some intermediaries, such as supermarkets, play the role of *aggregators*. That is, they offer thousands of products from hunderds of manufacturers to thousands and thousands of customers. This intermediary role is needed, but the existing intermediaries can be replaced by electronic intermediaries. These electronic replacements can improve the supply chain, reduce inventories, and deliver to the customer's door at lower cost, or in a more convenient way.

In response to this change, traditional intermediaries like retailers and some department stores have initiated online storefronts while still keeping their traditional way of doing business. Some manufacturers, like automakers, still need to cooperate with dealers, though in a different way. In addition, new electronic intermediaries—e-malls and product-selection agents—are emerging. Occurrence of a new breed of electronic intermediaries is called **reintermediation**. An example of reintermediation is that of Rosenbluth International (discussed in the opening case in Chapter 3). The company started to provide value-added services from which it derives its income rather than from commissions.

In some cases reintermediation is characterized by the shifting or transfer of the intermediary function, rather than the complete elimination of it. The new class of intermediaries includes e-malls, directory and search-engine services, market makers, and comparison-shopping agents.

IMPACT OF EC ON MANUFACTURERS' DISTRIBUTION STRATEGY. As the distribution channels undergo change, the strategies by which products are moved from manufacturers to customers also are changing. Distribution strategies in the digital era include the following:

1. ***Avoiding channel conflicts.*** In the late 1990s, Levi Strauss did not allow anyone else to sell the Levi's product on the Internet. The company wanted customers to have a single contact point in cyberspace for purchasing. By this decision, the company entered into a *channel conflict* with its major retailers. In this case, the conflict was between the new online channel and the traditional distribution channels. Levi Strauss decided to allow retailers to sell online. In spring 2000, the company decided to close its own Levi's online site.
2. ***Coexistence with the dealers.*** This is the case in car distribution. Auto-makers need to keep the traditional dealers to sell to non-Internet buyers and to provide services such as test-drives, financing, and maintenance. So, customized cars are sold on the Internet with dealers' participation (see the Jaguar case in Chapter 7).
3. ***Regionally mixed strategy.*** In certain regions a company may sell on the Internet, while in other regions it sells only through traditional retailers. For instance, Nike sells on the Internet, but only in the United States and a few other countries.

4. ***Restraint of competition by powerful distributors.*** Home Depot tried to pressure its suppliers not to market direct online. The company reminded its major suppliers, such as *Whirlpool.com,* that Home Depot has the right not to distribute products of suppliers who are actually competitors.
5. ***In-company channel conflicts.*** The creation of an online distribution channel may create a conflict with the same company's offline marketing and sales. Potential conflict areas are online versus offline product (service) pricing, resource allocation to advertisement, and handling of order fulfillment (see Turban et al., 2002).

5.3 CONSUMER BEHAVIOR, MARKET RESEARCH, AND CUSTOMER SUPPORT

In this section, we explore several issues related to consumers. First, it is important to know *who* the potential cyberconsumers are and *how* they make purchasing decisions. This knowledge can be gained through understanding consumer behavior and through market research. It is also important to understand the role of customer service.

Consumers and Their Behavior on the Internet

Two major types of consumers buy EC products and services: individuals and organizations. Most of the discussion in this section concentrates on the individual B2C shopper.

A key activity in EC implementation is finding out who are the actual and potential customers. Several studies used to be conducted periodically at Georgia Tech University (see *gtech.edu/gvu.user_surveys*) and are conducted today by several companies such as Ernst & Young (*ey.com/industry/consumer/internetshopping*) and *emarketer.com*. These surveys attempt to assess the demographics of Internet users and the activities of EC shoppers. They initially found that the vast majority of Internet users were mostly 15- to 35-year-old males. Now the situation is changing. The number of female users nearly equals that of males, and both younger and older surfers have joined the party. However, it may take several years before the Internet population exactly matches the general population mix.

The largest group of Internet users are married and highly educated; almost 90 percent are white. Most users are working in educational institutions, the computer industry, or professional jobs. The surfers have high household incomes. The amount of money spent on the Internet is increasing with users' experience. Men tend to buy more expensive items, usually computers. For those who do not buy over the Internet, the two major reasons cited are fear of inadequate security and quality uncertainty. (Both are discussed later.)

Online purchasing constitutes a fundamental change for customers. If the customer has previously used mail-order catalogs or television shopping, the change will not be so drastic. But moving away from a physical shopping mall to an electronic mall may not be simple. Furthermore, shopping habits keep changing as a result of innovative marketing strategies. Finding out what certain groups of consumers (such as teenagers or residents of certain geographical zones) want is the role of market research. And even if we know what consumers in general want, each individual consumer is very likely to want something different.

Market Research

Learning about customers is extremely important for any successful business, especially in cyberspace. Such learning is facilitated by market research. Market research has been conducted for decades in order to find out what motivates consumers to buy.

MODELS OF MARKET RESEARCH. Researchers have developed models (frameworks) that explain consumer behavior regarding purchasing decisions. We have developed a similar model for explaining consumer buying decisions on the Internet, as shown in Figure 5.3.

The purchasing process starts on the left, where factors that stimulate a consumer to think about buying are shown. As the consumer considers the need to buy, two types of factors influence the decision-making process (center): individual characteristics (top left), and environmental factors (top right). In EC there are several others factors that influence shoppers' decision making. These are shown at the bottom of the figure. These factors, which are controlled by the seller and/or the intermediary, range from technology to customer service. The model shows us that cybershopping is a complex process. It is clear from this model that there is much that sellers need to know about customers, since the seller controls all of the factors shown at the bottom of the figure, as well as being able to influence some of the stimuli factors (for example, through advertisement). Such knowledge is provided by market research.

The Internet is a powerful and cost-effective tool for conducting market research regarding consumer behavior, for identifying new markets, for investigating competitors and their products, and for testing consumer interest in new

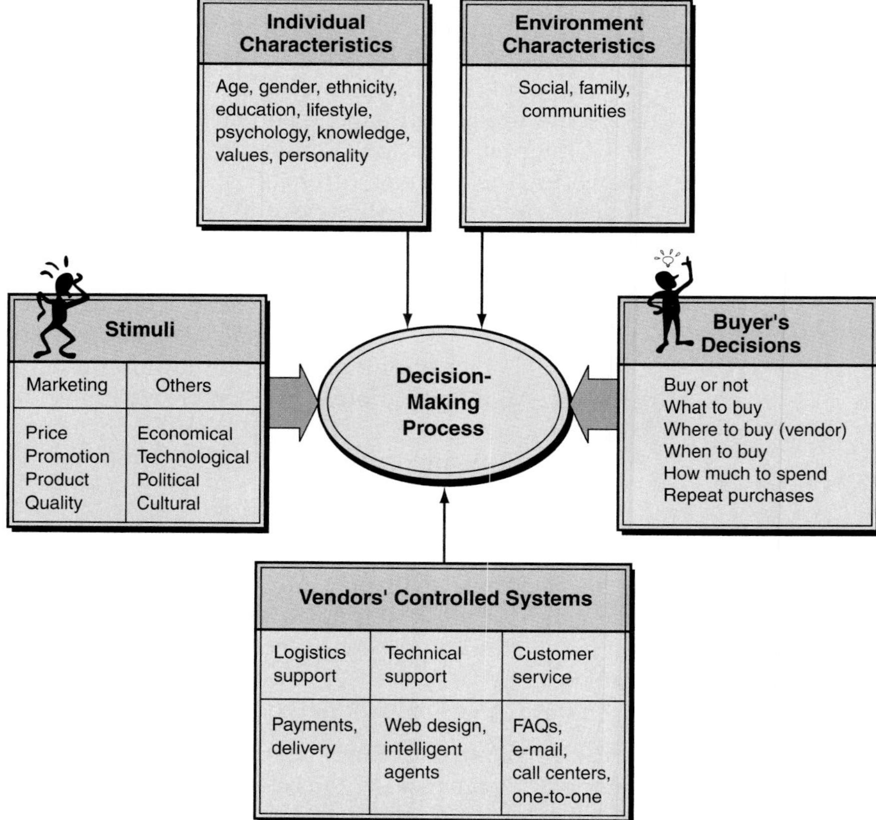

FIGURE 5.3 Model of EC consumer behavior. (*Source: Electronic Commerce: A Managerial Perspective,* by Turban/Lee/King/Chung, © 2000. Reprinted by permission of Pearson Education, Inc., Upper Saddle River, N.J.)

A CLOSER LOOK
5.1 HOW MARKET RESEARCH IS CONDUCTED ON THE INTERNET

PROCESS OF CONDUCTING THE RESEARCH

1. Define the target market.
2. Identify newsgroups to study.
3. Identify topics for discussion.
4. Subscribe to the pertinent groups.
5. Search discussion group topic and content lists to find target market.
6. Search e-mail discussion group lists.
7. Subscribe to filtering services that monitor groups (such as *reference.com*).
8. Read FAQs and other instructions.

CONTENT OF THE RESEARCH INSTRUMENT

1. Post strategic queries to groups.
2. Post surveys on your Web site.
3. Post strategic queries on your Web site.
4. Post relevant content to groups, with a pointer to your Web site survey.
5. Post a detailed survey in special e-mail questionnaires.

TARGET AUDIENCE OF THE STUDY

1. Identify the demographics of your Web site visitors. Compare them with the population demographics.
2. Determine your editorial focus.
3. Determine your content.
4. Determine what Web services to create for each type of audience.

Source: Compiled from T. Vassos, *Strategic Internet Marketing.* Indianapolis, IN: Que Publishing Company, 1996, pp. 66–68.

products. The findings of such research are essential for **one-to-one marketing**. This new interactive style of marketing allows one-to-one personal contact with customers, and it provides marketing organizations with greater ability to understand the consumers, market, and competition. For example, it can identify early shifts in consumer tastes and trends, enabling marketers to design products, services, and marketing opportunities that match these shifts. Market research also tells management when a product or a service is no longer popular. For a suggested process for market research, see *A Closer Look* 5.1.

HOW TO FIND OUT WHAT CUSTOMERS WANT. There are basically two ways to find out what customers want. The first is to ask them, and the second is to infer what they want by observing what they do on the Web.

Asking Customers What They Want. The Internet provides easy, fast, and relatively inexpensive ways for vendors to directly interact with consumers to find out what they want. The simplest way is to ask potential customers to fill in electronic questionnaires. To do so, vendors need to use some inducements. For example, in order to play a free electronic game, or participate in sweepstakes, you are asked to fill in a form and answer some questions about yourself. Frequently you are asked to "sign" an electronic agreement. Be sure to *read it very carefully even if it is very long.* From your direct answers, marketers learn what you say you want. They also try to infer from your answers about preferences in music, for example, what type of books, clothes, or movies you may be likely to prefer. This is done with the help of *intelligent agents,* as we will describe later.

Asking customers what they want may not be feasible in some cases. Customers may refuse to answer questionnaires, or they may provide false information (in about 40 percent of the cases, per Georgia Tech University Studies). Also, the administration of questionnaires can be lengthy and costly. Therefore, it may be necessary to use a different approach.

Tracking Customer Activities on the Web. Today it is possible to learn about customers by observing what they *do* on the Internet. Many companies offer site-tracking services, based on cookies or other approaches. For example, Internet Profile Corporation collects data from client/server logs and provides periodic reports that include demographic data such as which URLs customers are coming from, and where these URLs are located, or how many customers have gone straight from the home page to ordering. The company translates Internet domain names into real-company names and includes general and financial corporate information. Armed with this information, market researchers can make educated guesses about customers' interests and the kinds of products and services they can afford to buy. However, tracking customers' activities without their knowledge or permission may be unethical, or even illegal in some countries, even though the tracker does not know the name of the customer. This is an issue we'll discuss in Section 5.8.

Customer Service

THE PROCESS OF CUSTOMER SERVICE. In many cases, a competitive edge is gained by providing superb customer service. In electronic commerce, customer service becomes even more critical, since customers and merchants do not meet face to face (see Sterne, 1999). According to Ives and Learmouth (1984) and to McKeown and Watson (1998), customer service should be approached as a product life-cycle with the following four phases:

- ***Phase 1—Requirements:*** Assisting the customer to determine needs (providing photographs of a product, video presentations, textual descriptions, articles or reviews, sound bites on a CD, and downloadable demonstration files).
- ***Phase 2—Acquisition:*** Helping the customer to acquire a product or service (online order entry, negotiations, closing of sale, and delivery).
- ***Phase 3—Ownership:*** Supporting the customer on an ongoing basis (interactive online user groups, online technical support, FAQs and answers, resource libraries, newsletters, and online renewal of subscriptions).
- ***Phase 4—Retirement:*** Helping the client to dispose of a product or end a service (online resale, classified ads).

EXAMPLES OF CUSTOMER SERVICE. Many activities are conducted in each of the above phases. A few examples follow.

...in Marketing

- American Airlines (*aa.com*) offers flight and fare information such as flight schedules, fare quotes, and much more. This is an example of support for phases 1 and 2.

...in Production and Operations Management

- Dell, Compaq, and other computer vendors provide an electronic help desk for their customers. This is an example of supporting phase 3.
- Fidelity Investments (*fidelity.com*) provides investors with "the right tools to make their own best investment decisions." The site has several sec-

...in Finance

tions, which include daily updates of financial news, information about Fidelity's mutual funds, material for inteactive investment and retirement planning, and brokerage services. This is an example of support given to phase 1.

- Dell will help you to auction your obsolete computer, and Amazon will help you to sell used books (phase 4).

FACILITATING CUSTOMER SERVICE. Several tools are available for facilitating online customer service. The major tools, with their functionalities, are:

- ***Personalized Web pages.*** Customers build individualized pages at the vendor's site, and vendors provide customized information for them there. For example, some airlines will place your frequent-flier mileage status on a personalized page, eBay will show you your auction history, and E*Trade will show you your stock-trading history.
- ***A chat room.*** Customers can interact with each other and with the vendor's personnel, who monitor the chat room.
- ***E-mail.*** Vendors send confirmation, product information, and instructions to customers. They also can take orders, complaints, and other inquiries by this method.
- ***FAQs.*** Vendors provide online answers to questions customers ask.
- ***Tracking capabilities.*** Customers can track the status of their orders, services (such as FedEx shipments), or applications. Customers can find the status of their banking and stock activities, and more.
- ***Web-based call centers.*** A comprehensive communications center takes customers' inquiries in any form they come (fax, telephone, e-mail, letters) and answers them quickly. The service provides for quick problem resolution.

An application of Web-based call centers is becoming very popular, as shown in the case of Canadian Tire, in the *IT at Work* on page 192.

5.4 BUSINESS-TO-BUSINESS APPLICATIONS

In **business-to-business (B2B)** applications, the buyers and the sellers are organizations. B2B composes the majority of EC volume, and it covers a broad spectrum of applications that enable an enterprise or business to form electronic relationships with their distributors, resellers, suppliers, customers, and other partners. (Note that B2B applications also include those between government entities and the businesses they buy from or sell to.) B2B covers all activities along the supply chain (see Handfield and Nichols, 1999), including all internal operations. However, when using B2B e-commerce, organizations may need to redesign their business processes along the supply chain, as discussed in Chapter 6.

B2B Models

There are three primary B2B models: **sell-side**, **buy-side**, and **exchanges**.

1. ***Sell-side model.*** A sell-side model refers to a situation in which one company sells electronically to many (*one-to-many*). There are two primary methods of

IT at Work

www.canadiantire.com

CANADIAN TIRE PROVIDES SUPERB CUSTOMER SERVICE VIA INTEGRATED CALL CENTER

Canadian Tire Acceptance Ltd. (CTAL), the financial services division of the $4 billion Canadian Tire Corp., Ltd., serves 4 million Canadian Tire credit card holders. In 1998 it became the primary call center of the company. It expects to increase sales and enhance customer retention systematically through a new effort to develop an integrated call center. It intends to eliminate annoying and time-consuming call transfers, ensuring that customers are treated on an individual basis. "The call center is a strategic asset," says Mary Turner, vice president of customer services at CTAL. "This is our main point of contact with the customer. We have to maximize it."

Canadian Tire Corp. had operated 10 call centers, each dealing with a different subject area (general information and retail, wholesale, service, etc.) or geographical zone. The demands on the call centers were heavy. CTAL's 10 call centers operated 24 hours a day, 7 days a week, and responded to more than 16 million calls each year. Call center representatives were expected to provide personalized service while handling a diverse set of customer needs—responding to more than 200 types of customer requests.

"When we began the project, we took a look at our operations and saw too many independent call centers," Turner continues. "It seemed that every time we introduced a new product or service, we set up a new call center. We decided to streamline operations to make it possible for customers to reach the right representative whenever they called." CTAL's new, integrated system ensures that any representative can resolve any customer need without handing it off to another department or departments.

CTAL has several key business objectives:

- Greater customer loyalty to Canadian Tire as a result of enhanced service
- Personalized customer attention and reduced transfers
- Rapid introduction of new products or changes to existing business services
- Reduced training requirements for customer-service representatives
- Integration of all customer "touch points" via a single system capable of handling Web, e-mail, and call center interactions

The call center integrates telephone, fax, e-mail, and the Web. One of its major capabilities is to build customer profiles and act on them when needed, providing one-to-one relationships. The new call center can be viewed as an *interaction center* that immediately recognizes the individual customer and integrates data that reflect on the relationship. The Web-based call center is expected to pay for itself quickly.

For Further Exploration: Why did the company have several call centers? What are the capabilities of the Web-based system, and what are its advantages?

Sources: Compiled from D. Peppers et al., *The One to One Fieldbook* (New York: Currency & Doubleday, 1999), and *canadiantire.com.*

---

selling: The seller may sell (1) direct from catalogs, or (2) direct via auctions (usually via *forward auctions*). The seller in this model can be either a manufacturer, a distributor, or a retailer (e.g., *bigboxx.com* and *marshall.com*). (See Timmers, 1999, for details.)

2. ***Buy-side model.*** In a buy-side model, one organization (usually large) buys from many vendors (*many-to-one*). There are several methods of buying: (1) The buyer may buy via a tendering system, also known as an RFQ method, or *reverse auction.* (2) The buyer may buy from approved suppliers at predetermined prices. In this case, all suppliers' catalogs are aggregated and organized on the buyer's Web site. Or, (3) the buyer may join a group-purchasing scheme.
3. ***Exchanges.*** Exchanges are e-marketplaces in which many buyers and sellers meet. There are several types of exchanges: (1) those that are owned and operated by a neutral third party (such as *ChemConnect.com*); (2) those that are owned and operated by one large company (such as *patents.ibm.com*); and (3) those that are owned by a consortium of either large buyers (such as *cor-*

procure.com, or *myaircraft.com*) or large sellers (such as *rooster.com* and *rubbernetwork.com*).

Let's look at each of these models in closer detail and examine some examples of them as well.

SELL-SIDE MARKETPLACE. In the *sell-side marketplace* model, organizations attempt to sell their products or services to other organizations electronically. This model is similar to the B2C model in which the buyer is expected to come to the seller's site (or a mall), view catalogs, and place an order.

In the B2B case, the buyer is an organization that may be a regular customer of the seller. The key mechanism in such a model is electronic catalogs that can be customized for each large buyer. Sell-side marketspaces provide an ordering system, a payment system, and integration of the incoming orders with the vendor's logistics system. Examples of companies that each sell billions of dollars using the sell-side model are Cisco, IBM, and Dell Computer. This model is used by thousands of companies, and it is especially powerful for companies with superb reputations, such as Intel. Large sellers sell directly from their Web sites. Alternatively, catalogs can be placed in industry malls or in distributors' Web sites.

EC is used in this seller-oriented model to increase sales, reduce selling and advertisement expenditures, increase delivery speed, reduce administrative costs (for example, by using electronic catalogs), and provide electronic-based customer service. An example is Cisco Systems, as described in the *IT at Work* example on page 194.

Another mechanism used in the sell-side model is auctions.

Forward Auctions. **Forward auctions** refer to auctions in which items are placed for sale and the bidders increase their bids sequentially until no one else raises the bid. At that point, the highest bidder gets the item. Several variations of such auctions exist (see Turban et al., 2002, Chapter 9). Sellers such as Dell Computer (*dellauction.com*) use this method extensively.

In addition to selling direct from their Web site, organizations can use auction sites, such as eBay, to liquidate items. Companies such as *freemarkets.com* are helping organizations to auction obsolete and old stuff (asset recovery programs). We will return to auctions later in the chapter.

Let's move now to the buy-side models.

BUY-SIDE MODELS FOR PROCUREMENT. The most popular buy-side model for large companies is the reverse auction. In **reverse auctions**, a company places an item for bid (or *tender*). Suppliers then submit offers to provide the item. In reverse auctions, bid prices *decline* as the auction continues, and the lowest bidder wins the job. Formerly, this method was done manually, either as a *sealed-bid* approach, in which bidders do not know what the other bidders submit, or where the pricing information was disclosed, resulting in several rounds of bidding. Reverse auctions are now done on the Internet, and these electronic reverse auctions function very efficiently.

Via the Internet, EC technology is used to improve the bidding and procurement processes. One variation of this model involves the buyer placing a *request for quotation (RFQ)* on its Web site, or in a bidding, at a third-party auction place. Once RFQs are posted, sellers (usually approved bidders) submit bids electronically. Information is visible, and the auctions take usually a short time (30

IT at Work

CISCO SYSTEMS ONLINE—A BILLION-DOLLAR BUSINESS

www.cisco.com

Cisco Systems is the major producer of routers, switches, and related network products sold to information systems departments worldwide. Cisco decided to go online since virtually all its customers were regular Web users. The company started to sell its products online in 1996 via Cisco Connection Online (CCO), and reached over $1 billion of business in 1997. By the end of 1996 more than 8,000 customers had registered for online trading. By 2001 more than 15,000 customers were buying about $7 billion a year.

Cisco Connection Online is delivered over an extranet, enabling customers to buy, communicate, and collaborate regarding any issue related to their orders, such as checking current purchasing order status. Customers can configure, price, and submit orders online with direct access to Cisco's database for pricing and configuration information. By correctly configuring and pricing equipment before submitting orders, customers eliminate rework, which can delay order processing. Submitted orders are deposited directly into Cisco's procurement database, where they are quickly queued for production scheduling. Built-in security features ensure that orders cannot be changed or deleted without authorization. Customers' credit lines are preapproved offline, and payments are settled electronically.

Customers like Cisco's electronic purchasing for its:

- Up-to-the-minute price information (available 24 hours a day)
- Quick replies to queries (hours, compared to days)
- Ability to configure the needed system and price it very quickly
- Easy order status and invoice checking
- Easy accessibility to maintenance contracts
- Availability of online technical support

The main benefits to Cisco of the electronic purchasing system are: (1) reduced customer service cost and improved service, (2) reduced marketing costs, and (3) reduced order-handling administrative costs.

For Further Exploration: Compare Cisco Connection to Disney Online. What are the similarities and differences?

Sources: Industry Week, April 21, 1997, pp. 69–70, and *cisco.com* (2001).

minutes to 2 hours). The lowest bids are then routed via the buyer's intranet to the engineering and finance departments for evaluation. Clarifications, if needed, are made via e-mail. The winner is notified electronically. In some cases, there is no need for evaluation, and the winner is notified a few minutes after the close of the auction.

This type of bidding procedure attracts large pools of suppliers because these bids are cheaper to prepare. General Electric (*gegxs.com;* see tpn post), the originator of the concept, saves 10 to 15 percent on the cost of the items placed for bid and up to 85 percent on the administrative cost. In addition, cycle time is reduced by about 50 percent. ChemConnect provides private rooms for conducting this type of bidding.

GE has also organized a market for small companies that use GE's trading process network (TPN) to post their RFQs (*gegxs.com;* find tpn). These companies pay GE a fee for this service and for handling support services like payments. In this capacity, GE acts as an intermediary. Likewise, General Motors uses a Web site (*covisint.com*) to buy both direct manufacturing materials and parts, and indirect materials (e.g., office supplies) via reverse auctions.

Buyer's Internal Marketplace. In this model suppliers' catalogs are aggregated in a master catalog on the buyer's server. The *buyer's internal marketplace* model is best suited for large companies and for government entities. It is mostly suitable for *maintenance, replacement, and operations* (MRO) indirect items, such as office supplies. In this model, a company has many suppliers, but the quantities purchased are relatively small.

Here is how the internal marketplace model works at MasterCard International: MasterCard buys large numbers of MRO items from many vendors. Once prices are agreed upon, the items are approved for purchase and placed on MasterCard's internal procurement system. About 10,000 items, from dozens of vendors, are listed in the company's catalog. Over 2,300 purchasers at various MasterCard offices around the world can view the catalog, select the appropriate products, electronically place orders, and pay with a MasterCard procurement card. This model enabled MasterCard to consolidate buying activities from many corporate locations and reduce the administrative processing costs. Also, procurement cycle time has been reduced in many cases from 20 days to just one. Finally, since MasterCard now has a smaller supplier base to buy from, the quantities purchased from each vendor are larger, so MasterCard has been able to negotiate larger purchase discounts.

Group Purchasing. A third buy-side purchasing model is group purchasing. In **group purchasing**, orders of small buyers are aggregated by a third-party vendor, such as *shop2gether.com* and *demandline.com*. Once buyers' orders are aggregated, they can be placed on a reverse auction, or a volume discount is negotiated.

EXCHANGES. *Electronic exchanges* (in short, *exchanges*) refer to e-marketplaces in which there are many sellers and many buyers. Sometimes these are referred to as *e-hubs*, or *portals*. There are basically four types of exchanges, according to Kaplan and Sawhney (2000):

1. ***Vertical distributors.*** These are B2B marketplaces where direct materials are traded in an environment of long-term relationship, known as **systematic sourcing**. Examples are *plasticsnet.com* and *commerxplasticsnet.com*. Negotiated and fixed prices are common in this type of exchange.
2. ***Vertical exchanges.*** Here direct materials are purchased on a "when needed" basis. Buyers and sellers may not even know each other. *ChemConnect.com* and *e-steel.com* are online examples. On vertical exchanges, prices are continually changing, based on the matching of supply and demand. This is called **dynamic pricing**. Auctions are typically also used in this kind of B2B marketplace.
3. ***Horizontal distributors.*** These are "many-to-many" e-marketplaces for indirect materials (MRO), when systematic sourcing is used. Prices are fixed or negotiated. Examples are *globalsources.com* and *alibaba.com*.
4. ***Functional exchanges.*** Here, needed services such as temporary help or extra space are traded on an "as needed" basis. Prices can be negotiated, and they vary, depending on supply and demand.

In all types of exchanges, one can find lots of services, ranging from payments to logistics. Vertical exchanges are frequently owned and managed by a group of big players in the industry. For example, Marriott and Hyatt own a procurement consortium, and Texaco and Chevron own an energy e-marketplace. The vertical e-marketplaces offer lots of e-community services (see Chapter 16). (To learn more about exchanges, see Schully and Woods, 2000.)

Since B2B activities involve many companies, specialized network infrastructure is needed. Such infrastructure works either as an EDI or as extranets. We will return to these topics in Section 5.7.

Organizational Buyers and Their Behavior

Although the number of organizational buyers is much smaller than the number of individual buyers, their transaction volumes are far larger and the terms of negotiations and purchase are more complex. In addition, the purchasing process may be more important than advertising activities in making sales to organizational buyers. In general, factors that affect individual consumer behavior and organizational buying behavior are quite different.

A BEHAVIORAL MODEL OF AN ORGANIZATIONAL BUYER. The behavior of an organizational buyer can be described by a model similar to that of the individual buyer we showed in Figure 5.3 (page 188). However, the specific variables may differ. (For example, the family and the Internet communities may have no influence.) What is added in this model is an *organizational module* that includes the organization's purchasing guidelines and constraints, the relationship among various buyers, the possibility of group decision making, and the organizational structure. Also important are interpersonal variables of the organizational buyer and the seller, such as authority, status, empathy, and persuasiveness. (For a detailed discussion of organizational buying, see Chapter 6 in Kotler and Armstrong, 1999.)

5.5 Using EC in Service Industries

Selling books, computers, toys, and most other products on the Internet reduces the cost to the customers by 20 to 40 percent. Further reduction is difficult to achieve since physical products must be physically manufactured and delivered. Unfortunately, only a few products such as software and CDs can be digitized to be delivered online for substantial savings. On the other hand, delivery of services, such as buying stocks or insurance online, can be done close to 100 percent electronically, with cost reduction of as much as 99 percent. Therefore, online delivery of digitizable services is growing very rapidly, with millions of new customers added annually.

In this section we describe several types of e-commerce used in service industries. These applications are not strictly B2C or B2B e-commerce; the buyers can be individuals (B2C) *or* organizations (B2B). The major online services to be discussed here are: banking, personal finance, investing in stocks, job matching, travel, and real estate. In addition to these, many other services are becoming available online. Examples are dating services (try *match.com*) and learning.

Cyberbanking

Cyberbanking is also known as **electronic banking**, virtual banking, home banking, and online banking. It includes all major banking activities (from paying bills to securing a loan) conducted from home, a business, or on the road instead of going to a physical bank location. Electronic banking saves time and is convenient for customers. For banks, it offers a chance to enlist remote customers and is an inexpensive alternative to branch banking (costing about 2 cents per transaction vs. $1.07 at the physical branch). Many banks now offer home banking, and some use EC as a major competitive strategy. Electronic banking offers several of the benefits of EC in Section 5.1, such as expanding the customer base and saving the cost of paper transactions. In addition to regular banks with added online services, we see the emergence of virtual banks, such as netbank.com, dedicated solely to Internet transactions. Many banks offer both B2C and B2B services.

...in Finance

An example is Wells Fargo, a large California Bank (over 1,700 branches). The bank has been known for generations for its financial services, dating back to the days of the Wild West. Wells Fargo's declared competitive strategy is cyberbanking. It plans to move millions of customers to the Internet and close hundreds of branches. A visit to the Wells Fargo Web site (*wellsfargo.com*) indicates the richness of services offered by the bank.

The services are divided into five major categories: online (personal) banking, personal finance services, small business banking, commercial banking, and international trade. In addition, there are employment opportunities listed, and even a virtual mall in which you can buy from the Wells Fargo Museum Store or be linked to other virtual stores such as Amazon.com. The bank offers many services in all categories. Most interesting are the services that cover all the needs of small businesses. These small-business services are extremely user friendly and can run even on an old 386 computer. The bank also saves money for small-business customers by offering lower loan rates.

...in Finance

THE CYBERBANKING PIONEER: SFNB. The Security First Network Bank (SFNB) was the first virtual bank, offering secure banking transactions on the Web (*sfnb.com*). The home page (see Figure 5.4) looked like the lobby of a bank. The bank offered regular banking services: savings and checking accounts, certificates of deposit, money market accounts, joint accounts, check imaging, loans, and other services. To attract customers, SFNB also offered relatively high interest yields for CDs and money market accounts. You could transfer money between accounts, review past statements and credit card transactions, pay bills, check balances in all your accounts and credit cards, and calculate the interest to be

FIGURE 5.4 Security First Network Bank.

paid on loans and credit cards. If you had a joint account with your parents and you were away from home, both you and your parents could view the account and add or withdraw funds. SFNB's operations were so successful that in March 1998 it accepted an attractive buyout offer for its online banking operations from Royal Bank of Canada, which continues to operate the virtual bank. The Canadian bank needed the online services in order to serve its customers while they are vacationing in the United States. The original company is now a software company that is marketing online banking software to many banks.

INTERNATIONAL AND MULTIPLE-CURRENCY BANKING. International banking and the ability to handle trading in multiple currencies is critical for international trade. Although some international retail purchasing can be done by giving your credit card number, other transactions may require international banking support. Two examples of such cross-border support follow:

1. Citicorp, in its corporate/institutional banking, offers a large number of internationally oriented banking services (see *citibank.com/e-business/homepage*). The bank also provides e-procurement solutions, billing, and much, much more.
2. Hong Kong Bank has developed a special system (called HEXAGON) to provide electronic banking across Asia. Using this system, the bank has leveraged its reputation and infrastructure in the developing economies of Asia to become a major international bank rapidly, without developing an extensive new branch network. For details, see the HEXAGON case on our Web site.

Online Bill-Paying and Personal Finance

PAYING BILLS ONLINE. One of the most popular electronic banking features is the ability to pay bills online. In August 1998, 90 percent of people surveyed in the Bay Area in California indicated a desire to pay bills on the Internet. Mostly, people prefer to handle as online payments their recurring monthly bills, such as rent or mortgage, telephone, utilities, credit cards, and cable TV. The recipients of such payments are even more eager than the payers to use online payment systems, since they can reduce processing costs significantly.

The following are the major existing billing presentation and payment systems in common use:

1. ***Automatic payment of mortgages.*** This method has been in existence since the 1980s. The customer authorizes its bank to automatically pay the mortgage, including property tax, every month.
2. ***Automatic transfer of funds to pay monthly utility bills.*** Since fall 1988 the city of Long Beach, California, has allowed its customers to pay their gas and water bills automatically from their bank accounts. Many utility companies, worldwide, also offer such services.
3. ***Paying bills from online banking account.*** Monthly bill payments can be made from the customer's bank account to creditors' accounts. Many people pay their credit card and other bills directly to the payees' bank accounts. Many people set up a list of companies with which they regularly do business and then each month direct the necessary amount to be paid directly into each payee's bank account.
4. ***Merchant-to-customer direct billing.*** Under this model, a merchant like American Express posts bills on its Web site, where customers can privately view

their account status and approve a funds transfer to pay it. However, in this system, customers have to go to many Web sites to retrieve their bills.

5. ***Using an intermediary.*** In this model, a third party like Microsoft's Money-Center consolidates all of a customer's bills in one site and in a standard format. Collecting a certain commission for its services, the intermediary makes it convenient both to the payee and payer to complete transactions. The payer pays all bills in one place.
6. ***Customer-to-customer payment.*** Let's say you need to pay someone for an item you purchased in an electronic auction, or you want to return money you borrowed from a friend. In these and other cases, you can use customer-to-customer payment services such as *paypal.com.* You can charge the payment to your credit card and (for a small fee) the money is transferred to the payee's bank account. For an interesting example of C2C payments, see *achex.com.*
7. ***Prepaid Internet purchasing.*** For people who do not have a credit card, or who do not trust the security system of the vendor, you can prepay purchases at 7-Eleven stores in Japan (for a small fee). Similar prepayment is available in some other countries in 7-Eleven stores (a joint project with American Express). With a prepaid e-shopping card, you get a PIN number, and then you can use the money, like a debit card, in participating online stores. For details see *cashx.com.*

PERSONAL FINANCE. Electronic banking is also often combined with personal finance and portfolio management. Specialized personal finance vendors offer a variety of diversified services. For example, both Quicken (from Intuit) and Money (from Microsoft) offer the following capabilities:

- Bill paying and electronic check writing
- Tracking bank accounts, expenditures, and credit cards
- Budget management and organization
- Record keeping of cash flow and profit and loss computations
- Portfolio management, including reports and capital gains (losses) computations
- Investment tracking and monitoring of securities
- Quotes and tradelines, historical and current prices
- Tax computations
- Retirement goals, planning, and budgeting

In addition, brokerage firms such as Schwab offer personal finance services such as retirement planning, in addition to stock transactions.

Online Stock Trading

It is estimated that in the year 2001, about 30 million people in the United States alone were using computers to trade stocks, bonds, and other financial instruments. In Korea, 60 percent of all stock trading was done online in 2000. Why? An online trade typically costs between \$5 and \$30, compared to an average fee of \$100 from a full-service broker or \$35 from a discount broker. There is no waiting on busy telephone lines, and the chance of making mistakes is small since there is no oral communication that may take place in a very noisy physical environment. Orders can be placed from anywhere, any time, and you can find a considerable amount of information regarding investing in a specific company or in a mutual fund. (See Internet Exercise 4.)

Integrating IT ...in Finance

How does online trading work? Let's say you have an account with Schwab. You access Schwab's Web site (*schwab.com/schwabonline*), enter your account number and password, and click on stock trading. Using a menu, you enter the details of your order (buy, sell, margin or cash, price limit, or market order, etc.). The computer tells you the current "ask" and "bid" prices of the stock, much as a broker would do on the telephone, and you can approve or reject the transaction. In the United States, Schwab, E*Trade, and other brokers are authorized to operate as stock exchanges. They can electronically match buy and sell orders and complete transactions in about one second (for most stocks).

Some well-known companies that offer online trading are E*Trade, Ameritrade (see Figure 5.5), and Suretrade. E*Trade offers many services and also challenges you to participate in a simulated investment portfolio. (See Internet Exercise 1.) The ability to trade financial securities online may have a major impact on individual investors: They now have tools that enable them to perform as well as, and sometimes even better than, some financial institutions.

In addition to stocks and bonds, online trading is expanding to include mutual funds, financial derivatives, commodities, and more. Futures exchanges around the world are positioning themselves for a market that many participants now agree will be dominated by electronic trading. In the near future we may see multicountry or even global exchanges, trading 24 hours a day.

INVESTMENT INFORMATION. There is an almost unlimited amount of investment information, mostly available for free, on many Web sites. Here are some examples:

- For municipal bond pricing, see *bondmarkets.org*.
- For overall market information and many links, see *cyberinvest.com* and *bloomberg.com*.
- For free advice from investment gurus, see *upside.com*.
- For stock screening and evaluation, try *marketguide.com*.

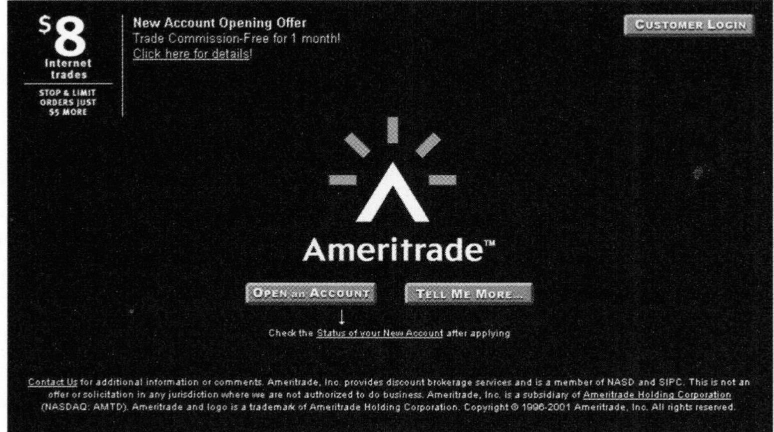

FIGURE 5.5 Trading stocks electronically.

- Articles from the *Journal of the American Association of Individual Investors* can be read online at *aaii.com.*
- For chart lovers, try *bigcharts.com.*
- For mutual fund evaluation and other related interesting investment information, see *morningstar.com.*
- Almost any investment information that you need will be provided to you by *yahoo.com.*
- Earnings estimates and much more can be found on *firstcall.com.*
- For current financial news and much more, try *cnnfn.com, hoovers.com,* and *yahoo.com/finance.*

Most of these services are provided free, together with financial news, global investment information, portfolio tracking, investor education, and much more. However, special reports are sold for a fee.

INITIAL PUBLIC OFFERINGS AND THE INTERNET. An *initial public offering (IPO)* is the first public sale of a company's stock. IPOs are attractive to investors because of the possibility of buying, at a low price, a stock that hopefully will experience significant price increases. IPOs typically are offered by large brokerage houses which charge a 7.5 to 10 percent commission.

Integrating IT ...in Finance

The first successful IPO offered for sale on the Internet was that of a beer-making company called Spring Street Brewing. The owner created a special company, Wit Capital Corporation (*witcapital.com*), to offer initial securities over the Internet and to allow for online trading in the shares once the initial offer was completed. Several other successful offerings followed. For example, Internet Venture Inc. raised $5 million in the spring of 1998 (*perki.net* and *ivn.net*). Also, directipo.com is active in this area. Virtual Wall Street brings together investors and companies interested in raising capital via direct public offering rather than using an underwriting syndicate. Auctions on IPOs also are being conducted by openipo.com.

The Online Job Market

The Internet offers a perfect environment for job seekers and for companies searching for hard-to-find employees. The job market is especially effective for technology-oriented jobs. However, thousands of companies and government agencies advertise available positions in all types of jobs, accept resumes, and take applications via the Internet.

THE PARTICIPANTS IN THE JOB MARKET. The job market is used by the following parties:

Integrating IT ...in Human Resources

1. ***Job seekers.*** Job seekers can reply to employment ads posted online. Alternatively, they can take the initiative and place resumes on their own home pages or on others' Web sites, send messages to members of newsgroups asking for referrals, and use recruiting firms such as Job Center (*jobcenter.com*) and Monster Board (*monster.com*). For entry-level jobs and internships for newly minted graduates, job seekers can try *job-direct.com.* Need help to write your resume and post it on the Net? Try *resume-link.com* or *jobweb.com.* To find the salary range that matches one's skills and experience, in major U.S. metropolitan areas, see *monsterjobs.com.* You can even learn how to use your voice in an interview (*greatvoice.com*).

2. ***Job offerers.*** Many organizations advertise openings on their own Web sites. Others use other sites ranging from popular portals to newspaper services, bulletin boards, and recruiting firms.
3. ***Recruiting firms.*** Thousands of job placement brokers are active on the Web. They use their own Web pages to post available job descriptions and to advertise their services in electronic mail and in others' Web sites. Recruiters use newsgroups, online forums, bulletin boards, and chat rooms. Job-finding brokers help candidates write their resumes and get the most exposure. Matching of candidates and jobs is done by companies such as *discoverme.com,* and *resumix.com*.
4. ***Newsgroups.*** Job finding is of interest to many newsgroups. These forums post jobs in certain categories or locations, conduct discussions about employment and employers, and allow readers to send resumes to potential employers. (Visit *1a.job* for examples.)

Smart Business Supersite (*smartbiz.com*) provides links to many sources for conducting further research, for accessing job listings, and for getting assistance from job counselors for a fee.

ADVANTAGES OF THE ELECTRONIC JOB MARKET. The major advantages of the electronic job market are:

FOR JOB SEEKERS

- Ability to find information on a large number of available jobs and employing companies worldwide
- Ability to quickly communicate with potential employers
- Ability to write and post resumes for large-volume distribution
- Ability to customize resumes quickly and at no cost
- Ability to search for jobs quickly from any place at any time
- Several support services available at no cost

FOR EMPLOYERS

- Ability to advertise to a large number of job seekers
- Ability to save on advertisement costs
- Ability to post job openings quickly
- Lower cost of processing applications (using electronic application forms)
- Ability to provide "equal opportunity" for job seekers
- Ability to find highly skilled employees, including those outside the area

LIMITATIONS OF THE ELECTRONIC JOB MARKET. Possible lack of security of one's employment information and of privacy about the job search are limitations of the electronic job market. Occasional stories surface about employers seeing (or worse, receiving) resumes of current employees who are looking for new jobs. But these problems are diminishing with security improvements. The electronic job market may also accelerate people's movements to better jobs, creating high and expensive turnover for employers. There is also a problem of information overload. In 2001, it was estimated that over 5 million resumes are on the Internet, as well as 2 million job openings. The problem of how to deal with so many listings may be addressed by use of intelligent agents (e.g., see *resumix.com*).

Travel and Tourism

Any experienced traveler knows that good planning and shopping around for the best rates can save a considerable amount of money. The Internet is an ideal place to plan, explore, and arrange almost any trip. Potential savings are available through special sales, auctions, name-your-price intermediaries, and the elimination of travel agents. Comprehensive travel online services can be found at *expedia.com, travelocity.com, travelweb.com,* and *orbitz.com*. Services are also provided online by all major airline vacation services, large conventional travel agencies, car rental agencies, hotels, and tour companies. Their online travel services allow you to purchase airline tickets, reserve hotel rooms, and rent cars. Most sites also support an itinerary-based interface, including a fare-tracker feature that periodically sends you e-mail messages about low-cost flights to your favorite destinations.

Travel Dispatch (from Expedia) is a digest of news stories that may affect your travel plans, including links to weather sites, currency converters, adventure magazines, and chat forums where users can share travel tips. Links to city maps, events, and ticket agencies online (such as ticketmaster.com) are also available. Some sites also include frequent-flier deals and special discounts. An interesting travel-related site is *priceline.com,* which allows you to set a price you are willing to pay for an airline ticket and hotel accommodations. The company then attempts to find a vendor that is willing to fulfill your wish.

Real Estate

Real estate transactions are an ideal arena for electronic commerce, for the following reasons. First, you can view many properties on the screen, saving time for you and the broker. Second, you can sort and organize properties according to your criteria and preview the exterior and interior design of the properties, shortening the search process. Finally, you can find detailed information about the properties and frequently get even more detail than brokers will provide. In some locations brokers allow the use of such databases only from their offices, but considerable information is now available on the Internet. For example, at *realtor.com* you can search a database of over 1 million homes all over the United States. The database is composed of local "multiple listings" of all available properties, in hundreds of locations. You also can apply for a mortgage online (*eloan.com*) or bid on a loan (*priceline.com*).

Home builders now use virtual-reality technology on their Web sites to demonstrate three-dimensional floor plans to potential home buyers. They use "virtual models" that enable buyers to "walk" through mockups of homes that can be built.

A Non-Internet Application

The applications presented so far have all been Internet-based. E-commerce is also being conducted on private lines (usually EDI) and increasingly offline, mainly with the use of smart cards (Section 5.6). Here is an example of a smart-card based, B2C non-Internet service.

Integrating IT ...in Production and Operations Management

THE HIGHWAY 91 PROJECT. Route 91 is a major eight-lane, east–west highway east of Los Angeles. Traffic is especially heavy during rush hours. To address this problem, the state of California allowed a private company, California Private Transportation Company (CPT), to build six express toll lanes along a 10-mile stretch in the median of the existing Highway 91. The express lanes system has only one entrance and one exit, and it is totally operated with e-commerce technologies. Here is how the system works:

Tollway commuters use transponders inside their cars to ease traffic and pollution problems on busy highways.

1. Only subscribers can drive the road. They receive an automatic vehicle identification (AVI) device that is placed on the rearview mirror of the car. The device, about the size of a thick credit card, includes a microchip, an antenna, and a battery.
2. A large sign over the tollway tells drivers the current fee for cruising the express lanes, which varies depending on traffic conditions. In 2001 it ranged from $0.50 in light traffic hours to $3.00 during rush hours.
3. Sensors in the pavement let the tollway computer know that a car has entered; the car does not need to slow or stop.
4. The AVI makes wireless radio contact with a transceiver installed above the lane.
5. The transceiver relays the car's identity through fiber-optic lines to the control center, where a computer deducts the fee from the driver's prepaid account. A monthly statement is sent to the subscriber's home.
6. Surveillance cameras record the license numbers of cars without AVIs. These cars can be stopped by police at the exit or fined by mail.
7. Video cameras along the tollway enable managers to keep tabs on traffic, for example, sending a tow truck to help a stranded car. Also, through knowledge of the traffic volume, pricing decisions can be made. Raising the price ensures the tollway will not be jammed.

The system saves commuters between 40 and 90 minutes each day, so it is in high demand. An interesting extension of this system is the use of the same AVIs for other purposes. For example, they can be used in paid parking lots. And one day you may be recognized when you enter the drive-through lane of McDonald's and a voice asks you, "Mr. Smart, do you want your usual meal today?"

5.6 M-Commerce, Auctions and Other Applications, and EC Failures

In the previous sections we mentioned auctions, wireless commerce, and other topics related to EC. Here we will elaborate on a few of these in more detail.

M-Commerce (Mobile Commerce)

Use of wireless and mobile networks and devices is growing quickly. Their widespread adoption creates an opportunity not only to transact applications that had been possible only from a PC, but also to conduct new applications online. **M-commerce (mobile commerce)** refers to the conduct of e-commerce via wireless devices. According to the GartnerGroup, the number of mobile devices in use worldwide is projected to top 1.5 billion by 2004. Furthermore, these devices can be connected to the Internet, enabling the conduct of transactions from anywhere the users are.

THE ECONOMIC ADVANTAGES OF M-COMMERCE. Besides the prospect of a large number of users, and the possibility of inexpensive Internet access, the following characteristics are driving the interest in m-commerce:

Mobility. M-commerce is appealing because wireless offers customers information from any location. Mobility implies that the Internet access travels with the customer. This enables customers to instantly act on any shopping impulse. Mobility is a benefit that appeals to vendors as well as customers.

Reachability. Reachability means that people can be contacted at any time. Of course, you can block certain times or certain messages.

These two characteristics—mobility and reachability—break the geographic and time barriers, resulting in the following value-added attributes:

Ubiquity. A mobile terminal in the form of a smart phone or a communicator can fulfill the need both for real-time information and for communication anywhere, independent of the user's location. It creates easier information access and provides a real-time environment.

Convenience. Convenience characterizes a mobile terminal. These devices store data, are always at hand, and are increasingly easy to use.

Localization of Products and Services. Localization of services and applications adds significant value to mobile devices. Location-based commerce, also known as **l-commerce**, delivers information about goods and services based on where you (and your mobile device) are located. For example, in San Francisco, passengers with a wireless device can instantly find when their bus is due to arrive. In this case, NextBus service knows, by the use of GPS, where the buses are in real time; when you call, the system will compute when the bus will be at any particular bus stop. Other localization systems will find where you are located, and based on this information will send you appropriate advertisements. For example, if you are in a mall, you will be notified of a sale that matches your shopping profile and desires with the ads. Knowing where the user is physically located at any particular moment is key to offering relevant services. (Note that there is some question as to whether this is an invasion of privacy.)

APPLICATIONS OF M-COMMERCE. Here are some representative applications of m-commerce.

...in Finance

- ***Online stock trading.*** Online stock trading is done all over the world, from I-MODE in Japan to E*Trade in several countries. Dagens Industri of Sweden allows subscribers to trade on the Stockholm Exchange and receive financial data using a personal digital assistant (PDA—a hand-held palmtop computer that uses a stylus pen for input). Stock trading from any place is important for traders and investors alike.
- ***Online banking.*** Mobile banking is rapidly taking off. Here are some examples: The Swedish Postal Bank allows customers to make payments from their headsets, and MaritaNordabanken in Sweden allows several other types of banking transactions. Citibank has mobile banking services in Singapore, Hong Kong, and other countries.
- ***Micropayments.*** Consumers in Japan can use their mobile phones to pay for purchases in vending machines. In Scandinavian countries, consumers pay for parking in unattended parking lots, for car washes, for gasoline, and even

for soft drinks in vending machines. Similar capabilities exist in France (Carte Bancaire) and in several other countries worldwide. In Germany, customers pay for transportation, including taxis, from their mobile phones.

- ***Online gambling.*** Eurobet, a large U.K. vendor, allows online gambling. In Hong Kong you can use your cell phone to bet on horse races.
- ***Ordering and service.*** Barnes and Noble Inc. created a service directed to PDA devices and cell phones that allows users to listen to personalized music clips by downloading the music to the devices.

Integrating IT ...in Marketing

- ***Online auctions.*** QXL.com, a U.K. online auction company, lets users open accounts on its Web sites and bid for items using cell phones. E-Bay conducts online auctions that can be accessed by cell phone as well.
- ***Messaging systems.*** The e-mail of mobile Internet is referred to as *short messaging service (SMS)*. In 2000, it was possible to send or receive up to 160 characters. In August 2000, about 10 billion messages were sent worldwide, doubled by early 2001. SMS can also be used for *advertisement*. Given that advertisers know something about a user, a personalized message can be sent to the users wherever they are.
- ***B2B applications.*** M-commerce can empower professionals to collect and evaluate data to make faster and better decisions. Remote employees can handle tasks such as checking inventory or submitting orders while in the field. The Internet thus becomes a repository of corporate information, acting as a virtual warehouse of goods and services.

SUCCESSFUL VENDORS: I-MODE. To illustrate the potential spread of m-commerce we will look at a particular successful vendor, I-MODE (*nttdocomo.com*). This pioneering wireless service took Japan by storm in 1999 and 2000. With a few clicks of a handset, I-MODE users can conduct a large variety of m-commerce activities ranging from online stock trading and banking to purchasing travel tickets and booking karaoke rooms. You can also send and receive color images via I-MODE. The service was launched in February 1999, and had over 15 million users by the beginning of 2001. Here are some interesting applications available on I-MODE:

- Access train and bus timetables, guides to shopping areas, and automatic notification of train delays.
- Get discount coupons for shopping and restaurants.
- Purchase music online.
- Send or receive photos.
- Buy airline tickets.
- Find information about best selling books and then buy the books.
- Receive Tamagotchi's characters, every day, for only $1/month.

I-MODE was taken international in late 2000, so it will soon begin appearing in other countries.

Auctions and Bartering

Electronic auctions started in the 1980s on private networks. But their use was very limited (cars in Japan, pigs in Singapore, and flowers in the Netherlands). The Internet opens many new opportunities for electronic auctions, and millions of shoppers participate. Auctions, reverse auctions (bidding), and bartering are rapidly growing on the Internet. B2B auctions are described next. After that, we discuss individual consumer (B2C and C2C) auctions and bartering.

BUSINESS-TO-BUSINESS AUCTIONS. As described earlier, are several types of electronic auctions (see Taylor and Cooney, 2000). In the ChemConnect case, for example, we introduced the reverse auction, where the buyer puts out a notice requesting bids. Another popular type is the forward auction, in which the seller (or seller's agent) lists items for sale and accepts bids for those items. An increasing number of organizations are utilizing auctions as a substantial business model. The U.S. federal government, for example, conducts auctions of houses and apartments to real estate brokers.

Two major options exist for conducting auctions: to use the organization's own Web site, as in the case of Dell Computer or Ingram Micro, or to use an auction site of an intermediary. In either case companies can reduce commissions by 50 to 80 percent and can also sell, and especially liquidate, products quickly. Corporations use auctions mainly as a B2B tool, but an increasing number use them also as a direct marketing channel to both companies and individuals.

The major benefits of such auctions are:

1. ***Generating revenue.*** As a new sales channel, auctions support existing online sales. For example, Weirton Steel Corp. doubled its customer base when it started auctions (Fickel, 1999). Auctions also offer a new venue for disposing of excess, obsolete, and returned products quickly and easily.
2. ***Increasing page views.*** Auctions give sites "stickiness." That is, auction users spend more time on a site and generate more page views than other users, so companies can sell ad space at auction sites for higher prices.
3. ***Acquiring and retaining members.*** All bidding transactions result in additional registered members, which increases the value of companies.

Types of B2B Auctions. There are four basic categories of B2B auctions: independent, commodity, private, and those conducted at a company's Web site. Within these categories, one can find examples of both forward and reverse auctions.

1. ***Independent auctions.*** In independent auctions companies use a third-party auctioneer to create the site and to sell the goods. Examples of such third-party sites are *fairmarket.com, imxexchange.com, ebay.com/business,* and *auctiongate.com.* Such an arrangement can be fairly complex, as shown in the *IT at Work* case about FreeMarkets, Inc. on page 208.
2. ***Commodity auctions.*** In commodity auctions, many buyers and sellers come together to a third-party Web site to buy and sell commodities (large lots of relatively undifferentiated products, such as copper, electricity, sugar, and crude oil). For example, energy access, utilities, and telecommunications are sold at *band-x.com.* Typical intermediaries are *metalsite.net* and *fastparts.com.*
3. ***Private auctions.*** Private auctions take place by invitation only. Several companies bypass the intermediaries and auction their products by themselves directly to buyers. For example, Ingram Micro has its own site, auctionblocktx.com, for selling obsolete computer equipment to its regular business customers.
4. ***Auctions at the company Web site.*** A growing number of companies build an auction capability on their own Web site. Dell Computer is an example (*dellauction.com*). Companies such as *opensite.com* and *fairmarket.com* provide software for such auctions, host them, and provide consulting services if needed.

IT at Work

HOW FREEMARKETS OPERATES: A NEW B2B MODEL

www.freemarkets.com

Imagine this scenario: United Technologies Corp. needs suppliers to make $24 million worth of circuit boards. Twenty-five hundred suppliers, found in electronic registries and directories, were identified as possible contractors. The list was submitted to FreeMarkets, Inc. FreeMarkets' experts reduced the list to 1,000, based on considerations ranging from plant location to the size of the supplier. After further analysis of plant capacity and customers' feedback, the list was reduced to 100. A detailed evaluation of the potential suppliers resulted in 50 qualified suppliers who were invited to bid.

Three hours of online competitive bidding was conducted. FreeMarkets divided the job into 12 lots, each of which was put up to bid. At 8:00 A.M., the first lot, valued at $2.25 million, was placed on the Net. The first bid was $2.25 million, which was seen by all. Minutes later, another bidder placed a $2.0 million bid. Using the reverse auction method, the bidders further reduced the bids. Minutes before the bid closed, at 8:45 A.M., the 42nd bidder placed a $1.1 million bid. When it all ended, the bids for all 12 lots totaled $18 million (which would represent about a 35 percent savings to United Technologies on its purchases).

To finalize the process, FreeMarkets conducted a very comprehensive analysis on several low bidders of each lot, attempting to look at other criteria in addition to cost. FreeMarkets then recommended the winners and collected its fees.

For Further Exploration: What are the unique aspects of this B2B model?

Source: Based on information from *freemarkets.com.*

B2C AND C2C AUCTIONS. Millions of people, all over the globe, sell to and buy from each other. The primary difference between B2B auctions and B2C and C2C auctions is that the items being bought and sold are products and services that appeal to individual consumers. Most B2C and C2C auctions are forward auctions, and most are independent (third-party) auctions. Examples of auctions focused on individual consumers are the following.

1. ***Specialized auction sites.*** There are hundreds of sites that specialize in auctions. The best known is *eBay.com*. The company started to serve collectors of stamps, dolls, and toys, but rapidly grew to a huge business (including a special section for businesses). eBay offers hundreds of thousands of different items in several types of auctions. The company provides all the necessary support services, such as payment, insurance, and delivery. Similarly, Onsale (*onsale.com*) conducts live online auctions, mostly of computers and electronic consumer products. It, too, offers several types of auctions. A detailed list of all the product specifications, warranties, and so forth is included, and purchases are made using a credit card. Over 300 other companies, including Amazon.com, offer online auctions as well.
2. ***Auctioning cars.*** In fall 1999, several Web sites (notably *autobytel.com* and *autoweb.com*) started to auction new and/or used cars. Manheim Online (*manheim.com*) brings the Web to the used-car supply chain—auto dealers, banks, leasing companies, rental companies, and users of fleet vehicles—by conducting dealers-only auctions. Dealers visit "cyberlots" where they see pictures of the cars. A buyer in city A can buy a car in city B, with transportation costs also quoted online. Aucnet conducts auctions on the Internet for used cars in Japan.

3. ***Art auctions.*** Artwork is sold online at various sites, including *onlineart.com* and Internet Liquidators. The large offline art auction houses, such as Christie's, offer limited online auctions.
4. ***Airlines.*** Several airlines auction tickets on their Web sites. See American Airlines (*aa.com*) and Cathay Pacific (*cathay-usa.com*).

As eBay's history demonstrates, interest in B2C and C2C auctions seems nearly unlimited. Indeed, eBay is now active in several countries, competing with local auction sites.

BARTERING. Related to auctions is **electronic bartering**, the *exchange* of goods and/or services without a monetary transaction. In addition to the individual-to-individual bartering ads that appear in some newsgroups, bulletin boards, and classified ads, there are several companies that arrange for corporate bartering (e.g., see *barterbrokers.com*). These companies try to find partners to a barter. Barter exchanges give you points in exchange for your products and services. You can then redeem these points to acquire products or services from participating members.

Consumer-to-Consumer (C2C) E-Commerce

An increasing number of individuals are using the Internet to conduct business or to collaborate with other individuals. Auctions are by far the most popular C2C e-commerce activity. As discused earlier, eBay is the best-known auction site. Some other illustrative C2C activities are:

1. ***Classifieds.*** Individuals used to sell items by advertising in the classified section of newspaper. Now they are using the Internet for this purpose. Some of the classified services are provided free (see *classifieds2000.com*).
2. ***Personal services.*** A variety of personal services are offered on the Internet, ranging from tutoring and astrology to the "oldest profession on earth." Personal services are advertised in the classified areas, in personal Web pages, on Internet communities' bulletin boards, and more. Be very careful before you buy any personal services. Fraud and crime may be involved.
3. ***Peer-to-peer (P2P) and bartering.*** An increasing number of individuals are using the P2P services of companies such as napster.com. Individuals can exchange products and services as well.

Intrabusiness and Business-to-Employees (B2E)

Many companies use EC activities. Any two departments or units can be considered as business units. So, buying, selling, and collaborative EC can be conducted within the company, usually using the company intranet and corporate portal (Chapter 4). Similarly, many EC activities are done with employees, starting from selling products and services to employees to managing fringe benefits online. These activities fall under the category of **intrabusiness** or B2E (business-to-employees) e-commerce.

E-Government

As e-commerce matures and its tools and applications improve, greater attention is given to its use to improve the business of public institutions and governments (country, state, county, city, etc.)

E-government is the use of information technology in general and e-commerce in particular to provide citizens and organizations with more convenient access to government information and services, and with delivery of public services to citizens, business partners and suppliers, and those working in the public sector. It is also an efficient way of conducting business transactions with citizens and business and within the governments themselves.

The potential benefits of e-government are to:

- Improve the efficiency and effectiveness of the executive functions of government, including the delivery of public services.
- Enable governments to be more "transparent" to citizens and businesses, by giving access to more of the information generated by government.
- Facilitate fundamental changes in the relationships between the citizens and the state, and among nation-states, with implications for the democratic process and structures of government.
- Provide people with more convenient access to government information and services, to improve the quality of the services, and to provide greater opportunities to participate in democratic institutions and processes.

E-government applications can be divided into the following major categories: *government-to-citizens (G2C), government-to-business (G2B),* and *government-to-government (G2G).* Government agencies are increasingly using the Internet to provide various services to citizens (G2C). An example would be **electronic benefits transfer (EBT)** in which government transfers Social Security, pensions, and other benefits directly to recipients' bank accounts or to smart cards. Governments also are using the Internet to conduct business with businesses (sell to or buy from). For example, electronic tendering systems are becoming mandatory.

E-Commerce Failures

In this and other chapters of the book we presented dozens of examples that illustrate the success of the new economy and EC. Yet, failures of EC initiatives are fairly common. Furthermore, beginning in spring 2000, large numbers of dot-com companies started to fail. The failure accelerated in the second half of 2000 and continued into 2001. In this section we will look at some examples of failures and their causes. We will also look into some success factors that can be used to prevent failure.

PRE-INTERNET FAILURES. Failures of e-commerce systems should not seem surprising, since we have known about failures of EDI systems for more than 10 years. A typical example involved the attempt of the U.S. Food and Drug Administration (FDA) to install an online collaboration system to reduce drug-review time (Williams et al., 1997). It was basically an electronic submission system and then an intranet-based internal distribution and review system. The system failed because:

- No standards were established for submitted documents.
- There was resistance to change to the new system, and the FDA did not force reviewers to work electronically.
- The system was an electronic version of existing documents. No business process reengineering (BPR) was undertaken in planning the new system.
- The FDA lacked technical expertise in interorganizational information systems and in collaborative commerce.
- No training or even information was provided to the FDA's end users.
- There were learning curve difficulties, and no time allowed to learn different document systems.

- Pharmaceutical companies were not encouraged to make electronic submissions.
- There was no IS planning. The FDA knew that a business process design study was needed, but it did nothing.

However, the FDA learned from its mistakes. An improved EDI-based system was installed in 1998/1999—after a BPR was done, training was completed, and standards were provided. The system became a full success in 1999.

INTERNET-BASED EC FAILURES. Failures of e-commerce initiatives started as early as 1996. Early on, pioneering organizations saw the potential for EC, but expertise and market models were just developing. However, the major wave of failures started in 2000, as secondary funding that was neded by Internet-based EC began to dry up. Here are some examples.

- PointCast, a pioneer in personalized Web-casting, folded in 1998 due to an incorrect business model.
- An Internet mall, operated by Open Market, was closed in 1996 due to an insufficient number of buyers.
- Several toy companies—Red Rocket (a Viacom Company), eparties.com, and babybucks.com—were failing due to too much competition, low prices, and lack of cash. Even E-toys, a virtual toy retailer that impacted the entire toy industry, folded in 2001 due to inability to generate profit and the need for additional funding for expanding its logistics infrastructure. It was sold to kbkids.com.
- A British advertising company Advertexpress.com failed due to lack of second-round funding.
- Garden.com closed its doors in December 2000 due to lack of cash. (Suppliers of venture capital were unwilling to give the company any more money to "burn.")
- Dr. Koop, a medical portal, was unable to raise the needed advertisement money, so the company folded. The diagnosis: death due to incorrect business model.
- Living.com, the online furniture store, closed in 2000. The customer acquisition cost was too high.
- Easier.co.uk, a U.K. property dealer, folded due to inability to find a buyer.
- PaperX.com, an online paper exchange in the U.K., folded due to lack of second-round funding.

Even Amazon.com, considered by many as one of the most successful e-commerce sites, had still not recorded a profit (as of this writing).

The major lessons of the Internet-based EC failures were summarized by Useem (2000) in his "12 truths" and by Agrawal et al. (2001). The major reasons for failure are incorrect revenue model, lack of a strategy and contingency planning, inability to attract enough customers, lack of funding, channel conflict with distributors, too much online competition in standard (commodity) products (e.g., CDs, supermarkets), poor order fulfillment infrastructure, and lack of qualified management.

To learn more about failures, visit *whytheyfailed.com* and *techdirt.com.*

Analyzing successful companies, researchers have suggested that if they do careful planning to reach profitability quickly, many click-and-mortar companies are likely to succeed. Joint ventures and partnerships are very valuable, and planning for satisfactory infrastructure and logistics to meet high demand is needed. In short, do not forget that e-business has a "business" side!

Finally, let us not forget that history repeats itself. When the automobile was invented there were 240 startup companies between 1904 and 1908. In 1910 there was a shakeout, and today there are only three U.S. automakers. However, the auto industry has grown by hundredfolds.

5.7 E-Commerce Infrastructure: EDI, Extranets, and E-Payments

In order for electronic commerce applications to succeed, it is necessary to provide them with all the needed infrastructure as shown in Figure 5.1.

E-commerce transactions must be executable worldwide without any delays or mistakes. Infrastructure may be of many types, and their description is outside the scope of this book. Here we deal with only three infrastructures: EDI, extranets, and electronic payments. An additional topic, supply chain management and order fulfillment, is discussed in Chapter 6.

E-Commerce Infrastructure

Electronic commerce infrastructure requires a variety of hardware and software. The major components are summarized in Table 5.4. (Technology Guide 4 provides explanations of many of these components.)

TABLE 5.4 Electronic Commerce Infrastructure

Component	Description and Issues
Networks	A shift from VANs to the Internet. Increased use of VPNs to enhance security and capabilities over the Internet.
Web servers	Specialized servers are usually superior to dual-purpose servers. They are available for rent. Interface to legacy systems may be a problem.
Web server support and software	**1.** Web site activity tracking. **2.** Database connectivity. **3.** Software for creating electronic forms. **4.** Software for creating chat rooms and discussion groups.
Electronic catalogs	Product description, multimedia use, customized catalogs, inclusion in Web site design and construction, templates for construction.
Web page design and construction software	Web programming languages (HTML, JAVA, VRML, XML).
Transactional software	**1.** Search engines for finding and comparing products. **2.** Negotiating software. **3.** Encryption and payment capabilities. **4.** Ordering (front office), inventory, and back office software.
Others	Firewalls, e-mail, HTTP (transfer protocols), smart cards.
Internet-access components	TCP/IP package, Web browsers, remote access server, client dial-in software, Internet connection device, leased-line connection, connection to leased line, Internet kiosks.
Intelligent agents	Programs to help users search and retrieve information, support decision making, and act as consulting experts. Provide assistance in finding products and vendors, and in negotiation.

First we will look at EDI networks, which are essential in connecting the participants in EC transactions.

ELECTRONIC DATA INTERCHANGE (EDI). As discussed briefly in Chapter 2, **EDI** is the electronic movement of specially formatted standard business documents, such as orders, bills, and confirmations sent between business partners. Figure 5.6 shows the order-delivery cycle with and without EDI. Like e-mail, EDI allows sending and receiving of messages between computers connected by a communication link. However, EDI has the following special characteristics:

- ***Business transactions messages.*** EDI is used primarily to electronically transfer *repetitive* business transactions. These include various transactions essential in EC: purchase orders, invoices, approvals of credit, shipping notices, confirmations, and so on.
- ***Data formatting standards.*** Since EDI messages are repetitive, it is sensible to use some formatting (coding) standards. Standards can shorten the length of the messages and eliminate data entry errors, since data entry occurs only once. In the United States and Canada, data are formatted according to the

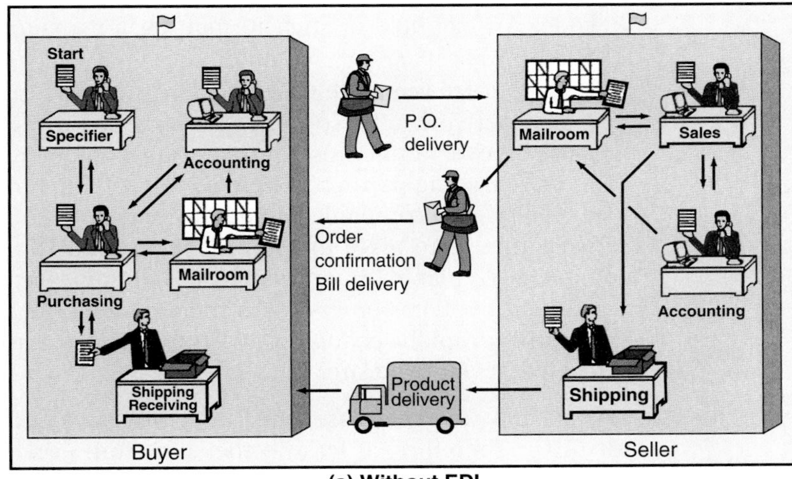

FIGURE 5.6 Order-delivery cycle with and without EDI. (*Source: Business Data Communications,* 2/E by Stallings/VanSlyke, © Reprinted by permission of Pearson Education, Inc., Upper Saddle River, NJ.)

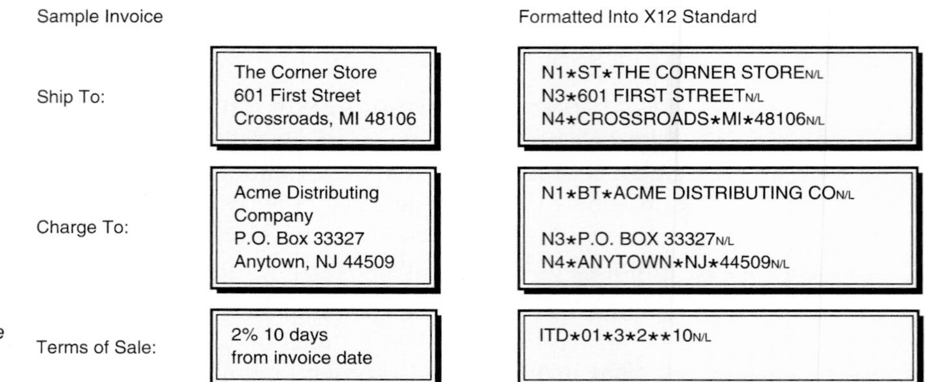

FIGURE 5.7 Translating data to an EDI code. (*Source:* C. Guglielmo, "Global Transport," *Corporate Computing*, June–July 1992, p. 242.)

ANSI X.12 standard. An international standard developed by the United Nations is called EDIFACT.

- ***EDI translators.*** An *EDI translator* converts data into standard EDI format code. An example of such formatting for a shipping company is shown in Figure 5.7.
- ***Private lines versus the Internet.*** In the past, EDI ran on expensive value-added networks. These networks provided a high level of security and capacity. However, because of cost, their implementation was confined mainly to large trading partners. There were also some problems of compatibility. As a result, large companies doing business with thousands of other companies were unable to place most of them on the EDI. For example, Boeing Commercial Airplane Group, which sells aircraft parts, was using EDI with only 30 out of 500 customers. With the emergence of Internet-based EDI, this situation is rapidly changing, as shown in the case of Hewlett-Packard, discussed at our Web site.

Note that Internet-based EDI does not have the same capabilities as VAN-based EDI. Therefore, at least in the short run, it is viewed as supplementary to the VAN, permitting more companies to use EDI. Also, Internet EDI may be cheaper, but it still requires coordination and integration with the company's back-end processing systems. In cases of high use of EDI, such as in financial services, the traditional EDI must be used. But in many cases where low volume of transactions is involved, EDI/Internet is becoming the chosen solution.

HOW DOES EDI WORK? *A Closer Look* 5.2 illustrates how EDI works. Information flows from the hospital's information systems into an EDI station that includes a PC and an EDI translator. From there the information moves, using a modem if necessary, to a VAN. The VAN transfers the formatted information to a vendor(s) where an EDI translator converts it to a desired format.

ADVANTAGES AND DISADVANTAGES OF EDI. Many companies use EDI to foster relationships with their suppliers and/or customers. The major advantages of EDI are summarized in Table 5.5.

A CLOSER LOOK

5.2 HOW EDI CUTS COSTS OF ORDERING SUPPLIES

An average hospital generates about 15,000 purchase orders each year at a processing cost of about $70 per order. The Health Industry Business Communication Council estimates that EDI can reduce this cost to $4 per order—potential yearly savings of $840,000 per hospital. The required investment ranges between $8,000 and $15,000, which includes purchase of a PC with an EDI translator, a modem, and a link to the mainframe-based information system. The hospital can have two or three ordering points. These are connected to a value-added network (VAN), which connects the hospital to its suppliers. (See figure.) The system also can connect to other hospitals, or to centralized joint purchasing agencies.

Source: Based on G. Nussbaum, "EDI: First Aid for Soaring Hospital Cost," *Corporate Computing,* August–September 1992.

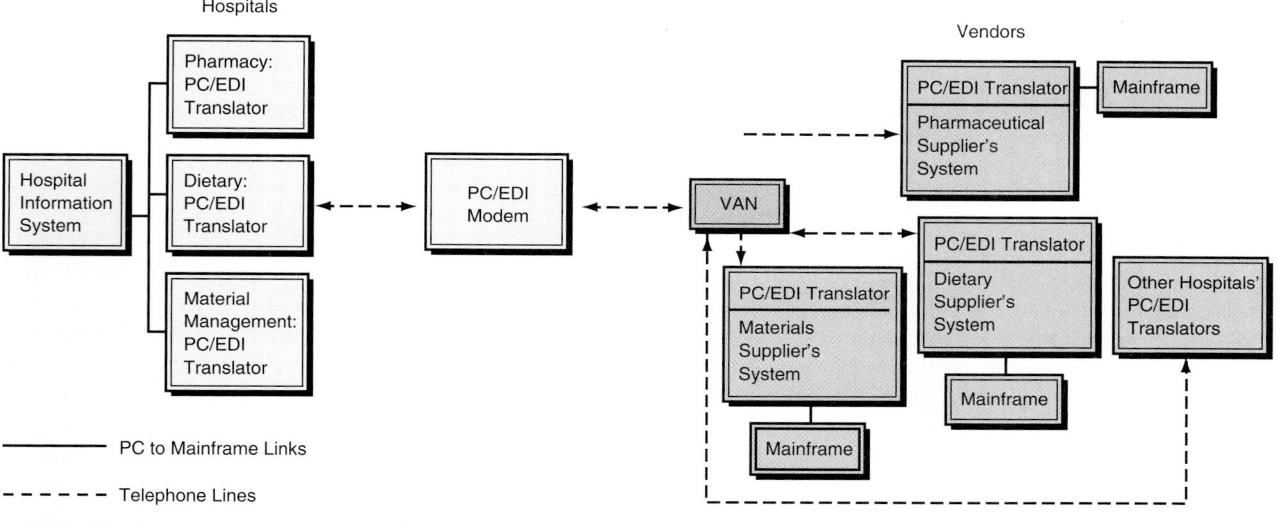

TABLE 5.5 The Benefits of EDI

- EDI enables companies to send and receive large amounts of routine transaction information quickly around the globe.
- There are very few errors in the transformed data as a result of computer-to-computer data transfer.
- Information can flow among several trading partners consistently and freely.
- Companies can access partners' databases to retrieve and store standard transactions.
- EDI fosters true (and strategic) partnership relationships since it involves a commitment to a long-term investment and the refinement of the system over time.
- EDI creates a paperless environment, saving money and increasing efficiency.
- Payment collection can be shortened by several weeks.
- Data may be entered offline, in a batch mode, without tying up ports to the mainframe.
- When an EDI document is received, the data may be used immediately.
- Sales information is delivered to interested parties almost in real time.
- EDI can save a considerable amount of money.

INTERNET-BASED EDI. There are several reasons for firms to create EDI ability over the Internet:

- The Internet is a publicly accessible network with few geographical constraints.
- The Internet global internetwork connections offer the potential to reach the widest possible number of trading partners of any viable alternative currently available.
- The Internet's largest attribute—large-scale connectivity (without the need to have any special networking architecture)—is a seedbed for growth of a vast range of business applications.
- Using the Internet can cut EDI communication costs by over 50 percent.
- Using the Internet to exchange EDI transactions is consistent with the growing interest of businesses in delivering an ever-increasing variety of products and services electronically, particularly through the Web.
- Internet-based EDI can complement or replace current EDI applications.
- Internet tools such as browsers and search engines are very user-friendly, and most users today know how to use them.

B2B Extranets

As discussed in earlier chapters (Chapters 2 and 4), an *extranet* is a network that links business partners to one another over the Internet by tying together their corporate intranets. The use of an extranet as a B2B infrastructure is growing rapidly. In contrast with electronic data interchange (EDI), which mostly supports *transaction processing* between two business partners, an extranet can be used for collaboration, discovery of information, trading support, and other activities. Also, EDI is mostly used to support company-centric transactions, where relationships are fairly permanent, whereas extranets are used also in exchanges where relationships may be of a "one-deal-only" nature.

The main goal of extranets is to foster collaboration between organizations. Extranets may be used, for example, to allow inventory databases to be searched by business partners, or to transmit information on the status of an order. An extranet typically is open to selected suppliers, customers, and other business partners, who access it on a private wide-area network, or usually over the Internet with a virtual private network (VPN) for increased security and functionality. In Figure 5.2 we showed two extranets. On the right side was the toy industry extranet, and on the left side a company's extranet with its major business partners.

Extranets allow the use of capabilities of both the Internet and intranets among business partners. External partners and telecommuting employees can use the extranet to place orders, access data, check status of shipments, and send e-mail. The Internet-based extranet is far more economical than the creation and maintenance of proprietary networks. Extranets support all types of the B2B models described earlier, but especially many-to-many exchanges. Buy-side and sell-side e-marketplaces are supported frequently by EDI/Internet. Extranets are especially useful in supporting **collaborative commerce (c-commerce)**. In c-commerce, the browser is used as the collaboration medium. An example of c-commerce is provided in the following *IT at Work* case.

IT at Work

HOW AN EXTRANET FACILITATES HOME LOANS

...in Finance

www.countrywide.com

Countrywide Home Loans of Pasadena, California, is the nation's largest independent mortgage lender, with nearly 330 branch offices nationwide. It is using extensive Internet, intranet, and extranet solutions to serve its employees, business partners, and consumers.

Every day, Countrywide processes thousands of transactions that are influenced by continuous fluctuations in lending rates and product offerings. To improve processing, the company has embarked on a long-term project to eliminate paper from its operating environment. The system provides a completely open, networked environment that seamlessly ties into the mountains of legacy data that must be accessed by people using various computer platforms, both inside and outside the organization.

Countrywide's IS department has developed a corporatewide intranet system servicing more than 5,000 employees at the company's headquarters and branch locations. This far-reaching network provides employees with online access to product guidelines, forms, and corporate information. Countrywide programmers develop intranet applications for such corporate functions as mortgage origination, mortgage servicing, and back-office operations.

The company has also developed a powerful extranet accessible only to Countrywide's lending partners, brokers, and real estate agents. These parties require secure access to valuable information, such as account and transaction status, loan status, company contacts, and company announcements. A total of 500 Countrywide lenders use Netscape Navigator client software to access the extranet, which uses a sophisticated routing program. This program automatically identifies each lender and provides it with customized information on premium rates, discounts, and special arrangements.

The same server deployed for the extranet is also used to develop a host of customer-oriented applications on a publicly accessible Internet site. These applications come online as part of a Web service offered free by Countrywide. For example, consumers can calculate home mortgage rates based on any number of market variables and product offerings. Countrywide integrated its consumer Web services with massive legacy databases that contain pertinent information on loan offerings, loan rates, and mortgage products.

For Further Exploration: Identify the collaboration and communication activities that are facilitated by the extranet. Why is this so beneficial? What aspects of the system increase Countrywide's business? What aspects of the system strengthen relationships with lending partners and real estate agents?

Sources: Compiled from Netscape Corporation news release No. 220 (1996) available at *home.netscape.com*; also see *Computer World*, August 12, 1996, and *countrywide.com* (2001).

Electronic Payment Systems

Payments are an integral part of doing business, regardless of how the business is done. In most cases, traditional payment systems are not effective for EC.

LIMITATIONS OF TRADITIONAL PAYMENT INSTRUMENTS. Nonelectronic payment methods such as paying cash, writing a check, sending a money order, or paying by giving your credit card number over the telephone have many limitations in EC. First, cash cannot be used since there is no face-to-face contact. Second, if a payment is sent by mail, it takes time for it to be received. Even if a credit card number is provided by phone or fax, it takes time to process it. It is inconvenient and less secure for the online buyer to stop surfing and use the telephone or "snail mail" to send a payment, especially to another country, than to finish the transaction on a computer. Also, not everyone accepts credit cards or checks. Finally, some buyers do not have credit cards or checking accounts.

Another issue is that many electronic commerce transactions are valued at only a few dollars or cents. The cost of processing such **micropayments** needs to be very low. You would not want to pay $5 to process a purchase valued at only a few dollars, and many payments are even less than $1. The cost of making micropayments offline is just too high.

For all the above reasons it is clear that a better way is needed to pay in cyberspace. This better way is referred to as *electronic payment systems.* As in a marketplace, a diversity of payment methods in cyberspace allows customers to choose how they wish to pay. Before we describe the various payment methods, we will describe the *security requirements* necessary for conducting EC.

SECURITY REQUIREMENTS. There are several security requirements for conducting electronic commerce:

1. ***Authentification.*** The buyer, seller, intermediary, and paying institutions need to be assured of the *identity* of the party with whom they are dealing.
2. ***Privacy.*** Many customers want their identity to be secured. They want to make sure others do not know what they buy. Some prefer complete anonymity, like they have when they pay with cash.
3. ***Integrity.*** It is necessary to assure that data and information transmitted in EC, such as orders, replies to queries, payment authorization, and so on, are not accidentally or maliciously altered or destroyed during transmission.
4. ***Nonrepudiation.*** Merchants need protection against the customer's unjustifiable denial of placing an order. On the other hand, customers need protection against the merchants' unjustifiable denial of orders or payments received.
5. ***Safety.*** Customers want to be sure that it is safe to provide a credit card number on the Internet. They also want protection against fraud by sellers or by criminals posing as sellers.

Several methods and mechanisms can be used to fulfill the above requirements. One of the primary mechanisms is encryption, which is used in some of the most useful security schemes. **Encryption** is a process of making messages indecipherable except by *those who have an authorized decryption key.* A **key** is a code composed of a very large collection of letters, symbols, and numbers. For example, the letter "A" might be coded as: ABQ8iF + 73 Rjbj/83 ds + 22 mx 3 SP × Qqm2z. Two basic encryption methods exist: a single key and two keys.

SINGLE-KEY (SYMMETRIC) ENCRYPTION. In early encryption technologies only one key was used. The sender of the message (or payment) encrypted the information with a key. The receiver used an identical key to **decrypt** the information to a readable form. Therefore, the same key had to be in the possession of both the sender and the receiver. This created problems. For example, if a key were transmitted and intercepted illegally, the key could have been used to read all encrypted messages or to steal money. Since keys are changed frequently, the problem becomes even more difficult in cyberspace. Single-key encryption is fast, but not secure enough. Therefore it may be used only as a component in a comprehensive payment security scheme known as *public-key infrastructure.*

PUBLIC-KEY INFRASTRUCTURE. A **public-key infrastructure (PKI)** is a comprehensive security system that is based on three elements: two encryption keys, a digital signature, and a security certificate.

Public and Private Keys. PKI uses two different keys. One key is called *public,* the other one, *private.* Each sender or receiver of communication has a set of

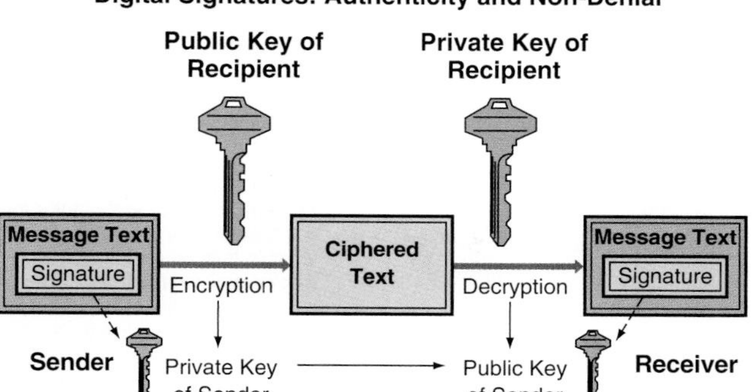

FIGURE 5.8 Two-key encryptions with digital signature.

the two keys. The public-key information is posted on the Internet or can be e-mailed to anyone who needs it. But only its owner knows the **private key**. Encryption and decryption can be done with either key. If encryption is done with the public key, the decryption can be done only with the private key, and vice versa (see Figure 5.8). There are several public key encryption algorithms; the most well known is RSA (*rsa.com*).

Here are some examples of the use of the two keys:

1. Adam (A) wants to be sure that Barbara (B) will be the only one able to read a message he sends to her. A encrypts the message with B's public key. B decrypts it with her private key.
2. Alicia (A) wants to assure Brent (B) that she is the author of a message. A encrypts a signature (as a message) in her own private key. B uses A's public key to decrypt the signature. The use of a private key to encrypt a signature is called a *digital signature.*

Digital Signatures. Encryption provides for privacy and safety but not for authentication or nonrepudiation. Therefore, in a PKI we add to encrypted messages a **digital signature**. The process of a digital signature is shown in Figure 5.9 (page 220). The digital signature provides for authentication. (For more information, see *signonline.com.*)

While a combination of encryption of the message and attaching it to a signature seems to be very safe, it is really not. The reason is that it is necessary to verify to whom a public key belongs. This is done by providing *certification.*

Electronic Certificates. **Electronic certificates** are issued by a trusted third party, called a *certificate authority (CA).* Their purpose is to verify that a specific public key belongs to a specific individual. In addition to a name, a certificate may verify age, gender, and other attributes of the individual to whom the public key belongs. Also, if the CA is not well known to the user of the certificate, it may be necessary to certify the CA by another, more trustworthy legal body. Thus, there could be several levels of certification. Certificates are valid until an expiration date and are signed by the CA. A major issuer of certificates is VeriSign, Inc. (*verisign.com*). In many countries the post office acts as a certificate authority. An example is Hong Kong Post e-Cert (see *hongkongpost.gov.hk*).

The PKI is the backbone of some of the payment mechanisms that are described later. Before we consider those mechanisms, however, we'll briefly look at the topic of payment standards, called *protocols,* which are necessary in order

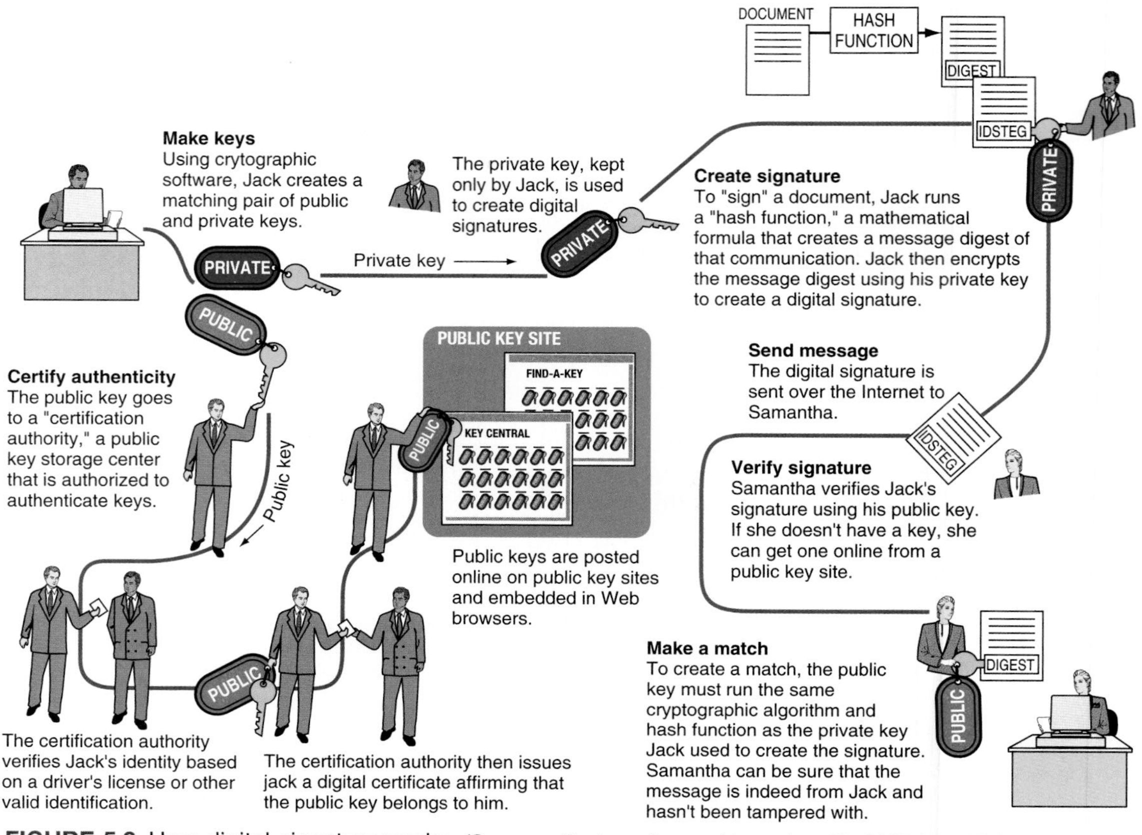

DOCUMENT
HASH FUNCTION
DIGEST
IDSTEG
Make keys
Using crytographic software, Jack creates a matching pair of public and private keys.
The private key, kept only by Jack, is used to create digital signatures.
PRIVATE
Private key
PRIVATE
Create signature
To "sign" a document, Jack runs a "hash function," a mathematical formula that creates a message digest of that communication. Jack then encrypts the message digest using his private key to create a digital signature.
PRIVATE
PUBLIC
PUBLIC KEY SITE
FIND-A-KEY
KEY CENTRAL
PUBLIC
Certify authenticity
The public key goes to a "certification authority," a public key storage center that is authorized to authenticate keys.
Public key
Send message
The digital signature is sent over the Internet to Samantha.
IDSTEG
Verify signature
Samantha verifies Jack's signature using his public key. If she doesn't have a key, she can get one online from a public key site.
Public keys are posted online on public key sites and embedded in Web browsers.
PUBLIC
Make a match
To create a match, the public key must run the same cryptographic algorithm and hash function as the private key Jack used to create the signature. Samantha can be sure that the message is indeed from Jack and hasn't been tampered with.
DIGEST
PUBLIC
The certification authority verifies Jack's identity based on a driver's license or other valid identification.
The certification authority then issues jack a digital certificate affirming that the public key belongs to him.

FIGURE 5.9 How digital signature works. (*Sources:* Business2.com, November 28, 2000 from Verisign.com, Thomas Smedinghoff).

to assure the acceptance of payments anywhere in the world. In 2001 there was no single PKI nor even a single agreed-upon standard (protocol) for setting up a PKI.

PROTOCOLS. A **protocol** is a set of rules and procedures that govern the transfer of information on the Internet. It is the software that also helps in authentication, security, and privacy. Two major protocols are used in EC payments: SSL and SET.

Secure Socket Layer (SSL). The *secure socket layer (SSL)* is the most common protocol used in EC. Its main capability is to encrypt messages. For example, any time you order merchandise from Wal-Mart Online, Amazon.com, or most other large vendors on the Internet, your order is automatically encrypted by the SSL in your computer browser *before* being sent over the Internet. (Both Netscape Navigator and Internet Explorer support SSL.) This includes the encryption of credit card numbers. SSL is also used in other payment methods such as electronic checks. SSL is using a single key, and it can be recognized by the "https" instead of the "http" in the URLs that use it.

Secure Electronic Transaction Protocol (SET). A proposed comprehensive standard for credit card processing is *secure electronic transaction (SET)* protocol. It is designed to allow consumers to shop anywhere as conveniently and securely as possible by incorporating digital signatures, certification, encryption, and an agreed-upon payment gateway (to banks). In 2001, SET was still under development; only a very few large companies were utilizing it. Due to its complexity, SET was temporarily abandoned by VISA in June 1999. (For details, see *setco.org*. You also can read all about SET at *ibm.com/software* and *visa.com*.)

ELECTRONIC CREDIT CARDS. The most common method of paying in B2C e-commerce is by means of **electronic credit cards**, which can be used as follows: Using SSL encryption, credit card details are encrypted for security. This is automatically done at the buyer's browser when an order is placed. So far, this method is used only by major vendors (e.g., Amazon.com). The encrypted payment process involves the buyer's and seller's banks and sometimes, for added security, an intermediary. (For details, see *e-credit-ability.com, card-processing.com,* and *visa.com*.)

ELECTRONIC CHECKS. **Electronic checks (e-checks)** are similar to regular checks. They are secured by public-key encryption and are usually used in B2B transactions. E-checks contain the same information as a paper check, can be used wherever paper checks are used, are based on the same legal framework, and work essentially the same way that a paper check works.

A company named eCheck Secure (*echecksecure.com*) is one third-party vendor that provides software that enables the purchase of goods and services with an e-check. The processes that are supported by its software illustrate how e-checks work at most B2C sites. When a consumer elects to pay for purchases with an e-check, he or she is asked to enter the check's routing number, the account number, and the check number. The process is shown in Figure 5.10. (For more information, see *echecksecure.com,* and *echeck.org*.)

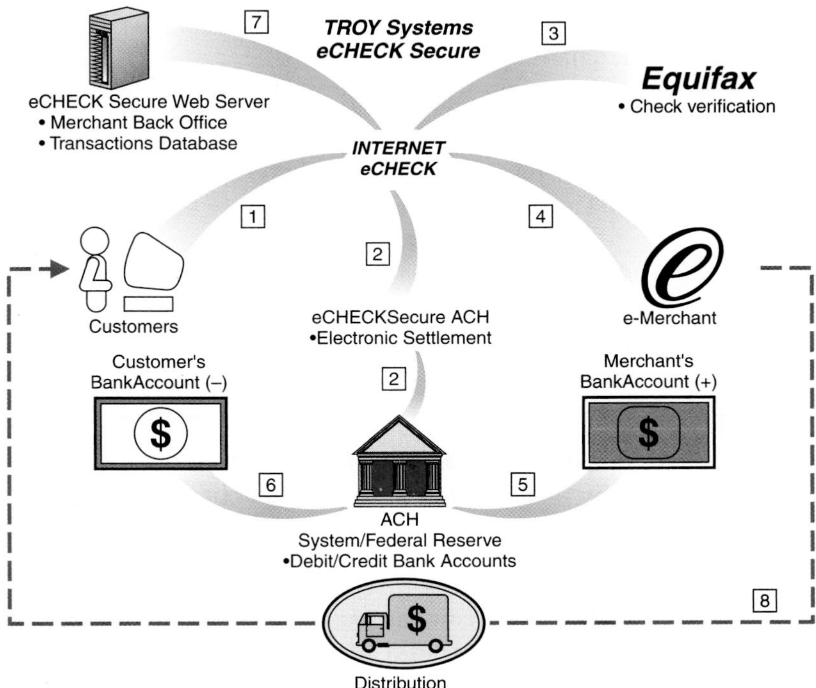

FIGURE 5.10 E-check processing. (*Source: echecksecure.com.*)

ELECTRONIC CASH. Cash is the most prevalent non-Internet consumer payment instrument. Merchants prefer cash since they do not have to pay commissions to credit card companies, and they can put the money to use as soon as it is received. Also, some buyers pay with cash because they do not have checks or credit cards, or because they want to preserve their anonymity. Banks like cash because it is inexpensive to process, more secure than checks or credit cards, and if used instead of credit cards, costs the bank less. Finally, due to the low processing cost, cash can be used for paying even small amounts of money (micropayments). It is logical, therefore, that EC sellers, some buyers, and banks prefer **electronic cash (e-cash)**.

Conceptually, e-cash makes a lot of sense. It's secure, it's anonymous, and it can be used to support micropayments that can't be economically supported with payment cards. From a practical standpoint, the inconvenience of opening an account and downloading software or installing special e-commerce systems and the difficulty of obtaining a critical mass of users seem to have outweighed the benefits of e-cash. However, in spite of these hurdles, new e-cash alternatives, or at least alternatives to payment cards, appear with some regularity. These alternatives can be grouped into a series of categories: e-cash, stored-value cards, e-loyalty and rewards programs, and person-to-person (P2P) payments.

Electronic Coins in Your Computer. eCoins, run by eCoin.Net (*ecoin.net*), is typical of many e-cash systems. The system consists of three participants. The first participant is the user. The user opens an account with eCoin.Net and downloads a special e-wallet to his or her PC. The user then purchases some eCoins with a credit card. An *eCoin* is a digital string that is worth 5 cents (U.S.). Each string is 15 bytes long and is unique so that it can be easily identified. The eCoins are downloaded into the e-wallet. The second participant is the merchant. To use eCoins, the merchant simply has to have embedded a special eCoin icon in its payment page. The final participant is the eCoin.Net server. The eCoin server operates as a broker that keeps customer and merchant accounts, accepts payment requests from the customer's wallet, and computes embedded invoices for the merchant.

An eCoin purchase consists of the following steps:

1. The user downloads eCoins from his or her online account to an e-wallet.
2. The merchant contacts the broker to get an embedded invoice tag.
3. The merchant inserts the invoice tag into the HTML page and sends it to the customer's browser.
4. The e-Wallet Manager plug-in interprets the embedded invoice.
5. The customer clicks on an embedded invoice displayed by Wallet Manager.
6. The plug-in sends the invoice data and eCoins to the broker.
7. The broker decodes the invoice and verifies the eCoins.
8. The broker transfers the eCoins to the merchant account.

E-Cash for Micropayments. One micropayment system that avoids some of the problems of micropayment and has enjoyed some success is Qpass (*qpass.com*). Qpass is used primarily to purchase content from participating news services and periodicals like the *New York Times, Wall Street Journal, Forbes,* and so on. With Qpass the user sets up a Qpass account, creating a user name and password and specifying a credit card against which purchases will be charged. Then, when a purchase is made at a participating site, the user simply enters his or her Qpass user name and password and confirms the purchase. Instead of immediately billing the user's credit card account, the charges are aggregated into a single monthly transaction and that transaction is billed to the user's credit card.

Stored-Value Cards. Electronic payment cards have been in use for several decades. The best known are credit cards, which use magnetic strips that contain limited information, such as the card's ID number. A more advanced form of payment card is the **stored-value card** that you use in your library to pay for photocopies, or to pay for telephone calls. Such cards store a fixed amount of prepaid money; each time you use the card, the amount is reduced. A successful example is used by the New York Metropolitan Transportation Authority (MTA), which operates buses, trains, interstate toll bridges, and tunnels. Nearly 5 million customers use these cards on buses, subways, and road tollbooths each day. Similar cards are in use in many other cities, including Chicago and Tokyo, where one card is used for all types of transportation, including taxis. Some of these cards are reloadable. In Hong Kong travelers use about 6 million cards on the subway, buses, and ferrys. These cards can be used to pay in vending machines as well. VisaCash is another example of such a card. If offers a disposable or a chargeable (loadable) option.

Enhanced Smart Cards. A more enhanced card, also referred to as a **smart card**, is a card that contains a microprocessor. This type of card can store a considerable amount of information (100 times more than a credit card). Smart cards also allow money to be stored in quantities that can be increased (reloaded) as well as decreased. These cards contain diversified additional information about the cardholder and can be used for several purposes, such as a loyalty card as at Takashimaya, in Japan, as described in the *IT at Work* on page 224.

Person-to-Person (P2P) Payment. **Person-to-person (P2P) payments** are one of the newest and fastest-growing payment schemes. They enable the transfer of funds between two individuals for a variety of purposes, like repaying money borrowed from a friend, paying for an item purchased at an online auction, sending money to students at college, or sending a gift to a family member. One of the first companies to offer this service was PayPal (*paypal.com*). PayPal claims to have 4.5 million customer accounts, to handle 25 percent of all transactions on eBay, and to funnel $2 billion in payments, annualized, through its servers (*BusinessWeek,* 2000). Although PayPal has not made a profit, this kind of activity has drawn the attention of a number of other companies who are trying to get in on the action. Citibank C2IT (*c2it.com*), AOL QuickCash (*aol.com*), which is a private branded version of c2it, BankOne eMoneyMail, Yahoo! PayDirect, and WebCertificate (*webcertificate.com*) are all PayPal competitors.

Virtually all of these services work in exactly the same way. Assume you want to send money to someone over the Internet. First, you select a service and open up an account with the service. Basically, this entails creating a user name, a password, giving them your e-mail address, and providing the service with a payment card or bank account number. Next, you add funds to your account with your payment card or bank account. Once the account has been funded you're ready to send money. You access the account with your user name and password. Now you specify the e-mail address of the person to receive the money, along with the dollar amount that you want to send. An e-mail is sent to the specified e-mail address. The e-mail will contain a link back to the service's Web site. When the recipient clicks on the link, he or she will be taken to the service.

IT at Work

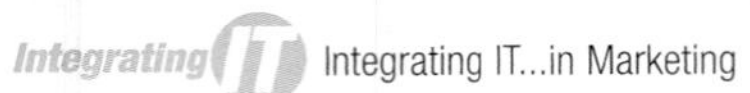

Integrating IT...in Marketing

SMART CARDS MOVE SHOPPERS TO THE TWENTY-FIRST CENTURY

www.takashimaya.co.jp

Takashimaya is a giant retailer based in Japan, with stores in Asia, Europe, and the United States. The company was the first to introduce (in Singapore) an international "loyalty" smart credit card. The card, called Takashimaya VISA Smart Card, can be used as a regular VISA credit card worldwide. It also features a microchip that stores a wealth of information, ranging from a customer's age and address to bonus points earned by shopping at Takashimaya stores. Holders of this loyalty card can redeem these bonus points for such privileges as free car parking, free delivery, lucky drawings, gifts, and gift coupons. The card also stores information about the cardholder's shopping habits and target direct mail programs.

The smart card system consists of an electronic data capture terminal, a card reader, and a printer. It is integrated with the point-of-sale (POS) terminal and a hand-held scanner. The information collected at the POS is used to create a customer information system. The card includes the customer's shopping preferences, which are transferred via an intranet to the corporate databases. Mr. Chen Seong Leng, the MIS Manager at Takashimaya Singapore, explained, "In today's competitive environment, a retailer has to find a better means of identifying shopping trends and habits." Retailers must know exactly who has bought what merchandise.

The smart card system saves time for store personnel, who now make one entry instead of two (one at the POS, the other one for a credit payment). The Singapore store is located on Orchard Road, one of the most competitive shopping streets in the world. Since the introduction of smart cards, business has been booming as never before. The information collected is also processed by a decision-support system for pricing, designing advertisements, and other promotional decisions.

For Further Exploration: Newer smart cards that are issued to students in universities include additional features such as keys to the dormitory and the computer room. What is the logic of such an inclusion? What other information can be stored on smart cards?

Sources: Based on a story in *ITAsia*, December 1993, and on communications with VISA International, Spring 1998.

The recipient will be asked to set up an account to which the money that was sent will be credited. The recipient can then credit the money from this account to either his or her credit card or bank account.

Electronic Wallets. Most of the time when you make a purchase on the Web you're required to fill out a form with your name, shipping address, billing address, credit card information, and so on. Doing this a few times is fine, but having to do it every time you shop on the Web is an annoyance. Some merchants solve the problem by having you fill out a form once and then saving the information on their servers for later use. For instance, this is what Amazon.com has done with its "one-click" shopping. It utilizes information that you entered at the Amazon site on an earlier date. Of course, even if every merchant provided "one-click" shopping, you would still have to set up an account with every merchant. This would also increase the possibility that the information might fall into the hands of a merchant who wanted to use this information for some other purpose.

One way to avoid the problem of having to repeatedly fill out purchase information, while at the same time eliminating the need to store the information on a merchant's server, is to use an **electronic wallet (e-wallet)**. An e-wallet is a software component that a user downloads to his or her PC and in which the user stores credit-card numbers and other personal information. When a user shops at a merchant who accepts the e-wallet, the e-wallet allows the user to perform one-click shopping, with the e-wallet automatically filling in the necessary information.

Credit card companies like Visa (*visa.com/pd/ewallet/main.html*) and MasterCard (*mastercard.com*) offer e-wallets. So does Yahoo!, America Online (called Quick Checkout), and Microsoft (Passport). Of these, Yahoo! has the largest number of merchant participants with over 10,000. As of 2001, many banks around the globe offer this service.

PURCHASING CARDS. In some countries, such as the U.K., the United States, and Hong Kong, companies are paying other companies by means of *purchasing cards.* Unlike credit cards, where credit is provided for 30 to 60 days, for free, before payment is made to the merchant, payments made with purchasing cards are settled within a week (see *visa.com*). Purchasing cards are used for unplanned purchases, and corporations generally limit the amount per purchase (usually $1,000 to $2,000). Purchasing cards can be used on the Internet much like regular credit cards.

ELECTRONIC PAYMENT FROM CELLULAR PHONES. New technology enables people to make payments from their cell phones. In Japan you can pay vending machines this way, and in Finland you can pay for gasoline in some areas from your cell phone. For more detail, see *mobileinfo.com.*

ELECTRONIC FUNDS TRANSFER. **Electronic funds transfer (EFT)** is the electronic transfer of money to and from financial institutions using telecommunication networks. Electronic funds transfer is now widely used. It enables funds, debits and credits, and charges and payments to be electronically routed via clearinghouses among banks and between banks and customers. Examples of EFT include:

- Interbank transactions around the globe
- Payment of university tuition using an ATM
- Direct deposit of salaries in employees' accounts
- Payment of mortgages, utility bills, or car loans through monthly bank account deductions

EFT is fast. It reduces delays associated with sending hard-copy documents, and it eliminates returned checks. It has become the only practical way to handle the large volume of financial transactions generated daily in the banking industry. EFT-based ATMs are increasingly available in shopping centers and business areas, allowing individuals to make deposits, withdrawals, and money transfers 24 hours a day. While most EFTs are done on private lines, a growing number of financial institutions are moving to extranets, which are cheaper to use.

Intelligent Agents in E-Commerce

A final topic relating to EC infrastructure is the use of intelligent agents for finding products and vendors on the Internet (as well as helping in negotiations). **Intelligent agents** are computer programs to help users conduct routine tasks, to search and retrieve information, to support decision making, and to act as consulting experts. Intelligent software agents play an increasingly important role in EC. For example, they match individuals whose preferences (profiles) are known, with certain products, using a technology called *collaborative filtering.* An

TABLE 5.6 Intelligent Agents in Electronic Commerce

Process	Representative Agents
Need identification (stimuli to buy)	*likemind.com*—what to look at, sample *gifts.com, shopping.ninesmsn.com*—matches gifts with people *salesmountain.com*—matches sales with people
Product brokering (which specific product to buy)	*mysimon.com*—prioritize your criteria, and the agent will find an appropriate product
Merchant brokering (who to buy from)	*pricescan.com*—where to buy computers *allbookstores.com*—where to pay the least for books *buyerzone.com*—find lowest prices in B2B Others: *compare.net, mysimon.com*
Negotiations	*AuctionBot.com* at *auction.eecs.umich.edu*—agent will do the bidding for you
Purchase and delivery	*UPS.com*—optimizes deliveries
After-sale service	*brightware.com*—automatic response to customers
Others	*Resumix.com* (now part of TMP Worldwide)—matches candidates to jobs *webassured.com*—increases trust level *eFalcon.com*—a fraud detection agent

interesting way to view the role of intelligent agents is to follow the process the customer goes through while shopping online. For each step in this process there are several intelligent agents, as shown in Table 5.6. On the left side are the steps in the process and on the right are representative agents that can guide the customer's shopping effort online. For further information see Chapter 12 and Maes et al., 1999.

5.8 LEGAL, ETHICAL, AND PUBLIC POLICY ISSUES

Several legal, ethical, and public policy issues are associated with the implementation of EC. Representative issues are discussed in this section.

Market Practices and Consumer/Seller Protection

When buyers and sellers cannot see each other (they may even be in different countries), there is a chance for dishonest people to commit fraud and other crimes over the Internet. During the first few years of EC, we witnessed many of these, ranging from the creation of a virtual bank that disappeared together with the investors' deposits, to manipulating stocks on the Internet.

FRAUD ON THE INTERNET. Internet fraud and its sophistication have grown as much as and even faster than the Internet itself, as can be seen in the following examples.

Internet Stock Fraud. Fraudulent stock promoters specifically target small investors who are lured by the promise of fast profits. Such actions trigger frantic buying. When prices go up, the promoters sell the stocks they purchased at a low price. Consequently prices decline significantly, and many investors lose money. In fall 1998, the SEC brought charges against 44 companies and individuals who illegally promoted stocks on computer bulletin boards, online newspapers, and investment Web sites. (See details on both settled and pending cases at *sec.gov.*) In many cases, stock promoters falsely spread positive rumors about the prospects of the companies they touted. In other cases the information provided might have been true, but the promoters did not disclose that they were paid to talk up the companies.

Fraud in Electronic Auctions. There are more complaints about fraud in electronic auctions than in all other areas combined. Visit *eBay.com* to see all the measures this leading auction site takes to counter this problem.

Other Financial Fraud. Stocks and auctions are only two of the many areas in which swindlers are active. Other areas include selling bogus investments and phantom business opportunities. Financial criminals have access to far more people than ever before, due mainly to the availability of the Web and electronic mail. An example is provided in *A Closer Look* 5.3, below.

THE FEDERAL TRADE COMMISSION CONSUMER ALERTS. The Federal Trade Commission (FTC) provides a list of 12 scams most likely to arrive via e-mail or the Web. They are:

1. ***Business opportunities.*** These are promoted as "easy-to-start" businesses that will earn you a fortune. Usually they don't. Also illegal pyramid schemes are being offered.
2. ***Bulk mail solicitors.*** These offer to sell you lists of e-mail addresses. If you use them, you usually violate the terms of service of your Internet service provider.

A CLOSER LOOK
5.3 HOW FRAUD IS COMMITTED ON THE INTERNET

David Lee, a 41-year-old Hong Kong resident, replied to an advertisement in a respected business magazine that offered him free investment advice. After he replied, he received impressive brochures and a telephone sales speech. Then he was directed to the Web site of Equity Mutual Trust (Equity) where he was able to track the impressive daily performance of a fund that listed offices in London, Switzerland, and Belize. From that Web site he was linked to sister funds and business partners. He was linked to what he believed was the famous fund evaluator company Morningstar (*morningstar.com*). Actually, the site was an imitation that replicated the original site. The imitation site provided a very high, but false, rating on the Equity Mutual Trust funds. Finally, Lee was directed to read about Equity and its funds in the respected *International Herald Tribune*'s Internet edition; the article appeared to be news but was actually an advertisement. Convinced that he would receive super short-term gains, he mailed US$16,000, instructing Equity to invest in the Grand Financial Fund. Soon he grew suspicious when letters from Equity came from different countries, telephone calls and e-mails were not answered on time, and the daily Internet listings dried up.

When Lee wanted to sell, he was advised to increase his investment and shift to a Canadian company, Mit-Tec, allegedly a Y2K-bug troubleshooter. The Web site he was directed to looked fantastic. But this time Lee was careful. He contacted the financial authorities in the Turks and Caicos Islands—where Equity was based at that time—and was referred to the British police.

Soon he learned that chances were slim that he would ever see his money again. Furthermore, he learned that several thousand victims paid a total of about $4 billion to Equity. Most of the victims live in Hong Kong, Singapore, and other Asian countries. Several said that the most convincing information came from the Web sites, including the "independent" Web site that rated Equity and its funds as safe, five-star funds.

Source: Based on a story in the *South China Morning Post* (Hong Kong), May 21, 1999.

3. ***Chain letters.*** You are asked to send money to some people and your name and e-mail address are placed on a list. There is no guarantee that you will receive money, and your name and e-mail address become available to everyone to whom the list is forwarded. Also, chain letters are usually illegal.
4. ***Work-at-home schemes.*** These are usually worthless and cost you money for "startup."
5. ***Health and diet schemes.*** You usually get worthless products with no proven benefits.
6. ***"Effortless income."*** Do not believe these "easy-to-make-money" opportunities. Most will take your money and produce little or no income.
7. ***"Free goods."*** You pay to join a club and recruit others. It is usually an illegal pyramid scheme.
8. ***Investment opportunities.*** Do not believe in "investment with no risk" and "high return." High return with no risk simply does not exist. There are many scams to watch for.
9. ***Cable descrambler kits.*** These kits usually do not work, and it is illegal to use them.
10. ***Guaranteed loans or credit, on easy terms.*** You usually pay application fees and then are turned down.
11. ***Credit repair.*** Again, you pay a service fee, but get no help in repairing your credit rating.
12. ***Vacation prize promotions.*** These electronic certificates are usually scams. You will be asked to upgrade, and it will be very expensive.

The FTC shows examples in each of these categories at its Web site (*ftc.gov/bcp/conline/pubs/alerts/doznalrt.htm*). Lately, the FTC has been trying to deal with fraud in electronic auctions. A good rule of thumb in any financial dealing on the Internet (or otherwise) is: If it seems too good to be true, it probably is.

There are several ways buyers can be protected against EC fraud. The major methods are described below.

BUYER PROTECTION. Buyer protection is critical to the success of any commerce, and especially of electronic commerce, where buyers do not see the sellers. Here are some tips for safe electronic shopping:

1. Look for reliable brand names at sites like Wal-Mart Online, Disney Online, and Amazon.com. (Make sure that the sites are authentic. It is best to go to the URL site directly. As *A Closer Look* 5.3 showed, if you are linked to a site, it may not be what its name shows!)
2. Search any unfamiliar selling site for the company's address and phone and fax numbers. Call up and quiz the employees about the business.
3. Check the seller with the local Chamber of Commerce and/or Better Business Bureau (*bbbonline.org*), or look for seals of approval such as TRUSTe.
4. Investigate how secure the seller's site is and how well it is organized.
5. Examine the money-back guarantees, warranties, and service agreements.
6. Compare prices with those in regular stores. Too-low prices are usually too good to be true and some catch is probably involved.
7. Ask friends what they know. Find testimonials and endorsements.
8. Find out what you can do in case of a dispute.

9. Consult the National Fraud Information Center (*fraud.org*).
10. Check *consumerworld.org* for other useful resources.
11. Be aware that you have shopper's rights. These are outlined on the book's Web site.

SELLER PROTECTION. Sellers, too, need safeguards. They must be protected against consumers who refuse to pay or who pay with bad checks. They must have protection against buyers' fraudulent claims that the merchandise did not arrive. Sellers also have the right to protect themselves against the use of their name by others as well as the use of their unique words and phrases, product names, slogans, and Web address (trademark protection). Another seller protection particularly applies to electronic media: Sellers should have legal recourse against customers who download copyrighted software, music, and/or knowledge and sell it to others. This practice is mainly done in auctions and classified electronic ads, both of which are difficult to control.

Legal Issues Specific to E-Commerce

Many legal issues relate to e-commerce. Here are the most important ones:

DOMAIN NAME. Internet addresses are known as **domain names**. Domain names appear in levels. A *top-level* name is *www.wiley.com,* or *www.stanford.edu.* A *second-level* name will be *www.wiley.com/college/turban.* Top-level domain names are assigned by central nonprofit organizations that check for conflicts and possible infringement of trademarks. Problems arise when several companies that have similar names compete over a domain name that is not a registered trademark. Several cases are already in court. An international arbitration system is now available to settle disputes out of court. This system saves considerable time and money. The problem of domain names was alleviated somewhat in 2001 after several upper-level names (such as "firm" and "web") were added to "com".

TAXES AND OTHER FEES. Federal, state, and local authorities are scrambling to figure out how to get a piece of the revenue created electronically. The problem is particularly complex for interstate and international trades. For example, some claim that even the state where a *server* is located deserves some tax. Others say that the state where the *seller* is located deserves the entire tax. In addition to sales tax, there is a question about where to pay business license tax, income tax, value-added tax, franchise fees, gross-receipts tax, excise tax, privilege tax, and utility tax. Furthermore, how should tax collection be controlled?

Legislative efforts to enact taxes on Internet transactions are opposed by the Internet Freedom Fighters. At the moment there is a ban on taxing business done on the Internet (sales tax) in the United States and many other countries. The U.S. ban will remain valid until fall 2001, at which point Congress will decide whether to extend the ban or authorize various taxing authorities to begin collecting taxes. (If you have a strong opinion either way, contact your elected representatives.)

COPYRIGHT. Legal systems in many countries provide creators of *intellectual property* with protection of that property through copyrights. Nevertheless, protecting software and other intangible creations is difficult over the Web. Copyright issues and protection of intellectual property are discussed in Chapter 16 and in the ethics appendix to Chapter 1.

OTHER ISSUES. Several other legal issues are a challenge to the existing system:

- What are the rules of *electronic contracting*, and whose *jurisdiction* prevails when buyers, brokers, and sellers are in different states and/or countries?
- When are electronic documents admissible evidence in courts of law? What alternative evidence does one have if they are not admissible?
- The use of multiple networks and trading partners makes the documentation of responsibility difficult. How is such a problem overcome?
- Liability for errors, malfunction of software, and theft and fraudulent use of data may be difficult to prove. How is such liability determined?
- What is considered misrepresentation? Where should one take legal action against misrepresentation?
- Much of the law hinges on the physical location of files and data. With distributed databases and replication of databases, it is difficult to say exactly where data are stored at a given time. How is electronic storage related to existing legalities?
- Online corporate reports are difficult to audit since they can be frequently changed. How should such auditing be conducted, and what legal value does it have?

Ethical Issues

Many of the ethical issues related to IT in general apply also to electronic commerce. Some particular issues are the following.

1. ***Privacy and Web tracking.*** Privacy issues are related to both customers and employees. On the customer side, most electronic payment systems know who the buyers are; therefore, it may be necessary to protect the buyers' identities. Businesses certified by TRUSTe have adopted personal privacy policies that require customers to give "informed consent" to the sharing of any personal information. Other privacy issues may involve tracking of Internet users' activities by intelligent agents and cookies. Companies that use Web-tracking technology extensively, such as *doubleclick.com*, have had some legal challenges relating to customer privacy. Another privacy issue is companies' in-house monitoring of employees' Web activities. Many companies feel that it is reasonable to be able to monitor how employees use company resources, on company time. If you want to use Web-tracking technology in your business, check its state-of-the-art situation and also check any legal restrictions that may apply.
2. ***The human element.*** A possible difficulty in implementing EC relates to human nature. The technology is new to many IS directors and employees and so they may require new sets of skills. Another human factor is related to the nature of sales. The implementation of EC may lead to loss of salespeople's income as customers bypass the salesperson and revenues become more widely distributed within the company. Also, moving away from commissions to profit-sharing may be rejected by salespeople.
3. ***Disintermediation.*** As noted earlier, the use of EC may result in the elimination of a company's employees as well as brokers and agents (disintermediation). How these people, especially employees, are treated may raise ethical issues, such as how to handle the displacement.

Chapter 16 further discusses ethical issues as they relate to IT in general.

The Future of Electronic Commerce Some EC applications grew by 25 percent per month in the late 1990s—an astounding phenomenon! Some e-commerce activities are still growing at an average rate of 10 percent per month. Predictions on the total size of e-commerce vary, depending on the methods and assumptions used. For 2003, the total B2C and B2B are estimated to be in the range of $2,000 to $4,000 billion ($4 trillion). For predictions about EC volume in the future, see *forrester.com* and *emarketer.com*. There's a huge difference between $2 trillion and $4 trillion, but one thing we do know is that EC will be big!

MANAGERIAL ISSUES

1. ***Managing resistance to change.*** Electronic commerce can result in a fundamental change in how business is done, and resistance to change from employees, vendors, and customers may develop. Education, training, and publicity over an extended time period offer possible solutions to the problem.
2. ***Integration of e-commerce into the business environment.*** E-commerce needs to be integrated with the rest of the business. Integration issues involve planning, competition for corporate resources with other projects, and interfacing EC with databases, existing IT applications, and infrastructure.
3. ***Lack of qualified personnel and outsourcing.*** Very few people have expertise in e-commerce. There are many implementation issues that require expertise, such as when to offer special promotions on the Internet, how to integrate an e-market with the information systems of buyers and sellers, and what kind of customer incentives are appropriate under what circumstances. For this reason, it may be worthwhile to outsource some e-commerce activities. Yet, as shown in Chapter 13, outsourcing decisions are not simple.
4. ***Alliances.*** It is not a bad idea to join an alliance or consortium of companies to explore e-commerce. Alliances can be created at any time. Some EC companies (e.g., Amazon.com) have thousands of alliances. The problem is which alliance to join, or what kind of alliance to form and with whom.
5. ***Implementation plan.*** Because of the complexity and multifaceted nature of EC, it makes sense to prepare an implementation plan. Such a plan should include goals, budgets, timetables, and contingency plans. It should address the many legal, financial, technological, organizational, and ethical issues that can surface during implementation.
6. ***Responding to e-mail.*** Some companies are flooded by e-mail queries, requests, or complaints. It may be expensive to answer them quickly, and slow response may be damaging to the company. Many companies develop a strict response time policy (e.g., within 24 or 48 hours). Intelligent agents can be useful for automated reply.
7. ***Choosing the company's strategy toward e-commerce.*** Generally speaking there are three major options:

   - ***Lead.*** Conduct large-scale innovative e-commerce activities.
   - ***Watch and wait.*** Do nothing, but carefully watch what is going on in the field in order to determine when EC is mature enough to enter it.
   - ***Experiment.*** Start some e-commerce experimental projects (learn by doing). Each of these options has its advantages and risks (see Exercise 2).

8. ***Privacy.*** In electronic payment systems, it may be necessary to protect the identity of buyers. Other privacy issues may involve tracking of Internet user activities by intelligent agents and cookies, and in-house monitoring of employees' Web activities.
9. ***Justifying e-commerce by conducting a cost-benefit analysis is very difficult.*** Many intangible benefits and lack of experience may produce grossly inaccurate estimates of costs and benefits. Nevertheless, a feasibility study must be done, and estimates of costs and benefits must be made. For example, see the proposal for assessing EDI investment presented by Hoogewelgen and Wagenaar (1996).
10. ***Order fulfillment.*** Taking orders in EC may be easier than fulfilling them. To learn about the problems and solutions related to order fulfillment, see Chapter 6.
11. ***Managing the impacts.*** The impacts of e-commerce on organizational structure, people, marketing procedures, and profitability may be dramatic. Therefore, establishing a committee or organizational unit to develop strategy and to manage e-commerce is necessary.

ON THE WEB SITE... Additional resources, including the Virtual Company, quizzes, cases, updates, additional exercises, links, demos, and activities, can be found on the book's Web site.

KEY TERMS

Advocacy marketing *183*
Affiliate programs *184*
Business-to-business EC (B2B) *191*
Business-to-consumer EC (B2C) *176*
Buy-side models *191*
Channel conflict *177*
Click-and-mortar retailers *177*
Collaborative commerce (c-commerce) *216*
Company-centric e-marketplace *167*
Cookie *185*
Cyberbanking (electronic banking) *196*
Cybermall (electronic mall) *175*
Decryption *218*
Digital signature *219*
Disintermediation *186*
Domain names *229*
Dynamic pricing *195*
e-business *168*
e-government *209*
e-marketplace *168*
e-tailer *176*
Electronic banking *196*
Electronic bartering *209*
Electronic benefits transfer (EBT) *210*
Electronic cash (e-cash) *222*
Electronic certificates *219*
Electronic checks (e-checks) *221*
Electronic commerce (EC) *168*
Electronic credit cards *221*
Electronic data interchange (EDI) *213*
Electronic exchange *167*
Electronic funds transfer (EFT) *225*
Electronic mall *175*
Electronic marketplace *168*
Electronic wallet (e-wallet) *224*
Electronic retailing (e-tailing) *175*
Electronic storefront *175*
Encryption *218*
Exchanges *191*
Forward auction *193*
Group purchasing *195*
Intelligent agents *225*
Internet communities *181*
Interorganizational information systems (IOS) *170*
Intrabusiness EC *209*
Key (in encryption) *218*
Keyword banner *178*
l-commerce *205*
m-commerce *205*
Metamalls *176*
Micropayments *217*
One-to-one marketing *189*
Online (electronic) catalogs *184*
Permission marketing *182*
Person-to-person (P2P) payments *223*
Private key *219*
Protocol *220*
Public-key infrastructure (PKI) *218*
Push technology *182*
Random banners *180*
Reintermediation *186*
Reverse auction *193*
Sell-side models *191*
Smart cards *223*
Spamming *180*
Stored-value card *223*
Systematic sourcing *195*
Viral marketing *183*

CHAPTER HIGHLIGHTS (Numbers Refer to Learning Objectives)

1 Electronic commerce can be conducted on the Web, by e-mail, and on other networks.

1 E-commerce offers many benefits to the organization, consumers, and society.

1 Electronic commerce is divided into three major areas: business to consumer (B2C), business to business (B2B), and intrabusiness.

1 Electronic commerce limitations are technical and nontechnical. The current technical limitations are expected to lessen with time.

2 The major pure business-to-consumer (B2C) applications are direct marketing and e-tailing.

3 Customer behavior is critical to B2C electronic commerce; it can be studied by questionnaires or by automatic observation of people's movements on the Internet. Market research can also be done utilizing newsgroups, Web sites, and "cookies."

3 Customer service occurs before purchase, during purchase, after purchase, and during disposal of products.

3 Electronic commerce (software) agents help customers find products and services, monitor events and notify customers, and negotiate on behalf of the customer.

4 The major B2B models for a single company are sell-side (one seller, many buyers), buy-side (one buyer, many sellers), collaborative commerce (a company with business partners). Auctions and reverse auctions can be used.

4 The major types of many-to-many e-marketplaces are third-party markets, consortia trading exchanges, information portals, and dynamic marketplaces.

5 The major service industries for EC are electronic banking and personal finance, electronic stock trading, travel, job market, and real estate. EC activities in these industries are both B2B and B2C operations.

6 Auctions are popular in C2C, B2C, and B2B e-commerce due to their dynamic pricing. Other C2C applications are classified sales and sale of personal services. EC that is done in a wireless environment is referred to as m-commerce. Finally, increasing attention is given to various EC activities in government services.

7 Electronic data interchange (EDI) deals with predetermined standard transactions (such as placing purchasing orders and billing) among regular trading partners.

7 The major electronic commerce infrastructure components are networks, Web servers, Web tools, programming languages, transactional software, and security devices.

7 An extranet connects the intranets of business partners. Its security is enhanced with VPN. It is a flexible, scaleable, and relatively inexpensive infrastructure for B2B and especially for exchanges.

8 Nonelectronic payment systems are insufficient or inferior for doing business on the Internet. Therefore, electronic payment systems are used.

8 Electronic payments can be made by e-cash (several methods), e-card (credit, debit, purchasing), e-checks, and smart cards.

8 Security is a major issue in e-commerce. Secure transactions and payments receive most attention, but protection of privacy must also be addressed. Security is provided by SSL protocols and PKI systems.

9 Many unresolved legal issues surround e-commerce implementation. Protection of customers and intellectual property is a major concern, but so are the value of contracts, domain names, and how to handle legal issues in a multicountry environment.

10 Implementing e-commerce is not simple, and multiple financial, organizational, technological, and managerial issues must be addressed.

10 E-commerce companies and initatives fail due to lack of enough buyers and sellers, wrong revenue models, poor planning, strong competition, and lack of cash.

QUESTIONS FOR REVIEW

1. Define electronic commerce and e-business.
2. List the major e-commerce infrastructure elements.
3. List the benefits of e-commerce to organizations.
4. List the benefits of e-commerce to consumers.
5. List the benefits of e-commerce to society.
6. Define business-to-consumer (B2C), business-to-business (B2B), and intrabusiness EC.
7. Describe an electronic mall.
8. List the different Internet advertisement options.
9. Describe banners and their use.
10. Define "cookies."
11. Define disintermediation and reintermediation.
12. Define market research for EC.
13. Describe the four phases of the customer service life cycle.
14. Define channel conflict.
15. Define a B2B exchange.
16. Describe a reverse auction.

17. Define EDI and describe its capabilities.
18. Define private and public keys in a PKI.
19. Define digital signature and certificate.
20. Describe electronic cash systems.
21. Define micropayments.
22. Define smart cards.
23. Define electronic funds transfer (EFT).

QUESTIONS FOR DISCUSSION

1. Compare and contrast electronic markets and interorganizational information systems; be sure to describe the major characteristics of each.
2. Discuss the major limitations of e-commerce. Which of them are likely to disappear? Why?
3. Describe the advantages of electronic home shopping over regular shopping.
4. Describe the benefits of electronic stock trading.
5. Why is the electronic job market so popular, especially among the high-tech professions?
6. Discuss the relationship between digital signature, certification, and the public-key system.
7. Compare company-centric B2B with exchanges. Discuss isssues such as buyers, sellers, ownership, and infrastructure.
8. Why is EDI moving from VANs to the Internet? What are some of the limitations of such a move? In what ways can VAN-based and Internet-based EDI complement each other?
9. Identify the e-commerce elements in the Highway 91 project.
10. If you had a chance to select between an electronic auction and a face-to-face auction, which one would you select and why?
11. Compare the following advertisement effectiveness measures: ad view, clickthrough, and actual purchase. What are the advantages and disadvantages of each?
12. Describe the benefits of a smart card.
13. Explain how electronic credit cards work. How can a third-party intervention be useful in electronic card payments?
14. What might be the impact of widely accepted electronic banking on the banking industry? (Try *ramresearch .com/crdflash/cf12_6e.html*.)
15. Why might people object to the use of a cookie to build their marketing profile? After all, no one knows whose profile is being constructed.
16. Discuss the major issues related to electronic payments.
17. Describe the role of intelligent agents in EC.
18. Compare and contrast EDI and e-mail.
19. The Highway 91 Express system is centered around a transponder and a prepaid account. Could a debit smart card be used instead? What are the advantages and disadvantages of each?
20. Why is it so difficult to measure the effectiveness of advertisements on the Internet?
21. Relate push technology to mass customization.
22. Why it is necessary to use different keys for a message and for its attached signature?

EXERCISES

1. Examine the customer service life-cycle model. Find one real-life example for each phase.
2. Compare B2B and B2C auctions. Also, find information about auction brokers (such as *auctionwatch.com*). Why is eBay at odds with such brokers?
3. Contact PictureTalk (*picturetalk.com*) and find information about its products. Discuss their advantages.
4. General Electric saved $240,000 in 1996 in printing costs by using its intranet to publish a simple directory of company information. How is this possible? Explain.
5. You want to open a baby diaper factory in China. You consider the following alternatives.
   a. Organize a partnership between an existing small diaper manufacturer in another country and a Chinese partner that will provide the facilities in China and do the marketing and sales. You will be the organizer. Your first mission is to find on the Web a suitable diaper manufacturer. How would you go about it?
   b. Buy the necessary machines and knowledge required for such a factory. Then organize a company in China. Locate such machines on the Web. Identify sources of the required knowledge.
   c. You are considering expansion from baby diapers to adult diapers, dog diapers (*dog-diaper.com*), and more. Explore and report.
6. Find information about how to conduct a new business. Go to *catalog.com*, and to *bankmag.com/guide/c090/ c090162.htm*. Report on your findings.

7. Find information on the Web about:
   a. Getting an MBA degree at a virtual university.
   b. Going public on the Internet with stocks.
   c. Business credit verification.
8. Describe how public and private keys are used in the following instances:
   a. A wants to send a secure message to many, but only authorized people.
   b. A pays B in digital cash via a digital bank's currency server. How can security be assured?
   c. A received an e-check from B. How can he or she be sure it is real?
9. Relate Clinton and Gore's (1997) paper to Figure 5.1.

GROUP AND ROLE-PLAYING ACTIVITIES

1. Wells Fargo Bank (*wellsfargo.com*) is well on its way to becoming a cyberbank. Hundreds of branch offices are being closed. Research the bank's strategy and its benefits and limitations and report on your findings.
2. Studying consumer behavior can be done with the consumer's cooperation, such as asking the consumer to answer a questionnaire and then analyzing it. Likewise, it can be done without the consumer's knowledge (using a cookie or other methods such as those used by DoubleClick). Divide the class into two groups; each will research one approach. Each group should present its report, and then the two groups should discuss and compare the differences between the two approaches.
3. Research the various measures that are available to protect customers shopping on the Internet. Prepare a list of such measures; include at least five not listed in this book. Prepare a report.
4. Surf the Internet to find articles, cases, and vendors related to Internet-based EDI.
   a. Join a newsgroup whose interest is EDI on the Internet. Identify the major issues of concern.
   b. Find the benefits and limitations of EDI/Internet.
5. The giant bookstore Amazon.com lists over 10,000,000 titles in its electronic catalog, yet it does not have much physical book inventory.
   a. Enter the company site at *amazon.com*.
   b. Print a list of books on the topics of m-commerce and EDI.
   c. Find out what professional advice on buying books you can get at the site.
   d. What other services do you get there that you normally do not get in a leading bookstore?

INTERNET EXERCISES

1. Access *etrade.com* and register for the Internet stock game there. You will be bankrolled with (hypothetical) $100,000 in a trading account every month. Try to win the game! Alternatively, try the $200,000 game available on *marketplayer.com*.
2. Access the Web site of Computer Associates (*cai.com*) and search for information on Kiplinger's Simple Money. Then access Microsoft's site (*msn.com*) and find information about Money. Compare the capabilities of the two. Finally, find information about Quicken (*quicken.com*). Why is Quicken's market share the largest?
3. Take an electronic tour of Wells Fargo bank (*wellsfargo.com*). Examine its services and fees. Assuming it is cheaper to do business there, would you open an account? Why or why not?
4. You want to invest in a semiconductor industry in Taiwan and Korea, and are looking for one U.S. mutual fund and one Asian mutual fund to put your money in. Use information at the following sites: *morningstar.com*, *funds-sp.com/win/en*, and *uneedtrust.com*. Which specific high-tech companies are the mutual funds investing in?
5. Access *realtor.com*. Prepare a list of services available on this site, then prepare a list of advantages derived by the users and the advantages to realtors. Are there any disadvantages? To whom?
6. Visit the following sites and prepare a research report on the current status of electronic commerce: *forrester.com*, *nielsenmedia.com*, and *zonaresearch.com*.
7. Discuss the status of the proposed Internet Tax Freedom Act by visiting *house.gov/republicanpolicy. global.html*.
8. Access the Web sites of CyberCash (*cybercash.com*) and Visa (*visa.com*). Find out the latest developments of e-cash and e-credit. What are they offering to the merchants? What other services do they provide?
9. Access *mondex.com*. Discuss the Mondex card and its benefits.
10. Access the Web site of Happy Puppy (*happypuppy.com*). Examine the various features offered. Download a

demo and play it. What do you like most about visiting this site? What do you not like? Why?

11. Try to find a unique gift on the Internet for a friend. Several sites can help you do it. For example, try *shopping.com* or *amazon.com*. Describe your experience with your online gift search.

12. Enter *echecksecure.com*. Take the demo and read all about electronic checks. Write a report.

Minicase 1

How Does Interactive Marketing Work? The DoubleClick Approach

www.doubleclick.net

Interactive marketing can take many forms. Assume that 3M Corporation wants to sell its $10,000 multimedia projectors. It knows that potential buyers are people who work in advertising agencies or in IS departments of large corporations, or are companies that use Unix as their operating system. 3M approaches DoubleClick Inc. and asks the firm to identify such potential customers. How does DoubleClick find them? Clever and simple.

In 1997, DoubleClick (*doubleclick.net*) monitored people browsing the Web sites of about 100 cooperating companies such as Quicken and Travelocity. In 2001 it monitored more than 300 sites. By inspecting Internet addresses of the visitors to the Web sites of these 300 companies and matching them against a database with 70,000 Internet domain names that include a line-of-business code, DoubleClick can find those people working for various types of companies, say, advertising agencies. By checking the browsers, it can also find out which visitor is using a Unix system. While DoubleClick cannot find out your name, it can build a dossier on you, attached to an ID number that was assigned to you during your first visit to any of the 300 cooperating sites. As you continue to visit the 300 sites, an intelligent software agent builds a relatively complete dossier on you, your spending, and your computing habits. This process is done with a device known as a *cookie*, a file created at the request of a Web server and stored on the user's hard drive. So, the Web site can "remember" your past behavior on the Internet.

DoubleClick then prepares an ad for 3M projectors. The ad is targeted for people whose profile matches what is needed for 3M. So, if you are a Unix user or employed by an advertising agency, on your next browsing trip to any of the 300 participating Web sites you will be surprised to find exactly what you wanted: information about the multimedia projector.

How is all this financed? 3M pays DoubleClick for the ad. The fee is then split with the Web sites that carry the 3M ads, based on how many times the ad is matched with a visitor.

Note: You can avoid the creation of a cookie on your hard drive if you elect to do so, using software such as Cookie Cutter or by turning off cookies in your browser. However, only a few people know this fact. In most cases the cookie is placed on your hard drive without your knowledge. You can also try to disable cookies yourself by making them read-only.

Source: Based on information from *doubleclick.net.*

Questions for Minicase 1

1. Is this a B2C or a B2B? Explain why.
2. Visitors' names are not known to any participating party, yet many object to this method. Why?
3. Discuss the revenue splitting. Can you suggest a better way to do it?
4. DoubleClick does not face much direct competition. Why not?

Minicase 2

Grocery Supermarket Keeps It Fresh

www.woolworths.com.au

Perishable goods such as fruit, vegetables, meat, and milk are significant in any retail marketplace. Online startup grocery companies like Peapod.com (U.S.) and Green-grocer.com (Australia) have found new ways to satisfy customers.

How is a well-established major player to respond? With huge investments in brick-and-mortar stores, Woolworths of Australia found itself dealing with just this question. The

(continued)

grocery market in Australia is dominated by three major players: Coles-Myers, Woolworths, and Franklins. Between them they control some 80 percent of the marketplace. Franklins, which is Hong Kong–owned, takes a low-cost minimum-service approach. The others, both Australian-owned, provide a full range of products, including fresh foods and prepared meals.

Woolworths' initial approach was to set up a standard Web site, offering a limited range of goods but excluding perishable items. This approach was test-marketed in areas near major supermarkets. The company felt that it had to respond to the emerging approaches from online entrepreneurs. If those organizations were allowed to take over a sizable segment of the market, recovering market share could be difficult.

Management soon realized that this was not an attractive approach. Woolworths' staff in the store nearest to the customer had to walk the aisles, fill the baskets, pack the goods, and deliver them. For an organization that had optimized its supply chain in order to cut costs, here was a sudden explosion in costs. With gross margins only 10 percent and net margins around 4 percent, it looked very easy to become unprofitable using this new approach.

Furthermore, Woolworths was known as "the fresh food people"—with fruit and vegetables, freshly baked bread, meat, and prepared meals being heavily promoted. By ignoring these at its home shopping site, Woolworths was avoiding its strengths.

Therefore, Woolworths retooled its approach. Its second-generation home shopping site, Homeshop, is designed with freshness in mind, and all the fresh food is available for delivery. Deliveries are arranged from major regional supermarkets, rather than from every local store. There is a $50 minimum order, a 7.5 percent surcharge for home delivery, and a $6 delivery charge. These charges help in recovering the additional costs, yet an average order of around $200 still returns little profit.

New users can register only if deliveries are possible to their postal address. On first use of the system, customers are guided to find the products that they want and are offered suggestions from the list of best-selling items. Alternatively customers can browse for items by category or search by keyword. Items are accumulated in the "shopping trolley" (cart). The first order can form a master list for future orders, as can subsequent orders.

When customers have selected the required items, they select "checkout," where the total value is computed and the customer confirms that delivery is required. Payment is made only at time of delivery, using cash or a mobile electronic funds transfer terminal (EFTPOS) and either a credit card or a debit card. In this way, precise charges can be made based on weight of meat or fish, as well as allowing credit for out-of-stock items. The customer sets the delivery time and day, and will bear an additional charge if not at home to accept the delivery.

Additional services that are available include dietary advice, recipes, and recording of preferred food items. At present, these do not link directly into the shopping trolley.

Source: Written by Professor Ernie Jordan, Macquarie Graduate School of Management, Sydney, Australia.

Questions for Minicase 2

1. Visit the Woolworths Homeshop site, and find any new activities now offered that were not mentioned above.
2. Who would be the target customers for this site?
3. How might this service disrupt the previously highly tuned supply chain?
4. Compare the advantages and disadvantages of the EFTPOS payment mechanism with the more usual "credit card at time of order."
5. Should the newer startups such as *greengrocer.com.au* and Peapod be threatened by this service? How about traditional local grocery stores, such as Dewsons Wembley (*dewsons.com.au*)?

REFERENCES AND BIBLIOGRAPHY

1. Adam, N., and Y. Yesha, *Electronic Commerce: Current Research Issues and Applications.* New York: Springer, 1996.
2. Agrawal, V., et al., "E-performance: The Path to Rational Exuberance," *The McKinsey Quarterly,* Vol. 1, No. 2, 2001.
3. Aronson, B., et al., *Advertising on the Internet.* New York: Wiley, 1999.
4. Asokan, K., et al., "The State of the Art in Electronic Payment Systems," *Computer,* September 1997.
5. Bernard, R., *Corporate Intranet.* New York: Wiley, 1997.
6. Chase, R. D., et al., *Production Operations Management,* 8th ed. Homewood, IL: Richard D. Irwin, 1998.
7. Choi, S. Y., et al., *The Economics of Electronic Commerce.* Indianapolis, IN: Macmillan, technical publication, 1997.
8. Clark, T. H., "Financial Times: Reengineering Logistics Using the Internet," *Proceedings of the 31st Hawaiian International Conference on Systems Sciences (HICSS),* January 1998.
9. Clinton, W. J., and A. Gore Jr., "A Framework for Global Electronic Commerce," www.iitf.nist.gov/eleccomm/ecomm.htm, July 1997.

10. "Electronic Commerce on the Internet," Special issues of *Communications of the ACM,* June 1996.

11. Farrell, P. B., *Investor's Guide to the Net.* New York: Wiley, 1996.

12. Fickel, L., *Big Business,* CIO Web Business, June 1, 1999.

13. Guglielmo, C., "Global Transport," *Corporate Computing,* June–July 1992.

14. Guglielmo, C., "Toys 'R' Us: Special Report," *Interactive Week,* November 1, 1999.

15. Handfield, R., and E. Nichols, *Supply Chain Management.* Upper Saddle River, NJ: Prentice-Hall, 1999.

16. Helm, S., "Viral Marketing: Establishing Customer Relationship by Word of Mouse," *Electronic Markets,* Vol. 10, No. 3, 2001.

17. Hills, M., *Intranet Business Strategy.* New York: Wiley, 1996.

18. Hoogewelgen, M. R., and R. W. Wagenaar, "A Method to Assess Expected Net Benefits of EDI Investments," *International Journal of Electronic Commerce,* Fall 1996.

19. Hutheeing, N., "HP's Giant ATM," *Forbes,* February 9, 1998.

20. Ives, B., and G. P. Learmouth, "The Information System as a Competitive Weapon," *Communications of the ACM,* December 1984.

21. Jarvenpaa, S. L., and P. A. Todd, "Consumer Reactions to Electronic Shopping on the WWW," *International Journal of Electronic Commerce,* Winter 1996/1997.

22. Kalakota, R., and A. B. Whinston, *Electronic Commerce: A Manager's Guide.* Reading, MA: Addison-Wesley, 1997.

23. Kaplan, S., and M. Sawhney, "E-hubs: The New B2B Marketplaces," *Harvard Business Review,* May–June 2000.

24. Kimbrough, S. O., and R. M. Lee, "Formal Aspects of Electronic Commerce: Research Issues and Challenges," *International Journal of Electronic Commerce,* Summer 1997.

25. Kosiur, D., *Understanding Electronic Commerce.* Redwood, WA: Microsoft Press, 1997.

26. Kotler, P., and G. Armstrong, *Principles of Marketing,* 8th ed. Upper Saddle River, NJ: Prentice-Hall, 1999.

27. Maes, P., et al., "Agents that Buy and Sell," *Communications of the ACM,* March 1999.

28. McElroy, D., and E. Turban, "Using Smart Cards in Electronic Commerce," *International Journal of Information Systems,* February 1998.

29. McGonagle, J., Jr., and C. Vella, *A New Archetype for Competitive Intelligence.* Westport, CT: Greenwood Publishing Group and Quorum Books, 1997.

30. McKeown, P. G., and R. T. Watson, *Metamorphosis—A Guide to the WWW and Electronic Commerce,* 2nd ed. New York: Wiley, 1998.

31. McLaughlin, T., "Electronic Benefits Transfer: Should Banks Be Interested?" *Banker's Magazine,* March–April 1996.

32. Meeker, N., *The Internet Advertising Report.* New York: Morgan Stanley Corp., 1997.

33. Mowen, J. C., and M. Minor, *Consumer Behavior.* Upper Saddle River, NJ: Prentice-Hall, 1998.

34. Moukheiber, Z., "DoubleClick Is Watching You," *Forbes,* November 4, 1996.

35. Nussbaum, G., "EDI: First Aid for Soaring Hospital Cost," *Corporate Computing,* August–September 1992.

36. O'Keefe, S., *Publicity on the Internet.* New York: Wiley, 1997.

37. Panurach, P., "Money in Electronic Commerce," *Communications of the ACM,* June 1996.

38. Pawar, B. S., and R. Sharda, "Obtaining Business Intelligence on the Internet," *Long Range Planning,* Vol. 30, No. 1, 1997.

39. Peffers, K., and V. K., Tunnainen, "Expectation and Impacts of Global Information Systems: The Case of a Global Bank from Hong Kong," *Journal of Global IT Management,* Vol. 1, No. 4, 1998.

40. Peppers, D., et al., *The One to One Fieldbook.* New York: Currency & Doubleday, 1999.

41. Perry, T. S., "Electronic Money: Toward a Virtual Wallet," Special Issue, *IEEE Spectrum,* February 1997 (13 papers).

42. Porter, M. E., "Strategy and the Internet," *Harvard Business Review,* March 2001.

43. Randall, D., "Consumer Strategies for the Internet: Four Scenarios," *Long Range Planning,* Vol. 30, No. 2, 1997.

44. Rose, L., "Internet Shopping Rights," *Internet Shopper,* Spring 1997, p. 104.

45. Schully, A. B., and W. Woods, *B2B Exchanges.* New York: ISI Publications, 2000.

46. Senn, J. A., "Capitalization on Electronic Commerce," *Information Systems Management,* Summer 1996.

47. Selz, D., and P. Schubert, "Web Assessment—A Model for the Evaluation of Successful Electronic Commerce Applications," *Proceedings HICSS 31,* Hawaii, January 1998.

48. Seybold, P. B., *Customers.com.* New York: Random House, 1998.

49. Stalling, W., *Business Data Communications.* New York: Macmillan, 1990.

50. Sterne, J., *WWW Marketing,* 2nd ed. New York: Wiley, 1999.

51. Taylor D., and S. M. Cooney, *The E-Auction Insider.* New York: Osborne McGraw Hill, 2000.

52. Timmers, P., *Electronic Commerce.* Chichester, U.K.: Wiley, 1999.

53. Tucker, J. M., "EDI and the Net: A Profitable Partnering," *Datamation,* April 1997.

54. Turban, E., et al., *Electronic Commerce: A Managerial Perspective,* 2nd ed. Upper Saddle River, NJ: Prentice-Hall, 2002.

55. Useem, J., "Dot.coms: What Have We Learned?" *Fortune,* October 2000.

56. Vassos, T., *Strategic Internet Marketing.* Indianapolis, IN: Que, 1996.

57. Waltner, C., "EDI 'Travels the Web,'" *Communications Week,* June 16, 1997.

58. Wang, S., "Analyzing Agents for Electronic Commerce," *Information Systems Management,* Winter 1999.

59. Wayner, P., *Digital Cash.* Boston: AP Professional, 1997.

60. Williams J., et al., "IT Lessons Learned from FDA," *Failures and Lessons Learned in IT Management,* Vol. 1, No. 1, 1997.

61. Zwass, V., "Electronic Commerce: Structures and Issues," *International Journal of Electronic Commerce,* Fall 1996.

CHAPTER

6

Supply Chain Management and Enterprise Resource Planning

LEARNING OBJECTIVES

After studying this chapter, you will be able to:

1. Understand the concept of the supply chain, its importance, and management.
2. Describe the problems of managing the supply chain and some innovative solutions.
3. Trace the evolution of software that supports activities along the supply chain.
4. Understand the relationships among enterprise resource planning (ERP), supply chain management (SCM), and e-commerce.
5. Describe order fulfillment problems and solutions in e-commerce and how EC solves other supply chain problems.

HOW DELL REENGINEERED AND MANAGES ITS SUPPLY CHAIN

THE PROBLEM

Michael Dell started his business as a student, from his university dorm, by using a mail-order approach to selling PCs. This changed the manner by which PCs were sold. The customer did not have to come to a store to buy a computer, and Dell was able to customize the computer to the specifications of the customer. The direct mail approach enabled Dell to underprice his rivals, who were using distributors and retailers, by 10 percent. For several years the business grew slowly, but Dell constantly captured market share. In 1993, Compaq, the PC market leader at that time, decided to drastically cut prices to drive Dell out of the market. As a result of the price war, Dell Computer Inc. had a $65 million loss from reduced sales and inventory writedowns in the first six months of 1993 alone. The company was on the verge of bankruptcy.

www.dell.com

THE SOLUTION

Dell realized that the only way to win the marketing war was to introduce fundamental changes, termed *business process reengineering* (Chapter 8), in its own business, and along the supply chain, from its suppliers all the way to its customers. In addition to competing on *price* and *quality,* Dell started competing on *speed.* Since 2000, if you order a customized PC on any working day, the computer will be on the delivery truck the next day; a complex custom-made PC will be delivered in 5 days or less. Among the innovations used to reengineer the business were:

- Dell uses an approach called *mass customization,* meaning that it produces large quantities of customized products, at a low cost. Though the approach wasn't a new one, Dell was the first to use it in marketing computers.
- Dell builds many computers only after they are ordered. This is done by using just-in-time manufacturing, which also enables quick deliveries, low inventories, little or no obsolescence, and lower marketing and administrative costs.
- Component warehouses, which are maintained by Dell's suppliers, are located within 15 minutes of Dell factories. Not only can Dell get parts quickly, but it can get parts that are up to 60 days newer than those of its major competitors.
- Most orders from customers and to suppliers are done on the Web.
- Shipments, which are done by UPS and other carriers, are all arranged electronically.
- Dell collaborates electronically with its major buyers to pick customers' brains for new product ideas.
- Dell's new PC models are tested at the same time as the networks that they are on are tested. This cooperation with another vendor reduced the testing period from 60 or 90 days to 15.
- Dell's employees constantly monitor productivity and rate of return on investment (ROI), on all products.

Most significant for Dell has been the emergence of *electronic commerce.* In 2001, Dell was selling more than $4.0 million worth of computers each day on its Web site, and this amount was growing by 6 percent per month! In 1999 Dell added electronic auctions (*dellauction.com*) as a marketing channel. Dell is aiming to sell most of its computers from its Web site (*dell.com*).

Dell is frequently cited as an example of a top customer relationship management (CRM) provider. The CRM activities are integrated with customers' ordering and order fulfillment. Customers can track their orders online, to see if the computers are in production or already on the shipping track. They also can access detailed diagrams of the computers and get information about troubleshooting. By using viewer-approved configurations and pricing for its customers and by eliminating paperwork, Dell has been able to cut administrative-process expenses by 15 percent.

In addition, Dell created customized home pages for its biggest corporate customers, such as Eastman Chemical, Monsanto, and Wells Fargo. These sites, known as Premier Pages, enable customers' employees to use Dell's provided configuration and workflow software to design computers, get an order approved inside the client organization, and place orders quickly and easily. These employees can also order PCs for their own homes and receive the corporate price! The electronic ordering makes customers happy, but it also enables Dell to collect payments very quickly.

Once orders are received they are transferred electronically to the production floor. Intelligent systems prepare the required parts and components list for each computer, and check availability. If not in stock, components are ordered electronically directly from suppliers who can sometimes deliver in less than 60 minutes. Dell uses several other information technologies, including e-mail, EDI, video teleconferencing, electronic procurement, computerized faxes, an intranet, DSS, and a Web-based call center. Computerized manufacturing systems tightly link the entire demand and supply chains from suppliers to buyers. This system is the foundation on which the "build-to-order" strategy rests.

Dell also passes along data about its defect rates, engineering changes, and product enhancements to its suppliers. Since both Dell and its suppliers are in constant communication, the margin for error is reduced. Also, employees are now able to collaborate in real time on product designs and enhancements. In turn, suppliers are required to share with Dell sensitive information, such as their own quality problems. It was easy to get suppliers to follow Dell's lead because they also reap the benefits of faster cycle times, reduced inventory, and improved forecasts.

Dell also uses the Internet to create a community around its supply chain. Dell's corporate portal has links to bulletin boards where partners from around the world can exchange information about their experiences with Dell and its value chain.

THE RESULTS

By 2000, Dell had become the number-one PC seller. It is considered one of the world's best-managed and most profitable companies.

Sources: Compiled from several articles in *Business Week* (1997–2001), *Information Week* (1998–2001), *cio.com* (2001), and *dell.com*.

LESSONS LEARNED FROM THIS CASE

The Dell case demonstrates the following points:

1. By introducing a new business model, a firm can change the manner in which business is done and may even capture the leadership in an industry.
2. To implement this model on a large scale (mass customization), one needs to build superb supply chain management that includes suppliers and customers.
3. Another major success factor in Dell's plans was the improvements made in its logistics system along the entire supply chain. Using Web technologies, Dell integrated its own suppliers into its supply chain efficiently and effectively.
4. By introducing major customer-related changes, Dell enables customers to order what they like, do it from home, and get it quickly, at a competitive price and with high quality. Improved communications and customer service, which are part of Dell's CRM program, are the cornerstones of its success.
5. In addition to trading, Dell was using c-commerce with its business partners.
6. Dell created flexible and responsive IT manufacturing systems that are integrated with the supply chain.

Dell successfully implemented the concepts of *supply chain management, enterprise resource planning, supply chain intelligence,* and *customer relationship management.* The first three topics are the subject of this chapter. CRM is described in Chapter 7.

6.1 ESSENTIALS OF THE SUPPLY AND VALUE CHAINS

Definitions and Benefits

Initially, the concept of a *supply chain* referred to the flow of materials from their sources (suppliers) to the company, and then inside the company to places where they were needed. There was also recognition of a *demand chain,* which described the process of taking orders. Soon it was realized that these two concepts are interrelated, so they were integrated under the single concept of *extended supply chain,* or just *supply chain.*

DEFINITION. A **supply chain** refers to the flow of materials, information, payments, and services from raw material suppliers, through factories and warehouses, to the end customers. A supply chain also includes the *organizations* and *processes* that create and deliver products, information, and services to the end customers. It includes many tasks such as purchasing, payment flow, materials handling, production planning and control, logistics and warehousing inventory control, and distribution and delivery.

The function of **supply chain management (SCM)** is to plan, organize, and coordinate all the supply chain's activities. Today the concept of SCM refers to a total systems approach to managing the entire supply chain.

BENEFITS. The goals of modern SCM are to reduce uncertainty and risks in the supply chain, thereby positively affecting inventory levels, cycle time, business processes, and customer service. All these benefits contribute to increased profitability and competitiveness. The benefits of supply chain management have long been recognized both in business and in the military. Clerchus of Sparta said, as early as 401 B.C., that the survival of the Greek army depended not only upon its discipline, training, and morale, but also upon its supply chain. The same idea was echoed later by famous generals such as Napoleon and Eisenhower.

In today's competitive business environment, the efficiency and effectiveness of supply chains in most organizations are critical for their survival and are greatly dependent upon the supporting information systems.

The Components of Supply Chains

The term *supply chain* comes from a picture of how the partnering organizations in a specific supply chain are linked together. Figure 6.1 shows a relatively simple supply chain, which links a company with its suppliers (on the left) and its distributors and customers (on the right). The upper part of the figure shows a generic supply chain; the lower part shows the chain of a toy manufacturer. Notice that suppliers may have their own suppliers. In addition to flow of material there is a flow of information and money as well. The flow of money goes in the opposite direction to the flow of materials.

Note that the supply chain involves three parts:

1. ***Upstream supply chain.*** This part includes the organization's *first-tier* suppliers (which themselves can be manufacturers and/or assemblers) and their

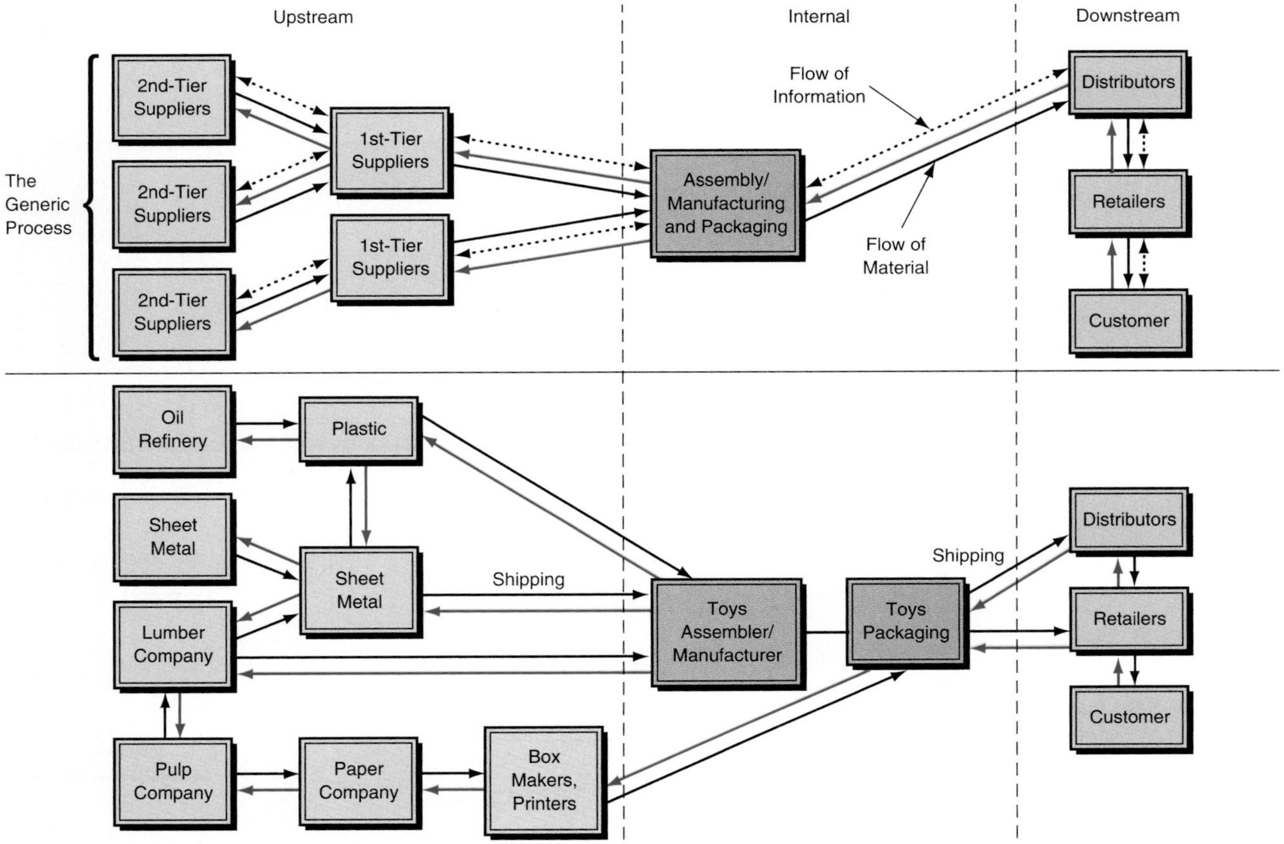

FIGURE 6.1 Supply chains. Not shown in the figure is the flow of money, which goes opposite to the flow of materials.

suppliers. Such a relationship can be extended, to the left, in several tiers, all the way to the origin of the material (e.g., mining ores, growing crops).

2. ***Internal supply chain.*** This part includes all the processes used by an organization in transforming the inputs shipped by the suppliers to outputs, from the time materials enter the organization to the time that the product goes to distribution, outside the organization.
3. ***Downstream supply chain.*** This part includes all the processes involved in delivering the product to final customers. Looked at very broadly, the supply chain actually ends when the product reaches its after-use disposal—presumably back to Mother Earth somewhere.

As you can see, a supply chain involves a *product life cycle* from "dirt to dust." However, a supply chain is more than just the movement of tangible inputs, since it also includes the movement of information and money and the procedures that support the movement of a product or a service. Finally, the organizations and individuals involved are part of the chain as well.

Supply chains come in all shapes and sizes and may be fairly complex, as shown in Figure 6.2. As can be seen in the figure, the supply chain for a car manufacturer includes hundreds of suppliers, dozens of manufacturing plants

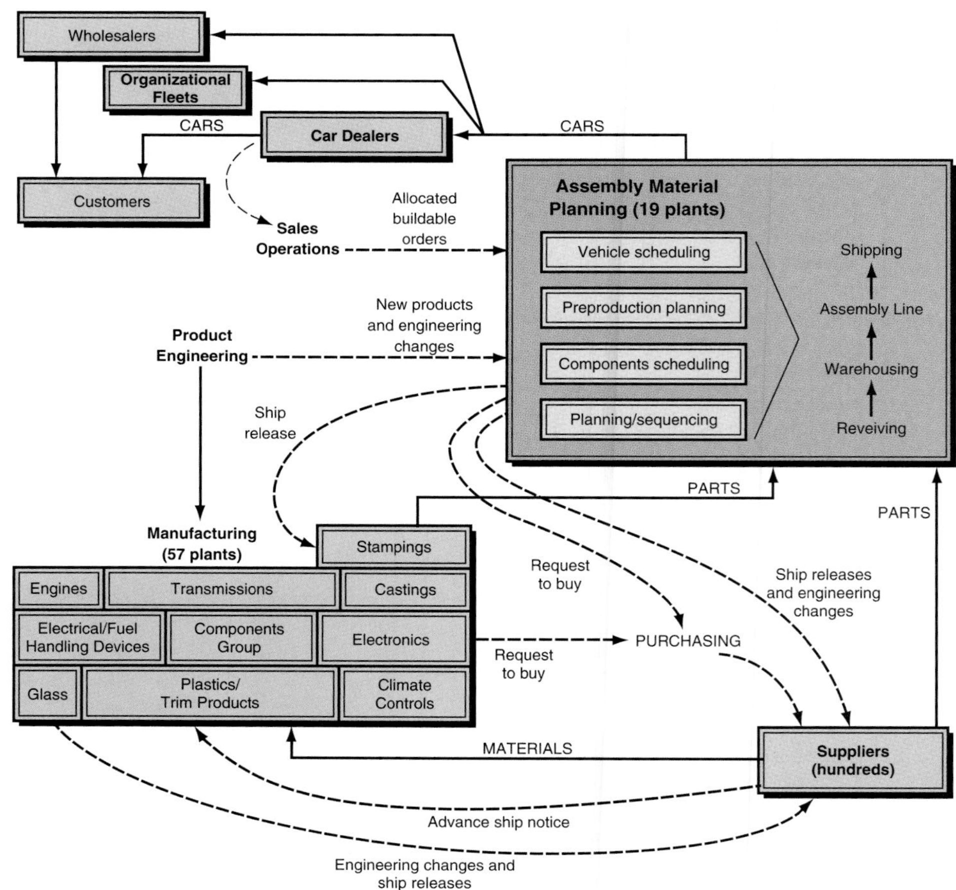

FIGURE 6.2 An automotive supply chain. (*Source:* Modified from *Introduction to Supply Chain Management* by Handfield/Nichols, © 1999. Reprinted by permission of Pearson Education, Inc., Upper Saddle River, N.J.)

(parts) and assembly plants (cars), dealers, direct business customers (fleets), wholesalers (some of which are virtual), customers, and support functions such as product engineering and purchasing.

Notice that in this case the chain is not strictly linear as it was in Figure 6.1. Here we see some loops in the process. In addition, sometimes the flow of information and even goods can be bidirectional. For example, not shown in this figure is the *return* of products (known as **reverse logistics**). For the automaker, that would be cars returned to the dealers in cases of defects or recalls by the manufacturer. Also notice that the supply chain is much more than just physical. It includes both information and financial flows. As a matter of fact, the supply chain of a service or a digitizable product may not include *any* physical materials.

The flow of goods, services, information, and financial resources is usually designed not only to effectively transform raw items to finished products and services, but also to do so in an efficient manner. Specifically, the flow must be followed with an increase in value, which can be analyzed by the *value chain*.

The Supply Chain and the Value Chain

In Chapter 3 we introduced the concepts of the *value chain* and the *value system*. A close examination of these two concepts shows that they are closely related to the supply chain. The *primary activities* of the value chain, corresponding to the model shown in Figure 6.1, were shown as a chain in Figure 3.6. Some of the support activities of the value chains can be identified in Figure 6.2. Note also that the *value system* concept corresponds to the concept of an *extended supply chain*, which includes suppliers, warehousing, distribution, and other business partners.

Porter's value chain (1985) emphasized that values are added as one moves along the chain. One of the major goals of supply chain management is to maximize this value, and this is where IT in general and electronic commerce in particular enter the picture, as will be shown in Sections 6.3 and 6.4. But let us first see why it is difficult to maximize or optimize the value chain.

6.2 Supply Chain Problems and Solutions

Background

Adding value along the supply chain is essential for competitiveness or even survival. Unfortunately, such addition is limited by many potential problems along the chain.

Supply chain problems have been recognized both in the military and in business operations for generations. Some even caused armies to lose wars and companies to go out of business. The problems are most evident in complex or long supply chains and in cases where many business partners are involved. For example, a well-known military case is the difficulties the German army in World War II encountered in the long supply chain to its troops in remote Russian territories, especially during the winter months. These difficulties resulted in a major turning point in the war and the beginning of the Germans' defeat. Note that during the 1991 Gulf War, the allied armies had superb supply chains that were managed by the latest computerized technologies (including DSS and EIS applications). These chains were a major contributor to the swift victory in this war.

In the business world there are numerous examples of companies that were unable to meet demand, had too large and expensive inventories, and so on. Some of these companies paid substantial penalties; others went out of business. On the other hand, some world-class companies such as Wal-Mart, Federal Express, and Dell have superb supply chains with innovative applications.

A recent example of a supply chain problem was the difficulty of fulfilling orders received electronically for toys during the 1999 holiday season. During the last months of the year, online toy retailers, including eToys (now kbkids.com), Amazon.com, and ToysRUs, conducted a massive advertising campaign for Internet ordering. This included $20 to $30 discount vouchers for shopping online. Customer response was overwhelming, and the retailers that underestimated it were unable to get the necessary toys from the manufacturing plants and warehouses and deliver them to the customers' doors by Christmas Eve. ToysRUs, for example, offered each of its unhappy customers a $100 store coupon as a compensation. Despite its generous gift, over 40 percent of the unhappy ToysRUs customers said they will not shop online at ToysRUs again.

These and similar problems create the need for innovative solutions. For example, during the oil crises in the 1970s, Ryder Systems, a large trucking company, purchased a refinery to ensure availability of gasoline for its trucks. Such vertical integration is effective in some cases but ineffective in others. In the remaining portion of this section we will look closely at some of the major problems in managing the supply chain and some of the proposed solutions, many of which are supported by IT.

Problems Along the Supply Chain

The problems along the supply chain stem mainly from two sources: (1) from uncertainties and (2) from the need to coordinate several activities, internal units, and business partners.

A major source of supply chain uncertainties is the *demand forecast*, as demonstrated by the 1999 toy season. The demand forecast may be influenced by several factors such as competition, prices, weather conditions, technological development, customers' general confidence, and more. Other supply chain uncertainties exist in delivery times, which depend on many factors, ranging from machine failures to road conditions and traffic jams that may interfere with shipments. Quality problems of materials and parts may also create production delays.

A major symptom of ineffective SCM is poor customer service, which hinders people or businesses from getting products or services when and where needed, or gives them poor-quality products. Other symptoms are high inventory costs, loss of revenues, extra cost of expediting shipments, and more. One of the most persistent SCM problems is known as the *bullwhip effect*.

THE BULLWHIP EFFECT. The **bullwhip effect** refers to erratic shifts in orders up and down the supply chain (see Lee et al., 1997). This effect was initially observed by Procter & Gamble with its disposable diapers product (Pampers). While actual sales in stores were fairly stable and predictable, orders from distributors had wild swings, creating production and inventory problems for P&G. An investigation revealed that distributors' orders were fluctuating because of poor demand forecast, price fluctuation, order batching, and rationing within the supply chain. All this resulted in unnecessary inventories in various areas along the supply chain, fluctuations of P&G orders to their suppliers, and flow of inaccurate information. Distorted information can lead to tremendous inefficiencies, excessive inventories, poor customer service, lost revenues, ineffective shipments, and missed production schedules (Lee et al., 1997).

The bullwhip effect is not unique to P&G. Firms ranging from Hewlett-Packard in the computer industry to Bristol-Myers Squibb in the pharmaceutical field have experienced a similar phenomenon (Handfield and Nichols, 1999).

Basically, even slight demand uncertainties and variabilities become magnified when viewed through the eyes of managers at each link in the supply chain. If each distinct entity makes ordering and inventory decisions with an eye to its own interest above those of the chain, stockpiling may be simultaneously occurring at as many as seven or eight places across the supply chain, leading in some cases to as many as 100 days of inventory—which is waiting, "just in case."

A 1998 industry study projected that $30 billion in savings could materialize in the grocery industry supply chains alone, by sharing information. Thus, companies may avoid the "sting of the bullwhip." Such sharing is facilitated by EDI, extranets, and groupware technologies, and it is part of interorganizational EC or c-commerce. One of the most notable examples of information sharing is between Procter & Gamble and Wal-Mart. Wal-Mart provides P&G access to sales information for every item P&G makes for Wal-Mart. The information is collected by P&G on a daily basis from every Wal-Mart store. Then, P&G is able to manage the inventory replenishment for Wal-Mart. By monitoring the inventory level of each P&G item in every store, P&G knows when the inventories fall below the threshold that triggers a shipment. All this is done automatically. The benefit for P&G is accurate demand information. P&G has similar agreements with other major retailers. Thus, P&G can plan production more accurately, avoiding some of the problem of the "bullwhip effect." (In fact, P&G implemented a Web-based "Ultimate-Supply System," which replaced 4,000 different EDI links to suppliers and retailers in a more cost-effective way.) Later on we will show how Warner-Lambert and other manufacturers are sharing information with wholesalers and retailers in order to solve the bullwhip effect problem.

Solutions to Supply Chain Problems

Over the years organizations have developed many solutions to the supply chain problems. One of the earliest solutions was *vertical integration*. For example, Henry Ford purchased rubber plantations in South America in order to control tire production for his cars. Undoubtedly, the most common solution used by companies is *building inventories* as an "insurance" against supply chain uncertainties. This way products and parts flow smoothly through the production process. The main problem with this approach is that it is very difficult to correctly determine inventory levels for each product and part. If inventory levels are set too high, the cost of keeping the inventory will be very large. If the inventory is too low, there is no insurance against high demand or slow delivery times, and revenues (and customers) may be lost. In either event the total penalty cost, including lost sales opportunities and bad reputation, can be very high. Thus, companies make major attempts to control inventory, as shown in the *IT at Work* example on page 248.

Proper supply chain and inventory management requires coordination of all different activities and links of the supply chain. Successful coordination enables goods to move smoothly and on time from suppliers to manufacturers to customers, which enables the firm to keep inventories low and costs down. Such coordination is needed since companies depend on each other but do not always work together toward the same goal. As part of the coordination effort, business partners must learn to trust each other. Both suppliers and buyers must participate together in the design or redesign of the supply chain to achieve their shared goals.

To properly control the uncertainties mentioned earlier, it is necessary to identify and understand the causes of the uncertainty, determine how uncertainties in some activities will affect other activities up and down the supply

IT at Work
HOW LITTLEWOODS STORES IMPROVED ITS SCM

Integrating IT ...in Marketing and Production and Operations Management

www.littlewoods.co.uk

Littlewoods Stores is one of Britain's largest retailers of high-quality clothing. It has 136 stores around the U.K. and Northern Ireland (*littlewoods.co.uk*). The retail clothing business is very competitive, so in the late 1990s the company embarked on an IT-supported initiative to improve its supply chain efficiency. A serious SCM problem for the company was *overstocking.*

In order to get better SCM, the company introduced a Web-based performance reporting system. The new system analyzes, on a daily basis, marketing and finance data, and space planning, merchandising, and purchasing data. For example, merchandising personnel can now perform sophisticated sales, stock, and supplier analyses to make key operational decisions on pricing and inventory. Using the Web, analysts can view sales and stock data in virtually any grouping of levels and categories. Furthermore, users can easily drill down to detailed sales and other data.

The system uses a data warehouse–based decision support system and other end-user-oriented software to make better decisions. Here are some of the results:

- The ability to strategically price merchandise differently in different stores saved $1.2 million in 1997 alone.
- Reducing the need for stock liquidations saved $1.4 million in a single year.
- Marketing distribution expenses were cut by $7 million a year.
- The company was able to reduce staff from 84 to 49 people, a saving of about $1 million annually.
- Back-up inventory expenses were cut by about $4 million a year. For example, due to quick replenishment, stock went down by 80 percent.

Within a year the number of Web-based users grew to 600, and the size of the data warehouse grew to over 1 gigabyte. In November 1999 the company launched its Home Shopping Channel (*shop-i.co.uk*) and other e-commerce projects. Improvements in SCM were recorded by fall 2000.

For Further Exploration: Explain how integrated software solved the excess inventory problem. Also, review the role of data warehouse decision support in this case.

Sources: Compiled from *microstrategy.com* (January 2000, Customers' Success Stories), and from *littlewoods.co.uk* (March 2001).

chain, and then formulate specific ways to reduce or eliminate the uncertainties. Combined with this is the need for an effective and efficient communication environment among all business partners. A rapid flow of information along the supply chains makes them very efficient. For example, computerized point-of-sale (POS) information can be transmitted once a day, or even in real time, to distribution centers, suppliers, and shippers. This enables firms to achieve optimal inventory levels.

Here are some other solutions to solve SCM problems:

- Use outsourcing rather than do-it-yourself during demand peaks.
- Similarly, buy rather than make production inputs whenever appropriate.
- Configure optimal shipping plans.
- Create strategic partnerships with suppliers.
- Use the *just-in-time approach* to purchasing, in which suppliers deliver small quantities whenever supplies, materials, and parts are needed. (See the Dell opening case.)
- Reduce the lead time for buying and selling.
- Use fewer suppliers.
- Improve supplier-buyer relationships.

- Manufacture only after orders are in, as Dell does with its custom-made computers.
- Achieve accurate demand by working closely with suppliers.

Most of the above solutions are enhanced by IT support. For specific IT solutions see Table 6.1.

Two tools in particular, supply chain teams and performance measurement, are especially potent in helping to solve supply chain problems.

SUPPLY CHAIN TEAMS. The change of the linear supply chain to a hub (Chapters 1 and 5) points to the need sometimes to create **supply chain teams**. According to Epner (1999), a supply chain team is a group of tightly integrated businesses that work together to serve the customer. Each task is done by the member of the team who is best positioned, trained, and capable of doing that specific task. For example, the team member that deals with the delivery will handle a delivery problem even if he or she works for a delivery company rather

TABLE 6.1 IT Solutions to Supply Chain Problems

Supply Chain Problem	IT Solution
Linear sequence of processing is too slow.	Parallel processing, using workflow software.
Waiting times between chain segments are excessive.	Identify reason (DSS software) and expedite communication and collaboration (intranets, groupware).
Existence of non-value-added activities.	Value analysis (SCM software), simulation software.
Slow delivery of paper documents.	Electronic documents and communication system (e.g., EDI, e-mail).
Repeat process activities due to wrong shipments, poor quality, etc.	Electronic verifications (software agents), automation; eliminating human errors, electronic control systems.
Batching; accumulate work orders between supply chain processes to get economies of scale (e.g., save on delivery).	SCM software analysis, digitize documents for online delivery.
Learn about delays after they occur, or learn too late.	Tracking systems, anticipate delays, trend analysis, early detection (intelligent systems).
Excessive administrative controls such as approvals (signatures). Approvers are in different locations.	Parallel approvals (workflow), electronic approval system. Analysis of need.
Lack of information, or too-slow flow.	Internet/intranet, software agents for monitoring and alert. Bar codes, direct flow from POS terminals.
Lack of synchronization of moving materials.	Workflow and tracking systems. Synchronization by software agents.
Poor coordination, cooperation, and communication.	Groupware products, constant monitoring, alerts, collaboration tools.
Delays in shipments from warehouses.	Use robots in warehouses, use warehouse management software.
Redundancies in the supply chain. Too many purchasing orders, too much handling and packaging.	Information sharing via the Web, creating teams of collaborative partners supported by IT (see Epner, 1999).
Obsolescence of parts and components that stay too long in storage.	Reducing inventory levels by information sharing internally and externally, using intranets and groupware.
Scheduling problems, manufacturing lack of control.	Intelligent agents for B2B modeling (see *gensym.com*).

than for the retailer whose product is being delivered. This way, redundancies will be minimized. If the customer contacts the delivery company about a delivery problem, he or she will be dealt with, rather than passing the problem along to the retailer, and the retailer will not have to spend valuable resources following up on the delivery. The task assignment to team members as well as the team's control is facilitated by IT.

MEASUREMENT AND METRICS. Measuring the supply chain performance is necessary for making decisions about SCM improvements. IT provides for the data collection needed for such measurement. Some potential metrics for supply chain operations are delivery on time (%), quality at unloading area (number of defects), cost performance, lead time for procurement, inventory levels (or days of turning an inventory), shrinkage (%), obsolescence (% of inventory), cost of maintaining inventory, speed of finding needed items in the storeroom, availability of items when needed (%), the percentage of rush orders, percentage of goods returned, and a customers' complaints rate. Establishing such metrics and tracking them with business partners is critical to the success of one's business. Companies that use such measures have the needed data to minimize supply chain problems.

6.3 COMPUTERIZED SYSTEMS: MRP, MRPII, ERP, AND SCM

The concept of the supply chain is interrelated with the computerization of its activities, which has evolved over 50 years.

The Evolution of Computerized Aids

Historically, many of the supply chain activities were managed with paper transactions, which can be very inefficient. Therefore, since the time when computers first began to be used for business, people have wanted to automate the processes along the supply chain. The first software programs, which appeared in the 1950s and early 1960s, supported short segments along the supply chain. Typical examples are inventory management systems, scheduling, and billing. The major objectives were to reduce cost, expedite processing, and reduce errors. Such applications were developed in the functional areas, independent of each other, and they became more and more sophisticated with the passage of time (as will be shown in Chapter 7). Of special interest were transaction processing systems and decision support procedures such as management science optimization and financial decision-making formulas (e.g., for loan amortization).

In a short time it became clear that interdependencies exist among some of the supply chain activities. One early realization was that production scheduling is related to inventory management and purchasing plans. As early as the 1960s, the **material requirements planning (MRP)** model was devised. This model essentially integrates production, purchasing, and inventory management of interrelated products (see Chapter 7). It became clear that computer support could greatly enhance use of this model, which may require daily updating. This resulted in commercial MRP software packages coming on the market.

While MRP packages were useful in many cases, helping to drive inventory levels down and streamlining portions of the supply chain, they failed in as many (or even more) cases. One of the major reasons for the failure was the realization that schedule-inventory-purchasing operations are closely related to both financial and labor resources. This realization resulted in an enhanced MRP methodology

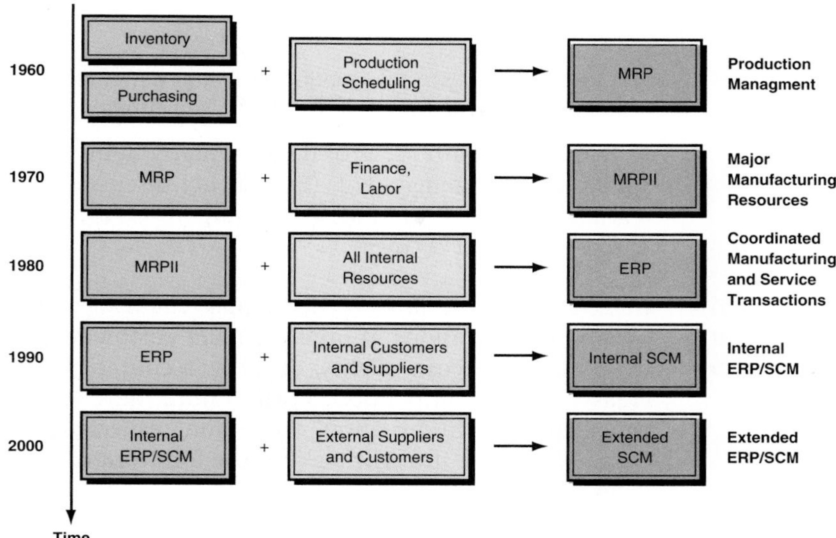

FIGURE 6.3 The evolution of integrated systems.

(and software) called **manufacturing resource planning (MRP II)**, which adds labor requirements and financial planning to MRP.

During this evolution there was more and more integration of functional information systems. This evolution continued, leading to the *enterprise resource planning (ERP)* concept, which integrates the transaction processing activities of all functional areas in the entire enterprise. ERP was initially expanded to include internal suppliers and customers and later to incorporate external suppliers and customers in what is known as *extended ERP/SCM software*. This evolution is shown in Figure 6.3. The next step in this evolution, which is just beginning to make its way into business use, is the inclusion of markets and communities. (See *mySAP.com* for details.) We'll look at ERP again in a bit more detail later in this section.

Notice that throughout this evolution there have been more and more integrations along several dimensions (more functional areas, combining transaction processing and decision support, inclusion of business partners). Therefore, before we describe the essentials of ERP and SCM software it may be beneficial to analyze the reasons for software and activities integration.

Why Systems Integration?

Creating the twenty-first-century enterprise cannot be done effectively with twentieth-century computer technology, which is *functionally* oriented. Functional systems may not let different departments communicate with each other in the same language. Worse yet, crucial sales, inventory, and production data often have to be painstakingly entered manually into separate computer systems every time a person who is not a member of a specific department needs ad hoc information related to the specific department. In many cases employees simply do not get the information they need, or they get it too late.

Sandoe et al. (2001) list the following major benefits of systems integration (in order of importance):

Tangible benefits: Inventory reduction, personnel reduction, productivity improvement, order management improvement, financial-close cycle improvements, IT cost reduction, procurement cost reduction, cash management improvements, revenue/profit increases, transportation logistics cost reduction, maintenance reduction, and on-time delivery improvement.

Intangible benefits: Information visibility, new/improved processes, customer responsiveness, standardization, flexibility, globalization, and business performance.

Notice that in both types of benefits many items are directly related to improved supply chain management. (For further discussion of the improvements that integration provided to SCM, see "Competition's New Battleground: The Integrated Value Chain," at *ctp.com*.)

Integrating the Supply Chain and the Value Chain

Integration of the links in the supply chain has been facilitated by the need to streamline operations in order to meet customer demands in the areas of product and service cost, quality, delivery, technology, and cycle time brought by increased global competition. Furthermore, new forms of organizational relationships and the information revolution, especially the Internet and electronic commerce, have brought SCM to the forefront of management attention. Upper-level management has therefore been willing to invest money in hardware and software that are needed for seamless integration.

TYPES OF INTEGRATION: FROM SUPPLY TO VALUE CHAIN. The most obvious integration is that of the segments of the supply chain, and/or the information that flows among the segments. We discussed this topic earlier and will discuss it further in this chapter. But there is another type of integration, and this is the integration of the value chain. Traditionally, we thought of supply chain in terms of purchasing, transportation, warehousing, and logistics. The *integrated value chain* is a more encompassing concept. It is the process by which multiple enterprises within a shared market channel collaboratively plan, implement, and (electronically as well as physically) manage the flow of goods, services, and information along the entire chain in a manner that increases customer-perceived value. This process optimizes the efficiency of the chain, creating competitive advantage for all stakeholders in the value chain. While the supply chain is basically a description of flows and activities, the value chain expresses the *contributions* made by various segments and activities both to the profit and to customers' satisfaction.

Another way of defining the value chain integration is as a *process of collaboration* that optimizes all internal and external activities involved in delivering greater perceived value to the ultimate customer. A supply chain transforms into an integrated value chain when it:

- Extends the chain all the way from subsuppliers (tier 2, 3, etc.) to customers
- Integrates back-office operations with those of the front office (see Figure 6.4)
- Becomes highly customer-centric, focusing on demand generation and customer service as well as demand fulfillment and logistics
- Is proactively designed by chain members to compete as an "extended enterprise," creating and enhancing customer-perceived value by means of cross-enterprise collaboration
- Seeks to optimize the value added by information and utility-enhancing services

Presently only a few large companies are successfully involved in a comprehensive collaboration to reengineer the supply chain or some of its segments. One such effort is described in the *IT at Work* case that begins on the opposite page.

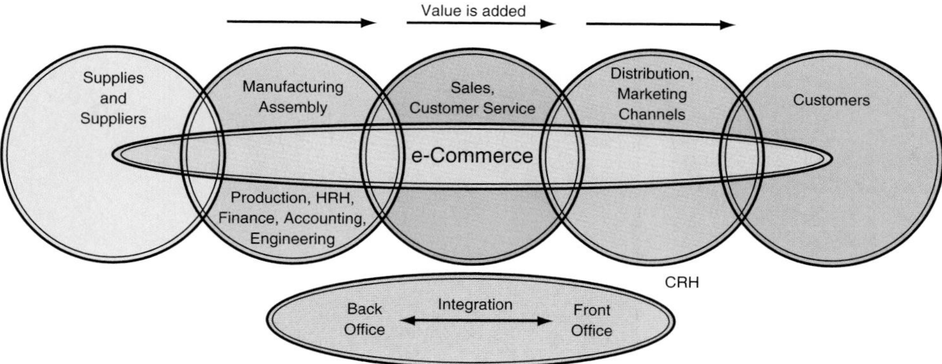

FIGURE 6.4 Back office and front office integration in a value chain.

IT at Work

HOW WARNER-LAMBERT APPLIES AN INTEGRATED SUPPLY CHAIN

Integrating IT ...in Production and Operations Management

www.warner-lambert.com

One of Warner-Lambert's major products is Listerine antiseptic mouthwash. The materials for making Listerine come from eucalyptus trees in Australia and are shipped to the Warner-Lambert (WL) manufacturing plant in New Jersey, U.S.A. The major problem there is to determine how much Listerine to produce. Listerine is first purchased by wholesalers and by thousands of retail stores, some of which are giants such as Wal-Mart. The problem that the manufacturing plant faces is to *forecast* the *overall demand*. A wrong forecast will result either in high inventories at WL, or in shortages. Inventories are expensive to keep, and shortages may result in loss of business.

Warner-Lambert forecasts demand with the help of Manugistic Inc.'s Demand Planning Information System. (Manugistic is a vendor of IT software for SCM.) Used with other software in Manugistics' Supply Chain Planning suite, the system analyzes manufacturing, distribution, and sales data against expected demand and business climate information. Its goal is to help WL decide how much Listerine (and other products) to make and how much of each raw ingredient is needed, and when. For example, the model can anticipate the impact of seasonal promotion or of a production line being down. The sales and marketing group of WL also meets monthly with WL employees in finance, procurement, and other departments. The group enters the expected demand for Listerine into a Marcam Corp. Prism Capacity Planning system (another SCM software), which schedules the production of Listerine in the amounts needed and generates electronic purchase orders for WL's suppliers.

WL's supply chain excellence stems from the Collaborative Planning, Forecasting, and Replenishment (CPFR) program. This is a retailing industry project for which piloting was done at WL (see *Datamation,* November 1996, and *Interactive Week,* February 23, 1999). In the pilot project, WL shared strategic plans, performance data, and market insight with Wal-Mart over private networks. The company realized that it could benefit from Wal-Mart's market knowledge, just as Wal-Mart could benefit from WL's product knowledge. In CPFR, trading partners collaborate on demand forecast using *collaborative e-commerce* (Chapter 5). The project includes major SCM and ERP vendors such as SAP and Manugistics (see figure, next page). During the CPFR pilot, WL increased its products' shelf-fill rate—the extent to which a store's shelves are fully stocked—from 87 percent to 98 percent, earning the company about $8 million a year in additional sales (the equivalent of a new product launch) for much less investment. WL is now using the Internet to expand the CPFR program to all its suppliers and retail partners.

Warner-Lambert is involved in another collaborative retail industry project, the Supply-Chain Operations Reference (SCOR), an initiative of the Supply-Chain Council in the United States. SCOR divides supply chain operations into parts, giving manufacturers, suppliers, distributors, and retailers a framework within which to evaluate the effectiveness of their processes along the same supply chains.

For Further Exploration: For what industries, besides retailing, will c-commerce beneficial? Why was Listerine a target for the pilot SCM collaboration?

Sources: Compiled from *CIO,* August 15, 1998; *Store,* June 1998; and *Logistics Management and Distribution Report,* October 1998, November 1999.

In a pilot project, Wal-Mart has used the Collaborative Forecasting and Replenishing (CFAR) standard to link up with one of its key suppliers, Warner-Lambert, manufacturer of consumer products like Listerine. Through CFAR workbenches (spreadsheet-like documents with ample space for collaborative comments), Wal-Mart buyers and Warner-Lambert planners are able to jointly develop product forecasts.

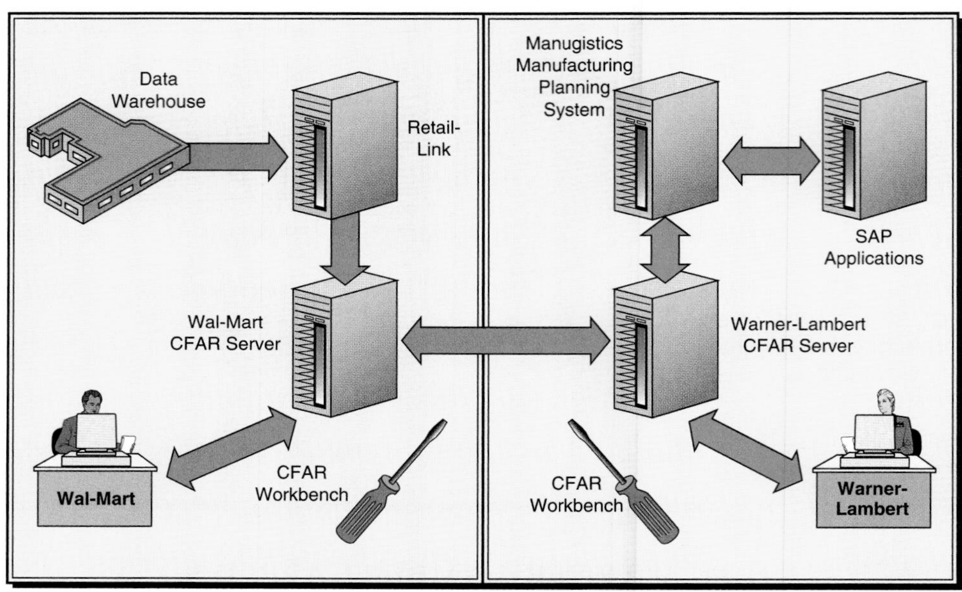

For a special report on this collaboration project, see ASCET (2000), where the name of such collaboration is **collaborative commerce networks**, or **collaborative commerce** (see Chapter 5).

Another example of supply chain integration is product-development systems that allow suppliers to dial into a client's intranet, pull product specifications, and view illustrations and videos of a manufacturing process. (For further discussion, see Selland, October 1999 and January 1999; and Andersen Consulting's white paper, 2000.)

Enterprise Resource Planning (ERP)

With the advance of enterprisewide client/server computing comes a new challenge: how to control all major business processes with a single software architecture in real time. The integrated solution, known as **enterprise resource planning (ERP)**, is a process of planning and managing all resources and their use in the entire enterprise. It promises benefits ranging from increased efficiency to improved quality, productivity, and profitability. (See Appleton, 1997, for details.) The name enterprise resource planning is misleading because the software does not concentrate on either *planning* or *resources*. ERP's major objective is to *integrate all departments and functions across a company* onto a single computer system that can serve all of the enterprise's needs. For example, improved order entry allows immediate access to inventory, product data, customer credit history, and prior order information. This availability of information raises productivity and increases customer satisfaction. ERP, for example, helped Master Product Company increase customers' satisfaction and, consequently, sales by 20 percent and decrease inventory by 30 percent, thus increasing productivity (Caldwell, 1997). ERP systems are in use in thousands of large and medium companies worldwide. Some ERP systems are producing dramatic results.

For businesses that want to use ERP, one option is to self-develop an integrated system by using existing functional packages, or by programming one's own systems. The other option is to use commercially available integrated ERP software. The leading software for ERP is **SAP R/3**.* Oracle, J.D. Edwards, Computer Associates, and PeopleSoft also make similar products. These products include Web modules. Another alternative is to lease systems from *application service providers (ASPs)*. This option is described later in this chapter and at length in Chapters 13 and 14.

The ERP software crosses functional departments. An ERP suite provides a single interface for managing all the routine activities performed in manufacturing—from entering sales orders, to coordinating shipping and after-sales customer service. As of the later 1990s, ERP systems have begun to be extended along the supply chain to suppliers and customers. They can incorporate functionality for customer interaction and for managing relationships with suppliers and vendors, making the system less inward-looking.

Companies have been successful in integrating several hundred applications using ERP software, saving millions of dollars and significantly increasing customer satisfaction. For example, ExxonMobil consolidated 300 different information systems by implementing SAP R/3 in its U.S. petrochemical operations alone. ERP forces discipline and organization around business processes, making the alignment of IT and business goals more likely. Such change is related to business process reengineering (BPR) (Chapter 8). Also, by implementing ERP a company can discover all the "dusty corners" of its business.

However, SAP and other ERP software can be extremely complex to implement; companies often need to change existing business processes to fit SAP's format; and some companies require only some of R/3's 70 software modules, yet must purchase the entire package. For these reasons, SAP may not be attractive to everyone. For example, Caldwell and Stein (1998) reports that Inland Steel Industries, Inc., opted to write its own ERP system (containing 7 million lines of code), which supports 27 integrated applications, rather than use commercial ERP. Also, some companies, such as Starbucks, decided to use a *best of breed* approach, building their ERP with ready-made components from several vendors.

In whatever form it is implemented, ERP has played a critical role in getting small- and medium-sized manufacturers to focus on business processes, thus facilitating business process changes across the enterprise. By tying together multiple plants and distribution facilities, ERP solutions have also facilitated a change in thinking that has its ultimate expression in an enterprise that is better able to expand operations and in better supply chain management. (For a comprehensive treatment of ERP, its cost, implementation problems, and payback, see Koch et al., 1999).

But ERP was never meant to fully support supply chains. ERP solutions are centered around business transactions. As such, they do not provide the computerized models needed to respond rapidly to real-time changes in supply, demand, labor, or capacity. This deficiency has been overcome by the second generation of ERP.

---

*SAP R/3 is described in the FoxMeyer case at *wiley.com/college/turban*, Chapter 3.

Post-ERP (Second-Generation ERP)

First-generation ERP aimed at automating key office processes. And indeed ERP projects do save companies millions of dollars. A report by Merrill Lynch noted that nearly 40 percent of all U.S. companies with more than $1 billion in annual revenues have implemented ERP systems. However, by the late 1990s the major benefits of ERP had been fully exploited. It became clear that with the completion of the Y2K projects that were an integral part of many ERP implementations, the first generation of ERP was nearing the end of its useful life. But the ERP movement was far from over. A second, more powerful generation of ERP development started. Its objective is to leverage existing systems in order to increase efficiency in handling transactions, improve decision making, and further transform ways of doing business. Let's explain:

The first generation of ERP basically supported routine business transactions. In other words, ERP has traditionally excelled in the ability to manage administrative activities like payroll, inventory, and order processing. For example, an ERP system has the functionality of electronic ordering or the best way to bill the customer—but all it does is automate the transactions. Palaniswamy and Frank (2000) cite examples of five case studies indicating that ERP significantly enhances the performance of manufacturing organizations as a result of automating transactions.

The reports generated by ERP systems gave planners statistics about what happened in the company, costs, and financial performance. However, the planning systems with ERP were rudimentary. Reports from first-generation ERP systems provided a snapshot of the business at a point in time. But they did not support the *continuous* planning that is central to supply chain planning, which continues to refine and enhance the plan as changes and events occur, up to the very last minute before executing the plan. Attempting to come up with an optimal plan using first-generation ERP-based systems has been compared to steering a car by looking in the rear-view mirror.

This created the need for planning systems oriented toward *decision making*, and this is what the *SCM software* vendors provided. To illustrate, consider how ERP and SCM approach an order-processing problem. There is a fundamental difference: The question in SCM becomes "Should I take your order?" instead of the ERP approach of "How can I best take or fulfill your order?"

Thus SCM systems have emerged as a *complement* to ERP systems, to provide *intelligent decision support* capabilities. An SCM system is designed to overlay existing systems and to pull data from every step of the supply chain. Thus it is able to provide a clear, global picture of where the enterprise is heading. An example of a successful SCM effort is that of IBM. IBM reengineered its global supply chain in order to achieve quick responsiveness to customers with minimal inventory. To support this effort, it developed an extended-enterprise supply-chain analysis tool, called the Asset Management Tool (AMT). AMT integrates graphical process modeling, analytical performance optimization, simulation, activity-based costing, and enterprise database connectivity into a system that allows quantitative analysis of extended supply chains. IBM has used AMT to study such issues as inventory budgets, turnover objectives, customer-service targets, and new-product introductions. The system was implemented at a number of IBM business units and their channel partners. AMT benefits include over $750 million in material costs and price-protection expenses being saved each year. (For details see Yao et al., 2000.) Creating a plan from an SCM

www.ibm.com

system allows companies to quickly assess the impact of their actions on the entire supply chain, including customer demand. Therefore, it makes sense to integrate ERP and SCM.

How is such integration done? One approach is to work with different software products from different vendors. For example, a business might use SAP as an ERP and add to it Manugistics' manufacturing-oriented software, as shown earlier in the Warner-Lambert case. Such an approach requires fitting different softwares, which may be a complex task, unless special interfaces exist.

The second approach is for the ERP vendors to add decision support and **business intelligence** capabilities. Business intelligence refers to analysis performed by DSS, EIS, data mining, and intelligent systems (see Chapters 10–12). These added capabilities solve the integration problem. But as is the case with integration of database management systems and spreadsheets in Excel or Lotus 1-2-3, the result can be a product with some not-so-strong functionalities. However, most ERP vendors are adding such functionalities for another reason: It is cheaper for the customers. The added functionalities, which create the *second-generation ERP*, include not only decision support but also customer relationship management (CRM) (Chapter 7), electronic commerce (Section 6.4), and data warehousing and mining (Chapter 11). Some systems include a *knowledge management* component (Chapter 9) as well. Another approach that is related to integration is componentization.

SUPPLY CHAIN INTELLIGENCE. The inclusion of business intelligence in supply chain software solutions is called by some **supply chain intelligence (SCI)**. SCI applications enable strategic decision making by analyzing data along the entire supply chain. This so-called intelligence is provided by the tools and capabilities discussed in Chapters 10 to 12.

To better understand SCI, it is worthwhile to compare it with SCM. Such a comparison is provided in Table 6.2 on page 258.

How Are SCI Capabilities Provided? The following are common ways to provide SCI capabilities:

- Use an enhanced ERP package that includes business intelligence capabilities. For example, see Oracle and SAP 2001 products.
- Integrate the ERP with business intelligence software from a specialized vendor such as Brio, Cognus, or Comshare.
- Create a best-of-breed system by using components from several vendors that will provide the required capabilities. (For component-based applications, see Chapter 14.)

COMPONENTIZATION. *Componentization* refers to breaking large ERP systems into individual components that work together. By breaking up large applications into components, ERP vendors such as SAP, Oracle, PeopleSoft, and J. D. Edwards are able to more quickly fix or add functionalities. The accounts payable component, for example, could be enhanced without having to touch the other financial components or any other components such as planning or logistics. And once the ERP vendor has established a component architecture, it becomes easier and safer for IT to customize the systems.

TABLE 6.2 Comparing SCM and SCI

Supply Chain Management	Supply Chain Intelligence
Largely about managing the procurement and production links of the supply chain.	Provides a broad view of an entire supply chain to reveal full product and component life cycle.
Transactional.	Analytic.
Tactical decision making.	Strategic decision making.
Helps reduce costs through improved operational efficiency.	Reveals opportunities for cost reduction, but also stimulates revenue growth.
Usually just the SCM application's data (as a vertical stovepipe).	Integrates supplier, manufacturing, and product data (horizontal).
Records one state of data, representing "now."	Keeps a historic record.
Assists in material and production planning.	Does what-if forecasting based on historic data.
Quantifies cost of some materials.	Enables an understanding of total cost.
Shows today's yield but cannot explain influences on it; thus provides no help for improvements.	Drills into yield figures to reveal what caused the performance level, so it can be improved.
Simple reporting.	Collaborative environment with personalizable monitoring of metrics.

Source: P. Russom, "Increasing Manufacturing Performance Through Supply Chain Intelligence," *DM Review*, September 2000. Reprinted by permission from Sage Tree, Inc.

Componentization not only makes it easier for ERP vendors to enhance their solutions but also makes it easier for customers to upgrade the software. A customer could selectively upgrade some components without having to upgrade the entire ERP solution, which usually entails a substantial effort and expense. Componentization also helps the vendors extend the core ERP system with supply chain, sales force automation solutions, and customer relationship management (CRM).

ERP Failures

Despite all the improvements, ERP projects, especially large ones, may fail. The *IT at Work* on the opposite page discusses some examples of ERP failures.

In order to avoid failures and ensure success, it is necessary, according to *thespot4sap.com*, for the partners involved in ERP implementation to hold open and honest dialogue at the start of each project, and to nail down the critical success factors of the implementation. Included in this initial dialogue should be consideration of the following factors:

- The customer's expectations
- The ERP product capabilities and gaps
- The level of change the customer has to go through to make the system fit
- The level of commitment within the customer organization to see the project through to completion
- The fit between the customer's organization and culture and the project organization and culture
- The risks presented by politics within the customer organization
- The consultant's capabilities, responsibilities, and role (if applicable)

Application Service Providers and ERP Outsourcing

A popular option today for businesses that want ERP functions is to lease applications rather than to build systems. In leasing applications, the ERP vendor takes care of the functionalities and the integration problems. This approach is known

IT at Work

EVEN THE BEST-PLANNED ERP SOMETIMES FAILS

The complexity of ERP projects causes some of them to fail. Here are some examples:

- Hershey's chocolate bars and its other products were not selling well in late 1999. Hershey Foods Corporation reported a 19 percent drop in third-quarter net earnings, due to computer problems. The problems continued for several months, causing Hershey to lose market share and several hundred million dollars. The major problem, according to the company, was its new order-and-distribution system, which uses software from both SAP (the ERP) and Siebel Systems (the CRM). Since the integrated system went live in July 1999, Hershey had been unable to fill all orders and get products onto shelves on time. It took many months to fix the problem.
- In November 1999, Whirlpool Corp. reported major delays in shipment of appliances due to "bugs" in its new ERP. Orders for quantities smaller than one truckload met with snags in the areas of order processing, tracking, and invoicing. According to *cnet.com,* SAP gave Whirlpool the red light twice prior to the date on which the project would go live, saying the supply chain was not ready, but Whirlpool ignored the signals.
- FoxMeyer, a major distributor of drugs to hospitals and pharmacies, which filed for bankruptcy in 1996, sued both SAP and Andersen Consulting for $500 million each, claiming that the ERP system they constructed led to its demise. See the complete case on the book's Web site at *www.wiley.com/college/turban.*
- W. L. Gore and Associates filed a lawsuit against PeopleSoft and Deloitte & Touche, because the ERP project that the two companies developed for the company cost twice the original estimate. In both the W. L. Gore and FoxMeyer cases, the ERP vendors and consultants blamed their clients' poor management teams for the ERP problems. Both cases were in court at the time this was written.

For Further Exploration: Why do even the best-planned ERPs fail? If planning doesn't help, what can you do? Can you identify similarities in the four incidents cited here?

Sources: T. H. Davenport, *Mission Critical: Realizing the Promise of Enterprise Systems,* Cambridge, MA: Harvard Business School Press, 2000; *cnet.com; cio.com; Business Courier* (miscellaneous dates).

as the "ASP alternative." An **application service provider (ASP)** is a software vendor that offers to lease ERP-based applications to other businesses. The basic concept is similar to that of the old-fashioned computer *time share.* The outsourcers set up the systems and run them for you. ASP is considered a product risk-management strategy, and it best fits small- to mid-size companies. (See Chapters 13 and 14 for details.) The delivery of the software can be done effectively via the Internet.

The ASP concept is especially useful in ERP projects, which are expensive to install and take a long time to implement, and for which staffing is a major problem. However, ASP offerings are also evident in ERP-added functions such as electronic commerce, CRM, datamarts, desktop productivity, human resource information systems (HRIS), and other supply-chain-related applications.

The use of ASP has its downside. First, ERP vendors typically want a five-year commitment. Some companies may not want to lock themselves in for that long, reasoning that within five years ERP may be simplified and easy to get and implement. Second, you lose flexibility with the use of ASP. Rented systems are fairly standard and may not fit your needs. (For further discussion of ASPs, see *Datamation,* July 1999.)

Global Supply Chains

The major reasons why companies go global are: lower prices of material, products, and labor; availability of products that are unavailable domestically; the firm's global attitude; advanced technology available in other countries; high quality of products available; intensification of global competition, which drives companies to cut costs; the need to develop a foreign presence; and fulfillment of counter trade. Supply chains that involve suppliers and/or customers in other countries are referred to as *global supply chains.* E-commerce has made it much easier to find suppliers in other countries (e.g., by using electronic bidding) as well as to find customers in other countries (see Turban et al., 2002).

Global supply chains are usually longer than domestic ones, and they may be complex. Therefore, additional uncertainties are likely. Some of the issues that may create difficulties in global supply chains are legal issues, customs fees and taxes, language and cultural differences, fast changes in currency exchange rates, and political instabilities. An example of difficulties in a global supply chain can be seen in the Lego case below.

IT at Work

LEGO STRUGGLES WITH GLOBAL ISSUES

www.lego.com

Lego Company of Denmark is a major producer of toys, including electronic ones. In 1999 the company decided to market its Lego Mindstorms on the Internet. This product is a unique innovation. Its users can build a Lego robot using more than 700 traditional Lego elements, program it on a PC, and transfer the program to the robot. Lego sells its products in many countries using several regional distribution centers. When the decision to do global electronic commerce was made, the company had the following concerns:

- Choice of countries. It does not make sense to go to all countries, since sales are very low in some countries, and some countries offer no logistical support services.
- A supportive distribution and service system would be needed.
- Merging the offline and online operations or creating a new centralized unit seemed to be a complex undertaking.
- Existing warehouses were optimized to handle distribution to commercial buyers, not to individual customers.
- It would be necessary to handle returns around the globe.
- Lego products were selling in different countries in different currencies and at different prices. Should the product be sold on the Net at a single price? In which currency? How would this price be related to the offline prices?
- How should the company handle the direct mail and track individual shipments?
- Invoicing must comply with the regulations of many countries.
- Should Lego create a separate Web site for Mindstorms? What languages should be used there?
- Some countries have strict regulations regarding advertisement and sales to children. Also laws on consumer protection vary among countries.
- How to handle restrictions on electronic transfer of individuals' personal data.
- How to handle the tax and import duty payments in different countries.

In the rush to get its innovative product to market, Lego did not solve all of these issues before the direct marketing was introduced. The resulting problems forced Lego to close the Web site for business. It took almost a year to solve all global trade-related issues and eventually reopen the site. By 2001 Lego was selling online many of its products, priced in U.S. dollars, but the online service was available in only 15 countries.

For Further Exploration: Visit Lego's Web site and see the latest EC activities. Also, investigate what the competitors are doing. Is the Web the way to go global?

Sources: Compiled from *lego.com,* and from L. Damsguard and J. Horluck, "Designing www.LEGO.com/ shop: Business Issues and Concerns," case 500-0061, European Case Clearing House, 2000.

Information technologies are found to be extremely useful in supporting global supply chains. For example, TradeNet in Singapore connects sellers, buyers, and government agencies via electronic data interchange (EDI). (TradeNet's case is described in detail on the Web site of this book.) A similar network, TradeLink, operates in Hong Kong, using both EDI and EDI/Internet to connect about 70,000 trading partners.

IT also facilitates global SCM. It provides not only EDI and other communication options, but also online expertise in sometimes difficult and fast-changing regulations. IT also can be instrumental in helping businesses find trade partners (via electronic directories and search engines as in the case of alibaba.com). Finally, IT facilitates outsourcing of products and services, especially IT programming, to countries with a plentiful supply of labor, at low cost.

6.4 Electronic Commerce and SCM

E-commerce is emerging as a superb approach for providing solutions to problems along the supply chain. As seen in Dell's example at the beginning of the chapter, many supply chain activities, from taking customers' orders to parts procurement, can be conducted as part of an EC initiative. In general EC can make the following contributions to supply chain management:

1. Digitize products such as software. This expedites the flow of materials in the chain. It is also much cheaper to create and move electronic digits than physical products.
2. Replace with electronic documents all paper documents that move physically. This change improves speed and accuracy, and the cost of document transmission is much cheaper.
3. Replace faxes, telephone calls, and telegrams with an electronic messaging system. A single transaction could involve many messages, totaling thousands of messages per week or even per day at a minimal cost.
4. Change the nature and structure of the supply chain from linear to a hub (see the Orbis case in Chapter 1). Such restructuring enables faster, cheaper, and better communication, collaboration, and discovery of information.
5. Enhance several of the activities discussed in the previous sections, such as collaboration and information sharing among the partners in the supply chain. This can improve cooperation, coordination, and demand forecasts.
6. Shorten supply chain and minimize inventories. Production changes from mass production to build-to-order as a result of the "pull" nature of EC. The auto industry, for example, is expected to save billions of dollars annually in inventory reduction alone by moving to build-to-order strategy.
7. Facilitate customer service. Of special interest is the reduction of information flow between companies and customers due to innovations such as FAQs and the self-tracking of shipments.
8. Introduce efficiencies into buying and selling through the creation of e-marketplaces, as we saw in Chapter 5.

Let's look now at some specific activities and cases.

Buying and Selling Along the Supply Chain

A major role of EC is to facilitate buying and selling along the supply chain. The major activities are: upstream, internal SCM, downstream, and combined upsteam/downstream activities.

UPSTREAM ACTIVITIES. There are many innovative models of EC that improve the upstream activities. These models are generally described as *e-procurement*. Several were presented in Chapter 5: reverse auctions, aggregation of vendors' catalogs at the buyer's site, and procurement via consortia and group purchasing. (For others, see Mitchell, 2000; Adamson, 2000; and Varley, 2000.)

INTERNAL SCM ACTIVITIES. Internal SCM activities include different *intrabusiness EC* activities. These activities, from entering orders of materials, to recording sales, to tracking shipments, are usually conducted over a corporate intranet. Details and examples are provided in Chapters 5 and 7.

DOWNSTREAM ACTIVITIES. Typical EC models of downstream activities are provided in Chapters 5 and 7. Some examples follow.

Selling on Your Own Web Site. Large companies such as Intel, Cisco, and IBM use this model. At the company's own Web site, buyers review electronic catalogs from which they buy. Large buyers get their own pages and customized catalogs (see the Dell opening case).

Auctions. As discussed in Chapter 5, large companies such as Dell conduct auctions of products or obsolete equipment on their Web sites. Electronic auctions can shorten cycle time and save on logistics expenses. For example, electronic auctions sell over 2.5 million cars each year, supplied by car rental companies, government agencies, banks, and some large organizations. One online B2B auctioneer, for example, is Autodags. The buyers are car dealers who then resell the used cars. Traditional car auctions are done on large lots, where the cars are displayed and physically auctioned. In the electronic auction, the autos do not need to be transported to a physical auction site, nor do buyers have to travel to an auction site. Savings of $500 per car are realized.

UPSTREAM AND DOWNSTREAM COMBINED. It is sometimes advisable to combine upstream and downstream EC activities. These can be done in *exchanges*, where many buyers and sellers meet, as discussed in Chapter 5. Most of these exchanges are centered on specialized products or services, so they are referred to as **vertical portals**. A typical vertical portal is the one organized by ChemConnect. Similar markets exist for metals, electricity (which is sold among electricity-generating companies), and many commodities. Some vertical marketplaces use auctions and reverse auctions, offering *dynamic pricing*, as described in Chapter 5.

INTEGRATION OF EC WITH ERP. Since most middle-sized and large companies already have an ERP system, or are installing one, and since EC needs to *interface* with ERP, it makes sense to connect the two. These efforts are still in their infancy in many organizations. ERP vendors started to integrate EC with ERP only since 1997 on a small scale and only in 2000 as a major initiative. For example, SAP started building some EC interfaces in 1997, and in 1999 introduced mySAP.com as a major initiative. The mySAP initiative is a multifaceted Internet product that includes EC, online trading sites, an information portal, application hosting, and more user-friendly graphical interfaces (see *A Closer Look* 6.1).

A CLOSER LOOK
6.1 mySAP.com

As a complement to existing SAP products (i.e., R/3, New Dimensions products, and Knowledge Management), mySAP.com offers four building blocks:

- Workplace—a personalized interface
- Marketplace—a one-stop destination where business professionals can collaborate
- Business Scenarios—products for the Internet and intranets
- Application hosting—hosting of Web applications for SEMs

Together, these building blocks create a strategy that extends the reach of the Internet to empower employees and improve competitive advantage by participating in the EC marketplace. As part of Web-enabled applications, they can break down functional and geographic barriers while encouraging a high level of individual and collaborative performance.

The capabilities of the four component areas are as follows:

1. ***Workplace.*** The Workplace is a role-based *enterprise portal* solution. Via an easy-to-use and personalized Web browser–based front end, users are presented with all of the information, applications, and services they need to get their jobs done.

   Targeted information is presented to users immediately when they log on, a feature that can help to alleviate information overflow. The Workplace comes with approximately 150 role templates that customers are free to use or modify, or they can define their own.
2. ***Marketplace.*** The Marketplace is a one-stop destination for business and industry professionals. It enables SAP collaborative business scenarios, allowing many buyers and sellers to come together and do business. It is an integration site for enterprises and business professionals to collaborate, conduct commerce, access personalized content, and interact in professional communities. (See *www.sap.com/solutions/marketplace/index.*) The Marketplace provides:
   - The complete infrastructure, security, commerce-enabling applications, value-added services, and interoperability required to enable one-stop business anytime, anywhere, with anyone.
   - A cross-industry horizontal marketplace as the basis for collaborative commerce for business professionals in general.
   - A number of vertical and regional marketplaces for specialized commerce among user groups with similar interests, such as the oil and gas industry.
3. ***Business scenarios.*** The Business Scenario component offers the specific knowledge, functions, and services that one or more users may need to succeed in their business tasks with other businesses, partners, channels, and communities. mySAP.com provides a variety of e-business-enabled solutions, including purchasing, collaborative planning, employee self-service, direct customer servicing, and interbusiness knowledge management, to support the scenarios. The major areas of the Business Scenario are:
   - Effective B2B buying and selling with multiple buyers and sellers.
   - Customer relationship management(CRM). Core CRM functions include Internet sales and service, field sales and service, collaborative bidding, and Web-enabled customer service applications. mySAP.com supports catalog maintenance and ordering, and both integrate seamlessly with back-end systems. The CRM component of mySAP.com integrates customer news, background information, and vendor data.
   - Collaborative planning forecasting. mySAP.com provides supply chain management (SCM) solutions, including scenarios in collaborative forecasting and planning.
4. ***Application hosting.*** The mySAP.com strategy is to target small- and mid-size companies with Web-based application hosting services, which offer a more cost-effective and faster approach for companies to leverage SAP business scenarios and engage in Internet collaborative markets.

Source: Based on information from *mySAP.com.*

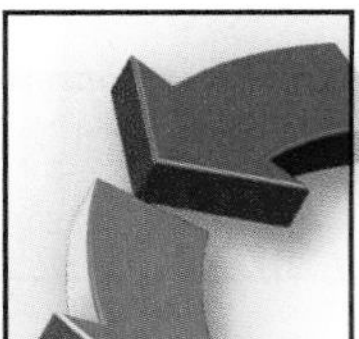

IT at Work

SMOOTHING THE SUPPLY CHAIN OF PLUMBING MATERIALS USING THE WEB

Integrating IT ...in Production and Operations Management

www.daviswarshow.com

Davis & Warshow (*daviswarshow.com*) is a plumbing and heating wholesaler in New York City. This is a very competitive business, where a medium-size company ($50 million annual sales) like Davis & Warshow (D&W) can survive only by being innovative. And indeed, the 75-year-old company survived mainly by positioning itself as a technology first mover in its industry. For example, in 1945 it used a billing machine, computerized its payroll in the 1950s, and in the mid-1980s introduced EDI and voice mail. In 2000, the company embarked on automated warehousing and e-commerce, to smooth its supply chain.

With New York's old buildings it is very difficult for plumbers to know in advance what parts they will need. They are usually on the job sites when they find out what parts are needed. Calling in for parts and materials and then waiting for delivery cost lots of money in terms of lost time. D&W's mission is to provide parts as quickly as possible to its customers, who are retailers and plumbing contractors.

The company has a large warehouse, six distribution centers (branches), and 20 delivery trucks, each equipped with a wireless communication system. But delivery was slow at times. In addition, inventories at the distribution centers were very high, since the delivery from the central warehouse was not fast enough. This has all changed now, thanks to the *automated warehouse*.

Using Mincron's Warehouse Management System, Davis & Warshow built an automated 120,000-square-foot warehouse. To begin with, all products that are not bar-coded by the manufacturers are labeled as they enter the warehouse. Then, all employees at the warehouse had to learn to use radio-frequency bar-code scanners, and unlearn many years of the traditional ways of putting away, picking, and shipping orders. Employees worried that scan guns would eliminate their jobs along with the paper documents that were being replaced. Employees' cooperation was achieved when job and salary levels were guaranteed. (New employees, however, are paid less, since they do not need the same level of training and experience.) Using the scan guns, employees can find items in a few minutes. Before, it took much longer, in some cases a few hours.

Another problem was order entry. Customers used to order by fax, phone, or by dropping in to a distribution branch. Now, the customer can order on the Web, and the orders go directly to the warehouse. From there, they are routed to the nearest distribution center, which gets parts for special orders, when needed.

Linking its Web site to eBay's Web site allows D&W to auction surplus faucets and other parts. The company was amazed to find that plumbing-hungry Web surfers were bidding up prices sometimes to as much as 100 percent over the normal price.

The electronic catalogs of D&W are used by the customers (plumbing contractors and builders) not only to place orders, but also to prepare their proposals to their clients. This coordination makes it easier for the customers to sell a job. D&W views it as a customer service. Using passwords, the contractors and builders can access information on the electronic catalogs that they can't get anywhere else.

The company also helped its customers solve another problem. Many of the customers do not keep their pricing information up-to-date. D&W has created a customized Excel spreadsheet for each customer, with a Web site password, and loaded updated pricing information on a CD-ROM. Contractors can use the CD-ROM to make sure prices are current. The Web site and the CD-ROM are synchronized.

Adoption was slow at the beginning, but it started to accelerate in 2001. D&W expects a major portion of its business to be online by 2005. Some of the system's benefits are:

- Employees can quickly find any item with the scan guns.
- Employees' stress has gone down dramatically, since they no longer need to hunt around the warehouse for products or pieces of paper.
- Customer-service and customer satisfaction have improved dramatically.
- The system paid for itself in two years, just from inventory reduction at the distribution branches.

For Further Exploration: Will D&W be disintermediated if manufacturers start to sell direct to contractors? Also, what if its competitors duplicate the system?

Sources: Compiled from B. Miodonski, "Davis & Warshow Hit 75 Running," *Supply House Times*, July 2000; and from *daviswarshow.com* (2001).

The logic behind integrating EC and ERP is that by extending the existing ERP system to support e-commerce, organizations not only leverage their investment in the ERP solution, but also speed up the development of EC applications. The problem with this approach is that the ERP software is very complex and inflexible (difficult to change), so it is difficult to achieve easy, smooth, and effective integration. One other potential problem is that ERP systems deal more with back-office (administrative) applications, whereas EC deals with front-office applications such as sales and order taking, customer service, and other customer relationship management (CRM) activities.

An example of how EC can improve customer services and smooth the supply chain is given in the *IT at Work* case on the previous page (page 264).

INTEGRATION WITH CRM AND EC. The integration of ERP and EC is related to the integration with customer relationship management (CRM). As you will see in Chapter 7 (Section 7.4), several CRM activities are part of EC customer service. Furthermore, CRM is considered a value-added function for the ERP vendors. Integration provides a single data model for ERP, CRM, and EC, which enables strong operational efficiencies.

6.5 ORDER FULFILLMENT IN E-COMMERCE

In the previous section we described how e-commerce can solve problems along the supply chain. However, some applications of EC, especially B2C and sometimes B2B, may have problems with their own supply chains. These problems usually occur in order fulfillment. Let's explain.

When a company sells direct to customers it must:

1. Quickly find the products to be shipped, and pack them.
2. Arrange for the packages to be delivered quickly to the customer's door.
3. Collect the money from every customer, either in advance, in COD, or by individual bill.
4. Handle the return of unwanted or defective products.

It is very difficult to fulfill these activities both effectively and efficiently. For this reason, both online companies and click-and-mortar companies have difficulties in their online-related supply chain. Here we will analyze the situation and look at possible solutions.

Order Fulfillment and Logistics: An Overview

ORDER FULFILLMENT. **Order fulfillment** refers not only to providing the customers with what they ordered and doing it on time, but also to providing all related customer service. For example, the customer must receive assembly and operating instructions for a new appliance. This can be done by including a paper document with the product, or by providing the instructions on the Web. (A nice example is available at *livemanuals.com*.) In addition, if the customer is not happy with a product, an exchange or return must be arranged. Thus, while order fulfillment is basically a part of the *back-office* operations, it is strongly related to *front-office* operations as well.

During the last few years, e-tailers have faced continuous problems in order fulfillment, especially during the holiday season. The problems resulted in inability to deliver on time, delivering wrong items, paying too much for deliveries, and heavily compensating unhappy customers. Taking orders over the Internet could well be the easy part of B2C electronic commerce. Fulfillment to customers' doors is the sticky part. As a matter of fact, many e-tailers have experienced fulfillment problems since they started EC. Amazon.com, for example, which initially operated as a totally virtual company, added physical warehouses in order to expedite deliveries and reduce order fulfillment costs. Woolworths of Australia, a large supermarket that added online services, had serious difficulties with order fulfillment and delivery of fresh foods, and had to completely reengineer its delivery system.

Several factors can be responsible for delays in deliveries. They range from inability to accurately forecast demand, to ineffective supply chains of the e-tailers. Such problems exist also in offline businesses. One factor that is typical of EC is that it is based on the concept of "pull" operations, which begin with an *order*, frequently a customized one. This is in contrast with traditional retailing that begins with a production to *inventory*, which is then "pushed" to customers. In the pull case it is more difficult to forecast demand, due to unique demands of customized orders and lack of sufficient years of experience. Another factor is that in a B2C pull model, the goods need be delivered to the customer's door, with small quantities to each customer, whereas in brick-and-mortar retailing, the customers come to the stores.

Innovative Solutions to the Order Fulfillment Problem

During the last few years companies have developed interesting solutions to both B2C and B2B order fulfillment. Here are some examples:

- Many companies allow customers to view goods in real-time. Live video is designed to let traditional brick-and-mortar retailers enhance online shopping. For example, galleryfurniture.com used dozens of cameras, called **Webcams**, to demonstrate its product inventory on the Web. The innovation allowed the company to move inventory 70 times a year on the average (compared to five times in conventional stores), resulting in huge inventory reduction. FAO Schwartz, the large toy store, uses Webcams to demonstrate its world-famous Manhattan store in New York. Webcams are used by art galleries and real estate developers. They even are used to show beaches to surfers.
- A joint venture of Mail Boxes Etc., a fulfillment services company (Innotrac. Corp.), and Return.com developed a logistics system that determines whether a customer is entitled to a return and refund. The logistics system connects e-tailers and order management systems to Return.com's intelligent system. Customers have the option of making returns at kiosks in Mail Boxes Etc.'s physical franchises.
- Garden.com, a retailer of plants and flowers, developed proprietary software that allowed it to collaborate with its 70 suppliers efficiently and effectively. Orders were batched and organized in such a way that pullers were able to find, pack, and deliver the plants and flowers efficiently. Customers were able to track the status of their orders in real time (*CIO*, April 15, 2000). Despite their efficient supply chain, the company went out of business in December 2000 due to an insufficient number of customers.
- *Relysoftware.com* manages a marketplace that helps companies with goods to find "forwarders"—the intermediaries that prepare goods for shipping. The company also helps forwarders to find the best prices on air carriers and helps

the carriers to fill up empty cargo space by bidding it up. Similar services are offered by Electronic Freight Exchange, *efxit.com* (see Internet Exercise 10).

SAME DAY, EVEN SAME HOUR DELIVERY. In the digital age, next-morning delivery may not be fast enough. Today we talk about same-day delivery, and even delivery within an hour. Delivering groceries is an area where speed is important. An example is *groceryworks.com*, which is both an online grocer and a delivery company of B2C items. Quick delivery of pizza has been practiced for a long time (e.g., by Domino's Pizza). Today, pizza orders in many places are accepted online. Many restaurants use the same approach, which is known as "dine online."

Some companies offer aggregating services, which process orders for several restaurants (e.g., *XpressAsia.com* and *dialadinner.com.hk* in Hong Kong) and also make the deliveries. Here is how it works:

- Customers click on the online menu to indicate dishes they want, then submit their request electronically.
- Sometimes you can mix and match orders from two restaurants.
- Order processors at the aggregating company receive the order.
- For first-time customers, a staff member phones to check delivery details and to confirm that the order is genuine.
- The orders are forwarded electronically to the participating restaurants.
- Delivery staff receives a copy of the order by e-mail on their mobile phones, telling them which restaurant to go to. There they are handed the food and delivery details.
- Delivery is made in small cars or on bicycles.
- Customers receive their meal and pay cash on delivery. Average time from order to delivery is 30 to 40 minutes.

For another example of quick delivery, see *sameday.com*.

Automated Warehouses

Traditional warehouses are built to deliver *large quantities* to a *small number* of stores and plants. In B2C EC, companies need to send small quantities to a large number of individuals. The picking and packing process therefore is different, and usually more labor-intensive. Therefore, large-volume EC fulfillment requires special warehouses. Automated warehouses, for example, may include robots and other devices that expedite the pickup of products. Several e-tailers, such as Amazon.com, operate their own warehouses (see *Interactive Week*, July 26, 1999). However, most B2C is probably shipped via outsourcers. One of the largest EC warehouses in the United States is operated by a mail-order company, Fingerhut (*fingerhut.com*). This company handles the logistics of all types of mail orders (including online orders) for Wal-Mart, Macy's, and many others. The process used at the warehouse involves eight steps:

1. Retailers contract with Fingerhut to stock their products and also fulfill orders.
2. Retailers' merchandise is stored by SKU (stock-keeping unit) at the huge warehouse.
3. Orders that arrive by e-mail, fax, or phone are transferred to Fingerhut's mainframe computer.

4. To optimize the work of pickers, a special computer program consolidates the orders from all vendors (including Fingerhut itself) and organizes them into "picking waves." These waves are organized such that pickers don't have to run from one end of the warehouse to another for each order.
5. The picked items are moved by conveyors to the packing area. The computer configures the size and type of box (or envelope) needed for packaging, and it types special packaging and delivery instructions.
6. Packages pass on a conveyor belt through a scanning station where they are weighed. (The actual weight must match the SKU projected weight.)
7. A scanner reads a bar code to identify the destination, and each package is automatically pushed down into one of 26 destination conveyer belts that takes the packages directly to a waiting truck.
8. Once trucks are full, they depart for local postal offices in 26 major cities, thereby dramatically cutting shipping costs. (For details, see *Interactive Week*, September 13, 1999 and *Internet Week*, June 28, 1998.)

Other companies (e.g., *submitorder.com*) provide similar services. The key for all such services is *speed* and *efficiency*.

Dealing with Returns

Returning unwanted merchandise and providing for exchanges are necessary for maintaining customers' trust and loyalty. The Boston Consulting Group found that the "absence of good return mechanism" was the second-biggest reason shoppers cited for refusing to buy on the Web frequently. For their part, merchants face the major problem of how to deal with returns. Several options exist (e.g., see Trager, 2000):

1. Return an item to the place where it was purchased. This is easy to do in a brick-and-mortar store, but not in a virtual one. To return an item to a virtual store, you need to get authorization, pack everything up, pay to ship it back, insure it, and wait up to two billing cycles for a credit to show up on your statement. The buyer is not happy. Neither is the seller, who must unpack the item, check the paperwork, and resell the item, usually at a loss. This solution is good only if the number of returns is small.
2. Separate the logistics of returns from the logistics of delivery. Returns are shipped to an independent unit and handled separately inside the company. This solution may be more efficient from the seller's point of view, but the buyer is still unhappy.
3. Allow the customer to physically drop the returned items at collection stations (such as convenience stores or Mail Boxes Etc.), from which the returns can be picked up. In addition to 7-Eleven stores, this is done, for example, at BP Australia Ltd. (gasoline service stations), which teamed up with *wishlist.com.au* and at Caltex Australia in their convenience stores.
4. Completely outsource returns. Several outsourcers, including United Postal Service (UPS), provide such services. The services they offer deal not only with shipments, but with the entire logistics process of returns.

Dealing with supply chain problems, either in the regular or the virtual business, must include not only fulfillment but the so-called *demand chain*, namely the customer side.

MANAGERIAL ISSUES

1. ***Ethical issues.*** Conducting a supply chain management project may result in the need to lay off, retrain, or transfer employees. Should management notify the employees in advance regarding such possibilities? And what about those older employees who are difficult to retrain? Other ethical issues may involve sharing of personal information, which may be part of the new organizational culture. Finally, individuals may have to share computer programs that they designed for their personal use. Such programs may be considered the intellectual property of the individuals.
2. ***How much to integrate?*** While companies should consider extreme integration projects, including ERP, SCM, and electronic commerce, they should recognize that integrating long and complex supply chains may result in failure. Therefore, many times companies tightly integrate the upstream, inside-company, and downstream activities, and loosely connect these three.
3. ***Role of IT.*** Almost all major SCM projects use IT. However, it is important to remember that in most cases the technology plays a supportive role, and the primary role is organizational and managerial in nature. On the other hand, without IT, most SCM efforts do not succeed.
4. ***Organizational adaptability.*** To adopt ERP, an organization must conform to the software, not the other way around. When the software is changed, in a later version for example, the organization must change also. Some organizations are able and willing to do so; others are not.

ON THE WEB SITE... Additional resources, including the Virtual Company, quizzes, cases, updates, additional exercises, links, demos, and activities, can be found on the book's Web site.

KEY TERMS

Application service provider (ASP) *259*
Bullwhip effect *246*
Business intelligence *257*
Collaborative commerce networks, collaborative commerce *254*
Enterprise resource planning (ERP) *254*
Material requirements planning (MRP) *250*
Manufacturing resource planning (MRP II) *251*
Order fulfillment *265*
Reverse logistics (returns) *245*
SAP R/3 *255*
Supply chain *242*
Supply chain intelligence (SCI) *257*
Supply chain management (SCM) *242*
Supply chain teams *249*
Vertical portals *262*
Webcam *266*

CHAPTER HIGHLIGHTS (Numbers Refer to Learning Objectives)

❶ It is necessary to properly manage the supply chain to assure superb customer service, low cost, and short cycle time.

❶ The supply chain must be completely managed, from the raw materials to the end customers.

❷ It is difficult to manage the supply chain due to the uncertainties in demand and supply and the need to coordinate several business partners' activities.

❷ Innovative approaches to SCM require cooperation and coordination of the business partners, facilitated by IT innovations such as extranets, which allow suppliers to view companies' inventories in real time.

- ❸ Software integration has increased both in coverage and scope, from MRP to MRP II, to ERP, to enhanced ERP, and to an ERP/SCM integration.
- ❸ Today ERP software, which is designed to improve standard business transactions, is enhanced with decision-support capabilities as well as Web interfaces.
- ❹ Implementing SCM projects, or using ERP software, frequently requires changing organizational processes.
- ❺ Order fulfillment in EC is difficult due to the need to ship many small packages to customers' doors. Outsourcing the logistics and delivery jobs is common.
- ❺ Special large and automated warehouses help in improving the EC order fulfillment.
- ❺ Electronic commerce is able to provide new solutions to problems along the supply chain by integrating the company's major business activities with both upstream and downstream entities via an electronic infrastructure.

QUESTIONS FOR REVIEW

1. Define supply chain and supply chain management (SCM).
2. Define ERP.
3. List the major components of ERP.
4. What is an extended supply chain?
5. Define order fulfillment
6. List the major benefits of SCM.
7. Define reverse logistics.
8. Describe the bullwhip effect.
9. Define MRP.

QUESTIONS FOR DISCUSSION

1. Identify the supply chain(s) and the flow of information described in the opening case.
2. Relate the concepts of supply chain and its management to Porter's value chain and value system model.
3. Discuss the Warner-Lambert Listerine case, and prepare a chart of W-L's supply chain.
4. Distinguish between ERP and SCM software.
5. It is said that SCM software created more changes in logistics than 100 years of continuous improvement did. Discuss.
6. Discuss what it would be like if the registration process and class scheduling process at your college or university were reengineered to an online, real-time, seamless basis with good connectivity and good empowerment in the organization. (If your registration is already online, find another manual process.) Explain the supply chain in this situation.
7. Compare MRP to MRP II to ERP.
8. Discuss how cooperation between a company that you are familiar with and its suppliers can reduce inventory cost.
9. Find examples of how organizations improve their supply chains in two of the following: manufacturing, hospitals, retailing, education, construction, and shipping.
10. The normal way to collect fees from travelers on expressways is to use tollbooths. Automatic coin-collecting baskets can expedite the process, but not eliminate the long waiting lines during rush hours. About 80 percent of the travelers are frequent users of the expressways near their homes, and they complain bitterly. The money collection process on some highways has been reengineered by using smart cards that allow machines to read the car ID numbers, so cars do not have to stop. This reduces travelers' waiting time by 90 percent and money processing cost by 80 percent.
    - a. Identify the supply chain.
    - b. Several new information technologies including smart cards are used in the process. Find information on how this is accomplished.
11. Discuss the problem of reverse logistics in EC. What kind of companies may suffer the most?
12. Explain why UPS defines itself as a "technology company with trucks" rather than a "trucking company with technology."
13. Discuss the meaning of intelligence in "supply chain intelligence."
14. It is said that supply chains are essentially "a series of linked suppliers and customers; every customer is in turn a supplier to the next downstream organization, until the ultimate end-user." Explain. Use of a diagram is recommended.
15. Explain the bullwhip effect. In which type of EC business it is likely to occur most? How can the effect be controlled?
16. Draw the supply chain of the Davis & Warshow plumbing parts business. Show the use of IT in various places of the chain.

EXERCISES

1. Draw the supply chains of Dell Computer and Warner-Lambert. What are the similarities? The differences?
2. Draw the supply chain of Lego. Include at least two countries.
3. Automated warehouses play a major role in B2C order fulfillment. Find material on how they operate. (Start with the story by Duvall in *Interactive Week,* Sept. 13, 1999.)
4. Examine the functionalities of ERP software from SAP or other vendors.
5. Draw the supply chain of several SMEs that participate in a group purchasing plan (online).

GROUP AND ROLE-PLAYING ACTIVITIES

1. Each group in the class will be assigned to a major ERP/SCM vendor such as SAP, PeopleSoft, Oracle, J. D. Edwards, etc. Members of the groups will investigate topics such as:
   - **a.** Web connections
   - **b.** Use of business intelligence tools
   - **c.** Relationship to CRM and to EC
   - **d.** Major capabilities
   - **e.** Availability of ASP services

   Each group will prepare a presentation for the class, trying to convince the class why their software is best for a local company known to the students (e.g., a supermarket chain).
2. Universities and many other organizations regularly order periodicals for their libraries. New periodicals appear every day, people change their preferences, and the librarians are busy. Typically, the library will contact an agent to place the order. The agent, who is in contact with hundreds (thousands) of publishers, consolidates orders from several universities and then places orders with the publishers. This process is both slow and expensive to the library, which pays a 3 percent commission to the agent and loses a 5 percent discount that the publisher passes on to the agent.

   The University of California at Berkeley pioneered an electronic ordering system in 1996, which enabled the university to save about $365,000 per year on periodicals costs. Furthermore, the cycle time is cut by as much as 80 percent, providing subscribers with the magazine one to three months earlier.

   The electronic ordering is coordinated by Rowe.Com. The system, called Subscribe (see *rowe.com*), enables the university to electronically submit its encrypted orders and a secure payment authorization to a central computer via EDI. The program verifies the order and the authorization. It then transfers the order via EDI to the publisher and the payment authorization to the automated clearinghouse. Finally, the buyers' bank sends payment to the payers' bank via EFT.

   The cost to the university is $5 per order. For an average periodical with annual subscription fee of $400, the cost is more than 80 percent lower ($5 vs. $32).
   - **a.** Prepare a flowchart of how the new purchasing process works. Show all the business partners (the university, Rowe.Com, publishers) and the flow of information (orders, etc.), periodicals, and money.
   - **b.** Prepare a flowchart of the traditional process, which involves placing an order to an agent who places the order with the publishers and bills the university. The university pays the agent who pays the publisher. One agent works with many publishers and many universities.
   - **c.** What are the advantages of the new system to the university? What are the disadvantages?
   - **d.** Identify the various software programs that support the new system. Where are they located and what is the role of each program?
   - **e.** What other services related to the ordering of periodicals (not books!) could Rowe.Com offer to the university?
   - **f.** What will happen to the intermediary (the agent)?
   - **g.** What can Rowe.Com do to stay ahead of potential competitors in this market? What will be the cost of such a strategy?
   - **h.** Enter Rowe's Web site (*rowe.com*). Has Rowe.Com made any recent changes to its Subscribe program?
   - **i.** What are EDI and the Internet used for in Subscribe?
   - **j.** Enter *rowe.com* and report on the status of the company.

INTERNET EXERCISES

1. Enter *ups.com*. Examine some of the IT-supported customer services and tools provided by the company. Write a report on how UPS contributes to supply chain improvements.
2. Enter *supply-chain.org, cio.com,* and *findarticles.com,* and search for recent information on supply chain management. Also find information about SCOR.

3. Enter *logictool.com*. Find information on the bullwhip effect and on the strategies and tools used to lessen the effect.
4. Enter *coca-colastore.com*. Examine the delivery and the return options available there.
5. *Kozmo.com*. was a company that rented videos and delivered them to within 30 to 60 minutes. Find out what you can about why it failed. Was there a problem with the company's order-fulfillment promises? Were there any drawbacks in Kozmo's alliances with Starbucks and Amazon.com? Explain.
6. The U.S. post office is entering EC logistics. Examine its services and tracking systems at *uspspriorityrnail.com*. What are the potential advantages for EC shippers?
7. Enter *brio.com* and identify Brio's solution to SCM integration as it relates to decision making for EC. View the demo.
8. Enter *kewill.com*. Examine the various products offered there, including Commander WMS. Relate this to SCM.
9. Enter *rightfreight.com* and *e-fxit.com*. Compare the features in the two sites.

Minicase 1

Quantum Corporation Streamlined Its Supply Chain

www.quantum.com

Quantum Corporation (*quantum.com*) is a major U.S. manufacturer of hard-disk drives and other high-technology storage components.

Quantum faced two key challenges in its manufacturing process. The first was streamlining its component supply process in order to reduce on-hand inventory. Quantum's traditional ordering process was labor-intensive, involving numerous phone calls and manual inventory checks. To ensure that production would not be interrupted, the process required high levels of inventory. Quantum needed a solution that would automate the ordering process to increase accuracy and efficiency, reduce needed inventory to 3 days, and provide the company's purchasing agents with more time for nontransactional tasks.

Quantum's second challenge was to improve the quality of the component data in its material requirements planning (MRP) system. Incomplete and inaccurate data caused delays in production. Quantum's solution of manually reviewing reports to identify errors was labor intensive and occurred too late; problems in production were experienced before the reports were even reviewed. Quantum needed a technology solution that would enable it to operate *proactively* to catch problems before they caused production delays.

The solution that Quantum chose to automate its component supply process was an interenterprise system that automatically e-mails reorders to suppliers. Initiated in 1999, the system uses an innovative event detection and notification solution from Categoric Software (*categoric.com*). It scans Quantum's databases twice daily, assessing material requirements from one application module against inventory levels tracked in another. Orders are automatically initiated and sent to suppliers as needed, allowing suppliers to make regular deliveries that match Quantum's production schedule. The system not only notifies suppliers of the quantity of components required in the immediate orders, but also gives the supplier a valuable window into the amount of inventory on hand and future weekly requirements.

The system also provided other improvements. It enabled Quantum to tap into multiple data sources to identify critical business events. To elevate data quality, Quantum implemented Categoric Alerts to proactively catch any data errors or omissions in its MRP database. The systems' notifications are now sent whenever any critical MRP data fall outside the existing operational parameters.

The system has produced the desired results. For example, the estimated value of the improved ordering process using the new system is millions of dollars in inventory reductions each year. The buyers have reduced transaction tasks and costs, and both Quantum and its buyers get a lot more information with a lot less work. Before the implementation of Categoric Alerts, Quantum's analysts would search massive reports for MRP data errors. Now that the new system is implemented, exceptions are identified as they occur. This new process has freed the analysts from the drudgery of scanning reports and has greatly increased employee satisfaction.

Data integrity of the MRP increased from 10 percent to almost 100 percent, and Quantum is now able to quickly respond to changing customer demand. The system paid for itself in the first year.

Sources: Compiled from an advertising supplement in *CIO Magazine* (October 1, 1999), and from information at *categoric.com* (May 2000).

Questions for Minicase 1

1. Identify the internal and external parts of the supply chain that were enhanced with the system.
2. Enter *categoric.com* and find information about Categoric Alerts. Describe the capability of the product.
3. Explain how purchasing was improved.
4. Describe how Quantum's customers are being better served now.
5. Identify the EC solutions used in this case.

Minicase 2

Green Mountain Coffee Roasters Integrates Electronic Commerce and Supply Chain Management

www.gmcr.com

Green Mountain Coffee Roasters (GMCR), a medium-sized distributor of quality coffee in the United States, experienced a high growth rate in recent years (from $34 million in 1996 to about $80 million in 2000). Sales are made through over 5,000 wholesalers and resellers, including supermarkets, restaurants, and airlines. In addition, mail-order shipments are made to over 40,000 loyal individual customers.

The rapid expansion of the business made it necessary to provide all employees access to the latest data so they could make better decisions regarding demand forecast, inventory management, and profitability analysis. To meet this need the company decided to install ERP software.

In 1997, GMCR replaced its custom legacy information system with an ERP from PeopleSoft. The ERP includes functional modules such as production and inventory control, financial management, and human resources management. GMCR decided in 1998 to hook the ERP to the Internet for the following reasons:

- The company expected to double its sales to individual customers. This was going to be done by displaying the culture and image of the company, allowing customers to learn more about coffee, and creating a "GMCR coffee community."
- The existing coffee tours and coffee club were well adapted to the Internet.
- The company estimated that at least 30 percent of its 5,000 business partners prefer to do business online.
- The company needed a better mechanism for customer relationship (both with individuals and businesses). The company wanted to get quick feedback, be able to solve customer problems quickly, and provide an efficient and easy order-taking facility.

The integration of the Web with ERP provided the following capabilities:

- Many of the business customers are small proprietor-managed shops. They are busy during the day, so they prefer to place orders in the evenings when GMCR's call center is closed.
- The customers like to know, immediately, if a product is in stock and when it will be shipped.
- Customers want to see their order histories, including summaries such as a most-frequently ordered product list.
- Customers want to track the status of their orders.

All of the above can be done by customers themselves, anytime and from anywhere. In addition, the system can support the requests of GMCR's sales force for instant information about customers, inventory levels, prices, competition, overnight delivery services, and so forth.

PeopleSoft's eStore, an Internet storefront that is tightly integrated with the ERP suite from order fulfillment to the rest of the supply chain management, was implemented in 1999. GMCR benefited not only from improved customer service and efficient online marketing, but also from providing access to the latest data to all employees. Some of the results so far: Forecasts have improved, inventory is minimized (using the just-in-time concept), and profitability analysis by product and/or customer is done in minutes.

Sources: Condensed from customer success stories at *peoplesoft.com* (January 2000) and from *gmcr.com* (December 2000).

Questions for Minicase 2

1. Enter *gmcr.com* and identify the major customer-related activities. How are such activities supported by information technology?
2. Coffee club members make up about 90 percent of all the company's direct mail business. Why? (Check the Web site.)

3. How can the ERP system improve GMCR's inventory system?
4. It is said that "Internet sales data must be taken into account by enterprise planning, forecast demand, and profitability studies." Explain why.
5. It is said that "Because the customer's account and pricing information are linked to the order, accurate invoicing will flow automatically from the Internet transaction." Explain, and relate to the concept of the supply chain.

REFERENCES AND BIBLIOGRAPHY

1. Adamson, J., "E-Procurement Comes of Age," *Proceedings, E-Commerce for Transition Economy,* Geneva, June 2000.
2. Alt, R., et al., "Interaction of Electronic Commerce and Supply Chain Management: Insights from 'The Swatch Group,'" *Proceedings, 33rd Hawaiian International Conference on Systems Sciences,* Hawaii, January 2000.
3. Appleton, E. L., "How to Survive ERP," *Datamation,* March 1997.
4. ASCET, "From Supply Chain to Collaborative Network: Case Studies in the Food Industry," white paper, 2000, *http://Andersen_gASCET.com.*
5. Ayers, J., "A Primer on Supply Chain Management," *Information Strategy: The Executive's Journal,* Winter 2000.
6. Bussiek, T., "The Internet-Based Supply Chain—New Forms of Procurement Utilizing Standard Business Software," *Electronic Markets,* Vol. 9, No. 3, 1999.
7. Caldwell, B., "Taming the Beast," *Information Week,* March 10, 1997.
8. Caldwell, B., and T. Stein, "Beyond ERP: New IT Agenda," *Information Week,* November 30, 1998.
9. Chase, R. B., et al., *Production and Operations Management,* 8th ed. Homewood, IL: Irwin, 1998.
10. cio.com, "Supply Chain Integration: The Name of the Game Is Collaboration," Special Advertising Supplement, *CIO Magazine,* November 1, 1999.
11. Connoly, J., "ERP Corporate Cleanup," *Computerworld,* Vol. 33, 1999, pp. 74–78.
12. Davenport, T. H., *Mission Critical: Realizing the Promise of Enterprise Systems.* Cambridge, MA: Harvard Business School Press, 2000.
13. Epner, S., "The Search for a Supply Team," *Industrial Distribution,* December 1999.
14. Handfield, R. B., and E. L. Nichols, Jr., *Introduction to Supply Chain Management.* Upper Saddle River, NJ: Prentice-Hall, 1999.
15. Jacobs, F. R., and D. C. Whybark, *Why ERP?* Boston: McGraw-Hill, 2000.
16. Johnston, R. B., et al., "An Emerging Vision of Internet-Enabled Supply-Chain Electronic Commerce," *Inter-Journal of Electronic Commerce,* Summer 2000.
17. Kalakota, R., and M. Robinson, *E-Business: Roadmap for Success.* Reading, MA: Addison-Wesley, 1999, Chapter 5.
18. Koch, C., et al., "The ABCs of ERP," *CIO Magazine* (cio.com), December 22, 1999.
19. Lee, L. H., et al., "The Bullwhip Effect in Supply Chains," *Sloan Management Review,* Spring 1997.
20. Lin, F. R., and M. J. Shaw, "Reengineering the Order Fulfillment Process in Supply Chain Networks," *International Journal of Flexible Manufacturing,* March 1998.
21. Miodonski, B., "Davis & Warshow Hit 75 Running," *Supply House Times,* July 2000.
22. Mitchell, P., "E-Procurement Systems: Beyond Indirect Procurement," *Proceedings, E-Commerce for Transition Economy,* Geneva, June 2000.
23. Palaniswamy, R., and T. Frank, "Enhancing Manufacturing Performance with ERP Systems: Five Case studies," *Information System Management,* Summer 2000.
24. Peppers, D., et al., *The One-to-One Fieldbook.* New York: Currency and Doubleday, 1999.
25. Poirier, C. C., *Advanced Supply Chain Management: How to Build a Sustained Competition.* Berkeley, CA: Publishers' Group West, 1999.
26. Porter, M. E., *Competitive Advantage: Creating and Sustaining Superior Performance.* New York: Free Press, 1985.
27. Rigney, P., "Eliminate Fulfillment Problems," *E-Business Advisor,* March 2000.
28. Russell, R. S., and B. W. Taylor, *Operations Management,* 3rd ed. Upper Saddle River, NJ: Prentice-Hall, 2000.
29. Russom, P., "Increasing Manufacturing Performance Through Supply Chain Intelligence," *DM Review,* September 2000.
30. Sandoe, K., et al., *Enterprise Integration.* New York: Wiley, 2001.
31. Schwartz B., "E-Business: New Distribution Models Coming to a Site Near You," *Transportation and Distribution,* February 2000.
32. Selland C., "Extending E-Business to ERP," *E-Business Advisor,* January 1999.
33. Selland C., "The Key to E-Business: Integrating the Enterprise," *E-Business Advisor,* October 1999.
34. Trager, L., "Not So Many Happy Returns," *Interactive Week,* March 20, 2000.
35. Turban, E., et al., *Electronic Commerce. A Managerial Perspective,* 2nd ed. Upper Saddle River, NJ: Prentice-Hall, 2002.
36. Varley, S., "E-Procurement-Beyond the First Wave" (wmrc.com), *Proceedings, E-Commerce for Transition Economy,* Geneva, June 2000.
37. Yao, D. D., et al., "Extended Enterprise Supply-Chain Management at IBM," *Interfaces,* January–February 2000.

PART III

Organizational Applications

CHAPTER

7

Transaction Processing, Innovative Functional Systems, CRM, and Integration

LEARNING OBJECTIVES

After studying this chapter, you will be able to:

1. Relate functional areas and business processes to the value chain model.
2. Identify functional management information systems.
3. Describe the transaction processing system and demonstrate how it is supported by IT.
4. Describe the support provided by IT and the Web to each of these functional areas: production/operations, marketing and sales, accounting and finance, and human resources management.
5. Describe the role of IT in facilitating CRM.
6. Describe the benefits and issues of integrating functional information systems.

INTEGRATED SOLUTIONS HELP COLONIAL BUILDING SUPPLY STAY COMPETITIVE

THE PROBLEM

Colonial Building Supply in Centerville, Utah, is a small company that must compete with chains like Home Depot. Until a few years ago, Colonial and other lumberyards used to run by the "seat of their pants." Managers used to go out into the lumberyard and physically count what was there. In contrast, Home Depot uses sophisticated computers to monitor inventory and support related decisions. Colonial installed a proprietary computer point-of-sale accounting system in 1988, but it quickly reached its capacity. Without a large investment it was impossible to add hand-held units for remote data collection. Furthermore, to remain competitive, Colonial needed a technology to provide it with information about inventory levels and customer buying trends. Lumber is a commodity whose prices fluctuate daily, sometimes hourly. When prices are low, lumberyards want to keep large inventories, to meet all customer demand and to benefit when prices increase (that is, they will have stock on hand and not have to buy at the new, higher prices). When prices are high, they do not want to overstock items they could later buy at lower prices. Therefore, the timing of lumber purchases also is a critical need for Colonial.

THE SOLUTION

Colonial purchased an *integrated* system from Dimensions Software (Salt Lake City). The system included software modules for accounting, inventory control, purchasing/receiving, and employee time control and attendance, plus several other modules, such as truck scheduling. Colonial also purchased point-of-sale (POS) terminals and hand-held automatic product identification and data collection devices. The system runs on an IBM Pentium server that supports 25 terminals and several peripheral devices to execute the above capabilities. The entire system was installed in five days. The software ties different functions together under one system. Employees have access to only some designated menus, using a password.

When sales are made, items are instantly deducted from the inventory. The software examines past buying patterns and future business conditions and automatically determines amounts for reordering. For example, if building permits are up, the system will increase orders. Purchase orders are sent electronically via the Internet. The system is very user friendly and requires minimal training.

Recent additions to Colonial's systems are the following: (1) A document management system stores all documents electronically. It scans, categorizes, and archives every piece of paper for easy access. (2) Radio-frequency–based hand-held computers collect data and transmit them to the computer automatically. (3) Laptops plugged into a cellular phone allow field salespeople to tap into the store's computer and check availability while they meet with contractors at construction sites.

THE RESULTS

The system produced what Colonial hoped it would: lower costs for data-entry labor, reductions in inventory and storage space, fast access to information, better customer service, and higher employee satisfaction. All of these results contribute to Colonial's ability to stay competitive and to increase its market share and profitability.

Sources: Condensed from *Integrated Solutions*, July 1997, pp. 7–8, and from *dimensions.com* (1998).

LESSONS LEARNED FROM THIS CASE

The Colonial case makes some interesting points about implementing IT.

1. IT supports the routine processes of a retailer, enabling it to be *efficient* and *effective* and to satisfy its customers.
2. The software helped to modernize and redesign the company's major business processes.
3. The software supports several business processes, not just one.
4. The system's major applications are in logistics. However, the same software vendor provides ready-made accounting, marketing, and operations modules, which are *integrated* with the inventory module and with each other.
5. IT can be beneficial to a relatively small company.
6. The integration includes connection to business partners using the Internet.

This solution has proven useful for a company whose business processes cross the traditional functional departmental lines.

To offer service in the digital economy, companies must continuously upgrade their functional information system by using state-of-the-art technology. Furthermore, the functional processes must be improved as needed. Finally, as indicated in Chapter 6, SCM software is needed in segments of the supply chain. These segments are frequently functional information systems.

Functional information systems get much of their data from the organizational transaction processing systems (TPSs). Also, many IT solutions use data and information from two or more functional information systems. One such solution is CRM. Therefore, there is a need to integrate the functional systems applications among themselves and with the TPS and CRM. These relationships are shown in Figure 7.1 (page 278), which provides a pictorial view of the topics discussed in this chapter.

7.1 FUNCTIONAL INFORMATION SYSTEMS

The logistics/operations, marketing, and accounting and finance departments are major functional areas at Colonial and at other companies. Traditionally, information systems were designed within each functional area to support the functional areas by increasing their internal effectiveness and efficiency. However, as we will discuss in Chapter 8, the traditional functional hierarchical structure may not be best for some organizations, because certain business processes may involve activities that are performed in several functional areas. Suppose a customer wants to buy a particular product. When the customer's order arrives at the marketing department, the customer's credit needs to be approved by finance. Someone checks to find if the product is in the warehouse. If it is there, then someone needs to pack the product and forward it to the shipping department, which arranges for delivery. Accounting prepares a bill for the customer, and finance may arrange for shipping insurance.

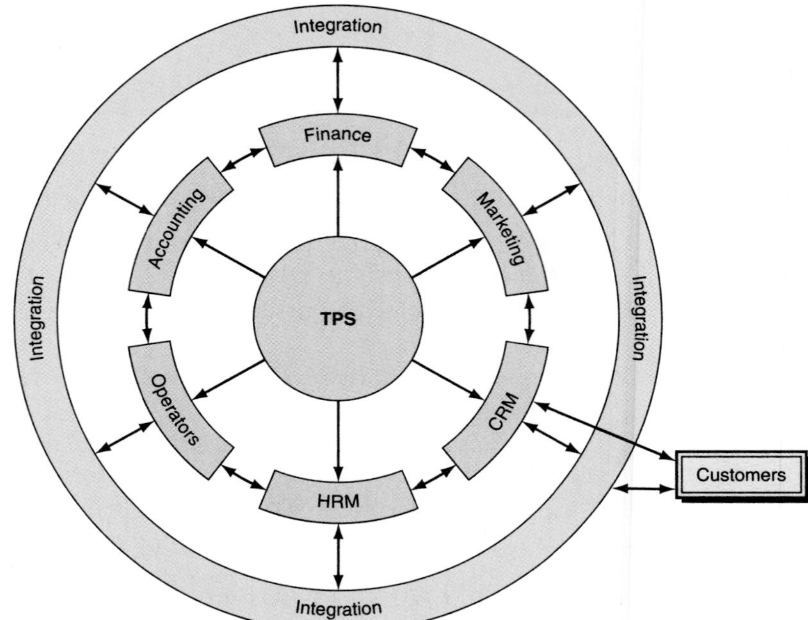

FIGURE 7.1 The functional areas, TPS, CRM, and integration connection. Note the flow of information from the TPS to the functional systems. Flow of information between and among functional systems is done via the integration component.

One possible solution is to reengineer or redesign the organization. For example, the company can create cross-functional teams, each responsible for performing a complete business process. Then it is necessary to create appropriate information systems applications for the reengineered processes. As we will discuss in Chapter 8, this can be an expensive solution. In other cases, the company can use IT to create minor changes in the business processes and organizational structure, but this solution may not solve problems such as lack of coordination or an ineffective supply chain. One other remedy may be an *integrated approach,* like the one used at Colonial. An integrated approach keeps the functional departments but creates a supportive information system to help communication, coordination, and control. Even if the company were to reengineer its organization, however, as suggested in Chapter 8, the functional areas might not disappear completely since they contain the expertise needed to run the business. Therefore, it is necessary to drastically improve operations in the functional areas, increasing productivity, quality, speed, and customer service, as we will see in this chapter.

Before we demonstrate how IT facilitates the work of the functional areas, and makes possible their integration, we need to see how they are organized and how they relate to the corporate value chain and the supply chain.

Porter's Value Chain Model and the Supply Chain

The *value chain* model, introduced in Chapter 3, views activities in organizations as either primary (reflecting the flow of goods and services) or secondary (supporting the primary activities). The organizational structure of firms is intended to support these activities. Figure 7.2 maps the typical *functional departments* onto the value chain structure.

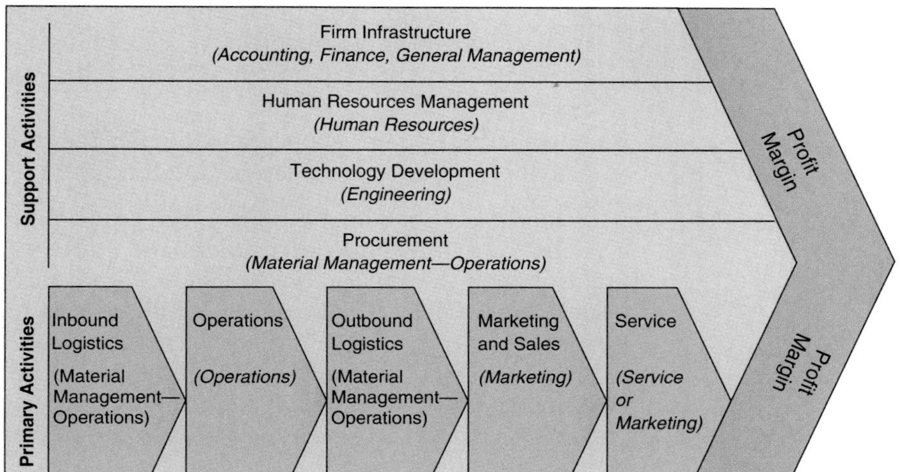

FIGURE 7.2 Typical functional areas mapped on the value chain of a manufacturing company.

As we saw in Chapter 6, the *supply chain* is a business process that links all the primary procurement activities inside a firm and may be extended to include customers, suppliers, wholesalers, retailers, and any other business partners. In this chapter we present innovative systems that increase internal functional efficiency, as well as examples of improved communication and collaboration with business partners. But, first, let us examine the characteristics of functional information systems.

Major Characteristics of the Functional Information Systems

The hierarchical organizational structure is built on functional areas. These functions, in turn, are supported by functional information systems. For example, a marketing information system supports the marketing department. Such systems mainly provide routine middle-management support to improve productivity and quality.

Functional information systems share the following characteristics:

1. A functional information system consists of several smaller information systems that support specific activities performed in the functional area. For example, computerized truck scheduling and inventory controls support the logistics system at Colonial Building Supply.
2. The specific IS applications in any functional area can be integrated to form a coherent departmental functional system, or they can be completely independent. Alternatively, some of the applications within each module can be integrated across departmental lines to match a business process. Several applications in the logistics information system of Colonial, for example, were integrated with the marketing information system.
3. Functional information systems interface with each other to form the organizationwide information system. A specific functional information system may be used as the core of this enterprisewide information system, as was the inventory information system in the case of Colonial.
4. Some organizational information systems interface with the environment. For example, a human resources information system can collect data about the

labor market and transmit information to federal agencies about compliance with safety and equal-opportunity regulations. Similarly, a manufacturing information system may be connected to the suppliers' logistics information systems.

5. Information systems applications support the three levels of an organization's activities: *operational, managerial,* and *strategic.*

A model of the IS applications in the production/operations area is provided in Figure 7.3. Other functional information systems have a similar basic structure. Note that the applications in Figure 7.3 are classified into operational, managerial, and strategic levels. Such classification is useful for understanding the support provided to different levels of managers.

In this chapter we describe IS applications in the major primary and support areas of the value chain. However, since information systems applications receive much of the data that they process from the corporate *transaction processing system,* we deal with this system first.

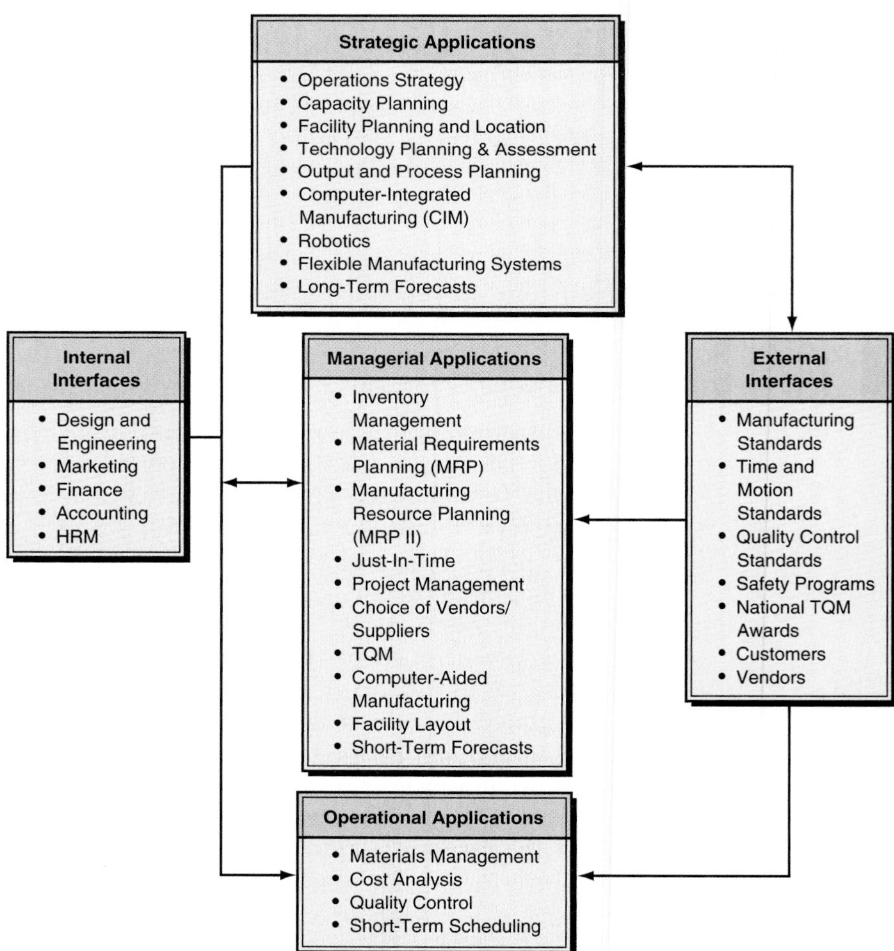

FIGURE 7.3 A model of information systems in the production/operations functional area.

7.2 TRANSACTION PROCESSING INFORMATION SYSTEMS

Computerization of Routine Transaction Processes

In every organization there are major business processes that provide the mission-critical activities. Business transactions occur when a company produces a product or provides a service. For example, to produce toys, a manufacturer needs to buy materials and parts, pay for labor and electricity, build the toys, ship them to customers, bill customers, and collect money. A bank that maintains the toy company's checking account must keep the account balance up-to-date, disperse funds to back up the checks written, accept deposits, and mail a monthly statement.

Every transaction may generate additional transactions. For example, purchasing materials will change the inventory level, and paying an employee reduces the corporate cash on hand. Because the mathematical manipulations of most transactions are simple and the volume is large and repetitive, such business transactions are fairly easy to computerize. As defined in Chapter 2, the information system that supports these *transaction processes* is the **transaction processing system (TPS)**. TPS mainly includes accounting and finance transactions, with some sales, personnel, and production activities as well.

The transaction processing system is the backbone of an organization's information systems. It monitors, collects, stores, processes, and disseminates information for all routine core business transactions. These data are input to functional information systems applications, DSS, and CRM. TPS provides critical data to e-commerce, especially data on customers and their purchasing history. An organization may have one integrated TPS or several, one for each specific business process. In the latter case, the systems should interface with each other.

Objectives of TPS

The primary goal of TPS is to provide all the information needed by law and/or by organizational policies to keep the business running properly and efficiently. To meet that goal, a TPS is constructed with the major characteristics listed in Table 7.1 (page 282).

Some specific objectives of a TPS include the following: to allow for efficient and effective operation of the organization, to provide timely documents and reports, to increase the competitive advantage of the corporation, to provide the necessary data for tactical and strategic systems such as Web-based applications, to ensure accuracy and integrity of data and information, and to safeguard assets and security of information. It should be emphasized that TPSs are the most likely candidates for reengineering and usually yield the most tangible benefits of IT investments. It also is important to remember that TPSs must closely interface with many EC initiatives, especially with e-procurement and direct marketing.

Activities and Methods of TPS

Regardless of the specific data processed by a TPS, a fairly standard process occurs, whether in a manufacturer, in a service firm, or in a government organization. First, data are collected by people or sensors and entered into the computer via any input device. Generally speaking, organizations try to automate the TPS data entry as much as possible because of the large volume involved.

Next, the system processes data in one of two basic ways: *batch* or *online processing*. In **batch processing**, the firm collects data from transactions as they occur, placing them in groups or batches. The system then prepares and processes the batches periodically (say, every night). In **online processing**, data are processed as soon as a transaction occurs.

TABLE 7.1 The Major Characteristics of a TPS

- *Typically, large amounts of data are processed.*
- *The sources of data are mostly internal, and the output is intended mainly for an internal audience.* This characteristic is changing since trading partners may contribute data and be permitted to use TPS output directly.
- *The TPS processes information on a regular basis:* daily, weekly, biweekly, and so on.
- *Large storage (database) capacity is required.*
- *High processing speed is needed due to the high volume.*
- *The TPS basically monitors and collects past data.*
- *Input and output data are structured.* Since the processed data are fairly stable, they are formatted in a standard fashion.
- *A high level of detail (raw data, not summarized) is usually observable,* especially in input data but often in output as well.
- *Low computation complexity* (simple mathematical and statistical operations) is usually evident in a TPS.
- *A high level of accuracy, data integrity, and security is needed.* Sensitive issues such as privacy of personal data are strongly related to TPSs.
- *High reliability is required.* The TPS can be viewed as the lifeblood of the organization. Interruptions in the flow of TPS data can be fatal to the organization.
- *Inquiry processing is a must.* The TPS enables users to query files and databases (even online and in real time).

To implement online transaction processing, *master files* containing key information about important business entities are placed on hard drives, where they are directly accessible. The *transaction files* containing information about activities concerning these business entities, such as orders placed by customers, are also held in online files until they are no longer needed for everyday transaction processing activity. This ensures that the transaction data are available to all applications, and that all data are kept up-to-the-minute.

Alternatively, a *hybrid system* (a combination of batch and online processing) can collect data as they occur but process them at specified intervals. For example, sales at POS terminals would be entered into the computer as they occur, but would be processed only at a certain time (say, in the evening).

The flow of information in a typical TPS is shown in Figure 7.4. An event, such as a customer purchase, is recorded by the TPS program. The processed information can be either a report or an activity in the database. In addition to a scheduled report, the user can query the TPS. The system will provide the appropriate answer by accessing the database (see Chapter 11).

Client/Server and Web-based TPS

CLIENT/SERVER SYSTEMS. Transaction processing systems may be fairly complex, involving customers, vendors, telecommunications, and different types of hardware and software. Traditional TPSs are centralized and run on a mainframe. However, innovations such as **online transaction processing (OLTP)** require a matching client/server architecture. With such architecture and Web technologies such as an extranet, suppliers can use the OLTP system to look at the firm's inventory level or production schedule. The suppliers can then assume responsibility for inventory management and ordering, as discussed in Chapter 6. Customers too can enter data into the TPS to track orders and even query it directly, as described in the *IT at Work* example (on page 284).

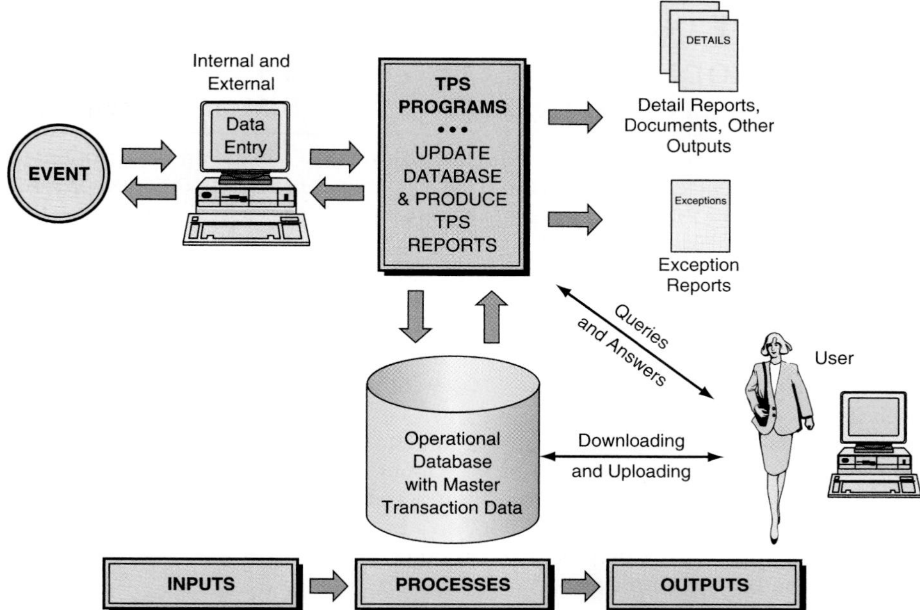

FIGURE 7.4 The flow of information in transaction processing.

OBJECT-ORIENTED TRANSACTION PROCESSING. The recent merging of distributed object technology and transaction-processing monitors has created a new class of technology known as *object transaction monitors (OTMs)*. OTMs typically contain a comprehensive set of features that make it possible to build enterprise-scale, high-performance transaction processing systems.

As more systems based on OTMs are built, there's a need for understanding the concepts and features of the available OTM technologies. It is also necessary to appreciate the important issues that drive a project's architecture, detailed design, and programming. For details on OTM and other TPS recent developments, see Gorton (2000).

WEB-BASED TRANSACTION PROCESSING. Rather than isolated exchanges of simple text and data over private networks, such as traditional EDI and EFT, transactions are increasingly conducted over the Internet and intranets. As a result, OLTP has broadened to become *interactive Internet TPS*. Internet transaction processing software and servers (see Internet Exercise 4) allow multimedia data transfer, fast response time, and storage of large databases of graphics and video—all in real time and at low cost. Here are some of the benefits:

- Flexibility to accommodate unpredictable growth in processing demand
- Cost effectiveness for small dollar amounts
- Interactive automatic billing, enabling companies to offer services to anyone, not just subscribers
- Timely search and analysis of large databases
- Ability to handle multimedia data such as pictures and sound effectively and efficiently
- High data throughput to support inquiries requiring massive file size

IT at Work
MODERNIZING THE TPS CUTS DELIVERY TIME AND SAVES MONEY

Integrating IT ...in Marketing and Production & Operations Management

Grossman's Bargain Centers, a retailer in Braintree, Massachusetts, replaced all its point-of-sale terminals with a network of 700 PCs. The network rings up sales, updates inventory, and keeps customers' histories at 125 stores. The PCs automatically record stock from a remote database and trace out-of-stock items available at other stores. This way, customers can locate unavailable items within hours. Employees no longer have to count inventory or order merchandise. The $3 million investment paid for itself in less than two years.

Several companies *outsource* their transaction processing. For example, Citgo Petroleum must process about 2.5 million credit card transactions each year. These transactions are transferred to J.C. Penney's Business Services subsidiary for processing. J.C. Penney has 40,000 other customers for whom they perform transaction processing.

Using an object-oriented approach, Sprint Inc. has improved its ordering processing for new telephones. In the past it took a few days for a customer to get a new telephone line; with the new system, it now takes a few hours. The order application is fast (10 minutes), experiences fewer errors, and can be executed on electronic forms on the salesperson's laptop computer.

For Further Exploration: How do you feel about outsourcing transaction-processing activities? Why is the back-ordering cycle usually reduced with a networked TPS? Why would a company like J.C. Penney be in the business of information services?

Sources: JC Penney.com, citgo.com, and *sprint.com.*

- Fast response time
- Effective storage of huge graphics and video databases

New software is needed in order to process transactions on the Web. *Object transaction monitors* (*OTMs*) are software tools that combine traditional transaction processing, which executes a series of steps in the right order, with the ability to manage independent software modules (known as objects) that encapsulate data (see Technology Guide 2). Leading vendors are Sybase (*sybase.com*) BEA Systems (*beasys.com*), and GemStone (*gemstone.com*).

Typical Tasks in Transaction Processing

Transaction processing exists in all functional areas. However, it has a major impact in the accounting and finance areas. Here we describe in some detail the first step in the marketing/accounting process—order processing.

ORDER PROCESSING. Orders for goods and/or services may flow to a company electronically, by phone, or on paper. Many companies have provided systems for their salespeople that enable them to enter orders from the client's site using portable, wireless devices and Web-enabled telephones. Orders can also be internal—from one department to another. However, as orders are entered, a computerized system receives, summarizes, and stores the orders.

Fast and effective order processing is recognized as a key to customer satisfaction. Using object-oriented software, for example, Sprint Inc. reduced the waiting time for telephone hookups from days to hours. In some cases, orders to warehouses and/or manufacturing are automatically issued following receipt of an order. An extranet system would be especially useful in processing orders involving several medium-to-large business partners. A computerized system can track sales by product, by zone, or by salesperson, for example. Some companies spend millions of dollars reengineering their order processing as part of an ERP system.

Orders can be for services as well as for products. Otis Elevator Company, for example, tracks orders for elevator repair. The processing of repair orders is done via wireless devices that allow effective communication between repair crews and Otis physical facilities. Orders also can be processed by using innovative IT technologies such as global positioning systems, as shown in the *IT at Work* example on page 286.

Other typical TPS activities are summarized in Table 7.2. Most of these routine tasks are computerized.

Transaction Processing Software

There are hundreds of commercial TPS software products on the market. Many are designed to support Internet transactions. For example, Compaq offers the following products:

- ***Pathway Transaction Services Software.*** This includes NonStop™ Transaction Manager/MP, NonStop™ Transaction Services/MP, Pathway/TS, Pathway/XM, and Pathway/ITS.
- ***Compaq NonStop™ TUXEDO Software.*** Cluster and transaction services for the Compaq platform and modifications to the BEA TUXEDO product are used to create the Compaq NonStop™ TUXEDO® product.
- ***NonStop™ Distributed Computing Environment (DCE) Software.*** DCE software provides comprehensive services for the development, use, and

TABLE 7.2 Typical TPS Activities

Activities	Description
The ledger	The entire group of an organization's financial accounts. Contains all of the assets, liabilities, and owner's equity accounts.
Accounts payable and receivable	Records of all accounts to be paid and those owed by customers. Automated system can send reminder notes about overdue accounts.
Receiving and shipping records	Transaction records of all items sent or received, including returns.
Inventory on hand records	Records of inventory levels as required for inventory control and taxation. Use of bar codes improves ability to count inventory periodically.
Fixed-assets management	Records of the value of an organization's fixed assets (e.g., buildings, cars, machines), including depreciation rate and major improvements made in assets, for taxation purposes.
Payroll	All raw and summary payroll records.
Personnel files and skills inventory	Files of employees' history, evaluations, and record of training and performance.
Reports to government	Reports on compliance with government regulations, taxes, etc.
Other periodic reports and statements	Financial, tax, production, sales, and other routine reports.

IT at Work

TAXIS IN SINGAPORE ARE DISPATCHED BY SATELLITES

Integrating IT ...in Production & Operations Management

Taxis in Singapore are tracked by a *global positioning system (GPS),* which is based on the 24 satellites originally set up by the U.S. government for military purposes. The GPS allows its users to get an instant fix on the geographical position of each taxi (see figure).

Here's how the system works: Customer orders are usually received via telephone, fax, and e-mail. Frequent users enter orders from their offices or homes by keying in a PIN number over the telephone. That number identifies the user automatically, together with his or her pickup point. Customers can also dispatch taxis from special kiosks located in shopping centers and hotels. Other booking options include the Internet and portable taxi-order terminals placed in exhibition halls. Infrequent customers use an operator-assisted system.

The computerized ordering system is connected to the GPS. Once an order has been received, the GPS finds a vacant cab nearest the caller, and a display panel in the taxi alerts the driver to the pickup address. The driver has five seconds to push a button to accept the order. If he does not, the system automatically searches out the next-nearest taxi for the job.

The system completely reengineered taxi order processing. First, the transaction time for processing an order for a frequent user is much shorter, even during peak demand, since there is no need for a human operator. Second, taxi drivers are not able to pick and choose which trips they want to take, since the system will not provide the commuter's destination. This reduces the customer's average waiting time significantly, while minimizing the travel distance of empty taxis. Third, the system increases the capacity for taking incoming calls 1,000 percent, providing a competitive edge to the cab companies that use the system. Fourth, frequent commuters get priority, since they are automatically identified. Finally, customers who use terminals do not have to wait a long time just to get a telephone operator (a situation that exists during rush hours, rain, or any other time of high demand for taxis).

For Further Exploration: What tasks do computers execute in this system? What kinds of priorities can be offered to frequent taxi customers?

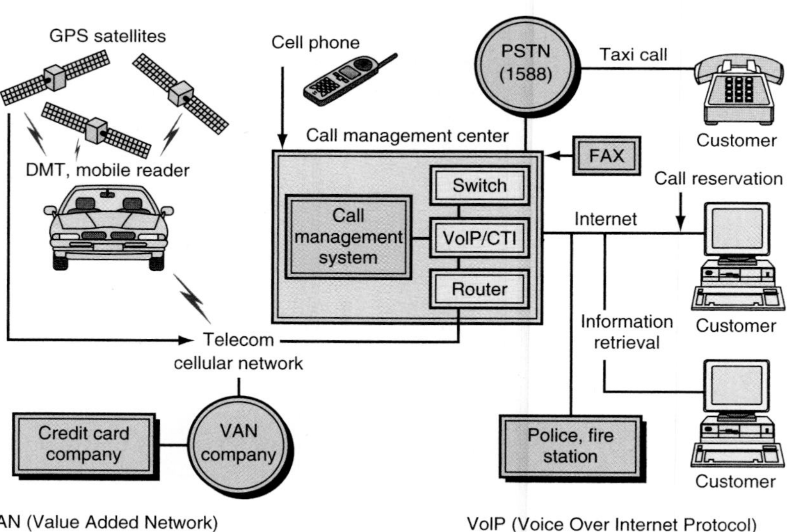

Location tracking of taxicabs.

maintenance of applications for open, heterogeneous, distributed computing environments.

- ***Compaq NonStop™ Remote Server Call/MP (RSC/MP) Software.*** RSC software combines the power and convenience of graphical desktop systems with the performance and reliability of Compaq NonStop™ Himalaya servers.
- ***Transaction Internet Protocol (TIP) Software.*** TIP is a heterogeneous, two-phase commit protocol that ensures the integrity of Internet transactions.

IBM, Unisys, and other mainframe and large computers offer a variety of products and so do several companies that provide middleware. In addition there is functional TPS software for payments (e.g., credit card processing), manufacturing (e.g., from Quantum software and HP), and much more. Then, there is software for online transaction processing (OLTP), such as the one from Unisys (Unisys TransIT Open/OLTP for MCP/AS), which is a client/server approach to computing that preserves the business-critical reliability of enterprise transaction processing systems. It offers the best of both worlds: enterprise dependability and client/server flexibility.

SOFTWARE SELECTION. The problem, then, is how to evaluate so many software packages. In Chapter 14, there is a discussion on software selection that applies to TPS as well. But, the selection of a TPS has some unique features. Therefore, one organization, the Transaction Processing Performance Council (*tpc.org*), has been trying to assist in this task. This organization is conducting benchmarking for TPS. It checks hardware vendors, database vendors, middleware vendors, and so forth. Recently it started to evaluate e-commerce transactions (*tpc.org/tpcw;* transactional Web e-commerce benchmark).

7.3 INNOVATIVE IT AND WEB APPLICATIONS IN THE FUNCTIONAL AREAS

In this and the following sections we present some innovative applications as they relate to five major functional areas: (1) production/operations management and logistics, (2) marketing/sales, (3) accounting, (4) finance, and (5) human resources.

Managing Production/Operations and Logistics

The *production and operations management (POM)* function in an organization is responsible for the processes that transform inputs into useful outputs (see Figure 7.5 on page 288). The POM area is very diversified, in comparison to the other functional areas, and so are its supporting information systems. It also differs considerably among organizations. For example, manufacturing companies use completely different processes than do service organizations, and a hospital operates much differently from a university. An example of the complexity of the field can be seen in Figure 7.3 (page 280). Note the internal interfaces on the left and the external ones on the right.

We present here four IT-supported POM topics. The first two relate to supply chain management (SCM), and the last two to production management:

1. In-house logistics and material management
2. Planning production/operations
3. Automating design work and manufacturing
4. Computer-integrated manufacturing (CIM)

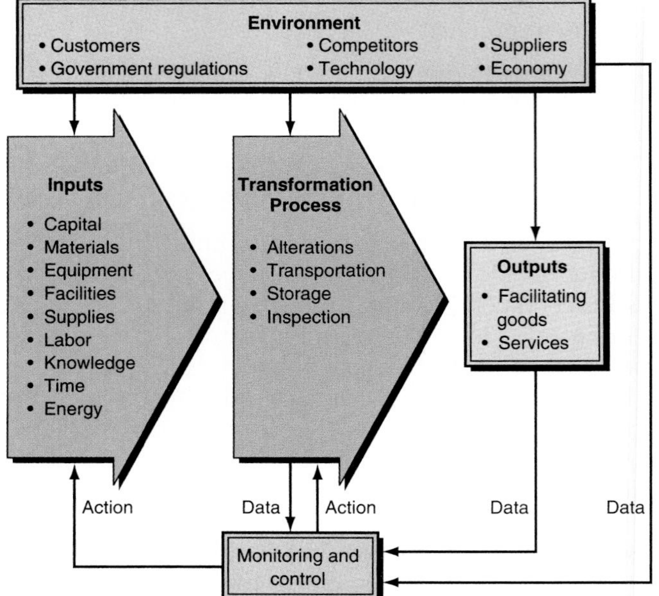

FIGURE 7.5 The operations process transforms inputs into useful outputs. (*Source:* J. R. Meredith, *Operations Management.* New York: Wiley. 1998. Reprinted by permission of John Wiley & Sons, Inc.)

IN-HOUSE LOGISTICS AND MATERIAL MANAGEMENT. Logistics management deals with ordering, purchasing, inbound logistics (receiving), and outbound logistics (shipping) activities. In-house logistics activities are a good example of processes that cross several primary and support activities in the value chain. Both conventional purchasing and e-purchasing result in incoming materials and parts. The materials received are inspected for quality and then stored. While in storage, they need to be maintained until distributed to those who need them. Some materials are disposed of when they become obsolete or when their quality becomes unacceptable.

All of these activities can be supported by information systems. For example, many companies today are moving to some type of e-procurement (Chapter 5). Scanners and voice technologies, including wireless ones, can support inspection, and robots can perform distribution and material handling. Large warehouses use robots to bring materials and parts from storage, whenever needed. The parts are stored in bins, and the bins are stacked one above the other, similar to the way safe deposit boxes are organized in banks. Whenever a part is needed, the storekeeper keys in the part number. The mobile robot travels to the part's "address," takes the bin out of its location (e.g., using magnetic force), and brings the bin to the storekeeper. Once a part is taken out of the bin, the robot is instructed to return the bin to its permanent location. In intelligent buildings in Japan, robots bring files to employees and return them for storage. In some hospitals, robots even dispense medicine.

Inventory Management. *Inventory management* determines how much inventory to keep. Overstocking can be expensive; so is keeping insufficient inventory. Three costs play important roles in inventory decisions: the cost of maintaining inventories, the cost of ordering (a fixed cost per order), and the cost of not having inventory when needed (the shortage or opportunity cost).

Two basic decisions are made by operations: when to order and how much. Inventory models such as the economic order quantity (EOQ) model support these decisions. Dozens of models exist, because inventory scenarios can be diverse and complex. A large number of commercial inventory software packages to automate the application of these models are available at low cost.

Once management has made decisions about how much to order and when, an information system can track the level of inventory for each item that management wants to control. When the inventory falls to a certain level, called the *reorder point,* the computer automatically generates a purchase order. The order is transferred electronically either to a vendor, or to the manufacturing department if restocking is done in-house. In Chapter 6 we demonstrated how IT and EC help in reducing inventories.

Quality Control. Quality-control systems can be standalone systems or part of an enterprisewide total quality management (TQM) effort. They provide information about the quality of incoming material and parts, as well as the quality of in-process semifinished and finished products. Such systems record the results of all inspections. They also compare actual results to standards. Quality-control data may be collected by sensors and stored in a database for analysis. Periodic reports are generated (such as percentage of defects, percentage of rework needed), and management can compare performance among departments.

Web-based quality control information systems are available from several vendors (e.g., HP and IBM) for executing standard computations such as preparing quality control charts. After manufacturing data, which are collected for quality-control purposes by sensors and other instruments, have been recorded, it is possible to use Web-based expert systems to make interpretations and recommend actions (e.g., to adjust production lines).

PLANNING PRODUCTION/OPERATIONS. The POM planning in many firms is supported by IT. Some major areas of planning and their computerized support are these:

Material Requirements Planning (MRP). Inventory systems that use an EOQ approach are designed for individual items, for which the demand is completely independent. However, in manufacturing systems, the demand for some items can be interdependent. For example, a company may make three types of chairs that all use the same legs, screws, and bolts. Thus, the demand for legs, screws, and bolts depends on the shipment schedule of all three types of chairs. The software that facilitates the plan for acquiring (or producing) parts, subassemblies, or materials in such a case is called **material requirements planning (MRP)**. MRP is computerized because of the complex interrelationship among many products and their components, and the need to change the plan each time that a delivery date or the order quantity is changed. Several MRP packages are commercially available. As mentioned in Chapter 6, MRP deals only with production scheduling and inventories. But a more complex process will also involve allocation of related resources. In such a case, more complex, integrated software is available—MRP II.

Manufacturing Resource Planning (MRP II). A POM system called **manufacturing resource planning (MRP II)** connects the regular MRP to other functional areas. In addition to the output similar to that of MRP, MRP II determines the costs of parts and the cash flow needed to pay for parts. It also estimates costs of labor, tools, equipment repair, and energy. Finally, it provides a detailed, computerized budget. Several MRP II software packages are commercially available.

Just-in-Time Systems. As discussed in Chapter 5, EC facilitates customization (build-to-order) production, in which the just-in-time concept is frequently used. **Just-in-time (JIT)** is an approach that attempts to minimize waste of all kinds (space, labor, materials, energy, and so on) and continuously improve processes and systems. For example, if materials and parts arrive at a workstation *exactly when needed,* there is no need for inventory, there are no delays in production, and there are no idle production facilities or underutilized workers.

JIT systems have resulted in significant benefits. At Toyota, for example, these included reducing production cycle time from 15 days to 1 day, reducing cost by 30 to 50 percent, and achieving these cost savings while increasing quality. Many JIT systems are supported by software from vendors such as HP, IBM, CA, and Cincom Systems.

JIT is especially useful in supporting Web-based mass customization, as in the case of Dell Computer. There, computers are assembled only after orders are received. To ship computers quickly, components and parts are provided just in time. As of 2001, car manufacturers are rapidly adopting make-to-order cars. To deliver these customized cars quickly, manufacturers will need a JIT system.

Project Management. A *project* is usually a one-time effort composed of many interrelated activities, costing a substantial amount of money, and lasting for weeks or years. The management of a project is complicated by the following characteristics.

- Most projects are unique undertakings, and participants have little prior experience in the area.
- Uncertainty exists due to the long completion times.
- There can be significant participation of outsiders, which is difficult to control.
- Extensive interaction may occur among participants.
- Projects often carry high risk but also high profit potential.

The management of projects is enhanced by project management tools such as the *program evaluation and review technique (PERT)* and the *critical path method (CPM)*. These tools are easily computerized, and indeed there are dozens of commercial packages on the market.

Developing *Web applications* is an example of a major project. Several IT tools are available to support and help manage such activities (see *citadon.com*).

Work Management Systems. **Work management systems (WMS)** automatically manage the prioritization and distribution of work. These systems deal with resource allocation, an activity that is missing from *workflow systems* (see Chapter 4). For example, if an operator is unavailable, WMS recalculates the process and reallocates human resources to meet the business need. For details and a case study in the U.K., see Collins (1999).

Troubleshooting. Finding what's wrong in the factory's internal operations may be a lengthy and expensive process. Intelligent systems can come to the rescue. Bizworks, from InterBiz Solutions, is an example of a successful software product that tackles thorny POM problems, such as interpretion of data gathered by factory sensors. The product is useful for quality control, maintenance management, and more. Similar products cut diagnosis time from hours to seconds. Several detecting systems are Web-based (see *gensym.com*).

AUTOMATING DESIGN WORK AND MANUFACTURING. An important activity in the value chain is the design of products, services, or processes. IT has been successfully used in reducing the time required for design. Following are descriptions of representative information technologies that can be used to facilitate design:

Computer-Aided Design. **Computer-aided design (CAD)** is a system that enables industrial drawings to be constructed on a computer screen and subsequently stored, manipulated, and updated electronically. Most CAD systems allow the designer to draw a model of the design using a set of simple 2-D geometric figures (such as lines and circles) that form a 3-D image. Images can be brought to the screen and resized, reoriented, partially trimmed, or otherwise adjusted to create the desired drawing. Different colors in the display help make drawings even clearer and easier to understand. The ability to rotate or create movement in the design allows testing for clearances and frequently reduces the cost of prototyping.

Having access to a computerized design database makes it easy for a designer to quickly modify an old design to meet new design requirements—an event that occurs quite frequently. This capability enhances designer productivity; speeds up the design process; reduces design errors resulting from hurried, inaccurate copying; and reduces the number of designers needed to perform the same amount of work. It also means that designers can focus on doing work that is mostly nonroutine, while the CAD system does most of the routine work.

Computer-Aided Engineering. Once CAD work has been completed, a designer can use **computer-aided engineering (CAE)** software to analyze the design and determine whether it will work the way the designer thought it would. With any kind of CAE, detailed engineering analysis provides data that may be useful when actually manufacturing the product. Such data include not only product specifications but also information about the design of tools or molds and programs used for controlling the motions of numerical control machines or robots. Thus, a database created as a result of CAD/CAE may then be used to support computer-aided manufacturing (CAM).

Computer-Aided Manufacturing. **Computer-aided manufacturing (CAM)** encompasses computer-aided techniques that facilitate planning, operation, and control of a production facility. Such techniques include computer-aided process planning, robotics programming, computer-generated work standards, MRP II, capacity requirements planning, and shop-floor control. When CAD feeds information to CAM, the combined system is referred to as *CAD/CAM.*

Web-based Collaborative Manufacturing. A new development in collaborative technologies utilizing the Internet is the **enhanced product realization (EPR) system**. EPR is a Web-based, distributed system that allows U.S. manufacturers to make product modifications anywhere in the world in as few as five days—instead of the typical industry response time of up to several months. The EPR system also accelerates the time-to-market for new products and services. EPR integrates and leverages the Internet with other existing and emerging information technologies, to enable a host of collaborative manufacturing and e-commerce applications, such as CAD/CAM, electronic whiteboarding, and multipoint desktop videoconferencing. By utilizing the Internet and its nonproprietary, open-standards environment, EPR brings collaborative computing to the entire supply chain, even when trading partners are using different and traditionally incompatible brands of hardware, software, and networking products and services. EPR was developed by participating members of InfoTEST International (*infotest.com,* Denver, Colorado). InfoTEST members can use Web browsers to access multiple corporate intranets for collaborative product development, data tracking, videoconferencing, and business process applications.

COMPUTER-INTEGRATED MANUFACTURING. Computer-integrated manufacturing (CIM) is a concept or philosophy about the implementation of various integrated computer systems in factory automation. CIM has three basic goals.

1. ***Simplification*** of all manufacturing technologies and techniques.
2. ***Automation*** of as many of the manufacturing processes as possible by the integration of many information technologies. Typical technologies are: flexible-manufacturing systems (FMS), JIT, MRP, CAD, CAE, and group technology (GT).
3. ***Integration and coordination*** of all aspects of design, manufacturing, and related functions via computer hardware and software.

The CIM Model. All the hardware and software in the world will not make a computer-integrated manufacturing system work if it does not have the support of the people designing, implementing, and using it. According to Kenneth Van Winkle, manager of manufacturing systems at Kimball International, a furniture manufacturer, "Computer technology is only 20 percent of CIM. The other 80 percent is the *business processes* and *people*." In order to bring people together and formulate a workable business process, CIM must start with a plan. This plan comes from the CIM model, which describes the CIM vision and architecture. The basic CIM model is shown in Figure 7.6.

The CIM model is derived from the CIM *Enterprise Wheel* developed by the Technical Council of the Society of Manufacturing Engineers. Its outer circle represents general business management. The inner circles represent four major families of processes that make up CIM: (1) *product* and *process definition,* (2) *manufacturing planning and control,* (3) *factory automation,* and (4) *information resource management.* Each of these five dimensions is a composite of more specific manufacturing processes, and each dimension is interrelated with the others. Thus, when managers plan a CIM system, no dimension can be ignored.

The hub of the wheel (the solid gold circle and the lighter gold circle around it) represents the IT resources and technologies necessary for the integration of CIM. Without an integrated plan, trying to implement CIM would be next to impossible. There must be communication, data sharing, and cooperation among the different levels of management and functional personnel.

The major advantages of CIM are its comprehensiveness and flexibility. These are especially important in business process reengineering, in which processes are completely restructured or eliminated. Without CIM, it may be necessary to invest large amounts of money to change existing information systems to fit the new processes. For an example of how a furniture company uses CIM, see *kimball.com* (click on Electronic Manufacturing Services).

Managing Marketing and Sales Through Channel Systems

In Chapters 1 through 6 we emphasized the increasing importance of a customer-focused approach and the trend toward customization and consumer-based organizations. How can IT help? First we need to understand how products reach customers, which takes place through a series of marketing entities known as *channels.*

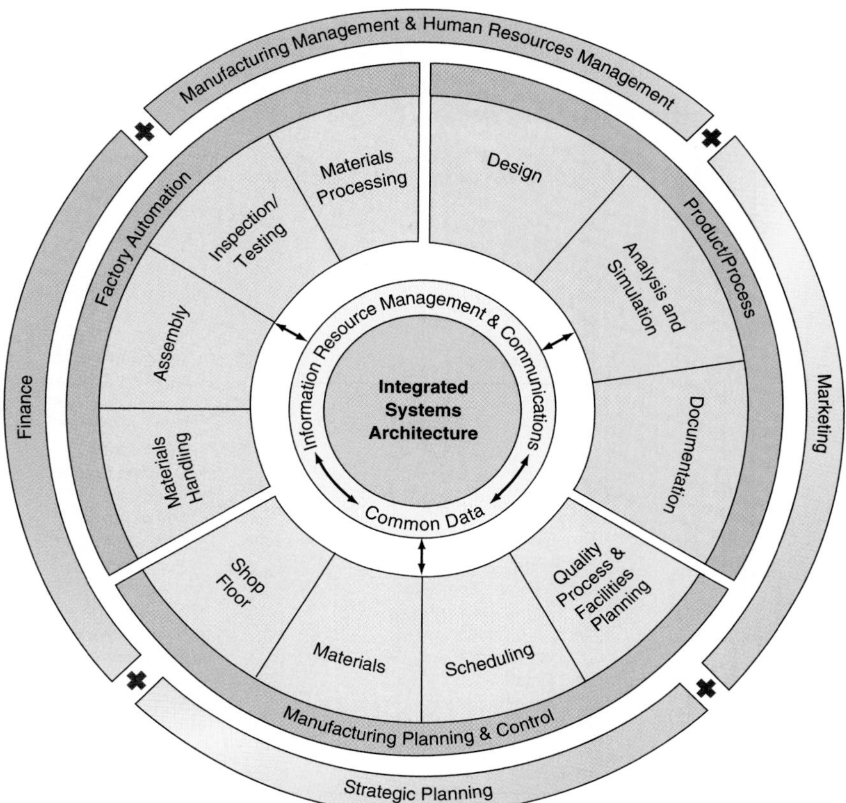

FIGURE 7.6 The CIM model: integration of all manufacturing activities under unified management. (*Source:* Reprinted from the CASA/SME Manufacturing Enterprise Wheel, with permission from the Society of Manufacturing Engineers, Dearborn, Michigan. © 1999, Third Edition.)

Channel systems are all the systems involved in the process of getting a product or service to customers and dealing with all customers' needs. The complexity of channel systems can be observed in Figure 7.7 (page 294), where seven major systems are interrelated.

Channel systems can link and transform marketing, sales, supply, and other activities. Added market power comes from the integration of channel systems with the corporate functional areas. The problem is that a change in any of the channels may affect the other channels. Therefore, the supporting information systems must be coordinated or even integrated. We describe only a few of the many channel systems' activities here, organizing them into four groups:

1. The customer is king/queen.
2. Telemarketing.
3. Distribution channels.
4. Marketing management.

THE CUSTOMER IS KING/QUEEN. It is essential for companies today to know who their customers are and to treat them like royalty. New and innovative products and services, successful promotions, and superb customer service are becoming a necessity for many organizations. In this section we will briefly describe

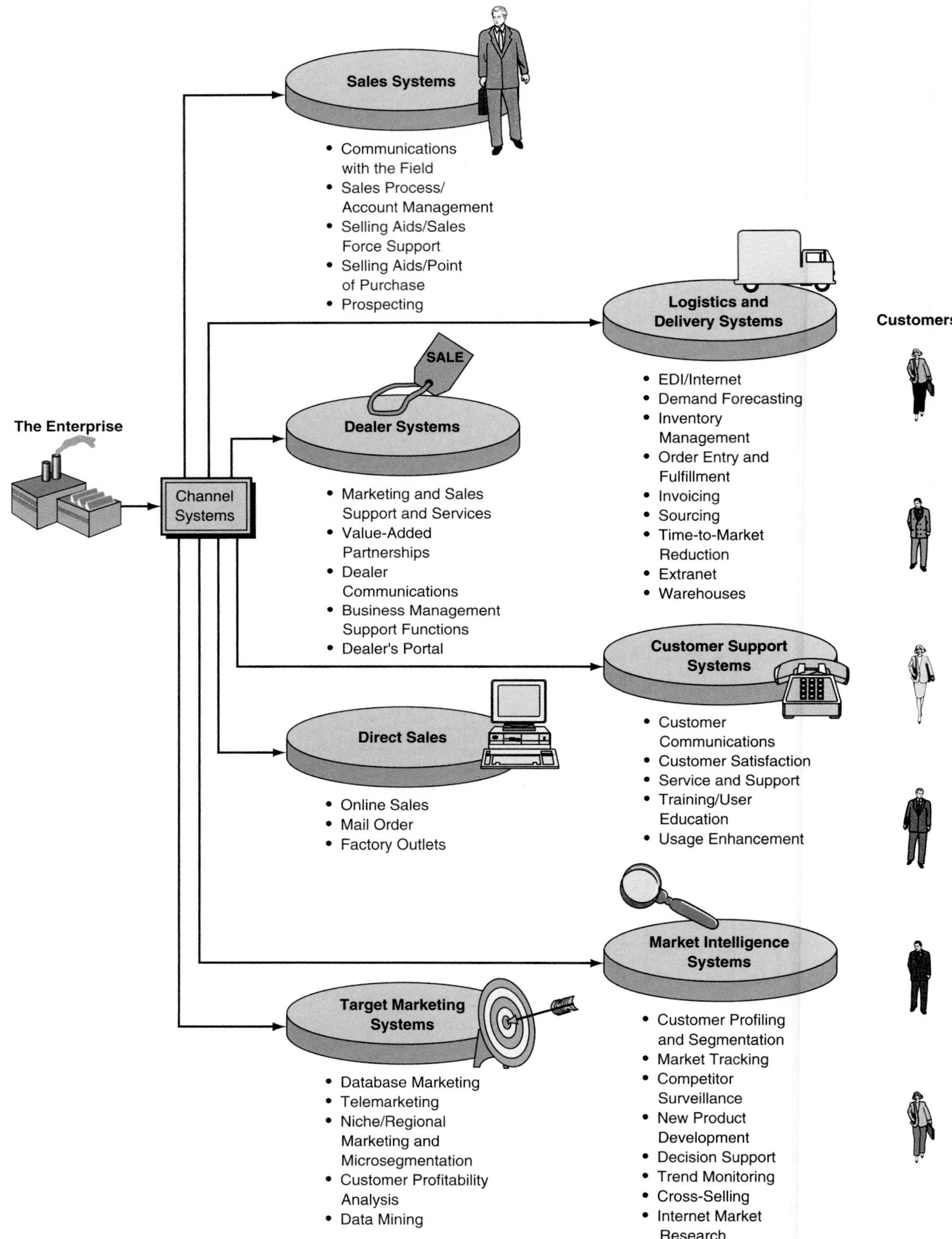

FIGURE 7.7 Marketing channel systems.

a few activities related to customer-centric organizations. More are described in Section 7.4, where customer relationship management (CRM) is presented.

Customer Profiles and Preference Analysis. Information about existing and potential customers is critical for success. Sophisticated information systems are being developed to collect data on customers, demographics (ages, gender, income level), and preferences.

Consumer online behavior can be tracked by *cookies,* and then (as explained in Chapter 5) it can be used for one-to-one advertising and marketing. By checking the demographics of its millions of customers and their locations, America Online (AOL) can match appropriate ads of advertisers with specific customers. The effectiveness of such ads is very high (and so are the fees charged by AOL to the advertising companies). Even more powerful is the combination of offline and online data (e.g., see *doubleclick.com*). Another approach for targeted marketing and/or advertising is intelligent agents in electronic commerce, as described in Chapter 5.

Prospective Customer Lists and Marketing Databases. All firms need to know who their customers are. IT can help create customer databases of both existing and potential customers. It is possible today to purchase computerized lists from several sources and then merge them electronically. Once prospective customer lists have been electronically stored, they can be easily accessed and sorted by any desired classification for direct mailing, e-mailing, or for telemarketing. Customer data are stored in a corporate database or in special marketing databases for future analysis and use. (We discuss database marketing in Chapter 11.)

Several U.S. retailers ask customers to tell them only the zip code in which they live. This way the retailers do not get involved in privacy issues, yet they gather valuable locational information. They then can match the geographical information with the items purchased in order to do sales analysis and make various marketing decisions. For example, software called *geographical information systems (GIS)* uses prestored maps at various levels of detail. With this software, retailers can learn a lot about the company's customers and competitors and can experiment with potential strategies, such as decisions about where to open new branches and outlets. (See Chapter 11 for more on GIS.)

Mass Customization. Increasingly, today's customers want customized products. Some manufacturers offer different product configurations, and in some products dozens of options are available. The result is **mass customization**, as practiced successfully by Dell Computer and many other companies. The Web can be used to expedite the ordering of customized products, as demonstrated in the *IT at Work* example on page 296.

Personalization. Using cameras, retailers can find what people are doing while they visit physical stores. Similarly, tracking software can find what people are doing in a virtual store. This technology provides information for real-time marketing and is also used in m-commerce (see Turban et al., 2002). Personalized product offers are made based on where the customer spent the most time, and what he or she purchased. A similar approach is used in Web-based *cross-selling* (or *up selling*) efforts, in which advertisement of related products is provided. For example, if you are buying a car, car insurance is automatically offered (see Strauss and Frost, 2001).

TELEMARKETING AND ONLINE SHOPPING. *Telemarketing* is a process that uses telecommunications and information systems to execute a marketing program for

IT at Work
BUILD YOUR JAGUAR ONLINE

Integrating IT ...in Marketing
www.jaguar.com

Prospective Jaguar car buyers can build, see, and price the car of their dreams online. As of October 2000, you can configure the car, at jaguar.com, in real time. Cars have been configured online since 1997; however it is an industry first to offer a comprehensive service, delivered in many languages.

Using a virtual car, users can view more than 1,250 possible exterior combinations in real time, rotating the car through 360 degrees, by moving directional arrows. As you select the model, color, trim, wheels, and accessories, both image and price information automatically update. The design choices are limited to current models. Up to 10 personalized car selections per customer can be stored in a "virtual garage." Customers can test virtual cars and conduct comparisons of different models. Once the buyer makes a decision, the order is forwarded to a dealer of your choice.

Like most other car manufacturers, Jaguar will not let you consummate the purchase online. To negotiate prices customers can go to a Jaguar dealer or use Auto By Tel (*autobytel.com*), which connects nearby dealers to the customer. However, Jaguar's system helps get customers to the point of purchase. It helps them *research* their purchases online, and explore, price, and vizualize options. They thus familiarize themselves with the Jaguar before even visiting a showroom. The innovation transforms the buying experience. The ability to see a 3-D photo of the car is an extremely important customer service. Finally, once configured online, the order can be transmitted electronically to the production floor, reducing the time-to-delivery cycle.

The IT support for this innovation includes a powerful configuration database integrated with Jaguar's production system (developed by Ford Motor Company and Trilogy Corp.), and the "virtual car" (developed by Global Beach Corp.).

Jaguar believes that the Web offers a way to market to customers features they might not normally purchase. However, delivery may take a few weeks, and it is not yet clear if online customers will mind waiting for product delivery. Jaguar is betting that many customers will be willing to wait in exchange for the chance to have a customized car.

By mid-2000, most car manufacturers had introduced Web-based make-to-order systems. In order to avoid channel conflicts, these systems typically involve the dealers in the actual purchase.

Jaguar is only one of many companies that allow you to customize products. How about customizing your next purchase of Nike runnings shoes (see Exercise 4)?

For Further Exploration: Why would manufacturers be interested in the Web if the actual purchase is done at the dealers' site?

Sources: jaguar.com, press releases (October–November, 2000); *ford.com* (2000) (go to Services); and *autobytel.com* (2000).

customers who want to shop from their homes. The process can be divided into five major activities: advertisement and reaching customers, order processing, customer service, sales support, and account management. All five activities are supported by IT and can be done on the Web, even in a wireless environment. Telemarketing can be done by telephone calls generated by computer programs and by computer-generated messages delivered by voice technologies. It can also be done by personalized e-mail. Lately, telemarketing has been moving to cell phones, using SMS systems. **Short message service (SMS)** consists of messages you can receive on your cell phone. With 2001 technology they are limited to 160 characters. In the near future, they will be longer (see *nttdocomo.com/imode*).

Home shopping via television grew very fast in the 1980s and 1990s. Shoppers watch a TV channel that displays products and, when interested, call and order, using a credit card to pay. The orders are entered into computers as soon as the telephone operators receive them. Such entry helps to determine whether to continue with the advertisement of an item or to discontinue advertising. (Because TV time is very expensive advertisers want to make use of it; therefore, if an item is not selling well, the advertising is stopped.) After a customer places an order, the computer entry triggers an order to the warehouse, instructions regarding shipment, and a bill to the credit card company.

Telemarketing benefits include generating sales leads, gathering information, providing information, improving cash flow, selling, and enhancing customer service. On the other hand, telemarketing has some limitations. But as Table 7.3 shows, the capabilities and benefits of telemarketing outweigh its limitations. Telemarketing is growing very fast. The Internet is becoming a prime telemarketing vehicle.

Through online shopping, described in Chapter 5, shoppers can also find information about *any* desired products from electronic catalogs, and then purchase them online. This is in contrast to home shopping via TV, where you can buy only what is displayed on the TV screen. In the near future, TV and computer shopping will be combined. Once you see a product on TV, you can get more details on your PC, and then place the order there. Also, interactive TV (or TV on demand) is available in some countries, enabling customization of customers' wishes.

TABLE 7.3 Capabilities and Limitations of Telemarketing

CAPABILITIES

- Telemarketing uses a targeted marketing strategy and personalized contact with the customers.
- Telemarketing's order processing allows customers to buy at their convenience.
- Message-on-hold feature is effective in informing customers about a company's products and services. This feature plays information about the company's products while the customer is waiting, on hold. This is the least expensive form of company advertisement, but it can be the most effective.
- Telemarketing reduces operating costs and cuts the number of salespeople, along with travel expenses, entertainment costs, and travel time.
- Telemarketing is a versatile and cost-effective method to increase sales, manage accounts, and make the outside sales force more productive.
- Telemarketing sales support improves the effectiveness and efficiency of the sales force.
- Customer service features allow customers to voice their concerns and gain ongoing support after purchasing products. The result is a positive image and a loyal customer.
- Telemarketing can collect information about customer needs and wants quickly, inexpensively, and accurately.
- Telemarketing is done primarily by phone, but computers support it. The computer is starting to be used as a communications tool with customers.

LIMITATIONS

- Cost of telemarketers, commissions, training, equipment, and telephone can be very high, depending on the scope of the operation and its overall objectives.
- It is difficult to find good telemarketers.
- Telemarketing is seen by many as a nuisance.
- Unlisted telephone numbers, devices that enable people not to accept calls, and telephone answering machines present telemarketing companies with challenges in reaching people.

DISTRIBUTION CHANNELS. Organizations can distribute their products and services through several available delivery channels. For instance, a company may use its own outlets or distributors. In addition, the company needs to decide on the delivery mode (trains, planes, trucks). Deliveries can be accomplished by the company itself, by a trucker, or by a subcontractor. Web-based DSS models are frequently used to support this type of decision.

Distribution Channels Management. Once products are in the distribution channels, firms need to monitor and track them, since only fast and accurate delivery times guarantee high customer satisfaction and repeat business. FedEx, UPS, and other large shipping companies use some of the most sophisticated tracking systems.

Improving Sales at Retail Stores. The home-shopping alternative puts pressure on retailers to offer more products in one location and provide better service. The increased number of products, and the customers' desire to get more information while at the store, results in a need to add many salespeople. This increases costs. Also, long lines are in evidence in some stores. Using information technology, it is possible to improve the situation by reengineering the checkout process. Here are some examples:

- Several companies use hand-held wireless devices that scan the bar code UPC of the product you want to buy, giving you all product information, including options such as maintenance agreements. The desired purchase is matched with the customer's smart card (or credit card), and an order to send the product(s) to the cashier is issued. By the time the customer arrives at the cashier, the bill and the merchandise are ready.
- Several supermarkets use machines that enable customers to check themselves out. Security devices make sure that all items are indeed scanned. For regular customers an automatic charge is made; others pay human cashiers.
- An alternative to the hand-held computer is the information kiosk. Kiosks at 7-Eleven stores in some countries, for example, can be used to place orders on the Internet.

MARKETING MANAGEMENT. Many marketing management activities are supported by computerized information systems (see Figure 7.8). Here are some representative examples of how this is being done.

Pricing of Products or Services. Sales volumes are largely determined by the prices of products or services. Price is also a major determinant of profit. Pricing is a difficult decision, and prices may need to be changed frequently. For example, in response to price changes made by competitors, a company may need to adjust its prices or take other actions. Three pricing models for retailers with thousands of items to price were developed by Sung and Lee (2000). Many companies are using online analytical processing (OLAP) to support pricing and other marketing decisions. Web-based comparison engines enable customers to select a vendor at the price they want, and they also enable vendors to see how their prices are compared with others.

Salesperson Productivity. Salespeople differ from each other; some excel in selling certain products, while others excel in selling to a certain type of customer or in a certain geographical zone. This information, which is usually collected in the marketing TPS, can be analyzed, using a comparative performance system, in which sales data by salesperson, product, region, and even the time of day can be analyzed. Actual current sales can be compared to historical data and to stan-

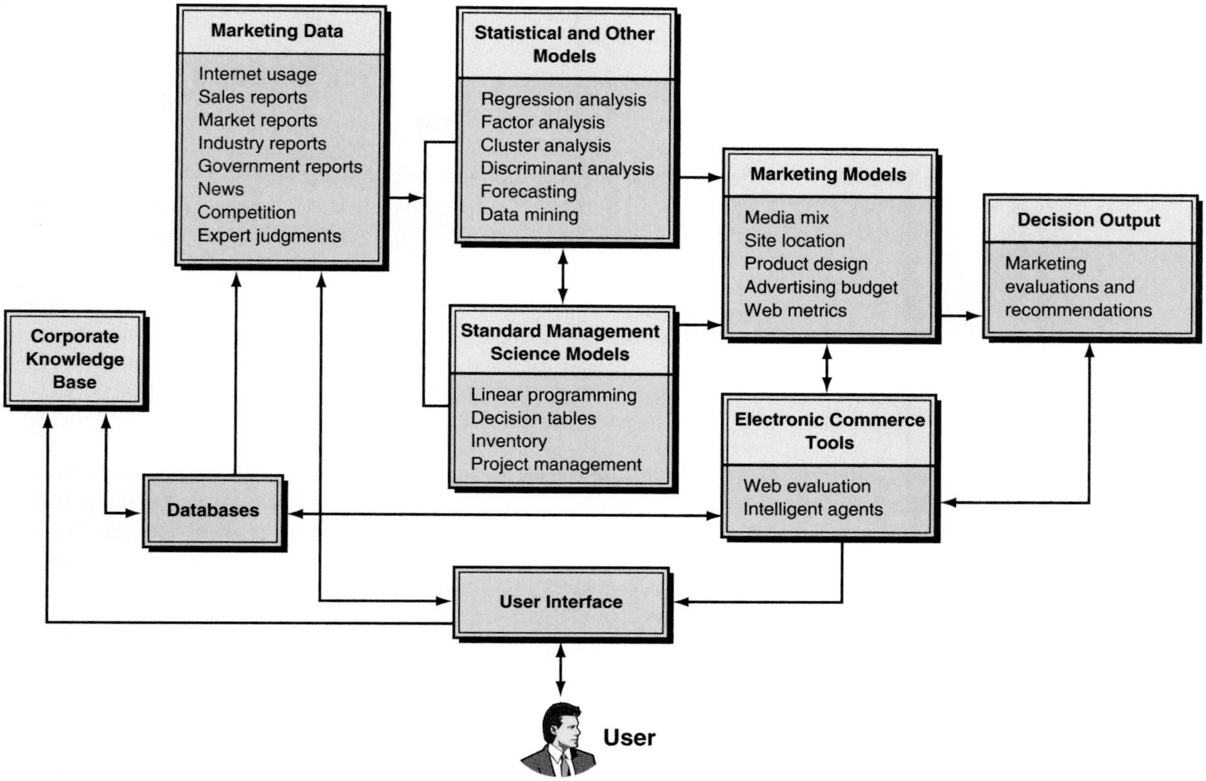

Marketing Data
Internet usage
Sales reports
Market reports
Industry reports
Government reports
News
Competition
Expert judgments

Statistical and Other Models
Regression analysis
Factor analysis
Cluster analysis
Discriminant analysis
Forecasting
Data mining

Marketing Models
Media mix
Site location
Product design
Advertising budget
Web metrics

Decision Output
Marketing evaluations and recommendations

Corporate Knowledge Base

Standard Management Science Models
Linear programming
Decision tables
Inventory
Project management

Electronic Commerce Tools
Web evaluation
Intelligent agents

Databases

User Interface

User

FIGURE 7.8 Marketing decision support framework.

dards. Multidimensional spreadsheet software facilitates this type of analysis. Assignment of salespeople to regions and/or products and the calculation of bonuses can also be supported by this system.

Sales productivity can be boosted by Web-based systems. For example, in a Web-based call center, when a customer calls a sales rep, the rep can look at the customer's history of purchases, demographics, services available where the customer lives, and more. This information enables reps to work faster, while providing better customer service. Customers' information can be provided by marketing customer information file technology (MCIF) (see Totty, 2000).

The productivity of salespeople in the field also can be greatly increased by what is known as **sales-force automation**, namely, providing salespeople with portable computers, access to databases, and so on. It empowers the field sales force to close deals at the customer's office and configure marketing strategies at home (for details see Schafer, 1997). For other uses of the Web by the sales force, see Varney (1996).

Productivity Software. **Sales automation software** is especially helpful to small businesses, enabling them to rapidly increase sales and growth. Such Web-based software can manage the flow of messages and assist in writing contracts, scheduling, and making appointments. Of course it provides word processing and e-mail; and it helps with mailings and follow-up letters. Electronic stamps (e.g., *stamp.com*) can assist with mass mailings.

Sales force automation can be boosted in many ways by using Web-based tools. Here are a few examples:

...in Marketing

- Netgain (from *netgainservices.com*) lets sales teams collaborate over the Web, passing off leads, bringing in new sales reps to clinch different parts of a deal, and tracking reports on sales progress.
- National Semiconductor uses a package developed in-house that lets sales reps easily set up major customers with a Web-based view of all their dealings with National Semiconductor, including contracts, project status, product availability, and emergency contact numbers. This capability leads to better customer services, as well as utilization of cross selling.
- Selectria.com provided an advanced configurator that let a remote sales rep configure a complex customer order through a browser-based form with rules and database connectivity built in. This ensured both correct pricing and compatibility with customers' existing equipment.

Product-Customer Profitability Analysis. In deciding on advertisement and other marketing efforts, managers often need to know the profit contribution of certain products, services, or customers. Profitability information can be derived from the cost-accounting system. Identification of profitable customers and the frequency with which they interact with the organization can be derived from special promotional programs, such as hotels' frequent stayer programs.

Both the operations and the analysis of such programs are fully computerized. For example, profit performance analysis software is available from Comshare (*comshare.com*). It is designed to help managers assess and improve the profit performance of their line of business, products, distribution channels, sales regions, and other dimensions critical to managing the enterprise. Northwest Airlines, for example, uses expert systems and DSS to check the profitability of more than 40,000 special agreements for calculating commissions to travel agents.

Sales Analysis and Trends. The marketing TPS collects sales figures that can be segregated along several dimensions for early detection of problems and opportunities, by searching for trends and relationships. For example, if sales of a certain product show a continuous decline in certain regions but not in other regions, management needs to investigate the declining region. Similarly, an increasing sales volume of a new product, if it is found to be statistically significant, calls attention to an opportunity. This application demonstrates the reliance of decision making on the TPS. Also, data mining can be used to find relationships and patterns in large databases (see Chapter 11).

New Product, Service, and Market Planning. The introduction of new or improved products and services can be expensive and risky. An important question to ask about a new product or service is, "Will it sell?" An appropriate answer calls for careful analysis, planning, and forecasting. These can best be executed with the aid of IT because of the large number of determining factors and the uncertainties that may be involved. Market research also can be conducted on the Internet, as described in Chapter 5.

Web-based Systems in Marketing. The use of Web-based systems in support of marketing and sales has grown rapidly. A summary of some Web-based impacts is provided in Figure 7.9.

Marketing concludes the primary activities of the value chain. Next we look at the functional systems that are secondary (support) activities in the value chain: accounting/finance, and human resources management.

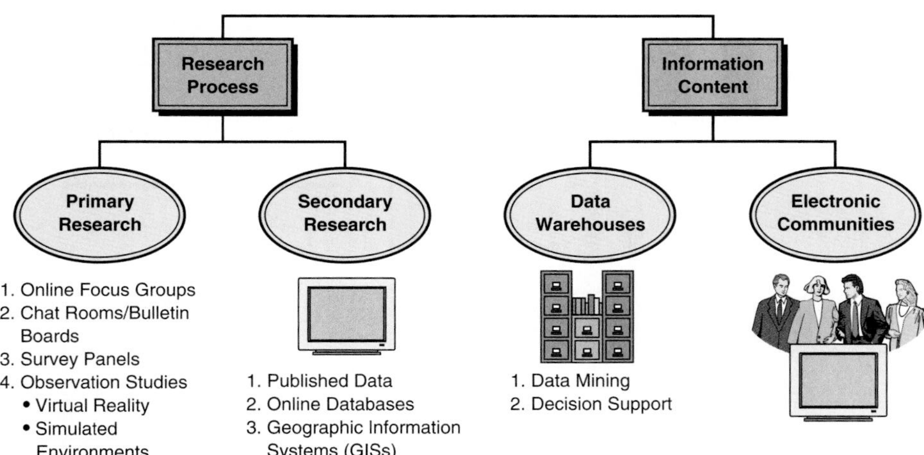

FIGURE 7.9 The impact of the Web on marketing information services. Channel-driven advantages are (1) transaction speed (real-time response) because of the interactive nature of the process, (2) global reach, (3) reduced costs, (4) multimedia content, and (5) reliability. (*Source:* P. K. Kannan et al., "Marketing Information on the I-Way," *Communications of the ACM,* 1999, p. 36. P. K. Kannan © 1998 Association for Computing Machinery, Inc. Reprinted by permission.)

Managing the Accounting and Finance Systems

A primary mission of the accounting/finance functional area is to manage money flows into, within, and out of organizations. This is a very broad mission since money is involved in all functions of an organization. Some repetitive accounting/financing activities such as payroll, billing, and inventory were computerized as early as the 1950s. Today, accounting/finance information systems are so diverse and comprehensive that to describe them would require several books.

The general structure of an accounting/finance system is presented in Figure 7.10 (page 302). It is divided into three levels: strategic, tactical, and operational. Information technology can support all the activities listed, as well as the communication and collaboration of accounting/finance with internal and external environments. We describe some selected activities in the rest of this section.

FINANCIAL PLANNING AND BUDGETING. Appropriate management of financial assets is a major task in financial planning and budgeting. Managers must plan for both the acquisition of financial resources and their use. Financial planning, like any other functional planning, is tied to the overall organizational planning and to other functional areas. It is divided into short-, medium-, and long-term horizons, much like activities planning. The best-known part of financial planning is the annual budget, which allocates the financial resources of an organization among participants and activities.

Prior to discussing the budget, though, we will discuss IT support for two related activities, financial and economic forecasting, and planning for incoming funds. We then turn to the key finance topics of budgeting and capital budgeting. Financial analysts use Web resources and computerized spreadsheets to accomplish these financial planning and budgeting activities.

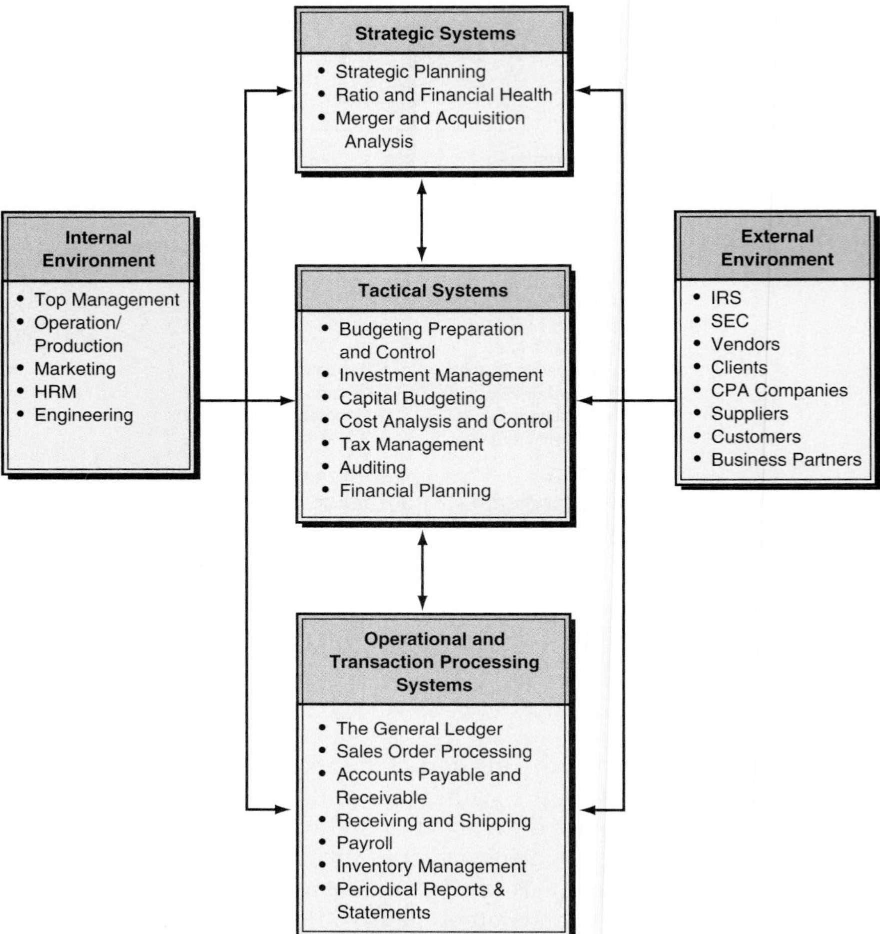

FIGURE 7.10 Major activities of the accounting/finance system.

Financial and Economic Forecasting. Knowledge about the availability and cost of money is a key ingredient for successful financial planning. Especially important is the projection of cash flow, which tells organizations what funds they need and when, and how they will acquire them. This function is important for all firms, but is especially so for small companies, which tend to have little financial cushion. Inaccurate cash flow projection is the major reason many small businesses go bankrupt. Availability and cost of money depend on corporate financial health and the willingness of lenders and investors to infuse money into the corporation.

Financial and economic analysis is facilitated by intelligent systems such as neural computing (Chapter 12). Many software packages are available for conducting business, for economic (using econometric models) and financial forecasting, and for planning. Economic and financial forecasts are also available for a fee, frequently over the Internet.

Planning for Incoming Funds. Funds for organizations come from several sources, including shareholders' investments, sale of bonds, loans from banks, and corporate sales and investments. Using the information generated by financial and economic forecasts, the organization can build a decision support model for planning incoming funds. For example, if the forecast indicates that interest rates will be high, the company can defer borrowing until the interest rates drop. Decisions about when and how much to refinance can be supported by expert systems.

Budgeting. The budget is the financial expression of the organization's plans. It allows management to allocate resources in the way that best supports the organization's mission and goals.

Several software packages are available to support budgeting (e.g., Budget 2000 from EPS Consultants and Comshare BudgetPlus from Comshare Inc.) and to facilitate communication among all participants in the budget preparation. For example, daily file updates can be sent via an intranet to all those who request funds and submit proposals. Since budget preparation can involve both top-down and bottom-up processes, modeling capabilities in some packages allow the budget coordinator to take the top-down numbers, compare them with the bottom-up data from the users, and reconcile the two.

Software also makes it easier to build complex budgets that involve multiple sites, including foreign countries. Budget software also allows various internal and external comparisons. The latest trend is industry-specific packages such as for hospitals, banks, or retailing. Budgeting software is frequently bundled with financial analysis and reporting functions.

The major benefits of using budgeting software according to Freeman (1997) are that it can:

- Reduce the time and effort in the budget process.
- Explore and analyze the implications of organizational and environmental changes.
- Facilitate the integration of the corporate strategic objectives with operational plans.
- Maintain data integrity of budgets and planning.
- Make planning an ongoing, continuous process.
- Explore and analyze across various planning and reporting dimensions.
- Automatically monitor exceptions for patterns and trends.

Capital Budgeting. Capital budgeting is the financing of planned acquisitions or the disposal of major organizational assets. It usually includes a comparison of options, such as keep the asset, replace it with an identical new asset, replace it with a different one, or discard it. The capital budgeting process also evaluates buy-versus-lease options. Capital budgeting analysis uses standard financial models such as net present value (NPV), internal rate of return (IRR), and payback period to evaluate these alternative investment decisions. Most spreadsheet packages include built-in functions of these models. Consolidating loans, deferring payments, and leasing instead of buying are all related to capital budgeting.

MANAGING FINANCIAL TRANSACTIONS. An accounting/finance information system is responsible for gathering the raw data necessary for the accounting/finance TPS, transforming the data into information, and making the information available to users, whether aggregate information about payroll or external reports to government agencies.

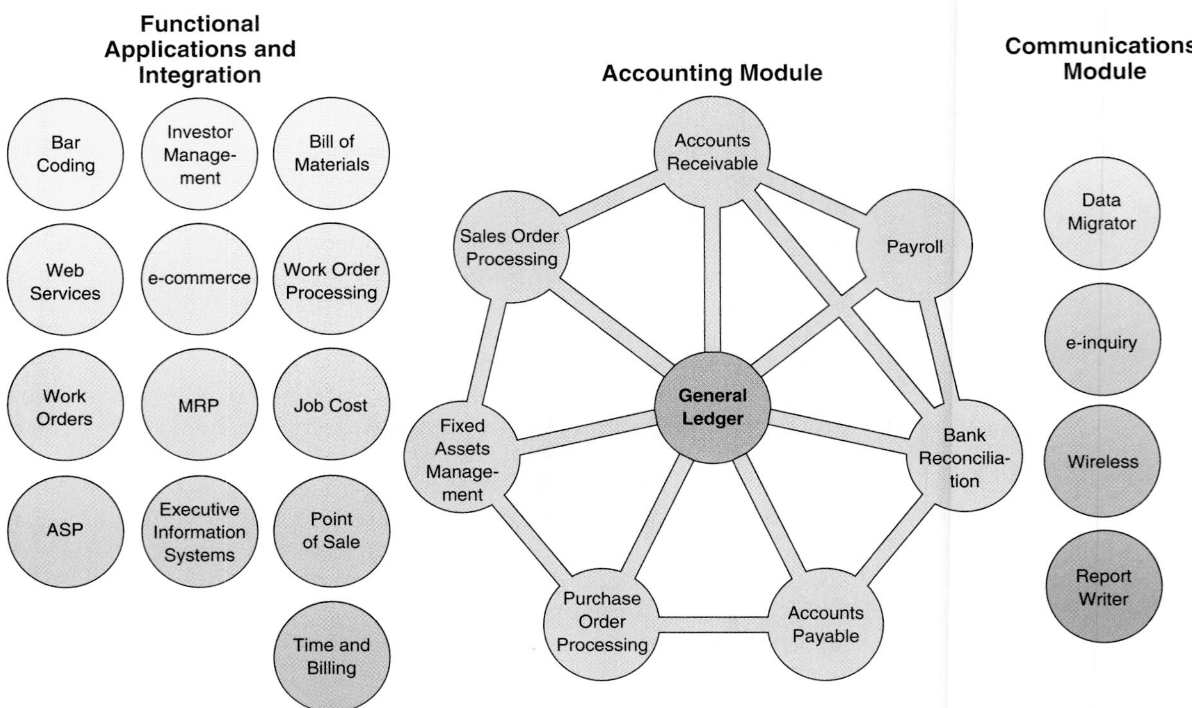

FIGURE 7.11 Integrated accounting/business software.

Many packages exist to execute routine accounting transaction processing activities. Several are available free on the Internet (try *tucows.com*). Many software packages are integrated, such as MAS 90 and MAS 200 (from *us.sage.com/MAS90*). This is a collection of standard accounting modules as shown in Figure 7.11 (the "wheel" in the diagram). Communication and inquiry modules (right side) support the accounting modules. The user can integrate as many of the modules as needed for the business. On the left side is a list of other business processes and functional applications that can interface with accounting applications. Note that the software includes an e-commerce module, which provides dynamic Web access to MAS 90. This module includes account and order inquiry capabilities as well as a shopping cart for order entry.

Another integrated accounting software package is *peachtree.com* (from Sage Corp.), which offers a sales ledger, purchase ledger, cash book, sales order processing, invoicing, stock control, job casting, fixed-assets register, and more. Another vendor is Great Plains (*solomon.com*), a subsidiary of Microsoft (see their demos). In these integrated systems, the accounting/finance activities are combined with other TPSs such as those of marketing and production and operations management.

The accounting/finance TPS also provides a complete, reliable audit trail of all transactions transmitted through the network. This feature is vital to accountants and auditors. The data collected and managed for the accounting/finance transaction processing system are input for the various functional information systems.

Companies doing e-commerce need to access financial data of customers (e.g., credit line), inventory levels, and manufacturing (to see available capacity, to place orders, etc.). Great Plains (*solomon.com*) offers 50 modules to choose from, to meet the most common financial, project, distribution, manufacturing, and e-business needs.

Integration of Financial Transactions with E-Commerce Applications. ACCPAC International (*accpaconline.com*) integrated its financial accounting software with e-business solutions (software, system building, consulting, and integration) to help traders in Asia. Called e.Advantage Suite, the e-commerce module is tightly integrated with AACPAC for Windows, offering a single, unifying financial and business management system.

INVESTMENT MANAGEMENT. Organizations invest large amounts of money in stocks, bonds, real estate, and other assets. Some of these investments are short-term in nature; others are long term. If you examine the financial records of publicly traded corporations, you will see that some of them have billions of dollars of assets. Furthermore, organizations need to pay pensions to their employees, so they need to manage the pension funds as an asset. Investment management is a difficult task for the following reasons:

- There are thousands of investment alternatives. As an example, there are more than 2,000 stocks on the New York Stock Exchange, and millions of possible combinations for creating portfolios.
- Investment decisions are based on economic and financial forecasts—which are frequently unreliable.
- The investment environment includes opportunities in other countries, providing both high potential rewards and high risks.
- Investments made by many organizations are subject to complex regulations and tax laws.
- Investment decisions need to be made quickly and frequently. Decision makers can be in different locations, and they need to cooperate and collaborate.
- Several multiple and conflicting objectives exist in making investments, including high yield, safety, and liquidity.

Computerization is especially popular in financial institutions that are involved in investments, as illustrated in the *IT at Work* example on page 306.

Neural networks (Chapter 12) are an important tool of *data mining*. Data mining tools are used by many institutional investment managers to analyze historical databases, so they can make better predictions. For a data mining tool, see *wizsoft.com*.

The following are the major areas of support that IT can provide to investment management.

Access to Financial and Economic Reports. Investment decisions require managers to evaluate financial and economic reports and news provided by federal and state agencies, universities, research institutions, financial services, and corporations. There are hundreds of Web sources, many of which are free; a sampling is listed in Table 7.4 on page 307. Most of these services are useful both for professional investment managers and for individual investors.

To cope with the large amount of online financial data, investors use three supporting tools:

IT at Work

Integrating IT ...in Finance

MATLAB MANAGES EQUITY PORTFOLIOS AT DAIWA SECURITIES

www.daiwa.co.jp

Daiwa Securities of Japan is one of the world's largest and most profitable multinational securities firms. Many of the company's traders are engineers and mathematicians who use computers to constantly buy and sell securities for the company's own portfolio. Daiwa believes that identifying mispricings in the stock markets holds great profit potential. Toward this end the company uses leading-edge computerized quantitative analysis methods. The software compares stock price performance of individual companies to that of other companies in the same market sector. In an attempt to minimize risk, the model then suggests a buy, sell, or sell-short solution for each investigated security.

The company is using an arbitrage approach. It may own undervalued stocks, but it sells short overvalued stocks and futures. The recommendations are generated by a system (coded in MATLAB, from mathworks.com), which is based on modern portfolio theory. The system uses two models: one for the short term (3 to 10 days) and one for the longer term (3 to 6 weeks). IT follows over 1,200 stocks and includes many variables, some of which are very volatile. Changes in the MATLAB model can be made quickly on the Excel spreadsheet it uses. Complex statistical tools, such as *symmetric correlation,* are used for the computations. The system attempts to minimize the risk of the portfolio yet maximize its profit. Since these two goals usually contradict each other, trade-offs must be considered.

The system is based on neural networks and fuzzy logic. The advantage of neural networks is that they can closely approximate the underlying processes that may be moving the financial markets in a particular direction.

To motivate the traders to use the system, as well as to quickly build modifications using Excel, the company pays generous bonuses for successful trades. As a matter of fact, some young MBA and Ph.D. traders are commanding bonuses of hundreds of thousands of dollars each year.

For Further Exploration: What is the logic of the arbitrage strategy? Why would bonuses be used to motivate employees to use the system?

Sources: A. Pittaras, "Automated Modeling," *PC AI,* January–February 1996; and *daiwa.co.jp* (press releases 2000).

1. Internet search engines for finding financial data
2. Internet directories and yellow pages
3. Software for monitoring, interpreting, analyzing financial data, and alerting management

Financial Analysis. Information analysis can be executed with a spreadsheet program, or with commercially available ready-made decision support software. Or, it can be more sophisticated, involving intelligent systems. Other information technologies can be used as well. For example, Morgan Stanley and Company uses virtual reality on its intranet to display the results of risk analysis in three dimensions. Seeing data in 3-D makes it easier to make comparisons and intuitive connections than would seeing a two-dimensional chart.

To illustrate the diversity of financial analyses, we examined the use of an emerging tool, neural computing. Here are typical financial applications of neural computing, per Trippi and Turban (1996):

- Analyzing the financial health of corporations in which one plans to invest
- Analyzing business failures and bankruptcies of companies, banks, and thrift institutions

TABLE 7.4 Online Financial Sources: A Sampler

GOVERNMENT ECONOMIC AND MONETARY STATISTICS
- U.S. Census Bureau (*census.gov*)
- University of Michigan economic bulletin board (*umich.edu/libhome/Documents.center stecom/html*)
- U.S. Dept. of Commerce (*stat-usa.gov*)
- World Bank (*worldbank.org*)

INDUSTRY SECTOR AND COMPANY ANALYSIS FUNDAMENTALS
- Dun & Bradstreet corporate and industry research (*dnb.com*)
- Value Line's electronic publishing (*valueline.com*)
- Dow Jones News/Retrieval (*dowjones.com*)
- CompuServe's Company and Industry Sector Analysis (*compuserve.com*)

SECURITY FILING
- EDGAR (*sec.gov/edgar.shtml*)
- The Disclosure Database (*ustreas.gov/usss/proc/finance.htm*)

SECURITY EXCHANGES
- The Chicago Mercantile Exchange (*cme.com*)
- The New York Stock Exchange (*nyse.com*)
- International Stock Exchanges (*ino.com/chart-html*)

SPECIAL INTERNET SERVICES
- Bloomberg (*nando.net*)
- Knight-Ridder (*kri.com*)
- Microsoft Network (*msn.com*)
- CNN (*cnn.com*)
- Dow Jones (*dowjones.com*)
- Hoover's (*hoovers.com*)
- Reuters (*reuters.com*)

INVESTMENT ADVISORY NEWSLETTERS ON THE INTERNET
- *Ameritrade.com Quicken.com/investments Suretrade.com*
- Investor Home (includes financial analysts' exams) (*investorhome.com*)

NEWS SERVICES: DIGEST AND CLIPPING SERVICES
- CompuServe (Executive News Service) (*compuserve.com*)
- NewsNet (*newsnet.co.jp*)
- CNN's financial channel (*cnnfn.com*)
- Newswire services (many)

FINANCIAL NEWSPAPERS
- The Wall Street Journal Online (*wsj.com*)
- London's Financial Times (*ft.com*)
- Investor's Business Daily (*investors.com*)
- New York Times Business Page (*nytimes.com*)
- Los Angeles Times Business Page (*latimes.com*)
- Time Warner (*time.com/time.com*)

NEWSGROUPS FOR INVESTORS
- Miscellaneous investments, miscellaneous stocks, miscellaneous funds

- Conducting risk analysis of bonds, mortgages, real estate, and other financial instruments
- Ranking companies by creditworthiness
- Predicting economic and financial performance
- Designing stock market investment strategies such as arbitrage
- Pricing initial public offerings
- Developing commodities trading models
- Pricing and hedging financial derivatives
- Recommending an appropriate investment mix
- Predicting foreign exchange rates

Several financial analyses can be supported by custom-made or commercially available software.

CONTROL AND AUDITING. The major reason organizations go out of business is their inability to forecast and/or secure sufficient cash flow. Underestimating expenses, overspending, fraud, and financial mismanagement can lead to disaster. Good planning is necessary but not sufficient and must be supplemented by skillful control. Control activities in organizations take many forms, including controls on the information systems themselves (see Chapter 15). Information systems play an extremely important role in supporting controls, as we show throughout the text. Specific forms of financial control are control of budgets and both internal and external audits.

Budgetary Control. Once the annual budget has been decided upon, it is divided into monthly allocations. Managers at various levels then monitor corporate expenditures and compare them against the budget and operational progress of the corporate plans. Simple reporting systems summarize the expenditures and provide exception reports by flagging any expenditure that exceeds the budget by a certain percent or that falls significantly below the budget. More sophisticated software attempts to tie expenditures to program accomplishment. Numerous software programs can be used to support budgetary control; most of them are combined with budget preparation packages such as Comshare BudgetPlus (from Comshare, Inc.). (For further details see Freeman, 1997.)

Auditing. The major purpose of auditing is to ensure the accuracy and condition of the financial health of an organization. Internal auditing is done by the accounting/finance department, which also prepares for external auditing by CPA companies. There are several types of auditing, including financial, operational, concurrent, and internal design systems. In *financial auditing* the accuracy of the organization's records are verified. The *operational audit* attempts to validate the effectiveness of the procedures of collecting and processing the information, for example, the adequacy of controls and compliance with company policies. When the operational audit is ongoing (all the time) it is called a *concurrent audit.*

IT can facilitate auditing. For example, intelligent systems can uncover fraud by finding financial transactions that significantly deviate from previous payment profiles.

Financial Ratio Analysis. A major task of the accounting/finance department is to watch the financial health of the company by monitoring and assessing a set of financial ratios. The collection of data for ratio analysis is done by the transaction processing system, and computation of the ratios is done by simple financial analysis models. The *interpretation* of the ratios, and especially the prediction of their future behavior, requires expertise and is sometimes supported by expert systems.

Financial ratio analysis is done not only on the company itself, but also on its partners, potential merger and acquisition candidates, and companies whose stocks are considered for purchase.

Profitability Analysis and Cost Control. Many companies are concerned with the profitability of individual products or services as well as with the financial health of the entire organization. Profitability analysis DSS software (see Chapter 10) allows accurate computation of profitability. It also allows allocation of overheads.

Product Pricing. Product pricing is an important corporate decision since it determines competitiveness and profitability. The marketing department may wish to reduce prices in order to increase market share, but the accounting/finance system must check the relevant cost in order to provide guidelines for such price reductions. Decision support models can facilitate product pricing. Accounting, finance, and marketing, supported by integrated software and intranets, can team up to jointly set appropriate product prices.

CONCLUSION. Several applications in the financial/accounting area described earlier are demonstrated in the *IT at Work* examples on page 310.

Managing Human Resources Systems

Developments in Web-based systems increased the popularity of human resources information systems (HRISs) as of the late 1990s. (For examples see James, 1997; Thomas and Ray, 2000; and Jandt and Nemnich, 1999.) Initial HRIS applications were mainly related to transaction processing systems. In the last decade we have seen considerable computerization in the managerial and even strategic areas.

Managing human resources (HR) is a complex job that starts with the hiring of an employee and ends with his or her retirement or departure. It includes several business processes, a few of which are described next.

RECRUITMENT. Recruitment is finding employees, testing them, and deciding which ones to hire. While some companies are flooded with applicants, in other cases it is difficult to find the right people. Information systems can be helpful in both cases. Here are some examples.

Using the Web for Recruitment. With millions of resumes available online, it is not surprising that companies are trying to find appropriate candidates on the Web, usually with the help of specialized search engines. Also, hundreds of thousands of jobs are advertised on the Web (see Thomas and Ray, 2000). Many matching services exist (see Internet Exercise 3). The benefits of online recruitment for employers are:

- Companies find employees faster.
- Companies reach more candidates by "casting a wider net," which results in finding better people.
- The life of the recruitment ad is much longer than paper-based ads. Also, the ad can be changed any time.
- Recruiting costs are significantly lower with online recruitment.
- Companies can post very detailed descriptions of the available jobs as well as answers to FAQs. This additional information attracts more applicants and saves time for recruitment personnel.
- Applications can be made electronically, saving processing time and reducing errors.

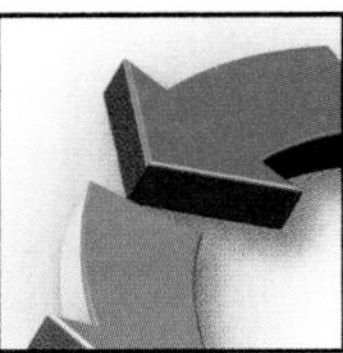

IT at Work

Integrating IT ...in Finance, Accounting, and Government

HOW THE WEB AND IT ARE USED TO ENHANCE ACCOUNTING/FINANCE TASKS

Fraud in the government health care systems of Medicare and Medicaid has been estimated to cost U.S. taxpayers about $100 billion per year. The U.S. General Accounting Office uses neural computing to facilitate detection of fraud and abuse against the health care system. The system detects subtle patterns of collusion associated with fraud.

Air Canada Vacations used a computer-based fax to send invoices and confirmations to travel agents. A substantial savings was achieved in billing, booking, payment cycle time, and customer service over the manual system. In 2000 the system was moved to Web-based e-commerce, resulting in further savings.

Toro Company shelters itself from seasonal and economic fluctuations by tracking and analyzing data from 175 units by division, product line, geographical location, and distribution channels. Using Comshare's executive information system (Chapter 10) and financial software, the company successfully predicted economic shifts and took appropriate actions to minimize negative effects on the company and enhance positive trends.

Plantation Resorts Management Inc. manages its Gulf Shores Plantation resort in Alabama with a fully integrated accounting system. The system facilitates standard transaction processing and provides information on cost control, resource allocation, and scheduling.

Union Bank of California uses a Web-based system to accept and process car loan applications generated at 20 car dealerships in southern California. Using imaging technologies, large databases, and decision support systems, bank loan officers evaluate loan applications so quickly that in some cases a response is provided in a minute. Related to this is the automation of an administrative environment of 120,000 business accounts and 1,200,000 regular bank accounts.

The City of Philadelphia was heading toward bankruptcy in the early 1990s. One problematic area was the management of the 1,500 contractors with whom the city did business. Using a client/server-based decision support system, the city was able to reduce the contract review from 44 to 13 steps and increase reliability. An intranet that connects the 40 departments and agencies in 21 locations allows information sharing and collaboration. Using imaging systems and query tools, the city improved vendor management drastically in less than three years, and the city's financial health was restored.

For Further Exploration: Does the increasing use of automation imply that fewer accounting and financial analysts will be needed?

Source: Miscellaneous news items and press releases.

Some of the disadvantages of online recruitment are:

- Companies cannot reach job seekers who are not on the Web.
- It is not useful for jobs for which the relevant labor market is local.
- The competition for candidates increases, since it is easy for other companies to find the same candidates.

Recruitment online is beneficial for candidates as well. They are exposed to a larger number of job offerings, can get details of the positions quickly, and can begin to evaluate the prospective employer. To check the competitiveness of salary offerings, or to see how much one can make elsewhere in several countries, job candidates can go to *monster.com*.

For a complete analysis of and guidelines for e-recruitment, see Thomas and Ray (2000) and Borck (2000).

Position Inventory. Large organizations frequently need to fill vacant positions. To do so, they maintain a file that lists all open positions by job title, geographical area, task content, and skills required. Like any other inventory, this position inventory is updated each time a position is added, modified, and so on.

In some cases, position inventories are used to improve national employment conditions. The government of the Philippines, for example, provides a list of available positions in that country. This list is accessible via the Internet. For those people without Internet access, the government provides access via computers in kiosks in public places and government facilities.

An advanced intranet-based position inventory system keeps the position inventory list current, matches openings with available personnel, and allows data to be viewed by an employee over the corporate portal from any location at any time. Outsiders can view openings from the Internet. In addition, it is possible to match openings to available personnel. By analyzing the position inventory and its changes over time, human resources personnel can find other useful information, such as those jobs with high turnover. Such information can support decisions about promotions, salary administration, and training plans.

Employee Selection. The human resources department is responsible for screening job applicants, evaluating, testing, and selecting them in compliance with state and federal regulations. To expedite the testing and evaluation process and ensure consistency in selection, companies use information technologies such as expert systems.

HUMAN RESOURCES MAINTENANCE AND DEVELOPMENT. Once recruited, employees become part of the corporate human resources pool, which needs to be maintained and developed. Some activities supported by IT are the following:

Performance Evaluation. Most employees are periodically evaluated by their immediate supervisors. Peers or subordinates may also evaluate others. Evaluations are usually recorded on forms and can be keyed in or scanned into the information system. Once digitized, evaluations can be used to support many decisions, ranging from rewards to transfers to layoffs. Using such information manually is a tedious and error-prone job. Managers can analyze employees' performances with the help of expert systems, which provide an unbiased and systematic interpretation of performance over time. Many universities evaluate professors online. The evaluation form appears on the screen, and the students fill it in. Results can be tabulated in minutes.

Wage review is related to performance evaluation. For example, Hewlett-Packard's Atlanta-based U.S. Field Services Operations Group (USFO) has developed a paperless wage review (PWR) system. The Web-based system uses intelligent agents to deal with quarterly reviews of HP's 15,000 employees. The agent software lets USFO managers and personnel access employee data from both the personnel and functional databases. The PWR system tracks employee review dates and automatically initiates the wage review process. It sends wage review forms to first-level managers by e-mail every quarter.

Training and Human Resources Development. Employee training and retraining is an important activity of the human resources department. Major issues are planning of classes and tailoring specific training programs to meet the needs of the organization and employees. Sophisticated human resources departments build a career development plan for each employee. IT can support the planning, monitoring, and control of these activities by using workflow applications.

IT also plays an important role in training. Some of the most innovative developments are in the areas of *intelligent computer-aided instruction (ICAI)* and application of multimedia support for instructional activities. Instruction is provided

IT at Work

TRAINING OVER THE NETS

Training salespeople is an expensive and lengthy proposition (which may cost as much as $8,000 per person). To save money on training costs, companies are providing sales-skills training over the Internet or intranet. Here are a few examples.

- Qantas Airways of Australia provides a Web-based Internet College that provides training to its 30,000 employees in over 30 countries. Many courses are available. Other airlines provide similar training.
- Cobe BCT, a large vendor of medical services, is training all its medical technicians on the Web, in order to keep up with the latest technology.
- DaimlerChrysler introduced Web-based training in every part of its organization, from purchasing to sales. The company initially used CD-ROMs, then moved to the Internet. The biggest obstacle in 2000 was the limited bandwidth.
- MCI Telecommunication offers close to 100 courses online to thousands of employees in many locations.
- Sun Microsystems is using Web-based training. Sun needs to train 5,000 distributors and 2,000 salespeople each time it comes up with a new product. Traditional classes can accommodate 25 people at a time; to train 7,000 people, Sun would need to run 250 such classes. This is big money. By using Web-based training, Sun saves money (about 50 percent) and shortens the training time by as much as 75 percent.
- KN Energy, a Lakewood, Colorado natural gas company, uses Internet-based courses to train remote employees on an array of Microsoft programs.
- At Hewlett-Packard, classes are delivered via Web-casting. Then, lab exercises are posted on the intranet so that trainees can review material as needed. Post-class discussions also take place on the intranet.
- Employees at Digital Equipment can search and browse through 11,000 training courses. Schedules and enrollment are also available on the intranet. Training is provided for business partners as well.
- Ernst & Young delivers multimedia training over the intranet, thus replacing CD-ROM-based training.

For Further Exploration: Why is CD-ROM-based training inferior to training over "the nets"?

Sources: Condensed from R. H. Kahn, and M. Sloan, "Twenty-First Century Training," *Sales and Marketing Management,* June 1997; *Training and Development,* February 1997 (several papers); *InternetWeek,* July 2000; and the *Asian Wall Street Journal,* February 2000.

online at 38 percent of all Fortune 1000 corporations, according to OmniTech Consulting. The *IT at Work* above provides examples of the variety of employee training available on the Internet and intranets.

Training can be improved using Web-based video clips. Using a digital video-editing system, Dairy Queen's in-house video production department produces a higher-quality training video at 50 percent lower cost than outsourcing. The affordability of the videos encourages more Dairy Queen franchisees to participate in the training program. This improves customer service as well as employee skill.

Finally, training can be enhanced by virtual reality. Intel, Motorola, Samsung Electronic, and IBM are using virtual reality (Chapter 11) to simulate different scenarios and configurations. The training is especially effective in complex environments where mistakes can be very costly (see Boisvert, 2000).

HUMAN RESOURCES PLANNING AND MANAGEMENT. Managing human resources in large organizations requires extensive planning. In some industries, labor negotiation is a particularly important aspect of human resources planning. For most companies, administering employee benefits is also a significant part of the human resources function. Here are some examples of how IT can help.

Personnel Planning. The human resources department forecasts requirements for people and skills. In some geographical areas and for overseas assignments it may be difficult to find particular types of employees. Then the HR department plans how to find (or develop from within) sufficient human resources.

Large companies develop qualitative and quantitative workforce planning models. Such models can be enhanced if IT is used to collect, update, and process the information.

Labor–Management Negotiations. Labor–management negotiations can take several months, during which time employees may present management with a large number of demands. Both sides need to make concessions and trade-offs. Large companies (like USX, formerly U.S. Steel, in Pittsburgh, Pennsylvania) have developed computerized DSS models that support such negotiations. The models can simulate financial and other impacts of fulfilling any demand made by employees, and they can provide answers to queries in a matter of seconds.

Another information technology that has been successfully used in labor–management negotiations is group decision support systems (see Chapter 10), which have helped improve the negotiation climate and considerably reduced the time needed for reaching an agreement.

Benefits Administration. Employees' contributions to their organizations depend on the rewards they receive, such as salary, bonuses, and other benefits. Managing the benefits system can be a complex task, due to its many components and the tendency of organizations to allow employees to choose and trade off benefits ("cafeteria style"). In large companies, using computers for benefits selection can save a tremendous amount of labor and time.

Providing flexibility in selecting benefits is viewed as a competitive advantage in large organizations. It can be successfully implemented when supported by computers. Some companies have automated benefits enrollments. Employees can register for specific benefits using the corporate portal and voice technology. Employees call in or use the intranet and select desired benefits from a menu. The system specifies the value of each benefit and the available benefits balance of each employee. Some companies use intelligent agents to assist the employees and monitor their actions. Expert systems can answer employees' questions and offer advice online.

INTRANET APPLICATIONS. Web applications facilitate the use of IS in the human resources department. As noted earlier, many corporations use their Web sites to advertise job openings and conduct online hiring and training. Here are some other examples:

- ***Edify Corporation***'s employee-service system allows users to access information via PCs, voice-recognition phone, kiosks, or faxes. The package offers intranet-based automation of company procedures, collective bargaining agreements, employees' handbooks, phone directories, pay scales, job banks, benefits, and training.
- ***Oracle Corporation*** conducts its flexible benefits enrollment program on its intranet. The employees give the program high marks because they feel it is simple and fast. Employees do not have to wait for a rigid companywide starting date, and forms do not get lost. Furthermore, employees can see the trade-offs between various benefits, since the system calculates the cost of each benefit. Oracle allows new hires to input benefits data online. Finally,

Oracle created links from its intranet pages to Fidelity Investments' 401(k) pages, so employees can learn about funds and pension plans online as well as register for the plans.

- ***Aetna Health Plan***'s directory of primary care physicians, hospitals, medical services, and health information is available to employees online around the clock. The company also offers insurance options online.
- ***Apple Computers, Inc.*** conducts extensive education and development activities on its intranet, including a remote management-training program.
- ***Merck & Company Inc.*** found that the cost of an HR transaction on the intranet is only $2.32 compared to $16.96 when done by HR employees. Also, when employees enrolled in benefits programs by themselves, changed address and other demographic data, and conducted other tasks electronically, there were very few errors. Finally, intelligent agents supervise employees' activities, calling their attention to existing or potential errors.

Perhaps the biggest benefit to companies is the release of HR staff from intermediary roles so they can focus on strategic planning and human resources organization and development.

Companies take strict measures to protect the privacy of their employees. Oracle, for example, allows employees to enroll in benefits programs over the Web, but the information is then encrypted and sent to headquarters over a secure T1 line.

For a comprehensive resource of HRM on the Web, see *shrm.org/hrlinks.*

7.4 Customer Relationship Management (CRM)

From Customer Service to CRM

Customer service is a series of activities designed to enhance the level of customer satisfaction—that is, the feeling that a product or service has met the customer's expectations. Customer service helps shoppers to resolve problems they encountered in any phase of the product life cycle. Whereas traditional customer service puts the burden on the customer to direct a problem or inquiry to the right place and receive information bit by bit, IT delivers improved customer service, frequently by automating and speeding it. As discussed in Chapter 5, customer service should be provided during the entire product life cycle, which is composed of the following four phases: identification of product requirements, acquisition, ownership, and disposal (McKeown and Watson, 1998). Due to the pressures in the business environment, today's customer service requires the best, most powerful IT support in order to be effective and to satisfy the increased expectations of customers. One relatively new form of IT support for customer service is e-service.

E-SERVICE. Customer service that is performed on the Web, sometimes automatically, is referred to as *e-service* (*searchhp.com*). It provides customer service to a sales transaction that is done either online or offline. For example, if you buy a product offline and you need expert advice on how to use it for an unusual application, you may get the instructions online. According to Voss (2000), most companies, even in the U.K. and the United States, are still providing fairly limited e-service. Voss distinguishes three levels of e-service:

- ***Foundation of service.*** This includes the minimum necessary services such as site responsibility, site effectiveness, and order fulfillment.
- ***Customer-centered.*** These services make the difference. These include order tracking, configuration and customization, and security.
- ***Value added.*** These are extra services such as dynamic brokering, online auctions, or training and education online.

RELATIONSHIP MARKETING. **Relationship marketing**, according to Mowen and Minor (1998), is the "overt attempt of exchange partners to build a long-term association, characterized by purposeful cooperation and mutual dependence on the development of social, as well as structural, bonds" (p. 540). It includes the concepts of *loyalty* and *trust.* In effect, part of what is being marketed in relationship marketing, in addition to the product or service for sale, is an ongoing relationship between the seller and the buyer.

THE NEXT STEP: CRM. The next step in customer relations is customer relationship management. **Customer relationship management (CRM)** means different things to different people. In general, it is an approach that recognizes that customers are the core of the business and that the company's success depends on effectively managing relationships with them. (See S. A. Brown, 2000.) It overlaps somewhat with the concept of relationship marketing, but not everything that could be called relationship marketing is in fact CRM. Customer relationship marketing is even broader, in that it includes a *one-to-one* relationship of customer and seller. To be a genuine one-to-one marketer, a company must be able and willing to change its behavior toward an individual customer, based on what it knows about that customer. So, CRM is basically a simple idea: *Treat different customers differently.* It is based on the fact that no two customers are exactly the same.

Therefore, CRM involves much more than just sales and marketing, because a firm must be able to change how its products are configured or its service is delivered, based on the needs of individual customers. Smart companies have always encouraged the active participation of customers in the development of products, services, and solutions. For the most part, however, being customer-oriented has always meant being oriented to the needs of the *typical* customer in the market—the average customer. In order to build enduring one-to-one relationships, a company must continuously interact with customers, *individually.* One reason so many firms are beginning to focus on CRM is that this kind of marketing can create high customer loyalty and, as a part of the process, help the firm's profitability.

How Is CRM Practiced?

There are many strategies by which to conduct CRM, and they appear under several names, such as customer service, customer asset management, help desk management, customer-centric systems, sales force automation, and more (e.g., see *crmassist.com, brint.com,* and *cio.com*).

To correctly manage customer relationships, a company must first know who its current and potential customers are, not just as groups or segments of customers, but as individuals. The company needs to know who is a good customer, and who are the most profitable customers for the business. Furthermore, it is important to know why a certain customer is in the market, why he or she does business with us, what the customers like and dislike about our business, and so forth.

With such knowledge companies can develop CRM programs, and there are many of them. (See *crmassist.com*; Kalakota and Robinson, 1999; Keen et al., 2000; and *crm.com*.) According to *CRM.forum.com*, an effective CRM approach will consist of the following 11 components: sales functionality, sales management functionality, telemarketing, time management, marketing, executive information, ERP integration, excellent data synchronization, e-commerce, field service, and customer service and support. Both the knowledge about customers and their behavior and CRM programs are greatly facilitated by several information technologies.

CRM IN ACTION. In order to understand the support of IT to CRM let's look at some specific CRM activities. According to Seybold and Marshak (1998), there are five steps in building IT-supported CRM:

1. Make it easy for customers to do business with you.
2. Focus on the end customer for your products and services.
3. Redesign your customer-facing business processes from the end customer's point of view.
4. Wire your company for profit: Design a comprehensive, evolving electronic business architecture.
5. Foster customer loyalty. In e-commerce, especially, this is the key to profitability.

To accomplish these steps it is necessary to take the following actions. (Note that although all of the following actions are Web-related, CRM does not have to be on the Web. But the trend is to move as much CRM activity to the Web as possible, because CRM generally is cheaper and/or more effective on the Web.)

- Deliver personalized services (e.g., *dowjones.com*).
- Target the right customers (e.g., *aa.com, national.com*).
- Help the customers do their jobs or accomplish their goals (e.g., *boeing.com*).
- Let customers help themselves (e.g., *iprint.com*).
- Stream business processes that impact the customers (e.g., *ups.com, amazon.com*).
- Own the customer's total shopping experience (e.g., *amazon.com, hertz.com*).
- Provide a 360-degree view of the customer relationship (e.g., *wellsfargo.com, bellatlantic.com*).

The Enabling Role of Information Technology in CRM

In order to better understand the contribution of IT to CRM, let's look at the areas in which IT supports CRM activities (Figure 7.12). As can be seen in the figure, the applications can be divided into two main categories: operational CRM and analytical CRM. The major supported activities in each are listed in the figure.

Let's look at some actual examples of operational CRMs:

- American Airlines generates personalized Web pages for each of about 800,000 registered travel-planning customers using intelligent agent technology.

FIGURE 7.12 Classification of the CRM field.

- Manchester Metropolitan University (U.K.) tracks a population of 30,000 students, manages modular courses, and keeps the student management system updated. The system is based on databases and parallel processing.
- Charles Schwab's call center effectively handles over 1 million calls from investments customers every day.
- State Farm Insurance Co. makes retaining customers its primary objective. Using a computerized incentives system, the company manages several initiatives for retaining customers.

For other examples, see S. A. Brown (2000), Peppers and Rogers (1999), Petersen (1999), and Gilmore and Pine (2000).

Typical CRM activities and their IT support are provided in Table 7.5 (page 318). As the table indicates, many organizations are using the Web to facilitate CRM.

CUSTOMER SERVICE ON THE WEB. Customer service on the Web can take many forms, such as answering customer inquiries, providing search and comparison capabilities, providing technical information to customers, allowing customers to track order status, and of course allowing customers to place an online order. We describe these different kinds of Web-based customer services below. (For fuller detail, see Chapter 4 in Turban et al., 2002.)

Providing Search and Comparison Capabilities. One of the major wishes of consumers is to find what they want. With the hundreds of thousands of online stores, and thousands of new ones being added every month, it is difficult for a customer to find what he or she wants, even inside a single electronic mall.

TABLE 7.5 CRM Activities and IT Support

CRM Activity	IT Support
Freedom of choice of doctors, hospitals, alternative medicine, etc. by HMOs.	Internet, online customer surveys, groupware, expert systems for giving advice.
Customized information and services in many languages; discounts based on life style. Appointments reminders, information on doctors, research. Help center to solve member problems. Offered by medical centers, hospitals, HMOs.	E-mails (push technology), data warehouse for customer information; data mining finds relationships; intelligent translating systems. Provide search engines on the Web help center.
Web-based integrated call centers; quick reply to customers' inquiries.	Facilitate help-desk activities; intelligent agents for answering FAQs.
Monitoring customers' orders inside the company.	Workflow software for planning and monitoring; intranets.
Appointment of account managers (BPR activity); creating specialized teams (BPR).	Expert systems for advice; groupware for collaboration.
Seminars and educational activities to customers (banks, hospitals, universities).	Online training, Internet.
Self-tracking of shipments, orders.	Web-based training software; workflow.
Segmenting customers.	Data mining in data warehouses.
Matching customers with products and services.	Web-based intelligent agents.
Customizing products to suit customers' specific needs.	Intelligent agents to find what customer wants, CAD/CAM to reduce cost of customization.
Customers' discussion forums.	Chat rooms, sponsored newsgroups.
Reward repeat customers (loyalty programs, e.g., frequent flyers and buyers of gas/oil companies; airlines, retailers)	Data warehouses and data mining of customers' activities; smart cards that record purchasers' activities.
Customer participation in product (service) development.	Online surveys, newsgroups, chat rooms, e-mails.
Proactive approach to customers based on their activity level.	Data warehouse, data mining.

Search and comparison capabilities are provided internally in large malls (e.g., *amazon.com*), or by independent comparison sites (*mysimon.com, compare.com*).

Providing Free Products and Services. One approach companies use to differentiate themselves is to give something away free. For example, compubank.com provides free bill payments and ATM services. Companies can offer free samples over the Internet, as well as free entertainment, customer education, and more. For further discussion, see Keen (2001), and Strauss and Frost (2001).

Providing Technical and Other Information and Service. Interactive experiences can be personalized to induce the consumer to commit to a purchase and remain loyal. For example, General Electric's Web site provides detailed technical and maintenance information and sells replacement parts for discontinued models for those who need to fix outdated home appliances. Such information and parts are quite difficult to find offline. Another example is *goodyear.com,* which provides information about tires and their use. The ability to download manuals and problem solutions at any time is another innovation of electronic customer service.

Allowing Customers to Order Customized Products and Services Online. Dell Computer has revolutionized purchasing of computers by letting customers design computers and then delivering them to customers' home. This process has been moved to the Internet, and now is used by hundreds of vendors for products ranging from cars (see the Jaguar case) to shoes (Nike). Such a process is known as *mass customization.* Consumers are shown prepackaged "specials" and are given the option to "custom-build" systems.

Other companies have found ways that are unique to their industries to offer customized products and services online. Web sites such as *hitsquad.com, musicalgreetings.com,* or *surprise.com* allow consumers to handpick individual titles from a library and customize a CD, a feature that is not offered in traditional music stores. Instant delivery of any digitized entertainment is a major advantage of EC. Web sites such as *gap.com* allow you to "mix and match" your entire wardrobe. Personal sizes, color and style preferences, dates for gift shipment, and so on, can be mixed and matched by customers, any way they like. This increases sales and the repeat business.

Letting Customers Track Accounts or Order Status. Customers can view their account balances at a financial institution and check their merchandise shipping status, at any time and from their computers or cell phones. For example, customers can easily find the status of their stock portfolio, loan application, and so on. FedEx and other shippers allow customers to track their packages. If you ordered books from Amazon or others, you can find the anticipated arrival date. Amazon even goes one step further; it notifies you by e-mail of the acceptance of your order, the anticipated delivery date, and later, the actual delivery date. Many companies follow the Amazon model and provide similar services.

All of these examples of customer service on the Web demonstrate an important aspect of CRM: a focus on the individual customer.

TOOLS FOR CUSTOMER SERVICE. There are many innovative Web-related tools to enhance customer service and CRM. Here are the major ones:

Personalized Web Pages. Many companies allow customers to create their own individual Web pages. These pages can be used to record purchases and preferences. Also, customized information can be efficiently delivered to the customer, such as product information, add-on purchases, and warranty information. The information is easily disseminated when the customer logs on to the vendor's Web site. Not only can the customer pull information as needed or desired, but also the vendor can push information to the customer. The customer's Web page records purchases, problems, and requests. The vendor can then utilize this information to enhance sales and facilitate service to the customer. Information that formerly may have been provided to the customer one to three months after a transaction was consummated is now provided in real or almost real time, and it can be traced and analyzed for an immediate response or action. Transaction information is stored in the vendor's database, and then accessed and processed to support marketing of more products and to match valuable information about product performance and consumer behavior.

FAQs. Frequently asked questions (FAQs) (see Chapter 4) is the simplest and least expensive tool to deal with repetitive customer questions. Customers use this tool by themselves, which makes the delivery cost minimal. However, any nonstandard question requires an e-mail. Also, FAQs are usually not customized. Therefore, FAQs produce no personalized feeling nor do they contribute to CRM. (They may do so one day; the system will know the customer's profile and be able to present customized FAQs and answers.)

Tracking Tools. Similar to FAQs, delegating to customers the task of tracking orders can save the vendors money, and satisfy the customer's need for quick and easy-to-obtain information about particular shipments. FedEX initiated this concept, saving millions of dollars.

Chat Rooms. Another tool that provides customer service, attracts new customers, and increases customers' loyalty is a chat room (see Chapter 4). For example, retailer QVC (see Minicase 2) offers a chat room, where customers can discuss their experiences shopping with QVC.

E-mail and Automated Response. The most popular tool of customer service is e-mail. Inexpensive and fast, e-mail is used to disseminate information (e.g., confirmations), to send product information, and to conduct correspondence regarding any topic, but mostly to answer inquiries from customers.

The ease with which e-mails can be sent results in a flood of e-mails. Some companies receive tens of thousands of e-mails a week, or even a day. To answer these e-mails manually is too expensive and time-consuming. Customers want quick answers, usually within 24 hours (a policy of many organizations). Priced at about $50,000 (in 2000), you can buy from several vendors an automated e-mail reply system that provides answers (e.g., see *eGain.com, brightware.com,* and *avaya.com*). The eGain system, for example, looks for certain phrases or words such as "complaint" or "information on a product" and then taps into a knowledge base to generate a matched response. In cases in which human attention is needed, the query is assigned an ID number and passed along to a customer service agent for a reply. The eGain system is just one feature in eGain's Web-based call center initiatives.

Rather than using automatic response, many companies send only automatic acknowledgment of receiving the inquiry. The queries are classified in a decision support repository until a human agent logs in and responds. This is usually a part of a call center.

Help Desks and Call Centers. One of the most important tools of customer service is the *help desk.* Customers can drop in or communicate by telephone, fax, or e-mail, which are integrated into a call center.

A *call center* is a comprehensive customer service entity in which companies take care of their customer service issues, communicated through various contact channels. New products are extending the functionality of the conventional call center to e-mail and to Web interaction. For example, *epicor.com* combines Web channels, such as automated e-mail reply, Web knowledge bases, and portal-like self-service, with call center agents or field service personnel. Such centers are sometimes called *telewebs.*

For both consumers and businesses, the Internet is a medium of instant gratification. Delays could easily send customers or potential customers elsewhere. More and more Internet users demand not only prompt replies but proactive alerts. For example, Travelocity sends out to a customer's cell phone or PC a message with updated gate and time information if a customer's flight is delayed. Online mortgage lender loanshop.com, focused on the teleweb center sales and support in a natural language–based application. To use the system, customers submitted structured e-mail messages in which they answered a number of questions. If the system could not answer a query automatically, the e-mail was routed to an integrated queue of phone calls, e-mails, and faxes in the teleweb center. A comprehensive description of Web-based call centers, including information on leading vendors, is available at Orzech (1998).

Some of the hurdles a call center needs to address include deploying technologies such as e-mail management software; creating knowledge bases for FAQs; integrating phone and e-mail into a single center; training customer service representatives who can manage such a function in an effective way; and dealing with foreign languages whenever necessary.

Providing well-trained customer service representatives who have access to data such as customer history, purchases, and previous contact with the call center agents is another way to improve service. In this way a company can maintain a personal touch with the online customer. An example is Bell Advanced Communication in Canada, whose subscribers can submit requests to resolve technical questions over the Web. Consumers fill out an e-mail form with drop-down menus that help to pinpoint the problem. The e-mail is picked up by the call center, which either answers the question immediately or tries to respond within one hour. "From a customer service perspective, it provides good context. It keeps the personal aspect alive," says Maggi Williams, director of business development. This form of online "managed comprehensive contact" also gives Bell insight into what kind of information customers are interested in, which may, in turn, generate selling or marketing opportunities.

Troubleshooting Tools. Large amounts of time can be saved by the customers if they can solve problems by themselves. Many vendors provide Web-based troubleshooting software to assist customers in this task. The vendors of course dramatically reduce their expenses for customer support when customers are able to solve problems without further intervention of customer service specialists.

Justifying Customer Service and CRM Programs

Customer service programs can be expensive and therefore they need to be justified in the budgeting process. Two major problems come up in attempting a justification. First is the fact that most of the benefits are intangible. Second is that substantial benefits can be reaped only from loyal customers who continue to buy. This of course is true for offline service as well. A study by Reichheld and Schefter (1992) showed that the high cost of acquiring customers renders many customer relationships unprofitable during their early years. Only in later years, when the cost of retaining loyal customers falls and the volume of their purchases rises, do CRM programs generate big returns (Reichheld and Schefter, 2000). Therefore companies are very careful in determining how much customer service to provide (see Petersen, 1999.)

METRICS. One way to determine how much customer service to provide is to compare your company against a set of standards known as **metrics**. Here are some metrics one can use to evaluate Web-related customer service:

- ***Response time.*** Many companies use 24 to 48 hours response time as a target. Using intelligent agents, response can be made in real time. At the least, acknowledgment of a customer's inquiry must be provided quickly.
- ***Site availability.*** Customers should be able to reach sites any time (24 hours). This means that downtime should be driven as close to zero as possible.
- ***Download time.*** Users usually will not tolerate more than a 20- to 30-second wait for material to download. (Some people will not wait longer than 6 to 8 seconds for a download.)
- ***Timeliness.*** Site information must be up-to-date.
- ***Security and privacy.*** A privacy statement and explanation of security measures are critical.

- ***Fulfillment.*** Fulfillment must be fast and delivery made when promised.
- ***Return policy.*** The ability to return purchased items is a standard accepted in the United States and only a few other countries. It increases trust and loyalty, and knowing they can return unwanted items makes customers somewhat more willing to buy.
- ***Navigability.*** Ease of navigability on the Web site is another "must" that pleases customers.

For more about metrics in CRM and other activities along the supply chain, see Dobbs (2000).

CRM Failures

In Chapter 6 we discussed the large number of ERP failures. In functional information systems there are failures as well. A large percentage of failures have been reported in CRM. For example, according to *Zdnetindia.com/news* of September 29, 2000, the founder and CEO of *24/7 Customer.com* estimated that 42 percent of the top 125 sites are e-CRM failures. A large number of failures is also reported by *thinkanalytics.com, cio.com, CRM-forum.com,* and many more. However, according to *itgreycells.com,* the CRM failure results have improved from a failure rate of up to 80 percent in 1998 to about 50 percent in 2000.

Some of the big issues relating to CRM failures are:

- Failure to identify and focus on specific business problems.
- Lack of active senior management (non-IT) sponsorship.
- Poor user acceptance, which can occur for a variety of reasons such as unclear benefits (i.e., CRM is a tool for management, but doesn't help a rep sell more effectively) and usability issues.
- Trying to automate a poorly defined process.

Strategies to deal with these and other problems are offered by many. (For example, see *CIO.com* for CRM implementation. Also see *conspectus.com* for "10 steps for CRM success.")

The failures of CRM mean poor customer services. CRM failures could create substantial problems. According to a Jupiter Communications study in 1999, response time took more than a day in 40 percent of shopping sites (vs. 28 percent that took that long in 1998). Companies are falling behind in their ability to handle the volume of site visitors and the volume of buyers. DeFazio (2000) provides the following suggestions for implementing CRM and avoiding CRM failure.

- Conduct a survey to determine how the organization responds to customers.
- Carefully consider the four components of CRM: sales, service, marketing, and channel/partner management.
- Survey how CRM accomplishments are measured; use metrics. Make sure quality, not just quantity, is addressed.
- Consider how CRM software can help vis-à-vis the organization's objectives.
- Decide on a strategy: refining existing CRM processes, or reengineering the CRM.
- Evaluate all levels in the organization, but particularly frontline agents, field service, and salespeople.

- Prioritize the organization's requirements as: must, desired, and not important.
- Select the CRM software. There are more than 60 vendors. Some (like Siebel) provide comprehensive packages, others provide only certain functions. Decide whether to use the best-of-breed approach or to go with one vendor.

It is interesting to note that ERP vendors such as PeopleSoft and SAP also offer CRM products.

Partner-Relationship Management (PRM)

Every company that has business partners has to manage the relationships with them. Partners need to be identified, recruited, and maintained. Communication needs to flow between the organizations. Information needs to be updated and shared. All of the efforts made to apply CRM to all types of business partners can be categorized under the term **partner-relationship management (PRM)**. Before the spread of Internet technology, there were few automated processes to support partnerships. Organizations were limited to manual methods of phone, fax, and mail. EDI was used by large corporations, but usually only with their largest partners. Also, there were no systematic ways of conducting PRM. Internet technology changes the situation by offering a way to connect different organizations easily, quickly, and affordably.

PRM solutions connect vendors with their business partners using Web technology to securely distribute and manage information. At its core, a PRM application facilitates partner relationships. Specific functions include: partner profiles, partner communications, lead management, targeted information distribution, connecting the extended enterprise, partner planning, centralized forecasting, group planning, e-mail and Web-based alerts, messaging, price lists, and community bulletin boards. (For more on PRM, see *channelwave.com,* and *it-telecomsolutions.com*.)

7.5 INTEGRATING FUNCTIONAL INFORMATION SYSTEMS

Reasons for Integration

For many years most IT applications were developed in the functional areas, independent of each other. Many companies developed their own customized systems that dealt with standard procedures to execute transaction processing/operational activities. These procedures are fairly similar, regardless of what company is performing them. Therefore, the trend today is to buy commercial, off-the-shelf functional applications. The smaller the organization, the more attractive such an option is. Indeed, several hundred commercial products are available to support each of the major functional areas. Development tools are also available to build custom-made applications in a specific functional area. For example, there are software packages for building financial applications, a hospital pharmacy management system, and a university student registration system.

However, to build information systems along business processes (which cross functional lines), requires a different kind of approach. Matching business processes with a combination of several functional off-the-shelf packages may be a solution in some areas, but not in all. For example, we saw in the Colonial Building Supply case that it is possible to integrate manufacturing, sales, and accounting software. However, combining existing packages may not be practical or effective in other cases. To build applications that will easily cross functional lines and reach separate databases often requires new approaches such as Web-based systems and integrated software.

Information systems integration tears down barriers between and among departments and corporate headquarters and reduces duplication of effort. Palaniswamy and Frank (2000) studied five ERP systems and found in all cases that better cross-functional integration was a critical success factor. A framework for an integrated information system was developed by Yakhou and Rahali (1992) and is shown in Figure 7.13. There is data sharing as well as joint execution of business processes across functional areas, allowing individuals in one area to quickly and easily provide input to another area. Various functional managers are linked together in an enterprisewide system.

Integrated information systems can be built not only in a small company like Colonial, but also in large organizations, and even in multinational corporations, as shown in the *IT at Work* example on page 325.

Another approach to integration of information systems is to use enterprise resources planning. However, ERP requires a company to fit its business processes

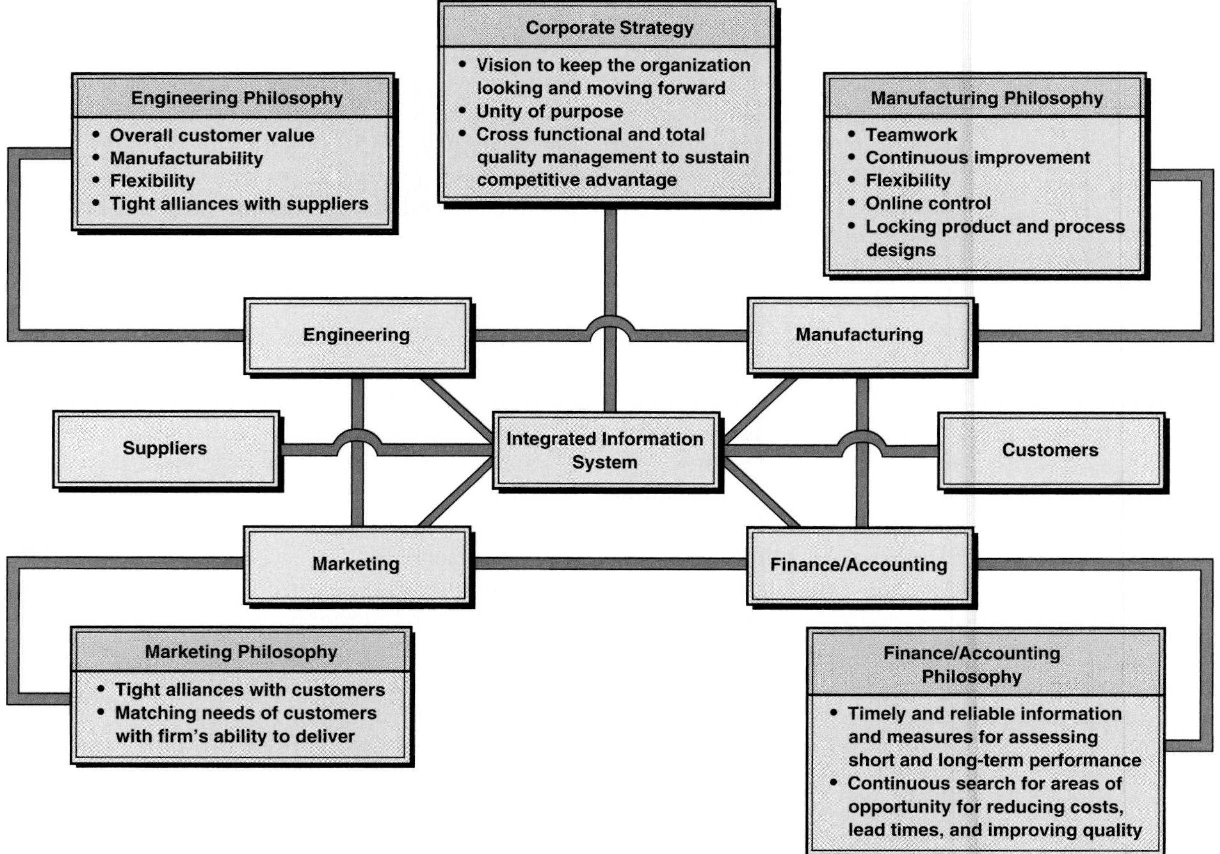

FIGURE 7.13 Integrated information systems—sharing data and business processes across functional lines. (*Source:* M. Yakhou and B. Rahali, "Integration of Business Functions: Roles of Cross-Functional Information Systems." Reprinted from *APICS—The Performance Advantage,* December 1992, p. 36. Copyright 1992 by APICS—The Educational Society for Resource Management. Copied from APICS—The Performance Advantage, December 1992.)

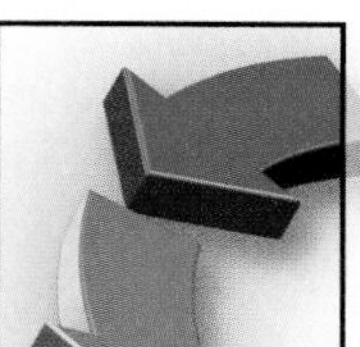

IT at Work
INTEGRATED CLIENT/SERVER SYSTEM AT EUROPCAR

...in Production & Operations Management, Marketing, and Accounting

www.europcar.com

Major reengineering of Europcar Internet, the largest European-based car rental agency, changed the structure of the entire organization, in addition to changing everyday work processes and methods. To support these changes, the company combined 55 different mainframe and minicomputer systems into a single client/server center known as Greenway. Located at corporate headquarters near Paris, the $400 million system initially combined data from nine different countries within Europe, and today it has expanded to a global system.

The 55 independent systems used various data types, many of which were incompatible and needed to be integrated. Europcar was interested in integrating the business practices, customer preferences, and related data into a single system. To complicate matters, the company had to simultaneously develop a uniform set of business practices, or corporate standards, to support the new single business entity. Furthermore, Europcar had to consider the variety of languages spoken in the nine countries involved, as well as different currencies and cultures.

Key business processes—including reservations, billing, fleet management, cost control, and corporate finance—were all integrated into Greenway. Customer-related benefits include (1) fast service since clerks no longer have to manually verify credit cards or calculate bills, (2) reservation desks linked to airline reservation systems like SABRE or Amadeus, and (3) corporate customers managed from one location.

Three thousand Europcar employees at 800 offices throughout the continent utilized Greenway at the time of its inception. Europcar originally grew through the acquisition of geographically and culturally disparate entities. Through reengineering, IT helps support these business alliances to present more of a multicountry team-based organization.

By 2000, Europcar had expanded to 100 countries worldwide. Its information system has expanded considerably. Reservations can be made on the Web, and a smart card is available to enable customers to check in and out rapidly.

For Further Exploration: What are some of the difficulties of integrating 55 systems from nine countries speaking different languages? What functional areas can you identify in the integrated system?

Sources: Based on J. Greenbaum, "A Bumpy Road for Europcar," *InformationWeek,* February 7, 1994; and *europcar.com/english* (2000).

to the software. As an alternative to ERP, companies can choose the best-of-breed systems on the market, or use their own home-grown systems and integrate them. The latter approach may not be simple, but it may be more effective.

By whatever method it is accomplished, integrating information systems helps to reduce cost, increase employees' productivity, and facilitate information sharing and collaboration, which are necessary for improving customer service.

Front-Office and Back-Office Integration

In Chapters 5 and 6 we discussed the need to integrate front-office with back-office operations. This is a difficult task. It is easier to integrate the front-office operations among themselves and the back-office operations among themselves (which is basically what systems such as MAS 90 are doing).

Oracle Corp. is continuously expanding its "Front Office" software. It offers front-office integration, with some capability of connecting with back-office operations. Among its capabilities are:

- ***Field sales online:*** a Web-based customer management application.
- ***Service contracts:*** contract management, service options (with ERP).
- ***Mobile sales and marketing:*** a wireless groupware for connecting different management groups.
- ***Call center and telephony suite:*** a Web-based call center.

- ***Internet commerce:*** an order-taking and payment unit interconnected with ERP back-office applications. It is also tightly connected to the call center for order taking.
- ***Business intelligence:*** identification of most-valuable customers, analysis of why customers leave, and evaluation of sales forecast accuracy.

MANAGERIAL ISSUES

1. ***Integration of functional information systems.*** Integration of existing stand-alone functional information systems is a major problem for many organizations. While client/server architecture (Chapter 2 and Technology Guide 4) solves some technical difficulties, there are still problems of integrating different types of data and procedures used by functional areas. Also, there is an issue of information sharing, which may contradict existing practices and cultures.
2. ***Priority of transaction processing.*** Transaction processing may not be an exotic application, but it deals with the core processes of organizations. It must receive top priority in resource allocation, balanced against innovative applications needed to sustain competitive advantage and profitability, because the TPS collects the information needed for most other applications.
3. ***The customer is king/queen.*** In implementing IT applications, management must remember the importance of the customer, whether external or internal. Some innovative applications intended to increase customers' satisfaction are difficult to justify in a traditional cost-benefit analysis. Corporate culture is important here, too. Empowering customers to enter into a corporate database can make customers happy (since they get quick answers to their queries) and can save money for a company. But it may raise security concerns. Everyone in the organization must be concerned about customers. Management should consider installing a formal CRM program for this purpose.
4. ***Finding innovative applications.*** Tools such as Lotus Notes, intranets, and the Internet enable the construction of many applications that can increase productivity and quality. Finding opportunities for such applications can best be accomplished cooperatively by end users and the IS department.
5. ***System integration.*** Although functional systems are necessary, they may not be sufficient if they work independently. It is difficult to integrate functional information systems, but there are several approaches to doing so. In addition to ERP (discussed in Chapter 6), one may consider a best-of-breed integration by finding the most suitable functional systems and tying them together.
6. ***Using the Web.*** Web-based systems should be considered in all functional areas. They are effective, cost relatively little, and are user friendly. In addition to new applications, companies should consider conversion of existing applications to Web-based ones.

7. ***Ethical issues.*** Many ethical issues are associated with the various topics of this chapter. Here are few examples:

- Professional organizations either of the functional areas (e.g., marketing associations), or in topical areas such as CRM have their own codes of ethics.

- In practicing CRM, companies may give priority to more valuable customers (e.g., frequent buyers). This may lead to perceived discrimination. For example, in one case a male customer found that Victoria's Secret charged him more than it did female buyers. He sued, and in court it was shown that he was buying less frequently than the specific female he cited. Companies need to be very careful with such CRM policies.
- Several organizations provide comparisons of privacy policies and other ethical-related topics. For an example, see *socap.org.*
- Training activities that are part of HRM and CRM activities may involve ethical issues, for example, in selecting participants and evaluating performance.
- TPS data processing and storage deal with private information about people, their performance, etc. Care should be taken to protect this information and the privacy of employees and customers.

For more on business ethics as it applies to CRM and other topics in this chapter, see *ethics.ubc.ca/resources/business.*

ON THE WEB SITE... Additional resources, including the Virtual Company, quizzes, cases, updates, additional exercises, links, demos, and activities, can be found on the book's Web site.

KEY TERMS

Batch processing *281*
Channel systems *293*
Computer-aided design (CAD) *291*
Computer-aided engineering (CAE) *291*
Computer-aided manufacturing (CAM) *291*
Computer-integrated manufacturing (CIM) *292*
Customer relationship management (CRM) *315*
Enhanced product realization (EPR) system *291*
Just-in-time (JIT) *290*
Manufacturing resource planning (MRP II) *289*
Mass customization *295*
Material requirements planning (MRP) *289*
Metrics *321*
Online processing *281*
Online transaction processing (OLTP) *282*
Partner-relationship management (PRM) *323*
Relationship marketing *315*
Sales automation software *299*
Sales-force automation *299*
Short message service (SMS) *297*
Transaction processing systems (TPS) *281*
Work management systems (WMS) *290*

CHAPTER HIGHLIGHTS (Numbers Refer to Learning Objectives)

❶ Information systems applications can support many functional activities. Considerable software is readily available on the market for much of this support.

❷ The major business functional areas are production/operations, marketing, accounting/finance, and human resources management.

❸ The backbone of most information systems applications is the transaction processing system, which is the routine, mission-central operations of the organization.

❹ The major area of IT support to production/operations management is in logistics and inventory management: MRP, MRP II, JIT, CAD, CAM, mass customization, and CIM.

❹ Channel systems deal with all activities related to customer orders, sales, advertisement and promotion, market research, customer service, and product and service pricing.

4 Accounting information systems cover many non-TPS applications in areas such as cost control, taxation, and auditing.

4 Financial information systems deal with topics such as investment management, financing operations, raising capital, risk analysis, and credit approval.

4 All tasks related to human resources development can be supported by human resources information systems. These tasks include employee selection, hiring, performance evaluation, salary and benefits administration, training and development, labor negotiations, and work planning.

4 Web-based systems are extremely useful for recruiting and training.

5 CRM is a corporatewide program that is composed of many activities aiming at fostering better relationships with customers. A Web-based call center is an example.

6 Integrated functional information systems are necessary to ensure effective and efficient execution of activities that cross functional lines or require functional cooperation.

QUESTIONS FOR REVIEW

1. What is a functional information system?
2. List the major characteristics of a functional information system.
3. What are the objectives of a TPS?
4. List the major characteristics of a TPS.
5. Distinguish between batch and online TPS.
6. Explain how the Web enables mass customization.
7. Describe MRP.
8. Describe MRP II.
9. Describe CAD. Explain CAE and CAM.
10. Define CIM, and list its major benefits.
11. Define channel systems.
12. What is telemarketing?
13. Define JIT, and list some of its benefits.
14. Describe some tactical and strategic accounting/finance applications.
15. Explain human resources information systems.
16. Describe CRM.
17. Describe PRM.
18. Describe a Web-based call center.

QUESTIONS FOR DISCUSSION

1. Why is it logical to organize IT applications by functional areas?
2. Describe the role of a TPS in a service organization.
3. Why are transaction processing systems a major target for reengineering?
4. Which functional areas are related to payroll, and how does the relevant information flow?
5. Relate CAD to CAE and to CAM.
6. It is said that in order to be used successfully, MRP must be computerized. Why?
7. The Japanese implemented JIT for many years without computers. Discuss some elements of JIT, and comment on the potential benefits of computerization.
8. Conduct some research on MRP and MRP II, and discuss the relationship between these two products.
9. Describe how IT can enhance mass customization.
10. Describe the role of computers in CIM.
11. Describe the benefits of an accounting integrated software such as MAS 90; compare it to MAS 2000.
12. Discuss how IT facilitates the budgeting process.
13. Why is risk management important, and how can it be enhanced by IT?
14. Explain how Web applications can make the customer king/queen.
15. Why are information systems critical to sales order processing?
16. Explain how IT can enhance telemarketing.
17. Geographical information systems are playing an important role in supporting marketing and sales. Provide some examples not discussed in the text.
18. Marketing databases play a major role in channel systems. Why?
19. How can the Internet support investment decisions?
20. Discuss the role IT plays in support of auditing.
21. Discuss the need for software integration.
22. Investigate the role of the Web in human resources management. Human resources information systems (HRISs) are a relatively new IT arrival.
23. Compare CRM to PRM. What PRM activities may not be found in CRM?
24. Discuss why Web-based call centers are critical for a successful CRM.

EXERCISES

1. Compare the way Colonial Building Supply integrated its software with an integration via ERP software such as SAP R/3.
2. The chart shown in Figure 7.6 portrays the flow of routine activities in a typical manufacturing organization. Explain in what areas IT can be most valuable.
3. Argot International (a fictitious name) is a medium-sized company in Peoria, Illinois, with about 2,000 employees. The company manufactures special machines for farms and food-processing plants, buying materials and components from about 150 vendors in six different countries. It also buys special machines and tools from Japan. Products are sold either to wholesalers (about 70) or directly to clients (from a mailing list of about 2,000). The business is very competitive.

   The company has the following information systems in place: financial/accounting, marketing (primarily information about sales), engineering, research and development, and manufacturing (CAM). These systems are independent of each other, and only the financial/accounting systems are on a local area network.

   Argot is having profitability problems. Cash is in high demand and short supply, due to strong business competition from Germany and Japan. The company wants to investigate the possibility of using information technology to improve the situation. However, the vice president of finance objects to the idea, claiming that most of the tangible benefits of information technology are already being realized.

   QUESTIONS. You are hired as a consultant to the president. Respond to the following:

   a. Prepare a list of ten potential applications of information technologies that you think could help the company. Prioritize them.
   b. From the description of the case, would you recommend any telecommunication arrangements? Be very specific. Remember, the company is in financial trouble.
   c. How can the Internet help Argot?
4. Enter *nike.com* and configure a pair of sneakers. Then enter *jaguar.com* and configure a car. Compare the two experiences.
5. Enter *resumix.com*. Take the tour of Resumix 6. Prepare a list of all the product's capabilities.

GROUP AND ROLE-PLAYING ACTIVITIES

1. Each group visits a large company in a different industry and identifies its channel systems. Prepare a diagram that shows the seven components in Figure 7.7. Then find how IT supports each of those components. Finally, suggest improvements in the existing channel system that can be supported by IT technologies and that are not in use by the company today. Each group presents its findings.
2. Preparing an advertising program for a client is a long process, involving many individuals and groups. The process starts with a work order generated by an account executive and distributed to a creative services department, which prepares the concepts of the program and layouts. The layouts must be approved, distributed, and filed. The art director, production manager, and media planner must prepare cost estimates. The client must approve the program and the cost. Then, final art must be prepared and again approved by the client. Finally, purchase orders must be created. Historically, all this has been done manually, creating a paper nightmare.

   Your group is acting as a consultant to Young & Rubicam, one of the nation's largest advertising agencies. The company wants to improve quality, productivity, and customer service by using IT. Online advertisement must be included. Prepare a report that includes:

   a. Material on the advertisement business and on Young & Rubicam.
   b. A diagram that shows how you envision the execution of an advertising program.
   c. A list of information technologies that can be used to improve the advertising program process.
   d. An explanation of how each of the technologies is going to be used. Be specific.
   e. For each technology proposed, the name of a vendor who distributes the technology. Get information about the cost and the possible integration of the various technologies.
3. The class is divided into groups of five. Each group member represents a major functional area: production/operations management, sales/marketing, accounting, finance, and human resources. Find and describe several examples of processes that require the integration of functional information systems in a company of your choice. Each group will also show the interfaces to the other functional areas.
4. Create groups to investigate the major CRM software vendors, their products, and the capabilities of those products in the following categories (each group represents a topical area or several companies):

   Sales force automation (Oracle, Onyx, Siebel, Saleslogix, Pivotal)

Call centers (Clarify, LivePerson, NetEffect, Inference, Peoplesoft)

Marketing automation (Annuncio, Exchange Applications, MarketFirst, Nestor)

Customer service (Brightware, Broadvision, Primus, Silknet)

Sales configuration (Exactium, Newtonian)

Start with *searchcrm.com* and *crmguru.com* (to ask questions about CRM solutions). Each group must present arguments to the class to convince class members to use the product(s) they investigated.

INTERNET EXERCISES

1. Surf the Net and find free accounting software (try *shareware.cnet.com, clarisys.ca/free, rkom.com.free, tucows.com, passthe shareware.com,* and *freeware-guide.com*). Download the software and try it.
2. Enter the site of Federal Express (*fedex.com*) and learn how to ship a package, track the status of a package, and calculate its cost.
3. Finding a job on the Internet is challenging; there are almost too many places to look. Visit the following sites: *headhunter.net, careermag.com, hotjobs.com, jobcenter.com,* and *monster.com.*
4. Enter the Web sites *tps.com* and *nonstop.compaq.com,* and find information about software products. Identify the software that allows Internet transaction processing. Prepare a report about the benefits of the products identified.
5. Enter the Web site *peoplesoft.com* and identify products and services in the area of integrated software. E-mail PeopleSoft to find out whether its product can fit the organization where you work or one with which you are familiar.
6. Examine the capabilities of the following financial software packages: Comshare BudgetPlus (from Comshare), Financial Analyzer (from Oracle), and CFO Vision (from SAS Institute). Prepare a report comparing the capabilities of the software packages.
7. Surf the Internet and find information from three vendors on sales-force automation (try *sybase.com* first). Prepare a report on the state of the art.
8. Enter *teknowledge.com* and review the products that help with online training. What are the most attractive features of these products?
9. Enter *comshare.com* and download the free whitepaper on management planning and control. Identify all relevant applications and their capabilities.
10. Enter *siebel.com.* View the demo on e-business. Identify all e-business–related initiatives. Why is the company considered as the leader of CRM software?
11. Enter *anntaylor.com* and identify the customer services activities.

Minicase 1

Chemical Customers Bond in Electronic Transactions via ChemConnect

www.chemconnect.com

At the beginning of Chapter 5 we presented the Internet markeplace ChemConnect (*chemconnect.com*), where buyers and sellers of chemicals and plastics can meet electronically. Global industry leaders, such as British Petroleum, Dow Chemical, BASF, Hyundai, and Sumitomo make transactions there every day, in real time, with trading partners around the globe.

As described in Chapter 5, ChemConnect provides an information portal for 12,000 members in 125 countries. It offers three trading places: (1) a *public exchange floor* where members can post items for sale or bid anonymously for all types of products at market prices; (2) the *commodities floor* where top producers, intermediaries, and end users buy, sell, and exchange commodity products through regional trading hubs; and (3) private *corporate trading rooms* where members negotiate contracts and spot deals in timed events managed by ChemConnect. Member-participants in any of the three trading spaces can obtain up-to-the-minute market information, translated into 30 different languages.

A large electronic catalog contains "offers to sell" and "requests to buy." Organized by category, the catalog shows starting prices and shipping terms, and buyers bid by changing the starting prices. Members pay transaction fees only for successfully completed transactions.

Business partners provide several support services. For example, Citigroup and ChemConnect offer several financial services for exchange members.

The corporate trading room allows a company to host private auction events for simultaneously negotiating online with several suppliers or buyers. ChemConnect can bring new potential partners into the trading rooms. The trading room allows companies to save up to 15 percent in just 30 minutes, instead of weeks or months in a manual method. For example, a company that placed an RFQ for 100 metric tons of acetic aid to be delivered in Uruguay with a starting price of $1.10 per kilogram reduced the price to $0.95, in six bids offered within 30 minutes. A demo for such reverse auction is available on the site (see CTR Demo).

As an independent intermediary, ChemConnect uses certain rules and guidelines that ensure an unbiased approach to the trades. There is full disclosure of all legal requirements, payments, trading rules, and so on (click on "Legal info and privacy issues"). ChemConnect is growing rapidly, adding members and trading volume.

Source: chemconnect.com press release.

Questions for Minicase 1

1. What marketing channels are used here?
2. What kind of EC model is this? (Consult Chapter 5.)
3. What functional areas, both at the buyer's site and the seller's site, may be involved in this process?
4. What kind of integration is necessary in this case?

Minicase 2

QVC Moving CRM from TV to the Web

www.qvc.com

QVC is known for its TV shopping channels. As a leading TV-based mail-order service, QVC is selling on the Web too. In 2000, QVC served more than 6 million customers, answered 125 million phone calls, shipped about 80 million packages, and handled more than a billion page views on its Web site. QVC's business strategy is to provide superb customer service in order to keep its customers loyal. QVC also appointed a senior vice president for customer service.

QVC's customer service strategy works very well for the TV business and is expected to work as well for the Web. For example, in December 1999, due to unexpected high demand, the company was unable to fulfill orders for gold NFL rings by Christmas Eve. When QVC learned about the potential delay, it sent an expensive NFL jacket, for free, and made sure the jacket would arrive before the holiday. This is only one example of the company's CRM activities.

To manage its huge business (about $3 billion a year), QVC must use the latest IT support. For example, QVC operates four state-of-the-art call centers, one for overseas operations. Other state-of-the-art technologies are used as well. However, before using technology to boost loyalty and sales, QVC had to develop a strategy to put the customers at the core of the corporate decision making. "Exceeding the expectations of every customer" is a sign you can see all over QVC's premises. As a matter of fact, the acronym QVC stands for Quality, Value, and Convenience—all from the customers' perspective. QVC created a superb service organization. Among other things, QVC provides education (demonstrating product features and functions), entertainment, and companionship. Viewers build a social relationship with show hosts, upon which the commercial relationship is built. Now QVC is attempting to build a social relationship with its customers on the Web (see *qvc.com*).

QVC knows that building trust on the TV screen is necessary, but not sufficient. So everyone in the company is helping. QVC's president checks customers' letters. All problems are fixed quickly. Everything is geared toward the long run. In addition, to make CRM work, QVC properly aligns senior executives, IT executives, and functional managers. They must collaborate, work toward the same goals, have plans that do not interfere with others' plans, and so forth. Also the company adopts the latest IT applications and offers training to its customer service reps in the new applications and in CRM continuously.

It is interesting to note that QVC is using metrics to measure customer service. These metrics used to be calls per hour, sales per minute, and profitability per customer. Now, the metrics are:

- Friendliness of the call center reps
- How knowledgeable the reps are about the products
- Clarity of the instructions and invoices
- Number of people a customer has to speak with to get a satisfactory answer
- How often a customer has to call a second time to get a problem resolved

Data on customer service are collected in several ways, including tracking of telephone calls and Web-site movements. Cross-functional teams staff the call center, so complete knowledge is available in one place. Corrective actions

(continued)

are taken quickly with attempts to prevent repeat problems in the future.

To get the most out of the call center's employees, QVC strives to keep them very satisfied. They must enjoy the work in order to provide excellent customer service. The employees are called "customer advocates," and they are handsomely rewarded for innovative ideas.

In addition to call centers, QVC uses computer-telephony integration technology (CTI), which identifies the caller's phone number and matches it to customer information in the database. This information pops up on the rep's screen when a customer calls. The rep can greet the customer by saying: "Nice to have you at QVC again, David. I see that you have been with us twice this year, and we want you to know that you are important to us. Have you enjoyed the jacket you purchased last June?"

To know all about the customer history, QVC maintains a large data warehouse. Customers' buying history is correlated by zip code with psychodemographics data from Experian, a company that analyzes consumer information. This way, QVC can instantly know whether a new product is a hit with wealthy retirees or with young adults. The information is used for e-procurement, advertisement strategy, and more. QVC also uses *viral marketing,* meaning the word-of-mouth of its loyal customers. In order not to bother its customers, QVC does not send any mail advertisements.

QVC is an extremely profitable business, growing at an annual double-digit rate since its start in 1986.

Sources: Compiled from *Darwin Magazine,* October 1, 2000, and from *qvc.com.*

Questions for Minicase 2

1. Visit the CRM learning center at *darwinmag.com/learn/crm,* and identify some CRM activities not cited in this case that QVC may consider to further increase customer loyalty.
2. Enter *qvc.com* and identify actions that the company does to increase trust in its e-business. Also, look at all customer-service activities. List as many as you can find.
3. What is the advantage of having customers chat live online?
4. List the advantages of buying online vs. buying over the phone after watching QVC. What are the disadvantages?
5. Enter the chat room and the bulletin board. What is the general mood of the participants? Are they happy with QVC? Why or why not?
6. QVC said that the key for its success is customer trust. Explain why.
7. Examine the new metrics that QVC uses to measure customer service. Can the company be successful by ignoring the productivity measures used before?

REFERENCES AND BIBLIOGRAPHY

1. Allamaraju, S., *Nuts and Bolts of Transaction Processing: A Comprehensive Tutorial, subrahmanyam.com...icles/transactions/NutsAndBoltsOfTP.html.*
2. Bhise, H., et al., "The Duel for the Doorstep," *McKinsey Quarterly,* No. 2, 2000.
3. Boisvert, L., "Web-based Learning," *Information Systems Management,* Winter 2000.
4. Borck, J. R., "Recruiting Systems Control Resumé Chaos," *Infoworld,* July 24, 2000.
5. Brown, L., *Integrating Models: Templates for Business Transformations.* Indianoplis, IN: SAMS Publishing, 2000.
6. Brown, S. A., *Customer Relationship Management: Linking People, Process, and Technology.* New York: Wiley, 2000.
7. Collins, P., "Harnessing IT for Sustainable Excellence," *Management Services,* March 1999.
8. DeFazio, D., "The Right CRM for the Job," Technologydecisions.com, November 2000.
9. Davenport, T. H., "Putting the Enterprise into the Enterprise System," *Harvard Business Review,* July–August 1998.
10. Dickson, G. W., and G. DeSanctis (eds.), *Information Technology and the Future Enterprise: New Models for Management.* Upper Saddle River, NJ: Prentice-Hall 2001.
11. Dobbs, J. H., *Competition's New Battleground: The Integrated Value Chain,* report from Cambridge Technology Partners, Boston, 2000.
12. Field, T., "Caller I.T.," *CIO Magazine,* February 1999.
13. Farrell, P. B., *Investor's Guide to the Net.* New York: Wiley, 1996.
14. Freeman, J., "Turn Your Budgeting Operations into a Profit Center," *Datamation,* 1997.
15. Gibney, F., "The Revolution in a Box," *Time,* July 31, 2000.
16. Gilmore, J., and B. J. Pine (eds.), *Markets of One: Creating Customer-Unique Value through Mass Customization.* Boston: Harvard Business School Press, 2000.
17. Gorton, I., *Enterprise TPS: Putting the CORBA OTS, ENGINA++, and OrbixOTM to Work.* Reading, MA: Addison Weley, 2000.
18. James, F., "IT Helps HR Become Strategic," *Datamation,* April 1997.
19. Jandt, E. F., and Nemnich, M. B. (eds.), *Using the Internet and the Web in Your Job Search,* 2nd ed. Indianoplis, IN: Jistwork, 1999.
20. Kalakota, R., and M. Robinson, *e-Business: Roadmap for Success.* Reading, MA: Addison-Wesley, 1999, Chapter 5.
21. Kannan, P. K., et al., "Marketing Information on the I-Way," *Communications of the ACM,* March 1999.
22. Keen, P., et al., *Electronic Commerce Relationship: Trust by Design.* Upper Saddle River, NJ: Prentice-Hall, 2000.
23. Keen, P., "The e-Commerce Imperative," in G. W. Dickson and G. DeSanctis (eds.), *Information Technology and the Future Enterprise: New Models for Management.* Upper Saddle River, NJ: Prentice-Hall, 2001.

24. King, J., "Teaching Over the Net," *Computerworld,* June 1997.
25. May, J. H., and L. G. Vargas, "SIMPSON: An Intelligent Assistant for Short-term Manufacturing Scheduling," *European Journal of Operational Research,* January 1996.
26. McKeown, P. G., and R. T. Watson, *Metamorphosis—A Guide to the www and Electronic Commerce.* New York: Wiley, 1998.
27. Mowen, J. C., and M. Minor, *Consumer Behavior.* Upper Saddle River, NJ: Prentice-Hall, 1998.
28. Orzech D., "Call Centers Take to the Web," *Datamation,* June 1998.
29. Palaniswamy, R., and T. Frank, "Enhancing Manufacturing Performance with ERP Systems," *Information Management Journal,* Summer 2000.
30. Peppers, D., and M. Rogers, *Enterprise One to One: Tools for Competing in the Interactive Age.* New York: Doubleday, 1999.
31. Petersen, G. S., *Customer Relationship Management Systems: ROI and Results Measurement.* New York: Strategic Sales Performance, 1999.
32. Rackham, N., *Rethinking the Sales Force.* New York: McGraw-Hill, 1999.
33. Reichheld, F., and P. Schefter, "Zero Defections: Quality Comes to Services," *Harvard Business Review,* September–October 1992.
34. Reichheld, F., and P. Schefter, "E-Loyalty—Your Secret Weapon on the Web," *Harvard Business Review,* July–August 2000.
35. Schafer, S., "Super Charged Sell," *Inc. Technology,* No. 2, 1997.
36. Seybold, P. B., and R. Marshak, *Customer.com: How to Create a Profitable Business Strategy for the Internet and Beyond.* New York: Times Books, 1998.
37. Snyder C. R., et al., "Use of Information Technologies in the Process of Building the Boeing 777," *Journal of Information Technology Management,* Vol. 9, No. 3, 1998.
38. Strauss J., and R. Frost, *E-Marketing,* 2nd ed. Upper Saddle River, NJ: Prentice-Hall, 2001.
39. Sung, N. H., and J. K. Lee, "Knowledge Assisted Dynamic Pricing for Large-Scale Retailers," *Decision Support Systems,* June 2000.
40. Thomas, S. L., and K. Ray, "Recruiting and the Web: High-Tech Hiring," *Business Horizons,* May–June 2000.
41. Totty, P., "MCIF Systems Are Gaining Broader Acceptance," *Credit Union Magazine,* May 2000.
42. Trippi, R., and E. Turban, *Neural Computing in Investment,* 2nd ed. Ridge Burr, IL: Richard D. Irwin, 1996.
43. Turban E., et al., *Electronic Commerce: A Managerial Perspective,* 2nd ed. Upper Saddle River, NJ: Prentice-Hall, 2002.
44. Varney, S. E., "Arm Your Salesforce with the Web," *Datamation,* October 1996.
45. Voss, C., "Developing an eService Strategy," *Business Strategy Review,* Vol. 11, No. 11, 2000.
46. Yakhou, M., and B. Rahali, "Integration of Business Functions: Roles of Cross-Functional Information Systems," *APICS,* December 1992.

CHAPTER

8

IT Planning and BPR

LEARNING OBJECTIVES

After studying this chapter, you will be able to:

1. Discuss the major issues addressed by information systems planning.
2. Demonstrate the importance of aligning information systems plans with business plans.
3. Explain the four-stage model of information systems planning.
4. Describe several different methodologies for conducting strategic information systems planning.
5. Identify the different types of information technology architectures and outline the processes necessary to establish an information architecture.
6. Distinguish the major Web-related issues and understand application portfolio selection.
7. Describe the need for process redesign and BPR.
8. Explain the IT support for BPR and for redesign.
9. Describe organizational transfomation and virtual corporations.

HOW TRUSERV PLANNED ITS INFORMATION TECHNOLOGY

 THE PROBLEM

TruServ Corp. (*truserv.com*) was created in 1997 by the merger of Cotter & Co. and Servistar Corp. TruServ, one of the largest hardware suppliers in the United States, has annual wholesale sales of about $5 billion, which supports sales of some $15 billion retail. A major challenge was to merge the information systems of the two companies. The two systems were completely different, so their integration was a major problem for TruServ.

www.truserv.com

 THE SOLUTION

To do the integration, Paul Lemerise, CIO of TruServ, relied on a *strategic IT plan*. Lemerise turned first to Ernst & Young, a major CPA/IT consultant with which he had worked before on external auditing. He created a planning team that included the consultants and executives from the two merging companies. Lemerise did not include IT executives because he wanted strong input from the business side. He felt that he and the consultants knew enough about IT.

The team decided to include both a short-term tactical plan and a long-term strategic plan. The short-term plan was aimed at supporting the immediate needs of TruServ. It ensured that projects such as the corporate intranet would be on track. It also established a help desk. The long-term plan examined such issues as e-procurement and other e-commerce applications.

The team examined the merger plans and the business plan of the new corporation. It conducted interviews with 30 top executives regarding business goals and technology wish lists. Of special importance were long meetings with the CEO, who got very excited about the possibilities the new system could offer, in particular, e-business.

Once the interviews were completed, Lemerise met with all the executives together, in an attempt to reach a consensus about the priorities of IT projects and the entire strategic plan. The formal IT strategic plan was completed in July 1997. It included all major initiatives for three years, such as the move to one common retail system, and delineated how the company would use the intranet and e-commerce. The topics ranged from the use of wireless technologies in the warehouses to collaboration with business partners.

 THE RESULTS

The plan has remained fluid. It has been reevaluated and updated with new business goals every six months since its inception. This has enabled TruServ to introduce new initiatives as needed. For example, in 2000 and 2001 the company embarked on several Web-based projects, including a Web-centric collaborative technology to streamline its supply chain and transportation networks. An e-commerce linkage with mid-market suppliers was announced in December 2000. TruServ decided not to plan for more than three years in the future ("anything beyond planning for three years often doesn't happen"), but every year the planning horizon is extended one year. The plan includes a return on investment

(ROI) section, which takes into account such intangible items as improving communication with customers.

Sources: Condensed from M. Blodgett, "Game Plans," *CIO,* January 1998, and from *truserv.com* (2001).

LESSONS LEARNED FROM THIS CASE

The case of TruServ demonstrates the benefits of a formal IT plan, especially for large corporations. It also demonstrates that there are different types of plans (e.g., tactical and strategic), and that end users as well as the CEO must be involved in the planning.

One of the major concerns of organizations today is how to transform yesterday's organization to a successful one in the digital economy. Many times, before e-commerce is undertaken, processes such as procurement must be redesigned or reengineered. Therefore IT planning frequently involves planning to redesign business processes as well (see El Sawy, 2001).

This chapter first describes the evolution and issues of information technology systems planning. Then it presents a four-stage model of information systems planning: strategic planning, requirements analysis, resource allocation, and project planning. Next, it discusses methodologies for operationalizing the model, with primary emphasis on the stages of strategic planning and requirements analysis. (Planning for developing individual applications is discussed in Chapter 14.) Moving to business process redesign and to organizational transformation, the chapter describes how IT supports such changes. Finally, the chapter deals with moving an organization and its IT to the digital economy.

8.1 IT PLANNING—A CRITICAL ISSUE FOR ORGANIZATIONS

IT planning is the organized planning of IT infrastructure and applications portfolios done at various levels of the organization. The topic of IT planning is very important for both planners and end users, for the following reasons:

- End users do IT planning for their own units.
- End users must participate in the corporate IT planning. Therefore they must understand the process.
- Corporate IT planning determines how the IT infrastructure will look. This in turn determines what applications end users can deploy. Thus the future of every unit in the organization will be impacted by the IT infrastructure.

Business Importance and Content

A survey of three hundred IT executives, conducted in October 1997 by *CIO Communication Inc.,* revealed that *IT strategy* was the number-one concern for CIOs. It has continued to be among the top issues in 2000 and 2001. Strategic planning used to rank at the top of the list in the late 1980s, then it retreated to the middle of the list. By 2000 it was back in style, with an increased emphasis on aligning IT, e-commerce, and business planning.

Why this renewed interest in formal strategic planning? According to Blodgett (1998), as the demands of an increasingly competitive workplace call for closer integration of IT goals and the business mission, strategic plans for the whole enterprise become more important. In addition, with advances in Web-based supply chain collaborations and integration of e-marketplaces with buyers, sellers, and service providers, a good business strategy involves an IT strategy that keeps in mind the internal customers as well as the external customers and vendors. IT has to work closely with the business side to make sure the company stays competitive.

What's in a strategic plan? Simply put, a *strategic information systems plan* identifies a set of computer-based applications that will help the company reach its business goals. To create a plan that is truly strategic, the CIO and the CEO must work together. Strategic planning is a complex process based on relationships and communications.

The Evolution of IT Planning

Initial efforts to establish planning and control systems for IT started in the late 1950s and early 1960s. During these early years, information technology resources went into developing new applications and then revising existing systems. These two areas became focal points for the first planning and control systems. Organizations adopted methodologies for developing systems, and they installed project management systems to assist with implementing new applications. These initial mechanisms addressed *operational* planning. As organizations became more sophisticated in their use of information systems, emphasis shifted to *managerial* planning, or resource allocation control.

Typically, annual planning cycles were established to identify potentially beneficial IT services, to perform cost-benefit analyses, and to subject the list of potential projects to resource allocation analysis. Often the entire process was conducted by an IT *steering committee* (see Chapter 15). The steering committee reviewed the list of potential projects, approved the ones considered to be beneficial, and assigned them relative priorities. The approved projects were then mapped onto a development schedule, usually encompassing a one- to three-year time frame. This schedule became the basis for determining IT resources requirements such as long-range hardware, software, personnel, facilities, and financial requirements.

Some organizations extend this planning process by developing additional plans for longer time horizons. They have a long-range IT plan, sometimes referred to as the *strategic IT plan* (see Ward and Griffiths, 1996, and Boar, 2000). This plan typically does not refer to specific projects; instead it sets the overall directions in terms of infrastructure and resource requirements for IT activities for five to ten years in the future. The next level is a *medium-term plan*. It identifies the **applications portfolio**, a list of major, approved IS projects that are consistent with the long-range plan. Since some of these projects will take more than a year to complete, and others will not start in the current year, this plan extends over several years. The third level is a *tactical plan*, which has budgets and schedules for current-year projects and activities. In reality, because of the rapid pace of change in technology and the environment, short-term plans may include major items not anticipated in the other plans.

The planning process just described is currently practiced by many organizations. Specifics of the IT planning process, of course, vary among organizations. For example, not all organizations have a high-level IT steering committee. Project priorities may be determined by the IT director, by his or her superior, by company politics, or even on a first-come, first-served basis.

Issues in IT Planning

Improving the planning process for information systems has long been one of the top concerns of information systems department (ISD) management. The Society for Information Management (SIM) (*simnet.org*) found this to be the number-one issue in surveys of senior IT executives.

Basic information systems planning addresses the following four general issues:

1. Aligning the IT plan with the organizational business plan (e.g., see Reich and Benbasat, 1996).
2. Designing an IT architecture for the organization in such a way that users, applications, and databases can be integrated and networked together.
3. Efficiently allocating information systems development and operational resources among competing applications.
4. Planning information systems projects so that they are completed on time and within budget and include the specified functionalities.

Let's look at each of these in more detail.

ALIGNMENT OF THE IT PLAN WITH THE ORGANIZATIONAL PLAN. The first task of IT planning is to identify information systems applications that fit the objectives and priorities established by the organization. Surprisingly, organizational strategies and plans are often not available in written form, or they may be formulated in terms that are not useful for IT planning. Therefore, it is often difficult to ascertain the strategies and goals to which the IT plan should be aligned. Clarification of the organization's plans and strategies may need to be carried out before or done simultaneously with the IT planning (as described in Minicase 1 at the end of the chapter). If selecting and scheduling information systems projects are based solely on proposals submitted by users, the projects will reflect existing computer-use biases in the organization, managers' aggressiveness in submitting proposals, and organizational power struggles, rather than the overall needs and priorities of the organization. Figure 8.1 graphically illustrates the

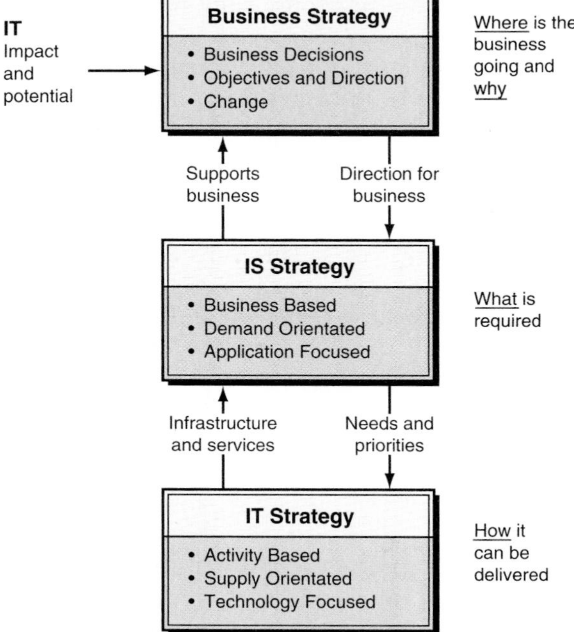

FIGURE 8.1 The relationship among business, IS, and IT strategies. (*Source:* J. Ward and P. Griffiths, *Strategic Planning for Information Systems*, 2nd ed. Chicester: Wiley, 1996, p. 31. Reprinted by permission of John Wiley & Sons, Inc.)

alignment of IS strategy, business strategy, and IT strategy and deployment. The *IT at Work* example below demonstrates how alignment is done.

DESIGN OF AN INFORMATION TECHNOLOGY ARCHITECTURE. The term **information technology architecture**, or **information architecture**, refers to the overall (high-level) structure of all information systems in an organization. This structure consists of applications for various managerial levels (operational control, management planning and control, and strategic planning) and applications oriented to various functional-operational activities such as marketing, R&D, production, and distribution. The information architecture also includes infrastructure (e.g., the databases, supporting software, and networks needed to connect applications together). An information architecture for an organization should guide the long-range development as well as allow for responsiveness to diverse, short-range information systems demands. The configuration of these architectures is discussed in Technology Guide 4.

ALLOCATION OF RESOURCES. Rational, optimal allocation of information systems resources among competing organizational units is difficult. This is especially true if the portfolio of potential applications does not mesh with an overall organizational plan, and if the functional or organizational unit requirements have not been integrated into a planning framework that establishes completeness and priority. Sometimes organizational dynamics, such as a manager's rela-

IT at Work
HEWLETT-PACKARD ALIGNS BUSINESS AND IT STRATEGIES

Integrating IT ...in All Functional Areas and Top Management

www.hp.com

Hewlett-Packard (H-P) developed a planning methodology in which business processes strategies and technologies are defined and aligned concurrently. This methodology was designed to allow the company to make process changes regardless of the limitations of the existing technology, and it gives visibility to the impacts that new technologies and processes have on each other.

In the past, H-P had used a sequential process. First, it defined the business strategy and the operations and supporting strategies, including technologies. Then, all these functions were aligned and replanned, taking into consideration the technologies available. In the new methodology, the planning is performed for all areas *concurrently*. Furthermore, the entire approach is complemented by a strong focus on teamwork, specialized and objective-driven functional areas and business units, and a commitment to quality and customer satisfaction. The approach links strategy and action. The business alignment framework takes into account the necessary process changes resulting from changes in the business environment, as well as potential technological developments. But, because major changes may result in a change in value systems as well as culture and team structures of the organization, H-P includes these factors within the planning methodology.

Target processes, technologies, and standards drive the selection of potential solutions. The participative management approach ensures effective implementation. According to the framework, business processes and information requirements are defined in parallel with technology enablers and models, which are then linked throughout the alignment process. Adjustments and refinements are made continuously.

For Further Exploration: Why is concurrent planning superior? What communication and collaboration support is needed?

Sources: Compiled from R. Feurer et al., "Aligning Strategies, Processes, and IT: A Case Study," *Information Systems Management,* Winter 2000; and from *hp.com*. For another example of alignment of business strategy and IT strategy, see Cale and Kanter (1998).

tive power and aggressiveness, are used in place of rational allocation. This can result in a precarious political situation for ISD management.

COMPLETION OF PROJECTS ON TIME AND WITHIN BUDGET. Many large IT projects (applications) are not completed on time or within budget. A common saying in the IT field is that projects often "take twice as long and cost four times as much" as originally planned. Consequently, organizational performance and ISD management's credibility suffer. Project plans are seldom accurate, as time and resource requirements are generally underestimated.

Often, under the pressure to finish a project on time and/or within budget, certain promised features are omitted. This reduction in functionality and/or quality frequently leads to user dissatisfaction with the resultant systems. Missing or inadequate features must be added later in what is usually called "system maintenance." Better project planning could avoid or reduce the impact of such mishaps. Chapter 14 discusses project planning methods and tools that can help control the schedule and budget of IT individual applications.

PROBLEMS WITH IT PLANNING. IT planning can be an expensive and time-consuming process. A study of five large-scale planning projects found that these projects may involve ten or more employees, on a half-time or full-time basis, for periods lasting from ten weeks to a year. The estimated costs of these projects ranged from $450,000 to $1.9 million. In addition, a survey reported by King (2000) disclosed that more than 50 percent of the companies surveyed were conducting IS planning with obsolete methodologies.

These research findings suggest that, although IT planning is desirable, organizations should be careful not to devote an excessive amount of resources to these efforts. In addition they should use up-to-date methodologies. Finally, they should also beware of the pitfall of allowing IT planning to become an end in itself. To overcome such problems a formal planning process may be useful. Lederer and Sethi (1998) advocate the following guidelines for developing a successful IT strategic plan: Prepare to implement, plan quickly, demonstrate the business value of the plan, understand top management, model only if time permits, do not expect a methodology to guarantee success, and manage outside consultants carefully.

PLANNING METHODOLOGIES. There are several methodologies that can be used to carry on IT planning and many tools to support them. Most of these methodologies start with some strategy investigation that checks the industry, competition, and competitiveness, and relates them to technology. Then alternative applications are uncovered and are checked for feasibility and risk. This is followed by an implementation plan that centers around allocating resources. Finally, after the project is implemented, project and strategy evaluation is done. For the success of such methods, see Doherty et al. (1999) and Sabberwal (1999).

A Four-Stage Model of IT Planning

Several models have been developed to facilitate IT planning (e.g., see Ward and Griffiths, 1996; Cassidy, 1998; and Papp, 2001). Of special interest is Wetherbe's (1993) **four-stage model of planning**. The model (depicted in Figure 8.2) consists of four major activities—*strategic planning, requirements analysis, resource allocation,* and *project planning*—and it is valid today. The stages involve the following activities:

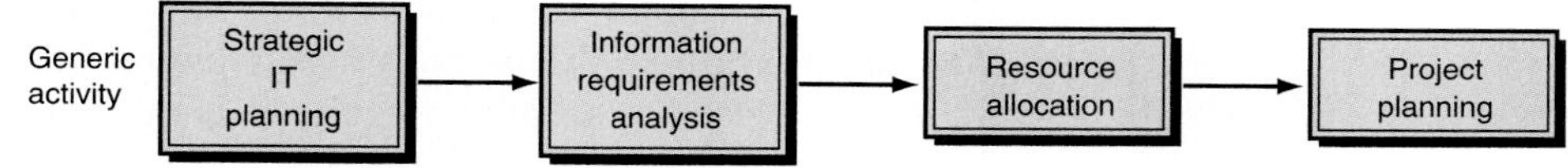

FIGURE 8.2 Basic four-stage model of IS planning.

- ***Strategic IT planning:*** Establishes the relationship between the overall organizational plan and the IT plan.
- ***Information requirements analysis:*** Identifies broad, organizational information requirements to establish a strategic information architecture that can be used to direct specific application development.
- ***Resource allocates:*** Allocates both IT application development resources and operational resources.
- ***Project planning:*** Develops a plan that outlines schedules and resource requirements for specific information systems projects.

Most organizations engage in all four stages, but their involvement in the specific stages tends to be sporadic and prompted by problems as they occur, instead of reflecting a systematic, stage-by-stage process. The four-stage model can be expanded to include major activities and outputs of the four stages, as shown in Figure 8.3. The model moves from a high level of abstraction to a more concrete formulation of IT planning activities. Some useful methodologies for conducting each planning stage are discussed later in this chapter.

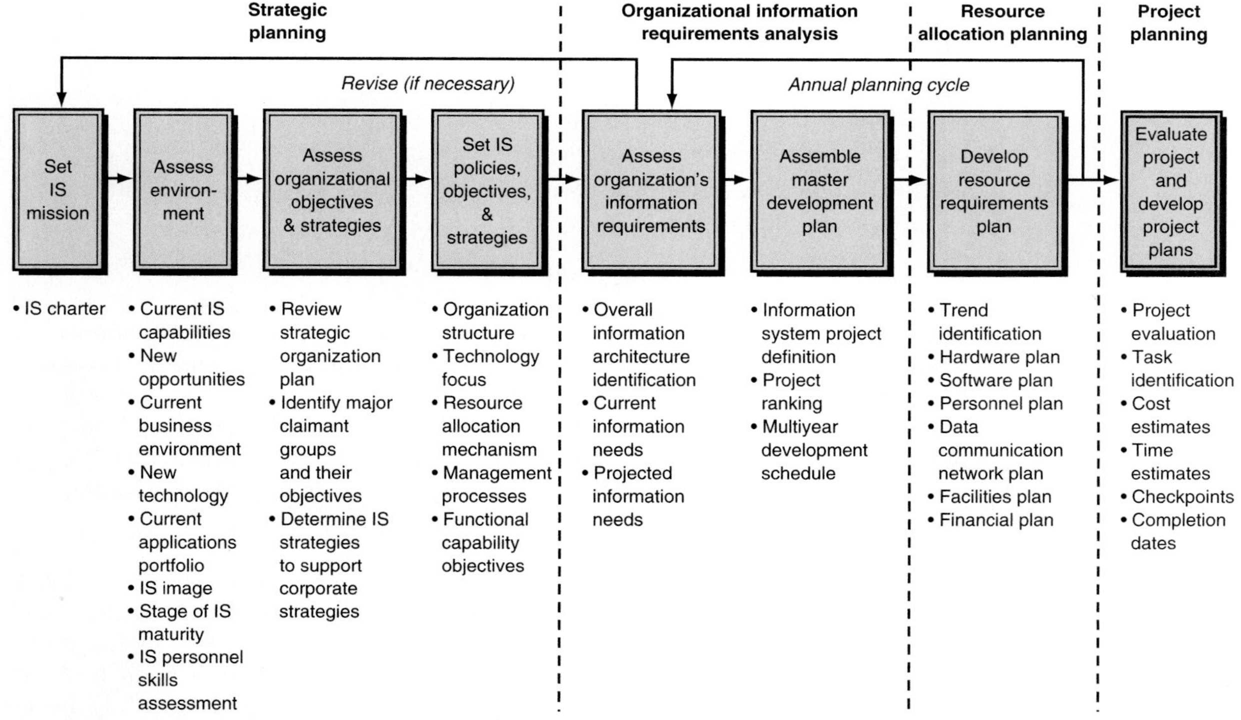

FIGURE 8.3 Major activities and outputs in the four stages of IT planning.

The four-stage planning model is the foundation for the development of a portfolio of applications that is both highly aligned with the corporate goals and has the ability to create an advantage over competitors. There is also a relationship between the four-stage planning model and the various versions of the system development life cycle (SDLC) described in Chapter 14. The four-stage planning model identifies projects and general resource requirements necessary to achieve organizational objectives. In the following two sections we describe the four stages in more detail.

8.2 STAGE 1: STRATEGIC INFORMATION SYSTEMS PLANNING

The first stage of the IT planning model is **strategic information planning (SIP)**. It includes several somewhat different types of activities. On the one hand, it refers to identifying a set of new applications—a *portfolio*—through which an organization will conduct its business. These applications make it possible for an organization to implement its business strategies in a competitive environment. This type of activity is evidenced in the opening case of this chapter.

On the other hand, SIP can also refer to a process of searching for *strategic information systems (SIS)* applications that enable an organization to develop a competitive advantage rather than just maintaining its position, as discussed in Chapter 3.

Strategic information planning (SIP) must be aligned with overall organizational planning (see Ward and Griffiths, 1996) and with e-business, whenever relevent (Pickering, 2000). To accomplish this alignment, the organization must execute the following:

1. Set the IT mission.
2. Assess the environment.
3. Assess existing systems' availabilities and capabilities.
4. Assess organizational objectives and strategies.
5. Set IT objectives, strategies, and policies.
6. Assess the potential impacts of IT.

An organization would conduct the same six steps for e-business.

The output from this process should include the following: a new or revised IT charter and assessment of the state of the ISD; an accurate evaluation of the strategic goals and directions of the organization; and a statement of the objectives, strategies, and policies for the IT effort.

Several methodologies exist to carry out the above tasks. The major ones are business systems planning (BSP), Nolan's stages of the IT growth model, ends/means (E/M) analysis, critical success factors (CSFs), and scenario planning. We look briefly at each of these methodologies next.

Business Systems Planning (BSP)

The **business systems planning (BSP)** model, which was developed by IBM, has influenced other planning efforts such as Andersen Consulting's *method/1* and James Martin and Clive Finkelstein's *information engineering*. BSP is a top-down approach that starts with business strategies. It deals with two main building blocks—*business processes* and *data classes*—which become the basis of an infor-

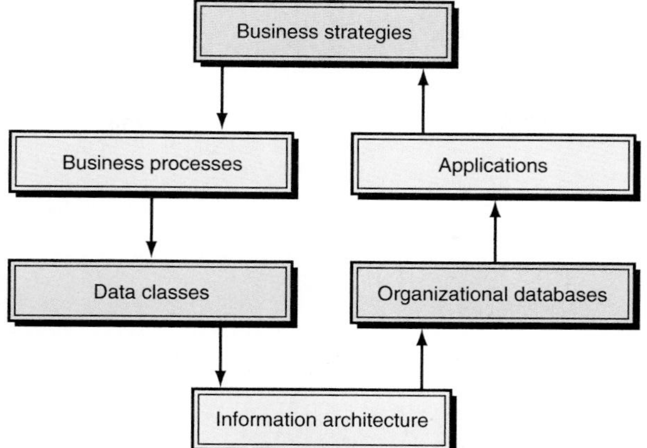

FIGURE 8.4 Business systems planning (BSP) approach. (*Source:* Derived from *Business Systems Planning—Information Systems Planning Guide,* Application Manual GE20-0527-3, 3rd ed., IBM Corporation, July 1981. Courtesy of the International Business Machines Corporation.)

mation architecture. From this architecture the planners can define organizational databases and identify applications that support business strategies, as illustrated in Figure 8.4.

Business processes are groups of logically related decisions and activities required to manage the resources of the business. The recognition that *processes* (such as filling a customer order) could be a more fundamental aspect of business than departments or other organizational arrangements broke new ground. That recognition is at the heart of much of the current business process reengineering activity discussed in Sections 8.7 through 8.10.

Figure 8.5 (page 344) shows the steps in a business systems planning study. Note that the study is conducted by a study team, which may include representatives from the IS group and representatives from end-user groups. The study team works under the sponsorship of a senior organizational executive. The process includes five control points, as identified in the figure. At each of these control points, the outputs of the process are subjected to a formal review prior to going on to the next steps.

BSP relies heavily on the use of metrics in the analysis of processes and data, with the ultimate goal of developing the information architecture. (For details see *Business Systems Planning,* 1981.)

Stages of IT Growth

Nolan (1979) indicated that organizations go through six **stages of IT growth** (called *IS* growth at that time). *A Closer Look* 8.1 (page 345) describes these six stages. In each stage, four processes are active to varying degrees. These are the applications portfolio, users' role and awareness, IT resources, and management planning and control techniques.

The *applications portfolio* is the mix of computer applications that the ISD has installed or is in the process of developing on behalf of the company. The *users' role and awareness* is the extent to which the user community is actively involved in identifying and promoting IT applications in areas of their responsibility. IT *resources* are the hardware, software, staff, and management available to provide information services to the company. Finally, *management planning and control* are the various tools and techniques, such as long-term or strategic planning, used to better manage information resources.

Step	Control point	Reviewer	Review content
Define business processes.			
Define data classes.			
	1	Study team	Review study to date, documentation standards, and team understanding of results. Confirm resource allocations for the next stage.
Define the information architecture.			
Analyze current systems support.			
	2	Executive sponsor	Results to date. Update the study plan. Review the executive interview objectives.
Interview executives.			
Define findings and conclusions.			
	3	Executive sponsor	Report on both qualitative and quantitative results of the executive interviews. Present and validate the assessment of business problems and benefits. Update the study plan.
Determine architecture priorities.			
Review information resource management.			
	4	Study team	Team agreement on all major issues. Review all supporting documentation to be completed. Confirm resource allocation. Update the plan.
Develop recommendations.			
	5	Executive sponsor	Review all major findings and recommendations. Demonstrate an understanding of the business and its requirements. Gain executive sponsor's agreement that the team is qualified to present the recommendations.
Report results.			

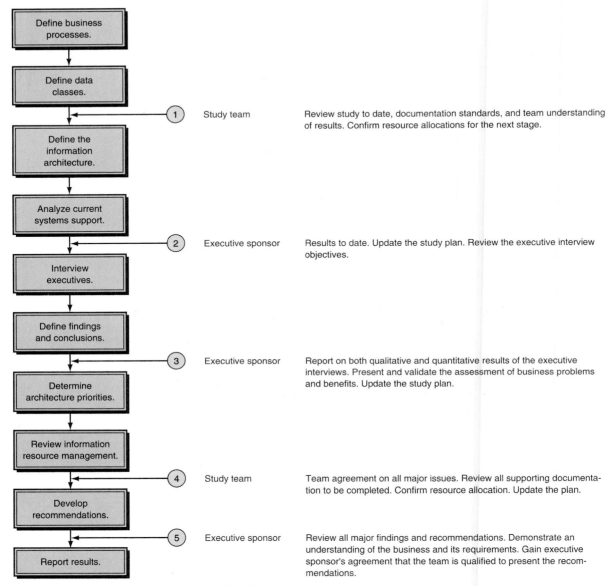

FIGURE 8.5 Steps in BSP study, including five control points.

The *y* axis in the figure in *A Closer Look* 8.1 (page 345) refers to IT expenditures. Note that the growth *rate* of IT expenses is low during data administration, medium during initiation and maturity, and high during expansion (contagion) and integration. In addition to serving as a guide for expenditure, the model helps in determining the seriousness of problems.

Nolan's model became the basis for a strategic information systems planning methodology, known as the *Nolan-Norton methodology,* and this model has been quite influential among IT practitioners. Academic researchers subsequently conducted studies to evaluate its validity, but they did not find a lot of support for specific aspects of the model (Benbasat et al., 1984).

A CLOSER LOOK
8.1 NOLAN'S SIX STAGES OF IS GROWTH

The six stages of IS growth (see figure) are:

1. ***Initiation.*** When computers are initially introduced to the organization, batch processing is used to automate clerical operations in order to achieve cost reduction. There is an operational systems focus, lack of management interest, and centralized ISD.
2. ***Expansion (contagion).*** Centralized rapid growth takes place as users demand more applications based on high expectations of benefits. There is a move to online systems as ISD tries to satisfy all user demands and little, if any, control. IT expenses increase rapidly.
3. ***Control.*** In response to management concern about cost vs. benefits, systems projects are expected to show a return, plans are produced, and methodologies/standards are enforced. The control stage often produces a backlog of applications and dissatisfied users. Planning and controls are introduced.
4. ***Integration.*** There is considerable expenditure on integrating (via telecommunications and databases) existing systems. User accountability for systems is established, and ISD provides a service to users, not just solutions to problems. At this time there is a transition in computer use and an approach from data processing to information and knowledge processing (transition between the two curves).
5. ***Data administration.*** Information requirements rather than processing drive the applications portfolio, and information is shared within the organization. Database capability is exploited as users understand the value of the information and are willing to share it.
6. ***Maturity.*** The planning and development of IT in the organization are closely coordinated with business development. Corporatewide systems are in place. The ISD and the users share accountability regarding the allocation of computing resources. IT has truly become a strategic partner.

Source: Compiled from R. L. Nolan, "Managing the Crises in Data Processing," *Harvard Business Review,* March–April 1979. Reprinted with permission of the *Harvard Business Review.*

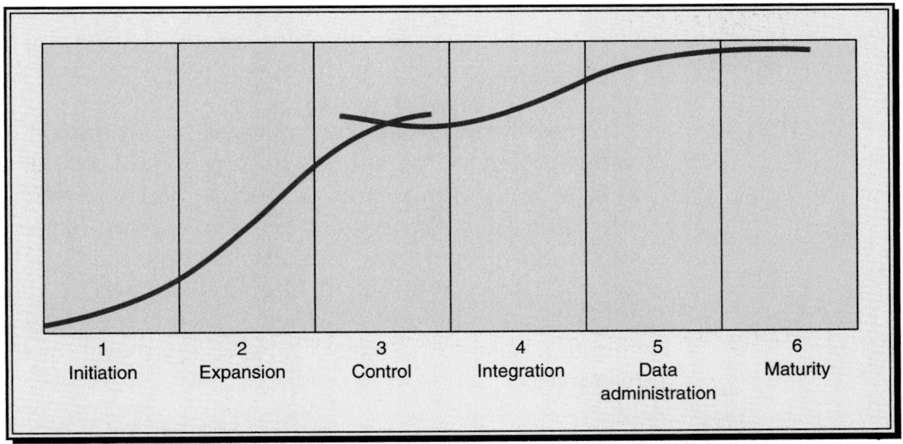

Nolan's six stages of IS growth.

King and Teo (1997) have taken Nolan's concept and applied it to the evolution of IT planning within organizations. Their research indicates that IT planning moves over time through the following four stages of growth:

1. ***Separate planning.*** There is a weak relationship between IT and business planning.
2. ***One-way linked planning.*** IT plans are based on business plans.

3. ***Two-way linked planning.*** Business and IT plans are coordinated.
4. ***Integrated planning.*** IT planning is an integral part of business planning.

WEB APPLICATIONS OF THE SIX STAGES OF GROWTH MODEL. Even if it does not have strong empirical support, Nolan's model does represent a useful perspective for conceptualizing how new information technologies develop and how they should be planned and managed. For example, the development of the Web in the 1990s seems to correspond in many organizations to the early stages of Nolan's model. The initiation stage extended through 1994. During this period, few organizations outside the academic and research worlds had any demand for Web sites. The expansion stage started around 1995 with a large increase in organizational activities on the Internet. In 1996 and 1997, some organizations expressed concern about the tremendous costs in relation to uncertain benefits, indicating an interest in moving on to the control stage. Development and use of organizational intranets and extranets in 1997/1998 and creation of exchanges in 1999/2000 corresponds to the integration stage.

Ends/Means Analysis

Ends/means (E/M) analysis is a planning technique that IT planners can use to determine information requirements at the organizational, departmental, or individual manager level. Based on general systems theory, this technique focuses first on the *ends,* or outputs (goods, services, and information), generated by an organizational process. Next, the technique is used to define the *means* (inputs and processes) used to accomplish these ends. The ends or outputs from one process—whether it is an organizational, departmental, or individual process—are the inputs to some other process. For example, the inventory process supplies parts to the production process, the accounting process generates budget information for other organizational processes, and the marketing process offers products to customer processes.

Ends/means analysis is concerned with both the effectiveness and the efficiency of generating outputs from processes. In this approach, *effectiveness* refers to how well outputs from a process match up with the input requirements of other processes. *Efficiency* refers to the amount of resources required to transform inputs into outputs. Most managers agree that it is more important to be effective than to be efficient. E/M analysis identifies effectiveness considerations in information requirements. Such considerations typically transcend departmental boundaries, so E/M analysis is especially useful for database and other shared IT resources.

Critical Success Factors

The **critical success factors (CSFs)** approach was developed to help identify the information needs of managers. The fundamental assumption is that in every organization there are three to six key factors. If these factors are done well, the organization also will do well. Therefore organizations should continuously measure performance in these areas, taking corrective action whenever necessary. CSFs also exist in business units, departments, and other organizational units.

Critical success factors vary by broad industry categories—manufacturing, service, or government—and by specific industries within these categories. For organizations in the same industry, CSFs will vary depending on whether the firms are market leaders or weaker competitors, where they are located, and what competitive strategies they follow. Environmental issues, such as the degree of regulation or amount of technology used, influence CSFs. In addition, CSFs change over time based on temporary conditions, such as high interest rates or long-term trends.

IT planners identify CSFs by interviewing managers in an initial session, and then refine these CSFs in one or two additional sessions. The first step is to determine the organizational objectives for which the manager is responsible, and then the factors that are critical to attaining these objectives. The second step is to select a small number of CSFs. Then, one needs to determine the information requirements for those CSFs and measure to see whether the CSFs are met. If they are not met it is necessary to build appropriate applications.

The critical success factors approach encourages managers to identify what is most important to their performance and then develop good indicators of performance in these areas. Conducting interviews with all key people makes it less likely that key items will be overlooked. On the other hand, the emphasis on critical factors avoids the problem of collecting too much data, or including some data just because they are easy to collect. Sample questions asked in the CSF approach are:

- What objectives are central to your organization?
- What are the critical factors that are essential to meeting these objectives?
- What decisions or actions are key to these critical factors?
- What variables underlie these decisions, and how are they measured?
- What information systems can supply these measures?

Scenario Planning

Scenario planning is a methodology used in planning situations that involve much uncertainty, like that of IT in general and e-commerce in particular. In this approach planners create several scenarios. Then a team compiles as many as possible future events that may influence the outcome of each scenario. It is a kind of what-if analysis. Scenario planning has been used by major corporations to facilitate IT planning (e.g., see customer lists at *ncri.com*, and *gbn.com*).

Recently scenario planning was adapted to e-commerce planning. For example, Hutchinson (1997) described four EC scenarios that can be used to accomplish EC strategy. The first is the open, *global commerce scenario*, where removal of intermediaries is a powerful force that flattens the value chain. The *members-only subnet* scenario applies mostly to B2B e-commerce. The *electronic middlemen* scenario is one in which suppliers in both business and consumer markets can make their products and services available through independent third-party distribution channels. Finally, in the new *consumer marketing channels* scenario, traditional broadcasting, advertising, and consumer telephony collapse into a unified consumer-centric EC medium on the Internet, for example, via a corporate portal. While EC proliferation would certainly allow any combination or variation of such scenarios, each company has to select the most appropriate model for its needs. The use of this model can help EC planners to determine the EC initiatives that best fit their organization. (See Minicase 1 for an example of implementation.)

8.3 STAGES 2–4: INFORMATION REQUIREMENTS ANALYSIS, RESOURCE ALLOCATION, AND PROJECT PLANNING

The goal of the second stage of the model, the *information requirements analysis,* is to ensure that the various information systems, databases, and networks can be integrated to support the requirements identified in stage 1 to enable decision making.

In the first step of **requirements analysis**, IT planners assess what information is needed to support current and projected decision making and operations in the organization. This is different from the detailed information requirements analysis associated with developing *individual* application systems (i.e., identifying required outputs and the inputs necessary to generate them, which we describe in Chapter 14). Rather, the stage 2 information requirements analysis is at a more comprehensive level of analysis. It encompasses infrastructures such as the data needed in a large number of applications (e.g., in a data warehouse) for the whole organization.

Conducting a Requirements Analysis

There are several alternative approaches for conducting the requirements analysis. One of them is presented as a five-step model in Figure 8.6. The steps of the process are discussed below.

- ***Step 1: Define underlying organizational subsystems.*** The first step of requirements analysis is to identify the underlying organizational processes, such as order fulfillment or product analysis.
- ***Step 2: Develop subsystem matrix.*** The next phase of the requirements analysis exercise is to relate specific managers to organizational processes. This relationship can be represented by a matrix. The matrix is developed by reviewing the major decision responsibilities of each middle-to-top manager and relating them to specific processes.
- ***Step 3: Define and evaluate information requirements for organizational subsystems.*** In this phase of the requirements analysis, managers with major

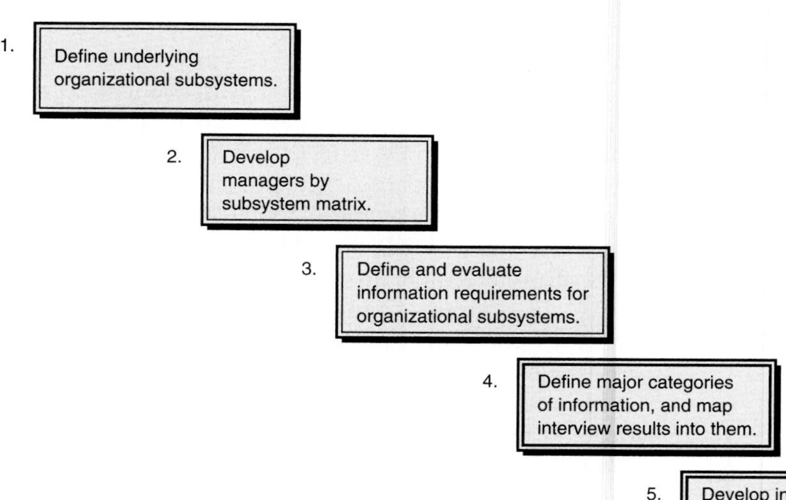

FIGURE 8.6 Planning model for information requirements analysis.

decision-making responsibility for each process are interviewed in groups by information analysts in order to obtain the information requirements of each organizational process.

- ***Step 4: Define major information categories and map interview results into them.*** The process of defining information categories is similar to the process of defining data items for individual application into entities and attributes.
- ***Step 5: Develop information/subsystem matrix.*** Mapping information categories against organizational subsystems creates an information-categories-by-organizational-process matrix. Information categories can be accounts receivable, customers' demographics, or products' warranties. In each cell of the matrix an important information category value is inserted.

Using the Requirements Analysis for Planning

The results of the requirements analysis exercise are threefold. It identifies high-payoff information categories, it provides a basis for the architecture of IT, and it guides in resource allocation. Also, remember that many times the managers are not aware of the day-to-day requirements. They see only the big picture.

IDENTIFYING HIGH PAYOFFS. To determine which IT projects will produce the highest organizational payoff, the organization can identify categories with high importance-value scores, and should consider them first for feasibility. Planners use an information-categories-by-organizational-process matrix to identify high payoff, but this matrix does not indicate whether it is technically, economically, or operationally feasible to develop systems for each information category. The matrix merely indicates the relative importance of information. Feasibility studies and other project-related tasks must still be performed, as described in Chapter 14. This step requires substantial creativity (e.g., see Ruohonen and Higgins, 1998). In Section 8.6 we demonstrate how this is done for Web-based systems.

PROVIDING AN ARCHITECTURE. Clearly defining the intersection of information and processes helps an organization avoid separate, redundant information systems for different organizational processes. When an organization decides to improve information for one process, other processes that need such information can be taken into consideration. By completing the conceptual work first, an organization can identify information systems projects that offer the most benefit and lead to cohesive, integrated systems. The resulting systems are far better than the fragmented, piecemeal systems that are continually being reworked or abandoned because they do not mesh with the organization's general requirements. To develop such integrated systems requires systematic planning from the top down, rather than randomly from the bottom up, and this is done in the architecture phase.

GUIDANCE IN RESOURCE ALLOCATION. Once high-payoff areas of IT have been identified it is reasonable to give those areas high priority when the organization allocates resources. Such an allocation is described next.

Resource Allocation

Resource allocation, the third stage of the model of IT planning, consists of developing the hardware, software, data communications, facilities, personnel, and financial plans needed to execute the master development plan as defined in the requirements analysis. This stage provides the framework for technology and labor procurement, and it identifies the financial resources needed to provide appropriate service levels to users. The financial aspect will be discussed briefly here (with a more in-depth discussion in Chapter 13).

Resource allocation is a contentious process in most organizations because opportunities and requests for spending far exceed the available funds. This can lead to intense, highly political competition between organizational units, which makes it difficult to objectively identify the most desirable investments.

Funding requests from the ISD fall into two categories. Some projects and infrastructure are necessary in order for the organization to stay in business. For example, it may be imperative to purchase or upgrade hardware if the network, or disk drives, or the processor on the main computer are approaching capacity limits. Obtaining approval for this type of spending is largely a matter of communicating the gravity of the problems to decision makers.

On the other hand, the IT planning process identifies an information architecture that usually requires additional funding for less critical items: new projects, maintenance or upgrades of existing systems, and infrastructure to support these systems and future needs. Approval for projects in this category may become more difficult to obtain because the ISD is already receiving limited funding for mandatory projects.

After setting aside funds for the first category, the organization can use the remainder of the IT budget for projects related mainly to the improved information architecture. The organization can prioritize spending among items in the architecture developed by using information requirements analysis. In addition to formally allocating resources through budgeting decisions, an organization can use chargeback mechanisms to fund corporate-level projects. In a *chargeback system*, some or all of a system's cost is charged to users (see Chapter 13). In addition, management may encourage individual units to make their own decisions about IT expenses. Chapter 13 discusses chargeback, cost-benefit analysis, and other, more sophisticated analyses that can also be used to assess investments in individual IT projects as well as infrastructure.

Project Planning

The fourth and final stage of the model for IT planning is **project planning**. It provides an overall framework within which specific applications can be planned, scheduled, and controlled. Since this stage is associated with systems development, it will be covered in Chapter 14.

The relationship between the four stages of the IT model, the execution methods, and the output of each stage are shown in Figure 8.7. The figure summarizes the discussion in the previous sections and ties it in with the remainder of this chapter and to Chapters 13 and 14. A major output of the planning process is the IT architecture, which is discussed next.

8.4 Planning Information Technology Architectures

Information technology architecture is the field of study and practice devoted to understanding and deploying information systems components in the form of an *organizational infrastructure*. In the simplest view, an IT architecture consists of a description of the combination of hardware, software, data, personnel, and telecommunications elements within an organization, along with procedures to employ them.

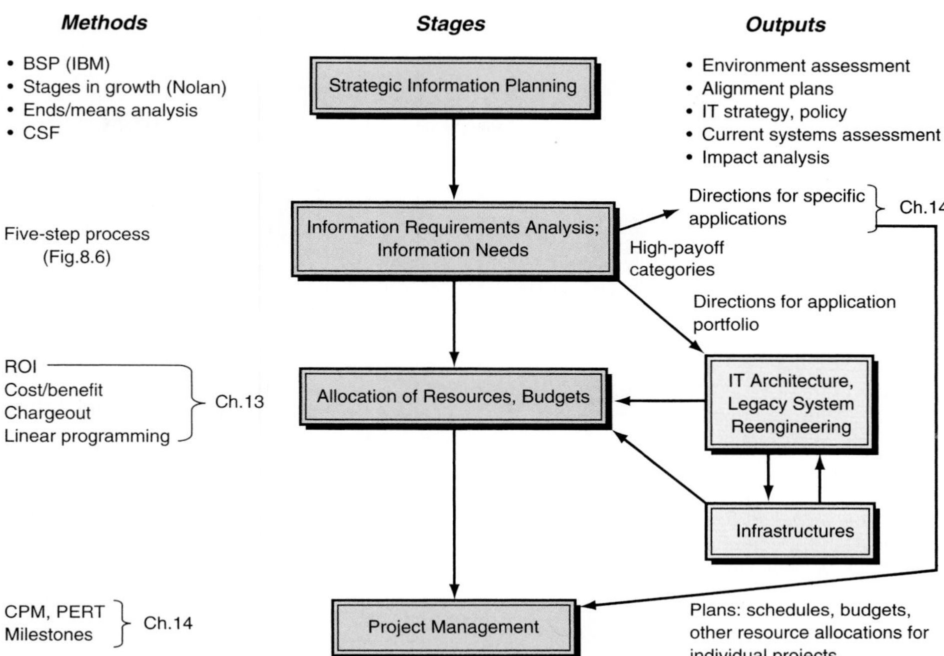

FIGURE 8.7 IT planning: methods, stages, and outputs.

An information architecture is a high-level, logical plan of the information requirements and the structures or integration of information resources needed to meet those requirements. An information technology architecture specifies the technological and organizational infrastructure that physically implements an information architecture.

Three types of technology architectures are described in Technology Guide 4: *centralized, noncentralized,* and *client/server.* In this section we discuss the general considerations relating to IT infrastructure and provide some guidelines for choosing among achitecture options. We conclude the section with a look at the issue of reengineering *legacy systems* (holdovers from earlier architectures).

IT Infrastructure Considerations

Different organizations have different IT infrastructure requirements. Broadbent et al. (1996) looked at how the characteristics and environments of organizations influenced their IT infrastructure. They identified several core *infrastructure services* provided in all of the firms, plus others provided by some of the firms. They also found the following four *infrastructure relationships* in a sample of 26 large firms:

1. ***Industry.*** Manufacturing firms use less IT infrastructure services than retail or financial firms.
2. ***Market volatility.*** Firms that need to change products quickly use more IT infrastructure services.
3. ***Business unit synergy.*** Firms that emphasize synergies (e.g., cross-selling) use more IT infrastructure services.
4. ***Strategy and planning.*** Firms that integrate IT and organizational planning, and track or monitor the achievement of strategic goals, use more IT infrastructure services.

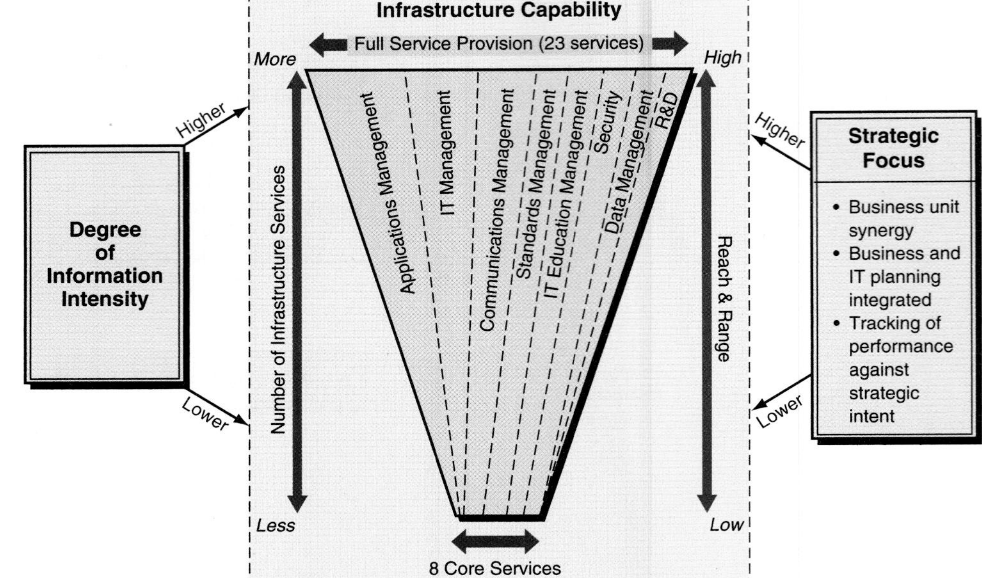

FIGURE 8.8 Model of relationship between firm context and IT infrastructure. (*Source:* Reprinted with permission from M. Broadbent, et al., "Firm Context and Patterns of IT Infrastructure Capability, *Proceedings of the 17th International Conference on Information Systems*, Cleveland, December 16–18, 1996, p. 186. Copyright © 1996/2001 IEEE.)

Based on analysis of their data, Broadbent et al. developed the model shown in Figure 8.8. This model indicates that two general factors influence infrastructure levels. The first factor is *information intensity,* the extent to which products or processes incorporate information. The second factor is *strategic focus,* the level of emphasis on strategy and planning. Firms with higher levels of these two factors use more IT infrastructure services, and have greater reach and range in their use of these services.

Choosing Among Architecture Options

A poorly organized IT architecture can disrupt a business by hindering or misdirecting information flows. Each organization—even within the same industry—has its own particular needs and preferences for information. Therefore each organization requires an IT architecture specifically designed and deployed for its use.

In today's computing environment, IT architectures are becoming increasingly complex, yet they still must be responsive to changing business needs. These requirements call for tough decisions about a number of architectural issues. The choices among *centralized computing, distributed computing,* and *blended computing* architectures are discussed below.

IN FAVOR OF CENTRALIZED COMPUTING. Centralized computing has been the foundation of corporate computing for over 30 years. **Centralized computing** puts all processing and control authority within one computer to which all other computing devices respond. With increasing use of **client/server** systems, however, the role of the mainframe computer has shifted toward a more collaborative relationship with other computing resources within an organization. Although some proponents of PCs claim that the mainframe is dead, many experts agree that the mainframe is likely to exist for many years, particularly as a repository for data that can be centrally maintained for enterprisewide use. Providing access to and analyzing very large quantities of data are uses for which mainframes are still very appropriate. This is especially important in banking, insurance, airlines, and large retailing. The Internet and intranets can be extremely useful in distributing information stored on mainframe (and smaller) computers.

Benefits of Centralized Computing. Centralized computing can exploit the economies of scale that arise whenever there are a large number of IT applications and users in an organization. It may be more cost-effective to have one large-scale computing resource that is used by many than it is to have many small-scale computing resources. The cost of a centralized facility can be divided among many users, usually reducing duplication of effort and more efficiently managing an operation (housing the computer, providing support services, etc.).

Centralized approaches can also offer easier control from an enterprise perspective. If important corporate data are stored on a centralized computing platform, a company is able to impose strict physical access controls to protect the data. When data are spread throughout an organization, securing and preserving data becomes much more difficult.

IN FAVOR OF DISTRIBUTED COMPUTING. A distributed approach argues that choices for computing are best handled at the point of the computing need; individual needs are best met with individualized computing. The rise in popularity of PCs, with their decreasing costs and increasing performance, has led many organizations to embrace **distributed computing**, giving users direct control over their own computing. Application data can be entered, verified, and maintained closer to its source.

Distributed computing can also offer a high degree of flexibility and desirable system redundancy. When an organization expands, it may be much easier and less expensive to add another local, distributed processor than to replace a centralized mainframe with an even larger mainframe. Moreover, a malfunctioning distributed computer ordinarily does not prevent other distributed computers from working, especially if data are partially or fully duplicated around the system, such as in the case of Lotus Notes/Domino or some intranets. (In contrast, a centralized approach has a single point of failure—the central computer. When it goes down, no one computes.) Consider an organization that sells from a catalog; if its order processing system goes down for a day in the holiday season, it could lose hundreds of thousands of dollars in sales. Also, a computer in a decentralized environment may be noticeably faster than a centralized computer very far away from a user.

IN FAVOR OF BLENDING CENTRALIZED AND DISTRIBUTED COMPUTING. As noted earlier, computing does not have to be entirely centralized or entirely distributed—it can be a blending of the two models. Many distributed systems are based on client/server architecture. In some circumstances, the mainframe (centralized resource) is viewed as a kind of peripheral device for other (distributed) computing resources. The mainframe can be a large file server that offers the economies of scale and data control that are desirable in most organizations, and yet still allows processing and handling of local needs via distributed computing resources. *What* to distribute *where* (and what *not* to distribute) then become key issues.

INFORMATION ARCHITECTURES AND END-USER COMPUTING. Like an automobile, a personal computer gives its user great flexibility, power, and freedom. But just as the user of an automobile needs access to an infrastructure of highways, the user of a personal computer needs access to an infrastructure of databases and communication networks, including the Internet and possibly intranets. Creating such an architecture for end-users invariably involves PC linkage issues.

There are five basic configurations of PCs for end users:

1. Centralized computing with the PC functioning as a "dumb terminal"
2. A single-user PC not connected to any other device
3. A single-user PC connected to other PCs or systems, using ad hoc telecommunications (such as dialup telephone connections)
4. Workgroup PCs connected to each other in a small *peer-to-peer network* (see Technology Guide 4)
5. Distributed computing with many PCs fully connected by LANs or an intranet

There are clear benefits and risks, but end-user computing with interconnected desktop PCs or network computers is inevitable. Given this inevitability, it is important that organizations maximize corporate business benefits and, at the same time, minimize risks and undue constraints on user initiative, business knowledge, and unity. (For more on the development of end-user computing, see Chapter 14.)

Reengineering Legacy Systems

Holdovers of earlier architectures that are still in use after an organization migrates to a new architecture are described as **legacy systems**. These systems may continue in use even after an organization switches to an architecture that is different from, and possibly incompatible with, the architectures on which they are based. They may still be capable of meeting business needs, and might not require any immediate changes. Or they may be in need of reengineering to meet some current business needs, requiring significant changes. Each legacy system has to be examined on its own merits, and a judgment made regarding the current and future value of the system to the organization. This type of decision—to keep, improve, or replace—can present management with agonizing alternatives. On one hand, keeping a legacy system active offers stability and return on previous investments ("If it ain't broke, don't fix it"). On the other hand, increasing processing demands and high operational costs make replacement attractive if not imperative. Newer systems, however, may be more risky and less robust.

Reverse engineering is the process of examining systems to determine their present status, and to identify what changes are necessary to allow the system to meet current and future business needs. The results of this process can then guide the redesign and redevelopment of the system. Some reverse engineering tools, when applied to legacy systems, automatically generate up-to-date documentation. Other tools in this category help programmers convert code in older programs into a more efficient form.

Legacy systems are not just mainframe systems. A legacy system might consist of PC programs that need to be reengineered and "ported" to a mainframe, a process that is called *upsizing* the system. Or a legacy system might be a mainframe application that needs to be reengineered and "rehosted" onto PCs, an example of *downsizing* a system. In each instance, a business is trying to effectively "rightsize" a legacy system to meet evolving business requirements.

Finally, but perhaps most importantly, organizations should reengineer legacy systems in concert with business process reengineering (refer to the "retooling" in Section 8.7). Changes to the computerized or automated side of a business should synchronize with changes in other business processes. While reengineering legacy systems might be justified solely on a cost or efficiency basis, significant business gains can also be made when this effort is a coordinated part of reengineering the entire business to improve efficiency and effectiveness.

8.5 SOME ISSUES IN IT PLANNING

IT planning is a complex process. Of the many special topics in this category, we have elected to focus on IT planning in interorganizational and international systems. Information technology planning may get more complicated when several organizations are involved, as well as when we deal with multinational corporations.

Planning for Interorganizational Systems

Internal information systems of business partners must talk with each other effectively and efficiently. In Chapter 4 we introduced IT technologies such as EDI, e-mail, and extranets that facilitate communication and collaboration between companies. IT planning that involves several organizations may be complex. The problem is that some information systems may involve hundreds or even thousands of business partners. IT planners in such a case should use focus groups of customers, suppliers, and other business partners, especially during the strategic information planning as well as during the information requirements analysis.

Planning for project management of interorganization systems (IOSs) can be fairly complex. IT planners may create virtual planning teams that will work together on projects such as extranets or EDI. Such cooperation is especially important in strategic planning that involves infrastructure. Questions such as who is going to pay for what can become critical factors in cost/benefit analysis and justification of information systems applications.

A comprehensive study of global IT strategic planning was conducted by Curry and Ferguson (2000). In order to increase the success of such planning, they suggest that organizations reduce the planning horizon to two to three years (from three to five) and that they increase the collaboration between the IT planners and end users.

Examples of joint planning for interorganizational systems can include using an extended supply chain approach and adopting the same enterprise software. If company A will use software from SAP and company B will use Oracle software, there could be additional expenses for connecting these softwares to each other.

IT Planning for Multinational Corporations

Multinational corporations face a complex legal, political, and social environment, which complicates corporate IT planning. Therefore, many multinational companies prefer to decentralize their IT planning and operations, empowering their local IT managers. However, such a policy may be self-defeating since communication, coordination, and collaboration among decentralized business units may require large expenses. ExxonMobil Corporation was forced to centralize its IT operations because of such high expenditures, as shown in the *IT at Work* example that follows on the next page.

IT at Work

IT PLANNING AND CENTRALIZATION AT EXXONMOBIL

Integrating IT ...in Production & Operations Management

www.exxonmobil.com

With sales over $234 billion a year and operations in over 125 countries, ExxonMobil is a true multinational corporation. The company, then Mobil Oil Corporation, originally preferred to decentralize its information resources. Spending $1 billion a year on IT, the company realized that in the distributed environment, local managers were making IT decisions independent of the decisions made in other business units. Communication among business units was poor, resources were wasted, and end users complained. It became clear that it was necessary to reengineer the corporate IT.

The process started with the establishment of a planning team that worked with IT consultants. Analysis of the existing system revealed many duplications and redundancies. The team recommended a new, centralized architecture based on one operating system and a standard set of applications. The planning team estimated a 40 percent reduction in the IS staff and a huge saving in software purchasing cost, due to the large quantity purchased (volume discounts). To move to the centralized system, Mobil consolidated six mainframe data centers into two. All pending IT projects were discontinued, and an evaluation of all IS staff was done to determine their competence levels. The IS staff was reduced from 4,400 to 2,400 in 1997. To ensure success, the company appointed its first-ever CIO, Ellen McCoy. She introduced a strict system for examining requests for nonstandard hardware and software. Furthermore, nonstandard items must be paid for only from end-user accounts.

By educating both functional managers and IS managers about IS and business issues, McCoy facilitated a better understanding and cooperation in the managerial ranks.

For Further Exploration: Why was it possible to reduce the IS staff? What are the benefits of the centralized architecture?

Source: Condensed from D. Gross, "Getting the Lead Out," *CIO,* April 15, 1997.

An important issue is information security, which is difficult to implement due to the long distances involved and the different legal aspects in different countries.

8.6 PLANNING FOR WEB-BASED SYSTEMS AND E-COMMERCE

Strategic planning for Web-based systems can be viewed as a subset of IT strategic planning. However, in many cases it is done independently of IT planning. Let's refer to this process as *e-planning* and examine some of its features.

IT planning in this chapter refers mostly to corporate planning of IT infrastructure rather than to applications planning. In contrast, e-planning may touch on EC infrastructure at times, but mostly it deals with uncovering opportunities and deciding on an applications portfolio (see Turban et al., 2002). One reason is that some of the infrastructure may be already in place, as part of the IT infrastructure. Other connections between IT planning and e-planning are:

- Web applications may replace traditional IT applications for improving their operations.
- Web applications must be integrated with legacy systems, ERP, etc.
- The e-commerce unit may report to the CIO.
- The ISD and the e-commerce project may compete for limited resources.
- Some Web-based applications are designed to directly support the IT strategy and goals.

Despite this strong connection, e-planning may be conducted as a separate planning exercise. In such a case, ISD people will participate in the steering committee together with end users. Of course, alignment between the two processes is needed. (For details, see Turban et al., 2002, Chapter 16.) One reason for such separation is that technology is an enabler of e-commerce, but the major objective of e-commerce is to rejuvenate organizations. If the process is controlled by IT people, the success of e-commerce may be constrained. Another reason for the separation is that e-planning is usually less formal, and it must be done quickly. Furthermore, due to rapid changes the e-planning must be more flexible.

Planning for Web-based individual applications is very similar to the planning of any IT application. However, in the macro level of planning, the emphasis is different. The areas where more attention is given in e-planning are the applications portfolio, risk analysis, and planning issues such as the use of metrics. Let's elaborate.

Applications Portfolio

The importance of the applications portfolio in regular IT planning may be declining. Most organizations have their mission-critical systems already in place, and IT activities are fairly distributed. In e-commerce, however, most organizations are starting from scratch. The cost of building systems is high, and so is the risk. Therefore it is advisable to conduct centralized EC planning and to select appropriate applications and prioritize them. A methodology to do just that was proposed by Tjan (2001).

TJAN'S PORTFOLIO STRATEGY. Tjan (2001) adopted a business project portfolio applications approach to create an Internet portfolio planning matrix. (Also see Boar, 2000.) However, instead of trading off industry growth and market position, here the strategy is based on *company fit,* which can be either low or high, and the project's *viability*, which can also be low or high. Together these create an *Internet portfolio map (matrix).*

A project's *viability* can be assessed by four criteria: market-value potential, time to positive cash flow, personnel requirements, and funding requirements. EC initiatives such as a B2B procurement site, a B2C store, or a portal for kids, for example, can be evaluated on a scale of 1 to 100, for each of the four metrics. Then, an average score (simple average) for each metric is computed. For *fit,* the following criteria are used: alignment with core capabilities, alignment with other company initiatives, fit with organizational structure, fit with company's culture and values, and ease of technical implementation. Again, each EC initiative is assessed on a scale of 1 to 100 (or on a qualitative scale of high, medium, low), and an average is computed. The various initiatives are then mapped on the *Internet portfolio matrix,* based on the two average scores. The Internet matrix is divided into four cells, as shown in Figure 8.9 (page 358). If both *viability* and *fit* are low, the project is killed. If both are high, then the project is adopted. If *fit* is high, but *viability* is low, the project is sent to redesign. Finally, if the *fit* is low but the *viability* is high, the project is to be sold, or spun off. The figure shows how several applications were rated for an e-marketplace company for toys in Hong Kong.

The method introduces a systematic approach to EC project selection. The assessment of the points per criterion can be done by several experts to ensure quality. Cases where there is more agreement can be considered with more confidence. Organizations can add their own criteria to the methodology.

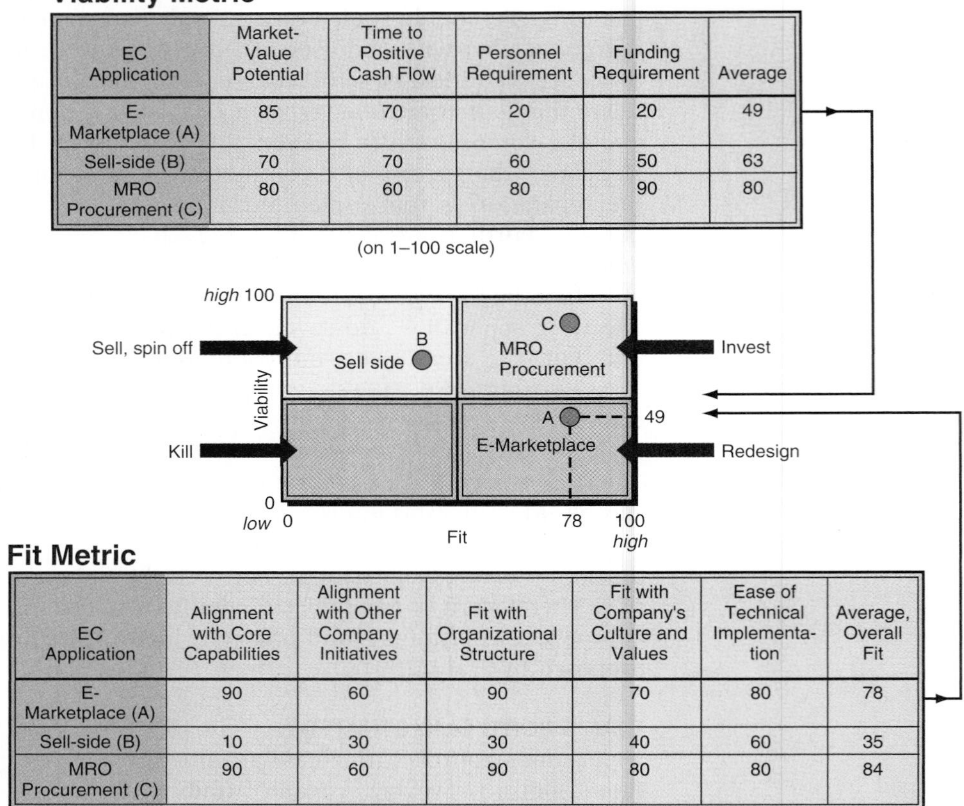

Viability Metric

EC Application	Market-Value Potential	Time to Positive Cash Flow	Personnel Requirement	Funding Requirement	Average
E-Marketplace (A)	85	70	20	20	49
Sell-side (B)	70	70	60	50	63
MRO Procurement (C)	80	60	80	90	80

(on 1–100 scale)

Fit Metric

EC Application	Alignment with Core Capabilities	Alignment with Other Company Initiatives	Fit with Organizational Structure	Fit with Company's Culture and Values	Ease of Technical Implementation	Average, Overall Fit
E-Marketplace (A)	90	60	90	70	80	78
Sell-side (B)	10	30	30	40	60	35
MRO Procurement (C)	90	60	90	80	80	84

(on 1–100 scale)

FIGURE 8.9 Application portfolio analysis for a toy distributor. Potential applications: (A) create e-marketplace; (B) direct sale (sell-side); and (C) MRO procurement. The average results determine the location on the grid. Results (at center): invest in project C; redesign project A so it will become viable; and sell the idea (B) to someone else since it does not pay to reengineer the company. (*Source:* Drawn by E. Turban.)

Risk Analysis

The degree of risk of some Web-based systems is very high, and such risk often leads to failure. For example, Disney Inc. aborted two major EC initiatives in 2000. First, Disney closed its e-toy company (*smartkid.com*). Second, it closed its company (*go.com*) that was managing all of Disney's EC initiatives. The loss was many millions of dollars. Failures of IT applications do not usually cost so much money, especially if they are not enterprisewide in nature. Conducting a risk analysis could reduce the chance of failures.

Planning Issues

Several strategic planning issues are unique to the Web environment. Each of these may involve IT infrastructure, but the market and organizational implications may be more important. Here are some examples:

- ***Who and where?*** Should the EC initiatives be conducted in a completely independent division or even a separate company?
- ***Use of metrics.*** EC planning is difficult because the field is evolving, the history is brief, and few planners have experience. Therefore it is desirable to

use industry standards, also known as **metrics**, for executing various steps of the planning process (see Plant, 2000).

- ***Learn from failures.*** During 2000/2001 there were many EC failures, both major initiatives and whole companies. Planners should study such failures, to learn what went wrong in the hopes of avoiding such problems in the future. (For lessons for planners, see Useem, 2000; Agrawal et al., 2001; and Chapter 5 of this book.)
- ***Use a different planning process.*** The Web environment requires a different planning process, as illustrated by Turban et al. (2002).
- ***Integration.*** Information systems strategic planning must integrate, in many cases, e-business and knowledge management (see Galliers, 1999, for details).

Planning in a Turbulent Environment

The Web environment is very turbulent. Some people question the validity of formal planning in such an environment. Others insist that the turbulence makes formal planning a necessity. Samela et al. (2000) investigated the issue in two organizations and concluded that a formal comprehensive approach may be more beneficial than not having a formal plan. Of course, generalizing from only two organizations may not tell the whole story.

Whether an organization uses formal planning for the Web environment or not, the planning of Web systems frequently requires redesign of business processes, our next topic.

8.7 THE NEED FOR BUSINESS PROCESS REENGINEERING AND THE ROLE OF IT*

The major environmental pressures described in Chapter 1 were summarized by Hammer and Champy (1993) as the *three C's*—customers, competition, and change.

1. ***Customers*** today know what they want, what they are willing to pay, and how to get products and services on their own terms.
2. ***Competition*** is generally increasing with respect to price, quality, selection, service, and promptness of delivery. Removal of trade barriers, increased international cooperation, and the creation of technological innovations cause competition to intensify.
3. ***Change*** continues to occur. Markets, products, services, technology, the business environment, and people keep changing, frequently in an unpredictable and significant manner.

Some of the old methods of organizational responses do not always work in this environment. Let's look at a typical example of a persistent organizational problem.

The Problem of the Stovepipe

All organizations have both horizontal and vertical dimensions. The organization's layers (usually top, middle, and supervisory management) define the horizontal dimensions; the organization's functional departments define the vertical dimensions.

*Note: A tutorial chapter about BPR and IT is available in Chapter 8 on our Web site.

The *vertical dimension* of the organization, primarily focused on functional specialization, has caused many problems in organizations as they have tried to move into the information-based economy. Such problems are sometimes referred to as "stovepipes," in recognition of their vertical nature. Because of the vertical structure of organizations, there is a lack of effective cooperation between functional areas. Interaction among vertical functions (across the stovepipes) turns out to be crucial in order for organizations to operate efficiently and effectively.

Often, the difference between duties of functional units and business processes in an organization is confused. Figure 8.10 illustrates how an organization can have vertical functions but have processes that transcend departmental boundaries. These are sometimes referred to as **cross-functional activities**. Product development, order processing, planning, sourcing, control, and customer service are processes that can transcend the functional boundaries of distribution, purchasing, research and development, manufacturing, and sales.

Here is an example of a stovepipe problem: A customer places an order with Sales. After a few days, she calls Sales to find out the status of the order. Sales calls various departments. Frequently, it is difficult to trace the order. People push the order from place to place and feel only a small sense of responsibility and accountability, so Sales may not be able to give the customer an answer in time, or may even give an incorrect answer. The problem of the stovepipe can intensify if the supporting information systems are improperly structured.

Focusing on vertical functions and their corresponding information systems to support the business has resulted in fragmented, piecemeal information systems that operate in a way in which the "left hand doesn't know what the right hand is doing." Integration of information is required for good decision making. Achieving it is one of the goals of *business process reengineering (BPR).*

WHAT IS BPR? **Business process reengineering (BPR)** refers to a situation in which an organization fundamentally and radically redesigns its business process to achieve dramatic improvement. Initially, attention was given to complete restructuring of organizations (Hammer and Champy, 1993). Later on, the con-

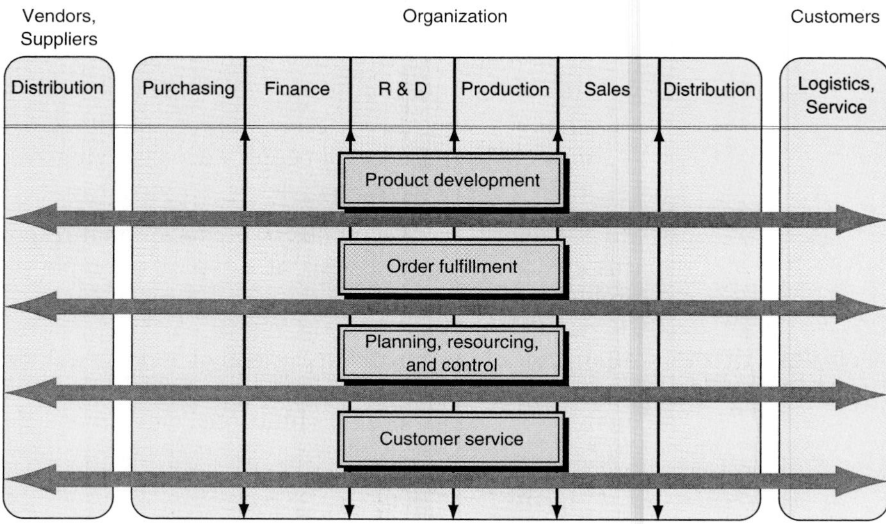

FIGURE 8.10 Business processes across functional areas and organizational boundaries.

cept was changed due to failures of BPR projects (e.g., Sarker and Lee, 1999) and the emergence of Web-based applications that solved many of the problems that BPR was supposed to solve. Today, BPR can focus on anything from complete restructuring of an organization to reengineering or at least the redesign of individual processes (see El Sawy, 2001). The reengineering of individual processes, especially of the procurement process, became a necessity for many companies aspiring to transform themselves to e-businesses.

The conduct of a comprehensive BPR, or even a one-process redesign, is almost always enabled by IT. One the major areas of related IT activities is the need for information integration.

Need for Information Integration

One objective of BPR is to overcome problems such as that of the stovepipe by redesigning and integrating the fragmented information systems. Let's explain.

Besides creating inefficient redundancies, information systems developed along departmental or functional boundaries cause difficulties in the *integration* of information that is required for decision making. A loan officer, for instance, may want to check information pertaining to a loan applicant's savings accounts. However, frequently there is no linkage to these data from the loan system. Indeed, the loan officer may have to ask the loan applicant if he or she has a savings account with the bank and what the account number is.

Or, consider a case where the management of a bank wants to offer more mortgage loans to utilize large savings deposits. Management decides to send letters encouraging specific customers to consider buying homes, using convenient financing available through the bank. Management also decides that the best customers to whom to send such letters are the following:

- Customers who do not currently have mortgage loans or who have loans for a very small percentage of the value of their homes
- Customers who have good checking account records (i.e., few or no overdrafts)
- Customers with sufficient funds in their savings accounts to make a down payment on a home
- Customers with good payment records on installment loans with the bank

Because the data necessary to identify such customers may be available in different files of different information systems, there may be no convenient or economical way to integrate them. Using innovations such as *data warehouses* and special integrated software can be helpful, but expensive. Therefore, extensive programming and clerical work are required to satisfy such an information request. The scenario of the bank can be translated into other organizational settings.

Integration should cross not only departmental boundaries but also organizational ones, reaching suppliers and customers. Namely, it should work along the *extended supply chain*. This is especially important in company-centric B2B markets and in B2B exchanges (see Chapter 5). An example of an internal integration followed by an integration with dealers is provided in the *IT at Work* case on page 362.

The integration of an organization's information systems enables BPR innovations such as the introduction of a single point of contact for customers, called a *case manager* or a *deal structurer*. We can see how this single point of contact

IT at Work

VW OF MEXICO SHIFTED TO E-PROCUREMENT

...in Production and Operations Management

www.vw.com.mex

Facing strong competition and the North American Free Trade Agreement (NAFTA) environment, Volkswagen of Mexico turned to IT. In 1996, VW implemented an enterprise resource planning system, using SAP R/3 software. By 1998, the company integrated its enterprise system, which was used to cut inventory and production costs, with an extranet, which streamlined spare-parts ordering by its dealers in Mexico. The major reason for the project is the increased demand that resulted from NAFTA and from VW's decision to market the Beetle (called the "New Beetle") in the United States and Canada. These cars are manufactured in Mexico, where labor and services are cheaper.

The integrated system allows people at every level of the company, from manufacturing to car servicing at the dealership, to take advantage of the SAP system. The SAP system integrates the manufacturing, finance, marketing, and other departments among themselves and, thanks to the extranet, now also links these departments with the dealers and business partners. Flora Lopez, production software manager, said that the R/3 system orchestrates all the different areas of the manufacturing and parts-ordering tasks, such as supplier orders, reception, warehousing, client orders, packing, and billing. By tapping into R/3 modules, the dealers can cut the turnaround time for ordering spare parts from 10 days to fewer than 5—a very important competitive advantage. The dealers can check the status of their orders on the computer.

One problem with the integrated system is that some of the dealers in Mexico are not ready to buy, install, and use computers. However, the fact that the new system means a low inventory level, which can save the dealers considerable money, is motivating them to join in. The company projects the application will result in $50 million in cost savings over three years for the dealers.

For Further Exploration: Can VW's suppliers be added to the system? What competitive advantage can be realized with such an addition?

Source: Condensed from *PC Week*, January 12, 1998, pp. 29, 39.

works by looking at a credit-approval process at IBM. The old process took seven days and eight steps. It involved creation of a paper folder that was routed, sequentially, through four departments (sales, credit check, business practices, finance, and back to sales). In the redesigned process, one person, the deal structurer, conducts all the necessary tasks. This one generalist replaces four specialists. To enable one person to execute the above steps, a simple DSS provides the deal structurer with the guidance needed. The program guides the generalist in finding information in the databases, plugging numbers into an evaluation model, and pulling standardized clauses—"boilerplate"—from a file. For difficult situations, the generalist can get help from a specialist. As a result, the turnaround time has been slashed from seven days to four hours!

The Enabling Role of Information Technology in BPR

IT has been used for several decades to improve productivity and quality by automating existing processes. However, when it comes to reengineering, the traditional process of looking at problems first and then seeking technology solutions for them needs to be reversed. Now it is necessary first to recognize powerful solutions that BPR makes possible, and then to seek the process that can be helped by it. Such an approach requires *inductive* rather than *deductive* thinking. It requires innovation, since a company may be looking for problems it does not even know exist.

IT can break old rules that limit the manner in which work is performed. Some typical rules are given in Table 8.1. IT-supported BPR examples can be found in any industry, private or public. The role of IT in redesigning business

TABLE 8.1 Changes in Business Processes Brought by IT

Old Rule	Intervening Technology	New Rule
Information appears in only one place at one time.	Shared databases, client/server architecture, Internet, intranets	Information appears simultaneously wherever needed.
Only an expert can perform complex work.	Expert systems, neural computing	Novices can perform complex work.
Business must be either centralized or distributed.	Telecommunications and networks: client/server, intranet	Business can be both centralized and distributed.
Only managers make decisions.	Decision support systems, enterprise support systems, expert systems	Decision making is part of everyone's job.
Field personnel need offices to receive, send, store, and process information.	Wireless communication and portable computers, the Web, electronic mail	Field personnel can manage information from any location.
The best contact with potential buyers is a personal contact.	Interactive videodisk, desktop teleconferencing, electronic mail	The best contact is the one that is most cost-effective.
You have to locate items manually.	Tracking technology, groupware, workflow software, search engines	Items are located automatically.
Plans get revised periodically.	High-performance computing systems, intelligent agents	Plans get revised instantaneously whenever needed.
People must come to one place to work together.	Groupware and group support systems, telecommunications, electronic mail, client/server	People can work together while at different locations.
Customized products and services are expensive and take a long time to develop.	CAD/CAM, CASE tools, online systems for JIT decision making, expert systems	Customized products can be made quickly and inexpensively (mass customization).
A long period of time is spanned between the inception of an idea and its implementation (time-to-market).	CAD/CAM, electronic data interchange, groupware, imaging (document) processing	Time-to-market can be reduced by 90 percent.
Organizations and processes are information-based.	Artificial intelligence, expert systems	Organizations and processes are knowledge-based.
Move labor to countries where labor is inexpensive (off-shore production).	Robots, imaging technologies, object-oriented programming, expert systems, geographical information systems (GIS)	Work can be done in countries with high wages and salaries.

Source: Compiled from M. Hammer and J. Champy, *Re-engineering the Corporation* (New York: Harper Business, 1993).

processes can be very critical and is increasing due to the Internet/intranet. Geoffrey (1996) provides several examples of how intranets have *rescued* BPR projects.

Retooling of IT for BPR

Redesign of business processes often means a need to change some or all of the organizational information systems. The reason for this is that information systems designed along hierarchical (vertical) lines are usually ineffective in supporting the redesigned organization. Therefore, it is often necessary to redesign the information systems. This process is referred to as *retooling*.

Retooling focuses on making sure the information systems are responsive to the processes-reengineering effort and to the use of e-commerce. Many organizations found that once they realized they had a problem and wanted to do something about it, their information systems function could not accommodate the desired changes. For example, a government agency in Singapore decided to defer a badly needed BPR project when it discovered that it would cost over $15 million just to rewrite the applicable computer programs.

To retool for reengineering, a key issue is getting a good understanding of the current installed base of information systems applications and databases. It is also important to understand the existing infrastructure in terms of computing equipment, networks, and the like, and their relationships to the current available software, procedures, and data. Another key issue is an assessment of what the ideal IT architecture would be for the organization in terms of hardware and software, as well as an appropriate information architecture.

During this stage, it is very important to *benchmark* the technology being used in the organization against what the best competitors are using. It is also imperative to find out what the latest technologies are and determine in what direction the organization needs to go. For an example of a massive IT retooling in a public agency where the technology enabled the company to reengineer all its major business processes, see Tung and Turban (1996).

IT INFRASTRUCTURE AND BPR. Business-process redesign is a challenging tool for transforming organizations. Information technology plays an important role by either enabling or constraining successful BPR. The links between firmwide IT infrastructure and business-process change were explored by Broadbent et al. (1999). They found that IT infrastructure is the base foundation of the IT portfolio, which is shared throughout the firm in the form of reliable services, and is usually coordinated by the IS group. Exploratory case analysis of four firms was used to understand the ways IT infrastructure contributes to success in implementing BPR. The researchers found that all firms needed a basic level of IT infrastructure capability to implement BPR. The firms that had developed a higher level of IT infrastructure capabilities, before or concurrent with undertaking business process redesign, were able to implement extensive changes to their business processes over relatively short time frames.

THE TOOLS FOR BPR. A large variety of IT tools can be used to support BPR and organizational transformation. The major categories of support tools are:

- ***Simulation and visual simulation tools.*** Simulation is essential to support the modeling activities of BPR. In addition to conventional simulation and visual simulation tools, there are simulation tools that are specifically oriented for BPR such as SIMPROCESS (from CACI), ProModel (from ProModel Corp.), BPSimulator (from Technology Economics), Witness (from Visual Interactive Systems, Inc.), and BPR Workflow (see El Sawy, 2001).
- ***Flow diagrams.*** Flow diagrams can be made with CASE tools or other systems development charting tools. They can also be made by specialized BPR tools that are usually integrated with other tools.
- ***Application development tools.*** BPR applications can be built with some of the tools described in Chapter 14.
- ***Work analysis.*** Analyzing both existing processes and proposed solutions can be accomplished with tools that conduct forecasting, risk analysis, and optimization, such as I-think (from Performance Systems, Inc.) and BizCase and Turbo SPR (from SRA International).

- ***Integrated tool kits.*** Several integrated tool kits are available to support BPR. ERP software such as SAP R/3 provides for BPR.
- ***Workflow software.*** In redesigning business processes, it is usually necessary to analyze the work to be done and the manner in which it flows from one place to another. A workflow system is a powerful business process automation tool that places system controls in the hands of end-user departments. Not only does workflow automate business processes, it also provides a quality interface between business systems. As a result, workflow installations have evolved into enterprisewide computing solutions at major companies. There are three types of workflow software: *administrative*—expense reports, travel requests, and messages; *ad hoc*—product brochures, sales proposals, and strategic plans; and *production*—credit card mailings, mortgage loans, and insurance claims.
- ***Business process design.*** New IT architecture is designed around business processes rather than around the traditional application hierarchy of most functional applications. (For details see *acc-sys.net.*)
- ***Comprehensive modeling tools.*** Several companies provide software products that model, simulate, and manage business processes.
- ***Other tools.*** Several special tools were designed to plan and manage the BPR process and the organization transformation. Information tools and technologies can also be part of the BPR solution itself. For example, CAD/CAM and imaging technologies contribute to cycle time reduction; expert systems support case managers and mass customization; and *cognitive maps* can support the redesign process (see Kwahk and Kim, 1999).

8.8 RESTRUCTURING PROCESSES AND ORGANIZATIONS

Reengineering efforts involve many activities, four of which are described in this section: redesign of processes, mass customization, cycle time reduction, and restructuring the entire organization. We also look at some BPR failures.

Redesign of Processes

BPR efforts frequently involve only one or a few processes. One of the most publicized examples of business process redesign is the accounts payable process at Ford Motor Company described in the *IT at Work* on page 366. Ford's example demonstrates changes in a simple process. Khan (2000) describes the reengineering of an air cargo process which was much more complicated and involved several IT tools. Let's look now at some impacts of BPR.

From Mass Production to Mass Customization

One of the most successful models of e-commerce is mass customization. It supplements or even replaces one of the most innovative concepts of the Industrial Revolution, *mass production.* In mass production, a company produces a large quantity of an identical standard product. The product is then stored for future distribution to many customers. Because the concept of mass production results in a low cost, products are relatively inexpensive; they are sold in department or specialty stores to unknown customers. The concept of mass production was adapted to thousands of products, ranging from simple watches to major appliances, vehicles, and computers.

IT at Work

REENGINEERING PROCESSES AT FORD MOTOR COMPANY

www.ford.com

As part of its productivity improvement efforts, the management of Ford Motor Company put its North American Accounts Payable Department under the microscope in search of ways to cut costs. Management thought that by streamlining processes and installing new computer systems, it could reduce the head count by some 20 percent, to 400 people.

But after visiting Mazda's payables department (Ford is part owner of Mazda), Ford managers increased their goal: perform accounts payable with only 100 clerks. Analysis of Ford's existing system revealed that when the purchasing department wrote a purchase order, it sent a copy to accounts payable. Later, when material control received the goods, it sent a copy of the receiving document to accounts payable. Meanwhile, the vendor also sent an invoice to accounts payable. If the purchase order, receiving document, and invoice matched, then accounts payable issued a payment. Unfortunately, the department spent most of its time on the many mismatches. To prevent them, Ford instituted "invoiceless processing." Now, when the purchasing department initiates an order, it enters the information into an online database. It does not send a copy of the purchase order to anyone. The vendor receives notification through an EDI.

When the goods arrive at the receiving dock, the receiving clerk checks the database to see whether the goods correspond to an outstanding purchase order. If so, he or she accepts them and enters the transaction into the computer system. (If there is no database entry for the received goods, or if there is a mismatch, the clerk returns the goods.)

Under the old procedures, the accounting department had to match 14 data items among the receipt record, the purchase order, and the invoice before it could issue payment to the vendor. The new approach requires matching only four items—part number, amount, unit of measure, and supplier code—between the purchase order and the receipt record. The matching is done automatically, and the computer prepares the check, which accounts payable sends to the vendor (or an electronic transfer is made). There are no invoices to worry about since Ford has asked its vendors not to send them. The reengineered system as compared to the old one is shown in the figure below.

Ford did not settle for the modest increases it first envisioned. Instead it opted for a radical change, and it achieved dramatic improvement: a 75 percent reduction in head count, not the 20 percent it would have achieved with a conventional improvement program. And since there are no discrepancies between the financial record and physical record, material control is simpler, receipts are more likely to be correct, and financial information is more accurate.

For Further Exploration: How did the EDI help attain the reduction? What other support was provided by IT?

Source: Condensed from Hammer and Champy, *Reengineering the Corporation* (New York: *Harper Business*, 1993).

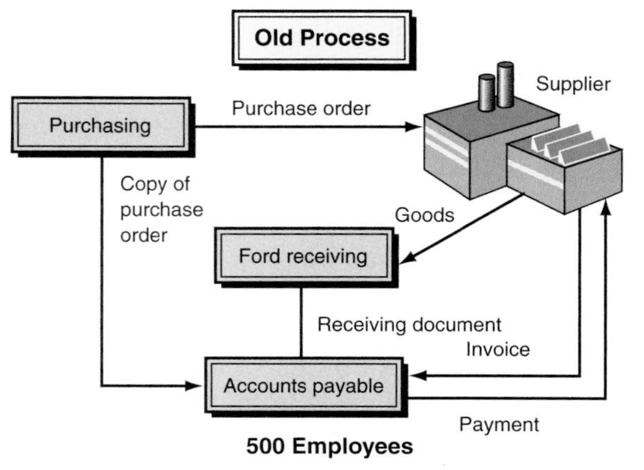

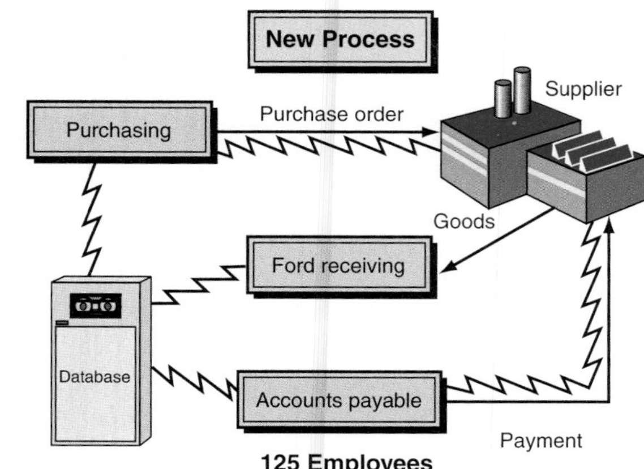

Reengineering processes at Ford Motor Company.

A major change in marketing started about 30 years ago with the increased competition between automobile manufacturers. Customers were able to select "options," such as an air conditioner or automatic transmission. Manufacturers collected the customized orders. Once they accumulated enough similar orders to justify manufacturing the customized product, they produced the items. The result was a waiting time of several months. A similar strategy was developed in other relatively expensive products. However, today's customers are not willing to wait so long, and to gain a competitive edge, companies are introducing mass customization.

The concept **mass customization** involves production of large quantities of customized items, as Dell is doing with personal computers (e.g., see Pine and Davis, 1999, and Gilmore and Pine, 2000). Mass customization enables a company to provide flexible and quick responsiveness to a customer's needs, at a low cost and with high quality. It is made possible by allowing fast and inexpensive production changes, by reducing the ordering and sales cycle time using e-commerce, and by shortening the production time (e.g., by using prefabricated parts and modules).

Mass customization, according to Pine and Gilmore (1997) and Gilmore and Pine (2000), can be facilitated by the Web in four different approaches, for which they give the following examples.

1. ***Collaborative customizers*** establish a dialogue with individual customers to help them figure out what they want to buy. For example, *Nike.com* allows you to customize sneakers, and at *Jaguar.com* you can customize a car. Dell (*dell.com*) uses this approach for its PCs, as do most car manufacturers. The Web is an ideal tool for such customization (see Chapter 5).
2. ***Adaptive customizers*** refers to offering one standard but customizable product that is designed so users can alter it themselves. A Web example might be an e-grocery that creates a learning relationship with its customers. With each interaction and service, the site becomes more tailored to the customer's needs.
3. ***Cosmetic customizers*** present a standard product differently to different customers. This approach is ideal when customers use a product the same way and differ only in how they want it presented. The product doesn't change—it's really the packaging or sizes that differ. A Web example is Interactive Custom Clothing (*ic3d.com*), which tailors jeans to your specifications over the Web.
4. ***Transparent customizers*** provide customers with unique goods or services without letting them know that these products have been customized for them. This involves adapting a product for you based upon observed behavior. One example is BOC Gases Americas (*boc.com*), of Murray Hill, New Jersey, whose parent company, The BOC Group, has been tailoring its Web catalog of gas products to clientele, utilizing knowledge of their previous purchases.

MASS CUSTOMIZATION AND E-COMMERCE. According to Turban et al. (2002), electronic commerce transforms the supply chain from a traditional *push model* to a *pull model*. In the push model, the business process starts with manufacturing and ends with consumers buying the products or services. In the pull model (see Figure 8.11 on page 368), the process starts with the consumer ordering the

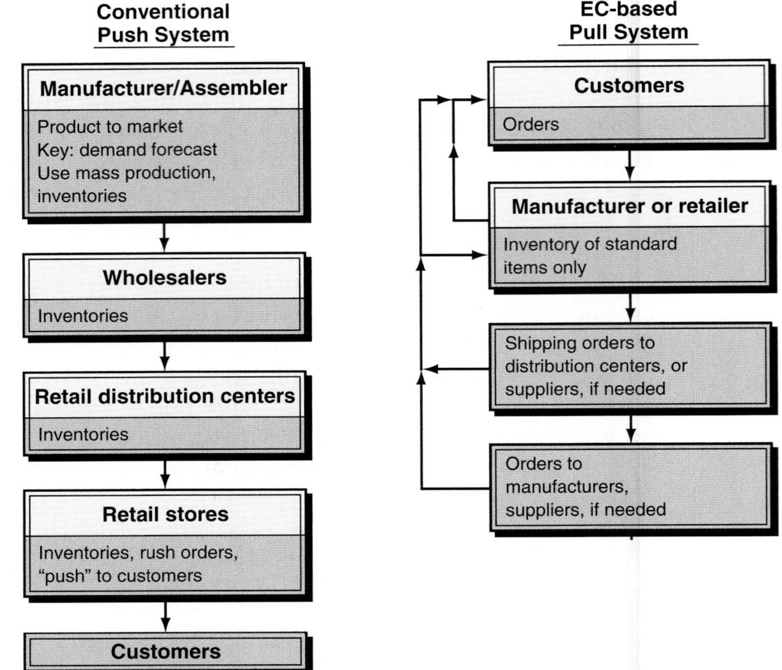

FIGURE 8.11 Push-based supply chain versus pull-based supply chain. (*Source:* Drawn by E. Turban.)

product (or service) and ends with the manufacturer making it. The pull model enables customization since orders are taken first. By organizing production to handle a large volume, mass customization is achieved. Dell Computer's success, for example, is basically due to reorganizing the supply chain as a pull system.

Cycle Time Reduction

Cycle time refers to the time it takes to complete a process from beginning to end. As discussed earlier, competition today focuses not only on cost and quality, but also on time. Time is recognized as a major element that provides competitive advantage, and **cycle time reduction** is a major business objective.

The success of Federal Express, for example, is clearly attributable to its ability to reduce the delivery time of packages. It does this by using complex computer-supported systems that allow flexible planning, organization, and control (see Wetherbe, 1996). The comeback of Chrysler Corporation and its success in the 1990s can be attributed largely to its "technology center," which brought about a more than 30 percent reduction in its time to market (the time from beginning the design of a new model to the delivery of the car). Boeing Corporation reengineered its design of airplanes by moving to total computerization. The first airplane designed in this manner was the Boeing 777. In a fundamental change to Boeing's processes, a physical prototype was never built. In addition to reducing the cycle time, Boeing was able to improve quality and reduce costs. Because of this, Boeing was better able to compete with Airbus Industries.

Notice that in both Boeing's and Chrysler's cases the change was fundamental and dramatic. First, the role of the computer was changed from a tool to a platform for the total design. Second, it was not just a process change, but a *cultural change* relative to the role of the computer and the design engineers. According to Callon (1996), the engineers are now a part of a computer-based design system. Computing also played a major communications role during the entire design process. As shown in the classic Ford case, IT makes a major contribution in shortening cycle times by allowing the combination or elimination of steps, and the expediting of various activities in the process.

There is an old saying that "time is money," so saving time saves money. But cycle time reduction does more than save money. If you beat your competitors with a new product, a product improvement, or a new service, you can gain a substantial market share. Pharmaceutical companies, for example, are desperately trying to reduce the cycle time of new drugs. If successful, they will be the first on the market, they may receive a patent on the innovation, and revenues will begin flowing sooner to repay their huge investments.

Additionally, telecommunications and especially the Internet and intranets provide a means of economically reducing cycle time by cutting communications time through the use of e-mail and EDI, and by allowing collaboration in design and operations of products and services.

Finally, an extreme example of cycle time reduction is same-day delivery, which has been revived by e-commerce. For example, restaurants in Hong Kong deliver meals to customers who order them using cell phones connected to the Internet. Also, one can order flowers for same-day delivery—a real help to people who forget birthdays and anniversaries until the day of the event (see *1800flowers.com* and *hallmark.com*).

Restructuring the Whole Organization

We've seen that one problem in many current organizations is vertical structures. How should a contemporary organization be organized? There are several suggestions of how to do it. Let's look at how it is done with BPR.

REDESIGNING THE ORGANIZATION. The fundamental problem with the hierarchical approach is that any time a decision needs to be made, it must climb up and down the hierarchy. If one person who does not understand the issues says "no," everything comes to a screeching halt. Also, if information is required from several "functions," getting all the right information coordinated can be a time-consuming and frustrating process for employees and customers alike.

So, how is organizational redesigning done? It all depends. For example, providing each customer with a single point of contact can solve the fundamental problem just described. In the traditional bank, for example, each department views the same customer as a separate customer. Figure 8.12 (page 370) depicts a redesigned bank. The customer deals with a single point of contact, the account manager. The account manager is responsible for all bank services, and provides all services to the customer, who receives a single statement for all of his or her accounts. Notice that the role of IT is to back up the account manager by providing her with expert advice on specialized topics, such as loans. Also, by allowing easy access to the different databases, the account manager can answer queries, plan, and organize the work with customers.

The bank example illustrates how a single-point contact provides a high level of customer service. A variation is one in which several people working in a networked structure can provide excellent service. In this structure, regardless of where and when a client contacts the company, the networked agents would have access to all customer data, so that any employee can provide customer service. This is

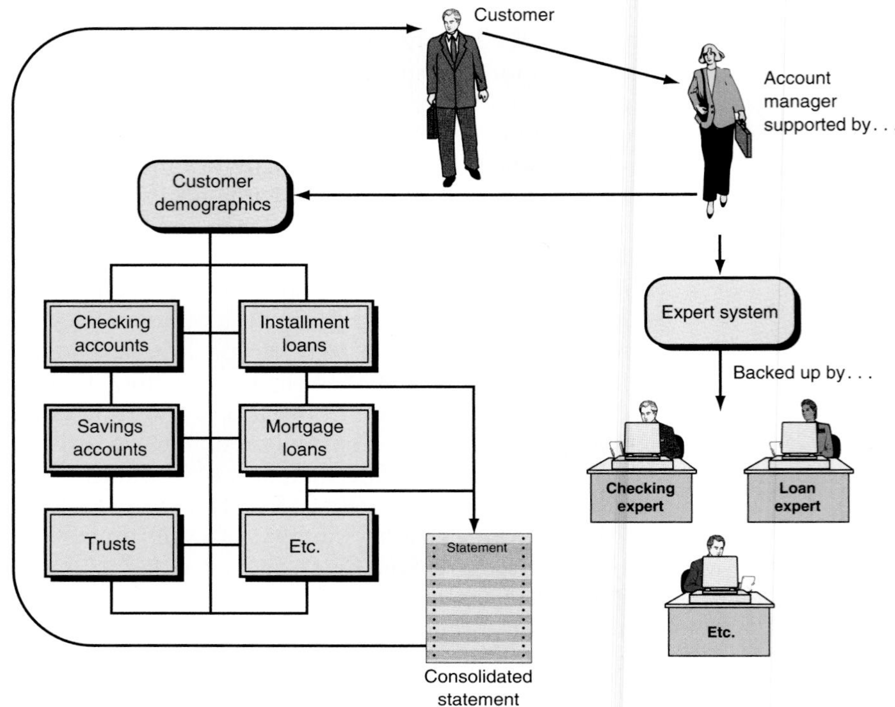

FIGURE 8.12 Reengineered bank with integrated system.

usually done by using a *call center,* which we described in Chapter 7. A variation used by companies such as USAA, Otis Elevator, and others is to have all agents located in one city and give customers a toll-free number or a centralized Web address. In this model, the company also can install a computer-based call-center technology, which brings up complete customer information (or information about a customer's elevator in the case of Otis) on the computer screen, whenever a customer calls. This means that anyone who answers the call would know all the information necessary to make a quick decision. There is no need to ask questions of the customer, and any agent can give personalized and customized service. This is especially important in reservation systems such as for hotels and airlines.

Reengineering and restructuring is not limited to a specific type of organization. As a matter of fact, studies indicate that 70 percent of all large U.S. corporations are reengineering or considering reengineering. In addition, the public sector, including the U.S. federal government, is implementing reengineering. (See the *IT at Work* on the opposite page).

BPR Failures

During the 1990s, there were many success stories of BPR, and just as many cases of failures. The PROSCI organization (*prosci.com*) conducted a survey of several hundred companies to learn the best practices and the reasons for BPR failures.

A summary of research into BPR failure is available at *managingchange.com/bpr/bprcult/4bprcult.htm*. The summary indicates a failure rate of 50 to 80 percent. Some of the reasons cited for failure are high risk, inappropriate change man-

IT at Work

...in Government

REENGINEERING THE FEDERAL GOVERNMENT WITH INFORMATION TECHNOLOGY

The U.S. federal government is using IT to streamline its bureaucracy and improve public services. The plan is to create an "electronic government," moving from the Industrial Age into the Information Age. It is also part of e-government, where redesign is done to enable e-purchasing and other EC activities.

Information technology is playing a key role in this reengineering of government operations and services. As in any project, top management support is vital.

The IT team describes the new e-government systems as a "virtual agency" in which information is shared throughout the government. The U.S. Department of Agriculture already distributes food stamps electronically. Medicare payments may be integrated into that system. Other e-government services being proposed include a national network serving law enforcement and public safety agencies; electronic linkage of tax files at federal, state, and local agencies; an international trade data system; a national environmental data index; government wide electronic mail; and an integrated information infrastructure, including consolidated data centers. Various IT teams are also looking at client/server networks and intranets to eliminate the need for large mainframe data centers. Tens of millions of U.S. citizens receive Social Security and other payments periodically. The distribution of these services is also moving to the Internet for greater savings and shorter cycle times.

For Further Exploration: Why is this system referred to as an electronic agency? Is so much computerization of the government beneficial? Why or why not?

Sources: Condensed from G. H. Anthes, "Feds to Downsize with IT," *Computerworld,* September 13, 1993; and *npa.gov* (1998). For more information, go to *fcw.com* and *govexec.com.*

agement, failure to plan, internal politics, high cost of retooling, lack of participation and leadership, inflexible software, lack of motivation, and lack of top management support. A highly detailed case study is provided by Sarker and Lee (1999). Highlights of the report are available at the organization's Web site, along with BPR tutorials, an article index, best practices, and more.

Despite the potential for failure, organizations should consider BPR. When successful, it has great potential to improve an organization's competitive position. The secret to success is to manage the BPR process thoughtfully and carefully.

8.9 THE NETWORKED ORGANIZATION

The examples in the previous section demonstrated some approaches that can be helpful in solving the stovepipe and other problems created by the new business environment. Such approaches can be part of an enterprisewide networked structure, which we discuss next.

The Structure of Networked Organizations

Many writers have advocated the concept of networked organizations (see Majcharzak and Wang, 1996). The term **networked organizations** refers to organizational structures that resemble computer networks and are supported by information systems. Figure 8.13 (page 372) shows the major characteristics of the networked organization (right side) and compares them with the characteristics of the hierarchical organization (left side).

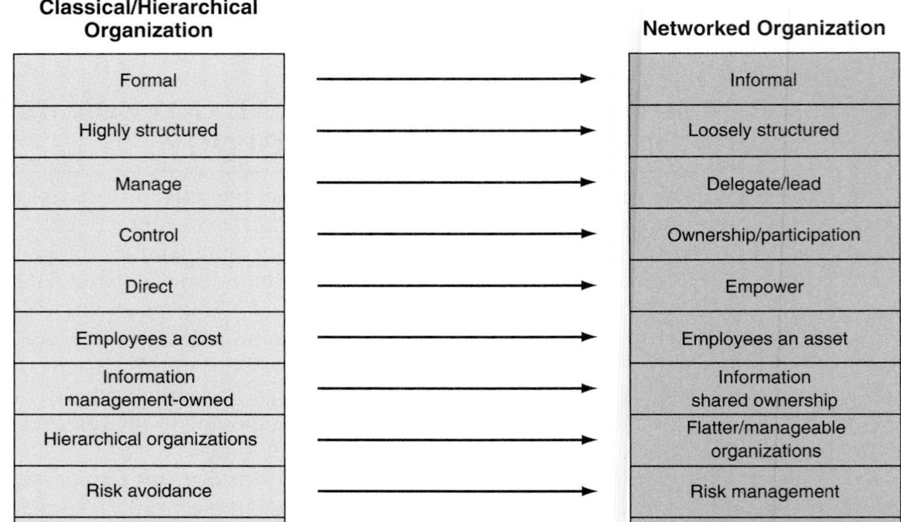

FIGURE 8.13 Networked versus hierarchical organization.

The hierarchical and network approaches to management obviously present significant contrast, and each has its successes and failures. There is, in fact, no single, best way to manage all organizations. Rather, the best management approach is *contingent* on characteristics of the organization being managed.

However, today some organizations are turning away from the hierarchical organization toward the networked organization. This trend is being brought about by the evolution from an industrial-based economy to an information-based economy. Today, most people do *knowledge work,* in which the intellectual content of the work increases to the point where the subordinate often has more expertise than the "hierarchical" supervisor. If managers knew "everything," they could use hierarchical methods to tell employees what to do, how to do it, and when to do it. But physicians, scientists, engineers, and similar employees in an organizational network are not just "cogs" in a hierarchical machine. Each employee that does knowledge work has special expertise and information. Therefore, it is better to view the information-based organization as a client/server network. The "node" that can best solve a problem is the one that should be used to do so.

Figure 8.14 portrays the continuum from the hierarchical approach to the networked approach. The nodes in the network can be individuals or teams. Note that in the middle is the **flattened organization**, which has fewer layers of management and a broader span of control than the hierarchical organization, and can be considered an improvement over the hierarchical one.

As a straightforward example of a network approach to problem solving, let us say a student in class begins to have cardiac arrest. What should happen? If one student in the class knows CPR, she should become a situational leader and configure a team to solve the problem. That person is the best-equipped "node" in the network. Note that she might be temporarily hierarchical in behavior. For example, she might tell one person to call 911, another to get some blankets, and another to keep the hallways clear for the ambulance personnel. The pro-

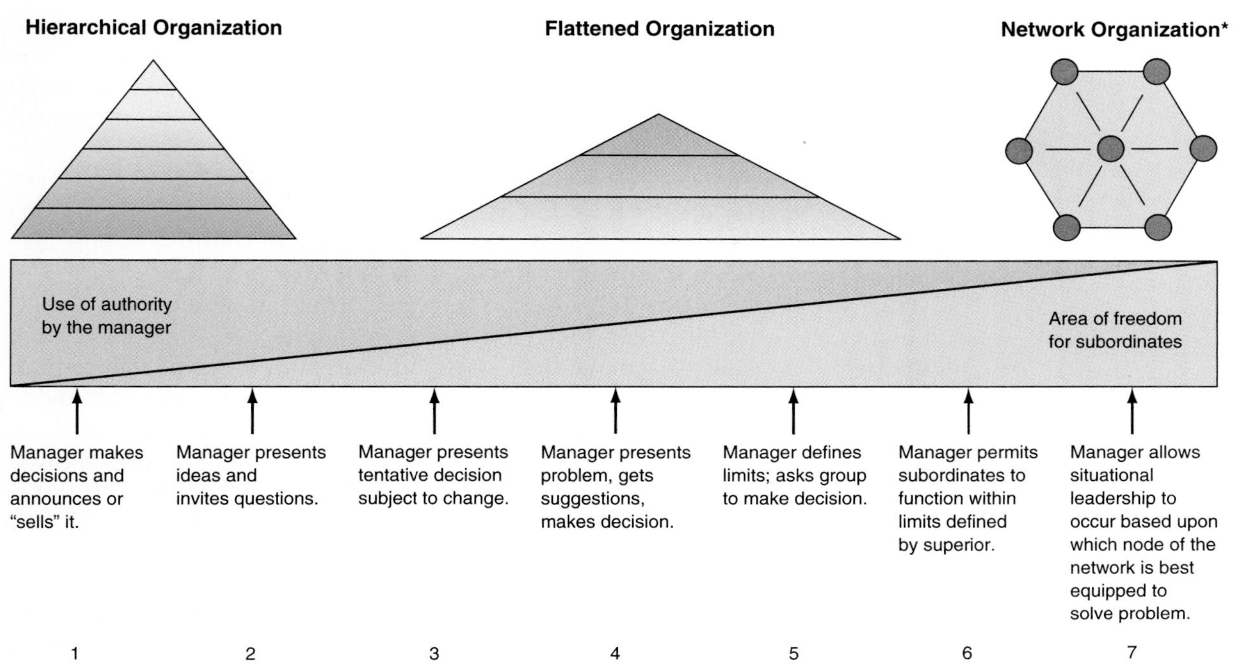
Hierarchical Organization
Flattened Organization
Network Organization*
Use of authority by the manager
Area of freedom for subordinates
Manager makes decisions and announces or "sells" it.
Manager presents ideas and invites questions.
Manager presents tentative decision subject to change.
Manager presents problem, gets suggestions, makes decision.
Manager defines limits; asks group to make decision.
Manager permits subordinates to function within limits defined by superior.
Manager allows situational leadership to occur based upon which node of the network is best equipped to solve problem.
1
2
3
4
5
6
7
* Multiple networks exist in organizations.

FIGURE 8.14 The roles of managers and subordinates in the different types of organizations.

fessor should relinquish authority, and those people assigned tasks by the CPR expert should not argue about who should call 911! The goal is to recognize the most important task. In this case, saving a life preempts teaching, and the situational leader needs to emerge from the network.

Empowerment Using IT

Empowerment is the vesting of decision-making or approval authority in employees where, traditionally, such authority was a managerial prerogative. As a philosophy and set of behavioral practices, empowerment means allowing self-managing teams and individuals to be in charge of their own career destinies, as they meet and exceed company and personal goals through a shared company vision (see Murrell and Meredith, 2000). As an organizational program, empowerment means giving permission to the workforce to unleash, develop, and utilize their skills and knowledge to their fullest potential for the good of the organization as well as for themselves. It also means providing the framework in which this can be done. Empowerment is done for individuals and for groups. Self-directed or autonomous teams make their own decisions. In order to do this, they must be empowered.

EMPOWERMENT'S RELATIONSHIP TO INFORMATION TECHNOLOGY. Empowerment can be enhanced through IT. Perhaps IT's most important contribution is the provision of the right information, at the right time, at the right quality, and at the right cost. Information is necessary, but it may not be sufficient. To be fully empowered means to be *able to make decisions,* and these require *knowledge.* Knowledge is scarce in organizations, and specialists usually hold it. Access to knowledge may not be easy or cheap. To empower employees means to increase the availability of such knowledge. Expert systems and other intelligent systems can play a major role in providing knowledge, as can the Internet and intranets.

Empowered employees are expected to perform better. To do so, they need new tools. Information technology can provide tools that will enhance the creativity and productivity of employees, as well as the quality of their work. These tools can be special applications for increasing creativity, spreadsheets for increasing productivity, and hand-held computers to improve communication. Examples are provided in Chapters 4 and 7.

Finally, empowerment may require training. People may need more skills and higher levels of skills. Self-directed teams, for example, are supposed to have all the necessary skills to achieve their goal. Once organized, teams will require training, which can be enhanced by IT. For example, many companies provide online training, use multimedia, and even apply intelligent computer-aided instruction. Many companies are using intranets to provide training. Levi Strauss & Company uses a program called Training for Technology, which aims at training people to use the skills and tools they need in order to be able to find information and use it properly.

EMPOWERMENT OF CUSTOMERS, SUPPLIERS, AND BUSINESS PARTNERS. In addition to empowering employees, companies are empowering their customers, suppliers, and other business partners. For example, Levi Strauss allows its textile suppliers to access its database, so they know exactly what Levi Strauss is producing and selling and can ship supplies just in time. The company is using a similar approach with all its suppliers. Federal Express is using the Internet to empower its customers to check prices, prepare shipping labels, find the location of the nearest drop box, and trace the status of packages. Finally, Dell empowers its customers to track orders and troubleshoot problems. Of special interest is the concept of using extranets, which allows companies to empower their business partners, as described in Chapter 5.

The networked organization is related to the concept of the virtual organization, which is presented next.

8.10 VIRTUAL ORGANIZATIONS

One of the most interesting organizational structures is the *virtual organization*, usually referred to as a *virtual corporation (VC)*. The creation, operation, and management of a VC is heavily dependent on IT and is especially facilitated by the Internet and e-commerce (see Venkatraman and Henderson, 1998).

Definition and Characteristics

A **virtual corporation** is an organization composed of several business partners sharing costs and resources for the purpose of producing a product or service. The virtual corporation can be temporary, with a onetime mission such as launching a satellite, or it can be permanent. The virtual corporation is usually composed of several components, each in a different location. Each partner contributes complementary resources that reflect its strengths and determine its role in the virtual corporation. VCs are not necessarily organized directly along the supply chain. For example, a virtual business partnership may include several partners, each creating a portion of a product or service, in an area in which they have special advantage such as expertise or low cost.

According to Goldman et al. (1995), permanent virtual corporations are designed to do the following:

- Create or assemble productive resources rapidly.
- Create or assemble productive resources frequently and concurrently.
- Create or assemble a broad range of productive resources.

The concept of virtual corporations is not new, but recent developments in IT allow new implementations that exploit its capabilities (see O'Leary et al., 1997). The modern virtual corporation can be viewed as a *network* of creative people, resources, and ideas connected via online services and/or the Internet, who band together to produce products or services.

The major attributes of virtual corporations are:

- ***Excellence.*** Each partner brings its core competency, so an all-star winning team is created. No single company can match what the virtual corporation can achieve.
- ***Utilization.*** Resources of the business partners are frequently underutilized, or utilized in a merely satisfactory manner. In the virtual corporation, resources can be put to use more profitably, thus providing a competitive advantage.
- ***Opportunism.*** The partnership is opportunistic. A virtual corporation is organized to meet a market opportunity.
- ***Lack of borders.*** It is difficult to identify the boundaries of a virtual corporation; it redefines traditional boundaries. For example, more cooperation among competitors, suppliers, and customers makes it difficult to determine where one company ends and another begins in the virtual corporation partnership.
- ***Trust.*** Business partners in a VC must be far more reliant on each other and require more trust than ever before. They share a sense of destiny. For example, Minicase 2 in Chapter 3 (the Dutch Flower Auctions) shows that trust is essential.
- ***Adaptability to change.*** The virtual corporation can adapt quickly to the environmental changes discussed in Chapter 1 because its structure is relatively simple or fluid.
- ***Technology.*** Information technology makes the virtual corporation possible. A networked information system is a must.

For an analysis of why virtual organizations work, see Markus et al. (2000). For strategies used by virtual organizations, see Venkatraman and Henderson (1998).

The Virtual Corporation and Interorganizational Information Systems

According to Goldman et al. (1995), in a VC the resources of the business partners remain in their original locations but are integrated. Since the partners are in different locations, they need information systems for supporting communication and collaboration (see Figure 8.15 on page 376). Such systems are a special case of interorganizational information systems (IOSs), information systems that cross organizational lines to one or more business partners (see Chapter 5).

How IT Supports Virtual Corporations

There are several ways for IT to support virtual corporations. The most obvious are those that allow communication and collaboration among the dispersed business partners. For example, e-mail, desktop videoconferencing, screen sharing, and several other groupware technologies described in Chapter 4 are frequently

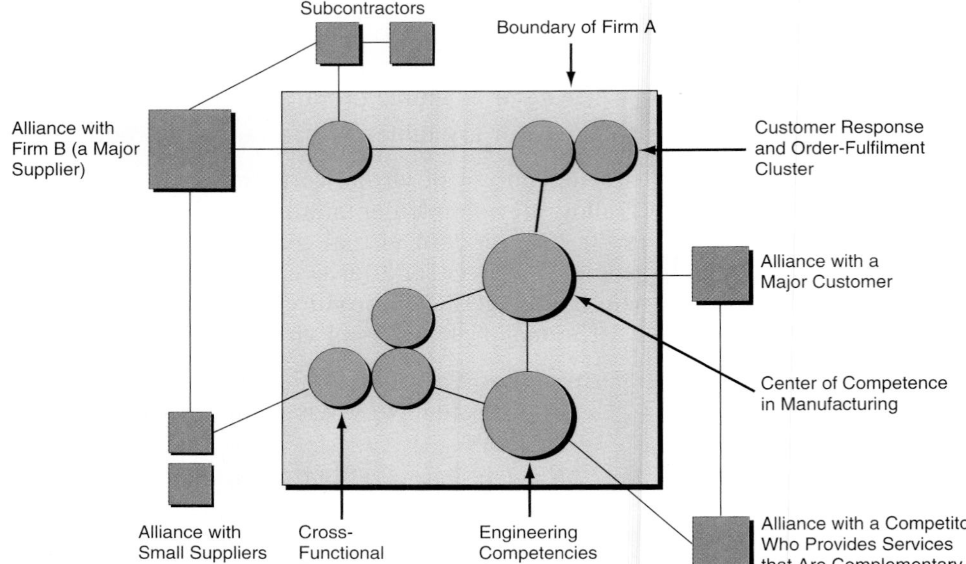

FIGURE 8.15 A network structure facilitates the creation of virtual companies. (*Source:* J. Cash et al., "A Network Structure Facilitates the Creation of Virtual Company," 1994, p. 34. J. Cash, Building the Information Age Organization. Reproduced with permission from McGraw Hill Publishing.)

used to support virtual corporations. Standard transactions in the interorganizational information systems are supported by electronic data interchange (EDI) and EFT (see Chapter 5).

The Internet is the infrastructure for these and other technologies. Virtual office systems, for example, can be supported by intelligent agents (see O'Leary et al., 1997, and Chapter 12). Modern database technologies and networking permit business partners to access each other's databases. Lotus Notes and similar integrated groupware tools permit diversified interorganizational collaboration. Turban et al. (2002) provide numerous examples of intranet/Internet applications. ERP software is extensively used to support standard transactions among business partners. In general, most virtual corporations cannot exist without information technology. (For a survey of other tools see Boudreau et al., 1999. For the effect of IT on VC, see Peng and Chang, 2000.)

MANAGERIAL ISSUES

1. ***Importance.*** Getting IT ready for the future—that is, planning—is one of the most challenging and difficult tasks facing all of management, including IS management. Each of the four steps of the IT strategic planning process—strategic planning, information requirements analysis, resource allocation, and project planning—presents its own unique problems. Yet, without planning, or with poor planning, the organization may be doomed.
2. ***Organizing for planning: Many issues.*** What *should* be the role of the ISD? How should IT be organized? Staffed? Funded? How should human resources issues, such as training, benefits, and career paths for IS personnel, be handled? What about the environment? The competition? The economy? Governmental regulations? Emerging technologies? What is the strategic direction of the

host organization? What are its key objectives? Are they agreed upon and clearly stated? Finally, with these strategies and objectives and the larger environment, what strategies and objectives should IS pursue? What policies should it establish? What type of information architecture should the organization have: centralized or not centralized? How should investments in IT be justified? The answer to each of these questions must be tailored to the particular circumstances of the ISD and the larger organization of which it is a part.

3. ***Fitting the IT architecture to the organization.*** Management of an organization may become concerned that its IT architecture is not suited to the needs of the organization. In such a case, there has likely been a failure on the part of the IT technicians to determine properly the requirements of the organization. Perhaps there has also been a failure on the part of management to understand the type and manner of IT architecture that they have allowed to develop or that they need.

4. ***IT architecture planning.*** IT specialists versed in the technology of IT must meet with business users and jointly determine the present and future needs for the IT architecture. In some cases, IT should lead (e.g., when business users do not understand the technical implications of a new technology). In other cases, users should lead (e.g., when technology is to be applied to a new business opportunity). Plans should be written and published as part of the organizational strategic plan and as part of the IT strategic plan. Plans should also deal with training, career implications, and other secondary infrastructure issues.

5. ***IT policy.*** IT architectures should be based on corporate guidelines or principles laid out in policies. These policies should include the roles and responsibilities of IT personnel and users, security issues, cost-benefit analyses for evaluating IT, and IT architectural goals. Policies should be communicated to all personnel who are managing or directly affected by IT.

6. ***Ethical and legal issues.*** Conducting interviews for finding managers' needs and requirements must be done with full cooperation. Measures to protect privacy must be taken.

   In designing systems one should consider the people in the system. Reengineering IT means that some employees will have to completely reengineer themselves. Some may feel too old to do so. Conducting a supply chain or business process reorganization may result in the need to lay off, retrain, or transfer employees. Should management notify the employees in advance regarding such possibilities? And what about those older employees who are difficult to retrain? Other ethical issues may involve sharing of computing resources (in a client/server environment, for example) or of personal information, which may be part of the new organizational culture. Finally, individuals may have to share computer programs that they designed for their departmental use, and may resist doing so because they consider such programs their intellectual property. Appropriate planning must take these and other issues into consideration.

   Implementing organizational transformation by the use of IT may tempt some to take unethical or even illegal actions. Companies may need to use IT to monitor the activities of their employees and customers, and in so doing may invade the privacy of individuals. When using business intelligence to find out what competitors are doing, companies may be engaged in unethical tactics such as pressuring competitors' employees to reveal information, or using software that is the intellectual property of other companies (frequently without the knowledge of these other companies).

7. ***IT strategy.*** In planning IT it is necessary to examine three basic strategies:
   a. Be a *leader* in technology. Companies such as FedEx, Dell, and Wal-Mart are known for their leading strategy. The advantages of being a leader are the ability to attract customers, to provide unique services and products, and to be a cost leader. However, there is a high development cost of new technologies and high probability of failures.
   b. Be a *follower*. This is a risky strategy because you may be left behind. However, you do not risk failures, and so you usually are able to implement new technologies at a fraction of the cost.
   c. Be an *experimenter*, on a small scale. This way you minimize your research and development investment and the cost of failure. When new technologies prove to be successful you can move fairly quickly for full implementation.
8. ***Integration: The role of IT in redesign and BPR.*** Almost all major supply chain management (SCM) and/or BPR projects use IT. However, it is important to remember that in most cases the technology plays a *supportive* role. The primary role is organizational and managerial in nature. On the other hand, without IT, most SCM and BPR efforts do not succeed.

9. ***Failures.*** A word of caution: One of the lessons from the history of IT is that very big projects have a tendency to fail when expectations exceed real capabilities. For example, many of the early material requirements planning (MRP) systems, artificial intelligence, and complex transaction processing systems never worked. BPR and some ERP projects are no exception. They too fail, for many reasons. One of the reasons for failure is a miscalculation of the required amount of IT. It simply may be too expensive to rebuild and retool the IT infrastructure and adjust applications that are necessary for BPR. The solution may be instead to defer the BPR and use incremental improvements, or to reengineer only the most critical processes.

ON THE WEB SITE... Additional resources, including the Virtual Company, quizzes, cases, updates, additional exercises, links, demos, and activities, can be found on the book's Web site.

KEY TERMS

Applications portfolio *337*
Business processes *343*
Business process reengineering (BPR) *360*
Business systems planning (BSP) *342*
Centralized computing *352*
Client/server *352*
Critical success factors (CSFs) *346*
Cross-functional activities *360*
Cycle time reduction *368*
Distributed computing *353*
Empowerment *373*
Ends/means (E/M) analysis *346*
Flattened organization *372*
Four-stage model of planning *340*
Information architecture *339*
Information technology architecture *339*
IT planning *336*
Legacy systems *354*
Mass customization *367*
Metrics *359*
Networked organization *371*
Project planning *350*
Requirements analysis *348*
Resource allocation *349*
Reverse engineering *354*
Scenario planning *347*
Stages of IT growth *343*
Strategic information planning (SIP) *342*
Virtual corporation (organization) (VC) *374*

CHAPTER HIGHLIGHTS (Numbers Refer to Learning Objectives)

1 Information technology and systems planning can help organizations meet the challenges of a rapidly changing business and competitive environment.

1 The major information systems planning issues are strategic alignment, architecture, resource allocation, and time and budget considerations.

2 Aligning IT plans with business plans makes it possible to prioritize IS projects on the basis of contribution to organizational goals and strategies.

3 The four-stage IT planning model includes strategic planning, requirements analysis, resource allocation, and project planning.

4 Strategic information systems planning involves methodologies such as business systems planning (BSP), stages of IT growth, ends/means (E/M) analysis, and critical success factors (CSFs).

5 Information technology architecture can be centralized or distributed. When it is distributed, it often follows the client/server architecture model.

5 Organizations can use enterprise architecture principles to develop an information technology architecture.

6 To prioritize an e-commerce applications portfolio, IT planners can use the validity of the application and its fit with the organization, plotting it on a grid that indicates company fit and project viability and suggests one of four strategies.

7 BPR is the fundamental rethinking and radical redesign of business processes to achieve dramatic improvements.

7 IT helps not only to automate existing processes, but also to introduce innovations which change structure (e.g., create case managers and interdisciplinary teams), reduce the number of processes, combine tasks, enable economical customization, and reduce cycle time.

8 Mass customization, which is facilitated by IT, enables production of customized goods by methods of mass production at a low cost.

8 Cycle time reduction is an essential part of many BPR projects and is usually attainable only by IT support.

9 One of the most innovative BPR strategies is the creation of business alliances and virtual corporations.

QUESTIONS FOR REVIEW

1. Briefly discuss the evolution of IT planning.
2. What are some of the problems associated with IT planning?
3. Define and discuss the four-stage model of IT planning.
4. Identify the methods used for strategic planning and review their characteristics.
5. What is information technology architecture and why is it important? List the major types.
6. What are the advantages and disadvantages of centralized computing architectures?
7. What is a legacy system? Why do companies have legacy systems?
8. Define applications portfolio.
9. Define BPR.
10. What are the limitations of the hierarchical structure in service organizations, such as banks, from a customer's perspective? What are the limitations from an organization's perspective?
11. What is meant by mass customization? Give examples.
12. What are the characteristics of a network? How would those characteristics be applied to an organization if it were trying to mirror networks?
13. Describe the enabling role of IT in BPR.
14. Describe the major characteristics of empowerment and describe its benefits.
15. Define cycle time reduction.
16. Define a virtual corporation.
17. Define scenario planning.

QUESTIONS FOR DISCUSSION

1. Discuss how strategic planning, as described in this chapter, could help an electric utility plan its future.
2. How might an organization with a good strategic idea be limited in its ability to implement that idea if it has an inferior or inappropriate information architecture? Provide an example.
3. What type of problems might an organization encounter if it focuses only on resource allocation planning and project planning?
4. Why is it so important to align the IT plan with organizational strategies? What could happen if the plan is not aligned with these strategies?

5. Discuss the advantages of using Tjan's approach to an applications portfolio.
6. Some organizations feel that IT planning is a waste of time, because the competitive environment and technologies are changing so rapidly. They argue that their plans will be obsolete before they are completed. Discuss.
7. Should there be a correlation between a firm's architecture structure (and chart) and its IT architecture (e.g., centralized IT for a centralized structure)?
8. Review the opening case. What approach was used to develop an information systems plan?
9. Relate the concepts of supply chain and its management to BPR and IT.
10. Explain why IT is an important BPR enabler.
11. Some people say that BPR is a special case of a strategic information system, whereas others say that the opposite is true. Comment.
12. Relate virtual corporations to networked organizations. Why is a VC considered to be a BPR activity?
13. What are some of the reasons for maintaining a functional structure of an organization?
14. Explain the role intranets can play in lessening the stovepipe problem.

EXERCISES

1. Using the CSF method of strategic planning, identify new strategic initiatives that a university might take using information technology.
2. In a computer publication, find an article that describes the IT architecture in a large multinational corporation. Evaluate the reasons behind the architecture. Do they seem to be valid?
3. Find a local organization that uses a mainframe for its core computing, and interview IT managers to determine the rationale. Are there plans to stop using a mainframe? If so, why? If not, why not?
4. What kind of IT planning is done in your university or place of work to ensure that the Internet demand in the future will be met? Does the university have a CIO? Why or why not?

GROUP AND ROLE-PLAYING ACTIVITIES

1. Divide the class into groups of six people or less. Each group will be entrepreneurs attempting to start some kind of nationwide company. Each group should describe the IT architecture it would build, as well as the expected benefits from, and potential problems with, the IT architecture it has chosen.
2. Have teams from the class visit IT project development efforts at local companies. The team members should interview members of the project team to ascertain the following information.
   a. How does the project contribute to the goals and objectives of the company?
   b. Is there an information architecture in place? If so, how does this project fit into that architecture?
   c. How was the project justified?
   d. What planning approach, if any, was used?
   e. How is the project being managed?
3. Assign groups to the following industries: banking, airlines, healthcare, insurance, and large retailing. Each group will investigate the use of the mainframe in one industry and prepare a report on the future of the mainframe. Also, include information on how client/server architecture is used in the industry.
4. Each group in the class will be assigned to a major ERP/SCM vendor such as SAP, PeopleSoft, Oracle, etc. Members of the groups will investigate topics such as:
   a. Web connections
   b. Use of business intelligence tools
   c. Relationship to BPR
   d. Major capabilities
   e. Use of ASP
   f. Low cost approaches

   Each group will prepare a presentation for the class.

INTERNET EXERCISES

1. Go to the Web page at *dwinc.com/strat.htm* and read the content. Compare and contrast the approach on this page to other approaches to strategic information systems planning.
2. Enter *cio.com*. Review the latest IT planning surveys and reviews reported. Start with the October 1997 survey conducted by CIO Communications Inc.

3. Find 10 to 15 examples of mass customization not cited in this book. Look for shoes, clothing, industrial products, etc.
4. There is an increased use of the Internet/intranets to enable employees to make their own travel arrangements. Several Internet travel companies provide opportunities for companies to reengineer their travel processes. Surf the Internet to find some vendors that provide such services. Prepare a report that summarizes all the various activities. Also discuss the potential impact on the travel agency industry.
5. Enter *truserv.com* and find "news" in the media relations section. Identify all IT-related plans announced by the company in the last six months. Comment on your findings.
6. Surf the Internet to find some recent material on the role IT plays in supporting BPR. Search for products and vendors and download an available demo.
7. Identify some newsgroups that are interested in BPR. Initiate a discussion on the role of IT in BPR.
8. Enter *gensym.com* and find their modeling products. Explain how they support BPR and redesign.
9. Enter *xelus.com/index.asp* and find how Xelus Corporation software can facilitate planning (e.g., see the Cisco case).

Minicase 1

Oregon Geographic Information System Plan

www.sscgis.state.or.us

Geographic information systems (GISs) are becoming increasingly important to governmental agencies in conducting their business and serving the public. Such systems use spatial data such as digitized maps and can combine these data with other text, graphics, icons, and symbols (see Chapter 11). The state government in Oregon recognized the increasing importance of GISs as a tool to support decisions that are related to data represented by maps. GISs also offer the potential benefit of coordination among agencies, to avoid duplicated efforts and incompatible data. The state therefore created a Geographic Information Council, consisting of 22 people from agencies at the federal, state, and local levels, to develop a strategic plan to promote the effective use of GISs in Oregon. The planning process commenced in 1995 and produced a comprehensive plan dated March 1996. The plan identified and prioritized goals and strategies, including leadership responsibilities and time frames for each major item. The Council circulated the draft plan to GIS personnel in different organizations, to obtain a peer review before finalizing the document.

The plan starts with a "vision for GIS," a scenario for potential types and levels of usage. This vision incorporates potential advances in technology such as multimedia, organizational structures including a statewide centralized GIS data administration function, a high-bandwidth telecommunications infrastructure, and adequate funding for GIS activities.

Benchmarks for Success

The plan identified criteria for evaluating its own validity:

- GIS integrated into governmental processes ("as common as word processing")
- Geographic data gathered and managed cooperatively and made available to the public
- Statewide standards for spatial data
- A centralized catalog of statewide GIS data
- GIS as an integral part of curriculum for K–12 and higher education throughout the state

Goals and Strategies

The plan also established specific goals, strategies for achieving them, agencies with lead responsibilities, and target dates. The goals include data requirements such as: (1) currency and completeness; (2) security; (3) ease of use and accessibility; (4) incorporation of metadata indicating applicability; (5) coordination of collection and maintenance; and (6) standardization.

For technology, the goals include: (1) network access for agencies and public; (2) compatible data exchange formats; (3) real-time update capability; (4) master contracts for hardware/software/training; (5) integration with global positioning system (GPS) technology; and (6) a centralized data repository.

For people and organizations, the goals include: (1) stable funding and resources; (2) recruitment and retention of GIS employees; (3) definition of a model GIS organizational structure; (4) development of an educational program; (5) effective marketing of Oregon's GIS program.

Follow-Up

The planning group recognized that this plan would lose its value if not maintained, or if there were no follow-up

(continued)

on its recommendations. Therefore the plan included the following ongoing strategies: (1) monthly meetings of the planning group; (2) workgroups to address specific recommendations; (3) development of GIS plans at other state agencies; (4) distribution of supplements and updates four times a year; and (5) measurement against benchmarks and revision of the plan for the next two-year period.

Source: Compiled from *sscgis.state.or.us/coord/orisplan.htm.* Adapted and reprinted with permission from Oregon Department of Administration and PlanGraphics, Inc.

Questions for Minicase 1

1. Which stage(s) and activities of the four-stage planning model is/are included in the Oregon GIS planning effort?
2. Based on material presented in this chapter and your own personal evaluation, identify things that the planners did well in this project.
3. Can you see any problems or weaknesses with this planning effort?
4. Discuss possible differences in IT planning for governmental agencies, as discussed in this minicase, versus planning in business organizations.
5. Identify businesses and other private organizations that might want to use GIS data created and maintained by public agencies in Oregon. Discuss how (and whether) public agencies should charge private organizations for such data.

Minicase 2

Scenario Planning at National City Bank Aligns IT with Business Planning

www.national-city.com

The banking industry is very competitive. National City Corp. of Cleveland (*national-city.com*) was confronting three challenges: (1) it needed new ways to generate earnings; (2) it faced increasing competition for market share; and (3) the bank was losing customers who wanted to do banking using the Internet.

National City saw the customer information system it was developing with IBM as a solution to these problems. The bank hoped to use this system to develop new, high-revenue products, tailor programs for customers, and cross-sell products to appropriate customers. But to design it, the bank had to know what kind of information the system would be aggregating. Would it track information about the products the bank offered or the people who bought them? If it was product-focused, it would have to include detailed descriptions of each financial service, whether credit cards or mortgages. If the system was customer-focused, it would track whether they used ATMs, branch offices, or call centers, and would indicate demographics in order to build customer profiles. Furthermore, the bank would need to set up business rules to determine customer profitability.

Management quickly realized that they simply could not answer these questions because the answers were linked to a larger issue: Management didn't have a clear sense of the bank's strategic direction. The required investment in technology was $40 million, so planning to invest it properly was critical.

To clarify the business direction, the bank hired a consulting company, *ncri.com,* to employ scenario planning. The planning process involved six phases used by an implementation team:

Phase I: Alternative Visions (Scenarios)

In this phase, a few possible visions of the future are selected. In the case of National City, the scenarios were:

- ***Utilize a CRM-based strategy.*** This was a major industry trend in which everything would be geared to individual customer need. This business model is complex and expensive to pursue.
- ***Specialize solely in certain financial services.*** This is a low-cost option, but may not bring new customers and may even result in losing existing customers.
- ***Create a separate online bank.***

Phase II: Events Generation

Next, a list of 150 internal and external events that might influence any of the outcomes was generated by the team. Events included new regulations and technological developments (e.g., wireless). These events were simulated as newspaper headlines (e.g., "Demand for real-time banking information via cell phones is skyrocketing"). These events were used later to create scenarios.

Phase III: The Workshop

A three-day workshop with the 24 top executives was conducted. The participants were divided into three groups. The first task was to rank all 150 events by the *chance that they will occur*. Once done, all participants met to discuss the rankings and, after appropriate discussion, reach a consensus. This process can be lengthy, but it is essential.

Then, each team was assigned one of the bank's three scenarios and was asked to analyze the impact of the most-likely-to-occur events on that scenario, within a five-year planning horizon.

Phase IV: Presentation

Each group made an oral presentation, in which their goal was to convince the other groups that their vision was the most feasible. This was a difficult task since some team members, who had to play the role of supporters, actually did not like the scenario they were suppose to "sell."

Phase V: Deliberation and Attempt to Reach a Consensus

The entire group of participants needed to agree on which alternative was the best for the bank. After long deliberation, the group decided to support alternative #1, the CRM-based strategy.

Phase VI: IT Support

To facilitate the IT planning, an IS plan was devised in which a data warehouse was planned, so that customers' profiles could be built. Data mining was planned for identifying the bank's most profitable customers, and a Web-based call center was designed to provide personalized services.

All in all, the scenario planning process was an exercise in contingency thinking that resulted in prosperity for the bank when the system was eventually deployed.

Sources: Condensed from M. Levinson, "Don't Stop Thinking About Tomorrow," *CIO Magazine*, January 1, 2000; *ncri.com*; and *national-city.com*.

Questions for Minicase 2

1. One critique of this approach is that some members who are asked to "sell" a specific scenario may not be enthusiastic to do so. Find information in the scenario planning literature on this issue, or e-mail to a scenario consultant (*ncri.com* or *gbn.com*). Write a report on your findings.
2. Can group decision support systems (Chapter 10) be used in this case? Why and what for, or why not?
3. How can the end users learn about technology in scenario planning?
4. What IT tools can be used to facilitate this scenario planning process, which was done manually?
5. How did the scenario planning help the IT people to better understand the business?
6. Why is scenario planning considered a risk-management tool?

REFERENCES AND BIBLIOGRAPHY

1. Agrawal, V., et al., "E-Performance: The Path to Rational Exuberance," *McKinsey Quarterly*, First Quarter, 2001.
2. Benbasat, I., et al., "A Critique of the Stage Hypothesis: Theory and Empirical Evidence," *Communications of the ACM*, Vol. 27, No. 5, May 1984.
3. Blodgett, M., "Game Plans" (Strategic Plans), *CIO Magazine*, January 1998.
4. Boar, B. H., *The Art of Strategic Planning for Information Technology*, 2nd ed. New York: Wiley, 2000.
5. "Bottom-Up GIS," *Journal of the American Planning Association*, Summer 2000.
6. Boudreau, M. C., et al., "Going Global: Using IT to Advance the Competitiveness of the Virtual Transactional Organization," *Academy of Management Executive*, Vol. 12, No. 4, 1998.
7. Broadbent, M., et al., "Firm Context and Patterns of IT Infrastructure Capability," *Proceedings of the 17th International Conference on Information Systems*, Cleveland, December 16–18, 1996.
8. Broadbent, M., et al., "The Implications of IT Infrastructure for Business Process Redesign," *MIS Quarterly*, June 1999.
9. *Business Systems Planning—Information Systems Planning Guide*, Application Manual GE20-0527-3, 3rd ed., IBM Corporation, July 1981.
10. Cale, E. G., and J. Kanter, "Aligning Information Systems and Business Strategy: A Case Study," *Journal of Information Technology Management*, Vol. 9, No. 1, 1998.
11. Callon, J. D., *Competitive Advantage Through Information Technology*. New York: McGraw-Hill, 1996.
12. Cash, J., et al., "A Network Structure Facilitates the Creation of Virtual Company, "*Building the Information Age Organizations: Structure, Control, and Information Technologies*. Burr Ridge, IL: R. D. Irwin, 1994.
13. Cassidy, A., *A Practical Guide to IT Strategic Planning*. Boca Raton, FL: CRC Press, 1998.
14. Clark, T. H., and D. B. Stoddard, "Interorganizational Business Process Redesign: Merging Technological and Process Innovation," *Journal of MIS*, Fall 1996.

15. Curry, J., and J. Ferguson, "Increasing the Success of IT Strategic Planning Process," *Proceedings, 33rd Hawaiian International Conference on Systems Sciences (HICSS)*, Hawaii, January 2000.
16. Doherty N. F., et al., "The Relative Success of Alternative Approaches to Strategic Information Systems Planning," *Strategic Information Systems*, Vol. 8, 1999.
17. El Sawy, O., *Redesigning Enterprise Processes for E-Business*. New York: McGraw-Hill, 2001.
18. Feurer, R., et al., "Aligning Strategies, Processes, and IT: A Case Study," *Information Systems Management*, Winter 2000.
19. Galliers, B., "Towards the Integration of E-Business, KM, and Policy Considerations Within an Information Systems Strategy Framework," *Strategic Information Systems*, Vol. 8, 1999.
20. Gardner, C., and C. Gardner, *The Valuation of Information Technology: A Guide for Strategy Development, Valuation, and Financial Planning*. New York: Wiley, 2000.
21. Geoffrey, J., "Intranets Rescue Reengineering," *Datamation*, December 1996.
22. Gilmore, J. H., and B. J. Pine (eds)., *Market of One: Creating Customer-Unique Value Through Mass Customization*. Boston: Harvard Business School Press, 2000.
23. Goldman, S. L., et al., *Agile Competitors and Virtual Organizations*. New York: Van Nostrand Reinhold, 1995.
24. Hammer, M., and J. Champy, *Re-engineering the Corporation*. New York: Harper Business, 1993.
25. Hutchinson A., "E-Commerce: Building a Model," *Communication Week*, March 17, 1997.
26. Intelle, M. J., "An Interactive Strategic Planning and Management Support Systems," *Proceedings, Western DSI*, Hawaii, 2000.
27. Jarrar, Y. F., and E. M. Aspinwall, "BPR: Learning from Organizational Experience," *Total Quality Management*, March 1999.
28. Ketting, W. J., et al., "Business Process Change: A Study of Methodologies, Techniques and Tools," *MIS Quarterly*, March 1997.
29. Khan, M. R. R., "BPR of an Air Cargo Handling Process," *International Journal of Production Economics*, January 2000.
30. King, W. R., "Assessing the Efficiency of IS Strategic Planning," *Information Systems Management*, Winter 2000.
31. King, W. R., and T. S. H. Teo, "Integration between Business Planning and Information Systems Planning: Validating a Stage Hypothesis," *Decision Sciences*, Spring 1997.
32. Kwahk, K. Y., and Y. G. Kim, "Supporting Business Process and Redesign Using Cognitive Maps," *Decision Support Systems*, March 1999.
33. Lampel, J., and H. Mintzberg, "Customization Customization," *Sloan Management Review*, Fall 1996.
34. Lederer, A. L., and V. Sethi, "Seven Guidelines for Strategic Information Systems Planning," *Information Strategy: The Executive Journal*, Fall 1998.
35. Levinson, M., "Don't Stop Thinking About Tomorrow," *CIO Magazine*, December 15, 1999–January 1, 2000.
36. Majcharzak, A., and Q. Wang, "Breaking the Functional Mind-Set in Process Organizations," *Harvard Business Review*, September–October 1996.
37. Markus, M. L., et al., "What Makes a Virtual Organization Work: Lessons from the Open-Source World," *Sloan Management Review*, Fall 2000.
38. Murrell, K. L., and M. Meredith, *Empowering Employees*. New York: McGraw-Hill, 2000.
39. Nolan, R. L., "Managing the Crises in Data Processing," *Harvard Business Review*, March–April 1979.
40. O'Leary, D., et al., "Artificial Intelligence and Virtual Organizations," *Communications of the ACM*, January 1997.
41. Papp, R., ed., *Strategic Information Technology: Opportunities for Competitive Advantage*. Hershey, PA: Idea Group, 2001.
42. Peng, K. L., and C. Y. Chang, "An Exploratory Study of the Virtual Organization from the Viewpoint of Information Science and Technology," *Proceedings, Western DSI*, Hawaii, 2000.
43. Pickering, C., *E-Business Success Strategies: Achieving Business and IT Alignment*. Charleston, SC: 2000 Computer Technology Research, 2000.
44. Pine, B. J., and S. Davis, *Mass Customization: The New Frontier in Business Competition*. Boston: Harvard Business School Press, 1999.
45. Pine, B. J., and J. Gilmore, "The Four Faces of Mass Customization," *Harvard Business Review*, January–February 1997.
46. Plant T., *E-Commerce: Formulation of Strategy*. Upper Saddle River, NJ: Prentice-Hall, 2000.
47. Reich, B. H., and I. Benbasat, "Measuring the Linkage between Business and Information Technology Objectives," *MIS Quarterly*, March 1996.
48. Ruohonen, M., and L. F. Higgins, "Application of Creativity Principles to IS Planning," *Proceedings HICSS*, Hawaii, January 1998.
49. Sabberwal, R., "The Relationship Between Information Systems Planning Sophistication and Information System Success," *Decision Sciences*, Winter 1999.
50. Samela, H., et al., "Information Systems Planning in a Turbulent Environment," *European Journal of Information Systems*, Vol. 9, No. 1, 2000.
51. Sarker, S., and A. S. Lee, "IT-Enabled Organizational Transformation: A Case Study of BPR Failure at TELECO," *Journal of Strategic Information Systems*, Vol. 8, 1999.
52. Tjan, A. K., "Finally, A Way to Put Your Internet Portfolio in Order," *Harvard Business Review*, February 2001.
53. Tung, L. L., and E. Turban, "The Reengineering of the ISD of the Housing Development Board in Singapore," in B. S. Neo, ed., *Exploring Information Technology for Business Competitiveness*. Reading, MA: Addison Wesley, 1996.
54. Turban, E., et al., *Electronic Commerce. A Managerial Perspective*, 2nd ed. Upper Saddle River, NJ: Prentice-Hall, 2002.
55. Useem, J., "Dot-coms: What Have We Learned?" *Fortune*, October 30, 2000.
56. Vedder, R. G., and M. T. Vanecek, "Competitive Intelligence for IT Resource Planning: Some Lessons Learned," *Information Strategy: The Executive Journal*, Fall 1998.
57. Venkatraman, N., and J. Henderson, "Real Strategies for Virtual Organizing," *Sloan Management Review*, Fall 1998.
58. Ward, J., and P. Griffiths, *Strategic Planning for Information Systems*, 2nd ed. Chichester: Wiley, 1996.
59. Wetherbe, J. C., "Four-Stage Model of MIS Planning Concepts, Techniques, and Implementation," in R. Banker, R. Kaufman, and M. Mahmood, eds., *Strategic Information Technology Management: Perspectives on Organizational Growth and Competitive Advantage*. Harrisburg, PA: Idea Group, 1993.
60. Wetherbe, J. C., *The World on Time*. Santa Monica, CA: Knowledge Exchange, 1996.
61. Wilson T., "Nike Model Shows Web's Limitations," *Interactive-Week*, December 6, 1999.

PART III
Organizational Applications

CHAPTER

9 Knowledge Management

This chapter was contributed by Professor Jay E. Aronson of The University of Georgia, Athens, Georgia, U.S.A.

LEARNING OBJECTIVES

After studying this chapter, you will be able to:

1. Define knowledge and describe the different types of knowledge.
2. Describe the characteristics of knowledge management.
3. Describe the knowledge management cycle.
4. Describe the technologies that can be utilized in a knowledge management system.
5. Describe the activities of the chief knowledge officer and others involved in knowledge management.
6. Describe the role of knowledge management in organizational activities.
7. Describe ways of evaluating intellectual capital in an organization.
8. Describe how knowledge management systems are implemented.
9. Describe the roles of technology, people, and management in knowledge management.
10. Describe how knowledge management can revolutionize the way an organization functions.

MITRE SHARPENS ITS CREATIVE SIDE THROUGH KNOWLEDGE MANAGEMENT

THE PROBLEM

The Mitre Corporation, a global, independent, not-for-profit, federally (U.S.) funded research and development center, provides federal agencies with system engineering and information technology expertise. Since incorporation in 1958, Mitre's mission has been to *use leading-edge technology to develop innovative, practical improvements for its customers' systems and processes.* The company's over 4,000 employees at 63 sites provide worldwide support for four primary customers: the Department of Defense, the Federal Aviation Administration, the U.S. intelligence community, and the Internal Revenue Service. In 1996, when Victor A. DeMarines took over its presidency, he believed that Mitre did not effectively leverage its expertise as well it could. At that time Mitre had a culture of *silos,* each with its own pocket of knowledge. Analagous to a grain silo on a farm, these are separate areas in which knowledge is developed and used independently. These silos functioned like rivals and compromised Mitre's ability to serve its clients. No one knew who Mitre's in-house experts were, how to find them, or how to access their knowledge.

www.mitre.org

THE SOLUTION

DeMarines intended to develop a culture for sharing knowledge, which would be enabled by information technology. To create and sustain such a culture shift, Mitre needed an information architecture that would not just enable but *encourage* sharing. In February 1997 DeMarines charged Andrea Weiss, the company's CIO, with developing an information system that would move away from the existing culture and allow Mitre executives to, as Weiss says, "know what we know, use what we know, and bring it all to bear on all of our customers' jobs."

In 1993, Mitre technologists developed the groundwork for MII (Mitre Information Infrastructure) through a wide-area information system. Mitre engineers built a rudimentary corporate intranet in 1994. By 1995, all employees had access to an intranet that included the employee directory, administrative policies, and corporate information. In 1997, Weiss wanted to expand this basic network to include information essential to employees' everyday work, from the mundane to the creative. Weiss and her team met with senior managers and others to develop a set of knowledge to incorporate including:

- A *corporate directory,* including personnel profiles, contact information, resumes, and publications
- A *"lessons learned" library,* whose purpose is to capture the organization's *best practices* and *lessons learned* (a knowledge repository)
- *Improved efficiency reports,* to handle *all* human resource documents
- A *facility-scheduling system* so users can locate, schedule, and set up meetings

A critical issue in deploying a knowledge management system is to motivate employees to contribute their knowledge and encourage them to use it. To get users to buy into Mitre's system, two approaches were taken. First, DeMarines, by then the CEO, often simply stated that he expected people to use MII. Second, Weiss made MII attractive to use. She initially put tedious paperwork and processes online (the company phone book, time cards, expense sheets, and technical information) to expedite work. As the system was prototyped, real expertise eventually came online, and MII became a *knowledge management system (KMS).*

 THE RESULTS

As MII was phased in, more and more employees started to use it. People became more aware of other Mitre projects that they were not actively involved in but in which they had some expertise, and people started to collaborate more. Their approach to work changed. MII has transformed Mitre's culture from a company that fostered intellectual fiefdoms and internal rivalry to one with an accessible corporate knowledge base and intellectual collaboration.

The MII has evolved into a state-of-the-art Web-based knowledge repository. It is a corporate intranet containing massive administrative and technical content, a corporate directory, access to corporate services and news, content relevant to leading technologies, and Mitre-sponsored research programs. MII is a single information system that stores and catalogues information about every significant task performed and can make it available to any employee, anywhere. Thus MII is an effective knowledge management system that enhances collaboration globally throughout the organization and among its clients. Globally, all 63 Mitre sites are connected to MII.

In 1998, Mitre performed a postimplementation audit of MII to determine both its tangible and intangible benefits. The hard financial benefits include:

- Reduced operating costs (estimated to be $16.6 million since 1996).
- Improved staff productivity (estimated to save $12.8 million).
- Cost avoidance. (Government contracts typically allow for revenue withholding when the paperwork is not delivered, even if the work is completed. Under MII, no revenue-withholding occurs.)

The soft (intangible) benefits include:

- Increasing the organization's knowledge base
- Sharing expertise

Since 1995 Mitre has invested $7.19 million in the system, netting a return on investment of $62.1 million (through 1998) in reduced operating costs and improved productivity. Internally, each of Mitre's business units has programs underway to further leverage MII companywide and to its clients.

Sources: Adapted from T. Field, "Common Knowledge," *CIO,* February 1, 1999; D. Young, "An Audit Tale," *CIO,* May 1, 2000; The Mitre Corporation, "Mitre Information Infrastructure," *mitre.org/mii/index.html* (2000); and The Mitre Corporation, "Project Showcase," *mitre.org/pubs/showcase/mii-page.html* (1999).

 LESSONS LEARNED FROM THIS CASE

This case illustrates the importance and value of identifying an organization's knowledge and sharing it throughout the organization. In a major initiative, The Mitre Corporation developed the MII knowledge management system to leverage its **intellectual assets** (also called *intellectual capital*), the valuable knowledge of the employees. The Mitre Corporation transformed its culture as the knowledge management system was deployed, leading to significantly lower operating costs and more collaboration throughout the global enterprise. Though hard to measure, organizations are beginning to recognize the value of their intellectual assets. Fierce global competition drives companies to better utilize their intellectual assets by transforming themselves into organizations that foster the development and sharing of knowledge.

In this chapter we describe the characteristics and concepts of knowledge management. In addition, we will explain how firms are using information technology to implement knowledge management systems and how these systems are transforming modern organizations. Furthermore, you will learn how knowledge management can revolutionize the way we collaborate and use computing, and why you should learn about it.

9.1 INTRODUCTION TO KNOWLEDGE MANAGEMENT

Concepts and Definitions

Conceptually ancient (e.g., see Cahill, 1996), knowledge management is a new form of organizational collaborative computing. Successful managers have always used intellectual assets and recognized their value. But these efforts were not systematic, nor did they ensure that knowledge gained was shared and dispersed appropriately for maximum organizational benefit. **Knowledge management (KM)** is a process that helps organizations identify, select, organize, disseminate, and transfer important information and expertise that are part of the organization's memory and that typically reside within the organization in an unstructured manner. This structuring of knowledge enables effective and efficient problem solving, dynamic learning, strategic planning, and decision making. Knowledge management focuses on identifying knowledge, explicating it in such a way that it can be shared in a formal manner, and thus leveraging its value through reuse. The system that makes knowledge management available throughout an organization is called a **knowledge management system (KMS)**.

Through a supportive organizational climate and modern information technology, an organization can bring its entire organizational memory and knowledge to bear upon any problem anywhere in the world and at any time. For organizational success, *knowledge, as a form of capital, must be exchangeable among persons, and it must be able to grow.* Knowledge about how problems are solved can be captured, so that knowledge management can promote organizational learning, leading to further knowledge creation.

KNOWLEDGE. Knowledge is very distinct from data and information in the information technology context (see Figure 9.1 on page 389). Whereas *data* are a collection of facts, measurements, and statistics, *information* is organized or processed data that are timely (i.e., inferences from the data are drawn within the time frame of applicability) and accurate (i.e., with regard to the original data) (McFadden et al., 1999; Watson, 1998). **Knowledge** is information that is *contextual, relevant,* and *actionable.* The implication is that knowledge has strong experiential and reflective elements that distinguish it from information in a given context. Having knowledge implies that it can be exercised to solve a problem, whereas having information does not carry the same connotation. An *ability to act* is an integral part of being knowledgeable. For example, two people in the same context with the same information may not have the same ability to use

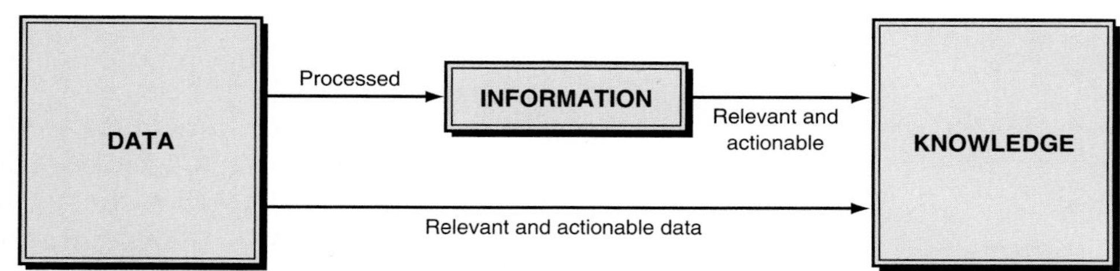

FIGURE 9.1 Data, information, and knowledge.

the information to the same degree of success. Hence there is a difference in the human capability to add value. The differences in ability may be due to different experiences, different training, different perspectives, and so on. While data, information, and knowledge may all be viewed as assets of an organization, knowledge provides a higher level of meaning about data and information. It conveys *meaning,* and hence tends to be much more valuable, yet more ephemeral.

There is a vast amount of literature about what knowledge and knowing means in epistemology (study of the nature of knowledge), the social sciences, philosophy, and psychology (Polanyi, 1958, 1966). Though there is no single definition of what knowledge and knowledge management specifically mean, the business perspective on them is fairly pragmatic. Information as a resource is not always valuable (i.e., information overload can distract from the important); knowledge as a resource is valuable because it focuses attention back toward what is important (McFadden et al., 1999). Knowledge implies an implicit understanding and experience that can discriminate between its use and misuse. Over time, information accumulates and decays, while knowledge evolves. *Knowledge is dynamic in nature.*

Intellectual capital is another term for knowledge, and implies there is a financial value to that knowledge. Though intellectual capital is difficult to measure, some industries have tried. For example, the value of the intellectual capital of the property-casualty insurance industry has been estimated to be between $270 billion to $330 billion (Mooney, 2000).

Knowledge evolves over time with experience, which puts connections among new situations and events in context. Given the breadth of the types and applications of knowledge, we adopt the simple and elegant definition that *knowledge* is *information in action* (O'Dell et al., 1998).

TACIT AND EXPLICIT KNOWLEDGE. Polanyi (1958) first conceptualized and distinguished between an organization's tacit and explicit knowledge. **Tacit knowledge** is usually in the domain of subjective, cognitive, and experiential learning. **Explicit knowledge** deals with more objective, rational, and technical knowledge (data, policies, procedures, software, documents, etc.), and is highly personal and hard to formalize (Nonaka and Takeuchi, 1995).

Explicit knowledge is the policies, procedural guides, white papers, reports, designs, products, strategies, goals, mission, and core competencies of the enterprise and the information technology infrastructure. It is the knowledge that has been codified (documented) in a form that can be distributed to others without requiring interpersonal interaction, or transformed into a process or strategy. For example, a description of how to process a job application would be documented in a firm's human resources policy manual. Explicit knowledge has also been called **leaky knowledge** because of the ease with which it can leave an individual, document, or the organization, since it can be readily and accurately documented (Alavi, 2000).

Tacit knowledge is the cumulative store of the experiences, mental maps, insights, acumen, expertise, know-how, trade secrets, skills set, understanding, and learning that an organization has, as well as the organizational culture that has embedded in it the past and present experiences of the organization's people, processes, and values. Tacit knowledge, also referred to as *embedded knowledge* (Madhaven and Grover, 1998), is usually either localized within the brain of an individual or embedded in the group interactions within a department or a branch office. Tacit knowledge typically involves expertise or high skill levels.

Tacit knowledge is diffused, unstructured, without tangible form, and therefore difficult to codify. Polanyi (1966) suggests that it is difficult to put tacit knowledge into words. For example, an explanation of how to ride a bicycle would be difficult to document explicitly, and thus is tacit. Successful transfer or sharing of tacit knowledge usually takes place through associations, internships, apprenticeship, conversations, other means of social and interpersonal interactions, or even through simulations (e.g., see Robin, 2000). Nonaka and Takeuchi (1995) claim that intangibles like insights, intuitions, hunches, gut feelings, values, images, metaphors, and analogies are the often-overlooked assets of organizations. Harvesting this intangible asset can be critical to a firm's bottom line and its ability to meet its goals. Tacit knowledge has been called **sticky knowledge** because it is relatively difficult to pull it away from its source.

Leonard and Sensiper (1998) suggest that most knowledge falls between the extremes of tacit and explicit. Some elements (explicit) are objective/rational, and others (tacit) are subjective/experiential and created in the "here and now." However, they say that its being tacit does not mean that such knowledge cannot be codified.

Historically, MIS has focused on capturing, storing, managing, and reporting explicit knowledge. Organizations now recognize the need to integrate both types of knowledge in formal information systems.

The Need for and Benefits of Knowledge Management

For centuries, the mentor-apprentice relationship has been a slow but reliable means of transferring tacit knowledge from individual to individual due to its experiential nature. When people leave an organization, they take their knowledge with them. One critical goal of knowledge management is to retain this valuable know-how that can so easily and quickly leave an organization.

Unlike other assets, knowledge has the following characteristics (Gray, 1999):

- ***Extraordinary leverage and increasing returns.*** Knowledge is not subject to diminishing returns. When it is used, it is not consumed. Its consumers can add to it, thus increasing its value.
- ***Fragmentation, leakage, and the need to refresh.*** As knowledge grows, it branches and fragments. Knowledge is dynamic; it is information in action. Thus, an organization must continually refresh its knowledge base to maintain it as a source of competitive advantage.
- ***Uncertain value.*** It is difficult to estimate the impact of an investment in knowledge. There are too many intangible aspects.
- ***Uncertain value sharing.*** Similarly, it is difficult to estimate the value of sharing the knowledge, or even who will benefit most.

Over the last few decades, the industrialized economy has been in the process of shifting from one based on natural resources to one based on intellectual assets (Hansen et al., 1999; Alavi, 2000; von Krogh et al., 2000). The **knowledge-based economy** is a reality. Rapid changes in the business environment cannot be handled in traditional ways. Firms are much larger, and in some areas turnover is extremely high, fueling the need for better tools for collaboration, communication, and knowledge sharing. Firms *must* develop strategies to sustain competitive advantage by leveraging their intellectual assets for optimum performance. To compete in the globalized economy and markets requires quick response to customer needs and problems.

To provide service, knowledge management is critical for consulting firms spread out over wide geographical areas, and for virtual organizations, as is demonstrated in the *IT at Work* example below.

Organizations are just beginning to recognize, develop, and deploy specific methodologies and technologies to *convert tacit knowledge into explicit knowledge*. They wish to do so in order to maintain ownership over the knowledge, even if the people who contribute the knowledge leave the organization (this is important

IT at Work

Integrating IT ...in Management

SIGMA SUMS IT ALL UP THROUGH KNOWLEDGE MANAGEMENT

Sigma, a German management consulting firm, needed a way for its employees to share knowledge throughout its large, geographically dispersed *virtual organization.* When Sigma first started, it was a small network of people who had come together to share ideas about collaboration and working practice. At this stage, the members of the consulting practice knew each other and collaborated with simple methods: telephone, fax, and face-to-face meetings. This was sufficient for people to identify who had appropriate problem-solving expertise as needed. As the organization grew in size and spread throughout Germany, and as freelance employees were brought into projects on an as-needed basis, forming a virtual organization, it became increasingly difficult for people to communicate, collaborate, and identify sources of expertise within the organization.

When the management of Sigma perceived a lack of information flow within the organization, they introduced a bulletin board system called SigSys. SigSys included threaded discussion groups, a means of linking continued e-mail discussions together sequentially. Even though the benefits of SigSys were clear, it took over a year for the system to be accepted by the employees. Tracking knowledge was fairly difficult in SigSys, but employees eventually learned the system and came to appreciate its benefits. Even after SigSys was deployed, e-mail and document sharing were still used throughout the organization. With both sets of technologies, computer-mediated communication and collaboration increased at Sigma.

However, a true knowledge repository (memory) cannot be created with these simple tools. Sigma's solution was to develop a Web-based knowledge management system, called Ariadne's Thread, to provide a knowledge source for all members. Ariadne's Thread includes information about the organization and its structure, and provides space for information about individuals, projects, and regional branches. Ariadne's Thread provides a knowledge repository that makes tacit knowledge explicit. Ariadne's Thread supports the distribution of information and know-how throughout the entire organization. The Web site functions as a knowledge repository, providing active knowledge to a dynamic, virtual workforce.

For Further Exploration: The SigSys, a bulletin board system, was adequate for a while but eventually proved ineffective. Why? What was different about how Ariadne's Thread enhanced knowledge storage and use versus the old system? Explain.

Source: Adapted from B. Lemken, H. Kahler, and M. Rittenbruch, "Sustained Knowledge Management by Organizational Culture," *Proceedings of the 33rd Annual Hawaii International Conference on Systems Sciences,* January 2000.

for virtual organizations). The fact that knowledge can be codified has fueled the development of knowledge management methodologies, tools, and applications.

Organizations are making major long-term investments in knowledge management. For example, through 1999, KPMG invested $100 million in its Global Knowledge Exchange KWorld (Madden, 1999). In a 2000 KPMG survey (McKellar, 2000) of 423 organizations, each with annual revenues exceeding $270 million in Europe, the United States, and elsewhere, nearly 75 percent were looking to knowledge management to play a significant role in improving competitive advantage, marketing, and customer focus; about 65 percent think that knowledge management would benefit product innovation, revenue growth, and profit; 71 percent believe that it leads to better decision making; and about 65 percent view it as achieving faster response to important business issues and better customer handling. Worldwide spending on knowledge management services is expected to grow from about $1.8 trillion in 1999 to over $8 trillion by 2003 (Dyer, 2000).

9.2 ORGANIZATIONAL LEARNING AND TRANSFORMATION

Knowledge management is rooted in the concepts of organizational learning and organizational memory. When members of an organization collaborate and communicate ideas, teach, and learn, knowledge is transformed and transferred from individual to individual.

The Learning Organization

The term **learning organization** refers to an organization's capability of learning from its past experience (DiBella, 1995). Before a company can improve, it must first *learn*. To build a learning organization, it must tackle three critical issues: (1) meaning (determining a vision of what the learning organization is to be); (2) management (determining how the firm is to work); and (3) measurement (assessing the rate and level of learning). A learning organization is one that performs five main activities well: systematic problem solving, creative experimentation, learning from past experience, learning from the best practices of others, and transferring knowledge quickly and efficiently throughout the organization (Garvin, 1993).

Organizational Memory

A learning organization must have an **organizational memory** and a means to save, represent, and share that organizational knowledge. Estimates vary, but it is generally believed that only to 10 to 20 percent of business data are actually used. Organizations "remember" the past in their policies and procedures. Individuals ideally tap into this memory for both explicit and tacit knowledge when faced with issues or problems to be solved. Human intelligence draws from the organizational memory and adds value by creating new knowledge. A knowledge management system can capture the new knowledge and make it available in its enhanced form.

Organizational Learning

Organizational learning is the development of new knowledge and insights that have the potential to influence an organization's behavior. It occurs when associations, cognitive systems, and memories are shared by members of an organization (Croasdell, et al., 1997). Establishing a corporate memory is critical for success (e.g., Brooking 1999; Hackbarth and Grover, 1999). Information technology plays a critical role in organizational learning, and management must place emphasis on this area to foster it (Andreu and Ciborra, 1996).

Since organizations are becoming more virtual in nature (see the *IT at Work* about Sigma), they must develop methods for effective organizational learning. Modern collaborative technologies can help in knowledge management initiatives. Organizational learning and memory depend less on technology than on the people issues, as we describe next.

Organizational Culture

The ability of an organization to learn, develop memory, and share knowledge is dependent on its culture. *Culture* is a pattern of shared basic assumptions (Schein, 1997, 1999). Over time organizations learn what works and what doesn't work. As the lessons become second nature, they become part of the **organizational culture**. New employees learn the culture from their mentors along with know-how.

The impact of corporate culture on an organization is difficult to measure. However, strong culture generally produces strong, measurable bottom-line results: net income, return on invested capital, and yearly increases in stock price (Hibbard, 1998). For example, Buckman Laboratories, a pharmaceutical firm, measures culture impact by sales of new products. Buckman undertook to change its organizational culture by making knowledge sharing part of the company's core values. After instituting a knowledge-sharing initiative, sales of products less than 5 years old rose to 33 percent of total sales, up from 22 percent (Hibbard, 1998).

Encouraging employees to use a knowledge management system, both for contributing knowledge and for seeking knowledge, can be difficult. The reasons people do not like to share knowledge are as follows (Vaas, 1999).

- Willing to share, but not enough time to do so
- No skill in knowledge management techniques
- Don't understand knowledge management and benefits
- Lack of appropriate technology
- No commitment from senior managers
- No funding for knowledge management
- Failure of culture to encourage knowledge sharing

Generally when a technology project fails, it is because the technology does not match the organization's culture. This is especially true for knowledge management systems, because they rely so heavily on individuals contributing their knowledge. Most KMSs that fail in practice do so because of organizational culture issues (e.g., see Drucker, 2001).

9.3 The Knowledge Management Process

Firms generate, transfer, and apply required knowledge, since markets are incapable of doing so. The cognitive capabilities of employees are the prime method of learning and memory. An organization performs three major steps: knowledge generation, knowledge codification, and knowledge utilization. Alavi (2000) describes organizations as *knowledge systems.*

Knowledge management formalizes organizational learning and memory into a nonconsumable resource, typically through a knowledge repository (described later). It is implemented through information, collaborative, and communication technologies. In a study at Xerox Corp., Barth (2000a) found that the top ten domains in which knowledge concepts are leveraged in organizations through knowledge initiatives are:

1. Sharing knowledge and best practices
2. Instilling responsibility for sharing knowledge
3. Capturing and reusing best practices
4. Embedding knowledge in products, services, and processes
5. Producing knowledge as a product
6. Driving knowledge generation for innovation
7. Mapping networks of experts
8. Building and mining customer knowledge bases
9. Understanding and measuring the value of knowledge
10. Leveraging intellectual assets

Primarily, knowledge management is a process of eliciting, transforming, and diffusing knowledge throughout an enterprise so that it can be shared and thus reused. Stated simply, knowledge management is making shared information useful (Bushko and Raynor, 1998).

The Goals and Objectives of Knowledge Management

Knowledge management involves a strategic commitment to improving the organization's effectiveness, as well as improving its opportunity enhancement. Its goal is not cost control (Davis, 1998). The goal of knowledge management as a process is to improve the organization's ability to execute its core processes more efficiently.

Davenport et al. (1998) describe four broad objectives of knowledge management systems in practice:

1. Create knowledge repositories.
2. Improve knowledge access.
3. Enhance the knowledge environment.
4. Manage knowledge as an asset.

Most firms have one primary KM objective. For example, in the opening case Mitre attempted to enhance the knowledge environment. While doing so, it achieved the other three goals as well. In the *IT at Work* on the facing page, we show how Xerox met its primary objective of creating knowledge repositories so that it would not be reinventing solutions to repetitive problems in its service department.

The Knowledge Management Cycle

A functioning knowledge management system follows six steps in a cycle (Figure 9.2, page 395). The reason for the cycle is that knowledge is dynamically refined over time. The knowledge in a good KM system is never finished because, over time, the environment changes, and the knowledge must be updated to reflect the changes. The cycle works as follows:

1. ***Create knowledge.*** Knowledge is created as people determine new ways of doing things or develop know-how. Sometimes external knowledge is brought in.

IT at Work

...in Marketing

KNOWLEDGE MANAGEMENT PREVENTS COPYING ERRORS OF THE PAST

www.xerox.com

In the past, Xerox Corporation shared stories among service technicians, but only in small groups, and their service manuals were very out of date. Technicians generally improvised in the field, and there was no mechanism for sharing solutions throughout the entire organization.

To better manage its corporate knowledge, Xerox Corp. developed Eureka. This knowledge management system for copier service technicians captures best practices and especially solutions to problems. Now, similar situations can be dealt with efficiently and effectively anywhere in the world. Eureka's effectiveness was demonstrated when Xerox had a situation with a leading copier that developed intermittent failures all over the world. Xerox was unable to identify the source of the problem and had already replaced six machines. The problem was occurring again in Rio de Janeiro, where Xerox estimated it would cost about $40,000 to replace machines, not to mention the cost of customer goodwill. Gilles Robert, a service technician at Xerox Canada in Montreal, had traced the problem to a 50-cent fuse holder that had a tendency to oxidize and needed to be swabbed with alcohol every so often. He had posted the tip on Eureka. When the copiers were failing in Rio, Eureka was just coming online in Brazil in Portuguese. The engineers there mentioned the problem, and Eureka provided the solution.

Personal recognition motivates technicians to submit tips to Eureka. Each tip has the author's name published with it. By early 2000, Eureka contained nearly 5,000 tips. Xerox has deployed it to over 44,000 technicians worldwide. One of Eureka's guiding principles is, "We should never create the same solution twice. If a solution already exists, it should be used rather than recreating a new solution. In addition, we should focus on continuously improving existing solutions." Eureka! It works!

For Further Exploration: How could a system like Eureka be used at your college or at work?

Sources: Adapted from S. Barth, "Knowledge as a Function of X," *Knowledge Management,* February 2000a; and C. Moore, "Eureka! Xerox Discovers Way to Grow Community Knowledge," *KMWorld,* October 1999.

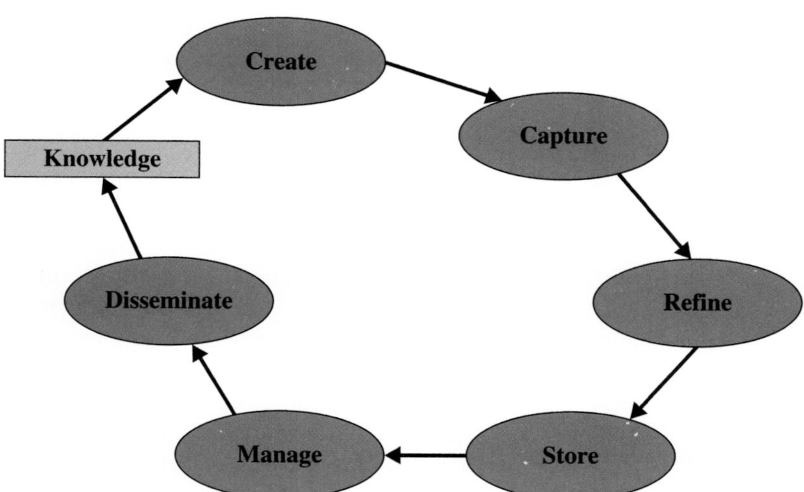

FIGURE 9.2 The knowledge management cycle.

2. ***Capture knowledge.*** New knowledge must be identified as valuable and be represented in a reasonable way.
3. ***Refine knowledge.*** New knowledge must be placed in context so that it is actionable. This is where human insights (tacit qualities) must be captured along with explicit facts.

4. ***Store knowledge.*** Useful knowledge must then be stored in a reasonable format in a knowledge repository so that others in the organization can access it.
5. ***Manage knowledge.*** Like a library, the knowledge must be kept current. It must be reviewed to verify that it is relevant and accurate.
6. ***Disseminate knowledge.*** Knowledge must be made available in a useful format to anyone in the organization who needs it, anywhere and anytime.

As knowledge is disseminated, individuals develop, create, and identify new knowledge or update old knowledge which they replenish into the system.

Knowledge is a resource that is not consumed when used, though it can age. (For example, driving a car in 1900 was different from driving one now, but many of the basic principles still apply.) Knowledge must be updated. Thus, the amount of knowledge grows over time.

9.4 ORGANIZATIONAL KNOWLEDGE REPOSITORIES

Once knowledge can be captured, the issue of where and how to store it arises. Explicit (structured, leaky) knowledge can easily be documented, and hence is often stored in a *knowledge repository,* a central location for documented knowledge. (Note that sometimes the term *organizational knowledge base* is used for a knowledge repository. This should not be confused with the *knowledge base* of an expert system.) Tacit (unstructured, sticky) knowledge, by its nature, is difficult to capture and so is sometimes left in its original state, with the information about how to find it recorded in a central location.

The effort that is used to capture organizational knowledge leads to the two *storage* models for knowledge management systems: the network model and the repository model.

The Knowledge Network Model

The **knowledge network model** does not attempt to codify and extract knowledge from individuals. Instead, the individual who has the knowledge transfers expertise through person-to-person contacts. Access to knowledge is generally enhanced through collaboration and communication methods rather than explicit storage of tacit knowledge. Intranet tools and specialized techniques can be used to categorize knowledge, but the knowledge itself is not stored in the system. For example, a directory (similar to phone-company "Yellow Pages"), listing people in an organization along with their expertise, is a simple, often-used approach to the network model. Just accessing information about who knows what is sufficient to get the ball rolling in solving a problem. This method can also be used to assemble virtual teams to attack a given problem. Many organizations (e.g., Sigma, British Petroleum) initially take this approach to knowledge management, partly because it is the easiest to do, and partly because it is the easiest to understand (see Alavi, 2000).

The Knowledge Repository Model

A knowledge repository is widely recognized as a key component of most knowledge management systems. In the **knowledge repository model**, knowledge contribution and use follow a two-step transfer procedure of person-to-repository and repository-to-person. Captured knowledge is stored in a knowledge repository. A **knowledge repository** is a collection in one place of both internal and external knowledge. Informal knowledge repositories seek to capture tacit knowledge that resides in the minds of experts within the organization in one place but has not been put into a structured format. Explicit knowledge has generally already been captured in some form, simply based on its definition. But, sometimes explicit knowledge must be filtered, organized, and stored in a central knowledge repository (e.g., HR forms and instructions at The Mitre Corporation) to make it available efficiently and effectively. We'll discuss the concept and contents of the knowledge repository in more detail, below.

The knowledge repository model is conceptually similar to the Arthur Andersen Subject Files created in the early 1960s. Recognized experts wrote white papers of best practices, which were stored and indexed in the Subject Files for future reference.

The Hybrid Model

Many organizations use a hybrid of the network and repository models. (In the next section, we shall explain how an 80/20 percent split works well.) Early in the development process it might not be clear how to extract tacit knowledge from its sources, so a repository is used to store explicit knowledge, because it is relatively easy to document. The tacit knowledge initially stored in the repository is contact information about experts and their areas of expertise. Such information is listed so that people in the organization can track down sources of expertise (e.g., the network model). From this beginning, best practices eventually can be captured and managed, so the knowledge repository will contain an increasing amount of tacit knowledge over time. Eventually, a true repository model may be attained. Regardless of the type of knowledge management system developed, a storage location for the knowledge—a knowledge repository—of some kind is needed.

The J. D. Edwards intranet-based Knowledge Garden helps its consultants share best practices (knowledge repository storage model) and find subject experts (network storage model) who can help them solve problems faster and more consistently. The application codifies the company's knowledge base using Site Server taxonomies and automatically delivers personalized updates based on user needs (Microsoft Corporation, 2001).

The Knowledge Repository

A knowledge repository is neither a database, nor a knowledge base in the strictest sense of the terms. Rather, a knowledge repository *stores knowledge,* which is often text-based and has very different characteristics.

Capturing knowledge is the objective of the knowledge repository. The structure of the repository is highly dependent upon the types of knowledge stored. The repository can range from simply a list of frequently asked (and obscure) questions and solutions, to a listing of individuals with their expertise and contact information, to detailed best practices for a large organization.

DATABASES. It is possible to structure part of a knowledge repository as a database, using any of the standard relational, networked, hierarchical, or object-oriented data storage models. (See Technology Guide 3.) Certainly, the search for knowledge is facilitated by using database technology. Further, intelligent database tools for search and interface can be utilized. Web deployment is almost automatic when a database is used. However, the structure and types of knowledge that databases can store are few.

DATA WAREHOUSES. *Data warehouses,* large repositories of important data, can also be used for knowledge management, especially in conjunction with customer relationship management (CRM) systems. Data warehouses have most of the advantages and disadvantages of databases. Data warehouses tend to be enterprisewide when deployed, which fits concepts underlying the repository model of knowledge management. For more on data warehouses, see Chapter 11.

SPECIALLY STRUCTURED DATABASES AND ELECTRONIC DOCUMENTS. Some systems have been developed in Lotus Notes/Domino Server and hence utilize the Notes database structure and collaboration mechanisms. Others have been developed around electronic document management systems (e.g., DocuShare by Xerox) primarily to store knowledge in text form (ideal for best practices, as described below). These specialized databases and documents are ideal for storing tacit knowledge because of its nature. It is vitally important to use relevant key words to indicate how the knowledge is to be identified and hence readily found.

New knowledge management technology released by Lotus Development Corp. (Domino Knowledge Discovery System) and Microsoft Corp. (Tahoe) in 2001 seem to be following the pattern that a knowledge management system can be developed on a collaborative computing platform with specialized database and document structures. As this book went to press, the Lotus and Microsoft products had not yet been released. Only recently have new "out-of-the-box" knowledge management systems that contain an existing knowledge repository structure been developed. These include the electronic document management system Xpedio by IntraNet Solutions. These systems should simplify the development of the system and the structuring of the knowledge repository.

PRACTICAL KNOWLEDGE REPOSITORY STRUCTURE. Most knowledge repositories are developed using several of the above storage mechanisms, depending upon the types and amount of knowledge to be maintained and used. Each has its strengths and weaknesses to be utilized for different purposes within a KM system. Finally, data mining and artificial intelligence techniques for automatic rule induction can be applied to databases, data warehouses, and textual data stored in an electronic document management system. We discuss this in a later section.

BEST PRACTICES. **Best practices** are the activities and methods that the most effective organizations use to operate and manage various functions. Chevron Corp., for example, recognizes four levels of best practices:

1. A good idea not yet proven but one that makes intuitive sense.
2. A good practice, implemented technique, methodology, procedure, or process that has improved business results.
3. A local best practice, a best approach for all or a large part of the organization based on analyzing hard data. In other words, the scope within the organization of the best practice is identified: Can it be used in a single department or geographical region, or can it be used across the organization, or anywhere in between?
4. An industry best practice, similar to level 3 but using hard data from industry (O'Dell et al., 1998).

Historically, the first knowledge repositories simply listed best practices and made them available within the firm. Now that knowledge repositories are electronic and Web accessible, knowledge repositories can have wide-ranging impact on the use of knowledge throughout a firm.

Constructing an Organizational Knowledge Repository

Constructing a knowledge repository is not an easy task. The most important aspects and difficult issues are making the contribution of knowledge relatively easy for the contributor, and determining a good method for cataloging the knowledge. The users should not be involved in running the storage and retrieval mechanisms of the knowledge repository. Typical construction approaches include developing a large-scale Internet-based system or purchasing a formal electronic-document management system. The structure and construction of the knowledge repository is a function of the specific technology used for the knowledge management system.

Managing the Knowledge Repository

Managing the knowledge repository typically requires a full-time staff (similar to a reference library staff). This staff examines, structures, filters, catalogues, and stores knowledge so that it is meaningful and can be accessed by the people who need it. The staff assists individuals in searching for knowledge, and performs "environmental scanning": If they identify specific knowledge that an employee or client might need, they send it directly to them, thus adding value to the organization. (This is standard procedure for Accenture knowledge management personnel.) Finally, the knowledge repository staff may create communities of practice (see Minicase 1) to gather individuals with common knowledge areas to identify, filter, extract, and contribute knowledge to a knowledge repository.

9.5 KNOWLEDGE MANAGEMENT SYSTEMS IMPLEMENTATION

We now turn to how knowledge management systems are implemented, and the types of technology that are implemented. First we discuss strategies for knowledge management. Then we turn to the processes and steps in developing KM systems. We describe how both the network and the repository storage models are implemented in practice, and knowledge management facilities.

Strategies for Knowledge Management

Hansen et al. (1999) studied KM practices at management consulting firms, health-care providers, and computer manufacturers and identified two very different strategies currently used in practice. These strategies are the *codification* strategy and the *personalization* strategy.

The **codification strategy** typically is adopted by companies that sell relatively standardized products that fill common needs. Under this strategy, knowledge is carefully codified and stored in knowledge repositories structured as databases, for repetitive use by anyone in the organization. Firms adopting the personalization strategy implicitly adopt the repository storage model in their knowledge management systems.

Most of the valuable knowledge in these firms is fairly explicit because of the standardized nature of the products and services. For example, a kazoo manufacturer has minimal product changes or service needs over the years, and yet there is steady demand and a need to produce the item. In these cases, the knowledge is typically static in nature.

Firms that adopt the codification strategy to store mostly explicit knowledge can obtain minimal benefits in attempting to capture tacit knowledge, because such knowledge, if available, is not very useful.

Even so, large firms that utilize tacit knowledge, like Ernst & Young, have invested heavily to ensure that the codification process works efficiently. The 250 people at Ernst & Young's Center for Business Knowledge manage the electronic repository and help consultants find and use information. Specialists write reports and analyses that many teams can use. And each of Ernst & Young's more than 40 practice areas has a staff member who helps codify and store documents. The resulting area databases are linked through a network (Hansen et al., 1999). Naturally, people-to-documents is not the only way consultants in firms like Ernst & Young and Accenture share knowledge; they talk with one another as well. But they do place a high degree of emphasis on the codification strategy (Hansen et al., 1999).

The **personalization strategy** typically is adopted by companies that provide highly customized solutions to unique problems. For these firms, knowledge is shared mostly through person-to-person contacts. Collaborative computing methods (for example, as in Lotus Notes/Domino Server or e-mail) help people communicate. The valuable knowledge for these firms is tacit in nature, which is difficult to express, capture, and manage. In this case, the environment and the nature of the problems being encountered are extremely dynamic. Because tacit knowledge is difficult to extract, store, and manage, the explicit knowledge that points to how to find the appropriate tacit knowledge (people contacts, consulting reports) is made available to an appropriate set of individuals who might need it. Consulting firms generally fall into this category. Firms adopting the codification strategy implicitly adopt the network storage model in their initial knowledge management systems (Alavi, 2000).

The challenge to firms that adopt the personalization strategy, and hence the network storage model, is to develop methods to make the valuable tacit knowledge explicit, capture it, and contribute it to and transfer it from a knowledge repository in a knowledge management system. Several major consulting firms are developing methods to do so. They store pointers to experts within the KMS, but they also store the tips, procedures, and best practices as well as the context in which they work. To make their personalization strategies work, firms like Bain invest heavily in building networks of people and communications technology such as telephone, e-mail, and videoconferencing. Also they commonly have face-to-face meetings (Hansen et al., 1999).

Hansen et al. (1999) indicate that firms that have attempted to straddle the two strategies (that is, to use about half of each) in their knowledge management efforts generally have failed. Management consulting firms run into serious trouble when they straddle the strategies. When firms use either strategy exclusively, they also run into trouble. The most successful efforts involve about an 80/20 percent split in the strategies. With the personalization strategy, there is a need to provide some codified knowledge in a repository so that people can access it on an as-needed basis. With the codification strategy, it is necessary to provide access to knowledge contributors, as additional advice and explanations might prove useful or even necessary.

Knowledge Management Systems Development

Forming a *knowledge strategy* is straightforward (Clarke, 1998). Generally, implementing a knowledge management methodology follows seven steps:

1. ***Identify the problem.*** Corporate knowledge is typically found in isolated systems or knowledge silos (as it was for Mitre Corp. described in the opening case). The access and technological barriers protecting this knowledge lead users to perceive that there is a lack of knowledge. The knowledge segments should be identified (see the minicases).

2. ***Prepare for change.*** This refers to change in terms of business efforts, especially in how the business is operated.
3. ***Create the team.*** Most organizations that have successfully implemented knowledge management have created a corporate-level knowledge management team charged with and responsible for implementing a pilot project. This is when a *chief knowledge officer* is appointed to lead the KM effort.
4. ***Map the knowledge.*** Identify what the knowledge is, where it is, who has it, and who needs it. Once the knowledge map is clear, define and prioritize the key features and identify appropriate technologies that can be used to implement the knowledge management system.
5. ***Create a feedback mechanism,*** indicating to management how the system is used, and report any difficulties.
6. ***Define the building blocks*** for a knowledge management system. The base structures of a viable KM system should consist of a knowledge repository, knowledge contribution and collection processes, knowledge-retrieval systems, a knowledge directory, and content management.
7. ***Integrate existing information systems*** to contribute and capture knowledge in an appropriate format.

Once the knowledge strategy is in place, it is time to develop the system. Zack (1999) suggests that knowledge assets should be analyzed in relation to their support of business strategy by performing a *SWOT* (strengths, weaknesses, opportunities, and threats) analysis. This makes intuitive sense in that knowledge management has strategic value; it identifies critically important intellectual assets of an organization. In a 1999 survey of 200 IT managers, 94 percent considered knowledge management strategic (Stahl, 1999).

Usually a prototyping process is used, starting with a small group in a pilot program. Once it has a demonstrated success, other members of the organization generally request access, and the system is expanded. For example, the Xerox Eureka system was initially deployed by a small group of researchers in France. Now, more than 40,000 technicians worldwide use Eureka (see the *IT at Work* example on page 402).

The Knowledge Audit

Early in the KMS development process, as part of the problem identification, a knowledge audit must be performed. A **knowledge audit** describes what knowledge an organization has, who has it, and how it flows (or doesn't) through the enterprise. A knowledge audit can show the needed changes in organizational and personal behavior, business processes, and enabling technologies so that knowledge can be applied to improve competitive advantage. A successful audit can identify intellectual assets of value to the company, but it is also valuable in identifying improvements to existing processes and identifying individuals acting as knowledge barriers. A knowledge audit also can clarify what information various people really need and locate its best sources. Most importantly, an audit determines whether an enterprise is socially ready to become a knowledge organization (see Stevens, 2000).

Create the KM Team

In the process of developing the KMS, a knowledge management team must be assembled. As mentioned earlier, a **chief knowledge officer (CKO)** at the senior level of management must be appointed early to lead the knowledge management project. Regardless of which storage model and strategy are identified as appropriate, a full-time operational staff will be needed to work either on tacit

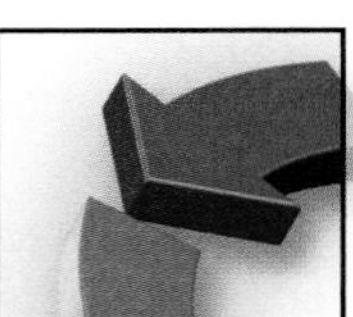

IT at Work

Integrating IT ...in Production & Operations Management

XEROX CORPORATION TRANSFORMS ITSELF INTO A KNOWLEDGE ENTERPRISE

www.xerox.com

Xerox Corporation has recognized that the bulk of the knowledge in an organization is contained in its documents and in how people collaborate and use these documents. The document becomes a focal point, while human collaboration results in new knowledge because people are able to interpret and act on a document's content. According to Rick Thoman, president and CEO, "In the digital age, knowledge is our lifeblood. And documents are the DNA of knowledge."

Xerox has transformed itself from a copy-machine developer and manufacturer into a developer of knowledge management. As part of the Xerox knowledge-work initiative, Xerox started by developing internal knowledge-sharing systems such as Eureka, a service-technician system (described earlier). The cultural infrastructure for sharing was in place when Xerox deployed AmberWeb, a community-of-practice Web site that started out as a solution for 500 researchers involved in the knowledge-capture integration and access initiative. In early 2000, AmberWeb was used by 30,000 Xerox employees.

Now that knowledge sharing has become a way of life at Xerox, the firm is attempting to keep track of innovations that can lead to viable products. Xerox developed DocuShare for in-house use. DocuShare is a knowledge management system that lets employees share information, collaborate on documents, and stay connected with coworkers. It is a Web-based knowledge management system. Eighteen months after DocuShare was developed for use by a small internal group of researchers, more than 10,000 Xerox employees with no training, administration, or technical support were using the system. DocuShare is used at thousands of organizations worldwide.

For Further Exploration: How can knowledge sharing become a way of life in a large organization? In a small organization?

Sources: Adapted from S. Barth, "Knowledge as a Function of X," *Knowledge Management,* February 2000; C. Moore, "Eureka! Xerox Discovers Way to Grow Community Knowledge," *KMWorld,* October 1999; and "Enterprise Knowledge Portals Wise Up Your Business," *InfoWorld,* Vol. 22, No. 49, December 4, 2000.

---

knowledge categorization and its management, or on facilitating the connections of individuals to others who have the needed knowledge.

Before the project can move into the system development phase, members of the organization who will be expected to contribute and/or use knowledge must be identified. Communities of practice are generally formed. A **community of practice (COP)** is a group of people in an organization with a common professional interest. A knowledge management effort succeeds only when cultural issues are dealt with, and when structured appropriately, communities of practice work fairly well. They apply pressure to break down the functional stovepipes in organizations. Members of communities of practice have a sense of ownership over the KMS, and especially of the knowledge contributed by its members.

Challenges to Knowledge Management Implementation

Major challenges to implementing knowledge management systems in practice were identified by Dyer (2000) as follows.

- Lack of understanding of knowledge management and its benefits (55 percent)
- Lack of time by employees for knowledge management (45 percent)
- Lack of skill in knowledge management techniques (40 percent)
- Failure of organizational culture to encourage knowledge sharing (35 percent)
- Lack of incentives to share (30 percent)

- Lack of funding of knowledge management initiatives (24 percent)
- Lack of appropriate technology (18 percent)
- Lack of commitment from senior management (15 percent)

To overcome these challenges, it is important that knowledge management not be seen as yet another business fad (KPMG, 2000). Knowledge management can succeed if an organization follows a careful, deliberate implementation path.

Eliciting Knowledge and Knowledge Requirements

In implementing a knowledge management project, the organization must identify the metaknowledge about the specific knowledge to be put into the system. Some of this identification may have taken place during the knowledge audit, but more detail will be needed before the system can be developed.

Since knowledge (unlike data) is "squishy," the CKO must identify experts in the organization and encourage them to become community leaders and promoters of the developing KM system. These experts should provide input and help the CKO develop maps of the knowledge. The best way to identify experts is by asking around and performing interviews. Appropriate knowledge sources will quickly surface. Samples of typical types of knowledge contributions should be obtained and examined. From these and the experts' advice on how the knowledge will be ideally used, the types of knowledge to be handled by the system can be established. The knowledge types will then determine which storage model is appropriate for the organization.

Also, once the experts are identified, they will ideally promote the KM project to others in the organization. Loose federations of individuals with common interests should be grouped into communities of practice. Details of how the communities of practice should function should be established, and ideally, these groups will contribute to establishing the knowledge requirements and provide more and more specific knowledge, thus automating the process of knowledge elicitation (see Minicase 1).

The Network Storage Model in Practice

The network storage model is a very effective approach to managing knowledge in an organization. In this case, firms utilize the personalization strategy, identifying where the knowledge is, and simply code where and how to find it (i.e., explicit knowledge about the tacit knowledge is maintained in a repository). Collaborative computing systems like Lotus Notes/Domino Server are used to link experts together with others to work on common problems.

For this model, the need for communities of practice is less critical in that much of their function generally involves evaluating knowledge such as best practices and determining whether or not to submit it to a knowledge repository. On the other hand, a community of practice led by a known expert can still provide advice in terms of best practices and so on, because even if the network storage model is the primary model, part of a successful knowledge management effort involves implementing a part of the alternative model (see Hansen et al., 1999). Also, the community mainly functions in a collaboration mode, rather than a contribution mode. Even when collaboration systems are available, once contact is established, people tend to bypass the formal system, because the needed knowledge is not in the system but in an individual's head. Instead, people tend to e-mail or telephone the experts (Cothrel and Williams, 1999a, 1999b). E-mail is a major technology used for firms adopting the network storage model.

Little knowledge is truly managed in firms using this model. Since the bulk of the knowledge is held in individuals' heads, the only contribution they typically make to the KMS is that of identifying their areas of expertise. There are tools, like TacitKnowledge Systems' KnowledgeMail (*tacit.com*), that unintrusively analyze e-mail to determine individuals' specific areas of expertise.

In the network storage model, the listing of expertise is stored in a repository, generally on an easy-to-use (Web-based) intranet. Keywords about the expertise must be established so that a search engine can be used to find it. This functions like the *Yellow Pages* telephone directory. Generally a small KMS staff is needed to maintain the explicit knowledge about the tacit knowledge. The first knowledge management system that Sigma used was a network storage model (see the earlier *IT at Work*).

The Repository Storage Model in Practice

The repository storage model is also a very effective approach to managing knowledge in an organization. In this case, firms utilize the codification strategy, attempting to identify tacit knowledge in best practices and so on, and store the tacit knowledge in a knowledge repository (e.g., see the opening case). This approach takes the network storage model a step further. Collaborative tools and e-mail are used, but for the most part, a major effort is made in storing and maintaining the knowledge itself.

An example of the repository storage model in practice can be found in the legal profession. This profession, worldwide, is structured with built-in inefficiencies, oral codes and methods, and sets of paper-based repositories (Montana, 2000). Though governments are slow to act to improve on this inefficiency, legal firms around the world are developing repository storage–based knowledge management systems. For example, Gottschalk (2000) found that Norwegian law firms are embracing KM systems in resounding numbers to combat inefficiencies of the legal system and to compete. The following *IT at Work* example on the facing page describes the experience at the Detroit law firm of Dickinson Wright.

Knowledge Management Facilities

No special facilities are needed for an organization that adopts the personalization strategy and uses the network storage model. Generally the same kinds of collaborative computing technologies that may be in place (or may be acquired) can be managed by an IT department as part of its routine set of tasks. However, since the 80/20 percent split is recommended in terms of the strategies (and storage models), there will be a need to have dedicated staff to manage the knowledge repository. For firms adopting the network storage model, the knowledge repository will be of minimal size, and needs to be reviewed from time to time. Knowledge contributions can be managed by the communities of practice, or by experts who work with the knowledge.

It is a much different situation for an organization that adopts the codification strategy, and hence uses the repository storage model. These become major efforts that do require dedicated staff, not only to develop the system but also to manage and maintain the knowledge repository. It is instructive to examine what the major consulting firms (Accenture, Ernst & Young, KPMG, and so on) have done in structuring their knowledge management efforts. Most of these firms have one or more Knowledge Centers. If there is one, it is open 24 hours per day, every day. If the firm has more than one, they are geographically dispersed so that at least one will be open at all times. These facilities are accessible via the Internet, as is the KMS. These centers function as a reference library would (see Sherman, 2000). The staff consists of the manager and reference

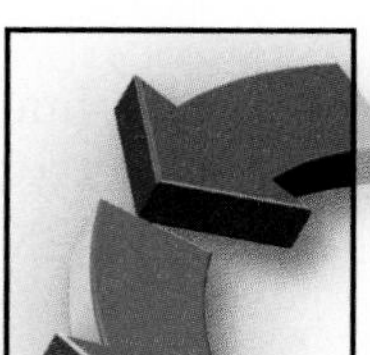

IT at Work

LAYING DOWN THE LAW OF KNOWLEDGE MANAGEMENT

...in the Legal Profession

www.dickinson-wright.com

In the age of knowledge management, there is no need for inefficiencies in access to expertise and legal information to plague law firms like Dickinson Wright of Detroit. To set a precedent for best-practice, expert, and collaboration systems, firms and lawyers must overcome hourly rate mindsets and other cultural barriers. To stay viable, the legal profession must change the way it has done business for hundreds of years.

Law firms face new competitive demands, and clients are starting to demand fixed-fee arrangements, electronic services, and lower prices. To achieve such change calls for the leveraging of technologies and knowledge assets to support the kinds of collaboration and innovation that translate into efficient, responsive services. Law has lagged behind other professional service sectors—and business in general—in these initiatives for a number of reasons. The two most significant barriers are economics and culture. The economics issue is simple: Most firms still make their money the old-fashioned way—by billing hourly for it—so the promise of increased efficiencies that drove many other sectors toward KM a few years ago has held little sway in law firms. The cultural barriers relate to the fact that law firms have highly individual personalities. Lawyers, as a group, have tended to be resistant to technology because their work processes are largely based on case law contained in bound volumes. Also, for territorial reasons, attorneys have generally shied away from widespread knowledge sharing with colleagues and have been motivated by the compensation structure to adopt a "me-first" attitude as opposed to a sharing one.

Nevertheless, Dickinson Wright felt the need to improve knowledge-sharing at the firm. The overhaul of its infrastructure and work processes began with the aim of increasing collaboration both internally and with clients. Now, three and a half years later, the firm has deployed the following programs and initiatives.

More than 130 Lotus Notes programs cover everything from individual applications for each practice group to human resources documents, scheduling conflicts, and client databases. Litigation gets a technical boost at Dickinson, not just in the capturing of discovery information but also in the online analysis of that information. The analysis is performed in order to identify commonalities, and then those common threads can be applied to the actual strategies that will be utilized in the firm's court case. Supporting technologies for these endeavors include Special Counsel, Case-Works, and Summation.

A document management system, based on Docs Open, a document assembly system based on Hot Docs, and an image retrieval and review system by IPRO support the production and storage of briefs and other legal documents. A workflow routing system constructs a workflow route based on information requests in the original document. The extranet utilizes a complex series of servers remotely and locally linked to partners connected via dedicated Internet lines through firewall buffers.

The firm's showcase is on the client extranets, where attorney knowledge is captured to fully automate the processes associated with loan transactions, creditor committees, and banking repositories. For example, using the extranet, clients can communicate through Dickinson's system to do the "paperwork" associated with the various stages of the loan-approval process. The systems cut down on the endless phone calls, faxes, overnight packages, and frustration that used to accompany large loan approvals.

Clients love the system because it has decreased the loan transaction processing time by 400 percent. The firm appreciates the fact that the system has increased the number of loans generated by the same number of employees by a whopping 500 percent. The overhaul of Dickinson's infrastructure and work processes began with the aim of increasing collaboration both internally and with clients, and ended with a major streamlining of efforts yielding substantial cost savings.

For Further Exploration: How can the entire legal profession (courts, and so on) adopt knowledge management, and what would be the impact?

Source: Adapted from E. Jones, "Remaking the Firm: How KM is Changing Legal Practice," *Knowledge Management,* December 9, 2000.

knowledge specialists. Ideally, the knowledge specialists have trained or worked in their areas of specialty. The specialists are part of the knowledge-contribution system. They filter and tag (assign key words to) knowledge contributions to ensure consistency, accuracy, and the ability to find it. The specialists assist clients by answering e-mail and telephone requests about knowledge. They aid clients in their search for knowledge (clients may also search on their own). The specialists have an understanding of how the knowledge is organized so that they can find knowledge quickly. They also will push process information to clients (internal and external) when they find it, even if the client has not specifically requested it.

9.6 THE ROLE OF INFORMATION TECHNOLOGY IN KNOWLEDGE MANAGEMENT

Knowledge management is more a methodology applied to business practices than a technology or product. Regardless, information technology is *crucial* to the success of every knowledge management system. Information technology enables every KMS by providing the enterprise architecture upon which it is built. Knowledge management systems are developed using three sets of technologies: *communication, collaboration,* and *storage.*

Communication, Collaboration, Storage

Communication technologies allow users to access needed knowledge, and to communicate with each other—especially with experts. E-mail, the Internet, corporate intranets, and other Web-based tools provide communication capabilities. Even fax machines and the telephone are used for communication, especially when the network storage model is adopted.

Collaboration technologies provide the means to perform group work. Groups can work together on common documents at the same time (synchronous) or at different times (asynchronous); in the same place, or in different places. This is especially important for members of a community of practice working on knowledge contributions. Other collaborative computing capabilities, such as electronic brainstorming, enhance group work, especially for knowledge contribution. Other forms of group work involve experts working with individuals trying to apply their knowledge. This requires collaboration at a fairly high level. Other collaborative computing systems allow an organization to create a virtual space so that individuals can work online anywhere and at any time.

Storage technologies originally meant using a database management system to store and manage knowledge. This worked reasonably well in the early days for storing and managing most explicit knowledge, and even explicit knowledge about tacit knowledge. However, capturing, storing, and managing tacit knowledge usually requires a different set of tools. Electronic document management systems and specialized storage systems that are part of collaborative computing systems like Lotus Notes fill this void. Note that systems like Lotus Notes also provide communication and collaboration technologies.

KMS Technology Integration

The KMS challenge is to identify and integrate these three technologies to meet the knowledge management needs of an organization. The earliest knowledge management systems were developed with networked technology (intranets), collaborative computing tools (groupware), and databases (for the knowledge repository). They were constructed from a variety of off-the-shelf IT components (e.g., see Ruggles, 1998). Many organizations, especially large management consulting firms like Accenture and J. D. Edwards, developed their knowledge architecture with a set of tools that provided the three technology types. Collaborative computing suites such as Lotus Notes/Domino Server provide many KMS capabilities. Other systems were developed by integrating a set of tools from a single or multiple vendors. For example, J. D. Edwards used a set of loosely integrated Microsoft tools and products to implement its Knowledge Garden KMS, as did KPMG.

In the early 2000s, KMS technology has evolved to integrate the three technologies into a single package. These include enterprise knowledge portals, knowledge management suites, and knowledge ASPs (application service providers). Knowledge servers provide centralized software to coordinate the knowledge management system operations. The newer tools include the capability to read and write standard XML documents, to provide for easy system integration (see Silver, 2000).

Knowledge Management Technologies and Tools

Technology tools that support knowledge management are called **knowware**. The areas of specific vendor tools include collaborative computing tools, knowledge management suites, knowledge servers, enterprise knowledge portals, electronic document management systems, knowledge management tools, application software providers, and knowledge management systems in XML. In most cases, one particular system may provide several tools because they are necessary in an effective knowledge management system. For example, most electronic document management systems may also be characterized as collaborative computing systems. We mention the consulting firms because they pioneered some of the most successful implementations.

COLLABORATIVE COMPUTING TECHNOLOGIES AND TOOLS. Collaboration tools, or groupware, were the first used to enhance collaboration for tacit knowledge transfer within an organization. One of the earliest collaborative computing systems, GroupSystems (*groupsystems.com*), provides many of the tools that support groupwork, including electronic brainstorming and idea categorization. Lotus Notes/Domino Server provides an enterprisewide collaborative environment. Some advantages of Notes include: (1) its internal documents are actually programs; (2) it includes a database management and document management system; and (3) it is accessible directly through an intranet or over the Internet with Web-browser clients. Three major disadvantages of Notes are: (1) it uses a proprietary system for its documents; (2) the documents must be programmed; and (3) it requires a knowledgeable, full-time staff. Despite the disadvantages, many firms have elected to use Notes as the fundamental building block of their knowledge management architecture. Other collaboration tools include MeetingPlace (Latitude), QuickPlace (Lotus Development Corp.), eRoom (eRoom Technology Inc.), and PlaceWare (PlaceWare Inc.).

KNOWLEDGE MANAGEMENT SUITES. **Knowledge management suites** are complete knowledge management solutions out-of-the-box. They integrate the communications, collaboration, and storage technologies into a single convenient package, generally controlled by a knowledge server on which the knowledge repository resides. A knowledge management suite must still access internal databases and other external knowledge sources, so some work is required to make the software truly functional. In some cases, vendors are repositioning their enterprise information system software by adding knowledge management capabilities. In other cases, they are repositioning their products as enterprise knowledge (or information) portals. Regardless, these packages are powerful approaches to developing a KMS.

A number of knowledge management suites have entered the market since late 2000 and early 2001. These include Microsoft Tahoe and Lotus Domino Knowledge Discovery System (also termed an *enterprise knowledge portal*, with a heavy emphasis on collaborative computing). See the respective corporation Web sites for details (*microsoft.com* and *lotus.com*).

Dataware Knowledge Management Suite provides a fairly comprehensive set of tools for a knowledge management initiative. It includes a Knowledge Audit, which leads to a Knowledge Map, a Knowledge Warehouse that is accessible via standard Web browsers, Expert Identification, Knowledge Map Navigator for knowledge contributors, and e-mail integration.

KnowledgeX (KnowledgeX, Inc.) is a suite of knowledge management tools that includes automatic document analysis to extract knowledge and categorize it. The Autonomy Knowledge Management Suite is a fairly comprehensive knowledge management system that integrates with a number of their other tools including ActiveKnowledge. Active delivers internal and external information without interrupting the work process. ActiveKnowledge analyzes the document, PowerPoint presentation, or e-mail an employee is composing and recommends real-time links to relevant documents. The Suite includes a server designed to automate categorization and hyperlinking of information and profiles of employee expertise, and Knowledge Update, a portal-like tool that pushes relevant developments to employees. Suites are often developed in conjunction with knowledge servers, and in early 2001, with enterprise knowledge portals.

KNOWLEDGE SERVERS. A *knowledge server* contains the main knowledge management software, including the knowledge repository, and it provides access to other knowledge, information, and data, both internal and external. Knowledge servers include the Hummingbird Fulcrum Knowledge Server, the Intraspect Software Knowledge Server, the Hyperwave Information Server, the Sequoia Software XML Portal Server, and the Delano Technology Knowledge Management Server.

The Delano Technology Knowledge Management Server integrates with the Delano e-Business Interaction Suite to include artificial-intelligence–assisted technology. This technology enables companies to automatically manage, capture, categorize, cross-reference, and route information across the enterprise. The server, built on Autonomy's pattern-matching technology, provides flexible, powerful natural language and language-independent search capabilities to interpret and manage free-form text from e-mail messages, wireless devices, or Web-based forms. The server provides a knowledge repository, a central location for searching and accessing information from many sources, such as the Internet, corporate intranets, databases, and file systems, thereby enabling the efficient distribution of time-sensitive information. The server seamlessly extends and integrates with the company's e-business suite, allowing rapid deployment applications that span the enterprise and leverage AI-assisted technology to harvest knowledge assets.

ENTERPRISE KNOWLEDGE PORTALS. **Enterprise knowledge portals (EKPs)** are the doorway into many knowledge management systems. They have evolved from the concepts underlying executive information systems, group support systems, Web-browsers, and database management systems. They are an ideal way to configure a knowledge management system. Most combine data integration, reporting mechanisms, and collaboration, while document and knowledge management is handled by a server. An enterprise information portal is a virtual place on a network of online users. The portal aggregates each user's total information needs: data and documents, e-mail, Web links and queries, dynamic feeds from the network, and shared calendars and task lists. The personal information portal has evolved into an enterprise knowledge portal (Silver, 2000).

EKPs dynamically create user profiles, gather data, and then push the information to users. Like KM systems, EKPs track all forms of institutional knowledge, whether formally recorded or not. An EKP is a kind of in-house research community. As with all portals, personalization is a key feature of an EKP. Some portals automatically build taxonomies for searching. Some EKPs even scan users' desktops, watch their actions, and simultaneously push related information to them in another window. EKPs automatically update information, and because all content is scanned and categorized for knowledge sharing, no one has to intervene to ensure that content is not lost.

When enterprise information portals first entered the market, they did not contain knowledge management features. Now, most do. Leading portal vendors include Autonomy, Brio, Corechange, DataChannel, Dataware, Epicentric, Glyphica, Intraspect, Hummingbird, InXight, KnowledgeTrack, IBM/Lotus, Knowmadic, OpenText, Plumtree, Portera, Sequoia Software, Verity, and Viador. Database vendors such as Microsoft, Oracle, and Sybase are also selling knowledge portals.

Microsoft's Digital Dashboard Portal Initiative integrates its Windows 2000, Office 2000, Exchange 2000, and Commerce Server technologies. OpenText's EKP (LiveLink) delivers a strong foundation for Internet collaboration.

The KnowledgeTrack Knowledge Center offers integrated business-to-business (B2B) functions and can scale from dot-coms to large enterprises. Knowledge Center can be built into the enterprise architecture instead of simply sitting on top, the way most intranet portals do. The Knowledge Center integrates with external data sources including ERP, online analytical processing (OLAP) (see Chapter 11), and CRM systems. Knowledge Center supports communities of practice and enables them for large project management, allowing information to be shared among all of the extended enterprise value chains.

Epicentric's Epicentric Portal lets companies build customized portals containing internal information as well as outsourced content and services. The portal offers a central place to access the applications and services an organization depends on the most: e-mail, databases, Microsoft Office, and so on.

Hyperwave's Hyperwave Information Portal (HIP) features dynamic, bidirectional link management, which verifies the quality of the link and hides links to unauthorized content. Built on the Hyperwave Information Server (HIS) infrastructure, HIP is designed to make structured and unstructured corporate information searchable via a browser-accessible networked environment. The HIP aggregates information from disparate sources. More importantly, it manages the connections between information sources. See the *IT at Work* on page 410 about how the Canadian law firm Smith Lyons developed a successful enterprise knowledge portal. For more on such portals, see Collins (2001), Liautaud and Hammond (2000), and "Enterprise Knowledge Portals Wise Up..." (2000).

ELECTRONIC DOCUMENT MANAGEMENT SYSTEMS. Electronic document management (EDM) systems focus on the document in electronic form as the collaborative focus of work. EDM systems allow users to access needed docu-

IT at Work
PORTAL OPENS THE DOOR TO LEGAL KNOWLEDGE

www.smithlyons.com

Richard Van Dyk, CIO of Smith Lyons, a Toronto-based international law firm, knew exactly what kind of system he was looking for to manage the firm's documents and knowledge. He had spent a year defining his requirements and had composed a complex flowchart on his whiteboard. Smith Lyons wanted to take thousands of pieces of information, give people different views into that information, and have a high level of link management. Van Dyk considered document management tools to be too inflexible for the way lawyers practice law. "We needed a flexible environment that we could massage and manipulate and that would allow people to continue working as they have," says Van Dyk.

"Lawyers are basically document generators," he says. "Due to time constraints, they spend more time collecting documents than organizing them." Because the firm's 550 attorneys and support specialists each had a distinct working methodology, often reflecting the requirements of a specific area of practice, Van Dyk knew they would resent having a rigid system they could not easily personalize.

The profusion of document management, knowledge management, and portal systems makes finding the right product difficult. Each has its strengths and weaknesses. Organizations coming from a document-centric perspective, like Smith Lyons, need to organize and manage content at the back end while developing highly customized individual user interfaces at the front end.

The solution that best met Van Dyk's criteria was the Hyperwave Information Portal from Hyperwave Information Management of Westford, Massachusetts. "What I liked about Hyperwave's portal environment was that as soon as we installed it, we had a framework to begin knowledge mapping—tagging and indexing documents by subject and key words and phrases—and for building the database structures in our repositories," says Van Dyk. The firm had definite ideas on how to structure templates and specific pieces of information that are unique to a legal practice. These issues included myriad legal forms and documents generated by the proprietary software applications used for different practice areas.

Once the portal was set up, Smith Lyons' developers began to customize the views for each desktop PC by creating wizards that connect users to their own secure information areas and to intranet pages containing company activity information. In development, too, is an extranet on which lawyers will be able to post status reports to clients and deliver confidential documents and contracts.

"That flexibility in building our DM portal allows our lawyers and specialists to be incredibly specific in their searches," says Van Dyk. Lawyers also can share their accumulated knowledge more easily with colleagues in the same practice areas, by referencing legal citations, court decisions, and winning strategies that have worked in the past.

For Further Exploration: How is the practice of law different from that of business? Investigate ways in which enterprise knowledge portal technology really helps a law firm.

Source: Adapted from P. Ruber, "Finding the Right Balance: A Canadian Law Firm Interrogated Its Requirements Before Selecting a Portal Solution," *Knowledge Management,* September 2000.

ments, generally via a Web-browser over a corporate intranet. EDM systems enable organizations to better manage documents and workflow for smoother operations. They also allow collaboration on document creation and revision.

Many knowledge management systems use an EDM system as the knowledge repository and access to it (see Minicase 2). There is a natural fit in terms of the purpose and benefits of the two. The key difference between a KMS and an EDM system is that a knowledge management system specifically stores knowledge in documents.

Integrating IT ...in Health Care

Pfizer uses a large-scale document management system to handle the equivalent of truckloads of paper documents of drug approval applications passed between Pfizer and the FDA, its regulating agency. The documents contain knowledge about how to use medications, interpretation of the testing, and so on. This

EDM system dramatically cut the time required for FDA submission and review, making Pfizer more competitive in getting new and effective drugs to market (Blodgett, 2000).

Systems like DocuShare (Xerox Corporation) and Lotus Notes (Lotus Development Corporation) allow direct collaboration on a common document. Other EDM systems include EDMS (Documentum Inc.), Enterprise Work Management (Eastman Software Inc.), FYI (Identitech), The Discovery Suite (FileNet Corporation), Livelink (Open Text Corporation), PageKeeper Pro (Caere Corporation), Pagis Pro (ScanSoft Inc.), Xpedio (IntraNet Solutions), and CaseCentral.com for the legal profession (Document Repository Inc.).

KNOWLEDGE MANAGEMENT TOOLS. Tools for capturing knowledge unobtrusively (with minimal effort and impact) are helpful since they allow a knowledge contributor to be minimally (or not at all) involved in the knowledge-harvesting efforts. Embedding this type of tool in a KMS is an ideal approach to knowledge capture. Tacit Knowledge Systems' KnowledgeMail is an expertise-location software package that analyzes users' outgoing e-mail to parse subject expertise. It maintains a directory of expertise and offers ways to contact experts, while maintaining privacy controls for those experts. Autonomy ActiveKnowledge performs a similar analysis on e-mail and other standard document types. Intraspect Software's Knowledge Server (*intraspect.com*) also offers an enhanced collaborative working environment by monitoring an organization's group memory through the information that has been put to use. It captures the context of its use, such as who used it, when, for what, how it was combined with other information, and what people said about it, and then it makes the information available for sharing and reuse. KnowledgeX (KnowledgeX, Inc.) does the same from a number of sources. Most of these tools are included in a knowledge management suite that publishes and distributes the knowledge obtained from the various sources. KnowledgeX also provides a visual knowledge map that shows the relationships among knowledge chunks. There are a number of other knowledge management tools with similar features that have been incorporated into various knowledge management suites, servers, and portals.

KNOWLEDGE MANAGEMENT SYSTEMS IN XML (EXTENSIBLE MARKUP LANGUAGE). A portal based on the eXtensible Markup Language (XML) technology standard (see Technology Guide 2) not only can automate processes and reduce paperwork, but also can unite business partners and supply chains for better collaboration and knowledge transfer. XML provides standardized representations of data structures so data can be processed appropriately by heterogeneous systems without case-by-case programming. This method suits e-commerce applications and supply chain systems that operate across enterprise boundaries. XML-based messages can be taken from back-end repositories and fed out through the portal interface and back again. A portal that uses XML allows the company to communicate better with its customers, linking them in a virtual demand chain where changes in customer requirements are immediately reflected in production plans. Although many portal-tools vendors claim to be XML-compliant, it often takes additional tools to embed XML capabilities within their applications. XML may become the universal language that all portal vendors embrace (see Ruber, 2001).

Vendors are quickly moving to integrate the advantages offered by XML standards. For example, Interwoven's content management software, Teamsite, now fully supports XML, enabling organizations to provide content available in any format across the enterprise. Sequoia Software's XML Portal Server (XPS) and Hummingbird's Enterprise Portal Suite support the XML standard for data exchange.

KNOWLEDGE MANAGEMENT APPLICATION SOFTWARE PROVIDERS (ASPs). Application software providers (ASPs) have evolved as a form of KMS outsourcing on the Web. There are many ASPs for e-commerce on the market. A recent trend is to provide a complete knowledge management suite, along with the consulting to set it up, via an ASP.

Communispace is a high-level ASP collaboration system. Communispace is a Web-based environment that focuses on connecting people to people (not just people to documents) to achieve specific objectives, regardless of geographic, time, and organizational barriers. As a hosted ASP solution, it is easy to rapidly deploy within organizations. Unlike conventional KM systems that organize data and documents, or chat rooms where people simply swap information, Communispace contains a rich assortment of interactions, activities, and tools that connect people to the colleagues who can best help them make decisions, solve problems, and learn quickly.

Communispace is designed to build trust online. It attempts to make a community self-conscious about taking responsibility for its actions and knowledge. Its Climate component helps participants to measure and understand how people are feeling about the community. The Virtual Café gives dispersed employees a way to meet and learn about each other through pictures and profiles. See the Communispace Web site, *communispace.com*, for details.

CONSULTING FIRMS. All of the major consulting firms (Accenture, IBM, and so on) have massive internal knowledge management initiatives. Usually these become products after they succeed internally and provide assistance in establishing knowledge management systems and measuring their effectiveness. (See, for example, KnowledgeSpace from Arthur Andersen, which you can try out at *knowledgespace.com*.) Consulting firms also provide some direct, out-of-the-box proprietary systems for vertical markets. Most of the major management consulting firms define their knowledge management offerings as a *service*. For more on consulting firm activities and products, see McDonald and Shand (2000).

The Role of Artificial Intelligence in Knowledge Management

In the definition of knowledge management, *artificial intelligence* (Chapter 12) is rarely mentioned. However, practically speaking, AI methods and tools are embedded in a number of knowledge management systems, either by vendors or by system developers. AI methods can assist in identifying expertise, eliciting knowledge automatically and semiautomatically, interfacing through natural language processing, and in intelligent search through intelligent agents. AI methods, notably expert systems, neural networks, fuzzy logic, and intelligent agents, are used in knowledge management systems to do the following:

- Assist in and enhance searching knowledge (e.g., intelligent agents in Web searches).
- Help establish profiles to determine what kinds of knowledge to scan for individuals and groups.
- Help determine the relative importance of knowledge, when knowledge is both contributed to and accessed from the knowledge repository.

- Scan e-mail, documents, and databases to perform knowledge discovery to determine meaningful relationships or to glean knowledge.
- Scan e-mail, documents, and databases to perform knowledge discovery to induce rules for expert systems.
- Identify patterns in data (usually neural networks).
- Forecast future results using existing knowledge.
- Provide advice directly from knowledge (neural networks or expert systems). (For example, use knowledge to construct an expert system for novices to use, perhaps for bank loan approvals.)
- Provide a natural language or voice command–driven user interface for a knowledge management system.

INTELLIGENT AGENTS. *Intelligent agents* are software systems that learn how users work, and provide assistance in their daily tasks. There are other kinds of intelligent agents as well (see Chapter 12). There are a number of ways that intelligent agents can help in knowledge management systems. Typically they are used to elicit and identify knowledge. Examples are:

- IBM (*ibm.com*) offers an intelligent data mining family, including Intelligent Decision Server (IDS), for finding and analyzing massive amounts of enterprise data.
- ProdeBeacon (*prode.com/index1.htm*) includes programmable agents designed to simplify the process of database access in data warehouses.
- Gentia (Planning Sciences International, *gentia.com*) uses intelligent agents to facilitate data mining with Web access and data warehouse facilities.
- Convectis (HNC Software Inc.) uses neural networks to search text data and images, to discern the meaning of documents for an intelligent agent. This tool is used by InfoSeek, an Internet search engine, to speed up the creation of hierarchical directories of Web topics.

Combining intelligent agents with enterprise knowledge portals is a powerful approach that can deliver to a user exactly what he or she needs to perform his or her tasks. The intelligent agent learns what the user prefers to see, and how he or she organizes it. Then, the intelligent agent takes over to provide it at the desktop like a good administrative assistant would. This is based on early work on monitoring and alerting (Web push technology) such as the monitoring and alerting agent NewsAlert (King and Jones, 1995).

Data Mining and Knowledge Discovery in Databases

Data mining is a tool used to search for and extract useful information from volumes of data. Data mining is used in a process called **knowledge discovery in databases (KDD)**. It includes tasks known as knowledge extraction, data archaeology, data exploration, data pattern processing, data dredging, and information harvesting. All of these activities are conducted automatically and allow quick discovery even by nonprogrammers. Data mining is ideal for eliciting knowledge from databases, documents, e-mail, and so on. Data are often buried deep within very large databases, data warehouses, text documents, or knowledge repositories, all of which may contain data, information, and knowledge gathered over several years. (For more on data mining, see Chapter 11.)

AI methods are useful data mining tools that include automated knowledge elicitation from other sources. Intelligent data mining discovers information within databases, data warehouses, and knowledge repositories that queries and reports cannot effectively reveal. Data mining tools find patterns in data and may even (automatically) infer rules from them. (For example, KnowledgeSEEKER from ANGOSS Software Corporation, *angoss.com*, can induce rules from patterns in databases and spreadsheet files. Try their demo software.) Patterns and rules can be used to guide decision making and forecast the effect of these decisions. Data mining can speed analysis by providing needed knowledge.

When a data warehouse is used as a knowledge repository, tags indicating the meaning of cleansed information can be used to express knowledge. Data mining, generally in text (electronic documents), data warehouses, and e-mail, can identify relationships among facts, identify patterns in data, create tags, and induce rules. These activities are powerful ways of identifying knowledge in data or documents. KDD can be used to identify the meaning of data or text, using KM tools that scan documents and e-mail to build an expertise profile of a firm's employees.

Extending the role of data mining and knowledge discovery techniques for knowledge externalization, Bolloju et al. (2001) propose a framework for integrating knowledge management into enterprise environments for next-generation decision support systems. Their framework, shown in Figure 9.3, includes **model marts** and **model warehouses**. Model marts and model warehouses are analogous for models to data marts and data warehouses. (See Chapter 11.) They act as repositories of knowledge created by employing knowledge-discovery techniques on past decision instances stored in data marts and data warehouses. The model marts and model warehouses capture operational and historical decision models, similar to the data in data marts and data warehouses. For example, a model mart can store decision rules corresponding to problem-solving knowledge of different decision makers in a particular domain such as loan approvals in a banking environment.

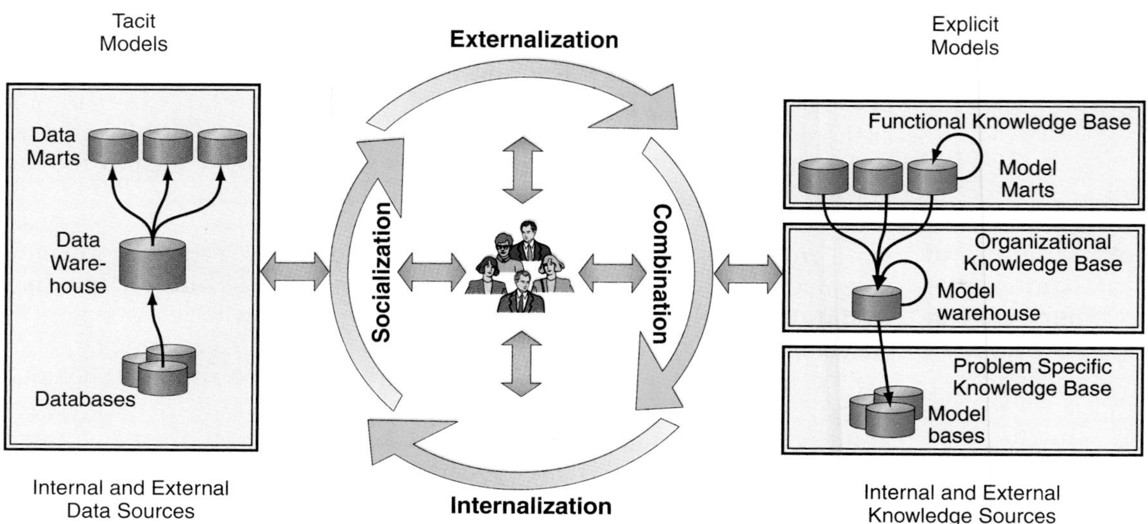

FIGURE 9.3 Framework for integrating decision support and knowledge management systems. (*Source:* N. Bolloju et al., "Integrating Knowledge Management into Enterprise Environments for the Next Generation of Decision Support," *Decision Support Systems,* 2001, forthcoming.)

This integrated framework accommodates different types of knowledge transformations proposed by Nonaka (1995). Systems built around this framework are expected to enhance the quality of support provided to decision makers; to support knowledge management functions such as acquisition, creation, exploitation, and accumulation; to facilitate discovery of trends and patterns in the accumulated knowledge; and to provide means for building up organizational memory.

9.7 MANAGING KNOWLEDGE MANAGEMENT SYSTEMS

Managing a knowledge management system requires great effort. Like any other information technology, getting it started, implemented, and deployed requires a champion's effort. Many issues of management, people, and integration must be considered to make a knowledge management system a success. In this section, we address those issues.

The major management issue is to determine the factors that lead to knowledge management success. Another one is to determine the value of the intellectual assets of an organization, and hence the value of a knowledge management system. Another major issue is to identify the causes of knowledge management system failures, that is, why a KMS did not deliver as promised. Another issue is buying and selling knowledge. Cultural and organizational challenges include encouraging system use and knowledge sharing, knowledge management in virtual organizations, and ethical issues.

Knowledge Management Success

Organizations can gain several benefits from implementing a knowledge management strategy. Tactically, they can accomplish some or all of the following: reduce loss of intellectual capital due to people leaving the company; reduce costs by decreasing the number of times the company must repeatedly solve the same problem, and by achieving economies of scale in obtaining information from external providers; reduce redundancy of knowledge-based activities; increase productivity by making knowledge available more quickly and easily; and increase employee satisfaction by enabling greater personal development and empowerment. The best reason of all may be a strategic need to gain a competitive advantage in the marketplace (Knapp, 1998).

Success indicators with respect to knowledge management are similar to those for assessing the effectiveness of other business-change projects. They include growth in the resources attached to the project, growth in the volume of knowledge content and usage (as at Mitre in the opening case), the likelihood that the project will survive without the support of a particular individual or individuals, and some evidence of financial return either for the knowledge management activity itself or for the entire organization (Davenport et al., 1998). The financial benefit might be perceptual, rather than absolute, but it need not be documented in order for the KM system to be considered a success. At Mitre and at Chevron, the return on investment was explicitly documented.

Major factors that lead to knowledge management project success (adapted from Davenport et al., 1998) include:

- A link to a firm's economic value, to demonstrate financial viability and maintain executive sponsorship.
- A technical and organizational infrastructure on which to build.

- A standard, flexible knowledge structure to match the way the organization performs work and uses knowledge. Usually, the organizational culture must change to effectively create a knowledge-sharing environment.
- A knowledge-friendly culture leading directly to user support. Mitre developed such a culture, for example.
- A clear purpose and language, to encourage users to buy into the system. Sometimes simple, useful knowledge applications need to be implemented first.
- A change in motivational practices, to create a culture of sharing, as was done at Mitre.
- Multiple channels for knowledge transfer—because individuals have different ways of working and expressing themselves. The multiple channels should reinforce one another. Knowledge transfer should be easily accomplished and be as unobtrusive as possible.
- A level of process orientation to make a knowledge management effort worthwhile. In other words, new, improved work methods can be developed.
- Nontrivial motivational methods, such as rewards and recognition, to encourage users to contribute and use knowledge.
- Senior management support. This is critical to initiate the project, to provide resources, to help identify important knowledge on which the success of the organization relies, and to market the project.

Effective knowledge sharing and learning requires cultural change within the organization, new management practices, senior management commitment, and technological support. All of these features are necessary to overcome the known barriers to implementation.

Establishing KM Value Metrics

Traditional ways of financial measurement may fall short when measuring the value of a KMS, because *they do not consider intellectual capital an asset.* Therefore there is a need to develop procedures for valuing the *intangible* assets of an organization, as well as to incorporate models of intellectual capital that in some way quantify innovation and the development and implementation of core competencies.

When evaluating intangibles, there are a number of new ways to view capital. In the past, only customer goodwill was valued as an asset. Now the following are included (adapted from Allee, 1999):

- ***External relationship capital:*** how an organization links with its partners, suppliers, customers, regulators, and so on
- ***Structural capital:*** systems and work processes that leverage competitiveness, such as information systems, and so on
- ***Human capital:*** the individual capabilities, knowledge, skills, and so on, that people have
- ***Social capital:*** the quality and value of relationships with the larger society
- ***Environmental capital:*** the value of relationships with the environment

Even though traditional accounting measures are incomplete for measuring KM, they are often used as a quick justification for a knowledge management initiative (e.g., Mitre in the opening case). Returns on investment (ROIs) are reported to range from 20:1 for chemical firms to 4:1 for transportation firms, with an average of 12:1, based on the knowledge management projects assisted on by one consulting firm (Abramson, 1998).

As more companies develop their knowledge management capabilities, some of the ground rules are becoming clearer. Success depends on a clear strategic logic for knowledge sharing, the choice of appropriate infrastructure (technical or nontechnical), and an implementation approach that addresses the typical barriers: motivation to share knowledge, resources to capture and synthesize organizational learning, and ability to navigate the knowledge network to find the right people and data.

In general, companies take either an asset-based approach to knowledge management or one that links knowledge to its applications and business benefits (Skyrme and Amidon, 1998). The former approach starts with the identification of intellectual assets and then focuses management's attention on increasing their value. The second uses variants of a *balanced scorecard,* where financial measures are balanced against customer, process, and innovation measures. Among the best-developed measurement methods in use are the balanced-scorecard approach, Skandia's Navigator, Stern Stewart's economic value added (EVA), M'Pherson's inclusive valuation methodology, the return on management ratio, and Levin's knowledge capital measure. See Skyrme and Amidon (1998) for details on how these measures work in practice.

Knowledge Management Failure

No system is infallible. There are many cases of knowledge management failing. Estimates of KM failure rates range from 50 percent to 70 percent, where a failure is interpreted to mean that *all* of the major objectives were not met by the effort (Ambrosio, 2000). Failures typically happen when the knowledge management effort mainly relies on technology and does not address whether the proposed system will meet the needs and objectives of the organization and its individuals (Swan et al., 2000). Other issues include lack of commitment (this occurred at a large Washington, D.C. constituent lobbying organization), and not providing incentive for people to use the system (as occurred at Pillsbury Co.; see Barth, 2000b, and Silver, 2000). An illustration of KM failure is presented in the *IT at Work* example on page 418.

Buying and Selling Knowledge

Most firms are reluctant to sell knowledge, unless they are expressly in the business of doing so. Generally a firm's knowledge is an asset that has competitive value, and if it leaves the organization, the firm loses its competitive advantage. However, it is possible to price the knowledge and access to the knowledge to make it worth a firm's while to sell it. For example, American Airlines' Decision Technologies Corp. grew from a small internal analysis team in the 1970s. Initially the team was created to solve problems and provide decision support to American Airlines only. As it grew, it became an independent corporation within AMR Corp., and it began to provide consulting and systems to other airlines, including American's competitors.

The major consulting firms are in the business of selling expertise. Therefore their knowledge management efforts, which began as internal systems, evolved into quite valuable systems that their clients use on a regular basis. In addition, their knowledge management staffs are available to their clients.

IT at Work

www.ford.com
www.firestone.com

KNOWLEDGE MANAGEMENT FAILS: FORD AND FIRESTONE SKID AND SPIN

The Ford Explorer was one of the most successful SUV automobiles in history, until a failure to share related knowledge scattered throughout both Ford and Firestone prevented both companies from discovering a major problem with the Explorer's tires in time to recall them in 2000. (See news reports from 2000 for more details on the tire problem and the recall.)

In 1995, well before the tire problem occurred, Ford had initiated a knowledge management system, the Best Practices Replication Process, that has produced a billion dollars in benefits. The system began as a manual process, which, as it succeeded, evolved into an online, Web-based knowledge repository model system on an intranet. Ford's knowledge management system has three simple procedural rules:

1. The process is managed, with distinct roles and responsibilities. Simple organisms don't need central nervous systems; complex ones can't live without them.
2. No practice would get into the system unless proven.
3. Every improvement would be described in both the technical language of the workgroup involved and its country's language(s): time, head count, gallons, quality. That way Mexican and French workers could easily compare manzanas with pommes, as well as pesos with francs.

Ford structures *communities of practice* around how vehicles are made. Each group has a companywide community administrator, selected by the director of manufacturing. At each plant, each community chooses an individual as the focal point. The focal point spends one to two hours a week working on knowledge management as part of his or her job.

From 1995 through 2000, about 3,000 proven best practices had been shared across Ford's manufacturing operations. The documented value of the shared knowledge in 2000 totaled $850 million, with another $400 million expected in 2001 from new ideas. The system is so successful that Royal Dutch/Shell and Nabisco have licensed the process, and parts of it have been patented.

Even though Ford shares knowledge extremely well, no one knew about the tremendous problem with the Explorer tires. This disaster happened because:

1. Knowledge is best shared *within* communities. People with something in common talk more than strangers do. Neither Ford's nor Firestone's social network was rich enough to support the kind of communication that might have uncovered the problem. Both companies were outside the communication loop in this matter—or rather, there was not even a loop.
2. The more widely dispersed knowledge is, the more powerful a force is needed to extract and share it. At Ford, managers are given improvement goals to meet, and they first look at the Best Practices Replication System for ideas that they know worked at least somewhere. The particular task pulls knowledge from wherever it is. Unfortunately, the knowledge at Ford and Firestone that indicated a potential problem was buried too deeply in and spread too far and wide throughout the organizations.

One lesson to be learned from the Firestone/Ford KM failure is this: Organizations should extract as much important knowledge as they can because they never know what might prove truly important, or when.

For Further Exploration: What can Ford and its vendors and Firestone and its customers do differently now to prevent such disasters from occurring again?

Source: Adapted from T. A. Stewart, "Knowledge Worth $1.25 Billion," *Fortune,* Vol. 142, No. 13, November 27, 2000.

Cultural and Organizational Challenges

Most of the cultural and organizational challenges have been discussed at sufficient length. We recognize that organizational culture must shift to a culture of sharing. This should be handled through strong leadership at the top, and by providing knowledge management tools that truly make people's jobs better. As far as encouraging system use and knowledge sharing goes, people must be *properly* motivated to contribute knowledge. The mechanism for doing so should be part of their jobs, and their salaries should reflect this. People must also be motivated to utilize the knowledge that is in the KMS. Again, this should be part of their jobs and their reward structures.

Early in the chapter, we discussed the use of knowledge management in Sigma, a virtual organization. Knowledge management systems contain the technologies of communications, collaboration, and storage. So, a KMS is an ideal platform on which to create or run a virtual organization (see Lemken et al., 2000). The Communispace system, the knowledge management suites, and portals provide ideal tools for the virtual environment.

People in the KM System

Most of the issues concerning the success, implementation, and effective use of a knowledge management system are people issues. And since a knowledge management system is an enterprisewide effort, many people are involved in it. They include the chief knowledge officer (CKO), the CEO, the other officers and managers of the organization, members and leaders of communities of practice, KMS developers, and KMS staff. Each person or group has an important role in either the development, management, or use of a KMS. By far, the CKO has the most visible role in a KMS effort, but the system cannot succeed unless the roles of all the players are established and understood.

THE CHIEF KNOWLEDGE OFFICER. Knowledge management projects that involve establishing a knowledge environment conducive to the transfer, creation, or use of knowledge attempt to build *cultural receptivity.* These attempts are centered on changing the behavior of the firm to embrace the use of knowledge management. Behavioral-centric projects require a high degree of support and participation from the senior management of the organization to facilitate their implementation. Most firms developing knowledge management systems have created a knowledge management officer, a *chief knowledge officer (CKO),* at the senior level. The objectives of the CKO's role are to maximize the firm's knowledge assets, design and implement knowledge management strategies, effectively exchange knowledge assets internally and externally, and promote system use.

A chief knowledge officer must do the following (adapted from Duffy, 1998):

- Set knowledge management strategic priorities.
- Establish a knowledge repository of best practices.
- Gain a commitment from senior executives to support a learning environment.
- Teach information seekers how to ask better and smarter questions.
- Establish a process for managing intellectual assets.
- Obtain customer satisfaction information in near real time.
- Globalize knowledge management.

The CKO is responsible for defining the area of knowledge within the firm that will be the focal point, based on the mission and objectives of the firm (Davis, 1998). The CKO is responsible for standardizing the enterprisewide vocabulary and for controlling the knowledge directory. This is critical in areas that must share knowledge across departments, to ensure uniformity. CKOs must get a handle on the company's repositories of research, resources, and expertise, including where they are stored and who manages and accesses them (e.g, perform a knowledge audit). Then the CKO must encourage pollination among disparate workgroups with complementary resources.

The CKO is responsible for creating an infrastructure and cultural environment for knowledge sharing. He or she must assign or identify the *knowledge champions* within the business units. The CKO's job is to manage the content their group produces (e.g., the Chrysler Tech Clubs; see Minicase 1), continually add to the knowledge base, and encourage their colleagues to do the same. Successful CKOs should have the full and enthusiastic support of their managers and of top management. Ultimately, the CKO is responsible for the entire knowledge management project while it is under development, and then for management of the system and the knowledge once it is deployed.

CEO, OFFICERS, AND MANAGERS OF THE ORGANIZATION. Briefly, the CEO is responsible for championing the KM effort. He or she must ensure that a competent and capable CKO is found, and that the CKO can obtain all the resources (including access to people with knowledge sources) needed to make the project a success. The CEO must also gain organizationwide support for the contribution to and use of the KMS. The CEO must also prepare the organization for the cultural changes that are about to occur. Support is the critical responsibility of the CEO.

The officers—the CFO, COO, CIO and others—generally must make resources available to the CKO so that he or she can get the job done. The chief financial officer (CFO) must ensure that the financial resources are available. The chief organization officer (COO) must ensure that people begin to embed knowledge management practices into their daily work processes. There is a special relationship between the CKO and chief information officer (CIO). Usually the CIO is responsible for the IT vision of the organization and for the IT architecture, including databases and other potential knowledge sources. The CIO must cooperate with the CKO in making these resources available. KMSs are expensive propositions, and it is wise to use existing systems if they are available and capable.

Managers must also support the KM effort and provide access to sources of knowledge. In many KMSs, managers are an integral part of the communities of practice.

COMMUNITIES OF PRACTICE. The success of many KM systems has been attributed to the active involvement of the people who contribute to and benefit from using the knowledge. Consequently, communities of practice have appeared within organizations that are serious about their knowledge management efforts. As discussed earlier, a *community of practice (COP)* is a group of people in an organization with a common professional interest. Ideally, all the KMS users should each be in at least one COP. Creating and nurturing COPs properly is one key to KMS success.

In a sense, a community of practice owns the knowledge that it contributes, because it manages the knowledge on its way into the system, and must approve modifications to it. The community is responsible for the accuracy and timeliness of the knowledge it contributes, and for identifying its potential use. A number of researchers have investigated how successful COPs form and function. We discuss several studies.

Storck and Hill (2000) investigated one of the earliest communities of practice at Xerox. When established at Xerox, the COP was a new organizational form. The word *community* captured the sense of responsible, independent action that characterized the group, which continued to function within the standard

TABLE 9.1 The Six Key Principles Supporting Communities of Practice at Xerox

Community Characteristic	Actions
Interaction format	Consists of meetings, collaborative computing, interaction structure, e-mail, etc.
Organizational culture	Leverages common training, experience, and vocabulary. Facilitates working around constraints.
Mutual interest	Builds commitment and promotes continuous improvement of processes.
Individual and collective learning	Recognizes and rewards knowledge contribution and use; leverages knowledge; provides a culture of knowledge sharing.
Knowledge sharing	Embeds knowledge sharing into work practices. Reinforces with immediate feedback the value of knowledge sharing.
Community processes and norms	Build trust and identity. Minimize linkage to the formal control structure. Motivate the community to establish its own governance processes.

Source: Reprinted from "Knowledge Diffusion Through Strategic Communities," by J. Storck and P. A. Hill. *Sloan Management Review*, Vol. 41, No. 2, Winter 2000.

boundaries of the large organization. Management sponsored the community, but did not mandate it. Community members were volunteers. In Table 9.1 we list the six key principles that support communities of practice at Xerox.

See *A Closer Look* 9.1 for methods for building a community of practice. Charitable organizations are a good metaphor for how to develop and run a community of practice. For example, Cothrel and Williams (1999b) present an interesting model for community-building based on the Willow Creek Community Church. For more on communities of practice, see Barth (2000a), Cothrel and Williams (1999a, 1999b), Eisenhart (2000), and Storck and Hill (2000).

KMS DEVELOPERS. These are the team members who actually develop the system. They work for the CKO. Some are organizational experts who develop strategies to promote and manage the organizational culture shift. Others are involved

A CLOSER LOOK
9.1 BUILDING A COMMUNITY OF PRACTICE

In a busy company where people are already fully occupied, a burdensome structure can doom their participation in a community of practice. Cliff Figallo, director of community development at Futurize Now of San Francisco, which advises companies on being responsive to their customers, says the success of any community of practice depends on how well management provides "convenience and commitment." *Convenience* entails making it as easy as possible for members to participate. These facilitations include choosing technological tools appropriate for the users; scheduling meetings, discussions, and other activities for minimal conflict with members' other duties; eliminating redundancy; and simplifying ways to access and archive knowledge.

"*Commitment* means that management has the patience to allow the community to build itself," Figallo says. "It also means providing incentives for members to use the community regularly. They should not feel conflicted about spending time to keep the community fresh and current. It should be a normal part of their work routines and deliverables."

Source: Modified from M. Eisenhart, "Around the Virtual Water Cooler: Sustaining Communities of Practice Takes Plenty of Persistence," *Knowledge Management*, October 2000.

in system software and hardware selection, programming, testing, deploying, and maintaining the system. Still others initially are involved in training users. Eventually the training function moves to the KMS staff.

KMS STAFF. Enterprisewide KM systems require a full-time staff to catalogue and manage the knowledge. This staff is either located at the firm's main IT facility or dispersed throughout the organization in the knowledge centers. Most large consulting firms have more than one knowledge center.

Earlier we described the function of the staff to be similar to that of reference librarians. They actually do much more. Some members are functional-area experts who are now cataloguing and approving knowledge contributions, and pushing the knowledge out to clients and employees who they believe can use the knowledge. These functional experts may also work in a liaison role with the functional areas of the communities of practice. Others work with users to train them on the system or help them with their searches. Still others work on improving the system's performance by identifying better methods with which to manage knowledge. For example, Ernst & Young has 250 people managing the knowledge repository and assisting people in finding knowledge at its Center for Business Knowledge. Some staff members disseminate knowledge, while others are liaisons with the forty practice areas. They codify and store documents in their areas of expertise (see Hansen et al., 1999).

Integration

Since a knowledge management system is an enterprise system, it must be integrated with other enterprise and other information systems in an organization. Obviously, when it is designed and developed, it cannot be perceived as an add-on system. It must be truly integrated into other systems. Through the structure of the organizational culture (changed if necessary), a knowledge management system and its activities can be directly integrated into a firm's business processes. For example, a group involved in customer support can capture its knowledge to provide help on customers' difficult problems. In this case, helpdesk software would be one type of package to integrate into a KMS, especially into the knowledge repository.

Since a KMS can be developed on a knowledge platform consisting of communication, collaboration, and storage technologies, and most firms already have many such tools and technologies in place, it is often possible to develop a KMS in the organization's existing tools (e.g., Lotus Notes/Domino Server). Or, an enterprise knowledge portal can provide universal access and an interface into all of an individual's relevant corporate information and knowledge. In this case, the KMS effort would provide the linkage for everyone into the entire enterprise information system.

INTEGRATION WITH DSS. Knowledge management systems typically do not involve running models to solve problems. This is typically done in decision support systems. However, since a knowledge management system provides help in solving problems by applying knowledge, part of the solution may involve running models. A KMS could integrate into an appropriate set of models and data and activate them, given that a specific problem may call for it.

INTEGRATION WITH ARTIFICIAL INTELLIGENCE. Knowledge management has a natural relationship with artificial intelligence (AI) methods and software, though knowledge management, strictly speaking, is not an artificial intelligence method. There are a number of ways in which knowledge management and artificial intelligence can integrate. For example, if the knowledge stored in a KMS is to be stored and used as a sequence of if-then-else rules, then an expert system becomes part of the KMS (see Rasmus, 2000). An expert system could also assist a user in identifying how to apply a chunk of knowledge in the KMS.

Much work is being done in the field of artificial intelligence relating to knowledge engineering, tacit-to-explicit knowledge transfer, knowledge identification, understanding, and dissemination, and so on. Companies are attempting to realign these technologies and resultant products with knowledge management. The AI technologies most often integrated with knowledge management are intelligent agents, expert systems, neural networks, and fuzzy logic. Several specific methods and tools were described earlier.

INTEGRATION WITH DATABASES AND INFORMATION SYSTEMS. Since a KMS utilizes a knowledge repository, sometimes constructed out of a database system or an electronic document management system, it can automatically integrate to this part of the firm's information system. As data and information updates are made, the KMS can utilize them. Knowledge management systems also attempt to glean knowledge from documents and databases (KDD—knowledge discovery in databases) through artificial intelligence methods as was described earlier. There are a number of products on the market to perform this task with minimal user involvement.

INTEGRATION WITH CUSTOMER RELATIONSHIP MANAGEMENT SYSTEMS. Customer relationship management (CRM) systems help users in dealing with customers. One aspect is the help-desk notion described earlier. But CRM goes much deeper. It can develop usable profiles of customers, and predict their needs, so that an organization can increase sales and better serve its customers. A KMS can certainly provide tacit knowledge to people who use CRM directly in working with customers.

INTEGRATION WITH SUPPLY CHAIN MANAGEMENT SYSTEMS. The supply chain is often considered to be the logistics end of the business. If products do not move through the organization and go out the door, the firm will fail. So it is important to optimize the supply chain and manage it properly. A new set of software called supply chain management (SCM) attempts to do so. SCM can benefit through integration with KMS because there are many issues and problems in the supply chain that require the company to bring to bear both tacit and explicit knowledge. Accessing such knowledge will directly improve supply chain performance.

INTEGRATION WITH CORPORATE INTRANETS AND EXTRANETS. Communication and collaboration tools and technologies are necessary for KMS to function. KMS is not simply integrated with the technology of intranets and extranets, but is typically developed on them as the communications platform. Extranets are specifically designed to enhance the collaboration of a firm with its suppliers and sometimes with customers. If a firm can integrate its KMS into its intranets and extranets, not only will knowledge flow more freely, both from a contributor and to a user (either directly or through a knowledge repository), the firm can also capture knowledge directly with little user involvement, and can deliver it when the system "thinks" that a user needs knowledge.

One advantage of a KMS integrated into an extranet is that when a problem occurs or is about to occur, individuals both from the firm and from suppliers and customers either can be alerted if the problem had been somehow detected before, or can collaborate to attempt to handle it. A KMS integrated with an extranet might have prevented the Ford Explorer/Firestone Tire problem (described in the *IT at Work* on page 418).

Closing Remarks

For millennia we have known about the effective use of knowledge and how to store and reuse it. Intelligent organizations recognize that knowledge is an intellectual asset, perhaps the only one that grows over time, and when harnessed effectively can sustain competition and innovation. Organizations can use information technology to perform true knowledge management. Leveraging an entire organization's intellectual resources can have tremendous financial impact.

With knowledge management, the definition is clear, the concepts are clear, the methodology is clear, the challenges are clear and surmountable, the benefits are clear and can be substantial, and the tools and technology—though incomplete and somewhat expensive—are viable. Key issues are organizational culture, executive sponsorship, and measuring success. Technological issues are minimal compared to these. Knowledge management is not just another expensive management fad. Knowledge management is a new paradigm for how we work.

MANAGERIAL ISSUES

1. ***Organizational culture change.*** This issue is how can we change organizational culture so that people are willing both to contribute knowledge to and use knowledge from a KMS? There must be strong executive leadership, clearly expressed goals, user involvement in the system, and deployment of an easy-to-use system that provides real value to employees. A viable reward structure for contributing and using knowledge must also be developed.
2. ***How to store tacit knowledge.*** This is extremely difficult. Most KMSs (based on the network storage model) store explicit knowledge about the tacit knowledge that people possess. When the knowledgeable people leave an organization, they take their knowledge with them. Since knowledge requires active use by the recipient, it is important for the person generating knowledge to articulate it in a way that another, appropriately educated person can understand it.
3. ***How to measure the tangible and intangible benefits of KMS.*** There are a number of ways to measure the value of intellectual assets and of providing them to the organization, as discussed in Section 9.7.
4. ***Determining the roles of the various personnel in a KM effort.*** This issue is described in Section 9.7.
5. ***The importance of knowledge management.*** Knowledge management is extremely important. It is not another management fad. If it is correctly done, it can have massive impact by leveraging know-how throughout the organization. If it is not done, or is not correctly done, the company will not be

able to effectively compete against another major player in the industry that does KM correctly.

6. ***Implementation in the face of quickly changing technology.*** This is an important issue to address regarding the development of many IT systems. Technology has to be carefully examined, and experiments done, to determine what makes sense. By starting now, an organization can get past the managerial and behavioral issues. As better and cheaper technology is developed, the KMS can be migrated over to it, just as legacy systems have migrated to the PC.
7. ***How can our organization develop a successful knowledge management system?*** All the experts in the field indicate that an organization must recognize that it must deal with managerial, behavioral, and cultural issues first. Technology issues have minimal impact.

ON THE WEB SITE... Additional resources, including the Virtual Company, quizzes, cases, updates, additional exercises, links, demos, and activities, can be found on the book's Web site.

KEY TERMS

Best practices *398*
Chief knowledge officer (CKO) *401*
Codification strategy *399*
Community of practice (COP) *402*
Data mining *413*
Electronic document management (EDM) *409*
Enterprise knowledge portal (EKP) *408*
Explicit knowledge *389*
Intellectual assets *387*
Intellectual capital *389*
Knowledge *388*
Knowledge audit *401*
Knowledge-based economy *391*
Knowledge discovery in databases (KDD) *413*
Knowledge management (KM) *388*
Knowledge management suites *407*
Knowledge management system (KMS) *388*
Knowledge network model *396*
Knowledge repository *397*
Knowledge repository model *396*
Knowware *407*
Leaky knowledge *390*
Learning organization *392*
Model marts *414*
Model warehouses *414*
Organizational culture *393*
Organizational learning *392*
Organizational memory *392*
Personalization strategy *400*
Sticky knowledge *390*
Tacit knowledge *389*

CHAPTER HIGHLIGHTS (Numbers Refer to Learning Objectives)

❶ Knowledge is different from information and data. Knowledge is information that is contextual, relevant, and actionable. It is dynamic in nature.

❶ Tacit (unstructured, sticky) knowledge is usually in the domain of subjective, cognitive, and experiential learning; explicit (structured, leaky) knowledge deals with more objective, rational, and technical knowledge, and is highly personal and hard to formalize.

❷❻ A learning organization has an organizational memory and a means to save, represent, and share it.

❷❻ Organizational learning is the development of new knowledge and insights that have the potential to influence behavior.

❷❻ The ability of an organization to learn, to develop memory, and to share knowledge is dependent on its culture. Culture is a pattern of shared basic assumptions.

❷ Knowledge management is a process that helps organizations identify, select, organize, disseminate, and transfer important information and expertise that typically reside within the organization in an unstructured manner.

❷❹ The fastest, most effective and powerful way to manage knowledge assets is through the systematic transfer of best practices.

2 6 10 Knowledge management requires a major transformation in organizational culture to create a desire to share (give and receive) knowledge, and a commitment to KM at all levels of a firm.

3 The knowledge management model involves the following cyclical steps: create, capture, refine, store, manage, and disseminate knowledge.

5 The chief knowledge office (CKO) is primarily responsible for changing the behavior of the firm to embrace the use of knowledge management and then managing the development operation of a knowledge management system.

5 6 Communities of practice (COPs) provide pressure to break down the cultural barriers that hinder knowledge management efforts.

6 10 Knowledge management is an effective way for an or ganization to leverage its intellectual assets.

7 It is difficult to measure the success of a KMS. Traditional methods of financial measurement fall short, as they do not consider intellectual capital an asset.

8 The two strategies used for knowledge management initiatives are the personalization strategy and the codification strategy.

8 The two storage models used for knowledge management projects are the repository storage model and the network storage model.

8 Standard knowledge management initiatives involve the creation of knowledge bases, active process management, knowledge centers, collaborative technologies, and knowledge webs.

9 A knowledge management system is generally developed using three sets of technologies: communication, collaboration, and storage.

9 A variety of technologies can make up a knowledge management system: the Internet, intranets, data warehousing, decision-support tools, groupware, and so on. Intranets are the primary means of displaying and distributing knowledge in organizations.

6 9 10 Knowledge management is not just another expensive management fad. It is a new paradigm for the way we work.

QUESTIONS FOR REVIEW

1. Define what is meant by an intellectual asset.
2. Define knowledge and knowledge management.
3. Define explicit knowledge. Why is it also called leaky?
4. Define tacit knowledge. Why is it also called sticky?
5. How can tacit knowledge be transferred or shared?
6. Define organizational learning and relate it to knowledge management.
7. Define organizational memory and relate it to the idea of a knowledge repository.
8. Define organizational culture.
9. List the ways that organizational culture can impact on a knowledge management effort.
10. What is the primary goal of knowledge management?
11. Describe the codification strategy for knowledge management.
12. Describe the personalization strategy for knowledge management.
13. Describe the repository storage model of knowledge management.
14. Describe the network storage model of knowledge management.
15. Describe the roles and responsibilities of the people involved in a knowledge management system, especially the CKO.
16. What is a community of practice?
17. List the steps in the cyclic model of knowledge management. Why is it a cycle?
18. List the steps of knowledge management implementation.
19. List the major knowledge management success factors.
20. Describe the role of IT in knowledge management.

QUESTIONS FOR DISCUSSION

1. Why is the term knowledge so hard to define?
2. Describe and relate the different characteristics of knowledge.
3. Explain why it is important to capture and manage knowledge.

4. Compare and contrast tacit knowledge and explicit knowledge.
5. Explain why organizational culture must sometimes change before knowledge management is introduced.
6. How does knowledge management attain its primary objective?
7. How can employees be motivated to contribute to and use knowledge management systems?
8. What is the role of a knowledge repository in knowledge management?
9. Explain the importance of communication and collaboration technologies to the processes of knowledge management.
10. Discuss the relationships among the personalization and codification knowledge management strategies, and the network and repository storage models.
11. Explain why firms adopt knowledge management initiatives.
12. Explain how the wrong organizational culture can reduce the effectiveness of knowledge management.
13. Explain the role of the CKO in developing a knowledge management system. What major responsibilities does he or she have?
14. What is meant by a culture of knowledge sharing?
15. Discuss the knowledge management success factors.
16. Why is it so hard to evaluate the impacts of knowledge management?
17. Explain how the Internet and its related technologies (Web browsers, intranets, and so on) enable knowledge management.
18. List three top technologies that are most frequently used for implementing knowledge management systems and explain their importance.
19. Explain the roles of a community of practice.
20. Describe an enterprise knowledge portal and explain its significance.

EXERCISES

1. Make a list of all the knowledge management methods you use during your day (work and personal). Which are the most effective? Which are the least effective? What kinds of work or activities does each knowledge management method enable?
2. Why did Sigma (in the *IT at Work*) choose the name Ariadne's Thread for its knowledge management system? Is this an appropriate name for such a system? Explain your answer in detail.
3. Investigate the literature for information on the position of CKO. Find out what percentage of firms with KM initiatives have CKOs and what their responsibilities are.
4. Investigate the literature for new measures of success (metrics) for knowledge management and intellectual capital. Write a report on your findings.
5. Describe how each of the key elements of a knowledge management infrastructure can contribute to its success.
6. Based on your own experience or on the vendor's information, list the major capabilities of a particular knowledge management product, and explain how it can be used in practice.
7. Describe how to ride a bicycle, drive a car, or make a peanut butter and jelly sandwich. Now, have someone else try to do it based solely on your explanation. How can you best convert this knowledge from tacit to explicit (or can't you)?
8. Examine the top five reasons that firms initiate knowledge-management systems, and investigate why these are important in a modern enterprise.
9. Read the article by E. Berkman titled "Don't Lose Your Mind Share," available at *cio.com*. Describe the major problems that Hill & Knowlton faced in February 1999, and what Ted Graham did to solve them.
10. Read the book by Thomas Cahill, *How the Irish Saved Civilization* (New York: Anchor, 1996), and describe how Ireland became a knowledge repository for western Europe just before the fall of the Roman Empire. Explain in detail why this was important in Western civilization and history.

GROUP AND ROLE-PLAYING ACTIVITIES

1. Compare and contrast the capabilities and features of electronic document management with those of collaborative computing and those of knowledge management systems. Each team represents one type of system.
2. Search the Internet for knowledge management products and systems and create categories for them. Assign one vendor to each team. Describe the categories you created and justify them.
3. If you are working on a decision-making project in industry for this course as part of the project (if not, use one from another class or from work), examine some typical decisions in the related project. How would you

extract the knowledge you need? Can you use that knowledge in practice? Why or why not?

4. Read the article by A. Genusa titled "Rx for Learning," available at *cio.com* (February 1, 2001), which describes Tufts University Medical School's experience with knowledge management. Determine how these concepts and such a system could be implemented and used at your college or university. Explain how each aspect would work, or if not, explain why not.

INTERNET EXERCISES

1. How does knowledge management support decision making? Identify products or systems on the Web that help organizations accomplish knowledge management. Start with *brint.com, decision–support.net,* and *knowledge.com.* Try one out and report your findings to the class.
2. Try the KPMG Knowledge Management Framework Assessment Exercise at *kmsurvey.londonweb.net* and assess how well your organization (company or university) is doing with knowledge management. Are the results accurate? Why or why not?
3. Access the Arthur Andersen Web site (*knowledgespace.com*) and look at the overview of services. Describe its features and how they can be used in practice.
4. Search the Internet to identify sites dealing with knowledge management. Start with *google.com, kmworld.com,* and *km-forum.org*. How many did you find? Categorize the sites based on whether they are academic, consulting firms, vendors, and so on. Sample one of each and describe the main focus of the site.
5. Identify five real-world knowledge management success stories by searching vendor Web sites (use at least three different vendors). Describe them. How did knowledge-management systems and methods contribute to their success? What features do they share? What different features do individual successes have?
6. Find a knowledge management product (such as KnowledgeSpace, which has a version running on the Web at *knowledgespace.com*), try out a demo, and write up your experience. Be sure to include a description of the features that make it a true knowledge management system.
7. Search the Internet for vendors of knowledge management suites, enterprise knowledge portals, and out-of-the-box knowledge management solutions. Identify the major features of each product (use three from each), and compare and contrast their capabilities.
8. J. D. Edwards (*jdedwards.com*) developed a knowledge management intranet initiative called the *Knowledge Garden.* Access both the J. D. Edwards and Microsoft Web sites and investigate its current capabilities.

Minicase 1

www.daimlerchrysler.com

DaimlerChrysler EBOKs with Knowledge Management

In 1980 Chrysler Corporation came back from near bankruptcy with innovative designs and a view of a shared culture in design, development, and manufacturing. The company began new ways of looking at its business, its suppliers, and its workers. After the acquisition of American Motors Corporation (AMC) in 1987, executives developed and deployed advanced, dedicated platform design and production methods, which showed enormous potential. Jack Thompson, the technology center development director, worked closely with Chairman Lee Iacocca on the development of a new, modern engineering and design facility. Thompson designed the center around knowledge-sharing and productivity principles: open air, natural light, and escalators (people don't talk on elevators).

In 1994 the tech center opened, providing a home for a transformed engineering culture. Two years later, the corporate headquarters was moved next to the tech center so executives could be nearby. By 2000, over 11,000 people were working at the Auburn Hills, Michigan, center. In November 1998, Daimler-Benz became the majority owner of Chrysler Corporation, renaming the company DaimlerChrysler. Chrysler's fast, efficient, and innovative nature, as a result of the extremely successful platform approach to design and engineering, led to the buy-in—the largest merger in manufacturing history.

Platform production at DaimlerChrysler has teams of engineers focused on a single type of car platform (small car, minivan, and so on), working on new models as a system from concept to production. Cars are designed by a single team considering customer needs and preferences, as opposed to the standard practice of organizing the new designs by organizational functions (silos). Platform teams of employees work and learn together focused on the product, with a payoff in market responsiveness, reduced cost, and increased quality. The Chrysler LH, the first model developed with the platform approach, took 39 months to produce; typically the time to market exceeds 50 months.

While the benefits were clear, Chrysler executives noticed that unexplained errors were popping up in the new platforms (like leaving a moisture barrier out of car doors). *There was an organizational memory problem:* Mentoring and peer support became limited. Informal and formal professional collaboration had stopped. The same mistakes were being made, corrected, and repeated. People were not learning about new developments in their core areas. The typical collaboration found among groups doing similar work was sharply reduced, and so problems and solutions were not being documented or shared.

Collaboration and communication needed to be reestablished within groups with common training, interests, and responsibilities (design, engineering, body, engine, manufacturing, and so on). The goal was to reestablish these links while becoming more competitive with even faster product-cycle times. Chrysler needed to institutionalize knowledge sharing and collaboration. In 1996 Chrysler Corporation made *knowledge management* a vital condition for design and engineering, leading to dramatic improvements in productivity.

First, engineers mapped out where the knowledge was within the organization (a knowledge audit). There were many categories, or "buckets of knowledge," ranging from product databases to CAD/CAM systems to manufacturing, procurement, and supply vehicle test data. Within each category, details were identified and codified. Sharing knowledge meant integrating these knowledge buckets, while resolving cultural issues that impeded sharing across platform boundaries. Chrysler created informal cross-platform *Tech Clubs,* functionally organized communities of practice to reunite designers and engineers with peers from other platform groups. Each community would then codify its knowledge and provide mentoring and apprenticing opportunities for learning.

The *Engineering Book of Knowledge (EBOK)* is Chrysler's intranet supporting a knowledge repository of process *best practices* and technical know-how to be shared and maintained. It was initially developed by two engineering managers but continues through encouraged employee participation in grassroots (i.e., supported at the lower levels of the organization) Tech Clubs. EBOK is written in GrapeVine (GrapeVine Technologies), running as a Lotus Notes application, and is accessed with the Netscape browser and NewsEdge.

Knowledge is explored and entered into the EBOK through an iterative team approach: the Tech Clubs. Best practices are identified, refined, confirmed, and finally entered into the EBOK in a secure interactive electronic repository. When an author proposes a best practice, users in the Tech Club responsible for that area of knowledge react by commenting on the knowledge through a discussion list. One manager, the *Book Owner,* is ultimately responsible for approving new entries and changes to the book. The Book Owner joins the conversation. The author can respond to the comments by either building a better case or going along with the discussion. Ultimately the Tech Club decides, and the Book Owner enters the new knowledge. The Book Owner is the individual who is ultimately responsible for the accuracy of the book, and therefore approves entries to, modifications to, and deletions from the book.

The EBOK is DaimlerChrysler's official design review process. The EBOK even contains best practices information about DaimlerChrysler's competitors. DaimlerChrysler has determined that EBOK is both a best practices tool (the codification strategy with a repository storage model) and a collaboration tool (the personalization strategy with a network storage model). DaimlerChrysler officials recognize that because the environment changes and new methods are being continually developed, the EBOK will never be fully complete. The EBOK is a *living book.* The EBOK *leverages* technology knowledge.

The EBOK is central to DaimlerChrysler's new way of working. The plan is to have more than 5,000 users with access to 3,800 chapters, of which just over half were completed by early 1999. Through the EBOK, DaimlerChrysler reconciled its platform problems and developed a technical memory while tracking competitive information, quality information, and outside standards. Even though there is no central budget for books of knowledge and associated processes, DaimlerChrysler is deploying knowledge in other departments such as manufacturing, finance, and sales and marketing.

Sources: Adapted from W. Karlenzig, "Chrysler's New Know-Mobiles," *Knowledge Management,* May 1999, pp. 58–66; and other sources.

Questions for Minicase 1

1. Platform design at DaimlerChrysler led directly to a reduction in the time to market and in costs for new vehicles. Explain how it caused new problems.
2. What is meant by a community of practice? How did DaimlerChrysler leverage the knowledge within such a community?
3. Describe the Engineering Book of Knowledge (EBOK). Explain how it is updated by adding new knowledge of practice.
4. It has been said that "the proper role for all knowledge management tools is to leverage technology in service to human thinking." Explain this statement.

5. How successful was the knowledge management initiative at DaimlerChrysler?
6. Consider how a book of knowledge could impact another organization, ideally one with which you are affiliated (e.g., your university, job, part-time job, family business). Describe the potential impacts, and list the benefits. Would there be any organizational culture issues to deal with? Why or why not?

Minicase 2

www.chevron.com

Chevron's Knowledge Management Initiatives Cook with Gas

Chevron wanted to explore, develop, adapt, and adopt knowledge management methods to leverage its expertise throughout the enterprise to maintain a competitive position in the marketplace. The improvements gained from identifying, sharing, and managing intellectual assets can impact positively on drilling, office work, safety, and refineries. Improvements were generated by focusing on process, culture, best practices, and technology, including Internet technology.

Chevron uses knowledge management in drilling, refinery maintenance and safety management, capital project management, and other areas. The electronic document-management system impacts on several different areas at Chevron.

Drilling. Chevron adopted an *organizational learning system (OLS)* that improves drilling performance by sharing information globally. The system uses a simple software tool to capture lessons from the first wells in a new area, and then uses that knowledge to drill the rest of the wells faster and cheaper. Well costs have dropped by 12 to 20 percent and cycle time has been reduced as much as 40 percent in some cases (offshore drilling vessels can cost up to $250,000 a day). Oil & Gas Consultants International developed the OLS for Amoco. Chevron found it through a best-practices survey.

Refineries. The company uses knowledge management IS to maintain six refineries. Sam Preckett, reliability-focused maintenance-system manager, is developing a process to improve information and knowledge sharing. Preckett and others realized that they were not effectively using the data and information already stored in Chevron's enterprise information systems. Preckett has been developing an informal best-practices methodology for maintenance by "trying to learn how we do things." Getting knowledge to users is only part of the system; another part captures the tacit knowledge and experiences of workers. Chevron is trying to motivate workers to participate. Preckett said that at Chevron creative thinking is promoted from the executive level, which "allows him to do interesting things" to achieve efficiency gains through knowledge sharing.

Electronic Document Management. Another specific need under the knowledge management umbrella was addressed by the DocMan system, initiated in December 1994 to improve the timeliness of document access, management, and integration, and sharing of information among individual divisions to meet regulatory compliances. A long-standing application, DocMan works for the Warren Petroleum Limited Partnership Mont Belvieu complex in Texas (of which Chevron is a joint owner).

To handle cultural resistance to change, management emphasized the benefits of the DocMan system: faster access to documents, elimination of wasted effort searching for documents, and assets protection. DocMan delivered a 95 percent return on investment over its 5-year project life. The investment payout period was 1.1 years based on an annual savings of $480,000.

Capital Project Management. Through knowledge management, Chevron implemented a new standard methodology for capital project management. In one case, 60 companies shared data and practices, and so it was possible to compare performance to determine which companies were best and why.

What have been the overall results? Improved management of knowledge was instrumental in reducing operating costs from $9.4 billion to $7.4 billion from 1992 to 1998 and in reducing energy costs by $200 million a year. During the 1990s, efforts like this were essential in reducing costs, achieving productivity gains of over 50 percent (in barrels of output per employee), and improving employee safety performance more than 50 percent. Chevron now calls itself a learning organization. Some gains from knowledge management at Chevron are qualitative: Employees' work is more interesting and challenging when it involves finding and applying new knowledge. Jobs are potentially more fulfilling and more personally rewarding.

Sources: Adapted from L. Velker, "Knowledge the Chevron Way," *KMWorld*, Vol. 8, No. 2, February 1, 1999, pp. 20–21; and "The Means to an Edge: Knowledge Management: Key to Innovation," *CIO*, September 15, 1999.

Questions for Minicase 2

1. What is meant by a learning organization?
2. Describe the gains that Chevron experienced through its knowledge management programs.
3. To what different areas did Chevron apply knowledge management, and how successful were they?
4. Why is it important to document cost savings of knowledge management systems?
5. If dramatic payoffs can be achieved through knowledge management (as with the DocMan system), why don't more companies do so?

REFERENCES AND BIBLIOGRAPHY

1. Abramson, G., "Measuring Up," *CIO,* June 15, 1998.
2. Alavi, M. "Managing Organizational Knowledge," Chapter 2 in Zmud, W. R. (ed.), *Framing the Domains of IT Management: Projecting the Future.* Cincinnati, OH: Pinnaflex Educational Resources, 2000.
3. Allee, V., "Are You Getting Big Value from Knowledge?" *KMWorld,* September 1999, pp. 16–17.
4. Ambrosio, J., "Knowledge Management Mistakes," *Computerworld,* Vol. 34, No. 27, July 3, 2000.
5. Andreu, R., and C. Ciborra, "Organisational Learning and Core Capabilities Development: The Role of IT," *Strategic Information Systems,* Vol. 5, No. 2, June 1996.
6. Barth, S., "Knowledge as a Function of X," *Knowledge Management,* February 2000(a).
7. Barth, S., "KM Horror Stories," *Knowledge Management,* October 2000(b).
8. Blodgett, M., "Prescription Strength," *CIO,* February 1, 2000.
9. Bolloju, N. et al., "Integrating Knowledge Management into Enterprise Environments for the Next Generation of Decision Support," *Decision Support Systems,* 2001, forthcoming.
10. Brooking, A., *Corporate Memory: Strategies for Knowledge Management.* London: International Thomson Business Press, 1999.
11. Bushko, D., and M. Raynor, "Knowledge Management: New Directions for IT (and Other) Consultants," *Journal of Management Consulting,* Vol. 10, No. 2, November 1998.
12. Cahill, T., *How the Irish Saved Civilization.* New York: Anchor, 1996.
13. Clarke, P., "Implementing a Knowledge Strategy for Your Firm," *Research Technology Management,* March–April 1998.
14. Collins, H., *Corporate Portals: Revolutionizing Information Access to Increase Productivity and Drive the Bottom Line,* AMACOM, 2001.
15. Cothrel, J., and R. L. Williams, "On-line Communities: Helping Them Form and Grow," *Journal of Knowledge Management,* Vol. 3, No. 1, 1999(a).
16. Cothrel, J., and R. L. Williams, "On-line Communities: Getting the Most Out of On-line Discussion and Collaboration," *Knowledge Management Review,* No. 6, January–February 1999(b).
17. Croasdell, D., et al., "Using Adaptive Hypermedia to Support Organizational Memory and Learning," *Proceedings, 30th Hawaiian International Conference on Systems Sciences (HICSS),* Hawaii, January 1997.
18. Davenport, T., et al., "Successful Knowledge Management Projects," *Sloan Management Review,* Vol. 39, No. 2, Winter 1998.
19. Davenport, T. H., and L. Prusak, *Working Knowledge: How Organizations Manage What They Know.* Boston: Harvard Business School Press, 1998.
20. Davis, M., "Knowledge Management," *Information Strategy: The Executive's Journal,* Fall 1998.
21. DiBella, A. J., "Developing Learning Organizations: A Matter of Perspective," *Academy of Management Journal,* Best Papers Proceedings, 1995.
22. Drucker, D., "Knowledge Mgm't Revised—Theory Doesn't Equal Practice," *InternetWeek,* No. 846, January 29, 2001.
23. Duffy, D., "Knowledge Champions," *CIO* (Enterprise-Section 2), November 1998.
24. Dyer, G., "Knowledge Management Crosses the Chasm," *Knowledge Management,* March 2000.
25. Eisenhart, M., "Around the Virtual Water Cooler: Sustaining Communities of Practice Takes Plenty of Persistence," *Knowledge Management,* October 2000.
26. "Enterprise Knowledge Portals Wise Up Your Business," *InfoWorld,* Vol. 22, No. 49, December 4, 2000.
27. Garvin, D. A., "Building a Learning Organization," *Harvard Business Review,* July–August 1993.
28. Gottschalk, P., "Knowledge Management in the Professions: The Case of IT Support in Law Firms," *Proceedings, 33rd HICSS,* January 2000.
29. Gray, P., "Tutorial on Knowledge Management," *Proceedings of the Americas Conference of the Association for Information Systems.* Milwaukee, WI, August 1999.
30. Gupta, B., et al., "An Exploration of Knowledge Management Techniques," *Proceedings of the Americas Conference of the Association for Information Systems.* Milwaukee, WI, August 1999.
31. Gupta, B., et al., "Knowledge Management: A Taxonomy, Practices and Challenges," *Industrial Management and Data Systems,* Vol. 100, Nos. 1 and 2, 2000.
32. Hackbarth, G., and V. Grover, "The Knowledge Repository: Organizational Memory Information Systems," *Information Systems Management,* Summer 1999.
33. Hansen, M., et al., "What's Your Strategy for Managing Knowledge?" *Harvard Business Review,* Vol. 77, No. 2, March–April 1999.
34. Herschel, R. T., and H. R. Nemati, "Chief Knowledge Officer: Critical Success Factors for Knowledge Management," *Information Strategy,* Vol. 16, No. 4, Summer 2000.

35. Hibbard, J., "Cultural Breakthrough," *InformationWeek*, September 21, 1998.

36. Holsapple, C. W., and A. B. Whinston, *Decision Support Systems*. St. Paul, MN: West Publishing, 1996.

37. Homburg, V., and A. Meijer, "Why Would Anyone Want to Share His Knowledge?" *Proceedings, 34th HICSS*, January 2001.

38. King, D., and K. Jones, "Competitive Intelligence, Software Robots, and the Internet: The NewsAlert Prototype," *Proceedings, 28th HICSS*, January 1995.

39. Knapp, E. M., "Knowledge Management," *Business and Economic Review*, Vol. 44, No. 4, July–September 1998.

40. KPMG Consulting (*kpmgconsulting.com/kpmgsite/service/km/publications.htm*), press release 2000.

41. Lane, P., and M. Lubatkin, "Relative Absorptive Capacity and Interorganizational Learning," *Strategic Management Journal*, Vol. 19, 1998.

42. Lemken, B., et al., "Sustained Knowledge Management by Organizational Culture," *Proceedings, 33rd HICSS*, January 2000.

43. Leonard, D., and S. Sensiper, "The Role of Tacit Knowledge in Group Innovations," *California Management Review*, Vol. 40, No. 3, Spring 1998.

44. Liautaud, B., and M. Hammond, *E-Business Intelligence: Turning Information into Knowledge into Profit*. New York: McGraw-Hill, 2000.

45. Madden, J. "KPMG Sharing Knowledge," *PCWeek*, August 9, 1999.

46. Madhaven, R., and R. Grover, "From Embedded Knowledge to Embodied Knowledge: New Product Development as Knowledge Management," *Journal of Marketing*, Vol. 62, No. 4, October 1998.

47. McDonald, M., and D. Shand, "Request for Proposal: A Guide to KM Professional Services," *Knowledge Management*, March 2000.

48. McFadden, F. R., et al., *Modern Database Management*. Reading, MA: Addison-Wesley, 1999.

49. McKellar, H., "KPMG Releases KM Report," *KMWorld*, March 8, 2000 (*www.kmworld.com*).

50. "The Means to an Edge: Knowledge Management: Key to Innovation," Special Supplement, *CIO*, September 15, 1999.

51. Microsoft Corporation, "Practicing Knowledge Management" (*Microsoft.com/business/km/casestudies/jdedward.asp*), 2001.

52. Montana, J. C., "The Legal System and Knowledge Management," *Information Management Journal*, Vol. 34, No. 3, July 2000.

53. Mooney, S. F., "P-C 'Knowledge Capital' Can Be Measured," *National Underwriter*, Vol. 104, No. 51/52, December 18–25, 2000.

54. Moore, C., "Eureka! Xerox Discovers Way to Grow Community Knowledge," *KMWorld*, October 1999.

55. Nonaka, I., and H. Takeuchi, *The Knowledge-Creating Company: How Japanese Companies Create the Dynamics of Innovation*. New York: Oxford University Press, 1995.

56. O'Dell, C., et al., *If Only We Knew What We Know: The Transfer of Internal Knowledge and Best Practice*. New York: Free Press, 1998.

57. Polanyi, M., *Personal Knowledge*. Chicago: University of Chicago Press, 1958.

58. Polanyi, M., *The Tacit Dimension*. London: Routledge & Kegan Paul, 1966.

59. Rasmus, D. W., "Knowledge Management: More than AI But Less Without It," *PC AI*, Vol. 14, No. 2, March–April 2000.

60. Robin, M., "Learning by Doing," *Knowledge Management*, March 2000.

61. Ruber, P., "Build a Dynamic Business Portal With XML," *Knowledge Management*, January 11, 2001.

62. Ruggles, R., "The State of the Notion: Knowledge Management in Practice," *California Management Review*, Vol. 40, No. 3, 1998.

63. Schein, E., *Organizational Culture and Leadership*, 2nd ed. San Francisco: Jossey-Bass, 1997.

64. Schein, E., *The Corporate Culture Survival Guide*. San Francisco: Jossey-Bass, 1999.

65. Sherman, L., "Creating Useful Knowledge Structures: Lessons from Library Science and Architecture Inform Today's Web Designs," *Knowledge Management*, October 2000.

66. Silver, C. A., "Where Technology and Knowledge Meet," *Journal of Business Strategy*, Vol. 21, No. 6, November–December 2000.

67. Skyrme, D. J., *Knowledge Networking: Creating the Collaborative Enterprise*. Woburn, MA: Butterworth-Heinemann, 1999.

68. Skyrme, D. J., and D. M. Amidon, "New Measures of Success," *Journal of Business Strategy*, Vol. 19, No. 1, January–February 1998.

69. Stahl, S., "Knowledge Yields Impressive Returns," *InformationWeek*, April 5, 1999.

70. Stevens, L., "Knowing What Your Company Knows," *Knowledge Management*, December 2000.

71. Storck, J., and P. A. Hill, "Knowledge Diffusion Through Strategic Communities," *Sloan Management Review*, Vol. 41, No. 2, Winter 2000.

72. Swan, J., et al., "Knowledge Management—When Will People Management Enter the Debate?" *Proceedings, 33rd HICSS*, January 2000.

73. Vaas, L., "Brainstorming," *PCWeek*, Vol. 16, No. 22, May 31, 1999.

74. Von Krogh, G., et al. (eds.), *Knowledge Creation: A Source of Value*. New York: St. Martin's Press, 2000.

75. Watson, R. T., *Data Management: Databases and Organizations*. New York: Wiley, 1998.

76. Zack, M. H., "Developing a Knowledge Strategy," *California Management Review*, Spring 1999.

CHAPTER

10

Supporting Management and Decision Making

LEARNING OBJECTIVES

After studying this chapter, you will be able to:

1. Describe the concepts of management, decision making, and computerized support for decision making.
2. Justify the role of models in decision making.
3. Describe the framework for computerized decision support, and classify problems and support according to the framework.
4. Describe decision support systems and their benefits, and analyze their role in management support.
5. Compare regular (personal) decision support systems with group and organizational decision support systems, and analyze the major differences.
6. Describe enterprise and executive information systems, and analyze their role in management support.
7. Explain how networks and the Web can enhance managerial decision making.

WEB-BASED DATA ANALYSIS AT SHOPKO

THE PROBLEM

ShopKo is a 130-store Wisconsin-based discount chain that is operating in an extremely competitive environment. The success of such companies depends on their ability to make quick decisions and on superb customer service and vendor (supplier) relations. The information systems that supported ShopKo's business in the past were highly fragmented, ineffective, and inflexible. It took a day to get an answer to a simple question, and reports were always late and had limited value. Financial and marketing analysts were frustrated. Forecasts were inaccurate, and wrong decisions were frequently made. With 130 stores and over 200,000 SKUs (stock-keeping units), it was difficult to know where profits were made and where money was lost.

www.shopko.com

THE SOLUTION

The company installed comprehensive decision support system (DSS) software (DSS Agent, from MicroStrategy). This system includes a data warehouse and online analytical processing (OLAP), which supports decision making, report generation, and query capabilities.

The system provides the following:

- Sales statistics for every SKU, at each store, on a daily basis.
- Summaries of sales data, by store, by regions, and so on.
- Analysis of the above and similar sales data (e.g., trend analysis, comparison to competitors).
- Inventory tracking and analysis.
- Sales and expenditures forecasts.
- Quick answers to ad-hoc managerial queries.
- Customized reports and detailed managerial analysis.
- Profitability analysis (by product, by store).
- A "drill-everywhere" component that automatically allows for exploration of information found along, above, within, or below the current level of details.
- Extensive market-basket analysis. For example, the company can look at whether customers coming into the stores are buying only items on sale.
- The ability to find the relationship between levels of advertisement and sales of each item.

Using software called DSS Web (from *microstrategy.com*), ShopKo permits its vendors to log onto its Web site and use standard browsers to see how well their products are selling. This facilitates *vendor partnerships* and ensures better customer service (the vendors quickly ship items that are depleted). Some parts of the DSS are integrated with other information systems, especially the pharmaceutical one that is now integrated with medical claim records. The system provides enterprisewide decision support services, including workbenches for sales/marketing, actuarial/claims, medical management, utilization, and government reporting. (See *shopko.com* for more information.)

Of special interest is the DSS application developed for ShopKo's pharmaceutical business. Costs can be compared over a wide range of variables, including health care providers, treatment protocols, specialties, care plans, patient demographics, and geographical distribution. At a global level, users can "slice and dice" data about a particular medicine or its generic equivalent, the day the drug was prescribed, the prescribing facility, or the physician involved. Complex set-math filtering criteria developed by MicroStrategy let analysts relate prescriptons to patient diagnoses, so that client firms' medical directors can determine which physicians are prescribing more brand-name than generic drugs for a particular diagnosis.

THE RESULTS

The competitive advantages provided by the DSS solution more than justified ShopKo's investment in the technology. The savings came from the corporate ability to use sophisticated analysis that enabled stores to carry the right merchandise at the right place and time. In 2000, however, competitive pressures in the industry plagued many retailers, including Shopko. The company responded in 2001 by installing e-procurements and other Web-based initiatives. Results from these new initiatives remain to be seen.

Sources: Compiled from *Stores Magazine,* 1996; *microstrategy.com* (2001); and *shopko.com* (2001).

LESSONS LEARNED FROM THIS CASE

The opening case illustrates that a solution to complex decisions can be enhanced with the use of computer programs called a decision support system (DSS). As a matter of fact, the DSS software supported several important decisions at Shopko. We also learned that decisions are supported both in the sales and inventory areas. Furthermore, much of the support is based around the concepts of data warehousing and online analytical processing (which we'll study in Chapter 11). Finally, the Web is playing an increasing role in facilitating purchasing.

This chapter is dedicated to the presentation of computer and Web support to managerial decision makers. We begin by reviewing the manager's job and the nature of today's decisions, which help explain why computerized support is needed. Then we present the concept and methodology of the computerized decision support system. Three cases of support are presented: supporting individuals, groups, and whole organizations. Finally, the topic of decision support in the Web environment is described.

10.1 MANAGERS AND DECISION MAKING

Decisions are being made by all of us every day. However, most major organizational decisions are made by managers. Our interest in this chapter is in managerial decision making, and therefore we begin with a brief description of the manager's job, of which making decisions is a major component.

The Manager's Job

Management is a process by which organizational goals are achieved through the use of resources (people, money, energy, materials, space, time). These resources are considered to be *inputs,* and the attainment of the goals is viewed as the *output* of the process. Managers oversee this process in an attempt to optimize it.

To understand how computers support managers, it is necessary first to describe what managers do in the above process. Managers do many things, depending on their position in the organization, the type and size of the organization, organizational policies and culture, and the personalities of the managers themselves. Mintzberg (1973) divided the manager's roles into three categories based on his classical studies:

1. ***Interpersonal roles:*** figurehead, leader, liaison
2. ***Informational roles:*** monitor, disseminator, spokesperson
3. ***Decisional roles:*** entrepreneur, disturbance handler, resource allocator, negotiator

Early information systems mainly supported informational roles. In recent years, however, information systems have been developed that support all three roles. In this chapter, we are mainly interested in the support that IT can provide to *decisional* roles. We divide the manager's work, as it relates to decisional roles, into two phases. Phase I is the identification of problems and/or opportunities. Phase II is the decision of what to do about them. Figure 10.1 provides a flowchart of this process and the flow of information in it.

Looking at Figure 10.1, we see that information comes from both internal and external environments. Internal information is generated from the functional areas. External information comes from sources such as the Internet, online databases, newspapers, industry newsletters, government reports, and personal contacts. Given the large amount of information available, it is necessary to scan the

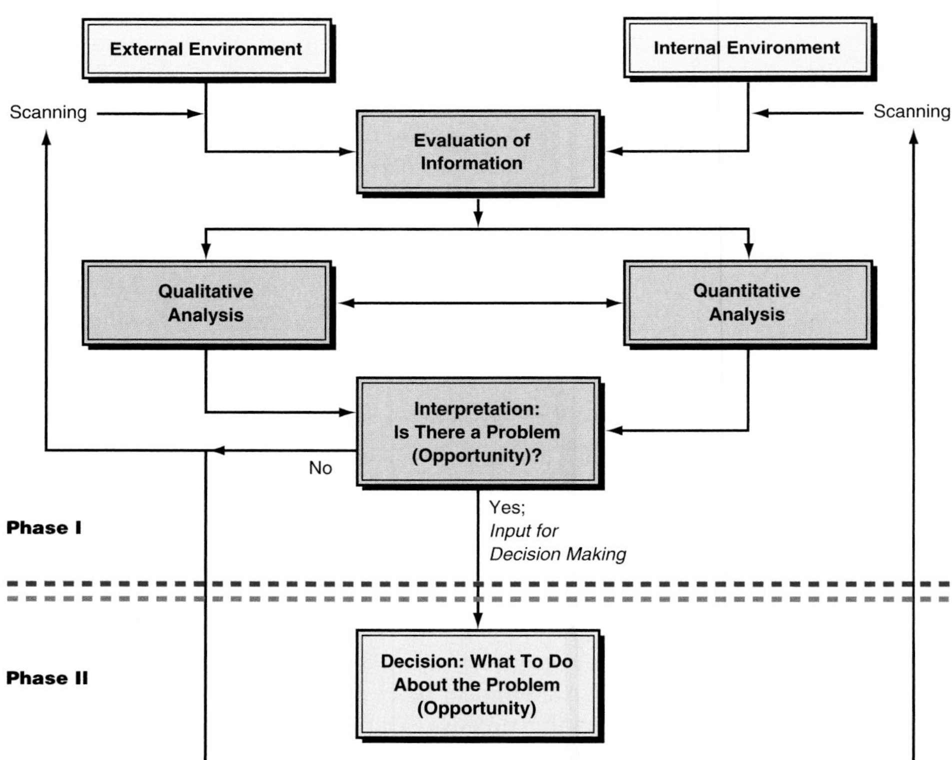

FIGURE 10.1 Two phases of a manager's decision role and the flow of information in the process.

environment and data sources to find the *relevant* information. Collected information is then evaluated for *importance,* and whenever appropriate it is channeled to quantitative and qualitative analysis, which is basically an interpretation of the information. Then, a decision by an executive or a group is made on whether a problem or opportunity exists. If it is decided that there is a problem (opportunity), then the problem is transferred as an input to Phase II. In Phase II, alternative solutions are evaluated and a choice of one alternative is made.

Executing this process manually is difficult. The major reasons for this are the information overload, the large number of alternatives that may be available, the continuous change in the business environment, and the need to make quick decisions. Therefore, computerized aid is provided for management support through various *management support systems (MSSs.).* These systems support the various tasks of the processes shown in Figure 10.1, such as scanning and analyzing, as well as supporting the three managerial roles described earlier. Why is such support needed?

Managerial Decisions and Computerized Support

The success of management depends on the skillful execution of managerial functions such as planning, organizing, directing, and controlling. To carry out these functions, managers engage in the continuous process of *making decisions.*

The ability to make crisp decisions was rated first in importance in a study conducted by the Harbridge House in Boston, Massachusetts. About 6,500 managers in more than 100 companies, including many large, blue-chip corporations, were asked how important it was that managers employ certain management practices. They also were asked how well, in their estimation, managers performed these practices. From a statistical distillation of these answers, Harbridge ranked "making clear-cut decisions when needed" as the *most important* of ten management practices. Ranked second in importance was "getting to the heart of the problems rather than dealing with less important issues." Most of the remaining eight management practices were related directly or indirectly to decision making. The researchers also found that only 10 percent of the managers thought management performed "very well" on any given practice, mainly due to the difficult decision-making environment. It seems that the trial-and-error method, which might have been a practical approach to decision making in the past, is too expensive or ineffective today in many instances.

Therefore, managers must learn how to use the new tools and techniques that can help them make decisions. Some techniques use a quantitative analysis approach, and they are supported by computers. Several of these are described in this chapter. Additional computerized techniques that support qualitative and quantitative analysis are described in Chapter 12. However, before we describe the specific techniques, let's look more closely at the process of decision making.

DECISION MAKING. When making a decision, either organizational or personal, the decision maker goes through a fairly systematic process. Simon (1977) described the process as composed of three major phases: *intelligence, design,* and *choice.* A fourth phase, *implementation,* was added later. Simon claimed that the process is general enough so that it can be supported by decision aids and modeling. A conceptual presentation of the four-stage modeling process is shown in Figure 10.2 (page 438), which illustrates what tasks are included in each phase. Note that there is a continuous flow of information from intelligence to design to choice (bold lines), but at any phase there may be a return to a previous phase (broken lines).

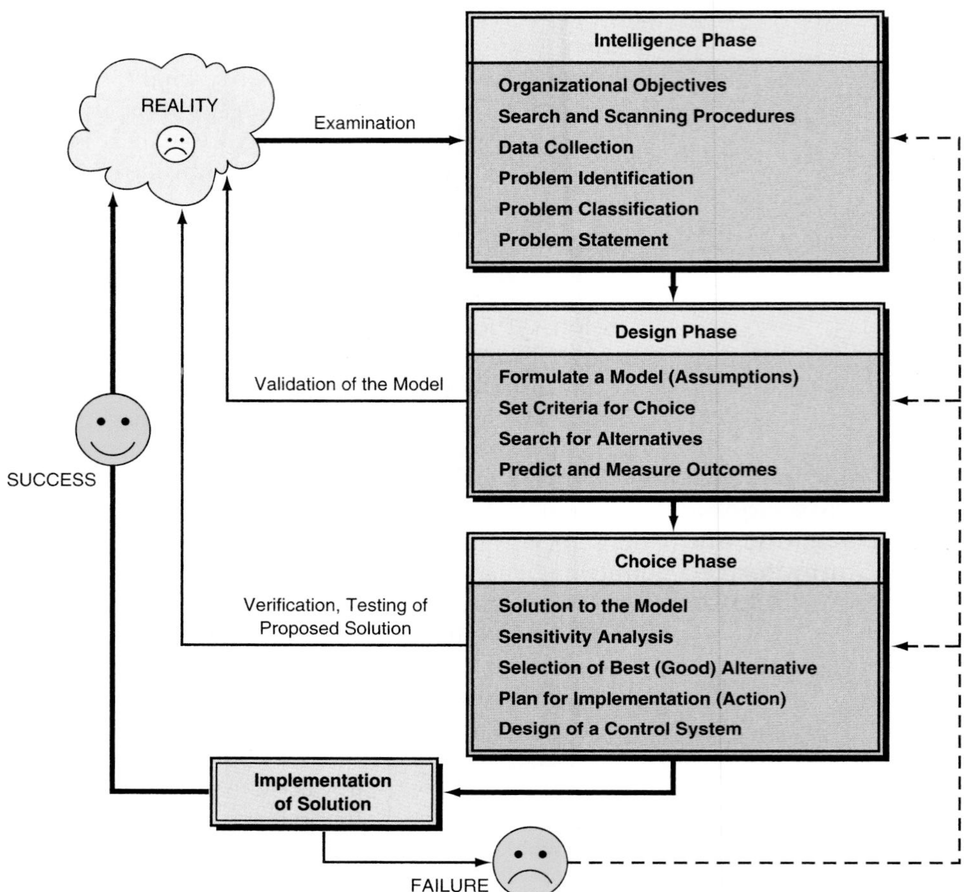

FIGURE 10.2 The process and phases in decision making/ modeling.

The decision-making process starts with the *intelligence phase,* in which managers examine a situation and identify and define the problem. In the *design phase,* decision makers construct a model that simplifes the problem. This is done by making assumptions that simplify reality and by expressing the relationships among all variables. The model is then validated, and decision makers set criteria for the evaluation of alternative potential solutions that are identified. The *choice phase* involves selecting a solution, which is tested "on paper." Once this proposed solution seems to be feasible, we are ready for the last phase—*implementation*. Successful implementation results in resolving the original problem. Failure leads to a return to the previous phases. A DSS attempts to automate several tasks in this process, in which *modeling* is the core.

Modeling and Models

A **model** (in decision making) is a *simplified representation* or abstraction of reality. It is usually simplified because reality is too complex to copy exactly, and because much of its complexity is actually irrelevant to a specific problem. With modeling, one can perform virtual experiments and an analysis on a model of reality, rather than on reality itself. The benefits of modeling are:

1. The cost of virtual experimentation is much lower than the cost of experimentation conducted with a real system.

2. Models allow for the simulated compression of time. Years of operation can be simulated in seconds of computer time.
3. Manipulating the model (by changing variables) is much easier than manipulating the real system. Experimentation is therefore easier to conduct, and it does not interfere with the daily operation of the organization.
4. The cost of making mistakes during a real trial-and-error experiment is much lower when models are used for virtual experimentation.
5. Today's environment holds considerable uncertainty. Modeling allows a manager to better deal with the uncertainty and calculate the risks involved in specific actions.
6. Mathematical models allow the analysis of a very large, sometimes infinite number of possible alternative solutions. With today's advanced technology and communications, managers frequently have a large number of alternatives from which to choose.
7. Models enhance and reinforce learning and support training.

Representation through models can be done at various degrees of abstraction. Models are thus classified into four groups according to their degree of abstraction: iconic, analog, mathematical, and mental. Brief descriptions follow.

ICONIC (SCALE) MODELS. An *iconic model*—the least abstract model—is a physical replica of a system, usually based on a different scale from the original. Iconic models may appear to scale in three dimensions, such as models of an airplane, car, bridge, or production line. Photographs are another type of iconic model, but in only two dimensions.

ANALOG MODELS. An *analog model,* in contrast to an iconic model, does not look like the real system but behaves like it. An analog model could be a physical model, but the *shape* of the model differs from that of the actual system. Some examples include organizational charts that depict structure, authority, and responsibility relationships; maps where different colors represent water or mountains; stock charts; blueprints of a machine or a house; and a thermometer.

MATHEMATICAL (QUANTITATIVE) MODELS. The complexity of relationships in many systems cannot conveniently be represented iconically or analogically, or such representations and the required experimentations may be cumbersome. A more abstract model is possible with the aid of mathematics. Most DSS analysis is executed numerically using mathematical or other quantitative models.

Mathematical models are composed of three types of variables (decision, uncontrollable, and result) and the relationships among them. These are shown in *A Closer Look* 10.1 (page 440).

With recent advances in computer graphics, there is an increased tendency to use iconic and analog models to complement mathematical modeling in decision support systems.

MENTAL MODELS. In addition to the three explicit models described above, people frequently use a behavioral mental model. A *mental model* of a situation provides a subjective description of how a person thinks about a situation. The model includes beliefs, assumptions, relationships, and flows of work as perceived by an individual. For example, a manager's mental model might say that it is

A CLOSER LOOK
10.1 ABOUT MODELING AND MODELS

Mathematical models are composed of three basic components: decision variables, uncontrollable variables (and/or parameters), and result (outcome) variables. (See figure below.) These components are connected by mathematical relationships. In a nonquantitative model, the relationships are symbolic or qualitative.

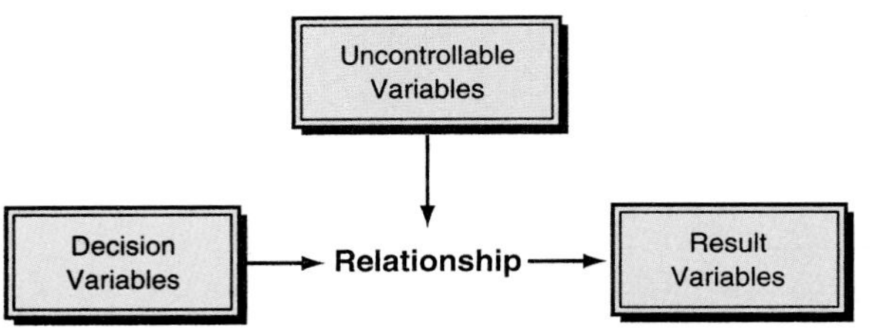

The results (or outcome) of decisions are determined by (1) the decision being made; (2) other factors that are uncontrollable by the decision maker; and (3) the relationships among variables.

Result Variables. The *result variables* reflect the level of effectiveness of the system. That is, they indicate how well the system performs or attains its goals. The result variables are considered, mathematically, to be *dependent variables.*

Decision Variables. *Decision variables* describe the alternative courses of action. For example, in an investment problem, how much to invest in bonds is a decision variable. In a scheduling problem, the decision variables are people and jobs. The *values* of these variables are determined by the decision maker. Decision variables are mathematically classified as *independent variables* (or unknown variables). An aim of a DSS is to find good enough, or possibly the best, values for these decision variables.

Uncontrollable Variables or Parameters. In any decision situation there are factors that affect the result variables but *are not under the control* of the decision maker. These factors can either be fixed (in which case they are called *parameters*), or they can vary (then they are called *variables*). Examples are the prime interest rate, a city's building code, tax regulations, and prices of utilities. Most of these factors are uncontrollable because they emanate from the environment surrounding the decision maker. These variables are classified as *independent variables* since they affect the dependent (result) variables.

Intermediate Variables. *Intermediate variables* are any variables necessary to link the decision variables to the results. Sometimes they reflect intermediate outcomes. For example, in determining machine scheduling, spoilage is an intermediate variable, while total profit is the result variable (spoilage affects the total profit).

The components of a quantitative model are tied together by sets of mathematical expressions such as equations or inequalities.

EXAMPLE: A simple financial-type model may look like this: $P = R - C$. P stands for profit, R stands for revenue, and C stands for cost. Another well-known financial-type model is a present-value model, which may look like this:

$$P = \frac{F}{(1 + i)^n}$$

where

P = the present value
F = a future single payment in dollars
i = interest rate
n = number of years

Using this model, one can calculate, for example, the present value of a payment of $100,000 to be made five years from today, considering 10 percent interest rate, to be:

$$P = \frac{100{,}00}{(1.1)^5} = \$62{,}110$$

better to promote older workers than younger ones and that such a policy would be preferred by most employees.

Mental models are a conceptual, internal representation used to generate descriptions of a problem structure and make predictions of future related variables. They determine the information we use and the manner in which people interpret (or ignore) information. Mental models are extremely useful in situations where it is necessary to determine which information is important.

Developing a mental model is usually the first step in modeling. Once people perceive a situation, they may then model it more precisely using another type of model. Mental models may frequently change, so it is difficult to document them. They are important not only for decision making, but also for human-computer interaction (see Saxby et al., 2000).

Computerized Decision Aids

We are now ready to explore four basic questions: (1) Why do managers need the support of information technology in making decisions? (2) How are the information needs of managers determined? (3) Can the manager's job be fully automated? (4) What IT aids are available to support managers?

WHY MANAGERS NEED THE SUPPORT OF INFORMATION TECHNOLOGY. It is very difficult to make good decisions without good information. Information is needed for each phase and activity in the decision-making process.

Making decisions while processing information manually is growing increasingly difficult due to the following trends:

- The *number of alternatives* to be considered is ever *increasing,* due to innovations in technology, improved communication, the development of global markets, and the use of the Internet and e-commerce. The more alternatives exist, the more information search and comparisons are needed.
- Many decisions must be made *under time pressure.* Frequently, it is not possible to manually process the needed information fast enough to be effective.
- Due to increased fluctuations and uncertainty in the decision environment, it is frequently necessary to *conduct a sophisticated analysis* to make a good decision. Such analysis usually requires the use of modeling. Processing models manually can take a very long time.
- It is often necessary to rapidly access remote information, consult with experts, or have a group decision-making session, all quickly and without large expense.

These trends cause difficulties in making decisions, but a DSS can be of enormous help. For example, a DSS can examine numerous alternatives very quickly, can provide a systematic risk analysis, can be integrated with communication systems and databases, and can be used to support group work. And, all this is done with relatively low cost. *How* all this is accomplished will be shown later. But first, let's consider how to find what information is needed by managers.

HOW TO DETERMINE THE INFORMATION NEEDS OF MANAGERS. An important key to the success of IT is its ability to provide users with the *right information* at the *right time.* Identifying the information needs of managers is not a simple task, but it is an essential one. Several approaches are available. For example, Wetherbe's approach (1991) consists of a two-phase process. In Phase I, a *structured interview* is conducted to determine managers' perceived information needs. In Phase II, a *prototype* of the information system is quickly constructed. The prototyped system is shown to the managers, who then make suggestions for improvements. The system is modified and again shown to the managers. Testing and modification go through several rounds until the detailed requirements are established. The *sources* of information are then identified, and the support system can be developed.

Another popular method for finding managers' information needs is the *critical success factor (CSF)* approach, described in Chapter 8.

The Watson and Frolick approach (1992) is based on the following strategies for determining information requirements: *asking* (the interview approach), *deriving* the needs from an existing information system, *synthesizing* from characteristics of the systems, and *discovering* via evolving systems (prototyping).

Several other approaches, some of which are intuitive, can be used to determine managers' information needs. Representative examples include the following.

1. Ask managers what questions they would ask upon their return from a three-week vacation.
2. List major objectives in the company's short- and long-term plans, and identify their information requirements.
3. Ask managers (and especially executives) what information they would least like their competition to see.
4. Either through an interview or by observation, determine what information is actually used by managers.
5. Provide more immediate online access to their current management reports, and then ask managers how you can better tailor the system to their needs. (Managers usually are much better able to tell you what is wrong with what you have given them than to tell you what they need.)

CAN THE MANAGER'S JOB BE FULLY AUTOMATED? The generic decision-making process involves specific tasks (such as forecasting consequences and evaluating alternatives). The process can be fairly lengthy, which is bothersome for a busy manager. Automation of certain tasks can save time, increase consistency, and enable better decisions to be made. Thus, the more tasks we can automate in the process, the better. A logical question that follows is this: Is it possible to completely automate the manager's job?

In general, it has been found that the job of middle managers is most able to be fully automated. Mid-level managers make fairly routine decisions, and these can be automated. Managers at lower levels do not spend much time on decision making. Instead, they supervise, train, and motivate nonmanagers. Some of their routine decisions, such as scheduling, can be automated; others that involve behavioral aspects cannot. But, even if we completely automate their decisional role, we cannot automate their jobs. The job of top managers is the least routine and therefore the most difficult to automate.

The Web provides an opportunity to automate certain tasks done by *frontline* employees. This topic is discussed in Section 10.5.

WHAT INFORMATION TECHNOLOGIES ARE AVAILABLE TO SUPPORT MANAGERS? Four major information technologies have been successfully used to support managers. They all can be facilitated by the Web. Collectively, they are referred to as **management support systems (MSSs)**. (See Turban and Aronson, 2001.) The four technologies are as follows: First, *DSSs,* which have been in use since the mid-1970s, provide support primarily to analytical, quantitative types of decisions. Second, *executive (enterprise) support systems* represent a technology developed in the mid-1980s, mainly to support the informational roles of executives. A third technology, *group decision support systems,* supports managers working in groups. The first three technologies are described in this chapter. A fourth technology, *intelligent systems,* is discussed in Chapter 12. These four technologies can be used independently, or they can be combined, each providing a different capability. They are frequently related to data warehousing. A simplified presentation of such support is shown in Figure 10.3.

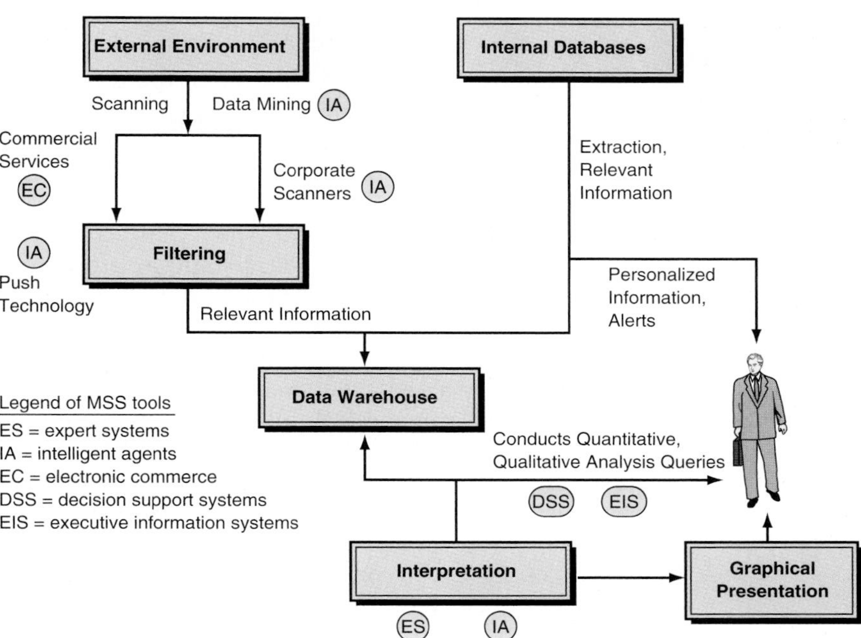

FIGURE 10.3 Computerized support for decision making.

As Figure 10.3 shows, managers need to find, filter, and interpret information to determine potential problems or opportunities and then decide what to do about them. The figure shows the support of the various MSS tools (circled) as well as the role of a data warehouse, which will be described in Chapter 11.

Several other technologies, either by themselves or when integrated with other management support technologies, can be used to support managers. One example is the **personal information manager (PIM)**. A set of tools labeled PIM is intended to help managers be more organized. A PIM can play an extremely important role in supporting several managerial tasks. Lately, the use of wireless PIM tools, such as personal Palm computers, is greatly facilitating the work of managers.

A Framework for Computerized Decision Support Analysis

A framework for decision support was proposed by Gorry and Scott-Morton (1971), based on the combined work of Simon (1977) and Anthony (1965). The details are as follows.

The first half of the framework is based on Simon's idea that decision-making processes fall along a continuum that ranges from highly structured (sometimes referred to as *programmed*) to highly unstructured (*nonprogrammed*) decisions. *Structured* processes refer to routine and repetitive problems for which standard solutions exist. *Unstructured* processes are "fuzzy," complex problems for which there are no cut-and-dried solutions.

In a *structured problem,* all phases—intelligence, design, and choice—are structured, and the procedures for obtaining the best (or at least a good enough) solution are known. Whether the solution means finding an appropriate inventory level or deciding on an optimal investment strategy, the solution's criteria are clearly defined. They are frequently cost minimization or profit maximization. Web-based **decision metrics** and online standard models are available to managers who input data and get suggested solutions (e.g., see Plant, 2000, Chapter 9).

In an *unstructured problem, none* of the three phases—intelligence, design, or choice—is structured, and human intuition is frequently the basis for decision making. Typical unstructured problems include planning new services to be offered, hiring an executive, or choosing a set of research and development projects for next year.

Semistructured problems, in which only some of the phases are structured, require a combination of standard solution procedures and individual judgment. Examples of semistructured problems include trading bonds, setting marketing budgets for consumer products, and performing capital acquisition analysis. Here, a DSS is most suitable. It can improve the quality of the information on which the decision is based (and consequently the quality of the decision) by providing not only a single solution but also a range of alternatives.

The second half of the decision support framework is based upon Anthony's taxonomy (1965). It defines three broad categories that encompass all managerial activities: (1) *strategic planning*—the long-range goals and policies for resource allocation; (2) *management control*—the acquisition and efficient utilization of resources in the accomplishment of organizational goals; and (3) *operational control*—the efficient and effective execution of specific tasks.

Anthony's and Simon's taxonomies can be combined in a nine-cell decision support framework (see Figure 10.4). The right-hand column and the bottom row indicate technologies needed to support the various decisions. Gorry and Scott-Morton suggested, for example, that for the semistructured and unstruc-

Type of Decision	Type of Control: Operational Control	Managerial Control	Strategic Planning	Support Needed
Structured	1 Accounts receivable, order entry	2 Budget analysis, short-term forecasting, personnel reports, make-or-buy analysis	3 Financial management (investment), warehouse location, distribution systems	MIS, management science models, transaction processing
Semistructured	4 Production scheduling, inventory control	5 Credit evaluation, budget preparation, plant layout, project scheduling, reward systems design	6 Building new plant, mergers and acquisitions, new product planning, compensation planning, quality assurance planning	DSS
Unstructured	7 Selecting a cover for a magazine, buying software, approving loans	8 Negotiating, recruiting an executive, buying hardware, lobbying	9 R & D planning, new technology development, social responsibility planning	DSS ES Neural networks
Support Needed	MIS, Management science	Management science, DSS, EIS, ES	EIS, ES, Neural networks	

FIGURE 10.4 Decision support framework. Technology is used to support the decisions shown in the column at the far right and in the bottom row.

tured decisions, conventional MIS and management science approaches are insufficient. Therefore, they proposed the use of a DSS.

Low-level managers usually perform the structured and operational control-oriented tasks (cells 1, 2, and 4), whereas tasks in cells 6, 8, and 9 are mainly the responsibility of top executives. Cells 3, 5, and 7 are usually the responsibility of middle managers and/or professional staff. This means that DSS, EIS, expert systems, and neural networks are often applicable for top executives and professionals tackling specialized, complex problems.

COMPUTER SUPPORT FOR STRUCTURED DECISIONS. Structured and some semistructured decisions, especially of the operational and managerial control type, have been supported by computers since the 1950s. Decisions of this type are made in all functional areas, especially in finance and operations management.

Problems that are encountered fairly often have a high level of structure. It is therefore possible to abstract, analyze, and classify them into standard classes. For example, a "make-or-buy" decision belongs to this category. Other examples are capital budgeting (e.g., replacement of equipment), allocation of resources, distribution of merchandise, and some inventory control decisions. For each standard class, a prescribed solution was developed through the use of mathematical formulas. This approach is called *management science* or *operations research* and is also executed with the aid of computers.

MANAGEMENT SCIENCE. The *management science* approach takes the view that managers can follow a fairly systematic process for solving problems. Therefore, it is possible to use a scientific approach to managerial decision making. This approach, which also centers on modeling, requires the following steps.

1. ***Defining*** the problem (a decision situation that may deal with a setback or with an opportunity)
2. ***Classifying*** the problem into a standard category
3. ***Constructing*** a standard mathematical model that describes the real-life problem
4. ***Finding*** potential solutions to the modeled problem and evaluating them
5. ***Choosing*** and recommending a specific solution to the problem

A list of representative structured management science problems and tools is given in Table 10.1 (page 446). Software packages are available, some on the Web, to solve such problems very quickly.

However, standard models cannot solve managerial problems that are not structured. These are usually more difficult and important problems of a managerial control and strategic planning nature. Such problems require the use of a DSS.

10.2 DECISION SUPPORT SYSTEMS

DSS Concepts

Broadly defined, a **decision support system (DSS)** is a computer-based information system that combines models and data in an attempt to solve semistructured problems with extensive user involvement. But the term decision support

TABLE 10.1 Representative Structured Management Science Problems and Tools

Problem	Tool
Allocation of resources	Linear and nonlinear programming
Project management	PERT, CPM
Inventory control	Inventory management models, simulation
Forecasting results	Forecasting models, regression analysis
Managing waiting lines	Queuing theory, simulation
Transporting and distributing goods	Transportation models
Matching items to each other	Assignment models
Predicting market share and other dynamically oriented situations	Markov chain analysis, dynamic simulation

system (DSS), like the terms MIS and MSS, means different things to different people. DSSs can be viewed as an *approach* or a *philosophy* rather than a precise methodology. However, a DSS does have certain recognized characteristics, which we will present later. First, let us look at a typical case of a successfully implemented DSS, shown in the *IT at Work* below.

The case demonstrates some of the major characteristics of a DSS. The risk analysis performed first was based on the decision maker's initial definition of the situation, using a management science approach. Then, the executive vice president, using his experience, judgment, and intuition, felt that the model should be modified. The initial model, although mathematically correct, was incomplete. With a regular simulation system, a modification of the computer pro-

IT at Work

USING A DSS TO DETERMINE RISK

Houston Oil and Minerals Corporation was interested in a proposed joint venture with a petrochemicals company to develop a chemical plant. Houston's executive vice president responsible for the decision wanted analysis of the risks involved in areas of supplies, demands, and prices. Bob Sampson, manager of planning and administration, and his staff built a DSS in a few days by means of a specialized planning language. The results strongly suggested that the project should be accepted.

Then came the real test. Although the executive vice president accepted the validity and value of the results, he was worried about the potential downside risk of the project, the chance of a catastrophic outcome. Sampson explains that the executive vice president said something like this: "I realize the amount of work you have already done, and I am 99 percent confident of it. But I would like to see this in a different light. I know we are short of time and we have to get back to our partners with our yes or no decision."

Sampson replied that the executive could have the risk analysis he needed in less than one hour. As Sampson explained, "Within 20 minutes, there in the executive boardroom, we were reviewing the results of his what-if questions. Those results led to the eventual dismissal of the project, which we otherwise would probably have accepted."

For Further Exploration: What were the benefits of the DSS? Why might it have reversed the initial decision?

Source: Information provided by Comshare Corporation.

gram would have taken a long time, but the DSS provided a very quick analysis. Furthermore, the DSS was flexible and responsive enough to allow managerial intuition and judgment to be incorporated into the analysis.

How can such a thorough risk analysis be performed so quickly? How can the judgment factors be elicited, quantified, and worked into the model? How can the results be presented meaningfully and convincingly to the executive? What are "what-if" questions? We answer these questions in the following sections. But first, let's close this section by reviewing some reasons for the increased use of DSSs. Many companies are turning to DSSs to improve decision making. Reasons cited by managers for the increasing use of DSSs include the following:

- New and accurate information was needed.
- Information was needed fast.
- Tracking the company's numerous business operations was increasingly difficult.
- The company was operating in an unstable economy.
- The company faced increasing foreign and domestic competition.
- The company's existing computer system did not properly support the objectives of increasing efficiency, profitability, and entry into profitable markets.
- The IS department could not begin to address the diversity of the company's needs or management's ad-hoc inquiries, and business analysis functions were not inherent within the existing systems.

In many organizations that have adopted a DSS, the conventional information systems, which were built for the purpose of supporting transaction processing, were *not sufficient* to support several of the company's critical response activities, described in Chapter 1, especially those that require fast and/or complex decision making. A DSS, on the other hand, can do just that.

Another reason for the development of DSS is the *end-user computing movement.* With the exception of large-scale DSSs, end users can build systems themselves. Using DSS development tools and the help of the IS department and vendors, many end users find that they can do this job.

Characteristics and Capabilities of DSSs

Because there is no consensus on exactly what constitutes a DSS, there obviously is no agreement on the characteristics and capabilities of DSSs. However, the following can be considered as an ideal set. Most DSSs have only some of the following attributes.

1. A DSS provides support for decision makers at all management levels, whether individuals or groups, mainly in semistructured and unstructured situations, by bringing together human judgment and objective information.
2. A DSS supports several interdependent and/or sequential decisions.
3. A DSS supports all phases of the decision-making process—intelligence, design, choice, and implementation—as well as a variety of decision-making processes and styles.
4. A DSS is adaptable by the user over time to deal with changing conditions.
5. A DSS is easy to construct and use in many cases.
6. A DSS promotes learning, which leads to new demands and refinement of the application, which leads to additional learning, and so forth.

7. A DSS usually utilizes quantitative models (standard and/or custom made).
8. Advanced DSSs are equipped with a knowledge management component that allows the efficient and effective solution of very complex problems.
9. A DSS can be disseminated for use via the Web.
10. A DSS allows the easy execution of *sensitivity analyses.*

SENSITIVITY ANALYSIS: "WHAT-IF" AND GOAL SEEKING. **Sensitivity analysis** is the study of the impact that changes in one (or more) parts of a model have on other parts. Usually, we check the impact that changes in input variables have on output variables.

Sensitivity analysis is extremely valuable in DSSs because it makes the system flexible and adaptable to changing conditions and to the varying requirements of different decision-making situations. It allows users to enter their own data, including the most pessimistic data, and to view how systems will behave under varying circumstances. It provides a better understanding of the model and the problem it purports to describe. It may increase the users' confidence in the model, especially when the model is not so sensitive to changes. A *sensitive model* means that small changes in conditions dictate a different solution. In a *nonsensitive model,* changes in conditions do not significantly change the recommended solution. This means that the chances for a solution to succeed are very high. Two popular types of sensitivity analyses are *what-if* and *goal seeking.*

What-If Analysis. A model builder makes predictions and assumptions regarding the input data, many of which are based on the assessment of uncertain futures. When the model is solved, the results depend on these assumptions. **What-if analysis** attempts to check the impact of a change in the assumptions (input data) on the proposed solution. For example, "*What* will happen to the total inventory cost *if* the originally assumed cost of carrying inventories is 12 percent, not 10 percent?" Or, "*What* will be the predicted market share *if* the initially assumed advertising budget increases by 5 percent?"

In a properly designed DSS, managers themselves can easily ask the computer these types of questions as many times as needed for sensitivity analysis.

Goal Seeking. **Goal-seeking analysis** attempts to find the value of the inputs necessary to achieve a desired level of output. It represents a "backward" solution approach. For example, let us say that a DSS solution yielded a profit of $2 million. Management wants to know what sales volume would be necessary to generate a profit of $2.2 million. This is a goal-seeking problem.

As an example, we look at the Goal Seek function of Excel. When you know the desired result of a single formula but not the input value the formula needs to determine the result, you can use the **Goal Seek feature**. When goal seeking, Microsoft Excel varies the value in one specific cell until a formula that's dependent on that cell returns the result you want (see Figure 10.5).

Structure and Components of a DSS

Every DSS consists of at least data management, user interface, and model management components, and users. A few advanced DSSs also contain a knowledge management component. What does each component (subsystem) consist of?

DATA MANAGEMENT SUBSYSTEM. The DSS data management subsystem is similar to any other data management system. It contains all the necessary data that

The value in cell B4 is the result of the formula = PMT (B3/12, B2, B1).

	A	B
1	Loan Amount	$100,000
2	Term in Months	180
3	Interest Rate	7.02%
4	Payment	($900.00)

Goal seek to determine the interest rate in cell B3 based on the payment in cell B4.

FIGURE 10.5 Goal-seeking with Excel.

flow from several sources and are *extracted* prior to their entry into a DSS database. In some DSSs, there is no separate DSS database, and data are entered into the DSS model as needed. In many DSS applications, data come from a *data warehouse.* A data warehouse (see Chapter 11) includes DSS-relevant data extracted from different sources and organized as a relational database.

MODEL MANAGEMENT SUBSYSTEM. Model management contains completed models and the models' building blocks necessary to develop DSSs applications. This includes standard software with financial, statistical, management science, or other quantitative models. An example is the many functions of Excel. A model management subsystem also contains all the custom models written for the specific DSS. These models provide the system's analytical capabilities. Also included is a **model base management system (MBMS)** whose role is analogous to that of a DBMS. (See Technology Guide 3.) The major functions (capabilities) of an MBMS are these:

- Creates DSS models easily and quickly, either from scratch, from existing models, or from the building blocks
- Allows users to manipulate DSS models so they can conduct experiments and sensitivity analyses
- Stores and manages a wide variety of different types of models in a logical and integrated manner
- Accesses and integrates the DSS model building blocks
- Catalogs and displays the directory of models
- Tracks models, data, and application usage
- Interrelates models with appropriate linkages through the database
- Manages and maintains the model base with management functions analogous to database management: store, access, run, update, link, catalog, and query

The model management subsystem of the DSS has several elements: model base; model base management system; modeling language; model directory; and model execution, integration, and command. (For details see Turban and Aronson, 2001.)

The model base may contain standard models (such as financial or management science) and/or customized models as illustrated in the *IT at Work* example at the top of the next page.

IT at Work

WEB-BASED DECISION SUPPORT SYSTEM HELPS A BREWERY TO COMPETE

www.guinness.com

Guinness Import Co. (a U.S. subsidiary of U.K.'s Guinness Ltd.) needed a decision support system for (1) executives, (2) salespeople, and (3) analysts. The company did not want three separate systems. Using infoAdvisor (from Platinum Technology Inc., now part of Computer Associates, *cai.com*), a client/server DSS was constructed. In the past, if manager Diane Goldman wanted to look at sales trends, it was necessary to ask an analyst to download data from the mainframe and then use a spreadsheet to compute the trend. This took up to a day and was error-prone. Now, when Diane Goldman needs such information she queries the DSS herself and gets an answer in a few minutes. Furthermore, she can quickly analyze the data in different ways. Over 100 salespeople keep track of sales and can do similar analyses, from anywhere, using a remote Internet access.

To expedite the implementation of the system, highly skilled users in each department teach others how to use the DSS. The DSS helped to increase productivity of the employees. ("There's constant pressure to do a lot with a minimum of head count at Guinness.") This improved productivity enables the company to compete against large companies such as Anheuser-Busch, as well as against microbrewers. The system reduced the salespeople's paperwork load by about one day each month. For 100 salespeople, this means 1,200 extra days a year to sell. And indeed, sales increased by 20 percent in 1997 versus 1996, and by a similar percentage in subsequent years.

Corporate financial and marketing analysts are also using the system to make better decisions.

For Further Exploration: What can a DSS do that other computer programs cannot do for this company?

Sources: Compiled from *Computerworld,* July 7, 1997; *platinum.com* (2000); and *dmreview.com* (2001).

THE USER INTERFACE. The term *user interface* covers all aspects of the communications between a user and the DSS. Some DSS experts feel that user interface is the most important DSS component because much of the power, flexibility, and ease of use of the DSS are derived from this component. For example, the ease of use of the interface in the Guiness DSS enables, and encourages, managers and salespeople to use the system. Most interfaces today are Web-based.

The user interface subsystem may be managed by software called *user interface management system (UIMS),* which is functionally analogous to the DBMS.

THE USERS. The person faced with the problem or decision that the DSS is designed to support is referred to as the *user,* the *manager,* or the *decision maker.* These terms fail to reflect, however, the heterogeneity that exists among users and usage patterns of DSSs. There are differences in the positions users hold, ways in which a final decision is reached, users' cognitive preferences and abilities, and ways of arriving at a decision.

The user is considered to be a part of the system. Researchers assert that some of the unique contributions of DSSs are derived from the extensive interaction between the computer and the decision maker. A DSS has two broad classes of users: managers, and staff specialists (such as financial analysts, production planners, and market researchers).

When managers utilize a DSS, they may use it via an intermediary person who performs the analysis and reports the results. There are four types of intermediaries, who reflect different types of support for the manager.

1. ***Staff assistant.*** This person has specialized knowledge about management problems and some experience with decision support technology.
2. ***Expert tool user.*** This person is skilled in the application of one or more types of specialized problem-solving tools. The expert tool user performs tasks for which the manager does not have the necessary skills or training.
3. ***Business (system) analyst.*** This person has a general knowledge of the application area, formal business administration education, and considerable skill in DSS construction tools.
4. ***Group facilitator.*** When group decisions are supported by IT, it is frequently beneficial to use a process facilitator (see Section 10.3).

With Web-based systems, the use of DSSs becomes even easier. Managers can use the Web-based system by themselves, especially when supported by an intelligent knowledge component.

KNOWLEDGE MANAGEMENT (KNOWLEDGE-BASED) SUBSYSTEMS. Many unstructured and semistructured problems are so complex that they require expertise for their solutions. Such expertise can be provided by a knowledge-based system, such as an expert system. Therefore, the more advanced DSSs are equipped with a component called a *knowledge-based subsystem.* Such a component can provide the required expertise for solving some aspects of the problem or knowledge that can enhance the operation of the other DSS components.

The knowledge component consists of one or more expert (or other intelligent) systems, or it draws expertise from the *organizational knowledge base* (see Chapter 9).

A decision support system that includes such a component is referred to as an *intelligent DSS,* a *DSS/ES,* or a *knowledge-based DSS (KBDSS).* An example of a KBDSS is in the area of estimation and pricing in construction. It is a complex process that requires the use of models as well as judgmental factors. The KBDSS inludes a knowledge management subsystem with 200 rules incorporated with the computational models. (For details, see Kingsman and deSouza, 1997.)

DSS CONSTRUCTION. The DSS components (see Figure 10.6 on page 452) are all software. They are housed in a computer and can be facilitated by additional software (such as multimedia). If the components are prepurchased they can be integrated by using special tools, or by writing a special connecting program. Tools like Excel include some of the components and therefore can be used for DSS construction by end users.

DSS VENDORS. Over 100 vendors offer DSS components, consulting services, ready-made DSS, integration tools, and so forth. For a list, see *dssresources.com.*

10.3 GROUP DECISION SUPPORT SYSTEMS

Although most business organizations have traditionally been hierarchical, decision making is frequently a shared horizonal process. Meetings among groups of managers from different areas are an essential element for reaching consensus. The group may be involved in making a decision or in a decision-related task, like creating a short list of acceptable alternatives or deciding on criteria for accepting

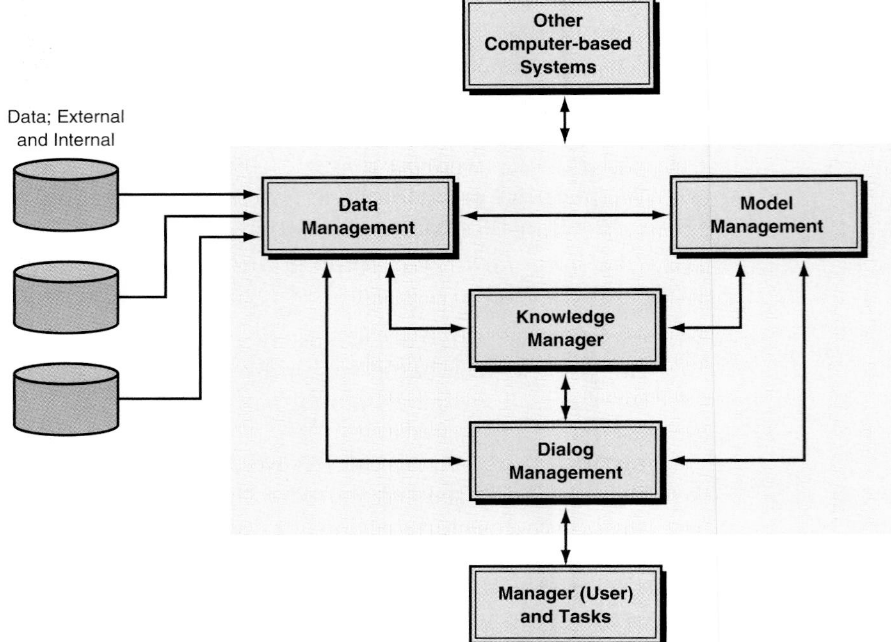

FIGURE 10.6 Conceptual model of a DSS shows four main software components facilitated by other parts of the system.

an alternative. When a decision-making group is supported electronically, the support is referred to as a *group decision support system (GDSS)*.

A **group decision support system (GDSS)** is an interactive computer-based system that facilitates the solution of semistructured and unstructured problems by a group of decision makers. Components of a GDSS include hardware, software, people, and procedures. These components are arranged to support the *process* of arriving at a decision. Important characteristics of a GDSS, according to DeSanctis and Gallupe (1987), are as follows:

- Designed with the goal of supporting groups of decision-makers in their work.
- Easy to learn and use. The GDSS accommodates users with varying levels of knowledge regarding computing and decision support.
- Can be designed for one type of problem or for a variety of group-level organizational decisions.
- Encourages generation of ideas, resolution of conflicts, and freedom of expression.
- Contains built-in mechanisms that discourage development of negative group behaviors, such as destructive conflict miscommunication and "groupthink."
- Is a specially designed information system, not merely a configuration of already-existing system components.

The goal of GDSSs is to improve the productivity of decision-making meetings, either by speeding up the decision-making process or by improving the quality of the resulting decisions, or both. This is accomplished by providing support to the exchange of ideas, opinions, and preferences within the group.

GDSSs can improve the decision-making process by:

- Supporting parallel processing of information and idea generation by participants.
- Enabling larger groups with more complete information, knowledge, and skills to participate in the same meeting.
- Permitting the group to use structured or unstructured techniques and methods.
- Offering rapid and easy access to external information.
- Allowing nonsequential computer discussion. (Unlike oral discussions, computer discussions do not have to be serial or sequential.)
- Producing instant, anonymous voting results.
- Providing structure to the planning process, which keeps the group on track.
- Enabling several users to interact simultaneously.
- Automatically recording all information that passes through the system for future analysis (it develops organization memory).

These gains can negate some of the dysfunctions of group processes described in Chapter 4, Table 4.2.

Supporting Collaborative Meetings

The first generation of GDSSs was designed to support face-to-face meetings in what is called a **decision room**. Such a GDSS is composed of hardware, software, people, and procedures.

HARDWARE. A group can use two basic types of hardware configurations. The first is a decision room, a GDSS facility designed for electronic meetings. An example is the facility at City University of Hong Kong. It is equipped with state-of-the-art workstations, a local-area network, a server, and a "facilitator station," which controls a large-screen projection system (see Figure 10.7). The system can also be used for group-to-group video teleconferencing.

The second configuration is basically a collection of PCs, each equipped with keypads for voting and other groupware activities. The machines can be in one

FIGURE 10.7 Decision room at City University of Hong Kong, equipped with state-of-the-art workstations, a local-area network, a server, and a "facilitator station."

location or in different locations. Simple to operate, such PCs are usually part of a network, and can be connected to the Internet. Most of the applications of GDSSs today are not for face-to-face meetings, but rather to support virtual (distributed) meetings.

SOFTWARE. Typical GDSS software is a collection of about a dozen tools or packages, which are integrated into a comprehensive system. GDSS software (such as GroupSystems and eroom.com) includes modules such as idea generation, idea organization, prioritizing (by votes), and policy formulation. This software can be used in a decision room or for a group of people who are at various locations, using Internet or intranet technology. Groupware such as Lotus Notes/Domino offers some of these capabilities (see Chapter 4).

Advanced software packages can support conflict resolution among participants, provide communication with commercial databases, and allow for execution of quantitative analysis. Advanced software includes artificial intelligence capabilities such as intelligent agents.

PEOPLE. The people component of the GDSS includes the group members and a facilitator. The facilitator is present in all face-to-face group meetings at a single site. He or she can also coordinate dispersed-participation groups, and serves as the group's "chauffeur," operating the GDSS hardware and software and displaying requested information to the group as needed. Distributed meetings usually require such a coordinator.

PROCEDURES. The final component of the GDSS consists of procedures that allow for ease of operation and effective use of the technology by group members. The procedures outline the role of the facilitator and members, the sequence of the various activities, and the support technologies to be used.

Some Applications of GDSSs

An increasing number of companies are using GDSSs. One example is the Internal Revenue Service, which used a GDSS to implement its quality-improvement programs based on the participation of a number of its quality teams. The GDSS was helpful in identifying problems, generating and evaluating ideas, and developing and implementing solutions. Another example is the European automobile industry, which used a GDSS to examine the competitive automotive business environment and make ten-year forcasts, needed for strategic planning.

Another GDSS application is described in the *IT at Work* example on the facing page.

10.4 ENTERPRISE DECISION SUPPORT SYSTEMS

Two types of enterprise decision support system are described here: systems that support a sequence of decision making within an organization, and systems that support decisions made by top-level managers and executives.

Organizational Decision Support Systems (ODSSs)

The term **organizational decision support system (ODSS)** was first defined by Hackathorn and Keen (1981), who distinguished among three levels of decision support: individual, group, and organization. They maintained that computer-based systems can be developed to provide decision support for *each* of

IT at Work
VIRTUAL MEETINGS AT THE WORLD ECONOMIC FORUM

...in Production & Operations Management

www.weforum.org

The World Economic Forum (WEF, *weforum.org*) is a consortium of top business, government, academic, and media leaders from virtually every country in the world. WEF's mission is to foster international understanding. Until 1998, the members conferred privately or debated global issues only at the forum's annual meeting in Davos, Switzerland, and at regional summits. Follow-up was difficult because of the members' geographic dispersion and conflicting schedules.

Bruno Giussani heads up WEF online strategy and operations. He developed a collaborative computing system to allow secure communication among members, making the nonprofit group more effective in its mission. Now WEF is making faster progress toward solutions for the global problems it studies. Called the World Electronic Community (WELCOM), the groupware and videoconferencing system gives members a secure channel through which to send e-mail, read reports in a WEF library, and communicate in point-to-point or multipoint videoconferences. Forum members now hold real-time discussions and briefings on pressing issues and milestones, such as, for example, when Hong Kong reverted to Chinese control.

USWeb Corporation worked with the WEF to develop the system, which is heavily based on a platform of Microsoft products. The system runs on a single Windows NT server. Also on the server are a Microsoft Exchange Server with scheduling and e-mail, as well as NetMeeting and NetShow. An Intel videoconferencing system is accessed via a browser. The client software running on the desktop of each of the 2,500 forum members consists of Windows and Internet Explorer.

The WELCOM system was designed with a graphical user interface (GUI) to make it easily accessible to inexperienced computer users, because many WEF members might not be computer-literate or proficient typists. The forum also set up a 24/5 "concierge service," based in Boston, Singapore, and Geneva, for technical support and to arrange videoconferences and virtual meetings. To handle any time/any place meetings, members can access recorded forum events and discussions that they may have missed, as well as an extensive library, which is one of the most heavily used features of the system.

By 2001 the system was completely on the Web. Using Webcasting, all sessions of the annual meetings can be viewed any time. The virtual meetings are done in a secured environment, and private chat rooms are also available.

For Further Exploration: Check the Netmeeting and Netshow products of Microsoft, and see how their capabilities facilitate the WEF virtual meetings. Does an environment such as *blackboard.com* and *eroom.com* enhance the process of group decision making? How?

Sources: Compiled from *weforum.org* (2001) and *PC Week*, August 17, 1998.

these levels. They defined an ODSS as one that focuses on an organizational task or activity involving a *sequence* of operations and decision makers, such as developing a divisional marketing plan or doing capital budgeting. Each individual's activities must mesh closely with other people's work. The computer support was primarily seen as a vehicle for improving communication and coordination, in addition to problem solving.

Some decision support systems provide support throughout large and complex organizations (see Carter et al., 1992). A major benefit of such systems is that many users of DSSs become familiar with computers, analytical techniques, and DSSs, as illustrated in the *IT at Work* example on page 456.

For further information on a very-large-scale ODSS, see El Sherif and El Sawy (1988) and Carter et al. (1992).

The major characteristics of an ODSS are:

- Affects several organizational units or corporate problems
- Cuts across organizational functions or hierarchical layers

IT at Work

BUILDING AN ODSS FOR KOREA TELECOM

Integrating IT ...in Finance and Production & Operations Management

www.kt.co.kt

Korea Telecom (KT) is Korea's largest telecommunications company. It employs 60,000 people in ten district offices and 360 local telephone offices. About half of the employees are in the Operations and Maintenance (O&M) division and work directly with the customers. For a high level of customer service, the company must invest about 15 percent of its annual budget for improvements and upgrades. The problem is that thousands of alternatives exist to accomplish this. Which alternative is best? The company realized the answer might require the reengineering of its Investment Performance Management activities.

At the core of Korea Telecom's organizational DSS model is the concept of quality of service. This is composed of four major indicators (operations quality, nonvoice service quality, transmission quality, and connection quality), each involving three to five specific measures. The model also checks the Context Difficulty Index (CDI), which evaluates each local or district office's operating environment.

The CDI evaluation, quality evaluation, and O&M performance determine the O&M budget in a complex model (called the Korea Telecom Operations & Management Model, KTOM-ODSS). The various organizational units that are involved and the connecting network are shown in the figure below. This DSS is basically a distributed, yet integrated system.

In addition to the budget allocation, the ODSS is used in decisions such as performance forecasting. The system cuts across functional areas and hierarchical layers (headquarters, districts, and local offices), and deals with many decision makers. The system was upgraded in 1998 with an intelligent component and a data warehouse for OLAP.

For Further Exploration: Why do the builders want to reengineer the allocation process first?

Sources: Y. G. Kim et al., "Building an Organizational DSS for Korea Telecom," *Decision Support Systems,* April 1997; and from the company's information (2000).

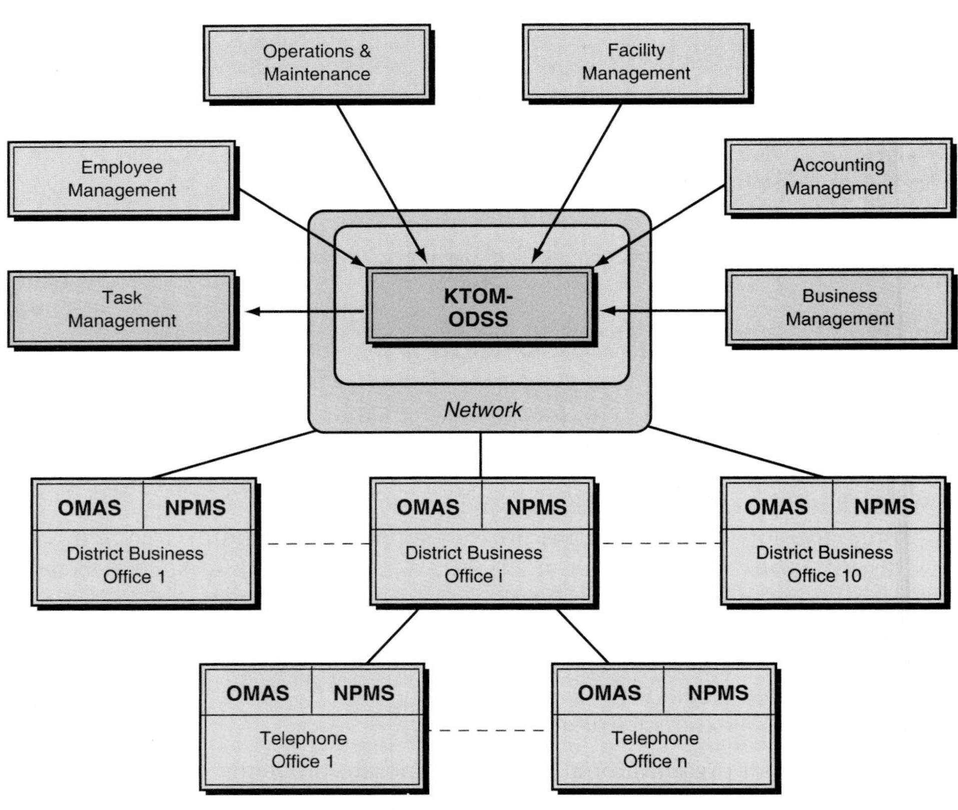

- Almost necessarily involves computer-based technologies and may also involve communication technologies

An ODSS often interacts or integrates with enterprisewide information systems such as an executive information system.

Executive Information (Support) Systems

The majority of personal DSSs support the work of professionals and middle-level managers. Organizational DSSs provide support primarily to planners, analysts, researchers, or to some managers. Rarely do we see a DSS used directly by top- or even middle-level executives. One of the reasons is that a DSS may not meet the executives' needs. An **executive information system (EIS)**, also known as an **executive support system (ESS)**, is a technology designed in response to managers' specific needs, as shown in the *IT at Work* below.

The terms *executive information system* and *executive support system* mean different things to different people, though they are sometimes used interchangeably. The following definitions, based on Rockart and DeLong (1988), distinguish between EIS and ESS.

- ***Executive information system (EIS).*** An EIS is a computer-based system that serves the information needs of top executives. It provides rapid access to timely information and direct access to management reports. An EIS is very

IT at Work

Integrating IT ...in Marketing and Finance

AN EXECUTIVE INFORMATION SYSTEM AT HERTZ CORPORATION

www.hertz.com

Hertz, the largest company in the car rental industry (and now a subsidiary of Ford Motor Company), competes against dozens of companies in hundreds of locations worldwide. Several marketing decisions must be made almost instantaneously (such as whether to follow a competitor's price discount). Marketing decisions are decentralized and are based on information about cities, climates, holidays, business cycles, tourist activities, past promotions, competitors' actions, and customers' behavior. The amount of such information is huge, and the only way to process it is to use a computer. The problem faced by Hertz was how to provide accessibility to such information and use it properly.

To address its decision-making needs, Hertz developed a mainframe DSS to allow fast analysis by executives and managers. But a marketing manager who had a question had to go through a staff assistant, which made the process lengthy and cumbersome. The need for a better system was obvious.

Therefore, the following year Hertz decided to add an EIS—a PC-based system used as a companion to the DSS. The combined system gave executives tools to analyze the mountains of stored information and make real-time decisions without the help of assistants. The system is extremely user-friendly and is maintained by the marketing staff. Since its assimilation into the corporate culture conformed to the manner in which Hertz executives were used to working, implementation was no problem.

With the EIS, executives can manipulate and refine data to be more meaningful and strategically significant to them. The EIS allows executives to draw information from the mainframe, store the needed data on their own PCs, and perform a DSS-type analysis without tying up valuable mainframe time. Hertz managers feel that the EIS creates synergy in decision making. It triggers questions, a greater influx of creative ideas, and more cost-effective marketing decisions.

In the late 1990s, the system was integrated with a data warehouse and connected to the corporate intranets and the Internet. Now local managers can know all competitors' prices, in real time, and by using supply-demand models, they can assess the impact of price changes on the demand for cars.

For Further Exploration: Why was the DSS insufficient by itself, and how did the addition of the EIS make it effective?

Sources: Condensed from M. O'Leary, "Putting Hertz Executives in the Driver's Seat," *CIO,* February 1990; and from *hertz.com* (1998).

user friendly, is supported by graphics, and provides "exception reporting" and "drill down" capabilities (see below). It is also easily connected with online information services and electronic mail.

- ***Executive support system (ESS).*** An ESS is a comprehensive support system that goes beyond EIS to include analysis support, communications, office automation, and intelligence.

Capabilities and Characteristics of EISs

Executive information systems vary in their capabilities and benefits. The following capabilities are common to most EISs.

DRILL DOWN. The **drill down** capability enables users to get details, and details of details, of any given information. For example, an executive may notice a decline in corporate sales in a weekly report. To find the reason, he or she may want to view (without the help of a programmer) a detail such as sales in each region. If a problematic region is identified, the executive may want to see further details (sales by product or by salesperson). In certain cases, this drill-down process may continue through several layers of details.

To provide such capability, the EIS may include several thousand menus, submenus, and sub-submenus. Drill down can be also achieved by direct query of databases, using a browser. New systems use intelligent agents to conduct the drill down and bring the results to the user.

CRITICAL SUCCESS FACTORS AND KEY PERFORMANCE INDICATORS. The factors that *must* be considered in attaining the organization's goals are called *critical success factors (CSFs)* (see Chapter 8). Such factors can be strategic, managerial, or operational. They are defined mainly according to three sources: organizational factors, industry factors, and environmental factors. They can exist at the corporate level as well as at a division, plant, and department level. Sometimes it is even necessary to consider the CSF of individual employees. Identifying critical success factors is important for executive decision making.

Critical success factors, once identified, are divided into *indicators* that can be monitored, measured, and compared to standards. A sample of indicators is provided in Table 10.2. The left side of the table lists CSFs; the right side lists the indicators.

TABLE 10.2 Illustrative Key Performance Indicators for Typical Critical Success Factors

CSF	Key Performance Indicators
Profitability	Profitability measures for each department, product, region, etc. Comparisons among departments, and product comparisons with those of competitors.
Financial	Financial ratios, balance sheet analysis, cash reserve position, rate of return on investment.
Marketing	Market share, advertisement analysis, product pricing, weekly (daily) sales results, customer sales potential.
Human resources	Turnover rates, skills analysis, absenteeism rate.
Planning	Corporate partnership ventures, growth/share analysis.
Economic analysis	Market trends, foreign exchange values, industry trends, labor cost trends.
Consumer trends	Consumer confidence level, purchasing habits, demographic data.

STATUS ACCESS. In a *status access mode,* the latest data or reports on the status of key indicators or other factors can be accessed at any time. The *relevance* of information is important here. The *latest data* may require daily or even real-time operational tracking.

TREND ANALYSIS. In analyzing data, it is extremely important to identify trends. Are sales increasing over time? Is market share decreasing? Is the competitor's share of the market declining against ours? Executives like to examine trends, especially when changes in data are detected. **Trend analysis** can be done using forecasting models, which are included in many ESSs, or the executive can activate a special adjacent DSS to conduct the trend analysis.

AD-HOC ANALYSIS. Executive support systems provide for **ad-hoc analysis** capabilities, in which executives can make specific requests for data analysis as needed, instead of merely having access to data produced periodically in a routine way. Executives can thus use the system to do creative analyses on their own. They may even select the analytical tools to be used, the outputs, and the desired model of information presentation. Several end-user tools provide for ad-hoc analysis.

EXCEPTION REPORTING. **Exception reporting** is based on the concept of *management by exception,* in which an executive gives attention to significant deviations from standards. Thus, in exception reporting, an executive's attention is directed only to cases of very bad (or very good) performance. This approach saves considerable time for both producers and readers of reports. Exceptions are signaled by a different color or by a voice (for online presentations).

EIS TYPES AND ISSUES. EIS can be enhanced with multidimensional analysis and presentation (Chapter 11), friendly data access, user-friendly graphical interface, imaging capabilities, hypertext, intranet access, e-mail, Internet access, and modeling. These are helpful to any executive. We can distinguish between two types of EISs: (1) those designed especially to support top executives (as described in the Hertz case) and (2) those intended to serve a wider community of users.

The latter type of EIS applications embrace a range of products targeted to support professional decision makers throughout the enterprise. For this reason, some people define the acronym EIS to mean **enterprise information systems**, or *everybody's* information systems.

INTELLIGENT EIS. In order to save the executive's time in conducting a drill down, finding exceptions, or identifying trends, an *intelligent EIS* has been developed. Automating these activities not only saves time but also ensures that the executive will not miss any important indications in a large amount of data. Intelligent EISs may include an intelligent agent for alerting management to exceptions. For further details, see King and O'Leary (1996) and Liu et al. (2000).

INTEGRATION WITH DSS. Executive information systems are useful in identifying problems and opportunities. Such identification can be facilitated by an intelligent component (see *A Closer Look* 10.2, page 460). In addition, it is necessary to do

A CLOSER LOOK
10.2 AN INTELLIGENT EIS

www.comshare.com

A pioneer in the EIS market, Comshare, Incorporated gives users highly effective, intelligent ways to obtain all the information they need. Comshare® Decision™ exploits Web technology so users can quickly make sense of organizational performance through powerful reporting and analysis capabilities anywhere, anytime, from any PC using only a Web browser.

For example, Decision's built-in proactive alerting capability filters through databases or other electronic sources to find irregularities, or exceptions, in the data (financial and nonfinancial) according to rules users set up themselves or are defined for the entire organization. The information is, then, delivered automatically in a form that is conducive for action.

Decision also includes advanced data visualization techniques that make it a truly powerful system for the unique, specialized OLAP (online analytical processing) solutions required by analysts, managers, and executives. The software uses 2-D and 3-D charts, color coding, and other techniques to make it easy to identify patterns, trends, and variances, even those buried deep within the data.

Both the exception alerting and the data visualization capabilities save a considerable amount of time in informing executives about organizational performance. The software can be designed to follow all the critical success factors and key performance indicators. It also provides answers to questions about why, where, and where exceptions are happening.

Source: Comshare Incorporated (*comshare.com*) (2001).

something if a problem or an opportunity was discovered. Therefore, many software vendors provide EIS/DSS integrated tools which are sold as business intelligence tools.

FROM EXECUTIVE INFORMATION, TO ENTERPRISE INFORMATION, TO BUSINESS INTELLIGENCE. Executive information systems lost their popularity in the late 1990s when it became clear that in only a few large corporations is it worthwhile to create a separate system for executives. Information that is useful to top-level executives is often also of use to lower-level executives and managers throughout the organization. With the introduction of the intranet and corporate portals, the traditional EIS has become a part of an *enterprise information system,* and it now often appears under the name of **business intelligence**. Business intelligence is now integrated with e-commerce and other Web-based systems.

Some of the capabilities discussed in this section are now part of a business intelligence system and report, as shown in Figure 10.8.

One of the most interesting examples of enterprise decision support is the corporate war room. This concept has been used by the military for a long time, and it has now been transformed by SAP for use in industry, as described in *A Closer Look* 10.3 (at the top of page 462).

10.5 WEB-BASED DECISION SUPPORT SYSTEMS

The Web is a perfect medium for deploying decision support capabilities on a global basis. Let's look at **Web-based decision support systems** from the point of view of a user and a developer.

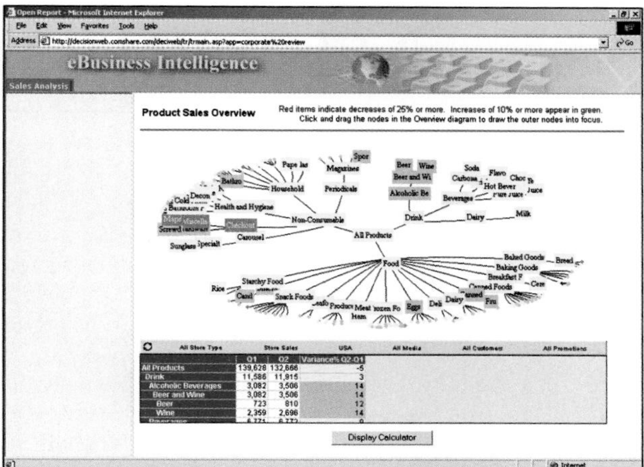

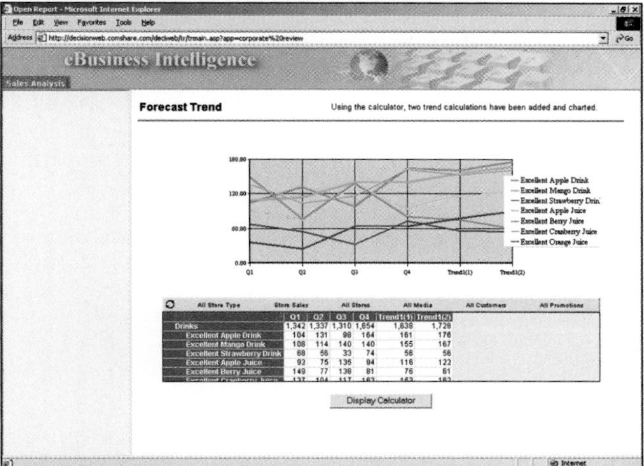

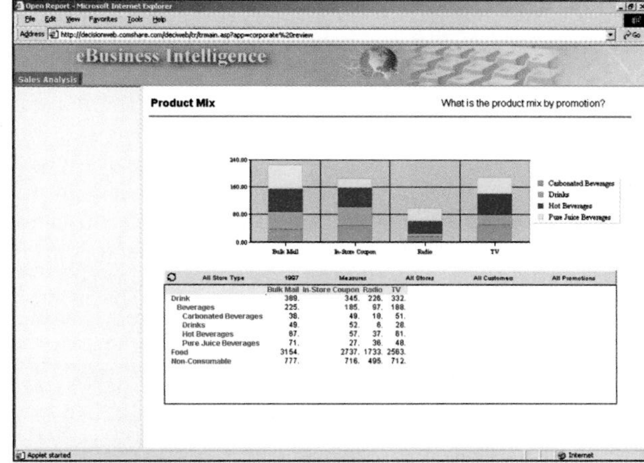

FIGURE 10.8 Sample screens from Comshare Decision—a modular system for generating a business intelligence report.

FOR THE DSS USER

1. Users can access DSSs from anywhere. In fact, remote employees can access a corporate DSS from clients' sites and can conduct analysis, do pricing, etc. This capability is now extended to wireless devices.
2. Many DSSs are now deployed on the corporate intranet, making them accessible to all employees.
3. The Web supports interactive DSS-related queries and ad-hoc report generation. Users can select a list of variables from a pull-down menu when executing a predefined query or report. This gives the DSS developer the ability to customize the DSS output.
4. Web-based application servers can download Java applets that execute functions on desktop DSS programs. (See Technology Guide 5.) This gives users the capabilities of advanced DSS applications without requiring client software to be loaded. All that users really need is a Web browser. A Web-based

A CLOSER LOOK
10.3 THE MANAGEMENT COCKPIT

www.management-cockpit.com

The Management Cockpit is a strategic management room that enables managers to pilot their businesses better. The aim is to create an environment that encourages more efficient management meetings and boosts team performance via effective communication. To help achieve this, key performance indicators and information relating to critical success factors are displayed graphically on the walls of a meeting room (see photo). The Management Cockpit supports top-level decision-makers by letting them concentrate on the essentials and conduct "what-if" scenarios. The cockpit-like arrangement of instrument panels and displays enables top managers to recognize whether corporate structures need changing and to grasp how all the different factors interrelate.

Executives can call up this information on their laptops, of course, but a key element of the concept is the Management Cockpit Room. There, on the four walls—Black, Red, Blue, and White—ergonomically designed graphics depict performance as reflected in mission-critical factors. The Black Wall shows the principal success factors and financial indicators; the Red Wall, market performance; the Blue Wall, the performance of internal processes and employees; and the White Wall, the status of strategic projects. The Flight Deck, a six-screen high-end PC, enables executives to drill down to detailed information.

Board members and other executives can hold meetings in this room. Typically, managers will also meet there with their comptrollers to discuss current business issues. For this purpose, the Management Cockpit can implement various scenarios. A major advantage of the Management Cockpit is that it provides a common basis for information and communication. At the same time, it supports efforts to translate a corporate strategy into concrete activities by identifying performance indicators, in addition to permitting appropriate monitoring.

The Cockpit environment is integrated with SAP's ERP products and reporting systems. External information can be easily imported to the room to allow competitive analysis.

Sources: Compiled from *management-cockpit.com, sap.com,* and from *origin-it.com.*

query model is shown in Figure 10.9. (CGI, common gateway interface, is a set of standard methods and routines used to write a stand-alone software

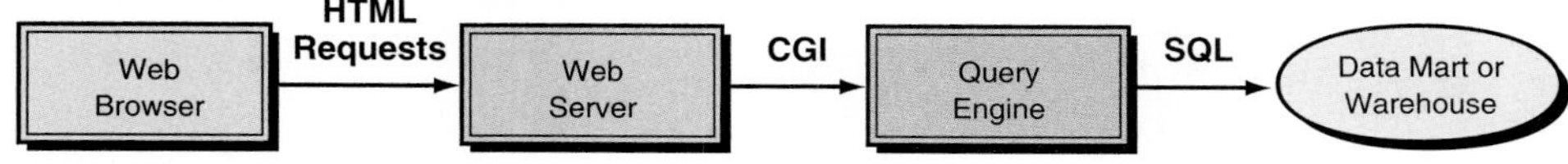

FIGURE 10.9 Web-based query.

program that enables users to send or receive data to or from a Web server. SQL, structured query language, as described in Technology Guide 3, is a query language that enables users to perform complicated searches with relatively simple statements.)

FOR THE DSS DEVELOPER (BUILDER)

1. A DSS developer (builder) can access Web pages with data related to the project, the software used, the users, and so on, thus cutting development time.
2. A DSS developer can collaborate with end users for quicker prototyping of DSS applications.
3. A DSS developer can collaborate with vendors over the Web. As discussed earlier, DSS software and applications are available from ASPs over the Web. In such a case there is no need to program the DSS, but the developer must work with the vendor.

FOR BOTH USERS AND DEVELOPERS. Several vendors offer services online that can benefit both a user and a developer. An example is *training*. For example, Promodel.com is introducing its new models by selling interactive CD-ROMs that include a refresher course on the software and answers to questions. User companies can place it on their intranets. Some companies provide similar free services online.

Most vendors of decision support applications have modified their tools in order for them to work across the Web. An example is Brio Technology Corporation, whose BrioQuery Enterprise, an online analytical processing tool, was converted to Brio's Web Warehouse. Brio's tool enables users to view and manipulate reports created with BrioQuery inside a browser. The user can employ the tool to drill down, pivot, or change the layout and content of the DSS output. Pilot Software and Comshare also offer DSS/Web products. An intranet-based DSS was proposed by Ba et al. (1997). This DSS is also related to intelligent decision support.

Web-based DSSs facilitate the use of these systems and are especially suitable to enterprise systems. An example is provided in the *IT at Work* example on page 464.

The Benefits of Web-based DSS

The following are some of the beneficial features of Web-based DSSs.

- ***Able to reach rich resources of data with simple data entry and analysis procedure.*** To attract customers, vendors try their best to enrich their resources of data and simplify the data entry and analysis procedure. A Web-based DSS helps users to obtain more benefits while they are using the system.
- ***Can easily retrieve data in sophisticated ways.*** Users can easily access the Web-based DSS from anywhere in the world. They need only a computer and a Web browser to do so. They can use the decision support applications

IT at Work

...in Finance

WEB-BASED DSS AT A LUXEMBOURG BANK

SEB Private Bank is the Luxembourg subsidiary of Swedish Bank SEB, an elite international bank that is quickly moving to take advantage of big growth opportunites in Europe with Internet banking. SEB is finding that customers on the Internet conduct more transactions than others, a trend that could deliver high profitability. The bank sees its greatest and most attractive opportunity in Europe, where SEB participates in a growing investment market and distinguishes itself with high-performance financial tools that empower managers to offer superior customer service. The bank has set an ambitious goal of having 5 million Internet customers by the end of 2004 with the help of a pan-European Internet model.

To move into real-time 24/7 operations, SEB Private Bank decided to investigate a DSS product called WebFOCUS from Information Builders. WebFOCUS Business Intelligence software allows users to quickly build self-service production reporting and business analysis systems. Everything from standard to customized reports can be developed quickly and delivered immediately, internally or externally, by intranets, extranets, and over the Internet. As a result, the entire *decision-making process* is shifted onto a real-time transaction platform. The bank developed over 600 reports, of which more than 150 are used by the bank's managers on a day-to-day basis.

Two core elements of SEB Private Bank's information system are the AS/400 hardware platform and Olympic, a Swiss-developed financial application. The combination of WebFOCUS and Information Builders' EDA (integration middleware that offers access to virtually any database) on the AS/400 has improved information access for account managers. EDA resides on the AS/400, interacting with the Olympic application and allowing access to any database application on the platform.

Olympic software generates SWIFT messages to leading stock exchanges, which in turn deliver a return message to the application, giving current financial updates. This streamlines the bank's reaction times with the outside world, giving up-to-the-minute information.

But having this intelligent information source is one thing; making full use of it is another.

SEB Private Bank sees the increasing use of its intranet, with its Web-based, thin-client architecture, as a move toward fewer paper reports. For example: Through this system, the bank's managers can easily check the inventory value of a client's assets; when the DSS is asked to evaluate a dossier, it can quickly produce a result.

With reliable security and high value-added services, SEB Private Bank feels well-positioned to expand its markets with new expatriate investor business.

For Further Exploration: What other applications can be developed with such a DSS?

Source: Compiled from *informationbuilders.com/applications/seb.html* (2001).

at any time. This is especially important to salespeople in the field and to employees on the road.

- ***Is easy to use.*** Since the Web-based a DSS is designed for helping decision makers to simplify the decision making and analysis processes, it is very user-friendly. Large data sets are stored in a relational database. Users can navigate the data merely by clicking a mouse button. Anyone who knows how to use the Internet can learn to use the Web-based DSS in a few minutes.
- ***Reduces paperwork.*** Since data for a DSS are stored in the data warehouse (in large companies) and can be transformed into information quickly and correctly, decision makers do not need to ask their employees, analysts, or consultants to provide them with information or suggestions via paperwork. Web-based DSSs save lots of paper, time, and money.
- ***Contributes to better decision making.*** The rich information provided by a Web-based DSS enables decision makers to chart the best future for their companies. The managers can make better decisions because they have better tools.

- ***Enables easier use of ready-made DSSs.*** The Web enables economic dissemination of ready-made DSSs by *application service providers (ASPs)*. As with other applications, there is a growing trend to rent (or lease) rather than to build (see Chapters 13 and 14). A large number of DSS packages for specific industries and applications is available from vendors such as Computer Associates and MicroStrategy.
- ***Cuts development costs.*** A company does not need to create its own decision support system if it employs Web-based DSS online from ASPs. To create a customized DSS is usually much more expensive than to subscribe to the services from a DSS vendor.

Requirements for Web-based DSS

A study by Business Objects Corporation (*businessobjects.com*) identified five key requirements for the successful delivery of Web-based, enterprise decision support solutions: self-service data access; high availability and performance; zero-administration clients; security; and unified meta data.

SELF-SERVICE DATA ACCESS. The most important characteristic of Web-based decision support tools is their ease of use. The Web opens up decision support to both occasional corporate users and users outside the organization (such as partners, suppliers, or customers). In many cases, little or no training is needed prior to using the tool. In order to deliver the ease of use necessary in this new environment, tools must offer:

- Autonomous access to information
- Easy navigation through enterprise reports
- Drill-down to access Web-based information sources

HIGH AVAILABILITY AND PERFORMANCE. To offer on-demand DSS access to a large or variable number of users, traditional two- or three-tier client/server technology is insufficient. Special improvements and optimizations are needed.

ZERO-ADMINISTRATION CLIENTS. Zero-administration clients can be achieved only by using true thin-client technology, such as Java applets.

SECURITY. An "information democracy," in which information is widely available to interested parties, offers organizations competitive advantage. But, opening up enterprise-critical information throughout an organization via an intranet, and especially when connection is made via the Internet, raises security risks that need to be addressed.

UNIFIED META DATA. Any decision support solution for the Internet must be standardized. Meta data integration can be of great help in this case.

10.6 Advanced Decision Support Topics

Several topics are involved in implementing DSS. Two of these are presented in this section. (For more details, see Turban and Aronson, 2001.)

Simulation for Decision Making

SIMULATION. *Simulation* has many meanings. In general, to *simulate* means to assume the appearance of characteristics of reality. In DSS, **simulation** generally refers to a technique for conducting experiments (such as "what-if") with a computer on a model of a management system.

Because a DSS deals with semistructured or unstructured situations, it involves complex reality, which may not be easily represented by optimization or other standard models but can often be handled by simulation. Therefore, simulation is one of the most frequently used tools of DSSs. (See Law and Kelton, 1999.)

Major Characteristics. To begin, simulation is not a regular type of model. Models in general *represent* reality, whereas simulation usually *imitates* it closely. In practical terms, this means that there are fewer simplifications of reality in simulation models than in other models.

Second, simulation is a technique for *conducting experiments.* As such it can describe and/or predict the characteristics of a given system under different circumstances. Once the characteristics' values are computed, the best among several alternatives can be selected. The simulation process often consists of the repetition of an experiment many, many times to obtain an estimate of the overall effect of certain actions. It can be executed manually in some cases, but a computer is usually needed. Simulation can be used for complex decision making, as illustrated in the *IT at Work* example below.

IT at Work

SIEMENS SOLAR INDUSTRIES SAVES MILLIONS BY SIMULATION

www.siemens.com

Siemens Solar Industries (SSI) is the world's largest maker of solar electric products. The German company operates in a global, extremely competitive market. Before 1994, the company suffered continuous problems in photocell fabrication, including poor material flow, unbalanced resource use, bottlenecks in throughput, and schedule delays. To overcome the problems, the company decided to build a *cleanroom* contamination-control technology.

Cleanrooms are standard practice in semiconductor businesses, but they had never been used in the solar industry. The new technology, in which there is perfect control of temperature, pressure, humidity, and air cleanliness, was shown in research to improve quality considerably. In addition, productivity is improved because of fewer defects, better material flow, and reduced cycle times. Because no one in the solar industry had ever used a cleanroom, the company decided to use a simulation. The simulation provided a virtual laboratory in which the engineers could experiment with various configurations of layouts and processes before the physical systems were constructed.

The simulation was constructed with a tool called ProModel (from ProModel Corp., *promodel.com*). This tool allowed the company to construct simulation models easily and quickly and to conduct what-if analyses. It also included extensive graphics and animation capabilities.

Computer simulation allowed SSI to compare numerous alternatives quickly. The company attempted to find the best design for the cleanroom. It also evaluated alternative scheduling, delivery rules, and material flows with respect to queue (waiting line) levels, throughput, cycle time, machine utilization, and work-in-progress levels.

The simulation involved the entire business process, the machines, equipment, workstations, storage and handling devices, operators, and material and information flows necessary to support the process. Using brainstorming, the builders came up with many innovative suggestions that were checked by the simulation. The solution identified the best configurations for the cleanroom, designed a schedule with minimum interruptions and bottlenecks, and improved material flow, while reducing work-in-progress inventory levels to a minimum.

All in all, the simulation enabled the company to significantly improve the manufacturing process of different solar products. The cleanroom facility has saved SSI over $75 million each year.

For Further Exploration: Relate this story to BPR (Chapter 8).

Sources: Condensed from J. R. Vacca, "Faking It, Then Making It," *Byte,* November 1995; *siemens.com* (2001); and *promodel.com* (2001).

Advantages of Simulation. Simulation is used for decision support because it:

1. ***Allows for inclusion of the real-life complexities of problems.*** Only a few simplifications are necessary. For example, simulation may utilize the real-life probability distributions rather than approximate theoretical distributions.
2. ***Is descriptive.*** This allows the manager to ask what-if type questions. Thus, managers who employ a trial-and-error approach to problem solving can do it faster and cheaper, with less risk, using a simulated problem instead of a real one.
3. ***Can handle an extremely wide variation in problem types,*** such as inventory and staffing, *as well as higher managerial-level tasks* like long-range planning. Further, the manager can experiment with different variables to determine which are important, and with different alternatives to determine which is best.
4. ***Can show the effect of compressing time,*** giving the manager in a matter of minutes some feel as to the long-term effects of various policies.
5. ***Can be conducted from anywhere*** using Web tools on the corporate portal or extranet.

Of the various types of simulation, the most comprehensive is visual interactive simulation, which is described in Chapter 11.

Specialized Ready-Made Decision Support

Initially, DSSs were custom-built. This resulted in two categories of DSS: The first type was small, end-user DSSs which were built by inexpensive tools such as Excel. The second type was large scale, expensive DSSs built by IT staff with tools such as those described in Minicase 2. For most applications, however, building a custom system was not justified. As a result, vendors started to offer DSSs in specialized areas such as financial services, banking, hospitals, or profitability measurements (or combinations of these areas). The popularity of these DSSs has increased since 1999 when vendors started to offer them online as ASP services.

Here are some examples, most of which are delivered via the Web:

- Business consultant PriceWaterhouseCoopers (*pwcglobal.com*) offers a large number of online DSSs in retailing, financial services, etc. (see Internet Exercise 8). Of special interest are the risk analyses (e.g., risk management and self-insurance decisions). They also analyze the effect of supply-chain decisions on product profitability.
- Microsoft's Office Small Business edition contains what-if wizards that can be used to view the financial impacts of decisions, such as price and inventory decisions. Also included are business charts and five-year projection reports (see *microsoft.com*).
- IBM offers many tools ranging from market-basket analysis to financial and manufacturing decision support (*-software.ibm.com*).
- Brio's "revenue optimization application" helps companies to identify and capture the full potential of revenue across product lines and market segments (*brio.com*).
- Hyperion provides a set of performance management solutions, supply chain analysis tools and solutions, financial analysis solutions, and more (*hyperion.com*).
- Comshare provides several management planning and control tools, ranging from budgeting to financial consolidation (*comshare.com*).

- A. C. Nielsen offers a variety of marketing analysis tools (*acnielsen.com*).
- SAS Institute and Decisioneering.com offers forecasting models to support a variety of decisions in several industries (*sas.com*).

These tools and many more can be customized, at additional cost. However, even when customizing ready-made DSS tools, the total cost to users is usually much lower than that of developing DSSs from scratch.

Frontline Decision Support Systems

Decisions at all levels in the organization contribute to the success of a business. But decisions that maximize a sales opportunity or minimize the cost of customer service requests are made on the front lines by those closest to situations that arise during the course of daily business. Whether it is an order exception, an upselling opportunity, or a contract that hangs on a decision, the decision maker on the front line must be able to make effective decisions rapidly based on context and according to strategies and guidelines set forth by senior management.

FRONTLINE SYSTEMS. **Frontline decision making** is the process by which companies automate decision processes and push them down into the organization and sometimes out to partners. It includes *empowering employees* by letting them devise strategies, evaluate metrics, analyze impacts, and make operational changes.

Frontline decision making automates simple decisions—like freezing the account of a customer who has failed to make payments—by predefining business rules and events that trigger them. At more complex decision points, such as inventory allocation, frontline decision making gives managers the necessary context—available alternatives, business impacts, and success measurements—to make the right decision.

Frontline decision making serves business users such as line managers, sales executives, and call-center representatives by incorporating decision making into their daily work. These workers need applications to help them make good operational decisions that meet overall corporate objectives. Frontline decision making provides users with the right questions to ask, the location of needed data, and metrics that translate data into corporate objectives and suggest actions that can improve performance. Analytic application products are now emerging to support these actions.

Frontline software that started to appear on the market in late 1999 can solve standard problems (such as what to do if a specific bank customer withdraws 100 percent more than the average withdrawal) by packaging in a single browser a self-service solution that requires business logic (including rules, algorithms, intelligent systems, and so on). Also provided are metrics such as life-cycle expectancy, decision workflow, and so on. Finally, to be successful, such systems must work hand in hand with transactional systems.

According to Forrester Research Inc., such systems are essential for the survival of many companies, but it is expected to take five years for the technology to mature. The major current vendors are Hyperion Solutions Corporation, NCR Corporation, SAS Institute Inc., and i2 Technology. However, almost all the SCM, ERP, and business intelligence vendors mentioned in this chapter may be involved in such systems. For further details see McCullough (1999) and Sheth and Sisodia (1999).

DSS Failures

Over the years there have been many cases of failures of all types of decision support systems. There are multiple reasons for such failures, ranging from human factors to software glitches. Here are a few examples:

- The ill-fated Challeger Shuttle mission was partially attributed to a flawed GDSS (see *http://frontpage/hypermall.com/jforrest/challenger/challenger_sts.htm*). NASA used a mismanaged GDSS session in which anonymity was not allowed and other procedures were violated.
- In an international congress on airports, failures in Denver, Hong Kong, and Malaysia airports were analyzed (*onera.fr/congress/jso2000airport*).
- The whitepapers of *visible.com/about/whitep.html* list many possible reasons for DSS failures and how to prevent them.
- Brezillon and Pomerol (1997) describe some failures in intelligent DSSs.

Despite the large number of failures, most DSS failures can be eliminated by using appropriate planning, collaboration, and management procedures.

MANAGERIAL ISSUES

1. ***Intangible benefits.*** Management support systems are difficult to justify because they generate mostly intangible benefits, such as the ability to solve problems faster. While the cost of small systems is fairly low and justification is not a critical issue, the cost of a medium-to-large MSS can be very high, and the systems must be economically justified.
2. ***Documenting personal DSS.*** Many employees develop their own DSSs to increase their productivity and the quality of their work. It is advisable to have an inventory of these DSSs and make certain that appropriate documentation and security measures exist, so that if the employee leaves the organization, the productivity tool remains.
3. ***Security.*** Decision support systems may contain extremely important information for the livelihood of organizations. Taking appropriate security measures, especially in Web-based distributed applications, is a must. The problem is that end-users who build a DSS frequently ignore appropriate security measures. Management must remember that end users are not professional systems builders. For this reason, there could be problems with data integrity and the quality of the systems developed.
4. ***Ready-made commercial DSSs.*** With the increased use of Web-based systems and ASPs, it is possible to find more and more DSS applications sold off the shelf, frequently online. The benefits of a purchased, or leased, DSS application (low cost, immediate use) sometimes make it advisable to change business processes to fit a commercially available DSS rather than to build a custom one. Some vendors are willing to modify their standard software to fit the customer's needs. Commercial DSSs are available both for certain industries (hospitals, banking) and for specific tasks (like profitability analysis).
5. ***Intelligent DSS.*** Introducing intelligent agents into a DSS application can greatly increase its functionality. The intelligent component of a system can be less than 3 percent of the entire system (the rest is models, a database, and telecommunications). Yet, the contribution of the intelligent component can be incredible.

6. ***Organizational culture.*** The more people recognize the benefits of a DSS and the more support is given to it by top management, the more the DSS will be used. If the organization's culture is supportive, dozens of applications can be developed.

7. ***Ethical issues.*** Corporations with management support systems may need to address some serious ethical issues such as privacy and accountability. For example, a company developed a DSS to help people compute the financial implications of early retirement. However, the DSS developer did not include the tax implications, which resulted in incorrect retirement decisions.

   Another important ethical issue is human judgment, which is frequently used in DSSs. Human judgment is subjective, and therefore, it may lead to unethical decision making. Companies should provide an ethical code for DSS builders. Finally, the possibility of automating managers' jobs may lead to massive layoffs. Some may ask whether companies should automate such decision making, as well as to what extent they should do so.

ON THE WEB SITE... Additional resources, including the Virtual Company, quizzes, cases, updates, additional exercises, links, demos, and activities, can be found on the book's Web site.

KEY TERMS

Ad-hoc analysis *459*
Business intelligence *460*
Decision metrics *443*
Decision room *453*
Decision support system (DSS) *445*
Drill down *458*
Enterprise information system *459*
Exception reporting *459*
Executive information system (EIS) *457*
Executive support system (ESS) *457*
Frontline decision making *468*
Goal Seek feature *448*
Goal-seeking analysis *448*
Group decision support system (GDSS) *452*
Management support system (MSS) *442*
Model (in decision making) *438*
Model base management system (MBMS) *449*
Organizational decision support system (ODSS) *454*
Personal information manager (PIM) *443*
Sensitivity analysis *448*
Simulation *465*
Trend analysis *459*
Web-based DSS *460*
What-if analysis *448*

CHAPTER HIGHLIGHTS (NUMBERS REFER TO LEARNING OBJECTIVES)

(1) Managerial decision making is synonymous with management.

(1) In today's business environment it is difficult or impossible to conduct analysis of complex problems without computerized support.

(2) Models allow fast and inexpensive virtual experimentation with systems. Models can be iconic, analog, or mathematical.

(2) Decision making is becoming more and more difficult due to the trends discussed in Chapter 1. Information technology enables managers to make better and faster decisions.

(3) To a degree, decisions can be structured and are either operational, managerial, or strategic.

(3) Decision making involves four major phases: intelligence, design, choice, and implementation.

(4) DSSs can improve the effectiveness of decision making, decrease the need for training, improve management control, facilitate communication, reduce costs, and allow for more objective decision making.

(4) The major components of a DSS are a database and its management, the model base and its management, and the friendly user interface. An intelligent (knowledge) component can be added.

4 The model base includes standard models and models specifically written for the DSS.

5 An organizational DSS deals with decision making across functional areas and hierarchical organizational layers, and it operates in a distributed environment.

6 Executive information systems are intended to support top executives. Initially these were standalone systems, but today they are part of enterprise systems delivered on intranets.

6 Organizational DSSs are systems with many users, throughout the enterprise. This is in contrast with systems that support one person or one functional area.

7 The Web can facilitate decision making by giving managers easy access to information and to modeling tools to process this information. Furthermore, Web tools such as browsers and search engines increase the speed of gathering and interpreting data. Finally, the Web facilitates collaboration and group decision making.

QUESTIONS FOR REVIEW

1. Describe the manager's major roles.
2. Define models and list the major types used in DSSs.
3. Explain the phases of intelligence, design, and choice.
4. What are structured (programmed) and unstructured problems? Give one example of each in the following three areas: finance, marketing, and personnel administration.
5. Explain what-if analysis, and provide an example.
6. What is goal-seeking analysis? Provide an example.
7. Give two definitions of DSSs.
8. List and briefly describe the major components of a DSS.
9. What is the major purpose of the user interface component in a DSS?
10. List the major classes of DSSs users.
11. Describe the relationship of DSSs and the Internet/intranet.
12. Define GDSS.
13. List some GDSS characteristics.
14. What is the difference between an EIS and an ESS?
15. What are the major benefits of an EIS?
16. Define drill-down, and list its advantages.
17. Relate DSS and EIS to the Internet.
18. Describe the benefit of simulation in decision support.
19. List the benefits of a Web-based DSS to the user.

QUESTIONS FOR DISCUSSION

1. What could be the biggest advantages of a mathematical model that supports a major investment decision?
2. Your company is considering opening a branch in China. List several typical activities in each phase of the decision (intelligence, design, choice, and implementation).
3. A hospital desires to know what level of demand for its services will guarantee an 85 percent bed occupancy. What type of sensitivity analysis should the hospital use and why?
4. Some experts believe that the major contribution of a DSS is to the implementation phase of the decision and not to the intelligence, design, or choice phases. Why?
5. How is the term *model* used in this chapter? What are the strengths and weaknesses of modeling?
6. List some internal data and external data that could be found in a DSS for a company's selection of an investment stock portfolio.
7. List some internal and external data in a DSS that will be constructed for a decision regarding the expansion of a university.
8. If a DSS is employed in finding answers to management questions, what is the EIS used for?
9. American Can Company announced that it was interested in acquiring a company in the health maintenance organization (HMO) field. Two decisions were involved in this act: (1) the decision to acquire an HMO, and (2) the decision of which one to acquire. How can a DSS and an EIS be used in each situation?
10. Why can't a conventional MIS fulfill the information needs of executives?
11. Relate the concept of knowledge subsystem to front-line decision support. What is the role of Web tools in such support?
12. Describe how critical success factors are measured in your company or in a company with which you are familiar.
13. Discuss how GDSSs can negate the dysfunctions of face-to-face meetings (Chapter 4).
14. Discuss the advantages of Internet-based DSSs.
15. Discuss the differences between an ODSS and a DSS.

EXERCISES

1. Susan Lopez was promoted to director of the transportation department in a medium-size university. She controlled the following vehicles: 17 sedans, 9 vans, and 3 trucks. The previous director was fired because there were too many complaints about not getting vehicles when needed. Susan is told not to expect any increase in budget for the next two years, which means there will be no replacement or additional vehicles. Susan's major job is to schedule vehicles for employees and to schedule maintenance and repair of the vehicles.

   Your job is to advise Susan regarding the possibility of using a Web-based DSS to improve her manually done job. Susan has a PC and Microsoft Office 2000, but she is using the computer only for word processing and for surfing the Internet.

   a. Justify use of the proposed DSS. What can this DSS do to improve Susan's job?

   b. Describe the decision variables, result variables, and independent variables of the DSS model.

   c. Which of the Microsoft Office components will you use for this DSS, and for what?

   d. How is the Web going to be used?

GROUP AND ROLE-PLAYING ACTIVITIES

1. Development of an organizational DSS is proposed for your university. Identify the management structure of the university and the major existing information systems. Then, identify and interview several potential users of the system. In the interview, you should check the need for such a system and convince the potential users of the benefits of the system.
2. Each group should identify current DSS tools in one area and go to a computer store or vendor's Web site, to examine some of these products. Then make a brief evaluation of at least four areas:

   a. An integrated spreadsheet (such as Excel)

   b. A Web-based DSS

   c. A data access tool (check with vendors like Comshare, Inc., Pilot Software, Brio, and Cognos)

   d. Multidimensional presentation, such as PowerPlay, or CA Compete

   Make a class presentation, stressing the superiority of your products.
3. Prepare a report regarding DSSs and the Web. As a start go to *http://dssresources.com*. (Take the DSS tour.) Each group represents one vendor such as *microstrategy.com*, *sas.com*, and *cai.com*. Each group should prepare a report that aims to convince a company why its DSS Web tools are the best.

INTERNET EXERCISES

1. Enter the site of *microstrategy.com* and identify its major DSS products. Find success stories of customers using these products. (Try *comshare.com/customers/customers.cfm*.) Also, find Comshare's Web-based strategy.
2. Find DSS-related newsgroups. Post a message regarding a DSS issue that is of concern to you. Gather several replies and prepare a report.
3. Several DSS vendors provide free demos on the Internet. Identify a demo, view it, and report on its major capabilities. (Try *microstrategy.com*, *sas.com*, *brio.com*, and *decisioneering.com*. You may need to register at some sites.)
4. Enter the Comshare site and find information about Comshare Decision. Explain the integration of EISs and DSSs in this product. E-mail Comshare and identify a successful real-world application using Comshare Decision. Submit a report.
5. Search the Internet for the major DSSs and business intelligence vendors. How many of them market a Web-based system? (Try *pilotsw.com*.)
6. Enter *asymetrix.com*. Learn about their decision support tool suite (Toolbook Assistant). Explain how the software can increase competitive advantage.
7. Find ten case studies about DSSs. (Try *microstrategy.com*, *sas.com*, *google.com*, and *comshare.com*.) Analyze for DSS characteristics.
8. Enter *pwcglobal.com* and find the e-Doctor. Take the test for your company, or a company you are familiar with. Review the score and the comment provided.
9. Enter *acxiom.com*, *ncr.com*, *hyperion.com*, and *ptc.com*. Identify their frontline system initiatives.

Minicase 1
A Decision Support System—Or Is It?

John Young, the general manager of a small electric utility company in Colorado, was concerned about the large number of customer complaints. Complaints were received by the customer relations department and distributed manually to the appropriate departments for consideration. Each complaint was investigated, and a response was provided either orally or in writing.

John completed a course in decision support systems and learned to program with Excel. As a part of the course, he constructed and installed a customers' complaint DSS in the utility company. Its database includes each complaint, information about it, who is handling it, when it was assigned to an individual department, when it was resolved, and how it was resolved (a copy of the letter or e-mail to the customer or a transcript of the telephone conversation with the customer).

John was very proud of the system. He felt that it increased his control and, because everything is documented, people would handle complaints more effectively. Furthermore, he placed the system on the company's intranet, so the internal paperwork was eliminated. One morning, he had the following conversation with his assistant, Nancy Gray, who also completed a DSS course.

John: What do you think about the success of my DSS?

Nancy: The system works fine, but I am not sure that this is a DSS.

John: You know that I designed it myself. The system is user friendly. I can find the status of any complaint and compute, if necessary, how long it took to solve the complaint.

Nancy: That is all great, but what specific decisions do you support?

John: Well, I can use this information to decide, for example, on rewards for those who handle the complaints most effectively.

Nancy: How?

John: I'm not sure. I may conduct comparisons.

Questions for Minicase 1

1. Is John's system a DSS? Why or why not?
2. If it is not a DSS, what changes would be necessary to make it a DSS?

Minicase 2
A DSS Reshapes the Railway in the Netherlands

More than 5,000 trains pass through 2,800 railway kilometers and 400 stations each day in the Netherlands. As of the mid-1990s, the railway infrastructure was hardly sufficient to handle the passenger flow. The problem gets worse during rush hours, and trains are delayed. Passengers complain and tend to use cars, whose variable cost is lower than that of using the train. This increases the congestion on the roads, adding pollution and traffic accidents. The largest railway company, Nederlandse Spoorweges (NS), was losing money in rural areas and agreed to continue services there only if the government would integrate the railways with bus and taxi systems, so commuters would have more incentives to use the trains. Several other problems plagued the system. Government help was needed.

Rail 21 is the name of the government project that aims to bring the system into the twenty-first century. It is a complex, multibillion-dollar project. The government wants to reduce road traffic among the large cities, stimulate regional economies by providing them with a better public transportation system, stimulate rail cargo, and reduce the number of short-distance passenger flights in Europe. NS wants to improve service and profitability. A company called Railned is managing the project, which is scheduled for completion in 2010.

Railned developed several alternative infrastructures (called "coctails"), and put them to analysis. The analysis involved four steps: (1) Use experts to list possible alternative projects. (2) Estimate passenger flows in each, using

(continued)

an econometric model. (3) Determine optimization of rail lines. (4) Test feasibility. The last two steps were complex enough that computerized DSSs were developed for their execution. These are:

- ***PROLOP:*** This DSS was designed to do the lines optimization. It involves a database and three quantitative models. It supports several decisions regarding rails, and it can be used to simulate the scenarios of the "coctails." It incorporates a management science model, called integer linear programming. PROLOP also compares line systems based on different criteria. Once the appropriate line system is completed, an analysis of the required infrastructure is done, using the second DSS, called DONS.
- ***DONS:*** This DSS is doing capacity checks, i.e., the feasibility of the desired lines systems. It contains a DSS database, graphical user interface, and two algorithmic modules. The first algorithm computes the arrival and departure times for each train at each station where it stops, based on "hard" constraints (must be met), and "soft" (can be delayed). It represents both safety and customer-service requirements. The objective is to create a feasible timetable for the trains. If a feasible solution is not possible, planners relax some of the "soft" constraints. If this does not help, modifications in the lines system are explored.
- ***STATIONS:*** Now it is time to route the trains through the railway stations. This is an extremely difficult problem that cannot be solved simultaneously with the timetable. Thus, STATIONS, another DSS, is used. Again, feasible optimal solutions are searched for. If these do not exist, system modifications are made.

The DSS solution is fairly complex due to conflicting objectives of the government and the railway company (NS), so negotiations on the final choices are needed. To do so, Railned developed a special DSS model for conducting cost-benefit evaluations. It is based on a multiple-criteria approach with conflicting objectives. This tool can rank alternative coctails based on certain requirements and assumptions. For example, one set of assumptions emphasizes NS long-term profitability, while the other one tries to meet the government requirements.

The DSSs were found to be extremely useful. They reduced the planning time and the cost of the analysis and increased the quality of the decisions. An example was an overpass that required an investment of $15 million. DONS came up with a timetable that required an investment of only $7.5 million using an alternative safety arrangement. The DSS solution is used during the operation of the system as well for monitoring and making adjustments and improvements in the system.

Source: Compiled from J. H. Hooghiemstra, et al., "Decision Support Systems Support the Search for Win-Win Solutions in Railway Network," *Interfaces,* March–April 1999.

Questions for Minicase 2

1. Why were management science optimizations by themselves not sufficient in this case?
2. What kind of a DSS is this?
3. Enter *NS.nl* and find information about NS's business partners and the system. (English information is available in some pages.)
4. Given the environment described in the case, which of the DSS generic characteristics described in this chapter are likely to be useful, and how?
5. In what steps of the process can simulation be used, and for what?
6. Identify sensitivity analysis in this case.

REFERENCES AND BIBLIOGRAPHY

1. Anderson, D. R., et al., *Quantitative Methods for Business,* 8th ed. Cincinnati, OH: South-Western, 2001.
2. Anthony, R. N., *Planning and Control Systems: A Framework for Analysis.* Cambridge, MA: Harvard University Graduate School of Business Administration, 1965.
3. Ba, S., et al., "Enterprise Decision Support Using Intranet Technology," *Decision Support Systems,* Vol. 20, 1997.
4. Bank J. (ed.), *Handbook of Simulation.* New York: Wiley, 1998
5. Bertsimas, D., and R. Freund, *Data Modeling and Decisions.* Cincinnati, OH: South-Western, 2000.
6. Brezillon, P., and Pomerol, J. C., "User Acceptance of Interactive Systems: Lessons from Knowledge-Based DSS," *Failure and Lessons Learned in IT Management,* Vol. 1, No. 1, 1997.
7. Carter, G. M., et al., *Building Organizational Decision Support Systems.* Cambridge, MA: Academic Press, 1992.
8. Cohen, H. D., et al., "Decision Support with Web-Enabled Software," *Interfaces,* March–April 2001.
9. DeSanctis, G., and B. Gallupe, "A Foundation for the Study of Group Decision Support Systems," *Management Science,* Vol. 33, No. 5, 1987.
10. Dutta, S., et al., "Designing Management Support Systems," *Communications of the ACM,* June 1997.
11. El Sharif, H., and O. A. El Sawy, "Issue-based DSS for the Egyptian Cabinet," *MIS Quarterly,* December 1988.
12. Foulds, L. R., and D. G. Johnson, "SlotManager: A Micro-

computer-based DSS for University Timetabling," *Decision Support Systems,* January 2000.

13. Gallegos, F., "Decision Support Systems: An Overview," *Information Strategy: The Executive's Journal,* Winter 1999.
14. Gorry, G. A., and M. S. Scott-Morton, "A Framework for Management Information Systems," *Sloan Management Review,* Vol. 13, No. 1, Fall 1971.
15. Gray, P., and H. J. Watson, *Decision Support in the Data Warehouse Systems.* Upper Saddle River, NJ: Prentice-Hall, 1998.
16. Hackathorn, R. D., and P. G. Keen, "Organizational Strategies for Personal Computing in Decision Support Systems," *MIS Quarterly,* September 1981.
17. Hooghiemstra, J. S., et al., "Decision Support Systems Support the Search for Win-Win Solutions in Railway Network," *Interfaces,* March–April 1999.
18. Kim, Y. G., et al., "Building an Organizational DSS for Korea Telecom: A Process Redesign Approach," *Decision Support Systems,* April 1997.
19. King, D., and D. O'Leary, "Intelligent Executive Information Systems," *IEEE Expert,* December 1996.
20. Kingsman, B. G., and A. A. deSouza, "A KBDSS for Cost Estimation and Pricing Decisions in Versatile Manufacturing Companies," *International Journal of Production Economics,* November 1997.
21. Law, A. M., and D. W. Kelton, *Simulation Modeling and Analysis.* New York: McGraw-Hill, 1999.
22. Leidner, D. E., et al., "Mexican and Swedish Managers' Perceptions of the Impact of EIS on Organizational Intelligence, Decision Making and Structure," *Decision Sciences,* Summer 1999.
23. Liu, S., et al., "Software Agents for Environmental Scanning in Electronic Commerce," *Information Systems Frontier,* Vol. 2, No. 1, 2000.
24. McCullough, S., "On the Front Lines," *CIO Magazine,* October 15, 1999.
25. Mintzberg, H., *The Nature of the Managerial Work.* New York: Harper & Row, 1973.
26. Nirchandani, D., and R. Pakath, "Four Models for Decision Support Systems," *Information and Management,* Vol. 35, 1999.
27. O'Leary, D. E., "Internet-based Information and Retrieval Systems," *Decision Support Systems,* December 1999.
28. Plant, R., *eCommerce Formulation of Strategy.* Upper Saddle River, NJ: Prentice-Hall, 2000.
29. Rockart, J. F., and D. DeLong, *Executive Support Systems.* Homewood, IL: Dow Jones–Irwin, 1988.
30. Sauter, V., "Intuitive Decision-Making," *Communications of the ACM,* June 1999.
31. Saxby, C. L., et al., "Managers' Mental Categorizations of Competitors," *Competitive Intelligence Review,* 2nd Quarter, 2000.
32. Scheer, A. W., *Aris: Business Process Modeling.* Berlin: Springer-Verlag, 2000.
33. Sheth, J. N., and R. S. Sisodia, "Are Your IT Priorities Upside Down?," *CIO,* November 15, 1999.
34. Simon, H., *The New Science of Management Decisions,* rev. ed. Englewood Cliffs, NJ: Prentice-Hall, 1977.
35. Singh, H., *Data Warehousing Concepts, Technologies, Implementation and Management.* Upper Saddle River, NJ: Prentice-Hall, 1998.
36. Skinner, D. C., *Introduction to Decision Analysis.* Gainseville, FL: Probabilistic Publishing, 1999.
37. Turban, E., and J. Aronson, *Decision Support Systems and Intelligent Systems,* 6th ed. Upper Saddle River, NJ: Prentice-Hall, 2001.
38. Vandenbosch, B., and S. L. Huff, "Searching and Scanning: How Executives Obtain Information from EIS," *MIS Quarterly,* March 1997.
39. Volbera, H. W., and A. Rutges, "FARSYS: A Knowledge-based System for Manaaging Strategic Change," *Decision Support Systems,* August 1999.
40. Watson, H. J., and M. Frolick, "Determining Information Requirements for an Executive Information System," *Information Systems Management,* Spring 1992.
41. Wetherbe, J. C., "Executive Information Requirements: Getting It Right," *MIS Quarterly,* March 1991.

PART IV

Managerial and Decision Support Systems

CHAPTER

11

Data Management: Warehousing, Analyzing, Mining, and Visualization

LEARNING OBJECTIVES

After studying this chapter, you will be able to:

1. Recognize the importance of data, their managerial issues, and their life cycle.
2. Describe the sources of data, their collection, and quality issues.
3. Relate data management to multimedia and document management.
4. Explain the operation of data warehousing and its role in decision support.
5. Understand the data access and analysis problem and the data mining and online analytical processing solutions.
6. Describe data presentation methods and explain geographical information systems, visual simulations, and virtual reality as decision support tools.
7. Discuss the role of marketing databases and provide examples.
8. Recognize the role of the Web in data management.

PRECISION BUYING, MERCHAND ING, AND MARKETING AT SEARS

THE PROBLEM

www.Sears.com

Sears, Roebuck and Company, the largest department store ch... largest retailer in the United States, was caught by surprise in th... d the third- pers defected to specialty stores and discount mass merchandis... s as shop- firm to lose market share rapidly. In an attempt to change the s... sing the used several response strategies, ranging from introducing its own sp... (such as Sears Hardware) to reengineering its mall-based stores. Rec... Sears has been moving to the Web. Accomplishing this goal required the r... res its information systems. ...rs

Sears had 18 data centers, one in each of 10 geographical regions as one each for marketing, finance, and other departments. The first proble... created when the reorganization effort produced only seven geographical reg... Frequent mismatches between accounting and sales figures and information sc... tered among numerous databases forced users to query multiple systems, eve... when an answer to a simple query was all that was required. Furthermore, users found that data that were already summarized made it difficult to conduct analysis at the desired level of detail. Finally, errors were virtually inevitable when calculations were based on data from several sources.

THE SOLUTION

To solve these problems Sears constructed a single sales information data warehouse. This replaced the 18 old databases which were packed with redundant, conflicting, and sometimes obsolete data. The new data warehouse is a simple depository of relevant decision-making data such as authoritative data for key performance indicators, sales inventories, and profit margins. Sears, known for embracing IT on a dramatic scale, completed the data warehouse and its IT reengineering efforts in under one year—a perfect IT turnaround story.

Using an NCR enterprise server, the initial 1.7 terabyte (1 terabyte equals 1 trillion bytes) data warehouse is part of a project dubbed the Strategic Performance Reporting System (SPRS). By 2001, the data warehouse had grown to over 10 terabytes. SPRS includes comprehensive sales data; information on inventory in stores, in transit, and at distribution centers; and cost per item. This has enabled Sears to track sales by individual items in each of its 1,950 stores (including 810 mall-based stores) in the United States and 1,600 international stores and catalog outlets. Thus, daily margin by item per store can be easily computed, for example. Furthermore, Sears now fine tunes its buying, merchandising, and marketing strategies with previously unattainable precision.

SPRS is open to all authorized employees, who now can view each day's sales from a multidimensional perspective (by region, district, store, product line, and individual item). Users can specify any starting and ending dates for special sales reports, and all data can be accessed via a highly user-friendly graphical interface. Sears staffers can now monitor the precise impact of advertising, weather, and other factors on sales of specific items. This means that buyers and other specialists can adjust inventory quantities, merchandising, and order placement, along with myriad other variables, almost immediately, so they can respond quickly to environmental changes. SPRS users can also group together widely divergent kinds of products, for example, tracking sales of items marked as "gifts under $25." Advertising staffers can follow so-called "great items," drawn from vastly different departments, that are splashed on the covers of promotional circulars.

By 2001 Sears also had the following Web initiatives: e-commerce home improvement center, a B2B supply exchange for the retail industry, a toy catalog (*wishbook.com*), an e-procurement system, and much more. All of these Web-marketing initiatives feed data into the data warehouse, and their planning and control are based on accessing the data in the data warehouse.

THE RESULTS

The ability to monitor sales by item per store enables Sears to create a sharp local market focus. For example, Sears keeps different shades of paint colors in different cities to meet local demands. Therefore, sales and market share have improved. Also, Web-based data monitoring of sales helps Sears to plan marketing and Web advertising.

At its inception, the data warehouse had been used daily by over 3,000 buyers, replenishers, marketers, strategic planners, logistics and finance analysts, and store managers. By 2001, there were thousands more, since users found the system very beneficial. Response time to queries has dropped from days to minutes for typical requests. Overall, the strategic impact of the data warehouse is that it offers Sears employees a tool for making better decisions, and Sears retailing profits have climbed more than 20 percent annually since SPRS was implemented.

Sources: Compiled from "Sears, Roebuck and Co.: Turning Technology into Advantage," *NCR Corp. Publications,* No. sp-6051-0396, 1996; from S. S. Beitler and R. Leary, "Sears' Epic Transformation," *Journal of Data Warehousing,* April 1997; and from press releases of Sears (2000, 2001).

LESSONS LEARNED FROM THIS CASE

The opening case illustrates the importance of managing data in the revitalization of a large retailer. Sears consolidated these data in one place, the data warehouse. The data warehouse is only one building block of effective data management. In this chapter we will look at several others, such as data analysis and visualization. For example, Sears created a *marketing database* that supported enterprise-level marketing analysis applications.

11.1 DATA MANAGEMENT: A CRITICAL SUCCESS FACTOR

In the previous chapter we saw that all decision support applications use some kind of data. In other words, without data you cannot make good decisions. However, there are increasing difficulties in acquiring, keeping, and managing data.

The Difficulties of Managing Data, and Some Solutions

THE DIFFICULTIES. Managing data in organizations is difficult for the following reasons:

- The amount of data increases exponentially. Much past data must be kept for a long time, and new data are added rapidly.
- Data are scattered throughout organizations and are collected by many individuals using several methods and devices.
- Only small portions of an organization's data are relevant for any specific decision.

- An ever-increasing amount of external data needs to be considered in making organizational decisions.
- Data are frequently stored in several servers and locations in an organization.
- Raw data may be stored in different computing systems, databases, formats, and human and computer languages.
- Legal requirements relating to data differ among countries and change frequently.
- Selecting data management tools can be a major problem because of the huge number of products available.
- Data security, quality, and integrity are critical yet are easily jeopardized.

SOLUTIONS TO MANAGING DATA. These difficulties, and the critical need for timely and accurate information, have prompted organizations to search for effective and efficient data management solutions. Historically, data management has been geared to supporting transaction processing by organizing the data in a hierarchical format in one location. This format supports efficient high-volume processing; however, it is inefficient for queries and other ad-hoc applications. Therefore, *relational databases* (based on organization of data in rows and columns, as explained in Technology Guide 3) were added to facilitate end-user computing and decision support. With the introduction of client/server environments, databases became distributed throughout organizations, creating problems in finding data quickly and easily. This was the major reason that Sears sought the creation of a data warehouse. As we will see later, the intranet and extranets can also be used to improve data management.

It is now well recognized that data are an asset, although they can be a *burden* to maintain. Thus the use of data, in terms of information and knowledge, is *power*. The purpose of appropriate data management is to ease the burden of maintaining data and to enhance the power from their use. Recently, intranets have been playing a greater role in the support of *information sharing* across the enterprise, and databases accessible through the Internet can be used by almost any organization.

Data Life Cycle Process

To better understand how to manage data, it is necessary to trace how and where the data flow in organizations. Businesses do not run on data. They run on *information* and on the *knowledge* of how to put that information to use successfully.

Knowledge fuels solutions. Everything from innovative product designs to brilliant competitive moves relies on knowledge. Therefore, knowledge has always been an underlying component of business. Knowledge is not readily available, however, especially in today's rapidly changing world. In many cases knowledge is continuously derived from data. However, because of the difficulties cited in Chapter 9, such a derivation may not be simple or easy.

Transformation of data into knowledge and solutions is accomplished in several ways. In general, it resembles the process shown in Figure 11.1 (page 480). It starts with data collection from various sources. These data are stored in a database(s). Then the data is preprocessed to fit the format of the data warehouse and stored in the data warehouse or data marts. Users access the warehouse or data mart and take a copy of the needed data for analysis. The analysis is done

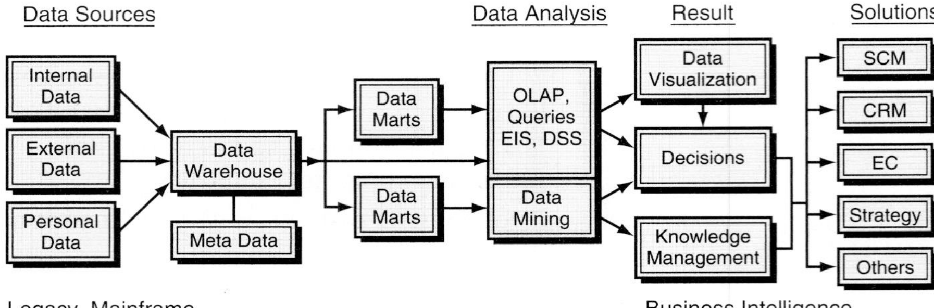

FIGURE 11.1 Data life cycle.

with data analysis and mining tools, which look for patterns, and with intelligent systems, which support data interpretation.

The result of all these activities is generation of decision support and knowledge. Both the data, at various times during the process, and the knowledge, derived at the end of the process, may need to be presented to users. Such a presentation can be accomplished by using different visualization tools. The created knowledge may be stored in an organizational *knowledge base* (as shown in Chapter 9) and used, together with decision support, to provide solutions to organizational problems. The elements and the process shown in Figure 11.1 are discussed in the remaining sections of this chapter.

Data Sources and Collection

The data life cycle begins with the acquisition of data from data sources. Data include concepts, thoughts, and opinions and can be raw or summarized. Data also include documents, pictures, maps, sound, and animation, and they can be stored and organized in different ways before and after use. Many IT applications use summary or extracted data. Data can also be classified as *internal, personal,* and *external.*

INTERNAL DATA. An organization's *internal data* are about people, products, services, and processes. Such data may be stored in one or more places. For example, data about employees and their pay are usually stored in the corporate database. Data about equipment and machinery may be stored in the maintenance department database. Sales data can be stored in several places—aggregate sales data in the corporate database, and details at each regional database, as in the Sears case. Internal data are usually accessible via an organization's intranet.

PERSONAL DATA. IS users or other corporate employees may document their own expertise by creating *personal data.* These include, for example, subjective estimates of sales, opinions about what competitors are likely to do, and certain rules and formulas developed by the users. These data can reside on the user's PC or be placed on departmental or business units' databases or on the corporate knowledge bases.

EXTERNAL DATA. There are many sources for *external data,* ranging from commercial databases to sensors and satellites. Government reports constitute a major source for external data. Data also are available on CD-ROMs, on Internet servers, as films, and as sound or voices. Pictures, diagrams, atlases, and television are other sources of external data. Hundreds of thousands of organizations worldwide place publicly accessible data on their Web servers, flooding us with data. Most external data are irrelevant to any single application. Yet much external data must be monitored and captured to ensure that important data are not overlooked. Large amounts of external data are available on the Internet.

THE INTERNET AND COMMERCIAL DATABASE SERVICES. Some external data flow to an organization on a regular basis through electronic data interchange (EDI), or through other company-to-company channels. Much external data are accessible via an extranet or the Internet, either for free or from commercial database services.

The Internet. Many thousands of databases all over the world are accessible through the Internet. Much of the database access is free. A user can access Web pages of vendors, clients, and competitors. He or she can view and download information while conducting research. The Internet, as discussed in Chapter 4, is becoming the major source of external data for many decision situations. Customized information may be pushed to you. (See Vassos, 1996, for a comprehensive list of Internet data sources.)

Commercial Online Publishing. An *online database publisher* sells access to specialized databases, newspapers, magazines, bibliographies, and reports. Such a service can provide external data to users in a timely manner and at a reasonable cost. Several thousand services are currently available, most of which are accessible via the Internet.

METHODS FOR COLLECTING RAW DATA. The diversity of data and the multiplicity of sources make the task of data collection fairly complex, creating quality and integrity problems. Sometimes it is necessary to collect raw data in the field. In other cases it is necessary to elicit data from people. Raw data can be collected manually or by instruments and sensors. Some examples of manual data collection methods are time studies, surveys, observations, and contributions from experts. Data can also be scanned or transferred electronically. **Clickstream data** are those that can be collected automatically from a company's Web site or from what visitors are doing on the site (see Turban et al., 2002).

Although a wide variety of hardware and software exists for data storage, communication, and presentation, much less effort has gone into developing software tools for data capture in environments where complex and unstable data exist. Insufficient methods for dealing with such situations may limit the effectiveness of IT development and use. One exception is the Web. The use of online polls and questionnaires is becoming very popular. For examples and discussion, see Lazar and Preece (1999) and Compton (1999).

The collection of data from multiple external sources may be an even more complicated task. One way to improve it, according to Roland (1994), is to use a *data flow manager (DFM),* which takes information from external sources and puts it where it is needed, when it is needed, in a usable form. A DFM consists of (1) a decision support system, (2) a central data request processor, (3) a data integrity component, (4) links to external data suppliers, and (5) the processes used by the external data suppliers.

Regardless of how they are collected, data need to be validated. A classic expression that sums up the situation is "garbage in, garbage out" (GIGO). Therefore, safeguards for data quality are designed to prevent data problems.

Data Quality

Data quality (DQ) is an extremely important issue since quality determines the data's usefulness as well as the quality of the decisions based on the data. Data are frequently found to be inaccurate, incomplete, or ambiguous, particularly in large, centralized databases. The economical and social damage from poor-quality data costs billions of dollars (see Redman, 1998). An example of typical data problems, their causes, and possible solutions is provided in Table 11.1. For a discussion of data auditing and controls, see Chapter 15.

Strong et al. (1997) conducted extensive research on DQ problems. Some of the problems are technical ones such as capacity, while others relate to potential computer crimes. The researchers divided these problems into the following four categories and dimensions (see also Wang, 1998).

- ***Intrinsic DQ:*** Accuracy, objectivity, believability, and reputation
- ***Accessibility DQ:*** Accessibility and access security
- ***Contextual DQ:*** Relevancy, value added, timeliness, completeness, amount of data
- ***Representation DQ:*** Interpretability, ease of understanding, concise representation, consistent representation

Strong et al. (1997) have suggested that once the major variables and relationships in each category are identified, an attempt can be made to find out how to better manage the data.

One of the major issues of DQ is **data integrity**. Data must be accurate, accessible, and up-to-date. Older filing systems may lack integrity. That is, a change

TABLE 11.1 Data Problems

Problem	Typical Cause	Possible Solutions (in Some Cases)
Data are not correct.	Raw data were entered inaccurately.	Develop a systematic way to ensure the accuracy of raw data. Automate (use scanners or sensors).
	Data derived by an individual were generated carelessly.	Carefully monitor both the data values and the manner in which the data have been generated. Check for compliance with collection rules.
Data are not timely.	The method for generating the data was not rapid enough to meet the need for the data.	Modify the system for generating the data. Move to a client/server system. Automate.
Data are not measured or indexed properly.	Raw data were gathered according to a logic or periodicity that was not consistent with the purposes of the analysis.	Develop a system for rescaling or recombining the improperly indexed data. Use intelligent search agents.
Needed data simply do not exist.	No one ever stored the data needed now.	Whether or not it is useful now, store data for future use. Use the Internet to search for similar data. Use experts.
	Required data never existed.	Make an effort to generate the data or to estimate them (use experts). Use neural computing for pattern recognition.

Source: Condensed from *Decision Support Systems* by Alter (1980). Reprinted by permission of Pearson Education, Inc., Upper Saddle River, N.J., 1980, p. 30. New material added in 1998–2001.

made in the file in one place may not be made in the file in another place or department. This results in conflicting data.

DATA QUALITY IN WEB-BASED SYSTEMS. Data are collected on a routine basis or for a special application on the Internet. In either case, it is necessary to organize and store them before they can be used. This may be a difficult task when media-rich Web sites are involved. This topic is discussed next.

Multimedia and Object-Oriented Databases

Data are organized and stored in files and databases. The major conventional, logical data organizations are *hierarchical, network,* and *relational*. These are described with other database topics in Technology Guide 3. The object-oriented database is the most widely used of the newest methods of data organization, especially for Web applications.

An **object-oriented database** is a part of the object-oriented paradigm, which also includes object-oriented programming, operating systems, and modeling. Its technical details are described in Technology Guide 3 and in Chapter 14. The object-oriented paradigm is used for complex applications, such as computer-integrated manufacturing or Web-based tutoring systems, that require accessibility to pictures, blueprints, and other images.

Object-oriented databases are sometimes referred to as **multimedia databases** (see Nwosu et al., 1997) and are managed by special *multimedia database management systems*. These manage data in a variety of formats in addition to the standard text or numeric fields (see Adjeroh and Nwosu, 1997). The formats include images such as digitized photographs or forms of bit-mapped graphics.

A considerable amount of corporate information resides outside the computer in the form of documents, maps, photos, images, and videotapes. For companies to build applications to take advantage of these rich data types, they must use a multimedia database management system. Database vendors are enhancing their offerings to include the ability to manage and manipulate multimedia data.

WEB-BASED SYSTEMS. There are many applications of a multimedia database. Most are Web-based, especially in such industries as newspapers and TV, where multimedia plays a critical role, as shown in the *IT at Work* case of Southam New Media on page 484. Electronic organization of data is interrelated with the issue of electronic document management.

Document Management

There are several major problems with paper documents. For example, in maintaining paper documents, we can pose the following questions: (1) Does everyone have the current version? (2) How often does it need to be updated? (3) How secure are the documents? and (4) How can the distribution of documents to the appropriate individuals be managed in a timely manner?

Electronic data overcome some of these problems. When documents are provided in electronic form from a single repository (typically a Web server), only the current version is provided. For example, many firms maintain their telephone directories in electronic form on an intranet to eliminate the need to copy and distribute hard copies of a document that requires constant corrections. Also, with data stored in electronic form, access to various documents can be restricted as required.

Document management is the automated control of electronic documents, page images, spreadsheets, word processing documents, and complex, compound

IT at Work
WEB-BASED NEWSSTAND AT SOUTHAM OF CANADA

...in Marketing
www.southam.com

Southam New Media, one of the largest newspaper chains in Canada, is a news agency that publishes information in its newspapers, and also creates and sells stories for other news providers. Southam has created a multimedia database called a *virtual newsstand*. The Southam Interactive Database allows the entry, filing, and retrieval of data in all formats used by Southam: wire service text, newspaper and magazine text, classified ads, photos, graphics, television, video and sound, software programs, and Web content. Any unit of data has identifiable attributes that can be stored and retrieved through a single access point. Southam's initial investment was only $500,000—much less than if its newspapers were prepared on conventional, non-Web systems.

According to Peter Irwin, president of Southam New Media, there is now a single access window for retrieval and input, with one export button, with which content can be exported onto the Web or, for example, to a commercial service provider such as America Online, for which Southam creates news and stories based on its own data. Basically, what the development team did was to write software that allowed extraction from all Southam's newspapers online and tried to make sense of what was in a newspaper's story. The information was then put into a relational database, which enabled flexibility. The system was set up on Southam's intranet.

Southam owns *Business World*, a Canadian television show. The company plans to put relevant videos from the program into the database using standard video-capturing technology. The videos then can be attached to any story published or sold. Future applications include a full electronic distribution of Southam's news.

For Further Exploration: Why is the database called interactive, and how is the Web related to this application?

Sources: Condensed from J. B. Cohen, "'Virtual Newsstand' Debuts Online," *Editor and Publisher*, Vol. 129, No. 24, pp. 86–87, June 15, 1996; and from *southam.com* ("Southam on the Web," 2001).

documents through their entire life cycle within an organization, from initial creation to final archiving. Document management offers various benefits: It allows organizations to exert greater control over production, storage, and distribution of documents, yielding greater efficiency in the reuse of information, the control of a document through a workflow process, and the reduction of product cycle times.

Document management technology grew out of the business community, where, according to the GartnerGroup, some 85 percent of corporate information resides in documents. The need for greater efficiency in handling business documents to gain an edge on the competition has fueled the increased availability of document management systems, also known as electronic document management.

Essentially, **document management systems (DMSs)** provide to decision makers information in an electronic format. The full range of functions that a document management system may perform includes document identification, storage, and retrieval; tracking; version control; workflow management; and presentation. The Thomas Cook Company, for example, uses a document management system to handle travel-refund applications. The system works on the PC desktop and has automated the workflow process, helping the firm double its volume of business while adding only about 33 percent more employees (see Cole, 1996). Another example is the Massachusetts Department of Revenue, which is using imaging systems to increase productivity of tax return processing by about 80 percent (see *civic.com/pubs*, March 2001).

Document management systems usually include computerized imaging systems that can result in substantial savings, as discussed in the *IT at Work* case below.

The major tools of document management are workflow software, authoring tools, scanners, and databases (object-oriented mixed with relational, known as object-relational database management systems; see Technology Guide 3).

IT at Work

THE IMAGING SYSTEM AT UNITED SERVICES AUTOMOBILE ASSOCIATION

Integrating IT ...in Production & Operations Management

www.usaa.com

United Services Automobile Association (USAA) is a large insurance company in San Antonio, Texas, serving about 2 million military officers, former officers, and their dependents. In 1998 the company processed about 130,000 documents every workday.

In the 1980s, the company employed 120 clerks whose only job was to search files (which occupied 39,000 square feet of office space) for information when needed. Searches for one document took anywhere from an hour to 2 weeks, and some documents were never found.

However, using an environment called Automated Insurance Environment, USAA has been transformed into a completely paperless company. Since 1993, employees have been able to scan over 50 million pieces of mail per year into a computer database. Using special imaging terminals, agents then access the database to process information and assist customers. Customers can now obtain *instant* answers to such questions as, "Is the car we bought an hour ago insured against theft?"

The system is also used to expedite the treatment of claims. When a customer calls to report a car accident, the telephone call is digitized and stored. Subsequently, all documents (photos, doctors' reports, appraisers' reports, and so on) are scanned into the computer. Once the case is closed, it is stored on a CD-ROM for future reference.

Here is how the data entry works: Every day the company receives almost 25,000 letters as well as thousands of telephone calls; every day the company sends over 60,000 letters and policies. All of these documents are indexed on an IBM mainframe and are scanned to create a digital electronic picture. The imaged documents can then be accessed from anywhere in the company for viewing or processing. Special high-resolution terminals are used for displaying and printing the imaged documents. The company uses *electronic forms* to expedite the preparation of standard documents.

The system reduces the cost of storing documents (most paper documents are destroyed), improves customer service, and improves productivity of employees. Employee productivity is improved because all pertinent data can be called to the user's screen within 6 minutes of the request's being issued (compared to an average of 0.5 work-hours under the old system). At an average hourly cost of $15 for document handlers, the savings are $7.05 per document, or $70,500,000 for the 10,000,000 documents handled annually.

Web-based Application. In the late 1990s the system became Web based. A search engine was developed and browsers are helping employees to navigate, so the system is even faster now.

Most users find the imaging system easier to work with than the old paper-clogged system. The system is also used for scheduling work and monitoring workflow.

For Further Exploration: In what other industries can such a system be beneficial?

Sources: Based on stories in *Best's Review Magazine,* May 1993; *Datamation,* May 15, 1990; *MIS Quarterly,* December 1991; *IBM Systems Journal,* Vol. 29, No. 3, 1990; and *usaa.com* (2001).

WEB-BASED DMS. In many organizations, documents are now viewed as multimedia objects with hyperlinks. The Web provides easy access to pages of information. DMSs excel in this area. Web-enabled DMSs also make it easy to put information on intranets, since many of them provide instantaneous conversion of documents to HTML. BellSouth, for example, saves an estimated $17.5 million each year through its intranet-enabled forms-management system. For a discussion of Web-enabled document management systems and a list of products and major vendors, see Haskin (1998).

McDonnell-Douglas (now part of the Boeing Company) distributed aircraft service bulletins to its customers around the world using the Internet. The company used to distribute a staggering volume of bulletins to over 200 airlines, using over 4 million pages of documentation every year. Now it is all on the Web, saving money and time both for the company and for its customers.

Motorola uses a DMS not only for document storage and retrieval, but also for small-group collaboration and companywide knowledge sharing. It develops virtual communities where people can discuss and publish information, all with the Web-enabled DMS.

Electronic delivery of documents has been around since 1999, with UPS and the U.S. Post Office playing a major role in such service. They deliver documents electronically over a secured system (e-mail is not secured), and they are able to deliver complex "documents" such as large files and multimedia videos (which can be difficult to send via e-mail). (See *exchange.ups.com* and take the test drive.)

One of the major vendors of document management is Lotus Development Corporation. Its *document databases* and their replication property provide many advantages for group work and information sharing (see *lotus.com*). For further discussion at *electron.doc.mgmnt* (EDM), see Chapter 9.

11.2 DATA WAREHOUSING

Transaction versus Analytical Processing

Data processing in organizations can be viewed either as transactional or analytical. The data in transactions processing systems (TPSs) are organized mainly in a hierarchical structure and are centrally processed. The databases and the processing systems involved are known as *operational systems,* and the results are mainly summaries and reports.

Today, the most successful companies are those that can respond quickly and flexibly to market changes and opportunities, and the key to this response is the effective and efficient use of data and information. This is done not only via transaction processing, but also through a supplementary activity, called *analytical processing,* which involves analysis of accumulated data, mainly by end users. Analytical processing includes DSS, EIS, Web applications, and other end-user activities. Placing strategic information in the hands of decision makers aids productivity and empowers users to make better decisions, leading to greater competitive advantage. A good data delivery system should be able to support:

- Easy data access by the end users themselves
- A quick decision-making process
- Accurate and effective decision making
- Flexible decision making

There are basically two options for conducting analytical processing. One is to work directly with the operational systems (the "let's use what we have" approach), using software tools and components known as front-end tools and middleware (see Technology Guide 3). This option can be optimal for companies that do not have a large number of end users running queries and conducting analyses against the operating systems. It is also an option for departments that consist mainly of users who have the necessary technical skills for an extensive use of "fourth-generation" (4GL) tools such as spreadsheets and graphics. (See Technology Guide 2.) Although it is possible for those with fewer technical skills to use the 4GLs as query and reporting tools, they may not be effective, flexible, or easy enough to use in many cases.

Since the mid-1990s, there has been a wave of front-end tools that allow end users to ease these problems by directly conducting queries and reporting on data stored in *operational databases*. The problem with this approach, however, is that the tools are only effective with end users who have a medium to high degree of knowledge about databases.

These limitations call for a second, improved option of *analytical processing,* which involves three concepts:

1. A business representation of data for end users
2. A Web-based environment that gives the users query and reporting capabilities
3. A server-based repository, the *data warehouse,* that allows centralized security and control over the data

The Data Warehouse

The Sears case illustrates the benefits of a single data repository, called a **data warehouse**. The major benefits are (1) the ability to reach data quickly, since they are located in one place, and (2) the ability to reach data easily, frequently by end users themselves, using Web browsers. Let's see what a data warehouse is and what its benefits are.

The purpose of a data warehouse is to establish a *data repository* that makes operational data accessible in a form readily acceptable for analytical processing activities such as decision support, EIS, and other end-user applications. As part of this accessibility, detail-level operational data must be transformed to a relational form, which makes them more amenable to analytical processing. Thus, data warehousing is not a concept by itself but is interrelated with data access, retrieval, analysis, and visualization. (See Gray and Watson, 1998.)

The process of building and using a data warehouse is shown in Figure 11.2 on page 488. The organization's data are stored in operational systems (left side of the figure). Not all data are transferred to the data warehouse, and frequently only a summary of the data is transferred. The data that are transferred are organized within the warehouse as a relational database, so it is easy for end users to access. Also, the data are organized by subject, such as by functional area, vendor, or product. In contrast, operational data are organized according to a business process, such as shipping, purchasing, or inventory control and/or according to the functional department.

Data warehouses provide for the storage of **metadata**, meaning data about data. Metadata include software programs about data, rules for organizing data, and data summaries that are easier to index and search, especially with Web

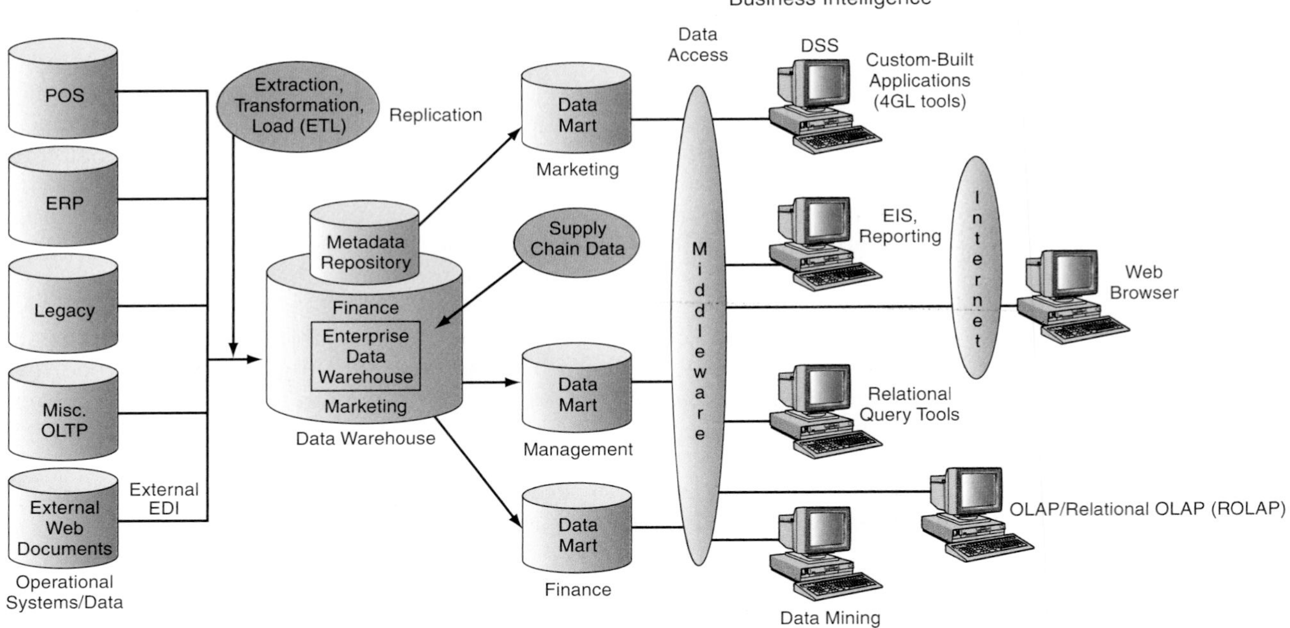

FIGURE 11.2 Data warehouse framework and views. (*Source:* Drawn by E. Turban.)

tools. Middleware tools enable access to the data warehouse (see Technology Guide 3).

CHARACTERISTICS OF DATA WAREHOUSING. The major characteristics of data warehousing are:

1. ***Organization.*** Data are organized by detailed subject (e.g., by customer, vendor, product, price level, and region), containing only information relevant for decision support.
2. ***Consistency.*** Data in different operational databases may be encoded differently. For example, gender data may be encoded 0 and 1 in one operational system and "m" and "f" in another. In the warehouse they will be coded in a *consistent* manner.
3. ***Time variant.*** The data are kept for five to ten years so they can be used for trends, forecasting, and comparisons over time.
4. ***Nonvolatile.*** Once entered into the warehouse, data are not updated.
5. ***Relational.*** Typically the data warehouse uses a relational structure.
6. ***Client/server.*** The data warehouse uses the client/server architecture mainly to provide the end user an easy access to its data.

BENEFITS. Moving information off the mainframe presents a company with the unique opportunity to restructure its IT strategy. Companies can reinvent the way in which they shape and form their application data, empowering end users to conduct extensive analysis with these data in ways that may not have been possible before. Another immediate benefit is providing a consolidated view of corporate data, which is better than providing many smaller (and differently formatted) views. For example, separate production systems may track sales and coupon mailings. Combining data from these different systems may yield insights into the cost efficiency of coupon sales promotions that would not be immediately evident from the output data of either system alone. Integrated within a data warehouse, however, such information can be easily extracted.

Another benefit is that data warehousing allows information processing to be offloaded from expensive operational systems onto low-cost servers. Once this is done, the end-user tools can handle a significant number of end-user information requests. Furthermore, some operational system reporting requirements can be moved to decision support systems, thus freeing up production processing.

These benefits can improve business knowledge, provide competitive advantage, enhance customer service and satisfaction, facilitate decision making, and help in streamlining business processes.

COST. The cost of a data warehouse can be very high, both to build and to maintain. Furthermore, it may difficult and expensive to incorporate data from obsolete legacy systems. Finally, there may be a lack of incentive to share data. Therefore, a careful feasibility study must be undertaken before a commitment is made to data warehousing.

ARCHITECTURE. There are several basic architectures for data warehousing. Two common ones are two-tier and three-tier architectures. (See Gray and Watson, 1998.) In three-tier architecture, data from the warehouse are processed twice and deposited in an *additional* multidimensional database, organized for easy multidimensional analysis and presentation, or replicated in data marts.

PUTTING THE WAREHOUSE ON THE INTRANET. Delivery of data warehouse content to decision makers throughout the enterprise can be done via an intranet. Users can view, query, and analyze the data and produce reports using Web browsers. This is an extremely economical and effective method of delivering data (see *Information Advantage*, 1997, and Eckerson, 1997).

SUITABILITY. Data warehousing is most appropriate for organizations in which some of the following apply.

- Large amounts of data need to be accessed by end users.
- The operational data are stored in different systems.
- An information-based approach to management is in use.
- There is a large, diverse customer base (such as in a utility company or a bank).
- The same data are represented differently in different systems.
- Data are stored in highly technical formats that are difficult to decipher.
- Extensive end-user computing is performed (many end users performing many activities).

Hundreds of successful applications are reported (e.g., see client success stories and case studies at Web sites of vendors such as Brio Technology Inc., Business Objects, Cognos Corp., Information Builders, NCR Corp., Platinum Technology, Software A&G, Comshare Inc., and Pilot Software). Some of the successful applications are summarized in Table 11.2. For further discussion see McFadden and Watson (1996), Barquin and Edelstein (1997), Gray and Watson (1998), and Inmon et al. (2000). Also visit the Data Warehouse Institute (*dw-institute.org*).

Data Marts and Stores: Alternatives to Data Warehouses

DATA MARTS. The high cost of data warehouses confines their use to large companies. An alternative used by many other firms is creation of a lower cost, scaled-down version of a data warehouse called a **data mart**. A data mart is a small warehouse designed for a strategic business unit (SBU) or a department.

The advantages of data marts are the following:

- The cost is low (prices under \$100,000 versus \$1 million or more for data warehouses).
- The lead time for implementation is significantly shorter, often less than 90 days.
- They are controlled locally rather than centrally, conferring power on the using group.
- They contain less information than the data warehouse. Hence they have more rapid response and are more easily understood and navigated than an enterprisewide data warehouse.
- They allow a business unit to build its own decision support systems without relying on a centralized IS department.

TABLE 11.2 Summary of Strategic Uses of Data Warehousing

Industry	Functional Areas of Use	Strategic Use
Airline	Operations and Marketing	Crew assignment, aircraft deployment, mix of fares, analysis of route profitability, frequent flyer program promotions
Apparel	Distribution and Marketing	Merchandising, and inventory replenishment
Banking	Product Development, Operations, and Marketing	Customer service, trend analysis, product and service promotions. Reduction of IS expenses
Credit Card	Product Development and Marketing	Customer service, new information service for a fee, fraud detection
Health Care	Operations	Reduction of operational expenses
Investment and Insurance	Product Development, Operations, and Marketing	Risk management, market movements analysis, customer tendencies analysis, portfolio management
Personal Care Products	Distribution and Marketing	Distribution decision, product promotions, sales decision, pricing policy
Public Sector	Operations	Intelligence gathering
Retail Chain	Distribution and Marketing	Trend analysis, buying pattern analysis, pricing policy, inventory control, sales promotions, optimal distribution channel
Steel	Manufacturing	Pattern analysis (quality control)
Telecommunications	Product Development, Operations, and Marketing	New product and service promotions, reduction of IS budget, profitability analysis

Source: Park, Y. T., "Strategic uses of data warehouses," *Journal of Data Warehousing,* April 1997, p. 19, Table 2.

There are two major types of data marts:

1. ***Replicated (dependent) data marts.*** Sometimes it is easier to work with a small subset of the data warehouse. In such cases one can replicate functional subsets of the data warehouse in smaller databases, each of which is dedicated to a certain area, as shown in Figure 11.2. In this case the data mart is *an addition to* the data warehouse.
2. ***Standalone data marts.*** A company can have one or more independent data marts without having a data warehouse. Typical data marts are for marketing, finance, and engineering applications.

OPERATIONAL DATA STORES. An **operational data store** is a database for transaction processing systems that uses data warehouse concepts to provide clean data. That is, it brings the concepts and benefits of the data warehouse to the operational portions of the business, at a lower cost. It is used for short-term decisions involving mission-critical applications rather than for the medium- and long-term decisions associated with the regular data warehouse. These decisions depend on much more current information. For example, a bank needs to know about all the accounts for a given customer who is calling on the phone. The operational data store can be viewed as situated between the operational data (legacy systems) and the data warehouse. A comparison between the two is provided by Gray and Watson (1998).

11.3 DATA ANALYSIS AND MINING

Once the data are in the data warehouse and/or data marts they can be accessed by end users. Users can then conduct several activities with the data, ranging from decision support and executive support analyses, which are discussed in Chapter 10, to ad-hoc query, online analytical processing (OLAP) and data mining, which are described here and are a part of knowledge discovery. The process of extracting useful knowledge from volumes of data is known as **knowledge discovery in databases (KDD)**, or just **knowledge discovery**, and it is the subject of extensive research (see Fayyad et al., 1996). KDD's objective is to identify valid, novel, potentially useful, and ultimately understandable patterns in data. KDD is useful because it is supported by three technologies that are now sufficiently mature: massive data collection, powerful multiprocessor computers, and data mining algorithms.

Tools and Techniques of KDD

Formal computer-based knowledge discovery has been done since the 1960s. However, the enabling techniques have been expanded and improved over time. KDD processes have appeared under various names and have shown different characteristics. The evolution of KDD tools over time can be divided into four major stages, which are shown in Table 11.3 (page 492). The table lists the enabling technologies and their characteristics. As time has passed, KDD has become able to answer more complex business questions. Data access techniques are discussed in Technology Guide 3. Online analytical processing and data mining are discussed in this section. Multidimensionality is discussed in Section 11.4, and massive databases, as employed in marketing databases, are the subject of Section 11.5.

TABLE 11.3 Stages in the Evolution of Knowledge Discovery

Evolutionary Stage	Business Question	Enabling Technologies	Characteristics
Data Collection (1960s)	What was my total revenue in the last five years?	Computers, tapes, disks	Retrospective, static data delivery
Data Access (1980s)	What were unit sales in New England last March?	Relational databases (RDBMS), structured query language (SQL)	Retrospective, dynamic data delivery at record level
Data Warehousing & Decision Support (early 1990s)	Drill down to Boston?	Online analytic processing (OLAP), multidimensional databases, data warehouses	Retrospective, dynamic data delivery at multiple levels
Intelligent Data Mining (late 1990s)	What's likely to happen to Boston unit sales next month? Why?	Advanced algorithms, multiprocessor computers, massive databases	Prospective, proactive information delivery

Source: Courtesy of Accrue Software.

AD-HOC QUERY. Ad-hoc queries allow users to request in real time information from the computer that is not available in periodic reports. Such answers are needed to expedite decision making. The system must be intelligent enough to understand what the user wants. Simple ad-hoc query systems are based on menus. More intelligent systems use SQL (structured query language) and query-by-example approaches, which are described in Technology Guide 3.

Web-based Tools. Web-based ad-hoc query tools let users access, navigate, and explore relational data to make key business decisions in real time. For instance, users can gauge the success of a Web marketing campaign according to the number of Web hits received last month, last week, or even yesterday, in relation to products or services purchased. This insight helps companies better target marketing efforts and forge closer, more responsive relationships with customers. Several vendors offer such tools. As an example, consider Cognos Corp. (see *cognos.com/products/query.html*). According to this company the following benefits can be derived from Web-based querying:

- Web users get an intuitive, easy-to-use interface for powerful ad-hoc navigation and exploration of corporate data assets.
- Query creation and modification is easy, with little or no user training needed.
- The tool offers feature-rich standard and customized queries to suit individual business requirements.
- Data sets are extended through calculations.
- Multiple heterogeneous data sources are supported, so users are not limited to one physical data source.
- Both general users and advanced users (who require features such as advanced calculations are filtering) are supported.
- Seamless integration is done with reporting, analysis, and other queries.

Advanced query tools can be connected to intranets and extranets for B2B and CRM querying. Also, a drill-down from multidimensional analysis to DSS and other tools is available. Answers to queries can be delivered to visualization tools.

ONLINE ANALYTICAL PROCESSING. Online analytical processing (OLAP) refers to such end-user activities as DSS modeling using spreadsheets and graphics, which are done online. Unlike *online transaction processing (OLTP)* applications, OLAP involves many data items (frequently many thousands or even millions) in complex relationships. One objective of OLAP is to analyze these relationships and look for patterns, trends, and exceptions. Another objective is to answer users' queries.

A typical OLAP query might access a multigigabyte, multiyear sales database in order to find all product sales in each region for each product type. After reviewing the results, an analyst might further refine the query to find sales volume for each sales channel within region or product classifications. As a last step, the analyst might want to perform year-to-year or quarter-to-quarter comparisons, for each sales channel. This whole process must be carried out online with rapid response time so that the analysis process is undisturbed.

OLAP queries can be characterized as online queries that:

- Access very large amounts of data, such as several years of sales data.
- Analyze the relationships between many types of business elements, such as sales, products, regions, and channels.
- Involve aggregated data, such as sales volumes, budgeted dollars, and dollars spent.
- Compare aggregated data over time—monthly, quarterly, yearly.
- Present data in different perspectives, such as sales by region versus sales by product or by product within each region.
- Involve complex calculations between data elements, such as expected profit as calculated as a function of sales revenue for each type of sales channel in a particular region.
- Are able to respond quickly to user requests so that users can pursue an analytical thought process without being stymied by the system.

READY-MADE WEB-BASED ANALYSIS. Many vendors provide ready-made analytical tools, mostly in finance, marketing, and operations. Such packages include built-in Web-based DSSs. Here is an example of a description of typical tools, provided at *cognos com:*

> *Cognos e-Applications* are complete end-to-end business intelligence solutions including defined extractions and data models, proven business content and *best practices* displayed through captured business metrics, and a full suite of key performance indicators (KPIs), reports and analyses. Built upon Cognos' operational framework and robust production environment, Cognos e-Applications help customers rapidly derive business value from their enterprise data and deploy it over the Web.
>
> *Cognos Finance* is a high-performance, enterprise-wide financial application that provides a complete framework for business professionals to understand and monitor the financial performance of their organization. It provides a single environment for completing financial processes in a timely manner: monthly and quarterly closes, the budget process inclusive of distributing and gathering budget information with budget suppliers, and integration of the lastest actual data with user-supplied forecasts. Users can also integrate Web information for a single view of the organization.

Although OLAP is very useful in many cases, it is retrospective in nature and cannot provide the automated and prospective knowledge discovery that is done by advanced *data mining* techniques.

Data Mining

Data mining derives its name from the similarities between searching for valuable business information in a large database, and mining a mountain for a vein of valuable ore. Both processes require either sifting through an immense amount of material or intelligently probing it to find exactly where the value resides. In some cases the data are consolidated in a data warehouse and data marts; in others they are kept on the Internet and intranet servers.

Given databases of sufficient size and quality, data mining technology can generate new business opportunities by providing these capabilities:

- ***Automated prediction of trends and behaviors.*** Data mining automates the process of finding predictive information in large databases. Questions that traditionally required extensive hands-on analysis can now be answered directly and quickly from the data. A typical example of a predictive problem is targeted marketing. Data mining can use data on past promotional mailings to identify the targets most likely to respond favorably to future mailings. Other predictive examples include forecasting bankruptcy and other forms of default, and identifying segments of a population likely to respond similarly to given events.
- ***Automated discovery of previously unknown patterns.*** Data mining tools identify previously hidden patterns in one step. An example of pattern discovery is the analysis of retail sales data to identify seemingly unrelated products that are often purchased together, such as baby diapers and beer. Other pattern discovery problems include detecting fraudulent credit card transactions and identifying *invalid* (*anomalous*) *data* that may represent data entry keying errors.

When data mining tools are implemented on high-performance parallel-processing systems, they can analyze massive databases in minutes. Often, these databases will contain data stored for several years. Faster processing means that users can experiment with more *models* to understand complex data. High speed makes it practical for users to analyze huge quantities of data. Larger databases, in turn, yield improved predictions. The data mining environment usually has a client/server architecture.

Data mining also can be conducted by nonprogrammers. The "miner" is often an end user, empowered by "data drills" and other power query tools to ask ad-hoc questions and get answers quickly, with little or no programming skill. Data mining tools can be combined with spreadsheets and other end-user software development tools, making it relatively easy to analyze and process the mined data. Data mining appears under different names, such as knowledge extraction, data dipping, data archeology, data exploration, data pattern processing, data dredging, and information harvesting. "Striking it rich" in data mining often involves finding unexpected, valuable results.

Data mining yields five types of information: (1) association, (2) sequences, (3) classifications, (4) clusters, and (5) forecasting. Data miners also can use several tools and techniques (see the list and definitions in *A Closer Look* 11.1).

A SAMPLER OF DATA MINING APPLICATIONS. According to a GartnerGroup report (*gartnergroup.com*), more than half of all the Fortune 1000 companies worldwide are using data mining technology. Data mining can be very helpful, as shown by the representative examples that follow. Note that the intent of most of these examples is to identify a business opportunity in order to create a sustainable competitive advantage.

A CLOSER LOOK
11.1 DATA MINING TECHNIQUES AND INFORMATION TYPES

The most commonly used techniques for data mining are the following.

- ***Case-based reasoning.*** The case-based reasoning approach uses historical cases to recognize patterns. For example, customers of Cognitive Systems, Inc., utilize such an approach for helpdesk applications. One company has a 50,000-query case library. New cases are matched quickly against the 50,000 samples in the library, providing more than 90 percent accurate and automatic answers to queries.
- ***Neural computing.*** Neural computing is a machine learning approach by which historical data can be examined for pattern recognition. These patterns can then be used for making predictions and for decision support (details are given in Chapter 12). Users equipped with neural computing tools can go through huge databases and, for example, identify potential customers of a new product or companies whose profiles suggest that they are heading for bankruptcy. Many practical applications are in financial services (Trippi and Turban, 1996), in marketing, and in manufacturing.
- ***Intelligent agents.*** One of the most promising approaches to retrieving information from the Internet or from intranet-based databases is the use of intelligent agents. As vast amounts of information become available through the Internet, finding the right information is more difficult. This topic is further discussed in Chapters 5 and 12.
- ***Association analysis.*** Association analysis is a relatively new approach that uses a specialized set of algorithms that sort through large data sets and express statistical rules among items. (See Moad, 1998, for details.)
- ***Other tools.*** Several other tools can be used. These include decision trees, genetic algorithms, nearest-neighbor method, and rule induction. For details, see Inmon et al., 2000.

INFORMATION TYPES:

- ***Classification:*** Infers the defining characteristics of a certain group (e.g., customers who have been lost to competitors).
- ***Clustering:*** Identifies groups of items that share a particular characteristic. Clustering differs from classification in that no predefining characteristic is given.
- ***Association:*** Identifies relationships between events that occur at one time (e.g., the contents of a shopping basket).
- ***Sequencing:*** Similar to association, except that the relationship exists over a period of time (e.g., repeat visits to a supermarket or use of a financial planning product).
- ***Forecasting:*** Estimates future values based on patterns within large sets of data (e.g., demand forecasting).

1. ***Retailing and sales.*** Predicting sales; determining correct inventory levels and distribution schedules among outlets.
2. ***Banking.*** Forecasting levels of bad loans and fraudulent credit card use, credit card spending by new customers, and which kinds of customers will best respond to (and qualify for) new loan offers.
3. ***Manufacturing and production.*** Predicting machinery failures; finding key factors that control optimization of manufacturing capacity.
4. ***Brokerage and securities trading.*** Predicting when bond prices will change; forecasting the range of stock fluctuations for particular issues and the overall market; determining when to buy or sell stocks.
5. ***Insurance.*** Forecasting claim amounts and medical coverage costs; classifying the most important elements that affect medical coverage; predicting which customers will buy new policies.
6. ***Computer hardware and software.*** Predicting disk-drive failures; forecasting how long it will take to create new chips; predicting potential security violations.

7. ***Policework.*** Tracking crime patterns, locations, and criminal behavior; identifying attributes to assist in solving criminal cases.
8. ***Government and defense.*** Forecasting the cost of moving military equipment; testing strategies for potential military engagements; predicting resource consumption.
9. ***Airlines.*** Capturing data on where customers are flying and the ultimate destination of passengers who change carriers in hub cities; thus, airlines can identify popular locations that they do not service and check the feasibility of adding routes to capture lost business.
10. ***Health care.*** Correlating demographics of patients with critical illnesses; developing better insights on symptoms and their causes and how to provide proper treatments.
11. ***Broadcasting.*** Predicting what is best to air during prime time and how to maximize returns by interjecting advertisements.
12. ***Marketing.*** Classifying customer demographics that can be used to predict which customers will respond to a mailing or buy a particular product (as illustrated in Section 11.5).

Text Mining and Web Mining

TEXT MINING. **Text mining** is the application of data mining to nonstructured or less-structured text files. Data mining takes advantage of the infrastructure of stored data to extract predictive information. For example, by mining a customer database, an analyst might discover that everyone who buys product A also buys products B and C, but does so six months later. Text mining, however, operates with less structured information. Documents rarely have strong internal infrastructure, and when they do, it is frequently focused on document format rather than document content. Text mining helps organizations to do the following:

- Find the "hidden" content of documents, including additional useful relationships.
- Group documents by common themes (e.g., identify all the customers of an insurance firm who have similar complaints).

WEB MINING. The previous discussion of data mining refers to data that are stored usually in a data warehouse. However, to analyze a large amount of data on the Web, such as what customers are doing on the Web—that is, to analyze *clickstream data*—one needs somewhat different mining tools. These were described in Chapter 4 under the topic of discovery.

Business Intelligence

The activities conducted during much of the process described in Figure 11.1 are generally referred to as **business intelligence**. The major reason for the name is that these activities not only collect and process data, but they also extract from it useful—intelligent—results that can be applied to business decision making. The concept of business intelligence originated from executive information system (EIS) activities, but it is used today to describe OLAP and data mining activities as well.

Failures of Data Warehouses and Data Mining

Since their early inceptions, data warehouses and mining have produced many success stories. However, there have also been many failures. Carbone (1999) defined levels of data warehouse failures as follows:

- Warehouse does not meet the expectations of those involved.
- Warehouse was completed, but went severely over budget in relation to time, money, or both.
- Warehouse failed one or more times but eventually was completed.
- Warehouse failed with no effort to revive it.

Carbone provided examples and identified a number of reasons for failures (which are typical for many other large information systems):

- Unrealistic expectations—overly optimistic time schedule or underestimation of cost.
- Inappropriate architecture.
- Vendors overselling capabilities of products.
- Lack of training and support for users.
- Omitted information.
- Lack of coordination (or requires too much coordination).
- Cultural issues were ignored.
- Using the warehouse only for operational, not informational, purposes.
- Not enough summarization of data.
- Poor upkeep of technology.
- Improperly managing multiple users with various needs.
- Failure to align data marts and data warehouses.
- Unclear business objectives; not knowing the information requirements.
- Lack of effective project sponsorship.
- Lack of data quality.
- Lack of user input.
- Using data marts instead of data warehouses (and vice versa).
- Inexperienced/untrained/inadequate number of personnel.
- Interfering corporate politics.
- Insecure access to data manipulation (users should not have the ability to change any data).
- Inappropriate format of information—not a single, standard format.
- Poor upkeep of information (e.g., failure to keep information current).

Suggestions on how to avoid data warhouse failure are provided by Griffin, at *datawarehouse.com* (July 18, 2000) and by Ferranti, at *sunworld.com* (July 30, 1998).

11.4 DATA VISUALIZATION TECHNOLOGIES

Once data have been processed, they can be presented to users as text, graphics, tables, and so on, via several data visualization technologies.

Data Visualization

Visual technologies make pictures worth a thousand numbers and make IT applications more attractive and understandable to users. **Data visualization** refers to presentation of data by technologies such as digital images, geographical information systems, graphical user interfaces, multidimensional tables and graphs, virtual reality, three-dimensional presentations, and animation. Visualization software

IT at Work
DATA VISUALIZATION HELPS HAWORTH TO COMPETE

...in Marketing and Production & Operations Management

www.haworth.com

Manufacturing office furniture is an extremely competitive business. Haworth Corporation operates in this environment and has been able to survive and even excel with the help of IT. To compete, Haworth allows its customers to customize what they want to buy. It may surprise you to learn that an office chair can be assembled in 200 different ways. The customization of all Haworth's products resulted in 21 million potential product combinations, confusing customers who were not able to visualize, until the item was delivered, how the customized furniture would look.

The solution was computer visualization software that allowed sales representatives with laptop computers to show customers exactly what they were ordering. Thus, the huge parts catalogs became more easily understood, and sales representatives were able to configure different options by entering the corporate database, showing what a product would look like, and computing its price. The customers can now make changes until the furniture design meets their needs. The salesperson can do all this from the customer's office by connecting to the corporate intranet via the Internet and using Web tools to allow customers to make the desired changes.

The program allows the company to reduce cycle time. After the last computer-assisted design (CAD) mockup of an order has been approved, the CAD software is used to create a bill of materials that goes to Haworth's factory for manufacturing. This reduces the time spent between sales reps and CAD operators, increasing the time available for sales reps to make more sales calls and increasing customer satisfaction with quicker delivery. By using this visualization computer program, Haworth has increased its competitive advantage.

WEB-BASED APPLICATION. As of 2000 the company operates on the Web a *design studio* in which customers can interact with the designers.

For Further Exploration: How can the intranet be used to improve the process? How does this topic relate to car customization at *jaguar.com*?

Sources: Condensed from *Infoworld*, January 27, 1997, p. 92 and from *haworth.com* (2001).

packages offer users capabilities for self-guided exploration and visual analysis of large amounts of data. By using visual analysis technologies, people may spot problems that have existed for years, undetected by standard analysis methods. Visualization technologies can also be integrated among themselves to create a variety of presentations, as demonstrated by the *IT at Work* above.

Data visualization is easier to implement when the necessary data are in a data warehouse. Our discussion here is focused mainly on the data visualization techniques of multidimensionality, geographical information systems, visual interactive modeling, and virtual reality. Related topics, such as multimedia and hypermedia, are presented in Technology Guide 2.

Multidimensionality

Modern data and information may have several dimensions. For example, management may be interested in examining sales figures in a *certain city* by *product*, by *time period*, by *salesperson*, and by *store* (i.e., in five dimensions). The more dimensions involved, the more difficult it is to present multidimensional information in one table or in one graph. Therefore, it is important to provide the user with a technology that allows him or her to add, replace, or change dimensions quickly and easily in a table and/or graphical presentation. Such changes are known as "slicing and dicing" of data. The technology of slicing, dicing, and similar manipulations is called **multidimensionality**.

Figure 11.3 shows three views of the same data, organized in different ways, using multidimensional software, usually available with spreadsheets. Part

(a) shows travel hours of a company's employees by means of transportation and by country. The "next year" column gives projections automatically generated by an embedded formula. In part (b) the data are reorganized, and in part (c) they are reorganized again and manipulated as well. All this is easily done by the end user with one or two clicks of the mouse.

Travel Hours

	Planes		Trains		Automobiles	
	This Year	Next Year	This Year	Next Year	This Year	Next Year
Canada	740	888	140	168	640	768
Japan	430	516	290	348	150	180
France	320	384	460	552	210	252
Germany	425	510	430	516	325	390

Country

(a)

Hours

		This Year	Next Year
Planes	Canada	740	888
	Japan	430	516
	France	320	384
	Germany	425	510
Trains	Canada	140	168
	Japan	290	348
	France	460	552
	Germany	430	516
Automobiles	Canada	640	768
	Japan	150	180
	France	210	252
	Germany	325	390

Travel Country

(b)

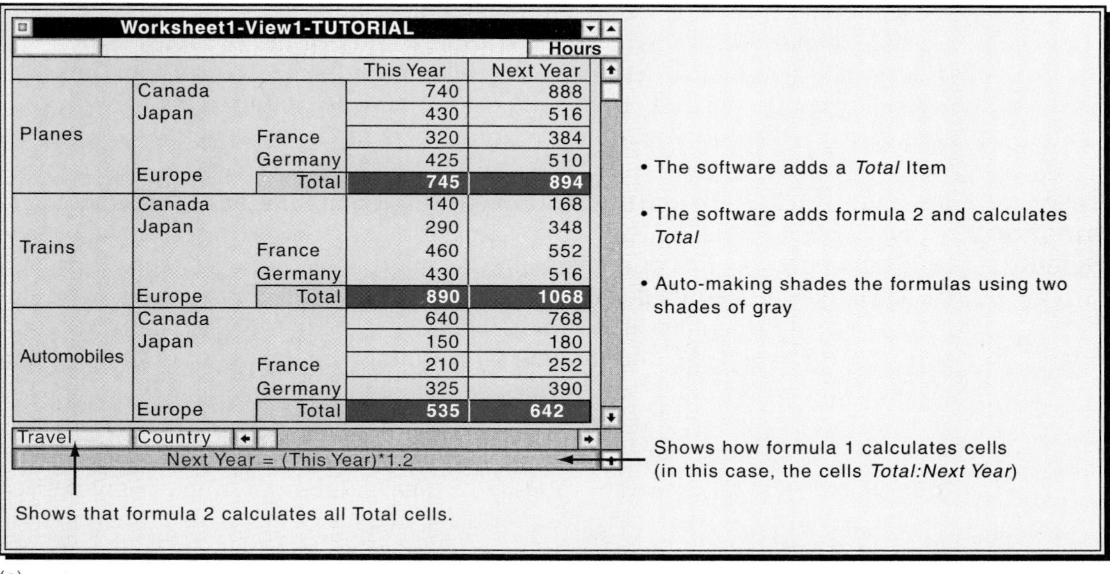

Worksheet1-View1-TUTORIAL

Hours

			This Year	Next Year
Planes	Canada		740	888
	Japan		430	516
		France	320	384
		Germany	425	510
	Europe	Total	745	894
Trains	Canada		140	168
	Japan		290	348
		France	460	552
		Germany	430	516
	Europe	Total	890	1068
Automobiles	Canada		640	768
	Japan		150	180
		France	210	252
		Germany	325	390
	Europe	Total	535	642

(c)

FIGURE 11.3 Multidimensionality views.

The major advantage of multidimensionality is that data can be organized the way managers like to see them rather than the way that the system analysts do. Furthermore, different presentations of the same data can be arranged and rearranged easily and quickly.

Three factors are considered in multidimensionality: dimensions, measures, and time.

1. ***Examples of dimensions:*** Products, salespeople, market segments, business units, geographical locations, distribution channels, countries, industries
2. ***Examples of measures:*** Money, sales volume, head count, inventory profit, actual versus forecasted results
3. ***Examples of time:*** Daily, weekly, monthly, quarterly, yearly

For example, a manager may want to know the sales of product M in a certain geographical area, by a specific salesperson, during a specified month, in terms of units. Although the answer can be provided regardless of the database structure, it can be provided much faster, and by the user himself or herself, if the data are organized in **multidimensional databases** (or data marts), or if the query tools are designed for multidimensionality. In either case, users can navigate through the many dimensions and levels of data via tables or graphs and then conduct a quick analysis to find significant deviations or important trends.

Multidimensional databases are typically more efficient than regular relational databases for sharing and processing many dimensions. There are several reasons for these advantages:

- Data can be presented and navigated with relative ease.
- Multidimensional databases are easier to maintain.
- Multidimensional databases are significantly faster than relational databases as a result of the additional dimensions and the anticipation of how the data will be accessed by users.

However, multidimensional databases do not replace the data warehouse, so there are additional costs of creating and maintaining them.

Multidimensionality is available with different degrees of sophistication and is especially popular in executive information and support systems. There are several types of software from which multidimensional systems can be constructed, and they often work in conjunction with OLAP tools.

Geographical Information Systems

A **geographical information system (GIS)** is a computer-based system for capturing, storing, checking, integrating, manipulating, and displaying data using digitized maps. Its most distinguishing characteristic is that every record or digital object has an identified geographical location. By integrating maps with spatially oriented (geographical location) databases (called *geocoding*) and other databases, users can generate information for planning, problem solving, and decision making, increasing their productivity and the quality of their decisions. The *IT at Work* case on page 501 illustrates how banks have used GIS.

GIS SOFTWARE. GIS software varies in its capabilities, from simple computerized mapping systems to enterprisewide tools for decision support data analysis (see Minicase 1). Clearly, a high-quality graphics display and high computation and search speeds are necessary, so most early GIS implementations were developed

IT at Work

BANKS USING GIS TO SUPPORT MARKETING

Integrating IT ...in Finance and Marketing

Banks are using geographical information systems (GISs) for plotting the following:

- Branch and ATM locations
- Customer demographics (e.g., residence, age, income level) for each product of the bank
- Volume and traffic patterns of business activities
- Geographical area served by each branch
- Market potential for banking activities
- Strengths and weaknesses against the competition
- Branch performance

A GIS is used as a geographical spreadsheet that allows managers to model business activities and perform what-if analyses (What if we close a branch or merge branches? What if a competitor opens a branch?). The maps consolidate pages of analysis. Representative pioneering banks are First Florida Banks (Tampa, Florida), Marion Bank (Philadelphia, Pennsylvania), and NJB Financial (Princeton, New Jersey).

For Further Exploration: How can a GIS indicate a bank's strengths and weaknesses against the competition?

Source: Condensed from A. Radding, "Going with GIS," *Bank Management,* December 1991.

Mapping Out a Strategy

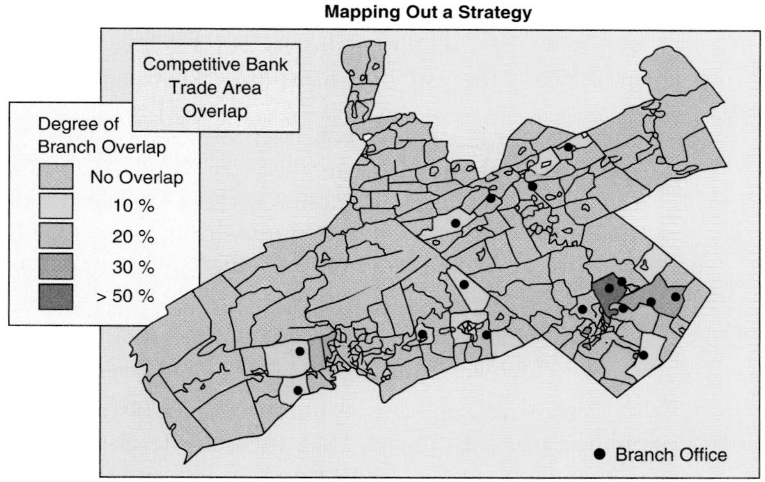

Source: Verdi Ryan Associates

An example of how banks can use geographical information systems (GIS) to support marketing efforts.

for mainframes. Initially, the high cost of GISs prevented their use outside experimental facilities and government agencies. Since the 1990s, however, the cost of GIS software and its required hardware has dropped dramatically. Now relatively inexpensive, fully functional PC-based packages are readily available.

GIS DATA. GIS data are available from a wide variety of sources. Government sources (via the Internet and CD-ROM) provide some data, while vendors provide diversified commercial data as well (such as CD-ROMs from MapInfo and FirstMap from Wessex Inc.).

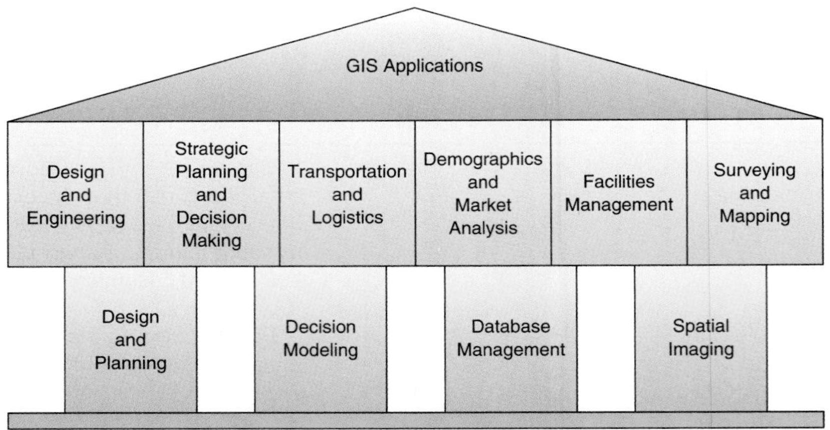

FIGURE 11.4 GIS functions and applications.

The field of GIS can be divided into two major categories: *functions* and *applications*. According to Mennecke et al. (1995), there are four major functions: design and planning, decising modeling, database management, and spatial imaging. These functions support six areas of applications as shown in Figure 11.4. Note that the functions (shown as pillars) can support all the applications. The applications they support most are shown closest to each pillar.

GIS AND DECISION MAKING. GISs provide a large amount of extremely useful information that can be analyzed and utilized in decision making. Its graphical format makes it easy for managers to visualize the data. For example, Janet M. Hamilton, market research administrator for Dow Elanco, a $2 billion maker of agricultural chemicals based in Indianapolis, Indiana, explains:

> I can put 80-page spreadsheets with thousands of rows into a single map. It would take a couple of weeks to comprehend all of the information from the spreadsheet, but in a map, the story can be told in seconds. (Hamilton, 1996, p. 21)

There are countless applications of GISs to improve decision making in the public or private sector. They include the dispatch of emergency vehicles, transit management (see Minicase 1), facility site selection, and wildlife management. GISs are extremely popular in local governments, where the tools are used not only for mapping but for many decision-making applications (see O'Looney, 2000).

For many companies, the intelligent organization of data within a GIS can provide a framework to support the process of decision making and of designing alternative strategies. Some examples of successful GIS applications are provided by Korte (2000) and Hamilton (1996). Other examples of successful GIS applications are summarized in *A Closer Look* 11.2 (page 503).

GIS AND THE INTERNET OR INTRANET. Most major GIS software vendors are providing Web access, such as embedded browsers, or a Web/Internet/intranet server that hooks directly into their software. Thus users can access dynamic maps and data via the Internet or a corporate intranet (see Jacobs, 1996). Big Horn Computer Services, in Buffalo, NY, has used a Web-adapted GIS to develop

A CLOSER LOOK
11.2 GIS SAMPLE APPLICATIONS

Company	Application of GIS
Pepsi Cola Inc., Super Value, Acordia Inc.	Used in site selection for new Taco Bell and Pizza Hut restaurants; combining demographic data and traffic patterns.
CIGNA (health insurance)	Uses GIS to answer such questions as "How many CIGNA-affiliated physicians are available within an 8-mile radius of a business?"
Western Auto (a subsidiary of Sears)	Integrates data with GIS to create a detailed demographic profile of a store's neighborhood to determine the best product mix to offer at the store.
Sears, Roebuck & Co.	Uses GIS to support planning of truck routes.
Health maintenance organizations	Tracks cancer rate and other diseases to determine expansion strategy and allocation of expensive equipment in their facilities.
Wood Personnel Services (employment agencies)	Maps neighborhoods where temporary workers live; for locating marketing and recruiting cities.
Wilkening & Co. (consulting services)	Designs optimal sales territories and routes for their clients, reducing travel costs by 15 percent.
CellularOne Corp.	Maps its entire cellular network to identify clusters of call disconnects and to dispatch technicians accordingly.
Sun Microsystems	Manages leased property in dozens of places worldwide.
Consolidated Rail Corp.	Monitors the condition of 20,000 miles of railroad track and thousands of parcels of adjoining land.
Federal Emergency Management Agency	Assesses the damage of hurricanes, floods, and other natural disasters by relating videotapes of the damage to digitized maps of properties.
Toyota (other car manufacturers)	Combines GIS and GPS as a navigation tool. Drivers are directed to destinations in the best possible way.

a custom application for a national television network that wants its affiliate stations to be able to access an intranet containing demographic information about their viewers. Using a Web browser, employees at each station can view thematically shaded maps, analyzing their market (see Swenson, 1996).

A number of firms are deploying GISs on the Internet for internal use or for use by their customers. For example, Visa Plus, which operates a network of automated teller machines, has developed a GIS application that lets Internet users call up a locator map for any of the company's 300,000 ATM machines worldwide. As GIS Web server software is deployed by vendors, more applications will be developed. Maps, GIS data, and information about GISs are available over the Web through a number of vendors and public agencies.

EMERGING GIS APPLICATIONS. The integration of GISs and *global positioning systems* (GPSs) has the potential to help reengineer the aviation, transportation, and shipping industries. It enables vehicles or aircraft equipped with a GPS receiver to pinpoint their location as they move (Steede-Terry, 2000). Emerging applications of GPSs include personal automobile mapping systems, railroad car tracking, and earth-moving equipment tracking. The price of these applications is dropping with improvements in hardware, increased demand, and the availability of more competing vendors. (A simple GPS cost less than $50 in 2001.) GPSs have also become a major source of new GIS data (see Group and Role-Playing Activity 1). Some researchers have developed intelligent GISs that link a GIS to an expert system.

L-COMMERCE. In Chapter 5 we introduced the concept of location-based commerce (l-commerce), a major part of m-commerce. In l-commerce, advertisement is targeted to an individual whose location is known (via a GPS and GIS combination). Similarly, emergency medical systems identify the location of a car accident in a second, and the attached GIS helps in directing ambulances to the scene. For other interesting applications, see Turban et al., 2002.

CONCLUSIONS. Improvements in the GIS user interface have substantially altered the GIS "look" and "feel." Advanced visualization (three-dimensional graphics) is increasingly integrated with GIS capabilities, especially in animated and interactive maps. GISs can provide information for virtual reality engines, and they can display complex information to decision makers. Object-oriented programming and databases are also likely to improve GISs. Multimedia and hypermedia will play a growing role in GISs, especially in help and training systems. Object linking and embedding will allow users to import maps into any document. More GISs will be deployed to provide data and access data over the Web and organizational intranets as "Web-ready" GIS software becomes available. See Korte (2000) for an overview of GISs, their many capabilities, and potential advances.

Visual Interactive Models

Visual interactive modeling (VIM) uses computer graphic displays to represent the impact of different management or operational decisions on goals such as profit or market share. VIM differs from regular simulation in that the user can intervene in the decision-making process and see the results of the intervention. A visual model is much more than a communication device, since it is used as an integral part of decision making and/or problem solving.

A VIM can be used both for supporting decisions and for training. It can represent a static or a dynamic system. Static models display a visual image of the result of one decision alternative at a time. (With computer windows, several results can be compared on one screen.) Dynamic models display systems that evolve over time; the evolution is represented by animation or motion pictures. These are also referred to as real-time simulation.

VIM has been used with DSSs in several operations management decisions (see Chau and Bell, 1996). The method consists of priming a virtual interactive model of a plant (or a business process) with its current status. The model is then rapidly run on a computer, allowing management to observe how a plant is likely to operate in the future.

One of the most developed areas in VIM is **visual interactive simulation (VIS)**, a decision simulation in which the end user watches the progress of the simulation model in an animated form using graphics terminals. The user may interact with the simulation and try different decision strategies. (See Pritsker and O'Reilly, 1999.) VIS is an approach that has, at its core, the ability to allow

IT at Work

COMPUTER TRAINING IN COMPLEX LOGGING MACHINES

The foresting industry is extremely competitive, and countries with high labor costs must automate tasks such as moving, cutting, delimbing, and piling logs. A new machine, called the "Harvester," can replace 25 lumberjacks.

The Harvester is a highly complex machine that takes six months to learn how to operate. The trainee destroys a sizeable amount of forest in the process, and terrain suitable to practice on is decreasing. In unskilled hands, this expensive machine can also be damaged. Therefore, extensive and expensive training is needed. Sisu Logging of Finland found a solution to the training problem by using a real-time simulation.

In this simulation, the chassis, suspension, and wheels of the vehicles have to be modeled, together with the forces acting on them (inertia and friction), and the movement equations linked with them have to be solved in real time. This type of simulation is mathematically complex, and until recently it required equipment investment running into millions of dollars. However, with the help of a visual simulations program, simulation training can now be carried out for only 1 percent of the cost of the traditional method.

Inside the simulator are the Harvester's actual controls, which are used to control a virtual model of a Harvester plowing its way through a virtual forest. The machine sways back and forth on uneven terrain, and the grapple of the Harvester grips the trunk of a tree, fells it, delimbs it, and cuts it into pieces very realistically in real time.

The simulated picture is very sharp: even the structures of the bark and annual growth rings are clearly visible where the tree has been cut. In traditional simulators, the traveling path is quite limited beforehand, but in this Harvester simulator, you are free to move in a stretch of forest covering two hectares (25,000 square yards).

In addition, the system can be used to simulate different kinds of forest in different parts of the world, together with the different tree species and climatic conditions. An additional advantage of this simulator is that the operations can be videotaped so that training sessions can be studied afterward. Moreover, it is possible to practice certain dangerous situations that cannot be done using a real machine.

For Further Exploration: Why is the simulated training time shorter?

Source: Condensed from *Finnish Business Report,* April 1997.

---

decision makers to learn about their own subjective values and about their mistakes. Therefore, VIS can be used for training as well as in games, as in the case of flight simulators, and as shown in the *IT at Work* above.

Animation systems that produce realistic graphics are available from many simulation software vendors (see *SAS.com*). The latest visual simulation technology is tied in with the concept of virtual reality, where an artificial world is created for a number of purposes—from training to entertainment to viewing data in an artificial landscape.

Virtual Reality

There is no standard definition of virtual reality. The most common definitions usually imply that **virtual reality (VR)** is interactive, computer-generated, three-dimensional graphics delivered to the user through a head-mounted display. Defined technically, virtual reality is an "environment and/or technology that provides artificially generated sensory cues sufficient to engender in the user some willing suspension of disbelief." So in virtual reality, a person "believes" that what he or she is doing is real even though it is artificially created.

More than one person and even a large group can share and interact in the same artificial environment. VR thus can be a powerful medium for communication, entertainment, and learning. Instead of looking at a flat computer screen, the virtual reality user interacts with a three-dimensional computer-generated environment. To see and hear the environment, the user wears stereo goggles and a headset. To interact with the environment, control objects in it, or move around within it, the user wears a computerized behavior-transducing head-coupled display and hand position sensors (gloves). Virtual reality displays achieve the illusion of a surrounding medium by updating the display in real time. The user can grasp and move virtual objects.

VIRTUAL REALITY AND DECISION MAKING. Most VR applications to date have been used to support decision making indirectly. For example, Boeing has developed a virtual aircraft mockup to test designs. Several other VR applications for assisting in manufacturing and for converting military technology to civilian technology are being utilized at Boeing. At Volvo, VR is used to test virtual cars in virtual accidents; Volvo also uses VR in its new model-designing process. British Airways offers the pleasure of experiencing first-class flying to its Web site visitors. For a comprehensive discussion of virtual reality in manufacturing, see Banerjee and Zetu (2001).

Another VR application area is data visualization. VR helps financial decision makers make better sense of data by using visual, spatial, and aural immersion virtual systems. For example, some stock brokerages have a VR application in which users surf over a landscape of stock futures, with color, hue, and intensity indicating deviations from current share prices. Sound is used to convey other information, such as current trends or the debt/equity ratio. VR allows side-by-side comparsions with a large assortment of financial data. It is easier to make intuitive connections with three-dimensional support. Morgan Stanley & Co. uses VR to display the results of risk analyses.

VIRTUAL REALITY AND THE WEB. A platform-independent standard for VR called **virtual reality markup language (VRML)** (*vrmlsite.com,* and Kerlow, 2000) makes navigation through online supermarkets, museums, and stores as easy as interacting with textual information. VRML allows objects to be rendered as an Internet user "walks" through a virtual room. At the moment, users can utilize regular browsers, but VRML browsers will soon be in wide circulation.

Extensive use is expected in e-commerce marketing (see Dalgleish, 2000). For example, Tower Records offers a virtual music store on the Internet where customers can "meet" each other in front of the store, go inside, and preview CDs and videos. They select and purchase their choices electronically and interactively from a sales associate. Applications in other areas are shown in Table 11.4 on the facing page.

Virtual supermarkets could spark greater interest in home grocery shopping. In the future, shoppers will enter a virtual supermarket, walk through the virtual aisles, select virtual products and put them in their virtual cart. This could help remove some of the resistance to virtual shopping. Virtual malls, which can be delivered even on a PC (*synthonics.com*), are designed to give the user a feeling of walking into a shopping mall.

Virtual reality is just beginning to move into many business applications. A three-dimensional world on the Internet should prove popular because it is a metaphor to which everyone can relate.

TABLE 11.4 Examples of Virtual Reality Applications

Industry	Application
Manufacturing	Training Design testing and interpretation of results Safety analysis Virtual prototyping Engineering analysis Ergonomic analysis Virtual simulation of assembly, production, and maintenance
Architecture	Design of building and other structures
Business	Real estate presentation and evaluation Advertisement Presentation in e-commerce Presentation of financial data
Medicine	Training surgeons (with simulators) Interpretation of medical data Planning surgeries Physical therapy
Research and education	Virtual physics lab Galaxy configurations Representation of complex mathematics
Amusement	Virtual museums Three-dimensional race car games (on PCs) Air combat simulation (on PCs) Virtual reality arcades and parks Ski simulator

11.5 MARKETING DATABASES IN ACTION

Data warehouses and data marts serve end users in all functional areas. However, the most dramatic applications of data warehousing and mining are in marketing, in what is referred to as **marketing databases** (also referred to as *database marketing*).

In this section we examine how data warehouses, their extensions, and data mining are used and what role they play in new marketing strategies, such as the use of Web-based marketing transaction databases in interactive marketing.

The Marketing Transaction Database

Success in marketing today requires a new kind of database, oriented toward targeting the personalizing marketing messages in real time. Such a database provides the most effective means of capturing information on customer preferences and needs. In turn, enterprises can use this knowledge to create new products and services. Such a database is called a **marketing transaction database (MTD)**. Most current databases are static: They simply gather and store information about customers. They fall under the following categories: operations databases, data warehouses, and marketing databases. The MTD combines many of the characteristics of these databases and marketing data sources into a new database that allows marketers to engage in real-time personalization and target every interaction with customers.

MTD'S CAPABILITIES. The MTD provides dynamic, or interactive, functions not available with traditional types of marketing databases. In marketing terms, a transaction occurs with the exchange of information. With interactive media, each exposure to the customer becomes an opportunity to conduct a marketing "transaction." Exchanging information (whether gathered actively through registration or use requests, or passively by monitoring customer behavior) allows marketers to refine their understanding of each customer continuously and to use that information to target him or her specifically with personalized marketing messages.

Comparing various characteristics of MTDs with other marketing-related databases shows the advantages of MTDs. For example, data warehouses lead to corporate decision making, and marketing databases focus on understanding customers' behavior, but do not target the individual customer nor personalize the marketing approach, as do MTDs. Additionally, data in MTDs can be updated in real time, as opposed to the periodic (weekly, monthly, or quarterly) updates that are characteristic of data warehouses and marketing databases. Also, the data quality in an MTD is focused, and is verified by the individual customers. It thus is of much higher quality than data in many operations databases, where legacy systems may offer only poor assurance of data quality. Further, MTDs can combine various types of data—behavioral, descriptive, and derivative; other types of marketing databases may offer only one or two of these types. Note that MTDs do not eliminate the traditional databases. They complement them by providing additional capabilities.

THE ROLE OF THE INTERNET. Data mining, data warehousing, and MTDs are delivered on the Internet and intranets. The Internet does not simply represent another advertising venue or a different medium for catalog sales. Rather, it contains new attributes that smart marketers can exploit to their fullest degree. Indeed, the Internet promises to revolutionize sales and marketing. Dell Computer (see Minicase 2) offers an example of how marketing professionals can use the Internet's electronic sales and marketing channels for market research, advertising, information dissemination, product management, and product delivery. For an overview of marketing databases and the Web, see Grossnickle and Raskin (2000).

Implementation Examples

Fewer and fewer companies can afford traditional marketing approaches, which include big-picture strategies and expensive marketing campaigns. Marketing departments are being scaled down, and new approaches such as one-to-one marketing, speed marketing, interactive marketing, and relationship marketing are being employed. The following examples illustrate how companies use data mining and warehousing to support the new marketing approaches.

- Alamo Rent-a-Car discovered that German tourists liked bigger cars. So now, when Alamo advertises its rental business in Germany, the ads include information about its larger models.
- Through its online registry for expectant parents, Burlington Coat Factory tracks families as they grow. The company then matches direct-mail material to the different stages of a family's development over time. Burlington also identifies, on a daily basis, top-selling styles and brands. By digging into reams

of demographic data, historical buying patterns, and sales trends in existing stores, Burlington determines where to open its next store and what to stock in each store.

- Au Bon Pain Company, Inc., a Boston-based chain of cafes, discovered that the company was not selling as much cream cheese as planned. When it analyzed point-of-sale data, the firm found that customers preferred small, one-serving packaging (like butter). As soon as the package size of the cream cheese was changed, sales shot up.
- Using U.S. census data along with its own internal data, Spalding Sports profiled thousands of golf courses and pro shops throughout the United States. Promotional materials for each golf course now match the customers' profiles (such as upscale golfers versus working-class tourists). They also found that buyers at pro shops were more interested in technical aspects than buyers at retail stores.
- Bank of America gets more than 100,000 telephone calls from customers every day. Analyzing customers' banking activities, the bank determines what may be of interest to them. So when a customer calls to check on a balance, the bank tries to sell the customer something in which he or she might be interested.
- Supermarket chains regularly analyze reams of cash register data to discover what items customers are typically buying at the same time. These shopping patterns are used for issuing coupons, designing floor layouts and products' location, and creating shelf displays.
- AT&T and MCI sift through terabytes of customer phone data to fine-tune marketing campaigns and determine new discount calling plans. (See Mattison, 1999.)
- A pharmaceutical company analyzes the results of its recent sales force activity to improve targeting of physicians who should be first contacted; it also determines which marketing activities will have the greatest impact in the next few months. The data include competitor market activity as well as information about the local health care systems. The results are distributed to the sales force via the Internet, intranets, or a private wide-area network.
- A diversified transportation company with a large direct sales force applied data mining to identifying the best prospects for its services. Using data mining to analyze its own customer experience, this company can build a unique segmentation identifying the attributes of high-value prospects. Applying this segmentation to a general business database, such as those provided by Dun & Bradstreet, can yield a prioritized list of prospects by region.
- A large consumer packaged-goods company applies data mining to improve its sales process to retailers. Data from consumer panels, shipments, and competitors' activity are examined to understand the reasons for brand and store switching. Through this analysis, the manufacturer can select promotional strategies that best reach its target customer segments.
- In its data warehouse, the *Chicago Tribune* stores information about customer behavior as customers move through the various newspaper Web sites. Data mining helps to analyze volumes of data ranging from what browsers are used to what hyperlinks are clicked on most frequently.

IT at Work
DATA MINING POWERS WAL-MART

Integrating IT ...in Marketing
www.walmart.co

With more than 35 terabytes of data (in 2000) on two NCR (National Cash Register) systems, Wal-Mart manages one of the world's largest data warehouses. Besides the two NCR Teradata databases, which handle most decision-support applications, Wal-Mart has another 6 terabytes of transaction processing data on IBM and Hitachi mainframes.

Wal-Mart's formula for success—getting the right product on the appropriate shelf at the lowest price—owes much to the company's multimillion-dollar investment in data warehousing. "Wal-Mart can be more detailed than most of its competitors on what's going on by product, by store, by day—and act on it," says Richard Winter, a database consultant in Boston. "That's a tremendously powerful thing."

The systems house data on point of sale, inventory, products in transit, market statistics, customer demographics, finance, product returns, and supplier performance. The data are used for three broad areas of decision support: analyzing trends, managing inventory, and understanding customers. What emerges are "personality traits" for each of Wal-Mart's 3,000 or so outlets, which Wal-Mart managers can use to determine product mix and inventory levels for each store.

Wal-Mart is using a data mining demand-forecasting application based on neural networking software and a 4,000-processor parallel computer. The application looks at individual items for individual stores to decide the seasonal sales profile of each item. The system keeps a year's worth of data on the sales of 100,000 products and predicts which items will be needed in each store and when.

Wal-Mart is expanding its use of market-basket analysis. Data are collected on items that comprise a shopper's total purchase so that the company can analyze relationships and patterns in customer purchases. The data warehouse is available over an extranet to store managers and suppliers. In 2001, 5,000 users made over 35,000 database queries *each day*.

"What Wal-Mart is doing is letting an army of people use the database to make tactical decisions," says consultant Winter. "The cumulative impact is immense."

For Further Exploration: Since small retailers cannot afford data warehouses and data mining, will they be able to compete?

Sources: This information is courtesy of NCR Corp., 2000, and *walmart.com*.

The data warehouses in some companies include several terabytes or more of data. They need to use supercomputing to sift quickly through the data. Wal-Mart, the world's largest discount retailer, has a gigantic database, as shown in the *IT at Work* above.

11.6 WEB-BASED DATA MANAGEMENT SYSTEMS

Business intelligence activities—from data acquisition, through warehousing, to mining—can be performed with Web tools or are interrelated with Web technologies and e-commerce. Users with browsers can log onto a system, make inquiries, get reports, and so on, in a real-time setting. This is done through intranets, and for outsiders via extranets (see *remedy.com*). (Also, for a comprehensive discussion of business intelligence on the Web, see the white paper at *businessobjects.com*).

E-commerce software vendors are providing Web tools that connect the data warehouse with EC ordering and cataloging systems. One such example is Tradelink, a product of Hitachi (*hitachi.com*). Hitachi's EC tool suite combines EC activities such as catalog management, payment applications, mass customization, and order management with data warehouses (marts) and ERP systems. *Oracle.com* and *SAP.com* offer similar products.

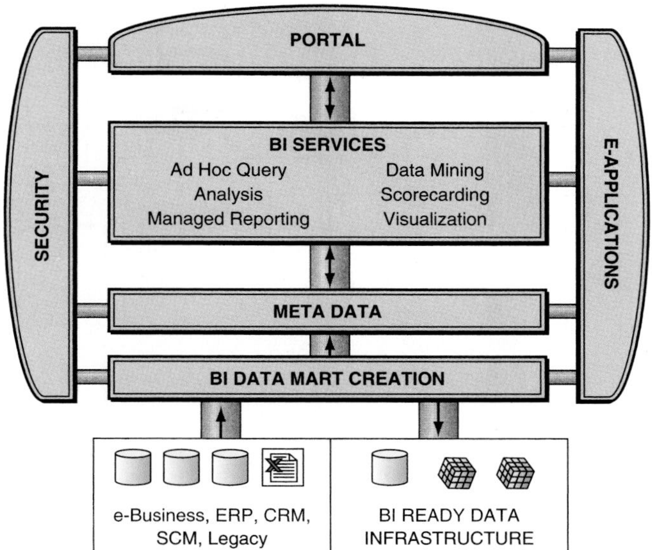

FIGURE 11.5 Web-based data management system. (*Source:* cognos.com. Platform for Enterprise Business Intelligence. © Cognos Inc. 2001.)

Data warehousing and decision support vendors are connecting their products or creating new ones to connect with Web technologies and EC. Examples are Comshare's Decision Web, Brio's Brio One (*brio.web.warehouse*), Web Intelligence from Business Objects, and Cognos's DataMerchant. Hyperion's Appsource "wired for OLAP" product connects OLAP with Web tools. IBM's Decision Edge and MicroStrategy's DSS Web are other tools that offer OLAP capabilities on the intranet from anywhere in the corporation using browsers, search engines, and other Web technologies. MicroStrategy offers DSS Agent and DSS Web for help in drilling down for detailed information, providing graphical views, pushing information to users' desktops, and more.

Bringing interactive querying, reporting, and other OLAP tasks to many users (both company employees and business partners) via the Web can also be facilitated by using Oracle's Financial Analyzer and Sales Analyzer, Hummingbird Bi/Web and Bi/Broker, and several of the products cited above.

The systems described in the previous sections of this chapter can be integrated among themselves and with the applications they are intended to generate. The integration is provided by Web-based platforms, such as the one shown in Figure 11.5. The Web-based system is accessed via a portal, and it connects the following parts: the business intelligence (BI) services, the data warehouse and marts, the corporate applications, and the data infrastructure. A security system protects the corporate proprietary data. Let's examine how all of these components work together via the corporate portal.

Corporate Portals

In Chapter 4 we introduced the concept of *corporate portals* as a Web-based gateway to data, information, and knowledge. In order to understand how the corporate portal works, examine Figure 11.6 (page 512). As seen in the figure, the portal integrates data from many sources. It provides end users with a single Web-based point of personalized access to business intelligence and other infor-

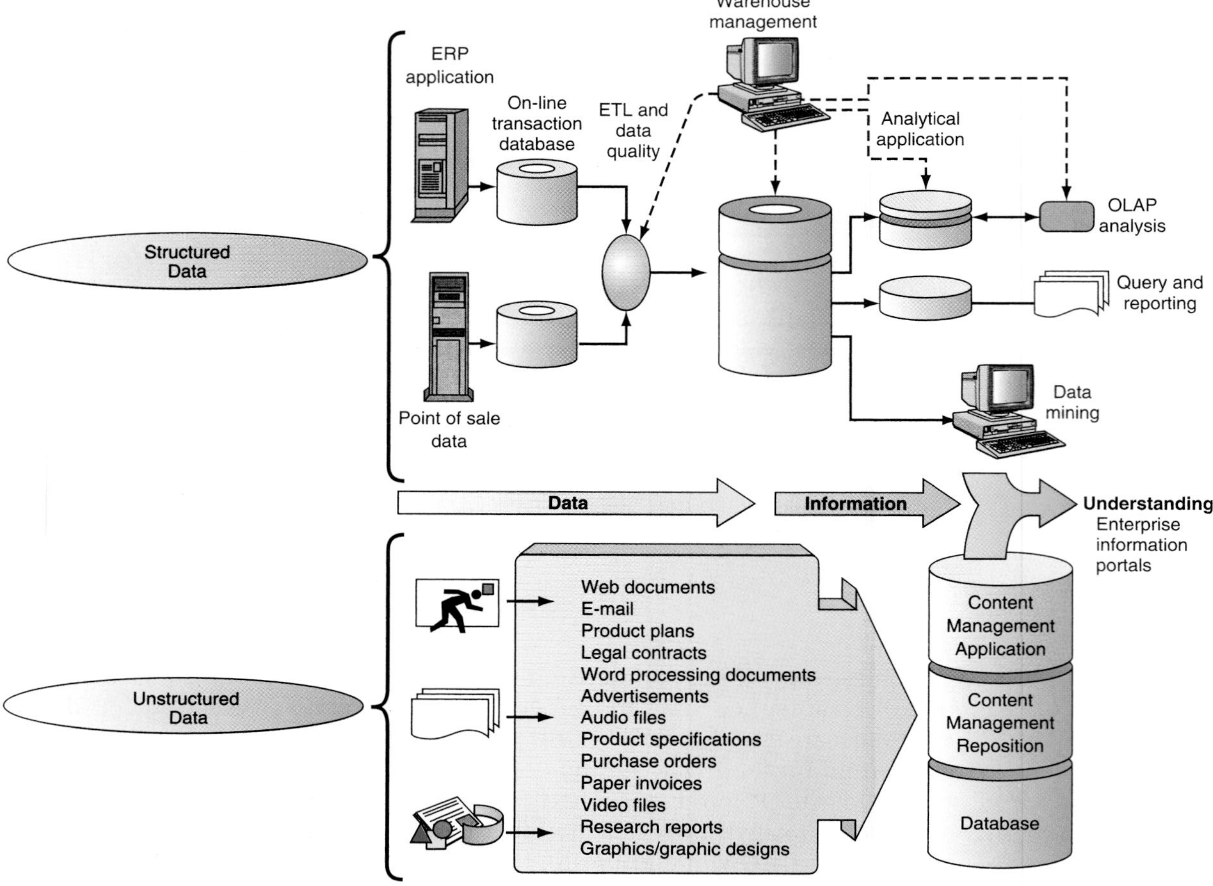

FIGURE 11.6 Sources of content for an enterprise information portal. (*Source:* Merrill Lynch, 1998.)

mation. Likewise, it provides IT with a single point of delivery and management of this content. Users are empowered to access, create, and share valuable information.

Web-based Data Acquisition

Traditional data acquisition has become a pervasive element in today's business environment. This acquisition includes both the recording of information from online surveys and questionnaires, and direct measurements taken in the manufacturing environment. However, most data-acquisition devices require software drivers and a user interface. But inserting a Web server inside a data-acquisition device (such as webDAQ from *cec488.com*) introduces the potential for a simple way to acquire data via a familiar user interface.

Intelligent Data Warehouse Web-based Agents

The amount of data in the data warehouse can be very large. While the organization of data is done in a way that permits easy search, it still may be useful to have a search engine for specific applications. Liu (1998) describes how an intelligent agent can improve the operation of a data warehouse in the pulp and paper industry. This application supplements the monitoring and scanning of external strategic data. The intelligent agent application can serve both managers' ad-hoc query/reporting information needs and the external data needs of a strategic management support system for forest companies in Finland.

MANAGERIAL ISSUES

1. ***Cost-benefit issues and justification.*** Some of the data management solutions discussed in this chapter are very expensive and are justifiable only in large corporations. Smaller organizations can make the solutions cost effective if they leverage existing databases rather than create new ones. A careful cost-benefit analysis must be undertaken before any commitment to the new technologies is made.
2. ***Where to store data physically.*** Should data be distributed close to their sources, thereby potentially speeding up data entry and updating but increasing problems of data security? Or should data be centralized for easier control, security, and disaster recovery, although they will be more distant from users and create a potential single point-of-failure location?
3. ***Legal issues.*** Data mining may suggest to a company to send catalogs or promotions to only one age group or one gender. A man sued Victoria's Secret because his female neighbor received a mail order catalog with deeply discounted items and he received only the regular catalog (the discount was actually given for volume purchasing). Discrimination charges can be very expensive.
4. ***Disaster recovery.*** Can an organization's business processes, which have become dependent on databases, recover and sustain operations after a natural or other type of information system disaster?
5. ***Internal or external?*** Should a firm invest in internally collecting, storing, maintaining, and purging its own databases of information? Or should it pay to subscribe to external databases, where providers are responsible for all data management and data access?

6. ***Data security and ethics.*** Are the company's competitive data safe from external snooping or sabotage? Are confidential data, such as personnel details, safe from improper or illegal access and alteration? A related question is, Who owns such personal data? (See Smith, 1997.)

7. ***Ethics: Paying for use of data.*** Compilers of public-domain information, such as Lexis-Nexis, face a problem of people lifting large sections of their work without first paying royalties. The Collection of Information Antipiracy Act (a pending bill in the U.S. Congress) will provide greater protection from online piracy. (See *Interactive Week,* February 16, 1998, for details.)

8. ***Privacy.*** Collecting data in a warehouse and conducting data mining may result in the invasion of individual privacy. What will companies do to protect individuals? What can individuals do to protect their privacy?
9. ***Data purging.*** When is it beneficial to "clean house" and purge information systems of obsolete or non-cost-effective data?
10. ***The legacy data problem.*** One very real problem is what to do with the mass of information already stored in a variety of formats, often known as the

legacy data acquisition problem. Data in older, perhaps obsolete, databases still need to be available to newer database management systems. Many of the legacy application programs used to access the older data simply cannot be converted into new computing environments without both transparent and procedural access to critical data remaining in the legacy environment. Basically, there are three approaches to solving this problem. One is to create a database front end that can act as a translator from the old system to the new. The second is to cause applications to be integrated with the new system, so that data can be seamlessly accessed in the original format. The third is to cause the data to migrate into the new system by reformatting it.

11. ***Data delivery.*** A problem regarding how to move data efficiently around an enterprise also exists. The inability to communicate among different groups in different geographical locations is a serious roadblock to implementing distributed applications properly, especially given the many remote sites and mobility of today's workers.

ON THE WEB SITE... Additional resources, including the Virtual Company, quizzes, cases, updates, additional exercises, links, demos, and activities, can be found on the book's Web site.

KEY TERMS

Business intelligence *496*
Clickstream data *481*
Data integrity *482*
Data mart *490*
Data mining *494*
Data quality (DQ) *482*
Data visualization *497*
Data warehouse *487*
Document management *483*
Document management system (DMS) *484*
Geographical information system (GIS) *500*
Knowledge discovery *491*
Knowledge discovery in databases (KDD) *491*
Marketing database *507*
Marketing transaction database (MTD) *507*
Metadata *487*
Multidimensional database *500*
Multidimensionality *498*
Multimedia database *483*
Object-oriented database *483*
Online analytical processing (OLAP) *493*
Operational data store *491*
Text mining *496*
Virtual reality (VR) *505*
Virtual reality markup language (VRML) *506*
Visual interactive modeling (VIM) *504*
Visual interactive simulation (VIS) *504*

CHAPTER HIGHLIGHTS (Numbers Refer to Learning Objectives)

1 Data are the foundation of any information system and need to be managed throughout their useful life cycle.

2 Data exist in internal and external sources. Personal data and knowledge are often stored in people's minds.

2 The Internet is a major source of data and knowledge.

2 Many factors that impact the quality of data must be recognized and controlled.

3 The newest types of data organization are object oriented and multimedia.

3 Electronic document management, the automated control of documents, is a key to greater efficiency in

handling documents in order to gain an edge on the competition.

4 Warehouses and data marts are necessary to support effective decision making. Relevant data are indexed and organized for easy access by end users.

5 Data mining for knowledge discovery is an attempt to use intelligent systems to scan volumes of data to locate necessary information and knowledge.

5 Online analytical processing is a data discovery method that uses analytical approaches to knowledge discovery.

6 Visualization is important for better understanding of data relationships and compression of information.

6 Multidimensional presentation enables quick and easy multiple viewing of information in accordance with people's needs.

6 A geographical information system captures, stores, manipulates, and displays data using digitized maps.

6 Virtual reality is 3-D, interactive, computer-generated graphics that provides users with a feeling that they are inside a certain environment.

7 Marketing databases provide the technological support for new marketing approaches such as interactive marketing.

7 Marketing transaction databases provide dynamic interactive functions that facilitate customized advertisement and services to customers.

8 Web-based systems are used extensively in supporting data access and data analysis. Also, Web-based systems are an important source of data. Finally, data visualization is frequently combined with Web systems.

QUESTIONS FOR REVIEW

1. List the major sources of data.
2. Briefly describe object-oriented and multimedia databases.
3. List some of the major data problems.
4. What is a terabyte? (Write the number.)
5. Review the steps of the data life cycle and explain them.
6. List some of the categories of data available on the Internet.
7. Define data quality.
8. Define document management.
9. Describe a data warehouse.
10. Describe a data mart.
11. Define online analytical processing (OLAP).
12. Define data mining and describe its major characteristics.
13. Explain the properties of multidimensionality.
14. Describe GIS and its major capabilities.
15. Define a marketing transaction database.
16. Define data visualization.
17. Define visual interactive modeling and simulation.
18. Define virtual reality.

QUESTIONS FOR DISCUSSION

1. Discuss the drivers of data warehousing.
2. Compare data quality to data integrity. How are they related?
3. Discuss some of the advantages of an object-oriented database. How does it relate to multimedia?
4. Discuss the factors that make document management so valuable. What capabilities are particularly valuable?
5. Relate document management to imaging systems.
6. Describe the process of knowledge discovery, and discuss the roles of the data warehouse, data mining, and OLAP in this process.
7. Discuss the major drivers and benefits of data warehousing to end users.
8. Discuss how a data warehouse can lessen the stovepipe problem. (See Chapter 8.)
9. A data mart can substitute for a data warehouse or supplement it. Compare and discuss these options.
10. Why is the combination of GIS and GPS becoming so popular? Examine some applications.
11. Discuss the advantages of terabyte marketing databases to a large corporation. Does a small company need a marketing database? Under what circumstances will it make sense to have one?
12. Discuss the benefits managers can derive from visual interactive simulation in a manufacturing company.
13. Why is the mass-marketing approach not effective any more? What is the logic of targeted marketing?

14. Distinguish between operational databases, data warehouses, and marketing data marts.
15. Relate the Sears case at the beginning of this chapter to the phases of the data life cycle.
16. Discuss the potential contribution of virtual reality to e-commerce.

EXERCISES

1. Review the list of data management difficulties in Section 11.1. Explain how a combination of data warehousing and data mining can solve or reduce these difficulties. Be specific.
2. Interview a knowledge worker in a company you work for or to which you have access. Find the data problems they have encountered and the measures they have taken to solve them. Relate the problems to Strong et al.'s four categories.
3. Ocean Spray Cranberries is a large cooperative of fruit growers and processors. Ocean Spray needed data to determine the effectiveness of its promotions and its advertisements and to make itself able to respond strategically to its competitors' promotions. The company also wanted to identify trends in consumer preferences for new products and to pinpoint marketing factors that might be causing changes in the selling levels of certain brands and markets. Ocean Spray buys marketing data from InfoScan (*infores.com*), a company that collects data using bar code scanners in a sample of 2,500 stores nationwide and from A. C. Nielsen. The data for each product include sales volume, market share, distribution, price information, and information about promotions (sales, advertisements).

   The amount of data provided to Ocean Spray on a daily basis is overwhelming (about 100 to 1,000 times more data items than Ocean Spray used to collect on its own). All the data are deposited in the corporate marketing data mart. In 1998, it was estimated to contain about 2 billion bytes. To analyze this vast amount of data, the company developed a DSS. To give end users easy access to the data, the company uses an expert system–based data-mining process called CoverStory, which summarizes information in accordance with user preferences. CoverStory interprets data processed by the DSS, identifies trends, discovers cause–effect relationships, presents hundreds of displays, and provides any information required by the decision makers. This system alerts managers to key problems and opportunities.

   a. Find information about Ocean Spray by entering Ocean Spray's Web site (*oceanspray.com*).
   b. Ocean Spray has said that it cannot run the business without the system. Why?
   c. What data from the data mart are used by the DSS?
   d. Enter *infores.com* or *scanmar.nl* and review the marketing decision support information. How is the company related to a data warehouse?
   e. How can one justify the cost of using Infoscan? (Read the report at *infoscan.com*.)
   f. How does Infoscan collect data? (Check the Data Wrench product.)

GROUP AND ROLE-PLAYING ACTIVITIES

1. Several applications now combine GIS and GPS.
   a. Survey such applications by conducting literature and Internet searches and query GIS vendors.
   b. Prepare a list of five applications, including at least two in e-commerce.
   c. Describe the benefit of such integration.
2. Prepare a report on the topic of "data management and the intranet." Specifically, pay attention to the role of the data warehouse, the use of browsers for query, and data mining. Also explore the issue of GIS and the Internet. Finally, describe the role of extranets in support of business partner collaboration. Each student will visit one or two vendors' sites, read the white papers, and examine products (Oracle, Red Bricks, Brio, Siemens Mixdorf IS, Comshare, NCR, SAS, and Information Advantage). Also, visit the Web site of the Data Warehouse Institute (*dw-institute.org*).
3. Companies invest billions of dollars to support database marketing. The information systems departments' (ISDs') activities that have supported accounting and finance in the past are shifting to marketing. According to Tucker (1997), some people think that the ISD should report to marketing. Do you agree or disagree? Debate this issue.
4. In 1996, Lexis-Nexis, the online information service, was accused of permitting access to sensitive information on individuals. Using data mining, it is possible not only to capture information that has been buried in distant courthouses, but also to manipulate and cross-index it. This can benefit law enforcement but invade privacy. The company argued that the firm was targeted

unfairly, since it provided only basic residential data for lawyers and law enforcement personnel. Should Lexis-Nexis be prohibited from allowing access to such information or not? Debate the issue.

INTERNET EXERCISES

1. Conduct a survey on document management tools and applications by visiting *dataware.com, documentum.com,* and *aiim.org/aim/publications.*
2. Access the Web sites of one or two of the major data management vendors, such as Oracle, Informix, and Sybase, and trace the capabilities of their latest products, including Web connections.
3. Access the Web sites of one or two of the major data warehouse vendors, such as NCR or SAS; find how their products are related to the Web.
4. Access the Web site of the GartnerGroup (*gartnergroup.com*). Examine some of their research notes pertaining to marketing databases, data warehousing, and data management. Prepare a report regarding the state of the art.
5. Explore a Web site for multimedia database applications. Visit such sites as *leisureplan.com, illustra.com,* or *adb.fr.* Review some of the demonstrations, and prepare a concluding report.
6. Survey some GIS resources such as *geo.ed.ac.uk/home/hiswww.html* and *prenhall.com/stratgis/sites.html.* Identify GIS resources related to your industry, and prepare a report on some recent developments or applications. See *http://nsdi.usgs.gov/nsdi/pages/what_is_gis.html.*
7. Visit the sites of some GIS vendors (such as MAP Info Systems at *mapinfo.com*). Join a newsgroup and discuss new applications in marketing, banking, and transportation. Download a demo. What are some of the most important capabilities and new applications?
8. Enter *websurvey.com, clearlearning.com,* and *tucows.com/webforms,* and prepare a report about data collection via the Web.

Minicase 1

GIS at Dallas Area Rapid Transit

www.dart.org

Public transportation in Dallas and its neighboring communities is provided by Dallas Area Rapid Transit (DART), which operates buses, vans, and a train system. The service area has grown very fast. By the mid-1980s, the agency was no longer able to respond properly to customer requests, make rapid changes in scheduling, plan properly, or manage security.

The solution to these problems was discovered using GISs. A GIS digitizes maps and maplike information, integrates it with other database information, and uses the combined information for planning, problem solving, and decision making. DART maintains a centralized graphical database of every object for which it is responsible.

The GIS presentation makes it possible for DART's managers, consultants, and customers to view and analyze data on digitized maps. Previously, DART created service maps on paper showing bus routes and schedules. The maps were updated and redistributed several times a year, at a high cost. Working with paper maps made it difficult to respond quickly and accurately to the nearly 6,000 customer inquiries each day. For example, to answer a question concerning one of the more than 200 bus routes or a specific schedule, it was often necessary to look at several maps and routes. Planning a change was also a time-consuming task. Analysis of the viability of bus route alternatives made it necessary to photocopy maps from map books, overlay tape to show proposed routes, and spend considerable time gathering information on the demographics of the corridors surrounding the proposed routes.

The GIS includes attractive and accurate maps that interface with a database containing information about bus schedules, routes, bus stops (in excess of 15,000), traffic surveys, demographics, and addresses on each street in the database. The system allows DART employees to:

- Respond rapidly to customer inquiries (reducing response time by at least 33 percent).
- Perform the environmental impact studies required by the city.
- Track where the buses are at any time using a global positioning system.
- Improve security on buses.
- Monitor subcontractors quickly and accurately.
- Analyze the productivity and use of existing routes.

For instance, a customer wants to know the closest bus stop and the schedule of a certain bus to take her to a certain

(continued)

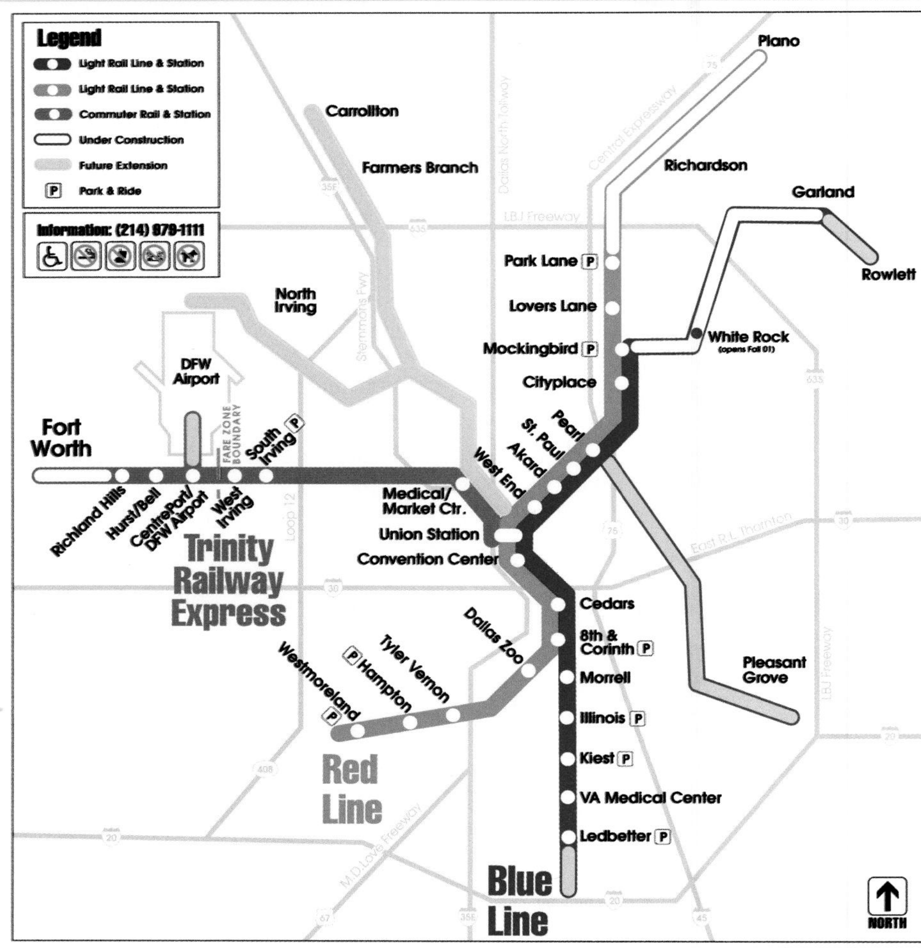

destination. The GIS automatically generates the answer when the caller says where she is by giving an address, a name of an intersection, or a landmark. The computer can calculate the travel time to the desired destination as well.

Analyses that previously took days to complete are now executed in less than an hour. Special maps, which previously took up to a week to produce at a cost of $13,000 to $15,000 each, are produced in 5 minutes at the cost of 3 feet of plotter paper.

In the late 1990s, the GIS was combined with a GPS. The GPS tracks the location of the buses and computes the expected arrival time at each bus stop. Many maps are on display at the Web site, including transportation lines and stops superimposed on maps.

Sources: Condensed from *GIS World*, July 1993; updated with information compiled from *dart.org* (2001).

Questions for Minicase 1

1. Describe the role of data in the DART system.
2. What are the advantages of computerized maps?
3. Comment on the following statement: "Using GIS, users can improve not only the inputting of data but also their use."
4. Speculate on the type of information provided by the GPS.

Minicase 2

Database Marketing Increases Dell's Sales

www.dell.com

Dell Computer Corporation has been the world's largest direct-sale vendor of personal computers. One way the company distinguishes itself from other suppliers of PCs is by acting quickly on the masses of data it gathers from customers. (The company receives over 50,000 telephone calls or electronic mail messages daily.) "Information is a valuable competitive weapon," says Tom Thomas, the chief information officer. "Our whole business system is geared to collect it."

Many of the 50,000 daily messages received by Dell are from potential customers who dial 800 numbers or send e-mail to reach the company's sales representatives. The rest are from current users of Dell machines, asking the technical support staff for help. The employees who take these calls work on PCs linked to a computer that contains the company's customer database, which has well over 1 million customer entries. The sales representatives enter information about each call as they receive it, recording names and addresses along with product preferences and/or technical problems. The company stores all this information and much more in a single database shared by employees in various departments, from marketing to product development to customer service.

The data yield significant marketing and sales guidelines. The company tailors its e-mails and advertisements to each recipient. The rate of response to its mailings to small businesses rose 250 percent once Dell used customer feedback to refine its pitch.

Dell organizes its sales by three types: individual consumers, businesses (small, medium, large, ISPs), and public (local government, federal, education, health). The marketing data are organized accordingly. Also, data by country are available. Data are kept by product. In 2000, Dell diversified to wireless products and greatly increased its server and storage products.

Experience from the database also guides the sales representatives who receive calls. As they enter information about each caller, sales suggestions automatically pop up on their computer screens using Dell's call center. Dell had a tenfold increase in sales of 3-year warranties after prompting representatives to pitch them to all callers buying systems costing more than a certain dollar amount.

Routine analysis of customer and sales data allows Dell to spot consumer trends such as a shift to larger hard disk drives. At one time, when Dell was shipping most of its systems with drives capable of storing over 120 MB, the customer database alerted management to the fact that new orders for drives with nearly twice the storage capability were rapidly climbing. Dell buyers rushed out, negotiated volume discounts from large disk drive manufacturers, and locked in deliveries before their competitors.

"Know your customer" is a tried and true business rule, and Dell gets the most it can out of it through customer databases.

Sources: Adapted from *Fortune 1994 Information Technology Guide,* August 1993, and from Dell's press releases 2000, 2001.

Questions for Minicase 2

1. What role do databases play in Dell's marketing strategies?
2. Can you identify any data mining necessary for the information described in the case?
3. Is there any possibility of invasion of privacy of Dell's customers? If so, how can this privacy be protected?
4. How can the company manage the data about so many products, in so many countries, sold to so many types of customers?
5. Is the paper catalog eventually going to disappear?

REFERENCES AND BIBLIOGRAPHY

1. Adjeroh, D. A., and K. C. Nwosu, "Multimedia Database Management—Requirements and Issues," *IEEE Multimedia,* July–September 1997.
2. Banerjee, P., and D. Zetu, *Virtual Manufacturing: Virtual Reality and Computer Vision Techniques.* New York: Wiley, 2001.
3. Barquin, R., and H. Edelstein, *Building, Using, and Managing the Data Warehouse.* Upper Saddle River, NJ: Prentice-Hall, 1997.
4. Beitler, S. S., and R. Leary, "Sears' Epic Transformation: Converting from Mainframe Legacy Systems to OLAP," *Journal of Data Warehousing,* April 1997.
5. Berry, M. J. A., and G. S. Linoff, *Mastering Data Mining.* New York: Wiley, 2000.
6. Carbone, P. L., "Data Warehousing: Many of the Common Failures," *Presentation, mitre.org/support/papers/tech...9_00/d-warehoulse_presentation.htm* (May 3, 1999).

7. Chau, P. Y. K., and P. C. Bell, "A Visual Interactive DSS to Assist in the Design of a New Production Unit," *INFOR*, May 1996.
8. Clarke, K. C., *Getting Started with Geographical Information Systems*. Upper Saddle River, NJ: Prentice-Hall, 1997.
9. Cole, B., "Document Management on a Budget," *Network World*, Vol. 13, No. 8, September 16, 1996.
10. Compton, J. "Instant Customer Feedback," *PC Computing*, December 1999.
11. Dalgleish, J., *Customer-Effective Web Sites*. Upper Saddle River, NJ: Pearson Technology Group, 2000.
12. Eckerson, W. W., "Web-based Query Tools and Architecture," *Journal of Data Warehousing*, April 1997.
13. Fayyad, U. M., et al., "The KDD Process for Extracting Useful Knowledge from Volumes of Data," *Communications of the ACM*, November 1996.
14. Gray, P., and H. J. Watson, *Decision Support in the Data Warehouse*. Upper Saddle River, NJ, Prenctice-Hall, 1998.
15. Grossnickle, J., and O. Raskin, *The Handbook of Marketing Research*. New York: McGraw-Hill, 2000.
16. Groth, R., *Data Mining*. Upper Saddle River, NJ: Prentice-Hall, 1998.
17. Hagel, J., and J. F. Rayport, "The Coming Battle for Customer Information," *Harvard Business Review*, January–February 1997.
18. Hamilton, J. M., "A Mapping Feast," *CIO*, March 15, 1996.
19. Haskin, D., "Leverage Your Knowledge Base" (Web-based document management systems), *Internet World*, February 1998.
20. *Information Advantage*, "Putting the Data Warehouse on the Intranet," a white paper, *inforadvan.com/1f.4_int.html*, 1997.
21. Inmon, W. H., et al., *Corporate Information Factory*, 2nd ed. New York: Wiley, 2000.
22. Jacobs, A., "Mapping Software Finds the Net," *Computerworld*, Vol. 30, No. 32, August 5, 1996.
23. Kaplan, D., et al., "Assessing Data Quality in Accounting Information Systems," *Communications of the ACM*, February 1998.
24. Kerlow, I. V., *The Art of 3D*, 2nd ed. New York: Wiley, 2000.
25. Korte, G. B., *The GIS Book*, 5th ed. Albany, NY: Onward Press, 2000.
26. Lazar, J., and J. Preece, "Designing and Implementing Web-based Surveys," *Journal of Computer Information Systems*, April 1999.
27. Liu, S., "Data Warehousing Agent: To Make the Creation and Maintenance of Data Warehouse Easier," *Journal of Data Warehousing*, Spring 1998.
28. Mattison, R., *Winning Telco Customers Using Marketing Databases*. Norwood, MA: Artech House, 1999.
29. Maybury, M. T., *Intelligent Multimedia Information Retrieval*. Boston: MIT Press, 1997.
30. McFadden, F., and H. J. Watson, "The World of Data Warehousing: Issues and Opportunities," *Data Warehousing*, Vol. 1, No. 1, 1996.
31. Mennecke, B. E., et al., "Using GIS as a Tool for Sensing and Responding to Customers," in S. P. Bradley and R. L. Nolan (eds.), *Multimedia and the Boundaryless World*. Boston: Harvard Business School Colloquium, 1995.
32. Moad, J., "Mining a New Vein," *PC Week*, January 5, 1998.
33. Nwosu, K. C., et al., "Multimedia Database Systems: A New Frontier," *IEEE Multimedia*, July–September 1997.
34. O'Looney, J. A., Beyond Maps: *GIS Decision Making in Local Governments*. Redlands, CA: Environmental Systems Research, 2000.
35. Park, Y. T., "Strategic Uses of Data Warehouses," *Journal of Data Warehousing*, April 1997.
36. Pritsker, A. A. B., and J. J. O'Reilly, *Simulation with Visual SLAM and Awesim*, 2nd ed. New York: Wiley, 1999.
37. Redman, T. C., "The Impact of Poor Data Quality on the Typical Enterprise," *Communications of the ACM*, February 1998.
38. Roland, D., "Data Flow Management Can Assist Underwriting," *National Underwriter*, August 29, 1994.
39. Smith, H. J., "Who Owns Personal Data?" *Beyond Computing*, November–December 1997.
40. Sprague, R. H., "Electronic Document Management: Challenges and Opportunities," *MIS Quarterly*, March 1995.
41. Steede-Terry, K., *Integrating GIS and GPS*. Redlands, CA: Environmental Systems Research (eSRI.com), 2000.
42. Strong, D. M., et al., "Data Quality in Context," *Communications of the ACM*, May 1997.
43. Swenson, J., "Maps on the Web," *Information Week*, July 8, 1996.
44. Trippi, R., and E. Turban (eds.), *Neural Networks in Finance and Investing*. Chicago: Irwin, 1996.
45. Tucker, M. J., "Poppin' Fresh Dough" (Database Marketing), *Datamation*, May 1997.
46. Turban E., et al., *Electronic Commerce: A Managerial Perspective*. Upper Saddle River, NJ: Prentice-Hall, 2002.
47. Varney, S. F., "Database Marketing Predicts Customer Loyalty," *Datamation*, September 1996.
48. Vassos, J., *Strategic Internet Marketing*. Indianapolis, IN: QUE Publishing, 1996.
49. Wang, R. Y., "Total Data Quality Management," *Communications of the ACM*, February 1998.

PART IV
Managerial and Decision Support Systems

CHAPTER

12 Intelligent Support Systems

LEARNING OBJECTIVES

After studying this chapter, you will be able to:

1. Describe artificial intelligence and compare it to conventional computing.
2. Identify the characteristics, structure, benefits, and limitations of expert systems.
3. Describe the major characteristics of natural language processing and voice technologies.
4. Describe neural computing and its differences from other computer-based technologies.
5. Define intelligent agents and their role in IT.
6. Describe the relationship between the Web and intelligent systems.
7. Understand the importance of creativity and how it is supported by IT.

LIFE IN THE DIGITAL AGE

 DRIVING TO WORK—IN ROYAL STYLE

Today when you drive to work or school, you follow a routine process. You start the car and move it into the street; you try to avoid accidents; you start fighting traffic ("all those people who don't know how to drive"); and finally, you are on the freeway, speeding, trying not to be late. "Sorry," the officer says. "You were speeding." ("Everybody is speeding. Why me?") Finally you arrive at your destination, tired and stressed. For a moment, you close your eyes and say to yourself, "My job is in the marketing department. I am not a paid driver. I wish I could afford a limo." Good news. Your wish may come true in the near future.

You will enter your autonomous land vehicle (ALV). You say, "Go to work, car," and slip into the back seat. The car will then start itself, open the garage door, back out into the street, and carefully drive itself to work. You can relax, watch TV, sip coffee, read a newspaper, or just take a nap.

 WIRELESS COMMERCE BRINGS YOU THE FOOD YOU LIKE

You're on the freeway and you are getting hungry. You think about the Japanese lunch you had a few days ago, but you do not know about the restaurants in the area you are driving through. As you continue to drive, hoping to see a billboard with restaurant ads, your cell phone rings, notifying you that a message was just posted on the cell phone. You push a button to hear the message. The message says: "Mr./Ms. Nice, you are approaching the Green exit, which will lead you to the Zen Japanese restaurant. Today's specials are. . . . If you push the replay button, we will reserve a table for you in 15 minutes and will display a map with driving instructions." You wonder: "How do they know that I am driving in this area? How do they know that I like Japanese food?"

 PLANNING A VACATION THE RIGHT WAY

It is time to take your annual vacation. How about a trip to Hawaii—a real trip, not a virtual one. You can call upon your *intelligent agent* for assistance, which will perfectly plan it for you in a Web-based, completely automated multiagent system. Here is how the system works:

- ***Step 1.*** On your PC, you enter onto an electronic form your desired destination, dates, available budget, special requirements, and desired entertainment.
- ***Step 2.*** Your computer dispatches an intelligent agent that "shops around," entering the Internet and communicating electronically with the databases of airlines, hotels, and other vendors.
- ***Step 3.*** Your agent attempts to match your requirements against what is available, negotiating with the vendors' agents. These agents may activate other agents to make special arrangements, cooperate with each other, activate multimedia presentations, or make special inquiries.
- ***Step 4.*** Your agent returns to you within minutes, with one or more suitable alternatives. You have a few questions; you want modifications. No problem. Within a few minutes, it's a done deal. No waiting for busy telephone operators and no human errors. Once you approve the deal, the intelligent agent will make the reservations, arrange for payments, and even report to you about any unforeseen delays in your departure.

How do you communicate with your agent? By voice, of course.

These scenarios are not as far off as they may seem. Prototype ALVs developed at Carnegie Mellon University and in Germany can already drive themselves through city traffic at about 30 mph. In California, ALVs can be seen on I-15 near San Diego (*aaai.org*, 1998). M-commerce on cell phones is currently being implemented in several countries (e.g., see *mobile.msn.com*, *nttdocomo.com/I*), and intelligent agents are rapidly moving to the commercial arena (*media.mit.edu*).

LESSONS LEARNED FROM THESE CASES

The incidents described earlier may seem like science fiction, but it is only a matter of time before they become reality. Many other scenarios are on the drawing boards of research institutions and technology-oriented corporations worldwide. Common to all these scenarios is the fact that each will include some intelligent component.

The three incidents illustrate some of the benefits the digital economy is bringing to our lives. For example, intelligent systems enable people to perform much better than ever before. Although these incidents illustrate improvements in business processes related to individual consumers, similar systems are available to improve business processes involving organizational transactions.

In this chapter we will illustrate many of the capabilities of intelligent systems or systems enhanced with intelligent components. We also will describe the major types of intelligent systems and how their intelligence is derived. Then, we will describe intelligent systems in Web infrastructure. Finally we will discuss how machines can facilitate humans' creativity.

12.1 INTELLIGENT SYSTEMS AND ARTIFICIAL INTELLIGENCE

Intelligent systems is the term that describes the various commercial applications of artificial intelligence (AI).

Artificial Intelligence and Intelligent Behavior

Artificial intelligence (AI) is a term that encompasses several definitions (see Cawsey, 1998, and Ramsay, 1996). Most experts agree that AI is concerned with two basic ideas. First, it involves studying the thought processes of humans; second, it deals with representing those processes via machines (computers, robots, and so on).

One well-publicized definition of AI is "behavior by a machine that, if performed by a human being, would be called *intelligent*." Let us explore the meaning of the term *intelligent behavior*. Several capabilities are considered to be signs of intelligence:

- Learning or understanding from experience
- Making sense of ambiguous or contradictory messages
- Responding quickly and successfully to a new situation
- Using reasoning to solve problems and direct actions effectively
- Dealing with complex situations
- Understanding and inferring in ordinary, rational ways
- Applying knowledge to manipulate the environment
- Recognizing the relative importance of different elements in a situation

AI's ultimate goal is to build machines that will mimic human intelligence. So far, the capabilities of current intelligent systems, exemplified in commercial AI products, are far from exhibiting any significant intelligence. Nevertheless, intelligent systems are getting better with the passage of time, and they are currently useful in efficiently conducting many tasks that require some human intelligence.

An interesting test to determine whether a computer exhibits intelligent behavior was designed by Alan Turing, a British AI pioneer. According to the **Turing test**, a computer could be considered "smart" only when a human interviewer, conversing with both an unseen human being and an unseen computer, cannot determine which is which.

So far we have concentrated on the notion of intelligence. According to another definition, artificial intelligence is the branch of computer science that deals with ways of representing *knowledge*, using symbols rather than numbers, and *heuristics*, or rules of thumb, rather than algorithms for processing information. Some of these properties are described next.

KNOWLEDGE AND AI. AI is frequently associated with the concept of knowledge. Although a computer cannot have experiences or study and learn as a human can, it can use knowledge given to it by human experts. Such knowledge consists of facts, concepts, theories, heuristic methods, procedures, and relationships. Knowledge is also information organized and analyzed to make it *understandable* and *applicable* to problem solving or decision making. The collection of knowledge related to a specific problem (or an opportunity) to be used in an intelligent system is organized and stored in a **knowledge base**. The collection of knowledge related to the operation of an organization is called an **organizational knowledge base** (see Chapter 9).

Comparing Artificial and Natural Intelligence

The potential value of AI can be better understood by contrasting it with natural (human) intelligence. AI has several important commercial advantages over natural intelligence, but also some limitations, as shown in Table 12.1.

The disadvantages of AI result in some limitations that will be pointed out later.

TABLE 12.1 Comparison of the Capabilities of Natural vs. Artificial Intelligence

Capabilities	Natural Intelligence	AI
Preservation of knowledge	Perishable from an organizational point of view.	Permanent.
Duplication and dissemination of knowledge	Difficult, expensive, takes time.	Easy, fast, and inexpensive once knowledge is in a computer.
Total cost of knowledge	Very high.	Can be very low.
Consistency of intelligence	Can be erratic and inconsistent. Incomplete at times.	Consistent and thorough.
Documentability of process and knowledge	Difficult, expensive.	Fairly easy, inexpensive.
Creativity	Can be very high.	Low, uninspired.
Use of sensory experiences	Direct and rich in possibilities.	Must be interpreted first; limited.
Recognizing patterns and relationships	Fast, easy to explain.	Machine learning still not as good as people in most cases, but in some cases can do better than people.
Reasoning	Making use of wide context of experiences.	Good only in narrow, focused, and stable domains.

BENEFITS OF AI. Despite their limitations, AI methods can be extremely valuable. They can make computers easier to use and can make knowledge more widely available. The major potential benefits of AI are that it:

- Significantly increases the speed and consistency of some problem-solving procedures
- Helps solve problems that cannot be solved or are difficult to solve by conventional computing
- Helps solve problems with incomplete or unclear data
- Helps in handling the information overload by summarizing or interpreting information and by assisting in searching through large amounts of data
- Significantly increases the productivity of performing many tasks
- Makes the use of some computer applications very friendly

Conventional versus AI Computing

Conventional computer programs are based on algorithms. An *algorithm* is a mathematical formula or sequential procedure that leads to a solution. The algorithm is converted into a computer program that tells the computer exactly what operations to carry out. The algorithm then uses data such as numbers, letters, or words to solve problems.

AI software is based on **symbolic processing** of knowledge. In AI, a symbol is a letter, word, or number that represents objects, processes, and their relationships. Objects can be people, things, ideas, concepts, events, or statements of fact. Using symbols, it is possible to create a knowledge base that contains facts, concepts, and the relationships that exist among them. Then various processes can be used to manipulate the symbols in order to generate advice or a recommendation for solving problems.

The major differences between AI computing and conventional computing are shown in Table 12.2.

DOES A COMPUTER REALLY THINK? Knowledge bases and search techniques certainly make computers more useful, but can they really make computers more intelligent? The fact that most AI programs are implemented by search and pattern-matching techniques leads to the conclusion that *computers are not really intelligent.* You give the computer a lot of information and some guidelines about how to use this information, and the computer can then come up with a solution. But all it does is test the various alternatives and attempt to find some combination that meets the designated criteria. The computer appears to be "thinking" and often gives a satisfactory solution. But Dreyfus and Dreyfus (1988) feel

TABLE 12.2 Conventional versus AI Computing

Dimension	Artificial Intelligence	Conventional Programming
Processing	Includes symbolic conceptualizations.	Primarily algorithmic.
Nature of input	Can be incomplete.	Must be complete.
Search approach	Frequently uses heuristics.	Frequently based on algorithms.
Explanation	Provided.	Usually not provided.
Focus	Knowledge.	Data, information.
Maintenance and update	Relatively easy; changes can be made in self-contained modules.	Usually difficult.
Reasoning capability	Yes	No

that the public is being misled about AI, whose usefulness is overblown and whose goals are unrealistic. They claim, and we agree, that the human mind is just too complex to duplicate. *Computers certainly cannot think,* but they can be very useful for increasing our productivity. This is done by several commercial AI technologies.

The Commercial Artificial Intelligence Field

The development of machines that exhibit intelligent characteristics draws upon several sciences and technologies, ranging from linguistics to mathematics (see the roots of the tree in Figure 12.1, on page 527). Artificial intelligence itself is not a commercial field; it is a collection of concepts and ideas that are appropriate for research but cannot be marketed. However, AI provides the scientific foundation for several commercial technologies.

The major intelligent systems are: expert systems, natural language processing, speech understanding, robotics and sensory systems, fuzzy logic, neural computing, computer vision and scene recognition, and intelligent computer-aided instruction. In addition, a combination of two or more of the above is considered a hybrid intelligent system. The major intelligent systems are illustrated in Figure 12.1 as the branches of the tree. Some are presented next.

EXPERT SYSTEMS. **Expert systems (ESs)** are computerized advisory programs that attempt to imitate the reasoning processes of experts in solving difficult problems. They are in use more than any other applied AI technology. Expert systems are of great interest to organizations because they can increase productivity and augment workforces in specialty areas where human experts are becoming increasingly difficult to find and retain or are too expensive to use. Expert systems are discussed in Section 12.2 of this chapter.

NATURAL LANGUAGE TECHNOLOGY. **Natural language processing (NLP)** gives computer users the ability to communicate with the computer in human languages. Limited success in this area is typified by systems that can recognize and interpret individual words or short sentences relating to very restricted topics. The field of natural language processing is discussed in detail in Section 12.3.

SPEECH (VOICE) UNDERSTANDING. *Speech understanding* is the recognition and understanding by a computer of a *spoken* language. Details are given in Section 12.3.

ROBOTICS AND SENSORY SYSTEMS. Sensory systems such as vision systems combined with AI define a broad category of systems generally referred to as *robotics*. A **robot** is an electromechanical device that can be programmed and reprogrammed to automate manual tasks.

Robots combine sensory systems with mechanical motions to produce machines of widely varying abilities. Robotics is used mainly in welding, painting, and simple material handling. Assembly-line operations, particularly those that are highly repetitive or hazardous, are also beginning to be performed by robots. Examples of robots' work are provided in Chapter 16.

Robots are becoming more and more capable, and they are being used today for conducting many new and useful tasks (see Wise, 1999). One increasing use of robots, for example, is for finding, moving, and packaging items in automated e-commerce warehouses. The rise in robot technology is accelerating due

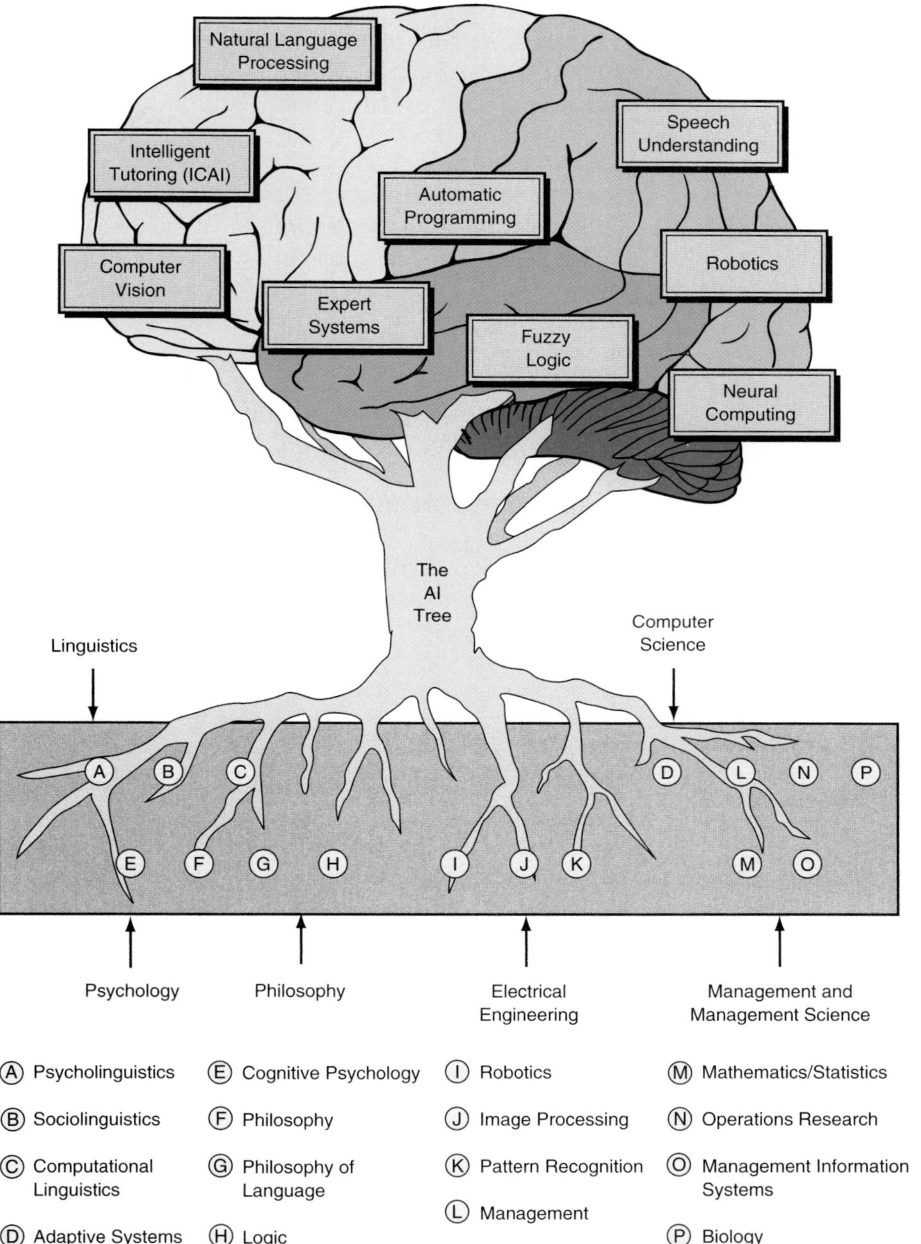

FIGURE 12.1 The disciplines of AI (the roots) and the major applications.

to advances in computer power, availability of inexpensive sonar, infrared and laser sensor, speech recognition, and the emergence of new paradigms for designing autonomous objects.

Robots can, of course, also be used for fun. In August 1997, the first World Cup Robot Soccer Competition was conducted in Nagoya, Japan. The robots included several AI technologies (see *robocup.org/*). To learn how to build your own robot, consult Lunt (2000). Many people are building robots, frequently for fun.

Using Lego's building blocks called Mindstorms, one can build a sophisticated robot. Marriott (2001) conducted comprehensive research on toy robots, whose capabilities have increased rapidly. According to his findings, real robot research and design can greatly benefit from toy robots. (See the 2001 movie *A.I.—Artificial Intelligence.*)

COMPUTER VISION AND SCENE RECOGNITION. **Visual recognition** has been defined as the addition of some form of computer intelligence and decision making to digitized visual information received from a machine sensor. The combined information is then used to perform, or control, such operations as robotics movement, conveyor speeds, and production-line quality control. The basic objective of computer vision is to interpret scenarios. Computer vision is used extensively in performing industrial quality control (such as inspection of products). Would you believe that *every* Tylenol or other brand-name pill is checked for defects by computers? Defective pills are removed.

INTELLIGENT COMPUTER-AIDED INSTRUCTION. *Intelligent computer-aided instruction (ICAI)* refers to the work of machines that can tutor humans. Such a machine can be viewed as an expert system. However, the major objective of an expert system is to render advice, whereas the purpose of ICAI is to teach.

Computer-assisted instruction (CAI), which has been in use for several decades, brings the power of the computer to the educational process. Now AI methods are being applied to the development of *intelligent* computer-assisted instruction systems. The purpose is to create computerized "tutors" that shape their teaching techniques to fit the learning patterns of individual students.

ICAI applications are not limited to schools. They also have found a sizable niche in the military and corporate sectors. ICAI systems are being used today for various tasks such as problem solving, simulation, discovery, learning, drill and practice, games, and testing. Such systems are also used to support people with physical or learning impairments. An increased number of ICAI programs are now offered on the Internet and intranets, creating virtual schools and universities. This application of artificial intelligence is used in **distance learning**, where teachers and students are in different locations. Another application of ICAI is *interpretive testing*. Using this approach the GMAT and other famously long tests have shortened their length of time. By being able to better interpret the answers, the test can more accurately pinpoint the strengths and weaknesses of the test takers, in fewer questions.

MACHINE LEARNING. Computers have long been used to solve structured problems with quantitative models. Such models, however, cannot solve complex problems in situations where specialized knowledge is needed. Such knowledge can be provided, in some cases, by an expert system (ES). However, the use of an ES is limited by such factors as difficulties in knowledge acquisition and the inability of the ES to learn from experience. For situations where an ES is inappropriate, we use a different approach called machine learning. **Machine learning** refers to a set of methods that attempt to teach computers to solve problems or to support problem solving by analyzing (learning from) historical cases (e.g., see Witten and Frank, 1999).

This task, however, is not simple. One problem is that there are many modes of learning. Sometimes it is difficult to match the learning mode with the type of problem that needs to be solved. Two methods of machine learning, *neural computing* and *fuzzy logic,* are described in Section 12.3. One application is the *learning agents,* described in Section 12.4.

HANDWRITING RECOGNIZERS. The dream of every post office in the world is to be able to automate the reading of all handwritten address characters, regardless of their shape. Today's scanners are good at "reading" typed or printed material, but they are not very good at handwriting recognition. Handwriting recognition is supported by technologies such as expert systems and neural computing and is available in some pen-based computers. (When you receive an overnight letter or a traffic violation ticket, you will probably sign for it on the screen of a pen-based computer.)

Scanners that can interpret handwritten input are subject to considerable error. To minimize mistakes, handwritten entries should follow very specific rules. Some scanners will flag handwritten entries that they cannot interpret or will automatically display for verification all input that has been scanned. Because handwritten entries are subject to misinterpretation and typed entries can be smudged, misaligned, erased, and so forth, optical scanners have an error rate considerably higher than the error rate for keyed data.

Handwriting interfaces are especially popular with people who are slow typists. Of special interest to them are products such as PDAs (personal digital assistants—handheld computers such as the Palm Pilot).

OTHER APPLICATIONS. AI can be applied to several other tasks such as automatic computer programming, news summaries, and translation from one language to another. The ultimate aim of automatic programming is to achieve a computer system that can develop programs by itself, in response to and in accordance with the specifications of a program developer. Some computer programs "read" stories in newspapers or other documents, including those available on the Internet, and make summaries in English or other languages. This helps handle the information-overload problem.

A pioneering project of summarizing financial news was conducted by General Electric's R&D center under the title SCISOR. The system was proven to be 100 percent effective in collecting information about corporate mergers. Another interesting application is reported by Wee et al. (1997), in which a Web-based personalized news system was developed to track news available in English, Chinese, and Malay, summarize it, and extract desired personalized news in one of these languages.

In later sections we describe the major business-related AI applications in more detail.

12.2 EXPERT SYSTEMS

When an organization has a complex decision to make or a problem to solve, it often turns to experts for advice. These experts have specific knowledge and experience in the problem area. They are aware of alternative solutions, chances of success, and costs that the organization may incur if the problem is not solved. Companies engage experts for advice on such matters as equipment purchase, mergers and acquisitions, and advertising strategy. The more unstructured the situation, the more specialized and expensive is the advice. *Expert systems (ESs)* are an attempt to mimic human experts. Expert systems can either *support* decision makers or completely *replace* them (see Edwards et al., 2000). Expert systems are the most widely applied and commercially successful AI technology.

Concepts of Expert Systems

In order to explore the concepts involved in ESs, review a well-known application at General Electric in the *IT at Work* illustration below.

Typically, an ES is decision-making software that can reach a level of performance comparable to a human expert in some specialized and usually narrow problem area. The basic idea behind an ES is simple: *Expertise* is transferred from an expert (or other source of expertise) to the computer. This knowledge is then stored in the computer. Users can call on the computer for specific advice as needed. The computer can make inferences and arrive at a conclusion. Then, like a human expert, it advises the nonexperts and explains, if necessary, the logic behind the advice. ESs can sometimes perform better than any single expert can.

EXPERTISE AND KNOWLEDGE. *Expertise* is the extensive, task-specific knowledge acquired from training, reading, and experience. It enables experts to make better and faster decisions than nonexperts in solving complex problems. Expertise takes a long time (usually years) to acquire, and it is distributed in organizations in an uneven manner. A senior expert possesses about 30 times more expertise than a junior (novice) staff member. (See Figure 12.2.)

IT at Work

Integrating IT ...in Production & Operations Management

GENERAL ELECTRIC'S EXPERT SYSTEM MODELS HUMAN TROUBLESHOOTERS

www.gc.com

David I. Smith, the top locomotive field service engineer at General Electric (GE), had been with the company for more than 40 years and was expert at troubleshooting diesel locomotive engines. Smith's job was to travel throughout the country to places where locomotives were in need of repair, to determine what was wrong and advise young engineers about what to do. The company was very dependent on Smith. The problem was that he was nearing retirement.

GE's traditional approach to such a situation was to create apprenticeship teams that paired senior and junior engineers for several months or even years. By the time the older engineers retired, the younger engineers had absorbed enough of their expertise to carry on. It was a good short-term solution, but GE still wanted a more effective and dependable way of disseminating expertise among its engineers and preventing valuable knowledge from retiring with people like David Smith.

GE decided, instead, to build an expert system to solve the problem by modeling the way a human troubleshooter works. The system builders spent several months interviewing Smith and transferring his knowledge to a computer. The computer programming was prototyped over a three-year period, slowly increasing the knowledge and number of decision rules stored in the computer. The new diagnostic technology enables a novice engineer or even a technician to uncover a fault by spending only a few minutes at the computer terminal. The system can also explain to the user the logic of its advice, serving as a teacher. Furthermore, the system can lead users through the required repair procedures, presenting a detailed, computer-aided drawing of parts and subsystems and providing specific how-to instructional demonstrations. It is based on a flexible, humanlike thought process, rather than rigid procedures expressed in flowcharts or decision trees.

The system, which was developed on a minicomputer but operates on PCs, is currently installed at every railroad repair shop served by GE, thus preserving Smith's expertise, eliminating delays, and boosting maintenance productivity.

For Further Exploration: If an expert system can replace David Smith, why not replace all experts in the world with expert systems?

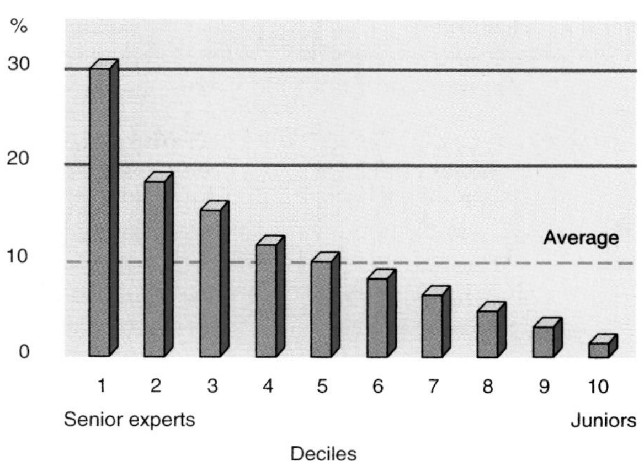

FIGURE 12.2 Distribution of expertise: percent successes achieved per decil. A senior expert possesses about 30 times more expertise than a junior expert. (*Source:* Adapted from N. R. Augustine, "Distribution of Expertise," *Defense Systems Management*, Spring 1979. Reprinted with permission from N. R. Augustine.)

The transfer of expertise from an expert to a computer and then to the user involves four activities: *knowledge acquisition* (from experts or other sources), *knowledge representation* (in the computer), *knowledge inferencing,* and *knowledge transfer* to the user.

Knowledge is acquired from experts or from documented sources. Through the activity of knowledge representation, acquired knowledge is organized as rules or frames (object-oriented) and stored electronically in a knowledge base. Given the necessary expertise stored in the knowledge base, the computer is programmed so that it can make inferences. The inferencing is performed in a component called the **inference engine** and results in a recommendation for novices. Thus, the expert's knowledge has been *transferred* to users.

A unique feature of an ES is its ability to explain its recommendation. The explanation and justification is done in a subsystem called the *justifier* or the *explanation subsystem.*

Benefits of Expert Systems

During the past few years, the technology of expert systems has been successfully applied in thousands of organizations worldwide to problems ranging from AIDS research to the analysis of dust in mines. Why have ESs become so popular? It is because of the large number of capabilities and benefits they provide. The major ones are listed in Table 12.3 (page 532).

The Limitations

Despite their many benefits, available ES methodologies are not always straightforward and effective. Here are some problems that have slowed the commercial spread of ES:

- Knowledge to be captured is not always readily available.
- Expertise is hard to extract from humans.
- The approach of each expert to a situation may be different, yet correct.
- It is hard, even for a highly skilled expert, to accurately assess situations when under time pressure.
- Users of expert systems have natural cognitive limits, so they may not use the benefits of the system to the fullest extent.
- ES works well only within narrowly defined subject areas such as diagnosing a malfunction in a machine.

TABLE 12.3 Benefits of Expert Systems

Benefit	Description/Example
Increased output and productivity	At Digital Equipment Corp. (now part of Compaq), an ES plans configuration of components for each custom order, increasing production preparation fourfold.
Increased quality	ESs can provide consistent advice and reduce error rates.
Capture and dissemination of scarce expertise	Physicians in Egypt and Algeria use an eye-care ESs developed at Rutgers University to diagnose and to recommend treatment.
Operation in hazardous environments	ESs that interpret information collected by sensors enable human workers to avoid hot, humid, or toxic environments.
Accessibility to knowledge and help desks	ESs can increase the productivity of help-desk employees (there are over 30 million in the U.S. alone), or even automate this function.
Reliability	ESs do not become tired or bored, call in sick, or go on strike. They consistently pay attention to details and do not overlook relevant information.
Increased capabilities of other systems	Integration of an ES with other systems makes the other systems more effective.
Ability to work with incomplete or uncertain information	Even with an answer of "don't know" or "not sure," an ES can still produce an answer, though it may not be a certain one.
Provision of training	Novices who work with an ES become more experienced thanks to the explanation facility which serves as a teaching device and knowledge base.
Enhancement of decision-making and problem-solving capabilities	ESs allow the integration of expert judgment into analysis. Successful applications are diagnosis of machine malfunction and even medical diagnosis.
Decreased decision-making time	ESs usually can make faster decisions than humans working alone. American Express authorizers can make charge authorization decisions in 3 minutes without an ES and in 30 seconds with one.
Reduced downtime	ESs can quickly diagnose machine malfunctions and prescribe repairs. An ES called Drilling Advisor detects malfunctions in oil rigs, saving the cost of downtime (as much as $250,000/day).

- Most expert systems have no independent means of checking whether their conclusions are reasonable or correct.
- The vocabulary, or jargon, that experts use for expressing facts and relations is frequently limited and not understood by others.
- Help in building ESs is frequently required from knowledge engineers who are rare and expensive—a fact that could make ES construction rather costly.
- Lack of trust by end users may be a barrier to ES use.
- Knowledge transfer is subject to perceptual and judgmental biases.
- Liability for bad advice provided by an ES is difficult to assess.

In addition, expert systems may not be able to arrive at conclusions (especially in early stages of system development). For example, even some fully developed expert configurators are unable to fulfill about 2 percent of the orders presented to it. Finally, expert systems, like human experts, sometimes produce incorrect recommendations.

Various organizational, personal, and economic factors can slow the spread of expert systems, or even cause them to fail, as shown in the *IT at Work* example that follows at the top of the next page.

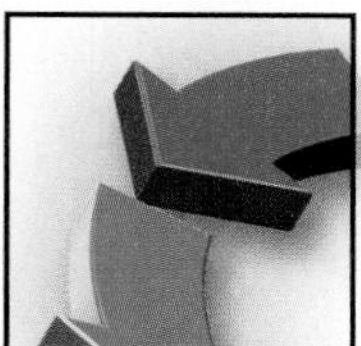

IT at Work
AN EXPERT SYSTEM THAT FAILED

...in Production & Operations Management

www.marykay.com

Mary Kay, the multinational cosmetics company, uses teams of managers and analysts to plan its products. This process attempted to iron out potential weaknesses before production. However, the company still faced costly errors resulting from such problems as product-container incompatibility, interaction of chemical compositions, and marketing requirements with regard to packaging and distribution.

An eclectic group of Mary Kay managers, representing various functional areas, used to meet every six weeks to make product decisions. The group's decision-making process was loosely structured: The marketing team would give its requirements to the product formulator and the package engineer at the same time. Marketing's design requests often proved to be beyond the allocated budget or technical possibilities, and other problems arose as a result of not knowing the ultimate product formulation. The result was more meetings and redesign.

Mary Kay decided to implement an expert system to help. In an effort to keep costs to a minimum, it engaged the services of a research university that developed a system that consisted of a DSS computational tool plus two ES components. The decision support tool was able to select compatible packages for a given cosmetic product and to test product and package suitability. The ES component used this information to guide users through design and to determine associated production costs.

At first the system was a tremendous success. There was a clear match between the abilities of the system technology and the nature of the problem. The director of package design enthusiastically embraced the system solution. The entire decision process could have been accomplished in two weeks with no inherent redesign. By formulating what previously was largely intuitive, the ES improved understanding of the decision process itself, increasing the team's confidence. By reducing the time required for new product development, executives were freed for other tasks, and the team met only rarely to ratify the recommendations of the ES.

However, without support staff to *maintain* the ES, no one knew how to add or modify decision rules. Even the firm's IT unit was unable to help, and so the system fell into disuse.

More importantly, when the director of package design left the firm, so did his enthusiasm for the ES. No one else was willing to make the effort necessary to maintain the system or sustain the project. Without managerial direction about the importance of the system to the firm's success, the whole project floundered.

For Further Exploration: What can a company do to prevent such failures? Can you speculate on why this was not done at Mary Kay?

Source: Condensed from R. G. Vedder et al., "An Expert System That Was," *Proceedings, DSI International,* Athens, Greece, July 1999.

Components and Processes of Expert Systems

The following components exist in an expert system: knowledge base, inference engine, blackboard (workplace), user interface, and explanation subsystem (justifier). In the future, systems will include a knowledge-refining component. The relationships among components are shown in Figure 12.3 (page 534).

THE COMPONENTS OF ES. A brief description of the major components follows:

- The *knowledge base* contains knowledge necessary for understanding, formulating, and solving problems. It includes two basic elements: (1) *facts*, such as the problem situation and theory of the problem area, and (2) *rules* that direct the use of knowledge to solve specific problems in a particular domain.
- The *blackboard* is an area of working memory set aside for the description of a current problem, as specified by the input data; it is also used for recording intermediate results. It is a kind of database.

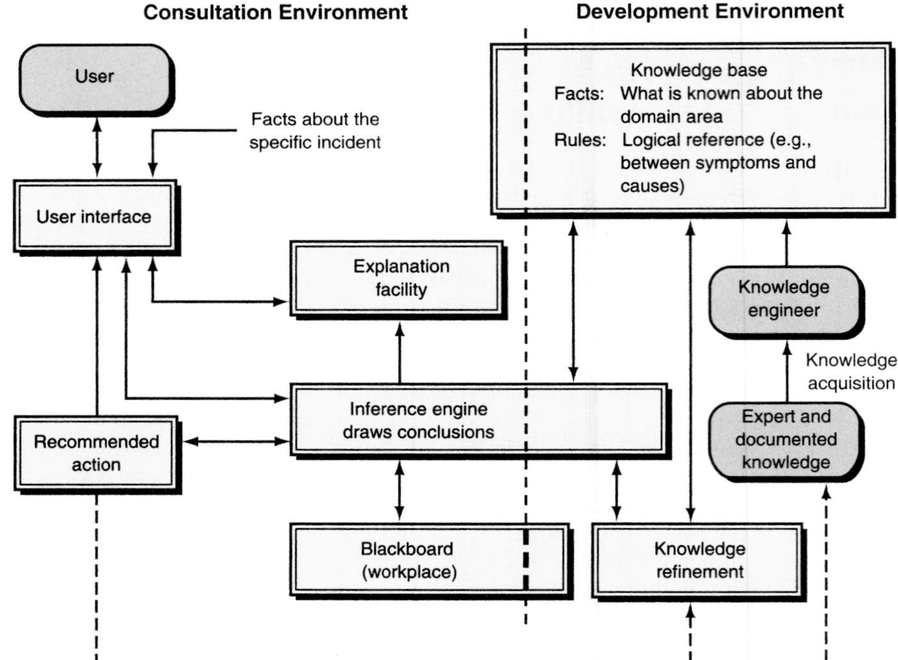

FIGURE 12.3 Structure and process of an expert system.

- The "brain" of the ES is the *inference engine*. This component is essentially a computer program that provides a methodology for reasoning and formulating conclusions.
- The *user interface* in ESs allows for user-computer dialogue, which can be best carried out in a natural language, usually presented in a questions-and-answers format and sometimes supplemented by graphics. The dialogue triggers the inference engine to match the problem symptoms with the knowledge in the knowledge base and then generate advice.
- The ability to trace responsibility for conclusions to their source is crucial both in the transfer of expertise and in problem solving. The *explanation subsystem* can trace such responsibility and explain the ES's behavior by interactively answering questions such as the following: *Why* was a certain question asked by the expert system? *How* was a certain conclusion reached? *Why* was a certain alternative rejected? *What* is the plan to reach the solution? (See the discussion by Gregor and Benbasat, 1999.)
- Human experts have a *knowledge-refining* system; that is, they can analyze their own performance, learn from it, and improve it for future consultations. Similarly, such evaluation is necessary in computerized learning so that the program will be able to improve by analyzing the reasons for its success or failure. Such a component is not available in most commercial expert systems at the moment, but it is being developed in experimental ESs.

Expert systems can provide management with inexpensive, innovative solutions to problems requiring expertise. For details see Jackson (1999), Giarratano (1998), and the next sections.

THE PROCESS OF BUILDING AND USING ES. The ES process can be divided into two parts: first, the system development (shown as development environment in Figure 12.3), in which the ES is constructed; and second, the consultation environment (left side of Figure 12.3), which describes how advice is rendered to the users.

The development process starts with the knowledge engineer (the system builder) acquiring knowledge from experts and/or documented sources. This knowledge is then programmed in the knowledge base as facts about the subject area (domain) and knowledge in terms of if-then rules.

The consultation environment includes the user, who contacts the system via a user interface to ask for advice. The ES provides advice by collecting information from the user, usually by asking questions, and then activating the inference engine. The engine searches the knowledge base for recommended actions based on the facts or symptoms provided by the user, and it can provide limited explanations. To execute its tasks, the inference engine uses a database for storing collected information, called the *blackboard*. Finally, the knowledge in the database may be refined as experience is accumulated through repetitive consultations. An example of a consultation is provided in the *IT at Work* illustration on page 536.

Some Illustrative Applications

Expert systems are in use today in all types of organizations. For many examples, by industry, see *exsys.com* (go to case studies). Expert systems are especially useful in ten generic categories, displayed in Table 12.4.

The following examples illustrate the diversity and nature of ES applications.

Integrating IT ...in Government

The U.S. Department of the Treasury Fights Criminals with an Expert System. One of the major tasks of the U.S. Financial Crime Enforcement Network (FinCEN) is to prevent and detect money laundering. One area of investigation is cash transactions over $10,000, which all banks must report. The problem is that there are over 200,000 such transactions every week (over 12,000,000/year). For well-trained analysts to examine all of this requires a large staff, which FinCEN is not budgeted for. By using an ES, the agency (*ustreas.gov*) can detect suspicious transactions and changes in transactions' patterns. Since its inception in 1993, the expert system has helped to uncover more than 100 cases of money-laundering activities each year.

TABLE 12.4 Generic Categories of Expert Systems

Category	Problem Addressed
1. Interpretation	Inferring situation descriptions from observations.
2. Prediction	Inferring likely consequences of given situations.
3. Diagnosis	Inferring system malfunctions from observations.
4. Design	Configuring objects under constraints.
5. Planning	Developing plans to achieve goal(s).
6. Monitoring	Comparing observations to plans, flagging exceptions.
7. Debugging	Prescribing remedies for malfunctions.
8. Repair	Executing a plan to administer a prescribed remedy.
9. Instruction	Diagnosing, debugging, and correcting student performance.
10. Control	Interpreting, predicting, repairing, and monitoring systems behavior.

IT at Work

Integrating IT ...in Marketing

HOW TO SELECT AN ADVERTISEMENT MEDIUM—A SAMPLE OF AN ES CONSULTATION

This prototype system attempts to provide recommendation(s) on an advertising mix so as to maximize the advertiser's product exposure in the market. For simplicity, the system makes recommendations on only two types of advertising media: television and newspaper.

The system will ask the user several questions, such as the one shown in the sample printout below, to find the requirements and/or symptoms of the problem.

```
EXSYS Pro ====== You may select ONLY ONE value ======

        Client prefer
          1   Only TV media
          2   Only Newspaper media
          3   More TV media
          4   More Newspaper media
          5   No preference indicated

                  ▶▶ Why_

Enter the value number<s> or select with arrow keys and press <ENTER>
WHY  QUIT  <H>-help  Memo <F10>
```

The user may ask the computer *why* (why you need this information). The computer answers by displaying the pertinent rule (rule number 1).

```
EXSYS Pro ====== RULE NUMBER: 1 ======

 IF:
    <1> Client prefer ONLY TV media
 THEN:
       All budget on TV - Confidence=8/10

 NOTE:  The client is always right. We should always try to meet the
 client's expectations. If the client prefers only TV as the
 advertising medium for product exposure, we should accomodate it.

IF line # for derivation <K>-known data  <C>-choices
↑or↓ - prev. or next rule <J>-jump  <H>-help <F10>-Memo <ENTER>-Done:
```

The computer continues with questions such as:

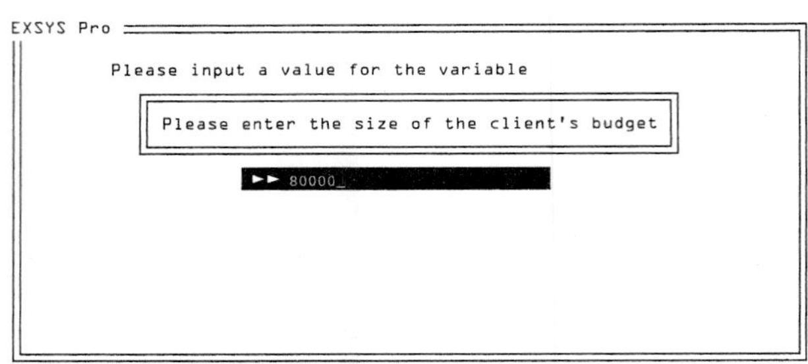

EXSYS Pro
Please input a value for the variable
Please enter the size of the client's budget
▶▶ 80000_
WHY QUIT <H>-help Memo <F10> <Ctrl-U>Undo

Once all questions have been answered by the user, the expert system displays the recommendations:

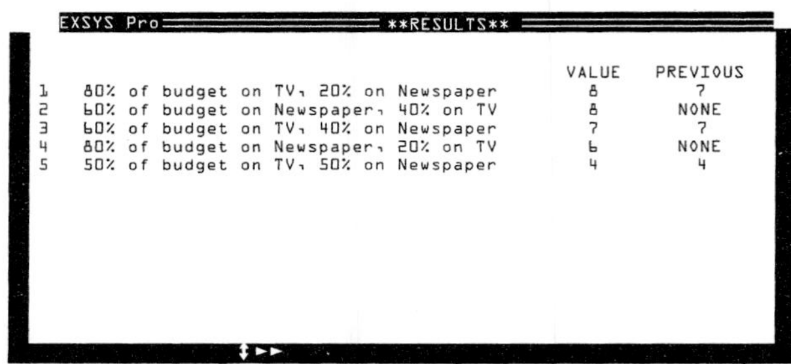

EXSYS Pro **RESULTS**
VALUE PREVIOUS
1 80% of budget on TV, 20% on Newspaper 8 7
2 60% of budget on Newspaper, 40% on TV 8 NONE
3 60% of budget on TV, 40% on Newspaper 7 7
4 80% of budget on Newspaper, 20% on TV 6 NONE
5 50% of budget on TV, 50% on Newspaper 4 4
All choices <A> only if >1 <G> Print <P> Change/rerun <C>
Rules used <line #> Quit/save <Q> Help <H> Memo <F10> Done <D>

Source: Printouts were generated with software from *exsys.com*.

...in Production & Operations Management

Visual Decision-Making System. Chevron Oil's refinery in El Segundo, California, uses a Web-based system for manufacturing enterprise and supply chain decision making. The system enables employees to visualize plant conditions over the intranet. The user needs only 15 minutes training. Real-time data from various plant databases are combined in graphical summaries. For more detail, users can drill down on selected objects in the Web browser. Interpretation is done by an expert system that analyzes historical data. By 2001 the system covered all the equipment of the company, and it conducts the troubleshooting along the entire internal supply chain.

...in Government

Helping The Navajo Nation. The states of Arizona, New Mexico, and Utah are transferring management of the welfare program to the Navajo Nation, which will self-administer the program for its own people. The program provides financial and human services to approximately 28,000 Navajo clients. An ES by Online Advisory Solution facilitates self-management of the welfare program. The interactive solution Case Worker Advisor (from *exsys.com*) integrates the tribe's unique cultural heritage while following complex federal, state, and tribal guidelines (*exsys.com*, October 1999).

Integrating IT ...in Production & Operations Management

China's Freight Train System. An expert system was developed in China to allocate freight cars and to determine what and how much to load on each car. The ES is integrated with the existing MIS, and the system is distributed to many users. (For details see Geng et al., 1999.)

Integrating IT ...in Production & Operations Management

Expert Configurator. Carrier Corporation (*carrier.com/*), a major air-conditioning manufacturer, introduced expert systems into its operations. The system, named Expert, configures a set of part numbers for each particular equipment order, based on customer requests. Not only is it necessary to compute the best design combination, but it is also necessary to procure all the parts and subsystems so the orders can be filled on time. Using an ES, Carrier was able to minimize both pricing and configuration errors, reduce cycle time, and increase customer satisfaction as well as profitability.

Integrating IT ...in Accounting

Expert Auditor. The State Street Bank and Trust Company operates in a highly competitive financial services field. To stay ahead of the competition, the bank is using expert systems to improve its daily operations. One application electronically audits daily and month-end data against the corresponding general ledger account balance, highlighting any exceptions. The client/server-based application provides online access to the audit exceptions via object-request broker technology. Accounting data are examined by audit and proofing processes. The expert system significantly increased the productivity of the auditors as well as the quality of error detection.

Embedded Expert Systems

One of the most useful applications of expert systems is as an embedded component in other systems, including intelligent agents. The ES components are so integrated that they have turned into parts of processes. Actually, many software and hardware products include embedded ESs or other intelligent systems, and we never know it. IT systems are sold based on their functionality, not on whether they include an intelligent component.

12.3 Other Intelligent Systems: From Voice Understanding to Neural Computing

An expert system's major objective is to provide expert advice. Other intelligent systems can be used to solve problems or provide capabilities in areas in which they excel. Four such technologies are described next.

Natural Language Processing and Voice Technology

Today, to tell a computer what to do, you type commands in the keyboard. In responding to a user, the computer outputs message symbols or other short, cryptic notes of information. Many problems could be minimized or even eliminated if we could communicate with the computer in our own languages. We would simply type in directions, instructions, or information. Better yet, we would converse with the computer using voice. The computer would be smart enough to interpret the input, regardless of its format. *Natural language processing (NLP)* refers to communicating with a computer in English or whatever language you may speak.

To understand a natural language inquiry, a computer must have the knowledge to analyze and then interpret the input. This may include linguistic knowledge about words, domain knowledge, common-sense knowledge, and even knowledge about the users and their goals. Once the computer understands the input, it can take the desired action.

In this section we briefly discuss two types of NLP:

- Natural language *understanding,* which investigates methods of allowing a computer to comprehend instructions given in ordinary English, via the keyboard or by voice, so that computers are able to understand people
- Natural language *generation,* which strives to allow computers to produce ordinary English language, on the screen or by voice (known as *voice synthesis*), so people can understand computers more easily

APPLICATIONS OF NATURAL LANGUAGE PROCESSING. Natural language processing programs have been applied in several areas. The most important are: human–computer interfaces (mainly to databases), abstracting and summarizing text, grammar analysis, translation of one natural language to another natural language, translation of one computer language to another computer language, speech understanding, and even composing letters by machine.

By far the most dominant use of NLP is in interfaces, or "front-ends," for other software packages, especially databases and database management systems. Such *front-end interfaces* are used to simplify and improve communications between application programs and the user. The natural language front-end allows the user to operate the applications programs with everyday language.

SPEECH (VOICE) RECOGNITION AND UNDERSTANDING. **Speech recognition** is a process that allows us to communicate with a computer by speaking to it. The term *speech recognition* is sometimes applied only to the first part of the communication process—in which the computer recognizes words that have been spoken without necessarily interpreting their meanings. The other part of the process, wherein the meaning of speech is ascertained, is called **speech understanding**. It may be possible to understand the meaning of a spoken sentence without actually recognizing every word, and vice versa. When a speech recognition system is combined with a natural language processing system, the result is an overall system that not only recognizes voice input but also understands it.

Advantages of Speech Recognition and Understanding. The ultimate goal of speech recognition is to allow a computer to understand the natural speech of any human speaker at least as well as a human listener could understand it. In addition to the fact that this is the most natural method of communication, speech recognition offers several other advantages:

- ***Ease of access.*** Many more people can speak than can type. As long as communication with a computer depends on typing skills, many people may not be able to use computers effectively.

- ***Speed.*** Even the most competent typists can speak more quickly than they can type. It is estimated that the average person can speak twice as quickly as a proficient typist can type.
- ***Manual freedom.*** Obviously, communicating with a computer through typing occupies your hands. There are many situations in which computers might be useful to people whose hands are otherwise occupied, such as product assemblers, pilots of aircraft, and busy executives. Speech recognition also enables people with hand-related physical disabilities to use computers (see Chapter 16).
- ***Remote access.*** Many computers are set up to be accessed remotely by telephones. If a remote database includes speech recognition capabilities, you could retrieve information by issuing oral commands into a telephone.
- ***Accuracy.*** In typing information, people are prone to make mistakes, especially in spelling. These are minimized with voice input.

American Express Travel Related Services (AETRS) is using a voice recognition system that allows its customers to check and book domestic flights by talking to a computer over the phone. The system asks customers questions such as: Where do you want to travel to?, from? when?, and so on. The system can handle 350 city and airport names, and lets callers use more than 10,000 different ways to identify a location. Compared to telephone served by an operator, reservation transaction cost is reduced by about 50 percent. The average transaction time is reduced from 7 to 2 minutes. AETRS offers a similar service on the Web.

Limitations of Speech Recognition and Understanding. The major limitation of speech understanding is its inability to recognize long sentences, or the need to accomplish it very slowly. The better the system is at speech recongition, the higher its cost. Also, in voice recognition systems, you cannot manipulate icons and windows, so speech may need to be combined with the keyboard entry, which slows it down.

VOICE PORTALS. Allowing customers to use an ordinary telephone as an Internet appliance is known as a **voice portal**. Customers dial a toll-free number and use voice to request information ranging from a traffic report to stock prices. That is, the site the customer reaches through the phone acts like an Internet portal (like Yahoo! or Lycos). The difference is that information is accessed by voice rather than by pointing and clicking a mouse. The major voice portal companies in 2000 were *heyanita.com, tellme.com, quack.com,* and *telsurf.networks.com*.

VOICE SYNTHESIS. The technology by which computers speak is known as **voice synthesis**. The synthesis of voice by computer differs from the simple playback of a prerecorded voice by either analog or digital means. As the term *synthesis* implies, sounds that make up words and phrases are electronically constructed from basic sound components and can be made to form any desired voice pattern.

The current quality of synthesized voice is very good, but the technology remains somewhat expensive. Anticipated lower cost and improved performance of synthetic voice should encourage more widespread commercial applications in the near future. Opportunities for its use will encompass almost all applications that can provide an automated response to a user, such as inquiries by employees pertaining to payroll and benefits. A number of banks already offer a

TABLE 12.5 Sample of Voice Technology Applications

Company	Applications
Scandinavian Airlines, other airlines	Answering inquiries about reservations, schedules, lost baggage, etc.[a]
Citibank, many other banks	Informing credit card holders about balances and credits, providing bank account balances and other information to customers[a]
Delta Dental Plan (CA)	Verifying coverage information[a]
Federal Express	Requesting pickups[b]
Illinois Bell, other telephone companies	Giving information about services,[a] receiving orders[b]
Domino's Pizza	Enabling stores to order supplies, providing price information[a,b]
General Electric, Rockwell International, Austin Rover, Westpoint Pepperell, Eastman Kodak	Allowing inspectors to report results of quality assurance tests[b]
Cara Donna Provisions	Allowing receivers of shipments to report weights and inventory levels of various meats and cheeses[b]
Weidner Insurance, AT&T	Conducting market research and telemarketing[b]
U.S. Department of Energy, Idaho National Engineering Laboratory, Honeywell	Notifying people of emergencies detected by sensors[a]
New Jersey Department of Education	Notifying parents when students are absent and about cancellation of classes[a]
Kaiser-Permanente Health Foundation (HMO)	Calling patients to remind them of appointments, summarizing and reporting results[a]
Car manufacturers	Activating radios, heaters, and so on, by voice[b]
Taxoma Medical Center	Logging in and out by voice to payroll department[b]
St. Elizabeth's Hospital	Prompting doctors in the emergency room to conduct all necessary tests, reporting of results by doctors[a,b]
Hospital Corporation of America	Sending and receiving patient data by voice, searching for doctors, preparing schedules and medical records[a,b]

[a]Output device.
[b]Input device.

voice service to their customers, informing them about their balance, which checks were cashed, and so on. Many credit card companies provide similar services, telling customers about current account balances, recent charges, and payments received. For a list of other voice synthesis and voice recognition applications, see Table 12.5.

VOICE PROCESSING SYSTEMS IN ELECTRONIC COMMERCE. Most of the existing voice technologies are designed to recognize or understand voice, but not to support dialogue. In e-commerce one may need both capabilities, in order to conduct a dialogue. Using IBM's Via Voice system, an expert system, and natural language processing, One Voice Technologies developed software that lets people interact with the Internet by voice rather than by pointing and clicking with a mouse. The first application was deployed at *autobytel.com*. Customers use it to find information and transact purchases. The system greets customers (by name if the company knows your name) and asks what kind of a car you are interested in buying. In the not-so-distant future voice systems will be deployed on many Web sites, and even attached to wireless devices.

Neural Computing

The tools of AI that we have discussed so far have been mostly restricted to sequential processing and only to certain representations of knowledge and logic. A different approach to intelligent systems is computing with architecture that mimics certain processing capabilities of the brain. The results are knowledge representations and processing based on massive parallel processing, fast retrieval of large amounts of information, and the ability to recognize patterns based on experiences. The technology that attempts to achieve these results is called **neural computing** or **artificial neural networks (ANNs)**.

BIOLOGICAL AND ARTIFICIAL NEURAL NETWORKS. Artificial neural networks are biologically inspired. Specifically, they borrow ideas from the manner in which the human brain works. The human brain is composed of special cells called *neurons*. Estimates of the number of neurons in a human brain cover a wide range (up to 150 billion), and there are more than a hundred different kinds of neurons, separated into groups called networks. Each network contains several thousand neurons that are highly interconnected. Thus, the brain can be viewed as a collection of neural networks.

Today's neural computing uses a very limited set of concepts from biological neural systems. The goal is to simulate massive parallel processes that involve processing elements interconnected in a network architecture. The artificial neuron receives inputs analogous to the electrochemical impulses biological neurons receive from other neurons. The output of the artificial neuron corresponds to signals sent out from a biological neuron. These artificial signals can be changed, like the signals from the human brain. Neurons in an ANN receive information from other neurons or from external sources, transform the information, and pass it on to other neurons or external outputs.

The manner in which an ANN processes information depends on its structure and on the algorithm used to process the information.

COMPONENTS AND STRUCTURE OF ANNs. ANNs are composed of artificial neurons; these are the *processing elements*. Each of the neurons receives input(s), processes the input(s), and delivers a single or a few outputs. This process is shown in Figure 12.4 (with a single output).

Note the following major components in the process:

Inputs. Each input corresponds to a single attribute. For example, if the problem is to decide on approval or disapproval of a loan, some attributes could

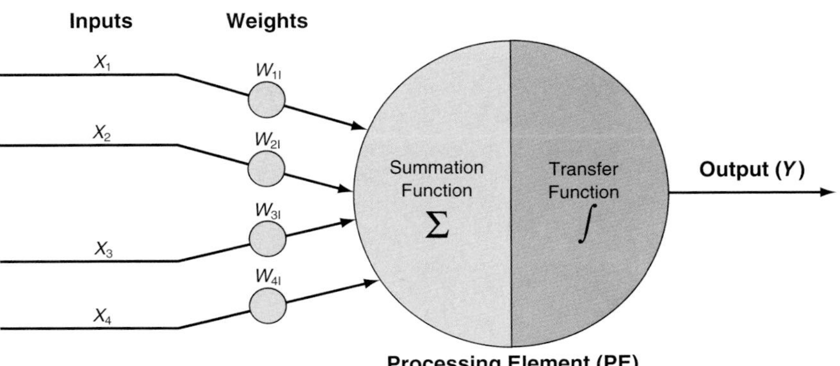

FIGURE 12.4 Processing information in an artificial neuron.

be the applicant's income level, age, and home ownership. Several types of data, such as text, pictures, and voice, can be used as inputs. Preprocessing may be needed to convert the raw data to meaningful inputs from symbolic data or to scale the data. The inputs are multiplied by weights—when they enter the processing elements (PEs).

Weights. Key elements in an ANN are the **weights**. Weights express the *relative strength* (or mathematical value) of the input data or the many connections that transfer data from layer to layer. In other words, in the case of a loan application, weights express the *relative importance* of each input applicant's attribute, based on past experiences. Weights are crucial in that they store learned patterns of information. It is through repeated adjustments of weights that the network learns.

Summation Function. The *summation function* (represented by the symbol Σ) calculates the weighted sum of all the input elements entering each processing element. A summation function multiplies each input value by its weight and totals the values for a weighted sum.

Transformation Function. A *transformation function* (represented by $\int$) integrates the information produced by all PEs, and transforms it to meaningful outputs.

Outputs. The outputs of the network contain the solution to a problem. For example, in the case of a loan application it can be "yes" or "no." The ANN assigns numeric values, like 1 for "yes" and 0 for "no." The purpose of the network is to compute the values of the output.

Often, *postprocessing* of the outputs is required. Outputs can be input to other decisions. For example, the decision to approve or reject a loan can be an input element in a decision regarding a mortgage approval. Therefore ANNs may be composed of several layers of processing elements.

In Figure 12.5 we show a three-layer situation with the input layer of PEs, an intermediate layer (called a hidden layer), and an output layer. The hidden

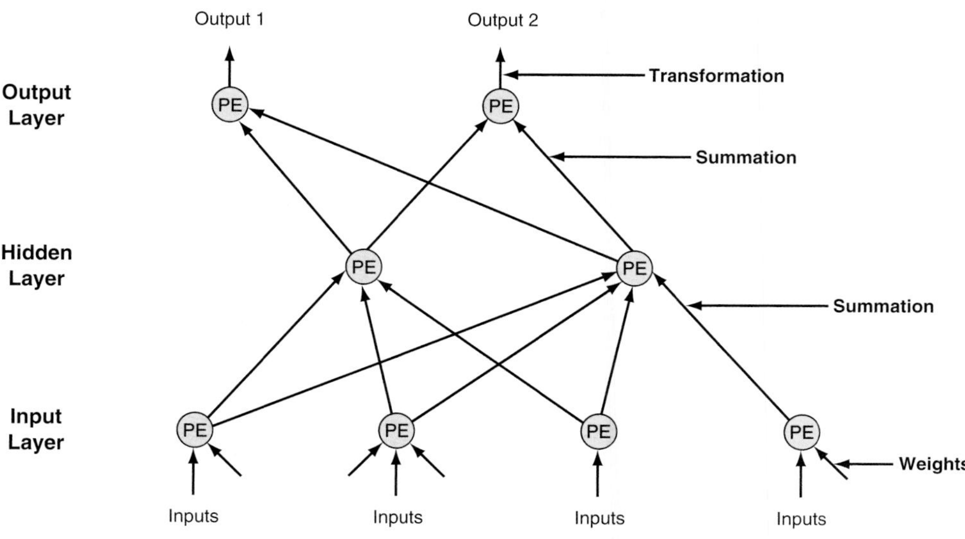

FIGURE 12.5 Neural network with one hidden layer.

layer (which could actually be several layers) indicates that additional processing is needed before a final output can be derived. Note the interconnections that exist between any PE and the various PEs at a forward layer.

Like biological networks, neurons can be interconnected in different ways. In processing information, many of the processing elements perform their computations at the same time. This **parallel processing** resembles the way the brain works, and it differs from the serial processing of conventional computing.

PROCESSING INFORMATION IN THE NETWORK. Once the structure of a network has been determined and the network constructed, information can be processed. Several concepts related to processing are important.

Each *input* corresponds to the value of a single attribute. All inputs—including qualitative attributes, voice, signals from monitoring equipment, or pictures—must be preprocessed into binary (0 and 1) equivalencies.

As noted earlier, the computed *output* of the network is the solution to a problem. Remember that the outputs may be part of a larger cycle, in which they become inputs for another stage of processing in the network.

HARDWARE AND SOFTWARE. Although neural computing is structured to run on mutiple processors (CPUs), it is considerably less expensive and simpler to run it on a single processor. Most current neural network applications use software simulations with a single processor expedited by the use of special acceleration computation boards. Thus, applications can even run on a PC. In the future, it will eventually become economically feasible to run some ANNs on mutiple processors.

BENEFITS AND APPLICATIONS OF NEURAL NETWORKS. The value of neural network technology includes its usefulness for pattern recognition, learning, and the interpretation of incomplete and "noisy" inputs.

Neural networks have the potential to provide some of the human characteristics of problem solving that are difficult to simulate using the logical, analytical techniques of DSS or even expert systems. One of these characteristics is **pattern recognition**. Neural networks can analyze large quantities of data to establish patterns and characteristics in situations where the logic or rules are not known. An example would be loan applications. By reviewing many historical cases of applicants' questionnaires and the decisions made (yes or no), the ANN can create "patterns" or "profiles" of applications that should be approved, or denied. A new application is matched against the pattern. If it comes close enough, the computer classifies it as a "yes" or "no"; otherwise it goes to a human for a decision. Neural networks are especially useful for financial applications such as determining when to buy or sell stock (see Trippi and Turban, 1996, for examples).

Neural networks have several other benefits:

- ***Fault tolerance.*** If there are many processing nodes, damage to a few nodes or links does not bring the system to a halt.
- ***Generalization.*** When a neural network is presented with an incomplete or previously unseen input, it can generalize to produce a reasonable response.
- ***Adaptability.*** The network learns in new environments. The new cases are used immediately to retrain the program and keep it updated.
- ***Forecasting capabilities.*** Similar to statistics, here, too, prediction is made based on historical data.

Beyond its role as an alternative computing mechanism, neural computing can be combined with other computer-based information systems to produce powerful hybrid systems, as we show later.

In general, ANNs do not do well at tasks that are not done well by people. For example, speedy arithmetic and transaction processing tasks are not suitable for ANNs and are best accomplished by conventional computers. Specific areas of business that are well suited to the assistance of ANNs include the following:

- ***Data mining:*** Finding data in large and complex databases, and in Web sites, as shown in Chapter 11
- ***Tax fraud:*** Identifying, enhancing, and finding irregularities
- ***Financial services:*** Identifying patterns in stock market data and assisting in stock and bond trading strategies; commodities selection and trading; mortgage underwriting; pricing IPOs; and foreign rate exchange forecast (see Trippi and Turban, 1996, and Peray, 1999)
- ***Loan application evaluation:*** Judging worthiness of loan applications based on patterns in previous application information (customer credit scoring)
- ***Solvency prediction:*** Assessing the strengths and weaknesses of corporations and predicting possible failures
- ***New product analysis:*** Sales forecasting and targeted marketing
- ***Airline fare management:*** Seat demand and crew scheduling
- ***Evaluation of personnel and job candidates:*** Matching personnel data to job requirements and performance criteria
- ***Resource allocation based on historical, experiential data:*** Finding allocations that will maximize outputs
- ***Identifying takeover targets:*** Predicting which companies are most likely to be acquired by other companies
- ***Signature validation:*** Matching signatures against those on file as valid
- ***Prediction:*** Anticipating employee performance, and behavior and personnel requirements
- ***Insurance fraud detection:*** Finding fraud patterns (see *hnc.com*)
- ***Credit card fraud detection:*** Analyzing purchasing patterns for fast detection of fraud (see the *IT at Work* on the facing page)

Neural computing is emerging as an effective technology in pattern recognition. This capability is being translated to many applications (e.g., see Haykin, 1998; Chen, 1996; and Medsker, 1995) and is sometimes integrated with fuzzy logic.

Fuzzy Logic

Fuzzy logic deals with uncertainties by simulating the process of human reasoning, allowing the computer to behave less precisely and logically than conventional computers do. Fuzzy logic is a technique developed by Zadeh (1994), and its use is gaining momentum (Nguyen and Walker, 1999). The rationale behind this approach is that decision making is not always a matter of black and white, true or false. It often involves gray areas where the term *maybe* is more appropriate. In fact, creative decision-making processes are often unstructured, playful, contentious, and rambling.

According to experts, productivity of decision makers can improve manyfold using fuzzy logic (e.g., see Nguyen and Walker, 1999). At the present time, there

IT at Work

BANKS ARE CRACKING DOWN ON CREDIT CARD FRAUD

www.visa.com

Only 0.2 percent of Visa International's turnover in 1995 was lost to fraud, but at $655 million it is a loss well worth addressing. Visa is now concentrating its efforts on reversing the number of fraudulent transactions by using neural network technology.

Most people stick to a well-established pattern of card use and only rarely splurge on expensive nonessentials. Neural networks are designed to notice when a card that is usually used to buy gasoline once a week is suddenly used to buy a number of tickets to the latest theater premiere on Broadway.

Visa's participating banks believe the neural network technology has been successful. Bank of America uses the cardholder risk identification system (CRIS) and has cut fraudulent card use by up to two-thirds. Toronto Dominion Bank found that losses were reduced, and overall customer service improved, with the introduction of neural computing. Another bank recorded savings of $5.5 million in six months. In 1994, Visa member banks lost more than $148 million to counterfeiters; by 1995, that figure was down to $124 million—a drop of more than 16 percent. With numbers like that, the $2 million Visa spent to implement CRIS certainly seems worth the investment. In fact, Visa says, CRIS had paid for itself in one year.

In 1995, CRIS conducted over 16 billion transactions. By 2000, VisaNet (Visa's data warehouse and e-mail operations) and CRIS were handling more than 5,250 transactions per second. By fall 2000, CRIS was able to notify banks of fraud within a few minutes of a transaction. The only downside to CRIS is that occasionally the system prompts a call to a cardholder's spouse when an out-of-the-ordinary item is charged, such as a surprise vacation trip or a diamond ring. After all, no one wants to spoil surprises for loved ones.

Sumitomo Credit Service Co., a credit card issuer in Japan, is using Falcon, a neural network–based system from HNC Corp. The product works well reading Japanese characters, protecting 18 million cardholders in Japan.

For Further Exploration: What is the advantage of CRIS over an automatic check against the balance in the account? What is the advantage of CRIS against a set of rules such as "Call a human authorizer when the purchase price is more than 200 percent of the average previous bill"?

Sources: Condensed from: "Visa Stamps Out Fraud," *International Journal of Retail and Distribution Management,* Vol. 23, No. 11, Winter 1995, p. viii; "Visa Cracks Down on Fraud," *Information Week,* August 26, 1996; and customer success stories at *hnc.com* (2001).

---

are only a few examples of pure fuzzy logic applications in business, mainly in prediction-system behavior (e.g., see Peray, 1999, for investment, and Flanagan, 2000, for project evaluation). An interesting application is available at *yatra.net/solutions,* where fuzzy logic is used to support services for corporate travelers (see *Information Week,* May 15, 2000).

HYBRID SYSTEMS. More often, fuzzy logic is used together with other intelligent systems. (As a matter of fact, intelligent systems are frequently integrated with other intelligent systems or with conventional systems such as decision support systems.) The following examples illustrate such *hybrid* systems.

Developing Marketing Strategy. Developing marketing strategy is a complex process performed by several people working as a team. The process involves many tasks that must be performed sequentially, with contributions from corporate experts. Numerous marketing strategy models were developed over the years to support the process. Unfortunately, most of the models support only one IT goal (e.g., to perform forecasting). A proposal to integrate expert systems, fuzzy logic, and ANN was made by Li (2000). The process of developing marketing strategy and the support of the three technologies in that process is shown in Figure 12.6 (page 546). The hybrid system is powerful enough to incorporate

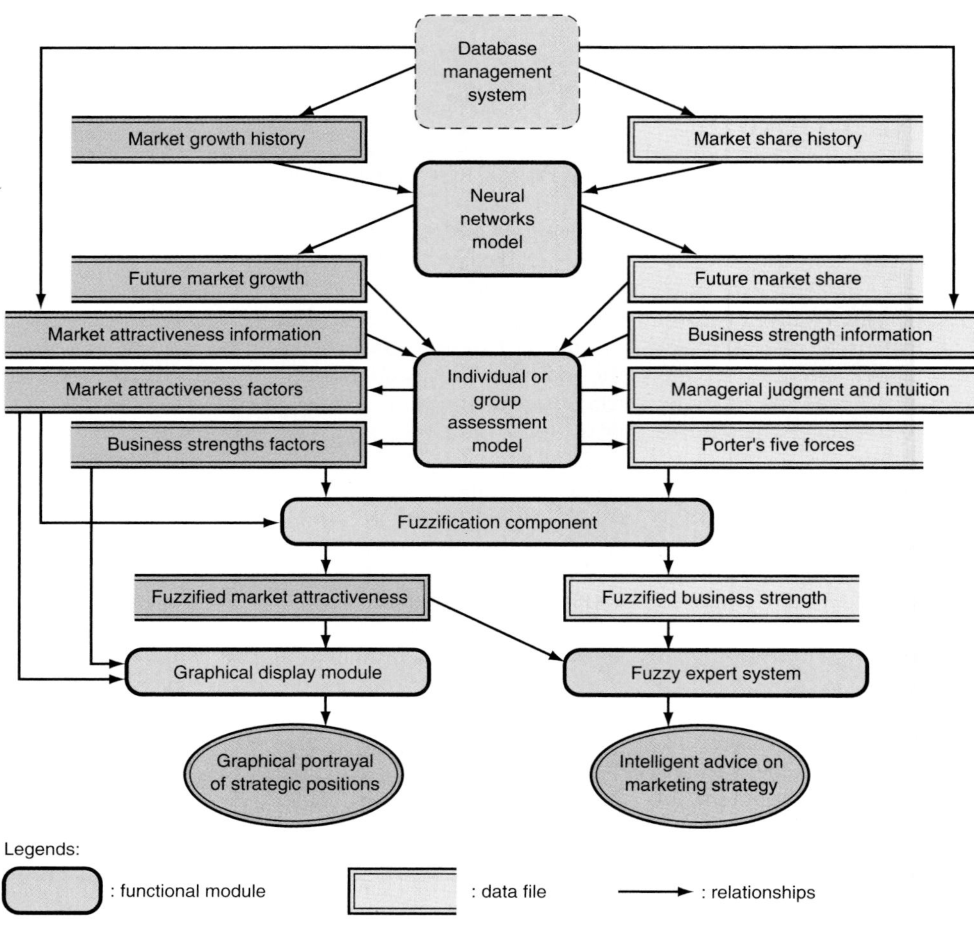

FIGURE 12.6 The architecture of a hybrid intelligent system. (*Source:* Reprinted from *Decision Support Systems*, January 2000, Fig. 1, p. 399. Reprinted from *Decision Support Systems*, January 2000, S. Li, "The Development of a Hybrid Intelligent System for Developing Market Strategy," p. 399. © 2000, with permission from Elsevier Science.)

strategic models such as Porter's five forces and the directional policy matrices model. The integrated technologies and their roles are:

- ***Neural networks.*** These are used to predict future market share and growth.
- ***Expert systems.*** These provide intelligent advice on developing market strategy to individuals and to the planning team.
- ***Fuzzy logic.*** This helps managers to handle uncertainties and fuzziness of data and information.

The integration of the technologies helps in sharing information, coordination, and evaluation. The system is designed to support both individuals and groups. It allows for inclusion of users' judgment in implementing the model.

Optimizing the Design Process. Another example of a hybrid system is one by Lam et al. (2000). They applied an integrated fuzzy logic, ANN, and algorithmic optimization to the design of a complex design process for ceramic casting manufacturing. The ANN estimates input needed by the fuzzy-rule base and also provides evaluation of the objective function of the optimization model. The system was successfully used, enabling fast and consistent production decision making.

12.4 INTELLIGENT AGENTS

Intelligent agents (IAs) represent a relatively new technology with the potential to become one of the most important tools of information technology in the twenty-first century (see Murch and Johnson, 1999, and Bigus et al., 2001). IAs can alleviate the most critical limitation of the Internet—information overflow—and facilitate electronic commerce. Before we look at their capabilities, let us determine what we mean by intelligent agents.

As indicated in Chapter 4, intelligent agents are known by several names. Notable are: *software agents, wizards, knowbots,* and *softbots.* The names sometime reflect the nature of the agent. Note that the term *agent* is derived from the concept of agency, referring to employing someone to act on your behalf.

There are several definitions of what an intelligent agent is. Each reflects the definer's perspective. Here are two examples:

- Intelligent agents are software entities that carry out some set of operations on behalf of a user or another program, with some degree of independence or autonomy, and in so doing, employ some knowledge or representation of the user's goals or desires. They do so to accomplish a task or a goal (e.g., see Levesque and Lakemeyer, 2001).
- Autonomous agents are computational systems that inhabit some complex dynamic environment, sense and act autonomously in this environment, and by doing so realize a set of goals or tasks for which they are designed (Maes, 1994, p. 108).

Characteristics of Intelligent Agents

While there is no single commonly accepted definition for the term "intelligent agent," there are several traits or abilities that many people think of when they are discussing intelligent agents. These are summarized in Table 12.6. Note that certain agents lack some of these characteristics.

TABLE 12.6 Characteristics of Intelligent Agents

Characteristic	Description
Autonomous	Capable of acting on its own, being goal-oriented and collaborative, able to alter its activity if needed (see Maes, 1994 and Maes et al., 1999).
Proactive response	The agents' response must be corrective (i.e., they must exhibit goal-directed behavior by taking the initiative).
Unobstructive	Must work without constant attention of its "master"; may be offsite (remote executions).
Modular	Transportable across different systems and networks. Many agents are not mobile (e.g., Wizards in spreadsheets).
Dedicated and automated	Usually designed to carry on a specific, usually repetitive, normally difficult task. Multifaceted jobs need a multiagent system.
Interactive	Designed to interact with human agents or software programs (see opening case). This is critical for a multiagent system.
Conditional processing, practice	Using rule-based or pattern-matching logic (supplied by the user), the agent can make decisions in choosing contexts in which they perceive changes in the environment or can send alerts to the user in a timely manner.
Friendly and dependable	To be effective, must be believable and exhibit easy interactivity with people.
Able to learn	Only a few agents can really do some learning, for example, observing the user and making predictions on his or her future behavior. Agent must be highly autonomous.

What Can Intelligent Agents Do?

The following are the major tasks that can be performed by IAs.

1. ***Information access and navigation*** are today's major applications of intelligent agents (see Chapter 4).
2. ***Decision support and empowerment.*** Knowledge workers need increased support, especially in decision making. IA can facilitate decision making and empower employees, as shown in the *IT at Work* illustration below.
3. ***Repetitive office activity.*** There is a pressing need to automate tasks performed by administrative and clerical personnel in functional areas, such as sales or customer support, to reduce labor costs and increase office productivity. Today, labor costs are estimated to be as much as 60 percent of the total cost of information delivery, and intelligent agents can help reduce those costs by eliminating some of the need for human labor or by expediting the work, so less labor is needed.
4. ***Mundane personal activity.*** In a fast-paced society, time-strapped individuals need new ways to minimize the time spent on routine personal tasks like booking airline tickets so that they can devote more time to professional activities. One specific form of intelligent agents is the voice-activated interface agent that reduces the burden on the user of having to explicitly command the computer.
5. ***Search and retrieval.*** It is not possible to directly manipulate a distributed database system in an electronic commerce setting with millions of data objects. Users will have to delegate the tasks of searching and of cost comparison to agents. These agents perform the tedious, time-consuming, and repetitive tasks of searching databases, retrieving and filtering information, and delivering results to the user (see Chapter 4).

IT at Work

...in Human Resources Management

EMPOWERING EMPLOYEES BY USING SOFTWARE AGENTS

Fringe benefits are frequently likened to a cafeteria—people mix and match what they like within the constraints of what is available and how much they can use. The management of fringe benefits is a very resource-intensive process, especially when thousands of employees are involved. Nike and Signet Bank both installed special software that empowers employees to directly manage their fringe benefits selections. Employees access the human resources databases by computer and conduct activities such as selecting and changing benefits or making charitable contributions through payroll deductions.

The software agent that supports these activities is called Electronic Workforce (from Edify Corp., *edify.com/products*). It enables employers to delegate to any employee supported by a computer some time-consuming and repetitive tasks that were previously conducted by human resources (HR) employees. Employees enter and delete data, command the computer to perform certain transactions, and interpret information. If they make mistakes or request benefits they are not eligible for, the agent automatically alerts them to the problem. Previously, paperwork would have to be routed to an employee for corrections and then back to the HR department. The use of the agents enables companies to increase benefits options, and employee satisfaction, with the same or even fewer human resources employees.

For Further Exploration: Can you imagine what would happen if there were no IAs to help in the choosing of benefits? How can an agent know that an employee made a mistake?

Source: Compiled from Edify Corporation, *edify.com/products* (2001).

6. ***Domain experts.*** It is advisable to model costly expertise and make it widely available. "Expert" software agents could be models of real-world agents, such as translators, lawyers, diplomats, union negotiators, stockbrokers, and even clergy.
7. ***Mobile agents.*** Some agents may be either static, residing on the client machine to manage a user interface, for instance, or mobile. **Mobility** is the degree to which the agents themselves travel through the network. **Mobile agents** can move from one Internet site to another and can send data to and retrieve data from the user, who can focus on other work in the meantime. This can be very helpful to users. For example, if users want to continuously monitor an electronic auction that takes a few days, they essentially would have to be online continuously for days. Software applications that automatically watch auctions and stocks for you are readily available. Another example of a mobile agent is one that travels from site to site, looking for information on a certain stock as instructed by the user. When the stock price hits a certain level, or if there is news about the stock, the agent alerts the user. What is unique about a mobile agent is that it is a software application that moves on its own to different computers to execute various tasks.
8. ***Clerical and management activities.*** Intelligent agents can even be used to assist clerks, professional staff, and managers in performing their activities. Some tasks that an agent can do are: advise, alert, broadcast, browse, critique, distribute, enlist, empower, explain, filter, guide, identify, match, monitor, navigate, negotiate, organize, present, query, report, remind, retrieve, schedule, search, secure, solicit, sort, store, suggest, summarize, teach, translate, and watch.

Applications of Intelligent Agents

We described some intelligent agent applications in Chapters 4, 5, and 9. Here are additional applications:

User Interface. For many users, a graphical user interface has been considered difficult to learn and use, especially its nonroutine functions. As capabilities and applications of computers improve, the user interface needs to accommodate the increases in complexity. Intelligent agents can help with both these problems. Intelligent agent technology allows systems to monitor the user's actions, develop models of user abilities, and automatically help out when interface problems arise.

Of special interest is Microsoft's animated family of agents (e.g., Merlin, Robby, Genie, and Peedy). They can appear in Web pages, displaying everything from simple idling activities such as yawning to attention-grabbing motions. Thus, even social interaction can be incorporated with the user interface. (For details see *microsoft.com/msagent; argolink.com/agent;* and Barker, 1998).

Operating Systems Agents. Agents can assist in the use of operating systems. For example, Microsoft Corp. has several systems agents (called Wizards) in its NT operating system. Some reside on the NT server, while others are on the workstations. These agents assist in the following tasks: add user accounts, manage file and folder access, add printer, add/remove programs, obtain licenses, and install new modems. They also assist with group management and network-client administration. (For details, consult *microsoft.com.*)

Spreadsheet Agents. Spreadsheet agents make the software more friendly. An example of an intelligent agent is the Wizard feature found in Microsoft's Excel. The Wizard is a built-in package capability that "watches" users and offers suggestions as they attempt to perform tasks by themselves. For example, suppose you are trying to format a group of spreadsheet cells or locations in a particular manner. If you are not skilled at using the spreadsheet package, you might try to format each cell individually. A much faster method is to select the entire group of designated cells and then conduct the format once for all the selected locations.

Suppose a friend of yours was watching you format the cells and noted that you worked on the individual cells. Suppose further that your friend was more of an expert on the software package than you were. Presumably, he or she would tell you that you were formatting unproductively. In a similar sense, the Wizard can detect your laborious, repetitive attempts and notify you that there is a better way, or even take the next step and offer to complete the remainder of the formatting task for you.

Workflow and Task Management Agents. Administrative management includes both workflow management and areas such as computer/telephone integration, where processes are defined and then automated. In these areas, users not only need to make processes more efficient, but also need to reduce the cost of human agents. Intelligent agents can be used to ascertain, then automate, user wishes or *business processes.*

Negotiation in Electronic Commerce. A challenging system is one in which agents need to negotiate with each other. Such systems are especially applicable to electronic commerce. Consider the vacation arrangement episode in the opening case. There, the scenario can be extended to one in which the user's agent will *negotiate* the best price for the car, hotel, airfare, and so on.

NETWORKED INTELLIGENT AGENTS. Although in 2001 most agents were working individually, there is a growing trend to have groups of agents working together, usually in a networked environment. This is called a *multiagent system,* an example of which follows:

Integrating IT ...in Production and Operations Management

Intelligent Agents Trim Papermaking Costs. Madison Paper Industries, a 282-employee company located in Maine, was struggling to compete against larger papermakers. Costs of transportation from suppliers and to customers seemed to be high, paper loss during production was cutting into profits, and scheduling work was difficult and lengthy. A multiagent system, initially developed at Carnegie Mellon University (*cs.smu.edu/~softagents/mas_interop.html*) and commercialized by IBM's cooperative decision support group (*research.ibm.com/coopds*), was implemented in an attempt to solve the problem. The knowledge for the system was solicited from human schedulers whose experience over the years created a pool of candidate scheduling solutions.

The agent-based system evaluates each of the solutions in light of multiple business objectives (cost, speed of delivery, and so on). The human schedulers now work with the system interactively, posting "what-if" questions to help find a solution that best fits a set of multiple business objectives that frequently conflict with each other. Working as an intelligent assistant, the system frees the schedulers of real-time computational tasks, giving them time to concentrate on more important tasks.

Traditional approaches to scheduling in the paper industry have involved scheduling each process independently, often using different software packages for each step. Because of the lack of interaction between applications, the combined schedules have been less than satisfactory in the past. They might, for instance, minimize trim waste at the expense of an inefficient, costly vehicle-loading schedule. In contrast, IBM's networked IA approach simultaneously considers numerous scheduling objectives and multiple manufacturing and distribution stages in a global multicriteria optimizing framework. The system cut paper trim losses by about 6 tons per day at Madison Paper, as well as 10 percent of freight costs, for annual savings of more than $5 million. (*Sources:* Compiled from *IEEE Intelligent Systems,* March–April 1999, and from the Carnegie Mellon University and IBM Web sites, March 2000.)

12.5 WEB-BASED EXPERTS AND INTELLIGENT SYSTEMS

The relationship between expert systems and the Internet and intranets is a two-way street. The Net supports expert systems (and other artificial intelligence) applications, and ESs support the Net.

Using Expert Systems on the Net

One of the justifications for an ES is the potential to provide knowledge and advice to a large number of users. By disseminating knowledge to many users, the cost per user becomes small, making ESs very attractive. However, according to Eriksson (1996), attaining this goal proved very difficult. Because advisory systems are used infrequently, they need a large number of users to justify their construction. As a result, a very few ESs were disseminating knowledge to many users. However, the widespread availability and use of the Internet and intranets now provide the opportunity to disseminate expertise and knowledge to mass audiences. By implementing expert systems (and other intelligent systems) as knowledge servers, it becomes economically feasible and profitable to publish expertise on the Net. This implementation approach is described in Eriksson (1996) and in Huntington (2000).

ESs can be transferred over the Net not only to human users, but also to other computerized systems, including DSSs, robotics, and databases. Another possibility is ES construction over the Net. Here, collaboration between builders, experts, and knowledge engineers can be facilitated by intranet-based groupware. (For example, end-user colloboration in developing, refining and testing hybrid intelligent systems is described in the journal *Database for Advances in Information Systems,* 1998.) Collaboration can reduce the cost of building an ES. Knowledge acquisition costs can be reduced, for example, in cases where there are several experts, or where the expert is in a different location from the knowledge engineer. Knowledge maintenance can also be facilitated by the use of the Net.

The Web also can support the spread of multimedia-based expert systems. Such systems, referred to as *intellimedia systems,* support the integration of extensive multimedia applications and ESs. Such systems can be very helpful for remote users, such as in the tourism industry and in remote equipment failure diagnosis (for details, see Fuerst et al., 1995). Examples of various types of Web-based ESs are described in the *IT at Work* box on page 552.

AUTOMATIC LANGUAGE TRANSLATION ON THE WEB. Translation of Web sites from one language to another has been attempted by intelligent systems since the mid-1990s (e.g., see *IEEE Expert,* 1996). Today it is done by many companies. Even Netscape 6 browser offers AutoTranslate, a feature that allows automatic translation of Web pages from one language to another. In fall 2000, the system was able to support 14 language pairs (e.g., from English to Japanese, Spanish,

IT at Work
WEB-BASED EXPERT SYSTEMS

Integrating IT ...in Government Production & Operations Management, Marketing, and Health Care

THE U.S. GOVERNMENT USES EXPERT SYSTEMS. Want to see the latest ES developments at the U.S. Department of Labor's Occupational Safety and Health Administration (OSHA)? Access the OSHA Web site at *osha.gov.* Try the Confined Spaces Advisor that provides guidance to help employers protect workers from the hazards of entry into permit-required confined spaces. The system, developed in the EXSYS Web Run Time Engine (WREN), helps determine if a space is covered by OSHA's Permit-Required Confined Spaces Regulation. OSHA also has many other systems (*osha.gov;* click on Expert Advisors). These include Hazard Awareness, Asbestos Advisor, Fire Safety, and Lead in Construction Advisor.

CUSTOMER SERVICE ONLINE IN JAPAN. Ebara Manufacturing, a Japanese pump manufacturer, produces several thousand kinds of pumps for many industries. Traditionally, customers would just ask for a pump. Sales personnel had to figure out what kind. As products got more numerous and sophisticated, this manual system started to break down. Ebara fixed this problem with an online expert system. The system takes customers through a series of questions that connect their needs to specific products, often in less than a minute.

CANSTOR—CANADIAN STORAGE GUIDELINES FOR CEREALS AND OILSEEDS. The Department of Agriculture and Agri-Food in Canada use an expert system to assist farmers and granary operators to make storage decisions for cereals and oilseeds, thus reducing losses from insects, contamination, and moisture. CanStor is available from the Web or as a *downloadable* application. With the Web version, the user fills out and submits a consultation to the intelligent system, which receives the input parameters and passes them to an ActiveX component registered in the Web server. The ActiveX component interacts with the necessary applications in the Web server and performs the computations. Once the computations are completed, the results, which may include recommendations from the system as well as pointers to a wealth of online supporting information, are returned to the user. (For details see *http://res2.agr.calwinnipeg/canstoronweb.*)

ISSUING INSURANCE POLICIES. On-the-spot policy issuing is becoming a reality thanks to auto-underwriting expert systems. A Web-based application entry, in electronic form, enables quick review of medical records and previous vehicle accidents. The results of the search are entered into the expert system, which configures the cost and prints a policy.

DIAGNOSIS FROM A DISTANCE. Reliant Energy HL&P of Houston, Texas, developed an ES to quickly diagnose energy distribution problems, using data collected by sensors and transmitted to the ES. The results of the ES's analysis are e-mailed to interested parties.

For Further Exploration: Placing expertise online reduces the cost to consumers. So why do experts do it? See *guru.com* or *allexpert.com.*

---

or Chinese). The browser identifies automatically the language on the screen, and asks the user to what language the translation should be done. Some search engines provide a similar service. For example, Altavista will make Web translations for you (*babefish.altavista.digital.com/translate.dyn*).

Other Web translation services are readily available. For example, a Korean ISP company provides automatic translation from Japanese to Korean, so potential shoppers in Korea can learn what's available in Japan. Several vendors provide translation online for free (*freetranslation.com*) or for a fee (*worldpoint.com*).

The major potential contributions of intelligent systems to the Internet are summarized in Table 12.7. (For details see O'Leary, 1996.) Information about the relationship of expert systems, intelligent agents, and other AI systems and the Internet is readily available on the Internet itself (e.g., see *primenet.com.pcai*).

TABLE 12.7 Artificial Intelligence Contributions to the Internet

Technology	Application
Intelligent agents	Assist Web browsing.
Intelligent agents	Assist in finding information.
Intelligent agents	Assist in matching items.
Intelligent agents	Filter e-mail.
Intelligent agents	Access databases, summarize information.
Expert systems	Improve Internet security.
Intelligent agents	Match queries to users with "canned" answers to frequently asked questions (FAQs).
WWW robots (spiders), Intelligent agents	Conduct information retrieval and discovery, smart search engines ("metasearch").
Expert systems	Conduct intelligent browsing of qualitative databases.
Expert systems	Browse large documents (knowledge decomposition).
Intelligent agents	Monitor data and alert for actions (e.g., looking for Web site changes), monitor users and usage.

A WEB-BASED INTELLIGENT TUTORING SYSTEM. Many companies are introducing Internet-based *intelligent tutoring systems (ITSs)* as a cost-effective approach to deliver training to wherever trainees are. This is especially beneficial in complex domains where students must master a variety of concepts and apply them in unique situations. For such cases regular training over the Internet is not enough. With ITS, programs can be customized, and instructors can monitor students' progress from a distance. Course developers can easily maintain and update training materials, and the instructor's productivity is enhanced by ITS. These systems also provide for customized training and for remediation, similar to one-to-one "private" tutoring. ITSs use different intelligent systems, ranging from expert systems to case-based reasoning (see Jackson, 1999, and Turban and Aronson, 2001), which contains realistic problem-solving situations and solutions.

The case base of examples and exercises captures realistic problem-solving situations and presents them to the student as virtual simulations. Each example or exercise includes the following:

- A multimedia description of the problem, which may evolve over time (such as in a tactical scenario)
- A description of the correct actions to take, including order-independent, optional, and alternative steps
- A multimedia explanation of why these steps are correct
- A list of methods for determining whether students have correctly executed the steps
- A list of principles that must be learned to take the correct action

Students solve the problems interactively, which gives them an opportunity to practice the necessary skills and also reveals any knowledge deficiencies. ITSs monitors students as they perform these simulations, diagnosing the strengths and weaknesses of their performance, and tailors instruction to correct weaknesses.

Web-based systems are a new paradigm for ITS education. An example is the ITS Authoring Tool from Stottler Henke Associates (*shai.com*), which helps build enterprise training programs that can be delivered on intranets and corporate portals. (For more on Web-based tutoring, see *PC AI*, July–August 1999, and Lance, 2000).

12.6 SUPPORTING CREATIVITY

The intelligent systems described so far in this chapter can increase productivity and quality—but are they really intelligent? If we check the definition of intelligent behavior, we would probably conclude that today's systems are not intelligent. However, let us look at computer programs that do exhibit what we might call *creative behavior.*

Rasmus (July 1995) gives an example of two creativity tools. The first one, called Copycat, is a program that seeks analogies in patterns of alphabetical letters. Identifying patterns is a property of intelligence. Copycat, which consists of several intelligent agents, can find analogies to sets or strings of letters, for example, transforming a sequence "aabc" to "aabd." This ability can be generalized to other problems that require conceptual understanding and the manipulation of things. The ability of the program to anticipate the meaning of the transformation and to find analogous fits provides evidence that computers can mimic a human being's ability to create analogies.

The second system, AARON, is a program that can draw. Its output can be considered to be art. Its developer, Harold Cohen, worked for 15 years to create a comprehensive knowledge base to support AARON. Similar programs have been developed to teach computers to write poems, compose music, and create works in other media. The increased size of knowledge bases, processing speed, and storage enables such programs to create artwork of good quality. However, we are still far away from having machines that exhibit more creativity and additional characteristics of intelligence, such as "use reason in solving problems" or "deal with perplexing situations."

Supporting Idea Generation and Creativity

As indicated earlier, intelligent systems by themselves are not very creative. Even the advanced systems such as Copycat exhibit limited creativity. Commerical attempts to automate creativity are available from companies such as Imagination-engines.com, which even received a U.S. patent (#5,659,666) on a neural network–based creativity machine. On the other hand, some software programs are fairly successful in *increasing* humans' creativity.

In the past, it was believed that an individual's creative ability stemmed primarily from personality traits such as inventiveness, independence, individuality, enthusiasm, and flexibility. However, several studies have now indicated that individual creativity is not so much a function of individual traits as was once believed, and that it can be learned and improved. This understanding has led innovative companies to recognize that the key to fostering creativity may be the development of an idea-nurturing work environment. Idea-generation methods and techniques for use by individuals or in groups, are consequently being developed.

Manual methods for supporting idea generation (such as brainstorming in a group) can be very successful in certain settings. However, there are circumstances where such an approach is either not economically feasible or not possible. For example, manual methods will not work or will not be effective in group creativity sessions when:

- There is a poor facilitator (or there is no facilitator).
- There is no time to conduct a proper idea-generation session.
- It is too expensive to conduct an idea-generation session.
- The subject matter is too sensitive for a face-to-face idea-generation session.
- There are not enough participants, the mix of participants is not optimal, or there is no climate for idea generation.

Thus, manual methods designed to facilitate individual creativity may not work for all individuals or in all types of situations. In such cases, it makes sense to try to electronically induce idea generation (see Marakas and Elam, 1997). Massetti (1996) demonstrated in experiments that computer-enabled people were more creative in problem solving. (For creativity and the Web see *ozemail.com.au/%7Ecareman/creative*.)

IDEA-GENERATION SOFTWARE. *Idea-generation software* is designed to help stimulate a single user or a group to come up with new ideas, options, and choices. The user does all the work, but the software encourages and pushes just like a personal trainer. Although idea-generation software is still relatively new, there are several packages on the market. Representative products are Brainstorm (from Mustang Software), Creative Whackpack (from Creative Think), IdeaFisher (from IdeaFisher Systems), and Think Tank (from Living Videotext).

Various approaches are used by idea-generating software to increase the flow of ideas to the user. One package (IdeaFisher) has an associative lexicon of the English language that cross-references words and phrases. These associative links, based on analogies and metaphors, make it easy for the user to be fed words related to a given theme.

Some software packages use questions to prompt the user toward new, unexplored patterns of thought. This helps users to break out of cyclical thinking patterns, conquer mental blocks, or deal with bouts of procrastination. Creative Whackpack provides techniques to "whack" the user out of habitual thought patterns.

Several products make use of visualization techniques to facilitate creativity. Examples are:

- The Brain (*thebrain.com*) can link topics or thoughts in a graphical environment that moves, depending on what thought you are focusing on. Similarly, spiderdiagrams, or *mind maps*, diagram information and supposedly mimic the layout of the brain, showing relationships among objects. This technique can help to organize thoughts. MindManager (from *mindjet.com*) replicates the mind mapping process.
- Another approach is for the computer to help people to visualize thoughts in 3-D (e.g., see *vizbang.com*).
- Yet another approach is to lay information on a map, where peaks represent the highest volume of information on any issue and the valleys link the issues together (*aurigin.com*).

Computer-assisted brainstorming (CAB) programs enhance creative thinking through the use of built-in creativity techniques along with a well-defined goal-oriented structure. Every CAB program incorporates creativity techniques that ask questions and urge the user to go on, thus shortening the incubation time for new ideas and creative problem solutions. The computer also assists in note-taking and reporting, freeing the user from these tasks. Brainstorming can be done alone, using the computer as a partner and "mind mirror." Or it can be done in an asynchronous group process: Group members do not have to participate at a certain time but can instead electronically transfer CAB workfiles (Trost, 2001).

Finally, Onestep (from *enfish.com*) is a free browser that among other things indexes your hard drive. Besides allowing you to retrieve data in seconds, it also suggests relationships between the files and other data that can lead to idea generation.

Idea-generation software for groups works somewhat differently from such software for individuals. Participants in groups create ideas simultaneously. Ideas generated by participants are shown to other participants, stimulating electronic discussion or generation of more ideas. A large number of ideas is usually generated in a short time. These ideas are then organized, debated, and prioritized by the group, all electronically, as shown in Chapter 10.

The benefits of creativity enhancement afforded by idea-generating software are numerous. A competitive advantage can be realized in all industries because of the many new ideas and approaches that can be facilitated electronically. Idea-generation software acts as a catalyst to generate alternative solutions that help operations run more efficiently and more competitively.

MANAGERIAL ISSUES

The implementation of intelligent systems is an extremely important yet difficult task in organizations. Here are some issues to be considered:

1. ***Cost-benefit and justification.*** While some of the benefits of intelligent systems are tangible, it is difficult to put a dollar value on the intangible benefits of many intelligent systems. Improved customer service, quality, cycle time, and safety could be more important than tangible benefits, but are difficult to measure quantitively.
2. ***Heightened expectations.*** When there is too much expectation and hope associated with intelligent technologies, management may get discouraged. There is currently a very high failure rate (some estimate it as high as 85 percent). More accurate and realistic goals will help increase the chance of success.
3. ***Acquiring knowledge.*** Intelligent systems are built on experts' knowledge. How to acquire this knowledge is a major problem, and not just a technical one. For example, how can an expert be motivated to contribute his or her knowledge?
4. ***System acceptance.*** The acceptance of intelligent systems by the IS department and the integration of such systems with mainstream IT is a critical success factor. There are psychological, social, technical, and political reasons for the IS department to reject the new technologies. Without the cooperation of the IS department, these systems are likely to fail.

5. ***System integration.*** Intelligent systems can succeed as standalone systems, but they have a broader area of applications when integrated with other computer-based information systems. This is another reason why the IS department must cooperate. Such hybrid systems are complex, but if they are successful, the rewards can be enormous.
6. ***Embedded technologies.*** Intelligent systems are expected to be embedded in at least 20 percent of all IT applications in about ten years. It is critical for any prudent management to closely examine the technologies and their business applicability.

7. ***Ethical issues.*** Finally, there can be ethical issues related to the implementation of expert systems and other intelligent systems. The actions performed by an expert system can be unethical, or even illegal. For example, the expert system may advise you to do something that will hurt someone, or invade the privacy of certain individuals.

   An example is the behavior of robots, and the possibility that the robots will not behave the way that they were programmed to. As a matter of fact there were many industrial accidents caused by robots that resulted in injuries and even deaths. The issue is, Should we employee productivity-saving devices that are not 100 percent safe?

   Another ethical issue is the use of knowledge extracted from people. The issue here is, Should a company compensate an employee when knowledge that he or she contributed is used by others? This issue is related to the motivation issue (see item 3 above). It is also related to privacy. Should people be informed as to who contributed certain knowledge?

   A final issue that needs to be addressed is that of dehumanization and the feeling that a machine can be smarter than some people (see Chapter 16). People may have different attitudes toward smart machines, which may be reflected in the manner in which they will work together.

ON THE WEB SITE... Additional resources, including the Virtual Company, quizzes, cases, updates, additional exercises, links, demos, and activities, can be found on the book's Web site.

KEY TERMS

Artificial intelligence (AI) *523*
Artificial neural network (ANN) *541*
Distance learning *528*
Expert system (ES) *526*
Fuzzy logic *544*
Inference engine *531*
Intelligent agent (IA) *547*
Knowledge base *524*
Machine learning *528*
Mobile agents *549*
Mobility (of agents) *549*
Natural language processing (NLP) *526*
Neural computing *541*
Organizational knowledge base *524*
Parallel processing *543*
Pattern recognition *543*
Robot *526*
Speech recognition *538*
Speech understanding *538*
Symbolic processing *525*
Turing test *524*
Visual recognition *528*
Voice portals *539*
Voice synthesis *539*
Weights *542*

CHAPTER HIGHLIGHTS (Numbers Refer to Learning Objectives)

- (1) The primary objective of AI is to build computers that will perform tasks that can be characterized as intelligent.
- (1) The major characteristics of AI are symbolic processing, use of heuristics instead of algorithms, and application of inference techniques.
- (1) AI has several major advantages: It is permanent; it can be easily duplicated and disseminated; it can be less expensive than human intelligence; it is consistent and thorough; and it can be documented.
- (1) The major application areas of AI are expert systems, natural language processing, speech understanding, intelligent robotics, computer vision, and intelligent computer-aided instruction.
- (2) Expert system technology attempts to transfer knowledge from experts and documented sources to the computer, in order to make that knowledge available to nonexperts for the purpose of solving difficult problems.
- (2) The major components of an ES are a knowledge base, inference engine, blackboard, user interface, and explanation subsystem.
- (2) The inference engine, or thinking mechanism, is a program of using the knowledge base, a way of reasoning with it to solve problems.
- (2) The ten generic categories of ES are interpretation, prediction, diagnosis, design, planning, monitoring, debugging, repair, instruction, and control.
- (2) Expert systems can provide many benefits. The most important are improvement in productivity and/or quality, preservation of scarce expertise, enhancing other systems, coping with incomplete information, and providing training.
- (3) Natural language processing (NLP) provides an opportunity for a user to communicate with a computer in day-to-day spoken language.
- (3) Speech recognition enables people to communicate with computers by voice. There are many benefits to this emerging technology.
- (4) Neural systems are composed of processing elements called artificial neurons. They are interconnected, and they receive, process, and deliver information. A group of connected neurons forms an artificial neural network (ANN).
- (4) Fuzzy logic is a technology that helps analyze situations under uncertainty. The technology can also be combined with an ES and ANN to conduct complex predictions and interpretations.
- (5) Software agents, some of which are called intelligent, can perform many mundane tasks, saving a considerable amount of time and improving quality.
- (6) The Web assists both in the development and dissemination of expertise worldwide. Automatic language translations and intelligent tutoring are two other applications of expert systems on the Web.
- (7) Intelligent systems can facilitate creativity and eventually will be embedded in machines that will exhibit creative behavior.

QUESTIONS FOR REVIEW

1. What is the Turing test?
2. List the major advantages that artificial intelligence has over natural intelligence.
3. List the major disadvantages of artificial intelligence when compared with natural intelligence.
4. Define a problem knowledge base and compare it with an organizational knowledge base.
5. List three major capabilities of an ES.
6. Explain how an ES can distribute (or redistribute) the available knowledge in an organization.
7. Define the major components of an ES.
8. Which component of ES is mostly responsible for the reasoning capability?
9. What is the function of the justifier?
10. Who are the potential users of ES?
11. List the ten generic categories of ES.
12. Describe some of the limitations of ES.
13. Describe a natural language and natural language processing.
14. What are the major advantages of NLP?
15. Distinguish between NLP and natural language generation.
16. List the major advantages of voice recognition.
17. What is an artificial neural network?
18. What are the major benefits and limitations of neural computing?
19. Define fuzzy logic, and describe its major features and benefits.
20. Define software agents. When can an agent be described as intelligent?
21. Describe the support that software can provide to creative thinking.

QUESTIONS FOR DISCUSSION

1. A major difference between a conventional decision support system and an ES is that the former can explain a "how" question whereas the latter can also explain a "why" question. Discuss.
2. What is the difference between voice recognition and voice understanding?
3. Compare and contrast neural computing and conventional computing.
4. Compare and contrast numeric and symbolic processing techniques.
5. Compare and contrast conventional processing with artificial intelligence processing.
6. Fuzzy logic is frequently combined with expert systems and/or neural computing. Explain the logic of such integration.
7. Why is it that ANNs can improve knowledge acquisition in cases where the experts are not available or not cooperating?
8. Review the various tasks that intelligent agents can perform. Do these tasks have anything in common?
9. How can an intelligent agent alleviate the information overload problem?
10. Deep Blue of IBM defeated the world chess champion, Kasparov, in 1997. If computers cannot think, how is such a defeat possible? Find some recent information about Deep Blue.
11. Explain why the Web is important to the future of expert systems.
12. Discuss the differences between supporting a human's creativity and creating programs that will behave creatively.
13. Explain how IT can facilitate idea generation. What are the advantages and disadvantages as compared with manual facilitation?

EXERCISES

1. Sofmic is a large software vendor. About twice a year, Sofmic acquires a small specialized software company. Recently, a decision was made to look for a software company in the area of neural computing. Currently, there are about 15 companies that would gladly cooperate as candidates for such acquisitions.

   Bill Gomez, the corporate CEO, asked that a recommendation for a candidate for acquisition be submitted to him within one week. "Make sure to use some computerized support for justification, preferably from the area of AI," he said. As a manager responsible for submitting the recommendation to Gomez, you need to select a computerized tool for conducting the analysis. Respond to the following points:

   a. Prepare a list of all the tools that you would consider.

   b. Prepare a list of the major advantages and disadvantages of each tool, as it relates to this specific case.

   c. Select a computerized tool.

   d. Mr. Gomez does not assign grades to your work. You make a poor recommendation and you are out. Therefore, carefully justify your recommendation.
2. Table 12.4 provides a list of ten categories of ES. Compile a list of ten examples from the various functional areas in an organization (accounting, finance, production, marketing, human resources, and so on) that will show functional applications as they are related to the ten categories.
3. Selecting projects for construction, research, or other purposes is a complex process.

   a. Find out why this is so.

   b. Explain why and how intelligent systems can help.

   c. Consult Machacha and Bhattacharya (2000) and Flanagan (2000) for the case of support by fuzzy logic. What contribution does fuzzy logic make?
4. *Debate:* Computers can be programmed to play chess. They are getting better and better, and in 1997 a computer beat the world champion. Do such computers exhibit intelligence? Why or why not?
5. *Debate:* Prepare a table showing all the arguments you can think of that justify the position that computers cannot think. Then, prepare arguments that show the opposite.
6. *Debate:* Bourbaki (1990) describes Searle's argument against the use of the Turing test. Summarize all the important issues in this debate.
7. *Debate:* Lance Eliot made the following comment in *AI Expert* (August 1994, p. 9):

   > When you log-on to the network, a slew of agents might start watching. If you download a file about plant life, a seed company agent might submit your name for a company mailing. Besides sending junk mail, such spying agents could pick up your habits and preferences and perhaps make assumptions about your private life. It could note what days you get onto the system, how long you stay on,

and what part of the country you live in. Is this an invasion of your privacy? Should legislation prevent such usage of intelligent agents? Perhaps network police (more intelligent agents) could enforce proper network usage.

Prepare arguments to support your perspective on this issue.

8. Give five examples not cited in this book where voice recognition can be applied, and list the benefit(s) in each case. Be specific.
9. Access the U.S. Department of Labor Web site on safety. Find the expert system at *osha.gov/*. Search for Web-based as well as Windows-based applications. Write a report on the capabilities of the ES and its advantages.
10. Refer to the American Express telephone-based voice-recognition system (AETRS) discussed in the chapter (page 539). Compare the telephone-based system with the Web-based system offered by the company (advantages and disadvantages).

GROUP AND ROLE-PLAYING ACTIVITIES

1. Find recent application(s) of intelligent systems in an organization. Assign each group member to a major functional area. Then, using a literature search, material from vendors, or industry contacts, each member should find two or three recent applications (within the last six months) of intelligent systems in this area. (*Primenet.pcai.com* is a good place to search. Also try the journals *Expert Systems* and *IEEE Intelligent Systems*.)
   - **a.** The group will make a presentation in which it will try to convince the class via examples that intelligent systems are most useful in its assigned functional area.
   - **b.** The entire class will conduct an analysis of the similarities and differences among the applications across the functional areas.
   - **c.** The class will vote on which functional area is benefiting the most from intelligent systems.
2. Each group member composes a list of mundane tasks he or she would like an intelligent software agent to prepare. The group will then meet and compare and draw some conclusions.
3. Investigate the use of NLP and voice recognition techniques that enable consumers to get information from the Web, conduct transactions, and interact with others, all by voice, through regular and cell telephones. Investigate articles and vendors of voice portals and find the state of the art. Write a report.

INTERNET EXERCISES

1. Prepare a report on the use of ES in help desks. Collect information from *ginesys.com*, *exsys.com*, *ilog.com*, and *pcai.com/pcai*.
2. Enter the Web site of Carnegie Mellon University (*cs.cmu.edu*) and identify current activities on the Land Vehicle. Send an e-mail to ascertain when the vehicle will be on the market.
3. At MIT (*media.mit.edu*) there is a considerable amount of interest in intelligent agents. Find the latest activities regarding IA. (Look at research and projects.)
4. Visit *sas.com/pub/neural/FAZ.html/*. Identify links to real-world applications of neural computing in finance, manufacturing, health care, and transportation. Then visit *hnc.com*. Prepare a report on current applications.
5. Enter *google.com*, *about.com*, and *looksmart.com*, and identify the latest managerial trends and issues related to applied AI technologies.
6. Enter *imagination-engines.com*. Find information about the process used, the patented machine, and the services offered by the company. Also learn about NLP creativity, musical creative machines, and virtual reality.
7. Visit *heyanita.com* and *tellme.com*, and find out what the companies are doing in the area of voice portals.
8. Enter *biocompsystems.com*. Download *BioComp profit*, and try its functionality. Summarize the benefits. Do the same with *imodel* and *Powerindicators*.

Minicase 1
Gate Assignment Display Systems

Gate assignment, the responsibility of gate controllers and their assistants, is a complex and demanding task at any airport. At O'Hare Airport in Chicago, for example, two gate controllers typically plan berthing for about 500 flights a day at about 50 gates. Flights arrive in clusters for the convenience of customers who must transfer to connecting flights, and so controllers must sometimes accommodate a cluster of 30 or 40 planes in 20 to 30 minutes. To complicate the matter, each flight is scheduled to remain at its gate a different length of time, depending on the schedules of connecting flights and the amount of servicing needed. Mix these problems with the need to juggle gates constantly because of flight delays caused by weather and other factors, and you get some idea of the challenges. The problem is even more complex because of its interrelationship with remote parking and constraints related to ground equipment availability and customer requirements.

To solve these problems, many airports are introducing expert systems. The pioneering work was done at Chicago O'Hare in 1987 and 1988. The Korean Air system at Kimpo Airport, Korea, won the 1999 innovative application award from the American Association of Artificial Intelligence (*aaai.org*). The two systems have several common features and similar architectures.

An intelligent gate assignment system can be set up and quickly rescheduled and contains far more information than a manual system. Its superb graphical display shows times and gate numbers. The aircraft are represented as colored bars; each bar's position indicates the gate assigned, and its length indicates the length of time the plane is expected to occupy the gate. Bars with pointed ends identify arrival-departure flights; square ends are used for originator-terminator flights. The system also shows, in words and numbers near each bar, the flight number, arrival and departure times, plane number, present fuel load, flight status, ground status, and more.

Each arriving aircraft carries a small radio transmitter that automatically reports to the mainframe system when the nose wheel touches down. The system immediately changes that plane's bar from "off," meaning off the field, to "on," meaning on the field. When the plane is parked at its gate, the code changes to "in." So gate controllers have access to an up-to-the-second ground status for every flight in their display.

The system also has a number of built-in reminders. For instance, it won't permit an aircraft to be assigned to the wrong kind of gate and explains why it can't. The controller can manually override such a decision to meet an unusual situation. The system also keeps its eye on the clock—when an incoming plane is on the field and its gate hasn't been assigned yet, flashing red lines bracket the time to alert the controller.

Three major benefits of the system have been identified. First, the assistant gate controller can start scheduling the next day's operations 4 or 5 hours earlier than was possible before. The Korean system, for example, produces a schedule in 20 seconds instead of in 5 manually worked hours. Second, the ES is also used by zone controllers and other ground operations (towing, cleaning, resupply). At O'Hare, for example, each of the ten zone controllers is responsible for all activities at a number of gates (baggage handling, catering service, crew assignment, and the rest). Third, superreliability is built into these systems.

Sources: Compiled from press releases from the American Association of Artificial Intelligence (1999) and Texas Instruments Data System Group (1988).

Questions for Minicase 1

1. Why is the gate assignment task so complex?
2. Why is the system considered a real-time ES?
3. What are the major benefits of the ES compared to the manual system? (Prepare a detailed list.)
4. Can a system be replicated for similar use in a non-airport environment? Give an example and discuss.

Minicase 2
How the United Nations Automated Its Payroll System

Over 15,000 employees work for the United Nations in more than a hundred countries and need to be paid in different currencies. The pay for each employee includes a base pay for the job and entitlements based on location, seniority, and special terms agreed on. The rules and regulations of these entitlements occupied about 1,000 pages in manuals. As a result, salary calculations were complex, lengthy, and error-prone, and they had resisted automation for decades.

Then the U.N. transferred the rules into an online knowledge base. An expert system was developed to determine which entitlements are relevant for each employee. A formula-based DSS calculates the salaries. The system maintains data on all U.N. employees and their dependents. It also monitors events such as promotions, relocations, and changes in dependents. The system contains an explanation mechanism that clarifies how it determines eligibility, and what the values of the related entitlements are. Explanations are also provided for why some employees are not eligible for certain entitlements.

The U.N. information system was recently converted from a legacy mainframe to a Unix-based client/server architecture. The entitlement application is only one of about 2,000 applications that run on the new $70 million Integrated Management Information System (IMIS). In addition to the entitlement applications, there are financial, accounting, procurement, payroll, and travel applications. The expert system was developed with an object-oriented software. It includes an easy-to-use graphical front end and links to databases as well as other applications. The system includes 20 LANs, and communication between locations is done via secured VANs.

The most difficult part of implementation was building the knowledge base. Previously, about 2,000 users at different locations worldwide applied the information requirements in different ways. The maintenance of the rules is now fairly simple since the rules are encapsulated into objects. All that needs to be done is to change the rule and check its consistency with other rules. The object-oriented programs also made it easy to compute backpay, a result of retroactive changes.

Several other ES applications were introduced in the U.N. financial area. For example, an ES analyzes financial data and determines which are debits and credits and which accounts should be consolidated into other accounts. Finally, the system recommends how to close out books at the end of designated financial periods.

The IMIS not only increases the productivity and accuracy of accountants, but it also facilitates planning. Management can make better decisions regarding the deployment of people and other resources. The determination of entitlements is consistent and therefore more equitable. Finally, the expertise of the U.N. experts at the headquarters in New York is now available online, all over the world.

Sources: Compiled from *Datamation,* November 1996, pp. 129–132, and from information provided by the IMIS administration at the U.N. (summer 2000).

Questions for Minicase 2

1. Why do employment rules and regulations fit an expert systems approach?
2. Why did the manual process defy automation until the ES approach was used?
3. Why are there links from the ES to databases and IT applications?
4. Today, the IMIS is praised by its users, those who are responsible for the payroll in all locations. Can you ascertain ways to make this system even better?
5. Management said the use of an ES forced them to make objective, rigorous definitions of the regulations. Why?
6. Identify other applications of ES in accounting. Start by searching customer stories at *exsys.com.* Also visit *pcai.com/pcai* and search at that site. Finally, search at *google.com.* Write a report to identify other IT applications at the U.N. that involve intelligent systems.

REFERENCES AND BIBLIOGRAPHY

1. Balentine, B., et al., *How to Build a Speech Recognition Application.* San Francisco: Enterprise Integration Group, 1999.
2. Barker, D., "Secret Agent Man," *PC AI,* January–February 1998.
3. Bigus, J. P., *Data Mining with Neural Networks.* New York: McGraw Hill, 1996.
4. Bigus, J. P., et al., *Constructing Intelligent Agents Using Java,* 2nd ed. New York: Wiley, 2001.
5. Bourbaki, N., "Turing, Searle, and Thought." *AI Expert,* July 1990.
6. Bradshaw, J. (ed.), *Software Agents.* Boston: MIT Press, 1997.
7. Cawsey, A., *The Essence of Artificial Intelligence.* Old Tappan, NJ: Pearson Printers, 1998.
8. Chen, C. H., *Fuzzy Logic and Neural Network Handbook.* New York, McGraw Hill, 1996.
9. Dreyfus, H., and S. Dreyfus, *Mind Over Machine.* New York: Free Press, 1988.
10. Edwards, J. S., et al., "An Analysis of Expert Systems for Decision Making," *European Journal of Information Systems,* March 2000.
11. Elofson, G., et al., "An Intelligent Agent Community Approach to Knowledge Sharing," *Decision Support Systems,* Vol. 20, No. 1, 1997.
12. Eriksson, H., "Expert Systems as Knowledge Servers," *IEEE Expert,* June 1996.
13. Flanagan, R., "A Fuzzy Stochastic Technique for Project Selection," *Construction Management and Economics,* January 2000.
14. Geng, G., et al., "Applying AI to Railway Freight Loading," *Expert Systems with Applications,* January 1999.
15. Giarratano, J. C., *Expert Systems: Principles and Programming.* Boston, MA: PWS Publishing, 1998.
16. Goralski, W. M., et al., *VRML: Exploring Virtual Worlds on the Internet.* Upper Saddle River, NJ: Prentice-Hall, 1997.
17. Gregor S., and I. Benbasat, "Explanations from Intelligent Systems," *MIS Quarterly,* December 1999.
18. Haykin, S., *Neural Networks: A Comprehensive Foundation.* Upper Saddle River, NJ: Prentice-Hall, 1998.
19. Hubms, M. N., et al., *Readings in Agents.* Palo Alto: Morgan Kaufmann, 1998.
20. Huntington, D., "Web-Based Expert Systems Are on the Way," *PC AI,* November–December 2000.
21. *IEEE Expert,* April 1996, pp. 12–18.
22. Jackson, P., *Introduction to Expert Systems,* 3rd ed. Reading, MA: Addison Wesley, 1999.
23. Knudsen, J. B., *The Unofficial Guide to Lego Mindstorm Robots.* Cambridge, MA: O'Reilly & Associates, 1999.
24. Lam, S. S. Y., et al., "Prediction and Optimization of a Ceramic Casting Process Using a Hierarchical Hybrid System of Neural Network and Fuzzy Logic," *IIE Transactions,* January 2000.
25. Lance, S., "Using Rule-Based Models for Training Complex Skills," *PC AI,* March–April 2000.
26. Levesque, H. J., and G. Lakemeyer, *The Logic of Knowledge Bases.* Boston: MIT Press, 2001.
27. Li, S., "The Development of a Hybrid Intelligent System for Developing Marketing Strategy," *Decision Support Systems,* January 2000.
28. Lunt, K., *Build Your Own Robot!* London: A. K. Peters, Ltd., 2000.
29. Machacha, L. L., and P. Bhattacharya, "A Fuzzy-Logic-based Approach to Project Selection," *IEEE Transactions on Engineering Management,* February 2000.
30. Maes, P., "Agents that Reduce Work and Information Overload," *Communications of the ACM,* July 1994.
31. Maes, P., et al., "Agents That Buy and Sell," *Communications of the ACM,* March 1999.
32. Marakas, G. M., and J. J. Elam, "Creativity Enhancement in Problem Solving: Through Software or Process," *Management Science,* August 1997.
33. Marriott, M., "Robots Can Learn Much from High-Tech Playthings," *New York Times,* March 22, 2001.
34. Massetti, B., "An Empirical Examination of the Value of Creativity Support Systems in Idea Generation, *MIS Quarterly,* March 1996.
35. Mendel, J. M., *Uncertain Rule-Based Fuzzy Logic Systems.* Upper Saddle River, NJ: Prentice-Hall, 2000.
36. Murch, R., and T. Johnson, *Intelligent Software Agents.* Upper Saddle River, NJ: Prentice-Hall, 1999.
37. Nguyen, H. T., and E. A. Walker, *A First Course in Fuzzy Logic.* Boca Raton, FL: CRC Press, 1999.
38. O'Leary, D., "AI and Navigation on the Internet and Intranet," *IEEE Expert,* April 1996.
39. Peppers, D., et al., *The One to One Fieldbook.* New York: Currency & Doubleday, 1999.
40. Peray, K., *Investing in Mutual Funds Using Fuzzy Logic.* Boca Raton, FL: CRC Press, 1999.
41. Ramsay, A. M., ed., *Artificial Intelligence: Methodology, Systems, and Applications,* 2nd ed. Amsterdam: IOS Press, 1996.
42. Rasmus, D. W., "Creativity and Tools," *PC AI,* Part 1: May–June 1995; Part 2: July–August 1995; Part 3: September–October 1995.
43. Reiter, E., and R. Dale, *Building Natural Language Generation Systems.* Cambridge U.K.: Cambridge University Press, 2000.
44. Robinson, A. G., and S. Stern, *Corporate Creativity: How Innovations and Improvement Actually Happen.* San Francisco, CA: Berrett-Koehler.
45. Sakellaropoulos, E. C., and E. C. Nikiforidis, "Prognostic Performance of Two Expert Systems," *Decision Support Systems,* January 2000.
46. Sutton, E., "Neural Networks Assist the Financial Auditor: Risk Reduction Going Concern Evaluations," *PC AI,* November–December 2000.
47. Trippi, R., and E. Turban (eds.), *Neural Computing Applications in Investment and Financial Services,* 2nd ed. Burr Ridge, IL: R. D. Irwin, 1996.
48. Trost, Robert, "Computer-Assisted Brainstorming and the Global Think Tank," *geocreate.com* (2001).
49. Turban, E., and J. Aronson, *Decision Support Systems and Intelligent Systems,* 6th ed. Upper Saddle River, NJ: Prentice-Hall, 2001.
50. Wee, L. K., et al., "DeNews—A Personalized News System," *Expert Systems with Applications,* November 1997.
51. Wise, E., *Applied Robotics.* Indianapolis: H. W. Sams, 1999.
52. Witten, I. H., and E. Frank, *Data Mining: Practical Machine Learning Tools.* San Francisco: Morgan Kaufmann, 1999.
53. Zadeh, L., "Fuzzy Logic, Neural Networks, and Self Computing," *Communications of the ACM,* March 1994.

CHAPTER 13
Information Technology Economics

LEARNING OBJECTIVES

After studying this chapter, you will be able to:

1. Identify the major aspects of the economics of information technology.
2. Explain the "productivity paradox."
3. Demonstrate how to define and measure tangible IT benefits.
4. Show how to evaluate intangible IT benefits.
5. Identify the advantages and disadvantages of approaches to charging end users for IT services.
6. Identify the advantages and disadvantages of outsourcing.
7. Describe causes of systems development failures.
8. Discuss the concept of "increasing returns" as it relates to the Internet and software production.
9. Describe economic issues related to Web-based technologies including e-commerce.

This chapter was revised by Narasimha Bolloju, City University of Hong Kong.

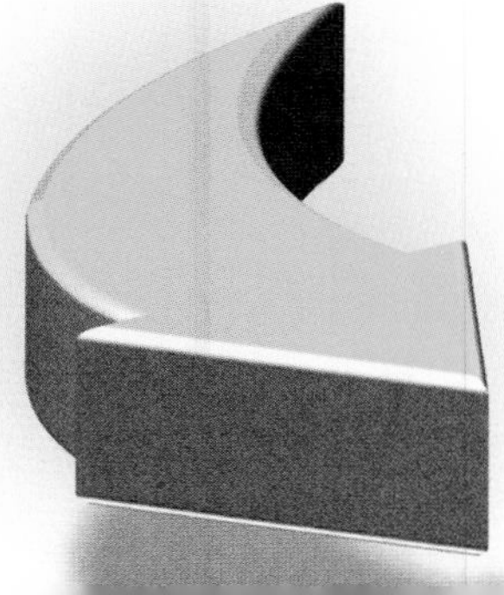

PILKINGTON PLC: TOTAL OUTSOURCING AT HEADQUARTERS

THE PROBLEM

Pilkington PLC is a major international supplier of glass products, with headquarters at St. Helens in Great Britain. In the early 1990s it downsized its headquarters staff in an effort to reduce costs in a period of declining profitability. Management needed to decide how to handle head office IT services in the context of this downsizing. Pilkington considered retaining the IT function (IS department) until after the downsizing, or spinning it off as a subsidiary that would sell services to outside organizations as well as to internal business units. Instead, it decided that most aspects of its IT were essentially commodities, and that a reasonable third option would be outsourcing them to a vendor.

www.pilkington.com

THE SOLUTION

Once it decided on outsourcing as a solution, Pilkington's next decision was whether to outsource IT on a piecemeal basis to multiple vendors, or to obtain all services from one vendor. Pilkington decided to use a single source, to minimize management involvement with the outsourcing. This approach would allow management to focus on strategic issues related to its core competencies. Using a single vendor would also facilitate a transition from a mainframe system to client/server systems.

Pilkington narrowed the choices to four vendors and, after extensive analysis, signed a contract with EDS-Scicon in January 1992. EDS offered support for IS technologies from multiple vendors and had strong technical capabilities, and its worldwide coverage paralleled Pilkington's multinational operations. Another consideration was the favorable working conditions and career opportunities for employees who would transfer to the vendor.

Pilkington's key concerns in the arrangement were to minimize risk and to maintain in-house capabilities related to the strategic management of IT. Pilkington negotiated a two-year contract with a renewal option. This flexible arrangement reduced the risk of outsourcing problems that other Pilkington units had experienced. Only six key IS professionals remained on Pilkington's payroll. Two managed the vendor contract, while the others were responsible for strategic policy and technology issues. In January 1994, EDS successfully replaced the head office mainframe with a local area network. Important financial reports are now available faster than before.

THE RESULTS

The outsourcing contract saved $1.85 million over two years. Pilkington renewed the contract for two more years, and has provided references to other companies considering contracts with EDS. Pilkington is satisfied with the current arrangement but faces additional questions for the future. Should it continue to use EDS? Should it bring the IT function back into the corporation now that the transition from the mainframe to a LAN is complete? Or should it outsource functions at its operating units that are still in-house?

So far it seems that the outsource strategy continues. For example, in 2000, Pilkington adopted cutting-edge technologies that enhance its ability to provide high-quality products to its customers around the globe. As part of a program,

Pilkington has signed an agreement to use FreeMarkets' e-Marketplace. This mechanism will be used to purchase selected goods and services for Pilkington's operations throughout the group. Again, Pilkington decided to outsource rather than build its own marketplace.

Sources: Condensed from L. Willcocks and G. Fitzgerald, "Pilkington PLC: A Major Multinational Outsources Head Office IT Function," 1996; and from *pilkington.com.* A full version of this case is available on *wiley.com/college/turban/cases.*

LESSONS LEARNED FROM THIS CASE

The opening case illustrates how a major corporation elected to outsource most of its headquarters' IT activities. Outsourcing is a very popular option, especially with networked computing and lately with e-commerce. Outsourcing is one of the major IT economic-related decisions corporations must make today. The unique aspects of IT make its economics different in many respects from the economics of other aspects of business. This chapter explores these issues and the factors that shape them.

In order to understand the factors that determine the outsourcing option, we need to understand the technological trends of increasing investment in technology, the first topic we address in the chapter. Next, we review the so-called "productivity paradox" and how it has been changed lately.

A major problem in making IT-related economic decisions is the measurement and comparison of performance under different options. This is done with approaches such as benchmarking and metrics. Other important issues are assessing intangible variables and dealing with costs, including accounting options. Outsourcing as a viable strategy is also explored in this chapter, especially for e-commerce, whose economic foundations are also explained here.

Finally, we discuss some failure issues. As pointed out throughout the book, failures are common in IT and can cost dearly.

13.1 ECONOMIC AND FINANCIAL TRENDS

Technological and Financial Trends

Information technology capabilities are advancing at a rapid rate, and this trend should continue for the forseeable future. Expanding power and declining costs enable new and more extensive applications of information technology, which makes it possible for organizations to improve their efficiency and effectiveness. However, the increasingly diverse uses of this new potential make it more and more difficult to get a true picture of the benefits relative to the associated costs.

On the hardware side, capabilities are growing at an exponential rate. **Moore's law**, named for one of the founders of Intel Corp., is illustrated in Figure 13.1. Moore suggested in a 1965 article that the number of transistors, and thus the power, of an integrated circuit (computer chip) would double every year, while the cost remained the same. Moore later revised this estimate to a slightly less rapid pace: doubling every 18 months (Moore, 1995). In Figure 13.1 power is measured in MIPS, or millions of (computer) instructions per second. Moore has also applied the law to the Web, electronic commerce, and supply chain management (see Moore, 1997).

At the current rate of growth in computing power, organizations will have the opportunity to buy, for the same price, twice the processing power in 1½

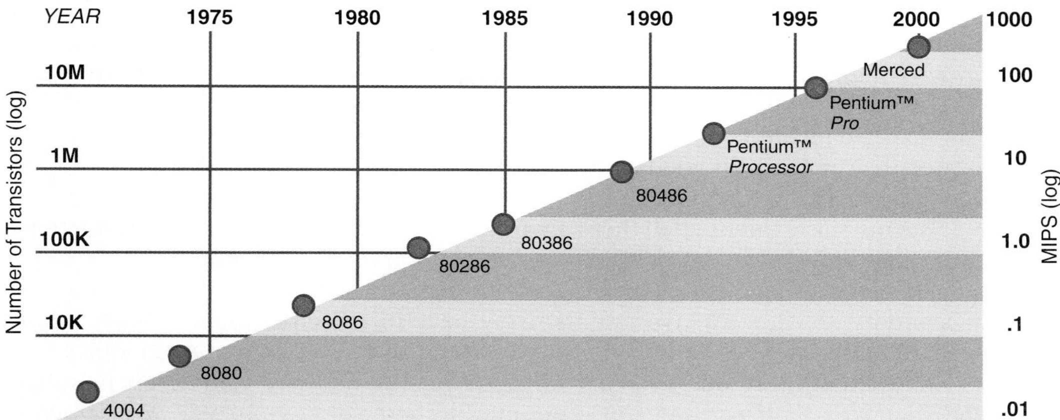

FIGURE 13.1 Moore's law as it relates to Intel microprocessors. (*Source:* Intel Corporation, *intel.com.research/silicon/mooreslaw.htm*. Reprinted by permission of Intel Corporation, ©Intel Corporation.)

years, four times the power in 3 years, eight times the power in 4½ years, and so forth. Another way of saying this is that the **price-to-performance ratio** will continue to decline exponentially. Limitations associated with current technologies could end this trend for silicon-based chips in 10 or 20 years (or possibly earlier; see Pountain, 1998), but new technologies will probably allow this phenomenal growth to continue. Advances in network technology, as compared to those in chip technology, are even more profound, as shown in Chapter 1.

What does this mean in economic terms? First, most organizations will perform existing functions at decreasing costs over time and thus become more efficient. Second, creative organizations will find new uses for information technology—based on the improving price-to-performance ratio—and thus become more effective. They will use the technology for new or enhanced products or services, or for operational activities, that are technically feasible only with higher levels of computing power. They will also apply technology to activities that are technically feasible at current power levels but will not be economically feasible until costs are reduced. Information technology will become an even more significant factor in the production and distribution of almost every product and service and will be physically embedded in many products, including commonplace low-technology items (for example, automobile tires).

These new and enhanced products and services will provide competitive advantage to organizations that have the creativity to exploit the increasing power of information technology. They will also provide major benefits to consumers, who will benefit from the greater functionality and lower costs. Moreover, applications of advanced information technologies are becoming increasingly diverse, with greater emphasis on intangible benefits. Increasing flexibility and ability to make better decisions are examples of *intangible benefits*—factors that are important but difficult to express in monetary values. These trends make it difficult to identify and evaluate the true financial impact of IT projects.

The remainder of this chapter focuses on evaluating the costs, benefits, and other economic aspects of information technology. First we address the so-called *productivity paradox,* the lack of evidence for a payoff from massive IT investments in the 1970s and 1980s.

The Productivity Paradox

Over the last 50 years, organizations have invested trillions of dollars in information technology. Total worldwide annual spending on IT in 2000 has surpassed two trillion dollars, and it is expected to be over three trillion dollars in four years (ITAA, 2000). These expenditures have unquestionably transformed organizations: The technologies have become an integral aspect of almost every business process. The business and technology presses publish many "success stories" about major benefits from information technology projects at individual organizations. It seems self-evident that these investments must have increased productivity, not just in individual organizations, but throughout the economy.

On the other hand it is very hard to demonstrate, at the level of a national economy, that the IT investments really have increased outputs or wages. Most of the investment went into the service sector of the economy which, during the 1970s and 1980s, was showing much lower productivity gains than manufacturing. Nobel prize winner in economics Robert Solow quipped: "We see computers everywhere except in the productivity statistics." The discrepancy between measures of investment in information technology and measures of output at the national level is described as the **productivity paradox**.

PRODUCTIVITY. To understand this paradox, we first need to understand the concept of productivity. Economists define *productivity* as outputs divided by inputs. Outputs are calculated by multiplying units produced (for example, number of automobiles) by their average value. The resulting figure needs to be adjusted for price inflation and also for any changes in quality (such as increased safety or better gas mileage). If inputs are measured simply as hours of work, the resulting ratio of outputs to inputs is **labor productivity**. If other inputs—investments and materials—are included, the ratio is known as **multifactor productivity**. *A Closer Look* 13.1 shows an example of a productivity calculation.

Explaining the Productivity Paradox

Economists have studied the productivity issue extensively in recent years and developed a variety of possible explanations of the apparent paradox. These explanations are grouped into the following three categories, which we discuss in more detail next.

1. Problems with data or analyses hide productivity gains from IT.
2. Gains from IT are offset by losses in other areas.
3. IT productivity gains are offset by IT costs or losses.

DATA AND ANALYSIS PROBLEMS HIDE PRODUCTIVITY GAINS. Productivity numbers are only as good as the data used in their calculations. For manufacturing, it is fairly easy to measure outputs and inputs. General Motors, Ford, and DaimlerChrysler produce motor vehicles, relatively well-defined products whose quality changes gradually over time. It is not difficult to identify, with reasonable accuracy, the inputs used to produce these vehicles. However, the trend in the United States and other developed countries is away from manufacturing and toward services.

In service industries, such as finance or health-care delivery, it is more difficult to define what the products are, how they change in quality, and how to allocate to them the corresponding costs. For example, banks now use IT to handle a large proportion of deposit and withdrawal transactions through automated

A CLOSER LOOK
13.1 CALCULATING LABOR PRODUCTIVITY AT THE DRISCOLL COMPANY

The Driscoll Company uses 10 employees who manually process 1,000 customer service inquiries per day. Unit sales are increasing at 5 percent per year, and the number of inquiries is increasing at about the same rate. Turnover among these customer service representatives is 20 percent: On the average, two of these employees leave the company every year.

The company purchased an automated call-answering and customer-service system, which should make it possible to increase output per employee by 50 percent. However, the Driscoll Company values its employees. Rather than having a layoff to achieve the 50 percent productivity gain right away, it will wait until there is a need to hire new employees to replace those who leave. The following calculations compare productivity with the previous system and new systems.

Productivity with the Manual System:

1,000 inquiries / 10 employees = 100 inquiries handled per employee per day

Productivity with the Automated System (One Year Later):

1,050 inquiries / 8 employees = 131 inquiries handled per employee per day

Productivity increase = 31%

Productivity will increase further as additional employees leave.

teller machines (ATMs). The ability to withdraw cash from ATMs 24 hours per day, 7 days per week is a substantial quality increase in comparison to the traditional 9 A.M. to 4 P.M. hours for live tellers. But what is the value of this quality increase in comparison with the associated costs? If the incremental value exceeds the incremental costs, then it represents a productivity gain; otherwise the productivity impact is negative.

The productivity gains may not be apparent in all processes supported by the information systems. Mukhopadhyay et al. (1997), in an assessment of productivity impacts of IT on a toll-collection system, found that IT had a significant impact on the processing of complex transactions, but not on simple transactions. Based on an investigation of IT performance in 60 construction-industry firms in Hong Kong, Li et al. (2000) found productivity improvements in architecture and quantity surveying firms (which perform a wide range of functions involved in the estimation and control of construction project costs) and no evidence of productivity improvement in engineering firms.

Another important consideration is the amount of time it takes to achieve the full benefits of new technologies. Economists point out that it took many decades to start achieving the productivity impacts of the Industrial Revolution. We all know that it takes time to learn to use new software: Productivity actually decreases during the initial learning period and then increases over a period of a year or longer. Economic analyses that fail to consider the *time lags* between IT investments and IT benefits may underestimate the productivity impacts.

Hitt and Brynjolfsson (1996) point out that answers to questions about the value of IT investments depend on how the issue is defined. They emphasize that productivity is not the same thing as profitability. Their research indicates that IT increases productivity and value to consumers but does not increase organizational profitability. Brynjolfsson and Hitt (1998) suggest using alternate measures, other than traditional productivity measures, for this purpose.

IT PRODUCTIVITY GAINS ARE OFFSET BY LOSSES IN OTHER AREAS. It is possible that IT produces gains in certain areas of the economy, but that these gains are offset by losses in other areas. One company's IT usage could increase its share of market at the expense of other companies. Total output in the industry, and thus productivity, remains constant even though the competitive situation may change.

Offsetting losses can also occur within organizations. Consider the situation where an organization installs a new computer system that makes it possible to increase output per employee. If the organization reduces its production staff but increases employment in unproductive overhead functions, the productivity gains from information technology will be dispersed.

IT PRODUCTIVITY GAINS ARE OFFSET BY IT COSTS OR LOSSES. The third possibility is that IT in itself really does not increase productivity. This idea seems contrary to common sense: Why would organizations invest tremendous amounts of money in something if it really does not improve performance? On the other hand, there are considerations that support this possibility. Figure 13.2 shows an analysis from Strassmann (1997) that suggests little or no relationship between IT spending and corporate profitability.

As mentioned earlier, productivity is the ratio of outputs divided by inputs. To determine whether IT increases productivity, it is not enough simply to measure changes in outputs for a new system. If outputs increase 40 percent but inputs increase 50 percent, the result is a decline in productivity rather than a gain. Or consider a situation where a new system is developed and implemented but then, because of some major problems, is replaced by another system. Even though the second system has acceptable performance, an analysis that includes

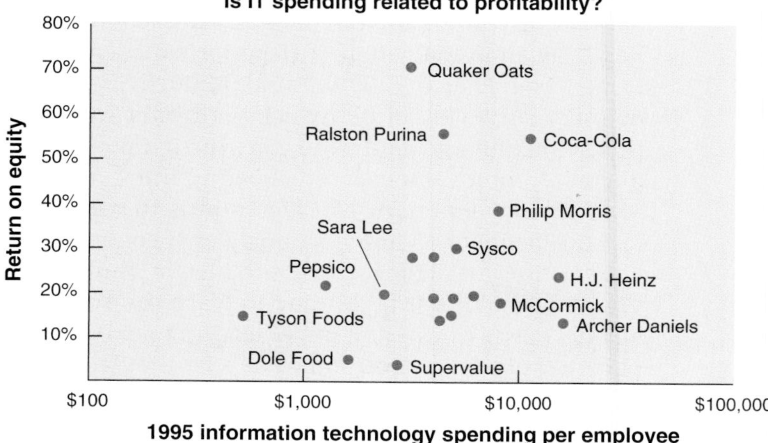

FIGURE 13.2 Comparing relative IT spending and profitability at a sample of corporations. (*Source: strassmann.com/ pubs/ datamation0297/*. Reprinted by permission of Paul A. Strassman, "The Squandered Computer," *Information Economics,* 1997.)

the costs of the unsuccessful system could indicate that IT did not increase productivity, at least in the short run.

Productivity evaluations must include changes in inputs, especially labor, over the total life cycle, including projects that are not implemented. These inputs need to include not just the direct labor required to develop and operate the systems, but also indirect labor and other costs required to maintain the system. Examples of factors that, under this broader perspective, reduce productivity include:

- ***Support costs.*** The GartnerGroup estimates the total cost of a networked PC can be as high as $13,000 per year (Munk, 1996). Technical support accounts for 27 percent of this cost, and administration for another 9 percent. The additional employees required for these support activities could offset a significant portion of the productivity benefits from the hardware and software.
- ***Wasted time.*** Personal computers make it possible to work more productively on some tasks but also result in nonproductive activities. A survey of 6,000 workers indicated the average PC user loses 5 hours per week waiting—for programs to run, reports to print, tech support to answer the phone, and so on—or "futzing" with the hardware or software (Munk, 1996). The GartnerGroup estimates that businesses lose 26 million hours of employee time per year to these nonproductive activities, and that they account for 43 percent of the total cost of a personal computer on a network. The cartoon in Figure 13.3 highlights the issue of wasted time.
- ***Software development problems.*** Some information systems projects fail and are not completed. Others are abandoned, completed but never used. Others are **runaway projects**, systems that are eventually completed but require much more time and money than originally planned. This is not an uncommon problem: A survey in 1997 (King, 1997) found that 73 percent of software projects at 360 U.S. corporations were canceled, over budget, or late. Labor hours associated with these projects can offset productivity gains from more successful projects.
- ***Software maintenance.*** The expense of software maintenance, which includes fixing bugs and modifying or enhancing system functionality, now accounts for up to 80 percent of IS budgets. Many of the modifications—for example, updates to payroll systems to reflect tax law changes—do not increase outputs. They are necessary just to keep the system at the same level of performance, so productivity declines because labor increases while output volumes do not.

FIGURE 13.3 Dilbert analyzes the productivity paradox. (*Source:* Dilbert; reprinted by permission of United Feature Syndicate, Inc.)

The "Year 2K Problem" is a notable example of software maintenance that did not add to productivity. The cost to update software throughout the world just to handle dates in the twenty-first century was estimated to be as high as $600 billion, which did not include legal liabilities for system failures. An estimated $100 billion was spent in the United States (Bennett and Dodd, 2000). To deal with this problem, Merrill Lynch in 1997 had an 80-person team working 24 hours per day in shifts seven days a week, even though "our return on investment [from the effort] is zero" (Vistica et al., 1997). The complexity of this problem is shown in Figure 13.1 at the book's Web site.

Most global organizations are also required to incur additional costs for acquiring and maintaining domain name registrations. GartnerGroup (2000) estimates that the average global organization has to register a total of at least 300 name variants by 2001, which amounts to $75,000. Many additional names are required because of the new high-level domains such as .biz, and .info. Companies want to register the variants of their company names to keep those variants out of the hands of others.

- ***Incompatible systems and workarounds.*** Although individual systems produce productivity gains, the increased labor required to get them to work together (or at all) could offset these benefits.

One other major phenomenon that can waste time and reduce productivity is known as *junk computing,* as described in *A Closer Look* 13.2 on the facing page.

These productivity-offsetting factors largely reflect problems with the administration of information technology, rather than with the technologies themselves. In many cases they are controllable through better planning or more effective management techniques. For organizations, the critical issue is not whether and how IT increases productivity in the economy as a whole, but how it improves their own productivity. Lin and Shao (2000) find a robust and consistent relationship between IT investment and efficiency, and they support evaluating IT investments in terms of organizational efficiency rather than productivity.

The next three sections cover ways organizations can evaluate IT benefits and costs and target their IT development and acquisition toward systems that will best contribute to the achievement of organizational goals.

13.2 Evaluating IT: Benefits, Costs, and Performance

Organizations face the ongoing problem of trying to most efficiently allocate their limited resources to maintain or improve performance. Information technology is very much a part of this problem, since IT is becoming a significant component of almost everything organizations do. Evaluating the costs and benefits of IT is therefore an important aspect of the allocation process.

The rapid rate of change contributes to the difficulty of making decisions about information technology. Newer technologies offer capabilities that are very different from what is currently available, and they make existing technologies obsolete. Costs of processing power per unit of computing are declining rapidly, which can have a great impact on the timing and nature of IT investment decisions.

A CLOSER LOOK
13.2 CONTROLLING JUNK COMPUTING

Guthrie and Gray (1996) coined the expression "junk computing" to describe "the use of information systems in a way that does not directly advance organizational goals." They created this expression as an analogy to the concept of junk mail. The subjects of their research identified 19 different types of junk-computing activities, and mentioned seven items most frequently. Two non-work-related items—***games*** and ***doing personal work*** on company time—were at the top of the list, followed by:

- ***Junk reporting***—creating unnecessary reports
- ***Excessive computerization***—automation that is not an improvement over manual systems
- ***Excessive detail***—for example, inputting minor activities into a scheduling system rather than focusing on milestones and higher priority projects
- ***Excessive attention to presentation,*** such as elaborate formatting for simple memos
- ***E-mail***—for example, sending copies to large distribution lists or responding to unimportant messages

The causes of junk computing include:

- ***Excessiveness.*** Employees may devote more time to computing than is necessary to achieve the desired result.
- ***Physical environment***—for example, incompatible hardware or systems that require manual effort to transfer or integrate data.
- ***Cultural or social pressures.*** Other employees or the organization may encourage excesses, for example, large reports or very elaborate presentations.
- ***Individual behavioral styles.*** Some employees are very oriented toward computers and try to do as much work as they can with them.
- ***Miscommunication and mismanagement.*** Managers may ask for or indirectly signal employees that they want elaborate work, or try to implement technical solutions instead of dealing with the people or procedures that are causing problems.

Guthrie and Gray note that junk computing is not always counterproductive. Experimentation—for example, using advanced features of a word-processing program to format a memo—may develop skills that the employee can subsequently use in a formal report that requires a more elaborate layout. Or playing a quick game of solitaire may provide a relaxing break to an employee, after which she or he can go back to work with renewed vigor.

The following recommendations can help managers control junk computing:

- ***Increase awareness.*** Recognize junk computing as an organizational productivity problem.
- ***Control environmental factors.*** Set policies against inappropriate use, mandate standard formats for documents and presentations to prevent excessive effort, and remove game software from computers.
- ***Control behavior*** through training that covers appropriate and inappropriate computer uses, and through chargeback of computing costs (see Section 13.4).
- ***Control mismanagement.*** Encourage appropriate computer usage through effective managerial communications, and by creating an environment that encourages employees to manage their own computer use consistent with organizational needs.

Note that with the advancement of the Web, the problem of junk computing has been accelerating because employees use corporate time for private viewing. Controlling this problem can be a major issue (see Chapter 15).

Source: Condensed from R. Guthrie and P. Gray, "Junk Computing: Is It Bad for an Organization?" *Information Systems Management*, Winter 1996, pp. 23–28.

A major problem in evaluating IT is that many of its benefits are intangible: They are real and important, but it is not easy to accurately estimate their value. The fact that organizations use IT for different purposes further complicates the evaluation process.

IT investments can be of different types, as categorized by Lucas (1999). Table 13.1 on the next page shows types of IT investments and the expected returns.

TABLE 13.1 IT Investment Types

Type of Investment	Comments
Infrastructure to support current business	Possible future benefits; hard to identify contribution.
Required for managerial control	No return is expected; considered as a cost of business.
No other way to do the job	Returns in terms of savings in labor or generation of new revenue.
Direct returns from IT	Returns can be identified and measured.
Indirect returns	Very hard to identify; has potential for considerable returns.
Competitive necessity	No return may be expected except for retaining market share.
Strategic application	Hard to identify return; has a high potential for upside; estimation possible only after implementation.
Transformational IT	Hard to identify specific returns tied to it; has a high potential for upside.

Source: Adapted from *Information Technology and the Productivity Paradox* by Henry C. Lucas, Jr. © 1999. Oxford University Press, Inc. Used by permission of Oxford University Press, Inc.

Lucas (1999) suggests that the following issues must be considered while assessing the value of investing in IT.

- There are multiple kinds of values, and the return on investment measured in dollar terms is only one of them.
- Different types of investments in IT are associated with different probabilities of providing returns.
- The probability of obtaining a return from an IT investment also depends on probability of conversion success. These probabilities reflect the fact that many systems are not implemented on time, within budget, and/or with all the features orginally envisioned for them.
- The expected value of the return on IT investment in most cases will be less than that originally anticipated.

Gray and Watson (1998) point out that managers often make substantial investments in projects like data warehousing by relying on intuition when evaluating investment proposals rather than on concrete estimates. A comprehensive list of over 60 different appraisal methods for IT investments can be found in Renkema (2000). These methods are categorized into the following four types.

1. ***Financial approach.*** These appraisal methods consider only impacts that can be monetary-valued. They focus on incoming and outgoing cash flows as a result of the investment made.
2. ***Multicriteria approach.*** These appraisal methods consider both financial impacts and nonfinancial impacts that cannot be, or cannot easily be, expressed in monetary terms. These methods employ quantitative and qualitative decision-making techniques.
3. ***Ratio approach.*** These methods use several ratios (e.g., IT expenditures vs. total turnover) to assist in IT investment evaluation.
4. ***Portfolio approach.*** These methods apply portfolios (or grids) to plot several investment proposals against decision-making criteria. The portfolio methods are more informative compared to multicriteria methods and generally use fewer evaluation criteria.

Methods of evaluating IT reflect the different types of uses, as we discuss below.

The Value of Information in Decision Making

People in organizations use information to help them make decisions that are better than they would have been if they did not have the information. Senior executives make decisions that influence the profitability of an organization for years to come; operational employees make decisions that affect production on a day-to-day basis. In either case, the value of information is the difference between the net benefits—benefits adjusted for costs—of decisions made using the information and decisions without the information. The value of the net benefits with information obviously needs to reflect the additional costs of obtaining the information. The value of information can be expressed as follows:

$$\text{Value of information} = \text{Net benefits with information} - \text{Net benefits without information}$$

It is generally assumed that systems that provide relevant information to support decision making will result in better decisions, and therefore they will contribute toward the ROI. However, Dekker and de Hoog (2000) found that the return on most knowledge assets created for loan revision decisions in a large bank was negative.

One way to estimate the value of information for complex decisions is to experiment, comparing decisions with and without information, either in real-world situations or in laboratory experiments that simulate some of the decision processes. Unfortunately, there are problems with both approaches, and it is difficult to accurately assign a value to the information. Organizations might experiment with small problems where the consequences of failure are limited, but for major decisions they usually cannot afford to test alternatives that are less likely to be successful. Laboratory experiments are much less risky, but it is not easy to translate the results into an accurate reflection of the value of information in real-world situations.

The remaining alternative is to have the decision maker subjectively estimate the value of the information. This person is most familiar with the problem and has the most to lose from a bad decision. If this person identifies a specific value for the information and it is obtainable for that cost or less, the organization probably should make the investment to acquire the information or develop a system to produce it. However, to make sure the estimates are not inflated in order to get an approval, the organization needs to hold the decision maker accountable for the cost of the information. Before we deal with such accountability we will examine the methodologies of evaluating automation of business processes with IT.

Evaluating Automation by Cost-Benefit Analyses

Automation of business processes is an area where it is necessary to define and measure IT benefits and costs. In automation, mechanical equipment under the control of information technology replaces or enhances human labor. For example, automation was implemented in the organization's business offices when word processing replaced typing and spreadsheet programs replaced column-ruled accounting pads and 10-key calculators. In the factory, robots weld and paint automobiles on assembly lines. In the warehouse, incoming items are recorded by bar-code scanners.

The decision of whether to automate is a capital investment decision. Such decisions can be analyzed by **cost-benefit analyses** that compare the total value

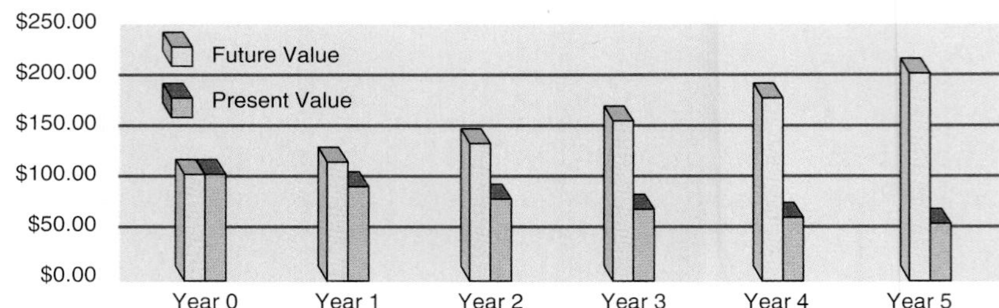

FIGURE 13.4 Future value and present value of $100 at 15 percent.

of the benefits with the associated costs. Organizations often use *net present value (NPV)* calculations for cost-benefit analyses. In an NPV analysis, analysts convert future values to their present-value equivalent by discounting them at the organization's cost of funds. Figure 13.4 illustrates the concept of future value and present value. The chart indicates that, in an organization earning a 15 percent return, $100 would grow to about $200 five years in the future. Similarly $100 five years in the future would be worth about $50 at present.

The NPV analysis works well in situations where the costs and benefits are well defined or "tangible," so that it is not difficult to convert them into monetary values. For example, if human welders are replaced by robots that produce work of comparable quality, the benefits are the labor cost savings over the usable life of the robots. Costs include the capital investment to purchase and install the robots, plus the operating and maintenance costs.

It would make life easier for financial analysts if all automation decisions were this simple. In many cases, however, the IT aspect of the new equipment generates benefits such as increased quality, faster product development, greater design flexibility, better customer service, or improved working conditions for employees. These are very desirable benefits, but it is difficult to place an accurate monetary value on them. The analyst could ignore intangible benefits, but this implies that their value is zero and may lead the organization to reject investments that could substantially increase its revenues and profitability. Therefore, financial analyses need to consider not just tangible benefits but also intangible benefits, in such a way that the decision reflects their potential impact.

HANDLING INTANGIBLE BENEFITS. The most straightforward solution to the problem of evaluating intangible benefits in cost-benefit analysis is to make *rough estimates* of monetary values for all intangible benefits, and then conduct the financial analysis. The simplicity of this approach is attractive, but in many cases the assumptions used in these estimates are debatable. If the technology is acquired because decision makers assigned too high a value to intangible benefits, the organization could find that it has wasted some valuable resources. On the other hand, if the valuation of intangible benefits were too low, the organization might reject the investment and then find that it is losing market share to competitors who did implement the technology.

Downing (1989) discusses these issues and suggests eight ways to evaluate intangible benefits. Here are three of them:

1. ***Use "concrete indicators."*** Instead of subjectively estimating the value, find some measurable effects resulting from the benefit. For example, automating a monotonous process could improve working conditions. Estimate how

much this could reduce employee turnover, and then use the savings in hiring and training costs as the value of this intangible benefit.

2. ***Solve for an unknown.*** Calculate the net present value without including any value for intangible benefits. If the net present value is negative, calculate the shortfall—the required value of the intangible benefits needed to make NPV positive. If the intangible benefits are worth at least this value, the project can be approved. With this approach, it is not necessary to accurately estimate the ultimate value of intangible benefits. Instead it is sufficient just to evaluate whether the shortfall is a reasonable estimate of the low end of the range of possible values of intangible benefits.
3. ***Prevent competitive disadvantage.*** The typical investment analysis assumes that the financial situation will not change if the investment is not made. In reality, however, competitors may adopt a new technology, which could reduce income for the organization that does not make an investment in that technology. Thus, it is necessary to include an estimate of not just the gain from the investment, but also the losses from failing to adopt the new technology.

Evaluating IT Infrastructure Through Benchmarks and Metrics

Information systems projects are usually not standalone applications. In most cases they depend for support on enabling technologies already installed in the organization. These *infrastructure technologies* include mainframe computers, operating systems, networks, database management systems, utility programs, development tools, and more. Since many of their benefits are intangible and are spread over many different present and future applications, it is hard to estimate their value or evaluate the desirability of enhancements or upgrades. In other words, it is much more difficult to evaluate infrastructure investment decisions than investments in specific information systems application projects.

One approach to evaluating infrastructure is to focus on objective measures of performance known as *benchmarks.* These measures are often available from trade associations within an industry or from consulting firms. The benchmark approach implicitly assumes that investments in infrastructure are justified if they are managed efficiently. A comparison of measures of performance or expenditures with averages for the industry, or with values for the more efficient performers in the industry, indicates how well the organization is using its infrastructure. If performance is below standard, corrective action is indicated.

Benchmarks come in two very different forms. **Metric benchmarks** provide *numeric* measures of performance, for example:

- IT expenses as percent of total revenues
- Percent of "downtime" (when the computer is not available)
- CPU usage (as percent of total capacity)
- Percent of IS projects completed on time and within budget

These types of measures are very useful to managers, even though sometimes they lead to the wrong conclusions. For example, a ratio of IT expenses to revenues that is lower than the industry average might indicate that a firm is operating more efficiently than its competitors. Or it might indicate that the company is investing less in IT than it should and will become less competitive as a result.

An illustration of typical support expected from benchmarking tools in complex IT environments is described at the book's Web site.

Metric benchmarks can help diagnose problems, but they do not necessarily show how to solve them. Therefore, many organizations also use **best-practice benchmarks**. Here the emphasis is on how information system activities are actually performed rather than numeric measures of performance. For example, an organization might feel that its IT infrastructure management is very important to its performance. It could obtain information about best practices in this area, such as the way other organizations—or its own more efficient units—operate and manage their IT infrastructure. The organization would then implement these best practices for all of its own IT infrastructure, to bring performance up to the level of the leaders.

Other Methods and Commercial Services

Several other methods can be used to assess the value of information. Table 13.2 lists some of the traditional methods with their advantages and disadvantages (including the NPV discussed earlier). However, traditional methods may not be useful in cases of some of the newest technologies (e.g., see Violino, 1997). (An example of one such case—acquiring expert systems—is shown at the book's Web site.) Because traditional methods may not be useful for new technologies, there are special methodologies for dealing with investment in IT and its special technologies. Also, there are many computerized models that help with investment decisions. (See Violino, 1997, for discussion of these methods.)

TOTAL COST OF OWNERSHIP. An interesting approach for evaluating the value of IT is the **total cost of ownership (TCO)**. TCO is a formula for calculating the cost of owning and operating a PC. The cost includes hardware, technical support, maintenance, software upgrades, and help-desk and peer support. By identifying such costs, organizations get more accurate cost-benefit analyses and also reduce the TCO. It is possible to reduce TCO of workstations in networked environments by as much as 26 percent by adopting best practices in workstation management (Kirwin et al., 1997).

TABLE 13.2 Traditional Methods of Evaluating Investments

Method	Advantages	Disadvantages
Internal rate of return (IRR)	Brings all projects to common footing. Conceptually familiar.	Assumes reinvestment at same rate. Can have multiple roots. No assumed discount rate.
Net present value or net worth (NPV or NW)	Very common. Maximizes value for unconstrained project selection.	Difficult to compare projects of unequal lives or sizes.
Equivalent annuity (EA)	Brings all project NPVs to common footing. Convenient annual figure.	Assumes projects repeat to least common multiple of lives, or imputes salvage value.
Payback period	May be discounted or nondiscounted. Measure of exposure.	Ignores flows after payback is reached. Assumes standard project cash flow profile.
Benefit-to-cost ratio	Conceptually familiar. Brings all projects to common footing.	May be difficult to classify outlays between expense and investment.

Source: Compiled from *Capital Budgeting and Long-Term Financing Decisions*. 2nd edition, by N. E. Seitz © 1995. Reprinted with permission of South-Western College Publishing, a division of Thomson Learning.

13.3 EVALUATING IT: PERSPECTIVES ON INTANGIBLE BENEFITS

Assessing Intangible Benefits

Some IT investment decisions are easy. Occasionally the benefits, especially cost savings, are quite measurable and carry little or no risk of failure. In other cases the project is necessary in order for the organization to stay in business: For example, the Internal Revenue Service is requiring businesses to switch to electronic systems for filing their tax returns. These types of investments do not require firms to do a lot of analysis.

Unfortunately, considerations related to most potential IT investments are not usually so well-defined. One possible way of dealing with this issue is to limit IT investments to situations where there is a compelling justification, such as regulatory compliance. However, the pressures of the competitive environment make this approach impractical for most organizations. They face a continuing need to improve their performance, and IT can produce many benefits that could improve performance. IT can speed up business processes, provide more accurate information for decision making and management control, improve communications, and make it easier for employees to work together.

These kinds of benefits are often difficult to measure by themselves, and their impact on organizational performance is even less measurable. For example, many people would agree that e-mail improves communications, but it is not at all clear how to measure the value of this improvement. A network administrator can provide statistics on the number of e-mail messages but cannot prove that communication within the organization is, say, 10 percent better because employees now receive an average of four e-mail messages per day. Managers are very conscious of the bottom line, but no manager can prove that e-mail is responsible for so many cents per share of the organization's total profits.

So, what is the solution? Even though the relationship between intangible IT benefits and performance is not clear, some investments should be better than others. How can organizations increase the probability that their IT investments will improve their performance? Several available methodologies are of special interest. They are: value analysis, information economics, management by maxim, and option valuation. Briefly:

- ***Value analysis*** allows users to evaluate intangible benefits on a low-cost, trial basis before deciding whether to commit to a larger investment.
- ***Information economics*** focuses on the application of IT in areas where its intangible benefits contribute to performance on key aspects of organizational strategies and activities.
- ***Management by maxim*** provides a means of rationalizing IT infrastructure investments.
- ***Option valuation*** takes into account potential future benefits that current IT investments could produce.

The remaining parts of this section describe how each of these methodologies works.

Value Analysis

Keen (1981) developed the **value analysis** method to assist organizations considering investments in decision support systems (DSSs). The major problem with justifying a DSS is that most of the benefits are not readily convertible into monetary values. Some—such as better decisions, better understanding of business situations, and improved communication—are difficult to measure even in nonmonetary

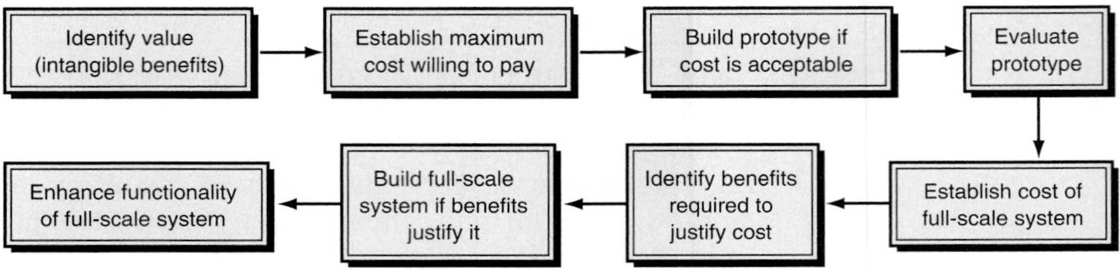

FIGURE 13.5 Steps in the value analysis approach.

terms. These problems in evaluating DSS are similar to the problems in evaluating intangible benefits for other types of systems. Therefore, value analysis should be applicable to other types of IT investments in which a large proportion of the value derives from intangible benefits.

The value analysis approach includes eight steps, grouped into two phases. The first phase works with a low-cost prototype, which, depending on the initial results, is followed by a full-scale system in the second phase. In the first phase the decision maker identifies the desired capabilities and the (generally intangible) potential benefits. The developers estimate the cost of providing the capabilities and, if the decision maker feels the benefits are worth this cost, a small-scale prototype of the DSS is constructed.

The results of the first phase provide information that helps with the decision about the second phase. After using the prototype, the user has a better understanding of the value of the benefits, and of the additional features the full-scale system needs to include. In addition, the developers can make a better estimate of the cost of the final product. The question at this point is: What benefits are necessary to justify this cost? If the decision maker feels that the system can provide these benefits, development proceeds on the full-scale system. Figure 13.5 illustrates these steps in the value analysis approach.

Though it was designed for DSSs, the value analysis approach is applicable to any information technology that can be tested on a low-cost basis before deciding whether to make a full investment. The current trend of buying rather than developing software, along with the increasingly common practice of offering software on a free-trial basis for 30 to 90 days, provide ample opportunities for the use of this approach. Organizations may also have opportunities to pilot the use of new systems in specific operating units, and then to implement them on a full-scale basis if the initial results are favorable.

Information Economics

The **information economics** approach is similar to the concept of critical-success factors in that it focuses on key organizational objectives. Information economics incorporates the familiar technique of scoring methodologies, which are used in many evaluation situations.

To use a **scoring methodology**, the analyst first identifies all the key performance issues and assigns a weight to each one. Each product in the evaluation receives a score on each factor, usually between zero and 100 points, or between zero and ten. These scores are multiplied by the weighting factors and then totaled. The item with the highest score is judged the best product. *A Closer Look* 13.3 on the facing page shows an example of using a scoring methodology to evaluate two different options.

The information economics approach uses organizational objectives to determine which factors to include, and what weights to assign, in the scoring

A CLOSER LOOK
13.3 SCORING WORKSHEET FOR EVALUATION OF OPTION *X* AND OPTION *Y*

Decision Participant Most Interested in Criteria	Criteria	Weight	Option *X* Grade	Option *X* Score	Option *Y* Grade	Option *Y* Score
	Intangibles (Benefits and Risks)					
CEO	Improve revenues, profits, and market share.	4	2	8	2	8
CEO	Integrate global operations.	4	3	12	5	20
CFO	Have flexibility for business changes and growth.	4	4	16	2	8
CFO	Have more end-user self-sufficiency.	4	3	12	3	12
VP, Human Resources (HR)	Improve employee morale.	2	2	4	1	2
CIO	Manage risk of organizational resistance to change.	2	−1	−2	−3	−6
CIO	Manage risk of project failure.	2	−1	−2	−2	−4
	Total Senior Management	**22**		**48**		**40**
CFO	Increase earnings per share.	2	2	4	2	4
CFO	Improve cash flow.	2	2	4	3	6
Dir. Acctg.	Close books faster.	2	3	6	2	4
Director, Fincl. Reporting	Expand profitability by better product line reporting.	2	3	6	3	6
	Total Finance	**8**		**20**		**20**
VP-HR	Improve employee productivity.	2	3	6	3	6
VP-HR	Attract, retain high-quality employees.	2	3	6	2	4
Dir. Employee Relations (ER)	Strengthen labor relations.	2	3	6	2	4
VP-HR	Enhance "employee service" image of HR.	2	3	6	2	4
Dir.-ER	Manage risk of insufficient communications with employees.	2	−2	−4	−3	−6
	Total Human Resources	**10**		**20**		**12**
CIO	Rapid implementation.	2	4	8	2	4
Director, Systems	Openness and portability.	2	4	8	3	6
Dir.-Sys	Easier software customization.	2	4	8	3	6
Dir.-Sys	Less software modification over time.	2	4	8	4	8
CIO	Global processing and support.	2	2	4	4	8
	Total Information Systems	**10**		**36**		**32**
	Total Intangibles	**50**		**124**		**104**
	Tangible Benefits					
CEO	Return on investment.	20	3	60	3	60
CEO	Payback period	20	3	60	2	40
	Total Tangibles	**40**		**120**		**100**
	Grand Total	**90**		**244**		**204**

Source: Compiled from "Peoplesoft Strategic Investment Model," *Peoplesoft.com* (August 1997).

methodology. The approach is flexible enough to include other factors in the analysis, such as impacts on customers and suppliers (the value chain). Executives in an organization determine the relevant objectives and weights at a given point in time, subject to revision if there are changes in the environment. These factors and weights are then used to evaluate IT alternatives; the highest scores go to the items that have the greatest potential to improve organizational performance.

Note that this approach can incorporate both tangible and intangible benefits. If there is a strong connection between a benefit of IT investment (such as quicker decision making) and an organizational objective (such as faster product development) the benefit will influence the final score even if it does not have a monetary value. Thus the information economics model helps solve the problem of assessing intangible benefits by linking the evaluation of these benefits to the factors that are most important to organizational performance. See Chou et al. (2000) for a discussion of the effectiveness of strategic IT investment decisions measured using a multicriteria analytical model. Wreden (1998) summarizes a discussion of how IT executives from different fields have attempted to measure IT value in practice.

Approaches like this are very flexible and can be carried out by software packages such as Expert Choice (*expertchoice.com*). The analysis can vary the weights over time; for example, tangible benefits might receive heavier weights at times when earnings are weak. The approach can also take risk into account, by using negative weights for factors that reduce the probability of obtaining the benefits. *A Closer Look* 13.4 on the opposite page shows an analysis of a decision of whether to develop a system in-house or buy it.

Management by Maxim for IT Infrastructure

Organizations that are composed of multiple business units, including large, multidivisional ones, frequently need to make decisions about the appropriate level and types of infrastructure that will be shared among and support their individual operating units. These decisions are important because infrastructure can amount to over 50 percent of the total IT budget, and because it can increase effectiveness through synergies across the organization. However, because of substantial differences among organizations—in their culture, structure, and environment—what is appropriate for one will not necessarily be suitable for others. The fact that many of the benefits of infrastructure are intangible further complicates this issue.

Broadbent and Weill (1997) suggest a method called **management by maxim** to deal with this problem. This method brings together corporate executives, business-unit managers, and IT executives in planning sessions to determine appropriate infrastructure investments through the following steps:

- ***Step 1. Consider strategic context.*** Identify long-term goals, potential synergies where sharing of services or data across units could improve performance, and degree of emphasis on autonomy or cooperation across business units.
- ***Step 2. Articulate business maxims.*** Develop short, well-defined statements of organizational strategies or goals in key areas such as costs, quality, flexibility, growth, human resources, and management philosophy.
- ***Step 3. Identify IT maxims.*** Develop statements of the IT strategies or goals required to support the business maxims. For example, a business maxim

A CLOSER LOOK
13.4 ANALYZING A BUILD VS. BUY DECISION

Tangible ROI with Enhanced Analysis
($ in thousands)

	Build Only (A)				Buy and Build (B)			
	2001	2002	2003	2004	2001	2002	2003	2004
Standard Tangible Savings								
(Reduced head count)	$ 0	$ 0	$ 75	$200	$ 0	$ 0	$175	$ 275
Overlooked Tangible Savings	0	0	375	575	0	275	600	625
Total Tangible Savings	$ 0	$ 0	$450	$775	$ 0	$275	$775	$ 900
Cost of new system	150	100	50	50	250	175	100	100
Net annual savings	($150)	($100)	$400	$725	($250)	$100	$875	$ 800
Cumulative savings	($150)	($250)	$150	$875	($250)	($150)	$525	$1,325
Gross four-year tangible savings		$1,225				$1,950		
Four-year cost of each choice		350				625		
Net Four-Year Saving from Each Choice		$875				$1,325		
Net Present Value (NPV) from Each Choice (at 6.5%)		$709				$1,100		
Internal rate of return (IRR)		150%				124%		
Choice Based on NPV Analysis: Buy and Build (choice B)								
Choice Based on IRR Analysis: Build Only (choice A)								

Source: Adapted from *Datamation,* January 7, 1994, p. 46.

might be "price products/services at lowest cost." A corresponding IT maxim could be "use IT to reduce costs by eliminating duplicated effort."

- ***Step 4. Clarify the firm's view of its IT infrastructure.*** Reach consensus on which category of infrastructure the business and IT maxims require. The four possibilities are:

  1. None—each business unit maintains its own infrastructure.
  2. Utility—sharing across units is done primarily to reduce costs.
  3. Dependent—primarily supports the requirements of current strategies of business units, including increasing revenues.
  4. Enabling—goes beyond current strategies of business units to support long-term goals.

- ***Step 5. Specify infrastructure services.*** Identify infrastructure services required to achieve the business and IT maxims, in the context of whichever of the above infrastructure categories is appropriate for the firm.

These steps are diagrammed in Figure 13.6 (page 584), which also shows a line at the bottom flowing through an item labeled "Deals." This represents a theoretical alternative approach in the absence of appropriate maxims, where the IT manager negotiates with individual business units to obtain adequate funding for

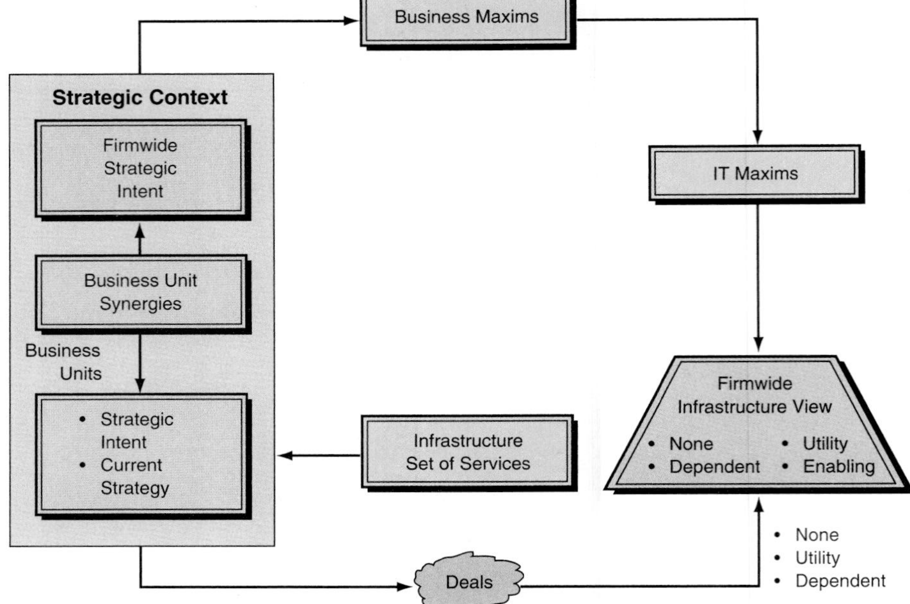

FIGURE 13.6
Management by maxim: linking strategy and infrastructure. (*Source:* M. Broadbent and P. Weill, "Management by Maxim," *Sloan Management Review*, Spring 1997, p. 79, by permission of publisher. ©2001 by Massachusetts Institute of Technology. All rights reserved.)

shared infrastructure. This approach can work where there is no shared infrastructure, or where the infrastructure category is a utility. However, Broadbent and Weill have not found any cases of firms that developed an enabling infrastructure via deals.

Option Valuation of IT Investments

A promising new approach for evaluating IT investments is to recognize that they can increase an organization's options in the future. Current IT investments, especially for infrastructure, make it possible to respond quickly to unexpected and unforeseeable challenges and opportunities in later years. If the organization waits until the benefits have been established, it may be very difficult to catch up with competitors that have already invested in the infrastructure and have become familiar with the technology.

The concept of **option valuation** is well known in the securities markets. In addition to stocks, investors can purchase options on stocks. These options give their owners the right to buy or sell the stock at a given price within a specified time period. For example, an investor could buy stock now in a major computer manufacturer at $80 per share, or he or she could pay around $8 now for the right to buy a share of that same stock at $80 any time in the next three months.

The key aspect of an option is that it offers an opportunity for a large profit in the future. If the stock in our example goes to $96—a 20 percent increase in value—the option to buy at $80 is now worth $16, which is a 100 percent gain over its original price. Therefore investors are willing to pay $8 for the option to pay $80 to buy a stock that is currently selling for $80, even though the actual value of the option at this point is zero.

Applying this concept to IT, the costs of a proposed investment could exceed the tangible benefits. However, if the project creates opportunities for additional projects in the future, the investment also has an options value that should be added to its other benefits.

The mathematics of option valuation are well established but unfortunately are too complex for many managers. (See Dixit and Pindyck, 1995, for details.) On the other hand, it is relatively easy to estimate **expected value (EV)** of possible future benefits by multiplying the size of the benefit by the probability of its occurrence. For example, an organization might consider investing in a corporate intranet. If there is a 50 percent probability that this would lead to better analyses, which would result in new business worth $10 million in additional profits, the value of this specific benefit would be 50 percent times $10 million, or $5 million. The calculations could also include an estimate of value for unspecified, totally unforeseeable benefits, based on the fact that they have occurred in the past. (For example, computerized airline reservation systems unexpectedly made it possible to establish "frequent flyer" and other yield-management marketing programs.)

The expected value approach does not, however, provide any estimate of the option value of an IT investment that makes it possible for the organization to either enter into or decide against other projects in the future. For a discussion on using *real-options pricing analysis* to evaluate a real-world IT project investment in four different settings, see Benaroch and Kauffman (1999). For an example of DSS evaluation using options theory, see Kumar (1999).

13.4 IT STRATEGIES: CHARGEBACK AND OUTSOURCING

In addition to identifying and evaluating the benefits of IT, organizations also need to account for its costs. Ideally the accounting systems will effectively deal with two issues. First, they should provide an accurate measure of total IT costs for management control purposes. Second, they should charge users for shared (usually infrastructure) IT investments and services in a manner that contributes to the achievement of organization goals. These are two very challenging goals for any accounting system, and the complexities and rapid pace of change make them even more difficult to achieve in the context of IT.

In the early days of computing it was much easier to identify costs. Computers and other hardware were very expensive and were managed by centralized organizational units with their own personnel. Most application software was developed internally rather than purchased. IT was used only for a few well-defined applications, such as payroll, inventory management, and accounts payable/receivable.

In contrast, nowadays computers are cheap, and software is increasingly purchased rather than made. The overwhelming majority of the total processing power is located on the collective desktops of the organization rather than in centralized computer centers, and it is managed by individual organizational units rather than a centralized IS department. A large proportion of the costs are in "hidden," indirect costs that are often overlooked.

These trends make it very difficult just to identify, let alone effectively control, the total costs of IT. As a practical matter, many organizations track costs associated with centralized IS and leave management and cost accounting for desktop IT to the user organizations. However, the trend toward attaching personal computers to networks, and the availability of network management software, make it easier to track and manage costs related to desktop IT. Some organizations indicate "six-digit" savings by using network management software to identify which computers use what software, and then reducing the site licenses to correspond to the actual usage (see Coopee, 2000, for details).

Chargeback

Although it is hard to accurately measure total IT costs, organizations can still use accounting systems to influence organizational IT usage in desirable directions. Large organizations typically require individual operating and support units to develop annual budgets and justify variances. Services from the central IS department represent a significant budget item for most of these units, so the way they are charged for these services will influence how much they use them.

In some organizations, the ISD functions as an *unallocated cost center.* All expenses go into an overhead account. The problem with this approach is that IT is a "free good" that has no explicit cost, so there are no incentives to control usage or avoid waste.

One alternative is to distribute all costs of IT to users as accurately as possible, based on actual costs and usage levels. This approach is one form of **chargeback** (also known as *chargeout,* or *cost recovery*). Although accurate allocation sounds desirable in principle, it can create problems in practice. The most accurate measures of use may reflect technological factors that are totally incomprehensible to the user. If fixed costs are allocated on the basis of total usage throughout the organization, which varies from month to month, charges will fluctuate for an individual unit even though its own usage does not change. These considerations can reduce the credibility of the chargeback system.

A third approach is to employ a **behavior-oriented chargeback** system. The primary objective of this type of system is influencing users' behavior. For example, it is possible to encourage (or discourage) usage of certain IT resources by assigning lower (or higher) costs. Although more difficult to develop, it recognizes the importance of IT—and its effective management—to the success of the organization. A behavior-oriented system not only avoids the unallocated-cost-center's problem of overuse of "free" resources; it can also reduce the use of scarce resources where demand exceeds supply, even with fully allocated costs.

In addition to increasing the organization's efficiency through better cost control, a behavior-oriented system can encourage more effective use of IT. Fully allocated costs often discourage the testing of new technologies—ones that could offer substantial benefits in the future—because the high initial costs are spread over a limited number of early users. On the other hand, behavior-oriented chargeouts can encourage experimentation and organizational learning of targeted technologies by offering them on a subsidized basis. Examples of behaviors that behavior-oriented chargeback systems may seek to influence are:

EFFICIENCY—DOING THINGS RIGHT

- Reduce wasted resources.
- Reduce use of scarce resources.
- Encourage use in off-peak hours (load leveling).
- Discourage "false economies" and suboptimizing behavior (actions that appear to help the individual unit but are bad for the organization as a whole).

EFFECTIVENESS—DOING THE RIGHT THINGS

- Encourage IT usage consistent with organizational strategies and goals.
- Encourage experimentation, technology assimilation, and organizational learning.
- Encourage more productive use of surplus resources.
- Encourage data sharing across organizational units.

- Encourage reuse of software instead of new development.
- Improve communications between users and IS department.

There are three steps in implementing a behavior-oriented chargeback system:

1. ***Determine objectives.*** This should involve IS staff, executives familiar with organizational plans, accounting personnel, and possibly consultants with related expertise. Within the context of organizational goals and plans, current and projected IT capabilities, and industry and technological trends, this group determines the general goals and specific behaviors that the chargeback system needs to encourage or discourage.
2. ***Determine appropriate measures.*** The success of a chargeback system depends on having measures that users can understand and control, and that they perceive as fair rather than arbitrary. It is better to use physical outputs (for example, number of invoices processed) rather than abstract computer jargon (such as "CPU seconds"). Calculations should be simple, verifiable, and consistent from month to month. However, caution is needed with measures that correspond to services offered by vendors, because they initially may provide lower quality or may price services at less than cost to attract business.
3. ***Implement and maintain the system.*** The final step is to put the new chargeback system into operation. Like other information systems, it will probably have initial bugs, and users will identify desirable features to add to the system. In addition, the system will need updates on a regular basis to reflect changes in technologies, organizational operations, strategies, and plans.

There are various methods of chargeback in addition to the regular and behavior-oriented methods. The reason is that it is very difficult to approximate costs, especially in companies where multiple independent operating units are sharing a centralized system. For a review of methods, see McAdam (1996). The difficulties in chargeback may be one of the drivers of IT outsourcing.

Outsourcing as an Economic Strategy

If organizations can effectively define and measure information technology costs and benefits, as we discussed in the preceding sections, they are in a better position to effectively manage their IT. On the other hand, they still may not be able to manage it as well as firms that specialize in managing IT. For such organizations, the most effective strategy for obtaining the economic benefits of IT and controlling its costs may be **outsourcing**, which is obtaining services from vendors rather than from within the organization.

Information technology is now a vital part of almost every organization and plays an important supporting role in most functions. However, IT is not the primary business of many organizations. Their *core competencies*—the things they do best and that represent their competitive strengths—are in manufacturing, or retailing, or services, or some other function. IT is complex, expensive, and constantly changing. It is difficult to manage IT, even for organizations with above-average management skills. Because of these considerations, some organizations decide to use outside vendors rather than internal IS units as their primary source of IT services.

The idea of outsourcing itself is not new. Organizations have always faced the choice of buying goods and services externally or producing them internally. The decision usually considers two factors: (1) which source is less expensive?

and (2) how much control is necessary? Most organizations buy their power from electric utilities because this is cheaper than operating their own generating equipment. However, a few (hospitals, for example) have their own emergency power-generating systems. These internal systems give them more control over their operations; they do not have to shut down if a disaster causes a power failure.

Outsourcing IT functions, such as payroll services, has been around since the early days of data processing. Contract programmers and computer timesharing services are longstanding examples. What is new is that, since the late 1980s, as illustrated in the opening case, *many* organizations are outsourcing the majority of their IT functions rather than just incidental parts. The trend became very visible in 1989 when Eastman Kodak announced it was transferring its data centers to IBM under a 10-year, $500 million contract. This example, at a prominent multibillion-dollar company, gave a clear signal that outsourcing was a legitimate approach to managing IT.

In a typical situation, the outsourcing firm hires the IS employees of the customer and buys the computer hardware. The cash from this sale is an important incentive for outsourcing by firms with financial problems. The outsourcer provides IT services under a five- to ten-year contract that specifies a baseline level of services, with additional charges for higher volumes or services not identified in the baseline.

Many smaller firms provide limited-scale outsourcing of individual services, but only the largest outsourcing firms can take over large proportions of the IT functions of major organizations. In the mid-1990s, IBM, EDS, and Computer Sciences Corp. were winning approximately two-thirds of the largest outsourcing contracts. PricewaterhouseCoopers (1999), in its 1998–99 survey of European private banks, found that nearly a quarter of survey respondents had either implemented or were considering implementing the outsourcing of their IT systems.

Offshore outsourcing of software development has become a common practice in recent years. About one-third of *Fortune* 500 companies have started to outsource software development to software companies in India. This trend of offshore outsourcing is largely due to the emphasis of Indian companies on process quality by adhering to models such as Software Engineering Institute's Software Capability Maturity Model (SW-CMM) and through ISO 9001 certification. India has fifteen of the twenty-three organizations worldwide that have achieved Level 5, the highest in SW-CMM ratings. For further details on offshore outsourcing, see Cusumano (2000) and Paulk (2000).

In addition to the traditionally outsourced services, Brown and Young (2000) identify two more scenarios for future outsourcing: creation of shared environments (e.g., exchanges, portals, e-commerce backbones), and providing access to shared environments (e.g., applications service providers (ASPs), Internet data centers). For example, Flooz.com, an online gift-currency store, outsourced its storage requirements to StorageNetworks, a storage service provider (Wilkinson, 2000). See *outsourcing-center.com* for details on advances and practices in outsourcing of various types of services such as ASPs and business process outsourcing (BPO).

OUTSOURCING ADVANTAGES AND DISADVANTAGES. Outsourcing advocates describe IT as a commodity, a generic item like electricity or janitorial services.

TABLE 13.3 Potential Outsourcing Benefits

FINANCIAL
- Avoid heavy capital investment, thereby releasing funds for other uses.
- Improve cash flow and cost accountability.
- Realize cost benefits from economies of scale, and from sharing computer housing, hardware, software, and personnel.
- Release expensive office space.

TECHNICAL
- Be freer to choose software due to a wider range of hardware.
- Achieve technological improvements more easily.
- Have greater access to technical skills.

MANAGEMENT
- Concentrate on developing and running core business activity.
- Delegate IT development (design, production, and acquisition) and operational responsibility to supplier.
- Eliminate need to recruit and retain competent IT staff.

HUMAN RESOURCES
- Draw on specialist skills, available from a pool of expertise, when needed.
- Enrich career development and opportunities for staff.

QUALITY
- Clearly define service levels.
- Improve performance accountability.
- Earn quality accreditation.

FLEXIBILITY
- Respond quickly to business demands.
- Handle IT peaks and valleys more effectively.

They note the potential benefits of outsourcing, in general, as listed in Table 13.3.

Clemons (2000) identifies the following risks associated with outsourcing contracts:

- ***Shirking*** occurs when a vendor deliberately underperforms while claiming full payment (e.g., billing for more hours than were worked, providing excellent staff at first and later replacing them with less qualified ones).
- ***Poaching*** occurs when a vendor develops a strategy and strategic application for a client and then uses them for other clients (e.g., vendor redevelops similar systems for other clients at much lower cost, or vendor goes into client's business).
- ***Opportunistic repricing or holdup*** occurs when a client enters into a long-term contract with a vendor and the vendor changes financial terms at some point or overcharges for unanticipated enhancements and contract extensions.

Organizations should consider the following strategies in managing the risks associated with outsourcing contracts (Clemons, 2000):

- ***Understand the project.*** Clients must have a high degree of understanding of the project, including its requirements, the method of its implementation, and the source of expected economic benefits. A common characteristic of successful outsourcing contracts is that the client was generally capable of developing the application but chose to outsource simply because of constraints on time or staff availability.

- ***Divide and conquer.*** Dividing a large project into smaller and more manageable pieces will greatly reduce programmatic risk and provides clients with an exit strategy if any part of the project fails.
- ***Align incentives.*** Designing contractual incentives based on activities that can be measured accurately can result in achieving desired performance.

The implementation of Internet-based technologies and especially of e-commerce encourages the use of outsourcing, as can be seen in the following *IT at Work* example below.

A special outsourcing consideration is the implementation of extranets. Implementing an extranet is very difficult due to security issues and the need to have the system be rapidly expandable. (Some companies report 1,000 percent growth for EC activities in a year; e.g., *seehotmail.com.*) General Electric Information Services (*geis.com*), an extranet outsourcer, charges between $100,000 and $150,000 to set up an extranet, plus a $5,000/month service fee. However, users of these services admit an ROI of 100 to 1,000 percent. For details see Duvall (1998).

OUTSOURCING RECOMMENDATIONS. Some organizations may decide to outsource because they just do not have the skills to manage the IT function, or because they need to sell off IT assets to generate funds. Various sources (e.g., Marcolin and McLellan, 1998) offer outsourcing recommendations, such as:

- ***Write short-period contracts.*** Outsourcing contracts are often written for five- to ten-year terms. Because IT and the competitive environment change so

IT at Work

...in Marketing

CANADIAN IMPERIAL BANK OF COMMERCE OUTSOURCES INTERNET TECHNOLOGIES

www.pcbanking.cibc.com

In the spring of 1996 the competitors of Canadian Imperial Bank of Commerce (CIBC) were ahead in implementing Internet banking, and CIBC was starting to lose market share. A decision was made to move quickly to implement the bank's own Internet capabilities.

Being a bank and not an IT expert, this was a challenge. So the bank decided to outsource the job to IBM's Global Services. Together, CIBC and IBM were able to implement home banking in six months. By 1998 the bank regained market share, having 200,000 online clients (see *pcbanking.cibc.com*).

IBM admits that CIBC's dilemma is becoming a familiar story in just about every industry. Time constraints brought on by competitive challenges, security issues, and a shortage of skilled system developers in the Internet/intranet field contribute to a boom in the outsourcing business. Implementing EC applications forces companies to outsource mission-critical applications. This was never done before on such a grand scale. This will result, according to the GartnerGroup, in the tripling of IT outsourcing in three years. Forrester Research found that 90 percent of the companies they polled use or plan to use Internet-related outsourcing.

For Further Exploration: What will happen to the outsourcers once the Internet/EC infrastructure is in place?

Source: Condensed from M. Duvall, "Companies Size Up Outsourcing," *Interactive Week,* January 12, 1998.

rapidly, it is very possible that some of the terms will not be in the customer's best interests after five years. If a long-term contract is used, it needs to include adequate mechanisms for negotiating revisions where necessary.

- ***Subcontracting.*** Vendors may subcontract some of the services to other vendors. The contract should give the customer some control over the circumstances, including choice of vendors, and any subcontract arrangements.
- ***Selective outsourcing.*** This is a strategy used by many corporations who prefer not to outsource the majority of their IT (like Kodak), but rather to outsource certain areas (such as connectivity or network security).

At this point, the phenomenon of large-scale IT outsourcing is approximately fifteen years old. The number of organizations that have used it for at least several years is still small, but it is growing. Business and IT-oriented periodicals have published numerous stories about their experiences. The general consensus of this anecdotal information is that the cost savings are not large—perhaps around 10 percent—and that not all organizations experience them. This still leaves the question of whether outsourcing IT can improve organizational performance by making it possible to focus more intensely on core competencies. Further research is necessary to answer this question.

An interesting example is the case of DuPont, the giant chemical concern. The magazine *Chemical Week* (March 12, 1997) reported that DuPont transferred its IT data center with 4,000 IT employees to Andersen Consulting and Computer Services Corp. This deal enabled DuPont and its outsourcers to form a partnership that markets IT services to others.

Finally, a new approach is that of *strategic outsourcing* (Garner, 1998), where you can generate new business, retain skilled employees, and effectively manage emerging technologies. Strategic outsourcing facilitates the leveraging of knowledge capabilities and investments of others by exploiting intellectual outsourcing in addition to outsourcing of traditional functions and services (Quinn, 1999).

13.5 ECONOMICS OF WEB-BASED SYSTEMS

As indicated earlier, Web-based systems can considerably increase productivity and profitability. In order to understand the reasoning for this, let us first examine the cost curves of digital products versus nondigital products, as shown in Figure 13.7. As the figure shows, for regular physical products the average cost declines up to a certain quantity, but then, due to increased production (e.g., adding a manager) and marketing costs, the cost will start to increase. For digital

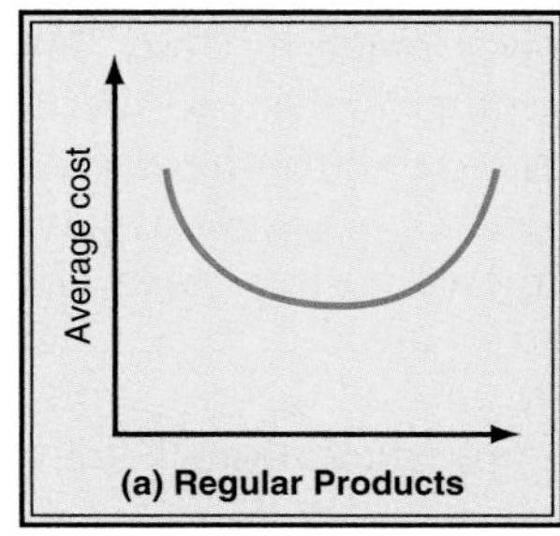

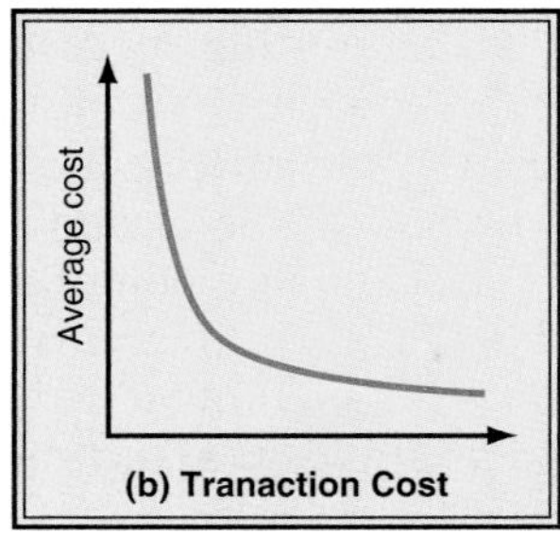

FIGURE 13.7 Cost curves of regular and digital products.

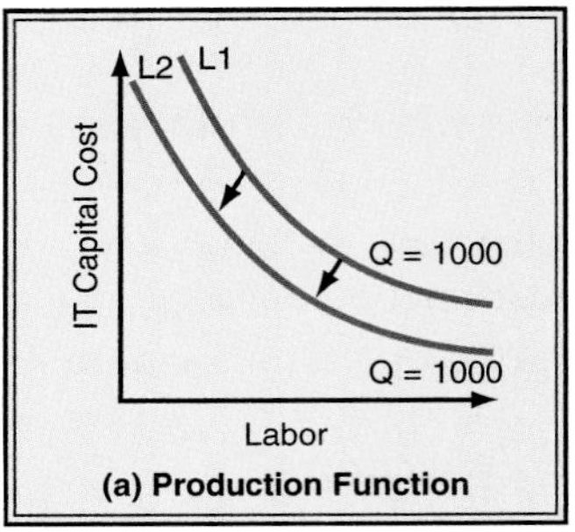

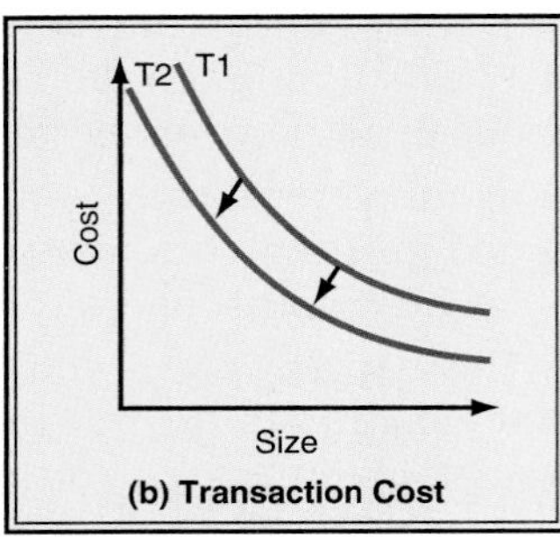

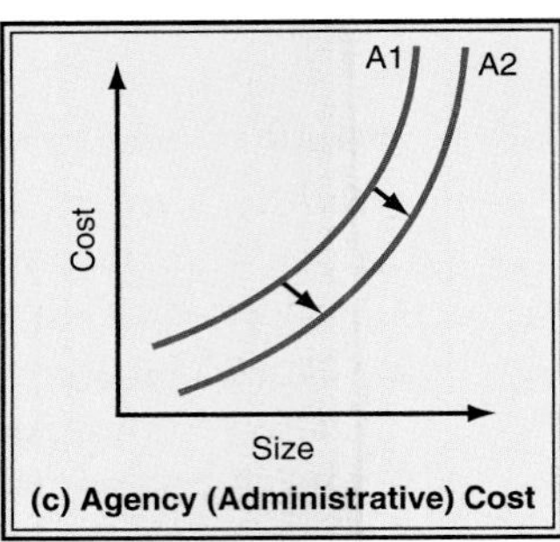

FIGURE 13.8 Economic effects of e-commerce.

products the cost will continue to decline with increased quantity. The variable cost in such a case is very little.

However, even for nondigital products electronic commerce can shift economic curves, as shown in Figure 13.8. The production function will decline (form L1 to L2) since you can get the same quantity with less labor and IT cost. The transaction cost for the same quantity (size) will be lower due to computerization. And finally, the administrative cost for the same quantity will be lower.

The justification of EC application is difficult. Usually one needs to prepare a *business case*. The purpose of the business case is not merely to justify an investment for the corporate leadership. A proper business case develops the baseline of desired results, against which actual performance can and should be measured. The business case should cover both the financial and nonfinancial performance metrics against which to measure the e-business implementation. These metrics must guide management of the implementation of all projects that fall within the e-business program.

The benefit and costs of EC depend on its definitions. But even when the applications are defined, we still have measurement complexities. Thomas Mesenbourg, from the Economic Programs of the U.S. Bureau of the Census, provides the following insights (summarized from *census.gov/epdc/www/ebusins.htm*), regarding these difficulties, by looking at a person buying a book online: The cost may include advertisement and marketing, cost of searching, cost of electronic payment and procurement, cost of security (authentication), shipping, customer support, accounting, and more. The bookseller may use vendors for fulfillment and support. It needs legal advice. It may have several business processes, involve many partners, and experience transaction-multiplier effects (positive or negative) of related transactions. As a result, it is difficult even to conduct risk analysis, not to mention cost-benefit analysis.

An interesting suggestion was made by Tjan (2001), who proposed to conduct an Internet portfolio planning analysis to identify appropriate EC applications. Using matrices, it is possible to find the *fit* of each project with the organizational objectives and the *viability* (potential payoff). Measures for viability are: market value potential, time to positive cash flow, personnel requirements, and funding requirements. Metrics for fit include: alignment with other company initiatives, alignment with core capabilities, fit with organization structure and culture, and ease of technical implementation. The fit and viability measures create a 2 × 2 matrix where initiatives can be placed to determine a recommended action. (See Figure 8.9, page 358.)

Web-based systems are being implemented by many organizations. However, hardly any efforts are being made to perform cost-benefit analysis or measure return on investment (ROI) on Web-based systems. There are various reasons for this lack of analysis: difficulties in quantifying expected benefits, limited time available for deployment, and so forth. Instead, most decisions to invest in Web-based systems are based on the assumption that the investments are needed for strategic reasons and that the expected returns cannot be measured in monetary values. Raskin (1999) advocates determining a return on investment (ROI) for extranet projects, though it is a difficult task, and suggests strategies for calculating ROI. The following *IT at Work* illustrates that some organizations calculate ROIs for their intranets and extranets, and others do not.

IT at Work

Integrating IT ...in Finance

INTRANET AND EXTRANET RETURNS ON INVESTMENT AND PROJECT JUSTIFICATION

Kinko's Inc., the copying and small-business-support retail chain, created an intranet document distribution and repository for information directed at its 900 retail branches. The intranet application resulted in savings of $500,000 per year in reduced paper, printing, and postage expenses. These savings gave the company a 50 percent ROI on the project, which cost $1 million to build.

Empire District Electric, a Missouri utility company with 140,000 customers, built an intranet-based customer information system (CIS) at a cost of $500,000 in one year, developed by only three programmers using Java programming language. The system handles customer information, usage records, rating charges, and other account-related information. A comparable off-the-shelf client/server or mainframe CIS system would have cost $3 million to $6 million. The CIS gave Empire District Electric an ROI of 100 percent, merely considering the savings on the lease for the mainframe to run the legacy CIS.

The American Medical Association (AMA) deployed 50 to 60 intranet applications for its 1,400 employees. These applications provide Web services such as telephone directories, policy and procedure sites, and self-service sites. The CIO of the AMA has not conducted any cost-benefits analysis for most of these applications, which cost $10,000 to $20,000 each to develop internally, because he felt that it is not worth his time.

Unilever Corp. is developing dozens of intranet applications to tie together its 300 subsidiaries operating in 88 countries. Most of these applications are not justified by ROI but by their ability to improve the information flow throughout the company, improve elements such as time to market, or increase local sales effectiveness. Some of these applications have resulted in direct ROI. For example, its Global Buying Service application brought down equipment costs by 20 to 40 percent by letting Unilever consolidate all its contracts with vendors, thus giving the company far greater purchasing power.

Heineken USA Inc. deployed an inventory-forecasting and sales extranet application to its network of 450 distributors. The application, apart from bringing significant savings from a reduction in manual data entry and paper shuffling, has also contributed to shrinking order-cycle time and has facilitated better inventory planning. With this extranet application, the distributors can order shipments of the Dutch beer only four to eight weeks ahead of time, rather than the previous ten to twelve weeks. The vice president of operations planning at Heineken, USA did not even try to calculate ROI.

Source: Compiled from C. Waltner, "Intranet ROI: Leap of Faith," *Information Week,* May 24, 1999.

13.6 OTHER ECONOMIC ASPECTS OF INFORMATION TECHNOLOGY

Negative Impacts of Failures and "Runaways"

Information technology is difficult to manage. One symptom of this problem is the trend to let somebody else manage IT through outsourcing. Another symptom is the high proportion of IS development projects that either fail completely or fail to meet some of the original targets for features, development time, or cost. The following definitions indicate the range of various types of failures:

- ***Outright failure.*** The system is never completed, and little or nothing is salvaged from the project.
- ***Abandoned.*** The system is completed, including some or all of the originally specified features, but it is never used or usage stops after a short period.
- ***Scaled down.*** The system is completed and used, but lacks much of the functionality of the original specifications.
- ***Runaway.*** The project requires much more money and time than planned, regardless of whether it is ever completed or used.

Many failures occur in smaller systems that handle internal processes within an organization, and they usually remain corporate secrets. The total investment is not large, the failure does not have a major economic impact, and the effects are generally not visible to outsiders. On the other hand, some IS failures result in losses in excess of ten million dollars and may severely damage the organization, as well as generating a lot of negative publicity. Failures in large public organizations such as the IRS or Social Security Administration are well advertised. One large-scale failure is described in the following *IT at Work.*

IT at Work

A LARGE-SCALE FAILURE AT DENVER INTERNATIONAL AIRPORT

www.flydenver.com

The Denver International Airport (DIA), at 53 square miles, was designed to be the largest U.S. airport. By 1992, it was recognized that baggage handling would be critically important and that this issue could not be off-loaded to the airlines that would be operating out of DIA. Consequently, an airportwide, IT-based baggage handling system was planned to dramatically improve the efficiency of airport luggage delivery. BAE Automated Systems, Inc., a world leader in the design and implementation of material handling systems, was commissioned by the City of Denver to develop the system. The system was composed of 55 networked computers, 5,000 electric eyes, 400 radio frequency receivers, and 56 bar code scanners. It was to orchestrate the safe and timely arrival of every suitcase and ski bag at DIA.

Problems with the baggage system, however, kept the new airport from opening as originally scheduled in October 1993. Soon the national and international media began to pick up the story, and the DIA came under investigation by various federal agencies. By the time the airport opened in late February 1995, it was 16 months behind schedule and close to $2 billion over budget. DIA eventually opened with two concourses served by a *manual* baggage system and one concourse served by a scaled-down semiautomated system.

For Further Exploration: Why do organizations keep investing money in projects in spite of clear evidence that they are failing? What are the issues in a decision to terminate a failing project?

Source: R. Monealegre and M. Keil, "De-escalating Information Technology Projects," *MIS Quarterly,* September 2000.

Spectacular, highly visible failures are evidence of problems in IS development. However, publicity on a few very large IT projects does not demonstrate how widespread these problems are throughout the field. The Standish Group International reports that a large majority of projects have experienced some form of failure. Its 1995 survey of 365 large organizations indicates that 31 percent of projects are not completed. Some 53 percent are completed, but with an average cost overrun of 189 percent; in other words, they cost almost three times the budget. Many of these completed projects did not contain all of the functionalities of the original specifications. Only 16 percent were completed on time and on budget (Standish Group, 1995).

These high failure levels are in marked contrast to experience with design and development in other areas of the economy. Architects and engineers design houses, buildings, and bridges, and then contractors construct them. Engineers design automobiles that are subsequently mass-produced in factories. Failures are rare, and they usually result from unusual situations such as natural disasters or gross negligence.

The number of system development problems is large enough to represent a market opportunity for consulting firms. A KPMG Peat Marwick survey in Britain provides another indicator of the magnitude of problems in this area. When using contractors to develop information systems, organizations threatened legal action on 20 percent of the projects and actually went into court on 4 percent. This level of legal involvement is much greater than in other types of business dealings.

What are the causes of the high failure rates? One problem is that computer systems are highly abstract and complex. Architects create drawings that eventually become houses or buildings, which are solid and visible and easily understandable by nontechnical people. In contrast there are two end results of programming: (1) code that requires a lot of effort even for other programmers to understand; and (2) systems that are comprehensible to users only in terms of a limited number of printouts and screen displays, rather than all the other things that need to occur within the hardware, software, and network to produce these outputs. Their inherent complexity means that systems development projects need more effective management than other organization activities.

Because of the complexity and associated risks, some managers refuse to develop systems beyond a certain size. The "one, one, ten rule" says not to develop a system if it will take longer than one year, has a budget over one million dollars, and will require more than ten people. Following this strategy, an organization will need to buy rather than develop large systems, or do without them.

Purchasing can be the safest strategy for very large and complex systems, especially those that involve multiple units within an organization. For example, the SAP AG software firm offers a family of integrated, "enterprise-level," large-scale information systems (see Chapter 8). These systems are available in versions tailored for specific industries, including aerospace, banking, utilities, retail, and so forth. Many organizations feel that buying from a good vendor reduces their risk of failure, even if they have to change their business processes to be compatible with the new system.

The economics of software production suggest that, for relatively standardized systems, purchasing can result in both cost savings and increased functionality. For example, if a large bank needs a system to handle a variety of customer checking and savings accounts, it has two options:

- Spend $5 million to internally develop its own system, which, *if the project is successful,* will match up exactly with the way it does business, or
- Spend $3 million to purchase a system from an outside vendor. The purchased system will require an additional $500,000 for customization and for changes within the organization to accommodate it. The new system includes desirable features that might not be available if the bank develops its own system, but it does not include certain other features that the bank views as important but not critical. The vendor spent $20 million developing the software, because it expects to sell the system to at least 10 banks. Several other banks are already using the system and recommend it, so there is very little risk of failure.

Execution of IT projects based on either purchased systems or developed systems is associated with different types of risks. Cule et al. (2000) categorize types of risk into four categories: two types of *inside* risks, associated with the project manager and the task, and two types of *outside* risks, related to the client and the environment. They suggest appropriate managerial behavior, in the directions of self-assessment, task control, client relationship, and environmental monitoring, respectively, to mitigate these four types of risks.

Liebowitz (1999) identified the following suggestions for managing development risks, based on the findings from a Delphi survey of IS managers in major U.S. organizations:

- All phases of development must be carefully planned out at the beginning of the project.
- Fear of failure of developing innovative IS projects has inhibited the creation and successful use of IS projects.
- The user interface design is a critical element in gaining acceptance of an information system.
- Accuracy and timeliness of information affects the level of confidence that the users and managers have in the information system.
- All interested parties including senior IS managers should be actively involved and informed throughout all phases of the system development.

The New Economics of IT

In the preceding sections, our focus has been on the economics of the *use of IT* in organizations to assist in performing other activities. In this section, we turn to the economics of IT *as a product in itself,* rather than in a supporting role.

In 1916, David Sarnoff attempted to persuade his manager that the American Marconi Company should produce inexpensive radio receivers to sell to the consumer market. Others in the company (which subsequently became RCA) opposed the idea because it depended on the development of a radio broadcasting industry. They did not expect this to happen, because they could not see how broadcasters could generate revenues by providing a service without any charges to the listeners. The subsequent commercial development of radio, and the even greater success of television, proved that Sarnoff was right. If it is possible to provide a popular service to a large audience at a low cost per person, there will be ways of generating revenues. The only question is, How?

The World Wide Web on the Internet resembles commercial broadcasting in its early days. Fixed costs—initial investments and production costs—can be high in themselves, but they are low in terms of average cost per potential customer. The incremental or variable costs of delivering content to individual customers, or processing transactions, are very low.

The market is large—at least one-half of the U.S. population, plus foreign markets, now have access to the Internet—and it is growing rapidly. Many people who do not have computers at home can access the Internet through computers at work, schools, or libraries. The arrival in 1995 of Web TV adapters for TV sets made it possible for homes without computers to get on the Internet for as little as $400. These trends could lead to a situation of "universal connectivity," in which almost every citizen in the industrialized countries has access to the Net.

The Web is also different from broadcasting in ways that increase its economic potential. At present, typical Web users have above-average incomes and education. Users can view most Web content at any time, rather than just at the scheduled times of broadcast programs. The Web can reach smaller, very specialized "niche" markets better than the mass media.

Chapter 5 provides detailed information on specific applications of e-commerce. These applications demonstrate how favorable economic factors are leading to a wide variety of approaches to generating income using the Web or other aspects of the Internet. We now turn to the economic concepts of increasing returns, which applies both to the Internet and to software production.

Increasing Returns

Stanford University economist Brian Arthur (1996) is the leading proponent of the economic theory of *increasing returns,* which applies to the Web and to other forms of information technology. He starts with the familiar concept that the economy is divided into different sectors, one that produces physical products, and another that focuses on information. Producers of physical products—e.g., foodstuffs, petroleum, automobiles—are subject to diminishing returns. Although they may have initial increasing economies of scale, they eventually reach a point where costs go up and additional production becomes less profitable.

Arthur notes that in the information economy the situation is very different. For example, initial costs to develop new software are very high, but the cost of producing additional copies is very low. The result is **increasing returns**, where profitability rises more rapidly than production increases. A firm with a high market share can use these higher profits to improve the product or to enhance the marketing, in order to strengthen its leading position. Figure 13.9 illustrates the difference between increasing and decreasing returns.

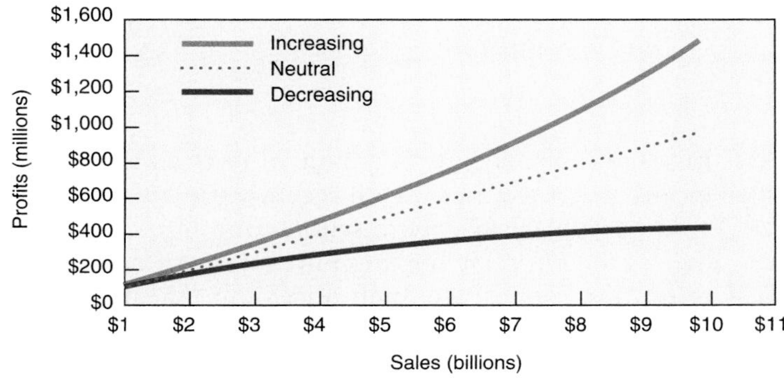

FIGURE 13.9 Increasing versus decreasing returns.

In addition to higher profitability, two other factors favor firms with higher market share. The first is **network effects**. Leading products in an industry attract a base of users, and this leads to development of complementary products. These users and products constitute a "network" that enhances the position of the dominant product. For example, the open architecture of the IBM PC made it possible to develop add-on hardware and to create clones that run the same software. The market for PCs became much larger than the market for Apple computers, which have a closed architecture. Software companies shifted production to PC versions of their products, which further enhanced the dominance of the PC. All this happened in spite of a substantial amount of evidence that Apple's computers really were better products.

The second factor is the **lock-in effect**. Most new software is hard to learn, so users typically will not switch to a different product unless it is much more powerful or they are forced into making the change. The end result of these factors is that when a firm establishes a clear lead over its competitors, it tends to become stronger and stronger in its market.

The potential for increasing returns requires management strategies that are very different from those in other industries. Arthur (1996) suggests the following strategies:

- ***Build up a large customer base through low prices.*** Netscape allows individual consumers (as opposed to organizations) to download its Web browser at no charge. This accelerated development of the Web and established Netscape's market position. It also increased the market for browsers and related software that Netscape sells to organizations as well as to individual consumers through retail outlets.
- ***Encourage development of complementary products.*** Novell provided support and assistance for developers to create applications or modify existing applications to run on its network operating system. The availability of this application software strengthened Novell's market position, which in turn increased the size of the market for the developers of these applications.
- ***Use "linking and leveraging."*** In addition to encouraging outside suppliers, firms can acquire or internally develop products that complement existing products. They can also capitalize on a large customer base for existing products. Microsoft's Windows operating system provides capabilities that make its word processing and spreadsheet software more competitive. The market for the Windows operating system is also enhanced because it is required in order to run these strong products. In addition, Microsoft generates a large proportion of its revenues by selling upgrades to customers who own previous versions of its products.

Market Transformation Through New Technologies

In some cases, IT has the potential to completely transform the economics of an industry. For example, until recently the encyclopedia business consisted of low-volume sales, primarily to schools and libraries. The physically very bulky product resulted in relatively high manufacturing and shipping costs, which made the price even higher. The high price, and the space required to store the books, reduced potential sales to the home market.

A CLOSER LOOK
13.5 THE ENCYCLOPEDIA ATLANTICA

The table below shows a financial analysis for an aggressive scenario in which the (hypothetical) *Encyclopedia Atlantica* immediately shifts all its production from the traditional hardbound book format to a CD-ROM version. Note that manufacturing and shipping costs drop from $150 to $10 per unit. The cost of the contents increases by $2 million, reflecting the addition of sound, greater use of graphics, and the effort required to set up hyperlinks between different sections. The price per unit is reduced by 50 percent, from $700 to $350, while unit sales more than double and marketing expenses increase in proportion to unit sales. Despite the lower price and higher costs for content and marketing, the profit margin on the CD-ROM version is projected at 19.6 percent versus 16.7 percent on the hardbound version.

In practice, some customers in *Atlantica*'s traditional markets will continue buying the hardbound version for many years to come. Additional scenarios are necessary to show a more gradual transition to a market dominated by CD-ROM versions.

The scenarios also need to include additional revenues from customers after the initial sale. Customers can receive annual updates for $25 per year, as well as the opportunity to buy new editions at a 50 percent discount every five years.

Some interesting questions may be raised regarding this situation:

- Should *Atlantica* cut the price of the CD-ROM version to reflect economies of production and shipping, and to dramatically increase the size of the total market? Or should it set the price at the same level as the hardbound version, and try to market the CD-ROM version as a low-volume, high-margin, premium product?
- What will happen if *Atlantica* starts to publish on the Web? Should it do so?

	Hardbound	CD-ROM
Unit sales	30,000	70,000
Price per unit	$700	$350
Gross revenue	$21,000,000	$24,500,000
− Cost of content	−10,000,000	−12,000,000
− Manufacturing & shipping costs	−4,500,000	−700,000
− Marketing costs	−3,000,000	−7,000,000
= Profit before taxes	$3,500,000	$4,800,000
Profit margin	16.7%	19.6%

Two things happened to change this situation. First, CD-ROM technology was adapted from storing music to storing other digital data, including text and images. Second, since the mid-1990s this technology has been a standard component of a majority of computers sold for the home market. Encyclopedia producers began selling their products on CD-ROMS, in some cases at reduced prices that reflected the lower production costs. These CD-ROM versions include new features made possible by the technology, most notably sound and hyperlink cross-references to related material in other sections. Lower prices and additional features have the potential to substantially increase the size of the total market. The hypothetical example in *A Closer Look* 13.5 shows how the economics of this business could change.

MANAGERIAL ISSUES

Information technology has certain characteristics that differentiate it, and its economics, from other aspects of the organizational world. Therefore IT requires management practices that are more effective than, and in some cases different from, those that are adequate for non-IT activities. For example, organizational resistance on many fronts can turn the most promising system into a failure (Watson and Haley, 1998). Managers need to be aware of and responsive to the following issues.

1. ***Constant growth and change.*** The power of the microprocessor chip doubles every two years, while the cost remains constant. This ever-increasing power creates both major opportunities and large threats as its impacts ripple across almost every aspect of the organization and its environment. Managers need to continuously monitor developments in this area to identify new technologies relevant to their organizations, and to keep themselves up-to-date on their potential impacts.

2. ***Shift from tangible to intangible benefits.*** Few opportunities remain for automation projects that simply replace manual labor with IT on a one-for-one basis. The economic justification of IT applications will increasingly depend on intangible benefits, such as increased quality or better customer service. In contrast to calculating cost savings, it is much more difficult to accurately estimate the value of intangible benefits prior to the actual implementation. Managers need to understand and use tools that bring intangible benefits into the decision-making processes for IT investments.

3. ***Not a sure thing.*** Although IT offers opportunities for significant improvements in organizational performance, these benefits are not automatic. Managers need to very actively plan and control implementations to increase the return on their IT investments.

4. ***Chargeback.*** Users have little incentive to control IT costs if they do not have to pay for them at all. On the other hand, an accounting system may allocate costs fairly accurately to users but discourage exploration of promising new technologies. The solution is to have a chargeback system that has the primary objective of encouraging user behaviors that correspond to organizational objectives.

5. ***Risk.*** Investments in IT are inherently more risky than investments in other areas. Managers need to evaluate the level of risk before committing to IT projects. The general level of management involvement as well as specific management techniques and tools need to be appropriate for the risk of individual projects.

6. ***Outsourcing.*** The complexities of managing IT, and the inherent risks, may require more management skills than some organizations possess. If this is the case, the organization may want to outsource some or all of its IT functions. However, if it does outsource, the organization needs to make sure that the terms of the outsourcing contract are in its best interests both immediately and throughout the duration of the agreement.

7. ***Increasing returns.*** Industries whose primary focus is IT, or that include large amounts of IT in their products, often operate under a paradigm of increasing returns. In contrast, industries that primarily produce physical outputs are subject to diminishing returns. Managers need to understand which paradigm applies to the products for which they are responsible and apply management strategies that are most appropriate.

ON THE WEB SITE... Additional resources, including the Virtual Company, quizzes, cases, updates, additional exercises, links, demos, and activities, can be found on the book's Web site.

KEY TERMS

Behavior-oriented chargeback *586*
Best-practice benchmarks *578*
Chargeback *586*
Cost-benefit analysis *575*
Expected value (EV) *585*
Increasing returns *597*
Information economics *580*
Labor productivity *568*
Lock-in effect *598*
Management by maxim *582*
Metric benchmarks *577*
Moore's law *566*
Multifactor productivity *568*
Network effects *598*
Offshore outsourcing *588*
Option valuation *584*
Outsourcing *587*
Price-to-performance ratio *567*
Productivity paradox *568*
Runaway project *571*
Scoring methodology *580*
Total cost of ownership (TCO) *578*
Value analysis *579*

CHAPTER HIGHLIGHTS (Numbers Refer to Learning Objectives)

1. The power of computer hardware should continue increasing at an exponential rate for at least 10 years, doubling every 18 months, while costs remain at the same levels as before.
2. Although organizations have spent tremendous amounts of money on IT, it is difficult to prove that this spending has increased national productivity.
3. Approaches to measuring IT benefits include: the value of information, cost-benefit analyses of automation projects, and benchmarking IT infrastructure performance.
4. Decision makers can evaluate intangible benefits of IT by using the value analysis, information economics, and option valuation methods.
5. Behavior-oriented chargeback systems, if properly designed, encourage efficient and effective usage of IT resources.
6. Outsourcing may reduce IT costs and can make it possible for organizations to concentrate their management efforts on issues related to their core competencies.
7. Computer systems are highly abstract and inherently very complex, which magnifies the impacts of weaknesses in the management of the development process.
8. Industries in the information sector of the economy experience increasing returns, which provide a major advantage to firms that have large shares of markets.
9. Web-based technologies may be approached differently for conducting cost-benefit analysis due to their different economic curves, lack of baseline data, frequent changes, etc. Modifying existing concepts, such as is done in portfolio selection, is advisable.

QUESTIONS FOR REVIEW

1. What are the impacts of exponentially increasing computer hardware power and declining price-to-performance ratios on business production activities and new product development?
2. What is the productivity paradox, and why is it important?
3. Why is it generally more difficult to evaluate the benefits of IT projects now than it was 20 years ago?
4. Write and explain the formula for calculating the value of information.
5. Identify examples of intangible benefits of IT.
6. Describe both metric and best-practice benchmarks, and give examples.
7. What are the results when an organization does not charge users for IT services?
8. Identify circumstances that could lead a firm to outsource its IT functions rather than continue with an internal IS unit.
9. Describe the different types of failure than can occur in IS development projects.
10. Identify some industries that operate with diminishing returns, and some that have increasing returns.

QUESTIONS FOR DISCUSSION

1. What are the general implications for managers, organizations, and consumers of constantly increasing computer capabilities and declining costs?
2. Discuss what is necessary to achieve productivity gains from IT investments.
3. Why is it more difficult to measure productivity in service industries?
4. Identify arguments for including estimated values for intangible benefits in net present value (NPV) analyses of IT investments, and contrast them with the arguments for excluding such estimates.
5. What is IT infrastructure, and why is it difficult to justify its cost?
6. Explain how a behavior-oriented chargeback system can be superior to an accounting system that charges users fairly accurate estimates of the costs of services they use.
7. Discuss the pros and cons of outsourcing IT, including alternatives to outsourcing.
8. How can an organization evaluate the quality of its customer service to make sure that the productivity gains of IT are not offset by poorer service?
9. Compare and contrast chargeback systems and outsourcing as alternative approaches for reducing costs and more effectively managing the IS function.
10. Identify and discuss reasons why IS projects are more vulnerable to failure than other types of projects.
11. Discuss how giving products away can be a profitable strategy in industries with increasing returns.
12. Is an NPV analysis appropriate for projects where there is a high risk of failure? If so, does the NPV model need to be modified? How?

EXERCISES

1. Conduct research on how long exponential growth in computer hardware capabilities (Moore's law) will continue.
2. Create a scoring methodology that reflects your personal requirements, and use it to evaluate two competing software products in the same category (for example, two Web browsers or two corporate portal development environments).
3. If you have access to a large organization, conduct research on the methods it uses to charge users for IT services and how the users feel about these charges.
4. Identify several large corporations that have outsourced major portions of their IT, and compare their stock market performance to the S&P 500 stock index over the same period.
5. Two companies, A and B, produce comparable software that sells for $325 a copy. Each invested $250 million to develop its version, and each has costs of $50 per copy for packaging, marketing, and so on. The only difference is that company A has 90 percent of a market of 10 million copies, and company B has 10 percent of that market. Calculate the profits and return on investment for these companies.

   Company A reduced the price of the software to $250 per copy, forcing its competitor to also lower its price, with unit sales rising to 12.3 million as a result of the lower price. What will be the effect of such a price change on profits and return on investment for these companies?
6. A small business invests $50,000 in robotic equipment. This amount is shown as a negative value in Year 0. Projected cash flows of $20,000 per year in Year 1 through Year 5 result from labor savings, reduced material costs, and tax benefits. The business plans to replace the robots with more modern ones after 5 years and does not expect them to have any scrap value. The equipment generates a total of $100,000 in savings over 5 years, or $50,000 more than the original investment. However, a dollar saved in the future is worth less than a dollar invested in the present. If the business estimates its return on investment as 15 percent, then $1.00 should be worth $1.15 in one year, $1.32 after 2 years with compound interest, and so on. Cash flows are divided by these "discount factors" to estimate what they are worth at present. Calculate the total cash flow after this discounting, and discuss whether the investment can be justified.

GROUP AND ROLE-PLAYING ACTIVITIES

1. Group members should use the Web and periodical indexes, such as ABI/Inform, to find information about IT failures with total losses of at least $50 million. Each group will produce a five-page report on at least three major failures. The report should identify the factors that led to each individual failure, emphasizing factors that were common to more than one project. The report should also identify management actions that could have prevented or reduced the impacts of these failures.

2. Considerable discussions and disagreements exist among IS professionals regarding outsourcing. Divide the group into two parts: One will defend the strategy of large-scale outsourcing. One will oppose it. Start by collecting recent material at *datamation.com* and *cio.com*.

INTERNET EXERCISES

1. Look at the work of Brynjolfsson and Hitt regarding the "productivity paradox" (two CACM papers) and at Paul Strassmann's article at *strassmann.com/pubs/datamation0297/*. Compare the different findings in these two sources, and prepare a summary report.
2. Read the *Information Week* article at *techweb.com/se/directlink.cgi?IWK19970630S0038*. Compare and contrast the approaches to evaluating intangible benefits in the article to those suggested in this textbook.
3. Enter the Web sites of the GartnerGroup (*gartnergroup.com*), The Yankee Group (*yankeegroup.com*), and *CIO* (*cio.com*). Search for recent material about outsourcing, and prepare a report on your findings.
4. Enter the Web site of IDC (*idc.com*) and find how they evaluate ROI on intranets, supply chain, and other IT projects.
5. Visit the Web site of Resource Management Systems (*rms.net*) and take the IT investment Management Approach Assessment Self-Test (*rms.net/self_test.htm*) to compare your organization's IT decision-making process with those of best-practices organizations.
6. Enter *compaq.com/tco* and *cosn.org/tco*. Find information about the total cost of ownership model. Write a report on the state of the art.

Minicase 1

Intranets: Invest First, Analyze Later?

The traditional approach to information systems projects is to analyze potential costs and benefits before deciding whether to develop the system. However, for moderate investments in promising new technologies that could offer major benefits, organizations may decide to do the financial analyses after the project is over. A number of companies took this latter approach in regard to intranet projects initiated prior to 1997.

Judd's

Located in Strasburg, Virginia, Judd's is a conservative, family-owned printing company that prints *Time* magazine, among others. Richard Warren, VP for IS, pointed out that Judd's "usually waits for technology to prove itself . . . but with the Internet the benefits seemed so great that our decision proved to be a no-brainer." Judd's first implemented Internet technology for communications to meet needs expressed by customers. After this it started building intranet applications to facilitate internal business activities. One indication of the significance of these applications to the company is the bandwidth that supports them. Judd's increased the bandwidth by a magnitude of about 900 percent in the 1990s without formal cost-benefit analysis.

Eli Lilly & Company

A very large pharmaceutical company with headquarters in Indianapolis, Eli Lilly has a proactive attitude toward new technologies. It began exploring the potential of the Internet in 1993. Managers soon realized that, by using intranets, they could reduce many of the problems associated with developing applications on a wide variety of hardware platforms and network configurations. Because the benefits were so obvious, the regular financial justification process was waived for intranet application development projects. The IS group that helps user departments develop and maintain intranet applications increased its staff from three to ten employees in 15 months.

Needham Interactive

Needham, a Dallas advertising agency, has offices in various parts of the country. Needham discovered that, in developing presentations for bids on new accounts, employees found it helpful to use materials from other employees' presentations on similar projects. Unfortunately, it was very difficult to locate and then transfer relevant material

(continued)

in different locations and different formats. After doing research on alternatives, the company identified intranet technology as the best potential solution.

Needham hired EDS to help develop the system. It started with one office in 1996 as a pilot site. Now part of DDB Needham, the company has a sophisticated corporate-wide intranet and extranet in place. Although the investment is "substantial," Needham did not do a detailed financial analysis before starting the project. David King, a managing partner explained, "The system will start paying for itself the first time an employee wins a new account because he had easy access to a co-worker's information."

Cadence Design Systems

Cadence is a consulting firm located in San Jose, California. It wanted to increase the productivity of its sales personnel by improving internal communications and sales training. It considered Lotus Notes but decided against it because of the costs. With the help of a consultant, it developed an intranet system. Because the company reengineered its sales training process to work with the new system, the project took somewhat longer than usual.

International Data Corp., an IT research firm, helped Cadence do an after-the-fact financial analysis. Initially the analysis calculated benefits based on employees meeting their full sales quotas. However, IDC later found that a more appropriate indicator was having new sales representatives meet half their quota. Startup costs were $280,000, average annual expenses were estimated at less than $400,000, and annual savings were projected at over $2.5 million. Barry Demak, director of sales, remarked, "We knew the economic justification . . . would be strong, but we were surprised the actual numbers were as high as they were."

Source: P. Korzenioski, "Intranet Bets Pay Off," *InfoWorld,* January 13, 1997, and the companies' Web site.

Questions for Minicase 1

1. Where and under what circumstances is the "invest first, analyze later" approach appropriate? Where and when is it inappropriate? Give specific examples of technologies and other circumstances.
2. How long do you think the "invest first, analyze later" approach will be appropriate for intranet projects? When (and why) will the emphasis shift to traditional project justification approaches? (Or has the shift already occurred?)
3. What are the risks of going into projects that have not received a thorough financial analysis? How can organizations reduce these risks?
4. Based on the numbers provided for Cadence Design System's intranet project, use a spreadsheet to calculate the net present value of the project. Assume a 5-year life for the system.
5. Do you see any relationship between the "invest first, analyze later" approach to financial analysis and the use of behavior-oriented chargeback systems?
6. Relate the Needham case to the concept of a repository knowledge base (see Chapter 9).

Minicase 2

Pfizer Japan Sharpens Its Competitive Edge

www.pfizer.co.jp

Pfizer Pharmaceutical, Inc. is a global research-based pharmaceutical company that discovers, develops, manufactures, and markets innovative medicines for people and animals. Pfizer Pharmaceutical Inc., Japan (Pfizer Japan), established in 1955, has its headquarters in Tokyo and oversees the operations of the branches located in major cities in Japan and its research center and laboratory in Nagoya. Its success in clinical research and the development of pharmaceutical products made it imperative that its enterprise computing infrastructure did not lag behind its product development and its flourishing sales, marketing, and delivery activities.

The current mixture of incompatible and disparate solutions was causing workflow problems at Pfizer Japan. The multiple IT vendors that were employed provided very little integration, causing operating costs to rise at an alarming rate and quality levels to take a significant dip. Recruiting specialized and suitable IT professionals proved an uphill task, as IT skills were not a core competency of pharmaceutical professionals. Pharmaceutical staff members were often side-tracked having to deal with IT functions, and this distracted them from Pfizer's core business objectives.

Pfizer Japan decided to outsource its IT operations to a single vendor so that it could concentrate fully on its core business of clinical research and product development, and could deliver quality customer service. The greatest challenge that CIO David Larkin faced was integrating the various computing functions to facilitate organizational workflow and achieve optimum efficiency.

Pfizer Japan selected Compaq Services, after assessing seven leading IT vendors who responded to its request. The solution that was proposed and implemented comprised scalable client/server systems on the Compaq *Tru64*™ UNIX and Microsoft Windows NT platforms with helpdesk, desktop, and server-management capabilities consolidated by Compaq. These capabilities aimed to improve Pfizer Japan's productivity and create a more homogeneous desktop environment across the organization.

Regulations in Japan demanded that clinical test results had to be strictly stored in a secure, controlled-access location and environment. As a result, it was critical that Pfizer move its computing hosting facility from the headquarters in Tokyo to a specially designed data center near Yokohama. The company had a tight deadline within which to shift its operations. Compaq was faced with the initial challenge of assisting Pfizer Japan with moving to the new computing hosting facility.

The lack of documentation of Pfizer's standard IT operating procedures was a major problem. Compaq has helped Pfizer in recovering from this to create a controlled and defined environment.

The scope of outsourcing services also included round-the-clock network monitoring and management, call-center staffing, catering to Pfizer Japan's operations, and IT maintenance. The tighter integration between the various components of Pfizer's business operations resulted in significant benefits for the company.

The deployment of the outsourcing project has considerably improved the overall efficiency of Pfizer's sales operation in Japan. The data mining solution implemented by Compaq has enabled the Pfizer sales force to develop customized sales programs that effectively target specific customers and identify hot leads. The targeted data mining has significantly increased the sales team's productivity above those of other Pfizer sales teams around the world. The solution implemented by Compaq has also opened possible avenues to expand Pfizer Japan's sales operations. According to Mr. Larkin, "We are experimenting with the possibility of establishing a parallel sales force that specializes in specific areas of healthcare. Now, with the essential IT functionality in place, the vision may soon materialize."

With the customer management database strategically integrated in call centers located all over Japan, Pfizer is able to identify customer needs more accurately and respond instantly to their needs. Compaq staffing of the Pfizer call centers in Japan has contributed to a faster response time to customer inquiries. The outsourcing contract has also permitted the call-center hours to be extended. The outsourced call-center operation has enabled Pfizer to free essential pharmaceutical expertise from handling customer inquiries to focusing on core business areas. Its operations have also taken a more global approach due to accessibility created by the enhanced call center.

Equipped with its current redefined computing model, Mr. Larkin envisions that advancements in applications development will assume greater forms at Pfizer Japan—applications that are ahead of the pharmaceutical market in the areas of sales, marketing, support, and delivery.

For companies exploring outsourcing, Mr. Larkin gives this advice: "The scope of outsourcing should be clarified at the onset. The agreement should also be flexible enough to accommodate revisions and adjustments in the future."

Source: Compiled from *www5.compaq.com/services/success/stories/ss_pfizer.html* (September 1999).

Questions for Minicase 2

1. What risks does Pfizer Japan incur by totally outsourcing its IT operations? Can you think of some organizations, or some types of operations, that should not be outsourced?
2. What considerations must there be in selecting an outsourcing vendor?
3. What were the major problems and difficulties faced by Pfizer Japan, and how did outsourcing of IT operations solve these problems?
4. What are the additional or unforeseen benefits to Pfizer Japan as a result of outsourcing?

REFERENCES AND BIBLIOGRAPHY

1. Arthur, W. B., "Increasing Returns and the New World of Business," *Harvard Business Review*, July–August 1996.
2. Benaroch, M., and R. J. Kauffman, "A Case for Using Real Options Pricing Analysis to Evaluate Information Technology Project Investments," *Information Systems Research*, Vol. 10, No. 1, March 1999.
3. Bennett, R. F., and C. J. Dodd, "Y2K Aftermath—Crisis Averted, Final Committee Report," The United States Special Committee on the Year 2000 Technology Problem. Washington, D.C.: Government Printing Office, February 29, 2000.
4. Broadbent, M., and P. Weill, "Management by Maxim: How Business and IT Managers Can Create IT Infrastrucures," *Sloan Management Review*, Spring 1997.
5. Brown, R. H., and A. Young, "Scenarios for the Future of Outsourcing," GartnerGroup, December 12, 2000.

6. Brynjolfsson, E., and L. M. Hitt, "Beyond the Productivity Paradox," *Communications of the ACM*, August 1998.

7. Choi, S. Y., and A. B. Whinston, *The Internet Economy: Technology and Practice*. Austin TX: SmartEcon, 2000.

8. Chou, T. C., et al., "Managing Strategic IT Investment Decisions: From IT Investments Intensity to Effectiveness," *Information Resources Management Journal*, October–December 2000.

9. Clemons, E. K., "The Build/Buy Battle," *CIO Magazine*, December 1, 2000.

10. Coopee, T., "Building a Strong Foundation," *Network World*, January 31, 2000.

11. Cule, P., et al., "Strategies for Heading Off IS Project Failure," *Information Systems Management*, Spring 2000.

12. Cusumano, M., "'Made in India'—A New Sign of Software Quality," *Computerworld*, February 28, 2000.

13. Dekker, R., and R. de Hoog, "The Monetary Value of Knowledge Assets: A Micro Approach," *Expert Systems with Applications*, Vol. 18, 2000.

14. Dixit, A. K., and Pindyck, R. S., "The Options Approach to Capital Investment," *Harvard Business Review*, May–June 1995.

15. Downing, T., "Eight New Ways to Evaluate Automation," *Mechanical Engineering*, July 1989.

16. Duvall, M., "Companies Size Up Outsourcing," *Interactive Week*, January 12, 1998.

17. Earl, M. J., "The Risks of Outsourcing IT," *Sloan Management Review*, Spring 1996.

18. Garner, R., "Strategic Outsourcing: It's Your Move," *Datamation*, February 1998.

19. GartnerGroup, *gartnerweb.com/public/static/aboutgg/pressrel/pr200001120b. html*, November 20, 2000.

20. Gray, P., and H. Watson, "Present and Future Directions in Data Warehousing," *Database*, Summer 1998.

21. Green, C. B., *Benchmarking the Information Technology Function*. New York: Conference Board, 1993.

22. Hitt, L. M., and E. Brynjolfsson, "Productivity, Business Profitability, and Consumer Surplus: Three Different Measures of Information Technology Value," *MIS Quarterly*, June 1996.

23. ITAA (Information Technology Association of America), "Skills Study 2000—Bridging the Gap: Information Technology Skills for a New Millennium," *uen.org/techday/html/technology.html*, April 2000.

24. Kappelman, L. A., et al., "Calculating the Cost of the Year-2000 Compliance," *Communications of the ACM*, February 1998.

25. Keen, P. G. W., "Value Analysis: Justifying DSS," *Management Information Systems Quarterly*, March 1981.

26. King, J., "IS Reins In Runaway Projects," *Computerworld*, February 24, 1997.

27. Kirwin, W., et al., "New Paradigms Challenge the PC LAN Topology," GartnerGroup, April 11, 1997 (*gartner3.gartnerweb.com/public/static/software/rn/00033861.html*).

28. Kumar, R. L., "Understanding DSS Value: An Options Perspective," *Omega*, June 1999.

29. Li, H., et al., "The IT Performance Evaluation in the Construction Industry," *Proceedings, 33rd Hawaiian International Conference on Systems Sciences (HICSS)*, January 2000.

30. Liebowitz, J., "Information Systems: Success or Failure?" *Journal of Computer Information Systems*, Fall 1999.

31. Lin, W. T., and B. M. Shao, "Relative Sizes of Information Technology Investments and Productivity Efficiency: Their Linkage and Empirical Evidence," *Journal of AIS*, September 2000.

32. Lucas, H. C., *Information Technology and the Productivity Paradox: Assessing the Value of Investing in IT*. New York: Oxford University Press, 1999.

33. Marcolin, B. L., and K. L. McLellan, "Effective IT Outsourcing Arrangements," *Proceedings, 31st HICSS*, January 1998.

34. McAdam, J. P., "Slicing the Pie: Information Technology Cost Recovery Models," *CPA Journal*, February 1996.

35. Montealegre, R., and M. Keil, "De-escalating Information Technology Projects: Lessons from the Denver International Airport," *MIS Quarterly*, September 2000.

36. Moore, G. E., "Cramming More Components on Integrated Circuits," *Electronics*, April 19, 1965.

37. Moore, G. E., *Inside the Tornado*. New York: HarperCollins, 1995.

38. Moore, G. E., "Moore's Law," *CIO*, January 1, 1997.

39. Mukhopadhyay, T., et al., "Assessing the Impact of Information Technology on Labor Productivity: A Field Study," *Decision Support Systems*, Vol. 19, February 1997.

40. Munk, N., "Technology for Technology's Sake," *Forbes*, October 21, 1996.

41. Paulk, M., "Indian Software Excellence: Education and Process Pay Off," *Cutter IT Journal*, February 2000.

42. Phelps, R., and M. Mok, "Managing the Risks of Intranet Implementation: An Empirical Study of User Satisfaction," *Journal of Information Technology*, Vol. 14, 1999.

43. PricewaterhouseCoopers, European Private Banking Survey, *pwcglobal.com/ch/eng/inssol/publ/bank/privatbanking.html*, 1999.

44. Pountain, D., "Amending Moore's Law," *Byte*, March 1998.

45. Quinn, J. B., "Strategic Outsourcing: Leveraging Knowledge Capabilities," *Sloan Management Review*, Summer 1999.

46. Raskin, A., "The ROIght Stuff," *CIO Web Business Magazine*, February 1, 1999.

47. Renkema, T. J. W., *The IT Value Quest: How to Capture the Business Value of IT-Based Infrastructure*. Chichester, England: Wiley, 2000.

48. Roberts, J., "Why an ERP Project Failed—A Valuable Case Study," *Inside GartnerGroup*, May 5, 1999.

49. Standish Group, "Chaos," Standish Research Paper, *standishgroup.com/visitor/chaos.htm*, 1995.

50. Strassmann, P. A., *The Squandered Computer*. New Canaan, CT: Information Economics Press, 1997.

51. Tjan A. K., "Put Your Internet Portfolio in Order," *Harvard Business Review*, February 2001.

52. Violino, B., "Return on Investment Profiles: The Intangible Benefits of Technology Are Emerging as the Most Important of All," *Information Week*, June 30, 1997.

53. Vistica, G. L., et al., "The Day the World Shuts Down," *Newsweek*, June 2, 1997.

54. Waltner, C., "Intranet ROI: Leap of Faith," *Information Week*, May 24, 1999.

55. Watson, H. J., and B. J. Haley, "Managerial Considerations," *Communications of ACM*, Vol. 41, No. 9, September 1998.

56. Wilkinson, S., "Phone Bill, Electricity Bill . . . Storage Bill? Storage Utilities Attract New Economy Companies with *Pay-as-you-go Service*," *Earthweb.com*, October 24, 2000.

57. Willcocks, L., and G. Fitzgerald, "Pilkington PLC: A Major Multinational Outsources Head Office IT Function," in E. Turban, et al., *Information Technology for Management*. New York: Wiley, 1996.

58. Willcocks, L., et al., "Risk Mitigation in IT Outsourcing Strategy Revisited: Longitudinal Case Research at LISA," *Journal of Strategic Information Systems*, Vol. 8, September 1999.

59. Wreden, N., "Proving the Value of Technology," *Beyond Computing*, July–August 1998.

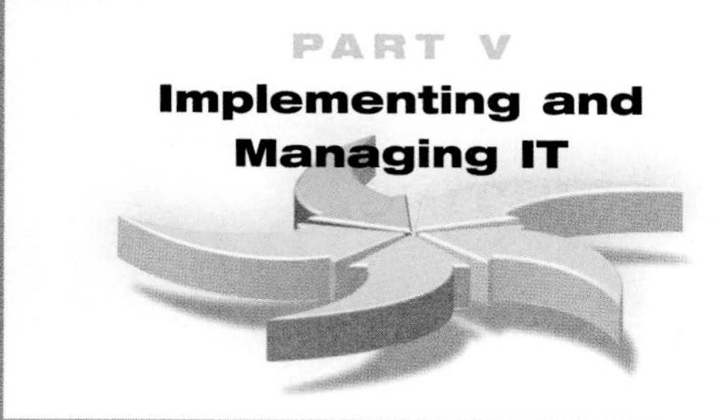

PART V

Implementing and Managing IT

CHAPTER 14

Building Information Systems

LEARNING OBJECTIVES

After studying this chapter, you will be able to:

1. Explain the concept of a systems development life cycle (SDLC).
2. Compare and contrast prototyping, rapid application development (RAD), joint application design (JAD), and traditional SDLC approaches to systems development.
3. Identify advantages and disadvantages of object-oriented (OO) development.
4. Describe component-based development.
5. Evaluate alternatives to in-house systems development.
6. Discuss the major strategies, methods, and tools for building e-commerce applications.
7. Identify advantages and disadvantages of CASE tools.
8. Describe alternative approaches to software process quality improvement.

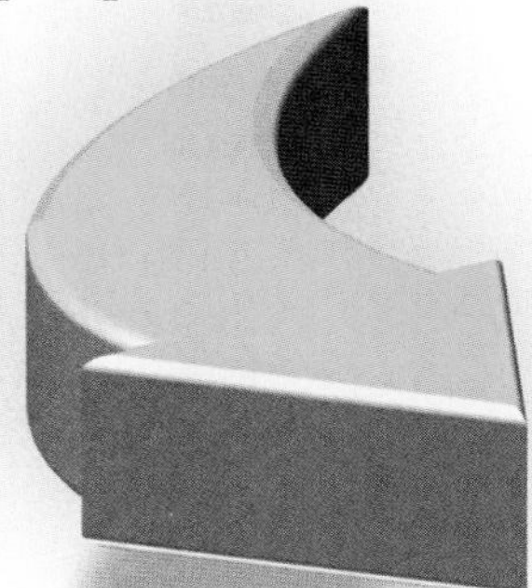

This chapter was revised by Linda Lai from the City University of Hong Kong.

SNAP-ON'S APPROACH TO SETTING UP AN E-COMMERCE SITE

THE PROBLEM

Snap-On, a tool and equipment maker in Washington state, wanted to set up an e-commerce site, and do so quickly. The problem the company faced was whether to build the site in-house, or buy the services of an outside contractor to set up the site.

THE SOLUTION

www.snap-on.com

Brad Lewis, e-commerce manager for Snap-On, decided to hire application service provider (ASP) OnLink Technologies to implement a catalog for the company's e-commerce site. Lewis wanted his industrial customers to navigate easily through the 17,000 products listed in Snap-On's paper catalog, and he wanted to integrate the site with Snap-On's ERP system. "If we developed this application in-house, we would have spent six to nine months just designing and implementing it," he said. By using an ASP, Snap-On was able to get the entire catalog up and running in four months.

What was unusual is that Lewis integrated his staff with OnLink's to help transfer those catalog-building skills. Lewis himself spent several days a week during the four-month development period at OnLink's headquarters, where he had his own office. He concentrated on developing application features and integration with back-end systems. "By spending so much time at OnLink, I became a member of their engineering group, and other members of my staff became temporary members of their professional services catalog group," Lewis says.

THE RESULT

The result was that Lewis created an in-house ASP consulting service for Snap-On, providing guidance to other departments and subsidiaries that want to put up catalogs on their own Web sites. "One of the first questions we pondered before we outsourced was whether we could later bring that expertise in-house," Lewis says. "We didn't want to do it any other way." The desire to have expertise in-house was fostered by Snap-On's desire for control of their Web site. "When e-commerce solutions become a mission-critical application, companies can become uncomfortable outsourcing them. If the outsourcer's site goes down, the company's business goes down," says Leah Knight, an analyst for the GartnerGroup. Snap-On found a way to both buy and build its e-commerce applications.

Sources: Compiled from *Internetweek,* January 10, 2000, and from *snap-on.com* (2001).

LESSONS LEARNED FROM THIS CASE

Snap-On.com is an example of what end users and analysts say is the newest trend in constructing e-commerce sites. With this approach, the site would already be in a host environment, and components are already there, so you can quickly add to the site. Most companies, feeling the "Internet-speed" pressure to get their sites up fast, need the experience and resources of outside vendors. At the same time, however, these end users are taking charge of those sites as soon as possible.

Local control enables them to make improvements faster and save money on expensive hourly fees each time they need to make a small change to the site. As Web sites evolve, e-businesses find that moving programming talent in-house is the way to go.

In this chapter we'll look at the topic of building information systems. The broad term **systems development** refers to all the activities used to create information systems in an organization and the processes of their accomplishment. Since organizational environments and general technologies change over time, organizations need new systems, or major revisions to existing systems, to continue to meet their objectives. Therefore, systems development is an ongoing process in all organizations that use IT.

In this chapter we discuss various approaches to development that can increase the probability of favorable outcomes. We initially discuss the concept of a systems development life cycle. We then discuss various system development alternatives (prototyping, rapid application development, joint application design, and object-oriented development). The subsequent two sections cover end-user development, acquiring systems from outside sources, and deciding between development approaches. Next is a section on the new approaches, methods, and techniques used in developing Web-based information systems. The final section looks at the use of quality management and project planning techniques to improve outcomes of the development process.

14.1 THE CONCEPT OF A SYSTEMS DEVELOPMENT LIFE CYCLE

In the early years of data processing, many software developers did not use any kind of formal approach. They would simply ask users a few questions about what the system was supposed to do and then start programming. Sometimes this approach resulted in desirable outcomes, and sometimes it failed. The failures were frequent enough to indicate that more formal approaches were necessary. The concept of a *systems development life cycle* provides a comprehensive framework for formal design and development activities.

To understand the concept of a systems development life cycle (SDLC), consider this analogy. A business firm moves from one city to another. Someone has to acquire property in the new city. Someone has to arrange for telephone and utility services at the new location. People need to pack, ship, unpack, and install furniture and equipment at the new location. The actual list of tasks will have many additional items.

The moving project therefore requires a very detailed plan. It should identify every significant task and assign each one to individuals or groups within or outside the organization. Every task needs a start date and a completion date, and some tasks cannot start until after the completion of others. Therefore the plan needs to coordinate the start and completion dates of the individual tasks within the limitation of the target completion date for the whole project.

Looking at the plans for several such moving projects, we would find many of the same tasks. With a little more effort, we could group the tasks into logically related categories and then arrange the categories in a sequence corresponding to the different phases of a moving project over time. These general categories would apply to most moving projects, even though the individual tasks could vary from project to project.

Substitute the words "information systems development" for the word "moving" in the above paragraphs and you have the concept of a **systems development life cycle (SDLC)**. An SDLC represents a set of general categories that show the major steps, over time, of an information systems development project. Within these general categories are individual tasks. Some of these tasks are present in most projects, while others would apply only to certain types of projects. For example, smaller projects may not require as many tasks as larger ones.

Note that there is no universal, standardized version of the SDLC. Consulting firms, as well as IS groups within organizations, develop individualized versions appropriate to their own operations. They may give their versions unique names. For example, Andersen Consulting calls its version Method/1. The Microsoft certification programs include training in its Solution Development Discipline (SDD) methodology. Most of the description of this chapter's version of an SDLC is relevant to other SDLCs.

Another consideration is that the phrase "systems development life cycle" has *two distinct meanings*. An SDLC can be a *general conceptual framework* for all the activities involved in systems development or acquisition. An SDLC can also be a very *structured and formalized design and development process.* The following discussion is from the perspective of the SDLC as a general conceptual framework. For a formal SDLC development methodology, see Kendall and Kendall (2001).

An Eight-Stage SDLC

Figure 14.1 provides a graphic model of an SDLC that has eight stages. That is, we placed all the major tasks into eight groups. Others group theirs into six, seven, eight, or even nine. Even if others use eight groups, the content of each stage may differ somewhat.

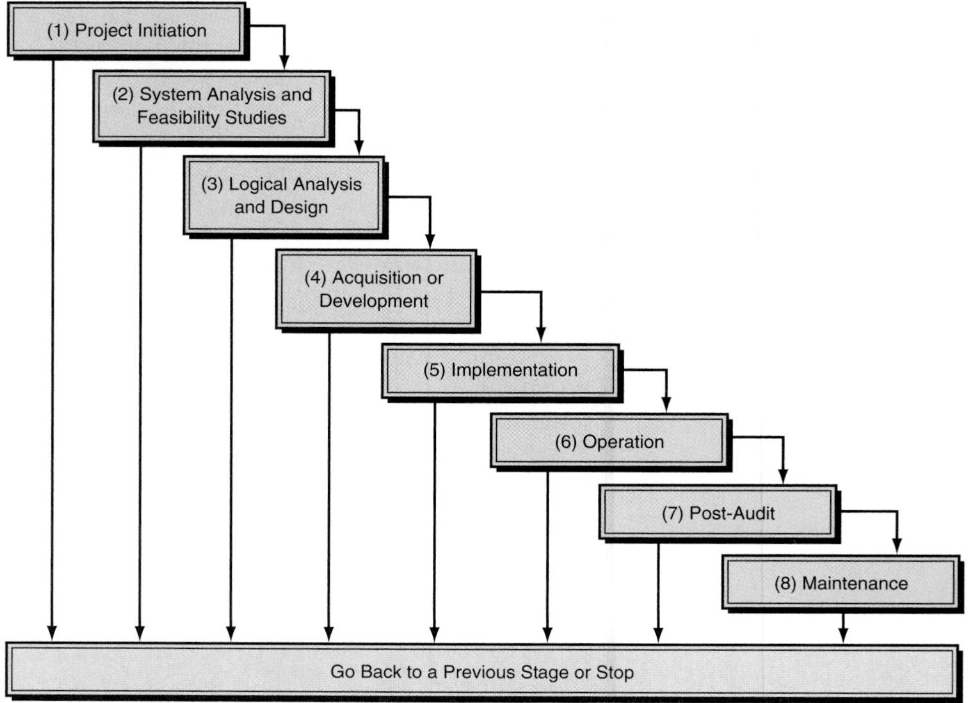

FIGURE 14.1 An eight-stage SDLC.

Note also that the stages overlap: A subsequent stage may start before the previous stage ends. This is in contrast to the traditional **waterfall method**, in which the work flows completely through the tasks in one stage before dropping down to the next stage. Also note that the process can go backward more than one stage, if necessary. These overlapping stages provide flexibility for adapting quickly to the volatile demands of the current business environment.

An organization can use this framework to develop its own comprehensive checklist of tasks and subtasks. Project managers can then use the checklist to identify activities required for specific projects. The following discussion outlines the individual stages and their major tasks.

STAGE 1: PROJECT INITIATION. Somebody needs to start the project. Usually it is a manager outside the IS organization who has a problem or sees an opportunity related to the area where he or she works. A formal planning process also may identify new systems that can help the organization meet its objectives. Sometimes the IS group initiates projects that will improve its own operations or deal with common problems among the user areas.

STAGE 2: SYSTEMS ANALYSIS AND FEASIBILITY STUDIES. Stage 2 consists of two phases of analysis: systems analysis and feasibility studies.

Systems Analysis. Once a project is initiated, the systems analysis phase begins. **Systems analysis** refers to the investigation of the existing situation. It may describe the status of a problem that the information system is expected to solve. It is a process that may take weeks, or months, involving many activities (see Kendall and Kendall, 2001, for details). Some of the major activities include isolating the symptoms of a problem and determining its cause. Other activities are the identification of the business processes and their interrelations and the flow of information related to these processes.

Systems analysis aims at providing a thorough understanding of the existing organization, its operation, and the situation relevant to the system one wants to build. Systems analysis deals also with the people and procedures involved, the existing IS technology, and the environment surrounding the problem area.

Systems analysis methods include observations, review of documents, interviews, and performance measurement. Several methods exist for the execution of systems analysis, and some of them are supported by software. Systems analysis also includes the concept of the proposed system and its anticipated contribution to the solution of the problem.

Feasibility Studies. To determine the probability of success of the proposed solution **feasibility studies** are conducted. Such studies may be conducted several times throughout the systems development life cycle. They are designed to determine whether the solution is achievable, given the organization's resources and constraints and the impact of the surrounding environment. The major areas of feasibility investigation are:

- ***Technology.*** Are the performance requirements achievable utilizing current information technologies? If not, are they attainable through capabilities that will be available by the time the project finishes? Will newer technologies supersede those in the proposed project before the organization recovers its investment?
- ***Economics.*** Are the expected benefits greater than the costs? Can the organization afford the costs, in terms of spending and personnel requirements?

Are the risks, including the possibility of cost and schedule overruns, acceptable for an investment of this size?

- ***Organizational factors.*** Is the proposed system reasonably compatible with the organizational culture, internal political considerations, and work rules? Are the skill levels needed to use the new system consistent with the employees who will operate it?

- ***Legal, ethical, and other constraints.*** Is the new or automated process ethical to employees and customers? Does it meet all regulatory requirements? Are any of the constraints in danger of being violated?

If the initial analysis indicates that the project could be feasible, the organization should conduct a more comprehensive analysis, using financial analysts and technology specialists as appropriate for the size and complexity of the project. This study needs to verify the findings of the initial analysis and develop more detailed information about costs and benefits for net present value or other formal financial analyses. If the detailed study verifies the feasibility (and the sponsors are still interested), the project can go on to the next stage.

STAGE 3: LOGICAL ANALYSIS AND DESIGN. At this point, one or more systems analysts determine two major aspects of the system: (1) what it needs to do, and (2) how it will accomplish these functions. The emphasis at this stage is on **logical design**, the design of an IS from the user's point of view. The analyst identifies *information requirements* and specifies processes and generic IS functions such as input, output, and storage, rather than writing programs or identifying hardware. Determining information requirements, as discussed in Chapter 8, may be a very difficult task. Then, the logical analysis and design process that lays out the components of the system and their relationships can start. The analysts often use modeling tools such as *data flow diagrams* (DFDs, see Figure 14.2) and *entity-relationship diagrams* (ERDs, see Figure 14.3, next page) to represent logical processes and data relationships.

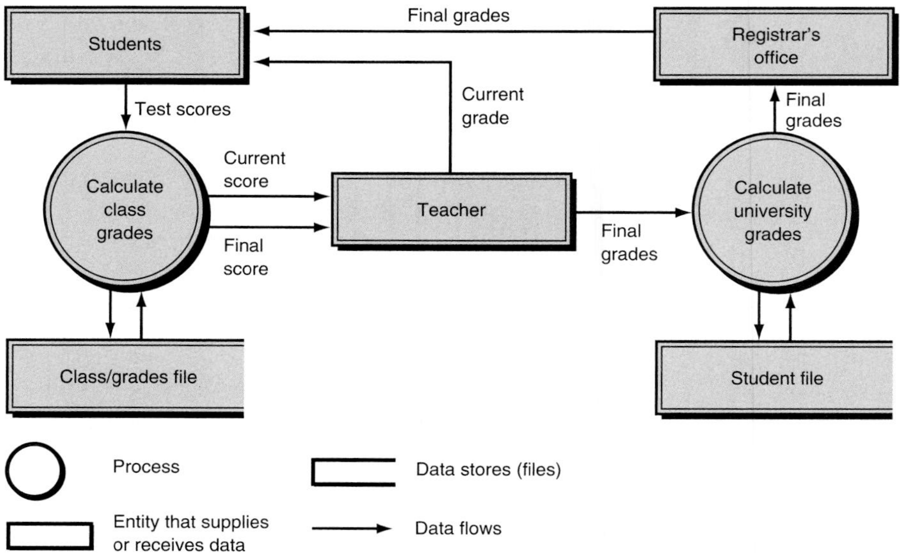

FIGURE 14.2 Data flow diagram for student grades example.

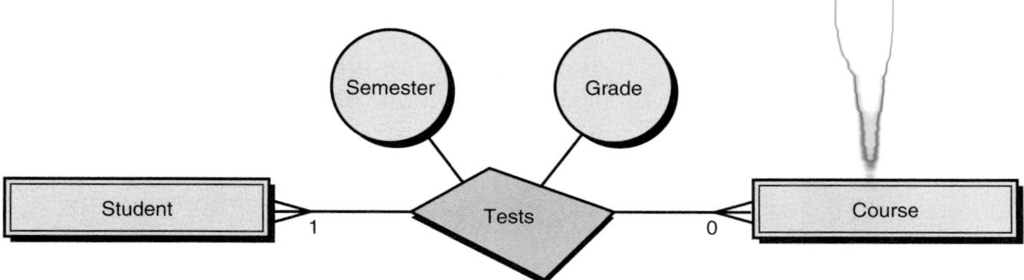

FIGURE 14.3 Entity-relationship diagram of students, courses, and grades.

The development team needs to involve the users in the process but not put a large burden on them. Users are a major source of information about the functional requirements of the system. Involving them can also increase their feelings of ownership of the system, which can lead to a more successful implementation. In contrast, the *IT at Work* illustration below shows how "insufficient senior staff on the team" could make a large-scale project fail.

Logical design is followed by a **physical design**, which translates the abstract logical model into the specific technical design (the "blueprints") for the new system.

The trend toward purchasing software, instead of developing it, is changing both the general emphasis and the specific tasks in the logical analysis and design

IT at Work

MASSIVE PROJECTS FAILURE AT ADIDAS

...in Production & Operations Management

www.adidas.com

In 1993, sportswear maker Adidas faced difficulties with its old distribution system that was responsible for distributing shipments of goods across the United States. Lack of standards, high coordinating complexity, late orders, slow response time, and market change were the main problems with the system. In fact, Adidas felt it was losing valuable customers as a result of its distribution system.

In January, top management approved the development of a new state-of-the-art distribution system. The goal of the new system was to centralize the bar-coded tracking system and link it to scanners, conveyor belts, lifting equipment, and chutes. The goal was to reduce the time needed for processing orders and merchandise, in order to be able to ship out orders within 24 hours.

The system became a nightmare when many of the key players involved with the initial system launch left the company and others were heading to the exit. There were no "appropriate staff" and management willing to take care of the avalanche of problems. First, Integrated Software Logistic Engendering (ISLE) Inc., the original software vendor, went out of business. This company had marketed the system to run under the UNIX platform, but Adidas had decided to use Stratus Computers, with which they were familiar. Also, ISLE left its creation without appropriate documentation and with many program bugs. Meanwhile, Adidas shot itself in the foot when it fired the lead integrator on the project. The system ran, but not well.

Eventually, Adidas decided to scrap the computer software and hardware (keeping the sorting equipment) and install an IBM RS/6000 server, running warehouse management software from Exeter Systems in North Billerica, Mass. That system brought Adidas's Spartanburg, South Carolina, facility to its knees. The business was down 90 percent of the time because of storage. Thanks to many of its other warehouses and facilities, Adidas managed to bypass the Spartanburg bottleneck by distributing workload among them. But it ended up paying double the price for another state-of-the-art system that finally met its needs.

For Further Exploration: How important are staff training and senior management capabilities to the success of an IS project?

Sources: Condensed from Robert L. Glass, *Software Runaways: Lessons Learned from Massive Software Projects Failure*, Upper Saddle River, NJ: Prentice-Hall, 1998; and from *adidas.com* (2001).

phase. Analysts still need to identify user requirements. However, they now spend more time comparing requirements to features of available software, and less time on designing systems. They need to prepare detailed specifications only when the functionality that users need is not available in software in the marketplace. They also have to identify configuration requirements for commercial packages that offer a wide range of customization options.

STAGE 4: ACTUAL ACQUISITION OR DEVELOPMENT. The logical design of the new system guides the actual development or acquisition, just as blueprints guide the construction of a new building. IS personnel use the specifications to purchase the hardware and software required for the system and then to configure it as needed. Programmers write code for parts of the system where commercial sources are not appropriate. Technical writers develop documentation and training materials. IS personnel *test* the system, and users should also do some testing prior to the actual implementation. The testing identifies bugs and also compares system performance to the specifications in the design.

STAGE 5: IMPLEMENTATION. Implementation is obviously an important stage; the system can fail here even if it has all the specified functionality. The project team should plan the implementation very carefully, to avoid problems that could lead to resistance. The users need training in the mechanics of the system, to reduce frustration and to minimize productivity losses in the transition period. In addition to developing technical skills, the training should also attempt to motivate users, for example, by stressing the benefits the system brings to the organization.

Even in the best circumstances, the implementation process will reveal bugs and other unexpected problems. The implementation team needs to resolve these as soon as possible, to retain its credibility with the users and maintain the progress of the conversion.

In most cases, implementing a new system requires a *conversion* from a previous system. Approaches to conversion include:

- ***Parallel conversion.*** The old and new systems operate concurrently for a test period, and then the old system is discontinued. **Parallel conversion** is the safest approach, but also the most expensive.
- ***Direct cutover.*** The old system is turned off, and the new system is turned on. This **direct cutover** is the fastest and least expensive approach, but also the most risky.
- ***Pilot conversion.*** The new system is implemented in a subset of locations—for example, some of the branches in a large banking chain—and extended to remaining locations over time. The **pilot conversion** approach is like a direct cutover for the pilot locations but, for the organization as a whole, it is similar to a parallel conversion. Both risks and costs are relatively low.
- ***Phased (or modular) conversion.*** Large systems often are built from distinct "modules." For example, an order-fulfillment system could have an inventory module, an order-processing module, and an accounts receivable module. If the modules were originally designed to be relatively independent, it may be possible to replace the modules one at a time. **Phased conversion** is probably safer than a direct conversion but takes longer and may require more testing, because it is necessary to test other parts of the system every time a new module is implemented.

STAGE 6: OPERATION. After a successful conversion, the system will operate for an indefinite period of time, until the system is no longer adequate or necessary, or cost effective.

STAGE 7: POST-AUDIT EVALUATION. An organization should evaluate all its larger systems projects after their completion. These **post-audits** introduce an additional element of discipline into the development process. If the implementation was successful, an audit should occur after the system's operations have stabilized. If the project failed, the audit should be done as soon as possible after the failure.

Many organizations do not conduct formal evaluations of their systems projects. They see no need for the extra effort if the project was successful, and would rather avoid the issue if it failed. Nevertheless, these evaluations are important. The feedback from comparisons of actual performance to specifications can help analysts learn to make better estimates on future projects. Identifying the causes of failures can help IS groups avoid the same problems on subsequent systems.

STAGE 8: MAINTENANCE. Every system needs two regular kinds of maintenance: fixing of bugs and regular updating. Bugs are more frequent in the beginning, but problems can appear even years later. In addition to fixing bugs, programmers need to *update* systems to accommodate changes in the environment. Examples include adjusting for tax law changes and dealing with the "Year 2000" problem. These corrections and updates usually do not add any additional functionality; they are just necessary to keep the system operating at the same level.

An additional form of maintenance adds new features to existing systems. This work is somewhat similar to the development of new systems; however, because the new features must be installed without disturbing the operation of the existing system, it is more difficult and less flexible.

Regardless of type, maintenance is expensive, accounting for up to 80 percent of organizational IS budgets. Therefore it is important that the design and development stages produce systems that include, in the initial versions, all the essential functionality. The developer should also use appropriate software engineering methodologies and produce good documentation for the system, to make the inevitable maintenance easier.

Traditional versus Modern SDLCs

There are two major problems with systems development life cycle methodologies. First, many systems projects fail, even though the project management incorporates a formal SDLC approach. Second, the environment is very different from what it was 30 years ago. Information technology is much more powerful and includes features such as graphical user interfaces and client/server architectures that are very different from earlier forms of programming.

Do these problems mean that project managers should abandon the SDLC concept? Not really. All the stages in Figure 14.1 (page 610) are still either absolutely necessary or highly desirable for larger projects. The benefits described above are still important. The increasing complexity of systems development means that some form of structure is even more necessary now than 30 years ago. However, the general organization of the SDLC needs to change to adjust to the realities of the current environment. IS groups considering the implementation of a formal SDLC methodology and associated tools for managing projects should today look for the following characteristics:

- ***Minimal overhead.*** One of the problems with older SDLCs and other project management techniques is that they require a great deal of record keeping and data entry. These tasks divert resources away from actual development activities. A modern SDLC needs to provide tools that capture most of this information automatically and that facilitate data entry for the rest.
- ***Flexibility and responsiveness.*** The traditional SDLC does not handle changes in specifications very well. However, the ability to handle change is more important now than ever before. The fast pace of the current world means that, for projects to be successful, systems developers need the flexibility to respond rapidly to environmental opportunities and threats even in the midst of the project.
- ***Concurrent tasks.*** The traditional life cycle is essentially sequential: Some stages focus on the early part of the project, while others occur toward the end. To meet the demands of the current environment, a new SDLC needs to allow developers to perform some tasks in different stages concurrently, or even to do tasks from "later" stages before tasks in "earlier" stages. For example, the developers may code, test, implement, and evaluate (post-audit) critical parts of the system before doing the logical analysis and design of other parts.
- ***Focused analysis.*** Another problem with the conventional approach is that it tends to emphasize analysis as an end in itself. Analysis is very important, but it needs to be focused on areas where it adds the most value to the project.

Yourdon (1989) proposes a modern "structured" project life cycle, which is pictured on the Web site for this chapter.

A Light SDLC Methodology for Web-based Systems Development

The SDLC (both traditional and modern) is a formal and disciplined approach to systems development. The time pressures for e-business development projects in the twenty-first century have tempted many project teams to simply abandon whatever degree of disciplined and formal process methodology they may have used in the 1980s and 1990s and simply proceed with an anarchical approach.

That "winging it" may have succeeded in first-generation e-business projects, but the risk of building a mission-critical system that's unstable, buggy, nonscalable, and vulnerable to hacker attacks is forcing more and more companies to look for a methodology that strikes a balance between rigor and speed (Yourdon, 2000). Such a so-called **light methodology** imposes discipline upon the most critical project activities, without wasting precious time on bureaucratic processes associated with old mainframe-era projects. It is less structured than the traditional SDLC and serves more as a framework or reference guide for skilled people than as a foolproof recipe for success.

14.2 Methods for Complex or Quickly Needed Systems

The traditional systems development life cycle approach works best on projects in which users have a clear idea about what they want. The typical automation project is a good example because, in this type of project, computer systems replace manual labor with only minimal changes in processes. Unfortunately, simple automation projects are becoming less common. Nowadays projects tend to require major changes in existing processes, through reengineering or through development of processes that are new to the organization. Furthermore, the need to build interorganizational and international systems using Web technologies such as extranets, and the need to build or modify systems quickly (see Minicases 1 and 2), created a major shift in the nature of information systems.

This shift in emphasis, along with the high failure rate in traditional systems development, indicates a need for alternatives to conventional SDLC methodologies. Prototyping, rapid application development, joint application design, and object-oriented development are four possible alternatives.

Prototyping

The **prototyping** approach to systems development is, in many ways, the very opposite of an old-style SDLC. Instead of spending a lot of time producing very detailed specifications, the developers find out only generally what the users want. The developers do not develop the complete system all at once. Instead they *quickly* create a prototype, which either contains portions of the system of most interest to the users, or is a small-scale working model of the entire system. After reviewing the prototype with the users, the developers refine and extend it. This process continues through several iterations until either the users approve the design or it becomes apparent that the proposed system cannot meet their needs. If the system is viable, the developers create a full-scale version that includes additional features.

In this approach, which is also known as *evolutionary development,* the emphasis is on producing something quickly for the users to review. To speed up the process, programmers may use a fourth-generation language (4GL) and other tools such as screen generators or spreadsheet software for parts of the prototype. After the users approve the prototype, the programmers can finish development, making whatever changes are necessary for acceptable performance and for meeting organizational standards for that type of system. This could involve programming it in a third-generation language, using the prototype as a model.

Prototyping can be a complete developmental methodology in itself. However, newer versions of the SDLC often incorporate it as an alternative, or supplement, to the analysis and design stage. Figure 14.4 (page 618) shows a flowchart of the prototyping process, using a relational database for the initial versions of the system. Note that in this version, the prototyping process creates the specifications, and the project then goes back into a conventional SDLC.

Neither the users nor the systems personnel know how many times the prototyping process will go through the loop of reviews and revisions. In a sense, prototyping is like a speeded-up version of the maintenance stage of a regular SDLC, in which users ask the IS group to add functionality to existing systems. However, it is much less expensive to make these changes over a short period on a model of the system, than to spread them over time on the operational version.

Prototyping is particularly useful for situations in which user interaction is especially important. Examples of such situations would be decision support (DSS), e-commerce "sell-sides," or executive information systems. Prototyping is also good for IS projects that substantially change business processes. For users of these types of systems, prototyping allows opportunities to work with the model, and to identify necessary changes and enhancements, before making a major commitment to development. Users should also consider prototyping if it is necessary to start using the system as soon as possible, even before it is complete.

Prototyping does have some disadvantages. It largely replaces the formal analysis and design stage of a conventional SDLC. As a result, the systems analysts may not need to produce much formal documentation for the programmers

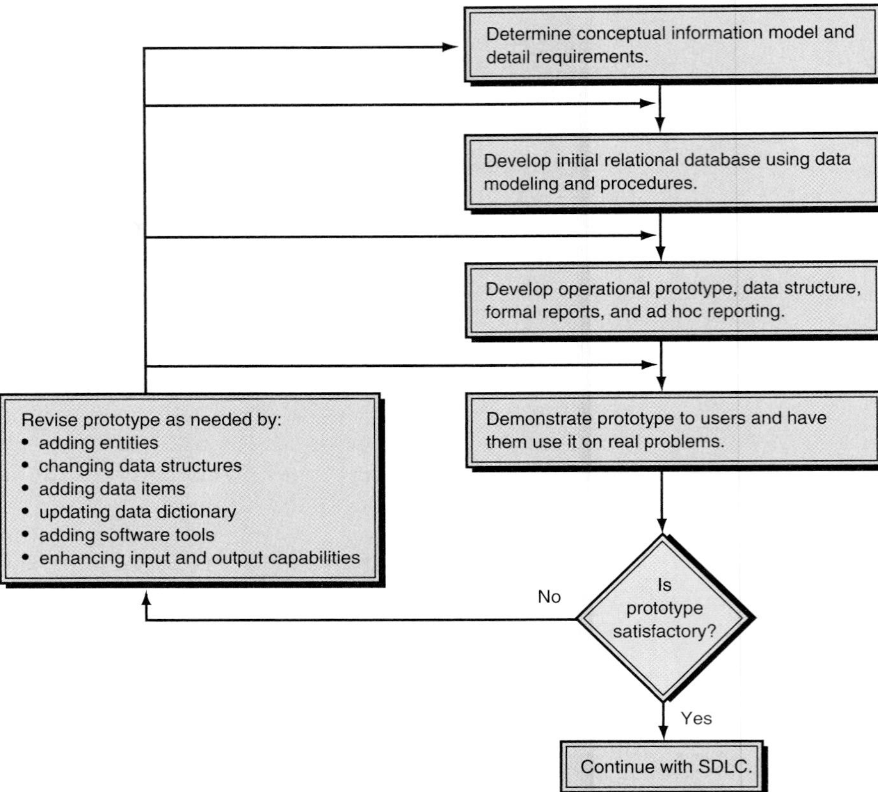

FIGURE 14.4 Model of prototyping process.

during the project. If managers do not follow up on this, the documentation may be inadequate years later when the system needs maintenance. Another problem is that users, after working with the final prototype, may not understand why additional work and associated charges are necessary to bring the system up to organizational standards.

Joint Application Design

Joint application design (JAD) is a group-based method for collecting user requirements and creating system designs. JAD is most often used within the systems analysis and systems design stages of the SDLC.

In the traditional SDLC, systems analysts interview or directly observe potential users of the new information system individually to understand each user's needs. The analysts will obtain many similar requests from users, but also many conflicting requests. The analysts must then consolidate all requests and go back to the users to resolve the conflicts, a process that usually requires a great deal of time.

In contrast to the SDLC requirements analysis, JAD has a group meeting in which all users meet simultaneously with analysts. During the meeting, all users jointly define and agree upon systems requirements. This process saves a tremendous amount of time.

The JAD approach to systems development has several advantages. First, the group process involves more users in the development process while still saving time. This involvement leads to greater support for and acceptance of the new system and can produce a system of higher quality. This involvement also may lead to easier implementation of the new system and lower training costs.

The JAD approach also has disadvantages. First, it is very difficult to get all users to the JAD meeting. For example, large organizations may have users literally all over the world; to have all of them attend a JAD meeting would be prohibitively expensive. Second, the JAD approach has all the problems caused by any group process (e.g., one person can dominate the meeting, some participants may be shy and not contribute in a group setting, or some participants may sit back and let others do the work). To alleviate these problems, JAD sessions usually have a facilitator, who is skilled in systems analysis and design as well in managing group meetings and processes.

JOINT APPLICATION DESIGN AND WEB SITE DESIGN. The emphasis now for e-business Web sites is to improve customer satisfaction and to make the users experience at the site simple, intuitive, and efficient. Companies that invest in designing solutions that make Web site navigation easy for their users are more likely to achieve customer retention—the key to the success or failure of any business on the Web.

Critical design features are those requirements that a Web site must support to allow a user to complete a task in an enjoyable and efficient way. For users to accept and adopt the interface of a Web site, it is useful to have them involved in its design. An electronic JAD session can be conducted offsite/online with technology support. This brings the key representatives of users (customers), managers, systems designers, and other stakeholders together for requirements determination. The initial set of requirements can serve as the basis for the development of a larger survey to determine user (customer) preferences and priorities. JAD is thus of particular interest to Web site designers (see Kendall and Kendall, 2001).

However, JAD may not be an easy task for Web site design since in some cases the stakeholders may be outside of an organization or may not know their own needs well. It is difficult to elicit a comprehensive list of requirements. An initial set of requirements can be generated from conducting focus groups, involving users' representatives offline as well as online. The initial set of requirements can serve as the basis for the development of a larger survey to determine the user preferences and priorities.

Rapid Application Development

Rapid application development (RAD) methodologies and tools make it possible to develop systems faster, especially systems where the user interface is an important component. Another area is the rewriting of legacy applications. An example of how quickly experienced developers can create applications with RAD tools is provided in the *IT at Work* illustration on page 620.

What are the components or tools and capabilities of a RAD system? Typical packages include the following.

- ***GUI development environment***—the ability to create many aspects of an application by "drag-and-drop" operations. For example, the user can create a report by clicking on file names, and then clicking and dragging fields from these files to the appropriate locations in the report.
- ***Reusable components***—a library of common, standard "objects" such as buttons and dialog boxes. The developer drags-and-drops these items into the application.
- ***Code generator.*** After the developer drags-and-drops the standard "objects" into the design, the package automatically writes computer programs to implement the reports, input screens, buttons, dialog boxes, and so forth.

IT at Work

Integrating IT ...in Marketing

BLUE CROSS & BLUE SHIELD DEVELOPS AN AWARD-WINNING APPLICATION USING RAD

A Y2K problem without a solution led to the development of an innovative customer-service application in less than a year at Blue Cross & Blue Shield of Rhode Island (BCBSRI). The new system is based on an internally developed architecture that the Application Development Trends' 2000 Innovator Awards judges lauded as modular and flexible enough to easily allow for system upgrades and the incorporation of new technology.

BCBSRI decided in mid-1998 to build a new customer-service system, a mission-critical application that monitors and records communications with policyholders. The internal work on the project began in January 1999 after the development plan and blueprint were validated by outside consultants.

The development team adhered to a phased-rollout approach and rapid application development (RAD) methodology. Developers used several productivity tools (including the Sybase EAServer, Sybase PowerBuilder, and Riverton HOW), as well as performance monitoring techniques and heavy user involvement to ensure the quality of the system throughout its life cycle. By September 1, 1999, the application was available to more than a hundred Windows 98-based clients. Since then, the customer-service unit has averaged about 1,800 daily calls and more than 20,000 transactions a day over the system.

By early 2000, the new customer-service system had already realized an ROI of $500,000, boosts in user productivity, significant strides in system performance, and increased data accuracy. The integration, power, and scalability of the BCBSRI solution is truly exemplary.

For Further Exploration: To what extent do you think the adoption of the RAD methodology contributed to the success of the BCBSRI project?

Sources: Condensed from *Application Development Trends,* April 2000 issue, and from paper published at *adtmag.com* (April 2000).

- ***Programming language***—such as BASIC (in Visual Basic), Object Pascal (in Delphi), or C++. This component includes an *integrated development environment (IDE)* for creating, testing, and debugging code. It may be possible to use drag-and-drop operations to create up to 80 percent of the code for a system.

The RAD process is similar to the prototyping process. Both are highly iterative and emphasize speed of development. Prototyping often uses specialized languages, such as 4GLs and screen generators, whereas RAD packages include different tools with similar capabilities. With RAD tools, developers enhance and extend the initial version through multiple iterations until it is suitable for operational use. The tools work together as part of an integrated package. They produce functional components of a final system, rather than mockups or limited-scale versions. Typical RAD products are suitable for development on a wide variety of platforms, especially the increasingly popular client/server and Web-based ones.

As Figure 14.5 shows, the same phases followed in the traditional SDLC are also followed in RAD, but the phases in RAD are combined to produce a more streamlined development technique. The emphasis in RAD is generally less on the sequence and structure of processes in the life cycle and more on doing different tasks in parallel with each other and on using prototyping extensively.

In addition to the benefits of speed and portability, RAD is used to create applications that are easier to maintain and to modify. However, RAD packages also have some disadvantages. Like prototyping, the iterative development process can continue indefinitely if there is no unambiguous criterion for ending it. RAD packages may have capabilities to document the system, but having these features does not guarantee that developers will produce appropriate documentation.

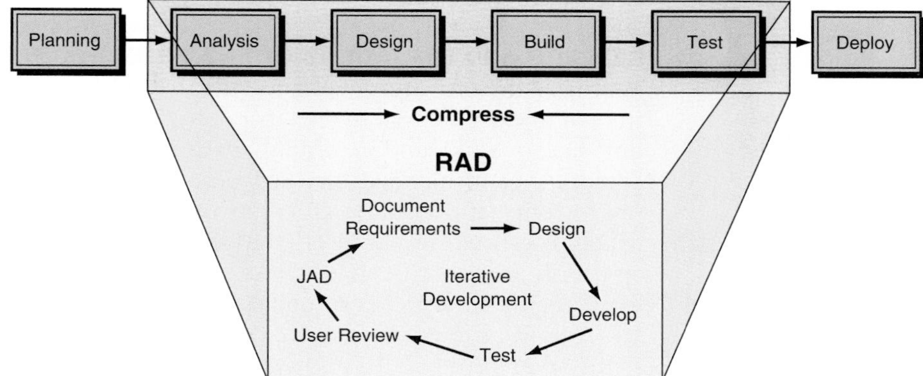

FIGURE 14.5 A rapid application development SDLC. (*Source: datawarehouse-training.com/ Methodologies/rapid-application-development.*)

RAPID APPLICATION DEVELOPMENT IN THE AGE OF THE INTERNET. RAD has been a key component of client/server systems development. According to Yourdon (2000), WWW applications are likely to accelerate the RAD process to the point where it becomes "FAD," or *frantic application development*. The technology-driven nature of the Internet is forcing developers to deliver applications that use these new technologies, such as streaming video and audio, in shorter and shorter time spans. This is spurred further by the development efforts of vendors, including Netscape and Microsoft, who continually release new versions of their Web browser software. Pressure arising from the constant introduction of new technology has introduced a FAD approach into organizations that are developing Web-based solutions. It appears that the FAD approach will become more prevalent as organizations become increasingly aware of the strategic value of an Internet presence.

Object-Oriented Development

SDLC development projects often run beyond schedule and over budget, and they result in systems that are too rigid, have too many defects, and do not meet user requirements closely enough. These problems illustrate the *software crisis* facing organizations today. An alternative approach is object-oriented development.

Object-oriented development (Technology Guide 2) is based on a fundamentally different view of computer systems than that found in traditional SDLC approaches. Traditional approaches provide specific step-by-step instructions in the form of computer programs, in which programmers must specify every procedural detail. They usually result in a system that performs the original task but may not be suited for handling other tasks, even when the other tasks involve the same real-world entities. For example, a billing system will handle billing but probably will not be adaptable to handle mailings for the marketing department or generate leads for the sales force, even though the billing, marketing, and sales functions all use similar data such as customer names, addresses, and current and past purchases.

An object-oriented (OO) system begins not with the task to be performed, but with the aspects of the real world that must be modeled to perform that task. Therefore, if a firm has a good model of its customers and its interactions with them, this model can be used equally well for billings, mailings, and sales leads. Object technology enables the development of purchasable, sharable, and reusable information assets (objects) existing in a worldwide network of interoperable interorganizational information systems.

BENEFITS AND LIMITATIONS OF THE OBJECT-ORIENTED APPROACH. The OO approach to software development can lead to many benefits. First, it reduces the complexity of systems development and leads to systems that are easier and quicker to build and maintain, because each object is relatively small, self-contained, and manageable. Second, the OO approach improves programmers' productivity and quality. Once an object has been defined, implemented, and tested, it can be reused in other systems. Third, systems developed with the OO approach are more flexible. These systems can be modified and enhanced easily, by changing some types of objects or by adding new types.

A fourth benefit is that the OO approach allows the systems analyst to think at the level of the real-world system (as users do) and not at the level of the programming language. The basic operations of an enterprise change much more slowly than the information needs of specific groups or individuals. Therefore, software based on generic models (the OO approach) will have a much longer life span than programs written to solve specific, immediate problems.

On the other hand, there are some disadvantages to the OO approach. OO systems, especially those written in Java, generally run more slowly than those developed in other programming languages. Many programmers have little skill and experience with OO languages, so retraining may be necessary in organizations that want to start using OO programming in their systems development projects.

By all appearances, object-oriented systems development (OOSD) is in the throes of a dilemma. Dozens of well-known experts claim the advantages of OOSD make it vastly superior to conventional systems development. But some of them also point to OOSD's disadvantages and question whether it will ever be a dominant approach to systems development. Tables 14.1 and 14.2 on the book's Web site indicate the belief strengths of both OO and non-OO developers in OOSD advantages and OOSD disadvantages. For a more detailed discussion of the ups and downs of the object-oriented approach, see Johnson (2000).

OBJECT-ORIENTED ANALYSIS AND DESIGN. The development process for an object-oriented system is in many respects similar to that for a conventional system. This process would include the same steps as the generic eight-stage SDLC presented in Section 14.1. The developers could use a formal SDLC methodology to manage this process, or use the prototyping or RAD approaches. The major difference is that, in the logical analysis and design stage, the analysts using an OO approach can use specialized modeling diagrams that are more appropriate for representing object-oriented concepts.

UNIFIED MODELING LANGUAGE. The techniques and notations that are incorporated into a standard object-oriented language are called *unified modeling language (UML)*. The UML allows the modeler to specify, visualize, and construct the artifacts of software systems, as well as business models. Figure 14.6 on the facing page provides an example of UML class and object diagrams.

Figure 14.6 (a) shows two object classes: Student and Course, along with their attributes and operations. Objects belonging to the same class may also participate in similar relationships with other objects. For example, all students register for courses, and therefore the Student class can participate in a relationship called "register-for" with another class called Course. Figure 14.6 (b) shows two

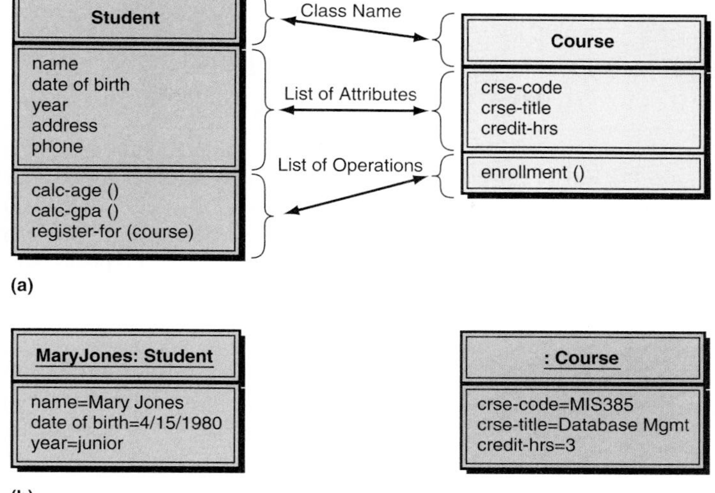

FIGURE 14.6 UML class and object diagrams. (*Source:* Valacich, et al., *Essentials of Systems Analysis and Design,* Prentice-Hall, 2001, p. 375. *Essentials of Systems Analysis and Design* by Valacich/Hoffer. Reprinted by permission of Pearson Education, Inc. Upper Saddle River, NJ.)

object instances, one for each of the classes that appears in Figure 14.6 (a). The object instance's attributes and their values are shown in the second compartment. An operation such as "calc-gpa" in the Student class (see Figure 14.6 (a)) is a function or a service that is provided for all the instances of a class. It is only through such operations that other objects can access or manipulate the information stored in an object.

OBJECT TECHNOLOGY AND WEB-BASED SYSTEMS DEVELOPMENT. The object-oriented approach is ideal for developing Web applications. First, the data and code of object-oriented systems are encapsulated into reusable components, each of which can be developed and enhanced independently. This increases development speed and flexibility, as well as reducing system maintenance. Object technology allows companies to share business applications on the Internet. An example of using object-oriented technology to speed up systems development is provided in the *IT at Work* example on page 624.

A second reason why the object-oriented approach is ideal for developing Web applications is that as the Web evolves from static data to active data, it is moving toward object-based software systems. Objects become useful in this context because, by definition, they join software code and data. Objects provide a modular way of organizing, configuring, and reusing code instead of "reinventing the wheel" each time a new routine is written. When users click on a Web page, for example, they are downloading objects into their client machines. This combination of data and code can be configured in new ways, manipulated, and operated actively.

Component-based Development

Object technology, however, does have its downside, including a steep learning curve. Business objects, though they represent things in the real world, become unwieldy when they are combined and recombined in large-scale commercial applications. What is needed are ensembles of business objects that provide major chunks of application functionality (e.g., preprogrammed workflow, transaction processing, and user event notification) that can be snapped together to create complete business applications.

IT at Work

CORNING DEVELOPS FLEXIBLE TOOLS TO PROVIDE SUPERB SERVICE

Integrating IT ...in Production & Operations Management

www.corning.com

Corning Inc.'s Telecommunication Product Division is the world's largest manufacturer of fiber-optic wavewires. The demand for the products has increased rapidly, so production must be expanded quickly (up 75 percent in 3 years). Due to technological development, the demand characteristics are constantly changing, and Corning must be very responsive in order to remain competitive.

Information technology supports the work of product developers, who must be very flexible in their work. They also must become productive quickly, which is difficult to do with all of the changes.

To build flexible information systems to support the product developers, and do it quickly, the company created a development team. The team decided that a distributed client/server environment for the applications would provide flexibility, and that object-oriented (OO) technology would yield the best IT tools.

The team decided to use an integrated tool set (from Forte Systems). The IS developers found that the training time for using the OO tools was only a few weeks. The team also purchased design and analysis tools to expedite the development. The OO tools led to improved programmers' productivity, since modules developed for one application could be used by several. The first application enabled collection and formatting of data needed to ship with fiber-optic cable orders. The system has the flexibility to provide customers with data they want within 24 hours. The second application was a factory-floor application that made production responsive to constantly changing demand requirements. To develop these applications, the team created a library of reusable objects and distributed OO services. These can be shared by future applications.

The first application was developed by a team of six in nine months, and the second by a team of two in three months. The larger the library of objects, the faster is the application development. In building the applications the team was able to use some off-the-shelf software. Also, integration with databases was needed. This was done with Visual C++ (from Microsoft). The second application won the 1997 Innovation award from *Application Development Trends* magazine.

For Further Exploration: Why is it hard to get developers to reuse software?

Sources: Condensed from J. Desmond, "Distributed Applications Built with OO Tools Get Corning's Waveguides to Customers," *Application Development Trends*, April 1997; and from *corning.com* (2001).

This approach is embodied in the next step in the evolution beyond objects, **component-based development.** *Components* are self-contained packages of functionality that have clearly defined, open interfaces that offer high-level application services. Components can be distributed dynamically for reuse across multiple applications and heterogeneous computing platforms. Components take the best features of objects to a higher level of abstraction that is learned more easily by mainstream commercial software developers.

Examples of components are user interface icons (small), word processing (a complete software product), a GUI, online ordering (a business component), inventory reordering (a business component), and so on. Components used on intranets include search engine, firewall, Web server, browser, page display, and telecommunication protocol.

The major reasons for using components-based development are:

- Code reusability, which makes programming faster, with fewer errors
- Support for heterogeneous computing infrastructure and platforms
- Rapid assembly of new business applications
- Ability of an application to scale

Components used in distributed computing need to possess several key characteristics to work correctly, and they can be viewed as an extension of the object-oriented paradigm. The two main traits are borrowed from the world of object-oriented technology: *encapsulation* and *data hiding*.

Components *encapsulate* the routines or programs that perform discrete functions. In a component-based program, one can define components with various published interfaces. One of these interfaces might be, for example, a date-comparison function. If this function is passed to two date objects to compare, it returns the results. All manipulations of dates are required to use the interfaces defined by the date object, so the complete function is encapsulated in this object, which has a distinct interface to other systems. Now, if the function has to be changed, only the program code that defines the object must be changed, and the behavior of the date comparison routine is updated immediately, a feature known as *encapsulation*.

Data hiding addresses a different problem. *Data hiding* places data needed by a component object's functions within the component, where it can be accessed only by specially designated functions in the component itself. Data hiding is a critical trait of distributed components. The fact that only designated functions can access certain data items, and outside "requestors" have to query the component, makes maintenance of component-oriented programs simpler.

COMPONENT-BASED DEVELOPMENT OF E-COMMERCE APPLICATIONS. Component-based EC development is gaining momentum. It is supported by Microsoft and the Object Management Group (OMG), which have put in place many of the standards needed to make component-based development a reality. A logical architecture for component-based development of e-commerce applications can be described in layers as shown in Figure 14.7.

Component-based development for e-commerce applications is a process of assembly and refinement. The process begins with *cross-application components* that provide functionality common to most types of e-commerce applications. Typical of such core components are user-profile management, authentication, authorization, data management, and so on. These cross-application components can be customized and extended to form *application-specific components*. For example, in a procurement application, a profiling component will contain attributes for identifying a user's role and buying power.

When applied to an I-market (Internet market) application, the profiling component will be extended to hold information that can be used to track customer

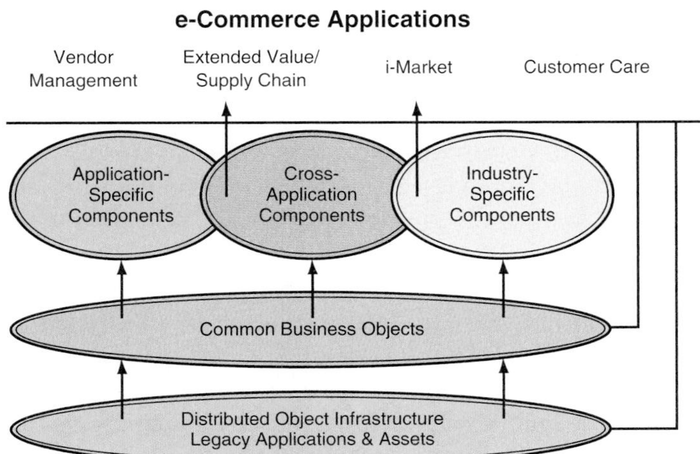

FIGURE 14.7 E-commerce applications and component logical architecture. (*Source:* Drawn by E. Turban.)

buying patterns. In addition to the tailored cross-application components, application-specific components will include best-of-breed search engines, shopping carts, catalogs, or other elements required for the application. These may be built in-house or purchased. Cross-application components also can be extended to develop *industry-specific components*. For example, in a manufacturing industry a workflow component can be extended to handle work-in-progress and integrate workflows across enterprises to make "just-in-time" a reality.

The final step in the component-based development process is the configuration of the components to incorporate the organization's unique business rules and user presentation and navigation. It is in this step that a company's competitive advantage is built on top of best-of-breed cross-applications, application-specific and industry-specific components, and embedded in its e-commerce applications.

14.3 SYSTEMS DEVELOPED OUTSIDE THE IS DEPARTMENT

The methodologies presented earlier are usually used by the IS department. Their execution requires highly skilled employees, and the methodologies are fairly complex. The result is a backlog in application development, and a high failure rate. Therefore, many organizations are using approaches that shift the construction task from the ISD to others. Of the various ways of doing this, three are most common: Let users build their own systems; outsource the entire systems development process; or let end users and/or the ISD use packages. These options are described next.

End-User Development

In the early days of computing, an organization housed its computer in a climate-controlled room, with locked doors and restricted access. The only people who interacted with the computer (most organizations had only one computer) were specialists: programmers, computer operators, and data entry personnel. Over the years, computers became cheaper, smaller, and more widely dispersed throughout the organization. Now almost everybody who works at a desk has a computer.

Along with this transfer of hardware, many computer-related activities shifted out into the work area. Users now handle most of their own data entry. They create many of their own reports and print them locally, instead of waiting for them to arrive in the interoffice mail after a computer operator has run them at a remote data center. They provide unofficial training and support to other workers in their area. And users also design and develop an increasing proportion of their own applications, sometimes even relatively large and complex systems.

TRENDS FAVORING END-USER DEVELOPMENT. The following list presents existing factors that lead to higher levels of end-user development. Note that many of these factors represent continuing trends; therefore this form of development could become even more important in the future.

- ***Increasingly powerful desktop hardware.*** This makes it possible to run powerful software that allows users, even with limited technical skills, to develop applications and systems.
- ***Declining hardware costs.*** In the early years, computers cost over a million dollars. Now for a few thousand dollars, users can acquire PCs that are much

more powerful than those old mainframes. Declining costs make it possible for almost everybody to have a computer, increasing the market potential for powerful software tools to support end-user developers.

- ***Increasingly diverse software capabilities.*** Early mainframes primarily handled accounting, finance, and inventory applications. Early PCs did word processing, spreadsheets, and databases. Although these categories still account for the majority of usage, the proportion and range of other applications is very large and growing. Many of the new packages are programmable: With macros and other features, users can automate activities for themselves or others in their work unit. Other packages, including the RAD tools discussed earlier, make it easier for users to develop even relatively large systems.
- ***Increasingly computer-literate population.*** Computers are becoming common at work, in homes, and at schools. Perhaps half the population in the United States under 65 now has some basic computer skills. With experience and study, some of these people move into the category of "power users," persons who are highly skilled with various kinds of software and able to develop applications.
- ***Backlog of IS projects.*** In most organizations, the internal IS unit has a large backlog of new systems-development projects. Unless they have a priority, users may have to wait years for work on their project to even start. This makes alternate sources, including end-user development, relatively attractive.
- ***Development speed.*** Even if the users have a priority, a formal systems-development project by the central IS unit may take longer than having an end user develop the system.
- ***Business orientation.*** One reason why end users may develop systems faster is that they understand their own business processes better than the technology-oriented staff in the IS unit.
- ***Small applications.*** Many office tasks can benefit from automation, even though they are far too small to be suitable for a formal systems project. For example, it is easier to enter a one-page table with 20 entries into a spreadsheet than it is to compute the total with a calculator and then type the table with a typewriter. It is far easier to update the same report when the data change the following month. End-user development is the only option for many small applications.
- ***Control.*** Managers often perceive the IS unit as unresponsive, and therefore they prefer to have the developers under their own direct control.
- ***Apparent cost savings.*** If the systems developer is already on the payroll of the user organization, the marginal costs may be negligible and far lower than a quotation from the central IS unit. Not recognizing the possibility of hidden costs, such as higher maintenance in the future, managers may bias their decisions in the direction of end-user development.

TYPES OF END-USER COMPUTING. Researchers have identified the six **end-user computing** categories shown in Table 14.1 on page 628 (see Rockart and Flannery, 1983; and Guimaraes, 1999). Note that the last four of these categories participate in some form of development. With experience, end users can migrate into the development categories, or advance from doing limited to more extensive development.

TABLE 14.1 Categories of End-User Computing

Category	Activities
1. Nonprogramming end users	Enter data, use application
2. Command-level users	Access data, print reports
3. End-user programmers	Develop applications for personal use
4. Functional support personnel	Develop applications for others to use
5. End-user computing support personnel*	Training, hotline, develop applications
6. Programmers*	Work on a contract basis

**Note:* Support personnel and programmers are typically not employees of user workgroups.

In the 1980s many large organizations set up **information centers** to help their employees learn how to use the emerging technology of personal computing. These information centers had their own office space and a variety of PC hardware and software, as well as employees in Category 5 in Table 14.1. Although some organizations have since closed their information centers, they typically continue to provide end users with help-desk and training functions from other locations or through outsourcing. The running of information centers in the twenty-first century is quite different from that of the 1980s. An innovative way of managing end-user computing is shown in the *IT at Work* on page 629.

PROBLEMS WITH END-USER DEVELOPMENT, AND SUGGESTED SOLUTIONS. Although the underlying trends and the advantages are favorable to end-user development, managers need to be aware of potential problems. End users who develop applications may claim that they need more expensive hardware and additional software. Although they tend to exaggerate their requirements, some additional spending will usually be necessary.

In addition to explicit costs, end-user developers can also incur hidden costs. Although the end user is already on the unit's payroll, developing systems takes time away from other responsibilities. The employee may also create support costs elsewhere in the organization, even if the unit does not receive charges for them. Different units may duplicate efforts by producing separate systems that do essentially the same thing. Development of localized systems and databases may conflict with organizational goals for increased data sharing among operating units.

Another problem is that managers outside the IS area generally have limited technical skills, which makes it difficult for them to evaluate end-user development activities. Although their managers may not realize it, some end-user developers are much less competent than others. In some cases a lack of competency may result in failed projects: systems that do not work at all. In other cases, applications that appear to function adequately may actually produce inaccurate outputs that lead to bad decisions.

End users often fail to produce adequate documentation for their systems, which can create maintenance problems later, especially if the developer leaves the organization. Security is also a potential problem area: End users may not understand, or be able to implement, organizational standards for data security. As a result, they may fail to appropriately safeguard confidential data or to properly back up data and programs. In some cases the maintenance or security problems revert back to the central IS unit.

IT at Work

...in Operations Management

www.ansett.com.au

ANSETT AUSTRALIA AND IBM SIGN END-USER COMPUTING DEAL

Ansett Australia—one of Australia's leading airlines—announced on January 4, 1999, that it had appointed IBM Global Services Australia to manage its end-user computing supports. Ansett, based in Melbourne, Australia, operates an extensive range of domestic airline services and also flies to Japan, Hong Kong, Taiwan, Bali, and Fiji.

Ansett Australia General Manager for IT Infrastructure and Operations, Hal Pringle, said, "IBM Global Services Australia's appointment would significantly improve desktop services to the airline's end users while at the same time delivering substantial cost savings." Such service was previously delivered by a mixture of external contractors and in-house staff.

Mr. Pringle said the decision to hire an external provider of end-user computing (EUC) support arose from a benchmarking study conducted by Ansett earlier this year. The study showed that a move to a single external provider of the caliber of IBM Global Services Australia would:

- Achieve a more consistent end-to-end delivery of applications.
- Assist the implementation of best-practice EUC support at the best cost.
- Deliver substantial cost savings.
- Allow Ansett to better manage EUC supply and demand.
- Deliver a more consistent and better quality support service to end users.

"The study highlighted the fact that Ansett had in effect 'outgrown' the level of end-user service provided at that time, and that a quantum leap in service was required to ensure a full return on our end-user computing investment," Pringle said.

"Improving delivery of services to end users and enhancing end-user productivity are becoming key focus areas for many Australian corporations. I am very pleased that we have been chosen to deliver these additional services to Ansett," said Mr. Bligh, General Manager of IBM Global Services Australia, Travel and Transportation Services.

For Further Exploration: What strategic advantages can Ansett Australia gain by ensuring consistent and reliable supports to its end-user computing? Is it worth it for a company to invest in end-user computing?

Sources: ibm.com/services/successes/ansett.html; and *ansett.com.au* (2001).

Research on End-User Computing Problems. Researchers who look at end-user computing applications have found alarmingly high errors rates. Panko and Halverson (1996) found that over 51 percent of the spreadsheets developed by experienced end users had at least one substantive error even though the user developers were confident their spreadsheets were correct. Panko and Sprague (1998) report error rates between 10 and 25 percent in real-world spreadsheet audits. These findings should be a red flag to managers because using spreadsheets is the leading activity of end-user computing.

Apart from spreadsheets, Edberg and Bowman (1996) also found more errors in database applications created by MBA students than in database applications created by senior MIS students. Davis (1998) warned about the risk of using applications that have not been thoroughly checked for correctness and that may not be consistently maintained.

Improving End-User Systems Development. It is suggested that end users should receive training in systems analysis and design in order to ensure the quality and success of the applications they develop (see Kreie et al., 2000). To prevent or control software errors, managers could consider applying or adapting the five-step program outlined in Table 14.2 (adapted from Panko and Halverson, 1996) with end-user development.

TABLE 14.2 Guidelines for Avoiding End-User Development Errors

1. Randomly audit a sample of 25 to 50 applications, especially mission-critical ones, and make corrections where necessary. If this initial review indicates substantial problems, extend the audit to other important applications.
2. Use the built-in security mechanisms of the software package to ensure its system integrity.
3. Establish organizational end-user computing policies regarding good coding style, identifying who is responsible for the validity of the outputs, and determining who will do the maintenance if the original author leaves the organization.
4. Check new applications manually, using existing data with known results (e.g., previous financial statements).
5. Application developers need to spend time creating detailed designs of their applications before plunging into development.

Source: Adapted from R. R. Panko and R. H. Halverson, "Are Two Heads Better than One (at Reducing Spreadsheet Errors)?" *Proceedings of the Second AIS Americas Conference on Information Systems,* August 16–18, 1996.

Dividing Computing Responsibilities. A management strategy to encourage the beneficial aspects of end-user computing and to minimize its risks is to divide computing responsibilities among groups—including IS groups. One approach is first to brainstorm a list of required computing activities, making the list as long as possible before eventually cutting it down to the most important activities. Each activity is then assigned either to an IS group or to end users. Some types of activities that should be examined for divisional responsibilities are listed in Table 14.3.

END-USER COMPUTING AND WEB-BASED SYSTEMS DEVELOPMENT. The development of client/server applications in the 1980s and 1990s was characterized by user-driven systems development. End users have been directly or indirectly making decisions for systems designers and developers on how the programs should operate. **Web-based systems** development in the twenty-first century, however, is application driven rather than user driven. The end user can still determine what the requirements will be and have some input into the design of the applications. But because of the nature of the technologies used in Web-based application design, the function, not the user, determines what the application will look like and how it will perform.

Outsourcing

As more and more organizations began to use computers, relying on internal IS units to develop applications and operate the hardware, they found that, at times,

TABLE 14.3 Computing Activities for Divided-Responsibility Decisions

- Standards for hardware and software acquisition
- Purchase authority for hardware and software
- Economic cost-justification standards and procedures
- Responsibility for developing and maintaining types of applications
- Data security, integrity, and privacy
- Electronic access to local and corporate data
- Authority and responsibility for entering and modifying data

the IS units needed additional staff or specialized skills for some projects. To meet these needs, they could hire experienced programmers who were willing to "moonlight" (work a second job) or who preferred to work on a project-by-project basis. These were the first contract programmers, and they represented the start of the outsourcing trend.

Outsourcing, it its broadest sense, is the purchase of any product or service from another company. In general, companies outsource the products and services they are unable or unwilling to produce themselves. IS departments have outsourced computer hardware, telecommunications services, and systems software (such as operating systems) for some time. They also purchase end-user software (e.g., Microsoft Office) because there is no reason to reinvent tools that a software company specializing in these products can provide more cheaply.

Recently, information technology has involved hiring outside organizations to perform functions that in the past have been performed internally by IS departments. Common areas for outsourcing have included maintaining computer centers and telecommunications networks. Some companies, however, outsource most of the IT functions—including systems and applications development—leaving only a very small internal information systems department. This department develops IS plans and negotiates with the vendors performing the outsourced functions.

Typically, the outsourcing firm hires the IS employees of the customer and buys the computer hardware. The outsourcer provides IT services under a contract that specifies a baseline level of services, with additional charges for higher volumes or services not identified in the baseline contract. Many smaller firms provide limited-scale outsourcing of individual services, but only the largest outsourcing firms can take over large parts of the IT functions of major organizations.

Firms that provide outsourcing cite numerous benefits that establish their claim that they can provide IT services at 10 to 40 percent lower cost, with higher quality. They note these reasons:

- ***Hardware economies of scale.*** With multiple customers, outsourcers can use larger, more cost-efficient computers or obtain discounts on volume purchase of hardware. They can also operate their computers with less excess capacity because peak loads from different customers will not all occur at the same time.
- ***Staffing economies of scale.*** A large customer base also makes it possible for outsourcers to hire highly skilled, specialized technical personnel whose salaries would be hard to justify in smaller IS groups.
- ***Specialization.*** Providing computer services is one of the core competencies of the outsourcing firm, rather than an incidental part of its business.
- ***Tax benefits.*** Organizations can deduct outsourcing fees from current income, in contrast to depreciating computer hardware purchases over three to five years.

However, outsourcing can create problems for companies, which include the following:

- ***Limited economies of scale.*** Although outsourcers can negotiate larger discounts on hardware, the advantage may not be significant, especially over the five-year life of a mainframe.
- ***Staffing.*** Typically, former employees, rather than the highly skilled vendor staff, serve customers. In some cases, the outsourcer shifts the better former employees to other accounts.

- ***Lack of business expertise.*** In addition to losing former employees to other accounts, the remaining staff members tend to become more technically oriented and have less knowledge of the business issues in the customer's industry.
- ***Contract problems.*** Some customers fail to adequately specify service levels in their contract with the outsourcer and so must pay excess fees for services not in the contract, or for volumes greater than the average written into the contract.
- ***Internal cost reduction opportunities.*** Organizations can achieve many of the cost savings of outsourcing by improving their own IT management. For example, these firms can achieve economies of scale by consolidating multiple data centers into one location.

Outsourcing can benefit public as well as private organizations. For example, government IT organizations are beginning to adopt outsourcing practices. Federal agencies, states, and local municipalities are hiring outside services firms for more than just specific system-integration projects. Some are outsourcing parts of their IT operations such as desktop and LAN management. Others are even more aggressive, turning over major IT functions to outside companies.

TRENDS TO OUTSOURCE WEB-BASED SYSTEMS DEVELOPMENT. There is a growing trend to outsource Web-based systems development, as illustrated in the opening case. This includes planning, Web site design and development, installation of the hardware and software, and more.

A principal reason for outsourcing all or part of a Web project is that few companies are fully equipped to do everything themselves, and many demand proof that their online presence will pay off before hiring additional staff. There are many skills needed to develop a Web site and get it up and running. You need people who know graphic design, marketing, networking, HTML, programming, copywriting, public relations, database design, account management, and sales. In addition, issues dealing with the back-end job of running a real business require office managers, accountants, lawyers, and so forth. Outsourcing provides a one-stop shopping alternative to customers who don't have the expertise or time to develop and maintain a commercial site. Consulting providers are broadening their skill sets and geographic reach to try to fill their clients' every need.

Outsourcing Web work means establishing a new, long-term relationship with a stranger. Careful questioning can minimize the risk of making a mistake. Look at the vendor's home page and the home pages it has created for others. Then ask questions:

ABOUT CAPABILITIES

- What portion of the work did you do? What was outsourced to subcontractors?
- What services can you provide?
- Who are your graphic designers, and what are their backgrounds?
- What can you do to publicize my Web site?

ABOUT TECHNICAL MATTERS

- What computer resources do you provide?
- Are your systems backed up?

- Do you have an alternate site in case of hardware failure?
- If you do the programming, how much of the code will be proprietary?
- What provisions do you make for security?

ABOUT PERFORMANCE

- What bandwidth do you provide? How much is dedicated to my home page?
- How much experience do you have managing high-traffic Web sites?
- How high is the volume at your most active site?

ABOUT THE BUSINESS RELATIONSHIP

- What statistical reports do you provide?
- What provisions do you make for handling complaints and problems?

External Acquisition of Software

The choice between developing proprietary software in-house and purchasing existing software is called the *make-or-buy decision*. Developing ("making") proprietary application software gives the organization exactly what it needs and wants, as well as a high level of control in the development process. In addition, the organization has more flexibility in modifying the software during the development process to meet new requirements. On the other hand, developing proprietary software requires a large amount of resources (time, money, personnel) that the in-house staff may have trouble providing. The large quantity of resources needed for this software increases the risk of the decision to "make" the software in-house.

The initial cost of off-the-shelf software is often lower because a software development firm can spread the cost over a number of customers. There is lower risk that the software will fail to meet the firm's business needs, because the software can be examined prior to purchase. The software should be of high quality, because many customers have used and helped debug it. However, buying off-the-shelf software may mean that an organization has to pay for features and functions that are not needed. Also, the software may lack necessary features, causing the buyer to have to make expensive modifications to customize the package. Finally, the buyer's particular IT infrastructure may differ from what the software was designed for, and require some additional modification to run properly.

SELECTING VENDORS AND COMMERCIAL SOFTWARE PACKAGES. Externally acquired systems should be evaluated to ensure that they provide the organization with the following advantages. If they do not provide most of these advantages, then the organizations may be better off developing proprietary systems. The most prominent considerations are:

- ***On-time.*** Completion and implementation of the system on or before the scheduled target date.
- ***On-budget.*** The system cost is equal to or less than the budget.
- ***Full functionality.*** The system has all the features in the original specifications.

These outcomes are very desirable, especially since fewer than half of all systems projects achieve all three. However, it is possible to succeed on each of these criteria but still have a system that does not increase the effectiveness of the organization. Therefore, the following outcomes are also important:

- ***User acceptance.*** Some systems perform poorly, or even fail, solely because of resistance from the users. One reason for resistance is a poor user interface that makes a system difficult to learn or use. Perceptions that the system shifts power from one part of the organization to another, or increases management control over employees, can also lead to resistance.
- ***Favorable costs-to-benefits ratio.*** A system may have all the specified functionality but still not help the organization because actual benefits and/or operating costs differ substantially from the initial estimates. This unfavorable outcome is becoming more common as organizations exhaust the possibilities for automation projects that replace manual labor with computer functionality. Decision makers must increasingly use intangible benefits, which are much harder to predict, to justify new systems.
- ***Low maintenance.*** Up to 80 percent of the operational ISD budget now goes for maintenance of existing systems. This implies that a more expensive system, which is easier to maintain or has greater functionality, could be more beneficial to an organization than one that is difficult to update or needs subsequent enhancements in its functionality.
- ***Scalability.*** Processing volumes can increase as usage levels expand and as organizations grow. It may therefore be necessary to migrate a system to another hardware platform with greater capabilities. If the original system is based on software that is portable to different platforms (for example, a common database management system), the migration should be cheaper and less difficult.
- ***Integration with other systems.*** A system may achieve all its own design objectives but not coordinate well with other systems in an organization. For example, some of its data may overlap files in other locations. The end result would be less organizational cost savings than available through more integrated systems.
- ***Minimal negative cross-impacts.*** A new system may be successful by itself but create major problems for an organization in other areas. For example, a new system could put unacceptably large demands on limited computing resources and result in unacceptable delays on other systems during peak demand.
- ***Reusability.*** Ideally, some of the more general code developed for the new system would be reusable. If so, it could save money in future systems development projects.

Criteria that may be used to select an application package to purchase include those listed in Table 14.4. Several independent organizations and magazines conduct software package comparisons from time to time. For smaller packages, you can use "trialware" from the Internet before purchase is made. Most vendors will give you the software for a limited testing time. Also, they will come and demonstrate the software. (Be sure to let them use *your* data in the demo.)

ENTERPRISE SOFTWARE. A recent trend in the software business is **enterprise software**, an integrated software that supports enterprise computing. One of the major attractions of enterprise packages is that they incorporate many of the "best practices" in the various functional areas. Organizations thus have the opportunity to upgrade their processes at the same time they install the new software. Major suppliers in this category include SAP/AG, Oracle, Baan, and PeopleSoft.

TABLE 14.4 Criteria for Selecting an Application Package

- Cost and financial terms
- Upgrade policy and cost
- Vendor's reputation and availability for help
- Vendor's success stories (visit their Web site, contact clients)
- System flexibility
- Ease of Internet interface
- Availability and quality of documentation
- Necessary hardware and networking resources
- Required training (check if provided by vendor)
- Security
- Learning (speed of) for developers and users
- Graphical presentation
- Data handling
- Environment and hardware

Since these companies sell their products to a large number of customers, they can hire more specialized personnel and spend more on development than an individual organization would spend to develop its own systems.

E-COMMERCE SOFTWARE. E-commerce software is a powerful yet affordable e-commerce solution that is geared toward Web entrepreneurs of varying skill levels and can greatly reduce the development time needed to launch an effective site. It can provide a comprehensive fix for the rapid construction and deployment of database-driven applications. Its back-end integration capabilities, combined with wizards and templates, make it both powerful and easy to integrate. E-commerce software also facilitates sales by sending orders to the warehouse, adjusting inventory tracking, and even e-mailing stock replenishment alerts to the merchant. Real-time credit card verification and processing is also a great advantage and can also be optimized for use with CyberCash. The software will also provide comprehensive detailed statistics on sales, users, product categories, and browser types.

With all these options and capabilities provided with just one software package, many companies opt to go with e-commerce software instead of developing their own system. Most e-commerce software is fully customizable for your particular company and is easily integrated into your business processes. This trend of using commercially available software will rapidly increase as more merchants go online. As illustrated in the *IT at Work* on page 636, an organization can set up its online store on the Web instantly and at minimal cost.

Management Considerations

Since organizations and their systems requirements vary along many dimensions, it is not possible to neatly match all types of systems projects with the acquisition approaches identified in this chapter. Therefore, in many cases it might be advisable to use a combination of approaches.

In this section we provide general considerations related to the different approaches. These considerations should be reviewed in the context of the desirable outcomes discussed earlier. If coupled with good judgment, these considerations may help managers make better decisions regarding new systems' acquisition.

IT at Work
BILL BROADBENT, THE T-SHIRT KING

Integrating IT ...in Marketing & Operations Management

www.t-shirtking.com

Bill Broadbent has been involved in the T-shirt business for over twenty years. Less than six months ago he opened his online store, T-Shirt King, and has already achieved startling results. In this interview Bill explains why he decided to take his bricks-and-mortar store online and how he went about it.

Interviewer: What made you decide to take your business online?

Broadbent: In discussing the advantages of cybersales we realized that we could show thousands of designs to anyone with Internet access. Also the Internet gave us the world as a market and the ability to bring any design we wanted into a huge online catalogue. Finally, the cost of overhead in a bricks-and-mortar store is sinful. The advantages of selling online are truly unfair. Bricks-and-mortar retailers are not prepared for the inevitable growth of online sales.

Interviewer: What server and shopping-cart software are you using and why?

Broadbent: We began T-Shirt King as a Yahoo! Store while we were still in the experimental mind. Launching the store cost less than $1,000, maintenance less than $500. Now that we are serious, our new site will be about $50,000 and our marketing and maintenance (hard to separate these on the Internet) will be in the six figures per month. We have still to choose an e-commerce software solution for this second phase.

Interviewer: What are your top tips for anyone considering opening his or her own Web store?

Broadbent: Start with Icat or Yahoo! to test the waters. Plan on growing, and go for it. This is the new frontier of retailing, and it is going to grow a lot over the next decade. New fortunes are being made right now. Cost of entry is minimal, and the opportunity to support growth through revenue created is a dream.

For Further Exploration: What are the advantages and disadvantages of buying instant e-commerce solutions from software vendors?

Source: Condensed from *http://sellitontheweb.com/ezine/mystore008.shtml* (2001) and *t-shirtking.com/* (2001).

TRADITIONAL SDLC METHODOLOGY. The SDLC approach often works well for large projects with well-defined requirements, where there is *not* a lot of pressure to finish the project quickly. Use of this approach requires appropriate and effective management, possibly including an end user as the leader if the project is not highly technical.

PROTOTYPING. Prototyping is especially useful in situations where the requirements (and therefore the costs) are poorly defined and/or when speed is needed. However, it requires effective management to make sure that the iterations of prototyping do not continue indefinitely. It is important to have tools such as 4GLs and screen generators when using this approach. If the project is large, it is probably better to establish the information requirements through prototyping and then use a more formal SDLC to complete the system.

RAPID APPLICATION DEVELOPMENT (RAD). This is an obvious candidate when new systems are needed very quickly. RAD tools can work well for developing client/server systems or front-ends for mainframe systems. RAD may be less appropriate than conventional programming languages for larger projects, or for developing systems with a lot of calculations or real-time processing.

JOINT APPLICATION DESIGN (JAD). JAD is easy for senior management to understand. The methodology also provides the needed structure to the process of collecting user requirements. However, it is difficult and expensive to get all people to the same place at the same time. Another disadvantage of JAD is its potential to have dysfunctional groups.

OBJECT-ORIENTED DEVELOPMENT. OO development is becoming increasingly popular, but usage is limited by a shortage of personnel with OO skills. Java is an OO language that is especially suitable for developing network applications. However, OO languages in general, and Java in particular, tend to run slowly. Reusability of code is a potential advantage of OO development, but reuse will not occur without appropriate cataloging, search engines, and experienced and motivated employees.

COMPONENT-BASED DEVELOPMENT. A component-based application architecture provides the business benefits of rapid applications development for quick time to market, enterprisewide consistency of business rules, and quick response to changing business requirements. And because major software vendors are committed to a component architecture, applications can mix and match best-of-breed solutions. Components suppress the complexity of the underlying systems technology. Plug-and-play business application components can be assembled or "glued together" rapidly to develop complex distributed applications needed for e-commerce. The execution of component-based development, however, requires special training and skill.

END-USER DEVELOPMENT. Although most appropriate for small projects, end-user development is also a possibility for larger projects whose priorities are not high enough to lead to a timely response from the central IS unit. Managers should beware of end-user development in situations where problems with the system can lead to significant risks for the organization, such as system failures, inaccurate results, disclosure of confidential data, inefficiency, incompatibility with other systems, and inability to maintain the system if the developer leaves.

PURCHASING OR OUTSOURCING. For large and complex systems with a significant risk of failure, organizations should *always* consider using an outside source. The exception to this rule is that in-house development may be necessary if the system is highly strategic or incorporates critical proprietary information. If scalability is important to the organization, it may be advisable to buy systems rather than make them, even for smaller systems. However, managers need to be aware of relatively high additional implementation costs when purchasing enterprise software packages.

14.4 BUILDING E-COMMERCE APPLICATIONS

The diversity of e-business models and applications, which vary in size from a small store to a global exchange, requires a variety of development methodologies and approaches. Small storefronts can be developed with HTML, Java, or other programming languages. They can also be quickly implemented with commercial packages or leased from application service providers (ASPs) for a small monthly fee. Some packages are available for a free trial period ranging from 30 to 90 days. Larger applications can be outsourced or developed in-house. Building medium to large applications requires extensive integration with existing information systems such as corporate databases, intranets, enterprise resource planning (ERP), and other application programs.

The Development Process of E-Commerce Applications

The development process of **e-commerce applications** consists of five major steps:

- ***Step 1: System analysis,*** as described earlier in the chapter.
- ***Step 2: Selection*** of one of several development options (which we will describe later). At the end of step 2, an application is ready to be installed.
- ***Step 3: Installation and connection*** to the corporate intranet and/or extranets, to databases, and to other applications. During step 3, the system is tested and users' reaction is examined.
- ***Step 4: Deployment.*** Once the applications pass the tests, they can be implemented. The procedures are similar to those conducted for any IT application (see Whitten and Bentley, 2001).
- ***Step 5: Operation and maintenance.*** As in any other IT application, operation and maintenance can be done in-house or can be outsourced (Kendall and Kendall, 2001).

An illustration of the development process of e-commerce applications is available at the book's Web site.

The five steps of the development process can be fairly complex and therefore they must be managed properly. A project team is usually created to manage the progress of the development and the vendors. Collaboration with business partners is critical. Some EC failures are the results of delays and lack of cooperation by business partners. For instance, you can install a superb e-procurement system, but if your vendors will not use it, the system will collapse.

Development Strategies for E-Commerce Applications

In step 2 of the system development process, there are several options for developing EC applications. The major applications are buy, lease, and develop in-house.

BUY THE EC APPLICATIONS. Standard features required by e-commerce applications can be found in commercial packages. Buying an existing package can be cost-effective and time-saving in comparison to in-house application development. The *buy* option should be carefully considered and planned for, to ensure that all critical features for current and future needs are included in the selected package. Otherwise such packages may quickly become obsolete.

In addition, organizational needs can rarely be fully satisfied by buying one single package. It is therefore sometimes necessary to acquire multiple packages to fulfill different needs. Integration may then be required among these packages as well as with existing software.

Major criteria for consideration in buying e-commerce applications are listed on the book's Web site.

The buy option may not be attractive in cases of high obsolescence rate or high software cost. In such a case, one should consider leasing.

LEASE THE EC APPLICATIONS. As compared to the buy option and to an in-house development (see next section), the *lease* option can result in substantial cost and time savings. Though the packages for lease may not always exactly fit with the application requirements (the same is true with the buy option), many common features that are needed by most organizations are usually included.

Leasing is advantageous over buying in those cases where extensive maintenance is required, or where the cost of buying is very high. Leasing can be especially attractive to SMEs (small to medium enterprises) that cannot afford major investments in EC. Large companies may also prefer to lease packages in order to test potential e-commerce solutions before committing to heavy IT investments. Also, since there is a shortage of IT personnel with appropriate skills for developing novel e-commerce applications, several companies lease instead of develop. Even those companies that have in-house expertise may decide they cannot afford to wait for strategic applications to be developed in-house. Hence they may buy or lease applications from external resources in order to establish a quicker presence in the market.

Types of Leasing Vendors. Leasing can be done in two major ways. One is to lease the application from an outsourcer and install it on the company's premises. The vendor can help with the installation, and frequently will offer to contract for the operation and maintenance of the system. Many conventional applications are leased this way. Vendors that lease EC applications are sometimes referred to as *commerce system providers (CSPs).* However, in e-commerce a second leasing option is becoming popular: leasing from an application service provider, which provides both the software and hardware at its site.

DEVELOP EC APPLICATIONS IN-HOUSE: INSOURCING. The third option to develop an e-commerce application is to *build it in-house.* Although this approach is usually more time-consuming and may be more costly than buying or leasing, it often leads to better satisfaction of the specific organizational requirements. Companies that have the resources to develop their e-commerce application in-house may follow this approach in order to differentiate themselves from the competition, which may be using standard applications that can be bought or leased. The in-house development of EC applications, however, is a challenging task, as most applications are novel, have users from outside of the organization, and involve multiple organizations.

Development Options. Three major options exist: Program from scratch, use components, or use enterprise application integration.

- ***Build from scratch.*** This is a rarely used option that should be considered only for specialized applications for which components are not available. It is expensive and slow. But it will provide the best fit.
- ***Build from components.*** Those companies with experienced IT staff can use standard components (e.g., a secure Web server), some software languages (e.g., C^{++}, Visual Basic, or Perl), and third-party APIs (application program interfaces) and subroutines to create and maintain an electronic storefront solely on their own.

  Alternatively, companies can outsource the entire development process using components. From a software standpoint, this alternative offers the greatest flexibility and is the least expensive. However, it can also result in a number of false starts and wasted experimentation. For this reason, even those companies with experienced staff are probably better off customizing one of the packaged solutions. (For details about using components, see Section 14.3.)
- ***Enterprise application integration.*** The **enterprise application integration (EAI)** option is similar to the previous one, but instead of components, one

uses an entire application. This is an especially attractive option when applications from several business partners need to be integrated.

OTHER DEVELOPMENT OPTIONS. Besides the three major options for developing EC applications (buy, lease, and develop in-house), several others are in use and are appropriate under certain circumstances.

Join an E-Marketplace. In this option the company "plugs" itself into an e-marketplace. For example, you can place your catalogs in Yahoo!'s marketplace. Visitors to Yahoo!'s store will find your products and will be able to buy from you. You will pay Yahoo! monthly space-rental fees. In such a case, Yahoo! is a hosting service for you as well. As far as development, you will use templates to build your store, and you can start to sell after only a few hours of preparation work.

Join an Auction or Reverse Auction Third-Party Site. Joining a third-party site is yet another alternative. Again the plug-in can be done quickly. Many companies use this option for certain e-procurement activities.

Joint Ventures. Several different joint-venture partnerships may facilitate EC application development. For example, four banks in Hong Kong developed an e-banking system. In some cases you team up with a company that has an application in place, so you can use it.

Join a Consortium. This option is similar to the previous one, except that you will be one of the e-market owners. Thus, you may have more say regarding the market architecture.

Hybrid Approach. A hybrid approach combines the best of what the company does internally with an outsourced strategy to develop contracted partnerships. Hybrid models work best when the outsourced partner offers a higher level of security, faster time to market, and service-level agreements. An example was shown in the opening case of this chapter.

Application Service Providers (ASPs)

An **application service provider (ASP)** is an agent or vendor who assembles functionality needed by enterprises, and packages it with outsourced development, operation, maintenance, and other services. Although several variations of ASPs exist, in general, monthly fees are paid by the end-user business, for services that include the application software, hardware, service and support, maintenance, and upgrades. The fee can be fixed, or based on utilization.

The essential difference between an ASP and an outsourcer is that an ASP will manage application servers in a centrally controlled location, rather than on a customer's site. Applications are accessed via the Internet or VANs through a standard Web browser interface. In such an arrangement, applications can be scaled, upgrades and maintenance can be centralized, physical security over the applications and servers can be guaranteed, and the necessary critical mass of human resources can be efficiently utilized.

ASPs are especially active in enterprise computing and e-commerce, areas in which it may be too complex to build and too cumbersome to modify and maintain on one's own (e.g., see Ward, 2000). Therefore, the major providers of ERP software, such as SAP and Oracle, are offering ASP options. Also IBM, Microsoft, and Computer Associates offer ASP services. Similarly, major vendors of e-commerce, such as Ariba, offer such services.

BENEFITS OF LEASING FROM ASPs. Leasing from ASPs is a particularly desirable option for SME businesses, for which in-house development and operation of e-commerce applications can be time-consuming and expensive. Leasing from ASPs not only saves various expenses (such as labor costs) in the initial development stage, but also helps to reduce software maintenance and upgrading and user training costs in the long run. A company can always select another software package from the ASP to meet its changing needs and does not have to further invest in upgrading the existing one. In this way, overall business competitiveness can be strengthened through reducing the time-to-market and enhancing the ability to adapt to changing market conditions. This is particularly true of e-commerce applications for which timing and flexibility are crucial. A detailed list of the benefits and potential risks of leasing from ASPs is provided in Table 14.3 at the book's Web site.

Leasing from ASPs is not without disadvantages. Many companies are particularly concerned with the adequacy of protection offered by the ASP against hackers, theft of confidential information, and virus attacks. Also, leased software may not provide a perfect fit for the desired application.

It is important to ensure that the speed of Internet connection is compatible with that of the application in order to avoid distortions to the performance of the application. For example, it is not advisable to run heavier-duty applications on a modem link below a T1 line or a high-speed DSL.

Here are some criteria for selecting an ASP vendor:

- ***Track record.*** In assessing the ASP's track record, one can look at how long the ASP has been in business, who its customers are, and how satisfied they are. However, it may be difficult to make such an assessment, as most ASPs are new to the business. To minimize the risk, minor applications can be leased first. This will provide an opportunity to perform a first-hand evaluation of the ASP before leasing major applications.
- ***Application and data storage.*** The client company should inquire how the application and its data are stored. Using dedicated servers may be more costly than sharing them with others, but dedicated servers reduce the security risk.
- ***Scope of service.*** The terms of fundamental services such as routine maintenance, availability of redundant servers, and default file backups should be clearly defined and agreed upon.
- ***Support services.*** User training is a very important support service, especially for complex applications. Other support services include phone, Web, and e-mail help hotlines, or sometimes a combination of these. However, not all of these services are always free of charge. It is also important to ascertain whether the services are actually rendered by the ASP itself or subcontracted to other companies.
- ***Integration.*** Integration is particularly important for applications such as enterprise resource planning (ERP), accounting, and customer relationship management (CRM). It is necessary to integrate such applications among themselves and with the EC applications. The effort required for integration and the assistance provided by the ASP for achieving the integration are critical selection factors.
- ***Database format and portability.*** The schema and physical structure of the databases of the ASP's application should be compatible with those of existing applications of the client company in order to facilitate the integration of the rented application with the existing ones.

Java, a Promising Tool

Internet and intranet Web pages are coded primarily in *HTML* (hypertext markup language), a simple language that is most useful for displaying static content to viewers. HTML has very limited capabilities for interacting with viewers, or for providing information that is continually being updated. It is not suitable for collecting information, such as names and addresses, or for providing animation or changing information such as stock quotes. To do these types of things it is necessary to add programs written in some form of programming language to the HTML for a Web site.

Java (see Technology Guide 2) is relatively new, but it has already established itself as the most important programming language for putting extra features into Web pages. It has many similarities to the C language, but omits some of the more complex and error-prone features of C. Java was specifically designed to work over networks: Java programs can be sent from a Web server over the Internet and then run on the computer that is viewing the Web page. It has numerous security features to prevent these downloaded programs from damaging files or creating other problems on the receiving computer.

Java is an object-oriented language, so the concepts of object-oriented development are relevant to its use. However, the Java Web-page programs, called **applets**, need to be relatively small to avoid delays in transmitting them over the Internet. Java programs run more slowly than other languages, such as C, which is another reason to keep them small. Therefore it is not necessary that Java developers use the very formal development methodologies appropriate for large system projects. Prototyping is probably the most suitable approach for developing Java applets, because it provides for a high level of interaction between the developers and users in regard to the critical issues of the appearance and ease-of-use of the Web page.

Managerial Issues in E-Commerce Applications

Several managerial issues apply specifically to building e-commerce applications:

- ***It is the business issues that count.*** When one thinks of the Web, one immediately thinks of the technology. Some of the most successful sites on the Web rely on basic technologies—freeware Web servers, simple Web-page design, and few bells and whistles. What makes them successful is not the technology but their understanding of how to meet the needs of their online customers.
- ***Build in-house or outsource.*** Many large-scale enterprises are capable of running their own publicly accessible Web sites for advertisement purposes. However, Web sites for online selling may involve complex integration, security, and performance issues. For those companies venturing into such Web-based selling, a key issue is whether the site should be built in-house, thus providing more direct control, or outsourced to a more experienced provider. Outsourcing services, which allow companies to start small and evolve to full-featured functions, are available through many ISPs, telecommunications companies, Internet malls, and software vendors who offer merchant server and EC applications.
- ***Consider an ASP.*** The use of ASPs is a must for SMEs and should be considered by any company. However, due to the newness of the concept, care must be used in selecting a vendor.

14.5 Some Important Systems Development Issues

Building information systems, either by the ISD or by end users, involves many issues not discussed in the preceding sections. Some additional issues that may be of interest to managers and end users are discussed here.

Case Tools

For a long time, computer programmers resembled the cobbler in the old story. He was so busy mending his customers' shoes that he didn't have time to repair the holes in his own children's shoes. Similarly, programmers were so busy developing systems to increase the productivity of other functions, such as accounting and marketing, that they didn't have time to develop tools to enhance their own productivity. However, this situation has changed with the emergence of **computer-aided software engineering (CASE)** tools. These are marketed as individual items or in a set (toolkit) that automates various aspects of the development process. For example, a systems analyst could use a CASE tool to create data-flow diagrams on a computer, rather than drawing them manually (see Technology Guide 2).

MANAGERIAL ISSUES REGARDING CASE. CASE can be used in two different ways. Individual system personnel or IS groups may use a variety of specific CASE tools to automate certain SDLC activities on a piecemeal basis. Or the IS group may acquire an integrated (I-CASE) package, whose components are tightly integrated and which often embodies a specific systems development methodology. (See Technology Guide 2.) These two approaches are quite different in terms of their implications for the organization.

Using tools independently can provide some significant productivity benefits. Since the tools are acquired on an individual basis, the organization has many options and can select the ones that offer the best performance for the cost and are best suited to the organization's needs. The tools can be used independently as needed, so users have the option of learning, at their own pace, the tools that are most helpful to them.

On the other hand, with integrated packages the components are specifically designed to work well together, and therefore they offer the potential for higher productivity gains. However, the learning pace for these packages is much slower than for individual tools. This means that after adoption, productivity will initially decline, which may be unacceptable for an organization with a large backlog of high-priority IS projects. Some components of an I-CASE package may not be as good as corresponding tools that can be purchased separately.

The relatively high turnover rate among systems personnel also creates problems for use of I-CASE systems. New employees will need to take the time to learn the integrated package. Existing employees may resist using the package, because they feel it will reduce their opportunities to move to other organizations that use either traditional development methods, or some other I-CASE package that is incompatible with the one at the present organization.

In addition to the costs of training and productivity losses, organizations need to purchase the actual I-CASE systems. In the past, this often required purchasing workstations in addition to software. Now, with the availability of much more powerful PCs and servers in client/server systems, many organizations may not find it necessary to buy any additional hardware (except possibly a plotter for printing large diagrams). On the other hand, buying an I-CASE system will cost more than buying a few of the most helpful individual tools.

Software Quality Improvement and ISO-9000

The success of quality management in manufacturing suggests that quality management might also be helpful in dealing with the problems of IS development. To implement this concept for systems development, the Software Engineering Institute at Carnegie Mellon University developed the *Capability Maturity Model (CMM)*. The original purpose of this model was to provide guidelines for the U.S. Department of Defense in selecting contractors for software development. The

TABLE 14.5 Levels of the Capability Maturity Model

Level	Characteristics
1. Initial	Processes are ad hoc, undefined, possibly chaotic. Success depends on individual efforts and heroics.
2. Repeatable	Basic project management tracks cost, schedule, and functionality. On similar applications, organization is able to repeat earlier successes.
3. Defined	Project management and software engineering activities are documented, standardized, and integrated into development through an organization-specific process (i.e., an SDLC).
4. Managed	Both software process activities and quality are measured in detail and are quantitatively understood and controlled.
5. Optimizing	Processes are improved continuously based on feedback from quantitative measures, and from pilot projects with new ideas and technologies.

Source: Compiled from J. Herbsleb et al., "Software Quality and the Capability Maturity Model," *Communications of the ACM*, June 1997, p. 32. ©1997 Association for Computing Machinery, Inc. Reprinted by permission.

CMM identifies five levels of maturity in the software development process, as summarized in Table 14.5.

As an organization moves to higher maturity levels of the CMM, both the productivity and the quality of its software development efforts should improve. Results of a case study, summarized in Table 14.6, verified substantial gains in both areas through software process improvement (SPI) programs based on the capability maturity model.

Organizations need to understand, however, that software process improvement efforts require significant spending and organizational effort. The case study mentioned above found costs ranging from $490 to $2,004 (median $1,375) per software engineer. Well over half the respondents found that SPI efforts cost more and took longer than expected (Herbsleb et al., 1997).

ISO 9000 Standards. Another approach to software quality is to implement the *ISO 9000* software development standards. The International Organization for Standardization (ISO) first published its quality standards in 1987, revised them in 1994, and then republished an updated version in 2000. The new standards are referred to as the "ISO 9000:2000 Standards." These international standards are very extensive: They identify a large number of actions that must be performed to obtain certification. However, the specifications do offer a substantial amount of leeway in many areas. (For an example, see the book's Web site.)

The ISO standards identify the responsibilities of the software developer, as well as the responsibilities of the purchaser or client, in developing quality soft-

TABLE 14.6 Improvements from Capability Maturity Model Implementations

Category	Range	Median	# of Cases
Productivity gain	9–67%	35%	4
Faster time to market	15–23%	NA	2
Reduction in defects	10–94%	39%	5

Source: Compiled from J. Herbsleb et al., "Software Quality and the Capability Maturity Model," *Communications of the ACM*, June 1997, pp. 30–40. ©1997 Association for Computing Machinery, Inc. Reprinted by permission.

ware. The purchaser needs to clearly identify the requirements and have an established process for requesting any necessary changes in these requirements.

An ISO 9000:2000 Quality Management System is made up of many processes, and these processes are glued together by means of many input-output relationships. These input-output relationships turn a simple list of processes into an integrated system. Under ISO standards, the supplier needs to have documented processes for developing software. The supplier's senior management is responsible for developing the *quality policy* document, a short statement that requires employees to use generally accepted quality practices in all areas of the organization. This quality policy is implemented through a *quality system,* which documents the development and quality-control processes that implement the quality policy. The quality system requires preparation of *quality plans* for types of products and processes. To ensure compliance with the plans, there needs to be an internal auditing process. ISO 9000 requires appropriate funding for quality activities, and appointment of personnel and assignment of responsibilities necessary to implement the program.

Project Planning

Chapter 8 provided a four-stage model for information systems planning for IT infrastructure projects. The final stage of this process, **project planning**, is also used in system development of individual applications. Project planning provides an overall framework with which the systems development life cycle can be planned, scheduled, and controlled. Some of the tools of project management are: milestones; critical path method (CPM) and its variant known as program evaluation and review technique (PERT); and Gantt charts.

MILESTONES. Milestone planning techniques allow projects to evolve as they are developed. Rather than try to predict all project requirements and problems in advance, management allows the project to progress at its own pace. **Milestones**, or checkpoints, are established to allow periodic review of progress so that management can determine whether a project merits further commitment of resources, requires adjustments, or should be discontinued.

Milestones can be based on time, budget, or deliverables. For example, a project's progress might be evaluated weekly, monthly, or quarterly. It might be evaluated after a certain amount of resources are used, such as $50,000. However, milestones are most effective when they identify that specific events have occurred, such as the completion of a feasibility study. Figure 14.8 illustrates the simplicity of a milestone chart.

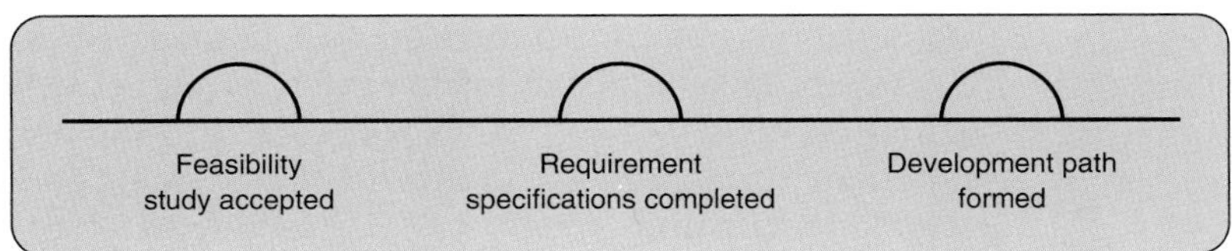

FIGURE 14.8 Milestones.

The *IT at Work* example on page 646 illustrates how Microsoft Corporation uses milestones in its software development projects.

CRITICAL PATH METHOD (CPM), PERT, AND GANTT CHARTS. These generic project management tools are suitable for systems development projects. Many

IT at Work
USING MILESTONES AT MICROSOFT

Integrating IT ...in Production & Operations Management

www.microsoft.com

Microsoft Corporation produces software packages that are extremely large and complex. Windows 95, for example, has over 11 million lines of code; its development team included over 200 programmers and testers.

For such large software projects, many companies use a very structured waterfall-type SDLC. The developers initially develop complete specifications and then "freeze" them so that they can focus on completing the remainder of the project.

Microsoft, however, finds that this approach is not flexible enough to meet the needs of the rapidly changing PC software market. Therefore its strategy is to use prototyping—namely to produce a workable product relatively early in the development process. Subsequent development adds more features to the limited functionality of this initial version.

Microsoft's projects have three major milestones. At the first milestone, the product has one-third of its features (the most important ones), plus the interface and any other shared components. At the second milestone, the developers add the next-most-important one-third of the features. The last milestone marks the completion of the remaining features. Individual programmers and small teams (three to eight developers) are responsible for developing individual features.

One key aspect of this approach is "synchronization and stabilization." The project "buildmaster" compiles a working version of the whole package, including any new or revised components from individual teams, at the end of every day. If it is not possible to compile this latest version, the team whose code caused the failure must correct the problem immediately. In this way, all teams are able to work with a copy of the latest version every morning. In addition, every day Microsoft has a working version that it can test with users, distribute to beta testers, or finalize for production at that level of functionality.

For Further Exploration: Would this development approach work for other companies in different industries? Is it possible to maintain as high a level of quality with this approach as with more structured approaches? What are the characteristics of the employees an organization would need in order to be successful with this approach?

Source: Based on M. A. Cusamono and R. W. Selby, "How Microsoft Builds Software," *Communications of the ACM,* June 1997, pp. 53–61; and on information from *microsoft.com* (2001).

off-the-shelf software packages are available for planning, organizing, and controlling projects.

PROJECT PROPERTIES AND PRIORITIES. Setting budget and time frames prior to defining the system design constraints is perhaps the greatest mistake made in project planning. For example, management may decide to install a new order entry system in nine months, for which it is willing to spend $1 million. This leaves one important issue undefined: What will the new system do? By default, management has constrained the functionality of the new system.

The proper sequence for managing a project is first to get a good functional definition of what the system is designed to do, and then to have people with experience and expertise in information systems and in project management develop a budget and schedule. If management cannot accept the schedule or budget, then the capabilities of the new system can be scaled down to meet the schedule and/or budget constraints.

In developing a budget, schedule, and specifications for a system, managers need to consider and understand several properties of projects and their management. The following five properties most significantly influence the overall nature of an IT project.

1. ***Predefined structure.*** The more predefined the structure of a project is, the more easily it can be planned and controlled.
2. ***Stability of technology.*** The greater the experience with a given technology to be used for a new system, the more predictable the development process.
3. ***Size.*** The larger the project, the more difficult it is to estimate the resources (time and costs) required to complete it.
4. ***User proficiency.*** The more knowledgeable and experienced users and managers are in their functional areas and in developing systems, the more proficient they will be relative to information technology and the easier it will be to develop systems for them.
5. ***Developer proficiency.*** The more knowledge and experience the systems analyst assigned to a project has, the easier the project will go, and vice versa.

Projects can possess variations of each of the preceding properties. For example, a project can have predefined structure but use unstable technology, or it can be a massive undertaking and have low user and developer proficiencies (e.g., most initial online airline reservations systems could be described this way).

Using appropriate project management concepts and tools could be critical to the success or failure of complex systems, as the *IT at Work* below shows.

IT at Work

IBM SUCCEEDED IN THE 1998 AND 2000 OLYMPICS WITH PROPER PROJECT MANAGEMENT

www.ibm.com

Above all, everyone with an interest in the Olympic Games—from organizers and athletes to officials and fans—wants immediate, accurate information. IBM MQSeries helped power the Sydney 2000 Games by enabling the exchange of information across each of the diverse computing platforms employed in an array of critical Olympic Games solutions. Providing dynamic access to real-time information across organizational, functional, and geographic boundaries was a massive task, even for IBM, which had experience in the Atlanta games and the Nagano Winter Olympics in February 1998.

Developing an Olympic IS and Web site is much more complex than many people think. The architecture of the Olympic IS for the 1998 Nagano games is illustrated on the next page. To begin with, the deadlines must be met; the games will not be delayed if the supporting IT is not in place. The users are from over 80 countries with diverse cultures and expectations. The 7,000 users speak many different languages, and the system must handle all the data of the games, including athlete accreditation, press feeds, results, housing arrangements, food, logistics, and more.

To improve project management IBM prepared a project plan as follows: Use proven technology, test the full system early, and foster tight communications with the diverse system users, ranging from Olympic committees to athletes. Finding the information requirements of these users was difficult.

For every sport a test was designed to find gaps between what users wanted and what the system delivered. Gaps were found with report generation, format of reports, names, and so on. The project management software planned all tests such that corrective actions could be made prior to the opening. Time was needed because different users (e.g., Olympic committees, sport federations, and the press) had different requirements that needed to be negotiated into an agreed-upon format.

To coordinate the entire project IBM created an end-to-end plan, using a CPM-based software management package. Actually, there were ten major projects, and they were interrelated. The software simulated the ripple-through effect when one piece falls behind. The software was also used to make adjustments in both simulated and real time. IBM also reviewed all potential changes in the ten projects and their impacts. Extensive testing was a key success factor. The testing found many requirements that were not included in the initial design.

On February 7, 1998, the Nagano games started. Over 100 million hits were recorded on the Web site. Everything worked as planned; IBM, the largest computer company

(continued)

in the world, did not fail. Most companies will never develop such enormous and complex systems.

What about cost/benefits? In the short run, IBM invested so much money that its earnings per share for the first quarter of 1998 declined by over $100 million. The benefits are difficult to measure, but IBM's reputation is the major one. IBM was also able to use the experience gained in 1998, along with parts of the 1998 system, for the Sydney games in 2000.

For Further Exploration: Find some information about IBM and the Sydney Olympic Games. Why was IBM willing to lose money on the 1998 system?

Sources: Condensed from R. Guth and L. Radosevich, "IBM Crosses the Olympic Finish Line," *InfoWorld*, February 9, 1998; and from paper published at *http://www-4.ibm.com/software/info/olympic/video/mqseries.html* (2001).

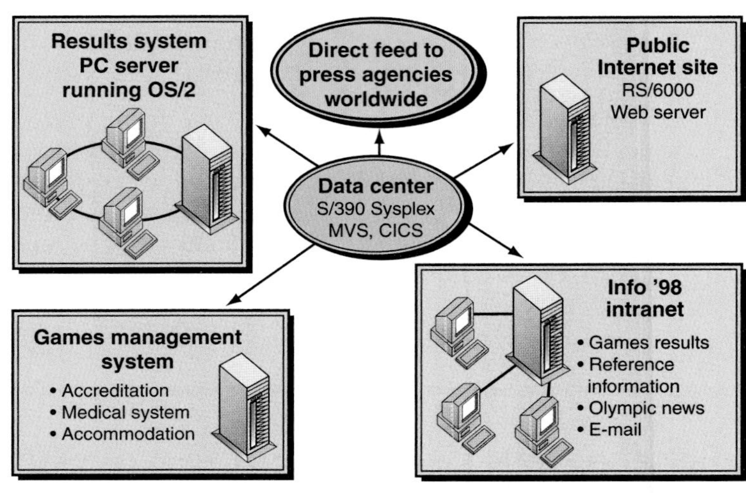

WEB-BASED PROJECT MANAGEMENT. Web-based project management solutions provide a central Web site, or project portal, where everyone involved in a project can get up-to-date project information, share documents, and participate in planning and problem-solving using such collaboration features as shared notebooks, threaded discussion groups, and chat forums. By making it easy for team members and managers to exchange information and ideas, Web-based project management solutions promise to reduce mistakes caused by poor communication. They also can minimize or eliminate delays due to the time it takes to move documents and people around for approvals and meetings. Examples of enterprise project management packages include: TeamCenter 3.0 (from Invoie Software), TeamPlay 1.6.4 (from Primavera Systems), and WebProject 3.1 (from WebProject).

MANAGERIAL ISSUES

1. ***Importance.*** Some general and functional managers believe that system development is a technical topic that should be of interest only to technical people. This is certainly not the case. Appropriate construction of systems is necessary for their success. Functional managers must participate in the development process and should understand all the phases. They must also participate in the make-or-buy decisions and software selection decisions. Inappropriate development methodologies can result in the system's failure.

2. ***Building interorganizational and international information systems.*** Building systems that connect two or more organizations, or one organization that operates in different countries, can be very complicated. (See Tractinsky and Jarvenpaa, 1995.) As seen in Chapter 8, you need to carefully plan for such systems, considering different requirements and cultures. In addition to planning, the analysis, design, and other phases of system development must take into account the information needs of the various parties. (See Minicase 2.) One of the major problems with international systems is that what is ethical or legal in one country may be unethical or illegal in another.

3. ***Ethical and legal issues.*** Developing systems across organizations and countries could result in problems in any phase of system development. For example, in developing the Nagano Olympics system in 1998, IBM found at the last minute that pro-North-Korea groups in Japan took offense at a reference to the Korean War written on the Web site. Although the material was taken from the *World Book Encyclopedia,* it offended some people. IBM had to delete the reference and provide an apology. IBM commented, "Next time we're going to do a ton of research first versus just do it and find out the hard way." A special difficulty exists with Internet-related projects, where legislation is still evolving.
4. ***User involvement.*** The direct and indirect users of a system are likely to be the most knowledgeable individuals concerning requirements and which alternatives will be the most effective. Users are also the most affected by a new information system. IS analysts and designers, on the other hand, are likely to be the most knowledgeable individuals concerning technical and data-management issues as well as the most experienced in arriving at viable systems solutions. The right mixture of user involvement and information systems expertise is crucial.
5. ***Traditional approaches vs. prototyping.*** The traditional development approach stresses detailed, lockstep development with established decision points. Prototyping stresses flexible development based on actual use of partially functional systems. Experience has shown that the traditional approach can be better for low-risk, environmentally stable, and technology-simple situations; prototyping is often better under the opposite conditions.
6. ***Tool use by developers.*** Development tools and techniques can ensure that developers consider all necessary factors and standardize development, documentation, and testing. Forcing their use, on the other hand, may unnecessarily constrain innovation, development efficiency, and personnel productivity.
7. ***Quality assurance vs. schedules.*** Quality counts in the short term and the long term, but it can lengthen development and increase developmental costs. Trying to meet tight development schedules can induce poor quality—with even worse schedule, cost, and morale problems.
8. ***Behavior problems.*** Information systems are primarily for people to use. People may react to new systems in unexpected ways, however, making even the best technically designed systems useless. Changes brought about by information systems need to be managed effectively. Of special interest is the issue of motivating programmers to increase their productivity by learning new tools and reusing preprogrammed modules.
9. ***Perpetual development.*** Information systems are designed to meet organizational needs. When they don't accurately meet these needs, or these needs

change, information systems need to be redeveloped. Developing a system can be a major expense, but perpetually developing a system to maintain its usefulness is usually a much larger expense.

ON THE WEB SITE... Additional resources, including the Virtual Company, quizzes, cases, updates, additional exercises, links, demos, and activities, can be found on the book's Web site.

KEY TERMS

Applets (Java) *642*
Application service provider (ASP) *640*
Component-based development *624*
Computer-aided software engineering (CASE) *643*
Direct cutover *614*
E-commerce application *638*
End-user computing *627*
Enterprise application integration (EAI) *639*
Enterprise software *634*
Feasibility study *611*
Information center *628*
Java *642*
Joint application design (JAD) *618*
Light methodology *616*
Logical design *612*
Milestones *645*
Object-oriented development *621*
Outsourcing *631*
Parallel conversion *614*
Phased conversion *614*
Physical design *613*
Pilot conversion *614*
Post-audit *615*
Project planning *645*
Prototyping *617*
Rapid application development (RAD) *619*
Systems analysis *611*
Systems development *609*
Systems development life cycle (SDLC) *610*
Waterfall method *611*
Web-based system *630*

CHAPTER HIGHLIGHTS (Numbers Refer to Learning Objectives)

❶ A systems development life cycle (SDLC) identifies the major steps, or stages, in the development or acquisition of an information system. Organizations may use a proprietary SDLC methodology to help manage systems projects.

❷ The prototyping approach is an iterative process that creates simple versions of a system to help users identify their requirements. Traditional SDLCs try to complete much of their analysis and design activities before starting development and are more appropriate where requirements are easier to identify.

❷ Rapid application development (RAD) packages can speed development. However, systems developed via RAD may not run as efficiently, or be as scalable, as systems developed with more conventional methodologies.

❷ Joint application design (JAD) is a structured process in which users, managers, and analysts work together for several days in a series of intensive meetings to specify or review systems requirements.

❸ Object-oriented development makes it easier to develop very complex systems rapidly and with relatively few errors. It is also easier to reuse code from object-oriented systems. However, object-oriented systems may not run as fast as those developed in other languages, and many programmers lack OO skills.

❹ Many e-commerce applications are assembled from a set of components, rather than being constructed from scratch. Components have evolved from the objects of object-oriented methodology. However, they are much larger, providing a kind of plug-and-play building blocks that help in developing large complex systems, such as ERP or e-commerce.

❺ Outsourcing custom development or purchasing generic systems are alternatives to in-house development.

❻ Web-based applications are easy to develop and implement. However, organizations need to establish consistent policies and practices to make sure that Web-page development activities support organizational goals. There are several options for developing EC applications. The major applications are buy, lease, and develop in-house.

❼ CASE tools can substantially increase programmer productivity. However, the more integrated packages are difficult to learn, which initially reduces productivity and can lead to resistance to implementation within IS groups.

❽ Software quality can be improved by implementing the capability maturity model (CMM) or ISO 9000:2000 standards.

QUESTIONS FOR REVIEW

1. Describe the major stages of the SDLC.
2. Explain why it is important to understand the concept of SDLC.
3. List four different approaches to converting from one system to another. Which is most risky? Least risky?
4. Describe post-audit activities. Why is it important to do an audit after a system has been completed and put into operation?
5. Describe the tools that are commonly included in rapid application development (RAD) packages. What capabilities can they provide?
6. Why do many companies use the prototyping approach to develop their e-commerce applications? What are the limitations of the prototyping approach?
7. Describe object-oriented development and its increasing importance.
8. Describe the architecture of component-based development of e-commerce applications.
9. Identify trends that encourage more systems development by end users.
10. What are the risks inherent in end-user development? How can they be minimized?
11. List the advantages and disadvantages of purchasing generic software versus using in-house staff or outsourcers to develop customized applications.
12. List the e-commerce application options.
13. Describe an application service provider (ASP).
14. Describe Java and its role in Internet development.
15. Identify and explain the five levels of the capability maturity model (CMM).
16. List the issues in controlling the quality of systems development. What is the role of IS-9000?

QUESTIONS FOR DISCUSSION

1. Why is it advisable in some systems development projects to use prototyping to find information needs? Why can't the analyst just ask the users what they want and use the SDLC?
2. What types of incentives could an IS group provide to its programmers to encourage reuse of objects and other software they develop?
3. What type of development approaches would be most appropriate for developing small systems? For very large systems? Why? What other factors need to be considered?
4. End-user systems developers usually work for managers whose IT knowledge is limited. Discuss the types of problems to which this situation could lead, and suggest possible ways of dealing with these problems.
5. Although the CASE concept—automated tools to increase programmer productivity—seems valid, many IS organizations do not use integrated (I-CASE) packages. Discuss the barriers to the increasing use of I-CASE.
6. Some programmers feel that implementing the capability maturity model (CMM) will make the development process too rigid and bureaucratic, thus stifling their creativity. Discuss the pros and cons of this issue.
7. Building Web-based systems such as intranets can be a fast and fairly easy process. Based on Chapters 4, 5, 6, and 14, can you explain why? What are the long-term implications of this for IS professionals? For end-user systems developers? For outsourcing firms?
8. Discuss the advantages of a lease option over a buy option in e-commerce applications development.
9. Compare component-based development to enterprise application integration.
10. A large company with a number of products wants to start selling on the Web. Should it use a merchant server or an electronic suite? Assuming the company elects to establish an electronic storefront, how would you determine whether it should outsource the site or run it itself?

EXERCISES

1. Contact a major information systems consulting firm and ask for literature on its systems development life cycle methodology (or search for it on the Internet). Compare and contrast the proprietary methodology to the eight-stage SDLC described in this chapter.
2. Identify and interview some end users who develop systems at their organizations. Ask them whether their organization has any standards for documenting and testing systems developed by end users. If it has such policies, are they enforced? If not, what do the end users do to ensure the accuracy and maintainability of the systems they develop?
3. Contact an administrator at your university or work place and find out what purchased systems, especially

larger ones, are in use. Do these systems meet the organization's needs, or are some important features missing that should be included in these packages?

4. Contact IS managers at some large organizations, and find out whether their IS developers use any CASE tools. If the IS units use an integrated (I-CASE) tool, what things do they like and dislike about it? If the units do not use I-CASE tools, what are the reasons for not using them?

GROUP AND ROLE-PLAYING ACTIVITIES

1. Divide the class into two teams. Have both teams collect information on SAP's integrated enterprise management software, and on Oracle's comparable software packages. After the teams analyze the data, stage a debate with one team arguing that the SAP products are the more desirable and with the other team supporting Oracle (or other vendor).
2. Study the IBM systems at the 1996, 1998, and 2000 Olympics. Find information about the two systems. Why did the 1996 system fail, and why were the 1998 and 2000 systems successful? Assign one group each to 1996, 1998, and 2000 and one to the comparisons.
3. Several vendors offer products for creating online stores. The Web sites of each vendor usually list those online stores using their software. Assign one or more vendors to each team member. Visit the online stores using each vendor's software. Prepare a report comparing the similarities and differences among the sites. Do the sites take advantage of the functionality provided by the various products?

INTERNET EXERCISES

1. Explore the General Electric site at *ge.com,* and then compare it to the Kodak site at *kodak.com.* Try to identify the organizational objectives for these two different types of sites. In the context of these objectives, discuss the advantages and disadvantages of having either: (1) a relatively simple site with limited graphics, or (2) a site that contains extensive graphics.
2. Go to the site at *geocities.com/~rfinney/case.htm.* Follow the links on the page to look at the features of several CASE tool packages. Prepare a report on the capabilities of one or two packages with multiple features.
3. Look at the Netron Corporation site (*netron.com*). Examine the tools they have for working with legacy systems (gap analysis) and for rapid application development. Write a report. Prepare a report on Netron's approach to and tools for renovating and maintaining legacy systems.
4. Open Market is the leading vendor of EC software. At their site they provide demonstrations illustrating the types of storefronts that they can create for shoppers. They also provide demonstrations of how their software is used to create a store.
   - Run either the Shopsite Merchant or Shopsite Pro demonstration to see how this is done.
   - What sorts of features are provided by Shopsite?
   - Does Shopsite support larger or smaller stores?
   - What other products does Open Market offer for creating online stores? What types of stores do these products support?

Minicase 1

Do or Die

www.quantum.com

A direct cutover from an existing system to a new one is risky. If the system is critical to the operations of the organization, the risks are magnified to an even higher level. Yet Quantum Corp., a Milpitas, California, disk-drive manufacturer, did just that—and lived to tell about it. The vendors and consultants on the project claim that this was one of the largest-ever direct cutovers of a distributed business system.

Quantum realized that it had to take action. The limitations of its existing systems were making it difficult for the company to compete in the disk-drive market. Sales representatives needed to determine how much of a specific item—in inventory or in production—had not yet been committed to other customers. However, because databases did not share information, it was very difficult for them to get this information.

Quantum was especially interested in a piece of information known as available-to-promise (ATP). This indicates how many units of a given item could be delivered, by what date, to specific locations throughout the world. Calculating these values requires coordination and real-time processing of sales, inventory, and shipping data. If Quantum implemented its new system by phasing in the modules one at a time, the conversion would take much longer. Furthermore, the system would not be able to provide this key information until the end of the transition.

Quantum felt that the business risks of this kind of delay were greater than the technical risks of a direct cutover. The company was also concerned about possible resistance in some departments if the full implementation took a long time. The departments had enough autonomy to implement other systems if they lost confidence in the new system and, if they did, Quantum would lose the benefits of having an integrated system.

Although the actual cutover took eight days, the planning and preparation required over three years. The initial analysis was in October 1992, and Quantum sent out requests for proposals in April 1993. In March 1994, the company chose Oracle, Hewlett-Packard, and Price Waterhouse as its business partners on the project.

Quantum created a project team of 100 people, composed of key employees from each business unit and the IS department, and moved them into a separate building. The purchase of the disk-drive business of Digital Equipment Corp. in October 1994, which brought in another set of legacy applications and assorted hardware platforms, set the project back by about four months.

In February 1995, Quantum started a public relations campaign with a three-day conference for the users. The following month, "project evangelists" made presentations at all organizational locations.

In August 1995, the team conducted a systems validation test. It failed. The team worked intensely to solve the problems and then tested the system again for four weeks starting in December 1995. This time, it was successful.

In March 1996, Quantum provided a very extensive and absolutely mandatory user-training program. In April, it conducted final briefings, tested the system at all locations throughout the world, and set up a "mission control" center.

At 5 P.M. on April 26, Quantum shut down the old system. Hank Delavati, the CIO, said, "Business as we know it stopped . . . we could not place an order, we could not receive material, we could not ship products. We could not even post cash." Data records from the old system were loaded into the new system. At 4 P.M. on May 5, the new system started up successfully.

Mark Jackson, an executive vice president at Quantum, noted afterward that the relatively large project budget was not the company's primary concern. He said, "We could have figured out how to save 10 percent of the project's cost . . . but that would have raised the risk to an unacceptable level. To succeed, you have to spend the money and take care of the details."

Source: Condensed from L. Radosevich, "Quantum's Leap," *CIO*, February 15, 1997, and from *quantum.com/* (2001).

Questions for Minicase 1

1. Estimate Quantum Corporation's chances of survival if this project failed. Provide some reasons to support your estimate.
2. What did Quantum do to minimize the risks of this direct cutover?
3. Evaluate the claim that, because of business and organizational issues, this direct cutover was less risky than a phased conversion.
4. Under what, if any, circumstances would you recommend this kind of direct cutover for critical operational systems?
5. Discuss the impact of this project on the internal power relationships between the IS department and the other departments in the organization.
6. It appears that Quantum spent a substantial amount of money on this project and was willing to increase spending when it seemed necessary for the success of the project. Discuss the risks of a "whatever it takes" approach.

Minicase 2
Implementing SAP R/3 at the University of Nebraska

www.uneb.com

On a Monday morning in August 1998, Jim Buckler, project manager of the University of Nebraska's Administrative System Project (ASP), was preparing for his weekly meeting with the project's steering committee, the Financial System Task Force (FSTF). The ASP is an effort charged with implementing SAP's R/3 client/server enterprise resource planning (ERP) product for the University of Nebraska's multicampus system.

As a result of mapping the University's future business processes to the SAP R/3 system, a number of gaps were identified between these processes and those offered by the SAP R/3 system. These critical gaps were tracked as one of the project's critical success factors. Project management and the FSTF had to consider all factors that could poten-

(continued)

tially be impacted by the critical gaps. Such factors include the scope of the project, resources (human and budgetary), the timeline, and previous configuration of the system, to name a few.

Four options have been developed as possible solutions to resolve the 14 critical gaps. Table 14.7 summarizes the options presented to the FSTF by project management.

With a number of constraints and issues in mind, Buckler contemplated which one or combination of the four options was the best course of action. Should SAP and IBM be working concurrently on resolving the gaps (i.e., options 1 and 2)? This seemed to be the safest course of action, but it would be very costly. Should the project timeline be extended until July 1, 1999? What if SAP could not resolve all the gaps by that time? Would that deter the University from transitioning smoothly into the new millennium? Should the implementation of the HR/Payroll module be delayed? These options would have to be carefully considered and a recommendation made at Buckler's meeting with the FSTF in a few hours' time.

Sources: Condensed from T. Sieber et al., "Implementing SAP R/3 at the University of Nebraska," *Proceedings of the 20th ICIS Conference,* December, 12–15, 1999; and from *sap.com* (2001).

Questions for Minicase 2

1. Which of the four options or combination of options would you recommend to project management and the steering committee? What are the risks involved in your recommendation? How would you manage the risks?
2. Discuss the advantages and disadvantages of a purchased system that forces different organizational units to change their business processes and policies to conform to the new system. Identify situations where this standardization would be desirable, and other situations where it would be undesirable.

TABLE 14.7 Possible Solutions to Critical Gaps

Option	Description	Gaps Affected	Risk	Costs
SAP provides on-site developer(s)	SAP provides on-site developers to edit the R/3 system's core program code and incorporate the changes in future R/3 system releases.	This option would resolve all gaps.	Moderate risk, as solutions will be incorporated in future R/3 system releases; however, developers must begin immediately.	Expected low cost to the University as SAP would be asked to absorb most of the costs.
IBM provides developers to create workarounds	IBM creates temporary workaround solutions that are "bolted on" to the system and are not part of the core SAP R/3 system code.	This option would resolve most gaps as attempts to develop workarounds for some gaps would not be feasible.	High risk, as solutions are not guaranteed to be in future R/3 system releases.	High cost to the University for the consulting resources. Needed to complete the workarounds.
Extend project timeline until July 1, 1999, to implement the next version of SAP R/3	Push project timeline three months, resulting in some implementation activities being conducted simultaneously to meet the July 1 "Go live" date.	SAP validates that all critical gaps are resolved in the next R/3 system release.	High risk, as new version must be delivered on time and resolution of critical gaps must be supported.	Moderate cost for some additional resources; potential for high cost if gaps are not resolved in new version.
University delays payroll until the next phase of implementing functionality	"Go live" with non-HR modules as outlined in the project scope and interface the R/3 system with the University's current human resource management system.	This option addresses only those gaps related to the human resources (HR) application module.	Low risk, as current payroll system is functional.	Moderate cost for some additional resources and to address change management issues; potential for high cost if payroll system has to be updated for Y2K compliance.

3. Can you think of circumstances where a company might want to install an enterprise management system, such as SAP's R/3, even though it appears that this would be significantly *more* expensive than developing a comparable system in-house? Discuss.

4. Go to the site at *sap.com*. Follow the links on the page to look at the features of some cross-industry solutions. Prepare a report on the capabilities of the SAP solutions.

REFERENCES AND BIBLIOGRAPHY

1. BenTov, S., "Transitioning IT Systems to the Web," *Electronic Business*, October 2000.
2. Beynon-Davies, P., "Rapid Application Development (RAD): An Empirical Review," *European Journal of Information Systems*, September 2000.
3. Biggs, M., "Why Choose a Web-based Project Management Solution?" *InfoWorld*, January 31, 2000.
4. Bolognesi, T., "Toward Constraint-Object-Oriented Development," *IEEE Transactions on Software Engineering*, July 2000.
5. Cooke, R., "Understanding and Performing Reviews of SDLC Project Software Products," *EDPACS*, January 2001.
6. Davis, G. B., "The Hidden Costs of End-User Computing," *Accounting Horizons*, February 1998.
7. "Developing E-Commerce Systems: Current Practices and State of Art," special issue, *Data Base*, December 2001.
8. Edberg, D. T., and B. J. Bowman, "User-Developed Applications: An Empirical Study of Application Quality and Developer Productivity," *Journal of Management Information Systems*, Summer 1996.
9. Fontoura, M., "Using Viewpoints to Derive Object-Oriented Frameworks: A Case Study in the Web-based Education Domain," *Journal of Systems and Software*, November 2000.
10. Guimaraes, T., "Empirically Testing the Relationship Between End-User Computing Problems and Information Center Success Factors," *Decision Sciences*, Spring 1999.
11. Hardgrave, B. C., "Toward a Contingency Model for Selecting an Information System Prototyping Strategy," *Journal of Management Information Systems*, Fall 1999.
12. Henderson, J. C., and J. G. Cooprider, "Dimensions of I/S Planning and Design Aids: A Functional Model of CASE Technology," *Information Systems Research*, September 1990.
13. Herbsleb, J., et al., "Software Quality and the Capability Maturity Model," *Communications of the ACM*, June 1997.
14. Johnson, R. A., "The Ups and Downs of Object-Oriented Systems Development," *Communications of the ACM*, October 2000.
15. Kendall, K. E., and J. E. Kendall, *Systems Analysis and Design*, 4th ed. Upper Saddle River, NJ: Prentice-Hall, 2001.
16. Kern, T., and J. Kreijger, "An Exploration of the ASP Outsourcing Option," *Proceedings, 34th Hawaiian International Conference on Systems Sciences (HICSS)*, Hawaii, January 2001 (0-7695-0981-9/01).
17. Kreie, J., et al., "Applications Development by End-Users: Can Quality Be Improved?" *Decision Support Systems*, August 2000.
18. Kreijger, T. K., "An Exploration of the ASP Outsourcing Option," *Proceedings, 34th HICSS, Hawaii*, January 2001.
19. Panko, R. R., and R. H. Halverson, "Are Two Heads Better than One (at Reducing Spreadsheet Errors)?" *Proceedings of the Second AIS Americas Conference on Information Systems*, August 16–18, 1996.
20. Panko, P. R., and Sprague, R. H., "Hitting the Wall: Errors in Developing and Code Inspecting for a Simple Spreadsheet Model," *Decision Support Systems* 22, 1998.
21. Praxiom Research Group Limited, *ISO 9004-2 Guidelines Translated into Plain English* (*http://www.connect.ab.ca/~praxiom/9004-2.htm*), 2001.
22. Ravichandran, T., "Quality Management in Systems Development: An Organizational System Perspective," *MIS Quarterly*, September 2000.
23. Rockart, J. F., and L. S. Flannery, "The Management of End-User Computing," *Communications of the ACM*, October 1983.
24. Seltsikas, P., "System Development: A Strategic Framework," *European Journal of Information Systems*, September 2000.
25. Sharman, V., and Sharma, R., *Developing E-Commerce Sites: An Integrated Approach*. Boston, MA: Addison-Wesley, 2000.
26. Szuprowicz, B., *Extranet and Intranet: E-commerce Business Strategies for the Future*, Computer Technology Research Corp. (*ctr.com*), 1998.
27. Tractinsky, M., and S. L. Jarvenpaa, "Information Systems Design Decisions in a Global vs. Domestic Context," *MIS Quarterly*, December 1995.
28. Treese, G. W., and Stewart, L. C., *Designing Systems for Internet Commerce*. Reading, MA: Addison-Wesley, 1998.
29. Valacich, J., et al., *Essentials of Systems Analysis and Design*, Upper Saddle River, NJ: Prentice-Hall, 2001.
30. Ward, L., "How ASPs Can Accelerate Your E-Business," *e-Business Advisor*, March 2000.
31. Weir, J., "A Web/Business Intelligence Solution," *Information Systems Management*, Winter 2000.
32. Whitten, J., and Bentley, L., *Systems Analysis and Design Methods*, 5th ed. New York: Irwin/McGraw Hill, 2001.
33. Yasin, R., "Project Management Meets Web," *Internetweek*, October 9, 2000.
34. Yourdon, E., "What's So Different About Managing E-Projects?" *Computerworld*, August 2000.
35. Yourdon, E., *Modern Structured Analysis*. Englewood Cliffs, NJ: Prentice-Hall, 1989.

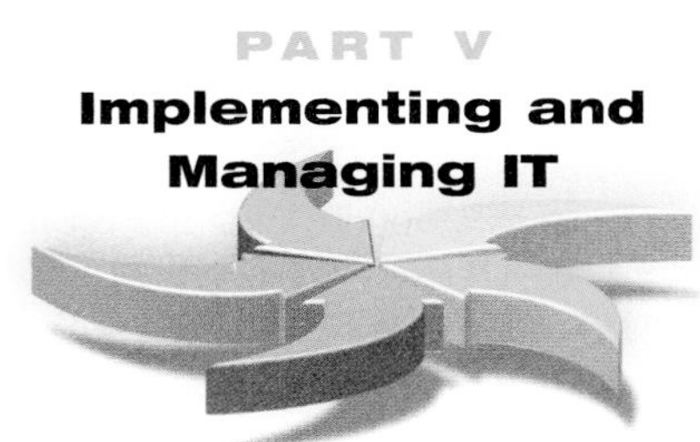

PART V

Implementing and Managing IT

CHAPTER

15

Managing Information Resources and Security

LEARNING OBJECTIVES

After studying this chapter, you will be able to:

1. Recognize the difficulties in managing information resources.
2. Understand the role of the IS department and its relationships with end users.
3. Discuss the role of the chief information officer.
4. Recognize information systems' vulnerability and the possible damage from malfunctions.
5. Describe the major methods of defending information systems.
6. Describe the security issues of the Web and electronic commerce.
7. Distinguish between security auditing and disaster recovery planning and understand the economics of security.

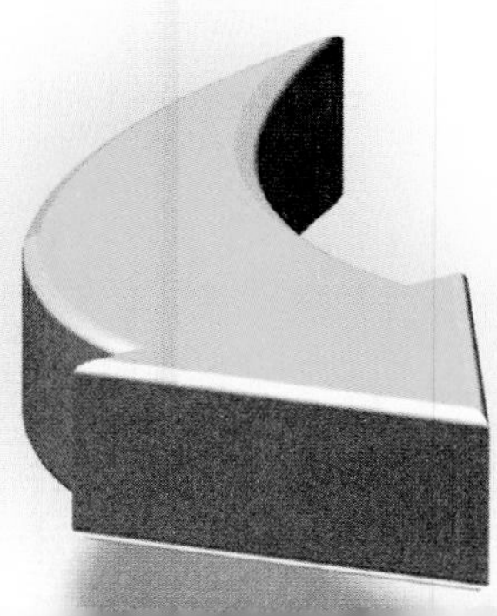

CYBERCRIME IN THE NEW MILLENNIUM

On January 1, 2000, the world was relieved to know that the damage to information systems due to the YK2 problem was minimal. However, only about six weeks into the new millennium, computer systems around the world were attacked, unexpectedly, by criminals.

On February 6, 2000, the biggest e-commerce sites were falling like dominos. First was Yahoo!, which was forced to close down for three hours. Next were eBay, Amazon.com, E*Trade, and several other major EC and Internet sites that had gone dark.

The attacker(s) used a method called *denial of service (DOS)*. By hammering a Web site's equipment with too many requests for information, an attacker can effectively clog a system, slowing performance or even crashing a site. All one needs to do is to get the DOS software (available for free in many hacking sites), break into unrelated unprotected computers and plant some software there, select a target site, and instruct the unprotected computers to repeatedly send a request for information to the target site. It is like constantly dialing a telephone number so that no one else can get through. It takes time for the attacked site to identify the sending computers and to block e-mails from them. Thus, the attacked site may be out-of-service for a few hours.

The magnitude of the damage was so large that on February 9, U.S. Attoney General Janet Reno pledged to track down the criminals and ensure that the Internet remains secure. This assurance did not last too long, as can be seen from the following story told by Professor Turban:

> When I opened my e-mail on May 4, 2000, I noticed immediately that the number of messages was larger than usual. A closer observation revealed that about 20 messages were titled I LOVE YOU, and most of them came from faculty, secretaries, and administrators at City University of Hong Kong. It was not my birthday and there was no reason to believe that so many people would send me love messages the same day. My initial thought was to open one message to find out what's going on. But, on second thought I remembered the "Melissa" virus and the instructions not to open any attachment of a strange e-mail. I picked up the telephone and called one of the senders, who told me not to open the attachment since it contained a deadly virus.

Although Professor Turban's system escaped the virus, thousands of users worldwide opened the "love" attachment and released the bug. The total damage worldwide was estimated at $5 billion to $10 billion (U.S.). It is interesting to note that the alleged attacker, from the Philippines, was not prosecuted because he did not break any law in the Philippines.

LESSONS LEARNED FROM THIS CASE

The opening incidents demonstrate the following:

- Information resources that include computers, networks, programs, and data are vulnerable to unforeseen attacks.
- Many countries do not have sufficient laws to deal with computer criminals.
- Protection of networked systems can be a complex issue.
- Attackers can zero in on a single company, or can attack many companies without discrimination.

- Attackers use different attack methods.
- Although variations of the attack methods are known, the defense against them is difficult and/or expensive.
- In both cases, the magnitude of the damage was the largest recorded until that time, for each attack method.
- Having a disaster recovery plan can be useful to restore business as quickly as possible.

The actions of people or of nature can cause an information system to function in a way different from what was planned. It is important, therefore, to know how to ensure the continued operation of an IS and to know what to do if the system breaks down. These and similar issues are of concern to the management of information resources, the subject of this chapter.

Information resources management (IRM) encompasses all activities related to the planning, organizing, acquiring, maintaining, securing, and controlling of IT resources. IT resources are very diversified; they include technology assets, personnel assets, and IT relationship assets (Ross et al., 1996). IRM activities are conducted both at the information systems department (ISD) level and in the end-user departments, units, and teams.

In this chapter we look at the following IRM issues: the distributions of IRM between the ISD and the end users; how the ISD and the end users work together; the role of the chief information officer; the issue of information security and control; and security of Web systems.

15.1 THE IS DEPARTMENT AND END USERS

Information Resources

Throughout this book, we have seen that information systems are used to increase productivity and help achieve quality. Most large, many medium, and even some small corporations around the world are strongly dependent on IT. Their information systems have considerable strategic importance. However, as the opening case showed us, information systems can become a dangerous and expensive problem when they break down.

The IS Department in the Organization

The management of information resources is divided between the information services department (ISD) and the end users, as discussed in Chapter 2. The division of activities between the two parties depends on many factors, beginning with the amount of IT assets and nature of duties involved in IRM, and ending with outsourcing policies. Decisions about the roles of each party are made during the IS planning and are not discussed here. (For some insights, see Wysocki and De Michiell, 1996, and Sambamurth et al., 2000.)

To show the importance of the IS area, some organizations call the director of IS a **chief information officer (CIO)**, similar to chief financial officer (CFO) and chief operating officer (COO). Typically, only important vice presidents or senior vice presidents receive this title. The actual title may be *vice president of IS, vice president of information technology,* or *vice president of information resources.* CIOs exist mainly in organizations that are heavily dependent on IT, such as banks, insurance companies, and airlines.

A major decision that must be made by senior management is where the ISD is to report. Partly for historical reasons, a common place to find the ISD is in the accounting or finance organization. In such situations, the ISD normally reports to the controller or the chief financial officer. The ISD might also report to one of the following: (1) a vice president of administration, (2) the senior executive of an operating division, (3) an executive vice president, or (4) the CEO. The four possibilities are marked and shown in Figure 15.1.

The *title* of CIO and the position to whom this person reports reflect, in many cases, the degree of support being shown by top management to the ISD. The *reporting relationship* of the ISD is important in that it reflects the focus of the department. If the ISD reports to the accounting or finance areas, there is often a tendency to emphasize accounting or finance applications at the expense of those in the marketing, production, and logistical areas. To be most effective, the ISD needs to take as broad a view as possible.

The *name* of the ISD is also important. Originally it was called the Data Processing (DP) Department. Then the name was changed to the Management Information Systems (MIS) Department and then to the Information Systems Department (ISD). Today we find, in addition to Information Services Department, names such as Information Technology Department, Corporate Technology Center, and so on. In very large organizations the ISD is a division, or even an independent corporation (such as at Bank of America and at Boeing Corp.).

The name of the ISD depends on the IT role, its size, and so forth. When the information systems function is given the title of information resources management or information technology, the organization often has the charter to do much more than just provide information system services. In these instances, the department usually involves itself in strategic corporate planning, in BPR, in e-commerce, and sometimes in selling IS services to other organizations. Some companies separate the e-commerce activities, creating a special online division, such as at Qantas Airways. In others, e-commerce may be combined with ISD in a technology department or division.

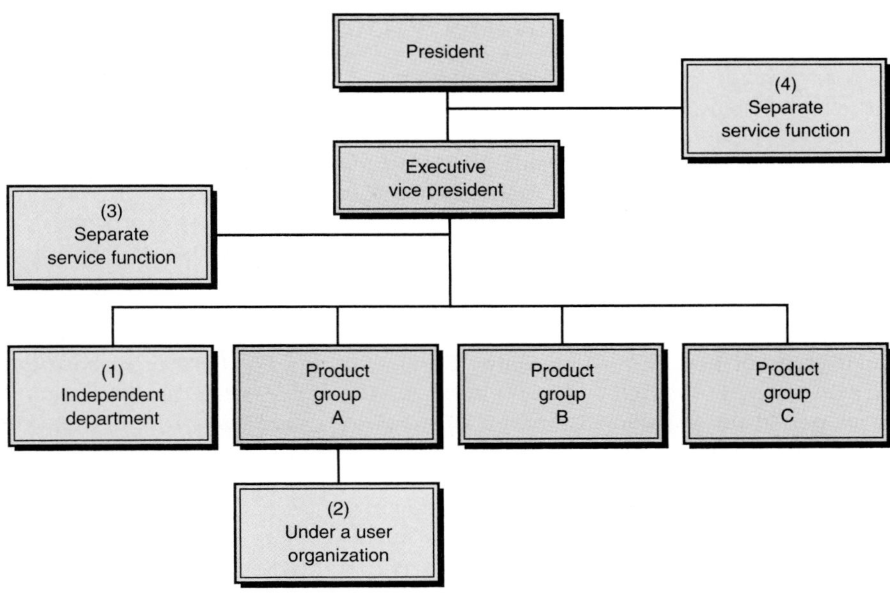

FIGURE 15.1 Four alternative locations for the ISD.

The increased role and importance of IT and its management both by a centralized unit and by end users require careful understanding of the manner in which ISD is organized as well as of the relationship between the ISD and end users. These topics are discussed next.

The IS Department and End Users

It is extremely important to have a good relationship between the ISD and end users. Unfortunately, though, this relationship is not always optimal. The development of end-user computing and outsourcing was motivated in part by the poor service that end users felt they received from the ISD. Conflicts occur for several reasons, ranging from the fact that priorities of the ISD may differ from those of the end users to a simple lack of communication. Also, there are some fundamental differences between the personalities, cognitive styles, educational backgrounds, and gender proportion of the end users versus the ISD staff (more males in the ISD) that could contribute to conflicts. An example of such conflict is illustrated in the *IT at Work* scenario below.

Generally, the IS organization can take one of the following four approaches toward end-user computing:

1. ***Let them sink or swim.*** Don't do anything—let the end user beware.
2. ***Use the stick.*** Establish policies and procedures to control end-user computing so that corporate risks are minimized.
3. ***Use the carrot.*** Create incentives to encourage certain end-user practices that reduce organizational risks.
4. ***Offer support.*** Develop services to aid end users in their computing activities.

IT at Work
MINNESOTA'S DEPARTMENT OF TRANSPORTATION VIOLATES PROCEDURES

www.dot.state.mn.us

The Department of Transportation in Minnesota had come across a hybrid PC system that would allow road surveys to be accomplished with less time and effort, and greater accuracy. The system would require two people to conduct a survey instead of the usual three, and because of the precision of the computer-based system, the survey could be done in half the time.

The department ran into a problem because the ISD for the State of Minnesota had instituted standards for all PCs that could be purchased by any state agency. Specifically, a particular brand of IBM PC was the only PC purchase allowed, without going through a special procedure. The red tape, as well as the unwillingness of the ISD to allow any deviation from the standard, caused a great deal of frustration.

As a last resort, the Department of Transportation procured the hybrid PC and camouflaged the transaction as engineering equipment for conducting surveys. From that point on, its staff decided they would do what they needed to do to get their jobs done, and the less the ISD knew about what they were doing, the better. When asked why they behaved this way, the administrator of the Department of Transportation simply said, "We have to do it this way because the ISD will either try to stop or hold up for a long period of time any decision we want to make, because they just are not familiar enough with the issues that we are facing in our department."

For Further Exploration: What are the organizational risks when the Transportation Department takes this attitude? How can the conflict be resolved?

Source: Author's experience.

Each of these responses presents the IS executive with different opportunities for facilitation and coordination, and each has its advantages and disadvantages.

Fostering the ISD/End-User Relationship

The ISD is a *service organization* that manages the IT infrastructure needed to carry on end-user IT applications. Therefore, a partnership between the ISD and the end-user is a must, as indicated by Wysocki and De Michiell (1996). This is not an easy task since the ISD is basically a technical organization that may not understand the business and the users. The users, on the other hand, may not understand information technologies.

In order to foster the relationship between the ISD and end users, organizations can employ several strategies. For example, the ISD of the Housing Development Board in Singapore uses the following strategies (per Tung and Turban, 1996):

- Introducing a special end-user support unit that coordinates quality assurance, data administration, and office systems
- Introducing an end-user training and development unit that is responsible for training and certification in IS software packages
- Giving high priority and visibility to end-user computing
- Training ISD employees to understand the business
- Implementing a special **conflict resolution team** that quickly handles ISD/ end-user conflicts
- Recognizing the CIO as a member of the top executive organizational team
- Empowering ISD employees to make decisions on the spot in order to minimize interferences and delays to end users
- Developing a malfunction *recovery plan* for each end-user unit to minimize interferences with work when a system fails

The ISD and end users also employ three common arrangements used in many other organizations: the steering committee, service-level agreements, and the information center.

The Steering Committee

The corporate **steering committee** is a group of managers and staff representing various organizational units that is set up to establish IT priorities and to ensure that the ISD is meeting the needs of the enterprise. The committee's major tasks are:

- ***Direction setting.*** In linking the corporate strategy with the IT strategy, planning is the key activity.
- ***Rationing.*** The committee approves the allocation of resources for and within the information systems organization.
- ***Structuring.*** The committee deals with how the ISD is positioned in the organization. The issue of centralization–decentralization of IT resources is resolved by the committee.
- ***Staffing.*** Key IT personnel decisions involve a consultation-and-approval process made by the committee. Notable is the selection of the CIO and major IT outsourcing decisions.
- ***Communication.*** It is important that information regarding IT activities flows freely.

- ***Evaluating.*** The committee should establish performance measures for the ISD and see that they are met. This includes the initiation of service-level agreements.

Service-Level Agreements

Service-level agreements (SLAs) are formal agreements regarding the division of computing responsibility among end users and the ISD. Such divisions are based on a small set of critical computing decisions that are made by *end-user management.* The way managers make these decisions commits them to accept certain responsibilities and to turn over others to the ISD. Since end-user management makes the decisions, they are free to choose the amount and kind of support they feel they need. This freedom to choose provides a check on the ISD and encourages it to develop and deliver support services to meet end-user needs.

An effective approach to managing end-user computing must achieve both facilitation and coordination. Service-level agreements do this by (1) defining computing responsibilities, (2) providing a framework for designing support services, and (3) allowing end users to retain as much control as possible over their own computing. A service-level agreement can be viewed as a *contract* between each end-user unit and the ISD. It is similar to an outsourcing contract. If a chargeback system exists, it is usually spelled out in the SLAs.

An approach based on SLAs offers several advantages. First, it reduces "finger pointing" by clearly specifying responsibilities. When a microcomputer malfunctions, everyone knows who is responsible for fixing it. Second, it provides a structure for the design and delivery of end-user services by the ISD. Third, it creates incentives for end users to improve their computing practices, thereby reducing computing risks to the firm. By clearly stating what has to be done to qualify for better IS service, end-user management is in a better position to make trade-offs in its computing decisions. Finally, an SLA provides a means for the ISD to coordinate end-user computing. The same staff people who provide support services also monitor and report on end-user IT activities. Some end-user computing will remain outside these coordination efforts, but those activities are recognized to be the responsibility of end-user managers.

Establishing SLAs requires four steps: (1) Define service levels. (2) Divide computing responsibility at each level. (3) Design the details of the service levels. (4) Implement service levels.

The process of establishing and implementing SLAs may be applied to each of the *major* computing resources: hardware, software, people, data, networks, and procedures.

Due to the introduction of Web-based tools for simplifying the task of monitoring enterprise networks, more attention has recently been given to service-level agreements, according to *Communications News* (June 2000). This is especially important when SLAs are made between outsourcing vendors and end users. Because most networks involve multivendor and multiproduct configuration, accurately measuring network performance by its components is critical. (For an overview of SLAs, see *Insurance and Technology,* July 2000.)

The Information Center

An interesting change in organizational structure related to computer technology is the introduction of the **information center (IC)**, also known as the user's service or help center. The concept was conceived by IBM Canada, as a response to the increased number of end-user requests for new computer applications.

This demand created a huge backlog in the IS department, and users had to wait several *years* to get their systems built. Today, the ICs concentrate on end-user support with PCs, client/server applications, and the Internet/intranet. The staff in the IC may work either as a team or as individuals to help end users.

The IC is set up to help users get certain systems built quickly and provide tools that can be employed by users to build their own systems. The concept of the IC, furthermore, suggests that the people in the center should be especially oriented toward the users in their outlook. This attitude should be shown in the training provided by the staff at the center and in the way the staff helps users with any problems they might have. There can be one or several ICs in an organization, and they report to the ISD and/or the end-user departments (see Fuller and Swanson, 1992).

The IC can also be used as a place to house a few "commandos" or "guerrilla warriors" who can be available to build important user systems very quickly. The staff of the IC can construct systems, such as standalone Web applications or decision support systems, much more quickly than such systems can be built with traditional software and systems development methods. Because of the impact of such systems and the rapidity with which they can be made available, the ISD often gets a very good reputation in the user community.

PURPOSES AND ACTIVITIES. The three main functions of an IC are (1) to provide assistance to end users in dealing with computing problems, (2) to provide general technical assistance, and (3) to provide general support services. Typical activities associated with these functions are shown at the book's Web site.

The importance of ICs may diminish in the future as users become more computer literate, end-user software development tools become more friendly, hardware becomes more reliable, and intelligent diagnostic and training tools provide some of the services provided by ICs. Finally, end-user help is increasingly provided via the corporate portal. Overall, management tends to view ICs as cost centers whose benefits are intangible and difficult to justify, and it attempts to keep them small.

The New IT Organization

To carry out its mission in the digital economy, the ISD needs to change. Rockart et al. (1996) proposed the following eight imperatives for ISDs in the digital age, which they call the "new IT organization."

1. ***Achieve two-way strategic alignment.*** As discussed in Chapter 7, it is necessary to align IT strategy with the organization's business strategy. This must be a two-way effort in which IT executives contribute.
2. ***Develop effective relations with line management.*** IT personnel at all levels must develop strong, ongoing *partnerships* with end-user managers. The goal is for both business and technology capabilities to be integrated into effective solutions for organizational problems, as shown in this chapter.
3. ***Quickly develop and implement new systems.*** Innovative applications must be developed *quickly* and *effectively* by the ISD, the users, and the outsourcers. System delivery includes effective system development, procurement, and integration. Firms are recognizing that they do not have time, money, expertise, or inclination to develop large integrated systems necessary for inhouse BPR or e-commerce, and so they increasingly rely on outsourcers and commercially integrated packages.

4. ***Build and manage infrastuctures.*** The ISD is responsible for creating and managing an effective infrastructure. As discussed in Chapters 7 and 13, an architecture must first be developed to guide infrastructure implementation. Because of the increased role of the network, a major component of the infrastructure is networked. As a result, some organizations create a new position—**chief network officer (CNO)**, who reports to the CIO.
5. ***Reskill the IT organization.*** The new role of the ISD, discussed in Chapter 2 and in this chapter, requires new skills. Retraining is one solution, some of which is available on the Web (for example, see *zdnet.com*). Finding employees with new technological skills becomes a difficult task that can be alleviated with the help of the Web, as described in Chapter 5.
6. ***Manage vendor relationships.*** Since outsourcing is an increasingly sensible option, especially for those activities that the ISD does not have the necessary time or skill to accomplish, it is important to properly manage the outsourced work and vendors. Vendor relationships must be not just transactional and contractual, but also strategic and joint.
7. ***Build high performance.*** Like any other unit in the organization, the ISD must strive to meet increasingly demanding performance goals. IT budgets are rising rapidly, and as shown in Chapters 13 and 14, justification is not a trivial thing. The ISD should use all modern management methods to improve its own operations. Systems must be developed quickly and in the most efficient manner, yet quality must be superb. Motorola, for example, has introduced Six-Sigma performance goals (about 99 percent accuracy) in their IT quality program.
8. ***Redesign and manage the "federal" IT organization.*** As stated earlier, the responsibility of managing information resources is divided between the ISD and end users. The exact locus of all or part of IT decision-making power is critical, and getting the right distribution of managerial responsibilities is thus imperative for IT management. This situation is analogous to power-sharing between the U.S. federal and state governments, and it has been long debated under the name of the "centralization-decentralization" issue.

Information technology, as shown throughout this book, is playing a critical role in the livelihood of many organizations, small and large, private and public, throughout the world. (For an extended example—how IT is responding to the conversion to Euro currency—see the book's Web site.) Furthermore, the trend is for even more IT involvement. Therefore, according to Rockart et al. (1996), the ISD will be even more critical to its firm's operations. Effective ISDs will help their firms apply IT to transform themselves to e-businesses, redesign processes, and access needed information on a tight budget. Following the eight imperatives suggested here is mandatory for an organization's survival in the fast-changing, digital world. (For more on managing IT in the digital era, see Sambamurthy et al., 2000.)

15.2 The CIO in Managing the IS Department

Managing the ISD is similar to managing any other organizational unit. The unique aspect of the ISD is that it operates as a service department in a rapidly changing environment, thus making the department's projections and planning difficult. The equipment purchased and maintained by the ISD is scattered over the entire en-

terprise, adding to the complexity of ISD management. Here we will discuss only one issue: the CIO and his or her relationship with other managers and executives. For more on the connection between the ISD and the organization, see the IRM feedback model at the book's Web site.

The Chief Information Officer

The changing role of the ISD highlights the fact that the CIO is becoming an important member of the organization's top management team (Ross and Feeny, 2000).

THE ROLE OF THE CIO. A survey conducted in 1992 found that the prime role of the CIO was to align IT with the business strategy. Secondary roles were to implement state-of-the-art solutions and to provide and improve information access (see details in *CIO Communications,* July 1992).

These roles are supplemented today by several strategic roles because IT has become a strategic resource for many organizations. Coordinating this resource requires strong IT leadership and ISD/end-user cooperation within the organization. In addition, the CIO–CEO relationships are crucial for effective, successful utilization of IT, especially in organizations that greatly depend on IT, where the CIO joins the top management "chiefs" group.

The chief information officer is a member of the corporate *executive committee,* the most important committee in any organization, which has responsibility for strategic business planning. Its members include the chief executive officer and the senior vice presidents. The executive committee provides the top-level oversight for the organization's information resources. It guides the IS steering committee, usually chaired by the CIO. Related to the CIO is the emergence of the chief knowledge officer (see Chapter 9). A CIO may report to the CKO, or the same person may assume both roles, especially in smaller companies. The major challenges facing CIOs are listed in Table 15.1.

TABLE 15.1 Major Challenges Facing the CIO

1. Understand the complexity of doing business in a competitive, global environment.
2. Manage the accelerating pace of technological change.
3. Understand that IT may reshape organizations to become technology driven.
4. Realize that IT often is the primary enabler of business solutions.
5. Know the business sector in which the company is involved.
6. Understand the company's organizational structure and operating procedures.
7. Use business, not technology, terms when communicating with corporate management.
8. Gain acceptance as a member of the business management team.
9. Establish the credibility of the IS department.
10. Increase the technological maturity of the company.
11. Create a vision of the future of IT and sell that vision.
12. Implement IT architecture that will support the vision.
13. Maintain technology competency.
14. Understand networking on a global basis.
15. Manage safety and security of IT systems.
16. Educate non-IS executives.

Sources: J. W. Ross and D. F. Feeny, "The Evolving Role of the CIO," in R. Zmud (ed.), *Framing the Domain of IT Management,* Cincinnati, OH: Pinnaflex, 2000; J. G. Sitonis and B. Goldberg, "Changing Role of the CIO," *Information Week,* March 24, 1997; and B. C. McNurlin and R. H. Sprague, Jr., *Information Systems Management in Practice,* 4th ed., Upper Saddle River, NJ: Prentice-Hall, 1998.

THE CIO IN THE WEB-BASED ERA. According to Ross and Feeny (2000) and Earl (1999–2000), the CIO's role in the Web-based era is influenced by the following characteristics.

- Technology and its management are changing: Companies are using Web-based new business models. Conventional applications are being transformed to Web based. There is increasing use of B2B e-commerce and extranet, supply chain, and knowledge management applications. The application portfolio includes more Web-based applications.
- Executives' attitudes are changing. Greater attention is given to opportunities and risks. At the very least, CIOs are the individuals to whom the more computer literate executives look for guidance, especially as it relates to e-commerce. Also, executives are more willing to invest in IT, since the cost-benefit ratio is improving with time.
- Suppliers of IT, especially the major ones (HP, Cisco, IBM, Microsoft, Sun, Intel, and Oracle), are influencing the strategic thinking of their corporate customers.

The above facts shape the roles and responsibilities of the CIO as follows:

- The CIO is taking increasing responsibility for defining strategic future.
- The increased networked environment may lead to disillusionment with IT (an undesirable situation that the CIO should help to avoid).
- The CIO needs to understand (with others in the organization) that the Web-based era is more about fundamental business change than about technology.
- The CIO needs to argue for a greater measure of central control. For example, placing inappropriate content on the Internet or intranets can be harmful and needs to be monitored and coordinated.
- The IT asset-acquisition process must be improved. The CIO and end users must work closer than ever before.
- The CIO is responsible for developing new Web-based business models and for introducing management processes that leverage the Internet, intranets, and extranets.
- The CIO is becoming a *business visionary* who drives business strategy, develops new business models on the Web, and introduces management processes that leverage the intranet.

These challenges place lots of pressure on CIOs. For this reason, and because demand is high, CIOs tend to have short tenure in organizations (e.g., see Earl, 1999–2000, and Minicase 2 at the end of this chapter).

CIOs earn very high salaries (up to $1,000,000/year in large corporations), and there is high turnover at this position (see McGee, 1996; and Sitonis and Goldberg, 1997). As technology becomes central to business, the CIO becomes a key mover in the ranks of upper management. For example, in a large financial institution's executive committee meeting, modest requests for additional budgets by the senior vice presidents for finance and for marketing were turned down after hours of debate. But, at the same meeting the CIO's request for a tenfold addition was approved in only a few minutes.

It is interesting to note that CEOs are acquiring IT skills. According to *InfoWorld* (June 16, 1997) and Duffy (1999), a company's best investment is a CEO who knows technology. If both the CIO and the CEO have the necessary skills for the information age, their company has the potential to flourish. For this reason some companies promote their CIOs to CEOs (e.g., Compaq Corp., in 2000).

Let's turn our attention now to one of the major areas of responsibility of the CIO—the security of information systems.

15.3 IS Vulnerability and Computer Crimes

Information resources are scattered throughout the organization. Furthermore, employees travel with and take home corporate computers and data. Information is transmitted to and from the organization and among the organization's components. IS physical resources, data, software, procedures, and any other information resources may therefore be vulnerable in many places at any time.

Before we describe the specific problems with information security and some proposed solutions, here is some of the key terminology in the field:

- ***Backup***—an extra copy of the data and/or programs kept in a secured location(s).
- ***Decryption***—transformation of scrambled code into readable data after transmission.
- ***Encryption***—transformation of data into scrambled code prior to its transmission.
- ***Exposure***—the harm, loss, or damage that can result if something has gone wrong in an information system.
- ***Fault tolerance***—the ability of an information system to continue to operate (usually for a limited time and/or at a reduced level) when a failure occurs.
- ***Information system controls***—the procedures, devices, or software that attempt to ensure that the system performs as planned.
- ***Integrity (of data)***—a guarantee of the accuracy, completeness, and reliability of data. System integrity is provided by the integrity of its components and their integration.
- ***Risk***—the likelihood that a threat will materialize.
- ***Threats (or hazards)***—the various dangers to which a system may be exposed.
- ***Vulnerability***—given that a threat exists, the susceptibility of the system to harm caused by the threat.

Most people are aware of some of the dangers faced by businesses that are dependent on computers. Information systems, however, can be damaged for many other reasons. The following incidents illustrate representative cases of breakdowns in information systems.

Information Systems Breakdowns

INCIDENT 1. On March 1999, a virus called Melissa spread throughout the world, paralyzing e-mail systems. Using a stolen AOL authorization code, David Smith, of New Jersey, entered a chat room called alt.sex, and left there a message with an attachment promising "free access codes to Internet Porn sites." Within minutes, dozens of visitors opened the attachment, releasing the deadliest computer virus the world had known up to that time.

INCIDENT 2. On February 29, 2000, in Japan, hundreds of ATMs were shut down, a computer system at a nuclear plant seized up, weather-monitoring devices malfunctioned, display screens for interest rates at the post offices failed, seismographs provided wrong information, and there were many other problems related to programming for "leap year." The problem was that years that end in "00" do not get the extra day, added every four years, unless they are divisible by 400 (2000 is a leap year, but not 1900, or 2100). This rule was not programmed properly in some old programs in Japan, thus creating the problems.

INCIDENT 3. In January 2000, a mysterious computer intruder tried to extort $100,000 from CD Universe Inc., claiming he had copied the company's list of more than 300,000 customers' credit card files. Because the company refused to pay the blackmail, the intruder released some of the credit card files on the Internet. The intruder claimed that he was from Russia. There is no extradition treaty between Russia and the United States regarding computer criminals, so it was difficult to investigate the crime. And of course, it was impossible to prosecute the criminal. The company notified the cardholders, who had to change their card numbers.

INCIDENT 4. For almost two weeks, a seemingly legitimate automated teller machine (ATM) operating in a shopping mall near Hartford, Connecticut, gave customers apologetic notes that said "sorry, no transactions are possible." Meanwhile, the machine recorded the card numbers and the personal identification numbers that hundreds of customers entered in their vain attempts to make the machine dispense cash. On May 8, 1993, while the dysfunctional machine was still running in the shopping mall, thieves started tapping into the 24-hour automated teller network in New York City. Using counterfeit bank cards encoded with the numbers stolen from the Hartford customers, the thieves removed about $100,000 from the accounts of innocent customers. The criminals were successful in making an ATM machine do what it was supposedly designed not to do: breach its own security by recording bank card numbers together with personal security codes.

INCIDENT 5. According to the *Wall Street Journal*, the Bank of Tokyo–Mitsubishi branch in New York and the National Westminster Bank in the U.K. reported losses of tens of millions of dollars in 1996 due to errors in their options and derivatives trading models. In both cases the losses went undetected for a long time. In the first case the trading model was found to be inaccurate; in the second case the model was fed inaccurate data.

INCIDENT 6. In 1996 the *Los Angeles Times* reported, "Computer makes $850 million error in Social Security." The glitch shortchanged about 700,000 Americans in retirement benefits and had been undetected for almost 23 years until it was discovered during an audit in 1994. While the newspaper blamed the computer, the fault was actually that of the programmers who were unable to properly automate the complex computations of the benefits. It took more than three years to fix the problem.

INCIDENT 7. Netscape security is aimed at scrambling sensitive financial data such as credit card numbers and sales transactions so they would be safe from break-ins, by using a powerful 128-bit program. However, using 120 powerful workstations and two supercomputers, in 1996 a French student breached the encryption program in eight days, demonstrating that no program is 100 percent secure.

INCIDENT 8. In 1994 a Russian hacker (who did not know much English) broke into a Citibank electronic funds transfer system and stole more than $10 million by wiring it to accounts around the world. Since then, Citibank, a giant bank that moves about a trillion dollars a day, increased its security measures, requiring customers to use electronic devices that create new passwords very frequently.

INCIDENT 9. On April 30, 2000, the London Stock Exchange was paralyzed by its worst computer system failure, before finally opening nearly eight hours late. A spokeman for the exchange said the problem, which crippled the supply of prices and firm information, was caused by corrupt data. He gave no further details. Dealers were outraged by the fault, which came on the last day of the tax year and just hours after violent price swings in the U.S. stock markets. The British Financial Services Authority said it viewed the failure seriously, adding it would insist any necessary changes to systems be made immediately and that lessons were "learned rapidly" to ensure the breakdown was not repeated.

These incidents illustrate the vulnerability of information systems and diversity of causes of computer security problems and the substantial damage that can be done to organizations anywhere in the world as a result.

Systems Vulnerability

Information systems are made up of many components that may be in several locations. Thus, each information system is vulnerable to many potential *hazards* or *threats*. Figure 15.2 presents a summary of the major threats to the security of an information system. That figure, along with the incidents just described, illustrates that information systems can be very vulnerable.

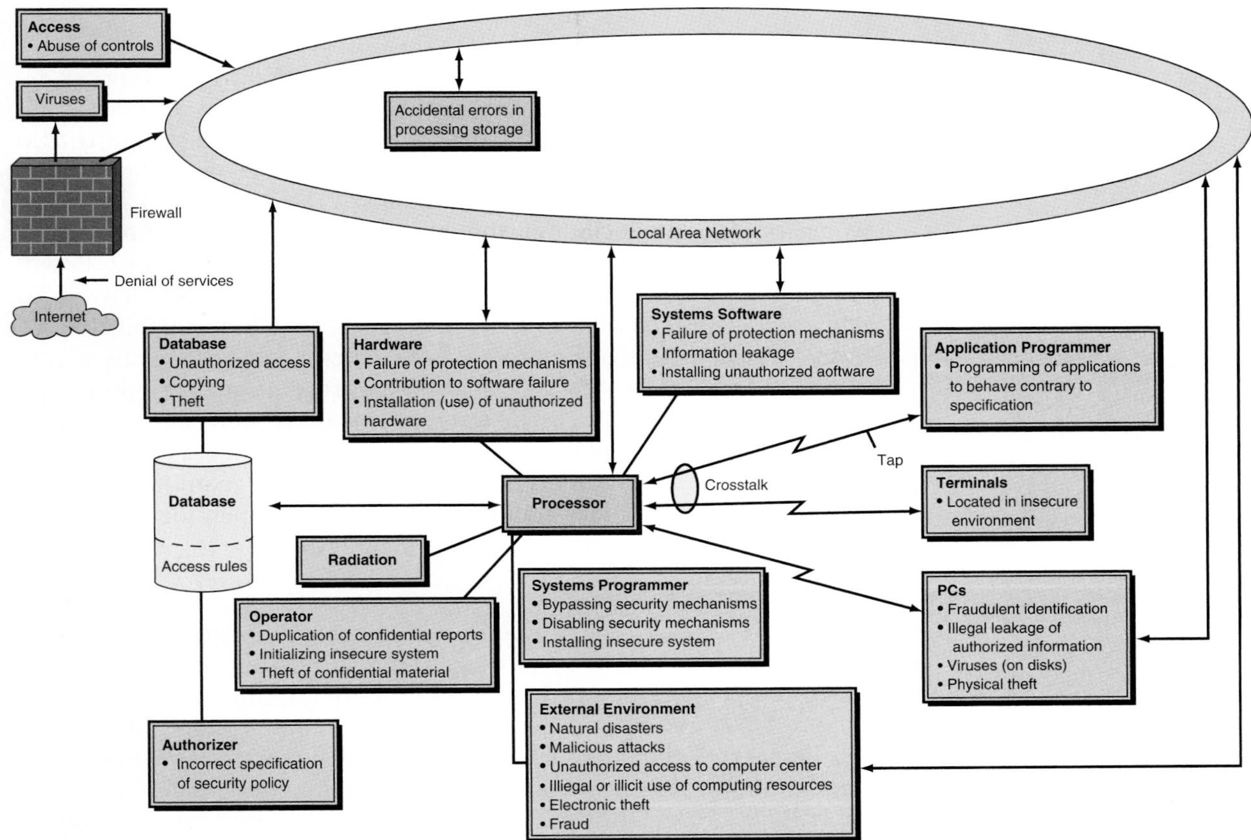

FIGURE 15.2 Security threats.

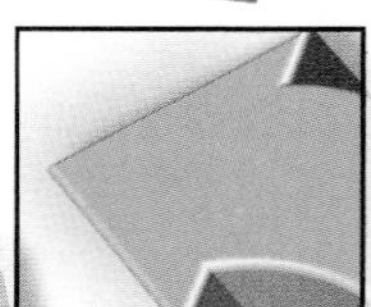

A CLOSER LOOK
15.1 COMPUTER GLITCHES DELAY AIRPORT OPENINGS

When the new multibillion-dollar airport was opened in Hong Kong on July 6, 1999, a combination of computer glitches and unprepared personnel turned the world's most expensive airport into chaos. Both travelers and cargo were affected. For example, one software bug erased all inventory records, leaving no clue as to who owned what. Another software bug erased flight information from monitors, preventing passengers from finding flights. Computer problems in the baggage system resulted in 10,000 lost bags. Fresh food and seafood being shipped to restaurants and hotels got spoiled, and considerable business was lost. In the United States, Denver's airport, which opened in 1995, had been plagued by computer glitches as well (see Chapter 13). Similarly, in Malaysia, when a new facility opened on July 1, 1999, a computerized total airport management system collapsed on the first day.

In all these airport cases, the problem was not external hackers' attacks or internal intentional acts. The bugs resulted from poor IS planning, lack of coordination, and insufficient testing.

The **vulnerability** of information systems is increasing as we move to a world of networked computing. Theoretically, there are hundreds of points in a corporate information system that can be subject to some threats. These threats can be classified as *unintentional* or *intentional.*

UNINTENTIONAL THREATS. Unintentional threats can be divided into three major categories: human errors, environmental hazards, and computer system failures (see *A Closer Look* 15.1, above).

Several computer problems result from *human errors.* Errors can occur in the design of the hardware and/or information system. They can also occur in the programming, testing, data collection, data entry, authorization, and instructions. Human errors contribute to the *vast majority* (about 55 percent) of control- and security-related problems in many organizations.

Environmental hazards include earthquakes, hurricanes, severe snow, sand and other storms, tornadoes, floods, power failures or strong fluctuations, fires (the most common hazard), defective air-conditioning, explosions, radioactive fallout, and water-cooling-system failures. In addition to damage from combustion, computer resources can incur damage from other elements that accompany fire, such as smoke, heat, and water. Such hazards may disrupt normal computer operations and result in long waiting periods and exorbitant costs while computer programs and data files are recreated.

Computer systems failures can occur as the result of poor manufacturing or defective materials. Unintentional malfunctions can also happen for other reasons, ranging from lack of experience to inappropriate testing.

INTENTIONAL THREATS. Computer systems may be damaged as a result of intentional actions as well. These account for about 30 percent of all computer problems, according to the Computer Security Institute, but the monetary damage from such actions can be extremely large. Here are some examples: theft of data; inappropriate use of data (e.g., manipulating inputs); theft of mainframe computer time; theft of equipment and/or programs; deliberate manipulation in handling, entering, processing, transferring, or programming data; labor strikes, riots, or sabotage; malicious damage to computer resources; destruction from viruses and similar attacks; and miscellaneous computer abuses and crimes.

Intentional threats can even be against whole countries. Many fear the possibility of *cyberattacks* by some countries against others.

Computer Crimes

According to the Computer Security Institute, 64 percent of all corporations experienced computer crimes in 1997. The figures in 1998 through 2000 were even higher. The number, magnitude, and diversity of computer crimes and abuse are increasing. Lately, increased fraud related to the Internet and electronic commerce is in evidence.

TYPES OF COMPUTER CRIMES AND CRIMINALS. In many ways, computer crimes resemble conventional crimes. They can occur in four ways. First, the computer can be the *target* of the crime. For example, a computer may be stolen or destroyed, or a virus may destroy data. Second, the computer can be the *medium* of the attack, by creating an environment in which a crime or fraud can occur. For example, false data are entered into a computer system to mislead individuals examining the financial condition of a company. Third, the computer can be the *tool* by which the crime is perpetrated. For example, a computer is used to plan a crime, but the crime does not involve a computer. Fourth, the computer can be used to *intimidate* or *deceive.* For instance, a stockbroker stole $50 million by convincing his clients that he had a computer program with which he could increase their return on investment by 60 percent per month.

Crimes can be performed by *outsiders* who penetrate a computer system (frequently via communication lines) or by *insiders* who are authorized to use the computer system but are misusing their authorization. **Hacker** is the term often used to describe outside people who penetrate a computer system. A **cracker** is a *malicious hacker,* who may represent a serious problem for a corporation. Computer criminals, whether insiders or outsiders, have a distinct profile and are driven by several motives (see *A Closer Look* 15.2). Ironically, many employees fit this profile, but only a few of them are criminals. Therefore, it is difficult to predict who will be a computer criminal. Criminals use various and frequently innovative attack methods.

A CLOSER LOOK
15.2 THE COMPUTER CRIMINAL—PROFILE AND MOTIVATION

THE PROFILE

Sex: White males between the ages of 19 and 30 with no criminal record. (Women tend to be accomplices.)

Occupation: Application programmer, system user, clerical personnel, student, or manager.

IQ: High IQ, bright, personable, and creative.

Appearance: Outwardly self-confident, eager, and energetic.

Approach to work: Adventurous, willing to accept technical challenge, and highly motivated.

THE MOTIVATION

Economic: Urgent need for money (e.g., due to extravagant lifestyle, gambling, family sickness, or drug abuse).

Ideological: Deceiving the establishment is viewed as fair game because "the establishment deceives everyone else."

Egocentric: Beating the system is fun, challenging, and adventurous. Egocentricity seems to be the most distinguishing motive of computer criminals.

Psychological: Getting even with the employer, who is perceived by the employee as cold, indifferent, and impersonal.

Joyriders: Getting a kick out of crashing systems, stealing passwords, etc. (called "black-hat hackers").

Other: The employee views himself as a "borrower" of software, for example, not a thief.

To learn more about the profile and motivations of computer criminals, see *nsca.com.*

TABLE 15.2 Methods of Attack on Computer Systems

Method	Definition
Virus	Secret instructions inserted into programs (or data) that are innocently run during ordinary tasks. The secret instructions may destroy or alter data, as well as spread within or between computer systems.
Worm	A program that replicates itself and penetrates a valid computer system. It may spread within a network, penetrating all connected computers.
Trojan horse	An illegal program, contained within another program, that "sleeps" until some specific event occurs, then triggers the illegal program to be activated and cause damage.
Salami slicing	A program designed to siphon off small amounts of money from a number of larger transactions, so the quantity taken is not readily apparent.
Superzapping	A method of using a utility "zap" program that can bypass controls to modify programs or data.
Trap door	A technique that allows for breaking into a program code, making it possible to insert additional instructions.
Logic bomb	An instruction that triggers a delayed malicious act.
Denial of services	Too many requests for service, which crashes the site.
Sniffer	A program that searches for passwords or content in a packet of data as they pass through the Internet.
Spoofing	Faking an e-mail address or Web page to trick users to provide information or send money.
Password cracker	A password that tries to guess passwords (can be very successful).
War dialing	Programs that automatically dial thousands of telephone numbers in an attempt to find a secret one.
Back doors	Invaders to a system create several entry points; even if you discover and close one, they can still get in through others.
Malicious applets	Small Java programs that misuse your computer resources, modify your file, send fake e-mail, etc.

METHODS OF ATTACK. Two basic approaches are used in deliberate attacks on computer systems: data tampering and programming fraud.

Data tampering ("data diddling") is the most common approach and is often used by insiders. It refers to entering false, fabricated, or fraudulent data into the computer or changing or deleting existing data. For example, to pay for his wife's drug purchases, a savings and loan programmer transferred $5,000 into his personal account and tried to cover up the transfer with phony debit and credit transactions.

Computer criminals also use *programming techniques* to modify a computer program, either directly or indirectly. For this crime, programming skills and knowledge of the targeted systems are essential. **Programming fraud** schemes appear under many names, as shown in Table 15.2. Several of the methods were designed for Web-based systems. Due to their frequency, viruses merit special discussion here.

VIRUSES. The most publicized attack method, the **virus**, receives its name from the program's ability to attach itself to ("infect") other computer programs, causing them to generate viruses themselves. A virus can spread throughout a computer system very quickly. Due to the availability of public-domain software, widely used telecommunications networks, and the Internet, viruses can spread to many organizations around the world, as shown in the incidents listed earlier. Viruses are known to spread all over the world. Some of the most notorious are "international," such as Michelangelo, Pakistani Brain, and Jerusalem.

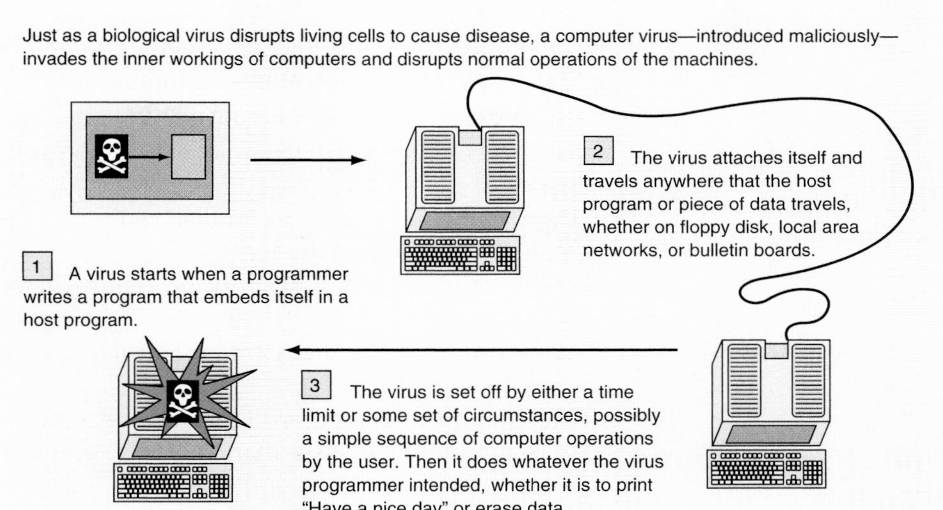

Just as a biological virus disrupts living cells to cause disease, a computer virus—introduced maliciously—invades the inner workings of computers and disrupts normal operations of the machines.
1 A virus starts when a programmer writes a program that embeds itself in a host program.
2 The virus attaches itself and travels anywhere that the host program or piece of data travels, whether on floppy disk, local area networks, or bulletin boards.
3 The virus is set off by either a time limit or some set of circumstances, possibly a simple sequence of computer operations by the user. Then it does whatever the virus programmer intended, whether it is to print "Have a nice day" or erase data.

FIGURE 15.3 How a computer virus can spread.

When a virus is attached to a legitimate software program, the program becomes infected without the owner of the program being aware of the infection (see Figure 15.3). When the software is used, the virus spreads, causing damage to that program and possibly to others. Thus, the legitimate software is acting as a *Trojan horse.*

We'll look at viruses and how to fight them later in the chapter, when we describe security on networks.

REPRESENTATIVE FEDERAL LAWS DEALING WITH COMPUTER CRIME. According to the FBI, an average robbery involves $3,000; an average white-collar crime involves $23,000; but an average computer crime involves about $600,000. The following are representative U.S. federal statutes dealing with computer crime.

- Counterfeit Access Device and Computer Fraud Act (passed in October 1984)
- Computer Fraud and Abuse Act (1986), 18 USC, section 1030
- Computer Abuse Amendment Act of 1994 (prohibits transmission of viruses)
- Computer Security Act of 1987
- Electronic Communications Privacy Act of 1986
- Electronic Funds Transfer Act of 1980
- Video Privacy Protection Act of 1988

For more on these laws, see *epic.org/security.*

15.4 PROTECTING INFORMATION SYSTEMS

Security and the Role of Controls

Knowing about major potential threats to information systems is important, but understanding ways to defend against these threats is equally critical (see *cert.org* and *sans.com*). Defending information systems is not a simple or inexpensive task for the following reasons:

- Hundreds of potential threats exist.
- Computing resources may be situated in many locations.
- Many individuals control information assets.
- Computer networks can be outside the organization and difficult to protect.
- Rapid technological changes make some controls obsolete as soon as they are installed.
- Many computer crimes are undetected for a long period of time, so it is difficult to learn from experience.
- People tend to violate security procedures because the procedures are inconvenient.
- Many computer criminals who are caught go unpunished, so there is no deterrent effect.
- The amount of computer knowledge necessary to commit computer crimes is usually minimal. As a matter of fact, one can learn hacking, for free, on the Internet.
- The cost of preventing hazards can be very high. Therefore, most organizations simply cannot afford to protect against all possible hazards.
- It is difficult to conduct a cost-benefit justification for controls before an attack occurs since it is difficult to assess the value of a hypothetical attack.

Therefore, organizing an appropriate defense system is one of the major activities of any prudent IS or functional manager who controls information resources.

Protection of IT is accomplished by inserting controls—defense mechanisms—intended to *prevent* accidental hazards, *deter* intentional acts, *detect* problems as early as possible, *enhance damage recovery,* and *correct* problems. Controls can be integrated into hardware and software during the system development phase (a most efficient approach). They can also be implemented once the system is in operation or during its maintenance. The important point is that defense should stress *prevention;* it does no good after the crime. Since there are many threats, there are also many defense mechanisms. In this section, we describe some representative controls.

Controls are designed to protect all the components of an information system, specifically data, software, hardware, and networks.

Defense Strategies: How Do We Protect?

The selection of a specific strategy depends on the objective of the defense and on the perceived cost-benefit. The following are the major objectives of *defense strategies:*

1. ***Prevention and deterrence.*** Properly designed controls may prevent errors from occurring, deter criminals from attacking the system, and better yet, deny access to unauthorized people. Prevention and deterrence are especially important where the potential damage is very high.
2. ***Detection.*** It may not be economically feasible to prevent all hazards, and deterrence measures may not work. Therefore, unprotected systems are vulnerable to attack. Like a fire, the earlier it is detected, the easier it is to combat and the less damage is done. Detection can be performed in many cases by using special diagnostic software.
3. ***Limitation.*** This strategy is to minimize (limit) losses once a malfunction has occurred. Users typically want their systems back in operation as quickly as

possible. This can be accomplished by including a *fault-tolerant system* that permits operation in a degraded mode until full recovery is made. If a fault-tolerant system does not exist, a quick (and possibly expensive) recovery must take place.

4. ***Recovery.*** A recovery plan explains how to fix a damaged information system as quickly as possible. Replacing rather than repairing components is one route to fast recovery.
5. ***Correction.*** Correcting the causes of damaged systems can prevent the problem from occurring again.

Any defense strategy may involve the use of several controls.

TYPES OF DEFENSE CONTROLS. The defense controls are divided into two major categories: general controls and application controls. Each has several subcategories, as shown in Figure 15.4.

Information systems controls can be divided into two major groups: general (system) controls and application controls. **General controls** are established to protect the system regardless of the specific application. For example, protecting hardware and controlling access to the data center are independent of the specific application. **Application controls** are safeguards that are intended to protect specific applications. In the next two sections, we discuss the major types of these two groups of information systems controls.

General Controls

The major categories of general controls are *physical controls, access controls, data security controls, communications (networks) controls,* and *administrative controls.*

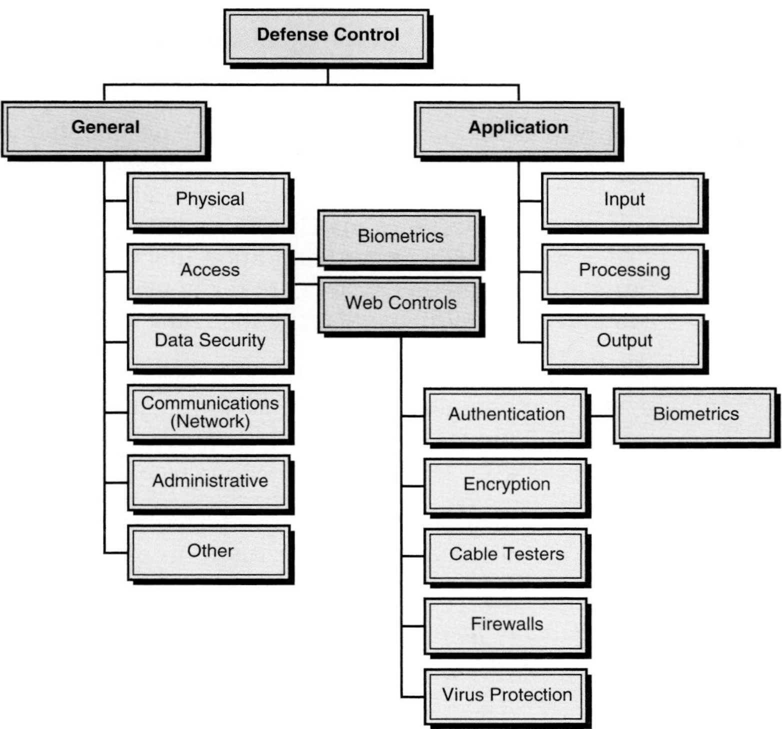

FIGURE 15.4 Major defense controls.

PHYSICAL CONTROLS. Physical security refers to the protection of computer facilities and resources. This includes protecting physical property such as computers, data centers, software, manuals, and networks. Physical security is the first line of defense and usually the easiest to construct. It provides protection against most natural hazards as well as against some human hazards. Appropriate physical security may include several controls such as the following:

- Appropriate design of the data center. For example, the site should be noncombustible and waterproof.
- Shielding against electromagnetic fields.
- Good fire prevention, detection, and extinguishing systems, including sprinkler system, water pumps, and adequate drainage facilities. A better solution is fire-enveloping Halon gas systems.
- Emergency power shutoff and backup batteries, which must be maintained in operational condition.
- Properly designed, maintained, and operated air-conditioning systems.
- Motion detector alarms that detect physical intrusion.

Protecting Portable Computers. Another example of physical controls is the need to protect against theft of portable computers. Such protection is important not only because of the loss of the computer but also because of loss of data. Several interesting protection devices are offered by *targus.com.*

ACCESS CONTROL. Access control is the restriction of unauthorized user access to a portion of a computer system or to the entire system. To gain access, a user must first be *authorized.* Then, when the user attempts to gain access, he or she must be *authenticated.*

Access to a computer system basically consists of three steps: (1) physical access to a terminal, (2) access to the system, and (3) access to specific commands, transactions, privileges, programs, and data within the system. Access control software is commercially available for large mainframes, minicomputers, personal computers, local area networks, and dial-in communications networks. Access control to the *network* is executed through firewalls and will be discussed later.

Access procedures match every valid user with a *unique user-identifier (UID).* They also provide an authentication method to verify that users requesting access to the computer system are really who they claim to be. User identification can be accomplished when the following identifies each user:

- Something only the user *knows,* such as a password.
- Something only the user *has,* for example, a smart card or a token.
- Something only the user *is,* such as a signature, voice, fingerprint, or retinal (eye) scan. It is implemented via biometric controls.

Biometric Controls. A **biometric control** is an automated method of verifying the identity of a person, based on physiological or behavioral characteristics. The most common biometrics are the following:

- ***Photo of face.*** The computer takes a picture of your face and matches it with a prestored picture. In 2000, this method was successful in correctly identifying users except in cases of identical twins.

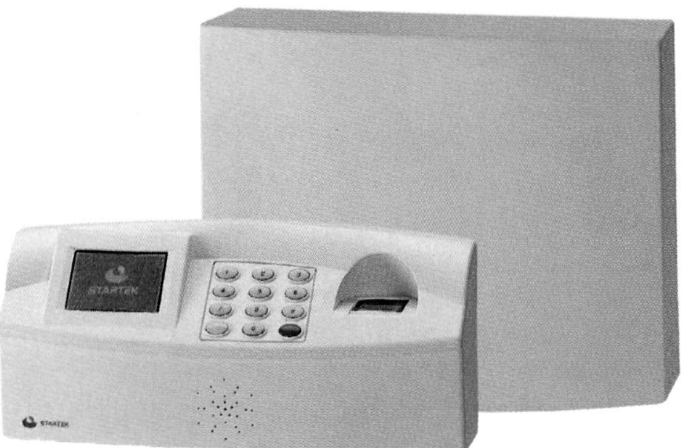

FIGURE 15.5 Biometric controls.

- ***Fingerprints.*** Each time a user wants access, matching a fingerprint against a template containing the authorized person's fingerprint identifies him or her (see Figure 15.5). Note that Microsoft introduced in 2001 a software program that will be part of Windows and will allow users to use Sony's fingerprint recognition device.
- ***Hand geometry.*** This biometric is similar to fingerprints except that the verifier uses a television-like camera to take a picture of the user's hand. Certain characteristics of the hand (e.g., finger length and thickness) are electronically compared against the information stored in the computer.
- ***Iris scan.*** This technology uses the colored portion of the eye to identify individuals (see Figure 15.5 and *iriscan.com*). It is a noninvasive system that takes a photo of the eye and analyzes it. It is a very accurate method.
- ***Blood vessel pattern in the retina of a person's eye.*** A match is attempted between the pattern of the blood vessels in the back-of-the-eye retina that is being scanned and a prestored picture of the retina.
- ***Voice.*** A match is attempted between the user's voice and the voice pattern stored on templates.
- ***Signature.*** Signatures are matched against the prestored authentic signature. This method can supplement a photo-card ID system.
- ***Keystroke dynamics.*** A match of the person's keyboard pressure and speed against prestored information.
- ***Other biometics.*** Several other methods exist such as *facial thermography.*

Biometric controls are now integrated into many e-commerce hardware and software products. (e.g., see *keywaretechnologies.com*). For an overview and comparison of technologies, see Jain et al. (1999 and 2000).

DATA SECURITY CONTROLS. Data security is concerned with protecting data from accidental or intentional disclosure to unauthorized persons, or from unauthorized modification or destruction. Data security functions are implemented through operating systems, security access control programs, database/data communications products, recommended backup/recovery procedures, application programs, and external control procedures. Data security must address the following issues: *confidentiality of data, access control, critical nature of data,* and *integrity of data.*

Two basic principles should be reflected in data security.

- ***Minimal privilege.*** Only the information a user needs to carry out an assigned task should be made available to him or her.
- ***Minimal exposure.*** Once a user gains access to sensitive information, he or she has the responsibility of protecting it by making sure only people whose duties require it obtain knowledge of this information while it is processed, stored, or in transit.

Data integrity is the condition that exists as long as accidental or intentional destruction, alteration, or loss of data *does not* occur. It is the preservation of data for their intended use.

COMMUNICATIONS (NETWORK) CONTROLS. Network protection is becoming extremely important as the use of the Internet, intranets, and electronic commerce increases. We will discuss this topic in more detail in Section 15.5.

ADMINISTRATIVE CONTROLS. While the previously discussed general controls were technical in nature, administrative controls deal with issuing guidelines and monitoring compliance with the guidelines. Representative examples of such controls include the following:

- Appropriately selecting, training, and supervising employees, especially in accounting and information systems
- Fostering company loyalty
- Immediately revoking access privileges of dismissed, resigned, or transferred employees
- Requiring periodic modification of access controls (such as passwords)
- Developing programming and documentation standards (to make auditing easier and to use the standards as guides for employees)
- Insisting on security bonds or malfeasance insurance for key employees
- Instituting separation of duties, namely dividing sensitive computer duties among as many employees as economically feasible in order to decrease the chance of intentional or unintentional damage
- Holding periodic random audits of the system

OTHER GENERAL CONTROLS. Several other types of controls are considered general. Representative examples include the following:

- ***Programming controls.*** Errors in programming may result in costly problems. Causes include the use of incorrect algorithms or programming instructions, carelessness, inadequate testing and configuration management, or lax security. Controls include training, establishing standards for testing and configuration management, and enforcing documentation standards.

- ***Documentation controls.*** Manuals are often a source of problems because they are difficult to interpret or may be out of date. Accurate writing, standardization updating, and testing are examples of appropriate documentation control. Intelligent agents can be used to prevent such problems.
- ***System development controls.*** System development controls ensure that a system is developed according to established policies and procedures. Conformity with budget, timing, security measures, and quality and documentation requirements must be maintained.

Application Controls

General controls are intended to protect the computing facilities and provide security for hardware, software, data, and networks. However, general controls do not protect the *content* of each specific application. Therefore, controls are frequently built into the applications (that is, they are part of the software) and are usually written as validation rules. They can be classified into three major categories: *input controls, processing controls,* and *output controls.*

INPUT CONTROLS. Input controls are designed to prevent data alteration or loss. Data are checked for accuracy, completeness, and consistency. Input controls are very important; they prevent the GIGO (garbage-in, garbage-out) situation.

Examples of input controls are the following:

- ***Completeness.*** Items should be of a specific length (e.g., nine digits for a Social Security number). Addresses should include a street, city, state, and Zip Code.
- ***Format.*** Formats should be in standard form. For example, sequences must be preserved (e.g., Zip Code comes after an address).
- ***Range.*** Only data within a specified range are acceptable. For example, Zip Code ranges between 10,000 to 99,999; the age of a person cannot be larger than say, 120; and hourly wages at the firm do not exceed $50.
- ***Consistency.*** Data collected from two or more sources need to be matched. For example, in medical history data, males cannot be pregnant.

PROCESSING CONTROLS. Processing controls ensure that data are complete, valid, and accurate when being processed and that programs have been properly executed. These programs allow only authorized users to access certain programs or facilities and monitor the computer's use by individuals.

OUTPUT CONTROLS. Output controls ensure that the results of computer processing are accurate, valid, complete, and consistent. By studying the nature of common output errors and the causes of such errors, security and audit staff can evaluate possible controls to deal with problems. Also, output controls ensure that outputs are sent only to authorized personnel.

COMBINING CONTROLS. Management should decide on the appropriate mix of controls. For example, a collection of controls can be assembled to combat viruses (see *A Closer Look* 15.3 on page 680).

A CLOSER LOOK
15.3 SOME GOOD ADVICE ON HOW TO MINIMIZE THE DAMAGE FROM VIRUSES

Take the following preventive actions against viruses:

1. Install a good antivirus program (e.g., Norton AntiVirus, McAfee, VirusScan).
2. Scan the hard drive for viruses at least weekly.
3. Write-protect your floppy disks and scan them before using them.
4. Write-protect your program disks.
5. Back up data fully and frequently.
6. Don't trust outside PCs.
7. Virus scan before "laplinking" or synchronizing files.
8. Develop an antivirus policy.
9. Identify the areas of risk in case of virus attack. These are:
   - **a.** Direct losses (e.g., time spent to restore systems)
   - **b.** Losses your customers and supplier suffer when your system is down
   - **c.** Losses to a third party to which your company had passed on a virus, possibly due to your employees' negligence
10. Minimize losses by the following measures:
    - **a.** Install strict employees' guidelines dealing with e-mail viruses.
    - **b.** Use a service provider to handle virus detection and control. This way you get the latest technology, make it more difficult for insiders to perform crimes, and may transfer the risk to the service provider.
    - **c.** Have contracts that will protect you from a legal action by your customers/suppliers who suffer damage when your systems are damaged (called a "force majeure" clause).
    - **d.** Instruct your employees on how to scan all outgoing e-mails to your business partners.
11. The SANS Institute (*sans.org*) is an IT cooperative research and education organization for system administrators and security professionals; it has more than 96,000 members. SANS recommends the following guidelines for action during virus attacks:
    - **a.** Preparation—establish policy, design a form to be filed when a virus is suspected (or known), and develop outside relationships.
    - **b.** Identification—collect evidence of attack, analyze it, notify officals (e.g., at *cert.org*).
    - **c.** Containment—back up the system to capture evidence, change passwords, determine the risk of continuing operations.
    - **d.** Eradication—determine and remove the cause, and improve the defense.
    - **e.** Recovery—restore and validate the system.
    - **f.** Follow up—write a follow-up report detailing lessons learned.
12. Get information and sometimes free software at the following sites:

Antivirus.com	*cert.org*	*pgp.com*
symantec.com	*ncsa.com*	*rsa.com*
mcafee.com	*iss.net*	*tis.com*

15.5 SECURING THE WEB AND INTRANETS

The incidents described at the beginning of the chapter point to the vulnerability of the Net. As a matter of fact, the more wired the world becomes, the more security problems we may have. Security is a race between "lock makers" and "lock pickers." Unless the lock makers have the upper hand, the future of the Internet's credibility and of e-commerce is in danger.

Security Measures

Over the Internet, messages are sent from one computer to another and not from one network to the other. This makes it difficult to protect, since at many points people can tap into the network and the users may never know that a breach had occurred. As described in Chapter 5, network security is needed to provide *integrity* of data, *confidentiality* and *privacy, availability* of systems, and nonreproduction. Here are the major security measures of the Internet and e-commerce. Security issues regarding the Internet are also discussed in Chapters 4 and 5.

ACCESS CONTROL. As applied to the Internet, an access control system guards against unauthorized dial-in attempts. Many companies use an access protection strategy that requires authorized users to dial in with a preassigned personal identification number (PIN). This strategy may be enhanced by a unique and frequently changing password. A communications access control system authenticates the user's PIN and password. Some security systems proceed one step further and accept calls only from designated telephone numbers. Access controls also include biometrics.

The Problem of Modems. In many companies employees who are on the road use modems for dial-in-access to the company intranet. Two types of modems exist: authorized and not authorized (known as rogue modems). The latter are installed by employees when there are no authorized modems, when it is inconvenient to use the authorized modems, or when the authorized modems provide only limited access.

Modems are very risky. It is quite easy for attackers to penetrate them, and it is easy for employees to leak secret corporate information to external networks. In addition, software problems may develop, such as downloading programs with viruses or with a "back door" to the system. Back doors are created by hackers to repenetrate a system, once a successful penetration is made. There are several ways to protect modems in the system. (See White, 1999.)

ENCRYPTION. As discussed in Chapter 5, **encryption** encodes regular digitized text into unreadable scrambled text or numbers, which are decoded upon receipt. Encryption accomplishes three purposes: (1) identification (helps identify legitimate senders and receivers), (2) control (prevents changing a transaction or message), and (3) privacy (impedes eavesdropping).

A widely accepted encryption algorithm is the Data Encryption Standard (DES), produced by the U.S. National Bureau of Standards. Many software products also are available for encryption. *Traffic padding* can further enhance encryption. Here a computer generates random data that are intermingled with real data, making it virtually impossible for an intruder to identify the true data.

Encryption is used extensively in e-commerce for protecting payments and for privacy. Public key/private key systems were described in Chapter 5. For further discussion see *sra.com.*

To ensure secure transactions on the Internet, VeriSign and VISA developed encrypted digital certification systems for credit cards. These systems allow customers to make purchases on the Internet without giving their credit card number. Cardholders create a digital version of their credit card, VeriSign confirms validity of the buyer's credit card, and then it issues a certificate to that effect—even the merchants do not see the credit card number. The secure electronic transaction (SET) protocol (see Chapter 5) is the standard for credit card transactions on the Internet.

TROUBLESHOOTING. A popular defense of local area networks (LANs) is troubleshooting. For example, a *cable tester* can find almost any fault that can occur with LAN cabling. Another protection can be provided by *protocol analyzers,* which allow the user to inspect the contents of information packets as they travel through the network. Recent analyzers use *expert systems,* which interpret the volume of data collected by the analyzers. Some companies offer integrated LAN troubleshooting (a tester and an intelligent analyzer).

PAYLOAD SECURITY. *Payload security* involves encryption or other manipulation of data being sent over networks. *Payload* refers to the contents of messages and communication services among dispersed users. An example of payload security is Pretty Good Privacy (PGP), which permits users to inexpensively create and encrypt a message.

COMMERCIAL PRODUCTS. Hundreds of commercial security products exist on the market. All major Internet vendors from Microsoft to IBM and Netscape offer inexpensive or free protection packages.

INTRUSION DETECTING. Because protection against denial of service (opening vignette) is difficult, the sooner one can detect an usual activity, the better. Therefore, it is worthwhile to place an *intrusion detecting* device near the entrance point of the Internet to the intranet (close to a firewall, discussed next). The objective is early detection, and this can be done by several devices (e.g., see Ranum, 1999, and *sans.org*). Examples of such devices are BladeRunner (from Raytheon), Praesidium (from HP), Caddx (from Caddx Controls, Inc.), and IDS (from Cisco).

Firewalls

A **firewall** is a system, or group of systems, that enforces an access-control policy between two networks. It is commonly used as a barrier between the secure corporate intranet, or other internal networks, and the Internet, which is assumed to be unsecured.

Firewalls are used to implement control-access policies. The firewall follows strict guidelines that either permit or block traffic; therefore, a successful firewall is designed with clear and specific rules about what can pass through. Several firewalls may exist in one information system (see Oppliger, 1997).

WHY FIREWALLS? Hacking is a growing phenomenon. Even the Pentagon's system, considered a very secure system, experiences more than 250,000 hacker infiltrations per year, many of which are undetected (*Los Angeles Times,* April 24, 1998). It is believed that hacking costs U.S. industry several billion dollars each year. Hacking is such a popular activity that over 80,000 Web sites are dedicated to it. Firewalls provide the most cost-effective solution against hacking.

Firewalls are also used as a place to store public information. While visitors may be blocked from entering the company networks, they can obtain information about products and services, download files and bug-fixes, and so forth.

WHAT FIREWALLS CANNOT DO. Useful as they are, firewalls do not stop viruses that may be lurking in networks. Viruses can pass through the firewalls, usually hidden in an e-mail attachment. Many viruses exist (about 35,000 in 2000, growing by 30 percent a year according to the National Computer Security Association). So the question is, What can you do to protect yourself against viruses? Some solutions against virus penetrations are provided in Table 15.3. As

TABLE 15.3 Protecting Against Viruses

Possible Mode of Entrance	Countermeasure
• Viruses pass through firewalls undetected (from the Internet).	• User must screen all downloaded programs and documents before use.
• Virus may be resident on networked server; all users are at risk.	• Run virus scan daily; comprehensive backup to restore data; audit trail.
• Infected floppy; local server system at risk; files shared or put on server can spread virus.	• Use virus checker to screen floppies locally.
• Mobile or remote users exchange or update large amounts of data; risk of infection is greater.	• Scan files before upload or after download; make frequent backups.

Source: Compiled from B. Nance, "Keep Networks Safe from Viruses," *Byte*, November 1996, p. 171.

described earlier, antivirus software is available (e.g., see *symantec.com*). However, antivirus software provides protection against viruses only after they have attacked someone and are known. New viruses are difficult to detect in their first attack (see *Internet World*, January 1998, pp. 37–40, and *Interactive Week*, January 19, 1998, p. 34).

COST. Firewalls may cost over $100,000. In comparison, less effective access control systems such as authentication cost only $20,000. But compared to the possible damage that hackers can cause, the cost of firewalls is not prohibitive for medium or large organizations.

15.6 IMPLEMENTING SECURITY

Implementing controls in an organization can be a very complicated task, particularly in large, decentralized companies where administrative controls may be difficult to enforce. Of the many issues involved in implementing controls, four are described here: auditing information systems, disaster recovery planning, risk analysis, and advanced systems.

Auditing Information Systems

Controls are established to ensure that information systems work properly. Controls can be installed in the original system; alternatively, the ISD, end users, or others (e.g., vendors) can add controls once a system is in operation. Installing controls is necessary but not sufficient. It is also necessary to answer questions such as the following: Are controls installed as intended? Are they effective? Did any breach of security occur? If so, what actions are required to prevent reoccurrence? These questions need to be answered by independent and unbiased observers. Such observers perform the information system *auditing* task.

An **audit** is an important part of any control system. In an organizational setting, it is usually referred to as a periodical *examination* and *check* of financial and accounting records and procedures. Specially trained professionals who may be internal employees or external consultants execute auditing. In the information system environment, auditing can be viewed as an additional layer of controls or safeguards.

TYPES OF AUDITORS AND AUDITS. There are two types of auditors (and audits): internal and external. An *internal auditor* is usually a corporate employee who is not a member of the ISD.

An *external auditor* is a corporate outsider. This type of auditor reviews the findings of the internal audit and the inputs, processing, and outputs of information systems. The external audit of information systems is frequently a part of the overall external auditing performed by a certified public accounting (CPA) firm.

IT auditing (which used to be called electronic data processing auditing) can be very broad, so only its essentials are presented here. Auditing looks at all potential hazards and controls in information systems. It focuses attention on topics such as new systems development, operations and maintenance, data integrity, software application, security and privacy, disaster planning and recovery, purchasing, budgets and expenditures, chargebacks, vendor management, documentation, insurance and bonding, training, cost control, and productivity. Several guidelines are available to assist auditors in their jobs. *SAS No. 55* is a comprehensive guide provided by the American Institute of Certified Public Accountants. Also, guidelines are available from the Institute of Internal Auditors, Orlando, Florida.

Auditors attempt to answer questions such as these:

- Are there sufficient controls in the system?
- Which areas are not covered by controls?
- Which controls are not necessary?
- Are the controls implemented properly?
- Are the controls effective; that is, do they check the output of the system?
- Is there a clear separation of duties of employees?
- Are there procedures to ensure compliance with the controls?
- Are there procedures to ensure reporting and corrective actions in case of violations of controls?

Two types of audits are used to answer these questions. The *operational audit* determines whether the ISD is working properly. The *compliance audit* determines whether controls have been implemented properly and are adequate.

HOW IS AUDITING EXECUTED? IT auditing procedures can be classified into three categories: auditing *around* the computer, auditing *through* the computer, and auditing *with* the computer.

Auditing around the computer means verifying processing by checking for known outputs using specific inputs. Therefore, it is assumed that there is no need to check the processing if the correct output is obtained. The best application of this approach is in systems that produce a limited range of outputs. It is fast and inexpensive, but it may give false results. For example, two errors may compensate for each other, resulting in correct output.

In *auditing through the computer,* inputs, outputs, and processing are checked. This approach is more complex and is usually supported by special tools. Some methods used by auditors are reviewing program logic, test data, and controlling processing and reprocessing.

Auditing with the computer means using a combination of client data, auditor software, and client and auditor hardware. It allows the auditor to perform tasks such as simulating payroll program logic using live data.

A CLOSER LOOK

15.4 "HACKERS" AUTHORIZED TO BREAK INTO THE STATE OF ILLINOIS INFORMATION SYSTEM

Auditors for the State of Illinois issued a public statement on July 1, 1993, in which they notified the State that they were successful in their mission of breaking into the Central Computer Facility which serves 109 state agencies. The auditors pulled off their mission with "disturbing ease." An authorized hacker, operating from a remote location, was able to break into the system, and read, modify, and delete data such as payroll and prison records. Real hackers could have altered the security structure and negated system integrity. The security system, which was thought to be satisfactory, was enhanced immediately, and all known security flaws were fixed.

Auditors use several tools to increase their effectiveness and efficiency. Typical tools are checklists, formulas, and charts. These can be executed manually or can be computerized. Several computer programs are available to support the auditor's job. These include programs for testing, summarizing, sampling, and matching. Generalized Audit Software (GAS) is a set of programs designed to support auditing. Expert systems and neural computing also can be used to facilitate IT auditing.

Often it is necessary to trace a transaction through each processing step (when, where, by whom, and so on). The procedure (or document) that describes such tracing is called an **audit trail**. In manual systems it is fairly easy to conduct an audit trail. However, in computerized systems, this may not be so easy. One task of auditing is to provide procedures for audit trails and to execute them when needed.

Auditors and security consultants may try to break into a computer system, in what is called a *simulated attack,* in order to find weak points in the system (see *A Closer Look* 15.4, above, and Steefora and Cheek, 1994). In some cases, companies hire famous hackers, acting as "white-hat hackers" in these instances, to do the job.

Auditing Web Systems. According to Morgan and Wong (1999), auditing a Web site is a good preventive measure to manage the legal risk. Legal risk is important in any IT system, but in Web systems it is even more important due to the content of the site, which may offend people or be in violation of copyright laws or other regulations (e.g., privacy protection).

Disaster Recovery Planning

As described, disasters may occur in many places without warning. According to Strassman (1997), the best defense is to be prepared. Therefore, an important element in any security system is the **disaster recovery** plan. Destruction of all (or most) of the computing facilities can cause significant damage. Therefore, it is difficult for many organizations to obtain insurance for their computers and information systems without showing a satisfactory disaster prevention and recovery plan.

Disaster recovery is the chain of events linking planning to protection to recovery. The following are some key thoughts about disaster recovery by Knoll (1986):

- The purpose of a recovery plan is to keep the business running after a disaster occurs. Both the IS department and line management should be

A CLOSER LOOK
15.5 PC-BASED SOFTWARE PROVIDES A USEFUL DISASTER RECOVERY

www.htfcu.org

Hurricane Hugo hit Charleston, South Carolina, on Friday, September 20, 1989. Electrical power was knocked out for nine days. However, Heritage Trust Credit Federal (a credit union) resumed normal operations by the following Tuesday.

The credit union had developed a disaster recovery plan supported by battery-operated, PC-based software (Recovery Pac, from Computer Security Consultants, Ridgefield, Connecticut). Both internal and external auditors were involved in the plan. When a disaster occurred, the software was to be activated. The software tracks the crisis and suggests the best method of handling it. The software is flexible enough to guide users through problems that have not been anticipated in the tests or the original plan. Other representative software products include the Total Recovery Planning System and PANAMAX.

involved in preparation of the plan. Each function in the business should have a valid recovery capability plan.

- Recovery planning is part of *asset protection.* Every organization should assign responsibility to management to identify and protect assets within their spheres of functional control.
- Planning should focus first on recovery from a total loss of all capabilities.
- Proof of capability usually involves some kind of what-if analysis that shows that the recovery plan is current.
- All critical applications must be identified and their recovery procedures addressed in the plan.
- The plan should be written so that it will be effective in case of disaster, not just in order to satisfy the auditors.
- The plan should be kept in a safe place; copies should be given to all key managers; and the plan should be audited periodically.

Disaster recovery planning can be very complex, and it may take several months to complete (see Devargas, 1999). Using special software, the planning job can be expedited (see *A Closer Look* 15.5).

BACKUP ARRANGEMENTS. In the event of a major disaster, it is often necessary to move a centralized computing facility to a far-away **backup** location. External *hot-site* vendors provide access to a fully configured backup data center. To appreciate the usefulness of such an arrangement, consider the following example.

On the evening of October 17, 1989, a major earthquake hit San Francisco, California, and Charles Schwab and Company was ready. Within a few minutes, the company's disaster plan was activated. Programmers, engineers, and backup computer tapes of October 17 transactions were flown on a chartered jet to Carlstadt, New Jersey. There, Comdisco Disaster Recovery Service provided a hot site. The next morning, the company resumed normal operations. Montgomery Securities, on the other hand, had no backup recovery arrangement. On October 18, the day after the quake, the traders had to use telephones rather than computers to execute trades. Montgomery lost revenues of $250,000 to $500,000 in one day. (For a review of how disaster recovery planning worked following the World Trade Center disaster, see pages 716–718.)

A less costly alternative arrangement is external *cold-site* vendors that provide empty office space with special flooring, ventilation, and wiring. In an emergency, the stricken company moves its own (or leased) computers to the site.

Physical computer security is an integral part of a total security system. Cray Research, a leading manufacturer of supercomputers (now a subsidiary of Silicone Graphics, Inc.), has incorporated a corporate security plan, under which the corporate computers are automatically monitored and centrally controlled. *Graphic displays* show both normal status and disturbances. All the controlled devices are represented as icons on floor-plan graphics. These icons can change colors (e.g., green means normal, red signifies a problem). The icons can flash as well. Corrective-action messages are displayed whenever appropriate. The alarm system includes over 1,000 alarms. Operators can be alerted, even at remote locations, in less than one second.

Of special interest is disaster planning for Web-based systems, as shown in the *IT at Work* example, below. For some of the latest methods of recovery, see the special issue of *Computers and Security* (Vol. 19, No. 1, 2000).

DISASTER AVOIDANCE. **Disaster avoidance** is an approach oriented toward *prevention*. The idea is to minimize the chance of avoidable disasters (such as fire or other human-caused threats). For example, many companies use a device called *uninterrupted power supply (UPS),* which provides power in case of a power outage.

Risk Management and Cost-Benefit Analysis

It is not economical to prepare protection against every possible threat. Therefore, an IT security program must provide a process for assessing threats and deciding which ones to prepare for and which ones to ignore, or provide reduced protection. Installation of control measures is based on a balance between the cost of controls and the need to reduce or eliminate threats. Such analysis is basically a **risk-management** approach, which helps identify threats and selects cost-effective security measures.

IT at Work

...in Finance

DISASTER PLANNING AND THE INTERNET AT REUTERS LTD.

www.reuters.com

Reuters is a multinational information-delivery corporation with great interest in the Web. One of its subsidiaries, Realty Online (*moneynet.com*), builds and operates online stock trading services for well-known brokerage houses, such as Paine Webber, Inc. If Reuters' information system were to fail outright, it would take more than 15 brokerage houses with it. The costs, not to mention the legal ramifications, can be tremendous.

There is very little experience in how to plan for Web-based disasters. Both traditional vendors, such as Comdisco Inc., and Internet-based specialists, such as Exodus Communications, are trying to grab a share of this developing market. Reuters implemented an Internet disaster recovery plan with SunGard Corp. In addition, the company operates three redundant Web sites in different locations from coast to coast. In case all of them were to fail, a hot site, which is constantly updated with information from the main Reuters server, would be used to ensure continuous operation.

For Further Exploration: How safe is this triple level of security? Are Web-based systems like this more vulnerable to disasters? Why?

Source: Condensed from *Interactive Week,* March 9, 1998, p. 7.

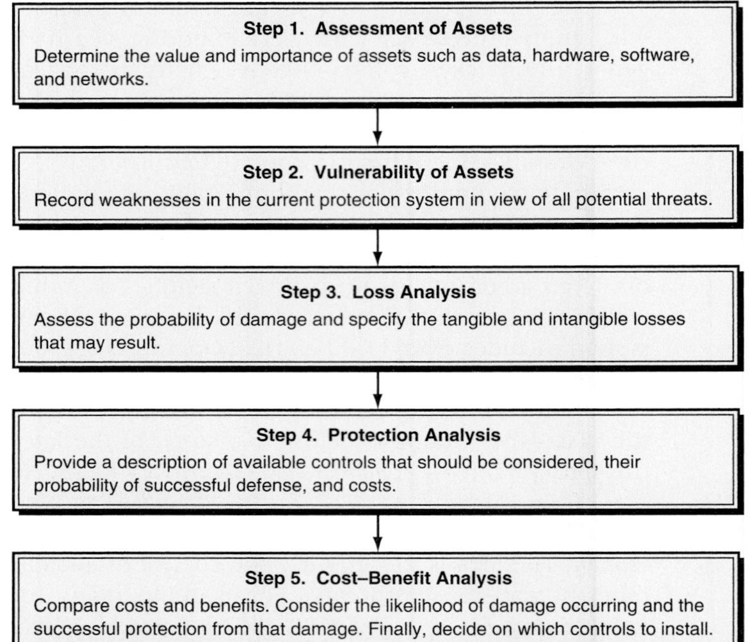

FIGURE 15.6 The risk management process.

Major activities in the risk-management process can be applied to existing systems as well as to systems under development. These are summarized in Figure 15.6.

RISK-MANAGEMENT ANALYSIS. Risk-management analysis can be enhanced by the use of DSS software packages. A simplified computation is shown here:

$$\text{Expected loss} = P1 \times P2 \times L$$

where:

P1 = probability of attack
P2 = probability of attack being successful
L = loss occurring if attack is successful

Example:

P1 = .02
P2 = .10
L = $1,000,000

Then, expected loss = P1 * P2 * L = 0.02 * 0.1 * 1,000,000 = $2,000.

The expected loss can then be compared with the cost of preventing it. The value of software programs lies not only in their ability to execute complex computations, but also in their ability to provide a structured, systematic framework for ranking both threats and controls.

HOW MUCH TO SECURE? The National Computer Security Center (NCSC) of the Department of Defense published guidelines for security levels. The government uses these guidelines in its requests for bids on jobs where vendors must

meet specified levels. The seven levels are shown at the book's Web site. Vendors are required to maintain a certain security level depending on the security needs of the job.

BUSINESS CONTINUITY PLAN. Risk management goes hand-in-hand with business-inpact analysis, vulnerability analysis, strategy development, and disaster planning recovery to form a **business continuity plan**. Such a plan outlines the process by which businesses should recover from a major disaster. The comprehensiveness of such a plan is shown in Figure 15.7. For a detailed step-by-step methodology, see Devargas (1999).

IT Security in the Twenty-First Century

As we entered the new millennium, computer control and security started receiving increased attention. For example, the story of the "I Love You" bug captured the headlines of most newspapers, TV, and computer portals in May 2000. Almost 80 percent of the world's major corporations battled computer viruses in 2000. Therefore, the latest technologies need to be employed to protect against viruses and other IT hazards. Several important trends are discussed in this section.

INCREASING THE RELIABILITY OF SYSTEMS. The objective relating to reliability is to use **fault tolerance** to keep the information systems working, even if some parts fail. Compaq Computer and other PC manufacturers provide a feature that stores data on more than one disk drive at the same time. So, if one disk fails or is attacked, the data are still available. Several brands of PCs include a built-in battery that is automatically activated in case of power failure.

INTELLIGENT SYSTEMS FOR EARLY DETECTION. Detecting intrusion in its beginning is extremely important, especially for classified information and financial data. Expert systems and neural networks are used for this purpose. For example, *intrusion-detecting systems* are especially suitable for local area networks

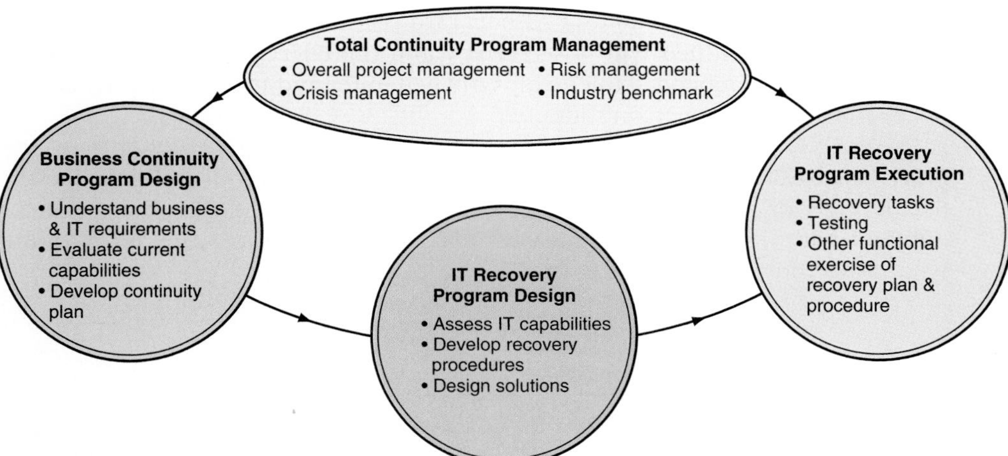

FIGURE 15.7 Business continuity services managed by IBM. (*Source:* IBM, Business Continuity and Recovery Services, January 2000, produced in Hong Kong. Courtesy of IBM.)

and client/server architectures. This approach compares users' activities on a workstation network against historical profiles and analyzes the significance of any discrepancies. The purpose is to detect security violations. The approach is pursued by several government agencies (e.g., Department of Energy and the U.S. Navy) and large corporations (e.g., Citicorp, Rockwell International, and Tracor). It detects other things as well, for example, compliance with security procedures. People tend to ignore security measures (20,000–40,000 violations were reported each month in a large aerospace company in California). The system detects such violations so that improvements can be made.

INTELLIGENT SYSTEMS IN AUDITING. Intelligent systems are used to enhance the task of IS auditing. For example, expert systems evaluate controls and analyze basic computer systems while neural networks are used to detect fraud.

ARTIFICIAL INTELLIGENCE IN BIOMETRICS. Expert systems, neural computing, voice recognition, and fuzzy logic can be used to enhance the capabilities of several biometric systems.

EXPERT SYSTEMS FOR DIAGNOSIS, PROGNOSIS, AND DISASTER PLANNING. Expert systems can be used to diagnose troubles in computer systems and to suggest solutions. The user provides the expert systems with answers to questions about symptoms. The expert system uses its knowledge base to diagnose the source(s) of the trouble. Once a proper diagnosis is made, the computer provides a restoration suggestion. Exec Express (*e-exec.co.uk*) sells intranet-based business recovery planning expert systems that are part of a bigger program called Self-Assessment. The program is used to evaluate a corporation's environment for security, procedures, and other risk factors.

SMART CARDS. Smart card technology can be used to protect PCs on LANs. An example is Excel MAR 10 (from MacroArt Technology, Singapore), which offers six safety levels: identification of authorized user, execution of predetermined programs, authentication, encryption of programs and files, encryption of communication, and generation of historical files. This product can also be integrated with fingerprint facility. The user's smart card is authenticated by the system, using signatures identified with a secret key and the encryption algorithm. Smart cards containing embedded microchips can generate unique passwords (used only once) that confirm a person's identity.

FIGHTING HACKERS. Several new products are available for fighting hackers. Secure Networks (*snc-net.com*) developed a product that is essentially a decoy network within network. The idea is to lure the hackers into the decoy to find what tools they use and detect them as early as possible.

➡ MANAGERIAL ISSUES

1. ***To whom should the IS department report?*** This issue is related to the degree of IS decentralization and to the role of the CIO. Reporting to a functional area may introduce biases in providing IT priorities to that functional area, which may not be justifiable. Responding to the CEO is very desirable.

2. ***Who needs a CIO?*** This is a critical question that is related to the role of the CIO as a senior executive in the organization. Giving a title without authority can damage the ISD and its operation. Asking the IS director to assume a CIO's responsibility, but not giving the authority and title, can be just as damaging. Any organization that is heavily dependent on IT should have a CIO.
3. ***End users are friends, not enemies, of the IS department.*** The relationship between end users and the ISD can be very delicate. In the past, many ISDs were known to be insensitive to end-user needs. This created a strong desire for end-user independence, which can be both expensive and ineffective. Successful companies develop a climate of cooperation and friendship between the two parties.

4. ***Ethical issues.*** The reporting relationship of the ISD can result in some unethical behavior. If the ISD reports, for example, to the finance department, the finance department may misuse information about individuals or other departments.
5. ***Responsibilities for security should be assigned in all areas.*** The more organizations use the Internet, extranets, and intranets, the greater the security issues. It is important to make sure that people know who is responsible and accountable for what. The vast majority of information resources is in the hands of end users. Therefore, functional managers must understand and practice IT security management and other proper asset management tasks.
6. ***Security awareness programs are important for any organization, especially if it is heavily dependent on IT.*** Such programs should be corporatewide and supported by senior executives. In addition, monitoring security measures and ensuring compliance with administrative controls are essential to the success of any security plan. For many people, following administrative controls means additional work, which they prefer not to do.
7. ***Auditing information systems should be institutionalized into the organizational culture.*** Organizations should audit IS not because the insurance company may ask for it, but because it can save considerable amounts of money. On the other hand, overauditing is not cost-effective.
8. ***Multinational corporations.*** Organizing the ISD in a multinational corporation is a complex issue. Some organizations prefer a complete decentralization, having an ISD in each country, or even several ISDs in one country. Others keep a minimum of centralized staff. Some companies, like Mobil Oil, prefer a highly centralized structure. Legal issues, government constraints, and the size of the IS staff are some factors that determine the degree of decentralization.

ON THE WEB SITE... Additional resources, including the Virtual Company, quizzes, cases, updates, additional exercises, links, demos, and activities, can be found on the book's Web site.

KEY TERMS

Application controls *675*
Audit *683*
Audit trail *685*
Backup *686*
Biometric control *676*
Business continuity plan *689*
Chief information officer (CIO) *658*
Chief network officer (CNO) *664*
Conflict resolution team *661*
Cracker *671*
Data integrity *678*
Data tampering *672*
Disaster avoidance *687*
Disaster recovery *685*
Encryption *681*

Fault tolerance *689*
Firewall *682*
General controls *675*
Hacker *671*
Information center (IC) *662*
Informations Resources Management (IRM) *658*
Information systems controls *675*
Programming fraud *672*
Risk management *687*
Service-level agreement (SLA) *662*
Steering committee *661*
Virus *672*
Vulnerability *670*

CHAPTER HIGHLIGHTS (Numbers Refer to Learning Objectives)

1 Information resources scattered throughout the organization are vulnerable to attacks, and therefore are difficult to manage.

1 The responsibility for IRM is divided between the ISD and end users.

2 Steering committees, information centers, and service-level agreements can reduce conflicts between the ISD and end users.

2 ISD reporting locations can vary, but a preferred location is to report directly to senior management.

3 The chief information officer (CIO) is a corporate-level position demonstrating the importance and changing role of IT in organizations.

4 Data, software, hardware, and networks can be threatened by many internal and external hazards.

4 The damage to an information system can be caused either accidentally or intentionally.

4 There are many potential computer crimes; some resemble conventional crimes (embezzlement, vandalism, fraud, theft, trespassing, and joyriding).

4 Computer criminals are driven by economic, ideological, egocentric, or psychological factors. Most of the criminals are insiders, but outsiders (such as hackers, crackers, and spies) can cause major damage as well.

4 A virus is a computer program hidden within a regular program that instructs the regular program to change or destroy data and/or programs. Viruses spread very quickly along networks worldwide.

5 Information systems are protected with controls such as security procedures, physical guards, or detecting software. These are used for *prevention, deterrence, detection, recovery,* and *correction* of information systems.

5 General controls include physical security, access controls, data security controls, communications (network) controls, and administrative controls.

5 Biometric controls are used to identify users by checking physical characteristics of the user (e.g., fingerprints and retinal prints).

5 Application controls are usually built into the software. They protect the data during input, processing, or output.

6 A detailed internal and external IT audit may involve hundreds of issues and can be supported by both software and checklists.

6 Encrypting information is a useful method for protecting transmitted data.

7 Disaster recovery planning is an integral part of effective control and security management.

7 It is extremely difficult and expensive to protect against all possible threats. Therefore, it is necessary to use cost-benefit analysis to decide how many and which controls to adopt.

QUESTIONS FOR REVIEW

1. What are possible reporting locations for the ISD?
2. Why has the ISD historically reported to finance or accounting departments?
3. List the mechanisms for ISD–end users cooperation.
4. Summarize the new role of the CIO.
5. List Rockart's eight imperatives.
6. What is a steering committee?
7. Define SLAs and the roles they play.
8. What are the services to end users that are usually provided by an information (help) center?
9. Define controls, threats, vulnerability, and backup.
10. What is the purpose of a control system?
11. What is a computer crime?
12. List the four major categories of computer crimes.
13. What is the difference between hackers and crackers?
14. Describe the profile of a computer criminal.
15. Describe the major motivations of computer criminals.
16. Explain a virus.
17. Describe prevention, deterrence, detection, recovery, and correction.
18. List five factors that make it difficult to protect an information system.

19. Distinguish between general controls and application controls.
20. What is the difference between authorized and authenticated users?
21. Explain encryption.
22. Distinguish between internal and external auditing.
23. Distinguish between auditing around, through, and within the computer.
24. What is a security policy?
25. Define and describe a disaster recovery plan.
26. What do "hot" and "cold" sites for recovery mean?
27. List and briefly describe the steps involved in risk analysis of controls.
28. Define firewalls.

QUESTIONS FOR DISCUSSION

1. What is a desirable location for the ISD to report to, and why?
2. What information resources are usually controlled by the ISD, and why?
3. Discuss the new role of the CIO and the implications of this role to management.
4. Why should information control and security be a prime concern to management?
5. Compare the computer security situation with that of insuring a house.
6. Explain what firewalls protect and what they do not protect.
7. Why is it important to have firewalls?
8. Describe how IS auditing works and how it is related to traditional accounting and financial auditing.
9. Why are authentication and authorization important in e-commerce?
10. Some insurance companies will not insure a business unless the firm has a computer disaster recovery plan. Explain why.
11. Explain why risk management should involve the following elements: threats, exposure associated with each threat, risk of each threat occurring, cost of controls, and assessment of their effectiveness.
12. It was suggested recently to use viruses and similar programs in wars between countries. What is the logic of such a proposal? How could it be implemented?
13. How important is it for a CIO to have an extensive knowledge of the business?
14. Why is it necessary to use SLAs with vendors? What are some of the potential problems in such situations?

EXERCISES

1. Examine Table 15.1. Read some new material on the CIO and add new roles. Which of the roles in the table seem to have gained importance and which seem to have lost importance?
2. The daily probability of a major earthquake in Los Angeles is 0.0007. The chance of your computer center being damaged during such a quake is 5 percent. If the center is damaged, the average estimated damage will be $1.6 million.
   a. Calculate the expected loss (in dollars).
   b. An insurance agent is willing to insure your facility for an annual fee of $15,000. Analyze the offer, and discuss it.
3. The theft of laptop computers at conventions, hotels, and airports is becoming a major problem. These categories of protection exist: physical devices (e.g., *targus.com*), encryption (e.g., *networkassociates.com*), and security policies (e.g., at *ebay.com*). Find more information on the problem and on the solutions. Summarize the advantages and limitations of each method.
4.  Expert systems can be used to analyze the profiles of computer users. Such analysis may enable better intrusion detection. Should an employer notify employees that their usage of computers is being monitored by an expert system? Why or why not?
5.  Ms. M. Hsieh worked as a customer support representative for the Wollongong Group, a small software company (Palo Alto, California). She was fired in late 1987. In early 1988, Wollongong discovered that someone was logging onto its computers at night via a modem and had altered and copied files. During investigation, the police traced the calls to Ms. Hsieh's home and found copies there of proprietary information valued at several million dollars. It is interesting to note that Ms. Hsieh's access code was canceled the day she was terminated. However, the company suspects that Ms. Hsieh obtained the access code of another employee. (*Source:* Based on *BusinessWeek*, August 1, 1988, p. 67.)
   a. How was the crime committed? Why were the controls ineffective? (State any relevant assumptions.)

b. What can Wollongong do in order to prevent similar incidents in the future?

6. Guarding against a distributed denial of service attack is not simple. Examine the major tools and approaches available. Start by downloading software from *nipc.gov*. Also visit *cert.org, sans.org,* and *ciac.llnl.gov*. Write a report summarizing your findings.

7. Twenty-five thousand messages arrive at an organization each year. Currently there are no firewalls. On the average there are 1.2 successful hackings each year. Each successful hacking results in loss to the company of about $130,000.

   A firewall is proposed at a cost of $66,000. The estimated life is three years. The chance that an intruder will break through the firewall is 0.0002. In such a case, the damage will be $100,000 (30 percent) or $200,000 (50 percent), or no damage. There is annual maintenance cost of $20,000 for the firewall.

   a. Should management buy the firewall?

   b. An improved firewall that is 99.9988 percent effective costs $84,000, with a life of three years, and annual maintenance cost of $16,000 is available. Should this one be purchased?

8. In spring 2000 the U.S. government developed an internal intrusion detection network (*fidnet.gov*) to protect itself from hackers. The Center for Democracy and Technology (*cdt.org*) objected, claiming invasion of privacy. Research the status of the project (FIDNet) and discuss the claims of the center. 

GROUP AND ROLE-PLAYING ACTIVITIES

1. With the class divided into groups, have each group visit an IS department. Then present the following in class: an organizational chart of the department; a discussion on the department's CIO (director) and her or his reporting status; information on a steering committee (composition, duties); information on any SLAs the department has; and a report on the extent of IT decentralization in the company.

2. Each group is to be divided into two parts. The first part will interview students and business people and record the experiences they have had with computer security problems. The second part of each group will visit a computer store (and/or read the literature or use the Internet) to find out what software is available to fight computer security problems. Then, each group will prepare a presentation in which they describe the problems and identify which of the problems could have been prevented with the use of commercially available software.

3. Create groups to investigate the latest development in IT and e-commerce security. Check journals such as *CIO* and *Datamation* (available free online), vendors, and search engines such as *techdata.com*.

4. Research the Melissa attack in 1999. Explain how the virus works and what damage it causes. Examine Microsoft's attempts to prevent similar future attacks. Investigate similarities between "I Love You" and Melissa. What preventive methods are offered by security vendors?

INTERNET EXERCISES

1. Explore some job-searching Web sites (such as *brassring.com,* and *headhunter.com*), and identify job openings for CIOs. Examine the job requirements and the salary range. Report your findings.

2. Access *datamation.com* and *cio.com,* and find some information regarding CIOs, their roles, salaries, and so forth.

3. Access the site of *comdisco.com*. Locate and describe the latest disaster recovery services.

4. Enter *epic.org/privacy/tools.html,* and examine the following groups of tools: Web encryption, disk encryption, and PC firewalls. Explain how these tools can be used to facilitate the security of your PC.

5. Access the Web sites of the major antivirus vendors (*symantec.com, mcafee.com,* and *antivirus.com*). Find out what the vendors' research centers are doing. Also download virusscan from McAfee and scan your hard drive with it.

6. Many newsgroups are related to computer security (*groups,google.com; alt.comp.virus; comp.virus; maous.comp.virus*). Access any of these sites to find information on the most recently discovered viruses.

7. Check the status of biometric controls. See the demo at *sensar.com*. Check what Microsoft is doing with biometric controls.

8. Access a good search engine (e.g., *google.com* or *findarticles.com*). Find recent articles on *disaster planning*. Prepare a short report on recent developments in disaster recovery planning.

9. The use of smart cards for electronic storage of user identification, user authentication, changing passwords,

and so forth is on the rise. Surf the Internet and report on recent developments. (For example, try the Web sites *microsoft.com/windows/smartcards*, *litronic.com*, *gemplus.com*, or *scia.org*.)

10. Surf the Internet to collect information about the following viruses: Concept, Airwolf, Hare, Good Times, and Jerusalem.
11. Access the Web site *www.2600.com* and read the *2600 Magazine*. Also try *waregone.com*, and *skynamic.com*. Prepare a report that shows how easy it is to hack successfully.
12. Enter *ncsa.com* and find information about "why hackers do the things they do." Write a report.

Minicase 1
Flyhigh Corporation B

Flyhigh is a large aerospace corporation (fictitious name, real incident) that regularly performs projects for the military and other government organizations. A virus attack that caused significant damage resulted in an investigation. The investigation revealed the following.

1. While there were clear instructions not to use common names (such as Smith, Lee, or Brown) as user ID or passwords, these names were in use.
2. While there were clear instructions to change passwords once a month, many people neglected to do so. In fact, some employees had not changed their password for more than a year.
3. There were clear instructions not to open strange Windows attachments. These instructions were repeatedly violated.
4. Violations were especially prevalent among top managers and top scientists. The higher the individuals were in the organizational hierarchy, the more likely it was that they would ignore the instructions.
5. In the past, notices had been mailed to violators, but most of the notices were ignored.
6. The responsibility for security issues was decentralized.

The database administrator was responsible for security in the IS department and for the LAN. Various individuals were assigned responsibility in users' departments, mainly for microcomputers. However, some departments do not have anyone formally assigned for computer security; others did not have any formal procedures regarding security management.

Questions for Minicase 1

1. What do you suggest should be done about the violators?
2. Would you change the responsibility scheme (structure)? How?
3. The actual loss to the corporation from the virus attack was estimated at $1,600,000. Should somebody be punished? Justify your answer, if punishment is recommended. What should it be, and who should be punished (the violators? their bosses? the security manager?, etc.).
4. Devise an improved security policy for this company.

Minicase 2

The CIO/CEO Connection at Xerox Paid Off

www.xerox.com

Xerox Corp., the "king" of copying, has been fighting for its life, facing challenges from new technologies and from strong competitors that are transforming the markets where Xerox does business. Electronic documents, which counted for only 10 percent of the business in 1990, captured 70 percent of the market by 2000 (*idcresearch.com*).

Xerox had to reengineer itself. In 1993, Xerox made history when it outsourced its IT operations, in the largest-ever and first global deal, in a $3.2 billion, 13-year contract. Despite the outsourcing, Xerox kept its CIO, Pat Wallington, at a very high vice presidential position, a member of the top management team. Wallington engineered the outsourcing and held her job until she retired from Xerox in 1999, a tenure of over six years. The average job tenure at the CIO position is less than three years. The CEO places lots of importance on the CIO's job, even though the IS area is small. The CEO said that Xerox gave Wallington long-term projects with long-term payoffs.

Wallington developed a strategic plan called IM 2000. (IM stands for Information Management.) The plan includes three key strategies: outsourcing, replacing proprietary infrastructure with a standard one, and creating an investment fund to support the reengineering of IT. Xerox reengineered four key areas: customer service, sale cycle (time-to market), integrated supply chain, and employee relations.

The key to Wallington's long-term success was considered to be her ability to create a roadmap for others to follow. She had a vision and she knew how to implement it through special teams, like the one that put together the outsourcing deal. People said that Wallington's success was also due to her ability in painting an accurate and compelling vision. It might have caused some controversy—nothing this important is easy—but she was able to sustain the vision and executive management support for it.

As IT continues to play an increasingly important role in enabling companies to become more competitive, CIOs and other IT executives must think beyond glass-house borders. But perhaps most important is the ability to find the right people both in the IS organization and among the end users to implement the visions.

Wallington worked with an IS steering committee (called IM Council) that included IS experts from each business unit. One of the major tasks of the committee was to review the IT project requests of the units, which were submitted annually. The IM Council met once a month to discuss IT strategy and implementation.

In addition, Wallington created the office of the CIO, consisting of herself and her two assistants, the director of IT operations, and the director of IT finance. This committee met almost daily to run the IM organization.

Sources: Condensed from A. Knowles, "CIO/CEO Spotlight on Xerox—Copy This," *Datamation*, June 1997; and from *xerox.com* and *cio.com*.

Questions for Minicase 2

1. Why is a CIO needed if the IS function is basically outsourced?
2. The CIO's job has a tenure of only three years. Find some research on why this is so, and why Wallington was able to last much longer on the job.
3. It is said that the CIO/CEO relations are critical, and that Wallington had the backing of the CEO to make bold decisions. Comment.
4. Wallington was extensively using the "IS by committee" approach. What are the major benefits of it?
5. Comment on the relationships between Wallington's strategy and Xerox's need for BPR.
6. People repeatedly said that Wallington's vision was the key to her success. What do they mean by that? Read "Shop Talk," written by Wallington, at *cio.com*, April 1, 1999.
7. Enter *cio.com* and learn more about the CIO/CEO relationship, and about Pat Wallington (who is now on the staff of *CIO*).

REFERENCES AND BIBLIOGRAPHY

1. Barnea, A., "IT Strategies for Migrating to the Euro," *Information Systems Management,* Winter 2000.
2. Chavez, G., "How Expert Systems Can Help Controllers," *Global Finance,* July 1996.
3. Denning, D. E., *Information Warefare and Security.* Reading, MA: Addison-Wesley, 1999.
4. Devargas, M., "Survival Is Not Compulsory: An Introduction to Business Continuity Planning," *Computers and Security,* Vol. 18, No. 1, 1999.
5. Dickson, G., and G. DeSanctis, *Information Technology and the Future Enterprise.* Upper Saddle River, NJ: Prentice-Hall, 2000.
6. Duffy D., "Chief Executives Who Get IT," *CIO Magazine,* July 15, 1999.
7. Earl, M. J., "Blue Survivors (the CIO's)," *CIO Magazine,* December 15, 1999–January 1, 2000.
8. Fuller, M. K., and E. B. Swanson, "Information Centers as Organizational Innovation," *Journal of Management Information Systems,* Vol. 9, No. 1, Summer 1992.
9. Jain, A., et al., "Biometric Identification," *Communications of the ACM,* February 2000.
10. Jain, A., et al. (eds.), *Biometrics: Personal Identification in Networked Security.* NewYork: Kluwer, 1999.
11. Jain, R., "Key Constructs in Successful IS Implementation: South-East Asian Experience," *Omega,* Vol. 25, No. 3, 1997.
12. Janczewski, L. (ed.), *Internet and Intranet Security Management.* Hershy, PA: Idea Group, 2000.
13. Kleinschrod, W. A., "Technology Transformations," *Beyond Computing,* July–August 1997.
14. Knoll, A. P., *Disaster Recovery: An Organization View.* Chicago, IL: IBM Information Systems Management Institute, 1986.
15. McGee, M. K., "Over the Rainbow (CIOs' salaries)," *InformationWeek,* July 8, 1996.
16. McNurlin, B. C., and R. H. Sprague, Jr., *Information Systems Management in Practice,* 4th ed. Upper Saddle River, NJ: Prentice-Hall, 1998.
17. Morgan, J. P., and N. A. Wong, "Conduct a Legal Web Audit," *e-Business Advisor,* September 1999.
18. Oppliger, R., "Firewalls and Beyond," *Communications of the ACM,* May 1997.
19. Palvia, P. C., and S. C. Basu, "Information Systems Management Issues: Reporting and Relevance," *Decision Sciences,* Winter 1999.
20. Ranum, M., "Intrusion Detecting Ideals, Expectations and Retailers," *Computer Security Journal,* Fall 1999.
21. Rockart, J. F., et al., "Eight Imperatives for the New IS Organization," *Sloan Management Review,* Fall 1996.
22. Ross, J. W., et al., "Develop Long-Term Competitiveness Through IT Assets," *Sloan Management Review,* Fall 1996.
23. Ross, J. W., and D. F. Feeny, "The Evolving Role of the CIO," in R. Zmud (ed.), *Framing the Domain of IT Management.* Cincinnati, OH: Pinnaflex Educational Resources, 2000.
24. Sambamurthy, V., et al., "Managing in the Digital Era," in G. Dickson and G. DeSanctis, *Information Technology and the Future Enterprise.* Upper Saddle River, NJ: Prentice-Hall, 2001.
25. Segev, A., et al., "Internet Security and the Case of Bank of America," *Communications of the ACM,* October 1998.
26. Sitonis, J. G., and B. Goldberg, "Changing Role of the CIO," *InformationWeek,* March 24, 1997.
27. Steefora, A., and M. Cheek, "Hacking Goes Legit," *Industry Week,* February 7, 1994.
28. Steinberg, R. M., and R. N. Johnson, "Implementing SAS No. 55 in a Computer Environment," *Journal of Accountancy,* August 1991.
29. Strassman, P., "What Is the Best Defense? Being Prepared," *ComputerWorld,* March 31, 1997.
30. Tung, L. L., and E. Turban, "Housing Development Board: Reengineering the IT Function," in B. S. Neo, *Exploiting Information Technology for Business Competitiveness.* Singapore: Addison-Wesley, 1996.
31. White, G. B., "Protecting the Real Corporate Networks," *Computer Security Journal,* Vol. 1, No. 4, 1999.
32. Wysocki, R. K., and R. L. De Michiell, *Managing Information Across the Enterprise.* New York: Wiley, 1996.
33. Zmud, R., (ed.), *Framing the Domain of IT Management.* Cincinnati, OH: Pinnaflex Educational Resources, 2000.

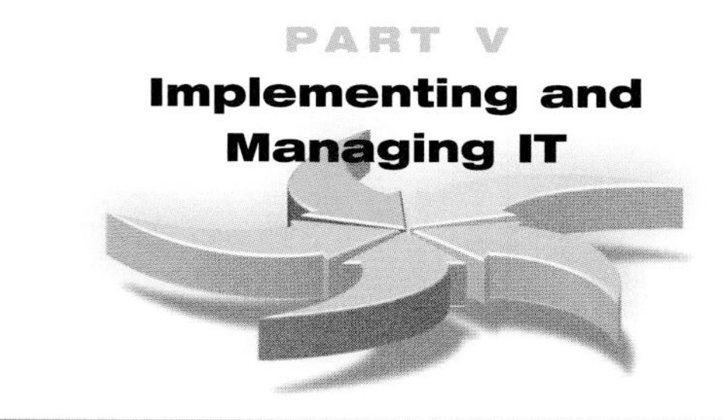

CHAPTER

16

Impacts of IT on Organizations, Individuals, and Society

LEARNING OBJECTIVES

After studying this chapter, you will be able to:

1. Understand the major impacts of information technology on organizations, individuals, and society.
2. Consider the potential dehumanization of people by computers and other potential negative impacts of information technology.
3. Identify the major impacts of information technology on organizational structure, power, jobs, supervision, and decision making.
4. Identify some of the major societal impacts of the Web.
5. Understand the role and impact of virtual communities.

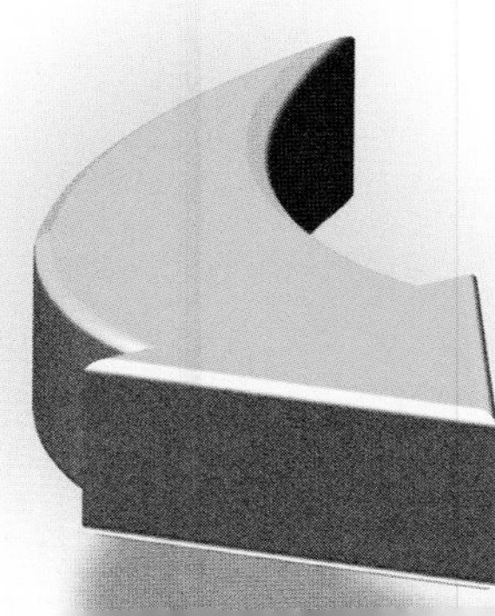

This chapter was updated with the assistance of Robert Davison of City University of Hong Kong.

WEARABLE COMPUTERS FOR WORKERS

THE PROBLEM

For years mobile employees, especially those that had to climb trees, electric poles, or tall buildings, were unable to enjoy the new technologies designed to make employees work or feel better. Thus their productivity and comfort were inferior, especially when computers were involved. But now the situation is changing.

THE SOLUTION

On a cold and damp November day in Toronto, Chris Holm-Laursen, a field technician with Bell Canada, is out and about as usual, but this time with a difference. A small but powerful computer sits in a pocket of his orange mesh vest, while a keyboard is velcroed to the vest's upper left side, and a flat-panel display screen hangs by his waist. A video camera attached to his safety hat enables him to take pictures without using his hands and to send them immediately to the office. A cell phone is attached too, connected to the computer, and then a battery pack—against his back—to keep everything going.

www.bci.ca

Holm-Laursen and 18 other technicians on this pilot project were equipped like this for ten weeks during fall 2000, enabling them to access work orders and repair manuals wherever they were. What is notable is that these workers are not typical of the group usually most wired up—that is, white-collar workers. However, as we move into the wireless age, applications of technology for front-line mobile workers are coming to the fore. Perhaps the most commonly seen example is at the car rental return, where employees carry handheld computers and printers that connect to central computer systems. Bicycle couriers, often seen on the streets of major cities such as London and New York, may have cell phones in their headsets, leaving hands free for steering. The hands-free aspect and the ability to communicate any time, from any place, represent major steps forward, and a wide variety of employees—technicians, medical practitioners, aircraft mechanics, and contractors—are using or testing these devices.

THE RESULTS

Known as an application of m-commerce (Chapter 5), the use of wireless devices that can communicate with each other and with remote information systems is increasing very rapidly, changing the manner in which people work and live.

Design guidelines for this technology are not necessarily intuitive; each type of user may need a different set of specifications. The Bell Canada employees, for example, often have to climb up poles or walk through forests. They don't want their wearable attachments to get caught—or worse still, to be dangerous. They need to be able to see clearly ahead; a head-mounted screen was problematic, so they prefer a flat-panel screen hanging by their sides.

Naturally there may be drawbacks too. Such systems could easily include GPSs (global positioning systems), which enable the company to know exactly where the employee is. This can be both practical and sensible; for instance, the nearest worker to an emergency call can be identified and instructed to take action. But a GPS could also be used to ensure that employees don't knock off work early. Would this be an unreasonable invasion of privacy?

So far, only a few companies make and sell wearables for mobile workers. Bell Canada's system was developed by Xybernaut, a U.S. company, which in

1. *Screen:* Wearers see what looks like a floating 15-inch display.
2. *Camera:* Without using their hands, workers can take digital photos and videos and transmit them wirelessly.
3. *Touch-panel display:* A flat-screen panel responds to the taps of a finger or stylus.
4. *Keyboard:* A wrist-mounted keyboard enables one-handed typing.

2000 had about a thousand of its units in use around the world, mostly in pilot programs. Minneapolis-based ViA is another supplier, most of whose systems are belt-worn.

Bell Canada meanwhile is impressed with initial results, and will equip most technicians with wearables over the next few years. Of course a practical problem in many countries is the weather: What happens when the temperature is minus 50 degrees, or the humidity is 99 percent? Other potential problems also exist: If you are wearing thick gloves, how can you use a keyboard? If it is pouring rain, will the battery short circuit? Various solutions are being developed, such as voice input, tapping on a screen instead of typing, and rainproof electrical systems.

Sources: Compiled from "Wearable Computers for the Working Class," *New York Times,* December 14, 2000; and from *xybernaut.com.*

 LESSONS LEARNED FROM THIS CASE

Wearable technologies are bringing changes to the way that people work—changes that for the most part are for the better. We will face many more of these new challenges as technological advances continue to spring up. IT is having an effect on private and public organizations as well as on employees, customers, clients, and society. Indeed, almost everyone, from the living room to the boardroom, has been touched in some way by IT.

People are working closer and closer with computers. Such relationships may have different impacts on people, organizational units, and work, as we have seen throughout the book, and as we will analyze and summarize in this chapter. For example, the opportunity to use a GPS to monitor employees' whereabouts is a tempting one but may not be welcomed by some employees. Also, we will highlight some of the impacts of e-commerce. Finally, we will end the book with some concluding thoughts.

16.1 DOES IT HAVE ONLY POSITIVE EFFECTS?

Concern about technology's effect on people, organizations, and society is not new. In the 1830s, English intellectuals expressed philosophical arguments about the effects on society of the Industrial Revolution that had begun some 60 to 70 years earlier. In Samuel Butler's 1872 book *Erewhon* (anagram for *nowhere*), a man loses his way in a strange land and wanders into a society that has rejected machines. The people have frozen technology at a predetermined level and outlawed all further technological development; they have made a conscious decision to reject new technology.

While there are many philosophical, technological, social, and cultural differences between society at the start of the Industrial Revolution and today, there are nevertheless many people who do believe that humankind is threatened by the evolution of technology. Our society, however, has so far not rejected technology, but rather has embraced it. Most of us recognize that computers and technology are essential to maintaining and supporting many aspects of our culture. We are involved in a symbiotic relationship with technology. All the same, we must be aware of its effect on us as individuals and as members of organizations and society.

Throughout this book, we have noted how information systems are being justified, constructed, used, and maintained. In all these discussions we have assumed that members of an organization will reap the fruits of new technology and that computers have no major negative impact.

But is this really true? There are people today who do reject the advances of technology—refusing to use the Internet, for example. A more critical issue, however, involves questions like, Will society have any control over the decisions to deploy technology? Where will technology critics be able to make their voices heard? Who will investigate the costs and risks of technologies, and who is going to pay for that investigation? For discussion on these and similar items, see the Roundtable discussion organized by *Interactive Week* on January 10, 2000, at *zdnet.com/intweek/filter/@online*.

Information technology *has* raised a multitude of negative issues, ranging from illegal copying of software programs to surveillance of employees' electronic mail files. Health and safety issues are also of major concern, as are the impact of IT on employment levels and the quality of life. One major area of concern is the impact of the Internet. For example, some people become "addicted" to the Web.

In this chapter, some of these issues will be discussed, especially the impact of IT on organizations, individuals, and society. Ethical issues, which are an important part of these impacts, have been discussed throughout the book as well as in the ethics primer in Appendix 1.1 (Chapter 1).

16.2 IMPACTS OF IT ON ORGANIZATIONS

The use of computers and information technology has brought many changes to organizations. These changes are being felt in areas like structure, authority, power, and job content; employee career ladders and supervision; and the manager's job. A brief discussion of these issues follows.

Structure, Authority, Power, and Job Content

Several issues are related to the changes in these areas. They include the following:

FLATTER ORGANIZATIONAL HIERARCHIES. IT allows for the increased productivity of and control of managers, an increased **span of control** (more employees per supervisor), and a decreased number of experts. IT allows organizations to harness expert knowledge, and reduces the need for technical experts in the organization. It is reasonable to assume, then, that *fewer* managerial levels will exist in many organizations; there will be fewer staff and line managers. This trend is already evidenced by the continuing phenomenon of the "shrinking size of middle management." (See Pinsonneault and Kraemer, 1993.)

Flatter organizational hierarchies will also result from reduction in the total number of employees, reengineering of business processes, and the ability of lower-level employees to perform higher-level jobs (e.g., by using expert systems). As one example, consider the reorganization of many companies during the 1990s, which made them "lean." This made them smaller in terms of the number of employees, with a larger span of control, and a flatter structure. The downsizing of many organizations is supported by the use of IT.

BLUE-TO-WHITE-COLLAR STAFF RATIO. The ratio of white- to blue-collar workers has increased in most organizations as computers replace clerical jobs, and as the need for information systems specialists increases. Further expansion of IT, and especially of intelligent and Web-based and knowledge-based systems, may reverse this trend. Specifically, the number of professionals and specialists could *decline* in relation to the total number of employees in some organizations.

SPECIAL UNITS. Another change in organizational structure is the possibility of creating a technology center, an e-commerce center, a decision support systems department, and/or an intelligent systems department. Such units may have a major impact on organizational structure, especially when they are well supported by top management or report directly to the president, CEO, or other senior manager.

CENTRALIZATION OF AUTHORITY. The relationship between computerized systems and the degree of centralization of authority (and power) in organizations that these systems serve has been debated extensively, especially since the introduction of microcomputers. It is still difficult, however, to establish a clear pattern. For example, the introduction of expert systems in General Electric's maintenance area increased the power of the decentralized units because they became less dependent on the company's headquarters. On the other hand, expert systems can be used as a means of increasing control and enhancing centralization. The Web permits greater empowerment, allowing for more decentralization.

Because of the trend toward smaller and flatter organizations, centralization may become more popular. However, this trend could be offset by specialization in more decentralized units. Whether extensive use of IT will result in more centralization or in decentralization of business operations and management may depend on top management's philosophy.

POWER AND STATUS. Knowledge is power—this fact has been recognized for generations in many different societies. The latest developments in computerized systems are changing the power structure within organizations, as well as between governments and citizens. The struggle over who will control the computers and information resources has become one of the most visible conflicts in many organizations, both private and public. Intelligent systems and knowledge bases, for example, may reduce the power of certain professional groups because their knowledge will be in the public domain. On the other hand, individuals who control e-commerce applications may gain considerable prestige, knowledge, power, and status.

As a result, there is a *power redistribution* in many organizations. Managers and employees who control information knowledge and IT are likely to gain power at the expense of others. Such shifts in power can prove dysfunctional, inducing further disruption in organizational practices.

Now consider the same issues at the country level. Who is fighting with whom to control IT and information more generally? In some countries, the fight may be between large corporations that seek to use this information to their own competitive advantage and the government (e.g., the case brought against Microsoft for unfair competition). In other countries, where IT has traditionally been less widely diffused, the government may be doing everything it can to ensure that it continues to hold onto these new reins of power—by not letting private citizens access some information. For example, about 20 countries, including

China, Saudi Arabia, and Singapore, try to block people from accessing certain Web sites. Certainly the widespread dissemination of reliable information could be a real threat to existing power structures in countries like China and North Korea. The establishment of new Internet-specific laws in China provides a case in point of how seriously concerned the Chinese government is about abuse of the Internet (see Group Activity 1).

JOB CONTENT. One major impact of IT is on the content of many jobs in both private and public organizations. **Job content** is important not only because it is related to organizational structure, but also because it is interrelated with employee satisfaction, compensation, status, and productivity. Changes in job content occur when work is redesigned, for example, when business process reengineering (BPR) is attempted or when e-commerce changes the marketing system (see Baatz, 1996). Furthermore, if job content changes, then people may need to change as well; they may need training, reskilling, or reallocating to a different part of the organization (or they may even be laid off). Changes in job skills are referred to as "staff upgrading" or "changing skill-set requirements" (see Routt, 1999). Resistance to such changes is common, and can lead to unpleasant confrontations between employees and management.

Personnel Issues

The IT revolution may result in many changes in personnel management and human resources management. These include the following:

EMPLOYEE CAREER LADDERS. Increased use of IT in organizations could have a significant and somewhat unexpected impact on career ladders. In the past, many highly skilled professionals have developed their abilities through years of experience, holding a series of positions that expose them to progressively more difficult and complex situations. The use of IT, and especially Web-based computer-aided instruction, may short-cut a portion of this learning curve. However, several questions remain unaddressed. How will high-level human expertise be acquired with minimal experience in lower-level tasks? What will be the effect on compensation at all levels of employment? How will human resource development programs be structured? What career paths will be offered to employees?

CHANGES IN SUPERVISION. The fact that an employee's work is performed online and stored electronically introduces the possibility for greater electronic supervision. For professional employees whose work is often measured by their completion of projects, "remote supervision" implies greater emphasis on completed work and less on personal contacts. This emphasis is especially true if employees, such as telecommuters, work in geographically dispersed locations, away from their supervisors. In general, the supervisory process may become more formalized, with greater reliance on procedures and measurable (i.e., quantitative) outputs than on interpersonal processes and the quality of work done.

OTHER CONSIDERATIONS. Several other personnel-related issues could surface as a result of using IT. For example, what will be the impact of IT on job qualifications, on training requirements, and on worker satisfaction? How can jobs that use IT be designed so that they present an acceptable level of challenge to users? How might IT be used to personalize or enrich jobs? What can be done to make sure that the introduction of IT does not demean jobs or have other negative impacts from the workers' point of view? What principles should be used to allocate functions to people and machines, especially those functions that can be performed equally well by either one? Should cost or efficiency be the sole or major criterion for such allocation? All these and more issues could be encountered in any system implementation.

An interesting area is *job mobility*. Today you can go on a Web site, such as *techjourney.com* and find out how much you can be paid in a job in any place in the United States. Using videoconferencing for interviews and intelligent agents to find jobs and new employers is likely to increase employee turnover.

The Manager's Job

The most important task of managers is making decisions. IT can change the manner in which many decisions are made and consequently change the managers' jobs. The most probable areas of change are:

- Automation of routine decisions (e.g., frontline employees, as discussed in Chapter 10)
- Less expertise required for many decisions
- Less reliance on experts to provide support to top executives
- Empowerment of lower and medium levels of management due to knowledge bases
- Decision making undertaken by nonmanagerial employees
- Power redistribution among managers, and power shifts down the organization
- Electronic support of complex decisions (the Web, intelligent agents, DSS)

Some organizational changes brought about by the use of computed-assisted communication technologies are listed at the book's Web site.

Many managers have reported that the computer has finally given them time to "get out of the office and into the field." They also have found that they can spend more time planning activities instead of "putting out fires." Another aspect of the management challenge lies in the ability of IT to support the process of decision making. IT could change the decision-making process and even decision-making styles. For example, information gathering for decision making will be done much more quickly. Web-based intelligent agents can monitor the environment, and scan and interpret information (see Liu et al., 2000). Most managers currently work on a large number of problems simultaneously, moving from one to another as they wait for more information on their current problem or until some external event interrupts them. IT tends to reduce the time necessary to complete any step in the decision-making process. Therefore, managers will work on fewer tasks during each day but complete more of them.

Another possible impact on the manager's job could be a change in leadership requirements. What are generally considered to be good qualities of leadership may be significantly altered with the use of IT. For example, when face-to-face communication is replaced by electronic mail and computerized conferencing, leadership qualities attributed to physical appearance and dress codes could be minimal.

Other Changes

Many other changes are expected in organizations. For example, the corporate culture in the Internet age is changing (see Kleiner, 2000), and IT managers are forced to assume a leadership role in making business decisions (see Dalton, 1999). For a comprehensive analysis of business leadership in the information age, see Nevins and Stumpf (1999).

16.3 IMPACTS OF IT ON INDIVIDUALS AT WORK

Information systems affect individuals in various ways. What is a benefit to one individual may be a curse to another. Some of the ways that IT may affect individuals, their perceptions, and behaviors are considered next.

Job Satisfaction

Although many jobs may become substantially more "enriched" with IT, other jobs may become more routine and less satisfying. For example, as early as 1970, researchers predicted that computer-based information systems would reduce managerial discretion in decision making and thus create dissatisfied managers.

Dehumanization and Psychological Impacts

DEHUMANIZATION. A frequent criticism of traditional data processing systems was their potential negative effect on people's individuality. Such systems were criticized as being impersonal; they were said to *dehumanize* and depersonalize the activities that have been computerized. Many people felt, and still feel, a loss of identity, a **dehumanization**, because of computerization; they feel like "just another number" because computers reduce or eliminate the human element that was present in the noncomputerized systems. People also feel this way about the Web. Some people have become so addicted to the Web that they have dropped out of their regular activities, at school or work or home, creating new social and organizational problems.

On the other hand, while the major objective of newer technologies, such as e-commerce, is to increase productivity, they can also create personalized, *flexible* systems that allow individuals to include their opinions and knowledge in the system. These technologies attempt to be people-oriented and user-friendly.

PSYCHOLOGICAL IMPACTS. The Internet threatens to have an even more isolating influence than has been created by television. If people are encouraged to work and shop from their living rooms, then some unfortunate psychological effects, such as depression and loneliness, could develop. Another example is distance learning. In some countries, it is legal to school children at home through IT, but the lack of social contacts could be damaging to their social, moral, and cognitive development.

Information Anxiety

One of the negative impacts of the information age is **information anxiety**. This disquiet can take several forms, such as frustration with our *inability to keep up with the amount of data* present in our lives. Other forms of information anxiety are:

- Frustration with the quality of the information available on the Web. This information is frequently not up-to-date, or is incomplete.
- Too many online sources.
- Frustration with the guilt associated with not being better informed, or being informed too late. "How come others knew before we did?"

Wurman (2000) identifies several types of information: internal, conversational, reference, news, and cultural. Between 60 and 80 percent of the people searching for specific information on the Web cannot find what they want. This adds to anxiety, as does the data glut that obscures the distinction between data and information, and between facts and knowledge. Wurman (2001) prescribes solutions to ease the problem of information anxiety, ranging from better access to data to better design of Web sites.

For some Internet users, anxiety resulting from information overload may even bring *insomnia*, the experience of inadequate or poor sleep. (For some possible solutions, see *sleepfoundation.org*.)

Impacts on Health and Safety

Computers and information systems are a part of the job environment that may adversely affect individuals' health and safety. To illustrate, we will discuss the effects of three issues: *job stress, video display terminals,* and *long-term use of the keyboard.* (For further discussion see the *Wall Street Journal,* April 9, 1996, p. 1.)

JOB STRESS. An increase in workload and/or responsibilities can trigger **job stress**. Although computerization has benefited organizations by increasing productivity, it has also created an ever-increasing workload. Some workers feel overwhelmed and start feeling anxious about their jobs and their performance. These feelings of anxiety can adversely affect workers' productivity. Management's responsibility is to help alleviate these feelings by redistributing the workload among workers or by hiring more individuals.

VIDEO DISPLAY TERMINALS. Exposure to video display terminals (VDTs) raises the issue of the risk of radiation exposure, which has been linked to cancer and other health-related problems. For example, lengthy exposure to VDTs has been blamed for miscarriages in pregnant women. However, results of the research done to investigate this charge have been inconclusive. It is known that exposure to VDTs for long periods of time can affect an individual's eyesight.

REPETITIVE STRAIN (STRESS) INJURIES. Other potential health and safety hazards are repetitive strain injuries such as backaches and muscle tension in the wrists and fingers. *Carpal tunnel syndrome* is a pernicious and painful form of repetitive strain injury that affects the wrists and hands. It has been associated with the long-term use of keyboards. Repetitive strain injuries can be very costly to corporations. According to Cone (1994), there have been more than 2,000 lawsuits against computer manufacturers and employers. For example, a large lawsuit was filed against IBM in the mid-1990s requesting $11.5 million because of the inappropriate design of a keyboard that supposedly caused carpal tunnel syndrome.

LESSENING THE NEGATIVE IMPACT ON HEALTH AND SAFETY. Designers are aware of the potential problems associated with prolonged use of computers. Consequently, they have attempted to design a better computing environment. Research in the area of **ergonomics** (or human factors) provides guidance for these designers. For instance, ergonomic techniques focus on creating an environment for the worker that is safe, well lit, and comfortable. Devices such as antiglare screens have helped alleviate problems of fatigued or damaged eyesight, and chairs that contour the human body have helped decrease backaches (see *A Closer Look* 16.1 on the facing page).

OTHER IMPACTS. Interactions between individuals and computers are so numerous that entire volumes can be written on the subject. An overview of such interactions is provided by Kanter (1992) and illustrated in Figure 16.1 (page 708). The figure shows the individual encircled by the electronic transfer of money (as in e-commerce and smart cards) that allows purchase of products and services. The intermediate rings identify six areas or systems of human activity affected by computers (consumerism, education, and so on). Finally, the outer

A CLOSER LOOK
16.1 ERGONOMIC PRODUCTS AND CORRECT SITTING PROTECT COMPUTER USERS

Many products are available to improve working conditions for people who spend much of their time with a computer. The following pictures are representative examples.

(a) Proper sitting position.

(b) Wrist support.

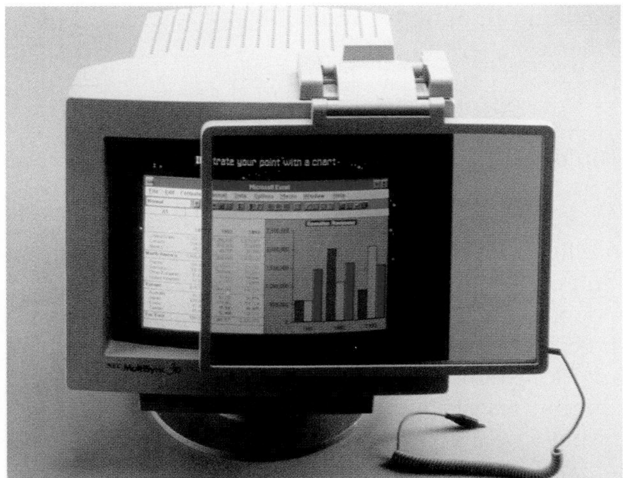

(c) Eye-protection filter (optically coated glass).

(d) Adjustable foot rest.

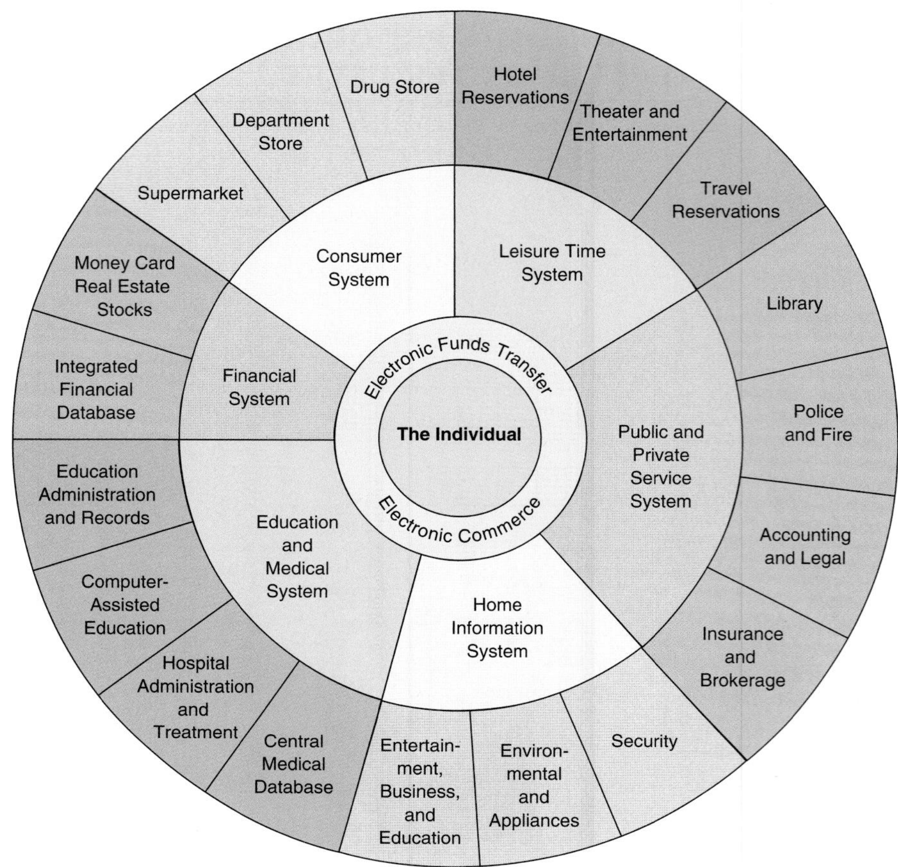

FIGURE 16.1 Information systems and the individual. (*Source:* Jerome Kanter, *Managing with Information*, 4th ed., 1992, p. 350. © Reprinted with permission of Pearson Education Inc., Upper Saddle River, NJ.)

ring gives some examples of specific products or services in each system. For a review of individual acceptance of information technologies, see Agarwal (2000).

16.4 Societal Impacts

The social implications of IT could be far reaching. This section describes several representative impacts.

Opportunities for People with Disabilities

The integration of artificial intelligence technologies, such as speech and vision recognition, into a computer and especially into Web-based information systems, can create new employment opportunities for people with disabilities. For example, those who cannot type are able to use a voice-operated keyboard, and those who cannot travel can work at home.

Adaptive equipment for computers permits people with disabilities to perform tasks they would not normally be able to do. Figure 16.2 shows a PC for a deaf user, a PC for a blind user, and a PC for a motor-disabled user. In Thailand, 18-year-old students at the Na Yai Arm Vocational School, in Chantaburi province, developed a special telephone for blind people because they wanted to help the sight-impaired to live on more equal terms with the rest of society and not need to depend on help from others (Boonnoon, 2000).

(a)

(b)

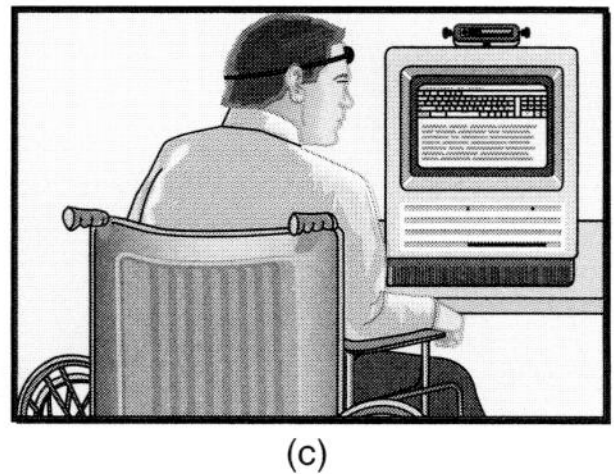
(c)

FIGURE 16.2 Enabling people with disabilities to work with computers. (*Source:* J. J. Lazzaro, "Computers for the Disabled," *Byte*, June 1993.)

(*a*) *A PC for a blind user,* equipped with an Oscar optical scanner and a Braille printer, both by TeleSensory. The optical scanner converts text into ASCII code or into proprietary word processing format. Files saved on disk can then be translated into Braille and sent to the printer. Visually impaired users can also enlarge the text on the screen by loading a TSR software magnification program.

(*b*) *The deaf user's PC* is connected to a telephone via an Ultratec Intele-Modem Baudot/ASCH modem. The user is sending and receiving messages to and from someone at a remote site who is using a telecommunications device for deaf people (right).

(*c*) *This motor-disabled person* is communicating with a PC using a Pointer Systems optical head pointer to access all keyboard functions on a virtual keyboard shown on the PC's display. The user can "strike" a key in one of two ways. He can focus on the desired key for a user-definable time period (which causes the key to be highlighted), or he can click an adapted switch when he chooses the desired key.

Some countries have developed more extensive legislative requirements than others so as to protect the rights of people with disabilities. In the United States, since the summer of 1994, companies with 15 employees or more must comply with the Americans with Disabilities Act. This act requires companies to take reasonable steps to ensure that employees with disabilities will be able to work with specially adapted computers as well as with other equipment. In many countries, however, notably those in the developing world, no such legislative measures exist, and those with disabilities are very much undervalued and underemployed members of society.

INTERNET IMPLICATIONS. E-commerce sites are studying how to handle people with disabilities, especially when several e-tailing stores were shut down for not complying with the law (*New York Times*, January 1, 2001). In the United States, 300,000 to 500,000 blind people rely on screen-reader software and a speech synthesizer, which turn words to sound and can interpret images. But many Web sites are not designed to be compatible with screen readers. People with impaired motor skills need a special mouse, and people with hearing impairments need to see messages. This can be done by using closed-captioning devices, but is usually not done.

Several organizations deal with IT and people with disabilities. An example is *able.towork.org* (see Exercise 5). For a comprehensive discussion of Web sites and the visually impaired, including software and hardware, see Rogers and Rajkumar (1999).

Quality of Life Improvements

On a broader scale, IT has significant implications for the **quality of life**. An increase in organizational efficiency may result in more leisure time for workers. The workplace can be expanded from the traditional nine-to-five job at a central location to twenty-four hours a day at any location. This expansion provides a flexibility that can significantly improve the quality of leisure time, even if the total amount of leisure time is not increased.

Of course there can be negative effects as well. None of us wants to work round the clock, twenty-four hours a day, seven days a week, 365 days a year, but the pressure to do so could be considerable if the facility exists. Indeed, another pressure may be to work antisocial hours—night shifts, for example, or weekends. Furthermore, not all of us necessarily want to spend more leisure time at home. One investigation showed that more time at home is a major contributory factor to increased domestic violence and the desire for divorce.

Nevertheless, our quality of life can be improved in various ways by IT. For example, Japanese auto manufacturers are leading the way in the development of onboard picture-map technology (e.g., see *toyota.com*), which makes it easier to drive to your destination. Some systems provide live data that is downloaded to you via a satellite link as you drive. Other systems require you to download information to a "card" before you start your trip, then to insert the card into the car's navigation system. For more details, see Kageyama (2000) and Flamma (1999). One way to improve quality of life with IT is to use robots to take over certain uncomfortable or dangerous tasks.

ROBOT REVOLUTION ON THE WAY. Robots will become ubiquitous, or so some people think. "Cyberpooches," nursebots, and more may be our companions before we know it. Around the world, quasi-autonomous devices have become increasingly common on factory floors, hospital corridors, and farm fields. Military applications are out there too: The Pentagon is researching self-driving vehicles and bee-like swarms of small surveillance robots, each of which would contribute a different view or angle of a combat zone.

Whether robots will be of R2D2 (the *Star Wars* android) quality is another issue. It will be a long time before we see robots making decisions by themselves, handling unfamiliar situations, and interacting with people. Nevertheless, robots that can do practical tasks do abound. Carnegie Mellon University, for example, has developed self-directing tractors that harvest hundreds of acres of crops around the clock in California, using global positioning systems combined with video image processing that identifies rows of uncut crops. Robots are especially helpful in hazardous environments, as illustrated in the *IT at Work* on page 711.

IMPROVEMENTS IN HEALTH CARE. IT has brought about major improvements in health-care delivery, ranging from better and faster diagnoses, to expedited research and development of new drugs, to more accurate monitoring of critically ill patients. One technology that has made a special contribution is artificial intelligence. For example, expert systems support diagnosis of diseases, and machine vision is enhancing the work of radiologists. Recently, surgeons started to use virtual reality to plan complex surgeries. And cardiologists can interpret patients' hearts' vital signs from a distance (see *micromed.com*).

The Internet cancer site (*cancer.med.upenn.edu*) features a huge array of documents, reviews, descriptions of personal experiences, suggested diets, and links to global resources for people who suffer from cancer, or who are interested in oncology. It offers information on the latest research studies and cancer pain management. It also helps families cope with emotional and financial burdens. The Web site has won numerous awards for its design and function-

IT at Work
THE WORKING LIVES OF ROBOTS

Integrating IT ...in Production & Operations Management ...in Public Service

LAYING FIBER OPTIC CABLES. Cities around the world are transforming themselves to the digital era by replacing copper wires with fiber-optic cables or by installing fiber optics where there were no wires before. Because fiber-optic cables are the choice method (in 2001) to deliver high-speed voice and data communication (see Technology Guide 4), demand for them is expanding. Cities know that in order to attract and hold on to high-tech business they must provide fiber-optic access to all commercial buildings. You may have seen this activity many times without realizing it: Workers cut up the street, creating noise, dust, and traffic problems. But the worst part of it is that the disruption to people may take weeks, or even months, just to complete one city block. Now, robots are changing it all.

One company that invented a technology to improve the situation is City Net Telecommunications (*citynettelecom.com*). The idea is to use the existing sewer system to lay the cables. This way no trenches need to be dug in the streets. Pioneering work has been done in Albuquerque, New Mexico; Omaha, Nebraska, and Indianapolis, Indiana (in spring 2001). How do the robots help? Robots are waterproof and do not have noses, and so they are not bothered by working in the sewer. They do not complain, nor do they get sick. As a matter of fact, they work faster than humans when it comes to laying the fiber-optic cables inside the sewer system.

What does it cost? The company claims that laying the fiber-optic cable with robots costs about the same as the old method. The major advantage is that it can be done 60 percent faster and without distruption to people's lives.

CLEANING TRAIN STATIONS IN JAPAN. With growing amounts of rubbish to deal with at Japanese train stations and fewer people willing to work as cleaners, officials have started turning the dirty work over to robots. Since May 1993, the Central Japan Railway Company and Sizuko Company, a Japanese machinery maker, have been using robots programmed to vacuum rubbish. A railway official said the robots, which are capable of doing the work of ten people each, have been operating at the Sizuko station in Central Japan. The robots measure about 1.5 meters wide and 1.2 meters long. The railway and Sizuko spent 70 million yen to develop the machines and are planning to program them for other tasks, such as sweeping and scrubbing.

For Further Exploration: If robots are so effective, what will be the impact on unemployment when more tasks are robotized? What will people do if robots take over?

Sources: Compiled from the *New York Times*, March 6, 2001; from the *Wall Street Journal*, November 21, 2000; and from "Robots Used to Clean Train Station in Japan," the *Sunday Times* (Singapore), June 6, 1993. See also "The Robot Revolution Is on the Way," *International Herald Tribune*, September 18, 2000.

ality. In 2001, the site had over 2 million visitors *each day* from all over the world.

Of the thousands of other applications related to health care it is interesting to point out the administrative systems, which range from insurance fraud detection (e.g., by IBM's Fraud and Abuse Management System) to nursing scheduling and financial and marketing management. Another interesting application is a small transistor that a sick person can wear on a necklace. If the person needs help, a computer chip automatically activates the telephone to notify an operator who can contact an emergency service or a physician.

On June 26, 1998, the first China-America Internet medical video teleconferencing was initiated. Doctors in Xian Medical University communicated over the Internet with American doctors at Stanford Medical School. Now, doctors can discuss complex medical cases not only on the telephone, but also with the support of pictures and sound. The issue of how to disseminate health-related (and other) information in developing countries is an important one. Furthermore, it is not just a question of bandwidth, but also of being able to identify which Web sites provide the kind of information likely to be of value. To this end, some Web pages in Hong Kong have been created that try to capture both country-specific and domain-specific information for developing countries. (You can explore these pages at *is.cityu.edu.hk/research/resources/itdc/itdc.htm*.)

...in Public Service

CRIME FIGHTING AND OTHER BENEFITS. Computer applications can benefit society in a variety of other ways. Here are some examples:

- Electronic sensors and computers reduce traffic congestion in many major cities from Los Angeles to Tokyo.
- A geographical information system helps the San Bernardino Sheriff's Department to better visualize crime patterns and allocate resources.
- A computerized voice-mail system is used in Rochester, New York, so that homeless and other needy people can find jobs, access health care resources, and gain independent living skills.
- IT provides many devices for disabled people. Examples include a bilingual notebook computer for blind students, a two-way writing telephone, a robotic page-turner, a hair-brusher, and a hospital-bedside video trip to the zoo or the museum.
- Since 1997, information about sex offenders has been available on the Internet, so that people can be aware of whether previously convicted offenders are living in their localities. (See Group Activity 2.)
- Los Angeles County has a sophisticated computer program for reporting evaluation and tracking of over 150,000 gang members in the county. The program significantly helps reduce gang crime.
- Electronic imaging and fax enhance searching for missing children. In addition to its Web site (*missingkids.com*), which attracts more than a million hits each day, the Center for Missing and Exploited Children can send high-quality photos plus text to many fax machines and to portable machines in police cars. Computers have improved the quality of fax transmission and increased the number of people exposed to the announcements.

Technology and Privacy

Throughout the book we have provided examples of invasion of privacy by IT applications. One of the major debates involves situations in which police are using technology to reduce crime. Here is an example:

Scanning Crowds for Criminals. It happened in January 2001, during the Super Bowl game in Tampa, Florida. Video cameras took a picture of each of 100,000 fans when they entered the stadium. No one knew about it, so permissions were not obtained. Within seconds, thousands of photos were compared with digital portraits of known criminals and suspected terrorists; several matches were found. The technology is not new, but its magnitude and speed is. Never before had such a large number of people been photographed and the photos analyzed in such a short time. The vendors of such systems are Visionics Corp, Viisage [*sic*] Technology, and Graphic Technologies.

Is this technology Big Brother watching over you, or just a friendly uncle? The ACLU says it is Big Brother. The police say it is the uncle, trying to protect the public. Who do you think is right?

Virtual Society

The term **virtual society** refers to all components that are part of a society's culture based on the functional rather than the physical structure. It includes significant IT-enhanced effects or actions, behavior of nonphysical entities, and remotely located members. Companies no longer talk about "work at home" programs. Rather, they talk about "work anywhere, anytime," with laptops, fax machines, mobile devices, networks, e-mail, and voice mail transforming work and communication into the virtual society. Societal changes are coming with the new generation who has grown up online (Roberts-Witt, 2000). (For the IT-related implications of the transformation to a virtual society, see Igbaria, 1999.)

Information Technology and Employment Level

During the last 30 years, there has been an ongoing debate regarding the possibility of massive unemployment resulting from the increased use of IT. The debate is between a group of economists that believe in massive unemployment and a group that believe that this will not occur. Both groups contain very prominent economists, including Nobel Prize recipients Leontief (1986) arguing for the massive unemployment and Simon (1977) arguing against it. The arguments are summarized in Table 16.1.

This debate about how IT will affect employment raises a few other questions: Is unemployment really socially undesirable? Should the government intervene more in the distribution of income and in the determination of the employment level? Can the "invisible hand" in the economy, which has worked so well in the past, continue to be successful in the future? Will IT make most of us idle but wealthy? (Robots will do the work, and people will enjoy life.) Should the issue of income be completely separated from that of employment?

The answers to these questions will be provided in part by the developments in future IT, but they must also be influenced by cultural differences. While some countries have governments rich enough to make income taxes a thing of the past (e.g., Brunei), this is not the case for most. Some countries (or communities within countries) have unemployment rates of 50 percent or more (e.g., East Timor, Kosovo). While the rates in others may seem low (typically 1.5 percent in Hong Kong), these must be measured against the need of people in society for work, as well as the ability or intention of the government to provide a social safety net. For example, Hong Kong lacks such a comprehensive safety net, and many eligible claimants believe it below their dignity to claim anyway—they would prefer to *earn* a living rather than to depend on the government. When

TABLE 16.1 Is Mass Unemployment Coming? Arguments on Both Sides of the Question

Massive Unemployment Will Come	No Massive Unemployment
• Benefit/cost advantage of computers increases with time. • Less skillful employees are needed. • Shifting displaced employees to services is getting difficult. • Many employees lost their jobs in the 1990s. • Hidden unemployment exists in many organizations. • Millions of help-desk employees will be replaced by intelligent agents. • E-commerce will cause millions of intermediaries and agents to lose their jobs. • The unemployment levels in certain countries is high and is increasing. • There is an upper limit to customer consumption.	• New occupations and jobs have always been created by automation. • There is much less unemployment in countries that use more automation. • Work can be expanded to accommodate everyone. • Conversion to automation is slow, and the economy can adjust. • There will always be some areas where people are better than machines. • People will work less but will have more money. • E-commerce reduces the cost of many goods and services; thus their consumption will increase, resulting in more buying and more jobs.

unemployment reaches 3 or 4 percent in Hong Kong, as during the recent Asian financial crisis, this is considered a very high rate. In other countries, for example, in North America and Western Europe, 3 to 4 percent may be considered unimaginably low.

Digital Divide

The term **digital divide** refers to the gap in computer technology in general, and now in Web technology in particular, between those who have such technology and those who do not. A digital divide exists both within and among countries. The problem, from a societal point of view, is that the gap is increasing rapidly. In 2001, for example, only 5 percent of the world's population used the Web, and the vast majority of this 5 percent was located in the developed economies of North America, Europe, South East and East Asia, and Australia. The issue is how to close the gap.

As technologies develop and become less expensive, the speed at which the gap can be closed will accelerate. For example, it is expensive to have a DSL-based broadband line to access the Internet today (2001), but it has been forecasted that it could cost as little as $10/month in 2005. Yet even this is expensive in some countries where wages are only several dollars a day. Cell phones will also increase inexpensive access to the Internet as well as Web TV.

According to Narayana Murthy, CEO of Infosys Technologies of India, IT and the Web can turn poor countries such as India into economic powerhouses. They can also help dissolve rigid social barriers (see Bodwo, 2000). One of the developments that can close the digital divide is the Internet kiosks in public places and cybercafés.

CYBERCAFÉS AND PUBLIC WEB TERMINALS. When you travel today, even to remote places such as the town of Shigatze in Tibet, or Phi Phi island in Thailand, you are likely to see a sign: *Internet café,* or *cybercafé.* **Cybercafés** come in all shapes and sizes, ranging from a chain of cafés (*easyeverything.com,* and *easy.com*) that include hundreds of terminals in one location (e.g., 760 in one New York setting), to a single computer in a corner of many restaurants. According to search engine *cybercaptive.com*, there were more than 6,000 cybercafés in more than 150 countries, in spring 2001. Computers have popped up in many other public locations: discos, laundromats, karaoke bars, bookstores, CD stores, hotel lobbys, and convenience stores. Some facilities give free access to patrons; others charge a small fee.

International Implications

As a result of advancements in information technology, such as the increased speed of communications and information flow, we are living in a shrinking world. In fact, more than 35 years ago, Marshall McLuhan coined the term "global village" to refer to this very concept. The power of the media is growing as a result of cable television, electronic publishing, and networking through computer modems.

Many countries, willingly or unwillingly, knowingly or unknowingly, are being westernized as a result of information about western ways of life and values flowing freely across borders. This has the potential to fuel the fires of political unrest, especially in nondemocratic countries. Access to IT equipment such as facsimile machines, computer disks, and electronic publishing, could be used to assist the masses in planning revolts and attempting to overthrow the government. Therefore, how these advancements in technology are viewed depends upon where one's affiliations lie.

As an example, in 1996, China blocked hundreds of western Web sites from being viewed on the Internet in China. This is not difficult to achieve, as the Chinese government maintains a strict control over Internet service providers (ISPs). Any ISP that failed to follow government guidelines about which Web sites to block would at the very least lose its licence to operate—and at the worst, its owners might be judged undesirable, reactionary, and antisocial elements. The punishment for such a charge varies from hard labor to execution, depending on the extent and severity of the crime.

Challenge to Free Speech versus Internet Indecency

Federal lawmakers in the United States and other countries are battling to protect children from being exposed to what is described by Senator James Exon, sponsor of the 1996 Communication Decency Act, as the "worst, most vile, and most perverse pornography." Immediately after passage, the act was ruled unconstitutional, as a violation of the First Amendment.

The problem of Internet pornography is very serious (see Elmer-Dewitt, 1995), since it is difficult to decide what is indecent and next to impossible to control what is delivered on Web sites from other countries. The U.S. Supreme Court was considering this issue at the time this book was written. In the meantime, it is clearly the responsibility of Internet companies and advertisers to do whatever they can to minimize the problem by issuing guidelines.

It is also valuable to consider that some countries take an entirely different line with respect to freedom of speech—for reasons that have much to do with culture. In many parts of Asia, for instance, the rights of the individual are subservient to those of society. In these countries, the lengthy and heated debate about communication decency and pornography is not even an issue. It is simply illegal to produce such information, let alone permit it to be distributed through a medium such as the Internet. In some countries, lengthy jail sentences or the death penalty are handed down to people for possessing these materials. In others, it may be permissable to view such material on Web sites abroad, but it is illegal to maintain Web sites that store such information.

In general, in many societies it is believed that the right to freedom of speech needs to be balanced by a duty to protect people, or not to harm them. If in doubt, or if it is difficult to identify what types of material are likely to be harmful, people tend to err on the side of caution. Fundamentally, constitutions and their amendments are valid only so long as the majority of people in a given society believe that they are reasonable. At some point, they are changed as the society evolves and moves in new directions. According to Lee (2001), about 20 countries are filtering Internet pornography.

Other Impacts

SOCIAL RESPONSIBILITY. Organizations need to be motivated to utilize IT to improve the quality of life in the workplace. This challenge relates not only to companies that produce IT hardware and software but also to companies that use these technologies. Increased exposure to the concepts and actual use of IT will bring pressure on public agencies and corporations to employ the latest capabilities for solving social problems outside the workplace as well. This is part of the organization's **social responsibility**, a willingness to take active measures to respond to social issues and to contribute to social improvements.

SOCIAL SERVICES AND PRIVACY. Conflicting public pressures may rise to suppress the use of IT because of concerns about privacy and "Big Brother" government. The absence of public pressure, or government intransigence, may see such concerns pushed aside. For example, for many years Hong Kong citizens have had to carry an identity card. One cogent justification for this requirement relates to the ongoing fight against illegal immigration into Hong Kong, as officers of the Hong Kong Police Force randomly spot-check ID cards in the street. The Hong Kong government now proposes to reissue all ID cards as smart ID cards — cards that will be able to capture significantly more data, such as driving permit and health information. Such a card may raise many privacy concerns. See the discussion at *pco.org.hk/*. While some can see many benefits, others are concerned about their privacy.

The World Trade Center Disaster: Implications for IT Management

The Sept. 11, 2001 terrorists' attack on the World Trade Center (WTC) brought to our attention the important role of several IT topics and their management. Here are the major ones.

THE ROLE OF THE INTERNET, SEARCH ENGINES, AND CHAT ROOMS. Following the disaster, the use of the Internet increased by about tenfold, with some sites (e.g., CNN) facing a volume increase of over 150-fold. The Internet and search engines were used for:

- Providing news to millions around the globe.
- Enabling people to find other people, public agencies, emergency services, and other important disaster relief information.
- Helping survivors, relatives, and other concerned individuals to feel somewhat encouraged that they were not suffering alone. People were trying to reach out to each other to share some sense of community. Many special chat areas were created.
- Allowing Americans and people from many other nations to vent fears, frustrations, and anger to a virtual community.
- Enabling people to search information about related topics such as WTC, Pentagon, Bin Laden, and Pearl Harbor. These replaced normal topics such as the NFL and perennial favorites like Pamela Anderson Lee and Britney Spears (usually among the top 10 terms searched on the Internet).

The front pages of search engines (e.g., Alta Vista, Lycos) and portals such as Yahoo! were drastically altered to meet the users' needs.

Several Web sites were virtually unavailable in the hours immediately after the attack, due to traffic overload. Several search engines were available but brought back no listings relevant to the WTC catastrophe.

PRIVACY VS. SECURITY. A dramatic shift in the debate over IT privacy was observed: Before it was a tug of war between protectors of civil liberties on one side and government intelligence gatherers on the other. In September 2001 it became an emotional weighing of personal rights vs. national security with a shift in favor of stepping up government eavesdropping.

Some of the immediate changes:

- The Data Protection Act was relaxed so ISPs were able to provide traffic data to the police in several countries.
- A global request was made for encryption software makers to let government authorities crack their tools.

- New anti-terrorist legislation was introduced in the U.S. that would make it easier for the FBI to wiretap phones and e-mails.
- The use of disposable cell phones (preloaded with a finite number of calling minutes and then useless) and telephone cards became a security risk since anonymous calls are difficult to track.
- ID smart cards, which are very difficult to forge, are becoming mandatory in some countries. The U.S. Congress is deliberating the issue.

WHY THE STOCK MARKETS WERE CLOSED FOR 4 DAYS. The IT operations of NYSE and Nasdaq were not damaged much because most of their facilities are outside New York and they had all the needed disaster recovery systems. Of special interest was Nasdaq. According to R. Yasin, "Nasdaq keeps systems up and running . . . . reliance on multiple communications carriers and a distributed IT infrastructure helped Nasdaq keep systems running after the attack." (*InformationWeek.com,* Sept. 21, 2001) However, the operation of many of the more than 100 trading companies located in Manhattan were disrupted. Many of these had network problems while others needed to relocate operations to backup centers. Therefore, despite the help provided by the exchanges to the trading partners, it took 5 days to restore the overall operations.

THE BENEFITS OF DISASTER-RECOVERY PLANNING AND ACTION. The WTC disaster highlighted the need for data storage and backup, for disaster recovery planning, and for operational communication systems. Large companies tend to have sophisticated disaster recovery plans as well as "hot" backups which enable them to roll the applications over in real time. Smaller firms may rely on backing up data to tape and sending the tapes off site. Here is how a medium-sized bank and a small legal office were affected.

> Singapore-based Overseas Union Bank (OUB) had its New York office on the 39th floor of the WTC. As soon as the CNN news reached Singapore (it was 9:30 pm there), the *business continuity* plan was placed into action. A recovery team was mobilized in minutes. An immediate attempt was made to find survivors. Fortunately all 13 employees survived. Second, it was necessary to recover as soon as possible and resume operation. The employees and the recovery team had been drilled for a disaster before, so they knew that they needed to move to the back-up site outside New York. But this was not possible. So, OUB solicited the help of a business partner and a new business recovery plan was drafted in hours. Using borrowed computers and phone lines, OUB employees extracted data from their computer back-up system reconstructing the business. It took a relatively short time to resume normal operation and the financial damage was minimal.
>
> But, many small businesses had no disaster planning and some did not even have backup files. An example is the Jan He Law office of China that operated from the 77th floor of the WTC. While all employees survived, all the firm client files stored in computers were gone. The firm was unable even to contact their clients, since all the telephone numbers were only in the computers. The damage was enormous. (*Source:* Compiled from S. S. Luh, "Preparing for the Worst," *Asia Wall Street Journal,* Sept. 21–23, 2001.)

BIOMETRIC SECURITY SYSTEMS. These systems grant or deny access to buildings and information by automatically verifying the identity of people through their distinctive physical or behavioral traits. Of special interest is the facial recognition, the same as that used during the 2001 Super Bowl, stirring a debate over invasion of privacy.

ONLINE CROOKS EXPLOIT WTC DISASTER. Several shameless con artists attempted to profit from the situation. Attempts were made to solicit donations for the survivors of the attacks and relatives of the victims. As an example, a widespread e-mail solicited donations for the Red Cross, but the link led to an imitation of the popular relief organization's Web site.

There were also unethical and offensive uses of the Internet for spinning the attacks into marketing events, for example, selling life insurance. Some even were selling commemorative products related to the disaster.

FOR THE FUTURE. In the future computers will be able to better track and detect in advance suspicious activities. Surveillance will be made even from tiny, non-manned, computerized planes. Immediately after the attack, the MIT Artificial Intelligence Laboratory brainstormed ideas such as designing buildings that can heal themselves, personal black boxes that could help locate disaster survivors, and detectors to track suspects by their nervous behavior or even smell (*ai.mit.edu*). One like MIT's ongoing project is development of software that will be able to detect unusual activities in parking lots, driveways, or areas around potential targets of terrorists. The software makes interpretations and alerts for anything that does not look normal. As the United States and the world adjust to life after the September 11 terrorist attacks, it is virtually certain that information technology will play an increasingly large role.

16.5 VIRTUAL COMMUNITIES

A *community* is a group of people who interact. A **virtual community** is one in which the interaction is done by using the Internet. Therefore it is also called an **Internet community** or an **electronic community**. Virtual communities parallel typical physical communities such as neighborhoods, clubs, or associations. Virtual communities offer several ways for members to interact, collaborate, and trade (see Table 16.2).

An Internet community may have millions of members. This is one of the major differences between Internet communities and physical communities, which are mostly smaller. Internet communities could have significant effects on e-markets. Another difference is that offline communities are frequently in geographical proximity, whereas only a few online communities are of this type. Geographical proximity, of course, is not significant for Internet communities—in terms of making contact, they are only as far away as one's computer. Many thousands of communities exist on the Net.

Types of Communities

In order to understand the economic impact of electronic communities, let us look more deeply into what they are. Hagel and Armstrong (1997) recognize four types of virtual communities: communities of transactions, of interest or purpose, of relations, and of fantasy.

COMMUNITIES OF TRANSACTIONS. *Communities of transactions* facilitate buying and selling. Members include buyers, sellers, intermediaries, and so on. An example is Virtual Vineyards (*evineyards.com*), which, in addition to selling wines,

TABLE 16.2 Elements of Interactions in Virtual Communities

Category	Element
Communication	Bulletin boards (discussion groups) Chat rooms/threaded discussions (string Q&A) E-mail and instant messaging Private mailboxes Newsletters, "netzines" (electronic magazines) Web postings Voting
Information	Directories and yellow pages Search engines Member-generated content Links to information sources Expert advice
E-commerce element	Electronic catalogs and shopping carts Advertisements Auctions of all types Bartering online Classified advertisement

provides expert information on wines and a place for wine lovers to chat with each other. The fishing community (see Minicase 1) is another example.

COMMUNITIES OF INTEREST OR PURPOSE. In *communities of interest or purpose*, people have the chance to interact with each other on a specific topic. For example, if you are interested in gardening, try *gardenweb.com*. The Motley Fool (*fool.com*) is a forum for individual investors. *Planet-rugby.com/index.html/rugby365* gets rugby fans, and music lovers go to *mp3.com*. *City411.com* provides comprehensive information about local physical communities where many topics such as entertainment, traffic, and weather reports are displayed.

Geocities' (*geocities.com*) millions of members are organized into thousands of clubs. These clubs are merged with Yahoo!'s discussion list (Geocities is not part of Yahoo!). Members have a marketplace for buying and selling goods and services. *Webchatting.com* serves a cyber-community of millions of women affiliated with *womantoday.com*. Members congregate there to chat, as they also do at *chat.yahoo.com*.

COMMUNITIES OF RELATIONS OR PRACTICE. *Communities of relations or practice* are organized around certain life experiences, situations, or vacations. For example, the cancer forum on CompuServe contains information and exchange of opinions regarding cancer. Parent Soup is a favorite gathering spot for parents, seniors like to visit "SeniorNet" (*seniornet.com*) and *ivillage.com* is a well-known online community aimed at women, with regular celebrity chats and discussions.

Many communities of practice are organized according to professional business interests. For example, *plasticsnet.com* is used by thousands of engineers in the plastics industry. A related exchange, *commerx.com*, provides a cybermarket for the industry. These communities offer opportunities for the translation of the community interest into commercial revenue.

COMMUNITIES OF FANTASY. In *communities of fantasy,* participants create imaginary environments. For example, AOL subscribers can pretend to be medieval barons at the Red Dragon Inn. On ESPNet, participants can create competing teams and "play" with Michael Jordan. Other communities of fantasy offer large numbers of games that thousands of people play simultaneously. For $10 a month, you can join a team at Aliens online; at Politike you can plot with and against other players; and Kingdom of Drakkar allows you to play various roles.

Business Aspects of Internet Communities

Virtual communities can create value in several ways, as summarized in Figure 16.3. Members input useful information to the community in the form of comments, feedback, and information needs. This input is retrieved and used by other members of the community or by marketers. The community organizers may also establish for-fee services. For example, at *espn.com,* a community of sports lovers, you pay a subscription fee that allows you to view certain events in real time.

Another possibility for value creation in virtual communities arises from the fact that the community brings together consumers of specific demographics and interests. This presents opportunities for transacting business, and for communicating messages about products and services, which marketers and advertisers value and are willing to pay for.

Other opportunities arise from the marketing information that is generated within communities, which marketers and advertisers find valuable. Such information includes demographics and psychographics of members; their attitudes and beliefs about products, services, and issues; their behavior data with regard to business transactions within communities; and information on their interactions and interaction dynamics. Such information, which is collected from chat rooms, questionnaires, or e-mail communications, could be sold to marketers and advertisers if the members do not object. For a look at the ways companies can benefit by using communities to make connections with members and exploit such opportunities, see Hagel and Armstrong (1997), Preece (2000), and Bressler and Grantham (2000). For ways to manage Internet communities, see McWilliam (2000).

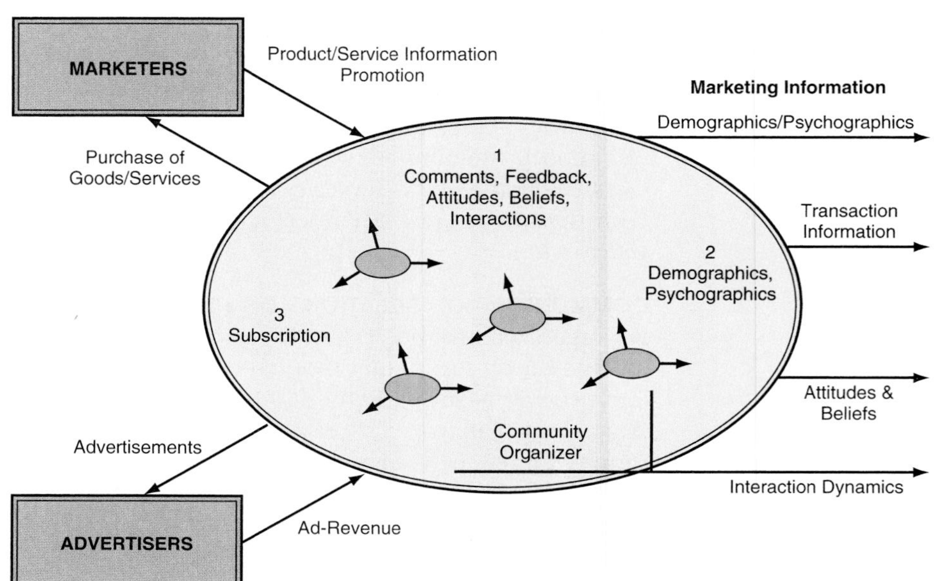

FIGURE 16.3 Value creation in virtual communities. (*Source:* Kannan et al., 1998, *Communications of the ACM.* P. K. Kannan © 1998 Association for Computing Machinery, Inc. Reprinted by permission.)

16.6 CONCLUDING THOUGHTS

Throughout this book we demonstrated how the new or digital economy is changing the manner in which business is done and how IT helps organizations to transform themselves so they can survive and prosper. Now that you are familiar with the IT technologies, applications, and implementation, we can summarize the major lessons learned from this book.

As stated earlier, the major concern of most organizations today is how to transform themselves into a "new organization" adaptable to the new economy. It seems that everyone recognizes Darwin's proposition for survival: the ability to properly and quickly adapt to changes in the environment. Therefore, it is necessary first to understand how the environment is changing. As we showed in this book, change in the business environment is demonstrated not only in the increased competition and globalization, but also in fundamental changes that are occurring in industry structures, distribution channels, production systems, and more. The creation of vertical and horizontal exchanges, for example, may place organizations in a position such that they must make critical decisions in order to survive.

IT is the major driver of the new economy. But IT can also save organizations, helping them to adjust and survive. Let's revisit Rosenbluth's case in Chapter 3. IT caused the major pressures on the travel-agency industry, threatening its survival. The company devised a survival strategy that could have been implemented only with IT support. While for most companies such a radical change is not needed, a do-nothing strategy can lead to disaster.

Here are some of the actions demonstrated in this book that should be considered by organizations, so they can transform themselves to be "digital-economy ready":

- Build strategic information systems and use innovations such as electronic auctions and exchanges to sustain competitive advantage (Chapters 3 and 5).
- Create effective and efficient communication and collaboration networks. Use groupware and intelligent agents to enable your systems to support your rapidly changing operations (Chapter 4).
- Examine possible new models and initiatives of e-commerce. There exist many opportunities in B2B, B2C, B2E, and more (Chapter 5). But you need to carefully plan the new systems and their introduction into the organization (Chapters 8 and 14).
- Examine supply chains. For most organizations, the contribution of IT is mainly along the supply chain. IT will help you to buy, sell, collaborate with supply chain partners, and make your customers happy. The extended supply chain concept implies the need for extreme integration. It must take place not only along the supply chain inside a company but also along the entire chain including customers and suppliers, as well as initiatives such as CRM and e-commerce. Such integration is possible only with support of software such as second-generation ERP (Chapter 6).
- Make a continuous effort to increase productivity, quality, security, and effectiveness in every facet of the organization's operations. Traditional functional areas such as finance, manufacturing, and marketing are changing—but not disappearing. Therefore, efforts to improve functional operations are needed. It is mostly IT innovations that enable continuous improvement ef-

forts. In addition, integration of functional activities is often required, especially in undertakings such as CRM (Chapter 7).

- In moving to a digital-economy-ready status, carefully plan IT systems in coordination with the business plans they intend to support (Chapter 8). Furthermore, the transformation to a new-economy organization will, in some cases, require you to fundamentally change many of your business processes, organizational structure, and organization climate. Such changes require a BPR approach (Chapter 8).
- Increase recognition of knowledge, and its creation, preservation, storage, and dissemination. An increased focus on knowledge is a major characteristic of the new economy. Knowledge management (Chapter 9) enables organizations to properly handle the ever-increasing amount of knowledge in organizations.
- Support managerial decisions with IT and especially the Web. In the new economy the importance of managerial decision making is increasing. It is critical for many organizations, especially medium and large ones, as shown in Chapter 10.
- Have the ability to process a large amount of data, especially for e-commerce and Web-based initiatives. Two important innovations, data warehousing and data mining, are extremely useful (Chapter 11). These can be supported by innovative computer-based visualization technologies.
- Facilitate innovation and creativity in digital economy applications by using intelligent systems. Different kinds of computer-based intelligent systems help us to improve productivity and sustain competitive advantage (Chapter 12).
- Carefully address the economies of IT in general and e-commerce in particular, including outsourcing, when moving to the new economy. While IT is necessary for survival for many organizations, an overdose or an incorrect mix of applications can be unhealthy or even dangerous. The methods of how to achieve a correct mix of applications are outlined in Chapter 13.
- Properly build and deploy information systems that will provide for internal efficiency and connect to the many business partners. This is a must for survival (Chapter 14).
- Manage the increasing information resources in both business units and a centralized IS department. Careful cooperation and coordination are essential. Furthermore, as the importance of information systems increases, so does the need for security (Chapter 15).
- Finally, address organizational, personal, and socioeconomic issues associated with the increased use of IT. These issues must be addressed especially when large-scale transformations are involved (Chapter 16).

Participants in Beyond Computing's 1997 Executive Forum discovered that they had a lot in common (Kleinschrod, 1997). Most notably, they found that information technology was helping to *reshape* their organizations in *dramatic ways*. The more you understand the issues involved in IT, the better able you will be to manage and lead organizations in their transformation.

This book is about IT use and its management throughout the organization and beyond. IT provides a comprehensive view of the most important issues in IT management. It is our hope that the knowledge presented here will prepare you to be an effective manager in the digital age.

MANAGERIAL ISSUES

1. ***Supporting people with disabilities.*** Lawsuits against employers for repetitive strain injuries are on the increase under the U.S. Federal Disabilities Act. Because this law is relatively new, court cases may be very costly.

2. ***Culture is important.*** Multinational corporations face different cultures in the different countries in which they are doing business. What might be ethical in country A may be unethical in country B—even if it is technically legal in both. Therefore, it is essential to develop a country-specific ethics code in addition to a corporatewide one. Also, managers should realize that in some countries there is no legislation specifically concerned with computers and data.
3. ***The impact of the Web.*** The impacts of e-commerce and the Internet can be so strong that the entire manner in which companies do business will be changed. Impacts on procedures, people, organizational structure, management, and business processes may be significant.
4. ***IT can cause layoffs.*** The spread of IT may result in massive layoffs in some companies. Management should be aware of this possibility and have a contingency plan regarding appropriate reaction.
5. ***Making money from electronic communities.*** Electronic communities are not just a social phenomena. Many of these communities provide an opportunity for a business to generate sales and profits.
6. ***Information anxiety may create problems.*** Make sure that your employees do not suffer from information anxiety. Companies provide considerable onsite recreational facilities to ease stress and anxiety.

ON THE WEB SITE... Additional resources, including the Virtual Company, quizzes, cases, updates, additional exercises, links, demos, and activities, can be found on the book's Web site.

KEY TERMS

Cybercafés *714*
Dehumanization *705*
Digital divide *714*
Electronic community *718*
Ergonomics *706*
Information anxiety *705*
Internet community *718*
Job content *703*
Job stress *706*
Quality of life *709*
Social responsibility *715*
Span of control *701*
Virtual community *718*
Virtual society *712*

CHAPTER HIGHLIGHTS (Numbers Refer to Learning Objectives)

❶ IT has significant impacts on organization (structure, operations, etc.), on individuals (negative and positive), and on society (positive and negative).

❷ The major negative impacts of IT are in the areas of invasion of privacy, unemployment, and dehumanization.

❷ Dehumanization is a major concern that needs to be overcome by proper design and planning of information systems.

❸ Because of IT, organizational structure is changing, organizations are getting flatter, teams play a major role, power is redistributed (more power to those that control IT), jobs are restructured, supervision can be done from a distance, and decision making is supported by computers.

3 Computers can increase health risks to eyes, back, bones, and muscles. Ergonomically designed computing facilities can greatly reduce the health risks associated with computers.

3 Information technology can change lines of authority, job content, and status of employees. As a result, the manager's job and methods of supervision and decision making may drastically change.

4 Many positive social implications can be expected from IT. They include providing opportunities to people with disabilities, improving health care, fighting crime, increasing productivity, and reducing people's exposure to hazardous situations.

4 In one view, IT will cause massive unemployment because of increased productivity, reduced required skill levels, and the potential reduction of employment in all sectors of the economy.

4 In another view, IT will increase employment levels because automation makes products and services more affordable, thus increasing demand; and the process of disseminating automation is slow enough to allow the economy to adjust to information technologies.

4 Quality of life, both at work and at home, is likely to improve as a result of IT.

5 Virtual communities of different types are spreading over the Web, providing opportunities to some companies to increase revenues and profit.

QUESTIONS FOR REVIEW

1. Describe how IT can have negative effects on people.
2. What are some of the major impacts of IT on individuals?
3. Describe some of the potential risks to human health caused by extensive use of computers.
4. List the major societal impacts of IT that are described in this chapter, and categorize each of them as either negative or positive.
5. Present three major arguments of those who believe that IT will result in massive unemployment.
6. Present three major arguments of those who believe that IT will *not* result in massive unemployment.
7. Define information anxiety.
8. Define digital divide.
9. Define virtual society.
10. Discuss the following organizational impacts: flatter organizations, increased span of control, power redistribution, supervision, and decision making.
11. Define the Internet community and list its four types.

QUESTIONS FOR DISCUSSION

1. Consider the design features for a picture-map–based navigation system for private car owners. What kind of constraints exist? Is there a universal standard for user-friendliness? How safe is such a system—that is, do you have to stop concentrating on driving in order to use it? What ethical concerns might be raised through such a system? How could it be abused?
2. Clerks at 7-Eleven stores enter data regarding customers (gender, approximate age, and so on) into the computer. These data are then processed for improved decision making. Customers are not informed about this nor are they asked for permission. (Names are *not* keyed in.) Do you see any problems with the clerks' actions?
3. Many hospitals, health maintenance organizations (HMOs), and federal agencies are converting, or plan to convert, all patients' medical records from paper to electronic storage (using imaging technology). Once completed, electronic storage will enable quick access to most records. However, the availability of these records in a database and on networks may allow people, some of whom are unauthorized, to view one's private data. To protect privacy fully may cost too much money and/or may considerably slow accessibility to the records. What policies could health-care administrators use in such situations? Discuss.
4. Northeast Utilities (Hartford, CT) has its meter readers gather information about services needed on its customers' homes, such as a driveway or fence requiring repairs. It sells the data to companies that would stand to gain from the information. Customers are then solicited via direct mail, telemarketing, and so on for the services that the meter readers record as being needed. While some customers welcome this approach, others consider it an annoyance because they are not interested in the particular repairs. Assess the value of the company's IT initiative against the potential negative effects of adverse public reaction.
5. IT may have both positive and negative societal effects in the same situation. Give two examples, and explain how to reconcile such a case.
6. It is said that IT has raised many new privacy issues. Why is this so?

7. Relate virtual communities to virtual society.
8. Several examples in this book illustrate how information about individuals can help companies improve their businesses and also benefit customers. Summarize some examples, and explain why they may result in invasion of privacy.
9. Robots take jobs away from people. Describe the considerations that management will be faced with when it needs to decide whether to use robots in an organization.
10. Explore the effects of the U.S. Americans with Disabilities Act on productivity and cost as it relates to IT. Should this act also exist in all other countries around the world? Discuss.
11. Explain why organizations are becoming flatter and what the implications are for management practices.
12. Discuss the benefits of a virtual community to its members, society, and agents of e-commerce.

EXERCISES

1. Review the opening case regarding wearable computers.
   a. Identify all the issues in this case that involve changes to the way people work.
   b. Advise Bell Canada's president as to any sensitivities that she or he may need to consider if extending this pilot program to the whole company.
2. Schafer (1996) pointed out that companies in industries such as the fishing industry must take advantage of IT to become intensely efficient. But as a result, they simply may run out of scarce natural resources. So, the technology that was a savior may wipe many people out of business. Discuss the dilemma, and examine the situation in other industries such as oil and coal. What are the possible solutions?
3. Visit the following virtual communities: *wbs.net, geocities.com, well.com, electricminds.com,* and *espn.go.com/malu.html.* Join one of the communities. Become a member of the community and report on your experiences.
4. Will the Web eat your job? Read Baatz's (1996) paper. What types of jobs are most likely to disappear or be drastically reduced? Why?
5. Research the status of IT helping people with disabilities. Visit the following sites: *abletowork.org, usdoj.gov./crt/ada/adahom1.htm, halftheplanet.com,* and *ican.com.* Write a status report on the latest innovations in this area.

GROUP AND ROLE-PLAYING ACTIVITIES

1. China has strengthened its control of the Internet with an extension of its criminal laws to cover the revealing of state secrets and spreading of computer viruses. The new laws were drafted in order "to promote the healthy development of the Internet and protect national security." They also make it an offense "to use the Internet to promote religious cults, hurt national unity, or undermine the government." (*Source:* William Kazer, writing for the *South China Morning Post,* December 30, 2000.)

   These laws raise as many concerns as they solve existing problems. Clearly governments have a strong need to protect their vital interests, but the new laws seem quite sweeping. The vagueness of expressions like "hurting national unity" may be particularly awkward—the intention is to prevent secession, but what constitutes a "nation" is itself arguable.
   a. What impacts do you think these new laws will have for citizens of China?
   b. Are the laws really enforceable? (Check the products of Safe Web Corporation that allow you to break Internet blockades.)
   c. Do we need laws to promote the healthy development of the Internet? What aspects of Internet development do you find unhealthy? Would you want to regulate the Internet's development? Create groups that will debate these issues.
2. The State of California maintains a database of people who allegedly abuse children. (The database also includes names of the alleged victims.) The list is made available to dozens of public agencies, and it is considered in cases of child adoption and employment decisions. Because so many people have access to the list, its content is easily disclosed to outsiders. In 1996, an alleged abuser and her child, whose case was dropped but whose names had remained on the list, sued the State of California for invasion of privacy.

   With the class divided into groups, debate the issues involved. Specifically:
   a. Is there a need to include names of people on the list in cases that were dismissed or declared unfounded?
   b. Who should make the decision about what names should be included, and what should the criteria be?
   c. What is the potential damage to the abusers (if any)?
   d. Should the State of California abolish the list? Why or why not?

INTERNET EXERCISES

1. There is considerable talk about the impact of the Internet on society. Concepts such as a global village, an Internet community, the Internet society, and the like are getting much attention (e.g., see *Harvard Business Review*, May/June 1996, and *Business Week*, May 5, 1997). Surf the Internet (e.g., try *google.com*), and prepare a report on the topic. How can companies profit from Internet communities?
2. The Internet and intranets are playing an important role in providing opportunities to people with disabilities. Find more about the topic by surfing the Internet.
3. Enter *internetwk.com/links*.
   a. Get a listing of industry organizations with privacy initiatives.
   b. Check out the W3C's Privacy Preferences Project (*w3c.org*).
4. Enter communities such as the following: *earthweb.com*, *dobedo.co.uk*, *hearme.com*, and *webmed.com*. Find common elements.
5. Investigate the services provided at *clubs.yahoo.com*.
6. Enter *google.com* and go to sources that deal with the "digital divide." Prepare a report on activities done within three countries.

Minicase 1
The Australian Fishing Community

Recreational fishing in Australia is popular both for residents and for international visitors. Over 700,000 Australians regularly fish. The Australian Fishing Shop (AFS) (*ausfish.com.au*) is a small e-tailer, founded in 1994, initially as a hobby site carrying information about recreational fishing. During the last few years the site has evolved into a fishing portal, and it has created a devoted community behind it.

A visit to the site will immediately show that the site is not a regular storefront, but that it actually provides considerable information to the recreational fishing community. In addition to sale of products (rods, reels, clothing, boats, and fishing-related books, software, and CDROMs) and services (fishing charters and holiday packages), the site provides the following information:

- Hints and tips for fishing
- What's new
- A photo gallery of people's catches
- Chat boards—general and specialized
- Directions of boat builders, tackle manufacturing, etc.
- Recipes for cooking fish
- Information about newsgroups and a mailing list
- Free giveaways, competitions
- Links to fishing-related government bodies, other fishing organizations (around the globe and in Australia), and daily weather maps and tides reports
- General information site and FAQs
- List of fishing sites around the globe
- Contact details by phone, post, and e-mail
- Free e-mail Web page hosting

In addition there is an auction mechanism for fishing equipment, and answers are provided to inquiries.

The company is fairly small (gross income of about AU$500,000 a year). How can such a small company survive? The answer can be found in its strategy of providing value-added services to the recreational fishing community. These services attract over 1.6 million visitors each month, from all over the world, of which about 1 percent make a purchase. Also, several advertisers sponsor the site. This is sufficient to survive. Another interesting strategy is to aim at the *global market*. Most of the profit is derived from customers in the United States and Canada who buy holiday and fishing packages.

In terms of products, the company acts basically as a referral service to vendors, so it does not have to carry an inventory. When AFS receives an order, it orders the products from its suppliers. It then manually aggregates the orders from the suppliers and packs and sends them via a service delivery to customers. Some orders are shipped directly from vendors to the customers.

Source: Based on information at *ausfish.com.au*.

Questions for Minicase 1

1. Why is this considered an Internet community?
2. How does the community aspect facilitate revenue?
3. What is the survival CSF (critical success factor) of this company?
4. What is the advantage of being a referral service? What is the disadvantage?
5. Compare the services offered at the AFS Web site with services offered by companies in other countries such as: *daytickets.co.uk*, *fishing-boating.com*, *pvisuals.com/fishing/online*, and *fishingtackleonline.co.nz*.

Minicase 2

American Stock Exchange Seeks Wireless Trades

For about 120 years, traders at the American Stock Exchange (Amex) have used hand signals to relay information about their trades. But in April 1993 Amex introduced a pilot project to test the use of handheld computers in trading. Previous attempts by the Chicago Board of Trade and by the Chicago Mercantile Exchange were not successful. Amex is using simple, off-the-shelf equipment instead of the highly customized terminals used by the Chicago exchanges. The project was the first in a series designed to make Amex a paperless trading floor.

Omer F. Sykan, director of technical planning at Amex, said that the biggest benefit is to get a real-time position analysis to the 462 members of the exchange. Experiments are being done with two different devices. One device is used by market specialists to transmit option trades to a PC-based risk-analysis system. The second device is used for equity (stocks) trading.

Wireless technologies are expected to be faster and more cost-effective than hand signals and the paper-and-pencil trading mechanism that has been in use for the past 70 years. In the old system, specialists receive orders by hand signals and scribble their trades on an order slip. Then a clerk manually enters the data into the computer. If the markets are moving rapidly, the information that the clerk gathers from the floor is often obsolete by the time it is put into the computers. Handheld devices transmit information instantaneously.

While the devices are extremely easy to use, many traders do not welcome them. "We old guys are faster than most of these computers," says Jack Maxwell, a veteran of 26 years with Amex. "To hell with it; I don't need the handhelds." Attitudes of traders like Maxwell are a big problem facing expanded use of computers.

By 1996, the Amex was in the process of implementing the system, first on a voluntary basis. In summer 1998, Amex agreed to merge with NASDAQ, moving to complete automation.

Sources: Based on *Computerworld*, May 17, 1993, p. 6; *Wall Street Journal*, July 19, 1993, p. C1; and *Fortune*, October 28, 1996, p. 52.

Questions for Minicase 2

1. As a consultant to Amex, you need to identify the problems of implementing the handheld computers. How would you approach your task?
2. The president of Amex was considering laying off traders like Maxwell. Would you support such a decision or not?
3. Find the status of the computerization that is going on in several stock and commodity exchanges in several countries.
4. How would you convince a trader, who may soon lose his or her job, to use the new device?

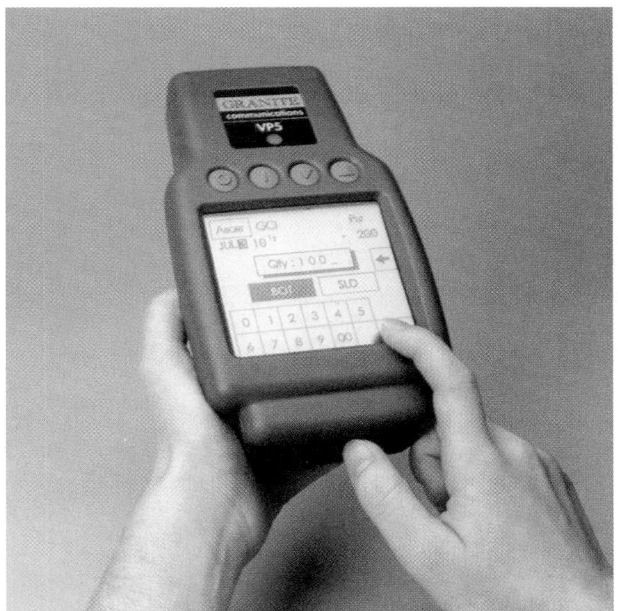

The American Stock Exchange's handheld computer.

REFERENCES AND BIBLIOGRAPHY

1. Agarwal, R., "Individual Acceptance of Information Technology," in R. Zmud (ed.), *Framing the Domain of IT Management*, Cincinnati, OH: Pinnaflex Educational Resources, 2000.
2. Baatz, E. B., "Will the Web Eat Your Job?," *Webmaster*, May–June 1996.
3. Bodow, S., "Murthy's Law," *Business 2.0 (business2.com)*, November 28, 2000.
4. Boonnoon, J., "Phone Technology Is Boon for the Visually Impaired," *The Nation (Thailand)*, March 28, 2000.
5. Bressler, S. E., and C. E. Grantham, *Communities of Commerce*. New York, McGraw Hill, 2000.
6. Butler, S., *EREWHON, or Over the Range* (1923), Shrewsbury Edition. New York: AMS Press; reprinted in 1972.
7. Cone, E., "Keyboard Injuries: Who Should Pay?," *Information Week*, January 27, 1994.
8. Dalton, G., "E-Business Revolution," *Information Week*, June 7, 1999.
9. Davison, R., et al., "Technology Leapfrogging in Developing Countries—An Inevitable Luxury? *City University of Hong Kong*, Working Paper, 2001.
10. Dertougos, M., *The Unfinished Revolution: Human Centered Computers, and What They Can Do for Us*. New York: HarperCollins, 2001.
11. Elmer-Dewitt, P., "On the Screen Near You: Cyberporn," *Time*, July 3, 1995.
12. Flamma, G. "Online Maps: Help or Hindrance?," *IEEE Intelligent Systems*, March–April 1999.
13. Good, D. J., and R. J. Schultz, *Strategic, Organizational and Managerial Impacts of Business Technologies*. New York: Quorum Books, 2000.
14. Gruenwold, J., "Global Disorder," *Interactive Week*, November 27, 2000.
15. Hagel, J., III, and A. G. Armstrong, *Net Gain: Expanding Markets through Virtual Communities*. Boston: Harvard Business School Press, 1997.
16. Hearst, M., "The Changing Relationship Between IT and Society," *IEEE Intelligent Systems*, January–February 1999.
17. Huber, G. P., "A Theory of the Effects of Advanced Information Technologies on Organizational Design, Intelligence, and Decision Making," *Academy of Management Review*, Vol. 15, No. 1, 1990.
18. Igbaria, M., "The Driving Forces in The Virtual Society," *Communications of the ACM*, November 1999.
19. Interactive Week Roundtable, "What Changes Remain for The Web to Work?," *Interactive Week*, January 10, 2000.
20. Jain, R., "Key Constructs in Successful IS Implementation: South-East Asian Experience," *Omega*, Vol. 25, No. 3, 1997.
21. Kageyama, Y., "CyberCars Hit Streets," *Associated Press Release*, July 26, 2000.
22. Kaltnekar, Z., "Information Technology and the Humanization of Work," in *Management Impacts of IT: Perspectives on Organizational Change and Growth*. Harrisburg, PA: Idea Group, 1991.
23. Kanter, J., *Managing with Information*, 4th ed. Englewood Cliffs, NJ: Prentice-Hall, 1992.
24. Kleiner, A., "Corporate Culture in Internet Time," *Strategy-Business* (Booz-Allen & Hamilton Quarterly, *strategy-business.com*), First Quarter, 2000.
25. Kleinschrod, W. A., "Technology Transformation," *Beyond Computing*, July–August 1997.
26. Kraut, R., et al., "Social Impact of the Internet: What Does It Mean?," *Communications of the ACM*, December 2000.
27. Lazzaro, J. J., "Computers for the Disabled," *Byte*, June 1993.
28. Lee, J., "Web Firms Strive to Get Around Governments' Internet Bans," *Herald International Tribune*, April 27, 2001, p. 1.
29. Leontief, W., *The Future Impact of Automation on Workers*. Oxford: Oxford University Press, 1986.
30. Liu, S., et al., "Software Agents for Environmental Scanning in Electronic Commerce," *Informations Systems Frontiers*, Vol. 2, No. 1, 2000.
31. Marshall, K. P., "Has Technology Introducted New Ethical Problems?," *Journal of Business Ethics*, March 1999.
32. McLeod, R. J., "Systems Theory and IRM: Integrating Key Concepts," *Information Resources Management*, Spring 1995.
33. McWilliam, G., "Building Stronger Brand Through Choice Communities," *Sloan Management Review*, Spring 2000.
34. Nevins, M. D., and S. A. Stumpf, "21st Century Leadership: Redefining Management Education," *Strategy-Business* (Booz-Allen & Hamilton Quarterly, *strategy-business.com*), Third Quarter, 1999.
35. O'Connor, C., "Planetary Visions," *Business 2.0 (business2.com)*, December 12, 2000.
36. Ogburn, W. F., "Cultural Lag as Theory," *Sociology and Social Research*, 1957, pp. 167–174.
37. Pickering, C., "Ready, Willing, and Able," *Business 2.0 (business2.com)*, August 22, 2000.
38. Pinsonneault, A., and K. Kraemer, "The Impact of Information Technology on Middle Managers," *MIS Quarterly*, September 1993.
39. Preece, J., *Online Communities*. Chichester, UK: Wiley, 2000.
40. Rifkin, J., *The End of Work*. New York: G. P. Putnam and Sons, 1995.
41. Roberts-Witt, S. L., "The Internet Generation," *Interactive Week*, November 6, 2000.
42. Rogers, M., and T. M. Rajkumar, "Developing E-Commerce Web Sites for the Visually Impaired," *Information Systems Management*, Winter 1999.
43. Routt, C., "The Jobs They Are A-Changing," *The Banker*, December 1999.
44. Schafer, S., "Fished Out," *Inc. Technology*, November 3, 1996.
45. Schwartz, J., "A Robot That Works in the City Sewer," *New York Times*, March 8, 2001.
46. Simon, H., *The New Science of Management Decision*. Englewood Cliffs, NJ, Prentice Hall, 1977.
47. Stellin, S., "Michael Dertouzos: Predicting How Technology Will Connect the Global," *Interactive Week*, November 27, 2000.
48. Toth, K., "The Workless Society," *The Futurist*, May–June 1990.
49. Wurman, R. S., "Redesign the Data Dump," *Business 2.0 (business2.com)*, November 28, 2000.
50. Wurman, R. S., *Information Anxiety 2*. Indianapolis: Macmillan, 2001.

TECHNOLOGY GUIDE

3

Data and Databases

This guide was updated by Linda Lai, at City University of Hong Kong.

T3.1 FILE MANAGEMENT

A computer system organizes data in a hierarchy that begins with bits, and proceeds to bytes, fields, records, files, and databases (see Figure T-3.1). A **bit** represents the smallest unit of data a computer can process (i.e., a 0 or a 1). A group of eight bits, called a **byte**, represents a single character, which can be a letter, a number, or a symbol. A logical grouping of characters into a word, a group of words, or a complete number is called a **field**. For example, a student's name would appear in the name field. A logical group of related fields, such as the student's name, the course taken, the date, and the grade, comprise a **record**. A logical group of related records is called a **file**. For example, the student records in a single course would constitute a data file for that course. A logical group of related files would constitute a **database**. All students' course files could be grouped with files on students' personal histories and financial backgrounds to create a students' database.

Another way of thinking about database components is that a record describes an **entity**. An entity is a person, place, thing, or event on which we maintain data. Each characteristic or quality describing a particular entity is called an **attribute** (corresponds to a field).

Every record in a file should contain at least one field that uniquely identifies that record so that the record can be retrieved, updated, and sorted. This identified field is called the **key field**. For example, a student record would probably use the Social Security number as its key field.

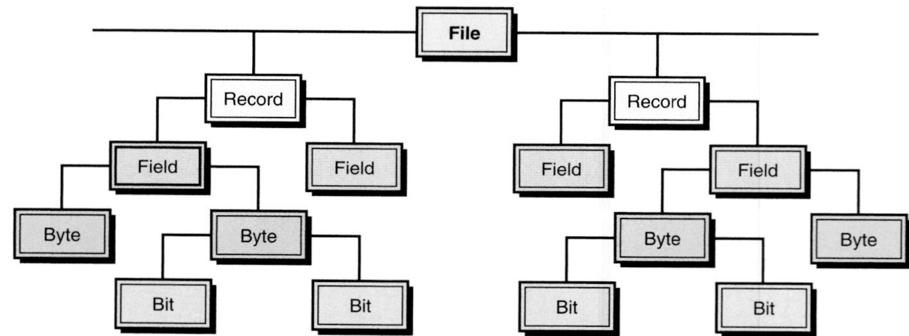

FIGURE T-3.1 Hierarchy of data for a computer-based file.

Accessing Records from Computer Files

Records can be arranged in several ways on a storage medium, and the arrangement determines the manner in which individual records can be accessed. In **sequential file organization**, data records must be retrieved in the same physical sequence in which they are stored. In **direct** or **random file organization**, users can access records in any sequence, without regard to actual physical order on the storage medium. Magnetic tape utilizes sequential file organization, whereas magnetic disks use direct file organization.

Problems Arising from the File Environment

Organizations typically began automating one application at a time. These systems grew independently, without overall planning. Each application required its own data, which were organized into a data file. This approach led to many problems. Figure T-3.2 uses a university file environment as an example.

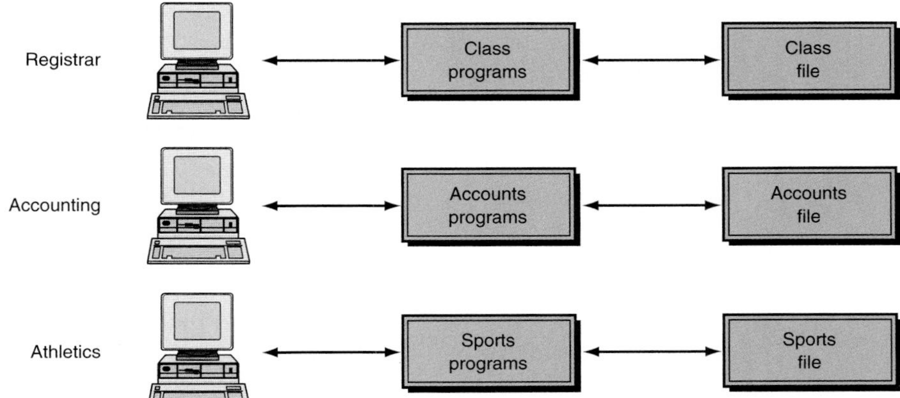

FIGURE T-3.2 Computer-based files of this type cause problems such as redundancy, inconsistency, and data isolation.

The applications (e.g., registrar, accounting, or athletics) would share some common core functions, such as input, report generation, querying, and data browsing. However, these common functions would typically be designed, coded, documented, and tested, at great expense, for each application. Moreover, users must be trained to use each application. File environments often waste valuable resources creating and maintaining similar applications, as well as in training users how to use them.

Other problems arise with file management systems. The first problem is **data redundancy**: As applications and their data files were created by different programmers over a period of time, the same data could be duplicated in several files. In the university example, each data file will contain records about students, many of whom will be represented in other data files. Therefore, student files in the aggregate will contain some amount of duplicate data. This wastes physical computer storage media, the students' time and effort, and the clerks' time needed to enter and maintain the data.

Data redundancy leads to the potential for data inconsistency. **Data inconsistency** means that the actual values across various copies of the data no longer agree. For example, if a student changes his or her address, the new address must be changed across all applications in the university that require the address.

File organization also leads to difficulty in accessing data from different applications, a problem called **data isolation**. With applications uniquely designed and implemented, data files are likely to be organized differently, stored in different formats (e.g., height in inches versus height in centimeters), and often physically inaccessible to other applications. In the university example, an administrator who wanted to know which students taking advanced courses were also starting players on the football team would most likely not be able to get the answer from the computer-based file system. He or she would probably have to manually compare printed output data from two data files. This process would take a great deal of time and effort and would ignore the greatest strengths of computers—fast and accurate processing.

Additionally, **security** is difficult to enforce in the file environment, because new applications may be added to the system on an ad-hoc basis.

The file environment may also cause **data integrity** problems. Data values must often meet integrity constraints. For example, the students' Social Security data field should contain no alphabetic characters, and the students' grade-point-average field should not be negative. It is difficult to place data integrity constraints across multiple data files.

Finally, applications should not have to be developed with regard to how the data are stored. That is, applications and data in computer systems should have **application/data independence**—that is, they should be independent. In the file environment, the applications and their associated data files are dependent on each other.

Storing data in data files that are tightly linked to their applications eventually led to organizations having hundreds of applications and data files, with no one knowing what the applications did or what data they required. There was no central listing of data files, data elements, or definitions of the data. The numerous problems arising from the file environment approach led to the development of *databases*.

T3.2 DATABASES AND DATABASE MANAGEMENT SYSTEMS

Databases

A **database** is an organized logical grouping of related files. In a database, data are integrated and related so that one set of software programs provides access to all the data, alleviating many of the problems associated with data file environments. Therefore, data redundancy, data isolation, and data inconsistency are minimized, and data can be shared among all users of the data. In addition, security and data integrity are increased, and applications and data are independent of one another.

Database Management Systems

The program (or group of programs) that provides access to a database is known as a **database management system (DBMS)**. The DBMS permits an organization to centralize data, manage them efficiently, and provide access to the stored data by application programs. (For a list of capabilities and advantages of the DBMS, see Table T-3.1.) The DBMS acts as an interface between application programs and physical data files (see Figure T-3.3) and provides users with tools to add, delete, maintain, display, print, search, select, sort, and update data. These tools range from easy-to-use natural language interfaces to complex programming languages used for developing sophisticated database applications.

DBMSs are used in a broad range of information systems. Some are loaded on a single user's personal computer and used in an ad-hoc manner to support individual decision making. Others are located on several interconnected mainframe computers and are used to support large-scale transaction processing systems, such as order entry and inventory control systems. Still others are interconnected throughout an organization's local area networks, giving individual departments access to corporate data. Because a DBMS need not be confined to storing just words and numbers, firms use them to store graphics, sounds, and video as well.

There are many specialized databases, depending on the type or format of data stored. For example, a **geographical information database** (see Chapter 11) may contain locational data for overlaying on maps or images. Using this type of data, users are able to spatially view customer and vendor locations instead of simply reading the actual addresses. A **knowledge database** (knowledge base, see Chapters 9, 11, and 12) can store decision rules used to evaluate

TABLE T-3.1 Advantages and Capabilities of a DBMS
• Access and availability of information can be increased. • Data access, utilization, security, and manipulation can be simplified. • Data inconsistency and redundancy is reduced. • Program development and maintenance costs can be dramatically reduced. • Captures/extracts data for inclusion in databases. • Quickly updates (adds, deletes, edits, changes) data records and files. • Interrelates data from different sources. • Quickly retrieves data from a database for queries and reports. • Provides comprehensive data security (protection from unauthorized access, recovery capabilities, etc.). • Handles personal and unofficial data so that users can experiment with alternative solutions based on their own judgment. • Performs complex retrieval and data manipulation tasks based on queries. • Tracks usage of data. • Flexibility of information systems can be improved by allowing rapid and inexpensive ad hoc queries of very large pools of information. • Application-data dependence can be reduced by separating the logical view of data from its physical structure and location.

situations and help users make decisions like an expert. A **multimedia database** (see Chapter 11) can store data on many media—sounds, video, images, graphic animation, and text.

Database management systems are designed to be relatively invisible to the user. To interact with them, however, one needs to understand the procedures for interacting, even though much of their work is done behind the scenes and is therefore invisible or "transparent" to the end user. Most of this interaction occurs by using DBMS languages.

DBMS LANGUAGES. A DBMS contains three major components: a data definition language, a data manipulation language, and a data dictionary. The **data definition language (DDL)** is the language used by programmers to specify the content and structure of the database. It is essentially the link between the

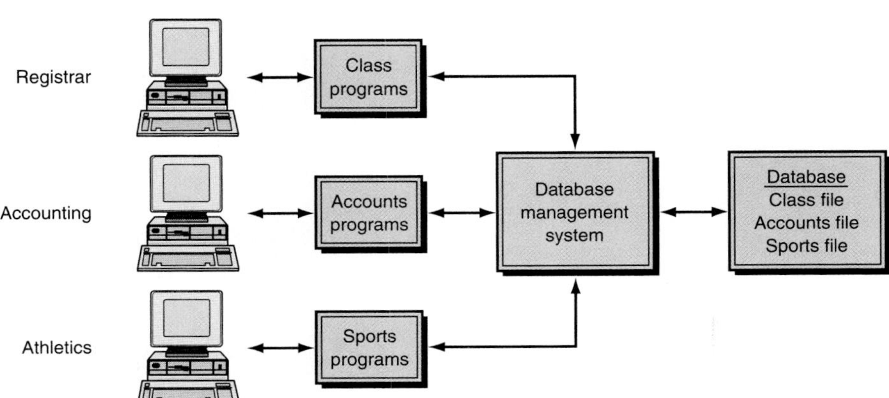

FIGURE T-3.3 Database management system provides access to all data in the database.

logical and physical views of the database. ("Logical" refers to the way the user views data, and "physical" to the way the data are physically stored and processed.)

A DBMS user defines views or schema using the DDL. The **schema** is the logical description of the entire database and the listing of all the data items and the relationships among them. A **subschema** is the specific set of data from the database that is required by each application.

The DDL is used to define the physical characteristics of each record, the fields within a record, and each field's logical name, data type, and character length. The DDL is also used to specify relationships among the records. Other primary functions of the DDL are the following:

- Provide a means for associating related data.
- Indicate the unique identifiers (or keys) of the records.
- Set up data security access and change restrictions.

The **data manipulation language (DML)** is used with a third- or fourth-generation language to manipulate the data in the database. This language contains commands that permit end users and programming specialists to extract data from the database to satisfy information requests and develop applications. The DML provides users with the ability to retrieve, sort, display, and delete the contents of a database. The DML generally includes a variety of manipulation verbs (e.g., CREATE, MODIFY, DELETE) and operands for each verb.

Requesting information from a database is the most commonly performed operation. Because users cannot generally request information in a natural language form, query languages form an important component of a DBMS. **Struc-**

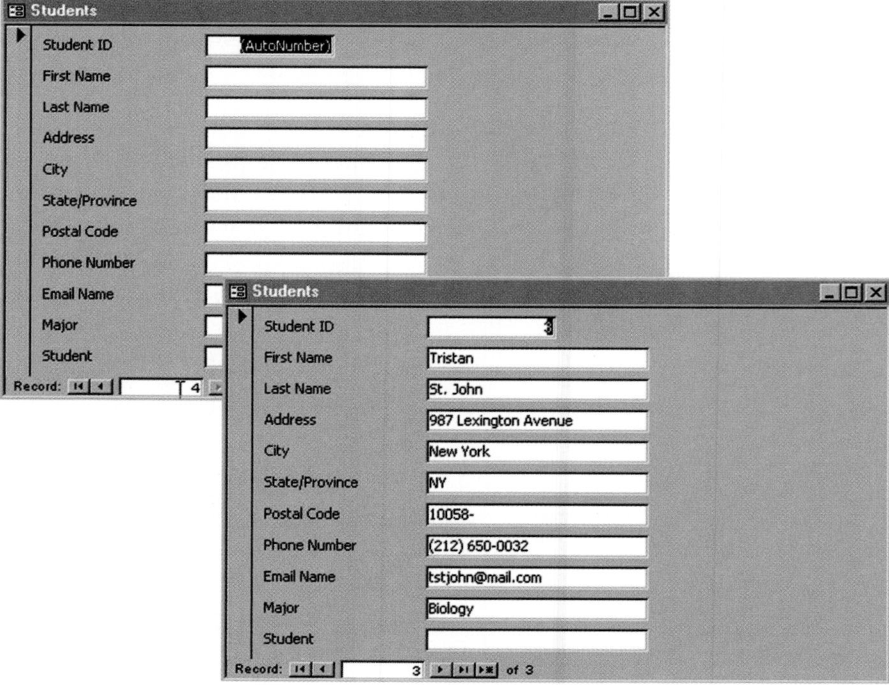

The QBE capabilities of Microsoft Access.

tured query language (SQL) is the most popular relational database language, combining both DML and DDL features. SQL offers the ability to perform complicated searches with relatively simple statements. Keywords such as SELECT (to specify desired attribute(s)), FROM (to specify the table(s) to be used), and WHERE (to specify conditions to apply in the query) are typically used for the purpose of data manipulation. For example, a state legislator wants to send congratulatory letters to all students from her district graduating with honors from a state university. The university information systems staff would query the student relational database with an SQL statement such as SELECT (Student Name), FROM (Student Table), WHERE (Congressional District = 7 and Grade Point Average > = 3.4).

When using a PC, the SQL is not normally used and instead an approach called **query-by-example (QBE)** is employed. The user selects a table and chooses the fields to be included in the answer. Then the user enters an example of the data he or she wants. The QBE provides an answer based on the example (see figure on page 734).

The third element of a DBMS is a **data dictionary**, which is a file that stores definitions of data elements and data characteristics such as usage, physical representation, ownership (who in the organization is responsible for maintaining the data), authorization, and security. A **data element** represents a field. Besides listing the standard data name, the dictionary lists the names that reference this element in specific systems and identifies the individuals, business functions, applications, and reports that use this data element.

T3.3 Logical Data Organization

Just as there are many ways to structure business organizations, there are many ways to structure the data those organizations need. A manager's ability to use a database is highly dependent on how the database is structured logically and physically. The DBMS separates the logical and physical views of the data, meaning that the programmer and end user do not have to know where and how the data are actually stored. In logically structuring a database, businesses need to consider the characteristics of the data and how the data will be accessed.

There are three basic models for logically structuring databases: *hierarchical, network,* and *relational*. Three additional models are emerging: *multidimensional, object-oriented,* and *hypermedia*. Using these models, database designers can build logical or conceptual views of data that can then be physically implemented into virtually any database with any DBMS. Hierarchical, network, and object-oriented DBMSs usually tie related data together through linked lists. Relational and multidimensional DBMSs relate data through information contained in the data. In this section we will present the three basic models. (Others are described in Chapter 11.)

The Hierarchical Database Model

The **hierarchical model** relates data by rigidly structuring data into an inverted "tree" in which records contain two elements:

1. A single root or master field, often called a *key*, which identifies the type location, or ordering of the records
2. A variable number of subordinate fields that defines the rest of the data within a record

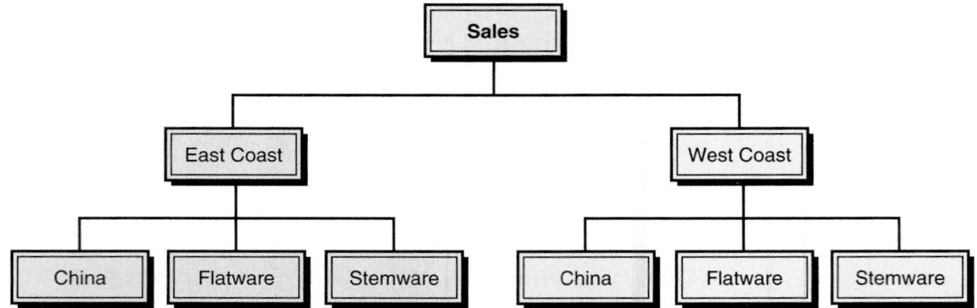

FIGURE T-3.4 Hierarchical database model.

As a rule, while all fields have only one "parent," each parent may have many "children." An example of a hierarchical database is shown in Figure T-3.4.

The hierarchical structure was developed because hierarchical relationships are commonly found in many traditional business organizations and processes.

The strongest advantage of the hierarchical approach is the speed and efficiency with which it can be searched for data. This speed is possible because so much of the database is eliminated in the search with each "turn" going down the tree. As shown in Figure T-3.4, half the records in the database (East Coast Sales) are eliminated once the search turns toward West Coast Sales, and two-thirds of the West Coast Sales are eliminated once the search turns toward stemware.

Finally, the explicit child/parent relationships in a hierarchical model mean that the integrity of the database is strongly maintained. Every child in a hierarchical database must belong to a parent, and if a parent is eliminated from the database, all its children automatically become children of the parent's parent.

But the hierarchical approach does have some deficiencies. In the hierarchical model, each relationship must be explicitly defined when the database is created. Each record in a hierarchical database can contain only one key field, and only one relationship is allowed between any two fields. This can create a problem because real-world data do not always conform to such a strict hierarchy. For example, in a matrix organization, an employee might report to more than one manager, a situation that would be awkward for a hierarchical structure to handle. Moreover, all data searches must originate at the top or "root" of the tree and work downward from parent to child.

Another significant disadvantage of the hierarchical model is the fact that it is difficult to relate "cousins" in the tree. In the example shown in Figure T-3.4, there is no direct relationship between china sales on the East Coast and china sales on the West Coast. A comparison of companywide china sales would entail two separate searches and then another step combining the search results.

The Network Database Model

The **network model** creates relationships among data through a linked-list structure in which subordinated records (called *members*, not children) can be linked to more than one parent (called an *owner*). Similar to the hierarchical model, the network model uses explicit links, called *pointers*, to link subordinates and parents. That relationship is called a *set*. Physically, pointers are storage addresses that contain the location of a related record. With the network approach, a member record can be linked to an owner record and, at the same time, can itself be an owner record linked to other sets of members (see Figure T-3.5). In this way,

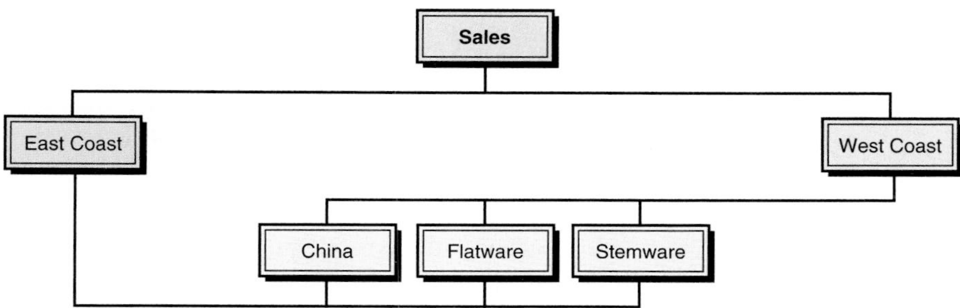

FIGURE T-3.5 Network database model.

many-to-many relationships are possible with a network database model—a significant advantage of the network model over the hierarchical model.

Compare Figure T-3.5 with Figure T-3.4. In Figure T-3.5, sales information about china, flatware, and stemware is in one subordinate or member location. Information about each has two parents or owners, East Coast and West Coast. The problem of getting a complete picture of nationwide china sales that exists with the hierarchical model does not occur with the network model. Moreover, searches for data do not have to start at a root—there may not even be a single root to a network—which gives much greater flexibility for data searches.

The network model essentially places no restrictions on the number of relationships or sets in which a field can be involved. The model, then, is more consistent with real-world business relationships where, for example, vendors have many customers and customers have many vendors. However, network databases are very complex. For every set, a pair of pointers must be maintained. As the number of sets or relationships increases, the overhead becomes substantial. The network model is by far the most complicated type of database to design and implement.

The Relational Database Model

While most business organizations have been organized in a hierarchical fashion, most business data, especially accounting and financial data, have traditionally been organized into tables of columns and rows. Tables allow quick comparisons by row or column, and items are easy to retrieve by finding the point of intersection of a particular row and column. The **relational model** is based on this simple concept of tables in order to capitalize on characteristics of rows and columns of data, which is consistent with real-world business situations.

In a relational database, the tables are called **relations**, and the model is based on the mathematical theory of sets and relations. In this model, each row of data is equivalent to a *record*, and each column of data is equivalent to a *field*. In the relational model terminology, a row is called a **tuple**, and a column is called an **attribute**. However, a relational database is not always one big table (usually called a *flat file*) consisting of all attributes and all tuples. That design would likely entail far too much data redundancy. Instead, a database is usually designed as a collection of several related tables.

One of the greatest advantages of the relational model is its conceptual simplicity and the ability to link records in a way that is not predefined (that is, they are not explicit as in the hierarchical and network models). This ability provides great flexibility, particularly for end users. The relational or tabular model of data can be used in a variety of applications. Most people can easily visualize the relational model as a table, but the model does use some unfamiliar terminology.

Division

Code	*Name*
01	Stemware

Title

Code	*Description*
01	Director

Employee

Name	*Title Code*	*Division Code*	*Age*
Smith, A.	01	01	42

FIGURE T-3.6 Relational database model tables.

Consider the relational database example on East Coast managers shown in Figure T-3.6. The table contains data about the entity called East Coast managers. Attributes or characteristics about the entity are name, title, age, and division. The tuples, or occurrences of the entity, are the two records on A. Smith and W. Jones. The links among the data, and among tables, are implicit, as they are not necessarily physically linked in a storage device but are implicitly linked by the design of the tables into rows and columns.

This property of implicit links provides perhaps the strongest benefit of the relational model—flexibility in relating data. Unlike the hierarchical and network models, where the only links are those rigidly built into the design, all the data within a table and between tables can be linked, related, and compared. This ability gives the relational model much more data independence than the hierarchical and network models. That is, the logical design of data into tables can be more independent of the physical implementation. This independence allows much more flexibility in implementing and modifying the logical design. Of course, as with all tables, an end user needs to know only two things: the identifier(s) of the tuple(s) to be searched and the desired attribute(s).

The relational model does have some disadvantages: Because large-scale databases may be composed of many interrelated tables, the overall design may be complex and therefore have slower search and access times (as compared to the hierarchical and network models). The slower search and access time may result in processing inefficiencies, which led to an initial lack of acceptance of the relational model. These processing inefficiencies, however, are continually being reduced through improved database design and programming. Second, data integrity is not inherently a part of this model as with hierarchical and network models. Therefore, it must be enforced with good design principles.

OBJECT-RELATIONAL DATABASE SYSTEMS. *Object-relational database* products are replacing purely relational databases. Object-relational database management systems (ORDBMSs) have some of the capabilities of object-oriented database systems as well as additional unique capabilities. (For details, see Katz, 1998.)

Comparing the Three Basic Database Models

The main advantage of the hierarchical and network database models is processing efficiency. The hierarchical and network structures are relatively easy for users to understand because they reflect the pattern of real-world business relationships. In addition, the hierarchical structure allows for data integrity to be easily maintained.

Hierarchical and network structures have several disadvantages. All the access paths, directories, and indices must be specified in advance. Once specified, they are not easily changed without a major programming effort. Therefore, these designs have low flexibility. Hierarchical and network structures are programming intensive, time consuming, difficult to install, and difficult to remedy if design errors occur. The two structures do not support ad-hoc, English-language-like inquiries for information.

The advantages of relational DBMSs include high flexibility in regard to ad-hoc queries, power to combine information from different sources, simplicity of design and maintenance, and the ability to add new data and records without disturbing existing applications. The disadvantage of relational DBMSs is their relatively low processing efficiency. These systems are somewhat slower because they typically require many accesses to the data stored on disk to carry out the select, join, and project commands. Relational systems do not have the large number of pointers carried by hierarchical systems.

Large relational databases may be designed to have some data redundancy in order to make retrieval of data more efficient. The same data element may be stored in multiple tables. Special arrangements are necessary to ensure that all copies of the same data element are updated together. A visual comparison of the three models is shown in Figure T-3.7. The lines with arrows in the relational models show the duplication of information.

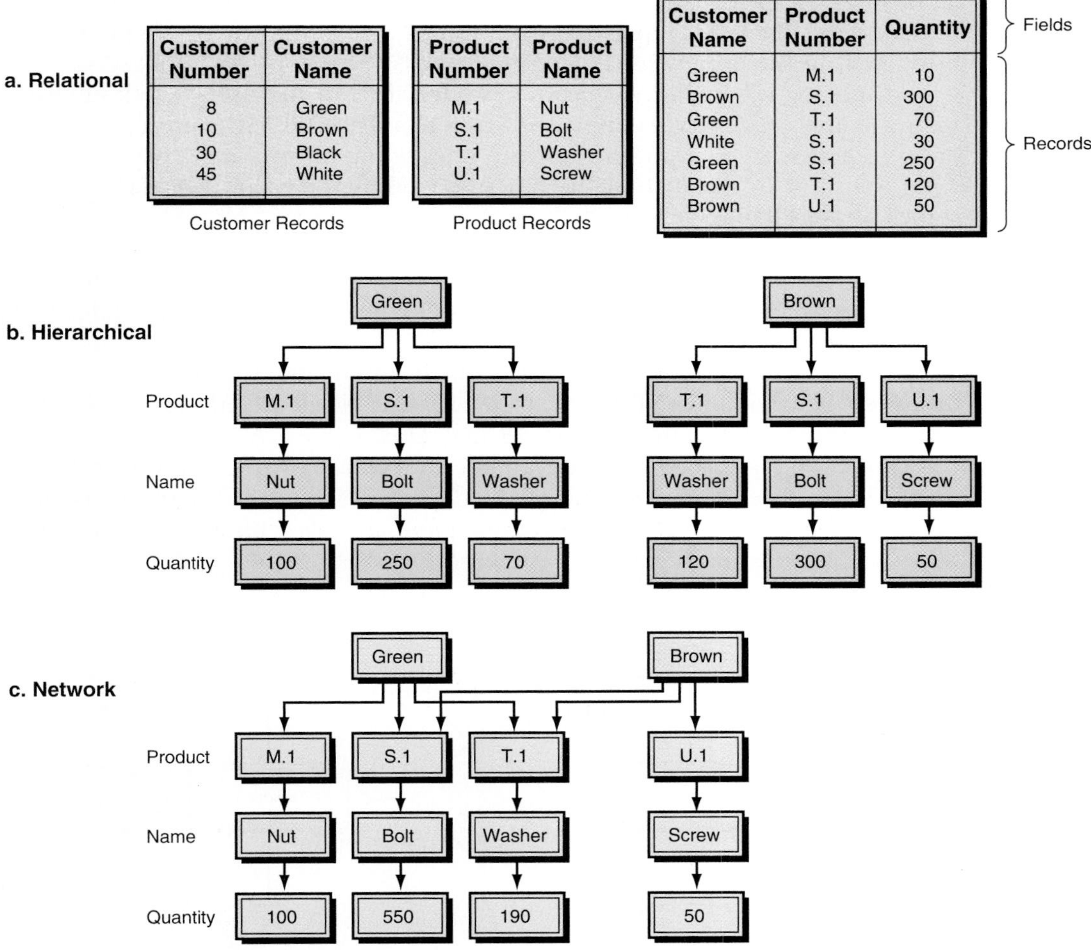

FIGURE T-3.7 Database structures.

T3.4 CREATING DATABASES

To create a database, designers must develop a conceptual design and a physical design. The **conceptual design** of a database is an abstract model of the database from the user or business perspective. The **physical design** shows how the database is actually arranged on direct access storage devices.

The conceptual database design describes how the data elements in the database are to be grouped. The design process identifies relationships among data elements and the most efficient way of grouping data elements together to meet information requirements. The process also identifies redundant data elements and the groupings of data elements required for specific applications. Groups of data are organized, refined, and streamlined until an overall logical view of the relationships among all of the data elements in the database appears. To produce optimal database design, entity-relationship modeling and normalization are employed. These are described next.

Entity-Relationship Modeling

Database designers often document the conceptual data model with an **entity-relationship (ER) diagram**. ER diagrams consist of entities, attributes, and relationships. In ER diagrams, the boxes represent entities, ovals represent attributes, and the diamonds represent relationships. The attributes for each entity are listed next to the entity (see Figure T-3.8).

An **entity** is something that can be identified in the users' work environment. In the university example, STUDENT and PROFESSOR are examples of entity. An **instance** of an entity is the representation of a particular entity, so John Smith is an instance of the STUDENT entity, and Sara Douglas is an instance of the PROFESSOR entity.

Entities have **attributes**, or properties, that describe the entity's characteristics. In our example, attributes for STUDENT would be Name, IDNumber, and Major. Examples of attributes for PROFESSOR would include Name, Department, and ClassTaught.

Entity instances have **identifiers**, which are attributes that identify entity instances. For example, STUDENT instances can be identified with IDNumber. These identifiers are underlined on ER diagrams.

Entities are associated with one another in **relationships**, which can include many entities. The number of entities in a relationship is the degree of the relationship. Relationships of degree 2 are common and are called **binary relationships**.

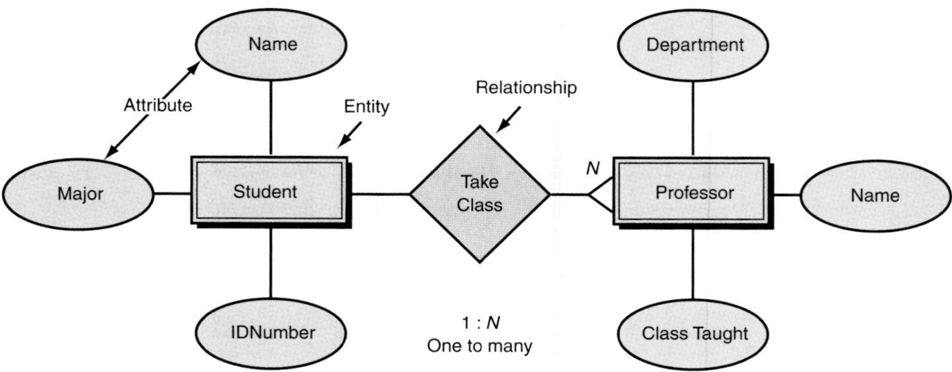

FIGURE T-3.8 Entity-relationship diagrams.

There are several types of binary relationships. For example, one student can take several classes as shown by the 1:N ($N > 2$) symbol in Figure T-3.8. We can expand the diagram to M:N relationships, meaning one student can take many classes from several professors, and each professor can teach several classes and have many students in each. Several other relationships can be shown on the diagram.

The ER diagrams are supported by tables. The diagrams help to ensure that the relationships among the data elements in the database are logically structured. When the database includes many files it is difficult to navigate and find data there. The ER acts like conceptual blueprints of the database. It represents all entity relationships. The ER diagrams are often consulted to determine a problem with a query or the complement changes.

Normalization of Relational Databases

In order to use a relational database model effectively, complex groupings of data must be streamlined to eliminate redundant data elements and awkward many-to-many relationships. The process of creating small, stable data structures from complex groups of data is called **normalization**.

Normalization is a method for analyzing and reducing a relational database to its most parsimonious or streamlined form for minimum redundancy, maximum data integrity, and best processing performance. Specifically, normalization has several goals:

- Eliminate redundancy caused by fields repeated within a file, fields that do not directly describe the entity, and fields that can be derived from other fields.
- Avoid update anomalies (i.e., errors from inserting, deleting, and modifying records).
- Represent accurately the item being modeled.
- Simplify maintenance and information retrieval.

Several levels of normalization exist, which build upon each other addressing increasingly specialized and complex normalization problems.

THE NORMALIZATION PROCESS. The concepts of functional dependency and keys are fundamental to normalization. A **functional dependency** is a relationship between or among attributes, where, given the value of one attribute, we can obtain (or look up) the value of another attribute. For example, in Figure T-3.9 if we know the value of IDnumber, we can find the student's major.

IDNumber	Major	Lab	Fee
3244	Management	Inorganic Chemistry	25
1697	Economics	Physics	25
9611	Accounting	Organic Chemistry	125
1234	Marketing	Physics	25

FIGURE T-3.9 Lab relation (single key)—first normal form.

Therefore, we say that a student's major is functionally dependent on the student's identification number, and that the student's identification number is a **determinant** of the student's major.

T3.5 Emerging Database Models

Many of today's applications require database capabilities that can store, retrieve, and process diverse media and not just text and numbers. Full-motion video, voice, photos, and drawings cannot be handled effectively or efficiently by either hierarchical, network, or relational databases and the DBMS. For multimedia and other complex data we use special data models.

The most common database models are:

- ***Multidimensional database.*** This is an additional database that enables end users to quickly retrieve and present complex data that involve many dimensions (see Chapter 11).
- ***Deductive databases.*** Hierarchical, network, and relational DBMSs have been used for decades to facilitate data access by users. Users, of course, must understand what they are looking for, the database they are looking at, and at least something about the information sought (like a key and some field or attribute about a record). This approach, however, may not be adequate for some knowledge-based applications that require deductive reasoning for searches. As a result, there is interest in what is called *deductive database* systems.
- ***Object-oriented databases.*** In order to work in an object-oriented environment, it is necessary to use OO programming and OO databases. This topic is presented in this section. Also see the description in Chapter 11.
- ***Multimedia and hypermedia databases.*** These are analogous to contemporary databases for textual and numeric data; however, they have been tailored to meet the special requirements of dealing with different types of media materials (see Chapter 11).

The Object-Oriented Database Model

www.wiley.com/college/turban

Although there is no common definition for *object-oriented database,* there is agreement as to some of its features. Terminology in the object-oriented model, similar to object-oriented programming languages, consists of objects, attributes, classes, methods, and messages (see Technology Guide 2).

Object-oriented databases store both data and procedures acting on the data, as objects. These objects can be automatically retrieved and processed. Therefore, the OO database can be particularly helpful in multimedia environments, such as in manufacturing sites using CAD/CAM. Data from design blueprints, photographic images of parts, operational acoustic signatures, and test or quality control data can all be combined into one object, itself consisting of structures and operations.. For companies with widely distributed offices, an object-oriented database can provide users with a transparent view of data throughout the entire system.

Object-oriented databases can be particularly useful in supporting temporal and spatial dimensions. All things change; sometimes keeping track of temporal and spatial changes, rather than just the latest version, is important. Related but slightly different versions of an object can easily be maintained in an object-oriented database. Object-oriented databases allow firms to structure their data and use them in ways that would be impossible, or at least very difficult, with other database models. An OO database is slow and therefore cannot be used efficiently for transaction-processing-type data. Therefore, as indicated earlier, it is sometimes combined with a relational database.

Hypermedia Database Model

The **hypermedia database model** stores chunks of information in the form of nodes connected by links established by the user. The nodes can contain text, graphics, sound, full-motion video, or executable computer programs. Searching for information does not have to follow a predetermined organizational scheme. Instead, users can branch to related information in any kind of relationship. The relationship between nodes is less structured than in a traditional DBMS. In most systems, each node can be displayed on a screen. The screen also displays the links between the node depicted and other nodes in the database. Like OO databases, this database model is slow.

T3.6 DATA WAREHOUSES

A **data warehouse** is an additional database that is designed to support DSSs, EISs, online analytical processing (OLAP), and other end-user activities, such as report generation, queries, and graphical presentation. It can provide an "executive view" of data and a unified corporate picture to the end users by combining the data from many operational systems and incompatible databases without affecting the performance of the running operational systems. It can also provide the decision support system environment in which end users can analyze timely information, and it increases the ability of end users to exploit such information effectively by using data-mining tools or OLAP. The topic is discussed at length in Chapter 11.

A **data mart** is smaller, less expensive, and more focused than a large-scale data warehouse. Data marts can be a substitution for a data warehouse, or they can be used in addition to it. In either case, end users can use the warehouse and/or the marts for many applications, such as query, DSS/EIS, reporting, OLAP, knowledge discovery, and data mining. It can increase the productivity of the end users. Also see the description in Chapter 11.

T3.7 PHYSICAL DATABASE ORGANIZATION

Once a database is logically structured based on its characteristics, relationships, and access methodology, it must be physically implemented with specific software and hardware so users can access data in real-world applications. Data organized into databases are usually stored and accessed through DBMSs, which are themselves organized under various processing arrangements or topologies. Each database management system uses one or more of the various digital storage and access methods, which can significantly affect the amount of required storage space and the speed of data retrieval.

Database Topology

A database is a collection of related files that need to be in one physical location. Where those related files are located can greatly affect user accessibility, query response times, data entry, security, and cost. In general, database files can be centralized or distributed.

A **centralized database** has all the related files in one physical location. Centralized database files on large mainframe computers were the main database topology for decades, primarily because of the enormous capital and operating cost of other alternatives. Not only do centralized databases save the expenses associated with multiple computers, but they also provide database administrators with the ability to work on a database as a whole at one location. Files can generally be made more consistent with each other when they are physically kept in one location because file changes can be made in a supervised and orderly fashion. Centralized files are not accessible except via the centralized host computer, where they can be protected more easily from unauthorized access or modification. Also, recovery from disasters can be more easily accomplished at a central location.

Like all centralized systems, however, centralized databases are vulnerable to a single point of failure. When the centralized database computer fails to function properly, all users suffer. Additionally, access speed is often a problem when users are widely dispersed and must do all of their data manipulations from great distances, thereby incurring transmission delays.

A **distributed database** has complete copies of a database, or portions of a database, in more than one location, which is usually close to the user. A **replicated database** has complete copies of the entire database in several locations, primarily to alleviate the single point-of-failure problems of a centralized database as well as to increase user access responsiveness. There is significant overhead, however, in maintaining consistency among replicated databases, as records are added, modified, and deleted. A **partitioned database** is subdivided, so that each location has a portion of the entire database (usually the portion meeting users' local needs). This type of database provides the response speed of localized files without the need to replicate all changes in multiple locations.

Physical versus Logical Data View

As mentioned earlier, the key benefits from a database, as opposed to multiple unrelated files, come from the ability of many different users to efficiently and effectively share data and process resources. But as there can be many different users, there are many different database needs. How can a single, unified database meet the differing requirements of so many users? For example, how can a single database be structured so that sales personnel can see customer, inventory, and production maintenance data while maintaining restricted access to private personnel data?

A DBMS minimizes these problems by providing two "views" of the database data: a physical view and a logical view. The **physical view** deals with the actual, physical arrangement and location of data in the *direct access storage devices (DASDs)*. Database specialists use this view to make efficient use of storage and processing resources. Users, however, may wish to see the data differently from how they are stored, and they do not want to know all the technical details of physical storage. After all, a business user is primarily interested in using the information, not in how it is stored.

The **logical view**, or user's view, of a database program represents data in a format that is meaningful to a user and to the software programs that process that data. One strength of a DBMS is that while there is only one physical view of the data, there can be an endless number of different logical views—one specifically tailored to every individual user, if necessary. This process allows users to see database information in a more business-related way rather than from a technical, processing viewpoint. Clearly, users must adapt to the technical requirements of database information systems to some degree, but DBMS logical views allow the system to adapt to the business needs of the users.

T3.8 Database Management

Database management, outside of purely technical hardware and software considerations, consists primarily of two functions: *database design and implementation,* and *database administration.*

In designing and implementing databases, specialists should carefully consider the individual needs of all existing and potential users in order to design and implement a database, which optimizes both processing efficiency and user effectiveness. The process usually starts by analyzing what information each user (or group of users) needs and then producing logical views for each. These logical views are analyzed as a whole for similarities that can lead to simplification, and then are related so that a single, cohesive logical database can be formed from all the parts. This logical database is implemented with a particular DBMS in a specific hardware system.

Database administrators are IT specialists responsible for the data as well as for ensuring that the database fulfills the users' business needs, in terms of functionality. User needs, like business in general, do not remain constant. As the business environment changes, and organizational goals and structures react, the database that the firm depends on must also change to remain effective. The computer hardware on which the DBMS software is installed must change to meet changing environments or to take advantage of new technology. This brings accompanying constraints and/or new opportunities for the DBMS's processing performance.

Further, database administrators need to ensure the reliability of databases under their care by managing daily operations, including planning for emergency contingencies by providing backup data and systems to ensure minimal loss of data in the event of a disaster. Security is always a data administration concern when there are multiple accesses to databases that contain all the corporate data. Administrators must balance the business advantages of widespread access with the threat of corporate espionage, sabotage by disgruntled employees, and database damage due to negligence. Database administrators play a significant role in training users about what data are available and how to access them. Finally, administrators are responsible for ensuring that the data contained in the database are accurate, reliable, verifiable, complete, timely, and relevant—a daunting task at best. Otherwise-brilliant business decisions, based on wrong information, can be disastrous in a highly competitive market.

T3.9 An Emerging Technology: IP-based Storage

Storage connected to servers over IP (Internet protocol) networks, also known as **IP storage**, enables servers to connect to SCSI (small computer system interface) storage devices and treat them as if they were directly attached to the server, regardless of the location. IP-based storage networking aims to eliminate problems of a fiber channel (FC) storage area network (SAN). An FC-SAN requires specially trained management personnel and uses relatively expensive hardware that may be incompatible among vendors. IP or Ethernet networks enable cost-effective SANs to be deployed by a broad market. Since IP storage runs over the existing Ethernet infrastructure, it retains all of the existing networking. This offers interoperability, manageability, compatibility, and cost advantages. People can use inexpensive, readily available Ethernet switches, hubs, and cables to implement low-cost, low-risk IP storage-based SANs.

Many vendors are seeking to offer their customers interoperable storage technologies that reduce the complexity of SANs. For example, the IBM TotalStorage IP Storage 200i is an iSCSI standard storage appliance that connects users to pooled storage on a network using IP. ISCSI is a "pure" IP over SCSI for storage and is an FC replacement. It provides storage that is directly attachable to an Ethernet LAN. The TotalStorage IP Storage 200i costs $20,000 and is available as of June 2001.

REFERENCES AND BIBLIOGRAPHY

1. Connolly, T. M., et al., *Database Systems,* 2nd ed. Reading, MA: Addison-Wesley, 1998.
2. Connor, D., "Start-up Plots Storage Over IP Coup," *Network World,* May 22, 2000.
3. Date, C. J., *An Introduction to Database Systems,* 7th ed. Reading, MA: Addison-Wesley, 1999.
4. Elmasri, R., and S. Navathe, *Fundamentals of Database Systems.* Reading, MA: Addison-Wesley, 1999.
5. Goodhue, D., et al., "The Impact of Data Integration on the Costs and Benefits of Information Systems," *MIS Quarterly,* Vol. 16, No. 3, September 1993.
6. Gray, P., and H. J. Watson, *Decision Support in the Data Warehouse.* Upper Saddle River, NJ: Prentice-Hall, 1998.
7. Gupta, A., and J. Ranesh, "Visual Information Retrieval," *Communications of the ACM,* Vol. 40, No. 5, May 1997.
8. Halper, M., "Welcome to 21st Century Data," *Forbes,* Vol. 157, No. 7, April 8, 1996.
9. Katz, M., ed., *Technology Forecast: 1998* (also 1999, 2000). Menlo Park, CA: Price Waterhouse World Technology Centre, 1998, 1999, 2000.
10. King, J., "Sorting Information Overload," *ComputerWorld,* December 2, 1996.
11. Kroenke, D., *Database Processing: Fundamentals, Design, and Implementation,* 7th ed. Upper Saddle River, NJ: Prentice-Hall, 2000.
12. Mearian, L., "Storage Conference: Long-term View Taking Precedence," *ComputerWorld,* April 10, 2001.
13. Ramakrishnan, R., and J. Gehrke, *Database Management Systems.* New York: McGraw Hill, 1999.
14. Silberschatz, A., et al., *Database Systems Concepts,* 4th ed. New York: McGraw Hill, 2001.
15. Sperley, E., *The Enterprise Data Warehouse: Planning, Building, and Implementation.* Upper Saddle River, NJ: Prentice-Hall, 1999.
16. Stonebreaker, M., and D. Moore, *Object-Relational DBMS: The Next Great Wave.* San Francisco: Morgan Kaufmann, 1996.
17. Ulman, J. D., and J. Widam, *A First Course in Database Systems.* Upper Saddle River, NJ: Prentice-Hall, 1997.
18. Zaniolo, C., et al., *Advanced Database Systems.* San Francisco: Morgan Kaufmann, 1997.

Technology Guides

TECHNOLOGY GUIDE

4

Telecommunications

This guide was updated by Joe Walls, University of Michigan.

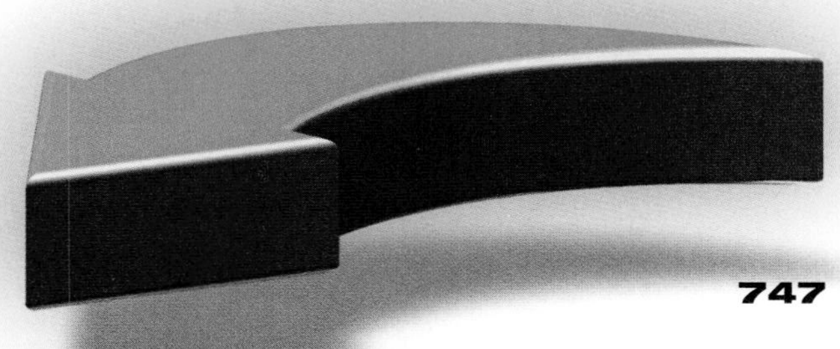

T4.1 TELECOMMUNICATIONS CONCEPTS

The term **telecommunications** generally refers to all types of long-distance communication that uses common carriers, including telephone, television, and radio. **Data communications** is the electronic collection, exchange, and processing of data or information, including text, pictures, and voice, that is digitally coded and intelligible to a variety of electronic devices. Today's computing environment is dispersed both geographically and organizationally, placing data communications in a strategic organizational role. Data communications is a subset of telecommunications and is achieved through the use of telecommunication technologies.

In modern organizations, communications technologies are integrated. Businesses are finding electronic communications essential for minimizing time and distance limitations. Telecommunications plays a special role when customers, suppliers, vendors, and regulators are part of a multinational organization in a world that is continuously awake and doing business somewhere 24 hours a day, 7 days a week ("24/7"). Figure T-4.1 represents a model of an integrated computer and telecommunications system common in today's business environment.

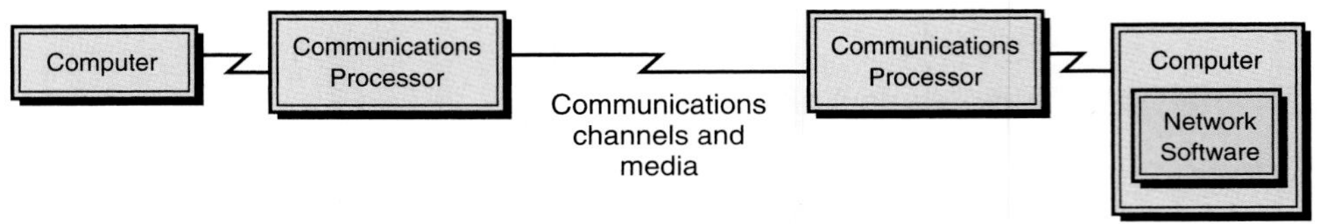

FIGURE T-4.1 An integrated computer and telecommunications system.

Telecommunications System

A **telecommunications system** is a collection of compatible hardware and software arranged to communicate information from one location to another. These systems can transmit text, graphics, voice, documents, or full-motion video information.

A typical telecommunications system is shown in Figure T-4.2. Such systems have two sides: the transmitter and the receiver.

The major components are:

1. ***Hardware***—host computers, PCs, wireless devices, and terminals for data input.
2. ***Communications media***—the physical media through which **electronic signals** are transferred; includes both wireline and wireless media.

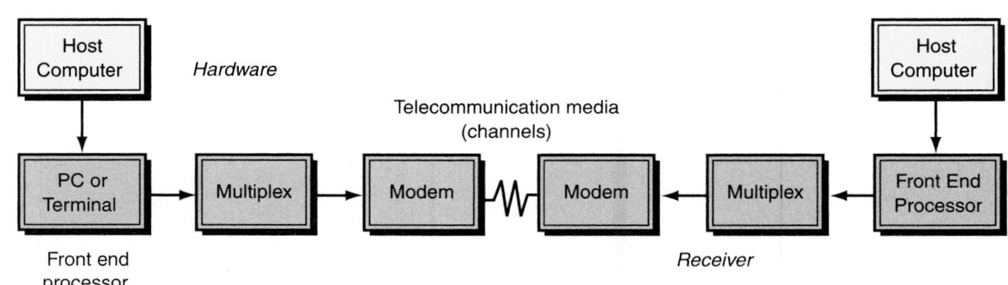

FIGURE T-4.2 A telecommunications system.

3. ***Communications networks***—the linkages among computers and communications devices.
4. ***Communications processors***—devices that perform specialized data communication functions; includes front-end processors, controllers, multiplexors, and modems.
5. ***Communications software***—software that controls the process.
6. ***Data communications providers***—either regulated utilities or private firms.
7. ***Communications protocols***—the rules for transferring information.
8. ***Communications applications***—examples include EDI, teleconferencing, electronic mail, facsimile, and electronic funds transfer.

To transmit and receive information, a telecommunications system must perform the following separate functions that are transparent to the user:

- Transmit information.
- Establish the interface between the sender and the receiver.
- Route messages along the most efficient paths.
- Process the information to ensure that the right message gets to the right receiver.
- Check for errors and rearrange the format if necessary.
- Convert messages from one speed to that of another communications line or from one format to another.
- Control the flow of information by routing messages, polling receivers, and maintaining information about the network.
- Secure the information at all times.

Electronic Signals

Telecommunications media can carry two basic types of signals, *analog* and *digital* (see Figure T-4.3). **Analog signals** are continuous waves that "carry" information by altering the *amplitude* and *frequency* of the waves. For example, sound is analog and travels to our ears in the form of waves—the greater the height (amplitude) of the waves, the louder the sound; the more closely packed the waves (higher frequency), the higher the pitch. Radio, telephones, and recording equipment historically transmitted and received analog signals, but they are beginning to change to digital signals.

Digital signals are discrete on-off pulses that convey information in terms of 1's and 0's, just like the central processing unit in computers. Digital signals have several advantages over analog signals. First, digital signals tend to be less affected by interference or "noise." Noise (e.g., "static") can seriously alter the information-carrying characteristics of analog signals, whereas it is generally easier, in spite of noise, to distinguish between an "on" and an "off." Consequently,

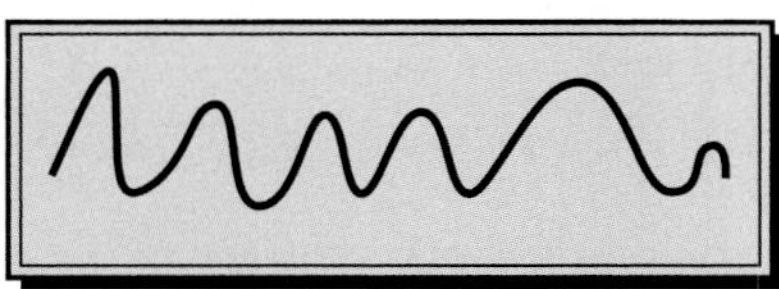

Analog data transmission
(wave signals)

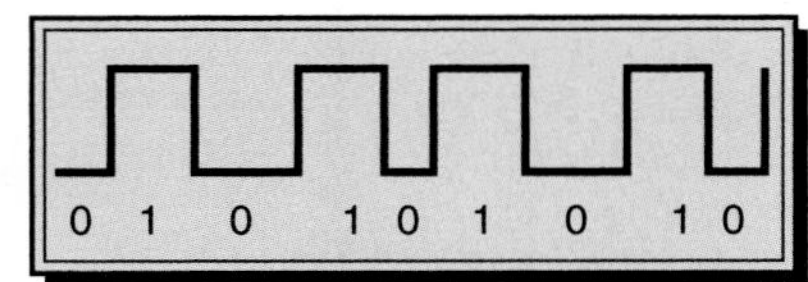

Digital data transmission
(pulse signals)

FIGURE T-4.3 Analog vs. digital signals.

digital signals can be repeatedly strengthened over long distances, minimizing the effect of any noise. Second, because computer-based systems process digitally, digital communications among computers require no conversion from digital to analog to digital.

Communications Processors

MODEM. The public telephone system (called POTS for "plain old telephone service") was designed as an analog network to carry voice signals or sounds in an analog wave format. In order for this type of circuit to carry digital information, that information must be converted into an analog wave pattern. The conversion from digital to analog is called **modulation**, and the reverse is **demodulation**. The device that performs these two processes is called a **modem**, a contraction of the terms *modulate/demodulate* (see Figure T-4.4). Modems are always used in pairs. The unit at the sending end converts digital information from a computer into analog signals for transmission over analog lines; at the receiving end, another modem converts the analog signal back into digital signals for the receiving computer. Like most communications equipment, a modem's transmission speed is measured in bits per second (bps). Today, typical modem speeds range from 28,800 to 56,600 bps.

The amount of data actually transferred from one system to another in a fixed length of time is only partially dependent on the transmission speed. Actual throughput speed, or the effective throughput speed (usually measured in characters per second), varies with factors such as the use of data compression or electrical noise interference.

NEWER ALTERNATIVES TO ANALOG MODEMS. **Digital subscriber line (DSL)** service allows the installed base of twisted-pair wiring in the telecommunications system to be used for high-volume data transmission. DSL uses digital transmission techniques over copper wires to connect the subscribers to network equipment located at the telephone company central office. *Asymmetric DSL (ADSL)* is a variety of DSL that enables a person connecting from home to upload data at 1 Mbps and download data at 8 Mbps. Clearly, this is many times faster than an analog modem. However, where it is available, ADSL service currently costs about $50 per month (which usually includes Internet service).

Cable modems are another alternative to analog modems. These are offered by cable television companies in many areas as a high-speed way to access a telecommunications network. These modems operate on one channel of the TV coaxial cable. Cost and transmission speed are comparable to that of an ADSL.

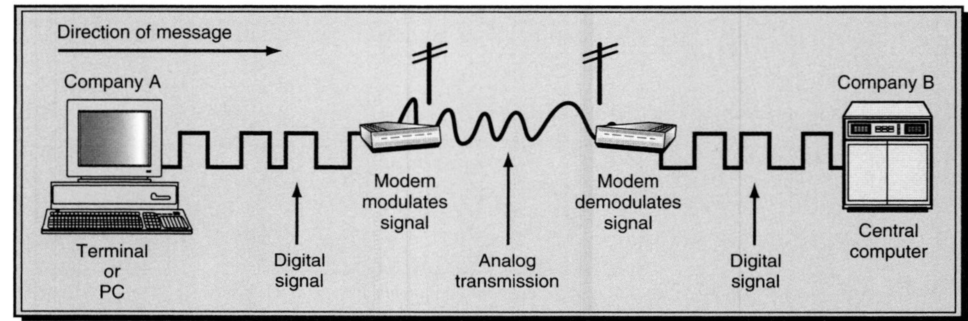

FIGURE T-4.4 A modem converts digital to analog signals and vice versa. (*Source: Computing in the Information Age*, Stern and Stern, © 1993 John Wiley & Sons, Inc.)

MULTIPLEXOR. A **multiplexor** is an electronic device that allows a single communications channel (e.g., a telephone circuit) to carry data transmissions simultaneously from many sources. The objective of a multiplexor is to reduce communication costs by maximizing the use of a circuit by sharing it. A multiplexor merges the transmissions of several terminals at one end of the channel, while a similar unit separates the individual transmissions at the receiving end. This process is accomplished through frequency division multiplexing (FDM), time division multiplexing (TDM), or statistical time division multiplexing (STDM). FDM assigns each transmission a different frequency. TDM and STDM merge together many short time segments of transmissions from different sending devices.

FRONT-END PROCESSOR. With most computers, the CPU has to communicate with several devices or terminals at the same time. Routine communication tasks can absorb a large proportion of the CPU's processing time, leading to degraded performance on more important jobs. In order not to waste valuable CPU time, many computer systems have a small secondary computer dedicated solely to communication. Known as a **front-end processor**, this specialized computer manages all routing communications with peripheral devices.

The functions of a front-end processor include coding and decoding data, error detection, recovery, recording, interpreting, and processing the control information that is transmitted. It can also poll remote terminals to determine if they have messages to send or are ready to receive a message. In addition, a front-end processor has the responsibility of controlling access to the network, assigning priorities to messages, logging all data communications activity, computing statistics on network activity, and routing and rerouting messages among alternative communication links and channels.

T4.2 COMMUNICATIONS MEDIA (CHANNELS)

For data to be communicated from one location to another, a physical pathway or medium must be used. These pathways are called **communications media (channels)** and are generally referred to as **wireline** (e.g., twisted pair wire, coaxial cable, and fiber optic cable) and **wireless** (e.g., cellular radio, microwave transmission, and satellite transmission) media. The advantages and disadvantages of various media are highlighted in Table T-4.1 on page 752. The essentials of these communications media are described below.

Wireline Media

Several wireline media exist, and in many systems a mix of media (e.g., fiber-coax) can be found. The major media are as follows.

TWISTED-PAIR WIRE. **Twisted-pair wire** is the most prevalent form of communications wiring, because it is used for almost all business telephone wiring. Twisted-pair wire consists of strands of insulated copper wire twisted in pairs to reduce the effect of electrical noise. (See Figure T-4.5, page 752) It is relatively inexpensive, widely available, easy to work with, and can be made relatively unobtrusive by running it inside walls, floors, and ceilings. However, twisted-pair wire has some important disadvantages. It emits electromagnetic interference, is relatively slow for transmitting data, is subject to interference from other electrical sources, and can be easily "tapped" to gain unauthorized access to data.

TABLE T-4.1 Advantages and Disadvantages of Communications Media

Medium	Advantages	Disadvantages
Twisted pair	• Inexpensive • Widely available • Easy to work with • Unobtrusive	• Emits electromagnetic interference • Slow (low bandwidth) • Subject to interference • Easily tapped (low security)
Coaxial cable	• Higher bandwidth than twisted pair • Less susceptible to electromagnetic interference	• Relatively expensive and inflexible • Somewhat difficult to work with • Easily tapped (low to medium security)
Fiber optic cable	• Very high bandwidth • Smaller and lighter than coaxial cable • Difficult to tap	• Difficult to work with (difficult to splice) • Expensive • Relatively inflexible
Microwave	• Very high bandwidth • Relatively inexpensive	• Must have unobstructed line-of-sight • Subject to interference from rain
Satellite	• Very high bandwidth • Large coverage on earth	• Must use encryption for security • Expensive • Must have unobstructed line-of-sight • Signals experience propagation delay

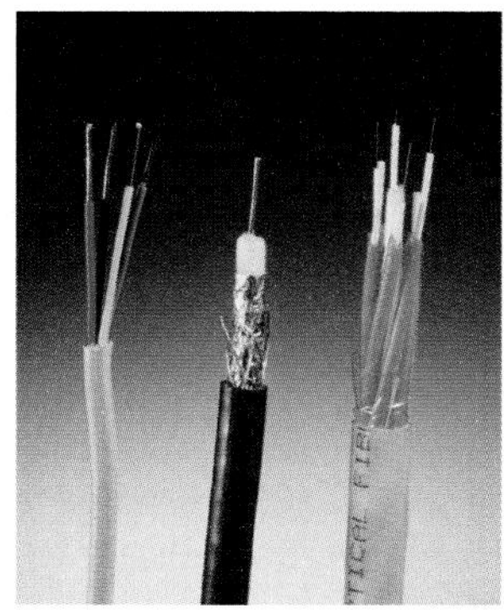

FIGURE T-4.5 Twisted pair telephone cable, coaxial cable, and fiber-optic cable.

COAXIAL CABLE. **Coaxial cable** consists of insulated copper wire surrounded by a solid or braided metallic shield and wrapped in a plastic cover. It is much less susceptible to electrical interference and can carry much more data than twisted-pair wire. For these reasons, it is commonly used to carry high-speed data traffic as well as television signals (i.e., in cable television). However, coaxial cable is 10 to 20 times more expensive, more difficult to work with, and relatively inflexible. Because of its inflexibility, it can increase the cost of installation or recabling when equipment must be moved.

FIBER OPTICS. Fiber-optic technology, combined with the invention of the semiconductor laser, provides the means to transmit information through clear glass fibers in the form of light waves, instead of electric current. **Fiber-optic cables** consist of thousands of very thin filaments of glass fibers. These fibers can conduct light pulses generated by lasers at transmission frequencies that approach the speed of light.

Besides significant size and weight reductions over traditional cable media, fiber-optic cables provide increased speed, greater data-carrying capacity, and greater security from interferences and tapping. A single hairlike glass fiber can carry up to 30,000 simultaneous telephone calls, compared to about 5,500 calls on a standard copper coaxial cable. Until recently, the costs of fiber and difficulties in installing fiber-optic cable slowed its growth.

The technology of generating and harnessing light and other forms of radiant energy whose quantum unit is the photon is called **photonics**. This science includes light emission, transmission, deflection, amplification, and detection by optical components and instruments, lasers and other light sources, fiber optics, electro-optical instrumentation, related hardware and electronics, and sophisticated systems. The range of applications of photonics extends from energy generation to detection to communications and information processing. Photons are used to move data at gigabit-per-second speeds across more than 1,000 wavelengths per fiber strand.

Wireless Media

Wireline media (with the exception of fiber-optic cables) present several problems, notably the expense of installation and change, as well as a fairly limited capacity. The alternative is **wireless communication**. Common uses of wireless data transmission include pagers, cellular telephones, microwave transmissions, communications satellites, mobile data networks, personal communications services, and personal digital assistants (PDAs).

MICROWAVE. **Microwave** systems are widely used for high-volume, long-distance, point-to-point communication. These systems were first used extensively to transmit very-high-frequency radio signals in a line-of-sight path between relay stations spaced approximately 30 miles apart (due to the earth's curvature). To minimize line-of-sight problems, microwave antennas were usually placed on top of buildings, towers, and mountain peaks. Long-distance telephone carriers adopted microwave systems because they generally provide about 10 times the data-carrying capacity of a wire without the significant efforts necessary to string or bury wire. Compared to 30 miles of wire, microwave communications can be set up much more quickly (within a day) and at much lower cost.

However, the fact that microwave requires line-of-sight transmission severely limits its usefulness as a practical large-scale solution to data communication needs, especially over very long distances. Additionally, microwave transmissions are susceptible to environmental interference during severe weather such as heavy rain or snowstorms. Although still fairly widely used, long distance microwave data communications systems have been largely replaced by satellite communications systems.

SATELLITE. A major advance in communications in recent years is the use of *communications satellites* for digital transmissions. Although the radio frequencies used by satellite data communication transponders are also line-of-sight, the enormous "footprint" of a satellite's coverage area from high altitudes overcomes the limitations of microwave data relay stations. For example, a network of just three evenly spaced communications satellites in stationary "geosynchronous" orbit 22,300 miles above the equator is sufficient to provide global coverage.

Currently, there are three types of orbits in which satellites are placed: geostationary earth orbit, medium earth orbit, and low earth orbit.

Geostationary earth orbit (GEO) satellites orbit 22,300 miles directly above the equator and maintain a fixed position above the earth's surface. These satellites are excellent for sending television programs to cable operators and broadcasting directly to homes. However, transmissions from GEO satellites take a quarter of a second to send and return (called *propagation delay*), making two-way telephone conversations difficult. Also, GEO satellites are large and expensive, and the equatorial orbit cannot hold many more GEO satellites than the 150 that now orbit there. In 2000, a system of eight GEO satellites was launched by Hughes Electronics at a cost of $3 billion.

Medium earth orbit (MEO) satellites are located about 6,000 miles above the earth's surface, in orbits inclined to the equator. While fewer satellites are needed to cover the earth than in LEO orbits (see below), telephones need more power to reach MEO satellites than to reach LEO satellites.

Low earth orbit (LEO) satellites are located 400 to 1,000 miles above the earth's surface. These satellites are much closer to the earth, reducing or eliminating apparent signal delay. They can pick up signals from weak transmitters, meaning that handheld telephones need less power and can use smaller batteries. They consume less power and cost less to launch than GEO and MEO satellites. However, moving data across constellations of many satellites is complex and the technology remains untested. In 1999, a system of 48 LEO satellites was launched by Loral and Qualcomm at a cost of $2.5 billion.

Satellites have a number of unique characteristics. Some of these characteristics are advantages while others are restrictions that render satellite use either impractical or impossible for other applications.

Advantages of Satellites

- Cost of transmission is the same regardless of the distance between the sending and receiving stations within the footprint of a satellite.
- Cost remains the same regardless of the number of stations receiving that transmission (simultaneous reception).
- They have the ability to carry very large amounts of data.
- They can easily cross or span political borders, often with minimal government regulation.
- Transmission errors in a digital satellite signal occur almost completely at random. Thus, statistical methods for error detection and correction can be applied efficiently and reliably.
- Users can be highly mobile while sending and receiving signals.

Disadvantages of Satellites

- Any one-way transmission over a satellite link has an inherent propagation delay of approximately one-quarter of a second. This delay makes the use of satellite links inefficient for some data communications needs (voice communication and "stepping-on" each other's speech).
- Due to launch-weight limitations, they carry or generate very little electrical power. Low power of signal coupled with distance can result in extremely weak signals at the receiving earth station.
- Signals are inherently not secure because they are available to all receivers within the footprint—intended or not.
- Some frequencies used are susceptible to interference from bad weather or ground-based microwave signals.

GLOBAL POSITIONING SYSTEMS. A **global positioning system (GPS)** is a wireless system that uses satellites to enable users to determine their position anywhere on the earth. GPS equipment has been used extensively for navigation by commercial airlines and ships and for locating trucks. GPS is supported by 24 U.S. government satellites that are shared worldwide. Each satellite orbits the earth once in 12 hours, on a precise path at an altitude of 10,900 miles. At any point in time, the exact position of each satellite is known, because the satellite broadcasts its position and a time signal from its on-board atomic clock, accurate to one-billionth of a second. Receivers also have accurate clocks that are synchronized with those of the satellites. Knowing the speed of signals (186,272 miles per second), it is possible to find the location of any receiving station (latitude and longitude) within an accuracy of 50 feet by triangulation, using the distance of three satellites for the computation. GPS software computes the latitude and longitude and converts it to an electronic map.

GPSs have many applications; several are discussed in this book. An interesting application is now available from several car manufacturers (e.g., Toyota, Cadillac) as a navigation system for finding your way to places such as gas stations. GPSs are also available on cell phones, so you can know where the caller is located. As of October 2001, cell phones in the United States must have a GPS embedded in them so that the location of a caller to 911 can be detected immediately. GPSs are now available to hikers in the form of handheld devices costing less than $100.

RADIO. **Radio** electromagnetic data communications do not have to depend on microwave or satellite links, especially for short ranges such as within an office setting. Radio is being used increasingly to connect computers and peripheral equipment or computers and local area networks. The greatest advantage of radio for data communications is that no wires need be installed. Radio waves tend to propagate easily through normal office walls. The devices are fairly inexpensive and easy to install.

However, radio can create reciprocal electrical interference problems—with other office electrical equipment, and from that equipment to the radio communication devices. Also, radio transmissions are susceptible to snooping by anyone similarly equipped and on the same frequency. (This limitation can be largely overcome by encrypting the data being transmitted.)

INFRARED. **Infrared light** is light not visible to human eyes that can be modulated or pulsed for conveying information. The most common application of infrared light is with television or videocassette recorder remote control units. With computers, infrared transmitters and receivers (or "transceivers") are being used for short-distance connection between computers and peripheral equipment, or between computers and local area networks. Many mobile phones have a built-in infrared (IrDA) port that supports data transfer.

Advantages of infrared light include no need to lay wire, equipment is highly mobile, no electrical interference problems, no Federal Communications Commission (FCC) permission required to operate an infrared transmitter, no certification needed before selling an infrared device, and fairly inexpensive devices with very high data rates. Disadvantages of infrared media include susceptibility to fog, smog, smoke, dust, rain, and air temperature fluctuations.

CELLULAR RADIO TECHNOLOGY. Mobile telephones, which are being used increasingly for data communications, are based on **cellular radio technology**. The basic concept behind this technology is relatively simple: The FCC has defined geographic cellular service areas; each area is subdivided into hexagonal cells that fit together like a honeycomb to form the backbone of that area's cellular radio system. Located at the center of each cell is a radio transceiver and a computerized cell-site controller that handles all cell-site control functions. All the cell sites are connected to a mobile telephone switching office that provides the connections from the cellular system to a wired telephone network and transfers calls from one cell to another as a user travels out of the cell serving one area and into another.

The cellular telephone infrastructure has primarily been used for voice transmission, but recent development of a transmission standard called *cellular digital packet data (CDPD)* has made it possible for the infrastructure to support two-way digital transmission.

MOBILE COMPUTING. **Mobile computing** refers to the use of portable computer devices in multiple locations. It occurs on radio-based networks that transmit data to and from mobile computers. Computers can be connected to the network through wired ports or through wireless connections. Mobile computing provides for many applications, including m-commerce (Chapter 5).

Another type of mobile data network is based on a series of radio towers constructed specifically to transmit text and data. BellSouth Mobile Data and Ardis (formerly owned by IBM and Motorola) are two privately owned networks that use these media for national two-way data transmission.

PERSONAL COMMUNICATION SERVICE. **Personal communication service (PCS)** uses lower-power, higher-frequency radio waves than does cellular technology. The lower power means that PCS cells are smaller and must be more numerous and closer together. The higher frequency means that PCS devices are effective in many places where cellular telephones are not, such as in tunnels and inside office buildings. PCS telephones need less power, are smaller, and are less expensive than cellular telephones. They also operate at higher, less-crowded frequencies than cellular telephones, meaning that they will have the bandwidth necessary to provide video and multimedia communication.

PERSONAL DIGITAL ASSISTANTS. **Personal digital assistants (PDAs)** are small, penbased, handheld computers capable of entirely digital communications transmission (see discussion in Technology Guide 1). They have built-in wireless telecommunications capabilities. Applications include Internet access, e-mail, fax, electronic scheduler, calendar, and notepad software.

NEWER WIRELESS TECHNOLOGIES. A relatively new technology for wireless connectivity is called **Bluetooth**. It allows wireless communication between mobile phones, laptops, and other portable devices. Bluetooth technology is currently being built into mobile PCs, mobile telephones, and PDAs.

Another new technology is "fiber optics without the fiber." With this technology, laser beams are transmitted through the air between two buildings or other points. Terabeam Corporation recently introduced such a service. Like other wireless media, the chief advantage of this technology is that there is no need to gain rights of way to lay cabling. However, weather can have a negative impact on transmission quality.

Characteristics of Communications Media

Communications media have several characteristics that determine their efficiency and capabilities. These characteristics include the speed, direction, mode, and accuracy of transmission.

TRANSMISSION SPEED. **Bandwidth** refers to the range of frequencies that can be sent over a communications channel. Frequencies are measured in the number of cycles per second (or *Hertz,* abbreviated Hz). Bandwidth is an important concept in communications because the transmission capacity of a channel is largely dependent on its bandwidth. Capacity is stated in bits per second (bps), thousands of bps (Kbps), millions of bps (Mbps), and billions of bps (Gbps). In general, the greater the bandwidth of a channel, the greater the channel capacity.

A **baud** is a detectable change in a signal (i.e., a change from a positive to a negative voltage in a wire). **Baud rate** refers to the rate at which signals can be transmitted through a communications channel. The baud rate is not always the same as the bit rate measured in bps. At higher transmission speeds, a single signal change can represent more than one bit, so the bit rate can be greater than the baud rate.

For many data communications applications (i.e, those that involve textual data), a low bandwidth (2,400 to 14,400 bps) is adequate. On the other hand, acceptable performance for transmission of graphical information requires bandwidth in the Mbps range.

Channel capacity is usually divided into three bandwidths: *narrowband, voiceband,* and *broadband* channels. Slow, low-capacity transmissions, such as those transmitted over telegraph lines, make use of **narrowband** channels, while telephone lines utilize **voiceband** channels. The channel bandwidth with the highest capacity is **broadband**, used by microwave, cable, and fiber-optic media.

Communications channels have a wide range of speeds based on the technology used. Transfer rates for various types of transmission media are shown in Table T-4.2.

OPTICAL NETWORKING. **Wave division multiplexing (WDM)** is a technique whereby different colors of light are transmitted on an optical fiber so that more than one message can be transmitted at a time. (This is actually a form of FDM.) Recent innovations have led to *dense wave division multiplexing (DWDM),* where hundreds of messages can be sent simultaneously. DWDM dramatically increases the capacity of existing optical fiber networks without laying any new cable.

TABLE T-4.2 Transmission Rates in Different Media

Medium	Capacity
Twisted pair	Up to 128 Mbps
Coaxial cable	Up to 200 Mbps
Fiber-optic cable	100 Mbps to 2 Gbps
Broadcast radio	Up to 2 Mbps
Microwave	45 Mbps
Satellite	50 Mbps
Cellular radio, 2 G cell phone	9600 bps to 14.4 Kbps
Cell phone, 3 G	Up to 2 Mbps
Cell phone, 2.5 G	GPRS, up to 115 Kbps EDGE, up to 384 Kbps
Infrared	1 to 4 Mbps

Eventually, an all-optical network, where signals coming into the network are immediately converted to colors of light and managed at an optical layer, will become economically feasible. The increased capacity will be very significant.

Transmission Direction

Data transmission can be simplex, half-duplex, or full-duplex.

Simplex data transmission uses one circuit in one direction only—similar to a doorbell, a public announcement system, or broadcast television and radio. Simplex transmission is simple and relatively inexpensive but very constraining, since communication is one way only.

Half-duplex transmission also uses only one circuit, but it is used in both directions—one direction at a time. Examples include an intercom or a citizen's band radio where users can receive or transmit, but cannot do both simultaneously. Two-way data transfer makes half duplex much more useful than simplex, but coordination of half-duplex communications could be difficult.

Full-duplex transmission uses two circuits for communications—one for each direction simultaneously (for example, a common telephone). Full-duplex is easier to use than half-duplex, but the cost of two circuits can be significant, especially over long distances. Most data devices can operate in both half- and full-duplex directions.

Transmission Mode

Data transmissions may be either asynchronous or synchronous. In **asynchronous transmission**, only one character is transmitted or received at a time. During transmission, the character is preceded by a start bit and followed by a stop bit that lets the receiving device know where a character begins and ends. There is typically idle time between transmission of characters, so synchronization is maintained on a character-by-character basis. Asynchronous transmission is inherently inefficient due to the additional overhead required for start and stop bits, and the idle time between transmissions. It is generally used only for relatively low-speed data transmission (up to 56 Kbps).

With **synchronous transmission**, a group of characters is sent over a communications link in a continuous bit stream while data transfer is controlled by a timing signal initiated by the sending device. The sender and receiver must be in perfect synchronization to avoid the loss or gain of bits; therefore, data blocks are preceded by unique characters called *sync bits* that are encoded into the information being transmitted. The receiving device recognizes and synchronizes itself with a stream of these characters. Synchronous transmission is generally used for transmitting large volumes of data at high speeds.

Transmission Accuracy

An electrical communications line can be subject to interference from storms, signals from other lines, and other phenomena that introduce errors into a transmission. Telephone line cables may be mishandled by repair personnel, accidentally cut by construction workers, or subjected to power surges while data are being transmitted. These events might cause one bit or several bits to be "dropped" during transmission, thus corrupting the integrity of the information. Because the loss of even one bit could alter a character or control code, data transmission requires accuracy controls. These controls consist of bits called *parity bits* that are like check sums added to characters and/or blocks of characters at the sending end of the line. Parity bits are checked and verified at the receiving end of the line to determine whether bits were lost during transmission.

T4.3 NETWORK SYSTEMS: PROTOCOLS, STANDARDS, INTERFACES, AND TOPOLOGIES

Network architectures facilitate the operation, maintenance, and growth of the network by isolating the user and the application from the physical details of the network. Network architectures include protocols, standards, interfaces, and topologies.

Protocols

Devices that are nodes in a network must access and share the network to transmit and receive data. These components work together by adhering to a common set of rules that enable them to communicate with each other. This set of rules and procedures governing transmission across a network is a **protocol**.

The principal functions of protocols in a network are line access and collision avoidance. Line access concerns how the sending device gains access to the network to send a message. Collision avoidance refers to managing message transmission so that two messages do not collide with each other on the network. Other functions of protocols are to identify each device in the communication path, to secure the attention of the other device, to verify correct receipt of the transmitted message, to verify that a message requires retransmission because it cannot be correctly interpreted, and to perform recovery when errors occur.

The simplest protocol is **polling**, where a master device (computer or communications processor) polls, or contacts, each node. Polling can be effective because the speed of mainframe and communications processors allows them to poll and control transmissions by many nodes sharing the same channel, particularly if the typical communications are short.

In the **token passing approach**, a small data packet, called a *token*, is sent around the network. If a device wants to transmit a message, it must wait for the token to pass, examine it to see if it is in use and pass it on, or use the token to help route its message to its destination on the network. After transmission is completed, the token is returned to the network by the receiving terminal if it is not needed. IBM token ring networks use this access method.

In another approach, called **contention**, which is part of the Ethernet protocol, a device that wants to send a message checks the communications medium (e.g., a twisted pair wire) to see if it is in use. If one device (e.g., a PC) detects that another device (e.g., a printer) is using the channel (i.e., a collision occurs), it waits a random time interval and retries its transmission.

The **Transmission Control Protocol/Internet Protocol (TCP/IP)** is a protocol for sending information across sometimes-unreliable networks with the assurance that it will arrive in uncorrupted form. TCP/IP allows efficient and reasonably error-free transmission between different systems and is the standard protocol of the Internet and intranets. (Further discussion of this protocol may be found in Technology Guide 5.)

Communication Standards

Networks typically have hardware and software from a number of different vendors which must communicate with each other by "speaking the same language" and following the same protocols. Unfortunately, commercially available data communication devices speak a variety of languages and follow a number of different protocols, causing substantial problems with data communications networks.

Attempts at standardizing data communications have been somewhat successful, but standardization in the United States has lagged behind other countries where the communications industry is more closely regulated. Various organizations, including the Electronic Industries Association (EIA), the Consultative Committee for International Telegraph and Telephone (CCITT), and the International Standards Organization (ISO), have developed electronic interfacing standards that are widely used within the industry. The major types of standards are *networking standards, transmission standards, and software standards.*

NETWORKING STANDARDS. Typically, the protocols required to achieve communication on behalf of an application are actually multiple protocols existing at different levels or layers. Each layer defines a set of functions that are provided as services to upper layers, and each layer relies on services provided by lower layers. At each layer, one or more protocols define precisely how software programs on different systems interact to accomplish the functions for that layer. This layering notion has been formalized in several architectures. The most widely known is the Open Systems Interconnection (OSI) Reference Model developed by the ISO. There is peer-to-peer communication between software at each layer, and each relies on underlying layers for services to accomplish communication.

The OSI model has seven layers, each having its own well-defined function:

- ***Layer 1: Physical layer.*** Concerned with transmitting raw bits over a communications channel; provides a physical connection for the transmission of data among network entities and creates the means by which to activate and deactivate a physical connection.
- ***Layer 2: Data link layer.*** Provides a reliable means of transmitting data across a physical link; breaks up the input data into data frames sequentially and processes the acknowledgment frames sent back by the receiver.
- ***Layer 3: Network layer.*** Routes information from one network computer to another; computers may be physically located within the same network or within another network that is interconnected in some fashion; accepts messages from source host and sees to it they are directed toward the destination.
- ***Layer 4: Transport layer.*** Provides a network-independent transport service to the session layer; accepts data from session layer, splits it up into smaller units as required, passes these to the network layer, and ensures all pieces arrive correctly at the other end.
- ***Layer 5: Session layer.*** User's interface into network; where user must negotiate to establish connection with process on another machine; once connection is established the session layer can manage the dialogue in an orderly manner.
- ***Layer 6: Presentation layer.*** Here messages are translated from and to the format used in the network to and from a format used at the application layer.
- ***Layer 7: Application layer.*** Includes activities related to users, such as supporting file transfer, handling messages, and providing security.

The SNA Standard. The *Systems Network Architecture (SNA)* is a standard developed by IBM that is widely used in private networks. Similar to OSI, SNA uses a layered approach; however, the layers are somewhat different.

TRANSMISSION STANDARDS. A number of network bandwidth boosters address the need for greater bandwidth on networks for advanced computing applications. These include FDDI (fiber distributed data interface), ATM (asynchronous transfer mode), LAN switches, and ISDN (integrated services digital network).

Like token-ring networks, the **fiber distributed data interface (FDDI)** passes data around a ring, but with a bandwidth of 100 Mpbs—far faster than a standard 10–13 Mbps token-ring or bus network. Although the FDDI standard can use any transmission medium, it is based on the high-speed, high-capacity capabilities of fiber optics. FDDI can significantly boost network performance, but this technology is about ten times more expensive to implement than most local area networks (LANs).

Asynchronous transfer mode (ATM) networks are based on switched technologies, allowing for almost unlimited bandwidth on demand. They are packet-switched networks, dividing data into uniform cells, each with 53 groups of eight bytes, eliminating the need for protocol conversion. ATM allows mixing of varying bandwidths and data types (e.g., video, data, and voice) and much higher speeds because the data are more easily "squeezed" in among other very small packets. ATM currently requires fiber-optic cable.

LAN switches are often used to boost local area network capacity. A switch can turn many small LANs into one big LAN. A network need not be rewired nor adapter cards replaced when changes are made; all that is needed is the addition of a switch. Switch technology can also add an ATM-like packet-switching capability to existing LANs, essentially doubling bandwidth.

Integrated services digital network (ISDN) is a high-speed data transmission technology that allows users to simultaneously transfer voice, video, image, and data at high speed. ISDN uses existing telephone lines and provides two levels of service: basic-rate ISDN and primary-rate ISDN. Basic-rate ISDN serves a single device with three channels. Two channels are B (bearer) channels with a capacity to transmit 64 Kbps of digital data. The third or D channel is a 16-Kbps channel for signaling and control information. Primary-rate ISDN provides 1.5 Mbps of bandwidth. The bandwidth contains 23 B channels and one D channel. A second generation of ISDN is *broadband ISDN (BISDN)*, which provides transmission channels capable of supporting transmission rates greater than the primary ISDN rate. BISDN supports transmission from 2 Mbps up to much higher, but as yet unspecified, rates.

SOFTWARE STANDARDS. Three types of software standards are necessary for an **open system**. An open system refers to the ability of different devices, from different vendors, to conveniently "talk" to each other.

Operating Systems. No single operating system standard exists. The result is many differing versions of operating systems, such as DOS, Unix, Windows 2000, OS/2, and Linux.

Graphical User Interface Standard. X Windows is the standard for GUI. It runs on all types of computers and is used with Unix and the DEC VAX/VMS operating systems. It permits one display of several applications on one screen and allows one application to use several windows.

Software Application Standards. The U.S. government is attempting to establish a standard for all its systems. It will cover operating systems, DBMSs, user interfaces, programming languages, electronic data interchange, and so on.

Interfaces

An **interface** is a physical connection between two communications devices. One important concept of interfacing concerns the types of data transfer—parallel or serial. **Parallel data transfer**, most often used for local communication, employs a communications interface with a series of dedicated wires, each serving one purpose. In parallel communication, both data and control signals are transmitted simultaneously.

A **serial data transfer**, most often used for long-distance communications, is bit by bit rather than many bits in parallel. Most data communications devices transmit in serial fashion. While much slower than parallel data transfer, serial transfer is simpler and requires much less on the part of the receiving system.

Network Topology

The **topology** of a network is the physical layout and connectivity of a network. Specific protocols, or rules of communications, are often used on specific topologies, but the two concepts are different. Topology refers to the ways the channels connect the nodes, whereas protocol refers to the rules by which data communications take place over these channels. Neither concept should be confused with the *physical cabling* of the network. There are three basic network topologies: bus, ring, and star (see Figure T-4.6).

BUS. In a *bus* topology, nodes are arranged along a single length of twisted-pair wire, coaxial cable, or fiber-optic cable that can be extended at the ends. Using a bus topology, it is easy and inexpensive to add a node to the network, and losing a node in the network will not cause the network to fail. The main disadvantages to the bus topology are that a defective bus causes the *entire network* to fail, and providing a bus with inadequate bandwidth will degrade the performance of the network.

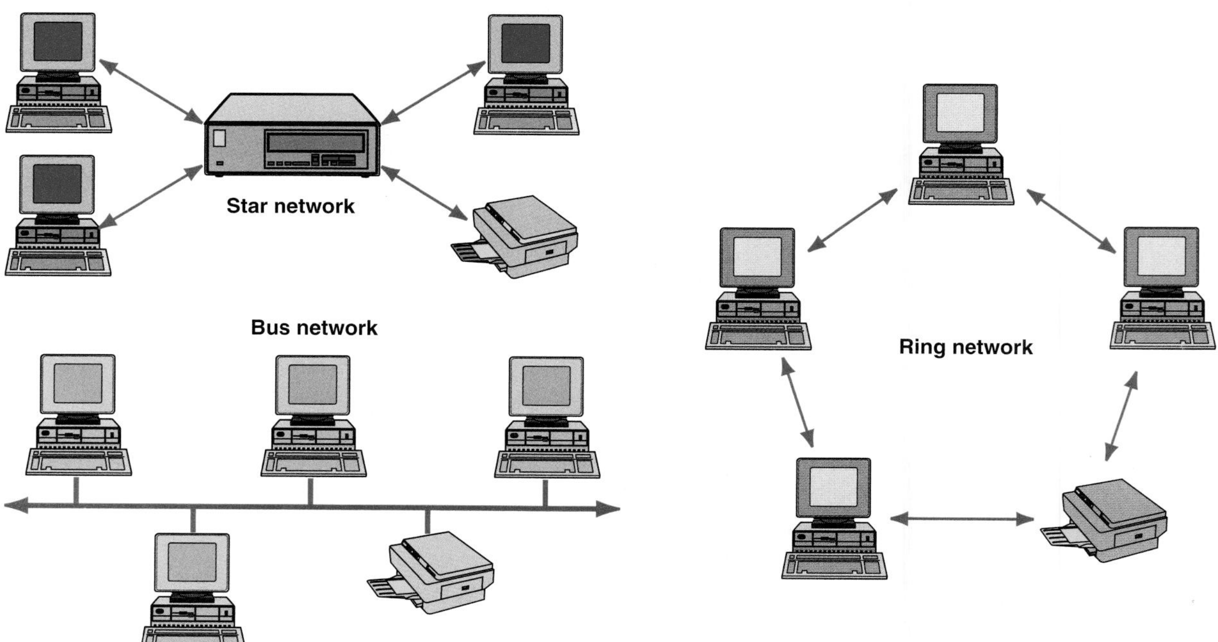

FIGURE T-4.6 The three main network topologies.

RING. In a *ring* topology, nodes are arranged along the transmission path so that a signal passes through each station one at a time before returning to its originating node. The nodes, then, form a closed circle. It is relatively easy and inexpensive to add a node to the network, and losing a node does not necessarily mean that the network will fail.

STAR. A *star* network has a central node that connects to each of the other nodes by a single, point-to-point link. Any communication between one node and another in a star topology must pass through the central node. It is easy to add a node in a star network, and losing a peripheral node will not cause the entire network to fail. However, the central computer must be powerful enough to handle communications in a star network. Too many devices in the star can overload the central computer and cause degradation in performance across the network. The star topology is typically used in low-cost, slow-speed data networks.

Each topology has strengths and weaknesses. When an organization is choosing a topology, it should consider such performance issues as delay, throughput, reliability, and the network's ability to continue through, or recover after, the failure of one or more of its nodes. A company should also consider such physical constraints as the maximum transmission speed of the circuit, the distances between nodes, the circuit's susceptibility to errors, and the overall system costs.

Network Size

Because people need to communicate over long as well as short distances, the geographic size of data communications networks is important. There are two general network sizes: local area networks and wide area networks. A "metropolitan" area network falls between the two in size.

LOCAL AREA NETWORKS. A **local area network (LAN)** connects two or more communicating devices within a short distance (e.g., 2,000 feet), so that every user device on the network has the potential to communicate with any other device. LANs are usually intraorganizational, privately owned, internally administered, and not subject to regulation by the FCC. LANs do not cross public rights-of-way and do not require communications hardware and software that are necessary to link computer systems to existing communications networks. A LAN allows a large number of its intelligent devices to share corporate resources (such as storage devices, printers, programs, and data files), and it integrates a wide range of functions into a single system. Many LANs are physically connected as a star, with every device connected to a hub or switch.

In an office, a LAN can give users fast and efficient access to a common collection of information while also allowing the office to pool resources, such as printers and facsimile machines. A well-constructed LAN can also eliminate the need to circulate paper documents by distributing electronic memos and other materials to each worker's terminal.

The network gateway connects the LAN to public networks or other corporate networks so that the LAN can exchange information with networks external to it. A **gateway** is a communications processor that can connect dissimilar networks by translating from one set of protocols to another. A **bridge** connects two networks of the same type. A **router** routes messages through several connected LANs or to a WAN.

A LAN consists of cabling or wireless technology linking individual devices, **network interface cards** (special adapters serving as interfaces to the cable), and software to control LAN activities. The LAN network interface card specifies the data transmission rate, the size of message units, the addressing information attached to each message, and the network topology.

Private Branch Exchange. A **private branch exchange (PBX)** is closely related to a LAN. The PBX is a special-purpose computer that controls telephone switching at a company site. PBXs can carry both voice and data and perform a wide variety of functions to make communications more convenient and effective, such as call waiting, call forwarding, and voice mail. PBXs also offer functions directed at decreasing costs, such as reducing the number of outside lines, providing internal extensions, and determining least-cost routings. Automatic assignment of calls to lines reduces the required number of outside lines. Providing internal extension numbers permits people to make calls within the same site using only extension numbers and without making a chargeable outside call.

WIDE AREA NETWORKS. **Wide area networks (WANs)** are long-haul, broadband, generally public-access networks covering wide geographic areas that cross rights-of-way where communications media are provided by common carriers. WANs include *regional networks* such as telephone companies or *international networks* such as global communications service providers. They usually have very large-capacity circuits with many communications processors to use these circuits efficiently.

WANs may combine switched and dedicated lines, microwave, and satellite communications. Switched lines are telephone lines that a person can access from his or her computer to transmit data to another computer, the transmission being routed or switched through paths to its destination. Dedicated (or leased) lines, or nonswitched lines, are continuously available for transmission, and a lessee typically pays a flat rate for exclusive access to the line. The lines can be leased or purchased from common carriers or private communications media vendors. Dedicated lines are often higher speed than switched lines and are used for high-volume transactions.

A leased line may handle data only, or it may be capable of handling both voice and data just as a standard telephone line does. When leased lines have been designed specifically for data transmission, they produce less noise and fewer transmission errors than regular telephone lines, and they are more secure from wiretapping and other security risks. Most importantly, the central processor is always accessible through the leased line, and the line usually transmits data at speeds (e.g., 1.544 Mbps) faster than a standard telephone line.

Some WANs are commercial, regulated networks, while others are privately owned, usually by large businesses that can afford the costs. Some WANs, however, are "public" in terms of their management, resources, and access.

Value-Added Networks. A **value-added network (VAN)** is a type of WAN. VANs are private, multipath, data-only, third-party-managed networks that can provide economies in the cost of service and network management because they are used by multiple organizations. VANs can add teleconferencing services and message storage, tracking, and relay services, and can more closely tailor communications capabilities to specific business needs.

VANs offer several valuable services; customers do not have to invest in network hardware and software or perform their own error checking, editing, routing, and protocol conversion. Subscribers realize savings in line charges and transmission costs because many users share the costs of using the network.

Value-added networks also provide economies through **packet switching**. Packet switching breaks up a message into small, fixed bundles of data called *packets*. The VAN continuously uses various communications channels to send the packets. Each packet travels independently through the network. Packets of data originating at one source can be routed through different paths in the network, and then may be reassembled into the original message when they reach their destination.

Frame Relay. **Frame relay** is a faster and less expensive version of packet switching. Frame relay is a shared network service that packages data into "frames" that are similar to packets. Frame relay, however, does not perform error correction, because modern digital lines are less error-prone than older lines and networks are more effective at error checking. Frame relay can communicate at speeds of 50 megabits per second.

Frame relay is essentially used for transmitting data. It is not recommended for any transmissions that are sensitive to varying delay, such as voice or digital video traffic, and it cannot easily control network congestion. Some companies do use voice-over frame relay, however, because of its low cost. Frame relay is rapidly replacing leased lines as the primary form of long-distance communication in WANs.

Virtual Private Networks. A **virtual private network (VPN)** is a network that exists on the hardware, software, and media of a communications carrier (e.g., Sprint) or an ISP (Internet service provider), but it looks to the customer as if he or she owns it. A VPN provides a link between a corporate LAN and the Internet and is a means for allowing controlled access to a private network's e-mail, shared files, or intranet via an Internet connection. The VPN provider handles security (e.g., authentication), thus permitting access from the Internet to an intranet. The data, from business partners or corporate commuters, travels over the Internet—but it is encrypted. To provide this level of security without a VPN it might otherwise be necessary to make a long-distance call to connect to a remote access service (RAS) dialup. With VPN, this cost is eliminated. In addition, VPN is less expensive than RAS and can provide more services.

There are several types of VPNs on the market, and they are priced differently. VPNs are especially suited for extranets, since they allow the use of the Internet between business partners instead of using a more expensive VAN. VPNs are especially important for international trade where long-distance calls, or VANs, are very expensive.

T4.4 NETWORK ARCHITECTURE: OPEN SYSTEMS AND ENTERPRISE NETWORKING

When two devices on a network are directly connected, there is a **point-to-point connection**. When the two devices have the same relative standing, as with two PCs, there is a **peer-to-peer connection**. If, however, there is a point-of-sale terminal dialing into a credit card checking mainframe via modem, there is a point-to-point, but not peer-to-peer connection. In this latter example, there is a client/server, point-to-point network.

Technology Architecture

CENTRALIZED ARCHITECTURE. *Centralized computer systems* are centered around a large computer, known as the *host,* that provides computational power and internal storage. Several devices that lack self-contained computer processors, such as dumb terminals and printers, are connected to the host. Information is entered, distributed, stored, or communicated through these devices. There are four basic types of these devices for direct, temporary interaction with people (usually via a typewriter-like keyboard and on an electronic monitor or screen): output devices such as printers and plotters for generating permanent outputs; input devices such as bar-code scanners for reading data; communications devices for exchanging data with other computer systems; and storage devices for electronically storing data. (See Technology Guide 1 for a review of computer hardware.) In each case, the host computer, usually a mainframe, is responsible for computer processing, and it is centrally connected to each device. All information processing is orchestrated by the host, and much of it is carried out by the devices. This arrangement (Figure T-4.7) is simple, direct, and easily controlled.

www.wiley.com/college/turban

Although mainframes have represented the dominant centralized form of computing for over 30 years, minicomputers, workstations, and powerful PCs are challenging that dominance. Centralized computing, as an architecture, can include all sizes of computer processors, including a conglomeration of computers acting in parallel. Mainframes, by themselves, no longer "rule the roost," but they are still an important part of an IT architecture, along with smaller computers ranging down to palmtops. Whereas architectural decisions were relatively simple with one computer—the mainframe—they are now much more varied and complex with a wide range of computers available.

Mainframes have traditionally been expensive to purchase, operate, and maintain. Indeed, the cost of mainframes is the primary reason industry analysts predict their demise. But the acquisition and operational costs of mainframes continue to decline, because of technological improvements (such as cheaper, more powerful processors and peripheral equipment) and production cost reductions. Operational costs are also declining through modern managerial techniques such as "lights out" automated operations, which reduce the need for personnel to operate and maintain the mainframe system. Built-in monitoring tools allow for control of the mainframe and problem detection without the need for any human presence.

There are still many business applications for which mainframes reign. For high-volume, rapid-pace, transaction-intensive applications—such as airline

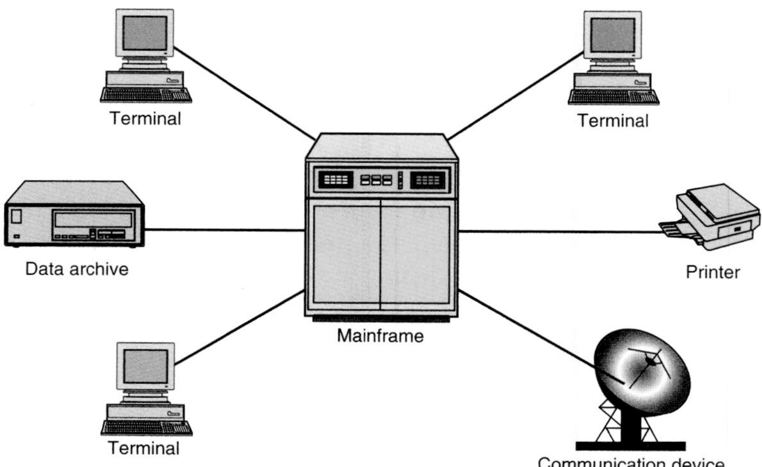

FIGURE T-4.7 An example of a centralized architecture. (*Source:* From *Systems Analysis and Design* Third Edition, Fourth Edition, by Wetherbe and Vitalare ©1988. Reprinted with permission of South-Western College Publishing, a division of Thomson Learning.)

reservation systems or stock trading systems—the mainframe still plays a vital role. Continuous availability and rapid response, as well as the benefits of reliability and security, are all available from the typical mainframe package, making it worthy of ongoing attention. Whether mainframe sales will continue at the same level, however, is still a controversial topic.

NONCENTRALIZED COMPUTING. *Noncentralized computing* architectures are decentralized or distributed. **Decentralized computing** breaks centralized computing into functionally equivalent parts, with each part essentially a smaller, centralized subsystem. Almost all telephone utilities operate this way. Local switching stations contain local, centralized computers for the telephones in their immediate areas—each switching center is functionally identical. **Distributed computing**, on the other hand, breaks centralized computing into many computers that may not be (and usually are not) functionally equivalent. For a bank with many regional centers, for example, one location may process loan applications, another foreign currency transactions, and another business and individual deposit accounts. All branches can access all data, but certain computing functions are distributed across different regional centers.

As smaller, midrange computers (commonly called *minicomputers*) appeared, and as businesses increasingly required systems capable of sharing information resources, computing evolved toward *peer-to-peer architectures*. In this architecture, which is basically distributed computing, one computing resource shares processing with other computing resources. As peers, they also share devices and data with each other, although one "peer" may be more important than another for certain tasks or for controlling devices such as printers. Such peer-to-peer relationships became even more common as PCs began to proliferate in offices, and as they were linked together for communications (see page 770).

There is nothing inherently good or bad about a decision to centralize versus a decision to distribute an IT architecture. Instead, there are benefits and limitations to each approach. Most organizations would normally be categorized somewhere along a continuum between the extremes of completely centralized and completely distributed.

Client/Server Architecture

The basic structure of **client/server architecture** is a client device(s) and a server device(s) that are distinguishable, but interact with each other. (That is, independent processing machines in separate locations perform operations separately, but can operate more efficiently when operating together.) This architecture divides processing between "clients" and "servers" (see Figure T-4.8). Both are on the network, but each processor is assigned functions it is best suited to perform. An example of a client might be a desktop PC used by a financial analyst to request data from a corporate mainframe. Or it might be a laptop used by a salesperson to get pricing and availability information from corporate systems, calculate and print an invoice, and order goods directly—all from a client's office.

In a client/server approach, the components of an application are distributed over the enterprise rather than being centrally controlled. There are three application components that can be distributed: the presentation component, the applications (or processing) logic, and the data management component. The *presentation component* is the application interface or how the application appears to the user. The *applications logic* is created by the business rules of the application.

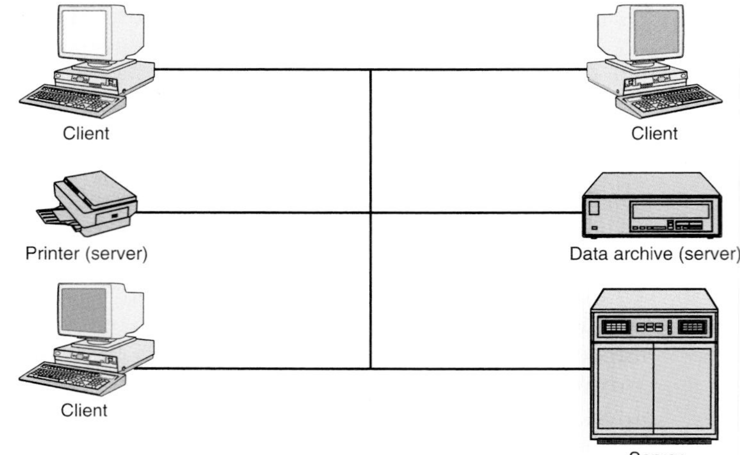

FIGURE T-4.8 An example of client/server architecture. (*Source:* From *Systems Analysis and Design:* Third Edition, Fourth Edition, by Wetherbe and Vitalare ©1988. Reprinted with permission of South-Western College Publishing, a division of Thomson Learning.)

The *data management component* consists of the storage and management of the data needed by the application. The exact division of processing tasks depends on the requirements of each application including its processing needs, the number of users, and the available resources.

There are five models of client/server implementation, depending on the partitioning of the three components between the server and the client.

1. With **distributed presentation**, all three components are on the server, but the presentation logic is distributed between the client and the server.
2. With **remote presentation**, applications logic and database management are on the server, and the presentation logic is located on the client.
3. With **distributed function**, data management is on the server and presentation logic is on the client, with application logic distributed between the two.
4. **Remote data management** means that database management is on the server, with the other two components on the client.
5. **Distributed data management** has all three components on the client, with database management distributed between the client and the server.

These models led to the ideas of "fat" clients and "thin" clients. **Fat clients** have large storage and processing power, and the three components of an application can be processed. **Thin clients** may have no local storage and limited processing power, meaning that thin clients can handle presentation only (such as in a network computer).

The client is the user point-of-entry for the required function, and the user generally interacts directly with only the client portion of the application, typically through a graphical user interface. Clients call on the server for services rendered by the application software. When a client needs information based on files in the server, the client sends a message (or remote procedure call) requesting the information from the server.

The server has the data files and the application software. The server stores and processes shared data and performs "back-end" functions not visible to users, such as managing peripheral devices and controlling access to shared databases. When a client makes a remote procedure call, the server processes file data and provides the information, not the entire file(s), to the client.

Early client/server systems were primarily used for non-mission-critical applications due to experiences with (or fears of) poor system stability and lack of robustness. More recently, studies have shown a significant increase in the number and size of installed business client/server systems—especially for critical online transaction processing.

When the client/server architecture first appeared, many analysts believed that it would lower costs because the typical servers were much less expensive (in relation to processing power) than mainframe computers. However, because of the complexities of linking many different types of hardware and software, as well as the relative immaturity of the technology, client/server applications may actually be substantially more expensive to operate than mainframe applications. The International Technology Group estimated that computing on a client/server system cost an average of $6,982 per user per year, versus $2,127 on a mainframe system. However, other experts provided substantially different results.

In summary, client/server architectures offer the potential to use computing resources more effectively through division of labor among specialized processing units. A client desktop PC can use its strengths for calculations and visually displaying results, but it can also access the specialized functionality of a file server for the required data. This configuration also facilitates sharing hardware such as printers and plotters, and sharing data throughout the organization via an intranet. The client/server model fits well in an environment of disparate computing needs that are distributed throughout an organization, in an environment that is unstable or changes frequently, and in an environment characterized by risk and uncertainty. In today's business environments, we can fully expect that client/server architectures will continue to increase in popularity and sophistication.

Peer-to-Peer Architecture

A **peer-to-peer network architecture** allows two or more computers to pool their resources together. Individual resources like disk drives, CD-ROM drives, and even printers are transformed into shared, collective resources that are accessible from every computer. Unlike client/server networks, where network information is stored on a centralized file server and made available to many clients, the information stored across peer-to-peer networks is uniquely decentralized. Because peer-to-peer computers have their own disk drives that are accessible by all computers, each computer acts as both a client and a server. Each computer has transparent access (as assigned for security or integrity purposes) to all files on all other computers (see Figure T-4.9).

Popular peer-to-peer network operating systems include Microsoft's Windows, Artisoft's LANtastic, and Netware Lite. Most of these operating systems allow each computer to determine which resources will be available for use by other users. When one user's disk has been configured so that it is "sharable," it will usually appear as a new drive to the other users.

There are several advantages of peer-to-peer architecture:

- There is no need for a network administrator.
- The network is fast and inexpensive to set up and maintain.

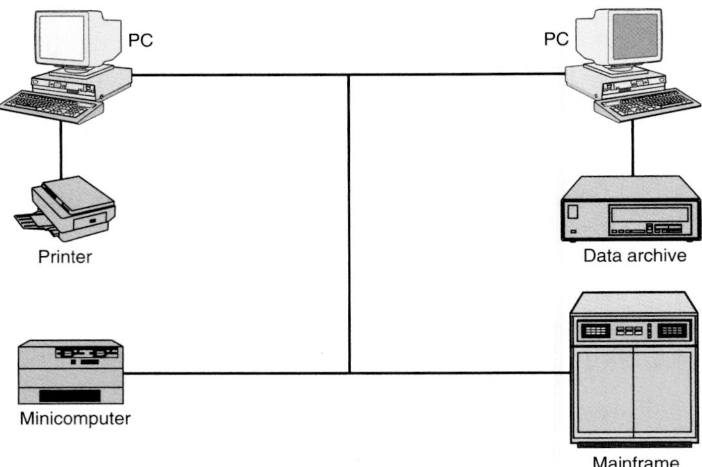

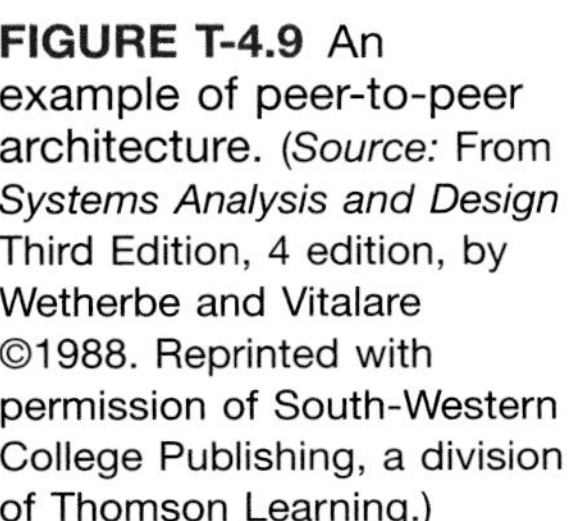

FIGURE T-4.9 An example of peer-to-peer architecture. (*Source:* From *Systems Analysis and Design* Third Edition, 4 edition, by Wetherbe and Vitalare ©1988. Reprinted with permission of South-Western College Publishing, a division of Thomson Learning.)

- Each computer can make backup copies of its files to other computers for security.
- It is the easiest network to build.

Peer-to-peer architecture, also known as P2P, is extremely popular on the Internet. Probably the best-known P2P application is music sharing managed by Napster.com.

Open Systems and Enterprise Networking

Open systems can provide flexibility in implementing IT solutions, optimization of computing effectiveness, and the ability to provide new levels of integrated functionality to meet user demands. Open systems require connectivity across the various components of the system.

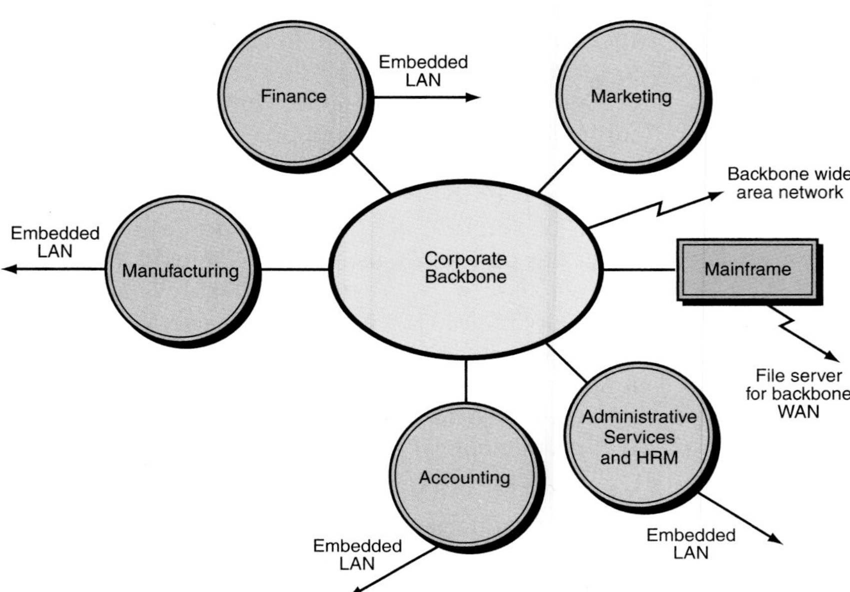

FIGURE T-4.10 Enterprisewide computing.

Connectivity is the ability of the various computer resources to communicate with each other through network devices without human intervention. Connectivity allows for application portability, interoperability, and scalability. **Portability** is the ability to move applications, data, and even people from one system to another with minimal adjustments. **Interoperability** refers to the ability of systems to work together by sharing applications, data, and computer resources. **Scalability** refers to the ability to run applications unchanged on any open system where the hardware can range from a laptop PC to a supercomputer.

Open systems and connectivity have enabled networks to completely span organizations. Most firms have multiple LANs and may have multiple WANs, which are interconnected to form an enterprisewide network (see Figure T-4.10). Note that the enterprisewide network shown in Figure T-4.10 has a backbone network composed of fiber-optic cable using the FDDI protocol. The LANs are called **embedded LANs** because they connect to the backbone WAN. These LANs are usually composed of twisted-pair wire.

REFERENCES AND BIBLIOGRAPHY

1. Baca, H., et al., *Local Area Networks with Novell.* Belmont, CA: Wadsworth, 1995.
2. Comer, D. E., and R. E. Droms, *Computer Networks and Internets.* Upper Saddle River, NJ: Prentice-Hall, 1996.
3. Dodd, A. Z., *The Essential Guide to Telecommunications,* 2nd ed. Upper Saddle River, NJ: Prentice-Hall, 2000.
4. Edwards, J., "Building the Optical Networking Infrastructure," *Computer,* March 2000, pp. 20–23.
5. Fitzgerald, J., *Business Data Communications: Basic Concepts, Security, and Design,* 5th ed. New York: Wiley, 1996.
6. Gauntt, J., et al., "Technology Forecast 2000," PricewaterhouseCoopers, 2000.
7. Goldman, R., *Business Data Communications,* 3rd ed. New York: Wiley, 2001.
8. Keen, P. G. W., and J. M. Cummings, *Networks in Action: Business Choices and Telecommunications Decisions.* Belmont, CA: Wadsworth, 1994.
9. Kim, B. G., and P. Wang, "ATM Network: Goals and Challenges," *Communications of the ACM,* Vol. 38, No. 2, February 1995.
10. Minoli, D., and A. Schmidt, *Internet Architectures.* New York: Wiley, 1999.
11. Mueller, M., "Universal Service and the Telecommunications Act: Myth Made Law," *Communications of the ACM,* Vol. 40, No. 3, March 1997.
12. Quelch, J. A., and L. R. Klein, "The Internet and International Marketing," *Sloan Management Review,* Spring 1996.
13. Rose, F., "New Modems Are Fast, Cheap," *Wall Street Journal,* February 11, 1997.
14. Simpson, D., "Cut Costs with Client/Server Computing? Here's How!" *Datamation,* October 1, 1995.
15. Stewart, T. A., "Managing in a Wired Company," *Fortune,* July 11, 1994.
16. Sullivan, D., *The New Computer User,* 2nd ed. Orlando, FL: Harcourt Brace, 1997.
17. Vetter, R. J., "ATM Concepts, Architectures, and Protocols," *Communications of the ACM,* Vol. 38, No 2, February 1995.
18. Wilson, C., "Optical Networking," White Paper, *Interactive Week,* February 21, 1998.

Glossary

Ad-hoc analysis The analysis of ad-hoc reports.

Ad-hoc reports Management reports that are issued in reply to a special request, in contrast with *periodic* reports.

Advocacy marketing See *Viral marketing.*

Affiliate marketing (programs) Programs in which companies pay a very small commission to other sites for "driving traffic" to their sites online. The target site uses its affiliate program to help acquire customers; the members of the program earn a commission every time a customer "clicks through" their site to the target site or makes a purchase.

Applets (of Java) Small programs written in Java for executing simple tasks such as developing a Web page or selecting a product that matches buyer's preferences.

Application controls Controls designed to protect specific applications.

Application portfolio The collection of corporate IT applications, sometimes including those under development.

Application program A set of computer instructions written in a programming language, the purpose of which is to provide functionality to a user.

Application service provider (ASP) Company that provides business applications (standard or customized) over the Internet for a per-use or fixed monthly fee. It is a form of outsourcing.

Artificial intelligence (AI) A subfield of computer science concerned with symbolic reasoning and problem solving.

Artificial neural network (ANN) A computer technology attempting to build computers that will operate like a human brain; ANN programs can work with ambiguous information.

Asynchronous communication The sending and receiving of messages in which there is a time delay between the sending and receiving; as opposed to *synchronous communication*.

Audit A regular examination or check of systems, their inputs, outputs, and processing.

Audit trail List of all changes made to a file, for checking or control purposes.

Backbone The long-distance, high-capacity, and high-speed network that links the major Internet computer nodes. Also may connect networks for an organization.

Backup A copy of software or data.

Batch processing Processing system that processes inputs at fixed intervals as a file and operates on it all at once; in contrast, *online* (or *interactive*) processing operates on a transaction as soon as it occurs.

Key terms from the Technology Guides are not included here, but can be found at the book's Web site (*wiley.com/college/turban*).

Behavior-oriented chargeback Accounting system that sets IS service costs in a way that encourages usage consistent with organizational objectives, even though the charges may not correspond to actual costs.

Best-practice benchmarks Activities and methods that the most effective organizations use to operate and manage various IS functions.

Best practices The best methods for solving problems; these are often stored in the knowledge repository.

Biometric controls Security controls that involve physically or behaviorally unique characteristics of people, such as fingerprints or voice.

Brick-and-mortar (organizations) Organizations that do business in old-economy style, basically offline.

Bullwhip effect Large fluctuations in inventories along the uncoordinated supply chain that result from small fluctuations in the demand for the finished products.

Business continuity plan A comprehensive plan for how the business and IT systems will operate in case a disaster strikes.

Business intelligence Computer-based decision analysis usually done online by managers and staff. It includes forecasting, analyzing alternatives, and evaluating risk and performance.

Business model A method by which a company generates revenue to sustain itself.

Business pressures Forces, such as global competition, in the organization's environment that create pressures on the organization's operations.

Business process A collection of activities that take one or more kinds of inputs and create an output.

Business process reengineering (BPR) A methodology for introducing a fundamental change in specific business processes, usually supported by an information system.

Business systems planning (BSP) Planning that concentrates on identifying problems and related decisions, based on business processes and data classes. (An IBM methodology.)

Business-to-business EC (B2B) E-commerce where both the buyers and the sellers are organizations.

Business-to-consumer EC (B2C) E-commerce in which a business is selling online to individual consumers.

Buy-side model (marketplace) A marketplace where one buyer buys from many sellers, frequently by using reverse auctions.

Byte A number of bits (usually eight) used to represent one alphanumeric character.

CD-ROM (**c**ompact **d**isc **r**ead-**o**nly **m**emory) A secondary digital storage medium that uses laser-made pits in plastic to represent bits.

Central processing unit (CPU) The "brain" of a computer — controlling all computational, input, output, and storage activities.

Centralized computing IS architecture that puts all processing and control authority at a single computer site to which all other computing devices respond.

Channel conflict The conflict between the existing distribution channels and the new channel of selling directly to customers, caused by bypassing traditional distribution partners.

Channel systems A network of the materials and product distribution system within an organization, and between the organization and its suppliers and customers.

Chargeback Systems that treat the MIS function as a service bureau or utility, charging organizational subunits for MIS services with the objective of recovering MIS expenditures.

Chargeout See *Chargeback.*

Chat room A Web page where people can interact ("chat") in real time; a virtual meeting place.

Chief information officer (CIO) The director of the IS department in a large organization, analogous to a CEO, COO, or CFO.

Chief knowledge officer (CKO) The title given to the director assigned to manage an organization's knowledge management program.

Chief network officer (CNO) The title given to the director of telecommunications; reflects the importance of the role in the organization.

Click-and-mortar (organizations) Organizations that employ both offline and online strategy, basically adapting the old economy to the new one rather than going 100 percent online; the most common e-commerce model.

Clickstream data The data collected on users' activities on a Web site, captured by various methods, including *cookies,* and mined by advertisers.

Client/server architecture A type of distributed architecture where end-user PCs (clients) request services or data from designated processors or peripherals (servers).

Code of ethics A set of ethical-behavior rules developed by organizations or by professional societies.

Codification strategy The knowledge management approach that attempts to identify tacit knowledge in best practices and so on, and store the tacit knowledge in a knowledge repository. The opposite is the *personalization strategy.*

Collaboration The mutual efforts by two or more individuals who perform activities in order to accomplish certain tasks.

Collaborative commerce networks Physical networks such as extranets or EDI, and the procedures of collaboration among them.

Community of practice (COP) A group of people in an organization with a common professional interest.

Company-centric EC (for B2B) E-commerce conducted on a company's server where either there is one seller and many corporate buyers (sell side), or one corporate buyer and many corporate sellers (sell side).

Competitive advantage An advantage over a competitor, such as lower cost or quicker deliveries.

Competitive forces model A business framework devised by Porter, depicting five forces in a market (e.g., bargaining power of customers).

Competitive intelligence The activities conducted by companies, frequently with the aid of IT and the Internet, to spy on their competitors and to collect marketing information.

Component-based development A strategy for developing applications from a preprogrammed component. A component can be a shopping cart in e-commerce or a statistical routine in a DSS.

Computer-aided design (CAD) software Software that allows designers to design and "build" production prototypes, "test" them as a computer object under given parameters, compile parts and quantity lists, outline production and assembly procedures, and then transmit the final design directly to milling and rolling machines.

Computer-aided engineering (CAE) Software that enables engineers to execute complex engineering analysis on a computer.

Computer-aided manufacturing (CAM) software Software that uses a digital design such as that from a CAD system to directly control production machinery.

Computer-aided software engineering (CASE) An integrated set of systems development tools.

Computer-based information systems (CBIS) Information systems that include a computer for their operation.

Computer-integrated manufacturing (CIM) Integrates several computerized systems, such as CAD, CAM, MRP, and JIT into a whole, in a factory.

Conflict resolution team A team that resolves conflicts between end users and the IS department.

Cookie A text string stored on the user's hard drive file to record the history of the user's computer visits to particular Web sites.

Cooperative processing Teams two or more geographically dispersed computers to execute a specific task.

Corporate portal The gateway for entering the corporate Web site. It is usually a home page, which allows for communication, collaboration, and access to diversified information. Companies may have separate portals for outsiders and for employees.

Cost-benefit analysis Study that helps in decisions on IT investments by determining if the benefits (possibly including intangible ones) exceed the costs.

Cost leadership The ability of a company to produce quality products at the lowest cost in its industry group.

Courseware Software support for distance learning; it includes collaboration tools and content.

Cracker A malicious hacker.

Critical response activities The major activities used by organizations to counter *business pressures.*

Critical success factors (CSFs) Those few things that must go right in order to ensure the organization's survival and success.

Cross-functional activities Activities that are performed in several functional areas along the same business processes.

Customer relationship management (CRM) The entire process of maximizing the value proposition to the customer through all interactions, both online and traditional. Effective CRM advocates one-to-one relationships and participation of customers in related business decisions.

Cyberbanking Banking conducted over the Internet or private networks, enabling people to bank from home or on the road.

Cybercafé A public place such as a coffee house or restaurant in which Internet terminals are available to users, usually for a small fee.

Cybermall An electronic shopping center on the Internet (may include thousands of stores).

Cycle time reduction The reduction of the time required to execute a task or produce a product. It is usually done by using information technologies.

Data Raw facts that can be processed into accurate and relevant information.

Data conferencing Data sent along with voice and/or video, enabling real-time communication.

Data integrity The accuracy of and accessibility to data.

Data mart A subset of the data warehouse, usually originated for a specific purpose or major data subject.

Data mining The process of searching for unknown information or relationships in large databases using tools such as neural computing or case-based reasoning.

Data quality (DQ) A measure of the accuracy, objectivity, accessibility, relevance, timeliness, completeness, and other characteristics that describe useful data.

Data tampering Deliberately entering false data, or changing and deleting true data.

Data visualization Visual presentation of data and information by graphics, animation, or any other multimedia.

Data warehouse A repository of historical data, subject-oriented and organized, summarized, and integrated from various sources so as to be easily accessed and manipulated for decision support.

Database A collection of files serving as a data resource for computer-based information systems.

Database management system (DBMS) A software program (or group of programs) that manages and provides access to a database.

Decision metrics See *Metric benchmarks.*

Decision room A face-to-face arrangement for a group DSS in which terminals are available to the participants.

Decision support system (DSS) A computer-based information system that combines models and data in an attempt to solve semistructured problems with extensive user involvement.

Decryption The restoration (uncoding) of scrambled data into the original format using some key.

Dehumanization A condition that makes people lose their personalities and sense of identity when working with computers and information systems.

Delphi method A qualitative forecasting methodology using anonymous questionnaires done in several iterations, to find consensus.

Differentiation (of product or service) A strategy of gaining competitive advantage by providing a product (or service) of the same cost and quality as a competitor, but with some additional attribute(s) that makes it different from the competition.

Digital divide The gap within a country, or between countries, between those that have information technology, particularly access to the Internet, and those that do not.

Digital economy Another name for today's Web-based, or Internet, economy.

Digital signature Authorizing signature added to electronic messages or electronic checks, usually encrypted in the sender public key for authentication purposes.

Direct cutover The option of converting to a new system by shutting off the old system and starting the new one at the same time.

Disaster avoidance plan A comprehensive plan to avoid a controllable catastrophe in the corporate information systems.

Disaster recovery plan A plan to operate an IS area after a disaster (such as an earthquake) and to restore the functioning of the systems.

Disintermediation The elimination of intermediaries; removing the layers of intermediaries between sellers and buyers.

Distance learning A learning approach in which teachers and students are in different locations.

Distributed computing Computing architecture that breaks centralized computing into many semiautonomous computers that may not be (and usually aren't) functionally equal.

Distributed processing See *Distributed computing.*

Document management The automated management and control of digitized documents throughout their life cycle.

Document management system (DMS) The system that provides document management.

Domain name The major (upper-level) category in an Internet name (URL).

Drill down The ability to investigate information in increasing detail; e.g., find not only total sales, but also sales by region, by product, or by salesperson.

Dynamic pricing The determination of prices based on supply and demand relationships at any given time, such as in auctions or stock markets; results in constantly changing prices.

E-business The broadest definition of e-commerce, including intrabusiness, IOS, and c-commerce; many use the term interchangeably with e-commerce.

E-commerce application An e-commerce program for a defined end-user activity such as e-procurement, e-auction, or ordering a product online.

E-government The use of e-commerce to improve the internal operation of the government as well as its communication and collaboration with citizens and businesses.

Electronic banking See *Cyberbanking.*

Electronic bartering The online exchange of commodities and/or services between business partners.

Electronic benefits transfer (EBT) Transfer of direct payments made by the government or other organization to recipients' bank accounts or smart cards.

Electronic cash (e-cash) A computerized stored value that can be used as cash; it is stored on a smart card or on a computer's hard drive.

Electronic certificates Verification, provided by a trusted third party, that a specific public encryption key belongs to a specific individual.

Electronic checks (e-checks) Payment mechanism made with electronic rather than paper checks.

Electronic commerce (e-commerce) The exchange of products, services, information, or money with the support of computers and networks; business conducted online.

Electronic communities Groups of people with similar interests who use the Internet to communicate or collaborate.

Electronic credit cards Payment mechanism that enables online payments with the characteristics of regular credit cards (e.g., pay within 30 days).

Electronic data interchange (EDI) Computer-to-computer direct communication of standard business transactions between or among business partners.

Electronic document management (EDM) See *Document management system.*

Electronic exchange See *Exchanges.*

Electronic funds transfer (EFT) The transmission of funds, debits and credits, and charges and payments electronically among banks and between banks and their customers.

Electronic mail (e-mail) Computer-based messages that can be electronically manipulated, stored, combined with other information, and exchanged with other computers.

Electronic mall An online shopping center with many (sometimes thousands) of stores in one Web site.

Electronic markets The networks of interactions and relationships where products, services, information, and payments are exchanged.

Electronic retailing Online selling of products or services to individuals, similar to regular retailing. Also known as *e-tailing.*

Electronic storefront A Web site of a single company in which orders can be placed. It includes a catalog, shopping cart, payment, search engine, shipment arrangements, etc.

Electronic surveillance The tracking of people's activities, online or offline. It is often done with the aid of computers (e.g., monitoring e-mail).

Electronic wallet (or purse) The storage and distribution of buying information, including credit card numbers, so buyers do not have to reenter information each time they buy.

E-mail agent Agent that manages users' e-mail by routing, deleting, prioritizing, or blocking e-mail.

E-marketplace (electronic markets) A place where buyers and sellers negotiate, submit bids, agree on orders, and if appropriate, finish the transactions electronically.

Encryption Scrambling of data so that they cannot be recognized by unauthorized readers.

Ends/means analysis (E/M analysis) Study that determines information requirements based on desired ends (effectiveness) and available means (efficiency) to achieve the ends.

End-user computing The use or development of information systems by the principal users of the systems' outputs or by their staffs.

Enhanced product realization (EPR) system System that allows manufacturers to make fast modifications by using collaborative tools over the Internet.

Enterprise application integration (EAI) The process that helps to integrate applications inside an organization (e.g., an ordering system with an inventory on hand), or applications of different organizations in a seamless fashion. It is done by EAI vendors with special software tools.

Enterprise computing (enterprisewide computing) The information system architecture that connects data that are used throughout the enterprise.

Enterprise information system See *Enterprise computing.*

Enterprise knowledge portal (EKP) An electronic doorway into a knowledge management system.

Enterprise resource planning (ERP) An integrated process of planning and managing of all resources and their use in the entire enterprise. It includes contacts with business partners.

Enterprise software An integrated software that supports enterprise computing and ERP. The most notable example is SAP R/3.

Enterprisewide system System that encompasses the entire enterprise, implemented on a companywide network.

Ergonomics The science of adapting machines and work environments to people.

E-tailers Electronic retailers, business-to-consumer (B2C) sellers in online stores; engaging in such activity is termed *e-tailing.*

Ethics A branch of philosophy that deals with what is considered to be right and wrong.

Exception reporting Management reporting system that calls attention only to results that deviate from a standard by a certain percentage or exceed a threshold.

Exchanges Many-to-many e-marketplaces. Some refer to an exchange only if dynamic pricing (e.g., auctions) is available there.

Executive information systems (EISs) Systems specifically designed to support executive work.

Executive support system (ESS) An executive information system that includes some analytical and communication capabilities.

Expected value A weighted average. It is achieved by multiplying values by their relative importance or frequencies and totaling the results.

Expert support system An expert system that supports problem solving and decision making.

Expert system (ES) A computer system that applies reasoning methodologies or knowledge in a specific domain to render advice or recommendations — much like a human expert.

Explicit knowledge The knowledge that deals with objective, rational, and technical knowledge (data, policies, procedures, software, documents, etc.).

Extranet A secured network that allows business partners to access portions of each other's intranets. It is usually Internet-based.

Fault-tolerance The ability to continue operating satisfactorily in the presence of faults.

Feasibility study Investigation that seeks an overview of a problem and a rough assessment of whether feasible solutions exist, prior to committing resources.

File A group of data with some form of commonality.

Firewalls Security devices that protect organizations' internal networks from hacking and other unauthorized access coming from the Internet.

Flaming Anonymous insulting or angry messaging on the Internet.

Flattened organizations Organizational structure that has fewer levels of management and a larger span of control than the hierarchical organization.

Forward auction An auction where the bidding price increases with time.

Four-stage model of planning A generic IS planning model based on four major, generic activities: strategic planning, information requirements analysis, resource allocation, and project planning.

Freeware Software available on the Internet for downloading, without the need to pay or get permission to use.

Frontline decision making The decision making of employees who are in direct contact with customers, suppliers, or other outsiders.

Functional MIS An information system for a functional area, such as a marketing information system.

Fuzzy logic A way of reasoning that can cope with uncertain or partial information; a characteristic of human thinking and some expert systems.

General controls Physical, access, communications, administrative, and data security controls aimed at protecting a system in general rather than protecting specific applications.

Geographical information system (GIS) Data visualization technoloy that uses spatial data such as digitized maps, and can combine this data with other text, graphics, icons, and symbols.

Global business drivers Entities that benefit from global economies of scale and add value to a global business strategy.

Goal-seeking (analysis) Study that attempts to find what values certain variables must have in order to attain desired goals.

Graphical user interface (GUI) An interactive, user-friendly interface in which icons and similar graphical devices enable a user to control a computer.

Group decision support system (GDSS) An interactive, computer-based system that facilitates finding solutions to semistructured problems by using a set of decision makers working together as a group.

Group purchasing The aggregation of purchasing orders from many buyers so volume discount (or negotiation, or reverse auction) can be achieved.

Group support systems (GSSs) Information systems that support the working processes of groups (e.g., communication and decision making).

Groupware A generic term for several computerized technologies and tools that aim to support people working in groups.

Hackers People who illegally or unethically access a computer system.

Hard disk A hard, metal platter coated with a material that can be magnetized in spots to represent bits, primarily for secondary storage.

Hardware The physical equipment, media, and attached devices used in a computer system.

Hierarchical model Data model that rigidly structures data into an inverted "tree" in which records refer to a senior field and any number of subordinate fields (i.e., one "parent" and several "children").

Hyperlink The links that connect data notes in hypertext and enable users to automatically move from one Web page to another by clicking on a highlighted word or icon.

Hypertext Markup Language (HTML) A programming language that uses hypertext to establish dynamic links (see *Hyperlink*) to other documents stored in the same or other computers on the Internet or intranets.

Increasing returns A concept in economics that expects increased benefits with the volume of operation (the larger, the better).

Inference engine The component of an expert system that performs a reasoning function.

Information Data that are processed or operated on by a computer.

Information anxiety The frustration resulting from some people's inability to cope with the quantity or quality of information.

Information architecture A conceptualization of the manner in which information requirements are met by the information system.

Information centers Facilities that train and support business users with end-user tools, testing, technical support information, and standard certification.

Information economics An approach to cost-benefit analysis that incorporates organizational objectives in a scoring methodology to assess more accurately the value of intangible benefits.

Information infrastructure The physical arrangement of hardware, software, databases, networks, and so forth.

Information intensity The amount of information that measures the actual, or planned, usage of information.

Information resources management All activities related to the planning, organizing, acquiring, maintaining, securing, and controlling of IT resources.

Information superhighway A national information infrastructure to interconnect computer users.

Information system (IS) A physical process that supports an organization by collecting, processing, storing, and analyzing data, and providing information to achieve organizational goals.

Information systems controls The procedures, devices, or software that are used to counter computer hazards (such as crime and human errors).

Information technology (IT) The technology component of an information system (a narrow definition); or the collection of the entire systems in an organization (the broad definition used in this book).

Information technology architecture The field of study and practice devoted to understanding and planning information systems components in the form of an organizational infrastructure.

Input device A computer system component that accepts data from the user (e.g., a keyboard or mouse).

Input/output (I/O) device A computer system component that transfers data into or out of a computer.

Inputs The resources introduced into a system for transformation into outputs.

Instant messaging Feature that allows users to identify partners and exchange realtime messages.

Integrated CASE tools Software engineering tools that support prototyping and reusable systems components, including component repositories and automatic computer code generation.

Intellectual assets The valuable knowledge of employees.

Intellectual capital See *Intellectual asset.*

Intelligent agents Expert or knowledge-based software systems embedded in computer-based information systems (or their components).

Intelligent systems Information systems that include a knowledge component, such as an expert system or neural network.

Internet A self-regulated network of computer networks connecting millions of businesses, individuals, government agencies, schools, and other organizations all over the world.

Internet communities See *Electronic communities.*

Internet economy See *Digital economy.*

Internet kiosks Public locations from which people can access the Internet.

Internet2 A U.S. government initiative supporting the creation of a high-speed computer network connecting various research facilities across the country.

Interorganizational information systems (IOSs) Information systems between two or more organizations that support efficient, routine flow of transaction processing data.

Intrabusiness EC An application of EC methods inside one organization, usually on its intranet, creating a paperless environment. Activities range from internal customer service to selling products to employees.

Intranet A corporate network that functions with Internet technologies, such as browsers and search engines, using Internet protocols.

IT planning The organized planning for IT infrastructure and applications portfolios done at various levels of the organization.

Java An object-oriented programming language used extensively for Internet applications. For example, a variation, Java Script, is used with HTML.

Job content The elements of a job as reflected in its description.

Job stress The discomfort experienced by individuals in performing their jobs.

Joint application design (JAD) A structured process for information gathering from a group of key stakeholders, mainly to find the information requirements of users.

Joint application development See *Joint application design.*

Just-in-time (JIT) An inventory scheduling system in which material and parts arrive at a work place when needed, minimizing inventory, waste, and interruptions.

Key (in encryption) The code in which a message is encrypted. Each letter or number of the original message is represented by a series of numbers and letters. It is necessary to know the key in order to decrypt the message.

Keyword banners Messages that appear when a predetermined word is queried from a search engine.

Knowledge The understanding, awareness, or familiarity acquired through education or experience.

Knowledge audit The process of identifying the knowledge an organization has, who has it, and how it flows (or does not flow) through the enterprise.

Knowledge base A collection of facts, rules, and procedures organized in one place.

Knowledge discovery See *Knowledge discovery in databases.*

Knowledge discovery in databases (KDD) The process of extracting knowledge from volumes of data in databases (e.g., in data warehouses); it includes data mining.

Knowledge management (KM) The comprehensive management of the expertise in an organization. It involves collecting, categorizing and disseminating knowledge.

Knowledge management suites Software packages that consist of a comprehensive set of tools.

Knowledge management system (KMS) A system that facilitates knowledge management by ensuring knowledge flow from those who know to those who need to know throughout the organization. KMSs are centered around a corporate knowledge base or depository.

Knowledge network model Model that describes the knowledge transfer process as occurring through person-to-person contacts.

Knowledge repository The software system that is a collection of both internal and external knowledge in a KMS.

Knowledge repository model Model that describes the two-step knowledge transfer procedure of person-to-repository and repository-to-person.

Knowledge workers People who use knowledge as a significant part of their work responsibilities.

Knowledge-based economy The new, global economy that is driven by what people and organizations "know" and not only by capital and labor.

Knowware A name for knowledge management (KM) software.

Labor productivity The ratio of the value of outputs to the quantity of labor required to produce those outputs.

L-commerce See *Location-based commerce.*

Leaky knowledge See *Explicit knowledge.*

Learning organization An organization with the capability of learning from its past experience, implying an organizational memory and a means to save, represent, and share it among its members.

Legacy systems Older systems that have become central to business operations and may be still capable of meeting these business needs; they may not require any immediate changes, or they may be in need of reengineering to meet new business needs.

Light methodology A simplified system development life cycle (SDLC) approach used mainly for Web-based systems. It strikes a balance between rigor and development speed.

Local area network (LAN) A system for interconnecting two or more closely located communicating devices supporting full connectivity so that every user device on the network has the potential to communicate with any other device.

Location-based commerce (l-commerce) A form of e-commerce that delivers information about goods and services based on where you (and your mobile device) are located.

Lock-in effect The difficulty of switching to a competing product because of the need to learn how to use a different product, or other factors that discourage change.

Logical design The design of information systems from the user's point of view.

Long-range planning A corporate or IT plan usually for five years or longer.

Lotus Notes (now Notes/Domino) An integrated groupware software package that also provides application developers an environment for quickly creating cross-platform client/server applications.

Machine learning A method by which a computer can learn from past experiences (e.g., from historical data).

Mainframe computers Relatively large computers built to handle very large computations and databases, thousands of user terminals with fast response times, and millions of transactions.

Management by maxim Approach that guides investment in IT infrastructure by identifying infrastructure requirements that correspond to organizational strategies and objectives.

Management information systems (MISs) Systems designed to provide past, present, and future routine information appropriate for planning, organizing, and controlling the operations of functional areas in an organization.

Management support systems (MSSs) Three major IT technologies designed to support managers: decision support systems, executive support systems, and groupware technologies.

Manufacturing resource planning (MRPII) A planning process that integrates production, inventory, purchasing, financing, and labor in an enterprise.

Marketing databases Large databases that contain marketing-related data and are used for determining advertisement and marketing strategies.

Marketing transaction database (MTD) An interactive marketing database oriented toward targeting messages and marketing in real time.

Mass customization The production of a very large quantity of customized products, such as computers (e.g., by Dell Computers).

Material requirements planning (MRP) A planning process (usually computerized) that integrates production, purchasing, and inventory management of interrelated products.

M-commerce (mobile commerce) E-commerce done with wireless devices including a GPS for location identification.

Metadata Data about data, such as indices or summaries.

Metamalls Online supermalls that serve several online malls by providing them with unified services, such as search engines.

Metcalfe's law Maxim that states that the value of a network grows roughly in line with the square of the number of its users.

Metric benchmarks Numeric measures of IS performance relative to other numerical factors such as organizational revenues, CPU capacity, etc.

Metrics See *Metric benchmarks.*

Microcomputers Small and relatively inexpensive general-purpose computers; also known as *micros* and *personal computers (PCs).*

Micropayments Small payments (a few dollars or less) for products or services purchased on the Internet.

Milestones Checkpoints established to allow periodic review of progress so that management can determine if a project merits further commitment of resources, if it requires adjustments, or if it should be discontinued.

Minicomputer A relatively smaller, cheaper, and more compact computer that performs the same functions as a larger, mainframe computer, but to a more limited extent.

Mobile agents Software agents that can move from one Internet site to another, access remote systems such as a database, perform tasks there, and send or retrieve data.

Mobile computing Information system applications in a wireless environment.

Mobility (of agents) The degree to which the agents themselves travel through the network.

Model base management system (MBMS) A software program to establish, update, and use a model base.

Model marts Small, generally departmental or topical repositories of knowledge created by employing knowledge-discovery techniques on past decision instances. Analogous to *data marts.*

Model warehouses Large, generally enterprisewide repositories of knowledge created by employing knowledge-discovery techniques on past decision instances. Analogous to *data warehouses.*

Modem A device that **mo**dulates and **dem**odulates signals.

Moore's law The expectation that the power of a microprocessor will double every 18 months, while the cost stays at the same level.

Multidimensional database A database organized by dimensions such as geographical region, time, product, or salesperson.

Multidimensionality The need to analyze data by looking at several dimensions. A dimension can be place, time, product, or customer.

Multifactor productivity The ratio of the value of outputs to the value of the inputs — including labor, investments, materials, etc. — used to produce these outputs.

Multimedia The combination of at least two media for input or output of data; these media can be audio (sound), voice, animation, video, text, graphics, and/or images.

Multimedia database A database in which data and procedures are stored as objects containing various multimedia (e.g., video clips).

Natural language processor (NLP) A knowledge-based user interface that allows the user to carry on a conversation with a computer-based system in much the same way as he or she would converse with another human.

Netiquette The rules of conduct over the Internet, especially in newsgroups, chat rooms, and bulletin boards.

Network A telecommunications system that permits the sharing of resources such as computing power, software, input/output devices, and data.

Network computer (NC) A network-based terminal, similar to a "dummy" terminal in a mainframe, that allows communication and use of information on the network, but does not have storage capability.

Network effects The support that leading products in an industry receive from their large user base and the complementary products marketed to these users.

Networked computing A corporate information infrastructure that provides the necessary networks for distributed computing. Users can easily contact each other or databases and communicate with external entities.

Networked organization (enterprise) Organizational structure that is a seamless network, extending the corporate contacts to all the entities a company does business with.

Neural computing The technology that attempts to achieve knowledge representations and processing based on massive parallel processing, fast retrieval of large amounts of information, and the ability to recognize patterns based on experiences.

New economy Productive system that is distinguished from the old economy by being Internet based.

Nominal group technique (NTG) A group-dynamic procedure to improve the process of people working in a group.

Nonrepudiation The property that the senders of a message cannot deny that they actually sent the message; ability to limit parties from refuting that a legitimate transaction has taken place.

Object technology Technology that includes object-oriented programming, object-oriented databases, and other object-oriented-based components and activities.

Object-oriented database A database that is organized and managed using an object-oriented approach for data presentation and management.

Object-oriented development System development based on interchangeable software components (objects) that model the behavior of persons, places, things, or concepts in the real world.

Object-oriented programming (OOP) Programming that models a system as a set of cooperating objects.

Office automation systems (OASs) Systems used to increase the productivity of office workers and the quality of office work.

Offshore outsourcing Use of vendors in other countries, usually where labor is inexpensive, to do programming or other system development tasks.

One-to-one marketing A new, interactive style of marketing that treats each customer in a unique way to match service with the customer's needs and other characteristics.

Online (electronic) catalogs Presentations of information about products (services) that traditionally were in paper catalogs. Electronic catalogs can include multimedia, such as voice and video clips.

Online analytical processing (OLAP) The processing of data as soon as transactions occur.

Online processing Analysis of databases to determine properties and complex relationships using DSS or other sophisticated software.

Online transaction processing (OLTP) A transaction processing system, created on a client/server architecture, that saves money by allowing suppliers to enter the TPS and look at the firm's inventory level or production schedule.

Operating system software The main system control program, which supervises the overall operation of a computer, including such tasks as monitoring the computer's status, handling executable program interruptions, and scheduling of operations.

Operational data store A database that provides clean data to the operational, mission-critical, short-term-oriented applications.

Optical character reader (OCR) An input device that scans textual data.

Optical scanners Devices that scan text and graphics forms for input to a computer system.

Option valuation The process of assigning a value to future benefits that could result from a current investment.

Order fulfillment All the activities needed to deliver a product (service) to a customer, after an order has been placed. This is done by the back-office operations.

Organizational culture The aggregate attitudes in an organization concerning a certain issue (such as technology, computers, and DSS).

Organizational decision support system (ODSS) A network DSS that serves people at several locations.

Organizational knowledge base The collection of knowledge related to the operation of an organization.

Organizational learning The process of organizations coping with major changes such as BPR. Such learning can be facilitated by knowledge bases.

Organizational memory What an organization "knows" and thus can apply.

Output device The part of a computer system that produces processed data or information.

Outputs The completed products or services of a system.

Outsourcing Acquiring IS services from an external organization rather than through internal employees.

Parallel conversion A process of converting to a new information system by using the old and new systems concurrently until the new system is demonstrably stable and reliable.

Parallel processing Executing several processing instructions at the same time (in parallel) rather than one at a time (serial or sequential processing).

Partner-relationship management (PRM) A strategy that focuses on providing quality service for business partners, facilitating communication and collaboration, and addressing problems quickly and effectively, while monitoring service levels provided by the partners.

Pattern recognition The ability of a computer to classify an item to a predetermined category by matching the item's characteristics with that of a stored category.

Peer-to-peer networks Network relationships that stress processing on an equal basis among all processors, sharing devices and data on a mutual basis.

Periodic reports Routine reports executed at predetermined times (in contrast with ad-hoc reports).

Permission marketing Efforts done once customers give their consent to receive advertisement and promotional material.

Personal information manager (PIM) A software package for a manager's personal use, combining the features of project management software and desktop organizers.

Personalization strategy The knowledge management approach that attempts to share knowledge mostly through person-to-person contacts. The opposite is the *codification strategy.*

Person-to-person (P2P) payments Payments between individual customers, made in C2C commerce, such as in e-auctions or e-classified sales. Innovative methods allow such payments to be made without the need for a credit card.

Phased conversion Switching from an old system to a new system in several phases.

Physical design The process of translating the logical design of a system into the technical design.

Pilot conversion Switching from an old system to a complete, new system in parts of an organization, one part at a time.

Portals The gateways to Web sites. They can be public (like Yahoo!), or private (corporate portals).

Post-audit The auditing conducted on information systems after their implementation and use.

Price-to-performance ratio The relative cost, usually on a per-mips (millions of instructions per second) basis, of the processing power of a computer.

Primary activities In Porter's value chain model, those activities in which materials are purchased and processed to products, which are then delivered to customers. Secondary activities, such as accounting, support the primary ones.

Primary storage Main memory, which stores data and code for the CPU.

Private key A security encryption/decryption code that is known *only* to its user/owner.

Processor A computer device that processes inputs into outputs.

Productivity paradox The seeming contradiction between extremely large IT investments in the economy, in contrast to indications of low productivity growth in the sectors that have received the largest IT investments.

Programming fraud A deliberate manipulation of a computer program so that a fraud can be committed.

Project planning The fourth stage of the model for information systems planning, providing an overall framework with which the system development life cycle can be planned, scheduled, and controlled.

Protocol A set of rules that determines how two computers communicate with one another over a network.

Prototyping An approach to systems development that exploits advanced technologies for using trial-and-error problem solving.

Public key A security code of a certain individual that is distributed to authorized people so they can encrypt or decrypt messages with it.

Public key infrastructure (PKI) A security schema based on public key encryption that is used to secure e-payments. It also includes a digital signature and certificates.

Push technology Software that delivers only information that users want, per their preference profile.

Quality of life The measure of how well we achieve a desirable standard of living.

Random-access memory (RAM) Digital storage or memory that can be directly written to and read.

Random banners Messages that appear at random, not as a result of the viewer's action.

Rapid application development (RAD) A methodology that enables the rapid construction of information systems applications by using special tools.

Read-only memory (ROM) Digital storage or memory that can be read directly.

Reintermediation The process of (1) redefining the role of traditional intermediaries, to provide value-added services that cannot be provided online; or (2) establishing new electronic intermediaries in place of disintermediated traditional intermediaries.

Relationship marketing See *One-to-one marketing.*

Requirements analysis The stage in a system development life cycle in which the goals (outputs) of a system are evaluated against the needs of the users.

Resource allocation The third stage of the model for information systems planning, consisting of developing the hardware, software, data communications, facilities, personnel, and financial plans needed to execute the master development plan.

Response management The strategy of responding to competitors or market developments rather than being a leader.

Return on investment (ROI) The percentage return on an investment in a project, computed as Net return ÷ Required investment.

Reverse auction An e-procurement mechanism in which sellers are invited to bid on the fulfillment of an order to produce a product or provide a service. During the auction, bid prices will decline, so the lowest bidder wins.

Reverse engineering The process of converting the code, files, and databases of legacy systems into components that can be used to create new (usually client/server) applications.

Reverse logistics (returns) The return of products by customers. The items flow in a reverse direction, from the buyer back to the seller.

Risk management The process of determining the potential risk associated with a project or a problem and considering this risk in cost-benefit analysis.

Robot An electromechanical device that can be programmed to automate manual tasks.

Runaway project A systems development project that requires much more spending or time to complete than budgeted or scheduled.

Sales automation software The software used to automate the work of salespeople.

Sales-force automation The hardware and software used by salespeople, usually in the field, to automate some of their tasks (e.g., using wireless computers to generate proposals at clients' sites).

SAP R/3 The leading EPR software (from SAP AG Corp.). It is a highly integrated package containing more than 70 modules.

Scenario planning A methodology of dealing with an uncertain environment by examining different scenarios; a what-if analysis.

Scoring methodology Methodology that evaluates alternatives by assigning weights and scores to various aspects and then calculating the weighted totals for comparison.

Screen sharing Technology that enables two or more participants to see the same screen and make changes on it that can be seen by all.

Search engines Software agents whose task is to find information by looking at keywords, or by following some guidelines.

Secondary storage Computer hardware that stores data in a format that is compatible with the data stored in primary storage, but provides space for storing and processing large quantities of software and data for long periods.

Sell-side models (marketplaces) Marketplaces with one seller and many buyers (one-to-many).

Sensitivity analysis Study of the effect of a change in one or more input variables on a proposed solution.

Server Any system or process that *provides* data, services, or access to other systems for clients.

Service-level agreements (SLAs) Contracts between the IS department and end users that specify what, when, and how IS services are expected to be rendered.

Shareware A downloadable software that the user can try without fee, but is expected to pay for if he or she wants to use it.

Short message service (SMS) The "e-mail" of the wireless environment, consisting of text messages up to 160 characters in length.

Simulation A process of imitation of reality. It is usually done for computerized experiments with proposed solutions.

Smart appliances Machines that react to communication over networks (including wireless) and perform tasks such as cooking. They can sense the environment and react like robots.

Smart cards Storage media the size of a credit card that contain a microprocessor capable of storing and processing information.

Social responsibility Concern of a corporation for social issues — for example, to improve the air pollution or health level in the community.

Softbot An abbreviation for **soft**ware ro**bot**s. Another name for *software agents.*

Software Instructional coding that manipulates the hardware in a computer system.

Software agents Autonomous software programs that execute mundane tasks for the benefit of their users. Also known as *intelligent agents.*

Spamming Indiscriminate distribution of messages (e.g., junk mail) without consideration for their appropriateness.

Span of control A measure of the number of employees who report to one supervisor or manager.

Speech recognition A process that allows people to communicate with a computer by speaking to it.

Speech understanding The ability of computers to understand the meaning of sentences, in contrast with *recognizing* individual words.

Stages of IT growth Six commonly accepted stages, suggested by Nolan, that all organizations seem to experience in implementing and managing an information system from conception to maturity over time.

Steering committee Group composed of key managers representing major functional units within the organization to oversee the IS function, to ensure that adequate planning and control processes are present, and to direct IS activities in support of long-range organizational objectives and goals.

Sticky knowledge See *Tacit knowledge.*

Stored-value card A smart card that stores electronic cash that can be used to purchase items or services.

Strategic alliances Business alliances among companies that provide strategic benefits to the partners.

Strategic information planning (SIP) The identification and planning of IT-based strategic applications.

Strategic information systems (SISs) Information systems that provide, or help to provide, strategic advantage.

Strategic planning The first stage of the planning model, which aligns IS strategic planning with overall organizational planning by assessing organizational objectives and strategies, setting the IS mission, assessing the environment, and setting IS policies, objectives, and strategies.

Strategic systems Those systems that *significantly* impact the operation of an organization, its success, or even its survival.

Supercomputers Computers that have the most processing power of computers generally available.

Supply chain All of the activities related to the acceptance of an order from a customer and fulfilling it. In its extended format, it also includes connections with suppliers, customers, and other business partners.

Supply chain intelligence (SCI) Software products that offer analysis of supply chain operations and their improvement.

Supply chain management (SCM) The management of all the activities along the supply chain, from suppliers, to internal logistics within a company, to distribution to customers. This includes ordering, monitoring, and billing.

Support activities Business activities that do not add value directly to a firm's product or service under consideration but support the primary activities that do add value.

Sustainable strategic advantage Strategic advantage that can last over a long period of time despite competitors' efforts to nullify it.

Symbolic processing The use of symbols, rather than numbers, combined with rules of thumb (or heuristics) to process information and solve problems.

Synchronous (real-time) communication The nearly simultaneous sending and receiving of messages.

System A set of elements that acts as a single, goal-oriented entity.

System development The structuring of hardware and software to achieve the effective and efficient processing of information.

System software A set of instructions that act as the intermediary between the computer hardware and application programs.

Systematic sourcing Purchases made from a supplier with whom a business maintains a long-term relationship and contracts.

Systems analysis In system development, the phase in which cost-benefit and feasibility studies are done.

Systems development life cycle (SDLC) A model for developing a system based on a traditional problem-solving process with sequential steps and options for revisiting steps when problems appear.

Tacit knowledge The knowledge that is usually in the domain of subjective, cognitive, and experiential learning. It is highly personal and hard to formalize.

Telecommunications All types of electronic, high-speed, long-distance voice and data communication, usually through the use of common carriers.

Teleconferencing The ability to confer with a group of people by telephone or computer systems.

Text mining The application of data mining analysis to nonstructured text files and documents.

Total cost of ownership (TCO) A formula for calculating the cost of owning and operating a PC.

Total quality management (TQM) An organizationwide effort to improve quality and make it the responsibility of all employees.

Transaction processing system (TPSs) An information system that processes an organization's basic business transactions such as purchasing, billing, and payroll.

Trend analysis The study of performance over time, attempting to show future direction using forecasting methods.

Turing test Named after the English mathematician Alan Turing, test designed to measure if a computer is intelligent or not. A computer is considered intelligent only when a human interviewer, conversing with both an unseen human being and an unseen computer, cannot determine which is which.

User interfaces Features that facilitate communications between a user (a person) and an information system and may be tailored uniquely for an individual.

Value analysis Study that facilitates decision making in situations where intangible benefits are important, by evaluating benefits and costs through an initial prototype prior to development of a complete system.

Value chain model Model developed by Porter that shows the primary activities that sequentially add value to the profit margin; also shows the support activities.

Value systems In Porter's value chain model, the producers, suppliers, distributors, and buyers (all with their own value chains).

Value-added networks (VANS) Networks that add communications services to existing common carriers.

Vertical marketplace (vertical exchange) An exchange whose members and activities are in one industry or segment of it (e.g., steel, rubber, or banking).

Vertical portals Electronic exchanges that combine upstream and downstream EC activities of specialized products or services (e.g., chemicals, metals, electricity).

Video mail Application that enables users to transmit photos, pictures, and documents among conversing people, including conferencing.

Video teleconferencing Teleconferencing with the added capability of the participants to see each other as well as documents or other objects.

Viral marketing Word-of-mouth advertisement in which customers promote your product or service without cost to you (or at a minimal cost). The advertising propagates itself the way viruses do.

Virtual communities See *Electronic communities.*

Virtual corporations Businesses that operate from various locations, usually through telecommunications, without a permanent headquarters.

Virtual reality A pseudo-3-D interactive technology that provides a user with a feeling that he or she is physically present in a computer-generated world.

Virtual Reality Markup Language (VRML) A platform-independent standard for virtual reality.

Virtual society A society in which all the components are based on some functional entities rather than physical ones.

Virus Software that can damage or destroy data or software in a computer.

Visual interactive modeling (VIM) A method of modeling situations for problem solving where users can interact with the system and the results of their actions are displayed.

Visual interactive simulation (VIS) A VIM where simulation is used as the problem-solving tool.

Visual recognition The computer's ability to interpret scenes. Also known as *computer vision.*

Voice mail Digitized spoken messages that are stored and transferred electronically to receivers.

Voice portals Gateways that allow customers to use an ordinary phone or a cell phone for requesting information about stocks or traffic, usually on portals such as Yahoo!.

Voice recognition The ability of a computer to understand the meaning of spoken words.

Voice synthesis The technology that transforms computer output to voice or audio output.

Vulnerability (in security) A system's exposure to potential hazards, either intentional or accidental.

Waterfall method The process of system development where work flows down from one stage to the next only after it is completed.

Web economy See *Digital economy.*

Web mining Finding ("mining") and analyzing data that are collected from the Web, such as clickstream data.

Web-based DSS A DSS that is supported by the Web, either for developing applications and/or disseminating and using them. Both the Internet and intranets can be used.

Web-based system An application delivered on the Internet or intranet using Web tools, such as a search engine.

Webcam A camera whose image information is uploaded to the Web site, sometimes every few seconds, so viewers can see up-to-the-minute showrooms.

Weights (in neural networks) Numbers assigned to express the relative importance of input data.

What-if analysis Study that determines the effect of changing some of the input data on solutions.

Wide area networks (WANs) Networks that generally span distances greater than one city and include regional networks such as telephone companies or international networks such as global communications services providers.

Work group Two or more individuals who act together to perform a task.

Work management systems (WMSs) Systems that distribute, route, monitor, and evaluate various types of work by controlling and managing all related information flow.

Workflow systems Systems that use group support software for scheduling, routing, and monitoring specific tasks throughout an organization.

WYSIWYG Acronym for "**w**hat **y**ou **s**ee **i**s **w**hat **y**ou **g**et," indicating that material displayed on a computer screen will look exactly (or almost exactly) as it will look on a printed page.

Photo Credits

Chapter 2
Page 50: ©Mugshots/Corbis Stock Market. Page 54: Courtesy Heimann Systems Co.

Chapter 4
Page 125 (top far left): ©Gabe Palacio/Leo de Wys, Inc. Page 125 (top left): ©James King-Holmes/Photo Researchers. Page 125 (top and center): Courtesy International Business Machines Corporation. Page 125 (top right): Courtesy Apple Computers. Page 125 (bottom left): Courtesy Sony Pictures Entertainment Company. Page 125 (bottom and center): Courtesy International Business Machines Corporation. Page 125 (bottom right): ©Blair Seitz/Photo Researchers.

Chapter 5
Page 197: Courtesy Security First Network Bank. Reproduced with permission. Page 200: Ameritrade is a trademark Ameritrade Holding Corporation. ©1996–2001 Ameritrade, Inc. All rights reserved. Page 204: Kari Rene Hall/Los Angeles Times Photo.

Chapter 10
Page 453: Courtesy City University of Hong Kong. Page 461: Courtesy Comshare, Inc. Page 462: The Management Cockpit ® is a registered trademark of SAP, created by Professor Patrick M. Georges and delivered by N.E.T. Research. Reproduced with permission.

Chapter 11
Page 485: Greg Pease/Stone. Page 518: Courtesy Dallas Area Rapid Transit (DART).

Chapter 13
Page 567: Courtesy Intel. Page 571: DILBERT reprinted by permission of United Feature Syndicate, Inc.

Chapter 15
Page 677: Courtesy Startek Engineering, Inc.

Chapter 16
Page 700: ©Brian Willer Photography. Page 707 (top right and bottom right): Courtesy WorkSmart. Page 707 (bottom left): Courtesy ErgoView Technologies. Page 727: Courtesy Granite Communications.

Tech Guide 1
Page TG1-4: Courtesy International Business Machines Corporation. Page TG1-6: Courtesy Cray, Inc. Page TG1-7: Courtesy International Business Machines Corporation. Page TG1-8 (top left and center): Courtesy International Business Machines Corporation. Page TG1-8 (top right): Courtesy Sony Electronics, Inc. Page TG1-8 (bottom): Courtesy Palm, Inc. Page TG1-9: Courtesy GEM Plus. Page TG1-10: Courtesy International Business Machines Corporation. Page TG1-15 (left): Courtesy Conner Peripherals. Page TG1-15 (right): Courtesy Sony Electronics, Inc. Page TG1-16: Courtesy International Business Machines Corporation. Page TG1-19: ©2001 Datadesk Technologies, Inc. Page TG1-21: David Young-Wolff/PhotoEdit. Page TG1-23: Courtesy Sony Electronics, Inc. Page TG1-24: Courtesy International Business Machines Corporation. Page TG1-25: Courtesy Fujitsu. Page TG1-25: ©Dick Luria/Photo Researchers.

Tech Guide 2
Pages TG2-3, TG2-4, TG2-6: Courtesy Microsoft.

Tech Guide 4
Page 752 (margin): Phil Degginger/Stone.

Global Index

Index page entries preceded by "T-" can be located on our Web site (*www.wiley.com/college/Turban*).

Name Index

Index page entries preceded by "T-" can be located on our Web site (*www.wiley.com/college/Turban*).

Subject Index

Index page entries preceded by "T-" can be located on our Web site (*www.wiley.com/college/Turban*).